T0185065

Computer Science Engineering and Emerging Technologies (ICCS-2022)

About the Conference

BOOTH100ICCS-2022

The year 2022 marks the 100th birth anniversary of Kathleen Hylda Valerie Booth, who wrote the first assembly language and designed the assembler and auto code for the first computer systems at Birkbeck College, University of London. She helped design three different machines including the ARC (Automatic Relay Calculator), SEC (Simple Electronic Computer), and APE(X). School of Computer Science and Engineering, under the aegis of Lovely Professional University, pays homage to this great programmer of all times by hosting "BOOTH100"—6th International Conference on Computing Sciences.

Computer Science Engineering and Emerging Technologies (ICCS-2022)

6th International Conference on Computing Sciences 2022

Chief Editor

Prof (Dr.) Rajeev Sobti

Professor & Dean,
School of Computer Science & Engineering
Lovely Professional University

Editor

Dr. Rachit Garg

Professor and CoS
School of Computer Science & Engineering
Lovely Professional University

Sub Editors

Dr. Ajeet Kumar Srivastava

Professor
School of Computer Science & Engineering
Lovely Professional University

Dr. Gurpreet Singh Shahi

Assistant Professor
School of Computer Science & Engineering
Lovely Professional University

Organised by

School of Computer Science and Engineering
Lovely Professional University
Phagwara, Punjab, India-144411

CRC Press
Taylor & Francis Group
Boca Raton London New York

CRC Press is an imprint of the
Taylor & Francis Group, an **informa** business

First edition published 2024
by CRC Press
4 Park Square, Milton Park, Abingdon, Oxon, OX14 4RN

and by CRC Press
2385 NW Executive Center Drive, Suite 320, Boca Raton FL 33431

© 2024 selection and editorial matter, Rajeev Sobti and Rachit Garg; individual chapters, the contributors

CRC Press is an imprint of Informa UK Limited

The right of Rajeev Sobti and Rachit Garg to be identified as the authors of the editorial material, and of the authors for their individual chapters, has been asserted in accordance with sections 77 and 78 of the Copyright, Designs and Patents Act 1988.

All rights reserved. No part of this book may be reprinted or reproduced or utilised in any form or by any electronic, mechanical, or other means, now known or hereafter invented, including photocopying and recording, or in any information storage or retrieval system, without permission in writing from the publishers.

For permission to photocopy or use material electronically from this work, access www.copyright.com or contact the Copyright Clearance Center, Inc. (CCC), 222 Rosewood Drive, Danvers, MA 01923, 978-750-8400. For works that are not available on CCC please contact mpkbookspermissions@tandf.co.uk

Trademark notice: Product or corporate names may be trademarks or registered trademarks, and are used only for identification and explanation without intent to infringe.

British Library Cataloguing-in-Publication Data
A catalogue record for this book is available from the British Library

ISBN: 978-1-032-52199-2 (pbk)
ISBN: 978-1-003-40558-0 (ebk)

DOI: 10.1201/9781003405580

Typeset in Times LT Std
by Aditiinfosystems

Contents

Computer Science Engineering and Emerging Technologies (ICCS-2022) – Prof (Dr.) Rajeev Sobti et al. (eds)
© 2024 Taylor & Francis Group, London, ISBN 978-1-032-52199-2

List of Figures

Computer Science Engineering and Emerging Technologies (ICCS-2022) – Prof (Dr.) Rajeev Sobti et al. (eds)
© 2024 Taylor & Francis Group, London, ISBN 978-1-032-52199-2

List of Tables

Computer Science Engineering and Emerging Technologies (ICCS-2022) – Prof (Dr.) Rajeev Sobti et al. (eds)
© 2024 Taylor & Francis Group, London, ISBN 978-1-032-52199-2

Message from the Honourable Chancellor, LPU

With immense pleasure I hereby extend warm welcome to the delegates of the International Conference on Computing Sciences (ICCS-2022) being jointly organized with University of Peradeniya, Sri Lanka. The deliberations of ICCS-2022 will take place in hybrid format on 11th November, 2022. Fast-moving inventions and developments in science and technology are continually raising the level of life and creating new knowledge, making the times we live in incredibly stimulating. The conference will offer a platform for recent developments and opportunities in technological solutions that aim to reach the common man.

The School of Computer Science and Engineering is making an effort through this conference to address workable and affordable technology solutions to the rising societal concerns. I am sure that the outcome of this conference will serve society and science to the fullest extent.

I wish the conference to be a grand success.

(Dr. Ashok Mittal)
Chief Patron, ICCS 2022

Computer Science Engineering and Emerging Technologies (ICCS-2022) – Prof (Dr.) Rajeev Sobti et al. (eds)
© 2024 Taylor & Francis Group, London, ISBN 978-1-032-52199-2

Message from the
Worthy Pro-Chancellor, LPU

It gives me great pleasure to extend a sincere welcome to the delegates and participants of ICCS- 2022 at Lovely Professional University, which brings together academia, researchers, and businesses. The School of Computer Science and Engineering is hosting this prestigious International Conference on Computing Sciences (ICCS-2022), offering a platform for top academicians, researchers, and industry practitioners to exchange innovative concepts, best practices, and cutting-edge research and technology. The conference will pave the way for technology to be used substantially by one and all.

The conference will deliberate on advancements and future trends in the field of computing. I firmly believe that this conference will serve as a catalyst for bringing about fundamental changes in how science and technology can help society and the ecosystem.

I extend my best wishes to the organizers and participants of ICCS-2022.

(Smt. Rashmi Mittal)
Patron, ICCS 2022

Computer Science Engineering and Emerging Technologies (ICCS-2022) – Prof (Dr.) Rajeev Sobti et al. (eds)
© 2024 Taylor & Francis Group, London, ISBN 978-1-032-52199-2

Message from the
Respected Pro-Vice Chancellor, LPU

We are pleased to announce the 6th hybrid edition of the BOOTH100 International Conference on Computing Sciences (ICCS 2022 on 11th November, 2022. This conference aims to bring together top academics, researchers, and scientists to discuss and share their ideas, concepts, opinions, trends, and issues, as well as the real-world problems being faced and the solutions formulated through IT, Computer Science, and Computer Engineering.

ICCS 2022 is the flagship conference of the School of Computer Science and Engineering of Lovely Professional University. The conference will address theoretical, computational, and experimental elements of research studies, taking into account the demands of academia and industry as of now and for the future as well. We are certain that the combination of a vibrant and varied mix of knowledgeable speakers and panelists will offer a thorough understanding as well as doable and useful brainstorming. Additionally, it will assist them in developing fresh ideas, enhancing their technical proficiency, and showcasing their abilities and discoveries through this platform for global audience.

The faculty members and students of the School of Computer Science and Engineering, Lovely Professional University deserve an applaud for their tireless efforts in giving shape to ICCS2022. I firmly believe that this conference will pave ways for new scientific and technological discoveries.

Wishing the very best to ICCS-2022.

(Dr. Lovi Raj Gupta)
General Chair, ICCS-2022

Message From the Executive Dean, Division of Research and Development

I extend warm greetings to all the delegates and resource person at the International Joint Conference on Computing Sciences (ICCCS-2022), being held at Lovely Professional University in Punjab on 11th November, 2022, organized by the School of Computer Science and Engineering. I'm pleased to hand out the conference abstract book that the school publication committee has produced for this occasion. For their rigorous planning and scheduling of ICCS-2022, the staff and students of the Lovely Professional University's School of Computer Science and Engineering are worthy of praise. I'd like to congratulate the conference organizers and extend a warm greeting to all the attendees, scientists, and young academics.

Dr. Monica Gulati
Executive Dean, Division of Research and Development
Lovely Professional University

Message from the Head of the School
School of Computer Science and Engineering, LPU

Dear Esteemed Delegates and Scientists,

It is my pleasure to welcome you to the 6th International Joint Conference on Computing Sciences (ICCS-2022), in association with University of Peradeniya, Sri Lanka. On behalf of the organizing committee, I extend a warm welcome to all the delegates, researchers, academicians, industrialists, and students from around the world.

The main objective of this conference is to provide a unique platform to facilitate the exchange of recent advancements and challenges in all aspects of Computer Science and Engineering. With a diverse group of attendees, we aim to create an environment that fosters collaboration and encourages the exchange of innovative ideas among researchers in the field.

Furthermore, this conference offers a wonderful opportunity for national and international experts and industry leaders to share their experiences and success stories. Through this sharing of knowledge, we hope to inspire and motivate the next generation of computer scientists and engineers. We believe that this exchange of ideas and knowledge will help us in our quest for continuous improvement and growth.

I am confident that the proceedings of this conference will lead to significant progress in the field of computer science and engineering. On behalf of the organizing committee, I wish all attendees a productive and enjoyable experience at ICCS-2022. I hope that you will find this conference to be a valuable experience and that you will return home with new insights, ideas, and collaborations.

Once again, I welcome you all to the International Conference of Computing Sciences and wish you all the best for a productive and enjoyable conference.

Thank you.

Dr. Rajeev Sobti,
Sr. Dean, School of Computer Science and Engineering
Lovely Professional University

Computer Science Engineering and Emerging Technologies (ICCS-2022) – Prof (Dr.) Rajeev Sobti et al. (eds)
© 2024 Taylor & Francis Group, London, ISBN 978-1-032-52199-2

Message from the Program Chair
KILBY 100 ICCS 2022

I would like to start by sending my warmest welcomes to each and every one of the attendees of the "International Joint Conference on Computing Sciences" (ICCS-2022), which is being held in the School of Computer Science and Engineering under the auspices of Lovely Professional University. This conference shall pave the way to strategically share the most recent developments and difficulties in multiple fields of computer science and technology for the attendees. I want to thank the programme committee members, the group of session chairs, and the session organizers in particular for their assistance in setting up this massive scientific exchange programme. Finally, I want to express my gratitude to the participants, reviewers, and honourable keynote speakers. I'm hoping that the ICCS-2022 conference will contribute to debate and discussion of the many aspects of science and technology in order to generate suggestions that will result in a more beneficial, wholesome, and sustainable society. I send the conference my very best wishes for success.

(Dr Rachit Garg)
Program Chair-ICCS 2022

Computer Science Engineering and Emerging Technologies (ICCS-2022) – Prof (Dr.) Rajeev Sobti et al. (eds)
© 2024 Taylor & Francis Group, London, ISBN 978-1-032-52199-2

Message from Conference Convenor

I am delighted that School of Computer Science & Engineering, Lovely Professional University, Phagwara (India) is organizing BOOTH100- 6th International Conference on Computing Sciences. It's a joint conference this time in collaboration with the renowned International Universities.

I am sure that the conference will provide an opportunity to participate & exchange the ideas and collaborative research in frontier interdisciplinary areas. I am happy to know that many distinguished professors and researchers from India and abroad are delivering the lectures.

I am hopeful that the conference will be a great success and benefit to all those concerned. I wish BOOTH100-ICCS a great success.

Prof. (Dr.) Prateek Agrawal,
Conference Convenor
Dy. Dean & Coordinator- School of Computer Science & Engineering,
Lovely Professional University, Phagwara, Punjab (India)

Computer Science Engineering and Emerging Technologies (ICCS-2022) – Prof (Dr.) Rajeev Sobti et al. (eds)
© 2024 Taylor & Francis Group, London, ISBN 978-1-032-52199-2

Message from Conference Convenor

Dear Participants of ICCS-2022,

It is my pleasure to welcome you to the 6th International Joint Conference on Computing Sciences. This conference provides an opportunity for scholars, researchers, practitioners, and students from around the world to discuss and exchange the latest advancements, challenges, and opportunities in various fields of computer science and technology.

I extend my gratitude to the program committee members, session chairs, and organizers for their hard work and dedication in bringing together this esteemed gathering. I would also like to thank the reviewers and keynote speakers for their contributions to this conference.

Through this conference, we hope to inspire innovative ideas, collaboration, and networking among the attendees. Our goal is to generate meaningful discussions and suggestions that will contribute to a more sustainable and wholesome society.

I wish all the participants a productive and enjoyable experience at ICCS-2022. I am confident that we will achieve our objectives and make this conference a resounding success.

Dr. Deepak Prashar
Professor, Coordinator of School School of Computer Science and Engineering,
Lovely Professional University, Phagwara, Punjab (India)

Computer Science Engineering and Emerging Technologies (ICCS-2022) – Prof (Dr.) Rajeev Sobti et al. (eds)
© 2024 Taylor & Francis Group, London, ISBN 978-1-032-52199-2

About the Editors

Dr. Rajeev Sobti,
Professor & Dean,
School of Computer Science & Engineering

Dr. Rajeev Sobti is a distinguished academic and administrative leader who currently serves as the Head of the School of Computer Science & Engineering at Lovely Professional University, India. With over two decades of experience in both academia and industry, Dr. Sobti has made significant contributions to the field of computer science. His expertise primarily lies in Network Security and System Architecture, and he has a keen interest in areas such as Cryptography, Cryptanalysis of Hash Functions, and Performance Analysis.

Dr. Sobti's impressive research portfolio includes numerous published research papers in reputed journals and conferences. He has also authored and reviewed various chapters in refereed books, showcasing his profound knowledge and scholarly contributions. Notably, his work on the RKC mode of operation had earned recognition as one of the thirteen recommended algorithms for authenticated encryption mode by NIST (National Institute of Standards and Technology), Security Division of the US Department of Commerce.

In addition to his research achievements, Dr. Rajeev Sobti is known for his dedication to education and student engagement. Over the past five years, he has conducted more than 100 counselling sessions, interacting with more than 10,000 students across India. His commitment to fostering academic growth extends to his role as a resource person in various faculty development and training programs.

Dr. Sobti's commitment to continuous learning is evident through his participation in approximately 20 relevant training programs and his memberships in several engineering and research societies and institutions. His expertise is also sought after on a global scale, as he has served on review boards for various journals and conferences both in India and abroad. He also holds several prestigious certifications in the field of computer science and network security, including:

GIAC Forensic Analyst (GFACT)

GIAC Security Essentials (GSEC)

GIAC Certified Incident Handler (GCIH)

Furthermore, Dr. Rajeev Sobti's mentorship has been instrumental in guiding the academic journeys of aspiring scholars. Under his supervision, two scholars have successfully defended their final viva and completed their doctorate, a testament to his guidance and commitment to nurturing future researchers.

These certifications further underscore his expertise and commitment to the field, solidifying his position as a leading figure in the realm of computer science and network security in India and beyond.

Dr. Rachit Garg
Professor and CoS,
School of Computer Science & Engineering

Dr. Rachit Garg is working as a COS (Coordinator of The School) of School of Computer Science and Engineering, Lovely Professional, Punjab, India. LPU is a young university having 30,000+ young minds in emerging areas of Science and Technology in a single campus. The university campus exhibits a rich diversity as the academic staff and students from all 29 states of India and more than 30 countries of the world.

He has 22+ years of teaching and administrative experience as Director and Principal to various institutions of repute in Lyallpur Khalsa College, Jalandhar; Universal Institute of Engg & Technology, Sri Sai College of Engg & Tehnology, Founder Director Pyramid College of Businss & Technology, where he has taught subjects like Distributed Mobile Computing, Software Engineering, System Analysis and Design, Operating System and Data Mining, Information Security, Information Systems, Health Informatics and Cyber Forensics.

He has organized 07 in series International conferences and chaired special sessions and delivered various technical sessions at the national and international level. He is currently guest editor to the JDMSC Talyor and Francis Journal. He is working in various capacities as Editor, Associate Editor, Guest Editor and is a member editorial board to many international journal and conferences. He has published more than 80 research paper(s) in reputed international journals and conferences, which are indexed in various international databases.

He has supervised many master and doctorate students in the various phases of dissertation. He has also edited books and authored book chapters with international and national publishers. He is a senior member to many international conferences in association with IEEE and a life member of CSI and IAENG. IEEE and SCRS student chapters have been initiated under his guidance. He is also associated with 02 International Universities of repute as Adjunct Professor.

Computer Science Engineering and Emerging Technologies (ICCS-2022) – Prof (Dr.) Rajeev Sobti et al. (eds)
© 2024 Taylor & Francis Group, London, ISBN 978-1-032-52199-2

Chapter

Potentiality of IOT in Resolving Failed Copulation

Shivam Tiwari[1], Niraj Kumar[2],
B. Tech CSE, Lovely Professional University

Gursharan Singh[3], Simarjit Singh Malhi[4]
Assistant Professor, Lovely Professional University

Abstract: Sex has always been a centered and significant part of human life since the beginning of civilizational augmentation. There always remained an upheaval side by side. But one challenge that the majority always encounters is female orgasm. The majority of the copulation is led and steered by the male counterpart. As per a number of surveys and research studies that we will discuss in this paper, female orgasm is remarkably low. The pursuit of these activities should be more focused on mutual benefits.

This study is based on analyzing the patterns, trends and body responses in various phases and finding a precise AI-based IOT solution to them so as to maintain gender equality. The aim is to suggest a probable solution by predicting the estimated time to achieve orgasm for both counterparts using multiple IOT sensors. It will help them switch rhythms. Certain types of flips and changes begin to take place in the body and it gradually increases as the person gets closer and closer to the peak. In this work, a detailed analysis of these changes is presented by the execution of machine learning, based on that, a probable solution using IOT is suggested. Furthermore, the working and applications of that solution have also been discussed in detail.

Keywords: Artificial Intelligence, Machine Learning, Internet of Things (IOT), Sex, Copulation, Orgasm, Sensors

1. Introduction

This paper is aimed to find pervasive and ubiquitous solutions to challenges in female orgasm with the help of IOT after analyzing the available data through its ingenuity. It will bring a paradigm shift and will open a new scope of innovation in a relatively less talked-about topic. According to multiple surveys and studies conducted across the world, it has been found that most females do not experience orgasm during intercourse. This data from a survey conducted in India is quite shocking. In a survey named "Durex Global Sex Survey 2017" conducted by Durex India, 70% of females in India do not experience orgasm in a heterosexual relationship. This gap is unrealistic and unfortunate. Further, it states that Indian women do not have an orgasm every time they have sex compared with the 80% of men who do. The reason behind it is the lack of understanding of female anatomy. They do not know how long they should go. In another study conducted, it was found that only 6 percent of women always had an orgasm and nearly 40 percent had nearly always. But 14 percent of females under 35 had never felt orgasm and 38 percent had very infrequent experiences (Kontula, 2016). Laurie Mintz, who is a professor at the University of Florida, in her book named "Becoming Cliterate: Why Orgasm Equality Matters – And How to Get It," calls it as "the orgasm gap" (Mintz, 2017). According to a 2016 study, 95 percent of men in the USA felt orgasm compared with 65 percent of heterosexual women. These data designate that there is a problem that persists and, from here, the role of artificial intelligence came into play (Frederick, 2017).

[1]Shivamtiwari2025@gmail.com,, [2]niraj7039@gmail.com, [3]gursharan.16967@lpu.co.in, [4]simarjit.28260@lpu.co.in

DOI: 10.1201/9781003405580-1

The involvement of artificial intelligence can guide both counterparts to manage the rhythm accordingly. Data regarding the changes in different phases while having sex is available, so the solution that we will suggest will be based on those studies. If succeeds, it will open a new market scope of IOT to explore deeper in this area. As the solution we have discussed will directly address a major day-to-day issue, the impact will prove to be revolutionary. In this research paper, we have analyzed the trends in changes in multiple vitals during intercourse in the human body and then suggested a probable solution by mapping real-time data with the use of sensors. That data will be analyzed using machine learning algorithms so that our solution can guide people in real time. The relevance of this work has increased a lot in today's context when we are working to find smart solutions to our day-to-day problems.

2. The Quandary

As discussed above, the disparity in frequency of orgasm during heterosexual activity is our area of focus. There can be multiple reasons depending upon social and emotional criteria, but the fact of the matter is that there is an imparity that should be addressed. We can say that the reason behind this imparity is the difference in anatomy between male and female simulations. Apart from the physiological measures, the psychological factors should also be addressed, particularly while considering the female simulation. We have discussed and analyze different data to came across a viable solution in this work.

3. Data Indagation

The human body experiences several physiological changes during sexual arousal and orgasm. These changes include:

(a) *Temperature:* Temperature in the genital area rises due to intense blood flow.
(b) *Heart rate:* Heart rate gradually increases and remains at its peak during orgasm. It is the result of the body's response to sex simulation.
(c) *Breathing:* Breathing often becomes faster and shallower during sex arousal and orgasm and the person may feel shortness of breath.
(d) *Muscle Tension:* Muscle tension in the genital, buttock and thigh muscles increases.
(e) *Blood Pressure:* Blood pressure also rises temporarily.

Though these changes are temporary and natural, they suggest us a trend of certain changes in the human body. These changes can be tracked using IOT sensors to predict the required time for orgasm to happen. There are multiple research studies that suggest us a generic range of data on these changes in the human body. These data on analyzing along with the real-time data obtained from sensors can easily predict how far the male or female is from the desired results. The data from various studies and researches we have considered for this work are as follows:

(a) In a study conducted to map the heart rate during sex, and it was found that the peak heart rate occurred at the beginning of the orgasm and dropped to the baseline level after 10–20 minutes. (Xui-Rui, 2008)
(b) In another study that was conducted over couples with age range between 24 and 40 years, the mean of heart rate for male on top (MOT) at orgasm was 114 compared with 117 for male at bottom (MOB). Mean BP at orgasm in the MOT was 163/81 and in MOB was 161/77. (Nemec, 1976)
(c) In another study conducted to analyze the impact of sex on cardiovascular disease, similar results were found. In that study, it was observed that both heartbeat and blood pressure peaked at orgasm and middled at heterosexual foreplays and stimulation. (Kostis, 2005)
(d) A study conducted by Hahn et al. (2012) found that facial and genital temperatures rise while having sex and can be mapped.
(e) Another study on analyzing genital temperature concluded that the genital temperature increased during the last 5 minutes of copulation. He has mapped the same using thermal imaging technology (Kukkonen, 2007).

After discussing the research and studies above, we can say that we can predict the expected time of orgasm if we have real time data with us. We can predict it using various machine learning methodologies by dissecting real-time data and data from existing sources.

4. Methods

The primary purposes of our research were to (a) develop a methodology to predict the estimated orgasm time so as to bridge the orgasm gap; (b) suggest ways to improve and achieve real-time data collection by the use of IOT devices. Thus, we had the following research questions:

(a) Is it possible to derive a trend or relationship between sex and time?

(b) Can we predict the expected time of orgasm?

(c) Can IOT sensors be used to get real-time data ?

On evaluating all the research mentioned, we have found the following trends. A graphical representation of those trends are as follows:

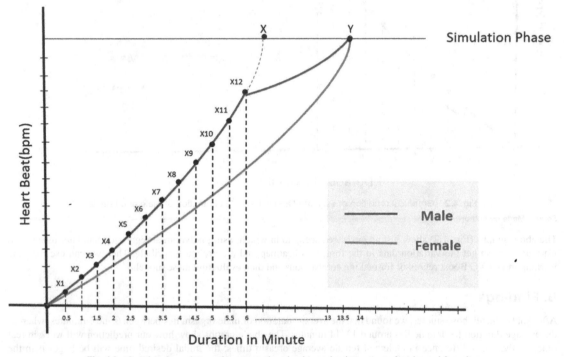

Fig. 1.1 Graphical rendition of estimated and achieved culmination of male and female

Source: Made by Author

One more slant that the proposed artefact should come to grips with is that every individual has a different metabolic edifice. Though we have the results that generalize the trends, we can extrapolate the broader postulations rather than considering them as parameters. The results that we have discussed are showing us a clear trend from the opacity that IOT can play its role. The graphs above and below show the expected orgasm times of both counterparts. After analyzing these trends, we will be able to suggest ways to orchestrate their rhythm. The parameters taken into account in these graphs are blood pressure and heart rate. The reason behind considering these two parameters out of many is that blood pressure and heart rate are easy to map and are more prominent. Orgasm increases blood pressure, heart rate, and noradrenaline and prolactin plasma concentrations. (Krüger, 1998).

In the graph shown in Fig. 1.1, the points X1, X2, X3....X are the points on the male simulation pattern and X is the expected orgasm point for the male, which is taking less time than the female counterpart. Point Y is the expected orgasm point of female counterpart. Meanwhile, as the female orgasm will take time, the real-time analysis of such data mapped from sensors can be conveyed to both counterparts to adjust their rhythm. These graphs will change in real time. Using the average time for orgasm and the average heartbeat and blood pressure during orgasm as initial parameters, the data in real time can be taken into consideration and updated later in the existing data for more accuracy.

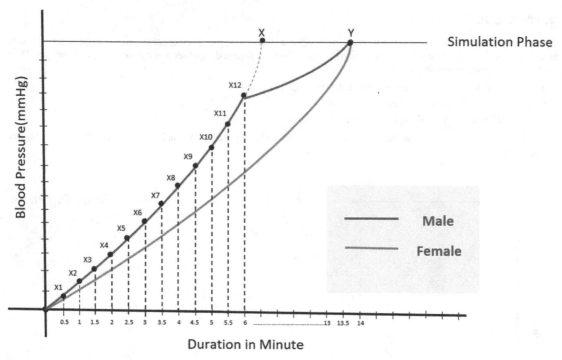

Fig. 1.2 Graphical rendition of estimated and achieved culmination of male and female

Source: Made by Author

The above graphs (Fig. 1.2) show just an envisaged scenario in which, using polynomial regression and later using deep learning, we can get the variation data in the form of a heatmap and a correlation attribute. Then we can use machine learning model XG Boost regressor for making comparisons and then evaluating these models.

5. Findings

After analyzing all those studies, we found that the average duration of male orgasm lies between 6 and 7 minutes, whereas the average duration for female lies around 13–14 minutes. The above graphs show how our prediction will work in real time. As there is a difference in male and female average orgasm times, the initial desired time will be larger than the average female orgasm time. Then, after analyzing the real-time data, it will suggest altering rhythm so as to achieve the peak simultaneously. We can take the mean data of the average baseline heartbeat/temperature/blood pressure and compare it with expected heartbeat/temperature/blood pressure as ideal, and any deviation from the ideal condition can be tracked by linear regression through a similar mechanism. The graph, as discussed, had two parameters: heartrate/blood pressure and average time of orgasm. It can easily predict and suggest both counterparts to manage the rhythm accordingly. The same can be analyzed through an increase in genital temperature also, if we have the data.

6. Recommendations

In this study, after analyzing the data, we have found that IOT can be a gamechanger in this area. The prediction can be done using real-time data and its accuracy will depend on the amount of data obtained from the sensors. The sensors, though required, are quite basic ones and are available. A lot of other research had been already done using those sensors. A similar sort of analysis can also be done using genital temperature data or muscular strain. Detection of these vitals is also possible with the use of sensors.

7. Future Scope, Limitations and Conclusion

We deduced from the analysis that different studies conducted so far have shown similar trends in heartbeat/blood pressure, which makes us to conclude that the trends thus obtained are reliable and if we have the data available, we can predict the orgasm time easily. Such predictions are done using deep learning, and similar sorts of research have been already done. All we need are quality sensors that will send real time data either on mobile or deploy them on cloud. If we have the real-time data, then prediction can also be done using cloud tools on which the data is being deployed like AWS Forecast.

We should not forget that every individual is different and has a different metabolic edifice. We cannot rely every time on the established trends and data. Moreover, it also depends on psychological parameters. It is also important to note that these topics are quite intimate and people may hesitate. It is also important to address potential risks like privacy and data security.

We can thus conclude from this study that IOT has enormous potential. The new technologies like smart condoms and other sensors will prove to be gamechanger. The trends that we obtained in this study are reliable, and the results can be improved further. The prediction in real time will help many to achieve orgasm and extend the intercourse timing so that the gap can be vanquished. This will substantiate the role of IOT further.

8. Acknowledgement

We would like to express sincere thanks to our families and friends for their unswerving support and encouragement throughout this research. Their love and patience have sustained us during the long hours and inevitable setbacks that come with any such research.

REFERENCES

1. Kontula, O., & Miettinen, A. (2016). Determinants of female sexual orgasms. *Socioaffective neuroscience & psychology*, 6, 31624. https://doi.org/10.3402/snp.v6.31624
2. Laurie, M. (2017). Becoming Cliterate: Why Orgasm Equality Matters--And How to Get It. HarperCollins
3. Frederick, D.A., John, H.K.S., Garcia, J.R. *et al.* (2018). Differences in Orgasm Frequency Among Gay, Lesbian, Bisexual, and Heterosexual Men and Women in a U.S. National Sample. *Arch Sex Behav* 47, 273–288. https://doi.org/10.1007/s10508-017-0939-z
4. Xue-Rui, T., Ying, L., Da-Zhong, Y., & Xiao-Jun, C. (2008). Changes of blood pressure and heart rate during sexual activity in healthy adults. Blood pressure monitoring, 13(4), 211–217. https://doi.org/10.1097/MBP.0b013e3283057a71
5. Nemec, E. D., Mansfield, L., & Kennedy, J. W. (1976). Heart rate and blood pressure responses during sexual activity in normal males. American heart journal, 92(3), 274–277. https://doi.org/10.1016/s0002-8703(76)80106-8
6. Kostis, J. B., Jackson, G., Rosen, R., Barrett-Connor, E., Billups, K., Burnett, A. L., Carson, C., 3rd, Cheitlin, M., Debusk, R., Fonseca, V., Ganz, P., Goldstein, I., Guay, A., Hatzichristou, D., Hollander, J. E., Hutter, A., Katz, S., Kloner, R. A., Mittleman, M., Montorsi, F., ... Shabsigh, R. (2005). Sexual dysfunction and cardiac risk (the Second Princeton Consensus Conference). The American journal of cardiology, 96(12B), 85M–93M. https://doi.org/10.1016/j.amjcard.2005.12.018
7. Hahn, A.C.; Whitehead, R.D.; Albrecht, M.; Lefevre, C.E.; Perrett, D.I. Hot or not? Thermal reactions to social contact. Biol. Lett. 2012, 8, 864–867. [Google Scholar] [CrossRef] [PubMed]
8. Kukkonen, T. M., Binik, Y. M., Amsel, R., & Carrier, S. (2007). Thermography as a physiological measure of sexual arousal in both men and women. The journal of sexual medicine, 4(1), 93–105. https://doi.org/10.1111/j.1743-6109.2006.00399.x
9. Krüger, T., Exton, M. S., Pawlak, C., von zur Mühlen, A., Hartmann, U., & Schedlowski, M. (1998). Neuroendocrine and cardiovascular response to sexual arousal and orgasm in men. *Psychoneuroendocrinology*, 23(4), 401–411.
10. Costanzo, S., Flores, A.M. (2021). IoT Non-contact Body Temperature Measurement System Implementing Access Control for COVID-19. In: Rocha, Á., Adeli, H., Dzemyda, G., Moreira, F., Ramalho Correia, A.M. (eds) Trends and Applications in Information Systems and Technologies. WorldCIST 2021. Advances in Intelligent Systems and Computing, vol 1368. Springer, Cham. https://doi.org/10.1007/978-3-030-72654-6_25
11. Charkoudian, N., Hart, E. C. J., Barnes, J. N., & Joyner, M. J. (2017). Autonomic control of body temperature and blood pressure: influences of female sex hormones. *Clinical Autonomic Research*, 27(3), 149–155. doi:10.1007/s10286-017-0420-z
12. Notley, S.R., Park, J., Tagami, K., Ohnishi, N. and Taylor, N.A.S. (2017), Variations in body morphology explain sex differences in thermoeffector function during compensable heat stress. Exp Physiol, 102: 545-562. https://doi.org/10.1113/EP086112
13. Finke, J. B., Hahn, S., Schächinger, H., & Klucken, T. (2023). Increased pupil and heart-rate responses to sexual stimuli in men after physical exertion. *Psychophysiology*, 00, e14254. https://doi.org/10.1111/psyp.14254

14. Brody, S., & Preut, R. (2003). Vaginal Intercourse Frequency and Heart Rate Variability. *Journal of Sex & Marital Therapy*, *29*(5), 371–380. doi:10.1080/00926230390224747

15. Alzate, H., Useche, B., & Villegas, M. (1989). Heart rate change as evidence for vaginally elicited orgasm and orgasm intensity. *Annals of Sex Research*, *2*(4), 345–357. doi:10.1007/BF00849751

16. Levin, R. J., & Wagner, G. (1985). Heart rate change and subjective intensity of orgasm in women. *IRCS Medical Science: Psychology & Psychiatry, 13*(9-10), 885–886.

17. Bohlen JG, Held JP, Sanderson MO, Patterson RP. (1984). Heart Rate, Rate-Pressure Product, and Oxygen Uptake During Four Sexual Activities. *Arch Intern Med.*, 144(9):1745–1748. doi:10.1001/archinte.1984.00350210057007

18. Littler, W. A., Honour, A. J., & Sleight, P. (1974). Direct arterial pressure, heart rate and electrocardiogram during human coitus. *Reproduction*, *40*(2), 321–331.

19. Rowland, D. L. (2010). Genital and heart rate response to erotic stimulation in men with and without premature ejaculation. *International Journal of Impotence Research*, *22*(5), 318–324.

20. Hoon, P.W., Wincze, J.P. and Hoon, E.F. (1976), Physiological Assessment of Sexual Arousal in Women. Psychophysiology, 13: 196-204. https://doi.org/10.1111/j.1469-8986.1976.tb00097.x

21. Britannica, T. Editors of Encyclopaedia (2023, January 4). *orgasm. Encyclopedia Britannica*. https://www.britannica.com/science/orgasm

22. Nasserzadeh S. (2018). Becoming Cliterate: Why Orgasm Equality Matters-and How to Get It, by Dr. Laurie Mintz. *Journal of sex & marital therapy*, *44*(3), 236–237. https://doi.org/10.1080/0092623X.2017.1384160

23. Fugl-Meyer, A. R., Sjögren, K., & Johansson, K. (1984). A vaginal temperature registration system. *Archives of sexual behavior*, *13*(3), 247–260. https://doi.org/10.1007/BF01541651

24. Jeong, H., Seong, M., Park, K., & Kim, J. G. (2020). Monitoring Differences in Vaginal Hemodynamic and Temperature Response for Sexual Arousal by Different Anesthetic Agents Using an Optical Probe. *Current Optics and Photonics*, *4*(1), 57–62. https://doi.org/10.3807/COPP.2020.4.1.057

25. Wang, N., Pugliese, G., Carrito, M. *et al.* (2022). Breath chemical markers of sexual arousal in humans. *Sci Rep* **12**, 6267. https://doi.org/10.1038/s41598-022-10325-6

26. https://www.psychologytoday.com/us/blog/body-sense/201004/male-and-female-orgasm-not-so-different

27. https://www.health.harvard.edu/healthbeat/is-sex-exercise-and-is-it-hard-on-the-heart

28. https://www.durex.co.uk/pages/global-sex-survey

29. https://www.durexindia.com/pages/global-sex-survey

30. https://theprint.in/talk-point/durex-sex-survey-is-the-land-of-kamasutra-not-adventurous-enough/322178/

31. https://www.desiblitz.com/content/durex-global-sex-survey-india-sex-lives

32. https://agentsofishq.com/post/makes-women-feel-hot-answers-may-surprise

33. https://www.intimina.com/blog/body-changes-when-horny/

34. https://www.visiotechsecurity.com/en/news/271-thermographic-cameras-measure-body-temperature

35. https://tipteh.com/sensors/process-sensors/contactless-body-temperature-measurement-with-a-thermal-imaging-camera/

Computer Science Engineering and Emerging Technologies (ICCS-2022) – Prof (Dr.) Rajeev Sobti et al. (eds)
© 2024 Taylor & Francis Group, London, ISBN 978-1-032-52199-2

Chapter **2**

A Comprehensive Review on Blockchain: Types, Techniques, Consensus Algorithms and Platforms

Bhupinder Kaur[1]
Research Scholar, Lovely Professional University, Phagwara, India

Deepak Prashar[2]
Associate Professor, Lovely Professional University, Phagwara, India

Arfat Ahmad Khan[3]
Khon Kaen University, Khon Kaen 40002, Thailand

Abstract: In WSN, during the process of localization various attacks could be performed, as a malicious node can send the wrong detail in the network related to the coordinates of the anchor node, and other nodes during the calculation of localization will use that detail, because they are not aware that we are using the malicious node's data, which will lead to the wrong position calculation. So, to solve this problem, we can use different approaches related to cryptography such as digital signature. But these increase the complexity, computation level. So, we can use the blockchain in the network to solve the problem of security, and when the interference of the malicious node is not there during the localization, it will also increase the accuracy. So, in this paper, we are understanding the basic architecture of blockchain, types, consensus algorithm and platforms, and later on, we will use this study to design a new localization algorithm with blockchain.

Keywords: Blockchain, Consensus, Platforms, Public, Private

1. Introduction

Although the concept of digital currency has been available since 1980, it took more than two decades to make it decentralize. In the past, there was a use of centralized authority to manage transactions-related data. To address the issue of keeping the order of transactions, Santoshi Nakamoto reported a blockchain technology, that is, distributed ledger [2] [6]. Distributed solutions to save the transactions of currencies were used to abolish the centralized authorities such as banks. Blockchain is a public ledger in which all the transactions are listed in the form of blocks. In a blockchain, all the transactions are stored in a sequence of blocks. The chain of these blocks increases when a new block concatenates with the previous chain of blocks after the transaction [14]. Transactions on the blockchain are proved and the entered details are immutable. This technology is usable in the financial and non-financial sectors. Blockchain was first used in cryptocurrency [4]. This technology is meant to provide security for transactions; it stores, reads and validates all the transactions in a distributed data base system [17]. Unlike the client-server model, in peer-to-peer network, data is stored in all the nodes that are participating in the network [17]. Blockchain is the foundation of the bitcoin [14] and it serves unchangeable ledger that allows all the transactions to take place in a decentralized manner [14]. In blockchain, ledger is a virtual book that stores all the past transactions and miner node in the network that is having the responsibility to validate transactions in the network [17].

[1]bhupinder.23626@lpu.co.in, [2]deepak.prashar@lpu.co.in, [3]arfatkhan@kku.ac.th

DOI: 10.1201/9781003405580-2

1.1 Properties of Blockchain

1. **Decentralization:** In a centralized system, transactions need to be validated by trust worthy central agencies such as BANK SYSTEM [14]. This central system results in bottleneck issues in central servers and cost also. But in blockchain, there is no need for a central system to validate the transactions. To maintain the consistency of data in blockchain, cryptographic algorithms/consensus algorithms are used [16].

2. **Persistency:** Validation of transactions is fast in blockchain and transactions that are not valid would not be accepted by the miners and will dropped off. Transactions that are already part of the bhlockchain are neither be deleted nor be rolled back [14][16].

3. **Immutability:** All the entries that are available on the blockchain are immutable. If an attacker changes any single node, it will be easily detected, so to avoid this detection, an attacker needs to compromise most of the nodes that are available in the blockchain, which is not an easy task because all the previously held records in the blockchain are also immutable [1].

4. **Anonymity:** In blockchain, the real identity of the user is not revealed; each user in the blockchain can interact with a generated id/address [14][15][16].

5. **Redundancy:** As blockchain technology relies on decentralization architecture, this means the data is replicated across all the writers, unlike the centralized in which to achieve the redundancy, there is need of backups and physical servers [16].

1.2 Architecture and Applications of Blockchain

The sequence of blocks is known as blockchain [14]. Blocks in a chain as a public ledger keeps the record of transactions. Figure 2.1 depicts the structure of basic blockchain in which every block contains two parts: the first one is the header part and the second one is the body part [1]. As shown in Fig. 2.1, transaction are stored in the body part of the block and the header part of the block contains the Hash of the Parent Block, Version of Block, Hash of Merkle Tree Root, Time Stamp, Nonce and nBits.

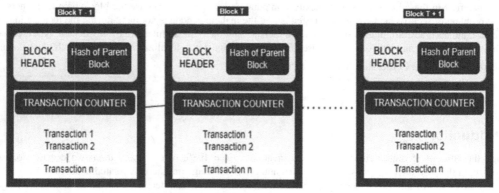

Fig. 2.1 Architecture of blockchain

Source: Made by Author

Version of Block: It specifies which set of block validation rules must be followed.

Hash of Merkle Tree Root: It contains the hash value of all the transaction in the block, as shown in Fig. 2.1.

Time Stamp: Time stamp when the block was published [7].

Nonce: 4-Byte Field, which starts with 0 and increases for each hash calculation [1].

nBits: Target threshold of a valid block hash.

Hash of Parent-Block: 256-bit hash value pointing to the preceding block. Identifier of each block, calculated by the cryptographic hash function. The chain's initial block is known as Genesis Block [1][14].To change a single block's details in a blockchain, an attacker must change the header in all subsequent blocks and propagate that change across the majority of network nodes in order for the peers to agree on the new blockchain. [1].

Validation of Blockchain: The process of finding the hash of block is known as block validation. Only the valid transaction needs to be added in the blockchain as per the property of persistency. Blocks can be added to the blockchain only after validation. Whenever a new transaction occurs in the blockchain, it will be added to the block: sometimes one transaction in one block or sometimes a number of transactions in one block; it depends upon the size of the block and the nature of the network as well.

Block Validators: Block validators are the nodes that participate in the validation of the block. These nodes get rewards for their efforts. Different blockchain protocols use different methods to select the validators for validation from the pool of nodes.

There are various applications in which we can use blockchain in our daily life such as in financial, business and industry, privacy and security, and the internet of things. In Fig. 2.2, different areas where blockchain is used are shown [18].

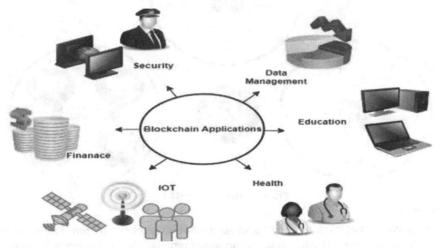

Fig. 2.2   Applications of blockchain

Source: Made by Author

Use of Blockchain in Localization: By 2021, every application uses sensors for sensing the target terrain and conveying that data towards base station that takes the appropriate actions as per the requirements of the phenomenon. In today's world, sensors are used in a variety of settings, including deep forest environment, military terrain, the medical field, smart watches, and human-tracking. But mostly in the hostile environment the challenge occurs when the deployment of sensors is not possible with human; for example, in dense forest areas, it is not possible for human being to go there and deploy the nodes. So, in those cases, we need to deploy the nodes randomly with an airplane, and we do not have any idea where the nodes are getting deployed. Nodes that are sensing the target terrain and conveying details to the base station, in that case that information will not be useful because the base station is unfamiliar with the position, where that particular node is residing. To solve this problem, we can connect the sensors with GPS but this makes the network costly. So, we can do one thing; we can connect some nodes with GPS, and other remaining nodes try to find out its locality with the help of GPS that are attached with nodes. Knowing the position of the node is known as localization. Public and private authors have done research, but challenges are there, such as accuracy in localization and security. Distance calculation between the nodes and security are two of the main reasons that affect the localization accuracy. Malicious nodes during the calculation of localization process can transmit the wrong information related to the nodes, which affects the results. Various attacks could also be performed as per the different layers of localization such as Sybil attack, wormhole attack, jamming, tempering and flooding. To solve the problem of malicious node intervention in localization, there is need for one secure approach that can do the localization and provide good results. Blockchain is a technology that is doing work in security with the use of ledger, miners, and decentralized technique. With the help of this technology, we can do the verification of malicious node, and only authenticated node will participate in the localization process.

2. Types of Blockchain

On the basis of how blockchain is used in various applications, it can be divided into different categories with different attributes. Figure 2.3 compares several forms of blockchain based on many factors and displays the different types of blockchain.

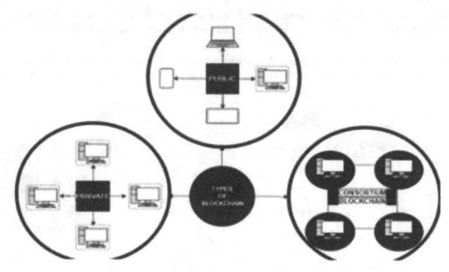

Fig. 2.3 Types of blockchain

Source: Made by Author

Public Blockchain: Public blockchains are really decentralized, where all nodes can take part in creating a new block and get access to the blockchain content. Public blockchains are named permissionless in that they permit anybody to keep a replica of the blockchain. Examples of this public blockchain are the cryptocurrency networks such as Bitcoin, Ethereum and so on. Publishing a new block in public blockchain includes either the computational puzzle solving or staking one's own currency.

Private Blockchain: In distinction of public blockchain, private blockchains are permissioned. Each node that is joined with network is a known member of the single organization. These are good for the solutions of a single enterprise and used as synchronized distributed database prepared to keep track of data transmission performing in different departments. There is no token or currency required to perform transactions, and there are no processing costs involved in transactions. In these, blocks get published by the delgated nodes. Example: Ethereum, Hyperledger.

Consortium Blockchain: Federated Blockchain or consortium blockchain is the same as private blockchain. It is a permissioned network. In this, multiple groups are involved. It serves as a distributed database that is consistently synced and audited to keep track of data transfers among consortium members. Similar to a private consortium blockchain, it does not include any processing fees. This is not entirely decentralized.

3. Literature Review

R. Goyat et al. (2021) The authors of this work offered a solution to the localization issue in WSN. Unwanted nodes may be present in hostile WSN areas; hence, the author employed a trust evaluation technique and blockchain construction. According to several trust measures, each known node's trust value is computed in this process, and the appropriate weights are dynamically changed. More reliable beacon nodes are thus solely chosen for the mining process This two-step process guarantees a blockchain that is reliable and consistently reflects the trust values of all known nodes. The authors used simulations to verify the efficiency and performance of the suggested approach. Based on localization accuracy, harmful activity detection, false positive rate (FPR), and false negative rates, the simulation results are compared. The results of this approach were better than those of existing algorithms [19]. **E. Alma et al. (2020)** In this paper, the authors designed a methodology that protects data from manipulation and the presence of data based on the security advantages provided by blockchain and the use of cryptography tool. The correctness of the designed methodology was checked on temperature and humidity sensing IOT based WSN. The outcome indicates that the idea satisfies the primary need of the IOT system. It is autonomous, safe to share and convey data among devices and users, has privacy, is dependable and the data is available in the infrastructure. This research shows that the proposal is less susceptible to the most recurring attacks against IOT systems, such as Man in the Middle, Linking attack and Distributed Denial of Service attack [23]. **N. Tariq et al. (2020)** In this paper, the authors have done the work to detect the within attacks for sensor device-powered IOT. Author worked on energy-efficient decentralized trust mechanism with the use of a blockchain-based multi-mobile code-driven solution. The new proposed approach yields better results over existing solutions, with 43.94% and 2.67% less message overhead in blackhole and grey hole attack scenarios, respectively. Similarly, the unauthenticated node detection time is decreased by 20.35% and 11.35% in black hole and grey hole attacks. Both of these factors play an important role in improving network lifetime [22].

Table 2.1 Comparison of blockchain on various parameter

Parameters	Public Blockchain [1,4,13]	Private Blockchain [5,7,10]	Consortium Blockchain [1,2,11]
Approach to Read	Publicly Accessible to Perform Read/Write	Restriction can be there	
Node involvement in Consensus	Involvement of All Nodes.	One Group	Designated Nodes in Multiple Groups.
Singularity	Pseudo-Anonymous	Accepted Nodes	Accepted Nodes
Rigorous	Allowed	Partially Allowed	Partially Allowed
Execution Speed	Slow	Fast	
Approval	Not Required	Required	Required
Decentralization	Entirely Decentralized	Centralized	Less Centralized

Source: Made by Author

Goyat et al. (2020): The authors of this study have developed a modern, range-free, secure positioning method for WSN. Because hostile nodes inside the network have an impact on localization accuracy, they have utilized blockchain technology to provide security during the positioning process. Blockchain was utilized by the authors to share the network's anchor node's trusted value in order to tackle that challenge. The network's anchors with high trust values are referred to as miners, and other non-intelligent nodes use the trust values of those miners for localisation. The accuracy of this approach has been improved; simulation findings indicate that it can separate hostile nodes from the network. The new technique has less average-localization error as compared to already available methods. [21][24]. **L. Qinghua et al. (2022)** In this research paper, authors proposed a new distributed positioning method built on intelligent nodes chosen and optimized by particle filters for solving the issue of localization. The analysis of error propagation using the least-squares localization method is the initial step in this process. Intelligent sensors were best chosen in real-time when mobile nodes were in motion, according to the proportional relationship between location inaccuracy and the propagation of uncertainty. The author then used the range and location of the known sensor that was appropriately chosen to obtain positional information for the mobile nodes. The particle filter (PF) approach was lastly employed to estimate location outcomes as accurately as possible. The experimental findings demonstrated that the new approach significantly improves the robustness and location accuracy of distributed systems [20].

4. Consensus Algorithms

Consensus is an algorithm required in Blockchain. Due to the lack of a central authority on the blockchain, some sort of protocol is required to guarantee the consistency of the ledger across dispersed nodes. In this section, we are defining several approaches to reaching a consensus in blockchain [14].

In Table 2.2, the comparison of different Consensus algorithms is done. POW (Proof of Work): This was used in the Bitcoin network. In decentralized systems, there is a need for a node (miner) who will be responsible to record the transaction. Random selection is an easy method. Because random selection is open to assault, as a result, every node that wants to create a block in the network for a transaction must put in a lot of effort to demonstrate through computation that it is unlikely to attack the network. POS (Proof of Stake): in this case, the selection of the miner to generate the block is

Table 2.2 Comparison of consensus algorithms on various parameters

Parameters	POW algorithm	POS algorithm	DPOS algorithm	PBFT algorithm	PAXOS/RAFT algorithm
Stability [1]		Fork		No Fork	No Fork
Capability [2,12]	Low	Best	Good	Better	Good
Usage of resources [3]	Vast	Slight Less		Very Less	Less
Fault tolerance [5]	Less than 50 percent			Less than 33 percent	Less than 50 percent
Extensible [4]	Poor	Fine		Poor	Fine
Application [5]	Bitcoin	PPCoin	Bitshares	Fabric	ZooKeeper
Types of blockchain [6,9]	Public			Consortium	Private

Source: Made by Author

different from POW. Validators are supposed to be selected based on the fraction of coins they own in the system. The node with a greater number of coins has more chances to be selected than the node with lesser number of coins. DPOS (Delegated Proof of Stake) In DPOS stakeholders choose their delegates to generate and validate the blocks. Significantly, if a smaller number of nodes validates the block, then the block could be confirmed fast, and as could quick confirmation of transactions as well. PBFT (Practical Byzantine Fault Tolerance): this is a replication algorithm for Byzantine faults. Hyperledger fabric uses the PBFT. It saves energy and the tolerated power of adversary is <33.3%. PAXOS/RAFT: these consensus algorithms use less resources and fault tolerance of these id less than 50 percent.

5. Platforms

In this section, we discuss the different 10 blockchain platforms, and the comparison is done in Table 2.3 [2].

Table 2.3 Comparison of platform on various parameters [2]

Platform for blockchain	Points need to check while selecting platform	Type of blockchain	Consensus Protocol	Need of Hardware	Open source
Bitcoin [1,8]		Public	POW		
Ethereum [3]		Public/Private	POW/Proof of State		
Zcash [2]	1. Type of blockchain		POW		
Litecoin [2]					
Dash (Digital Cash) [2]	2. Consensus protocol		POW/POS	NO	YES
Peercoin [2,4]		Public	POW/Proof of Stake		
Ripple [2]	3. Need of hardware		RPCA/Consensus and Confirmation		
Monero [2]	4. Language for script		POW		
Multichain [2]		Private	POW/Mining Diversity		
Hyperledger [5,6]			Not uses POW	Depends	

Bitcoin: This is the first cryptocurrency that is distributed and uses a peer-to-peer network without a central authority acting as a bank. It uses the POW and uses a huge amount of energy. With the help of this Bitcoin, other different consensus mechanisms and cryptocurrencies were also created. [2].

Ethereum: This is platform meant for decentralized applications and uses smart contracts that run on blockchain [2]. This Ethereum also adapts the consensus protocol – POS.

Zcash: this is a cryptocurrency that is decentralized and open source that provides anonymity in transactions and privacy. The challenge with bitcoin is that even though sender and receiver are represented by the hashed address and provide enough transaction data, transactions can still be traced with careful analysis; to solve this issue, Zcash uses an algorithm: A zero-knowledge proof [2].

Litecoin: this is a decentralized payment network. The major change in Litecoin as compared to bitcoin is that Litecoin provides faster transaction. It uses the Scrypt hash algorithm [2].

Dash: Digital cash is a fast-transaction digital money that prioritises privacy. It is based on the Bitcoin software and extends the Bitcoin blockchain on top with a "Masternode" network tier [2].

Peercoin: developed from Bitcoin with the intention of lowering the energy consumption associated with the mining of coins [2].

Ripple: is a low-latency blockchain network that atomically settles and records transactions on a distributed, secure database [2].

Monero: This cryptocurrency is safe, discrete, and untraceable. By utilising Confidential Ring transactions, it gives users privacy and anonymity [2].

Multichain: A platform for developing and deploying private or restricted blockchain. It benefits round robin consensus protocol Mining Diversity and Bitcoin Blockchain POW. Mining diversity is: As with private blockchain, all participants are already to some extent trusted because they are all identifiable entities [2].

Hyperledger: With numerous firms, Hyperledger has a number of international alliances. This is an open-source collective effort to provide advancement in permissioned/private, cross-industry blockchain technology.

6. Conclusion

In 2022, when most of the data is online, there is a need of security. In all the areas we talk about, such as medical field, industry area, agriculture, VANET, WSN, IOT and so on, a lot of data is there that demands security in terms of confidentiality, availability, and consistency. So, to provide security in all these areas, one new technology is there, that is, blockchain. In this paper, we have done work to understand the blockchain, techniques, platform and consensus algorithm. In the future, we will use the blockchain to solve the problems of WSN related to security and centralization.

REFERENCES

1. M. S. Ali, M. Vecchio, M. Pincheira, K. Dolui, F. Antonelli, and M. H. Rehmani, "Applications of Blockchains in the Internet of Things: A Comprehensive Survey," *IEEE Commun. Surv. Tutorials*, vol. 21, no. 2, pp. 1676–1717, 2019.
2. T. T. Kuo, H. Zavaleta Rojas, and L. Ohno-Machado, "Comparison of blockchain platforms: A systematic review and healthcare examples," *J. Am. Med. Informatics Assoc.*, vol. 26, no. 5, pp. 462–478, 2019.
3. S. Aggarwal, R. Chaudhary, G. S. Aujla, N. Kumar, K. K. R. Choo, and A. Y. Zomaya, "Blockchain for smart communities: Applications, challenges and opportunities," *J. Netw. Comput. Appl.*, vol. 144, pp. 13–48, 2019.
4. M. A. Uddin, A. Stranieri, I. Gondal, and V. Balasubramanian, "A survey on the adoption of blockchain in IoT: challenges and solutions," *Blockchain Res. Appl.*, vol. 2, no. 2, p. 100006, 2021.
5. M. N. M. Bhutta *et al.*, "A Survey on Blockchain Technology: Evolution, Architecture and Security," *IEEE Access*, vol. 9, pp. 61048–61073, 2021.
6. F. Casino, T. K. Dasaklis, and C. Patsakis, "A systematic literature review of blockchain-based applications: Current status, classification and open issues," *Telemat. Informatics*, vol. 36, no. November 2018, pp. 55–81, 2019.
7. K. Yue *et al.*, "A Survey of Decentralizing Applications via Blockchain: The 5G and beyond Perspective," *IEEE Commun. Surv. Tutorials*, vol. 23, no. 4, pp. 2191–2217, 2021.
8. G. S. Aujla, M. Singh, A. Bose, N. Kumar, G. Han, and R. Buyya, "BlockSDN: Blockchain as a Service for Software Defined Networking in Smart City Applications," *IEEE Netw.*, vol. 34, no. 2, pp. 83–91, 2020.
9. M. S. Christo, V. E. Jesi, U. Priyadarsini, V. Anbarasu, H. Venugopal, and M. Karuppiah, "Ensuring Improved Security in Medical Data Using ECC and Blockchain Technology with Edge Devices," *Secur. Commun. Networks*, vol. 2021, 2021.
10. M. Singh, G. S. Aujla, A. Singh, N. Kumar, and S. Garg, "Deep-Learning-Based Blockchain Framework for Secure Software-Defined Industrial Networks," *IEEE Trans. Ind. Informatics*, vol. 17, no. 1, pp. 606–616, 2021.
11. G. Bansal, A. Dua, G. S. Aujla, M. Singh, and N. Kumar, "SmartChain: A smart and scalable blockchain consortium for smart grid systems," *2019 IEEE Int. Conf. Commun. Work. ICC Work. 2019 - Proc.*, pp. 1–6, 2019.
12. Y. Ren, Y. Liu, S. Ji, A. K. Sangaiah, and J. Wang, "Incentive Mechanism of Data Storage Based on Blockchain for Wireless Sensor Networks," *Mob. Inf. Syst.*, vol. 2018, 2018.
13. L. Xie, Y. Ding, H. Yang, and X. Wang, "Blockchain-based secure and trustworthy internet of things in SDN-enabled 5G-VANETs," *IEEE Access*, vol. 7, pp. 56656–56666, 2019.

14. Z. Zheng, S. Xie, H. Dai, X. Chen, and H. Wang, "An Overview of Blockchain Technology: Architecture, Consensus, and Future Trends," *Proc. - 2017 IEEE 6th Int. Congr. Big Data, BigData Congr. 2017*, no. June, pp. 557–564, 2017.
15. J. Garcia-Alfaro *et al.*, "Data privacy management, autonomous spontaneous security, and security assurance," *Lect. Notes Comput. Sci. (including Subser. Lect. Notes Artif. Intell. Lect. Notes Bioinformatics)*, vol. 8872, no. September 2014, 2015.
16. Priyadarshini, "Cybersecurity in Parallel and Distributed Computing Techniques Introduction to Blockchain Technology," no. April, 2019.
17. N. Bozic, G. Pujolle, and S. Secci, "A tutorial on blockchain and applications to secure network control-planes," *2016 3rd Smart Cloud Networks Syst. SCNS 2016*, no. July 2019, 2017.
18. F. Casino, T. K. Dasaklis, and C. Patsakis, "A systematic literature review of blockchain-based applications: Current status, classification and open issues," *Telemat. Informatics*, vol. 36, no. May 2018, pp. 55–81, 2019.
19. R. Goyat, G. Kumar, M. Alazab, R. Saha, R. Thomas, and M. K. Rai, "A secure localization scheme based on trust assessment for WSNs using blockchain technology," *Futur. Gener. Comput. Syst.*, vol. 125, pp. 221–231, 2021.
20. Z. Zhou, "A Distributed Localization Method for Wireless Sensor Particle Filter," 2022.
21. R. Goyat, G. Kumar, M. K. Rai, R. Saha, R. Thomas, and T. H. Kim, *"Blockchain Powered Secure Range-Free Localization in Wireless Sensor Networks,"* *Arab. J. Sci. Eng.*, vol. 45, no. 8, pp. 6139–6155, 2020.
22. A. B. M. C. Trust, N. Tariq, M. Asim, F. A. Khan, T. Baker, and U. Khalid, "A Blockchain-Based Multi- Mobile Code-Driven Trust Mechanism for Detecting Internal Attacks in Internet of Things," pp. 1–27, 2021.
23. A. E. Guerrero-Sanchez, E. A. Rivas-Araiza, J. L. Gonzalez-Cordoba, M. Toledano-Ayala, and A. Takacs, "Blockchain mechanism and symmetric encryption in a wireless sensor network," *Sensors (Switzerland)*, vol. 20, no. 10, 2020.
24. Bhupinder Kaur, Deepak Prashar,"Localization in Wireless Sensor Network: Techniques, Algorithms Analysis and Challenges", 2021 9th International Conference on Reliability, Infocom Technologies and Optimization (Trends and Future Directions) (ICRITO), 2021.
25. B. Kaur and D. Prashar, "Analysis of Improved DV-Hop Algorithm with Distance Error," *2nd International Conference on Intelligent Computing, Instrumentation and Control Technologies ICICICT 2019*, pp. 1242–1246, 2019.
26. B. Kaur and D. Prashar, "Analysis and Comparison of Localization Approaches in WSN: A Review," *ICAICR 2018*, pp. 294–309, 2019.

Computer Science Engineering and Emerging Technologies (ICCS-2022) – Prof (Dr.) Rajeev Sobti et al. (eds)
© 2024 Taylor & Francis Group, London, ISBN 978-1-032-52199-2

Chapter

Biometrics and its Application in Parkinson's Disease Detection

Jatin Gupta[1]

Research Scholar, School of Computer Science and Engineering,
Lovely Professional University, Phagwara, India

Baljit Singh Saini[2]

Associate Professor, School of Computer Science and Engineering,
Lovely Professional University, Phagwara, India

Abstract: Computers are employed to handle and store delicate information, which must be protected from intruders. Biometric technology is a means of user authentication for which a number of viable technologies are used. Also, biometrics have various applications in medical field also. Especially various biometrics like keystroke, Gait, mouse dynamics, and voice recognition may be utilized to detect Parkinson's disease.

Keywords: Biometric, Recognition, Parkinson's disease, Authentication

1. Introduction

Computers have become an indispensable aspect of everyday life. Computers are used to store and process sensitive information (like government and military secrets or any company's plans, or bank accounts details, passwords, etc.) and personal data. The demand for reliable user authentication techniques is rising as a result of escalating security issues and rapid advancements in networking, communications, and mobility [1]. Biometrics are recognised as the most trustworthy and safe means for security. Biometrics is defined as the study of identifying people based on their legal means of establishing their identities [2].

Aspects of the human body's characteristics and behaviour are known as biometrics. From a cryptographic point of view, because they cannot be stolen or lost like a token or forgotten like a pin or a password, biometrics are suitable as an authentication element. Biometrics can assist in addressing cryptography's intrinsic security flaw by determining a legitimate user. However, biometrics have their own limitations and might be permanently lost if they are hacked. Additionally, legislative rules are in place to safeguard the privacy of biometrics. In order to overcome these issues, there is a paradigm shift toward privacy-preserving biometric authentication technologies [3].

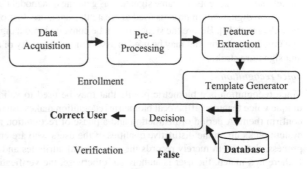

Fig. 3.1 Working of Biometric Authentication System

Source: Made by Author

[1]jatingupta8377@gmail.com, [2]baljitsaini28@gmail.com

DOI: 10.1201/9781003405580-3

Applications that utilise biometric technology and enable the automatic identification, verification, or authentication of a natural person are known as biometric systems. In theory, privacy experts believe that only locations needing a high level of security and strict identification processes may justify processing personal data using biometric technology. Similar systems should be implemented in a transparent manner, so staff should always be given the necessary information. Employers should choose a biometric system that offers a high degree of comfort within the confines of privacy laws when the deployment of such systems is essential [4]. Also, biometrics can be used in the detection of various diseases such as Parkinson's disease.

2. Types of Biometric

Biometric traits are distinct and particular to each individual. Some of these qualities are challenging to accurately reproduce or duplicate. The two main categories of biometric IDs are behavioural and physiological [5].

2.1 Behavioral Biometrics

Behavioural biometrics is the study of human behaviour patterns that may be utilised for uniquely recognizing and quantifying reasons. The types of behavioral metrics are:

- Signature recognition
- Voice recognition
- Keystroke dynamics
- Gait
- Mouse dynamics

Signature recognition

One of the most commonly used items in a variety of transactions, from official to commercial, is a signature. It is simple to fake a person's signature and use it inappropriately because it is one of the most extensively used formats for transactions in public. Identification of the signature and verification with a technology that can determine if it is a genuine or fake signature are done as a preventative precaution [6]. Signature recognition technology, as a broad definition, is a behavioural biometric way to identify people through either an online or offline procedure of verifying their written signatures. To put it another way, a signature can be handwritten on paper using the conventional method produced by typical ink (offline). The alternative method of delivering a handwritten signature is through the use of electronic tools such as mobile phones, iPads, and styluses (online) [7].

Various techniques used for signature recognition include convolution neural network (CNN), probabilistic neural network (PNN), support vector machine (SVM), and recurrent neural network (RNN).

Because signatures are inconsistent from time to time, signature recognition encounters several difficulties in real life [8]. It is difficult to develop a programme that can tell the difference between a real signature and a well forged one since this discrepancy depends on the circumstances and human behaviour at the moment. This issue can result in either a strict model that only accepts the same signature as genuine or a model that is very flexible and accepts diverse signatures as real. Due to the digitalization process used to create the signature, loss of data is another issue that offline signature recognition must deal with [9]. Before the signature can be converted into a digital picture, it must be scanned. This results in a loss of dynamic information that may be used to assess the authenticity of a signature, such as pen position and velocity, pressure, and signature stroke.

Voice recognition

Voice recognition is a biometric profile that may be used to validate a person's identification because each person has unique voice features [10]. Vocal biometric recognition makes use of a person's unique voice characteristics to identify and confirm them. A period of instruction and a phase of recognition are both present in the speech recognition system. The system picks up on the distinctive qualities of the users who are enrolled throughout training. Later on in the recognition process, the system merely records the user's vocal attributes and compares them to the registered voice measurements. If there is a match, the user is authorized; otherwise, the verification system rejects the user. The voice-based biometric system's key strength is that it simply uses sound recognition to verify identity; user speech is not recorded. The amount of airstream and airstream impediments such as the tongue, gums, and lips determine the type of sound that is generated.

Therefore, high-risk and security systems are suitable for the high-standard authentication technique. It is determined that there are three methods by which text-dependent speaker confirmation, text-prompted speaker authentication, and text-independent speaker verification often function for speech biometric recognition [11]. Various techniques used for voice recognition are the Extra-Trees algorithm, K-nearest-neighbor (KNN), SVC algorithm, and Gaussian NB algorithm.

Many significant applications, most notably user authentication on smart devices, have adopted voice biometric identification and authentication. Here, using the already-present device sensors, lip movement and voice authentication may function well even in loud surroundings. Intelligent speech bots can ensure remote user authentication in digital banking in a practical and affordable manner. The difficulty here is that technology must progress to store the distinct digital code while taking up less space. Additionally, as a person's voice changes, their accuracy declines (emotional or sick) [12].

Keystroke dynamics

The unique rhythmic and timing-based patterns that are created when someone types on an appropriate device, such as a keyboard, mobile phone, smart phone, or tablet, are referred to as keystroke dynamics, which is a behavioural biometric [13]. Keystroke dynamics is a method that quantifies a user's typing habits in terms of timing data, such as the length of time a key is pushed, the time it takes to switch to another key, etc., to create a signature or keystroke profile. Cognitive traits have been observed in abundance in these signatures, which are potential individual identifiers because of their unique nature. It is challenging to imitate typing behaviour since it is ballistic (semiautonomous), making it suitable as a biometric. Data can be acquired from text entry through various data acquisition methods, which can be broadly classified into two types – static and dynamic text. Static analysis or structured text examines a person's keyboard patterns on a predefined phrase or phrases at certain locations in the system. Systems that don't have room for additional text entry can use static text entry. In dynamic analysis, keystroke behaviour is continuously or sporadically monitored. Keystroke dynamics are significantly influenced by human–computer interactions [14]. The classification of users is carried out based on the similarities and differences among the templates once the characteristics have been retrieved and the templates have been constructed. To categorize typists, researchers have employed anything from basic patterns generated from statistics of the data, including the mean and standard deviations, to sophisticated pattern recognition algorithms. A mix of techniques has also occasionally been applied.

Various techniques used for keystroke dynamics are KNN, SVM, Hidden Markov Model (HMM), Euclidean distance, and Neural network.

The uniqueness lies in the computation of a keystroke event, which can be done with a precision of up to milliseconds, making it difficult to accurately recreate someone's keystroke routine. This method has a low cost of implementation because specialized hardware is not required; software can perfectly execute the procedure. One of the major drawbacks of keystroke dynamics is lower accuracy, which can be caused by a variety of external reasons, including injury, exhaustion, or any emotional state that affects the user's typing rhythm and may result in incorrect rejection or acceptance rates.

Gait

Humans can identify other persons based on their walking patterns. Gait is the name given to this person's gait pattern. This Gait can be utilised for a person's biometric authentication [15]. Gait may be described as a coordinated series of motions involving a number of cyclic acts that cause a person to move. The motions are coordinated so that they take place according to a predetermined temporal and geographical sequence. With alternate foot movements, these motions seem to cycle. Gait is an exclusive parameter in biometric identification systems because of the coordinated and cyclical structure of the motions. Here, characteristics can be captured in two ways: one is by recording through video camera (Vision-based approach) and the other is using a sensor (sensor-based approach). In vision-based techniques for gait analysis, frames are captured using a video camera. There are two ways to do this analysis: directly (with markers on the subject), or indirectly (without markers on the subject). Gait analysis makes use of digital or analogue cameras. The sensor can be put on the subject's body or on the ground to analyse their gait. Electromyography (EMG), inertial systems, and middle-or surface-based EMG are applied to the subject's body. Force Platform is also used to determine the kinetics of the subject's movement.

Various techniques used for gait recognition are backpropagation neural network, CNN, golden ratio segmentation method, and SVM.

Despite advances in data collection technology, the system is still unable to accurately record individuals' actual gait patterns. The study done so far has shown that its use is constrained by fixed views and hardware. A device that can analyse a subject's real walking pattern in three dimensions is urgently needed. Another pressing issue in gait analysis is the fact that a variety of external, internal, physical, psychological, and pathological variables influence walking patterns. Researchers are still struggling to determine how these two things are related to one another [16].

Mouse dynamics

Mouse dynamics is the term typically used to describe mouse use. The analysis of user mouse behaviour does not need sensitive information from the users, in contrast to keystroke dynamics. Furthermore, mouse use outpaces keyboard use in web-based contexts [17]. Static and dynamic authentications have already employed this kind of behavioural biometric. Because no specialised gear is required to acquire biometric data, there has been a rising interest in research on mouse dynamics-based user authentication. As a method of authentication, mouse dynamics includes watching the user's behaviour through how they use the mouse. In order to acquire active and continuous authentication, the problem of continuous user authentication is taken into consideration by continually evaluating the user's mouse movements. The mouse's movements may be divided into two categories: activities that include movement and quiet. The mouse's movements can vary in movement type, movement speed, distance travelled, and movement direction. Drag-and-Drop (DD), Point-and-Click (PC), and Mouse-Move (MM) actions are all included in the movement type. The quantity of mouse events as well as the sorts of mouse events affect how quickly a mouse may detect an intruder in mouse dynamics (click, move, and drag-and-drop) [18].

Various techniques used for mouse dynamics are Euclidean distance, Manhattan distance, KNN, K-Means, and SVM.

One of the mouse dynamic's main advantages over other biometric technologies is that it allows for both active and passive user monitoring. Thus, it may be used to continually monitor real and fake users throughout computing sessions.

2.2 Physiological Biometrics

The foundation of physiological biometrics is the behaviour of an individual. This encompasses all of the physical qualities [19]. The types of physiological biometrics are:

- Iris
- Face
- Fingerprint
- Finger veins
- Ear
- Footprint

Iris recognition

Iris recognition is a technique for verifying a person's identity by looking at an iris pattern that appears at random. Human authentication and identification via biometrics may be done using the iris texture of an eye. The central, vibrant, circular area of the eye is called the iris. An efficient method of identifying people is made possible by the uniqueness of iris patterns. Based on its biological makeup, the iris contains a distinct network of tissues that may be seen. But throughout the first year of life, when the iris cannot be genetically altered, a person's iris develops [20]. A typical iris-based biometric system consists of the following elements: iris picture acquisition, pre-processing, segmentation, texture normalization, feature extraction, feature codification, and matching.

Various techniques used for iris recognition are Euclidean distance, Hamming distance, Normalized correlation, and Nearest feature line.

It is the finest method for automated person authentication because iris scanners are widely used in many security domains. Additionally, the flexibility and convenience of scanning technology are driving up demand for this method. Additionally, this method attained a suitable degree of dependability by accumulating as many distinctive traits as feasible. There are several problems/factors that make iris recognition less accurate. Some of these variables include eyeglasses, contact lenses, and others. The high expense of implementing such an authentication method is another challenge when using iris-based biometrics [20].

Face recognition

The face is said to be the most important part of the body. Human facial features, including the eyes, nose, lips, and chin, have historically played a significant role in identifying individuals. It has been a common technique in the field of biometric recognition, taking into account each person's distinct facial features. A person's face is essential for identifying and authenticating them, which makes it useful in many aspects of daily life. Systems for facial recognition are becoming more and more important. The use of facial recognition systems is becoming increasingly popular due to their safe and dependable security solutions. It is the quickest biometric technique available to identify someone without having to interact with that individual [21].

Various techniques used for face recognition are PCA, LDA, Skin color-based algorithm, and ANN-based algorithm.

The advantages of facial recognition systems are the their simplicity of use and inexpensive setup costs. The effectiveness of face recognition based on biometrics is influenced by numerous factors such as those that convey happiness, anger, and other emotions, offer some difficulties for the automated identification of people's identities [20].

Fingerprint

The fingerprint is one of the most commonly used physiological biometrics in people. A fingerprint is the pattern or imprint made when a human finger encounters an object. This imprint represents the dermis (spaces between ridges) and epidermis (ridge lines) of a finger [22]. The use of the fingerprint as a biometric feature has been widespread and for many different purposes. Because of their individuality and simplicity of use, fingerprints are now often used for human verification and identification. People may be uniquely identified by their fingerprints, which have been discovered to have some uniqueness and consistency. The crucial elements in fingerprint identification are the minutiae. The shift in ridge structure is what it alludes to. Each fingerprint is thought to include roughly 70 minutiae details on average, with the most frequent being termination, bifurcation, crossover, lake, independent ridge, point, or island. Identity theft can be decreased, fraud can be prevented, and security can be increased with this biometric function.

The use of fingerprint identification for security measures has increased in many businesses for a variety of reasons. First, this approach is simpler for consumers to utilize than the previous one, which included physically inking a fingertip and afterwards having trouble removing the ink. Given that the optical sensor is a cheap component, the low implementation cost is the second consideration. Additionally, a fingerprint-based authentication method uses less electricity. This methodology for authentication is also used in mobile environments, particularly smart phones (like iPhones), which makes it more appealing. One of various techniques used for fingerprint recognition is Pattern-based Minutiae-based Fingerprint Recognition Algorithm.

Although fingerprint recognition technology has many great advantages, this method has certain downsides. In order to capture photographs of finger patterns of high quality, this biometric system requires significant sophistication. Because of the problems with filth, wounds, wear, and tear that may quickly affect the ridges and minute details of a fingertip [23].

Finger vein

The biometric recognition system now uses a new technology called finger vein identification. An individual can be authenticated for access to high-security apps using their finger vein patterns. To make the picture more stable for processing later, pretreatment techniques are applied to finger vein images. Finger vein identification was first proposed in the 1980s, but it has not yet been put into use, despite being a promising method for the human recognition system. The standard procedure is to get pictures of finger veins using near-infrared spectroscopy. The use of infrared light with a wavelength of 760 nm and the placement of fingers above it allow for the collection and absorption of vein patterns by deoxygenated hemoglobin [24]. Only the blood vessels can absorb light; hence, the resulting image of the veins seems more detailed than the other finger areas.

Various techniques used for finger vein recognition are Hausdorff distance matching, PCA, LDA, and CNN.

Finger vein characteristics deliver a variety of additional preferred benefits, including: Everybody, including identical twins, has unique finger vein patterns. As a result, it provides a clear contrast between each person. In order to reach the greater performance desired when it comes to biometric finger vein identification, there are still several issues that need to be fixed. First of all, the vein image capturing device determines the quality of the finger vein pictures. During the acquisition procedure, optical blurring may occur due to the close proximity of the finger to the camera. The illumination of the capturing device is another crucial component of the system. Poor lighting may make a picture noisy by making it look either very dark or very bright. Additionally, the erroneous alignment or location of the finger decreased the rate of identification. Therefore, the finger's direction is equally crucial. Thus, matching might not be accurate. Other than that, each person has a different range of skin and bone thickness. Because of this, light scattering may occur because the human skin layer is not coherent [25].

Ear recognition

In the last 10 years, the field of biometrics has paid considerable attention to the growing technology of ear recognition, which has been the focus of active study[26]. There are primarily 11 anatomical ear components in the human ear anatomy. The lobe that surrounds the ear makes up the bottom part of the ear, and the helix that is on the outside is part of the ear. An outer helix and the antihelix are parallel. The concha, which resembles a shell, is formed by the region between the bottom branch of the antihelix and the inner helix. A strong intertragic notch emerges from the concha's bottom portion. The point where the helix and antihelix converge is known as the crus of the helix. On the right-hand side of the intertragic notch, there is a little elevation called the antitragus. The tragus conceals the hole or ear canal. A triangular fossa is a little hole found between the helix and antihelix. The auricle, which is visible and has a complex structure of curves, is one of the distinguishing characteristics of the human ear, making it a suitable biometric modality. This trait has been found to be a reliable trigger for person recognition and may be highly useful in confirming a person's identity, even for identical twins. Additionally, the properties and structure of the ear are more stable and are not as heavily changed by external factors (such as ageing and facial emotions). However, a vital stage is good feature extraction and depiction of ear characteristics. On the other hand, a vital component that directly influences an identification system's efficiency is the accurate feature extraction and depiction of ear characteristics.

Various techniques used for ear recognition are PCA, LDA, and SURF algorithm.

A lot of development has been achieved in the field of ear recognition. However, the majority of the currently available work is done in laboratory-like settings, and just a small amount of work has reportedly been done in a natural setting. Images in the real world are compromised by posture adjustments, illumination changes, chaotic backgrounds, blockage from ear accessories, and hair. [27].

Footprint

A growing biometric characteristic is the ability to identify an individual by their footprint. Numerous forensic and medical investigations have focused on the human foot, which exhibits many of the same distinctive qualities as the human hand. Either statically or dynamically obtained footprint pictures are possible. Its application in industrial biometric systems is regarded as challenging. The absence of a habit and awkward data collection are among the causes [28]. Dactyloscopy or scanning the footprint are two methods for obtaining a footprint picture. The underside of a person's foot is inked during the dactyloscopy procedure, and the imprint is then written down on an A4 piece of paper. In the scanning method, the prominent edges of the footprint are scanned with a high-resolution flatbed image scanner to capture an imprint of the footprint.

Various techniques used for ear recognition are PCA, Euclidean Distance, Independent Component Analysis, Hidden Markov Model, and Correlation Method.

Footprints can be analyzed in forensic science to offer proof for crime scenes and to identify a subject's weight, height, gender, and other attributes depending on the size of the prints. Using a person's footprint to identify them is another growing biometric technique. This technique is also regarded as unique because it has been proven to work. Even though the human foot has indeed been widely studied and resembles the human hand in many ways, using it in a sophisticated biometric system is difficult because of the unfavorable or strange conditions under which data collection occurs. In order to improve accuracy, researchers are now concentrating on multimodal biometric systems, which combine two or more biometric traits. In order to perform better, the study of footprints may need to be combined with other biometric features, which will be tough [28].

3. Techniques

Various techniques used for biometric recognition are described here.

Euclidean distance

A section connecting two locations in a 2D plane or 3D space is measured by the Euclidean distance between them. This method of expressing the distance between two places is the most straightforward. This method is employed graphically and offers decent accuracy.

Hamming distance

The (XOR) operator has been used to separate any matched bits at hamming distance while making sure that none of the compared bits have been influenced by any external factors, such as eyelids, eyelashes, irregular illumination, or other sounds.

Hidden Markov model

A crucial statistical method for modelling data with sequential correlations in nearby instances, such as timeseries data, is the Hidden Markov Model (HMM). In statistical pattern identification and classification, it is frequently employed.

Support vector machines

Support-vector machines (SVM) look at data used for categorization in machine learning and have related learning methods. Utilizing SVM, feature matching is done.

Correlation method

As a statistical link between two variables, the correlation is stated. If one of the variables is connected to the other in some way, there is a correlation between the two.

Neural network

A neural network is composed of numerous simple processing units called neurons. Every neuron is linked to a few other neurons and perhaps to the input nodes. Each link has an actual weight attached to it to symbolise how strong it is.

Deep learning methods

The most well-known deep neural network, CNN, is insensitive to differences in age, luminance, lighting, and facial orientation and is capable of autonomously extracting high-level representative properties from large datasets.

Fuzzy recognition

An input dataset is non-linearly mapped onto linear data output in a fuzzy logic system. The fuzzifier, rules, inference engine, and defuzzifier are its four primary parts.

Principal component analysis

A statistical technique for analysing n-dimensional data is the PCA. This system is frequently used to process signals so that measurements may be taken or information can be connected. The orientation of the chosen item is ascertained using the eigenvector attributes.

4. Applications

In today's world, biometrics have become a very important part of every individual's life. Biometrics has a lot of applications. Since we are living in a digital era, most of the data is present on either computers or digital platforms. So, to protect important and sensitive data, biometrics are used.

For real-time user authentication, various biometric techniques like keystroke dynamics, mouse dynamics, and face recognition are used. Nowadays also mobile devices use fingerprint and facial recognition for user verification.

One of the latest applications of biometrics is in medical field. Various biometric features and data can be used in the detection of different diseases. One such example is the detection of Parkinson's disease. Parkinson's is a neural disease that slowly affects the patient's nervous system and body parts that are controlled by nerves. Parkinson's disease initially affects the hands and legs movement and also changes the voice, which makes it easier for Biometrics like keystroke dynamics, voice recognition, and Gait to detect Parkinson's disease. Additionally, the severity of Parkinson's disease may be evaluated using these biometrics. Also, keystrokes can be used to constantly monitor the condition of patients suffering from Parkinson's disease.

5. Proposed Work

Using keystroke dynamics, we are going to devise an algorithm using a keystroke dataset and detect if the user has Parkinson's disease and how severe it is if the patient is suffering from Parkinson's.

6. Conclusion

Computers have become an indispensable aspect of everyday life. Since we are so much dependent on computers to process and store sensitive and personal data, it is more critical and important to develop a method or technique to protect data from intrusions like identity theft. One such method developed and used worldwide is the biometric system. Biometrics are distinct traits of different individuals on the basis of which they can be identified. Biometrics are of two different types, namely behavioural biometric and physiological biometrics. Biometrics that rely on traits such as typing behaviour and the way a person walks are called behavioural biometrics and those that rely on the physical traits such as the face, eyes, and voice are known as physiological biometrics.

Nowadays, biometrics are widely used as a method for user authentication, which can be done using various biometric traits. To increase the accuracy of an authentication system, multiple recognition methods can be used together so that it is difficult for intruders and safer for the user. Also, biometrics can be used in the medical field. Biometrics can be used in the detection of various diseases. One of them is Parkinson's disease. Various biometric methods, such as keystroke dynamics, voice recognition, and Gait, can be used on the basis on different criteria to detect Parkinson's disease.

REFERENCES

1. Abhilash Kumar Sharma, Ashish Raghuwanshi, Vijay Kumar Sharma (2015) - Biometric System—A Review - Abhilash Sharma et al, /(IJCSIT) International Journal of Computer Science and Information Technologies, Vol. 6 (5), 4616–4619
2. Anil K. Jain, Arun Ross, and Sharath Pankanti (2005), "Biometrics: A Tool for Information Security", IEEE Transactions on Information Forensics and Security, vol. 1, no. 2, pp 21–38, June
3. Quang Nhat Tran, Benjamin P. Turnbull, And Jiankun Hu (2021) - Biometrics and Privacy-Preservation: How Do They Evolve? – IEEE Open Journal of the Computer Society - Received 25 February 2021; accepted 18 March 2021. Date of publication 23 March 2021; date of current version 12 April 2021. The review of this paper was arranged by Associate Editor P. Li.
4. Pooja Bansal (2018) - A Review On Scope Of Biometrics And Its Application - Ugc Approved Journal © Universal Research Reports | Refereed | Peer Reviewed ISSN : 2348–5612 | Volume : 05 , Issue : 05 | May 2018
5. Mohammad Al Rousan and Benedetto Intrigila (2020) - A Comparative Analysis of Biometrics Types: Literature Review – Journal of Computer Science – 24-12-2020
6. E. A. Soelistio, R. E. Hananto Kusumo, Z. V. Martan and E. Irwansyah (2021), "A Review of Signature Recognition Using Machine Learning," 2021 1st International Conference on Computer Science and Artificial Intelligence (ICCSAI), pp. 219-223, doi: 10.1109/ICCSAI53272.2021.9609732.
7. Impedovo D., Pirlo G. (2008) Automatic Signature Verification: The State of the Art. IEEE Transactions on Systems, Man, and Cybernetics, Part C (Applications and Reviews) [Internet]. Institute of Electrical and Electronics Engineers (IEEE);38(5):609–35. Available from: http://dx.doi.org/10.1109/tsmcc.2008.923866
8. A. B. Jagtap, R. S. Hegadi, and K. C. Santosh (2019), "Feature learning for offline handwritten signature verification using convolutional neural network," in Int. J. Technol. Hum. Interact., vol. 15, no. 4, pp. 54–62, doi:10.4018/IJTHI.2019100105.
9. L. G. Hafemann, R. Sabourin, and L. S. Oliveira (2017), "Learning features for offline handwritten signature verification using deep convolutional neural networks," in Pattern Recognit., vol. 70, pp. 163–176, doi: 10.1016/j.patcog.2017.05.012.
10. Gursimarpreet Kaur and Chander Kant Varma (2014), "Comparative Analysis of Biometric Modalities", International Journal of Advanced Research in Computer Science and Software Engineering, vol. 4, no. 4, pp. 603-613.
11. Princy Ann Thomas · K. Preetha Mathew, "A broad review on non-intrusive active user authentication in biometrics", Journal of Ambient Intelligence and Humanized Computing https://doi.org/10.1007/s12652-021-03301-x
12. S. Harakannanavar, Sunil & C. R., Prashanth & K. B., Raja. (2019). Comprehensive Study of Biometric Authentication Systems, Challenges and Future Trends. International Journal of Advanced Networking and Applications. 10. 3958-3968. 10.35444/IJANA.2019.10048.
13. Fabian Monrose and Aviel D. Rubin. (Feb. 2000), "Keystroke dynamics as a biometric for authentication". In: Future Generation Computer Systems 16.4 pp. 351–359. ISSN: 0167-739X.
14. R. V. Yampolskiy and V. Govindaraju (2008). Behavioural biometrics: a survey and classification. International Journal of Biometrics, 1(1): 81–113.
15. G1 Prof. Jaychand Upadhyay, Rohan Paranjpe, Hiralal Puorhit, Rohan Joshi (2020), Biometric Identification Using GAIT Analysis By Deep Learning, International Research Journal of Engineering and Technology (IRJET), Volume: 07, Issue: 02, Feb 2020
16. Prakash, C., Kumar, R. & Mittal (2018), N. Recent developments in human gait research: parameters, approaches, applications, machine learning techniques, datasets and challenges. Artif Intell Rev 49, 1–40 (2018). https://doi.org/10.1007/s10462-016-9514-6

17. Kratky, P., Chuda, D. (2018): 'Recognition of web users with the aid of biometric user model', J. Intell. Inf. Syst., 4, pp. 1–26.
18. Margit Antal, Elöd Egyed-Zsigmond (2019): Intrusion detection using mouse dynamics, IET Biom., Vol. 8 Iss. 5, pp. 285–294.
19. Patel, A. N., Howard, M. D., Roach, S. M., Jones, A. P., Bryant, N. B., Robinson, C. S., ... & Pilly, P. K. (2018). Mental state assessment and validation using personalized physiological biometrics. Frontiers in human neuroscience, 12, 221.
20. Dharavath, K.; Talukdar, F.A.; Laskar, R.H. (2013), "Study on biometric authentication systems, challenges and future trends: A review," in Computational Intelligence and Computing Research (ICCIC).
21. IEEE International Conference on, vol., no., pp. 1–7, 26–28 Dec. 2013
22. Maheen Zulfiqar, Fatima Syed, Muhammad Jaleed Khan, Khurram Khurshid (2019), "Deep Face Recognition for Biometric Authentication", Proc. of the 1st International Conference on Electrical, Communication and Computer Engineering (ICECCE) 24–25 July 2019, Swat, Pakistan, 978-1-7281-3825-1/19/$31.00 ©2019 IEEE
23. Maheswari, S. U., and Chandra, E. (2012): 'A review study on fingerprint classification algorithm used for fingerprint identification and recognition', IJCST, 3, (1), pp. 739–745
24. Faundez-Zanuy, M. (2006), "Biometric security technology," in Aerospace and Electronic Systems Magazine, IEEE, vol.21, no.6, pp. 15–26, June 2006
26. Madhusudhan, M. V., Basavaraju, R., & Hegde, C. (2019). Secured Human Authentication Using Finger-Vein Patterns. In Data Management, Analytics and Innovation (pp. 311–320). Springer, Singapore.
27. E. C. Lee and K. R. Park (2011), Image restoration of skin scattering and optical blurring for nger vein recognition, Optics and Lasers in Engineering, vol. 49, no. 7, pp. 816828.
28. Youbi Z, Boubchir L, Boukrouche A (2018) Human ear recognition based on local multi-scale LBP features with city-block distance. Multimedia Tools and Applications, 1–17
29. Kamboj, A., Rani, R. & Nigam, A. (2022) A comprehensive survey and deep learning-based approach for human recognition using ear biometric.VisComput38,2383–2416 https://doi.org/10.1007/s00371-021-02119-0
30. Khokher, R., Singh, R. C. (2021), Footprint Identification: Review of an Emerging Biometric Trait. Macromol. Symp., 397, 2000246. https://doi.org/10.1002/masy.202000246

Computer Science Engineering and Emerging Technologies (ICCS-2022) – Prof (Dr.) Rajeev Sobti et al. (eds)
© 2024 Taylor & Francis Group, London, ISBN 978-1-032-52199-2

Chapter **4**

Alzeimer's Detection Using Deep Learning: A Review

Suseel Kumar Gedela[1]
Student, School of Computer Science Engineering, Lovely Professional University, Phagwara, Punjab

Komal Arora[2]
Assistant Professor, School of Computer Science Engineering, Lovely Professional University, Phagwara, Punjab

Abstract: In the human brain, to know the changes in the functioning or the shape of internal parts, we need the help of magnetic resonance imaging (MRI) or positron emission tomography (PET) scans (images), as we cannot see them from outside. These images are very helpful to see the change from a regular functioning brain. Information regarding the unusual cell development in the brain is observable from MRI pictures. Support Vector Machine (SVM), Convolutional Neural Network (CNN), K-Nearest Neighbour (KNN), Naive Bayes, and Decision Tree are the five conventional classifiers we used in the conventional classifier section. For feature extraction, shape-based features are deployed. Finally, this article depicts the patient's current AD condition and uses machine learning and visual processing to determine if AD is present or not.

Keywords: CNN, Decision tree, Feature extraction, Hippocampus, KNN, Magnetic resonance imaging, Naïve Bayes, Positron emission tomography, Segmentation, SVM

1. Introduction

The brain is the most crucial part of the human body; it is the place where humans store memory, think, and are intellectual. So, it is very important to lead a good life. The brain is a complex organ that consists of a large number of nerves that are responsible for the functioning of other organs. A degenerative neurological state in the brain is called Alzheimer's disease (AD), which results in damage to brain cells and brain shrinkage. The most prevalent form of dementia, Alzheimer's disease, results in a steady loss in a person's cognitive, behavioural, and social abilities, which impairs their capacity for independent living. Early and precise AD diagnosis is crucial for the patient's care and upcoming treatment planning. The patient's hippocampus section of the brain shrinks and wrinkles, affecting thinking, memory, and reasoning [1]. This disease is thought to start progressing ten years or more prior to the onset of clinical symptoms. In order to give the essential therapies and stop the course of AD for a while, it is crucial to identify it in its early stages in patients.

There are two types of this disease. Early on-set and late on-set AD Early-onset AD occurs when the person is less than 65 years old, usually 40–50 years. It is very rare (5 out of 100). There are two types of onsets. The early-onset type also seems to be linked to a flaw in chromosome 14, a particular region of the person's DNA. Myoclonus, a kind of muscular spasm and twitching, is also frequent in those with early-onset Alzheimer's. Late onset AD is common and observed above 65 years. The precise genetic cause has not yet been found. However, scientists have identified a number of risk factors, and further study is continuing. Familial Alzheimer's disease is another subtype of AD. This is uncommon (1 out of 100 cases). Only when the precise genotypic pattern of the illness is described by family members and the exact risk can be anticipated can a person be diagnosed with FAD. Mild cognitive impairment is the intermediate stage between cognitive normal and AD [2].

---

[1]suseelkumargedela@gmail.com, [2]komal.17783@lpu.co.in

DOI: 10.1201/9781003405580-4

Alzheimer's disease and related dementia research organisations concentrated on identifying biomarkers for the condition from the early 2000s through 2010. The efficiency of many biomarkers for spotting early-stage Alzheimer's disease is being tested, including phosphorylated tau (ptau), beta amyloid plaque deposition, tau, fluorodeoxyglucose positron emission tomography (FDG-PET) absorption in PET, and hippocampus volume loss [9].

2. Related Work

Alzheimer's disease is thought to start progressing ten years or more prior to the onset of clinical symptoms. In order to give the essential therapies and stop the course of AD for a while, it is crucial to identify Alzheimer's disease in its initial phase in patients. The most precise categorization of AD is achieved with machine learning techniques. Support vector machine (SVM) presented a model using ranking based on feature algorithms to categorise the illness as AD and healthy controls, and it is the most common of these approaches (HC). SVM is beneficial for creating high-dimensional, predictive, and informative feature extraction models from MRI data. However, this necessitates manually building aspects of brain regions, which is time-consuming and arduous and necessitates the counsel of professionals.

Deep learning algorithms are a different class of machine learning techniques. Without human assistance, deep learning algorithms carry out autonomous feature extraction. Deep learning algorithms learn the high-level visualisation using unprocessed data since there are many hidden layers available. So, in the field of computer vision, it is prominent. [1]

Numerous deep learning architectures for early AD diagnosis were addressed by Ortiz et al. The human visual brain served as inspiration for convolutional neural networks (CNNs), which use a dense hierarchical structure to learn characteristics from simple edges to more complicated edges. It serves as the foundation for convolution and pooling layers. By combining the input picture with the kernel in a convolutional layer, feature maps are produced. The pooling layer then downsampled the image while maintaining common characteristics.

H. Fuse [10] used a support vector machine to do classification, utilising a mixture of several descriptors as features. The categorization accuracy of 87.5% found in the data was higher than the accuracy attained with the volume ratio to intracranial volume (81.5%), which is frequently employed for traditional evaluation of morphological alterations. This research indicates that, in comparison to the traditional volume ratio, shape details are more helpful in treatment.

R. Cui. [3] measured the longitudinal progression to address the sequential interpretation of an MRI scan along a time axis. A recurrent neural network (RNN) is used to train the spatial properties of the multi-layer perceptron (MLP). As a pre-processing task, this approach does need rigorous segmentation. The 2-way classification accuracy for AD and NC is 89.69%.

For four classes, Islam et al. presented a diffusion-convolution neural network (DCNN) model, where the proposed system contains five models that are trained and the output is combined to predict illness. This method is distinctive in that each model provides distinct traits that set it apart from the others, allowing it to be extended for the prediction of unknown data with an accuracy of 93.18%. Similar to this, S. S. Kundaram's [12] used the same model, DCNN, along with some inbuilt libraries like Keras, tensor-flow on GPU, and spyder software from the Anaconda package on the ADNI dataset. This method mainly focuses on identifying Alzheimer's disease (AD), moderate cognitive impairment (MCI), and normal control (NC) and achieved an accuracy of 98.57%. MRI scan images of NC, MCI, and AD can be seen in Fig. 4.1.

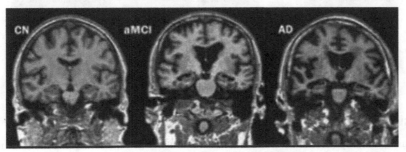

Fig. 4.1 MRI scan of NC, MCI and AD [3]

Cascaded CNNs were recommended in 2018 by Liu et al. due to their capacity to gradually identify various levels and features of MRI and PET scans. The proposed method did not need any extra segmentation for pre-processing, so the characteristics were extracted directly from ADNI data containing MCI, NC, and AD patients and fitted to the model. Through this model, the accuracy achieved was 93.26 percent.

A convolutional neural network (CNN) model and a deep neural network (DNN) model are combined in the approach presented by A. Basher [11]. A two-stage ensemble, Hough-CNN, has been used to automatically locate the left and right hippocampi. The 3-D patches and 2-D slices are then divided using axial, sagittal, and coronal perspectives. The derived volumetric characteristics assigned to the left and right hippocampi and the suggested technique obtained average weighted classification accuracies of 94.82% and 94.02%, respectively. It also attained area under the curve (AUC) values for the left and right hippocampi of 92.54% and 90.62%, respectively.

Convolutional neural networks (CNNs) without supervision are initially used by X. Bi [8] for feature extraction, and an unsupervised predictor is used to achieve the final diagnosis. Three orthogonal panels (TOP) of an MRI image and one slice of an MRI image are used, respectively, as input to the model in the suggested technique. The approach with one slice data gives the best prediction output for AD vs. MCI (accuracy is 95.52%) and MCI vs. NC (accuracy is 90.63%), and the proposed approach with TOP data gives the overall best prediction outputs for AD vs. MCI (accuracy is 97.01%) and MCI vs. NC (accuracy is 92.6%).

3. Methodology

Input data: Input data, or image acquisition, is the first step; it is collecting the images to train the machine. We can get the images from hospitals or from online websites.

Pre-processing: The pictures that are obtained from the devices are included in Digital Imaging and Communications in Medicine (DICOM), and these must be properly formatted (JPG, PNG, TIFF, etc.) after capture in order to be used for additional processing.

Segmentation: All Alzheimer's Disease data positions should match in order to compare photos between persons. Therefore, picture registration is carried out by converting each unique brain to the universal template of the brain. Grey matter and white matter are combined to create a unique brain extract during picture segmentation. Then, using re-slicing to adjust for position, we provide pictures for analysis.

Feature Extraction: This is a crucial stage in computer vision and the finest image solutions. Shape, picture location, composition, and size are taken into consideration while changing the specified parameters. The feature of the input image is changed at this stage.

Classification: Image classification is the process of identifying what an image depicts. An approach for classifying photos is taught to identify various image classes. After segmenting a hazy area, a selection scheme and feature extraction are used to extract the necessary data from the area, and a classification approach is then applied to arrive at the initial results based on the features that are available. We train modal to classify the images by using pre-existing images using CNN.

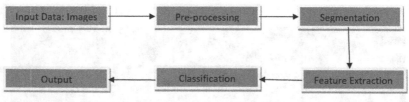

Fig. 4.2 Workflow of Model [5]

4. Conclusion

This article discusses the many studies that have been conducted on utilising deep learning to identify Alzheimer's disease. It can be observed that the hybrid models outperformed the conventional approaches and that taking the loss function into account may be quite helpful in lowering the error. The use of image processing can be quite helpful in detecting illnesses at an early stage. CNN is mainly used in various studies. They have used different data, i.e., MRI and PET images, for the identification of AD. This work offers a thorough analysis of several algorithms and novel combinations of techniques that were employed by numerous studies in this field utilising MRI images to develop the capacity to identify AD in the brain.

REFERENCES

1. H. A. Helaly, M. Badawy, and A. Y. Haikal, "Toward deep MRI segmentation for Alzheimer's disease detection," *Neural Comput Appl*, vol. 34, no. 2, pp. 1047–1063, Jan. 2022, doi: 10.1007/s00521-021-06430-8.
2. S. El-Sappagh, H. Saleh, F. Ali, E. Amer, and T. Abuhmed, "Two-stage deep learning model for Alzheimer's disease detection and prediction of the mild cognitive impairment time," *Neural Comput Appl*, vol. 34, no. 17, pp. 14487–14509, Sep. 2022, doi: 10.1007/s00521-022-07263-9.
3. R. Cui, M. Liu, and G. Li, "Longitudinal analysis for Alzheimer's disease diagnosis using RNN," in *Proceedings - International Symposium on Biomedical Imaging*, May 2018, vol. 2018-April, pp. 1398–1401. doi: 10.1109/ISBI.2018.8363833.
4. J. Venugopalan, L. Tong, H. R. Hassanzadeh, and M. D. Wang, "Multimodal deep learning models for early detection of Alzheimer's disease stage," *Sci Rep*, vol. 11, no. 1, Dec. 2021, doi: 10.1038/s41598-020-74399-w.
5. J. Islam and Y. Zhang, "Brain MRI analysis for Alzheimer's disease diagnosis using an ensemble system of deep convolutional neural networks," *Brain Inform*, vol. 5, no. 2, Dec. 2018, doi: 10.1186/s40708-018-0080-3.
6. M. Neethu and J. Roopa Jayasingh, "Effectiveness of AI techniques for the classification of Alzheimer's disease—A review," in *International Conference on Signal Processing and Communication*, May 2021, pp. 309–311. doi: 10.1109/ICSPC51351.2021.9451778.
7. A. Puente-Castro, E. Fernandez-Blanco, A. Pazos, and C. R. Munteanu, "Automatic assessment of Alzheimer's disease diagnosis based on deep learning techniques," *Comput Biol Med*, vol. 120, May 2020, doi: 10.1016/j.compbiomed.2020.103764.
8. X. Bi, S. Li, B. Xiao, Y. Li, G. Wang, and X. Ma, "Computer aided Alzheimer's disease diagnosis by an unsupervised deep learning technology," *Neurocomputing*, vol. 392, pp. 296–304, Jun. 2020, doi: 10.1016/j.neucom.2018.11.111.
9. X. Gao, F. Shi, D. Shen, M. Liu, and T. Alzheimer's Disease, "Task-Induced Pyramid and Attention GAN for Multimodal Brain Image Imputation and Classification in Alzheimer's Disease," *IEEE J Biomed Health Inform*, vol. 26, no. 1, 2022, doi: 10.1109/JBHI.2020.3097721.
10. H. Fuse, K. Oishi, N. Maikusa, and T. Fukami, "Detection of Alzheimer's Disease with Shape Analysis of MRI Images," 2018. [Online]. Available: https://humandbs.biosciencedbc.jp/en/hum0043-j-adni-authors.
11. A. Basher, B. C. Kim, K. H. Lee, and H. Y. Jung, "Volumetric Feature-Based Alzheimer's Disease Diagnosis from sMRI Data Using a Convolutional Neural Network and a Deep Neural Network," *IEEE Access*, vol. 9, pp. 29870–29882, 2021, doi: 10.1109/ACCESS.2021.3059658.
12. S. S. Kundaram and K. C. Pathak, "Deep Learning-Based Alzheimer Disease Detection," in *Lecture Notes in Electrical Engineering*, 2021, vol. 673, pp. 587–597. doi: 10.1007/978-981-15-5546-6_50.
13. S. Kim, S. Noh, and H. S. Ryoo, "Identifying Combinatorial Significance for Classification of Alzheimer's Disease Proteomics Expression with Logical Analysis of Data," in *IEEE International Conference on Bioinformatics and Biomedicine*, 2021, pp. 1661–1663. doi: 10.1109/BIBM52615.2021.9669835.
14. S. Al-Shoukry, T. H. Rassem, and N. M. Makbol, "Alzheimer's diseases detection by using deep learning algorithms: A mini-review," *IEEE Access*, vol. 8, pp. 77131–77141, 2020, doi: 10.1109/ACCESS.2020.2989396.

Chapter

5

Survey on Heart Diseases Prediction Using Machine Learning Algorithms

Saurav Kumar[1], Sudhanshu Prakash Tiwari[2]
School of Computer Science and Engineering,
Lovely Professional University, Punjab, India

Abstract: In today's world, people are letting themselves become preoccupied with the activities of their everyday lives, such as their jobs and other responsibilities, to the detriment of their health. There are many diseases that are caused by an unhealthy lifestyle, but cardiac disease is considered one of the most prominent and serious causes of death not just in India but all around the world. The number of patients with cardiovascular diseases is growing in India every year, and currently India has more than 30 million heart disease patients. The diagnosis of cardiovascular disease is both the medical field's most challenging and most crucial endeavour. The diagnosis of cardiovascular disease involves many risk factors and requires sensible approaches to make an early diagnosis. There are various approaches and procedures that require ideal information collection. Using recent datasets, different algorithms of machine learning can be applied to predict and diagnose whether a patient is affected or influenced by cardiovascular disease or not. This review highlights various machine learning techniques and algorithms like logistic regression, K-NN, A-NN, SVM, NB, and DT, all of which have been utilised for the prediction and diagnosis of cardiovascular (heart) disease.

Keywords: Heart disease, Machine learning, KNN, ANN, SVM

1. Introduction

Over the course of the last ten years, cardiovascular disease has become the primary cause of mortality around the globe. The World Health Organisation (WHO) has estimated that every year more than 17.9 million deaths occur because of heart disease (cardiovascular disease) [1]. On a global scale, heart-related disorders are a prominent cause of death, accounting for nearly 31% of all deaths. For the last 15 years, heart-related disorders have been the leading and most prominent cause of death [2]. The heart plays the most important and crucial role in the body's circulatory system. There are several different types of cardiovascular diseases.

1.1 Coronary Heart Diseases

Plaque is a waxy substance that forms inside coronary arteries as a result of coronary heart disease (CHD). The oxygen-rich blood that travels to the heart comes from arteries. Atherosclerosis is the medical term for the development of plaque in the arteries. The newly developed plaque has the potential to either harden or burst. Plaque that hardens over time might eventually cause narrowing of the arteries, which in turn limits the amount of oxygen-rich blood that can reach the heart. If the plaque bursts, the creation of a blood clot may occur. The blood flow via a coronary artery can almost always be fully obstructed when there is a significant blood clot present. And if the blocked blood flow is not rapidly restored, the coronary muscles begin to die, which can lead to a heart attack [3].

[1]sauravkr894@gmail.com, [2]sudhanshu.15813@lpu.co.in

DOI: 10.1201/9781003405580-5

1.2 Cardiomyopathy

In this, the structure of the muscles changes or the muscles of the heart get disabled, causing a change in the heart rate of pumping, usually a decrease in pumping rate. And ultimately, this can result in the heart failing [2]. As heart disease is the most serious disease, knowing how to spot the warning signs of it is essential. Most patients die because of the lack of accuracy of the instruments. So, computer technology and methods of machine learning are being employed to assist and become a system in support of the early detection and prognosis of cardiac disease. The early discovery of sickness might save many lives, and mortality can be decreased. Machine learning is an efficient technology for testing procedures [4]. ML (machine learning) is one of the subfields of AI (artificial intelligence) [5]. The term machine learning refers to a method for the manipulation of data as well as the extraction of hidden information that could be beneficial [6]. The area of data mining known as machine learning is able to handle enormous datasets that are appropriately prepared in an effective manner [7].

2. Literature Review

Table 5.1   Literature review [9, 1, 8, 4, 11, 6, 15, 16]

Source	Year	Author	Purpose	Dataset	Techniques	Accuracy
9	2015	T. Santhanamand, and E. P. E	Prediction of cardiovascular disorder utilizing a hybrid genetic fuzzy model	UCI ML repository	Hybrid genetic fuzzy model, fuzzy entropy-based method (NNTS), GAFL system	Method based on fuzzy entropy (NNTS) – 84.46%, proposed method (GAFL System) – 86%
1	2020	D. Shah, S. Patel, and S. Kumar. Bharti	Different ML techniques for the prognosis of heart disorder	Cleveland database of UCI repository	KNN (K-nearest neighbor), NB (Naïve Bayes), DT and RF	KNN – 83.16%, Naïve Bayes – 83.49%, Decision tree – 71.43%, random forest – 91.6%
8	2018	Aditi. G, I. Pandya, G. Kokkula, and Dr. K. Devadkar	ML algorithms for the prognosis of cardiovascular (heart) diseases	Cleveland dataset from UCI library	Multi-layer perceptron algorithm (a NN algorithm)	91%
4	2020	Archana. Singh, Rakesh K	Heart disorder prognosis using different ML algorithms	UCI repository datasets	SVM, DT, LR, KNN	Support vector machine – 83%, Decision tree – 79%, Linear regression – 78%, KNN – 87%
11	2017	Vidya K Sudarshan, U R. Acharyaa Oh S. L, M. Adam, T. J. Hongl, C. K. Chual, C. Kok Poo1 and T. Ru S.	Automated Diagnosis system of congestive heart failure/heart disorder	MIT-BIH NSR, Fantasia, and BIDMC CHF	Used dual tree complex wavelet transform	99.86%
6	2021	H. Jindal, S. Agrawal, R. Khera, R. Jain and P Nagrath	Cardiovascular disorder prognosis using machine learning algorithms	UCI repository	LR, RF classifier and KNN	87.5%
15	2019	Mr. S. Krishnan. J, Dr. Geetha.S	Algorithms of ML for cardiovascular disorder prognosis	UCI ML repository	Decision tree, Naïve Bayes	DT – 91%, NB – 87%
16	2021	Dr. M. K., G. Gnaneswar, Y. R. Sail R. D., and R. S. Suraj	Prediction of cardiovascular disorder utilizing a hybrid machine learning model	Cleveland dataset	DT, RF, hybrid (DT + RF)	DT – 79%, RF – 81%, Hybrid (DT + RF – 88%)

3. ML (Machine Learning)

The field of artificial intelligence includes a subfield known as ML (machine learning) [1]. The field of ML is vast and diverse, and its scope is increasing day by day. Machine learning can be defined as the ability of a machine to independently gain knowledge by extracting various patterns from data sets. [14] The determination of heart disease is profoundly dependable with ML. The foundation of ML in the field of medicine has seen relatively slow progress thus far. The prime focus of machine learning in heart prediction is to design the system; after that, it is allowed to learn and generate predictions based on its experiences [1]. Using a training dataset, the machine learning algorithms are trained so that they may be used to develop a model. The following three are the primary classifications of machine learning algorithms: Supervised, unsupervised, and reinforced.

4. Algorithms

4.1 (KNN) k-Nearest Neighbor

KNN is a form of ML that requires supervision [1]. In 1951, Hodges and colleagues presented the KNN rule to the scientific community as a nonparametric method for the classification of patterns [18]. The K-Nearest Neighbour approach is an excellent technique for classification. KNN is used for the task of classification when there is no previous information available about the distribution of the data. This is because KNN doesn't make assumptions regarding the data. KNN is an ML technique that is event-based and doesn't frame the entire theoretical model before beginning the training examples [11].

4.2 SVM (Support Vector Machines)

V. Vapnik is credited as being the one who originally introduced the SVM in his work on statistical learning [10]. It is the possession of a pre-defined target variable that is capable of serving both as a classifier and as a predictor [14]. It is based on the hyper-plane concept, and during the classification process, it locates the hyper-plane in the feature space that distinguishes between the different classes [12, 4]. In order to reduce the likelihood of an incorrect classification being made, SVM works to increase the space between the hyperplane and the two points of data belonging to each class that are physically closest to it [3]. The kind of support vector that is used is determined by the number of hyperplanes [4].

4.3 LR (Logistic Regression)

The algorithm of supervised machine learning known as logistic regression can be used to analyse data. It is possible to apply it in the process of problem classification and regression [2]. This methodology is predicated on the connection that exists between the two independent variables that are being considered [4]. The binary classification issues are where this logistic regression approach sees the majority of its application [7]. In this algorithm, instead of fitting the straight line or the hyperplane, the input values are linearly combined together by using a logistic or sigmoidal function and the coefficient values to make predictions for the outcome of the dataset and squeeze the output between 0 and 1 of the linear equation [2, 7]. It is a simple model to implement, and it is able to provide a reasonable expectation.

4.4 ANN (Artificial NN)

supervised form of ML, which is known as an artificial neural network and is a subset of neural networks. [2] A mathematical model is used to integrate the neurons that are responsible for passing on the message [10]. The functioning of ANN algorithms is often compared to that of the human brain. Similar to how human neuron cells are able to take in information and then respond to it, ANN is able to learn from data, classify it, and then use that information to predict the outcome [2]. ANN possesses components like input, output, transfer functions, and hidden layers. These components can be broken down further. The output consists of a number of nodes, each of which is analogous to a neuron found in the human brain. The hidden may be a solitary entity or a group. Multi-Layer Perception, sometimes known as MLP, is an artificial neural network (ANN) that has numerous hidden layers and uses backpropagation. ANN yields significantly more accurate results when used for prediction [10, 2].

4.5 NB (Naïve Bayes' Classifier)

Naïve Bayes' classifier is actually a type of supervised classification ML algorithm. This technique is utilised for categorization of the datasets, and it is based upon the law of Bayes; this is the reason why Bayes is in the name of the technique. This technique assumes strong independence among the features or attributes, which is why it is called "naive." It is one of the simplest and most effective algorithms that is used for making models of machine learning at a faster rate, which is useful in making quick and effective predictions. This model classifies the data on the basis of probability; it is basically a probabilistic classifier. The Bayes Theorem (BT) is mathematically represented as follows:

$$P[R/Q] = P[Q/R] \, P[R]/P[Q]$$

P[R] = Independent Probability of R [Priori of R], P[Q] = Independent probability of Q, P [Q/R] = Conditional Probability of Q given R. This model is an effective and efficient technique that is used for classification; it is able to deal with complex, dependent, large, and non-linear data sets. The term "naive" refers to both the first part of the term and the second component, which is "Bayes." Naive denotes that the occurrence of one feature is not dependent on the occurrence of any other feature [1, 7, 15].

4.6 RF (Random Forest)

The classification process also makes use of Random Forest, which is another supervised algorithm technique that has gained a lot of popularity recently. This technique can actually be used for classification as well as for regression tasks, but it accomplishes in a better way in the case of classification. This technique uses many different decision trees before coming up with an output. It takes the mean in order to solve and increase the accuracy of prediction of the dataset that has been provided; rather than relying wholly and entirely on a single decision tree, it actually takes into consideration each and every tree and, based upon the votes that are in majority, gives its final output. The accuracy of this RF algorithm is dependent upon the number of trees; if the number of trees is higher, there will be high accuracy, which will actually prevent the overfitting problem [15, 7, 1].

4.7 DT (Decision Tree)

The process of classification can be accomplished with the help of an algorithm called a DT. It can be used for numerical data as well as categorical data; it is basically used for making structures that are tree-like. This is a simple technique that is famously and commonly used to handle the case of medical data, as it is easy to implement and analyse data in graphs that are in the shape of trees. The analysis in the decision tree model is based upon three nodes: the root node, the interior node, and the leaf node. This technique first divides the data into two or more sets that are comparable in certain respects, and this is done on the basis of the level of importance. Following this step, the entropy of each individual attribute is calculated, and then the data is further segmented using predictors that either have a high quantity of information or have an entropy that is either minimal or close to it [2,7,10].

5. Conclusion and Future Work

Diseases of the heart pose a significant risk to one's life and are among the top causes of mortality on a global scale. Therefore, the early detection of cardiovascular disease can save a significant number of lives. If it were possible to accurately predict the risk or possibility of developing heart disease, it might have a significant impact on the overall death rate of humans. In addition, the computer-assisted heart disease prognosis system can be a useful tool for the doctor in the process of diagnosing and determining the prognosis for heart disease. There are a variety of methods for diagnosis that can be utilised in the field of medicine; however, the computer-assisted ML strategy provides the prognosis result with a higher level of precision. The primary objective of this survey was to conduct a thorough analysis of the effectiveness of the ML algorithm for the diagnosis of cardiovascular disorders (heart disease). Each ML method performed much better in some of the scenarios and significantly worse in other scenarios, depending on the scenario. According to the findings of the literature review, it is generally accepted that the development of a prognostic (predictive) model for the purpose of finding the likelihood of developing a heart disorder has only met with limited success. Deep learning algorithms are not only playing a significant role in the healthcare industry, but they are also being employed in a wide variety of other fields for the purpose of achieving superior results. Deep learning is just one of several ML algorithms that can be used to predict cardiac disease. In the future, we may also use other ML algorithms in addition to deep learning. In addition, a new algorithm could be implemented to achieve a result that is both more accurate and dependable.

REFERENCES

1. D. Shah, S. Patel, and S. K. Bharti, "Heart Disease Prediction using Machine Learning Techniques," *SN COMPUT. SCI.*, vol. 1, no. 6, p. 345, Nov. 2020, doi: 10.1007/s42979-020-00365-y.
2. R. Katarya and S. K. Meena, "Machine Learning Techniques for Heart Disease Prediction: A Comparative Study and Analysis," *Health Technol.*, vol. 11, no. 1, pp. 87–97, Jan. 2021, doi: 10.1007/s12553-020-00505-7.
3. A. Hazra, S. K. Mandal, A. Gupta, A. Mukherjee, and A. Mukherjee, "Heart Disease Diagnosis and Prediction Using Machine Learning and Data Mining Techniques: A Review," p. 24.
4. A. Singh, R. Kumar, "Heart Disease Prediction Using Machine Learning Algorithms," presented at the 2020 International Conference on Electrical and Electronics Engineering (ICE3), Gorakhpur, India, 2020.
5. V. Sharma, S. Yadav, and M. Gupta, "Heart Disease Prediction using Machine Learning Techniques," in *2020 2nd International Conference on Advances in Computing, Communication Control and Networking (ICACCCN)*, Greater Noida, India, Dec. 2020, pp. 177–181. doi: 10.1109/ICACCCN51052.2020.9362842.
6. H. Jindal, S. Agrawal, R. Khera, R. Jain, and P. Nagrath, "Heart disease prediction using machine learning algorithms," *IOP Conf. Ser.: Mater. Sci. Eng.*, vol. 1022, no. 1, p. 012072, Jan. 2021, doi: 10.1088/1757-899X/1022/1/012072.
7. A. Rajdhan and A. Agarwal, "Heart Disease Prediction using Machine Learning," *International Journal of Engineering Research*, vol. 9, no. 04, p.5.
8. A. Gavhane, I. Pandya, G. Kokkula, and K. Devadkar, "Prediction of Heart Disease Using Machine Learning," *IEEE Conference Record*, p. 4, 2018.
9. T. Santhanam and E. P. Ephzibah, "Heart Disease Prediction Using Hybrid Genetic Fuzzy Model," *Indian Journal of Science and Technology*, vol. 8, no. 9, p. 797, May 2015, doi: 10.17485/ijst/2015/v8i9/52930.
10. A. U. Haq, J. P. Li, M. H. Memon, S. Nazir, and R. Sun, "A Hybrid Intelligent System Framework for the Prediction of Heart Disease Using Machine Learning Algorithms," *Mobile Information Systems*, vol. 2018, pp. 1–21, Dec. 2018, doi: 10.1155/2018/3860146.
11. V. K. Sudarshan *et al.*, "Automated diagnosis of congestive heart failure using dual tree complex wavelet transform and statistical features extracted from 2 s of ECG signals," *Computers in Biology and Medicine*, vol. 83, pp. 48–58, Apr. 2017, doi: 10.1016/j.compbiomed.2017.01.019.
12. P. Ghosh *et al.*, "Efficient Prediction of Cardiovascular Disease Using Machine Learning Algorithms With Relief and LASSO Feature Selection Techniques," *IEEE Access*, vol. 9, pp. 19304–19326, 2021, doi: 10.1109/ACCESS.2021.3053759.
13. R. Bharti, A. Khamparia, M. Shabaz, G. Dhiman, S. Pande, and P. Singh, "Prediction of Heart Disease Using a Combination of Machine Learning and Deep Learning," *Computational Intelligence and Neuroscience*, vol. 2021, pp. 1–11, Jul. 2021, doi: 10.1155/2021/8387680.
14. Y. Khourdifi, M. Bahaj, "Heart Disease Prediction and Classification Using Machine Learning Algorithms Optimized by Particle Swarm Optimization and Ant Colony Optimization," *IJIES*, vol. 12, no. 1, pp. 242–252, Feb. 2019, doi: 10.22266/ijies2019.0228.24.
15. Mr.S. Krishnan.J, Dr.Geetha.S "Prediction of Heart Disease Using Machine Learning Algorithms.," p. 5.
16. M. Kavitha, G. Gnaneswar, R. Dinesh, Y. R. Sai, and R. S. Suraj, "Heart Disease Prediction using Hybrid machine Learning Model," in *2021 6th International Conference on Inventive Computation Technologies (ICICT)*, Coimbatore, India, Jan. 2021, pp. 1329–1333. doi: 10.1109/ICICT50816.2021.9358597.

Computer Science Engineering and Emerging Technologies (ICCS-2022) – Prof (Dr.) Rajeev Sobti et al. (eds)
© 2024 Taylor & Francis Group, London, ISBN 978-1-032-52199-2

Chapter **6**

Detection of Brain Tumor Using Machine Learning: An Overview

Chittem Harika[1], Ashu Mehta[2]

School of Computer Science Engineering, Lovely Professional University, Phagwara, Punjab

Abstract: During several years, it is very difficult for doctors to determine whether brain cancer is present or not in the patient. A brain tumor is an abnormal growth of one million or more brain tissues. By using MRI brain scans to detect the normal model brain tumor. From MRI images, information about the abnormal cell growth in the brain is recognised. In the conventional classifier part, we used five conventional classifiers: SVM, CNN, KNN, Naïve Bayes, and Decision-Tree. Shape-based features are used for feature extraction. Finally, this paper represents the present status of a brain tumor patient and how to detect whether the tumor is present or not, by means of image processing and machine learning.

Keywords: CNN, Decision tree, Feature extraction, KNN, Magnetic resonance imaging, Naïve Bayes, Pre-processing, Segmentation, SVM

1. Introduction

The brain is the most intricate and significant organ in the human body and is composed of a significant amount of nerve tissue that is responsible for the functioning of other organs. The more rapid multiplication of cells than the actual rate and the cells that do not die even after their maximum lifecycle cause the tumor, and the tumor that is developed on the brain tissue is known as an intracranial tumor. The two main categories of methods of brain tumors are primary and metastatic.

It is necessary for primary brain tumors to be brain tissue-derived cancers. Glial or non-glial primary tumors are classified as benign or malignant. Metastatic brain tumors are referred to as cancers that begin elsewhere in the body and spread to the brain, generally through the circulation. These tumors spread throughout the body quickly, have a terrible prognosis, and have a rapid evolution. They could be made up of oligodendrocytes, astrocytes, and other types of cells. GBM is more prevalent in individuals between the ages of 50 and 75 and is more common in men than in women [1].

Magnetic Resonance Imaging [2] gives details on the size, shape, and area of human cells. The images acquired are clear and accurate. The most prevalent form of brain tumor is gliomas, which account for 77 percent of malignant brain tumors. The origin of the helping cells of the brain is known as glia. Tissues are bisected into astrocytes, ependymal cells, and oligodendroglial cells (or oligos) [3]. Magnetic Resonance Imaging can be used to detect the brain tumor with the help of an MRI brain image, but this method is time-consuming and exhausting in a large number of cases. [4]

In certain cases, machine learning is a precise tool for small datasets when the significant features are extracted for the training model. Texture features provide detail that represents the arrangement of colours [5].

---

*harikachittem2000@gmail.com, [2]ashu.23631@lpu.co.in

DOI: 10.1201/9781003405580-6

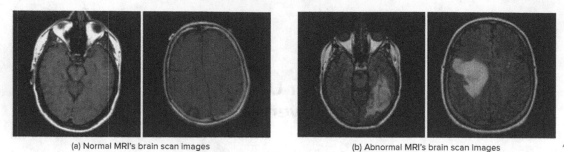

(a) Normal MRI's brain scan images   (b) Abnormal MRI's brain scan images

Fig. 6.1 Examples of brain scan images [1]

2. Related Work

One of the mass testing's as well as exacting tasks is to segment the region from an object, and segmenting the tumor from an MRI scan brain image is an aspiring one. Tonmoy Hussian proposed a method to transfer the brain tumor. 2D MRI was used to find higher accuracy than the existing method. It is used to help the patient catch the disease early. The fuzzy C-mean clustering algorithm was accompanied by the use of some classifiers to compare whether the accuracy was better or not. CNN achieved 97.87% accuracy. The dataset is brats2020 [6].

Sravanthi proposed a method that includes stages like converting an image into a grayscale image. To clean up the image's noise and other clogs, they use certain filters. The SVM, FCM, image segmentation procedure, and other filtering algorithms are among the findings. Furthermore, the SVM classifier's total accuracy is 97%. [7]

Hemanth suggests a method for detecting and segmenting affected brain tumor areas. G. Hemanth proposed modifying the parameters of an algorithm. In this project, they used some combination of algorithms: CNN, CRF, GA, and SVM. The technique is developed and applied in MATLAB by using image processing. Datasets are used from the UCI datasets. CNN achieved 91% accuracy [8].

Using CNN, DNN, RBF (radial basis function), and Decision Tree, these are the combinations of algorithms in this paper. For feature extraction, they used a first-order clustering algorithm. In the existing system, CNN (Soft Max) accuracy is 98.6%; in the proposed system, accuracy is 99.12%. [9]

The Brain Tumor Detection Model is proposed by Hein Tun Zaw and modifies MRI brain images as abnormal or normal. They suggested using a maximum entropy threshold with Naive Bayes categorization. This research makes use of the REMBRANDT database. The accuracy of the tumor detection rate on non-tumor brain imaging is 94%. This applies to all sites where a brain tumor may exist [1].

Chirodip Lodh Choudhary suggested work that involves the deep neural network and CNN-based model to classify the MRI brain image as to whether a tumor is present or not. MRI datasets are used. Findings are CNN (deep neural network). The 35-epoch CNN model produces results with a very small number of pre-processing stages. CNN's accuracy is 96.08%, while its f-score is 97.3%. [10]

Using CNN and 3D-CNN, these are the combinations of the algorithm. There is an application of the MRI brain tumor dataset. This research proposes the use of multimodal CNN in conjunction with 3-D MRI brain tumor detection. The three assessment indices used in this experiment—SN, SE, and a two-dimensional brain tumor detection network—are displayed in the results. The dataset is very small compared to other papers [2].

Mallem proposed a system to differentiate between the normal brain tumor patient and the abnormal brain tumor patient by using MRI brain images and also LGG and HGG tumors to classify the abnormal brain tumor. For clustering, K-means is used as the segmentation technique for principal component analysis, and discrete wavelet transforms are the feature reduction mechanisms for feature extraction. SVM is a main part of this suggested system. SVM classifiers HGG and LGG are used to reduce the features. [3]

Bhagyashri H. proposed two methods: image segmentation and image classification. To analyse the benefit of shape features in the classification of brain tumors and malignant tumors. When the shape is known, use some parameters to find the tumor or not. Shape plays a major role in brain tumor classification. By utilising shape feature classification and extraction with SVM and random forests. The accuracy of the random forest algorithm is 86.66%. In this paper, they utilise the MICCAI BraTS 2015 dataset. Findings include the random forest algorithm and SVM. In this paper, they used less classifiers. [11]

Ali Pashaei proposed two algorithms, and the results of each method are discussed. In the earliest method, they used CNN, which contained four convolution layers, four pooling layers, normalising data, and one fully connected layer. The accuracy of the model is 81.09% for this classification. An accuracy of 91.28% on the dataset [12].

Aaswad Sawant used TensorFlow to detect the brain tumor using MRI brain images. In TensorFlow, CNN is implemented with 5 layers. The accuracy of brain tumor detection was 98.6% in 35 epochs, indicating high accuracy and validation accuracy. The format of the dataset is dicom. By using the mango tool to obtain the equivalent PNG or JPG image [4],

Javeria Amin DWI, T2, T1, FLAIR, and T1c MRI are the suggested approaches. Pixel-based outcomes and feature-based findings from two studies were both assessed. A random forest classifier is classified into three subtumors regions, such as enhanced, enhancing tumor, and complete. The fivefold method and 0.5 holdout cross-validation are applied. It illustrates the effectiveness of the proposed strategy for a brain tumor [13].

Himaja Byale proposed various variations of neural networks that can be applied to detect brain tumors. Brain tumors grow accurately using tools. It helps the patient get good treatment in time because it detects the early stages. By using a neural network classifier, the accuracy is 93.33%. In this project, they used four-step segmentation using the Gaussian Mixture Model (GMM), an adaptive median filter, and a grey-level co-occurrence matrix using feature extraction. [14]

Heba Mohsen proposed efficient classifiers and methodologies that combine the deep NN and discrete wavelet transform to categorise the MRI brain. DNN classifiers have high accuracy compared to other classifiers. By using an MRI brain dataset to find high accuracy using neural network classifiers [15]

Lina Chato's proposed model of the noise in brain MRI images depends on the imaging system. It assumes the imaginary and real parts of the brain MRI image have a gaussian distribution uncorrelated with an equal variance and zero mean. Linear discriminant accuracy is high compared to support vector machines. [5]

B. Raj Pragathi proposed using image processing techniques with machine learning. By segmenting brain cancer using morphological operations and image pre-processing to extract tumor features like SVM classifiers and DWT. The RCB image is converted into a grayscale image, which helps identify the tumor in the MRI scan image. Feature extraction is done in three steps. DWT, statistical, PCA, and texture features [16].

Table 6.1   Currently developed methods and results

S. No.	Author name	Dataset	Method	Results	Limitation
1.	Tonmoy Hossain [6]	Brats 2020	CNN	Accuracy = 97.87%	Model contains too many learnable parameters.
2.	N. Sravanthi [7]	Brats12	SVM	Accuracy = 93%	Staging is not done
3.	G. Hemanth [8]	UCI dataset	CNN	Accuracy = 91% Efficiency = 92.7%	Area of the tumor is not computed
4.	Masoumeh Siar [9]	MRI dataset	CNN	Accuracy = 99.12% Sensitivity = 96.42%	So many systems are confines only segmentation.
5.	Hein Tun Zaw [1]	REMBRANDT dataset	Naïve Bayes	Accuracy = 94%	The algorithm wrongly identifies the bones and eyes as tumors
6.	Chirodip Lodh [10]	MRI brain dataset	CNN	Accuracy = 96.08% f-score = 97.3%	Not used many classifications.
7.	Ming Li [2]	MRI dataset	CNN	Accuracy = 94%	Dataset is small
8.	P. Mallem [3]	Brats 20	HGG and LGG	Accuracy = 99%	In this paper they used less classifiers, and effects of limited parameters.
9.	Bhagyashri H. [11]	BraTs 2015	Random Forest	Accuracy = 86.66%	In this paper they used less classifier.
10.	Ali Pashaei [12]	MR dataset	KE-CNN	Accuracy = 93.68%	Not used many classifications.
11.	Aaswad Sawant [4]	Tensorflow dataset	Convolutional neural network	Accuracy = 98.6%	Model contains too many learnable parameters

S. No.	Author name	Dataset	Method	Results	Limitation
12.	Javeria Amin [13]	BRATS 2012,	SFTA, Random Forest	Accuracy = 93.3%	Less classifier used
13.	Himaja Byale [14]	MRI brain dataset	Neural Network, K-means	Accuracy = 93.33%	Dataset is small
14.	Heba Mohsen [15]	MRI brain dataset	DNN (deep neural network)	Accuracy = 96.97%	Model contains too many learnable parameters
15.	Lina Chato [5]	BRATS 2017	Linear discriminant	Accuracy = 91%	Area of the tumor is not computed
16.	B.Raj Pragati [16]	MRI brain dataset	SVM	Accuracy = 90%	Staging is not done

3. Methodology

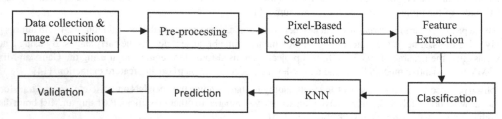

Fig. 6.2 Brain tumor detection methodology steps

Image Acquisition: Image acquisition is the formation of photographic images, such as the interior figure of an object or a physical scene image. The term is frequently assumed to include the compression, processing, display, and printing of images. Image processing is mainly defined as receiving an image from a source. Image processing is the first step in the workflow because, without an image, processing is not possible.

Pre-processing: In the pre-processing of this project, these developments contain corrective information on undesired noise in a region, send an image of a non-brain segment, and change the data. The pre-processing means are to change this input MRI brain image into an applicable form with further.

Pixel Based Segmentation: Pixel-based segmentation involves the technique of splitting an image into various segments. Image segmentation is a common method of digital image processing. Recently, brain tumor image separation in MRIs has stimulated famous research in the sector of medical imaging systems.

Feature Extraction: This is the main step in finding the best imaging solutions and computer vision. Shape, image location, composition, and size are taken into consideration while changing the specified parameters. The feature of the input image is changed at this stage. The image is analysed, and the tumor's location is identified in accordance with these characteristics.

Classification: Classification is an important step of the image analysis technique that requires sorting component data in an image into different classes. Later, after segmenting an uncertain region, a selection scheme and feature extraction are executed to extract the suitable information from the region, and a classification method is used so that the first results are attained on the basis of the available features and the tumor region.

4. Conclusion

Essentially, the ability to identify brain tumors from MRI is a rapidly evolving empirical challenge, and it's a demanding task nowadays. In order to increase the ability to detect the tumor in the brain. His paper provides a detailed review of various algorithms and new combinations of approaches that have been used by many researchers in this field using MRI images. Further, the proposed methods were compared based on architecture and performance metrics, i.e., accuracy, efficiency, and sensitivity f-score. The discussion also includes the limitations that were identified in each proposed system; this can help in the improvement of future models that can help in tumor detection in the brain.

REFERENCES

1. IEEE Thailand Section. and Institute of Electrical and Electronics Engineers, 5th ICEAST 2019: the 5th International Conference on Engineering, Applied Sciences, and Technology: conference proceeding: Luang Prabang, Lao PDR, 2–5 July, 2019.
2. M. Li, L. Kuang, S. Xu, and Z. Sha, "Brain Tumor Detection Based on Multimodal Information Fusion and Convolutional Neural Network," IEEE Access, vol. 7, pp. 180134–180146, 2019, doi: 10.1109/ACCESS.2019.2958370.
3. P. Mallam, Ashu, and B. Singh, "Business Intelligence Techniques Using Data Analytics: An Overview," in Proceedings - 2021 International Conference on Computing Sciences, ICCS 2021, 2021, pp. 265–267. doi: 10.1109/ICCS54944.2021.00059.
4. A. Sawant, M. Bhandari, R. Yadav, R. Yele, and S. Bendale, "BRAIN CANCER DETECTION FROM MRI: A MACHINE LEARNING APPROACH (TENSORFLOW)," International Research Journal of Engineering and Technology, vol. 9001, p. 2089, 2008, [Online]. Available: www.irjet.net
5. L. Aydin et al., "Is central origin of muscle fatigue distinguished solely in finger tapping performance?" in Proceedings - 2017 IEEE 17th International Conference on Bioinformatics and Bioengineering, BIBE 2017, Jul. 2017, vol. 2018-January, pp. 542–547. doi: 10.1109/BIBE.2017.00009.
6. East-West University, Institute of Electrical and Electronics Engineers, Institute of Electrical and Electronics Engineers. Bangladesh Section, and IEEE Robotics and Automation Society. Bangladesh Chapter, 2019 1st International Conference on Advances in Science, Engineering and Robotics Technology (ICASERT 2019): May 3–5, 2019, Dhaka, Bangladesh.
7. N. Sravanthi, N. Swetha, P. R. Devi, S. Rachana, S. Gothane, and N. Sateesh, "Brain Tumor Detection using Image Processing," International Journal of Scientific Research in Computer Science, Engineering and Information Technology, pp. 348–352, May 2021, doi: 10.32628/CSEIT217384.
8. SCAD College of Engineering and Technology and Institute of Electrical and Electronics Engineers, Proceedings of the International Conference on Trends in Electronics and Informatics (ICOEI 2019): 23–25, April 2019.
9. 2019 7th Iranian Joint Congress on Fuzzy and Intelligent Systems (CFIS). IEEE, 2019.
10. C. L. Choudhury, B. K. Mishra, C. Mahanty, and R. Kumar, "XXX-X-XXXX-XXXX- X/XX/$XX.00 ©20XX IEEE Brain Tumor Detection and Classification Using Convolutional Neural Network and Deep Neural Network," 2020.
11. Pimpri Chinchwad College of Engineering, Institute of Electrical and Electronics Engineers. Pune Section, and Institute of Electrical and Electronics Engineers, 2019 Fifth International Conference on Computing Communication Control and Automation (ICCUBEA): proceedings: (19th to 21st September, 2019).
12. 2018 8th International Conference on Computer and Knowledge Engineering (ICCKE). IEEE, 2018.
13. J. Amin, M. Sharif, M. Raza, and M. Yasmin, "Detection of Brain Tumor based on Features Fusion and Machine Learning," J Ambient Intell Humaniz Comput, 2018, doi: 10.1007/s12652- 018-1092-9.
14. H. Byale, L. G. M, and S. Sivasubramanian, "560054 3 Researcher, Research in Knowledge Management," 2018. [Online]. Available: http://www.ripublication.com11686
15. H. Mohsen, E.-S. A. El-Dahshan, E.-S. M. El-Horbaty, and A.-B. M. Salem, "Classification using deep learning neural networks for brain tumors," Future Computing and Informatics Journal, vol. 3, no. 1, pp. 68–71, Jun. 2018, doi: 10.1016/j.fcij.2017.12.001.
16. P. Raj, A. Mehta and B. Singh, "Stock Market Prediction Using Deep Learning Algorithm: An Overview," in International Conference on Innovative Computing and Communications, 2023, pp. 327–336.

Computer Science Engineering and Emerging Technologies (ICCS-2022) – Prof (Dr.) Rajeev Sobti et al. (eds)
© 2024 Taylor & Francis Group, London, ISBN 978-1-032-52199-2

Chapter

7

Development of Future Wireless Communication-based IoT System

Mintu Debnath[1]

Assistant Professor, Department of Physics, Chakdaha College, Chakdaha, West Bengal, India

C. A. Subasini[2]

Associate Professor, Department of Computer Science and Engineering,
St. Joseph's Institute of Technology, Old Mamallapuram Road, Chennai-119

D. Khalandar Basha[3]

Associate Professor, Department of ECE, Institute of Aeronautical Engineering Dundigal, Hyderabad

Adlin Sheeba[4]

Professor, Department of Computer Science and Engineering,
St. Joseph's Institute of Technology, Old Mamallapuram Road, Chennai-119

G. Shiva Kumari[5]

Associate Professor, Department of Electronics and Communication Engineering,
St Martin's Engineering College, Dhulapally, Secunderabad

Firos A.[6]

Assistant Professor, Department of computer Science and Engineering Rajiv Gandhi University
(A Central University), Rono-Hills, Doimukh, Arunachal Pradesh, India

Abstract: A revolutionary phenomenon known as the "Internet of Things (IoT)" is characterised by diverse components with smart, ubiquitous objects, all of which are connected to the web. Such technologies are often used in many contexts to provide cutting-edge programmes for varied commercial productions, like smart cities, healthcare, and so on. These IoT gadgets produce a lot of sensitive data. Securing access to IoT networks is a challenge since they have limited storage, processing power, and connectivity. Within the blockchain (BC) notion, if transferred content relates to monetary operations, sensor measures, or identity messages, most, if not all, networking nodes verify its legitimacy as well as reliability prior to receiving and storing it. N should agree upon a unique operation to assess the integrity of transmitted information, which considerably reduces the possibility of entering trades and recording erroneous contacts with the program. A novel access control based on BC has recently emerged to share and provide accessibility to IoT system content with a dispersed approach. It is stated that such a mechanism fulfils confidentiality while maintaining safety. The ubiquity and use of identity and authenticity methods to date are quickly expanding, but they still suffer from significant drawbacks. In order to ensure the program's effectiveness, it is crucial that these devices are protected. Under this study, a BC-based approach that facilitates identity and protects wireless communication involving IoT N is developed, as well as a decentralised authenticating and managing approach for lighter IoT networks. The recommended process surpasses a BC-dependent authenticity scheme, according to the examined results. The method relies on fog data systems with the concept of a BC system. Utilising the BC approach, an identification as well as validation mechanism is put through. This approach combines BC's obvious benefits with those of developer schemes. Visibility, stability, and traceability are all supported by recommended BC-relied methodology, architecture, and design, which further offer tamper-proof archives. The study is

[1]min22phcs@gmail.com, [2]subasiniaji@gmail.com, [3]bashavlsi@gmail.com, [4]adlinsheeba78@gmail.com, [5]sravikumarece@smec.ac.in,
[6]firos.a@rgu.ac.in

DOI: 10.1201/9781003405580-7

based on the performance of a real-world scenario, as only a conceptual model is outlined in the study along with the basic architecture of programs. The model is safeguarded so that it could send data using an encrypted channel with a low rate of errors owing to the inclusion of verification.

Keywords: Internet of things, Blockchain, Wireless communication, Verification

1. Introduction

IoT can be placed anywhere in a variety of sectors as well as forms. These devices can communicate to one another, gather, distribute, and analyse information that offer a service (Bouras et al., 2021). Until 2020, there'll be higher than forty-five billion linked gadgets, according to experts at CISCO, Ericsson, and other companies (Dadhania and Patel, 2020). IoT is employed in a number of sectors, namely home devices, medical equipment, besides accessory for people. To make these capacity possible, such devices should possess specific characteristics. They should be capable of communicating with few other heterogeneous networks and run on a reasonable energy premise. Additionally, if there is just one rear, they have to be ready to have a strong connectivity and get upgrades as required. A crucial concept for controlling operating system or communications securely is the authentication protocol. In contrast to earlier mentioned aspects, such classifications must be reformulated in the perspective of IoT. Identifying protocols and authorization guidelines should take the fact of resource constraints into account. The no. of networked devices is expected to surpass twenty billion in 2019 (Patil et al., 2021). IoT has already become ubiquitous in almost every part of our lives (such as healthcare and public transit), and many IoT apps make it easier to do routine activities. These solutions include integrating recycling programs, architecture for mobility, smarter grid, transport, weather forecasting, and traffic monitoring, as well as a number of other techniques (Xu et al., 2020). IoT devices create a lot of data, some of which may be confidential. Patient-attached sensors in smart hospital practises, for example, produce private data like a patient's current healthcare state (Zhai et al., 2021). The health centre receives such data and periodically checks it in order to turn on alarms in the event of an emergency. Because all of the IoT program's crucial choices are reliant upon its gathered information, the security of such an apparatus, in addition to a clear set of requirements, is essential for maintaining the IoT program's natural tendencies (Algarni et al., 2021). If a malicious gadget acquires control over a network architecture, it may disrupt a program's normal operation with dire repercussions. IoT security appears to include data management, confidentiality, validity, access, and unlinkability (Abdi et al., 2020). On the other side, the authentication method will be the initial line of defence, restricting data sharing to individuals who have the necessary rights. Protected IoT systems need an authenticating procedure between IoT systems as well as other networks in order to maintain data confidentiality and security. In the absence of such measures, these networks would've been vulnerable to a number of safety problems, such as illegal accessibility, data breaches, and information manipulation (Nyame et al., 2020).

The two types of blockchain (BC) technology—permissioned and non-permissioned—can be separated. Anyone who wishes to utilise it can browse a permission-nil BC, also referred to as a public ledger. Although it possesses huge potential and is identical to Bitcoin, entrepreneurs that wish to retain authority over the processing of transactions might not find it suitable. Business functions might well have unique requirements and intricate protocols that call for the use of adaptable options that restrict the involvement of other parties in these kinds of operations. In addition to such problems, non-permissioned BC also faces challenges with scaling, regulatory bodies, and evolutionary governance. These have given businesses a chance to look at alternative solutions, like permissioned BC, that might be discreetly controlled and will only allow well-known, reliable people to join the BC platform. A BC is referred to as a permissioned entity that has been given privileges, often termed a private BC. The subsequent execution of transactions would be fundamentally altered as a result of this. The BC approach is the core principle behind cryptocurrency (Liu and Li, 2020). It may be regarded as a communications system that is developing. Through design, the BC gained useful qualities like decentralised, tamper-proof chunks with data that can be seen equally from all nodes. Whatever service calls for verification of data or actions from a reliable third party may employ this idea. Through substituting the trustworthy third-party source by providing an available, unaltered chunk of data that exists in a dispersed form, the BC made an entire assurance to be transmitted network-wide. In fact, the smarter contract (SC) is a practical application of the BC approach. It is a great answer for recognition problems because of its enhanced reliability, informational fidelity, and adaptability. BC could also be connected with SC, which offers quite good network connectivity across IoT devices. Additionally, BC-dependent technology and fog computing both offer a strong basis for creating and maintaining decentralised credibility, along with secured solutions for time-sensitive fog-enabled IoT systems (Arunkumar and Kousalya, 2020). A robust yet potent cooperative fog-based IoT networking infrastructure had also been exhibited (Sultana et al., 2020). Taking into account the features of fog computing and the decentralised feature of BC, we propose a delay-sensitive BC-enabled secure authentication approach for IoT systems. In actuality, the following are the primary contributing reasons for the study:

- A ground-breaking decentralised method that provides identity and safety protocols across Internet of Things applications, enabling them to function in a secure and reliable environment.
- The recommended method's solid evidence indicates how well it can meet IoT safety objectives.
- Comparing the overall efficiency of the proposed technique to cutting-edge IoT biometric data

The remainder of the paper is organised as described herein. Section 2 covers the body of existing research. A statement of the problem is addressed in Section 3. The suggested framework and layout are explained in Section 4. The modelling approach is discussed in Section 5. Implementation is covered in Section 6. Section 7 of the paper includes a summary.

2. Related Works

Ethereum BC offers features like logs as well as transactions. An event is a deal's reaction to a customer journey, which communicates with that too. The primary objective of using event and log logging is to facilitate communication between commitments and programs that engage with them. The consumer initially requests access to a specific item or commodities with agreement. Second, the software program decides if the commodity is ready for usage before initially obtaining payment from the client. In that instance, the consumer used Ethereum, a digital currency, to make their purchase. The deal also reserves the services for existing customers. Lastly, the client uses the service appropriately. A smarter contract would then charge the customer as specified, following the assumption that all of the agreement's terms were fulfilled. According to Lone and Naaz (2021), it is important to keep in mind that the agreement could be entirely self-contained because owners might not have been involved with any of the four steps, which include: a) the consumer requests that somehow a commodity or product be made available to him via smarter contract (SC); b) the SC verifies if the commodity is accessible before recording the payment made by the client. In this instance, the consumer is paying with bitcoin Eths; c) SC guarantees that asset is only accessible to existing consumers; d) the consumer uses the asset in conformance with SC's permission; and e) if all goes smoothly, SC will start charging the consumer for the payment that's been agreed upon with party leaders.

2.1 Blockchain (BC)

As per Latchoumi and Parthiban (2022), BC was initially used in cryptocurrency before being developed to be utilised in financial transactions. On the contrary, its unforgeability, decentralised architecture, and failure tolerance make it suitable for setting up computer security. Access control systems are one example of a safety approach that makes use of BC premises and could offer essential safety requirements to protect services. In the ledger, a hashing algorithm and the number of linked blocks are noted. Each chunk is divided into two sections, the first of which lists the number of finished and confirmed actions. A transfer of funds, a financial graph, or a signal from a communication network are all instances of trades. To structure these networks, multiple data forms are employed. For example, Merkel's tree configuration includes an inverted hash method, keeping the centre core hash as the block identity. The second component of blocks, known as the "data block, contains network packets like transaction date stamps, block hashing, and prior block hashing. A hash-supported system is created as a consequence of the compilation of already-existing blocks. As the network lengthens, its ability to resist fabrication increases. Additionally, since all blocks after this one are related by hash, any changes or updates made by a malicious user to one block should be applied to all subsequent blocks as well. According to Kumar and Tripathi (2021), the BC system's nodes can consent to the inclusion of a novel block by using the unanimity technique. One of the consensus processes used by the Bitcoin system is proof-of-work (PW). The PW process utilises a mathematical mystery that mining nodes should solve in order for a block to be verified. The processing capabilities of mine nodes and the duration needed to validate newer blocks may be used to modify the puzzle's difficulty. In situations where computer power isn't a factor, the PW method is used.

2.2 IoT Verification Traditionalized Protypes

According to research by Hussain et al. (2019), IoT authentication is a way to establish faith in the identification of IoT devices and machines in order to safeguard information and regulate accessibility as it moves across an unprotected channel, like the Internet. Robust IoT authenticity is necessary in order for connected IoT equipment and devices to be entrusted to resist control instructions by unauthorised individuals or sources. IoT authorization must be solid. A second advantage of authenticating is that it stops hackers from impersonating IoT devices in order to obtain data kept on websites, including discussions that have been captured, pictures, and other possibly confidential material. According to Dehariya et al. (2016), solitary techniques are a considerably more advanced option than standard IoT devices. For instance, wherever OAuth2 (OA2) is employed as the authenticator, users seek to reach gadgets by checking in to a reliable OA2 source. One could utilise Google, Facebook, as well as other dependable third parties. If the user authenticates correctly and becomes in possession of the necessary authorization, the trusted organisation grants entry. Every gadget controlled by an identical individual could be accessed by verifying the trustworthy source. Step 2 is the customer giving permission for the application to communicate with OA2 suppliers, often called the authenticating server.

2.3 Statement of Problem

Verification

Assuring the validity of an equipment's identity whenever it links to a connection forms the basis of IoT protection (Hussain et al., 2016). A networking mechanism for figuring out if a consumer gets rights to particular resource assets is an authenticating system. Expertise, authority, and right-based verification are three different categories.

Safety

The security of the Internet of Things is ensured by preserving its consistency. Owing to programming or network flaws, it remains susceptible to threats by malicious people while completing the task. The intruder would typically update the gadget key file type (Shukla et al., 2012) that conflicts with the overall infrastructure, including altering the connectivity object, to flee from either a rear entrance or through the machine in order to gear up for yet more intrusion. We frequently check for modifications to important information in order to spot strong infractions as early as feasible.

Suppositions

(a) **Register validation:** Utilise authorised routes for which the web server controls privileges. Before getting connected to the networking system, something should first enrol in BC. Machines could only keep files in BC using lawful IDs, according to the rights channel allocation management plan (Saxena et al., 2017).

(b) **Safe route of communication:** To prevent intermediary assaults, think about using a secure network. As a consequence, nobody else could see the communications or alter things. The main goal of this type of safe method of connection is to ensure the reliability of information (Hussain et al., 2018). The node may exchange information as well as properly update the contents. The rapid development of voice activation technology has made it difficult to improve language processing reliability in several IoT industries. Understanding the setting of a speech scenario is a crucial difficulty in voice activation programs to overcome due to the wide variety of conversational settings. On the other end, reality is that there is never enough retraining evidence for language structures. Through the application of data pre-processing approaches, we principally tackle the problem of data imbalance in language structures under this work (Wang et al., 2020). The Los Alamos National Lab Enterprises (LANLE) network is being utilised, for instance, to record networking and computational (hosting) activities utilising a variety of databases. Such an assortment resulted in the development of the Unification Host (UH) and Networking Database (ND). Sampling nets and assaults are taken out of the UH and ND datasets (Turcotte et al., 2019).

(c) **Organizing in a limited period of time:** Just ask for the ledger to contain fewer knots rather than an additional one whenever a service is added to BC. It might be presumed that perhaps time nodes are trustworthy because they were chosen at random.

3. Prototype and Architecture of Proposed Model

In this study, a BC solution with a novel design process is proposed, which closes the holes left by earlier fixes. In contrast to blocking stacks, it ought to be flexible and operate across any network with very few prerequisites. This is made for IoT sensors with modest computational power. Also, it suggests using a smarter contract to execute OAuth (OA), which would let people access first and operate any authorised devices without needing to sign in sequentially for every IoT system. IoT devices could also carry out smarter contracts (SC), enabling devices to function independently. A prototype model will be utilised for evaluation, and the results from those trials are going to be considered. Performance appraisals and deliberate cyberattacks would be part of the test. This solution's utilisation of Ethereum (Eth) as its foundation provides a number of benefits. Eth. does have a robust implementation framework in place in addition to an inherent motive for young people to participate in problem-solving. Additionally, the suggested solution could be implemented using the Eth. light consumer interface for IoT gadgets that have limited processing and memory. Authenticating, validation, and safety phases come after the review procedure. Whenever a client submits an authenticator, the appeal is processed in multiple ways by SC, and privacy is verified at the protection sequence. Once the validation is complete, an individual is given a link to the dataset.

4. Assertions

Here's a listing of actions to put this notion into practise. Every individual has access across one single or multiple IoT systems, their secret key to the Ethereum (Eth.) key store hasn't been compromised, and they have become a member of the Eth. platform (iv). IoT gadgets and consumers are connected by Eth. BC (v) The system's overall functionality allows this to alter the final hypothesis by allowing users to incorporate their own SC. It is possible to create a centralised SC for client verification on specific IoT systems. But avoiding reliance on a single data frame is among the section's objectives. To have entire authority across existing networks, consumers must be urged to develop their own customised SC. Utilise an authorised channel where the web server controls permitted credentials.

5. System Framework

The communication sequence schematic in Fig. 7.2 describes the stages of the authenticating process.

1. The client verifies SC with their Eth. wallet address.
2. If indeed the consumer is sincere, SC gives the recipient an authorization code in addition to the distributor's Eth. location if the input data are obtained on a real-ttime basis from the consumer's end while accessing data. Both service users as well as IoT utilities are included in the intellectual contract particulars.
3. The person inserts together a plan that covers details like the person's IP locality, Eth. session key, accessibility to the token, and its expiration. This payload is signed using the Eth. secret key and transmitted accompanied by the appropriate key pair. The payload would be encoded if necessary, negating the necessity for the technique to function. The statement's validity is therefore important; thus, it is verified.
4. An IoT device manages the shipment information whenever it is collected. If everything goes well, the gadget gives the consumer access to the sender's IP address during the time frame specified. If any of said screenings are unsuccessful, the petition is rejected anyway.

6. Verifying Process Safety

Servers processing (SP) unit classifies this stage. The m-th input customer who requires permissions is chosen for data input rm. The client in question often has the id IDrm and is a member of GID m user community. In order to confirm authenticity using an SC and grant identification rights to authenticated accounts, the input processing element transmits a message to an IoT network utilising a confirmation code as well as the data of (IDr_m, GID_m, and r_m). A specific place serves as a gateway to all forty-eight interconnections among per-user and SP units over a security gateway. As indicated by eqn. (1), the computation of input is executed.

$$M_h = (IDr_m \oplus GID_m + r_m) \tag{1}$$

Processing element aired the inputs. Eqn. (2) represents the circumstance that verifies inputting consumer to IoT systems:

$$\sum Tj \ 1 < j < m \tag{2}$$

whereby eqns. (3) and (4) indicate the use of tags in SC inputs to validate the verification system.

$$NT_j = (M_h - (GID_m \oplus IDr_m)) \text{ V r T } j \tag{3}$$

$$QT_j = e_i \oplus (S_g \text{ V r T } j) \tag{4}$$

in which Sg stands for cohort mystery and ei for Ti sequencing no. Owing to reader Rm, the tagged Tj sends (NTj, QTj, and rTj) to Rm. Unless and only when NTj is valid, the reader could only retrieve ei, in whose instance ei = QTj (Sg rTj).

Identical to that, it gathers data out of each tagging connected to the grouping till time has run out or grouping is disbanded. The contents (IDr_m, GID m, rm, e1, e2..., ej) would then be transmitted by scanner via a safe channel link to SP unit. This is accomplished by contrasting data packet and answers (IDr_m, GIDm, rm, Re1, Re2, and Re3), wherein re1, Re2, and Re3 being independently generated pseudorandom nos. for every tagging. The scanner keeps a copy of crucial data necessary for verification in its storage. The scanner creates a temporary ID (Temp ID) for every tag in grouping so as to link with said original tag. Utilizing equations $r'T1 = rT1$ re1 and TempIDT1, the reader Rm calculates $r'T1 = rT1$ re1 and TempIDT1 = (GID j e1) (r' T1 IDR m). The reader sends Unit g (QT1, TempIDT1, 1st, re1), and the initial tagging in group is given that tag. The tagging also calculates TempIDT1 and contrasts it with that which was delivered. The tagging computes TempIDT1 = (re1 + ST1) and CT1 = (((e1 r' T1) NT1) and sends the results to scanner as (TempIDT1, CT1, ZGIDg). Once the validity of CT1 has been established, the scanner sends accompanying tagging to the corresponding tags in cohort: (QT2, TempoIDT2, ZGIDg, re2).

After learning the details of every tag in grouping or following downtime, the reader gets insider information regarding all of the current tags.

7. System's Stage of Validation

Reader gives following data to BPS so as to trigger tagging: (IDrm, GIDm, rm, e1...eq), in which e1...eq are indeed the series nos. of active tagging. The existence of asset is verified if specific tags are properly verified. BPS is informed of whatever labels that can't be satisfactorily confirmed using these details.

8. Input Assault

> A transmits to B a connectivity demand (ID A, M signed by A):
>
> // B confirm A's identity by using Key _ A;
>
> Validate A's identification if (Key_ A present in regional) is true;
>
> If Key _ A present in consensus nodes, then Else
>
> Confirm A's identification;
>
> Otherwise, decline A's demand for connectivity;

Algorithm 1 P2P identifying verification method

Algorithm 1 describes well how efficiently retrieve group secrecy (Sg) from supplied variables. Suppose the intruder does have a replica of every message exchanged among tags (T) and reading unit. Let 1jn be the total number of readers (r) and T, let rm and rTj be the bit matrices of length 1 for r and I-th T, accordingly. The extent of Sg is 1 characters, and NTj = Sg rRm rTj. The input conditions provided in eqn. (5) might affect the base attack.

$$\frac{Tja*C1}{TaC0} \tag{5}$$

Utilizing premise T_j and identifiability rule R_1,

$$\frac{Tj = \varnothing(r1),\ T \ni D1ID2}{Tj = \varnothing(h(D1ID2\|r1))} \tag{6}$$

Freshen rule is described in eqn. (7):

$$\frac{Tj/=\#(rm)}{Tj/=\#(h(D1ID2\|r1}) \tag{7}$$

T always has the authority to review that if any eqn. in wherein r0 is a constituent is also brand-new as soon as T deems r0 is novel. Therefore, G1 is completed. It is demonstrated that target G2 is successful in giving the r impression that T transmitted M1 and is up to date. This can be demonstrated utilising premises AR5 and possessing norm P1 in a way akin to target G1. Additionally, this guarantees that message M1 was not sent by r. We initially use P2 to show G3.

$$\frac{R1 \ni C5,\ R1 \ni RID\ m,\ R \ni r1}{R \ni OID} \tag{8}$$

We implement P1 and get the outcome utilizing the parser response M3 and outcome from earlier phase.

$$\frac{R1aM4}{R1 > T_{idm}} \tag{9}$$

Using R2, we obtain

$$\frac{CS|\equiv \phi \,(OID1 \oplus S_{Rm}), CS_{\ni} S_{Rm}}{CS1|\equiv \phi \,(OID1)} \tag{10}$$

Cloud system validates the r's identity as well as obtains OID, which in turn is employed to access additional data base stored data.

9. System Model

After verification, a device's vital information hashing would be examined for accuracy to look for potential invasion actions. The system's operation is depicted in Fig. 7.1, and the modelling approach is shown in Fig. 7.2. Nodes could be classified as consensual (CN) or non-consensual (NCN), depending on the various aims of the permit network. CN participates in the consensus procedure, produces blocks, and then transmits them to the opposing node. The duties of two nodal kinds are displayed in Table 7.1. BC should be used to collect data from every node in the IoT. Depending on its private key component, every gadget creates a set of keys. Whereas the public key is kept on the BC ledger, the confidential data is kept on a gadget and encrypted. Blocking is created as a consequence of CN treating data as a storage event. In order to be ready for future data protection accreditation, the registration process needs to keep the hash function of crucial BC data, including regional config files and software.

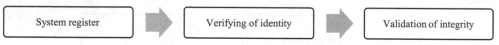

Fig. 7.1 System workflow (Liu et al, 2020)

Devolution and tamper-proof archives might well be provided through BC-based solutions that could be utilised to supplement current recordkeeping techniques. The authentication as well as access control of IoT devices might well be accomplished while using paper-based SC-based techniques. The system has the benefit of becoming portable as needed because it was developed and implemented in reality using widely available equipment and technologies. When the users' identities had been verified, the strategy worked well to grant them entry to the respective IOT systems. In addition, it was resistant to well-planned attacks that aimed to steal legitimate accounts or brute-force identities.

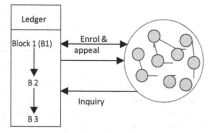

Fig. 7.2 System framework (Liu et al, 2020)

Table 7.1 Node incidents and vocations (Liu et al, 2020)

Careers	Actions
Nodes of contract	Blocks-development, inspecting, consensus method involvement
Nodes of non-consensus	Data transmission

10. Peer-wise ID Verifying Method

Validation of identification is performed in the manner described below, assuming that A submits a network-based demand to link to B that contains an M signal.

Whenever B gets the message, it searches the regional BC ledger using A's ID to find A's key pair. A's authenticity could be confirmed if A's key pair is located in a nearby BC ledger. While A searches for CN for the key pair of B. If B is able to get A's public key, A's authenticity is verified by B. Instead, B would reject A's demand for connectivity because A isn't a part of the BC network. In Alg. 1, the P2P authenticating method is displayed. Each piece of equipment's crucial data was hashed and stored on BC as part of the recording process. IoT nodes send a vital data consistency check request to the closest device while carrying out a task. In the event that validation is unsuccessful, a caution has indeed been issued, and a crucial installer has now been altered. The data gleaned as well as logging records created by devices throughout the course of the project could be added to a BC for security and safeguarding audits after the data has been hashed.

11. Results and Discussions—Implementation

11.1 Environ Discharge

For authentication, we choose to employ IoT application code. We developed BC connectivity utilising the Raspberry Pi (RP) and fully accessible Hyperledger Fabric (HF) software. Each RP connects to the BC connection as a node, in which the devices engage in a randomised fashion. BC could well be divided into several subnetworks relying on multicast and routing techniques, while IoT modules might generate different subnetworks according to company demands. There aren't any interruptions whenever a subdomain communicates with another subnet. Fig. 7.3 depicts the BC system's layout.

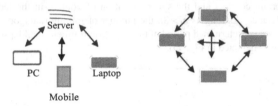

Fig. 7.3 Schematic of proposed BC configuration (Lone et al, 2021)

Entire transactions are recorded on BC, a decentralised ledger that spans the entire BC system. Blocks have similar data organisation as Bitcoins. Contrarily, transactions involve things like equipment licencing, approval, and identification verification. Figure 7.4 depicts the block's data architecture.

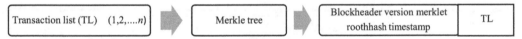

Fig. 7.4 Blocking information outline (Lone et al, 2021)

11.2 Operations in a Chain

The connection among BC and the periphery is made possible through transactional processes. SC and intellectual contracts (IC) were able to distinguish three distinct types of deals. ICs receive requests from sensors and react to them by executing different BC operations, such as read and write. Fig. 7.5 shows the connection between hardware and BC.

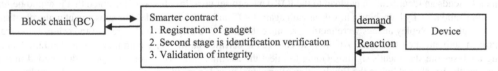

Fig. 7.5 Device and BC connection (Lone et al, 2021)

12. Cryptography (CR)—Based Key Generating Strategy

A secret key (SK) and a public key (PK) are employed to designate every IoT device. A randomised number is used as SK, while elliptic multiplication curving may be utilised to construct PK. The much more crucial step in creating SK is locating a safe and trustworthy entropy generator. To ensure that such generation of chosen randomised data is unexpected or nonrecurrent, a cryptographic pseudo-intellectual number generator (PNG) is frequently utilised as a randomised asset. Through the use of PNG, CR creates cryptographic hashing roles. Unlike stats with shorter PNGs, CR creates a safe cryptographic PN with enhanced pseudorandomized features. To create an anticipated randomised seeding in our solution, we gather numerous IoT device data points, including memory utilisation state, disc space availability, I/O, volume of operations, and CPU power. The elliptic curve phases allow PK to be computed using SK. K = k G is an irrevocable equation. In this case, k is the actual SK, G appears to be the generator spot's consistent spot, and K represents the generator spot's PK. If a PK; K is acquired, it is extremely difficult to identify the correct key by rigorously testing every potential value in order to gain a SK; K. Figure 7.6 demonstrates how to make keys. BC confirms the data's privacy. BC replaces conventional document signing with the dispersed ledger technique to certify things. Fraud and database manipulation are exceedingly difficult. The hashing is created by adding hash values (hv) that are initially stored for each document. Unless a core HV is found, the same process is continued. The resultant database schema is called a Merkle or hashing tree. The hash path from each file to core hashing is required in order to verify an item.

13. Performance Assessment

Since bandwidth as well as latency are system metrics heavily reliant on Hyper Ledger Fabric (HF) BC infrastructure, they won't be covered in this study. To ensure BC networking consistency, the PBF (Practical Byzantium Flaw) tolerance enables the recognition of aberrant conduct and the synchronisation of content in the ledger. Our system's reliability depends greatly on its PBF tolerance. As long as $n > 3t$, the number of mining (antagonising) nodes in a BF tolerance network having n nodes is t. After a predetermined period of time, the commitment shall lapse, and the loyal side (authentic nodes) will lastly come to a deal as depicted in Fig. 7.6.

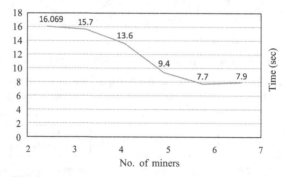

Fig. 7.6 Time is necessary to stop the malware (Hussain et al, 2016)

After the solution model had indeed been examined, the optimal scenario was first assessed. An authorised consumer can connect to the logon administrator SC functionality by using the MIST Eth browser. The customer and IOT device receive an authenticator as well as the person's Eth. address simultaneously from SC, reducing time and energy. Based on the exam's outcomes, the initial phase was completed on a personal BC in very little over four seconds. The client subsequently sends an identification payload to the IOT device to set up a link. It was determined that it would be feasible to get around validation by launching a hostile assault against IOT authenticating code. The subsequent malevolent assaults have been evaluated: Replay attacks were ineffective since the attacker's origin IP had to reflect the origin IP indicated in the approved authenticated statement. Attempts to change the certified authenticity communication also failed since this scripting analyses the statement's signing. Going to inject the assailant's personal verification module ended in quite an error because the PK should link to the Eth. location of an actual user. If a middle guy comes too close, he could be capable of detecting and authenticating packet data. Nevertheless, because one cannot alter the notarized validation document, its validity is protected. The consequent benefits of our technique are related to safety, such as:

1. Restrict accessibility for hostile nodes. Peer-wise verification is carried out via a sequence of permits, and the access control layer successfully keeps risky nodes out.

2. Resistance to DoS assaults. Given that every node shares a registry, the proposed scheme is distributed. The service would remain operational even if a few nodes were subject to cyber threats.

3. Disable the firmware's (fw) secret entrance. We are using BC due to its invulnerability to preserve crucial data hashes, including fw and configuration files. Most every node on a connection may instantly detect the fw back entrance by checking the information's validity.

Data input from consumer = Output: PK from consumer

Begin

- fork = 0to length (PK)
- q(j+1) = q(j)+L*cos (j)
- (j+1) = (j) + q(j+1)
- close for
- SC = int 0
- SC = SC percent length (SK)
- SK = checking SK
- fori = 0to length (SK)
- idx1 = i
- idx2 = key rate (i)
- swap (SC (idy1), SC (idy2))
- close for

Finish

Pseudocode (PC) 1: Verification PC.

The succeeding step is to verify if the proposed alternative is of outstanding calibre by comparing it to earlier solutions that have been presented. The evaluation criterion is dependent on the degree to which problems that had been encountered with the earlier verifying systems that were originally recommended for the IOT system were resolved by the provided authenticity scheme. In contrast to last comparability, analysing metrics in this instance is much more clearly defined. The capability to function with no need for a singular point of flaw and the elimination of a backlog are what are meant by reliability. The extra burden that arises as novel electronic features are indeed brought to an app's usage is referred to as virtualization. Devolution is the ability of an identification program to run independently of a centralised unit, which, if interfered with, can result in software glitches. Tramp proof ensures that activities and encrypted information won't be altered after being logged in the service's event logs.

14. Conclusion

The current study addresses the drawbacks of traditional IoT for identity and protection solutions. A BC approach for IoT authentication and safety was also described. Likewise, extensively discussed was the program's development, including the creation of a prototyping system that relies on Hyperledger Fabric to verify the suggested method. The suggested approach to research does have the potential to be more general and straightforward than other studies. Because of its low computational complexity, it is suitable for installation on portable devices like IoT. The multiple-chain topology also provides an additional level of protection across various zones of faith.

REFERENCES

1. Bouras, M. A., Xia, B., Abuassba, A. O., Ning, H., and Lu, Q. (2021). IoT-CCAC: a blockchain-based consortium capability access control approach for IoT. Peer J. Comput. Sci., 7: e455.
2. Dadhania, A. J., and Patel, H. B. (2020, December). Access control mechanism in Internet of Things using blockchain technology: a review. In 2020 3rd International Conference on Intelligent Sustainable Systems (ICISS) (pp. 45–50). IEEE.
3. Patil, P., Sangeetha, M., and Bhaskar, V. (2021). Blockchain for IoT access control, security and privacy: a review. Wirel. Pers. Commun., 117(3): 1815–1834.
4. Xu, R., Chen, Y., and Blasch, E. (2020). Decentralized access control for IoT based on blockchain and smart contract. Modeling and Design of Secure Internet of Things: 505–528.
5. Zhai, P., Zhang, L., and He, J. (2021). A review of Blockchain-based access control for the industrial IoT. Converter, 3: 308–316.
6. Algarni, S., Eassa, F., Almarhabi, K., Almalaise, A., Albassam, E., Alsubhi, K., and Yamin, M. (2021). Blockchain-based secured access control in an IoT system. Appl. Sci., 11(4): 1772.
7. Abdi, A. I., Eassa, F. E., Jambi, K., Almarhabi, K., and Al-Ghamdi, A. S. A. M. (2020). Blockchain platforms and access control classification for IoT systems. Symmetry, 12(10): 1663.

8. Nyame, G., Qin, Z., Obour Agyekum, K. O. B., and Sifah, E. B. (2020). An ECDSA approach to access control in knowledge management systems using blockchain. Information, 11(2): 111.

9. Liu, H., Han, D., and Li, D. (2020). Fabric-IoT: A blockchain-based access control system in IoT. IEEE Access, 8: 18207–18218.

10. Arunkumar, B., and Kousalya, G. (2020). Blockchain-based decentralized and secure lightweight e-health system for electronic health records. In Intelligent Systems, Technologies and Applications (pp. 273–289). Springer, Singapore.

11. Sultana, T., Almogren, A., Akbar, M., Zuair, M., Ullah, I., and Javaid, N. (2020). Data sharing system integrating access control mechanism using blockchain-based smart contracts for IoT devices. Appl. Sci., 10(2): 488.

12. Lone, A. H., and Naaz, R. (2021). Applicability of Blockchain smart contracts in securing Internet and IoT: A systematic literature review. Comput. Sci. Rev., 39: 100360.

13. Latchoumi, T. P., and Parthiban, L. (2022). Quasi oppositional dragonfly algorithm for load balancing in cloud computing environment. Wirel. Pers. Commun., 122(3): 2639–2656.

14. Kumar, R., and Tripathi, R. (2021). Scalable and secure access control policy for healthcare system using blockchain and enhanced Bell–LaPadula model. J Ambient Intell Humaniz Comput., 12(2): 2321–2338.

15. Hussain, N., Maheshwary, P., Shukla, P. K., and Singh, A. (2019). Detection of black hole attack in GPCR VANET on road network. In International Conference on Advanced Computing Networking and Informatics (pp. 183–191). Springer, Singapore.

16. Dehariya, H., Shukla, P. K., and Ahirwar, M. (2016). A survey on detection and prevention techniques for SQL injection attacks. Int. J. Microw. Wirel. Technol., 6(6): 72–79.

17. Hussain, N., Singh, A., and Shukla, P. K. (2016). In depth analysis of attacks & countermeasures in vehicular ad hoc network. Int. J. Softw. Eng. its Appl., 10(12): 329–368.

18. Shukla, P. K., Bhadauria, S. S., and Silakari, S. (2012). ARA-MAC: A qualifying approach to improving attack resiliency and adaptability in medium access control protocol for WLAN 802.11. Int. J. Comput. Appl., 49(19): 01–10.

19. Saxena, A. K., Sinha, S., and Shukla, P. (2017, October). A review on intrusion detection system in mobile ad-hoc network. In 2017 International Conference on Recent Innovations in Signal processing and Embedded Systems (RISE) (pp. 549–554). IEEE.

20. Hussain, N., Maheshwary, P., Shukla, P. K., and Singh, A. (2018). Mobility-aware GPCR-MA for vehicular ad hoc routing protocol for highways scenario. International Journal of Organizational and Collective Intelligence (IJOCI), 8(4): 47–65.

21. Wang, L., Chen, J., Peng, Y., and Zhang, L. (2020). physical layer security and wireless access control (QSHINE 2017). Mob. Netw. Appl., 25(1): 1–3.

22. Turcotte, M. J., Kent, A. D., and Hash, C. (2019). Unified host and network data set. In Data Science for Cyber-Security (pp. 1–22).

Computer Science Engineering and Emerging Technologies (ICCS-2022) – Prof (Dr.) Rajeev Sobti et al. (eds)
© 2024 Taylor & Francis Group, London, ISBN 978-1-032-52199-2

Chapter

8

A Comprehensive Review of Different Clustering Algorithms for IoT-Based Networks

Bishwajeet Kumar*

Research Scholar, LPU Phagwara, Lovely Professional University

A. Ranjith Kumar[1]

Associate Professor, Computer Science and Engineering,
Lovely Professional University, Phagwara, Punjab, India

Abstract: Because of the far and widespread utilization of IoT in different businesses, the pattern of its reception has expanded as of late. The Internet of Things (IoT) will be utilized in the up-and-coming age of advancements, empowering billions of brilliant items to convey and gather data all alone. We concentrate on the development of the Web of Things (IoT), in which genuine gadgets meet PCs and sensors and actuators meet the Web so they can have the information they produce on IoT-based networks. IoT-based networks are impacted by elements like gadget heterogeneity, energy productivity, and versatility, so adult IoT biological systems require enormous information streams, prompting bottlenecks. Grouping calculations had a significant impact on diminishing energy utilization and expanding network lifetime. This article surveys different bunching calculations and suggests the best calculations for IoT-based networks.

Keywords: Internet of things, Clustering, Wireless sensor networks

1. Introduction

The Web of Things decidedly affects individuals' lives and brings monetary advantages. Colleges, organizations, and legislatures are presently understanding the significance of IoT in encouraging the formation of state-of-the art items and administrations including current homes and endeavors, medical care, natural checking, and brilliant urban communities. For such an extensive variety of IoT applications, the found information should be shipped off the Base Station (BS) for additional tasks. Successful steering conventions, which are fundamental for helping information move, energy productivity, and versatility in IoT-based networks, ought to be utilized to achieve this. Subsequently, one of the main review regions is the making of a fitting steering framework. Bunching might be viewed as a reasonable methodology for settling this sort of issue.

Role of Clustering in IoT

- Energy consumption can be reduced in clustering at the expense of the cluster head (CH).
- Clustering improved the network's capacity for IoT applications.
- Clustering improves bandwidth use.

*bishwajeetit@gmail.com, bishwajeet.kumar@nshm.com, [1]ranjith.26108@lpu.co.in

DOI: 10.1201/9781003405580-8

2. Classification of Clustering Algorithm

On the basis of cluster head selection and cluster range computation, the algorithm can be classified into the following categories:

- Probabilistic
- Deterministic
- Fuzzy logic-based algorithm

2.1 Probabilistic Algorithms

As a rule, probabilistic-type grouping strategies are straightforward, fast, and request less messages. Albeit this kind of grouping calculation makes CHs indiscriminately and has practically no above, it tends to be upgraded by adding more customary elements, like hub thickness, lingering energy, etc. (Yick and Mukherjee 2008). Two classifications of probabilistic calculations exist. Factual gathering calculations for equivalent and inconsistent size gatherings.

1. **Equal Size Probabilistic Algorithms:** Equivalent size groups are created with the assistance of an equivalent size probabilistic calculation. These are a few significant probabilistic calculations.

   (b) **LEACH:** The low-energy versatile bunching calculation is called Drain. This WSN bunching technique is notable. A few hubs are picked as bunch heads and different hubs join the group as bunch hubs in the event that the bunch is in the CH range. Information transmission from sensor hubs to recipients and information movement between hubs are remembered for the CH extent of obligation. In this strategy, every Si hub creates an irregular number somewhere in the range of 0 and 1, which is then stood out from a gathering characterized edge.

   Hub Si is classified as the bunch chief for that round assuming that the produced count is under a foreordained limit; else, he is viewed as a non-group pioneer (Dada and Thiesse 2008).

   (c) **Stable Election Protocol (SEP):** High level hubs in the SEP cycle are hubs with more energy. These state-of-the-art hubs act as CHs and are set in unambiguous spots. With the guide of SEP, an almost three-overlay ascend in the length of the first and last hubs was noticed (Chatzigiannakis and Mylonas, 2011).

2. **Unequal Size Probabilistic Clustering Algorithm:** In this model, the clustering algorithm creates an unbalanced-sized cluster. This approach can be used to address the issue of energy holes. Location and energy both affect cluster size.

   (a) **Energy Driven Unequal Clustering (EDUC):** It is a type of distributed clustering method that successfully reduces energy consumption while preventing the issues associated with hotspot formation in clusters of different sizes. Data gathering and cluster formation are the two components of this technique (Jiazi et al 2015). During the cluster construction phase, CHs are picked at random, and they serve as cluster heads up until the network is terminated. During the data collecting phase, CHs send data straight to the base station, but such single-hop communication is not practical for large networks.

   (b) **Energy-Efficient Unequal Clustering (EEUC):** It is a particular hybrid algorithm that is regularly used for WSN data collection. In this case, cluster heads are chosen at random, but their depth is determined by how far away the CHs are from the BS (S.G et al 2012). This method may manage multi-hop routing while sending data packets from CHs to BS. In this instance, residual energy and the distance between the forwarding CH and the target CH are taken into consideration while selecting CHs.

2.2 Deterministic Algorithms

Deterministic calculations select CHs and structure groups relying upon factors like leftover energy, hub degree, hub centrality, distance from BS, and others. A hub can get this data by trading information with its neighbors. Due to the sensible way these bunches are shaped, it is known as a deterministic method.

There are two sorts of deterministic calculations to look over

- Equivalent size deterministic grouping calculations.
- Inconsistent size deterministic grouping calculation

1. **Equal Size Deterministic Clustering Algorithm:** Groups of a similar size are delivered by these calculations.

   Energy-Aware Routing Algorithm [ERA]: In this directing strategy, CH utilizes a huge amount of ensuing jump hubs to send its data, and the realities transmission is relative to their remaining strength. yet, age produces a bunch of a similar length, which reasons area of interest inconveniences.

2. **Unequal Size Clustering Algorithm:** Here are a few algorithms that produce clusters of different lengths.

   (a) **EADUC:** As a balanced distributed multi-hop routing protocol, it has a short message time and low complexity. The CHs of this paradigm are selected based on the relationship between the average energy of a node and its leftover energy in order to avoid the hot spot issue. In this method, unequal size clusters are produced by calculating the residual energy and the distance from BS (Lutando, 2015). Data is sent directly from the cluster head to the base station (BS) by CH if the distance between the cluster head and the defined threshold is less than the threshold; otherwise, data is sent to the BS via other nodes.

   (b) **Arranging Cluster Size and Data Transmission WSNs (ACT):** It is one sort of inconsistent bunch based directing convention which ready to adjust the issue of energy dissemination in CHs.

2.3 Fuzzy-Based Algorithms

Bunching for WSN is seen to be reliant upon a few qualities like leftover energy, hub degree, hub centrality, distance from BS, etc., as per a new report. Along these lines, we can say that idea of fluffy is extremely helpful for bunching in WSN. Fluffy based bunching approaches can be arranged into two classifications: equivalent size and inconsistent size grouping draws near.

3. Clustering Algorithm for IoT Based Networks

Aside from above examined grouping calculation number of bunching calculations are accessible which reasonable for IoT-based networks which are as per the following:

1. **Linked Cluster Algorithm (LCA):** The Connected Group Calculation was one of the main bunching calculations. It was first made for use with wired sensors but was subsequently adjusted for remote sensor organizations. By utilizing TDMA outlines for between hub correspondence, with each casing having a correspondence opening for every hub in the organization, this technique lessens correspondence clashes between hubs. In the event that a hub has the most noteworthy personality among all hubs inside one bounce of it or among all hubs inside one jump of one of its neighbors, it is assigned as the CH in the Connected Group Calculation. There are two methods for turning into a group head, and every hub in LCA is relegated an unmistakable ID number. The first is on the off chance that the hub has the most noteworthy ID number among both the hub and its adjoining hubs. On the off chance that its neighbors are not really group heads, it acquires subsequent bunch head status.

2. **LEACH and LEAC-C:** Drain makes reference to a disseminated low-energy versatile bunching order that isolates the organization into groups. Each hub decides that they are so prone to turn into a CH and communicates the outcomes. A hub chooses its bunch so that speaking with the CH requires minimal measure of energy. The method empowers energy balance among hubs by utilizing irregular pivot among CHs. As switches, CH hubs move data to the base station and perform information combination and collection on the data accumulated by the bunch. Drain diminishes energy utilization by commanding that every hub pick a bunch contingent upon which requires a minimal measure of correspondence energy. Also, on the grounds that every hub picks its own group head, there is no above in the choice cycle. Since Filter's CH determination is probabilistic, it is workable for a low-energy hub to be chosen as CH, jeopardizing the group overall. Furthermore, Drain could create a one-jump intra- and between-group geography in any event, when hubs can discuss straightforwardly with CH.

3. **Hybrid Energy Efficient Cluster Algorithm (HEEC):** A multi-jump WSN grouping strategy created by Younis and Fahmy, Mixture Energy-Proficient Conveyed Bunching, addresses the Filter calculation's weaknesses of unevenly circulated CH (Adnan et al 2021). The Regard calculation is particular from Filter concerning CH determination. The lingering energy of a hub is presented as a boundary in the CH political race. The typical lingering energy of chosen CHs in Notice is generally high when contrasted with part hubs.

4. Rather than Filter, which sent collected information to the BS in a solitary bounce design, Notice utilizes different jumps to send the information to the BS. This advances more noteworthy energy protection and adaptability rather than the single-bounce strategy for the Filter convention.

5. **Energy-Efficient Multi-level Clustering Algorithm for Large-Scale WSN(EEMC):** In this process, a time of group development is trailed by a period of information transmission. Hubs pass their remaining energy to the sink, and level-1 CHs are picked in light of their higher leftover energy and closer vicinity to the sink, while CH1 neighbors are picked in view of both distance and lingering energy. Different Chs are produced at various levels, and information is shipped utilizing a multi-jump system.

6. **Grid Clustering Routing Protocol for WSN(GROUP):** A lattice bunching steering procedure for enormous scope remote sensor networks that gives versatile and effective bundle directing Here, the sink builds a group framework geography proactively, powerfully, and haphazardly. A minuscule piece of all sensor hubs will take part in the appointment of group pioneers. To decrease how much information that should be conveyed to the sink, Gathering can circulate the energy trouble across the organization's sensors and proposition in-network handling. Table 8.1 shows the correlation (Adnan et al. 2014) between different routing protocol at various parameters

Table 8.1 Comparison of clustering algorithms (Adnan et al. 2014)

Algorithm	Control Manner	Energy Efficiency	Data Aggregation	Scalability	CH Selection	CH Rotation	Mobility	Network Type
EEDC	Centralized	High	No	No	Probabilistic	Yes	No	Homogeneous
GROUP	Hybrid	High	No	No	Weight Based	No	No	Homogeneous
HEED	Distributed	Medium	Yes	Yes	Probabilistic	Yes	Yes	Homogeneous
EEHCA	Distributed	High	Yes	Yes	Probabilistic	Yes	No	Homogeneous
WBCHN	Distributed	High	No	Yes	Weight Based	No	No	Homogeneous
EACLE	Distributed	Medium	Yes	No	Connectivity	Yes	No	Homogeneous
MWBCA	Distributed	High	Yes	Yes	Weight Based	Yes	No	Homogeneous

4. Conclusions

We examined various grouping calculations frequently utilized with regards to WSNs in this exploration. Artificial intelligence calculations were classified in light of energy proficiency, portability, information accumulation, and organization type. We additionally investigated the directing prerequisites of a few IoT spaces, like brilliant medical services, shrewd transportation, and ecological observation. It was found that applications like ecological observing, horticulture, and reconnaissance act much the same way as typical WSN applications, though applications like shrewd medical services, savvy home, and others experience deterrents, for example, differing hub types and versatility prerequisites. We suggested relevant grouping strategies reasonable for a specific space in view of the prerequisites of different IoT applications. Bunching calculations give off an impression of being a promising answer for the IoT's geography upkeep, energy prerequisites, and information total issues. Nonetheless, issues like adaptation to internal failure, administration quality, and secure correspondence should be addressed.

REFERENCES

1. Atzori, L.; Iera, A.; Morabito, G. "The internet of things: A survey. Computer. Network." 2010, 54, 2787–2805.
2. Akyildiz, I.; Su, W.; Sankarasubramaniam, Y.; Cerci, E. "Wireless sensor networks: A survey. Computer. Network". 2002, 38, 393–422
3. Yick, J.; Mukherjee, B.; Ghosal, D. "Wireless sensor network survey. Computer. Network." 2008, 52, 2292–2330.
4. Dada, A.; Thiesse, F. "Sensor applications in the supply chain: The example of quality-based issuing of perishables on Internet of Things "2008, 4592, 140–154.
5. Ilic, A.; Staake, T.; Fleisch, E. "Using sensor information to reduce the carbon footprint of perishable goods." IEEE Pervasive Computer. 2009, 8, 22–29.
6. Gao, T.; Greenspan, D.; Welsh, M.; Juang, R.; Alm," A. Vital Signs Monitoring and Patient Tracking over a Wireless Network." In Proceedings of the 27th Annual International Conference of the Engineering in Medicine and Biology Society, Osaka, Japan, 30 August–3 September 2006;pp. 102–105.
7. Chatzigiannakis, I.; Mylonas, G.; Vitaletti, "A Urban pervasive applications: Challenges, scenarios and case studies". Computer. Sci. Rev. 2011, 5, 103–118.

8. Sanchez, L.; Galache, J.; Gutierrez, V.; Hernandez, J.; Bernat, J.; Gluhak, A.; Garcia, T.SmartSantander: "The Meeting Point between Future Internet Research and Experimentation and the Smart Cities". In Proceedings of the 2011 IEEE Future Network & Mobile Summit, Warsaw,Poland, 15–17 June 2011; pp. 1–8.

9. Cuong Duc Truong, "Routing and Sensor Search in the Internet of Things", Ph. D Dissertation Report From the Institute of Computer Engineering of the University

10. Jiazi Yi, Thomas Clausen, Ulrich Herberg, "Depth-First Forwarding for Unreliable Networks: Extensions and Applications", IEEE INTERNET OF THINGS JOURNAL, VOL. 2, NO. 3, JUNE 2015.

11. Weisheng Tang, Xiaoyuan Ma, Jun Huang, JianmingWei, "Toward Improved RPL: A Congestion Avoidance Multipath Routing Protocol with Time Factor for Wireless Sensor Networks", Journal of Sensors, Article ID 264982.

12. Lutando Ngqakaza and Antoine Bagula, "Least Path Interference Beaconing Protocol (LIBP): A Frugal Routing Protocol for The Internet-of-Things", 12International Conference Proceedings, Wired/Wireless Internet Communications-WWIC 2014 Paris, France,vol: , May 26–28, 2014, PP: 148–161.

13. Adnan Aijaz and A. Hamid Aghvami, "Cognitive Machine-to-Machine Communications for Internet-of-Things: A Protocol Stack Perspective", IEEE INTERNET OF THINGS JOURNAL, APRIL 2015.VOL. 2, NO. 2.

Computer Science Engineering and Emerging Technologies (ICCS-2022) – Prof (Dr.) Rajeev Sobti et al. (eds)
© 2024 Taylor & Francis Group, London, ISBN 978-1-032-52199-2

Chapter 9

Review Paper on Real-time Speech Recognition for Augmentation of Class Room Learning

Neha[1]
Research Scholar, Computer Science, and Engineering,
Lovely Professional University
A. Ranjith Kumar[2]
Assistant Professor, Computer Science, and Engineering,
Lovely Professional University

Abstract: To enhance learning outcomes, as compared to learning by doing, we are now introducing technical ideas to support theoretical concepts in engineering and other fields of education. The use of AR as a tool for interactive learning in various engineering education areas and its function in increasing student engagement in educational settings are the major subjects of this essay [1]. In AR, the majority of existing AR technologies allow the combination of live reality with 3D virtual scenarios. Augmented reality (AR) users generally interact with 3D objects by using image recognition. Although users are now capable of communicating with the system because of advancements in image recognition technology, this interaction is typically limited by the number of patterns that were utilised to recognise the image. This paper integrates the voice-recognition technology that enables users to control 3D objects in an AR system simply by speech, in addition to giving a more adaptable interactive control mode.

Keywords: Augmented reality (AR), Speech recognition, Smart classroom, Education, Learning

1. Introduction

According to Cuendet et al. (2013) and Bacca et al. (2014), augmented reality (AR), a type of technology that augments or combines real-world things with virtual ones, is being explored more frequently for use in classrooms [2, 3]. With the development of information technologies, a lot of people utilise 3D AR technology. So "augmented reality" enhances users' senses using 3D virtualized technology so they can observe their surroundings. The technologies offer information about the real world as well as virtual information. The technologies provide both virtual and real-world information. Both forms of information may be combined and stacked to provide a comprehensive image of the surroundings where the users are located. 3D AR technology is applied in different areas, including the military, medicine, architecture, engineering, film and television, and entertainment.

1.1 The AR Technology Includes Three Characteristics

1. Combined both information of real and virtual worlds.
2. Immediate interactivity.
3. Capability to add the locations of 3D virtual objects in 3D space.

[1]neha1997125@gmail.com, [2]ranjith.26108@lpu.co.in

DOI: 10.1201/9781003405580-9

1.2 AR Technology Contains Three Main Display Devices

Table 9.1 Three Main Display Devices of AR technology [10]

Headgear (Microsoft HoloLens)	Mobile	Open-space devices
The Microsoft HoloLens is a vital part of putting Windows Holographic as smart glass into practice operating through Windows 10	Many cell phones today offer augmented reality capabilities	These gadgets come in different sizes from table size to room size
The user interface in AR enables people to connect through eye contact, speech or hand gestures	By merging 3D virtual objects, the depth camera in the dual-lens would monitor real data, which is utilized to create the necessary real scene and achieve augmented reality	It is generally applied in open work displays or other more interactive setups

Source: Made by Author

To make it more interactive, this paper imported speech recognition technology so that AR users could directly control the AR system.

The rest of the paper is structured as follows: Section 2 reviews the existing literature. Section 3 describes speech recognition for augmentation using machine learning and dataset sources. Section 4 summarises the paper.

2. Benefits of Augmented Reality and Speech Recognition in Education

2.1 Benefit of Using Augmented Reality

Augmented Reality and Student Motivation: Using AR to enhance the visualisation of the course material for a better grasp of their field, Tools in Classrooms increases student motivation [1].

Fig. 9.1 Benefit of Using Speech Recognition [10]

3. Literature Review

In this paper, researchers surveyed engineering and other domain students and analysed how many students are motivated. The idea behind AR is to increase student motivation by making course material easier to visualise for a deeper comprehension of their subject. A group of undergraduate students was used in this study to gauge their interest in adopting AR as a teaching and learning aid in classrooms. The ARCS model was used in that survey to determine how motivated students were based on the parameters assessing their attention (A), relevance (R), confidence (C), and satisfaction (S) for interactive learning. They found good results based on the results based on the RACS model. (1) Attention accuracy is 4.19; (2) relevance is 4.09; (3) confidence is 4.20; and (4) satisfaction is 4.26. Satisfactory results are more common with the use of augmented reality tools in classrooms [1].

Enhance cognitive engagement in the classroom for young language learners, according to Wen, Yun (2020) [4]. This study examines the effects of a Chinese character learning game enhanced by AR on students' cognitive engagement with traditional classroom instruction. Displays a comparison between children who participate in learning activities designed to assist self-generated scenarios more frequently, according to a study done with 53 grade 2 students and two Singaporean teachers. The findings indicate that pupils are now more cognitively engaged in activities made possible by AR. The study offers some guidance on how to analyze the learning process to explore the cognitive effects of AR-enabled learning design [4].

R. M. et al. [5] This study focuses on applications based on AR. The movie business continues to place a lot of importance on visually appealing movie posters even in the era of the internet advertising. This article examines how interactive movie information might be presented to viewers in a more practical way using technologies like speech recognition, AR, and image processing. Among other image-processing techniques, this model's activities comprised pre-processing, data augmentation, and feature extraction using convolutional neural networks. When compared to RNN and other methods for image pre-processing employing wavelet transformations over CWT, picture over-fitting and data augmentation, and feature extraction, it is clear that using CNN for image classification and object identification has produced better results. Ends speech recognition and AR integration [5].

Babaei, Hossein et al. [6]. In this paper, the researcher clarifies and discusses the purpose of developing an image-based Android application. Real-time image processing and detection form the foundation of this investigation. It's a new practical method that enables consumers to instantly learn about pictures. The purpose of this project is to address current technology issues and enable consumers to expand their mobile possibilities. The project cuts down on delays and enables consumers to obtain comments immediately. With the use of photographs that are already saved in some type of database, it provides a mobile user with the convenience of easily obtaining information from a single image captured. In this project, AR enables users to alter data and improve captured images with additional information (video, GPS tags) [6].

Nasser Alalwan et al. [7]. This study can shed light on how to use virtual reality and augmented reality to do a variety of contemplative and investigative tasks in the classroom. To learn more about the difficulties and potential benefits of integrating VR and AR technology into the teaching of science courses, a researcher conducted a semi-structured interview with primary school teachers. Based on an interview with 29 scientific instructors, a set of data and suggestions for using AR and VR to teach science were offered. It was discovered that common barriers to adopting VR and AR were a lack of knowledge, a lack of concentration, a lack of time, and a lack of available environmental resources. The study discovered that both technologies may be utilized to encourage curiosity, increase perceived value, and cultivate a positive outlook.

Akçayir, M. et al. [8]. In this study, approaches for mobile augmented reality (MAR) have been used as an instructional tool in academic settings. This article's objective is to describe the most recent developments in the usage of the MAR for educational purposes. Based on the chosen studies, the researcher examined which areas of knowledge the MAR techniques are applied to in educational environments. The methods, development and evaluation require to acquire reliable data that may be used to support decisions on the employment of such techniques and/or their ongoing refinement for educational purposes. Pedagogical problems and technical issues. Some difficulties with usability need more time. Large groups are not recommended. Moreover, mental exhaustion make it challenging to design. [8].

4. Speech Recognition for Augmentation Using Machine Learning and Datasets Sources

4.1 Machine Learning

The algorithms used in machine learning are the ones that allow the software to autonomously forecast results, discover hidden patterns in data, and enhance performance. For various purposes, machine learning uses a variety of algorithms.

Types of Machine Learning

1. **Supervised Machine learning:** The labeled dataset is used to train the supervised learning models. After training and processing, the model is put to the test by being given a sample set of test data to see if it predicts the desired result.

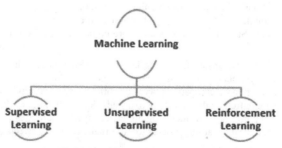

Fig. 9.2 Types of machine learning

Source: Made by Author

2. **Unsupervised Machine Learning:** The algorithm must operate on the data without any supervision and can be taught using an unlabeled dataset that is neither classified nor categorized. In unsupervised learning, the model searches through the vast quantity of data in search of meaningful insights rather than producing a predetermined result.

3. **Reinforcement Machine learning:** In reinforcement learning, a machine learns by generating behaviors in response to feedback from its surroundings. The agent receives feedback in the form of rewards; for example, he receives a positive reward for each good activity and a negative reward for each poor action.

4.2 Dataset Sources

1. Data.gov
2. Five Thiry Eight
3. Kaggle
4. Data. World
5. Google Dataset Search

4.3 Rating based on AR Model

1. Knowledge of AR
2. Interaction with AR
3. Use of AR Application
4. Functionality of AR Application

4.4 Applications of Augmented Reality

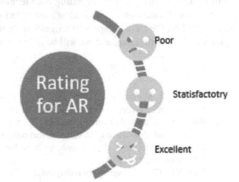

Fig. 9.3 Feedback rating wise
Source: Made by Author

Fig. 9.4 Block diagram showing applications of augmented reality [9]

5. Conclusion

Integrating AR with speech recognition in classrooms will improve traditional study methods, and our classroom learning will become smarter. After integrating both techniques into the smart classroom using a machine-learning model, It will help to understand how many students are able to learn or understand the concepts. In the future, a survey will also be conducted on the basis of speech recognition. In the future, image recognition will capture the picture and augment that picture into a virtual one, and we will be able to control it by speech as well as by touching the screen.

REFERENCES

1. Kaur, D. P., Mantri, A., & Horan, B. (2020). Enhancing Student Motivation with the use of Augmented Reality for Interactive Learning in Engineering Education. Procedia Computer Science, 172, 881–885, https://doi.org/10.1016/j.procs.2020.05.127
2. Bacca, J., Baldiris, S., Fabregat, R., Graf, S., & Kinshuk. . (2014). Augmented reality trends in education: A Systematic review of research and applications. Educational Technology & Society, 17(4), 133–149.
3. Cuendet, S., Bonnard, Q., Do-Lenh, S., & Dillenbourg, P. (2013). Designing augmented reality for the classroom. Computers & Education, 68, 557–569.
4. Wen, Yun. (2020). Augmented reality enhanced cognitive engagement: designing classroom-based collaborative learning activities for young language learners. Educational Technology Research and Development. 69 10.1007/s11423-020-09893-z.
5. R. M. Jayamanne and D. Shaminda, "Technological Review on Integrating Image Processing, Augmented Reality and Speech Recognition for Enhancing Visual Representations," 2020 International Conference on Image Processing and Robotics (ICIP), 2020, pp. 1-6, DOI: 10.1109/ICIP48927.2020.9367358.
6. Babaei, Hossein & Mohurutshe, Pagiel & Habibi Lashkari, Arash. (2012). Image-Processing With Augmented Reality (AR) 10.1117/12.2011323.
7. Nasser Alalwan, Lim Cheng, Hosam Al-Samarraie, Reem Yousef, Ahmed Ibrahim Alzahrani, Samer Muthana Sarsam,A Developing Country Perspective, Studies in Educational Evaluation, Volume 66, 2020, 100876, ISSN 0191-491X, https://doi.org/10.1016/j.stueduc.2020.100876.
8. Akçayir, M., Akçayir, G.: Advantages and challenges associated with augmented reality for education: a systematic review of the literature. Educ. Res. Rev. 20, 1–11 (2017)
9. Mekni, M., & Lemieux, A. (2014). Augmented Reality: Applications, Challenges, and Future Trends, Applied Computational Science, ISBN: 978-960-474-368-1 207 (BARS) by Julier et al.

Computer Science Engineering and Emerging Technologies (ICCS-2022) – Prof (Dr.) Rajeev Sobti et al. (eds)
© 2024 Taylor & Francis Group, London, ISBN 978-1-032-52199-2

Chapter

10

Applied Cryptography in Banking and Financial Services for Data Protection

Sarika Tanwar[1]
Assistant professor in Department of MBA,
The Technological Institute of Textile and Sciences, Bhiwani, Haryana

Roopa Balavenu[2]
Assistant professor, Department of MBA,
K. S. School of Engineering and Management, Bangalore

Ramesha H. H.[3]
Program Coordinator and Associate Professor,
Centre for Management, Muddenalli Post, Bangalore Region

Mohit Tiwari[4]
Assistant Professor, Department of Computer Science and Engineering,
Bharati Vidyapeeth's College of Engineering, Delhi A-4, Rohtak Road, Paschim Vihar, Delhi

K. K. Ramachandran[5]
Director/Professor, Management/Commerce/International Business,
Dr GRD College of Science, India

Dilip Kumar Jang Bahadur Saini[6]
Assistant Professor, Department of Computer Science and Engineering,
Himalayan School of Science & Technology, Swami Rama Himalayan University,
Dehradun, Uttarakhand, India

Abstract: The importance of security and privacy has increased in the banking and insurance industries. Online transactions require security at all times. Customers have access to all types of information and transactions online. But since information is not sufficiently encrypted, internet banking needs a lot of security and privacy. Online information on banks and their many services can be found through electronic banking. Nowadays, the fundamental component of banking services is electronic banking. The operational environment of the banking industry has undergone significant changes as a result of information technology. Banks have adopted cutting-edge methods in the form of automated teller machines, online banking, telephone banking, mobile banking, etc. The primary problem with all Internet banking methods is data security and privacy. The online banking system is also susceptible to user authentication-related assaults. This paper's goal is to review various banking security measures and explain various data encryption strategies based on cryptographic technologies.

Keywords: Banking, Security, Cryptography, Encryption, Decryption

[1]dr.sarikatanwar2427@gmail.com, [2]roopabalavenu2@gmail.com, [3]drhhramesh@gmail.com, [4]mohit.tiwari@bharatividyapeeth.edu,
[5]dr.k.k.ramachandran@gmail.com, [6]dilipsaini@gmail.com

DOI: 10.1201/9781003405580-10

1. Introduction

Banks are being compelled to invest in information security due to external threats, rising internet and mobile usage, and regulatory constraints (Gupta, 2007; Taherdoost, 2017). Comparing online banking and phone banking to other service delivery channels, managing security is more difficult. ATMs have developed into a lucrative target for robbers due to their abundance of cash. The ATM has evolved into the nation's primary banking facility, with many institutions using these devices to receive deposits, count money, dispense cash, and display account balances. The banking, financial services, and insurance (13FST) verticals are looking for scalability and reliability from their IT infrastructure in order to spur corporate growth, in addition to difficulties with data protection and risk mitigation. The use of cryptography is crucial for the protection of data. The types of cryptography techniques known as hash functions, secret key functions, and public key functions can be used to develop cryptography Matlab projects. These features may aid in the safe transfer of messages from intrusive parties. Utilizing a MATLAB program with a genetic algorithm allows for the optimization of these functions' quality attributes (Jain and Pandey, 2017).

One method used by banks and insurance companies to guarantee the security of all private and business transactions is cryptography. Because current cryptography includes the theory and application of hiding information by means of keys linked to web-based applications, ATMs, e-commerce, computer passwords, and the like, we commonly refer to cryptosystems when discussing modern cryptography. Many firms are incorporating powerful cryptographic techniques-based data encryption and data loss prevention measures into their strategic network security planning procedures. The word "cryptography" (Barker & Roginsky, 2011; Barker, 2017) almost entirely relates to the act of converting plaintext, or normal information, into nonsense (called ciphertext). Decryption is the process of recovering plaintext from unintelligible ciphertext. A cipher is an algorithm combination that performs both encryption and reversing decryption (or cypher). The algorithm and a unique "key" are both in responsible for the complicated workings of a cipher. This is a private parameter for a certain message exchange context that should be known only by the communicants. The development of a genetic algorithm might be facilitated by a mathematical framework created utilizing surface response techniques (Panwar, 2021). A "cryptosystem" is an ordered collection of items that includes the encryption and decryption methods that go with each key, as well as the finite possible plaintexts, cyphertexts, and keys. Keys are crucial because ciphers without them can be easily cracked using only the knowledge of the cipher that was employed, making them useless (or even counterproductive) for the majority of uses. In the past, ciphers were frequently employed for encryption and decryption without the need for extra steps like authentication or integrity checks.

Banks can utilize browsers that support Server Gated Cryptography (SGC) or 128-bit encryption. A browser using 40-bit encryption can operate with SGC as long as it has 128-bit encryption for the duration of the session (Barker and Roginsky, 2011; Barker, 2017). The maximum level of commercially available security for your financial transactions is offered by browsers with 128-bit encryption. Your online banking transactions are converted into code by encryption so that we can decipher them. Machine learning for process modeling can aid in improved performance (Jain and Pandey, 2019).

Technologies like the Internet, which have made it much easier to communicate and deal with all types of information, call for a high level of security to make these exchanges private and secure. Additionally, titanium-made metal cards are quickly becoming a must-have prestige symbol for people with excellent credit. Though they could be a more obvious target of card-present fraud, flashing a contactless metal card while making a purchase is nonetheless a sign of high credit limits. Titanium cards are affordable, gaining top-of-wallet status with sleek design and a heavyweight feel that signals to clients that they are receiving top-notch service (Jain et al., 2020). Data encryption is unavoidably necessary. Networks are used to transmit information about banks and insurance businesses. Transactions would be open to illegal meddling without strong encryption. Secure electronic transactions are implemented using cryptographic techniques that can be used with digital checks, debit cards, credit cards, and stored value cards, among other payment methods. Privacy, authenticity, and no repudiation are common security features for electronic transaction systems (prevention of subsequently denying having conducted a transaction). To achieve these security goals, digital signatures based on public key cryptography can be utilized. In such a cryptosystem, a public key and a secret key are employed. The public key is used to validate digital signatures, whereas the secret key is used to create them. Withdrawal, payment, and deposit are the three basic forms of electronic transactions. (Herrero-Collantes and Garcia-Escartin, 2017; Barker and Roginsky, 2011; Barker, 2017). The current focus is on using cryptography in banking and financial services to protect customer data.

2. Literature Review

Aaditya Jain and Sourabh Soni (2017) highlighted that the banks utilize biometric authentication technologies; however, the financial system's database is no longer safe owing to inevitable hostile behavior. Intelligent hackers can collect biometric information about consumers from the bank's database and then use it to commit fraud. A cryptography approach is utilized to avoid all of these dreadful consequences. Visual cryptography is a powerful encryption technology that hides information inside visuals and can only be deciphered by the human visual system.

Logashanmugam Edeswaran and Velumurugan Andi (2016) transmitted the image in a defined manner using visual cryptography, steganography, and AES encryption. On the cover sheet, Share One is embedded with the Least Significant Bit (LSB). The cipher key is used to encrypt embedded images with AES. DCT is used to generate the cipher key (Discrete Cipher Transform).

According to Jitendra Saturwar and D.N. Chaudhari (2013), a picture watermarking model based on progressive visual cryptography is presented to identify the appropriate number of shares. Research on the usage of meaningful shares in conjunction with a visual cryptography method for secret images is being done for algorithm implementation.

Nagham Hamid, Abid Yahya, R. Badlishah Ahmad, and Osamah M.Al Qershi (2012), in their research entitled "Image Steganography Techniques: An Overview," explain that in order to send secret information using steganographic techniques, an agent must select a suitable steganographic algorithm as well as a suitable cover image. The only thing that decides the best steganographic approach among all the known picture steganographic techniques is the application.

3. Methodology

This study primarily employed secondary data that was gathered from earlier literature. Martins et al. (2018) define secondary data as datasets that were previously gathered by a person other than the researcher and seem useful to meet the research issues of this study. Additionally, Ellram and Tate (2016) believe that secondary data is a valuable resource that may be used in a variety of sectors. Secondary data are much preferred due to the regularly provided well-established measurements that might greatly aid researchers in the clear investigation of real events (Hair et al., 2019). According to Johnston (2014), secondary data give researchers adaptable and reliable sources that are simple to gather, compile, and store.

4. Results and Discussion

4.1 E-Banking Security

According to Table 10.1, 29% of customers were obtained in rural areas, 33% were obtained in municipalities, followed by 14% customers obtained in various district towns, and 24% of customers accounted for various city corporations. Amongst the customers, 15% of the customers, who came from a variety of locations, said that online banking is very secure. Additionally, the data showed that 31% of the customers felt that e-banking security is insufficient, while 15% claimed it is highly secure. 11.5% of the entire population are unaware of the level of security in e-banking in India.

Table 10.1 Level of security in e-banking.

Location	Highly Secured (%)	Sufficiently Secured (%)	Not enough Secured (%)	Not secured at all (%)	Don't Know (%)	Total percentage
Rural Area	15	38	11	0	15	29
Municipality	7.5	40	42.5	2.5	7.5	33
District town	18	41	29	0	12	14
City Corporation	24	48	18	0	10	24
Total	15	42	31	.80	11.2	100

Source: Sadekin and Shaikh, 2016

4.2 Password Usage for Maintaining E-Bank Account

Among the total percentage, 31.7% of people use a combination of digits as their password. 13.3% of customers solely use names or letters, 18.3% use a combination of letters and numbers, and about 28.33% of customers do not hold any kind of e-banking account (Fig. 10.1).

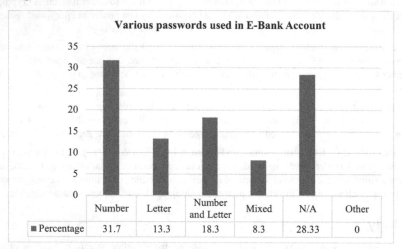

Fig. 10.1 Various passwords used in e-bank account

Source: Sadekin and Shaikh, 2016

Simple passwords that are easy for a user to remember, such as a person's name or other real terms, are poor from a security standpoint since they are susceptible to dictionary attacks. Strong passwords are mixed (for example, a5h! s$N7). Passwords are less attackable but also more challenging to remember. Figure 2 shows that, although this form of password is not sufficiently safe, 31.7% of respondents use only some "number" and 13.3% use only some "letter" as their e-banking passwords.

4.3 Logging-out from Bank Website

According to the results of Table 10.2, around 51.67% of customers tend to agree that they do not log off of their bank's website after a transaction, and about 85.83% of customers tend to agree that they do not restart their computers after finishing a transaction.

Table 10.2 Account holders' preference for log off from bank website after transaction

	Log-out from bank website (%)	Restart computerafter transaction (%)
Yes	48.33	14.17
No	51.67	85.83
Total	100	100

Source: Sadekin and Shaikh, 2016

The majority of customers, according to Table 10.2, do not log out of their accounts or from the bank's website. This might put the security of online banking at risk. Account holders must restart or log off if they utilize a shared computer. From the perspective of security, signing out is insufficient. Because hackers are skilled at logging in if people don't restart their computers or log out of the website.

5. Conclusion

In the upcoming years, the use of electronic payments will increase significantly. We anticipate being able to simply purchase goods online from the comfort of our homes. Debit cards, credit cards, and upcoming smart cards will be used for more and more in-person purchases. The development of strategies for ensuring privacy while carrying out electronic financial transactions has been a focus of ongoing research within the cryptography community. For instance, many bank-to-bank transactions currently include cryptography. Most people believe that more encryption will be used between customers and their banks as Internet commerce expands since it can easily reduce the hazards of plaintext transmission for a large number of financial transactions. Organizations can utilize cryptography for security objectives more frequently over time, such as by requiring rigorous authentication before giving access to private databases. There are significant economic, psychological, and other reasons why customers might decide not to behave anonymously, even though younger generations of users may be more accustomed to cryptography than present users. Key management issues will continue, consumers still need to disclose their names and credit scores in order to borrow money, and banks may still have strong incentives to reward clients who agree to divulge their unique identities by offering them better conditions.

REFERENCES

1. Brockman, P., French, D. and Tamm, C. (2014). REIT organizational structure, institutional ownership, and stock performance. J. Real Estate Portf. Manag. 20(1): 21–36.
2. Sadekin, M., and Shaikh, Md., (2016). Security of E-Banking in Bangladesh. Journal of Finance and Accounting. 4. 1. 10.11648/j. jfa.20160401.11.
3. Martins, F. S., da Cunha, J. A. C., & Serra, F. A. R. (2018). Secondary data in research–Uses and opportunities. Revista Ibero-Americana de Estratégia, 17(4), 1–4. https://doi.org/10.5585/ijsm.v17i4.2723
4. Ellram, L. M., & Tate, W. L. (2016). The use of secondary data in purchasing and supply management (P/SM) research. Journal of Purchasing and Supply Management, 22(4), 250–254. https://doi.org/10.1016/j.pursup.2016.08.005
5. Johnston, M. P. (2014). Secondary data analysis: A method of which the time has come. Qualitatve and Quantative Methods in Libraryes, 3, 619–626.
6. Gupta, P. K. (2007). Internet banking in India–Consumer concerns and bank strategies. Proceedings of Global Conference on Business and Finance, May 23-26, 2007, San Jose, Costa Rica, 2, 59.
7. Taherdoost, H. (2017). Understanding of e-service security dimensions and its effect on quality and intention to use. Information and Computer Security. 25, 535.
8. Barker E. and Roginsky A. (2011). Transitions: Recommendation for transitioning the use of cryptographic algorithms and key lengths, NIST Special Publication 800-131A; available at http://www.gocs.eu/pages/fachberichte/archiv/075-sp800-131A.pdf
9. Barker, E. (2017). "SP 800-67 Rev. 2, Recommendation for Triple Data Encryption Algorithm (TDEA) Block Cipher." NIST special publication 800, 67.
10. Herrero-Collantes M. and Garcia-Escartin, J. C. (2017). Quantum random number generators, Rev. of Mod. Phys. 89, 015004.
11. Nagham Hamid, Abid Yahya, R. Badlishah Ahmad & Osamah M. Al-Qershi, (2012). "Image Steganography Techniques: An Overview," International Journal of Computer Science and Security (IJCSS), Volume (6): Issue (3).
12. Aaditya Jain, Sourabh Soni, (2017). "Visual Cryptography and Image Processing Based Approach for Secure Transactions in Banking Sector," 2nd International Conference on Telecommunication and Networks (TEL-NET) 2017.
13. Jitendra Saturwar, D.N. Chaudhari, (2013). "Secure Visual Secret Sharing Scheme for Color Images Using Visual Cryptography and Digital Watermarking," IEEE Transactions on Cloud Computing, 1(1).
14. Velumurugan Andi and Logashanmugam Edeswaran, (2016). "An efficient steganography algorithm using visual cryptography and AES encryption", IIOABJ.
15. Panwar, V., Sharma, D. K., Kumar, K. P., Jain, A., & Thakar, C. (2021). Experimental investigations and optimization of surface roughness in turning of en 36 alloy steel using response surface methodology and genetic algorithm. Materials Today: Proceedings, 46, 6474–6481.
16. Jain, A., & Pandey, A. K. (2017). Multiple quality optimizations in electrical discharge drilling of mild steel sheet. Materials Today: Proceedings, 4(8), 7252–7261.
17. Jain, A., & Pandey, A. K. (2019). Modeling and optimizing of different quality characteristics in electrical discharge drilling of titanium alloy (Grade- 5) sheet. Materials Today: Proceedings, 18, 182–191.
18. Jain, A., Yadav, A. K., & Shrivastava, Y. (2020). Modelling and optimization of different quality characteristics in electric discharge drilling of titanium alloy sheet. Materials Today: Proceedings, 21, 1680–1684.

Computer Science Engineering and Emerging Technologies (ICCS-2022) – Prof (Dr.) Rajeev Sobti et al. (eds)
© 2024 Taylor & Francis Group, London, ISBN 978-1-032-52199-2

Chapter 11

A Study to Investigate the Methods of Enhancing Database Security in Web-based Environments through Big Data

Akash Saxena[1]

Compucom Institute of Information Technology and Management, Jaipur

Nagendra Prasad Krishnam[2]

Assistant Professor, School of Management and Commerce (SOMC) Malla Reddy University,
Hyderabad Telangana, India

Rahul Joshi[3]

Associate Professor, Department of CSE, Symbiosis Institute of Technology, Pune,
Symbiosis International (Deemed University), Pune, India

Namita Arya[4]

Assistant Professor, Galgotia University, Noida, UP, India

Shailendra M. Pardeshi[5]

Assistant Professor, R. C. Patel Institute of Technology, Shirpur, Maharashtra, India

Balaji Ramkumar Rajagopal[6]

Sr. Data Architect, Cognizant Technology Solutions, Chennai, Tamilnadu, India

Abstract: Web apps are now widely used by many different types of businesses, organisations, and commerce. This is due to its dependability and effective end-result response to a range of communication issues in Web of Things environments. It has obtained high-interest collections as well, much like some evolutionary architectures, as a result of unscrupulous users who wait to take advantage of their flaws and defects for their own ends. Given the volume of incidents reported on a regular basis, database security is critical and becoming a growing concern. The actual difficulty is the emergence of emerging threats and vulnerabilities given the rapid pace of innovation. Due to the web application's dependable and effective solutions to problems, it is now frequently used in a variety of applications. The computer operations are then executed on the user's query data following decryption. The customer can once more encrypt the result and store it on the cloud after performing the tasks. Secondary empirical analysis has been done based on the research topic to perform the analysis part.

Keywords: Database, Security, Big data, web-based, architecture, applications.

1. Introduction

Sophisticated data analytics platforms frequently function in very unpredictable and volatile situations. Due to the increased threats to confidential and important information in a smart environment, establishing protection for these kinds of structures is a significant task. Design and operation with more dependable rules can benefit from an appreciation of how

[1]akash27jaipur@gmail.com, [2]nagendra27.krishnam@gmail.com, [3]rahulj@sitpune.edu.in, [4]namita.usar@gmail.com, [5]pardeshishailendra1184@gmail.com, [6]balajiramkumar@gmail.com

DOI: 10.1201/9781003405580-11

the various security area aspects interact with one another. This research focuses on proposing certain security methods and strategies to enhance the trustworthiness of the incremental advancement of a high-performance big data analytic system [1]. As research is based on clinical information, the overall purpose is to methodically create a safe data analysis framework that can maintain safety towards its consumers and satisfy administrative compliance standards such as the "Health Insurance Portability and Accountability Act of 1996 (HIPAA)".

The data protection needs of the "Texas Tech University (TTU)" EXPOSOME big data research, subsidized by the NIH as well as NSF, is one of the specific situations that had an impact on this research. The goal of this study is to identify the various risks and how they influence the well-being of those who are impacted over the course of their lives. The various data structures, meanwhile, have made it difficult for data scientists to draw conclusions from actual data [2]. Regardless of the ongoing inclusion of new data, notably de-identified but yet safeguarded personal medical records, statistics must continue to be maintained and confidentiality guaranteed. For further evaluation of the data from the TTU EXPOSOME Experiment, a multidisciplinary team is now working to create a safe mechanism to translate this information and save these different data sources in the MongoDB database. Therefore, to protect the information and provide authorised researchers with unhindered accessibility, this initiative addresses four key aspects [3]. These four categories include security measures, network monitoring, custom application confidentiality, as well as information security (Server with LXCs). The provision of a robust integrative framework seems to be the overarching goal, as was before stated. In order to minimise efficiency deterioration while accessing even though unsecured techniques may be employed, this study will look into methods designed to protect information and accessibility towards the EXPOSOME data that might be safeguarded.

2. Background and Related Work

Researchers demonstrate a safety concept for the information storage in the MongoDB database system running in Singularity Linux containers in this part. Information is authenticated, authorized, and encrypted throughout transit whereas information is employed to guard against breaches. Additionally, by translating the real data structure to a numeric values description, a technique is suggested and put into practice for confidentiality information extraction procedure, transfers, and loadings [4]. Then, researchers provide a number of novel approaches that they plan to use to further research objectives while building a much more solid base to handle confidential material and adhere to laws like HIPAA.

2.1 Authentication

The current MongoDB version doesn't quite come with a verification scheme by default, despite the fact that it enables a number of methods, including "SCRAM-SHA-1", "MongoDB-CR", and "x.509 Certificate authentication". Consequently, until designers provide a more reliable, tougher technique utilizing Mongoose and bcrypt components with Backbone, researchers plan to develop a passcode security mechanism combining built-in technology. Mongoose is a sophisticated item database design framework for MongoDB networks that can organize and structure data. It also functions as a data model translation tool. Another choice is to employ distinct gateway verification methods like "*Kerberos and Lightweight Directory Access Protocol*" (LDAP), which can be a trickier procedure [5]. Since this approach may also be employed to protect the database at rest, designers want to utilize Mongoose to encrypt files (or other material) while storing these in the "*MongoDB database server*".

2.2 Authorization

Although MongoDB does not implement identity management by standard, the database's actions and the resources that are available to authorized individuals are determined by the sign-up process. After activation, MongoDB is equipped with the nine administrative functions that the system has specified. This study defines the fundamental information strategy that directs the execution of password protection. The network manager, who has complete access, and one normal user are the first emphasis [6]. The other individuals have lower authorizations because they adhere to the idea of minimum competence when creating responsibilities that govern the amount of access granted per account.

2.3 Privacy-preserving Data Extractions, Transmissions, and Loadings

While required to fulfil into MongoDB, scholar's suggested private information data processing technique turns the data header and file name into a quantitative data heading and file name interpretation, which makes it harder to interpret what a given column's contents and/or source file signify. Every document or folder that is imported into MongoDB has a pair of keys created for it, often in the format of "Header: its Content." These prefixes are typically "String" objects of various sizes. The "Header Formatter" generates a new numeric value to each distinct header at this stage, and this integer number serves as the header's network identification [7]. At this point, dispute resolution gets crucial since it frequently happens that the exact headline is employed to designate multiple metrics. Multiple flag use needs to be handled since leaving such headers in their current state will simply cause confusion and misunderstanding throughout selecting features. The system includes header structuring to address this repeated heading usage. Each distinct header is given a special numeric ID by the header's compiler. The header's related explanation is examined if it is not identical. The frequently viewed heading receives the very same result as the other corresponding element if the explanation of the frequently viewed heading fits the definition of any of the related non-unique headings [8].

A contradictory component is created and given a brand-new numerical ID if the content of the newly received heading differs from the specifications of all other matched headers. For any clashing headings, the framework likewise keeps a distinct set of information. Whereas the information sequence is creating the database schema, the computational step constructs as well as reproduces a collection to keep records of the headings and the documents in which they are contained [9, 10]. This metadata plays a crucial role in the extraction stage.

In accordance with the study security arrangements of this investigation, encrypting is begun at the software level [11, 12]. Considering that MongoDB substitutes unencrypted information in a document with encrypted files and its advanced version, encrypting information is conceptually simple, but practical challenges might arise. The secrets are at the protocol stack, distinct from the database layer, and the unencrypted material is never kept or sent at this stage, where the presentation layer has entire authority and decryption is independent of the host and the host system [13]. As a result, the data structure is incapable of disclosing the attack's actual unencrypted contents. The attack channel for encrypting at this stage is provided by widespread application flaws like cross-site scripting (XSS) or SQL injection. Implementation encrypting, one of several components of proper encryption, supports the system. Additionally, researchers utilise Mongoose as well as crypto modules with Node [14]. js for encryption software and storing in MongoDB, much like how it is used for password protection during verification. The AES-256-CBC technique of the Crypto component is employed for encryption, using a distinct randomized input value for each execution.

3. Research Methodology

Research methods are successful tactics, approaches, and procedures used to collect data for analysis of internal information and the development of a clearer knowledge. The topic at hand calls for the employment of a secondary qualitative data collection method. In accordance with the secondary data collecting approach, information was gathered from various journals, books, and peer-reviewed publications by accurately evaluating each component. In this context, empirical analysis has been done based on the data gathered from those secondary sources. Thus, a definite conclusion has been reached.

4. Analysis and Discussion

4.1 The Method of Enhancing Database Security in Web-based Environment through Big Data

A "dynamic detection system" for database activity monitoring is the "intrusion detection system" (IDS). Through the recognition of unlawful use of the database's information systems resources, it may discover unauthorised access operations from internal purposes. By correlating characteristic databases to recognize foreign harmful takeover and attacking behaviour, it can recognize potential risks [15]. In order to assist users in doing pertinent research, the system may also track the volume of network traffic passing through it and give users with information regarding congestion. Innovation for preventing intrusions is distinct from vulnerability scanning. It is a technique for bypassing identification.

$$(x) = b_{n-1}x^{n-1} + b_{n-2}x^{n-2} + \cdots + b_2n^2 + b_1x + b_0 \tag{1}$$

Alternative password encryption:

$$E((m) = (m + k) \ mod * n \tag{2}$$

M stands for the plaintext letter positions, n for the total number of letters, and K for the private key. inverse modulo components

$$ed = 1(mod \ \phi(n)) \tag{3}$$

$$ed - k(n) = 1 \tag{4}$$

A modulo inverse element is one for which the remainder of ed divided by $\phi(n)$ is an integer d such that the value of the result is 1.

System Integration of AI: Because this technique primarily employs the human brain to carry out simulated activities, it offers several distinct benefits. Additionally, AI can recognize in either the input mode or the output mode with effectiveness, and because the detection impact is stronger, it is commonly employed. Information is sent from the input layer to the hidden layer in the centre of a straightforward neural network before being output through the output nodes. The bottom neural network receives its output from the higher neural network in the hidden layer, and there are complete connections or local connections across network nodes. The convolution layer and the pooling layer are often superimposed to create the hidden layer [16]. A common predictor is a neural network. A SoftMax classifier and a whole connection layer are Randomised dispersion is established in the hidden state of the neural channel's final layer and contributes to it. The steps in the instructional procedure are as follows: (1) The specimen information is divided into training dataset, confirmation sets, and test sets; (2) instructional information is entered into the backbone network for forward instruction; (3) network output prognostication values and real label deficit value is computed; (4) the weight of every layer is modified through using erroneous value back transmission; (5) after many repetitions; (6) the network can be considered trained when the depreciation rate does not alter [17]. The formula in question is written as follows:

$$\frac{dJ}{dw} = -e_j \cdot sigmoi(\sum_j w_{jk} \cdot o_i)(1 - sigmoid(\sum_j w_{jk} \cdot o_i)) \cdot o_i \tag{5}$$

$$w_{jk} = w_{jk} - \alpha \frac{dJ}{dw} \tag{6}$$

where e_j, w_{jk}, and o_i are, respectively, the errors at the fifth neuron, the weight at the j neuron, and the output of the I neuron, $\frac{dJ}{dw}$ is the derivative of the cost function. Equation (7) may be written as follows:

$$\Delta w_{jk} = \alpha \cdot J_k \cdot o(1 - ok) \cdot o_j^T \tag{7}$$

The following equation is taken into consideration while determining the encryption rate of transmitted data. From similar work, researchers get the following equation:

$$E_n R_a = \frac{R_e D_{ata} - (T_r D_{ata} * NL_{ter})}{T_r T_{ime}} \tag{8}$$

The Abbreviation Meaning $E_n R_a$ Data Encryption Rate

$E_n D_{ata}$ Imported Data

$R_e D_{ata}$ Transferred Data

NL_{ter} Optimum Iterations

$T_r T_{ime}$ Data Transmission Time

Researchers have a very modest percentage of packet losses due to the enormous volume of data delivered.

$$P_a L_o = \frac{(P_a T_r - P_a R_e) - D_u P_a}{T_r T_{ime}} \tag{9}$$

$$\frac{P_a R_e}{T_r T_{ime}} = \frac{P_a T_r - P_a L_o - D_u P_a}{T_r T_{ime}} \tag{10}$$

Where,

$P_a L_o = Packet\ loss$

$P_a T_r = Packet\ transmitted$

$P_a R_e = Packet\ received$

$D_u P_a = Duplicate\ packet$

$T_r T_{ime} = Transmission\ time\ of\ packet\ sent$

The data packet of the data transmission across the suggested network is shown in (9). The quantity of data sent at each moment affects the rate of packet loss, which varies with time. On the other hand, (10) illustrates the relationship between the total packets transmitted, minus packet loss and duplicate packets, and the packets retrieved throughout the data transmission (time).

4.2 Innovative Database Security Mechanism

After decades of development, modern databases have proven to be extremely robust and have complex structures. Like many other evolving architectures, databases have become more popular recently. While the optimization algorithm in the current research work used the query attack and DI attack, a protected database in the web injects many threats in web servers. The database server side provides a controlled protection system as part of a decentralized cloud service to ensure the safe execution of all required queries without any database hijacking [18].

Database Interferences Problem

Sorting the database to draw a conclusion on a particular class of data security breaches is difficult. This may be explained by the way it uses a logical process and human personality to derive secure data. In order to protect a database, it must be current, intact, and private. The accessibility factor involves avoiding hardware and software [20]. When information is necessary, authenticity protects it from unauthorised data access and unlawful data modification. Confidentiality protects it from unauthorised data access to webpage data protection.

Query Preprocessing

The front-end limits the queries during query pre-processing to keep the aggregation outcomes in check. To ensure that only a permitted aggregate function is employed for each item, it is validated before it is selected. To aid in future study, a count is automatically recorded for each chosen item. The non-valuable inquiries from this preparation system are not sent to the webpage "data security model". Moreover, "query processing performance" can be significantly improved by reducing the amount of ON actions [21]. The likelihood of data risks rises when a large number of unidentified individuals access the data. Additionally, the database hacks are carried out in order to profit greatly by selling private information in illicit ways.

Query Optimization

DBCO executes the query optimization after the pre-processed SQL and DI queries have been secured. It is typically one of the most overlooked, yet while utilising blind SQL injections, it has important angles. Not only does an efficient SQL injection yield a quicker result, but it also eases network congestion, which lessens the server's workload. Without valid records, SQL queries may result in table exports, which may affect performance or locking [22].

SQL Injection Problem

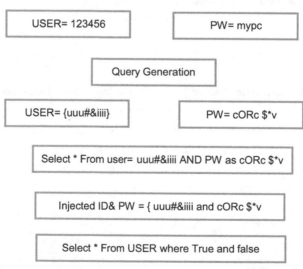

Fig. 11.1   Representation for SQL injection model

Source: Made by Author

According to reports, SQLIA is a system for code injection attacks that is typically used to target websites. In order to access the database in this system, an attacker substitutes some SQL codes for the original ones. Figure 11.1 depicts this injection technique. The strengths of both static and dynamic analysis approaches are utilised by merged static and dynamic analysing processes to evaluate SQL injection attacks. It examines internet pages and generates SQL queries to sample this model's simulation results [19].

Attack Injection

The private word and username sections are open to any malicious user to enter dangerous data. A user's single instruction can either obliterate the entire database or notify the administrator of a potential interruption. Many websites employ the user's input—such as their search keywords, their feedback, or their login and secret word—to create a SQL query that is subsequently sent to the database.

"Query: Choose * Customer ID = {2}

SQL Query = Choose*From Customer ID = 4121 = Valid

Valid Query = Choose attacked customer ID {4121} = 7896"

5. Conclusions

The investigation was carried out in three phases, as well as the outcomes are shown above. In the initial process, researchers suggested an information-analytical model with MongoDB and LXCs and basic security prerequisites. By utilising all of the above-said security measures, researchers have been able to add an added protection to this structure. Researchers then suggested a vulnerability assessment testing ground in the second stage to discover system-related vulnerabilities. Lastly, in the third part, researchers went into great depth on the sources of security flaws as well as some preventative measures. Using the abovementioned safety procedures, researchers propose to address the study issue via the research methods. Furthermore, the overall security needs rely on the security requirements of a certain individual or organisation and the available funding. Because of this, it is crucial to adjust the structure in order to comply with the company's or user's regulatory issues in order to add much more protection and achieve the highest intended secure communication of the suggested data analytical lens. However, it is important to emphasise that both teams of experienced and the program platform's users/clients share some responsibility for the program's general stability. Particularly, the user-related flaws are essential since they have the potential to undermine the system's safety if authenticated users are led astray and utilise it to their advantage. It is crucial to remember that threats to security may not necessarily be caused by the technical attributes of the system.

REFERENCES

1. Raj, R. J. S., Prakash, M.V., Prince, T., Shankar, K., Varadarajan, V. and Nonyelu, F., 2020. Web Based Database Security in Internet of Things Using Fully Homomorphic Encryption and Discrete Bee Colony Optimization. *Malaysian Journal of Computer Science*, pp. 1–14.
2. Talari, G., Cummins, E., McNamara, C. and O'Brien, J., 2021. State of the art review of Big Data and web-based Decision Support Systems (DSS) for food safety risk assessment with respect to climate change. *Trends in Food Science & Technology*.
3. Ahmad, K., Alam, M.S. and Udzir, N.I., 2019. Security of NoSQL database against intruders. *Recent Patents on Engineering*, *13*(1), pp. 5–12.
4. Mailewa, A., Mengel, S., Gittner, L. and Khan, H., 2022. Mechanisms and techniques to enhance the security of big data analytic framework with mongodb and Linux containers. *Array*, *15*, p. 100236.
5. Samaraweera, G.D. and Chang, J.M., 2019. Security and privacy implications on database systems in Big Data era: A survey. *IEEE Transactions on Knowledge and Data Engineering*, *33*(1), pp. 239–258.
6. Li, L. and Zhang, J., 2021. Research and analysis of an enterprise E-commerce marketing system under the big data environment. *Journal of Organizational and End User Computing (JOEUC)*, *33*(6), pp. 1–19.
7. Moutselos, K., Kyriazis, D. and Maglogiannis, I., 2018, July. A web based modular environment for assisting health policy making utilizing big data analytics. In *2018 9th International Conference on Information, Intelligence, Systems and Applications (IISA)* (pp. 1–5). IEEE.
8. Adnan, N. A. N. and Ariffin, S., 2018, August. Big data security in the web-based cloud storage system using 3D-AES block cipher cryptography algorithm. In *International Conference on Soft Computing in Data Science* (pp. 309-321). Springer, Singapore.
9. V. Panwar, D.K. Sharma, K.V.P.Kumar, A. Jain & C. Thakar, (2021), "Experimental Investigations And Optimization Of Surface Roughness In Turning Of EN 36 Alloy Steel Using Response Surface Methodology And Genetic Algorithm" Materials Today: Proceedings, https://Doi.Org/10.1016/J.Matpr.2021.03.642

10. A. Jain, A. K. Pandey, (2019), "Modeling And Optimizing Of Different Quality Characteristics In Electrical Discharge Drilling Of Titanium Alloy (Grade-5) Sheet" Material Today Proceedings, 18, 182-191. https://doi.org/10.1016/j.matpr.2019.06.292
11. Deibe, D., Amor, M. and Doallo, R., 2018, December. Big data storage technologies: a case study for web-based LiDAR visualization. In *2018 IEEE International Conference on Big Data (Big Data)* (pp. 3831–3840). IEEE.
12. A. Jain, A.K.Yadav & Y. Shrivastava (2019), "Modelling and Optimization of Different Quality Characteristics In Electric Discharge Drilling of Titanium Alloy Sheet" Material Today Proceedings, 21, 1680-1684. https://doi.org/10.1016/j.matpr.2019.12.010
13. A. Jain, A. K. Pandey, (2019), "Modeling And Optimizing Of Different Quality Characteristics In Electrical Discharge Drilling Of Titanium Alloy (Grade-5) Sheet" Material Today Proceedings, 18, 182-191. https://doi.org/10.1016/j.matpr.2019.06.292
14. Sonewar, P.A. and Thosar, S.D., 2016, August. Detection of SQL injection and XSS attacks in three tier web applications. In Computing Communication Control and automation (ICCUBEA), 2016 International Conference on (pp. 1–4). IEEE.
15. Katole, R.A., Sherekar, S.S. and Thakare, V.M., 2018, January. Detection of SQL injection attacks by removing the parameter values of SQL query. In 2018 2nd International Conference on Inventive Systems and Control (ICISC) (pp. 736–741). IEEE.
16. Basta, C., Elfatatry, A. and Darwish, S., 2016. Detection of SQL Injection Using a Genetic Fuzzy Classifier System. International Journal of Advanced Computer Science and Applications, 7(6), pp. 129–137.
17. A. Jain, A. K. Pandey, (2019), "Multiple Quality Optimizations In Electrical Discharge Drilling Of Mild Steel Sheet" Material Today Proceedings, 8, 7252–7261. https://doi.org/10.1016/j.matpr.2017.07.054
18. V. Panwar, D.K. Sharma, K.V.P.Kumar, A. Jain & C. Thakar, (2021), "Experimental Investigations And Optimization Of Surface Roughness In Turning Of EN 36 Alloy Steel Using Response Surface Methodology And Genetic Algorithm" Materials Today: Proceedings, https://Doi.Org/10.1016/J.Matpr.2021.03.642
19. Alwan, Z.S. and Younis, M.F., 2017. Detection and Prevention of SQL Injection Attack: A Survey. International Journal of Computer Science and Mobile Computing, 6(8), pp. 5–17.
20. Shankar, K. and Lakshmanaprabu, S.K., 2018. Optimal key based homomorphic encryption for color image security aid of ant lion optimization algorithm. International Journal of Engineering & Technology, 7(1.9), pp. 22–27.
21. A. Jain, C. S. Kumar, Y. Shrivastava, (2021), "Fabrication and Machining of Fiber Matrix Composite through Electric Discharge Machining: A short review" Material Today Proceedings. https://doi.org/10.1016/j.matpr.2021.07.288
22. K. Shankar, Mohamed Elhoseny, R. Satheesh Kumar, S. K. Lakshmanaprabu, Xiaohui Yuan, "Secret image sharing scheme with encrypted shadow images using optimal homomorphic encryption technique", Journal of Ambient Intelligence and Humanized Computing, December 2018. https://doi.org/10.1007/s12652-018-1161-0

Computer Science Engineering and Emerging Technologies (ICCS-2022) – Prof (Dr.) Rajeev Sobti et al. (eds)
© 2024 Taylor & Francis Group, London, ISBN 978-1-032-52199-2

Chapter | **12**

Challenges in Security and Privacy in Wireless Networks and Mitigation Methods Using Blockchain Technology

Vikas Nana Mahandule[1]
Head & Assistant Professor, Computer Application Department,
MIT Arts Commerce &Science College Alandi (D.), Pune, Maharashtra

Ankur Kulshreshtha[2]
Principal, NIMS School of Robotics and Artifical Intelligence,
NIET, NIMS University, Jaipur, Rajasthan

Babu Kumar S.[3]
Assistant Professor, Department of Computer Science and Engineering,
CHRIST (Deemed to be University), Bangalore, Karnataka

S. Shyni Carmel Mary[4]
Assistant professor, Business analytics,
Loyola institute of business administration

Ashim Bora[5]
5Principal, Kampur College, Kampur, Assam. India

Anilkumar Suthar[6]
Director & Professor, New L. J. Institute of Engineering and Technology,
Ahmadabad, Gujarat

Abstract: With blockchain technology, the digital database may be transferred via the internet without the need for duplicating any of the information. It serves as a public ledger accessible to anybody, decentralized from any one source of authority. It's a tool that can help businesses and individuals work together more effectively, build trust, and boost transparency in their digital dealings. With the advent of blockchain technology, businesses may now benefit from more openness, security, and traceability of their transactions. As a result, developers may create new marketplaces and transfer cash by predetermined guidelines. Blockchain's primary benefits are its decentralization, immutability, and accelerated transactions and confirmation times (measured in seconds). Blockchain's impressive problem-solving power in commercial contexts stems from its decentralized nature. All of a blockchain transaction's past and present interactions are encrypted using cryptography. Algorithms running on the nodes of a blockchain validate the legitimacy of transactions. Since a single party cannot initiate a transaction, blockchains enable transparency by giving each participant the ability to monitor the trade at any moment. Smart contracts enable encrypted exchanges, which protect users from fraudulent activities of third parties. The two decentralized features of blockchain, create dependability and reduce risk when joining a commercial partnership with an unknown party. To ensure its integrity, the blockchain is developed and maintained by a distributed network of computers using encryption that is both intelligent and decentralized.

Keywords: Blockchain technology, Security issues, Double spending, Mining attacks, Distributed techniques, Security, Privacy, Cryptocurrency, Decentralized system, Fraud, Transparency, Interference

[1]vikasmahandule@gmail.com, [2]ankurkulsh@nimsuniversity.org, [3]babukumar.sbk@gmail.com, [4]Shynipragasam@gmail.com, [5]ashim.bora@gmail.com, [6]sutharac@gmail.com

DOI: 10.1201/9781003405580-12

1. Introduction

The blockchain was used to introduce the world to Bitcoin, the most widely recognized cryptocurrency. It builds on the ideas of a P2P network by allowing for a shared source of information on which all consumers may depend, although they wouldn't respect each other. It creates a decentralized, reliable, & confidential transactional record or logs in which duplicate, encoded versions of material are maintained on every node. The system is made more resilient to errors and collisions by the use of financial incentives, such as native network tokens and so on.

To a lesser extent, blockchain technology has proven effective in other technological domains. The Internet of Things, for instance, has been used to improve the safety and performance of connected devices. For instance, studies have shown that food can be traced from fields to shops in a matter of seconds using Blockchain technology in the agricultural business. This helps in the fight against illicit harvesting and transportation schemes (Hackernoon, n.d.a). Overflowing goods inventory monitoring is another use. The premise on which this solution relies is that Blockchain prevents altering data, making hacking more difficult. There is a unique problem with using Blockchain with IoT. Blockchain data mining is computationally and processing-intensive. Most gadgets in the Internet of Things lack the juice to make it happen. It has been hypothesized that blockchain technology might potentially improve the safety and efficacy of cyber-physical systems. Recent research, for instance, has shown that Blockchain technology has applications in the growing field of driverless vehicles. Information on freshly manufactured automobiles may be recorded in a Blockchain-based database. Consequently, a digital wallet may be used to safely keep track of all the details of freshly made automobiles. The integrity of the data you save will be cryptographically guaranteed to remain unaltered. This will allow the car to pay its bills, tolls, and penalties by connecting to various networks. Social media and other network infrastructures have benefited greatly from the use of blockchain technology. False information may go as fast as legitimate stuff on social media. Blockchain's distributed ledger may be used to combat disinformation campaigns. At any moment, you may check your content and your identity. Data collection is also greatly facilitated by this. To further track data and see how users engage with the material, blockchain technology also allows for this. This improves the accuracy with which social media platforms can estimate the number of likes, shares, and views. Despite some concerns about privacy and other difficulties, the use of crowdsourcing platforms has skyrocketed in recent years. To address the issue of low-value transactions in crowdsourcing, blockchain-based technologies were used (Li et al., 2019). Crowdsensing, which involves the collection and processing of data via the use of a network of dispersed sensing devices, has also seen significant growth in recent years. Blockchain's qualities as a distributed, immutable database make it ideal for bolstering the safety of crowdsensing programs. Cloudlet is another significant use of Blockchain technology. Cloudlet is a collection of computers that can quickly provide cloud-based computing services to consumers, which may improve the efficiency of multimedia applications. With the growing demands of migrated tasks from users comes the need of ensuring the security or integrity of offloaded data handled by cloudlets. Blockchain's features are very useful in this context. Blockchain is also employed in cloud, fog, and edge computing environments to boost security and trust. The term "fog computing" refers to a kind of distributed computing architecture in which resources such as data, computing, storage, and applications are located between the cloud as well as the data source. Due to its dispersed nature, fog computing needs a method of safeguarding data transmissions and server assets. In a similar vein, the edge is a decentralized architecture in which computations are performed closer to the source of data creation (the network's periphery) than in a centralized data processing repository. Computing services like databases, storage, software, and analytics may now be accessed remotely through the internet thanks to cloud computing. In this case, a uniformly dispersed system of safety precautions is necessary. Blockchain is an immutable distributed ledger that guarantees the integrity of its data. As a result, it establishes a network where everyone can feel safe and trusted.

2. Literature Review

2.1 Issues and Challenges in Privacy and Security in Blockchain Technology

Akin to the adage, Every coin has two sides, the benefits of digital information's authentication and transparency also come with drawbacks. It's not uncommon for cyberattacks to be the result of the propagation of false information. Blockchain's primary focus is on the development of a system that can effectively combat fraudulent activity. How do we encourage individuals to provide their very best effort in a professional setting? How can we best find common ground to further everyone's goals?

(a) The increasing number of people using and interacting with well-known social media platforms is of immediate and pressing concern. Social media sites like Facebook and Twitter employ advertising to attract more users, but some of those users may be more comfortable remaining anonymous online.

(b) Second, incorrect data transmission is a problem. When sending sensitive data to a server, you don't know who may exploit it for his gain, and this becomes a serious problem.

(c) The third concern is crypto-jacking, a kind of malware that, although it may not steal money from members directly, nonetheless leaves the door open for criminals to access hostile software that might create issues for users.

(d) As a result, the whole process is flawed due to the fourth problem:

greedy mining that optimizes efficiency or profits by concealing its blocks and not exposing its genuine identity.

(e) The fifth problem is that, unlike linked lists, which carry the following block's hashing values, blocks in a blockchain do not contain that value.

(f) The sixth concern is that, contrary to popular belief, an attacker may make illicit profit via a rogue mining operation with as little as 25% operating capacity.

(g) Bitcoin wallets, the seventh problem, have become a primary target for cybercriminals.

(h) The eighth problem is double-spending; this has been an issue for some time, and the irreversibility of data renders the transaction invalid.

(i) The ninth problem is the security of the software being utilized. Although very effective, it is not immune to the kinds of minor flaws that might lead to significant transaction mistakes.

(j) The tenth problem is that they suggest utilizing a hardware token to safeguard the private key, which may be lost or stolen. The eleventh problem is that they cannibalize the data and cause undesired collisions via timestamp attacks.

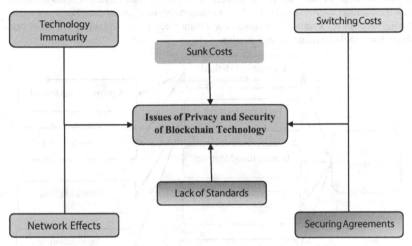

Fig. 12.1 Issues of privacy and security of blockchain technology

2.2 In a Consensus Algorithm for Reaching Agreement

A Consensus Algorithm for Reaching Agreement Intricate as they may be, these algorithms come in handy when operating a node or buying cryptocurrency. In networks when multiple nodes are present and follow the aforementioned standards, they ensure the network's dependability. In a Blockchain, the consensus is determined not by the miners but by the nodes. When determining a consensus, the chain with the most work is used. When the Proof of Work is changed, there will be no more miners to keep the Blockchain safe if the Blockchain splits. The transactions are accepted, validated, and replicated by the nodes. Together with providing and storing in the Blockchain, they also validate and reproduce the blocks. The nodes, and not the miners, decide on the proof-of-work algorithm. The reward of works was the initial Blockchain agreement method. This algorithm is what the Blockchain relies on to verify transactions and add new blocks. Competition amongst miners to verify transactions and earn rewards is the basis of proof of work. Each participant in a network is issued a digital token. All transactions in a distributed ledger are grouped into "blocks." Transactions should be properly validated at this stage.

This approach, called Proof of Stake, was developed to address various weaknesses in the more popular Proof of Work protocol. As stated, a user's ability to verify or mine block transactions is proportional to their currency holdings. As a result, a user's ability to mine increases in proportion to the number of coins he or she has.

Evidence of Interest Assigned is an example of an agreement technique that may be used to verify transactions and maintain the network's agreement on the truth. To arrive at a decision, our system takes into account past voting results and user reputation in real time. It is the most democratic consensus protocol since it has the fewest central points of control. Tolerating Byzantine Faults in Practice: A Practical Approach This is a method for a decentralized network to reach an agreement on the Blockchain even if some nodes are malevolent or fraudulent. This means that the majority of nodes must reach a consensus on a topic before the transaction can be 204 Issues and Verified Confidentiality, Protection, as well as Confidence Issues in Blockchain-Based Programs. The ability of the Blockchain to confirm a transaction even if some of the network's nodes disagree with it is essentially its defining feature.

The following are the two fundamental concepts on which the Raft Consensus method operates. Only one leader may be selected every term. A leader may only add new items to the log; it cannot modify or remove existing ones. When there are few servers available, this algorithm is employed. There are leader servers, follower servers, and candidate servers. In response to leaders' demands, followers express their appreciation. Every new term starts with a flurry of leadership elections.

2.3 Algorithms for Mining Cluster analysis

Sequence analysis and association rules are the three main subfields of data mining. Clustering and classification are processes that examine data sets to provide sets of rules for categorizing new sets of data. Sequence analysis is the process of looking at repeating trends over a certain time frame. For a database, an association rule is a set of rules that govern the proper way in which data should be related to one another.

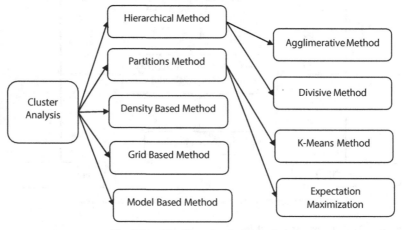

Fig. 12.2 Algorithms for cluster analysis

3. Data and Variables

3.1 Study Period and Sample

Algorithm for Creating a Chain of Traceability While new data is being gathered in the background to improve the efficiency of internal operations and to plan the efforts of each node in the chain, traceability validates the start and work after a transaction. This algorithm's goal is to quickly draw conclusions on traceability. This method is faster than a consensus algorithm since it includes an inference mechanism. The function of traceability in Blockchain is to reinforce and improve the coordination the chain already has, allowing more information to be gathered about the location and status of transactions taking place, which can then be utilized by the nodes to plan the chain's future endeavors. With this technique, we can track the provenance of every single digital item stored on the Blockchain. In this approach, nodes are labeled so that they may be quickly located and examined. Electronic information dissemination requires extensive scanning to provide rapid data retrieval. Connections are constructed so that information can be efficiently transferred across chains. Therefore, several current tools, methodologies, and algorithms for blockchain-based applications are discussed in depth in this section. In the next part, we will provide some suggestions on where future research may go (toward possible blockchain-based applications).

3.2 Mechanisms for Ensuring Safety in Wireless Networks

There are four main categories for wireless network security needs. These specifications must be met by any wireless network to ensure that it is safe against intrusion. Data confidentiality, data integrity, and data availability are the three pillars of information security that every control system should support. Major wireless network security needs are outlined in Table 12.1. It is useful to think about why these safeguards are simple to install in wired networks but seem more challenging in wireless ones. For instance, a wireless node employs supplementary DSSS (or FHSS) algorithms to counteract jamming assaults. Think about how permission, one of the security needs, might work in the context of Bluetooth technology. An essential part of any Bluetooth security architecture is the security manager, which handles all authentication, authorization, and encryption. Bluetooth has security features including encryption, authentication, and key generation built into it. The key is produced from a Bluetooth personal identification number (PIN) that must be input into both gadgets. A master key, also known as an initialization key, is produced during pairing using the E22 technique. When a Bluetooth device needs access to another, it uses an authorization mechanism to do so. Many positives have been attributed to Bluetooth technology; however, it can present certain difficulties. DDoS assaults, eavesdropping, man-in-the-middle attacks, tampering with messages, and so on are only a few examples.

4. Methodology and Model Specifications

Blockchain technologies are a potential utility for businesses, with future uses that will enable encrypted payments without the requirement for a centralized agency. The initial use was digital currency platforms, which distributed a worldwide database recording all payments. Cryptographic hashing is employed to encrypt the payments, while asymmetric key pairings are utilized to authenticate or validate them. The implementation of blockchain technologies remains in its initial stages, although it is centered on cryptographic ideas that are well-known as well as sound. A blockchain is based on current networking, cryptography, or record-keeping technology, but it employs these in a more sophisticated manner with modifications or upgrades.

Although it cannot be disputed that certain blockchain beginners would fight harder for understanding or knowledge on how to use these technologies. Persons may acquire new abilities, but traditional businesses must completely redesign their processes. Blockchain has been a fantastic innovation in the recent years because it supports various implementations, including hand bitcoin coin purchases, greater protection throughout exchanges, particularly responsive information, quicker as well as affordable exchanges, as well as almost any peers implementation, as well as extra advantages in its clarity as well as data integrity.

Table 12.1 Analysis of jamming attacks in wireless communication and mitigation (Ishengoma, 2022)

Years	Number of attacks	Complexity	Jamming effectiveness
2019	5	4.5	4
2020	8	9.3	5
2021	10	5.5	9
2022	13	11.2	10
2023	14	13.2	11
2024	15	12.3	13
2025	17	11.2	16
2026	19	14.9	18
2027	21	15.8	20
2028	22	16.8	21
2029	25	19.5	24

5. Empirical Results

5.1 Advancement of Wireless Communications in Blockchain Technology

The late 1800s and the pioneering work of M.G. Marconi, who successfully established a radio connection between a land-based station and a tugboat, are credited with the creation of wireless communications. Thereafter, Fessenden developed amplitude modulation (AM) for the radio transmission of music in 1906, and Edwin H. Armstrong introduced frequency modulation (FM) in 1933. There has been a veritable surge in the development of wireless technologies during the last two decades. First-generation (1G) wireless communications systems used narrow-band analog signaling for voice transmission in the 1980s, giving way to second-generation (2G) narrow-band systems in the 1990s that relied on digital communication techniques like time division multiple access (TDMA), frequency division multiple access (FDMA), and code division multiple access (CDMA). The GSM 900MHz frequency band and the General Packet Radio Service (GPRS) at 56 Kbps to 114 Kbps were used for the transmission of the 2G voice signal. In addition to the development of digital transmission systems, 2G technology also gave birth to the Global Systems for Mobility (GSM), personal digital cellular (PDC), IS-136, and IS-95. Various wireless technologies (e.g., GSM, CDMA, and TDMA) are now being used to build up 2G, 2.5G, and ultimately 3G networks throughout the globe. The 144 Kbps data rate provided by a 2.5G network is superior to that of a 2G network and may be utilized to transmit elementary data services like text messages. However, a PDA user would not be able to utilize 2.5G for picture downloads or web browsing. Because of its many shortcomings, 2G technology inspired the development of 3G technology. At the very least, this technology should provide more cutting-edge options, such as internet multimedia services. In addition, 3G technology should speed up the delivery of information services. The Universal Mobile Telecommunications System (UMTS) is a third-generation mobile network that is being upgraded to fourth-generation standards. Transmission of voice communications and multimedia services were both accomplished digitally by the use of 3G technology. The third-generation (3G) mobile network standard was succeeded by the higher-speed (3G+, or HSDPA) network that aimed to achieve between 7.2 and 14.4 Mbps on mobile phones for rapid mp3 downloads. Broadband wireless access with data speeds of 100 Mbps is the goal of the newly announced 4G technology, which aims to complete the cycle of technical improvement in wireless communication. A 4G network may provide coverage over a larger region and send data at a much quicker rate. It is expected that a 4G system, also known as Long Term Evolution (LTE) technologies, would be able to provide an all-encompassing and secure IP solution, allowing users to receive voice, data, and streaming multimedia on an "anytime-anywhere" a more frequent period as well as a higher information rate than prior versions.

Table 12.2 Analysis of security and privacy In various devices (Kar, 2022)

Percentages (%)	Value (0-350)	Security and privacy in devices
20	100-120	Wearable devices
45-55	150-250	Sensors, IoT devices
90	300-320	Mobile phones, tablets

6. Conclusion

The study states that an increasing number of sectors and institutions are making use of the benefits offered by Blockchain networks. Blockchain's decentralization, distributed ledger, and cryptographic hashing will cause it to disrupt every industry over the next decade or so (or using no intermediaries). Blockchain, a distributed, public ledger, has the potential to revolutionize both industries and societies. Short-term reality permits a blockchain-based change. Great transparency, better security, improved traceability, higher efficiency, and speed are some of the most well-known benefits of employing blockchain (using proof of work) in manipulations (such as cloudlet, the internet of things, cloud computing, edge computing, etc.) (with reduced cost). Our future success depends on advancing blockchain technology or eliminating its negative consequences. A widely accepted technology will be both inexpensive (easy to get) and harmless to humans and their natural surroundings. To lessen the potential drawbacks of using blockchain in our personal and professional lives, we may use this technology to build a more innovative and environmentally friendly way of living.

REFERENCES

1. Bolting, A. (2020). Introduction to blockchain technology. Cryptographic Primitives in Blockchain Technology, 199–240. doi:10.1093/Oso/9780198862840.003.0006
2. Applications of blockchain technology in different domains. (2020). Blockchain and the Digital Economy, 115–172. DOI: 10.2307/j.ctv16qjxg0.8
3. Applying blockchain technology to model-based systems engineering. (2020). DOI: 10.2514/6.2021-0093.vid
4. Baldoni, P., & Baraita, M. T. (2019). Legal aspects of Blockchain technology. Essentials of Blockchain Technology, 293–348. doi:10.1201/9780429674457-14
5. Blockchain technology. (2018). Blockchain Regulation and Governance in Europe, 1–33. doi:10.1017/9781108609708.001
6. Blockchain technology. (2018). Blockchain Regulation and Governance in Europe, 1–33. doi:10.1017/9781108609708.001
7. Kar, M. (2022). Blockchain technology and cryptocurrency. Blockchain Technology, 13–26. doi:10.1201/9781003138082-2
8. Pandey, M., & Singhal, B. (2022). Blockchain technology in biomanufacturing. Blockchain Technology for Emerging Applications, 207–237. doi:10.1016/b978-0-323-90193-2.00007-7
9. Subha, T. (2020). Assessing security features of Blockchain technology. Blockchain Technology and Applications, 115–138. doi:10.1201/9781003081487-7
10. Karim, R., & Sifat, I. (2022). Blockchain technology in the energy industry. Blockchain Technology, 109–126. doi:10.1201/9781003138082-7
11. Kovaleva'll, C., Saxena, D., & Laroiya, C. (2020). Overview of blockchain technology concepts. Handbook of Research on Blockchain Technology, 349–371. doi:10.1016/b978-0-12- 819816-2.00014-9
12. Kumar, R. (2021). Blockchain in Ehr. Blockchain Technology for Data Privacy Management, 275–293. doi:10.1201/9781003133391- 13
13. Sudha Sadasivam, G. (2021). A critical review on using blockchain technology in the education domain. Blockchain Technology for IoT Applications, 85–117. doi:10.1007/978-981-33-4122- 7_5
14. Thakur, A. (2022). A comprehensive study of the trends and analysis of distributed ledger technology and blockchain technology in the healthcare industry. Frontiers in Blockchain, 5. doi:10.3389/bloc.2022.844834
15. Treiblmaier, H., & Tumasjan, A. (2022). Editorial: Economic and business implications of Blockchain Technology. Frontiers in Blockchain, 5. doi:10.3389/bloc.2022.857247
16. Conclusion:. (2020). Blockchain and the Digital Economy, 173–178. doi:10.2307/j.ctv16qjxg0.9
17. Ishengoma, F. (2022). Blockchain technology as Enablement of Industry 4.0. Integrating Blockchain Technology Into the Circular Economy, 137–164. doi:10.4018/978-1-7998-7642- 7.ch009
18. Sudha Sadasivam, G. (2021). A critical review on using blockchain technology in the education domain. Blockchain Technology for IoT Applications, 85–117. doi:10.1007/978-981-33-4122- 7_5

Computer Science Engineering and Emerging Technologies (ICCS-2022) – Prof (Dr.) Rajeev Sobti et al. (eds)
© *2024 Taylor & Francis Group, London, ISBN 978-1-032-52199-2*

Chapter   **13**

Prediction of Suicide Ideation for Military Personnel Based on Deep Learning: A Review

Sapna Katoch[1]

Student, Department of Computer Science and Engineering, Lovely Professional University

Balwinder Kaur Dhaliwal[2]*, Gurpreet Singh[3]*, Navjot kaur[4]

Assistant Professors, Department of Computer Science and Engineering, Lovely Professional University

Abstract: There is a broad variety of risk factors for suicide, including individual physical, psychological and behavioural characteristics, as well as socioeconomic issues. Because of the greater amount of psychological stress they experience compared to the general population, members of the armed forces have a greater risk of attempting suicide. Suicide attempts may be fuelled by suicidal thoughts if a person is under a lot of mental stress. This may be done by mental health professionals by using traditional diagnostic procedures. Chatbots powered by artificial intelligence have been developed with the goal of reducing the number of deaths by suicide; nevertheless, their success rate is only around 75 percent. We employ machine learning and deep learning algorithms to predict suicide attempts with great accuracy in order to reduce the incidence of suicide in the future. Preliminary data analysis might help us better understand suicide rates and the numerous variables that contribute to them. There is a graphic depiction of suicide attempts available in order to better comprehend the tendencies. For the purpose of constructing suicide prediction models, this study provides a variety of current methodologies. In this review, there are three different algorithms used to find the accuracy of the model: Convolutional Neural Network (CNN), Recurrent Neural Network (RNN) and Multilayer perceptron (MLP).

Keywords: Pre-processing, Deep learning algorithms, CNN, RNN, MLP, Suicide ideation, Machine learning

1. Introduction

Suicide affects people of all races, ethnicities, faiths, genders, and socioeconomic backgrounds. To put it simply, the Centre's for Disease Control and Prevention says that suicide is becoming a major issue in our culture. Approximately 800,000 individuals commit suicide each year, or one person every 40 seconds, according to the CDC. Suicide affects people of all ages and all around the world. As a result, suicide has become the world's top non-natural cause of death and the fourth most common cause of death in the world. Suicide is more common among military members.

Anxiety, performance, physical condition, mental health and well-being, workplace performance, and overall life satisfaction are some of the other factors that should be taken into consideration in addition to the rates of depression, which are one factor that holds a significant amount of importance. Because of the strenuous physical training, the repeated deployments, and the duties, members of the military are more likely to suffer from psychological stress.

The percentage of active-duty members of the armed services who attempt suicide at a rate that is much higher than that of the general population has been gradually increasing over the last several years. According to the National Crime Record

*Corresponding authors: [2]balwinder.25673@lpu.co.in, [3]Gurpreet.17671@lpu.co.in
[1]sapnaktch@gmail.com, [4]navjot.20506@lpu.co.in

DOI: 10.1201/9781003405580-13

Bureau, the incidence of suicide among army personnel grew more than that of those in other armed services. The reason for this is despair, as well as more work and less time for sleep, all of which promote disease and melancholy. The number of service members in the armed forces who take their own lives is getting closer to 1.6 lakh per year and is continuing to rise. Predicting suicidal thoughts and behavior, as well as preventing suicidal behavior altogether, are both necessary and significant tasks for military personnel.

The fast growth of deep learning may be directly attributed to advances in technology that are directly connected to it as well as the availability of a wide variety of different sorts of enormous data sets from the actual world. Academics have devoted a significant amount of work into developing computerized algorithms to cope with large amounts of data. Deep learning is able to work on huge amounts of data. In this review, the algorithms used are CNN (Convolutional Neural Network), RNN (Recurrent Neural Network) and Multilayer Perceptron. In the upcoming paragraphs, there is some information regarding the given algorithms.

Convolutional Neural Networks, much like other kinds of neural networks, are built up of neurons that contain learnable weights and biases. Each neuron receives a number of inputs, does a weighted sum over those inputs, and then processes the result via an activation function before reacting with an output. RNN is predicated on the idea of "keeping the output of a particular layer and feeding this back to the input in order to anticipate the output of the layer." This is the fundamental idea behind RNN. RNN is built on this underlying structure, which is its basis. This is the fundamental idea behind RNN. This is the core concept that makes RNN function in the way that it does. A multilayer perceptron is a kind of feedforward artificial neural network. Its mode of operation involves the development of a collection of outputs that are reliant on the inputs that are provided. A multilayer perceptron's name comes from the fact that it is composed of many layers. In addition, you could hear people refer to it as MLP, which is an acronym for "multilayer perceptron." The existence of several layers of input nodes that are connected in the form of a directed graph between the input and output layers is one of the characteristics that may be used to identify a multilayer perceptron (MLP). Other characteristics include: One of the characteristics that sets an MLP apart is its ability to do this. Backpropagation is the method that is used by MLP when it comes to training the network.

As seen in Fig. 13.1, a schematic representation of the approach presented in this article is shown. There is an overview of the process shown in the figure. Using deep learning techniques and image processing, this model will take a photo with an active camera, analyze it to find symptoms of suicide thoughts, and then generate a prediction about what will happen next.

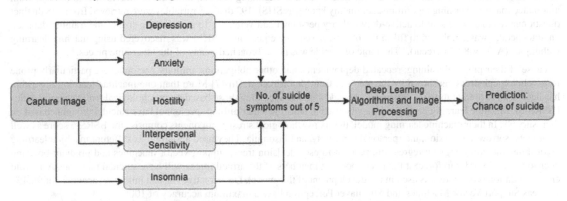

Fig. 13.1 Systematic diagram of proposed method

Source: Made by Author

2. Literature Review

Machine learning algorithms like Random Forest (RF) and Support Vector Machine (SVM) have been used by B. Srinu, P. N. L. Bhavana, B. Tarun Reddy, and B. Vaishnavi [1] to examine and predict whether or not a person has suicidal thoughts by considering the six most important domains of psychological stress and the messages people send to others. Next, we'll look at the similarities and differences between Random Forest (RF) and Support Vector Machine (SVM) outcomes. One of them, known as the Random Forest, has been shown to be more accurate than its counterpart, the Support Vector Machine.

S.S. Priyanka and colleagues [2] wanted to determine the key variables that influence the suicide rate in certain regions of India, so they concentrated their research on those regions. The R-squared value obtained from the Pearson correlation and the OLS regression was 0.998, and the corrected R-squared value was 0.991. Both of these values are quite close to one.

According to Abhishek Vichare, Karthik Ram Srinivas and Pratyaksh Jain [3] depression is the primary mental illness that contributes to suicidal ideation and behavior. They have used a variety of ML techniques, such as Naive Bayes and SVM, in order to forecast the suicide attempts. They have looked at two different subreddits, both of which have supplied us with relevant information that enables us to monitor individuals who are at danger. This is being done so that they can solve the research issue. The Naive Bayes model had the greatest accuracy with 77.29 percent and a f1-score of 0.77. This was followed by the Logistic Regression model and the Support Vector Machine model, both of which also achieved accuracy rates and f1-scores of 0.77. They also observed that Logistic Regression had the highest accuracy rates and f1-scores of 0.77.

In addition to using text analysis and feature engineering, Shaoxiong Ji and his colleagues [4] applied deep learning algorithms in their study. These tactics included CNN and RNN. They analyzed the user's social media postings by applying a keyword filter in order to acquire a better picture of the user's mental health. They have also used a method known as "reach-out," in which an automatic alert is sent to a mental health organization if the individual has a high risk of committing suicide. This approach was used in the event that the individual posed a significant threat to themselves. The 1990s saw the conception and development of this method. Inadequate data and an inability to comprehend the user's intentions are two of the many drawbacks.

A study conducted by F. Chiroma and colleagues looked at the computational efficiency of several classifiers for identifying suicidal messages on social media. The experiment used four different well-known machine classification approaches; Using the Decision Tree technique, the F-measure for suicidal interaction varied from 0.346 to 0.778, with the highest efficiency.

Researchers J. Don Richardson, Sinisa Colica, Kate St. Cyr, Jiang Chen He, Gary M. Hasey, and James P. Reilly [5] wanted to find out if an analysis using machine learning (ML) of data that could easily be collected in a clinic for operational stress injuries could provide new insights into the detection of suicidal ideation. Specifically, they were interested in whether or not this type of analysis could lead to the early identification of suicidal ideation. In particular, they were interested in discovering whether or not this kind of study may assist in recognizing suicidal thoughts in individuals. In order to train automated machine learning algorithms, commonly known as SHSI, 192 distinct variables were retrieved from 738 distinct questionnaires that were sent to active-duty military personnel and veterans. To increase the size of the training data set, an autoencoder was employed to fill in the blanks. Seventy-five percent of SHSI was discovered using machine learning techniques (AUC = 82.7 percent)." The topic of suicide was never broached in any of the other nine pieces.

Because of their physical training, repeated deployments, and other obligations, military personnel are particularly prone to psychological stress, as shown by the study of Gen Men Lin et al. [6]-[7] More than one machine learning algorithm has been used to predict military personnel's suicide ideation, including those based on psychological stress characteristics (BSRS-5). Machine learning algorithms may be used to detect whether military personnel have suicidal thoughts based on their surveys. In their machine learning model, the six psychological stress components comprise the BSRS-5 score as well as anxiety, sorrow, aggression, interpersonal sensitivity, and insomnia. They used a total of six different machine learning algorithms, including logistic regression, random forests, decision trees, support vector machines and gradient-boosting decision trees, in order to forecast the likelihood that members of the armed forces will have suicidal thoughts. A 10-fold cross-validation procedure was used in the development of this model. Decision trees have a minimum accuracy of 98.4%, whereas Support Vector Machines and Multilayer Perceptron have a maximum accuracy of 100%.

B. Ida Seraphim et al. [8] were able to detect impending suicide attempts with varied degrees of accuracy by using four distinct algorithms. They began by preprocessing the data and then normalizing it before moving on to evaluate the effectiveness of four distinct algorithms for machine learning. The Ada boost algorithm had the greatest results, as it attained an accuracy of 97.6 percent, followed by the Xg-boost algorithm, which yielded an accuracy of 96.35 percent. The accuracy provided by the decision tree was 91.67 percent, while the accuracy provided by the MLP classifier was 90 percent.

The sequential difficulty of spotting changes in suicide conduct from Reddit mental health discussions was solved by De Choudhury et al. [9]. They planned for the transition to ideation to take place in such a way that users would first post in other subreddits pertaining to mental health for a certain amount of time before posting in the SW subreddit. They correctly identify 77.5 percent of their users as having suicide thoughts.

Using logistic regression, random forest, and Nave-Bayes, Tarun Agarwal et al. [10]-[11] compared three machine learning algorithms for suicide prediction: Kaggle's "Forever Alone" dataset was used by them. According to their research, 77.65% of those who attempted suicide had 0 to 5 friends. As a result, this characteristic was taken into account while making the forecast. This phenomenon has never previously been seen. Also, 87.6 percent of those who attempt suicide are between the ages of 15 and 30. In terms of their models, Logistic Regression produced predictions that were 94.68% correct. 64.89 percent of the predictions made using naive Bayes were correct. 92.55 percent of the predictions made using Random Forest were correct. The class distribution and limited dataset were blamed for the low accuracy of Naive Bayes.

A model called AISA (Artificial Intelligence based Suicide Avert) was proposed in a study by S.A.S.A. Kulasinghe et al. [12] The goal of this model is to provide users the opportunity to freely communicate their thoughts and sentiments to an artificial companion in the form of a chatbot, which also monitors the users' behavior on social media and listens to what they have to say. The goal of this concept is to reduce the number of users who take their own lives. According to them, extroverts and introverts struggle with various issues related to their mental health, and there is a favorable correlation between depression and introversion. The needs of the users have been taken into consideration in the development of a helpful generative Chat-bot, which will act as a companion for the users and allow them to have conversations on any topic. Seq2Seq (Sequence-to-Sequence) is the model used by their Chat-bot. Users' social media feeds, such as Facebook postings and online browsing histories, are analyzed for sentiment. In addition, they employ speech analysis to determine the user's emotional condition. The data that is obtained from Facebook will be converted into binary, and the symbols that are used the most often will be taken into account throughout the process of analyzing and obtaining the data. To decide the tokens to be utilized, the topic modelling procedure uses the LDA (Latent Dirichlet Allocation) approach. NLP (Natural Language Processing) is used for opinion mining after each session with the user. Accordingly, the bot alters its conversational tone to fit the user's emotional condition. The model was able to accurately predict 75% of the time. Computer communication may further alienate certain people and increase their risk of taking their own life, among other consequences, in a small sample (53 rows). Suicide isn't always the result of depression, but it certainly plays a role.

Machine learning should be used to study suicide risk variables in at-risk groups. The researchers compared the effectiveness of "brief cognitive behavioral therapy" (BCBT) with that of "treatment as usual" (also known as "treatment as usual") for preventing suicide in outpatient mental health care for military personnel (TAU). The clinical and demographic information that was self-reported by 152 patients who had recently exhibited suicidal thoughts or behaviors before beginning treatment was analyzed by a machine learning program for the purpose of predicting whether or not a patient will attempt suicide during or after outpatient treatment. The patients had recently exhibited suicidal thoughts or behaviors before beginning treatment. 38% of patients who attempted suicide during the two-year follow-up period were correctly identified by worst-point suicidal ideation, a history of multiple suicide attempts, treatment group (BCBT or TAU), suicidogenic cognitions, and male sex. Other factors that correctly identified patients who attempted suicide include a history of multiple suicide attempts. The following are some other aspects that played a role in the identification process: This combination predicts suicidal thoughts and behavior better than other models. This study presents a collection of characteristics that may be tested clinically to identify suicide risk [13].

Although depression is one of the most frequent mental diseases among U.S. military communities, few prospective studies investigate a broad variety of variables across various domains for new onset (incident) depression in adulthood, as shown by the work of Laura Sampson and colleagues [14]. Some of the assumptions and limitations that underpin conventional regression studies are unnecessary when using supervised machine learning techniques to discover predictors of incident depression. The purpose of this research was to evaluate the efficacy of machine learning algorithms in predicting the occurrence of depression over a 5-year follow-up period.

The points raised above are the highlights of the review that has already been completed, but it is not always simple to read each and every review line by line. Therefore, in order to cover the main concepts presented in the papers, the table that is provided below should be read in order to comprehend each and every summary presented in the papers.

Table 13.1   Various algorithm used for the prediction of suicide

Authors	Inputs	Used algorithms	Predicted accuracy
B. Srinu et al.[1]	Test Dataset	Random Forest and Support Vector Machine	Accuracy of Random forest is 97 % and accuracy of Support Vector Machine is 96 %.
S.S. Priyanka and colleagues [2]	Text Dataset	Pearson correlation and the OLS regression	value of $R^2 = 0.998$ and an adjusted $R^2 = 0.991$

Authors	Inputs	Used algorithms	Predicted accuracy
Abhishek Vichare, Karthik Ram Srinivas and Pratyaksh Jain [3]	Text Dataset	Naive Bayes, SVM, Logistics regression and random forest	Logistic Regression had an accuracy of 77.29 Naive Bayes had an accuracy of 74.35 percent Support Vector Machine had 77.120 percent accuracy Random Forest had 77.298 percent accuracy
Shaoxiong Ji et al. [4]	Image Dataset	CNN and RNN	CNN accuracy 96 percent RNN accuracy 94.5 percent
F. Chiroma	Suicidal messages on social media.	Four different well-known machine classification approaches	Decision tree has maximum accuracy
Sinisa Colica et al. [5]	192 variables from 738 surveys	Automated machine learning algorithms (SHSI)	AUC = 82.7 percent
Gen Men Lin et al. [6]-[7]	Psychological stress dimensions (BSRS - 5)	Support Vector Machines, Decision trees, and Multilayer Perceptrons	Decision tree accuracy 98.4% Multilayer perceptron and Support Vector Machines accuracy 100%
Apoorv Ranjan, Subroto Das, and Mrs. B. Ida Seraphim [8]	Text Dataset	Ada boost, Xg-boost, decision tree, MLP classifier.	Ada boost accuracy 97.6 percent Xg-boost accuracy 96.35 percent Decision tree accuracy 91.67 MLP classifier accuracy 90 percent
De Choudhury et al. [9]	Reddit mental health discussions	Machine Learning algorithm	77.5 percent
Tarun Agarwal et al. [10]-[11]	"Forever Alone" dataset	logistic regression, random forest, and Nave-Bayes	Logistic Regression produced predictions 94.68% correct. 64.89 percent of the predictions made using naive Bayes were correct. 92.55 percent of the predictions made using Random Forest were correct.
S.A.S.A. Kulasinghe et al. [12]	Data from Facebook	Natural Language Processing and Artificial Intelligence (chat-bot)	Accurately predict 75% of the time.
Dartnell, N. and Rudd, M.D. et al. [13]	Text Dataset	Machine Learning algorithms	38 % classification shows suicide predictions.
Sampson, L., Jiang, T., Gradus, J.L., Cabral, H.J., Rosellini, A.J., Calabrese, J.R., Cohen, G.H., Fink, D.S., King, A.P., Liberzon, I. and Galea, S. [14]	Data were from Army National Guard personnel without a history of depression (n = 1951 males and 298 women).	Classification tree and random forest	Cross verified random forest methods were accurate (73 percent for men and 68 percent for women).

3. Methodology

3.1 Step 1: Importing the Libraries

The most essential step in beginning the implementation of an idea using a programming language is to import the libraries so that any library may be retrieved while working.

3.2 Step 2: Importing the dataset

It has been determined that the needed dataset of attempted suicides has been imported.

3.3 Step 3: Data Analysis

The dataset was analyzed with a variety of commands and functions, such as data, data.shape, type(data), data.head(), data.tail(), and data.sample, in order to get an overall picture of the entire dataset before beginning the data pre-processing and implementation of the deep learning models to predict the chances of suicide. This was done in order to get an overview of the entire dataset before beginning these processes. The Data.info() method is helpful for determining the number of null values included in the dataset, as well as the data type of the various characteristics contained inside the columns and the data itself. describe() is useful for determining fundamental mathematical parameters such as the mean, count, standard deviation, minimum, and maximum values, as well as information about quartiles.

The functions Data.isnull().any() and data.isnull.sum() provide accurate statistics on the number of null values present in the dataset. It is necessary to reduce the number of null values to zero before applying deep learning models to any dataset. even when it comes at the start of a phrase. When we use data.isnull().any(), it is easy to see that the HDI for the year column, description, contains null values. When we use the data.info() function, we learn that there are 19456 null values in the description column. Either these null values need to be normalized or they should be eliminated entirely. Here, we will go on to the fourth phase.

3.4 Step 4: Data Pre-processing

In order for the deep learning models to function properly, the data will need to be preprocessed in order to remove any null values that may be present in the dataset. Since we already knew from analyzing the dataset by using data that the HDI for year, which is description, included 19456 null values, we decided to remove this column from the dataset altogether by using the data.dropna(axis = 1) command.

At this point, our dataset does not include any null values at all anymore. Following the removal of all null values, our data has been completely preprocessed, as can be seen in the picture below. Our data is now ready to be divided into testing and training data.

3.5 Step 5: Splitting the Dataset for Training and Testing Data

Our dataset is now split into training data (80%) and test data (20%). That is, the deep learning model is trained using 80% of the dataset, and then tested using 20% of the dataset. Our dataset now includes X as a subset, which we have specified. One of the target subsets is Y.

X train accounts for eighty percent of the X subset, whereas X test takes up twenty percent of the X subset. In a similar vein, Y-train constitutes 80% of the Y subset, but Y test accounts for just 20% of the Y subset. Due to the fact that the data has now been partitioned, we are able to train a variety of DL models using the train dataset, then test them using the test dataset, and lastly forecast our needed outcome.

3.6 Step 6: Model Building & Trainig

We will use three different deep learning models to find the one with the highest accuracy to predict our desired output.

Convolutional Neural Network

A CNN model was created and trained with the X_train and Y_train dataset.

Now, the accuracy of this model was found on the test data and was found to be 96%. The confusion matrix was created for the same, and the corresponding heat map was plotted.

Recurrent Neural Network

Accuracy for Recurrent Neural Network was 94.5%.

Multilayer Perceptron

Accuracy for Multilayer Perceptron was 100%.

3.7 Step 7: Predicting the Comparison between Models

It was found that out of three multilayer perceptrons, one had an accuracy of 100%. So, we can use of multilayer perceptron to predict the rating of suicide.

4. Conclusion

According to the previous published research papers, I have seen that many researchers have used different machine learning algorithms, but there are very few researchers who have used deep learning algorithms for the prediction of suicide ideation. The most commonly used algorithms are Logistic Regression, SVM, Random Forest, Naive Bayes algorithm, Decision Tree and many more. This study uses the deep learning algorithms Convolutional Neural Network, Recurrent Neural Network, and Multilayer Perceptron to forecast suicide attempts, and after comparing their accuracy, Multilayer Perceptron predicts the greatest accuracy. According to this paper, deep learning algorithms show better accuracy and performance as compared to machine learning algorithms based on five different symptoms. In the future, we can use the deep learning algorithm with image processing to predict the percentage of suicide chances using a person's image. As we know, image processing is used to capture the movement and expression of the image. Further research may significantly aid in the identification of military members at high risk for suicide and in the model that will use both the dataset and user input. If users want to predict the rate of suicide, then they will directly use the provided dataset in the model. If they want to know about their own chances of suicide, then they have to simply put their information in the form made by the graphic interface, and they can check their chances of suicide and also learn how they can prevent suicide.

REFERENCES

1. Srinu, B., Bhavana, P.N.L., Reddy, B.T. and Vaishnavi, B., 2022, March. Machine Learning based Suicide Prediction. In 2022 6th International Conference on Computing Methodologies and Communication (ICCMC) (pp. 953–957). IEEE.
2. S.S. Priyanka, S. Galgali, S. S. Priya, B. R. Shashank and K. G. Srinivasa 2016. Analysis of suicide victim data for the prediction of number of suicides in India. 2016 International Conference on Circuits, Controls, Communications and Computing (I4C), pp. 1–5, DOI: 10.1109/CIMCA.2016.8053293.
3. Pratyaksh Jain1, Karthik Ram Srinivas1 and Abhishek Vichare2 Journal of Physics: Conference Series, Volume 2161, 1st International Conference on Artificial Intelligence, Computational Electronics and Communication System (AICECS 2021) 28–30 October 2021, Manipal, India Pratyaksh Jain et al 2022 J. Phys.: Conf. Ser. 2161 012034
4. Ji, S. 2020. Suicidal ideation detection: A review of machine learning methods and applications. IEEE Transactions on Computational Social Systems, 8(1), pp. 214–226.
5. Colic, S., He, J.C., Richardson, J.D., Cyr, K.S., Reilly, J.P. and Hasey, G.M., 2022. A machine learning approach to identification of self-harm and suicidal ideation among military and police Veterans. Journal of Military, Veteran and Family Health, 8(1), pp. 56–67.
6. Lin, G.M. et al., 2020. Machine learning based suicide ideation prediction for military personnel. IEEE journal of biomedical and health informatics, 24(7), pp. 1907–1916.
7. R. Acierno, L.K. Richardson and B. C. Frueh "Prevalence estimates of combat-related PTSD: critical review," Australian and New Zealand Journal of Psychiatry, vol. 44, no. 1, pp. 4–19, January 2010.
8. Subroto Das , Mrs. B. Ida Seraphim, Apoorv Ranjan, 2021, A Machine Learning Approach to Analyze and Predict Suicide Attempts, INTERNATIONAL JOURNAL OF ENGINEERING RESEARCH & TECHNOLOGY (IJERT) Volume 10, Issue 04 (April 2021),.
9. Dredze M, De Choudhury M, Coppersmith G, Kiciman E , Kumar M. Discovering Shifts to Suicidal Ideation from Mental Health Content in Social Media. Proc SIGCHI Conf Hum Factor Comput Syst. 2016 May;2016:2098-2110. doi:10.1145/2858036.2858207. PMID: 29082385; PMCID: PMC5659860
10. Agarwal, T., Dhawan, A., Jain, A., Jain, A. and Gupta, S., 2019, September. Analysis and prediction of suicide attempts. In 2019 International Conference on Computing, Power and Communication Technologies (GUCON) (pp. 650–665). IEEE.
11. Coppersmith G, Leary R, Crutchley P, Fine A. Natural Language Processing of Social Media as Screening for Suicide Risk. Biomed Inform Insights. 2018 Aug 27;10:1178222618792860. doi: 10.1177/1178222618792860. PMID: 30158822; PMCID: PMC6111391.
12. Kulasinghe, S.A.S.A., Jayasinghe, A., Rathnayaka, R.M.A., Karunarathne, P.B.M.M.D., Silva, P.S. and Jayakodi, J.A., 2019, December. AI based depression and suicide prevention system. In 2019 International Conference on Advancements in Computing (ICAC) (pp. 73–78). IEEE.
13. Rozek, D.C., Andres, W.C., Smith, N.B., Leifker, F.R., Arne, K., Jennings, G., Dartnell, N., Bryan, C.J. and Rudd, M.D., 2020. Using machine learning to predict suicide attempts in military personnel. Psychiatry research, 294, p. 113515.
14. Sampson, L., Jiang, T., Gradus, J.L., Cabral, H.J., Rosellini, A.J., Calabrese, J.R., Cohen, G.H., Fink, D.S., King, A.P., Liberzon, I. and Galea, S., 2021. A Machine Learning Approach to Predicting New-onset Depression in a Military Population. Psychiatric research and clinical practice, 3(3), pp. 115–122

Computer Science Engineering and Emerging Technologies (ICCS-2022) – Prof (Dr.) Rajeev Sobti et al. (eds)
© 2024 Taylor & Francis Group, London, ISBN 978-1-032-52199-2

Chapter

14

Machine Translation Models and Named Entity Recognition: Comprehensive Study

K. Soumya[1]
Research Scholar, School of Computer Science and Engineering,
Lovely Professional University, Punjab, India

Vijay Kumar Garg[2]
Associate Professor, School of Computer Science and Engineering,
Lovely Professional University, Punjab, India

Abstract: Human translation is no longer sufficient to meet society's needs as there are more regular international contacts. However, as computer technology advances, machine translation is becoming a practical option. Machine Translation (MT) is a tough and challenging process since natural languages differ in a multilingual environment. Named Entity Recognition is one of the major tasks of natural language processing because it recognizes predefined text meanings as language entities in the text in any language. Our inference from the examined literature is that a machine translation strategy along with named entity recognition is a more effective way in NLP than applying MT approaches alone. A hybrid technique, on the other hand, utilizes the advantages of two approaches to enhance the translation's overall quality and performance. This paper's objective is to provide a comprehensive report of machine translation models named entity recognition in general, and this article reviews the development of machine translation over time and examines its primary techniques before making recommendations for its design.

Keywords: Computational machine translation, Automatic translation, Computational languages, Named entity recognition

1. Introduction

Language is the only medium that people can communicate with. Also, people from different ethnic groups around the world speak more than 4000 different languages. And this explains the diversity of languages in the world. It is also difficult and impossible for all citizens to understand and communicate in all languages. So here comes the importance of language translation between two different languages. Language translation [5], with the help of an intermediary or a third party who understands both languages, was usually done before the development of automatic machine translation. Thus, machine translation is the automatic translation of words from one language to another using a computer system. So, for a fully functional system, it is important to have a good knowledge of the source and target language, the content and concepts of the language.

2. History of MT

Converting from one language to another without sacrificing any semantic connotations is both an art and a science of language. Since the 1940s, MT systems have existed, but have recently exploded because of the growth of the internet. The

[1]kothapallisowmya@gmail.com, [2]vijay.garg@lpu.co.in

DOI: 10.1201/9781003405580-14

earliest computer-based NLP application was called MT, and it has a lengthy history. According to some, the discipline acted as computer science's self-forcing function in the 1960s, when the cold war increased the need for automatic translation.

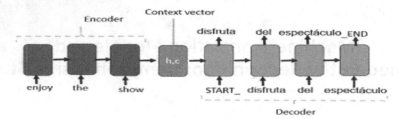

Fig. 14.1 The Machine Translation model

Source: Renu Khandelwal, Towards Data Science.

3. MT Approaches

3.1 Rule-based Approaches

Different rule-based approaches of MT are:

1. This type of direct machine translation (MT) [7] simply matches the input text against a stored sentence in a corpus or database and outputs the corresponding sentence.
2. Unlike direct machine translation, translation-based MT first analyzes the source text to determine its grammatical structure, phonological patterns, and semantics, and then creates intermediate forms that can be used to translate individual words and entire sentences.
3. An alternative to direct and translation-oriented MT is Interlingua MT. The word "interlingua" denotes a neutral, abstract, interconnected representation that can project the source language as well as represent the target language.

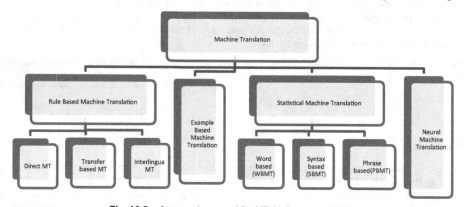

Fig. 14.2 Approaches used for MT (K. Soumya, 2020)

3.2 Example-based NMT

It is essentially a translation by association that only uses proportionate analogies as support. Both the target language corpus and the source language corpus are provided to the MT system in this. In order to translate between languages, correlation analysis is also performed. In other words, it is assumed that the translation will likely be the same if a sentence that has already been translated appears again. In other words, it creates a brand-new set of sequencing using examples from taught translations and earlier translations.

3.3 Statistical-based Machine Translation

This framework deciphers text chosen from bilingual equal text data sets or corpora. Furthermore, its fundamental thought is to involve an equal corpus as a preparation test for the deciphered text. Essentially, a basic SMT [7, 8] has an interpretation model and a language model. These two models, thusly, rely upon registering restrictive probabilities of closeness between texts or words in equal corpora.

1. Word-based MT

In word-based machine translation, the source words are first matched with the objective words and word matching changes are determined, where there might be a few comparable words with the objective words. Afterward, the words are acclimated to give the right interpretation.

2. Sentence-based Machine Translation

Not at all like word-based machine translation, sentence-based MT considers a gathering of words or strings or sentence matches between the source and target dialects.

3. Syntax-based Machine Translation

This machine translation model is fully based on the grammatical rules of the natural source and target languages. They are examined in terms of individual parts such as verbs, prepositions, adverbs, conjunctions, etc.

3.4 Neural Machine Translation

An artificial neural network is used in neural machine translation (NMT) [10], a method of machine translation, to forecast the likelihood of a word sequence, generally modelling full sentences in a single integrated model.

4. Named Entity Recognition

Unstructured text can be automatically tagged with Named Entities using the Named Entity Recognition (NER) tool [3], which is based on the principles of AI and NLP. The names of people, organizations, places, etc. can all be found in Named Entities, which are often proper nouns. A key component of natural language processing is named entity recognition. Information Extraction and Retrieval, Machine Translation, Text Summarization, and other fields of application for NER are a few examples.

Existing NER systems have a few drawbacks, including:

1. The NER systems' accuracy is not consistent and can change.
2. Rule-based systems are not resilient because they were developed by linguists for a particular domain, despite the fact that they provide comparatively high accuracy.
3. The relevant corpus must be derived—i.e. NER systems for languages such as English is very precise. This system has many advantages, annotated corpora and other linguistic resources. However, for Indic languages, which lack resources (missing annotated corpora), the development of NER systems with important assessment measures for these languages is a difficult task.
4. There is limited tag set considered by most systems.

Table 14.1 Pros and cons of statistical machine translation by considering challenges of SMT into consideration (K. Soumya, 2020)

Statistical Machine Translation	
Pros	**Cons**
• It is easy to train and add new languages to statistical MT models when compared to other MT models. • SMT requires less virtual space than other models of MT. • It is easy to operate and train smaller systems with SMT. • If the model is well trained, a customized corpus can consistently translate the source content to a target content more accurate than NMT.	• It is difficult to analyze and translate a source content to a target content in SMT, if the training corpora doesn't include more feasible and similar content. • In this case, SMT may have a strong fall in accuracy. • SMT models depends on bilingual content. • SMT is expensive too, because it takes more time in preprocessing and corpus creation. • It is difficult to fix problems in model once it is implemented.

Table 14.2 Pros and cons of rule-based machine translation by considering challenges of RBMT into consideration (K. Soumya, 2020)

Rule based machine translation	
Pros	**Cons**
• Based on morphological theories • Can be applied to languages with limited set of rules for forming language. • It is easy to verify errors with this method	• Must have complete knowledge of linguistic rules of languages • Inconsistency problem occurs because there is less possibilities for translations. • It is expensive to maintain and improve the translations.

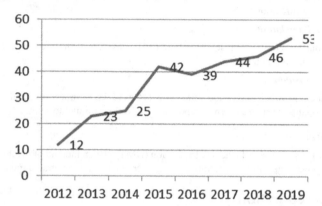

Fig. 14.3 Number of papers published and review (from 2012 to 2021) (K. Soumya, 2020)

Table 14.3 Comparison of various Machine Translation approaches (K. Soumya, 2020)

MT approach criteria	DMT	RBMT	CBMT	KBMT	NMT
Morphological analysis	Required	Required	Required	Required	Done by encoder
Syntactic and semantic analysis	Not required	Required	Required	Syntactic required not semantic	Encoder performs this task
Deep linguistic knowledge	Not required	Required	Not required	No, require inference engine	Training of encoder and decoder is required not simple, but less space is required than SMT
Simple to implement	Yes	No	Simple than RBMT	No	
Cost	Less costly	Costly in terms of time	Costly in terms of resources	Costly in terms of conceptualization	Costly in terms of computational power required (needs GPU)
Fast development	Yes	Time consuming	Faster than RBMT	Less than RBMT but less then CBMT	Once trained gives output in fractions of seconds
Efficiency	Better for simple and small translation	Most efficient	Better than DMT	Better than DMT and CBMT	Better than SMT
Large computation required	No	No	Yes	Yes	Yes
Word level translation	Yes	Yes	Yes	Yes	No
Sentence level translation	No	No	Yes	No	End-to-end translation

The quantity of journal articles on machine translation research in various years is depicted in Fig. 14.3. More articles emerged between 2012 and 2021 than in the first article search, although the figures given are taken into consideration. However, the quick increase in articles demonstrates how important and well-known this topic is to academics, professionals, particularly in the healthcare industry, and governments all over the world. This research subject is still evolving, despite the growing diversity and quantity of articles, and it appears that it needs additional in-depth conceptual studies in addition to empirical and analytical studies.

Table 14.4 Included databases (K. Soumya, 2020)

Database	Number of papers considered for final
PubMed & PubMed	52
CINAHL	11
ACMDigital Library	46
IEEE Xplore	51
MT Archive	65

The classification of reviewed articles according to the different types of publication is shown in Fig. 14.4. It is clear from the above data that the majority of the publications are research articles, followed by literature reviews, general reviews and then perspective publications. The growing number of research articles included in the review reinforces the importance of machine translation in different areas (e.g., health, public authorities, etc.). Several authors concluded that there is still room to improve their work by applying it to other bodies in the field of translation.

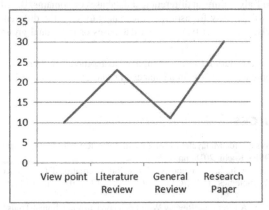

Fig. 14.4 Classification of publication types (K. Soumya, 2020)

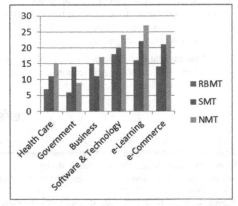

Fig. 14.5 Review of MT algorithms when applied to various domains (K. Soumya, 2020)

The statistics on the usage of machine translation techniques across many fields are shown in Fig. 14.5. It is evident from the data in the image above that neural machine translation and machine translation as a service are used in the majority of articles. In their articles, almost all of the authors came to the conclusion that there is still significant opportunity for development in translation in many areas.

Table 14.5 Glance of machine translation (MT) system evaluations and NER approaches (K. Soumya, 2020)

Name of the paper	Author(s)	Problem definition
A survey of machine translation techniques and systems for Indian languages	Sandeep Saini, Vineet Sahula	The main objective is to fill the language gap between people speaking two different languages, communities or countries, hence scope and need of language translation is immense.
An efficient English to Hindi machine translation system using hybrid mechanism	Jayashree Nair, Amrutha Krishnan K, Deetha R	Authors proposed an English to Hindi machine translation system design based on declension rules. This paper also describes the different approaches of Machine Translation.
Supervised speech separation based on deep learning an overview	DeLiang Wang, Jitong Chen	The recent introduction of deep learning to supervised speech separation has dramatically accelerated progress and boosted separation performance. This article provides a comprehensive overview of the research on deep learning based supervised speech separation in the last several years.

Name of the paper	Author(s)	Problem definition
Improving automatic call classification using machine translation	Tanveer A. Faruquie, Nitendra Rajput, Vimal Raj	Often the input speech is spontaneous and noisy which results in high word error rates. This results in unsatisfactory system performance. This paper described a method to improve the natural language call classification task using statistical machine translation (SMT).
Bilingual machine translation using RNN based deep learning	Janhavi R. Chaudhary, Prof. Ankit C. Patel	The proposed model here is a neutral machine translation that has an encoder–decoders architecture and encode a source sentence into a fixed-length vector from which a decoder generates a translation.
Neutral machine translation research based on the semantic vector of the tri-lingual parallel corpus	Xiao-Xue Wang, Cong-Hui Zhu, Sheng L13, Tie-Jun Zhao, De-Quan Zheng	RNN Encoder-Decoder and attentional mechanism have lately been used to improve neural machine translation (NMT) on bilingual parallel corpus

5. Conclusion

This paper provided a comprehensive overview of machine translation as well as named entity recognition and its importance in different fields. And the application of different MT algorithms in different text databases or domains. Based on the information obtained from existing research studies, it will be easy for aspiring researchers to learn the different advantages and disadvantages of applying different MT models to different types of text databases or individual group domains to perform entity recognition.

Various machine translation techniques are capable of performing translation from one language to another. And there exist various named entity recognition applications. A combined approach could be an advancement that can be brought into MT systems.

REFERENCES

1. A. P. Ajees and S. M. Idicula, "A Named Entity Recognition System for Malayalam Using Conditional Random Fields," 2018 International Conference on Data Science and Engineering (ICDSE), Kochi, 2018, pp. 1–5.
2. K. Bhattacharjee et al., "Named Entity Recognition: A Survey for Indian Languages," 2019 2nd International Conference on Intelligent Computing, Instrumentation and Control Technologies (ICICICT), 2019, pp. 217–220, doi: 10.1109/ICICICT46008.2019.8993236.
3. Wasnik, Vaibhavi B., and Archana R. Thool. "Ocular Gene Therapy: A Literature Review With Focus on Current Clinical Trials." *Cureus* 14.9 (2022).
4. Turner AM, et al. (2014). A comparison of human and machine translation of health promotions materials for public health practice: time, costs and quality, Journal of Public Health Management and Practice, 20(5): 523–9.
5. Oladosu E, Esan A, Edayanju I, et al. (2016). Approaches to Machine Translation: A review.
6. Journal of Engineering and Technology, 1(1): 120–126.
7. Weiss RJ, Chorowski J, Jaitly N, et al.(2017). Sequence-to-Sequence Models Can Directly Transcribe Foreign Speech. CoRR. abs/1703.08581.
8. Turner AM, Desai L, Dew K, Martin N, Kirchoff K. (2015). Machine Assisted Translation of Health Materials to Chinese: An Initial Evaluation. MEDINFO, 979.
9. Taylor RM, Crichton N, Moult B, et al. (2015). A prospective observational study of machine translation software to overcome the challenge of including ethnic diversity in healthcare research. Nursing Open,2(1): 14–23.
10. Liu W, Cai S, Ramesh BP, Chiriboga G, Knight K, Yu H. Translating Electronic Health Record Notes from English to Spanish: A Preliminary Study. ACL-IJCNLP 2015. 2015 Jul 30:134.
11. Greg P. Finley, Erik Edwards, Amanda Robinson et al. (2018). An automated medical scribe for documenting clinical encounters, in Proceedings of NAACL-HLT, Association for Computational Linguistics, pages 11–15.
12. DimitarShterionov, Riccardo Superbo, Pat Nagle et al. (Sep 2018). Human versus automatic quality evaluation of NMT and PBSMT.in Machine Translation, Volume32, Issue 3, pp 217–2 35.

Computer Science Engineering and Emerging Technologies (ICCS-2022) – Prof (Dr.) Rajeev Sobti et al. (eds)
© 2024 Taylor & Francis Group, London, ISBN 978-1-032-52199-2

Chapter

15

IOT-based Security and Surge Rescue—
A Modish Smart Bus System

Aniruddha Prabhu B. P.[1]
Assistant Professor, Computer Science,
Graphic Era Hill University, Dehradun, Uttarakhand

Ojas Misra[2]
Associate Analyst, Digital and Emerging Technology,
Ernst & Young, Hyderabad, Telangana

Sumeshwar Singh[3]**, Shiv Ashish Dhondiyal**[4]
Assistant Professor, Computer Science, Graphic Era Hill University,
Dehradun, Uttarakhand

Rajeev Gupta[5]
Assistant Professor, Electronics & Communication,
Graphic Era Hill University, Dehradun, Uttarakhand

Abstract: In this paper, we are demonstrating a method to solve the transportation security issue. As the crime rate is increasing day by day, to ensure the safety of the passengers and to avoid a surge in public transportation, we are developing an IOT-based application that tracks all the information about the nearby public transportation. The user could comfortably get the details of buses and real-time tracking for any particular route using RFID, GPS, and Raspberry PI technologies. Even counting the number of people and real-time tracking are done. Users will enter the source and destination while standing at the bus stop. With respect to the source and destination entered, the application is going to display the details of the buses that are running along that route. This will be free of confusion for the users about the buses in this way. The system would be obliging to people, particularly those who are strangers in town. It's an economically resourceful application for users, especially in metropolitan cities.

Keywords: IoT, Raspberry Pi, RFID, GPS, E-ticket, Real time tracking

1. Introduction

This paper aims to aid the people who travel in buses by providing the crowd in the bus so one could make an appropriate decision for him or her. Suppose a person already knows the details of the upcoming bus or buses before it reaches its stop. He or she could save his or her time. For instance, if a person is carrying some valuable asset that could get stolen, is commodious, or is breakable, using the application, one could easily determine what steps could be taken.

1.1 Problems and its Causes

A few times, some delays and gaps could easily happen, caused by unforeseeable issues in the scheduled service, with which the proposed application can deal tactically. The time management of the application is effective by taking the count

[1]aniprabhubp@gmail.com, [2]misraojas@hotmail.com, [3]singh.sumeshwar@gmail.com, [4]shivashish1234@gmail.com, [5]grajeev63@gmail.com

DOI: 10.1201/9781003405580-15

of passengers into consideration. Simultaneously helping the person to consider appropriate decisions builds on it. The people who have just arrived in the city would make the most of the application. There are a vast variety of applications present that utilise GPS technology [5]. The most widely used one is the vehicle tracking system. It consistently monitors them. One could easily track the live location of any vehicle along the route that it has, should, or would travel. This information is available at one's fingertips without requiring him or her to be at a nearby location or anything else. Plus, there is no stopping it, regardless of the weather condition or the route taken by the vehicle. It utilises GSM and GPS technologies [6].

Usually during peak hours, people face discomfort and uneasiness travelling in these overcrowded buses, which is mainly due to unavailability. Generally, people prefer travelling in transit vehicles rather than private ones, mainly due to the inexpensive fare and extended routes provided by them. The time buses take to conclude the trips is pretty much relative to the number of people boarding or descending at various stops. It results in deviating the load of passengers.

Several times, buses also get delayed, mainly due to crowds. The bus transportation system is the most feasible and flexible means of travelling between and within cities. One could, according to his or her needs, access this facility across any metropolitan city because of the wide variety of routes and networks. The universal design principle that the buses follow should be well maintained, which in turn would result in comfortable boarding for various people.

Industrial objectives should be incorporated well in advance before taking any final decisions regarding the bus network and connectivity. With community engagement and an upright feedback system, one can achieve better accessibility for buses. The urban side of the country mainly sustains all the economic growth.

The efficiency of any city highly depends on its convenient transport system. Poor conveyance stifles the economic growth of the place and impacts its development, so anyone could argue it is the backbone of the country. Traffic congestion is becoming a time-consuming issue in people's everyday lives [5]. On an estimated basis, people in metro cities spend millions of hours "stuck in traffic," i.e., a clear example of how poor our bus system is presently. On top of this, the bus fleet is old and rigid. This congestion is mainly caused by the acute rise in private vehicle ownership and its increasing usage. Along with it, people are unaware of the bus service timing and network. There have been various kinds of bottlenecks that need to be fixed [9], [10].

2. Literature Review

In this section, we discuss related works to this paper. Three different related projects are cited below.

1. Malaysia—Intelligent Bus Monitoring

This referred paper deals with the monitoring of buses in Malaysia with the help of a unique code, namely RFID, installed with a reader, a GPRS transmitter, and GPS. It is collectively stored in a box called the Black Box [1]. Whenever a bus approaches any terminal, the RFID tag present interacts with the reader. The data extracted with it is sent to a monitoring centre with the help of GPRS.

This data is then stored in a database [1]. GPRS sends data from GPS and RFID to the database, and the GPS module is activated, which in turn provides the real-time location of the bus, which is popularly known as "live tracking.

2. Saudi Arabia—Integrated Routing and Tracking System in University Buses

In the above work, they have proposed an app that students and drivers at Taibah University can utilize. Every time the app gets updated, if any kind of change is made in the schedule of buses [2], In cases relating to the delay or unavailability of any bus, instant alerts are sent to all users. With the help of Google Maps, one could easily track the buses. They have a machine framework named GIS (Geographic Information System) that's used for storing, catching, controlling, overseeing, investigating, and getting spatial information about any location [2].

3. GPS- and GSM-based Passenger Tracking System in India

The buses are installed with GPS and GSM in this Global Positioning System (GPS) and Global System for Mobile Communication (GSM)-based tracking system [3]. It tracks by using the ticket number of the passenger and shows the location in Google Maps. The GPS starts locating the coordinates when it gets locked, i.e., it acquires the latitude–longitude of that particular time and location. Then this fetched data is further sent to the Cloud via GPRS or an SMS, and the location gets displayed on Google Maps [3].

3. Data and Variables

In this section, we provide definitions for some of the terminologies used in the paper.

Raspberry Pi: The Raspberry Pi is a small computer that uses a different kind of processor. Microsoft Windows cannot be installed on it. But several versions of the Linux operating system that are pretty much like Windows can be installed.

RFID: It is a radio frequency identifier that uses electromagnetic or electrostatic coupling in the radio frequency portion of the electromagnetic spectrum to uniquely identify an object [1].

GPS: It is a global positioning system that determines the exact location of an object anywhere in the world and uses GIS to capture and manage geographical information [1].

WAMP Server: It consists of the Apache web server, OpenSSL for SSL support, the MySQL database system, and PHP programming. It is used to create dynamic web applications.

Python: Python is a high-level, general-purpose programming language. Here, Python coding is done for integrating the services and the WAMP database server.

4. Methodology and Model Specifications

The system capabilities are as follows [7][8]:

Crowd Manager: In the stated module, we extract the total count of passengers in the bus in addition to the male-female passengers' difference.

Bus-Route Manager: In the stated module, we extract different routes in the city that buses travel.

Timings, along with the source and destination of the buses, get updated in the system database. Information such as the bus's name, number, arrival timings, and details of the bus route is also handled. Security: It's a much simpler module that provides alert messages to the emergency numbers that are pre-fed into the system in case any discrepancy occurs.

The system architecture is as shown in Fig. 15.1. We have several tables holding passenger information like bus pass ID, number, gender, source, and destination. Now all these tables are stored in a database maintained by a WAMP server. There are only two categories of passengers: people with an issued Pass-ID card and others without it. All the RFID tag details of a passenger holding a Pass-ID are read by RFID readers. After which, the collected data gets updated in the database [4]. For finding whether the boarded person is male or female, the collected information about him or her is fetched. In a similar manner, people without a Pass-ID card are required to collect their e-ticket from the ticket collection centres. This involves another web interface with personal authentication facilities for the collector staff. Using this interface, the collector staff has to manually enter all details, similar to the Pass-ID cards of the passengers.

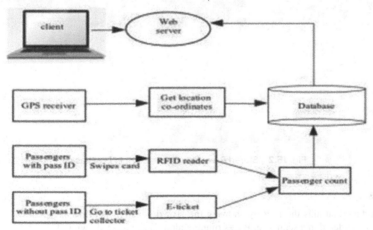

Fig. 15.1   System architecture

Source: Made by Author

The algorithm for the system implemented would be as follows:

Algorithm 1 Algorithm for system implementation

```
1:   Begin
2:       Initialize total_count to 0
3:       for ever do
4:               if commuter swipes Pass-ID card do
5:                       count_1 = count_1+1
6:               end if
7:               if commuter grabs E-ticket do
8:                       count_2 = count_2+1
9:               end if
10:              total_count = count1 + count2
11:      end for
12:  End
```

The algorithm above shows the workings of the system. The results from two modules of the system are integrated together to produce a precise result, so that there is no fault present.

5. Conclusion

Now we'll talk through the results of our effortless proposed system, which involves the integration of a GUI (graphical user interface) and a database. The programming language Python is used for integrating the front-end and back-end frameworks. For accessing data from the WAMP server, we have exploited PHP too. And for designing the pages of the user dashboard, HTML, Bootstrap, and CSS frameworks are utilised.

(i) Data-Base

Once a person swipes his or her Pass-ID card or takes an e-ticket, all the information gets stored in the database. Every person, regardless of card or e-ticket, is assigned a unique identification number. Fig. 15.2 shows the sample database system.

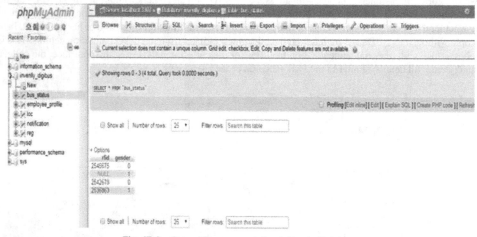

Fig. 15.2 Stored Passenger Information in Database

Source: Made by Author

(ii) View Bus Details

Consider a user interface that aids the user by showing the crowd density. The first page shows various buses for any particular route that are ordered in a sequence. Buses running along a route are shown in Fig. 15.3.

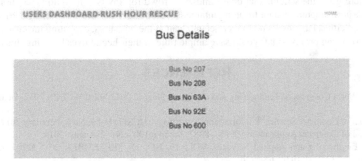

Fig. 15.3 Bus Details

Source: Made by Author

(iii) Bus Status

Considering a bus selected by any person, i.e., running on a route, one wants to know the crowd details. In Fig. 4, we have the count of all the travellers, along with male and female travellers.

These details get updated as and when a passenger boards or descends a bus.

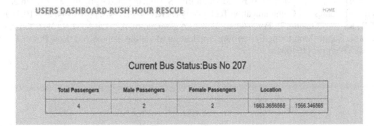

Fig. 15.4 Current bus status

Source: Made by Author

(iv) E-ticket

Now, take a look at the user interface for collector staff issuing e-tickets. Manual entry for issuing a e-ticket is shown in Fig. 15.5.

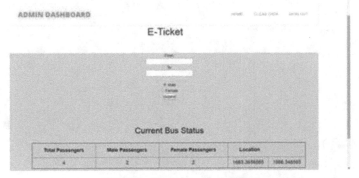

Fig. 15.5 Ticket Vending Interface

Source: Made by Author

The paper presented here gives the scheme that determines the crowd for any bus. It could be economically feasible and reliable since there is a low amount of data to be maintained. We strongly believe that this system could be effectively deployed in metropolitan cities. Passengers no longer need to wait at the bus stops, expecting the crowd of upcoming buses and their arrival time. Working professionals could save ample time in their hectic lives by using this application.

REFERENCES

1. Proceedings of the World Congress on Engineering and Computer Science 2012 Vol II WCECS 2012, October 24–26, 2012, San Francisco, USA.
2. International Journal of Computer Science & Information Technology (IJCSIT) Vol 9, No 1, February 2017.
3. International Journal of Computer Applications (0975 – 8887) Volume 100 – No. 2, August 2014.
4. ARPN Journal of Engineering and Applied Sciences. VOL. 10, NO. 17, SEPTEMBER 2015 ©2006–2015 Asian Research Publishing Network (ARPN). All rights reserved.
5. College bus management system. https://www.scribd.com/presentation/300037170/College-Bus-Management-System
6. Intelligent transport system. http://www.sutpindia.com/skin/pdf/event_31.pdf
7. B. P. Aniruddha Prabhu and S. Hebbal, "Small Unarmed Robot for Defense and Security:A Cost-Effective Approach Using Arduino Uno," 2017 2nd International Conference On Emerging Computation and Information Technologies (ICECIT), 2017, pp. 1–6, doi: 10.1109/ICECIT.2017.8453325.
8. Aniruddha Prabhu, B.P., Ashwini, B.P., Anwar Khan, T., Das, A. (2019). Predicting Election Result with Sentimental Analysis Using Twitter Data for Candidate Selection. In: Saini, H., Sayal, R., Govardhan, A., Buyya, R. (eds) Innovations in Computer Science and Engineering. Lecture Notes in Networks and Systems, vol 74. Springer, Singapore. https://doi.org/10.1007/978-981-13-7082-3_7
9. S. R. Prathibha, A. Hongal and M. P. Jyothi, "IOT Based Monitoring System in Smart Agriculture," 2017 International Conference on Recent Advances in Electronics and Communication Technology (ICRAECT), 2017, pp. 81–84, doi: 10.1109/ICRAECT.2017.52.
10. Senadeera, S.D.A.P.; Kyi, S.; Sirisung, T.; Pongsupan, W.; Taparugssanagorn, A.; Dailey, M.N.; Wai, T.A. Cost-Effective and Low Power IoT-Based Paper Supply Monitoring System: An Application Modeling Approach. J. Low Power Electron. Appl. 2021, 11, 46. https://doi.org/10.3390/jlpea11040046

Computer Science Engineering and Emerging Technologies (ICCS-2022) – Prof (Dr.) Rajeev Sobti et al. (eds)
© 2024 Taylor & Francis Group, London, ISBN 978-1-032-52199-2

Chapter

16

A Flexible Blockchain-dependent IoT Communication Framework

Jay Kumar Pandey[1]
Department of Electronics and Communication Engineering,
Shri Ramswaroop Memorial University, Dewa Road, Barabanki, Uttar Pradesh, India

Vivek Veeraiah[2]
Department of R & D Computer Science, Adichunchanagiri University,
Mandya, Karnataka, India

Vaibhav Ranjan[3]
Department of Computer Science, ABES Engineering College,
Ghaziabad, Uttar Pradesh, India

Dharmesh Dhabliya[4]
Department of Information Technology,
Vishwakarma Institute of Information Technology, Pune, Maharashtra, India

Krishna Nand Mishra[5]
Department of Computer Science and Engineering,
Khwaja Moinuddin Chishti University, Lucknow, Uttar Pradesh, India

Sarita Soni[6]
Department of Computer Science & Engineering,
Government Polytechnic Bighapur, Unnao, Uttar Pradesh, India

Ankur Gupta[7]
Department of Computer Science and Engineering,
Vaish College of Engineering, Rohtak, Haryana, India

Abstract: Numerous applications in people's everyday lives now have a high degree of trust and security thanks to the recent advancements in blockchain-based cryptocurrency technology. Traditional Blockchain design may provide trustworthy, decentralized financial service systems that are guaranteed to be persistent, anonymous, and auditable. IoT, the following prospective smart technology, has a decentralized topology similar to that of blockchain. Blockchain use in IoT systems is currently impractical in many ways. In this article, we first identify the practical challenges associated with implementing Blockchain technology in an IoT framework. Further, a dynamic Blockchain-dependent trust system is suggested to facilitate an IoT network with a scalable and dynamic communication framework. To address the security concerns and impart suggestions for impending research, the authors also give a case study.

Keywords: IoT, Security, Blockchain, Bitcoin, Privacy

[1]er.jay11@gmail.com, [2]Vivek@EdVista.in, [3]vaibhav.ranjan@abes.ac.in, [4]dharmesh.dhabliya@viit.ac.in, [5]knmishra24@gmail.com,
[6]saritasoni90@gmail.com, [7]ankurdujana@gmail.com

DOI: 10.1201/9781003405580-16

1. Introduction

In many ways, the blockchain has been a crucial tool for developing trust architecture. Since then, blockchain has been extensively used in other cryptocurrencies. Blockchain (Mukherjee et al., 2022) was initially announced in 2008 as the technological underpinning for a cryptocurrency called Bitcoin. Blockchain is the fundamental technology that underpins all cryptocurrencies. Decentralization is accomplished by installing every involved party to examine and approve fresh transactions. The transaction data is incapable of being changed retroactively after it has been verified, confirmed, and recorded since doing so would involve changing all blocks after them, which needs agreement from the majority of the network. All legitimate transaction records in the Bitcoin implementation are hashed and encoded into a Merkle tree (Khadse et al., 2022). Further, blocks are created from collections of valid transactions. Each block consists of the previous block's hash results, which connect the two subsequent blocks.

Blockchain refers to a network of connected blocks. Continuously adding new blocks to a current blockchain, often known as mining, is the process of creating a blockchain. The fundamental task of mining is solving a challenging arithmetic problem that is simple to verify (often a Proof of Work (PoW)). The engaging entities should supply a substantial computational resource that limits the number of blocks that may be mined, in order to solve this problem. With this method, malicious block mining may also be further prevented. Proof of Stake (PoS) is often the widely utilized problem in blockchain technology. High computing resources are required by POW, which is used in the Bitcoin protocol to find a certain value with a particular set of hash results. Both computational and memory resources will be used by POS. With the use of dynamic public keys, all messages sent between entities are encrypted to prevent eavesdropping.

Even though Bitcoin and other well-known cryptocurrencies employ blockchain technology, there are other possible uses for this core technology. Several financial services, including digital assets, remittance, and smart contracts, are being created as a result of the development of blockchain, which enables payments to be done without any trusted middleman. In reality, the development of the IoT and other future communication and interaction systems is increasingly utilizing blockchains.

The IoT idea is quickly becoming a reality with widespread acceptance and popularity because of the rapid expansion of smart devices and wireless network bandwidth. Today, it stands for a network of interconnected smart "things" with antennae and sensors. IoT possesses the scalability to constantly enable nodes to join and exit the network since it is such a highly dynamic network. In reality, the IoT paradigm acquires the standard privacy and security (Gupta et al., 2022) challenges of computer networks since it consists of a variety of linked devices and heterogeneous networks. IoT devices often have finite resources, like a restricted power supply, limited computing power, and limited storage space, in contrast to conventional PCs. As a result, it is challenging to integrate the usual security protocols used in computer networks built on blockchain into IoT networks.

The ID management of the devices in IoT networks is one issue. As a result of the many diverse connection characteristics of IoT devices, like connection duration and service requirements, it is challenging to create and maintain an ID that can consistently spot the "things" in the IoT. In actuality, the blockchain framework may be used as the cornerstone for enhancing IoT privacy and security. Every IoT node might be deployed as an engaging element of blockchain as part of the very basic architecture that can, moreover, establish a trustworthy digital ledger in IoT usage. Here, we initially identify the challenges associated with using blockchain in IoT networks. Later, a system architecture for IoT ID management with a labeled network topology is provided to show one approach to using a blockchain-dependent protocol in IoT networks.

2. Literature Review

Here, we highlight the challenge of developing a secured IoT system. It is highlighted how low functional overhead is needed in implementing IoT networks and how the expense of security solutions conflict. The new blockchain architecture with full and lightweight nodes is then shown.

2.1 An Illustration of an IoT Security Problem

IoT networks, as seen in Fig. 16.1, are made up of a variety of heterogeneous digital devices with widely varying hardware organizations that depend on the communication intermediate layer to link them. Two fundamental components for data transmission and collecting are included in many IoT devices. Some gadgets, like smartphones, are also fitted with powerful computation circuits that can investigate the collected data.

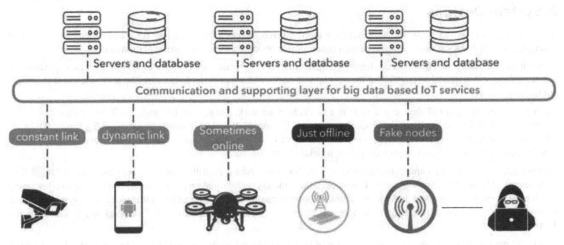

Fig. 16.1 IoT network having diverse devices

Source: Made by Author

IoT is inherited from conventional computer networks, which also inherit the security and privacy challenges, as is mentioned in Section 1; however, the old countermeasures are challenging to inherit. The primary cause is not just because of the heterogeneous devices with various hardware setups, but also because of the IoT concept's dynamic transmission capability.

One illustration of this is shown in Fig. 16.1, which shows both devices with continuous and dynamic connectivity as well as those that are always offline or often unite and abandon networks. Under these circumstances, it is considerably simpler for an intruder to trick a negotiated node into joining the communication environment using bogus IDs. With such dynamic networks, managing the ID in IoT is more challenging than it is in regular computer networks.

The work of Pramanik et al. (2022) contains a list of security risks. Authentication and secure communication in the Internet of Things are two risks. Every device in an IoT network has to be authorized before it can communicate, as illustrated in Fig. 16.1. However, actual implementations must reduce the overhead of security methods owing to limited hardware resources in order to take into account efficiency issues that might further result in security violations.

2.2 Scalable Nodes for Blockchain

The cornerstone of blockchain is that every transactional record is authenticated and affirmed in previous blocks, as stated in Section 1, which may prevent the use of deniable activities. Because of this approach, every participant in a blockchain network will have to keep track of and, more crucially, preserve the established and approved transaction records.

All history blocks must be downloaded. This characteristic, however, ended up being a barrier to the enactment of blockchain technology in IoT networks. It is not possible to retain or download the history blocks since the majority of devices have limited storage and computation capabilities, and the communication (Anand et al., 2022) linkages between IoT nodes are always changing.

Thankfully, new full node and lightweight node designs for blockchain nodes exist in the Bitcoin protocols (Zamani, 2022). Full nodes then provide lightweight nodes, which are simple to operate and maintain and don't have a high overhead, with connections to the blockchain network.

However, the widespread use of lightweight nodes might cause privacy (Pandey, et al., 2022) problems in the IoT. Because full nodes feed lightweight nodes, malevolent users who control full nodes will jeopardize the secrecy of lightweight node transactions. A full node leaving the network will also make it difficult for the matching lightweight nodes to use the blockchain network, similar to the dynamic connections of the Internet of Things. One study presented IoT architecture with smart home settings that leverage in-home electronics such as PCs as complete nodes to service the lightweight nodes. However, this architecture is appropriate for the topology of a smart home scenario in which personal computers are supposed to be present in each house and serve as the connecting hubs for each smart home's IoT sub-networks.

3. System Designs

To place the dynamic IoT network, we describe a multi-layered, blockchain-dependent ID management structure. For managing the whole blockchain network, several functions for nodes are explained and synchronized.

According to the connection duration and hardware, different roles will be allocated to the various IoT devices. Coordination techniques are also required to ensure that the backup full nodes will support the lightweight nodes in the event that their full nodes go down.

We begin by seeing each IoT device as a node in a blockchain network. Then, each IoT gadget will be given a unique ID that will also be linked to the ID of the blockchain wallet. This approach makes it simple to verify all legitimate IDs in an IoT network while making it challenging to detect and reject false IDs. Additionally, the ID will be associated with any harmful activity by IoT devices to protect against attackers in the future.

For instance, a surveillance camera like the one in Fig. 2 will be given a coordination node because it has a longer link lifetime and a low hardware requirement. The blockchain is mostly maintained on the machines used as the overlay layer, which have been given complete node names. Then, in order to enable their participation in this blockchain system without incurring the expense of full nodes, the devices that dynamically join and depart this IoT network are given labels for lightweight nodes.

An IoT ID management framework may be developed by fusing identity verification and recording with the decentralized blockchain architecture. By reducing harmful activity, this technology might increase security in IoT networks. It will become more difficult for any attackers using false IDs to keep a connection to the IoT network since repeatedly creating new IDs is more difficult and expensive. Furthermore, despite the challenging hardware configurations of IoT devices, realistic applications are feasible.

4. A Quick Case Study

The first step when a newer sensor node wishes to connect to this blockchain network is to submit a request with its label to the coordinating nodes. Whenever it is a complete node, excellent security authentication is necessary before it receives authorization to join the whole node group. The coordinating nodes disperse a complete node, which will help the novice if it is a lightweight node. The newcomer won't, however, get a legitimate ID until the true ID has been verified. The coordination nodes thereafter allocate newer full nodes to the lightweight nodes for preserving the interconnections after a full node goes down.

In this part, we make the assumption that a malicious person is trying to get access to the Internet of Things network by manipulating a single IoT node by fabricating a node ID. In the first scenario, an intruder can hack and take control of a single IoT node. Other nodes within the IoT network may then report many harmful acts. In this situation, the blockchain system will indicate and record the ID of the hacked node in the next block. High security verification (Pradhan et al., 2022) standards and a low degree of trust can be adjusted in the time windows that follow. As a result, it is harder for the intruder to later adjust to the same node.

In the other scenario, the attacker connects to the Internet of Things network using a phoney ID. The controller node's verification mechanism will reject the link to keep the intruder out if the fictitious ID belongs to an IoT node that is still in operation. The attacker will often need to modify the phoney ID in order to keep the connection if the ID management mechanism is effective. Higher security levels will be attained as a result of rising ID fraud costs.

5. Upcoming Works

We can track all device-related transactions on a blockchain-based IoT network and save them locally. For security purposes, this information may be quite beneficial. For instance, the label has to be issued before the attacker may pretend to be someone else to unite with the IoT network. The high-level security verification will identify the attacker if he poses as a complete node or will make the attack very costly. Alternatively, it is difficult for an attacker to simply pose as a lightweight node since all past attacks are tracked, necessitating a new set of false information for every attack attempt. Other circumstances, such as when entire nodes cannot be trusted, must also be taken into account.

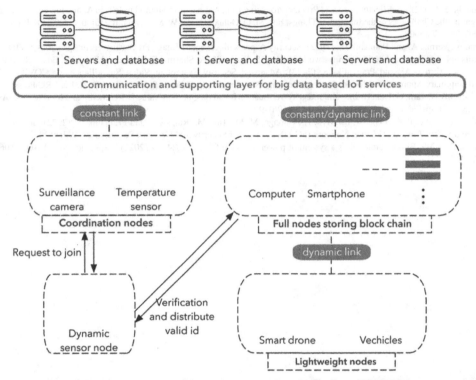

Fig. 16.2 Labeled endpoints and dynamic connectivity in an IoT network

Source: Made by Author

Managing the ID and securing the data shared in the IoT network should both be part of an additional blockchain-based IoT architecture. To further ensure the security of the IoT network, protocols for data exchange and authentication, for instance, should be developed. Verification and authentication are crucial for guaranteeing the security of data sharing since IoT devices have extremely diverse hardware configurations that make it challenging to adopt a consistent, simple encryption method. For certain specific use scenarios, lightweight encryption (Gupta et al., 2022) techniques should be included as additional security measures.

6. Conclusion

In this study, we discussed the challenges of integrating blockchain framework in IoT networks. We presented the architecture for an IoT framework that essentially labels every IoT component and maps them to ideas of complete nodes and lightweight nodes in the blockchain protocol. The authors next assessed whether the architecture may raise security by controlling IoT device IDs while making it more difficult for attackers to pose as legitimate IoT nodes.

REFERENCES

1. Anand, R., Singh, J., Pandey, D., Pandey, B. K., Nassa, V. K. and Pramanik, S. (2022). Modern Technique for Interactive Communication in LEACH-Based Ad Hoc Wireless Sensor Network", in Software Defined Networking for Ad Hoc Networks, M. M. Ghonge, S. Pramanik and A. D. Potgantwar, Eds, Springer.
2. Mukherjee, A., Singh, R.K., Mishra, R. et al. Application of blockchain technology for sustainability development in agricultural supply chain: justification framework. Oper Manag Res 15, 46–61 (2022). https://doi.org/10.1007/s12063-021-00180-5
3. Pandey, B. K., Pandey, D., Wairya, S., Agarwal, G., Dadeech, P., Dogiwal, S. R. and Pramanik, S. (2022). Application of Integrated Steganography and Image Compressing Techniques for Confidential Information Transmission", in Cyber Security and Network Security, https://doi.org/10.1002/9781119812555.ch8, Eds, Wiley.

4. Pramanik, S. (2022). An Effective Secured Privacy-Protecting Data Aggregation Method in IoT, in Achieving Full Realization and Mitigating the Challenges of the Internet of Things, Eds, M. O. Odhiambo and W. Mwashita, IGI Global, 2022, DOI: 10.4018/978-1-7998-9312-7.ch008

5. Gupta, A., Verma, A. and Pramanik, S. (2022). Security Aspects in Advanced Image Processing Techniques for COVID-19, in An Interdisciplinary Approach to Modern Network Security, S. Pramanik, A. Sharma, S. Bhatia and D. N. Le, Eds, CRC Press.

6. Gupta, A., Verma, A., and Pramanik, S. (2022). Advanced Security System in Video Surveillance for COVID-19", in An Interdisciplinary Approach to Modern Network Security, S. Pramanik, A. Sharma, S. Bhatia and D. N. Le, CRC Press.

7. Khadse, D.B., Swain, G. Data Hiding and Integrity Verification based on Quotient Value Differencing and Merkle Tree. Arab J Sci Eng (2022). https://doi.org/10.1007/s13369-022- 06961-9

8. Pradhan, D., Sahu, P. K., Goje, N. S., Myo, H., Ghonge, M. M., Tun, M., Rajeswari and Pramanik, S. (2022). Security, Privacy, Risk, and Safety Toward 5G Green Network (5G-GN)", in Cyber Security and Network Security,Eds, Wiley, 2022.

9. Zamani, E.D. The Bitcoin protocol as a system of power. Ethics Inf Technol 24, 14 (2022). https://doi.org/10.1007/s10676-022-09626-1

Computer Science Engineering and Emerging Technologies (ICCS-2022) – Prof (Dr.) Rajeev Sobti et al. (eds)
© 2024 Taylor & Francis Group, London, ISBN 978-1-032-52199-2

Chapter **17**

The Emerging Role and Application of Adopting Revolutionary Internet of Things (IoT) for Future Technology Sustainability

Ashutosh Singh[1]
Assistant Professor, Institute of Business Management,
GLA University, Mathura, U.P.

Deepali Virmani[2]
Vivekananda Institute of Professional Studies-Technical Campus,
School of Engineering and Technology

Nirzar Kulkarni[3]
Associate Director & Professor,
Dr. Ambedkar Institute of Management Studies and Research, Deekshbhoomi Nagpur-10

Mohit Tiwari[4]
Assistant Professor, Department of Computer Science and Engineering,
Bharati Vidyapeeth's College of Engineering, Delhi A-4, Rohtak Road, Paschim Vihar, Delhi

Geetha Manoharan[5]
Assistant Professor, School of Business, SR University, Telangana

Joel Alanya-Beltran[6]
Universidad Tecnológica del Perú

Abstract: The societal, environmental, and economic facets of future sustainable growth have been incorporated into national plans. The next phase of technology has been identified as the internet of things (IoT). Nevertheless, there is currently limited evidence that IoT is emerging in underdeveloped nations. One of the sectors with sustainable growth in many areas is healthcare. In order to achieve sustainable development, this research intends to produce an assessment of IoT in the healthcare industry. The research adopted an applied descriptive study methodology. The technique used was called the Fuzzy Analytical Hierarchy Process (FAHP). Following the collection of data, priority rankings for IoT utilization, weighted criterion allocation, and agreed-upon paired comparison matrices were established. The two factors with the highest importance for IoT's future technological sustainability in the healthcare sector were quality of life as well as economic success. IoT was reported to be heavily used in fields like fall identification and UV radiation.

Keywords: Sustainable technology, Applications, Internet of things, Healthcare sector

[1]assingh86@gmail.com, [2]deepali.virmani@vips.edu, [3]knirzar@gmail.com, [4]mohit.tiwari@bharatividyapeeth.edu, [5]geethamanoharan1988@gmail.com, [6]C18121@utp.edu.pe

DOI: 10.1201/9781003405580-17

1. Introduction

Technologies are essential for long-term economic success (Khorov, E., et al., 2015; Panwar, V., et al., 2021). The application of the revolutionary internet in recent years served as a signal that emerging technologies might have an impact on many facets of business (Ashibani, Y., and Mahmoud, Q. H. 2017). Without human interplay, they transform structures into autonomous, self-contained structures, such as homes, workplaces, industries, and perhaps entire cities (Jain, A., and Pandey, A. K. 2019). The global economy is being boosted by this technological automation pattern and the expanding utilization of cutting-edge technologies (Landaluce, H., et al., 2020). Modern network connectivity, wireless technology, and sensor advances have made it possible for ubiquitous communication (Jain, A., and Pandey, A. K. 2017). Communication within gadgets as well as between people and devices has greatly improved (Afifi, M. A. M., et al., 2020).

In this sense, the internet of things (IoT) has grown to be a new aspect of technology that should be taken into account when determining how to use it to accomplish various aims and objectives for corporate functions. IoT is a brand-new information and communication technology (ICT) innovation with enormous capability to impact numerous commercial facets (De Villiers, C., et al., 2021). The emerging role of IoT is as a cutting-edge future technology that is making life and business smarter through intelligent gadgets with improved connections, like smart agriculture, healthcare monitoring, environmental monitoring, smart homes, and energy management (Abbas, A., et al., 2022). Figure 17.1 implies the various applications of the adoption of the revolutionary IoT.

Due to the limited healthcare resources available, it is necessary to find efficient methods for handling the issue. Delivering healthcare services to everyone in society requires the development of a sustainable healthcare sector. For example, there aren't many individuals who use healthcare services in underdeveloped countries, and there aren't enough resources to

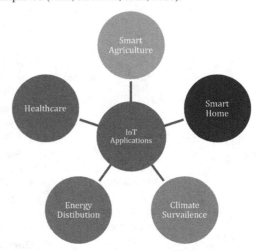

Fig. 17.1 IoT applications (Abbas, A., et al., 2022)

create systems that are very successful. The IoT can be employed in the healthcare sector to improve service delivery, as there are numerous variables at play as the industry grows (Jayavel, K., et al., 2017).

Setting IoT as a top priority is crucial for the future sustainability of the technological healthcare industry. While establishing solutions to be employed in the handling of various healthcare demands, communication across multiple devices is essential. The improvement of IoT applications across multiple healthcare platforms has been made possible by the emergence of smart technology. The necessity to develop and implement highly efficient and sustainable means of meeting the requirements of society in regards to lowering the accessibility and cost of healthcare facilities has been motivated by the growth in demand for healthcare services (Zanjal, S. V., and Talmale, G. R. 2016).

The way data is employed in the IoT is a crucial component. For the growth of IoT systems to be efficient in their application, data is essential. With the emerging applications of IoT, it is now possible to follow and trace any labeled mobile object as it travels through its setting or a stationary gadget that keeps an eye on its shifting settings (Tiwari, S., et al., 2022). This could involve instruments and equipment used in hospitals or factories, as well as items travelling via a value chain that produces unprecedented end-to-end visibility into supply chains. In short, big data analytics is required for the collection, fusion, and analysis of data from sensors, RFID tags, satellites, social media streams, photographs, videos, and mobile GPS signals in order to handle this degree of automation effectively (Jain, A., et al., 2020). As a result, big data and its analytics are essential to the establishment of a successful IoT application in the future sustainable technological healthcare industry (Riggins, F. J., and Wamba, S. F. 2015).

The objective of this investigation is to identify the operational areas in the medical industry where the adoption of IoT can improve the sector's long-term sustainability. The type of healthcare services that are provided to individuals in society has an impact on their level of economic success and quality of life.

This research includes five parts, including an introduction. In the following part two of the literature review, we explain smart healthcare and other related works between 2015 and 2022. Section 3 describes the materials and methods utilized in this research. The outcomes are presented and discussed in Section 4; Section 5 ends with the key findings, their implications, and recommendations for theory as well as practise.

2. Review of Literature

2.1 Smart Healthcare

E-health has a bright future owing to the IoT. In fact, certain IoT-based technologies have indeed been established, and they perform well in addressing various patient healthcare difficulties. In order to provide an effective method for achieving illness control, Aladwani, T. (2019) states that constant surveillance of individuals or patients is crucial. According to Verdejo Espinosa et al. (2021), the gadgets used to track people's health are crucial in creating a successful strategy for raising their quality of life. As there are numerous different ways to express different issues about the demands of patients, they contend that sustainable technology has been a crucial component in the healthcare industry. Patients are empowered since, as a consequence of controlling themselves, they are capable of creating a method of accessing various medical treatments. According to Chandy, A. (2019), the IoT offers a number of platforms that can be utiliZed to provide crucial data for the management of several healthcare conditions. It is easy for a patient to handle themselves and get the best results when they have access to various types of information. The next sections will explore the many services that are offered for IoT-sustainable technology for health.

Fall identification: The fall of patients is a typical occurrence. The adoption of IoT for vulnerable patients makes it simple to observe and handle them efficiently to reduce the chance of falls. Efficient, sustainable technologies that track impaired individuals can reduce the risk of patient falls.

Sportsmen's Nursing: Athletes' health should be observed, and this can be accomplished with the help of wearable gadgets that track their systems and look for any abnormalities. To achieve efficacy, several tools are essential.

Chronic Disease Management: Lowering the number of individuals in healthcare institutions is essential. This is accomplished via the distant monitoring of chronic diseases, where individuals may keep track of their own development and clinicians can receive information about it.

2.2 IoT Sustainable Indicators in Healthcare Sector

Due to the rising demand for these services, the healthcare industry must be developed sustainably. The IoTs will be utilized to deliver an efficient method of providing healthcare facilities that will be employed to handle various challenges in the healthcare industry (Tian, J., and Gao, L. 2021). The increase in a person's quality of life is essential for the quality to continue to rise. Since it will reduce the strain on healthcare establishments and improve the performance of various healthcare service suppliers, the deployment of sustainable technology in the healthcare industry is essential to creating a more sustainable healthcare sector. For sustainable growth, the healthcare industry must adopt technology, which is sustainable in every discipline (Ghazal, T. M, 2021).

3. Materials and Method

3.1 Research Model

Fuzzy Analytical Hierarchy Process (FAHP) is the theoretical model selected for this research that emphasizes the usage of IoT for future sustainable technological growth of the medical industry.

3.2 Research Methodology

This is a quantitative and descriptive analysis. The weighing of IoT priorities in the healthcare industry was done using FAHP. The initial scoring system gave equal weight to the factors of economic success, quality of life, and environmental preservation. For the purpose of understanding the healthcare setting, various parameters were used. For the purpose of analyzing the setting, comparative questionnaires were created and used. Employing several criteria, the revolutionary IoT application in every healthcare industry was evaluated. Following the results analysis, a choice matrix was created. The statistical group includes professionals who are familiar with the ways in which IoT is being used in the healthcare industry. The restricted pool of specialists employed in this study led to the snowball method's subsequent application.

3.3 FAHP

- Entails a decision-making procedure with several factors.
- This model was crucial to utilize for this investigation since it successfully addresses a variety of parameter concerns. The following is a description of the FAHP application procedure.
- Collection of data's to identify sustainability standards as well as the adoption of IoT applications in the health industry.
- Creating a decision-making unit to evaluate the validity of the data.
- Creating the matrix for matched comparisons.
- Evaluation of the criteria.

Table 17.1 Employing the FAHP approach and measure the IoT adoption in the healthcare industry (Tian, J., and Gao, L. 2021)

Intensity of Significance	Fuzzy Value	Factors	Function Membership
9	9	Extreme significance	(8,9,10)
7	7	Very strong significance	(6,7,8)
5	5	Strong significance	(4,5,6)
3	3	Moderate in significance	(2,3,4)
1	1	Equal significance	(1,1,2)

4. Result and Analysis

Employing FAHP, scores were acquired, the paired comparison criteria were used, and a decision matrix was created. To provide a suitable method for creating the matrix, the scores of each choice were implemented.

4.1 Ranking Options

The ultimate ranking for the IoT implementation in all of the healthcare sectors was produced employing the scores derived for sustainable development criteria and decision matrix.

Table 17.2 Sustainability criteria scores (Tian, J., and Gao, L. 2021)

Economic Success	Quality of Life	Environmental Preservation
45.32%	31.1%	23.63%

Table 17.3 The decision matrix, calculated from the average scores of each indicator (Tian, J., and Gao, L. 2021)

Factors	Economic Success	Quality of Life	Environmental Preservation
Fall identification	0.11	0.096	0.14
Medical Refrigerators	0.084	0.11	0.039
Sportsman Nursing	0.07	0.014	0.153
Surveillance of patients	0.12	0.095	0.121
Chronic diseasemanagerial	0.079	0.104	0.025
U-V radiation	0.113	0.132	0.18
Hand hygiene management	0.098	0.094	0.12
Sleep management	0.068	0.143	0.059

Table 17.4 Priority-based score (Tian, J., and Gao, L. 2021)

Factors	Rank	Score
UV radiation	1	0.057
Fall identification	3	0.0374
Surveillance of patients	4	0.0371
Hand hygiene management	5	0.0340
Sportsman nursing	6	0.031

Factors	Rank	Score
Sleep management	7	0.029
Medical refrigerators	8	0.027
Chronic disease managerial	9	0.024

Table 17.5   Industries compared pair-wise to a synthesized matrix (based on) quality-of-life standards (Tian, J., and Gao, L. 2021)

Matrix	Healthcaresector	Transport	Smart homes	Energy sectors	Retailing sector
Healthcare sector	1	3.464	5.5951	1.4142	7.416
Transport	0.289	1	0.8944	0.245	1.0000
Smart homes	0.179	1.118	1	0.1996	3.0274
Energy sector	0.7071	4.091	5.0100	1	2.646
Retailing sector	0.135	1.0000	0.3303	0.378	1

As the value 0.1 is considered to be the highest limit for CR, it was calculated that the pair-wise comparative synthesized matrix's CR was equivalent to 0.0509. In assessments, it demonstrates good compatibility.

5. Conclusion

It is clear from the research's findings that economic success is among the factors with the top rating, coming in at 45.32%. The other industries will automatically grow if this industry invests more in IoT. The enhancement of healthcare service delivery depends on hospital staff satisfaction. As IoT is adopted in the industry, it is vital to heed this fact in order to give successful healthcare services.

The application of revolutionary IoT in healthcare has been studied, and the results show that the adoption of technology is more prevalent in facilities that employ UV radiation. This is one method used in numerous tests to look for diseases or abnormalities in the body. Table 4 demonstrates the types of investments that should be made in the healthcare industry to enhance its efficiency by listing the sequence in which diverse IoT applications are adopted in hospitals.

6. Recommendations

It is clear that the IoT must be adopted, and policymakers must make certain that assets are managed well to provide people with efficient ways to make a variety of advances in the future sustainable technological healthcare industry. Developing sustainable growth in the industry would need adopting IoT in healthcare. This is due to a decrease in the amount of strain placed on healthcare resources. When patients are able to handle their own care remotely, medical centers can handle other urgent cases more efficiently.

REFERENCE

1. Khorov, E., Lyakhov, A., Krotov, A., & Guschin, A. (2015). A survey on IEEE 802.11 ah: An enabling networking technology for smart cities. *Computer communications, 58,* 53–69.
2. Panwar, V., Sharma, D. K., Kumar, K. P., Jain, A., & Thakar, C. (2021). Experimental investigations and optimization of surface roughness in turning of en 36 alloy steel using response surface methodology and genetic algorithm. *Materials Today: Proceedings, 46,* 6474–6481.
3. Ashibani, Y., & Mahmoud, Q. H. (2017). Cyber physical systems security: Analysis, challenges and solutions. *Computers & Security, 68,* 81–97.
4. Jain, A., & Pandey, A. K. (2019). Modeling and optimizing of different quality characteristics in electrical discharge drilling of titanium alloy (Grade-5) sheet. *Materials Today: Proceedings, 18,* 182–191.
5. Landaluce, H., Arjona, L., Perallos, A., Falcone, F., Angulo, I., & Muralter, F. (2020). A review of IoT sensing applications and challenges using RFID and wireless sensor networks. *Sensors, 20*(9), 2495.
6. Jain, A., & Pandey, A. K. (2017). Multiple quality optimizations in electrical discharge drilling of mild steel sheet. *Materials Today: Proceedings, 4*(8), 7252–7261.

7. Afifi, M. A. M., Kalra, D., Ghazal, T. M., & Mago, B. (2020). Information Technology Ethics and Professional Responsibilities. *International Journal of Advanced Science and Technology*, *29*(4), 11336–11343.

8. De Villiers, C., Kuruppu, S., & Dissanayake, D. (2021). A (new) role for business–Promoting the United Nations' Sustainable Development Goals through the internet-of-things and blockchain technology. *Journal of business research*, *131*, 598–609.'

9. Abbas, A., Khan, M. A., Latif, S., Ajaz, M., Shah, A. A., & Ahmad, J. (2022). A new ensemble-based intrusion detection system for internet of things. *Arabian Journal for Science and Engineering*, *47*(2), 1805–1819.

10. Jayavel, K., Nagarajan, V., & Sharma, G. (2017). An analysis of iot test beds with application in the field of medicine and health care. *Research Journal of Pharmacy and Technology*, *10*(12), 4155–4161.

11. Zanjal, S. V., & Talmale, G. R. (2016). Medicine reminder and monitoring system for secure health using IOT. *Procedia Computer Science*, *78*, 471–476.

12. Tiwari, S., Rosak-Szyrocka, J., & Żywiołek, J. (2022). Internet of Things as a Sustainable Energy Management Solution at Tourism Destinations in India. *Energies*, *15*(7), 2433.

13. Jain, A., Yadav, A. K., & Shrivastava, Y. (2020). Modelling and optimization of different quality characteristics in electric discharge drilling of titanium alloy sheet. *Materials Today: Proceedings*, *21*, 1680–1684.

14. Riggins, F. J., & Wamba, S. F. (2015). Research directions on the adoption, usage, and impact of the internet of things through the use of big data analytics. In *2015 48th Hawaii international conference on system sciences* (pp. 1531–1540). IEEE.

15. Aladwani, T. (2019). Scheduling IoT healthcare tasks in fog computing based on their importance. *Procedia Computer Science*, *163*, 560–569.

16. Verdejo Espinosa, Á., López, J. L., Mata Mata, F., & Estevez, M. E. (2021). Application of IoT in healthcare: keys to implementation of the sustainable development goals. *Sensors*, *21*(7), 2330.

17. Chandy, A. (2019). A review on iot based medical imaging technology for healthcare applications. *Journal of Innovative Image Processing (JIIP)*, *1*(01), 51–60.

18. Tian, J., & Gao, L. (2021). Using data monitoring algorithms to physiological indicators in motion based on Internet of Things in smart city. *Sustainable Cities and Society*, *67*, 102727.

19. Ghazal, T. M. (2021). Internet of things with artificial intelligence for health care security. *Arabian Journal for Science and Engineering*, 1–12.

Computer Science Engineering and Emerging Technologies (ICCS-2022) – Prof (Dr.) Rajeev Sobti et al. (eds)
© 2024 Taylor & Francis Group, London, ISBN 978-1-032-52199-2

Chapter **18**

Forecasting of Stock Market Data Frame Analysis Using Relative Strength Index (RSI) and Deep Learning

Anuj Pratap Singh[1]
Scholar Student, Computer science and engineering,
Lovely Professional University, Phagwara, Punjab, India

Ranjith Kumar Anandan[2]
Assistant Professor, Computer science and engineering,
Lovely Professional University, Phagwara, Punjab, India

Rajat Rana[3], Harsh Prakash Dwivedi[4], Avinash P.[5], Akshat Narendra Sakharkar[6]
Scholar Student, Computer science and engineering,
Lovely Professional University, Phagwara, Punjab, India

Abstract: The stock market has a significant impact on our daily lives. It plays an important role in a country's GDP growth. Exact forecasting of stock market returns is a particularly challenging task due to the unstable and indirect nature of money markets. The share price is an important indicator of a company, and the factors will affect their prices. Because of its great learning ability to solve indirect situations in time series prediction problems, machine learning has been used in this research project. You can use supervised learning models such as bagging, ensemble classifier boosting, and deep learning neural networks to predict whether to buy, sell, or keep. Feature engineering is the key to building high-performance models and allows for feature selection (random forest)/feature extraction (PCA) techniques. The accuracy of these models depends on two factors: the input data used and the type of algorithm chosen. The model can be used to predict stock price movements at any point in time. We propose an approach that combines an LSTM (long short-term memory) network with an RSI (relative strength index).

Keywords: Gross domestic product (GDP), Principal component analysis (PCA), LSTM (long short-term memory), RSI (relative strength index)

1. Introduction

The use of techniques to predict stock charges early by analysing overall performance over the last few years may be beneficial. The technical evaluation approach also uses the inventory rate history, which includes the last and opening rates, extent traded, and close to inventory charges, to predict the future rate of the stock marketplace. Analysis is quality; it's based totally on outside factors, including corporation profile, marketplace situation, political and financial elements, textual knowledge of tendencies in new economic topics, verbal exchange media, and financial evaluation theory. The aim of this project is to investigate the functioning of traditional emotional networks, i.e., long-short-term memory (LSTM) networks, in the predictive nature of stock market changes. Evaluate their performance in terms of accuracy with other

---
[1]anujkannauj002@gmail.com, [2]aranjithkumar.dr@gmail.com, [3]rajat15121998@gmail.com, [4]harshprakash2211@gmail.com,
[5]avinashp0201@gmail.com, [6]akshatsakharkar28@gmail.com

DOI: 10.1201/9781003405580-18

metrics using real-world data in testing and see if they offer any advantages to standard machine learning techniques (Navale et al., n.d.).

2. Literature Review

The debate over the forecast of the proposed inventory cross has returned to the green marketplace speculation, which states that the progressive asset charge is the simplest value. It asserts that the stock price fluctuates beyond its base; in other words, the price of the future might be determined best with the aid of the knowledge of destiny. straight-backslide models work act is that they are continuously fitted with the least amount of material. Because they do not consistently deliver specified results, it is critical to develop ways to increase the accuracy of your gauge. Wang et al. (2019) introduced artificial neural networks to stock market price prediction in 2003 and focused on volume as a specific element of the stock market. In (Liu et al., 2017), we introduced a convolutional neural network (CNN) and a long short-term memory (LSTM) neural network-based model to examine different quantitative strategies in stock markets and used a wavelet neural network (WNN) to forecast stock price changes (Nelson et al., 2017). Lee (Selvin et al., 2017) predicted stock movements using the support vector machine (SVM) and a hybrid feature selection strategy. For stock market forecasting, Urlam & Al (2021) analysed stock market behaviour and used a number of classical models. We determined the best model among the machine learning methods and SoftMax. Pimenta et al. [9] applied a multi-objective genetic programming-based automated investment system to the stock market. In Liu et al. (2017), Hassan and Nath used the Hidden Markov Model (HMM) to anticipate stock prices for four different airlines. They divide the model's states into four categories: opening price, closing price, maximum price, and lowest price. There are a variety of approaches to determining the most effective method. For each, all approaches don't operate in the same manner, and yield varies.

3. Methodology and Model Specifications

In this project, the estimate of the stock exchange is done with LSTM and RSI.

Long Short-Term Memory (LSTM): An extraordinary sort of RNN, which can figure out how to depend for quite a while, is called long-short-term memory (LSTM) (Le et al., 2019). LSTM causes RNN to recollect long-haul input.

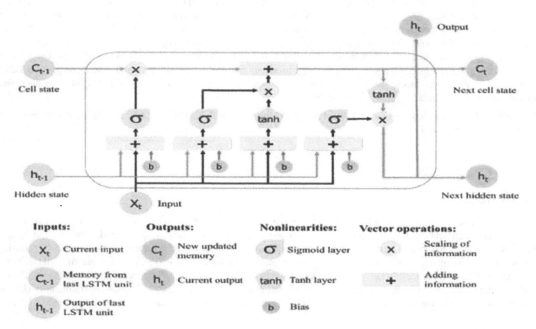

Fig. 18.1 LSTM Cell

Source: Available from: https://www.researchgate.net/figure/The-structure-of-the-Long-Short-Term-Memory-LSTM-neural-network-*Reproduced-from-Yan_fig8_334268507 [accessed 7 Jul ,2023]*

Contains data on memory, like PC memory. It knows how to read, compose, and erase data from its memory. This memory should be visible as a shut cell, with a shut importance, if the cell chooses to store or erase data. In LSTM (Hari & Dewi, n.d.), there are three entryways: input, neglecting, and leave door. In an entryway cell, LSTMs store data without the typical progression of a nonstop organization. Like information in a PC memory, data can be put away in a cell and composed and perused in the cell (Pramod & Pm, 2021). The cell comes to conclusions about when to permit perusing, composing, and erasure and what to keep with the entryways shut and open. In contrast to computerized putaway on PCs, notwithstanding, these simple entryways, which are utilized for savvy duplication by sigmoid, are all 0-1. Simple is more profitable than advanced for parting, and therefore it merits backpropagation. Those doors work on the signs they get, block, or communicate data as far as its abilities and information sources; they channel themselves by their weight sets, like hubs in the brain organization. The learning system of dull organizations has such loads, as well as data sources that control inputs and secret circumstances (Wang et al., 2019).

Forget gate: Forget gate determines when to insert a specific part of a cell with information newer than subtracts almost one part of the cell state to keep and the value to ignore, zero.

Input gate: It determines the extent to which records are written directly to the inner cellular state.

Output gate: Relying on the input mode and cellular, this factor determines the data to be transferred to the subsequent factor within the network (Le et al., 2019).

The Relative Strength Index (RSI) is one of the most widely used technical analysis indicators. After adjusting the RSI to the trading quantity, the lookup will check its new type on the same set of records. Eventually, it'll compare the consequences obtained from the use of the vintage version of the index with the ones acquired from the use of the changed shape (Yu et al., 2019). The RSI indicator of dynamics works to show us how the marketplace depends on one asset or every other, how the pressure pushes a specified asset, and what the predicted changes need to be.

Relative Strength Index

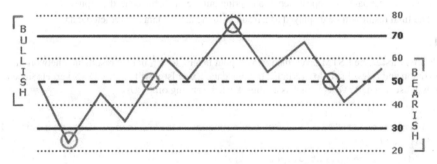

Fig. 18.2 RSI Pattern

Source: This figure took from https://forex-forex-jednoduse.cz/rsi/

RSI may have a cost anywhere between 0 and 100, but it rarely hits any of these marks.

3.1 Proposed Model

In the implementation part, the data we are using are given below:

1. *Historic Data:* In this historic data, we mean the raw data that we use for the purpose of training the model. For collecting the raw data, we used the API key of Yahoo Finance, through which we are taking all the entries for the company's stock prices.
2. *Processing the data:* In this step, the data will be forwarded for training purposes, and there it will be correctly arranged in the sequence if there are any mistakes or missing entries. so it will be corrected at that time.
3. *Function Selection:* In this step, data attributes are chosen that are going to be fed to the neural network. In this research, date and close price are chosen as selected features.
4. *Training the Neural Networks:* In the step the LSTM model will fetch the processed inputs and train them in the network layer of LSTM architecture.

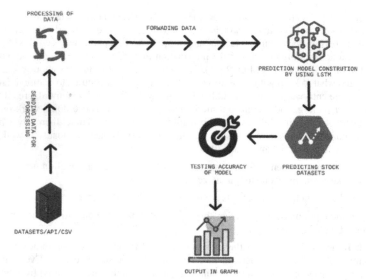

Fig. 18.3 Model training process

Source: Created by Author

5. *The Output Generation:* The neural network will generate the results using the algorithm. And reprocess the output data to get an accurate result.

6. *Test Output:* The test data will repeat step 2 to filtering out the disturbance in the inputs.

7. *Result:* The final result will be displayed as a result with the actual data or predicted data.

3.2 Model

We used six layers. First is the LSTM layer, then two dropout layers, which in turn results in a network that is capable of better generalization and is less likely to overfit the training data. Layer lstm will not use DNN kernels since it doesn't meet the criteria. It will use a generic GPU kernel as a fallback when running on GPUs.

```
model = Sequential ()

model.add(Bidirectional(LSTM(512 , return_sequences=True , rec urrent_dropout=0.1,
input_shape=(32, 2))))

model.add(LSTM(256 , recurrent_dropout=0.1))
model.add(Dropout(0.3))
model.add(Dense(64 , activation='elu'))
model.add(Dropout(0.3))
model.add(Dense(32 , activation='elu'))
model.add(Dense(1 , activation='linear')) #Final Layer
```

3.3 Predicted Graph

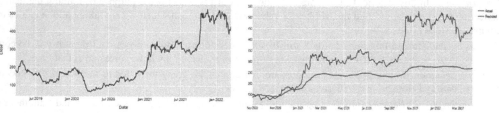

Fig. 18.4 Actual or Predicted Graph

Source: Author's generated results

Closing value factors are considered to control their effect on the stock return.

3.4 Statistics

	Open	High	Low	Close	Adj close	Volume
Count	742.000000	742.000000	742.000000	742.000000	742.000000	7.420000e+02
Mean	235.122237	239.586388	230.417992	234.827359	234.827359	5.200314e+07
Std	128.876168	130.677005	126.750171	128.678659	128.678659	4.058689e+07
25%	66.500000	66.900002	63.500000	65.300003	65.300003	5.531940e+06
50%	133.674995	184.099998	176.449997	180.300003	180.300003	4.092467e+07
75%	314.787491	320.000000	309.575005	315.112511	315.112511	6.445397e+07
Max	531.450012	536.700012	520.250000	530.150024	530.150024	3.905778e+08

Source: Author's Compilation

4. Conclusion

There are now various models for predicting the stock market; however, they are not particularly accurate. We've suggested a model that employs LSTM to forecast stock price patterns with greater accuracy. The memory cell is a unit of estimation introduced by LSTM, which substitutes typical neurons with a concealed network topology. By using its higher and lower graph lines, the RSI indicator can even assist us in taking precise actions to invest in stocks. The effectiveness of the forecast is improved in this work by raising the epoch and collection size. We use predictive value test data in the suggested plan to get the most accurate outcomes using the training dataset. The proposed approach can track and forecast the stock market, and the forecasting will be high-quality and dependable. We acquire accurate results from our model above, which will be highly valuable for analysts and investors, industry experts, and stock traders.

REFERENCES

1. Hari, Y., & Dewi, L. P. (n.d.). *Forecasting System Approach for Stock Trading with Relative Strength Index and Moving Average Indicator*. *10*(2), 5.
2. Le, X. H., Ho, H., Lee, G., & Jung, S. (2019). Application of Long Short-Term Memory (LSTM) Neural Network for Flood Forecasting. *Water*, *11*, 1387. https://doi.org/10.3390/w11071387
3. Liu, S., Zhang, C., & Ma, J. (2017). *CNN-LSTM Neural Network Model for Quantitative Strategy Analysis in Stock Markets*. 198–206. https://doi.org/10.1007/978-3-319-70096-0_21
4. Navale, G. S., Pune, S. P., Dudhwala, N., Pune, S. P., Jadhav, K., Pune, S. P.,
5. Gabda, P., Pune, S. P., Vihangam, B. K., & Pune, S. P. (n.d.). *SITS Narhe, Pune-411041*.
6. Nelson, D. M. Q., Pereira, A. C. M., & de Oliveira, R. A. (2017). Stock market's price movement prediction with LSTM neural networks. *2017 International Joint Conference on Neural Networks (IJCNN)*, 1419–1426. https://doi.org/10.1109/IJCNN.2017.7966019
7. Pramod, & Pm, M. (2021). Stock Price Prediction Using LSTM. *Test Engineering and Management*, *83*, 5246–5251.
8. Selvin, S., Vinayakumar, R., Gopalakrishnan, E. A., Menon, V. K., & Soman, K. P. (2017). Stock price prediction using LSTM, RNN and CNN-sliding window model. *2017 International Conference on Advances in Computing, Communications and Informatics (ICACCI)*, 1643–1647. https://doi.org/10.1109/ICACCI.2017.8126078
9. Urlam, S., & Al, E. (2021). Stock Market Prediction Using LSTM and Sentiment Analysis. *Turkish Journal of Computer and Mathematics Education (TURCOMAT)*, *12*(11), Article 11.
10. Wang, J., Sun, T., Liu, B., Cao, Y., & Zhu, H. (2019). CLVSA: A Convolutional LSTM Based Variational Sequence-to-Sequence Model with Attention for Predicting Trends of Financial Markets. *Proceedings of the Twenty-Eighth International Joint Conference on Artificial Intelligence*, 3705–3711. https://doi.org/10.24963/ijcai.2019/514

Computer Science Engineering and Emerging Technologies (ICCS-2022) – Prof (Dr.) Rajeev Sobti et al. (eds)
© 2024 Taylor & Francis Group, London, ISBN 978-1-032-52199-2

Chapter 19

Enablement of Blockchain in Healthcare: A Systematic Review

Rishabh Srivastava[1], Deepak Prashar[2]
School of Computer Science and Engineering,
Lovely Professional University, Phagwara, Punjab, India

Abstract: Blockchain technology is considered disruptive because no central authority is involved. Because of its decentralized and disruptive nature, it is bringing transformations in various domains. This paper studies the potential and need for blockchain applications in healthcare systems. The main aim is to highlight the main causes of the requirement for blockchain in healthcare. The review presents the benefits of digitizing medical records in terms of better storage and management of patient records, providing secured and greater access, enhanced quality of treatments, and better patient care. The introduction to technology and its applications is discussed, followed by the benefits of the electronic health system, the need for blockchain, and the basic features of electronic health record systems.

Keywords: Blockchain Technology, Electronic health record, Healthcare, Electronic medical record

1. Introduction

Blockchain is the latest technology that is changing the world around us. Satoshi Nakamoto created the blockchain in 2008. To act as a public transaction ledger for the cryptocurrency bitcoin (S. Nakamoto, 2008), blockchain applications can be found in every domain, like finance, government, real estate, voting, supply chain management, biomedical sciences, and healthcare. On a simpler note, a blockchain is a transaction ledger open to anyone. Once data is added, it will prevent previous information from changing as it is recorded. Blockchain mainly comprises a growing blockchain connected by cryptography, so every block becomes immutable when chained. These blocks are accessible to anyone. This feature makes the blockchain system both secure and efficient. Blockchain helps increase safety and accessibility and is highly secure when connected with patient data according to decentralized standards, which might disturb the functionality of medical processes.

Blockchain can be used as a specific technology for healthcare as it can improve the interoperability of patient records stored in healthcare databases, facilitating their increased access, device tracking, and all-time access to patient records for providing the right medication and superior healthcare outcomes. We can say that blockchain is the main technology that can improve the framework of healthcare services (S. Tanwar *et al.,* 2020).

2. Benefit of Digitization of Medical Records

Blockchain should be used for more than just the financial industry, including applications in the public health sector and beyond bitcoin. In the past, medical information was written down on paper, which was prone to damage and alteration. Consequently, electronic data preservation was required (S. Arijit *et al.,* 2019). When a patient transfers from one hospital

[1]rishabhcolvin@gmail.com, [2]deepak.prashar@lpu.co.in

DOI: 10.1201/9781003405580-19

to another, they must carry their records and show them to the new doctors. Techniques for transmitting or exchanging data were developed to decrease this inconvenience. The issue's major constraint is that each doctor or institution keeps its records in a different format. Some general hospitals have created web-based information exchange systems to connect with their linked clinics and do away with manual processes to overcome this obstacle. However, these kinds of systems are more suited to their connected medical facilities than the national standard model (Kim N.H. *et al.,* 2005).

Healthcare systems can develop comprehensive patient views and better communication, enhance the quality of treatment and care, and enhance the outcomes of medical practices through proper management and safe retrieval of patient data (Attaran Mohsen, 2022). To efficiently exchange histories of patients' treatment records dispersed throughout medical institutions, the EHR (Electronic Healthcare Record) is the information system that combines the EMRs (Electronic Medical Records) kept by separate medical facilities (EHR Seoul, 2008).

EHRs offer several advantages in terms of increased patient safety, accessibility, and medical service quality. The healthcare sector might greatly benefit from electronic medical records. By allowing it to be used with only authorized access, storing scans and other digital images, and facilitating improved departmental communication, these types of systems might help save healthcare expenditures, improve patient care quality, reduce paper-related confusion, and improve overall system efficiency. The ability to identify and treat high-risk people with some disease, perform important research, uncover abuse or fraud, and assess and improve the quality of care can all be improved through electronic medical data (Steward Melissa, 2005). E-health records can be used for patient care, research, health education, and disease surveillance to maintain public health. However, it also increases patient-provider communication, which leads to more effective health monitoring and treatments, increased access to medical care, and reduced strain on the public healthcare system. The value of eHealth is found in its capacity to provide patients with access to their medical records and real-time health monitoring with the development of IoT and connected gadgets (Rifi, Nabil, *et al.,* 2017).

3. Literature Review

A medical record-sharing EHR system was proposed (Su Qianqian *et al.,* 2020) using blockchain based on a scheme for signatures that use attributes involving attribute revocation; for hiding the real identity of users, mainly doctors, it uses the KUnodes algorithm for generating keys and uses the concept of attribute revocation. Another paper (Mettler, Matthias, 2016) talks about the applicability of blockchain outside financial segments; it discusses various healthcare-based start-ups running in different countries on the blockchain; at the end, a counterfeit medicine project based on Hyperledger technology is discussed as being jointly developed by companies like Bloomberg, Block Stream, IBM, Intel, Accenture, and Cisco. The author (Azaria Asaph *et al.,* 2016) proposed a new record-managing system for managing EMR implemented via blockchain technology. This system enables patients to have full and easy access across various medical service providers and treatment entities. This system enables medical data sharing among patients, which maintains confidentiality, authentication, and accountability of the data. Further, it structures patients' medical records on blockchain by implementing them in different formats.

The authors (Liang, Xueping, *et al.,* 2017) have designed a mobile blockchain-based system of healthcare for collecting personal medical data and a sharing interface controlled by users. Health data is collected from wearable medical devices that monitor health conditions like sleeping, heartbeat, and walking distance. This data is recorded and uploaded to a cloud database via a mobile application; medical data is stored off-chain using the IPFS mechanism; the implementation uses language solidity. JavaScript testing is done using the Raspberry Pi platform. This paper introduces an architecture based on blockchain for EHR systems that incorporates a blockchain solution for enhancing the interoperability of the existing EHR systems, preventing malicious use and tampering of EHRs, and tracing all events that happen to data in databases. This suggested architecture also includes a fresh incentive system for adding new blockchain blocks (Rifi, Nabil, *et al.,* 2017). Another paper (Y. Guang &C. Li., 2018) suggests a platform built on Blockchain BlocHIE to exchange information in healthcare. Its system architecture uses two loosely coupled blockchains named EMR-Chain and PHD-Chain to store PHD and EMRs separately.

The author has given a direction for blockchain technology in cloud applications. This application can be useful to patients, medical practitioners, pharmacies, insurance companies, research agencies, and governments. As a result, this can be used in analysing diseases for research by generating authorized access and insurance policy management by patients and insurance providers (Jiang Shan *et al.,* 2018). This paper discusses interoperability in healthcare data exchange controlled by patients using blockchain technology. First, it discusses the benefits of interoperability in healthcare and why medical institutions have not adopted EHR systems; further, it discusses the challenges and opportunities of patient-based interoperability (Kaur Harleen *et al.,* 2018). This paper talks about an entire ecosystem consisting of EMR, PHR, and EHR used to share patients' data in real-time via the cloud and how blockchain technology can be applied in this ecosystem for the privacy, safety, and security of the patient's data. The limitation of the paper is presenting an automated and proper patient management system that enhances the quality of care given to patients and reduces its cost at the same time (Gordon, W. J., and Christian C., 2018). In this paper, a system for "Bindaas Blockchain-Based Deep Learning as a Service" is proposed. In this Bindaas framework, blockchain combines deep learning techniques for EHR record sharing among healthcare users. It is a two-phase system; in the first phase, a signature and authentication scheme is suggested, which relies on lattice-based cryptography, while in the second phase, DaaS (deep learning as a service) is applied to saved EHR records for predicting future diseases (Bhattacharya P. et *al.,* 2019).

This paper (Tripathi G. et *al.,* 2020) implements a secure and smart healthcare system using blockchain technologies. S2HS explores different issues and challenges related to transparency, privacy, and security of data and users, so first, it discusses various expert views, including basic concepts, challenges, and issues involved in blockchain using healthcare, so it does a thorough research gap analysis. This paper (Tran Quy et *al.,* 2019) gives a comparative analysis of Hyperledger frameworks. First, it gives an overview of Hyperledger Frameworks and their properties, then gives a performance evaluation by setting up a model configuration and using metrics like throughput and latency. In this paper, the author has given a comparison between the Sawtooth and Fabric frameworks, and this comparative analysis can be used by developers when choosing between different frameworks.

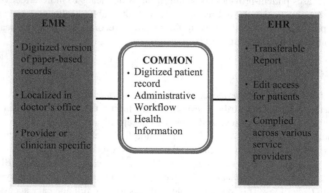

Fig. 19.1 Comparison of various forms of digitized health records [29]

4. Need for Blockchain in Healthcare

The private medical information of a patient frequently needs to be exchanged between various healthcare providers and made available to the public. With advanced technology in the past few years, most healthcare records have moved online to facilitate storage and improve accessibility for patients and healthcare professionals. However, such a development also raises the possibility of data breaches, which are terrible issues in terms of the privacy of patients and financial damage. According to a recent Forbes article, the healthcare sector loses roughly $380 for every patient's data hacked (Chen H., Huang X. W., 2018). As a result, blockchains are a necessary and effective means for storing and transmitting such data. Multiple healthcare professionals and the patient can access the data as a single, consolidated record when it is stored on blockchains, which is one of the many benefits of doing so. For example, when a patient is moved from one medical facility to another, this offers a useful way to transfer the medical record. Additionally, when the data is recorded in the system, the existing data cannot be changed; only new data may be added. This change-tracking system is crucial for the healthcare industry since it's imperative that any alterations to the records can be tracked, for instance, if a patient receives medication more than once (Chen H., Huang X. W., 2018). All the medical data in a blockchain system is encrypted and shielded from any possible data breach. Personal healthcare information must be highly protected because it is incredibly sensitive, and blockchain offers the required level of security (Chen H., Huang X. W., 2018). In the medical field, blockchain can improve daily life applications like exchanging clinical data in electronic form, observing devices, data stock protection, basic clinical information, etc. It also ensures the security and safety of patient information through its decentralization and can further disturb the functionality of the medical system. Currently, research in blockchain is very limited, but blockchain is on the verge of changing the entire medical care ecosystem (Srivastava R. and Deepak P., 2021). Blockchain is thought to improve the use of healthcare-related data. Data, process improvement, cost reduction, patient outcomes improvement, and compliance improvement A study by IBM covering executives of 200 life sciences companies across 18 countries shows that blockchain will enable them to overcome legacy systems and inefficient administrative procedures that limit their ability to innovate and adapt (Attaran Mohsen, 2022).

Table 19.1   Key Enablers and Challenges BC-Healthcare [3]

Healthcare challenges	How BC addresses these challenges
Data Security	• Cryptographic keys • Hashing Function
Fragmented Data	• Decentralization • Interoperability
System Interoperability	• Data immutability • Digital access rules • Data aggregation
Timely Access to Data	• Cloud Technology • IoT
Patient generated data	• Sensors • IoT-based healthcare devices

5. Countries that have Fully Digitized their Healthcare Management System

Modern medical record digitization has raised more questions about healthcare data security and privacy. In various countries like Denmark, Estonia, and Norway, over the past 20 years, the government and medical institutions have steadily developed national electronic health records and e-health services. With countries going for digitization for medical records, concerns related to the security and privacy of health records are also increasing daily.

In 2007, when the national repository of record information from all public hospitals in Denmark, known as E-Record (or E-Journal in Danish), was established, it served as the foundation for the exchange of EHR data among hospitals (Rahbek-Nrgaard J., 2013). The Estonian eHealth Foundation was established in 2005. The Estonian Health Insurance Fund introduced the country's electronic prescription system in 2010. 99.9% of prescriptions are issued digitally as of now (Karin Kõnd and Anett Lilleväli, 2019). Work in healthcare started in Norway in the year 1984, and after almost 20 years, the rate of adoption of EHR in Norway has risen to 80% in various hospitals and medical centres. To develop and deploy a national Electronic Health Record (EHR) system in Norway, the Norwegian Directorate of Health and Accenture inked a five-year agreement in October 2012 (Heimly V. et al., 2011).

6. Results and Conclusion

This study was conducted to list the benefits of digitization of medical records and their advantages over traditional healthcare records, identify the main points that enable blockchain usage in healthcare management systems, and also show how blockchain technology is helping in the creation and management of electronic health records.

This study helps determine the root causes for choosing blockchain in healthcare and also studies the structure and components of an electronic health record system. For future works, I will find out the tools used for creating electronic health record systems in blockchain, their comparisons, and the factors used for selecting particular tools.

So, from the above survey, I can conclude that by using blockchain in healthcare, patients' data will be:

- Safe, secure and tamper-proof.
- The patient will have authority over his well being.
- Healthcare providers will be to digitize, store and integrate patients' data across various hospitals, doctors, and clinics by using a single application.
- Interoperability of patient data across various hospitals, clinics, and healthcare providers.

• Patients will also be able to trace their medication costs and check the duplicity of their records, and traceability of medicines will also be there.

REFERENCES

1. Tanwar, Sudeep, Karan Parekh, and Richard Evans. "Blockchain-based electronic healthcare record system for healthcare 4.0 applications." Journal of Information Security and Applications 50 (2020): 102407.
2. Angraal, Suveen, Harlan M. Krumholz, and Wade L. Schulz. "Blockchain technology: applications in health care." Circulation: Cardiovascular quality and outcomes 10.9 (2017): e003800.
3. Attaran, Mohsen. "Blockchain technology in healthcare: Challenges and opportunities." International Journal of Healthcare Management 15.1 (2022): 70–83.
4. Azaria, Asaph, et al. "Medrec: Using blockchain for medical data access and permission management." 2016 2nd international conference on open and big data (OBD). IEEE, 2016.
5. Ban, Tran Quy, et al. "Survey of Hyperledger blockchain frameworks: case study in FPT university's cryptocurrency wallets." Proceedings of the 2019 8th International Conference on Software and Computer Applications. 2019.
6. Bhattacharya, Pronaya, et al. "Bindaas: Blockchain-based deep-learning as-a-service in healthcare 4.0 applications." IEEE Transactions on Network Science and Engineering 8.2 (2019): 1242–1255.
7. Chen H, Huang X. Will, Blockchain Technology Transform Healthcare and Biomedical Sciences? EC PharmacolToxicol. 2018 Nov; 6(11): 910–911. Epub 2018 Oct 29. PMID: 31460519; PMCID: PMC6711478.
8. EHR. Seoul: Center for Interoperable EHR; c2008- [cited at 2010 Dec 15]. Available from: http://www.ehrkorea.org
9. Esposito, Christian, et al. "Blockchain: A panacea for healthcare cloud-based data security and privacy?" IEEE Cloud Computing 5.1 (2018): 31–37.
10. Gordon, William J., and Christian Catalini. "Blockchain technology for healthcare: facilitating the transition to patient-driven interoperability." Computational and structural biotechnology journal 16 (2018): 224–230.
11. Heimly V, Grimsmo A, Faxvaag A. Diffusion of Electronic Health Records and electronic communication in Norway. Appl Clin Inform. 2011 Sep 7; 2(3): 355–64. doi: 10.4338/ACI-2011-01-IE-0008. PMID: 23616882; PMCID: PMC3631929.
12. Hölbl, Marko, et al. "A systematic review of the use of blockchain in healthcare." Symmetry 10.10 (2018): 470.
13. Jiang, Shan, et al. "Blochie: a blockchain-based platform for healthcare information exchange." 2018 ieee international conference on smart computing (smartcomp). IEEE, 2018.
14. Karin Kõnd and AnettLilleväli, "E-prescription success in Estonia: The journey from Paper to Pharmacogenomics", National success in digital health, Eurohealth, Vol.25, No.2, 2019. https://apps.who.int
15. Kaur, Harleen, et al. "A proposed solution and future direction for blockchain-based heterogeneous medicare data in cloud environment." Journal of medical systems 42.8 (2018): 1–1
16. Kim NH, Kim HR, Nah JY, Choi HJ, Lee HR, Jung HJ, Choi MR. Designing electronic medical record using health level 7 development framework. J Korean Soc Med Inform 2005; 11: 273–278.
17. Liang, Xueping, et al. "Integrating blockchain for data sharing and collaboration in mobile healthcare applications." 2017 IEEE 28th annual international symposium on personal, indoor, and mobile radio communications (PIMRC). IEEE, 2017.
18. Mettler, Matthias. "Blockchain technology in healthcare: The revolution starts here." 2016 IEEE 18th international conference on e-health networking, applications and services (Healthcom). IEEE, 2016.
19. RahbekNørgaard J. E-record - access to all Danish public health records. Stud Health Technol Inform. 2013; 192: 1121. PMID: 23920895.
20. Rifi, Nabil, et al. "Towards using blockchain technology for eHealth data access management." 2017 fourth international conference on advances in biomedical engineering (ICABME). IEEE, 2017.
21. S Nakamoto. "Bitcoin: A Peer-to-Peer Electronic Cash System" (2008).
22. Saha, Arijit, et al. "Review on "Blockchain technology based medical healthcare system with privacy issues"." Security and Privacy 2.5 (2019): e83.
23. Srivastava, Rishabh, and Deepak Prashar. "A Secure Block-chain Enabled Approach for E-Heath-care System." 2021 International Conference on Computing Sciences (ICCS). IEEE, 2021.
24. Steward, Melissa. "Electronic medical records: privacy, confidentiality, liability." The Journal of legal medicine 26.4 (2005): 491–506.
25. Su, Qianqian, et al. "Revocable attribute-based signature for blockchain-based healthcare system." IEEE Access 8 (2020): 127884–127896.
26. Tripathi, Gautami, Mohd Abdul Ahad, and Sara Paiva. "S2HS-A blockchain based approach for smart healthcare system." Healthcare. Vol. 8. No. 1. Elsevier, 2020.
27. Yang, Guang, and Chunlei Li. "A design of blockchain-based architecture for the security of electronic health record (EHR) systems." 2018 IEEE International conference on cloud computing technology and science (CloudCom). IEEE, 2018.
28. Zhang, Jie, Nian Xue, and Xin Huang. "A secure system for pervasive social network-based healthcare." Ieee Access 4 (2016): 9239–9250.
29. Samikshan Sarkar.Types of Electronic Health Record (EHR)System.ehr.medicalsoftware.selecthub https://www.selecthub.com/medical-software/ehr/types-of-ehr/

Computer Science Engineering and Emerging Technologies (ICCS-2022) – Prof (Dr.) Rajeev Sobti et al. (eds)
© 2024 Taylor & Francis Group, London, ISBN 978-1-032-52199-2

Chapter **20**

An Empirical Analysis in Understanding the Transformative Effect of Application of Internet of Things in Business and Society

Franklin John Selvaraj[1]

Department of Marketing, Vignana Jyothi Institute of Management, Hyderabad, India

Neeru Sidana

Assistant professor –III, Amity school of Economics, Amity University, Noida

Roop Raj[2]

Lecturer in Economics, Education Department, Government of Haryana (India)

Seema Sharma

Department of Management, Assam Down Town University Guwahati, Assam

Geetha Manoharan[3]

Assistant Professor, School of Business, SR University, Telangana

Firos A.[4]

Assistant Professor, Department of computer Science and Engineering,
Rajiv Gandhi University (A Central University), Rono-Hills, Doimukh-791112, Arunachal Pradesh, India

Abstract: The Internet of Things is a rapidly growing sector used in an enormous number of physical devices that are featured with software and technologies based on locations, which helps in connecting the network and data transmission among people. IoT has influenced many people by attracting them to information systems, which helps in the rapid growth of the market and huge demand from a wide range of stakeholders that include business organizations, society, government agencies, and consumers. In the next industrial revolution, IoT will play a major role in the interconnection of physical devices for the automation of tasks and skills. IoT in the hyperconnected economy of hyperconnection helps transform society and businesses with the help of enhanced transparency, a decrease in operation expenses, and the process of optimising production. The IoT has an impact on business as well as society's services. The proposed study analyses the transformative effect of IoT in business and society using various parameters.

Keywords: Transformative effect, Internet of things, Business and society, Operational cost

1. Introduction

The network connects the devices for computing, mechanical devices, digital items, animals, and people for the exchange of information across the network without the requirement of computer-to-human interaction. Any artificial or natural object that is provided with the address of Internet Protocol is referred to as a "thing that has the ability to transfer

[1]dr.sfranklinjohn@vjim.edu.in, [2]rooprajgahlot@gmail.com, [3]geethamanoharan1988@gmail.com, [4]firos.a@rgu.ac.in

DOI: 10.1201/9781003405580-20

information over the network. This includes people who are fixed with implanted heart monitors, biochip transponders off farm animals, and pressure monitors present in cars. The range of industries and organizations that start to utilise IoT for running their businesses in a smooth way and to understand consumers for providing the best customer service It helps in raising the company's value as well as boosting decision-making.

The Internet of Things is the new paradigm that has transformed traditional living into a highly technological lifestyle. The changes brought by the IoT include smart industries, smart transportation, energy conservation, pollution control, smart homes, and smart cities. Most of the researchers who investigated the yeah food of advanced technology through IoT found that it can be completely realised with a promising IoT, which has a number of problems and obstacles that are able to be resolved. The problems as well as difficulties are taken into account from many perspectives of the IoT, which include environmental and social implications, enabling technologies, difficulties, and applications (Kumar et al., 2019).

The Internet of Things is the ever-increasing collection of multiple physical objects that are equipped with location-based technologies and software for communication with one another over networks and exchanging data. Due to the nature of fast-growing demand in the business market, the IoT has a diverse variety of stakeholders that include government agencies, consumers, and corporate organisations. The Internet of Things has attracted substantial attention to those information systems. IoT will play a key role in the upcoming industrial revolution by automating operations and talents. IoT can drastically change society and business through a hyperconnected economy by enhancing transparency, streamlining manufacturing, and decreasing operational costs. (Shim et al., 2019).

IoT is the linking of various sorts of wearable and non-wearable devices. Technology significantly affects business. Businesses must adapt to emerging technologies in order to be competitive in the face of a significant shift in the technological world. Between digital and physical realities, it has closed the gap. IoT's ability to provide real-time communication between systems and devices that are far apart is a critical feature. By 2020, it is expected that the IoT market will be worth roughly $9 trillion. This illustrates how quickly this technology is developing. Users frequently believe that the Internet of Things is closely tied to the IT (information technology) industry. IoT, on the other hand, is a more general term that is connected to practically everything in some way. IOT application concepts include everything from tiny businesses to massive data analytics. Consequently, it is wise to be knowledgeable about how the internet affects society and business.

2. Materials and Methods

The interconnection of numerous "things" is giving rise to a number of problems with the security and privacy of IoT platforms. Many e-businesses and brick-and-mortar retailers are utilizing IoT-based solutions due to technological advancements for their sales, marketing, productivity, and promotions. These IoT-based solutions are quite beneficial, giving owners and customers a variety of advantages.

2.1 Transformative Effect in Business

Reduction of Operational Cost

IoT devices have the ability to provide real-time data, which helps the organization streamline its workflow and cut down on operational costs. IoT devices are proactively notified by the personnel in the state for maintenance, which can be scheduled and promote production. The operational effectiveness and contributions to cost savings are increased by the integration of a bigger system. IoT devices help in controlling, monitoring, and tracking the building systems that run to track the usage of the building and adapt with the benefit of lowering expenses in time of use.

Enhanced the Output and Security in Workplace

Devices of the IoT notify, monitor, and assist unmanaged staff for changes in productivity or workflow and assist them in making more decisions in their employment. Most industries are specialized in IoT technologies for tracking the body using sensor technology and safeguarding employees from overexertion. It helps improve their performance in the workplace. The information can be used by ergonomists and engineers for improving the workstation for effective movement, and it also helps in reducing injuries.

Improved Client Experiences

Tools of the IoT can make the experiences of clients like Maurizio easier than ever for other businesses to monitor, track, and analyse. Business helps in anticipating patterns or changes in customer behaviour and tailoring the prior experiences through advanced technologies of the IoT for the improvement of the client experience. The personalised instructions are considered through a mobile app for the clients who use smart devices when they visit the business or store to track the location of the shipment vehicles. The devices of the IoT assist the companies in transmitting and collecting the person's data, which is already provided by the customers. It helps in boosting the loyalty of the clients and providing a superior customer experience.

Business Information

IoT devices assist businesses with data collection and insights discovery about their operations. Externally and internally, establishments like retail are rebuilt as stores, depending on the traffic patterns at present. It is optimised for the people who use Kamal logistics trucks for delivery coordination, hot schedules, and locations using IoT devices that are connected to the Internet.

Businesses and employees use IoT for acceleration of organisation modernization and speeding up return on investment for new services and products. Because more actionable data from the devices is freely available, they will be able to offer value to the organization faster and more effectively. For a better customer experience, IoT technology is assisting businesses in collecting and analysing more data. There are also many other uses. Here are some instances of how the Internet of Things is enhancing many industries:

2.2 Manufacturing and Industrial Production

Thanks to automation and the IoT, the industrial industry has undergone a significant transformation. By offering the following options, smart sensors boost productivity and decrease downtime: Remote control of autonomous units allows them to operate on an array of product production lines. The Internet of Robotic Things (IoRT) is an Internet of Things that is used for the creation of toys, components of vehicles, electronics, and aeroplanes worldwide.

Prevention of Future Problems

Continuous equipment health monitoring is done using IoT sensors. IoT data is used to develop routine maintenance schedules that have a minimal effect on the continuity of manufacturing lines.

Moreover, enabled data by the operator helps in the prediction of needs and maintenance. Sensors in the IoT forecast the probabilities of equipment failure and help in planning maintenance. These anticipation projections help minimise the impact of machines during production hours.

To automate maintenance schedules, large companies employ networked sensors. Take Volvo as an example; the corporation makes use of IoT to track equipment flaws and anticipate repair requirements. As a result, diagnosis time is cut by 70%, and repair time is decreased by 20%.

Logistics and the Supply Chain

Supply chain management and logistics have always been highly capital-intensive and congested enterprises. Customers desire dependability, and firms are constantly expected to be more open. IoT supports companies in achieving both objectives.

Improved Tracking Techniques

The moment a customer places an order, they want to know everything about their packages. IoT-based solutions give customers a wealth of information about the environment the package is in, delighting and enticing them.

IoT is being used by several delivery services to provide up-to-the-minute information on a package's condition. Suppliers and shippers can provide exceptional client support and quick dispute resolution.

Delivery and Pick-up on Demand

Customers adore ease, especially when it alleviates a major complaint. The logistics and delivery processes for the e-commerce industry are improved by smart pick-up locations. For instance, businesses can transport goods using a network of smart lockers connected to the Internet of Things. Smart lockers that are online-connected alert customers when a shipment arrives. With the help of IoT software one of the Internet of Things projects, we made package delivery simpler for users who work in big offices. Customers can access their locker at any time via a smartphone app. If they can't be there to pick up the package from the courier, they don't have to postpone crucial meetings or worry that they won't receive their delivery.

Automated Production Units

Industrial robots enabled by the internet of things minimise the losses that are brought about due to human errors. Robots have the ability to work without rest. Assist manufacturers in lowering operating expenses while increasing production output. IoT is used by logistics to make smart deliveries and streamline package collection in big offices. Find out how logistic services make package distribution in big offices simpler.

Optimizing Mileage and Driving Routes

By optimizing routes, fleet management systems driven by the Internet of Things enable administrators to cut operational costs. Employing driver behaviour, fuel economy, and maintenance prediction, businesses may design the most cost-effective delivery routes.

Analytics help track problems like employee use of personal vehicles and cut expenditures.

Healthcare

IoT is being used by hospitals and physicians for patient monitoring and preventive healthcare. IoT may be utilized to make wise decisions across the diagnostic and therapeutic cycles by:

- Critical data of health that include blood sugar, heartbeat rate and blood pressure can be tracked by IoT systems. Through equipment with smart sensors, doctors may access extensive information about a patient's health.
- The telemedicine sector will benefit from the upcoming IoT device generation. Accurate clinical forecasts can be produced by programmes like TeleICU. Algorithms examine IoT data and forecast when a patient will require emergency medical care.

Production of Media

IoT is a useful tool in the media and production sectors, among other creative businesses. The dynamic and efficient production environment can be enhanced through the Internet of Things. It takes careful planning to get the ideal lighting for video production. Gaffers can use mobile devices to operate lighting equipment and improve light adjustment with IoT. All lighting fixtures are DMX-connected with Apollo Control. Amateurs and professionals alike in lighting can rapidly set up their scenarios and define the tiniest aspects of light.

Agriculture

Interconnected solutions that let farmers have better control over their surroundings have become more prevalent in agriculture in recent years. One manufacturer of products for measuring important agricultural parameters is John Deere. The soil temperature, moisture content, air temperature, and wind speed can all be measured to provide farmers with useful data.

3. Results and Discussion

The section explains the analysis and findings of the transformative effect of the IoT in business and society. Various parameters are considered for the evaluation to find out the report for analysis for the transformative effect.

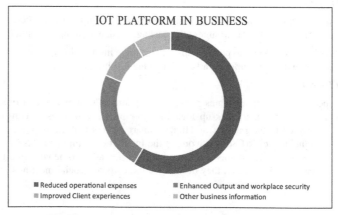

Fig. 20.1 IoT platform in businesses (Shim et al., 2019)

Table 20.1 Level of IoT in transformation (Shim et al., 2019)

IoT in Business Transformation	Score
Prevention of future problems	8
Logistics and supply chain	9
Improvement in tracking techniques	10
Delivery and pick-up	8.3
Automated production unit	7.2
Healthcare	8.5
Media productions	9.6
Agriculture	6.9

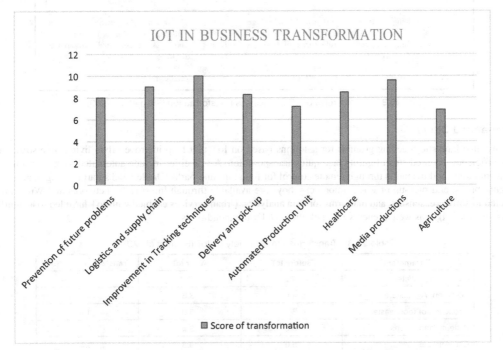

Fig. 20.2 Transformation score of IoT in Businesses (Shim et al., 2019)

Table 20.2 Various roles of IoT in Business Transformation (Shim et al, 2019)

Sl. No	Role of Iot in business transformation	Percentage
1	IoT playing major role in collecting and gathering information	92%
2	IoT in increasing the profit of business	95%
3	IoT giving personalized preferences as preferred by consumers	90%
4	IoT helps in automation of business	98%
5	IoT empowers business models	80%
6	IoT helps in posting business ads in social media platform	78%
7	IoT helps in reducing operational costs	94%
8	IoT helps in providing workplace security	82%

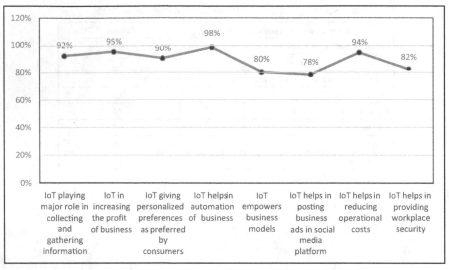

Fig. 20.3 Various roles of IoT in business transformation (Shim et al., 2019)

3.1 Enhanced Cities

Cities are also fantastic breeding grounds for solutions based on IoT that help improve urban living, like structures of energy efficiency, secured street lighting, and quick transportation. A few cities include automated street lighting, smart water technology, and irrigation through remote control for fountains and parks. On-demand smart parking metres, routes for digital buses, and pick-up of waste among city boys are available through information networks and Wi-Fi that are connected to software, sensors, and platforms for data analytics. Urban services enabled with IoT have led to a significant decrease in water light as well as energy use, pollution, and traffic conditions.

Table 20.3 Transformation of society by IoT (Byun et al., 2016)

Parameters	Before IoT	After IoT	Transformative effect
Pure Air and Water	4.2	7.3	3.1
Intelligent Agriculture	4.1	8.6	4.5
Reduction of food waste	5	6.9	1.9
Patient connections	3.8	9.5	5.7
Cab services	5.6	9.3	3.7

Calculation for Transformative effect of IoT:

Transformative effect of Internet of things in society can be calculated by the following formula:

$$\text{Transformative Effect} = \text{After IoT} - \text{Before IoT} \tag{1}$$

3.2 Purer Water and Air

Cities can enhance public health using the Internet of Things. According to a recent study, unclean air and water were responsible for a startling 9 million fatalities in just 2015 alone. Sensor networks are being introduced in chronically polluted cities like Delhi in order to warn locals when pollution levels are too high. Use of Google Street View of vehicles outfitted with special sensors, sensor networks that apply the concept to multiple cities could assist decision-makers in locating and reducing pollution hotspots.

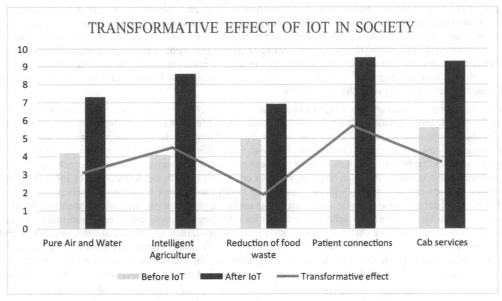

Fig. 20.4 Transformative effect on society (Byun et al., 2016)

3.3 Intelligent Agriculture

All over the world, farmers use the Internet of Things to minimise the use of fertiliser and water, cut down waste, and increase the quantity and quality of their products, from tiny organic forms to large-scale agribusinesses. A few examples include temperature variations monitoring and level of humidity for the perishable commodities and migration from the field to the warehouse run to the shop for increasing shelf life and waste reduction, as well as tracking microclimates across agriculture.

3.4 Reduce Food Waste

The Food and Agriculture Organization of India estimates that somewhere in the supply chain, about 1/3 of the food produced each year for human consumption is lost or wasted. For a globe that is expanding, that is 1.4 billion tonnes of wasted nutrients. The Internet of Things can boost productivity and reduce crop losses. Automation in a greenhouse setting using the IoT The work is concentrated on the small-scale deployment of agricultural greenhouses and converting them into smart greenhouses. They are to support the administration of water irrigation systems, picture gathering using installed cameras, and disease prediction in plants utilizing datasets of collected leaves. This study focuses on the development of a system architecture and design for an appropriate Internet of Things-based monitoring system for environmental conditions, controlling water irrigation systems, and an efficient approach for spotting plant illnesses inside a greenhouse atmosphere (Khan et al., 2020).

3.5 Patient Connections

Facility for speedy access to patient data for   medical practitioners IoT has the potential to make a revolution in the healthcare sector. The accuracy, size, and cost of sensor devices connected to the Internet for monitoring the blood pressure, pulse, and heart rate of patients are improved using IoT. The most promising application of IoT is wearables in healthcare, but there is still significant disagreement regarding the collection, transmission, and usage of data.

4. Discussion

In the upcoming IoT for healthcare and other businesses, various devices will be distributed for collection, analysis, and transmission of real-time data through hybrid, private, or open clouds that enable analyses, storage, and collection of streams of big data in different forms, as well as the activation of alarms sensitive to context. A revolutionary health application ecosystem develops as a result of this ground-breaking data collection paradigm, which enables continuous and ubiquitous access to medical data from any connected device over the Internet. Healthcare has evolved thanks to the Internet of Things (IoT) revolution. Health management has replaced treatment as the primary focus of healthcare. As a result, as healthcare develops towards patient-oriented and analytical applications, more data is being collected and pooled than ever before. This essay examines the various facets of healthcare using IoT that include data related to health and patient-centered health management (Zhu et al., 2019).

Conflicts over natural resources are becoming more intense as a result of climate change and society's impact on the planet, which is also endangering our infrastructure, food systems, and way of life. We have made enormous strides in the past few decades in the fight against sickness, illiteracy, and poverty. We must now use the same inventiveness to solve the global warming issue and other issues brought on by human activity. To resolve these difficulties in business and society, adopt the new philosophies that prioritise the well-being of people over profit. It also requires cutting-edge technology. IoT links common devices with the Internet, which helps improve our environment. With the development of IoT technology and the beginning of a new era, the problems with the conventional supply chain, which travels from suppliers of raw materials to final consumers, have become apparent. Additionally, the entire supply chain path necessitates the implementation of a few strategies that include green and agile supply chains for achieving smartness due to environmental issues and the speed at which customer needs are changing across a variety of industries, including retail and wholesale, which undergo more changes after the emergence of IoT. Therefore, new technologies like the Internet of Things have a big impact on how flexible and environmentally friendly the entire retail supply chain is. The use of blockchain technology in supply chain operations powered by the Internet of Things ensures the security of big data and supports optimum data performance.

Data gathering, analysis of data, assessment of corporate development, and improvement in performance are reasons businesses are increasingly investing in tools and solutions that enable their processes, machines, personnel, and even the goods themselves to be integrated into a single integrated network (Nagy et al., 2018). The Internet of Things is not just a game-changing technology for all industries; it has also demonstrated promise in operations like supply chain management. With the development of technology and the beginning of a new era, the problems with the conventional supply chain, which travels from suppliers of raw materials to final consumers, have become apparent. The use of blockchain technology in supply chain operations powered by the Internet of Things ensures the security of big data and supports optimum data performance (Nozari, H., & Nahr, J. G., 2022).

The evidence for trunk transportation is still maximized by the location button, grading impact in optimization of integers, and evaluation of overall benefits in economic transportation. A specific reference is offered by the logistics of the cold chain in the design of the network for transforming transportation. It is thought to be based on an enhanced IoT data model and the proposed framework of predictive data transfer technology. a paradigm for the Internet of Things study that evaluates overall performance. Results from simulations support this method's effectiveness. To stop food from being transferred through the logistics of the cold chain, like monitoring the freezing temperature and removing tracking from the containers, fried locations are also required. As a result, the integration of wireless sensor networks, the point of access of the GPS system, and the system of 5G communication is extensive and developed (Li et al., 2021).

IoT helps in enhancing many businesses such as food supply, agriculture, logistics, and other industries. It also helps in monitoring air pollution in the largest cities in the country and all over the world through devices enabled with IoT and sensors, which is the added crown to modern data analytics. IoT status, which has recently become a popular IT issue, and in providing relevant IoT business models to assist businesses and research organizations involved in related projects in creating a smart city that reflects the new information paradigm of IoT (Byun et al., 2016).

5. Conclusion

The proposed study helps in understanding the applications of IoT in businesses and society and its transformative effect. In the present scenario, IoT plays a significant role in different domains; it has a vast number of advantages for enhancing the business by increasing the production profit and decreasing the operation cost, and it also provides safety in the workplace. The transformative effect in society of applications of IoT can be visualised through different parameters and compared. IoT can speed up development and provide fresh commercial prospects in every sector. However, the key to that development is how rapidly you can integrate IoT and establish yourself as a leader in the sector. Thus, the transformative effect of the application of IoT in business as well as society is empirically analysed.

REFERENCES

1. Kumar, S., Tiwari, P., & Zymbler, M. (2019). Internet of Things is a revolutionary approach for future technology enhancement: a review. Journal of Big data, 6(1), 1–21.
2. Shim, J. P., Avital, M., Dennis, A. R., Rossi, M., Sørensen, C., & French, A. (2019). The transformative effect of the internet of things on business and society. Communications of the Association for Information Systems, 44(1), 5.
3. Byun, J., Kim, S., Sa, J., Kim, S., Shin, Y. T., & Kim, J. B. (2016). Smart city implementation models based on IoT technology. Advanced Science and Technology Letters, 129(41), 209–212.
4. Nozari, H., & Nahr, J. G. (2022). The Impact of Blockchain Technology and The Internet of Things on the Agile and Sustainable Supply Chain. International Journal of Innovation in Engineering, 2(2), 33–41.
5. Li, G. (2021). Development of cold chain logistics transportation system based on 5G network and Internet of things system. Microprocessors and Microsystems, 80, 103565.
6. Nagy, J., Oláh, J., Erdei, E., Máté, D., & Popp, J. (2018). The role and impact of Industry 4.0 and the internet of things on the business strategy of the value chain—the case of Hungary. Sustainability, 10(10), 3491.
7. Zhu, H., Wu, C. K., Koo, C. H., Tsang, Y. T., Liu, Y., Chi, H. R., & Tsang, K. F. (2019). Smart healthcare in the era of internet-of-things. IEEE Consumer Electronics Magazine, 8(5), 26–30.
8. Khan, F. A., Ibrahim, A. A., & Zeki, A. M. (2020). Environmental monitoring and disease detection of plants in smart greenhouse using internet of things. Journal of Physics Communications, 4(5), 055008.

Computer Science Engineering and Emerging Technologies (ICCS-2022) – Prof (Dr.) Rajeev Sobti et al. (eds)
© *2024 Taylor & Francis Group, London, ISBN 978-1-032-52199-2*

Chapter

21

MORSE: Social Networking Platform that Enables Connecting with Alumni, Teachers, and Students

Samir Akthar[1], Kambam Sindhuja Priya[2], Mayank Shekhar[3], Gauri Mathur[4]

Student, Department of Computer Science and Engineering,
Lovely Professional University Phagwara, Punjab 144411, India

Abstract: The network technology concept has been continuously improved and developed, which is why online social networks have been around for a long time. It puts system users in control and overcomes the limitations imposed by the conventional model of a Web network. Any user can become the publisher, disseminator, and creator of information at this time by registering. Morse is an online social networking platform that helps to connect with alumni, co-workers, teachers and students. Over the past era, the Internet has extremely influenced higher education by empowering the phenomenal magnification of online learning. To provide an innovative touch to education, our group has developed a social networking platform that effortlessly connects with teachers, students, and alumni. The main appliance used for the buildout of the MORSE is Tailwind.css, vs code, next.js. The new technologically innovative learning environments manufactured by web-based technologies, not only put an end to the barriers of time, space, and learning methods, but provide exceptionally increased access to higher education, where they dare the traditional notions of teaching and learning.

Keywords: Online learning, VScode, Tailwind.css, Social networking

1. Introduction

A social networking site where individuals can discuss, and share information. The way people communicate with one another has changed as a result of the global phenomenon of social networking. It affects almost every aspect of our lives: Personal productivity, education, communication, and social connections are all important. People use online platforms known as social networking services (SNS) to establish and maintain relationships with other people. It enables users to connect online with people who share their interests, whether for dating or social purposes. People can use it to share blog posts, digital photos and videos, emails, instant messages, wikis, and more (Miguéns, J., 2008). Some websites allow users to write blogs, upload pictures, comment on posts, change the look and feel of their profiles, add multimedia content, make and share a list of contacts, and so on (Gu, Y., 2019). Social networks are content providers and consumers at the same time. They let the user choose who can see their profile. Frequently use a type of network structure known as a "small world network" to re-enact actual scenes. However, in actuality, group structures frequently shift. Students and teachers' participation in education is changing as a result of social media. They are currently utilized for educators' professional development, content sharing, and learning. Knowledge is shared by scientific communities via social media. Researchers and librarians frequently use social media to share ideas and maintain professional relationships. Networks for research and education can be formed through social media. Each university uses social networking sites like Facebook, Twitter, and Instagram and has at least one page on its website (Wang, M., 2021). Social media has changed how information is created, processed, and disseminated. Various fields, including business management, industrial chains, virtual teams,

---

[1]akhtarsamir242@gmail.com, [2]sinduja9676@gmail.com, [3]shekharmayank2001@gmail.com, [4]gauri.mathur@lpu.co.in

DOI: 10.1201/9781003405580-21

educational knowledge chains, and healthcare, have utilized social network analyses. It's a place where people can talk to each other, interact, and give feedback on the content of other people. Any kind of content—text, images, sounds, or a combination of the three—can be stored, arranged, labeled, edited, and recommended by them. Consequently, social media facilitates collaboration, community, and creativity (Asmi, 2018). Users can like, rate, remix, friend, and trend on social media platforms. As a consequence of this, there is a link between these apps and an increase in the tendency of people who rely on and do multitask "digital juggling" of regular responsibilities and activities. With an education based on social networking, privacy, genuine friendship, time consumption, and miscommunication are all issues. However, the primary advantages are accessibility, repeatability, adaptability, and user-friendliness.

2. Literature Review

Sadiku, M. (2019) stated Facebook, Twitter, and LinkedIn are the major social networking sites (SNSs) in today's time.

Facebook: In 2004, Harvard students were the first to be able to use Facebook as a social networking platform. From there, it spread to other universities and eventually everyone. In 2009, it became the most widely used social networking site, and it continues to be the most widely used website for sharing photos. Marketing strategists can use Facebook to their advantage because it caters to a wide range of personal and professional interests. stream processing's application framework of Facebook, which supports declarative and imperative APIs, is used by application developers to build a data processing pipeline.

Twitter: Odeo, Inc. founded Twitter in 2006. At first, only employees of Odeo, Inc. and their families were eligible to participate. Twitter is a real-time, Web-based service that lets users post short messages and comment on other people's posts. In 2006, it became a public network. can be used to extract tweets. A tweet is a short message of 140 characters that people use to share their thoughts. A more recent type of blogging is microblogging, which gained popularity thanks to Twitter.

Kennedy, P., (2004) **LinkedIn:** A place for professionals to network with other professionals in this professional network. By creating an account on LinkedIn, you can connect with professionals who share your interests. LinkedIn continues to be the most widely used social networking site for businesses seeking new employees.

2.1 Problems with Existing Social Networking Platforms

In the existing platforms, users are not able to get connected with the relevant users. Anyone can create a fake or a bot account and can perform any illegal activities. How social media sites like Twitter and Facebook have become increasingly used for communication. It is being utilized by numerous individuals and businesses for various purposes. Twitter has become very popular among various networks, with young adults and government users using it as a way to instantly connect with their audience and easily convey messages (Awan, 2022). The size of an organization or individual's audience in online social media networks is a crucial indicator of that entity's popularity. Due to the fake profiles on the social site, tailoring can be biased. To address this issue, the authors of this paper examined 62 million publicly accessible profiles to detect fake profiles. An analysis of these fake accounts' profile creation times and URLs against a ground truth data set revealed distinct behavior. This method and well-established social graph analysis made it possible to quickly identify fake profiles. However, it only identified a small number of fake accounts. Lots of privacy issues like stalking, false information, and cyberbullying (Salmivalli, C., 2012). According to a report, 15% of students who is bullied at school are bullied online (Chen, J., 2021). In the recent years, due to social media's apparent growth, people's mental and physical safety are in concerns.

2.2 MORSE is the Solution for the Existing Social Networking Platform's Problems

People's thoughts and actions are changing as a result of social media (Guo, Y., 2020). High-quality output meets the needs of the intended recipient (Ramkumar, G., 2016). To get connected with relevant users, we will use a new data structure and algorithms which will only show the people who are currently available in your university and your location and will not get any users who are far from those users (Kim, J.S., 2020). Many studies have focused on location-based social networks, such as location recommendation, "next-location" prediction, potential "social-link". No one will be able to create a fake account in MORSE they will have to provide their university registration id number to get register and later on they have to upload the same id in document submission which will verify the user is genuine and this process will be done by the application itself, the application will scan the id uploaded by the users and it will match the id number (Registration number) with the registration number is been provided by the user (O'Reilly, T., 2011). To prevent stalking, we will be given an option to make an account private as well as users will get a notification to whoever visits their profile. Users can report accounts who will try to do something irrelevant things and their account will be permanently removed from the platform and that user will never be able to join again.

2.3 Data Structure Graph for the Existing Social Networking Platform

As stated in Fig. 21.1 how the existing platform users are connected because of this type of data structure users are not able to get connected with the relevant users.

2.4 Data Structure Graph for MORSE Platform

As stated in Fig. 21.2, each university has its database which makes it easier to connect with the people in their location and can make new friends take help from the alumni of their university as well as they can get in touch with teachers. Users will also have an option to merge with other colleges and it will have all the features of existing platforms so they can get in touch with anyone they want.

3. Applications

Social Interaction: Computer-mediated social interaction and the ability to connect with similar interests. They are used by people to make new friends and reconnect with old ones (Masden, C., 2015). They also offer a place online where people can talk to each other and share personal information. When looking for work, some job seekers use social media, which can help them get offers and find work that pays well.

Education: How educators and students engage in learning is being affected by social networks (Ghaisani, A.P., 2017). Social media are used by scientific communities to share knowledge. Researchers and librarians frequently use social media to share ideas and maintain professional relationships. Networks for learning and research can emerge from social media.

Data Sharing: MORSE has the potential to quickly share data with students, teachers, and alumni in real time.

4. Methodology

MORSE as social site attempts to fulfil affective, personal, educational, and social needs, it is affecting the everyday life of teachers, co-workers, students, and alumni (Hargittai, E., 2011). Although the minimum age should be greater than thirteen is required for joining MORSE, every student can join with their educational email id and registration number. We have used MS Visual Studio Code as one of our platforms, which is a desktop-based, lightweight editor for different types of OS (Klimm, M.C., 2021). Tailwind CSS is a framework of CSS which is used to build custom user interfaces and has a rich ecosystem of extensions for another language (18, Aggarwal, S., 2018). It also comes with built-in support for JavaScript, Typescript, and Node.js. GitHub on the other hand use to store source code for a project and track the completion by providing tools for managing conflicting changes

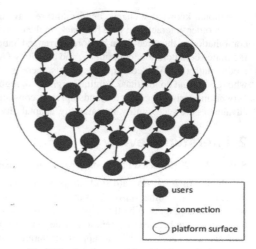

Fig. 21.1 Existing social networking platform

Source: Made by Author

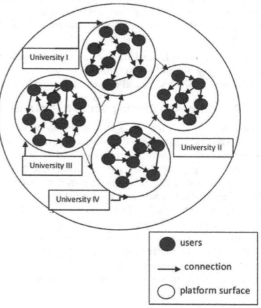

Fig. 21.2 Morse platform

Source: Made by Author

from multiple developers, it makes it possible for developers to work together more effectively on a project (Geewax, J.J.J., 2018). We managed the database in Google Cloud Platform (GCP), which functions similarly to other public cloud providers, to store it safely and make it simple to access (Masinde, N., 2020). The management of the various network loads is the primary focus of GCP.

As stated in Fig. 21.3 given below shows how the user data flow while logging into the MORSE. It explains what happens after the entry of the login credential if it is the right one, it will redirect to the platform if not then will be given 3 more chances before showing the password reset option.

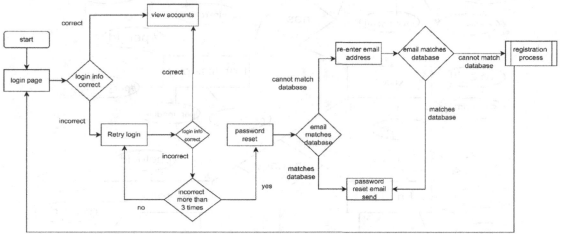

Fig. 21.3 User data flow while logging into the morse

Source: Made by Author

As stated in Fig. 21.4, after taking the user credential, it validates and verifies the account and it will check the user belonging to which university and will be redirected to that university database.

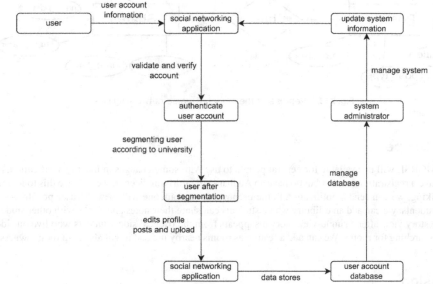

Fig. 21.4 Validates and verifies the account

Source: Made by Author

As stated in the Fig. 21.5, this E-R diagram represents the model of our social media networking sites, entities and their attributes.

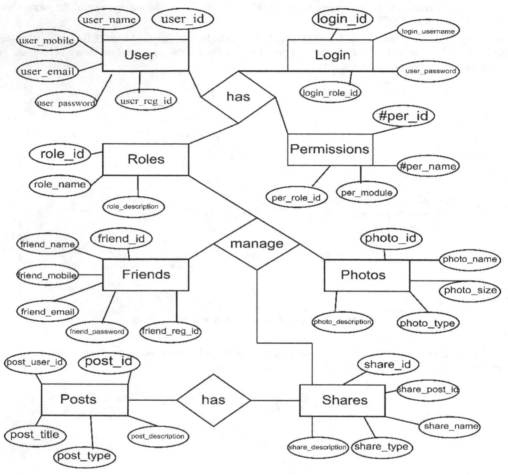

Fig. 21.5 Represents the model of morse networking site

Source: Made by Author

5. Future Scope

In the future, MORSE will be available for general people to use with some changes in identity verification. As common people don't have a registration number but do have an Aadhar card or driving license, we will use this to identify the user. To prevent stalking, we can send a notification to the user whenever someone will view the user profile. As most of the users will be students, we can add an e-library where students can share their notes and books with other students. We can add a one-time story view after a single-view story disappears from the friends' side. Students who live outside the hostel face problems searching for rooms. We can add a feature as rooms nearby me and it will also help room owners to get their rooms listed.

6. Conclusion

Many students and universities in our country are looking for smaller platforms that do not use algorithms to filter information and serve a greater purpose than simply allowing users to chat and post videos to have more authentic interactions with friends, co-workers, classmates, teachers, and alumni. Through this platform, schools, colleges, and universities can now connect with members based on their core values. The objective is to make things safer and more personal, which is exactly what internet users want when they switch from large to smaller social media platforms.

REFERENCES

1. Miguéns, J., Baggio, R. and Costa, C., 2008. Social media and tourism destinations: TripAdvisor case study. Advances in tourism research, *26*(28), pp. 1–6.
2. Gu, Y. and Zhang, B., 2019, June. Social network public opinion evolution model based on node intimacy. In 2019 Chinese Control And Decision Conference (CCDC) (pp. 4496–4500). IEEE.
3. Wang, M., Nimmolrat, A. and Khamaksorn, A., 2021, March. Knowledge flows through social networks in new-born intensive care units. In 2021 Joint International Conference on Digital Arts, Media and Technology with
4. ECTI Northern Section Conference on Electrical, Electronics, Computer and Telecommunication Engineering (pp. 102–107). IEEE.
5. Asmi, N. A., 2018, February. Engaging research scholars in social media a new way to innovative research. In 2018 5th international symposium on emerging trends and technologies in libraries and information services (ETTLIS) (pp. 188–192). IEEE.
6. Sadiku, M., Omotoso, A. and Musa, S., 2019. Social networking. International Journal of Trend in Scientific Research and Development, *3*(3), pp. 126–128.
7. Kennedy, P., 2004. Making global society: friendship networks among transnational professionals in the building design industry. Global networks, *4*(2), pp. 157–179.
8. Awan, M. J., Khan, M.A., Ansari, Z. K., Yasin, A. and Shehzad, H. M. F., 2022. Fake profile recognition using big data analytics in social media platforms. International Journal of Computer Applications in Technology, *68*(3), pp. 215–222.
9. Salmivalli, C. and Pöyhönen, V., 2012. Cyberbullying in finland. Cyberbullying in the global playground: Research from international *perspectives*, pp. 57–72.
10. Chen, J., 2021, September. The Method of Information Communication of Online Social Network Based on Communication Algorithm. In 2021 IEEE 4th International Conference on Information Systems and Computer Aided Education (ICISCAE) (pp. 489–493). IEEE.
11. Guo, Y., Cao, J. and Lin, W., 2020, January. Social network influence analysis. In 2019 6th International Conference on Dependable Systems and Their Applications (DSA) (pp. 517–518). IEEE.
12. Ramkumar, G., Vigneshwari, S. and Roodyn, S., 2016, March. An enhanced system to identify mischievous social malwares on Facebook applications. In 2016 International Conference on Circuit, Power and Computing Technologies (ICCPCT) (pp. 1–5). IEEE.
13. Kim, J. S., Jin, H., Kavak, H., Rouly, O. C., Crooks, A., Pfoser, D., Wenk, C. and Züfle, A., 2020, June. Location-based social network data generation based on patterns of life. In 2020 21st IEEE International Conference on Mobile Data Management (MDM) (pp. 158–167). IEEE.
14. O'Reilly, T. and Milstein, S., 2011. The twitter book. " O'Reilly Media, Inc."
15. Masden, C. and Edwards, W. K., 2015, April. Understanding the role of community in online dating. In Proceedings of the 33rd annual ACM conference on human factors in computing systems (pp. 535–544).
16. Ghaisani, A. P., Handayani, P. W. and Munajat, Q., 2017. Users' motivation in sharing information on social media. Procedia Computer Science, 124, pp. 530–535
17. Hargittai, E., Schultz, J. and Palfrey, J., 2011. Why parents help their children lie to Facebook about age: Unintended consequences of the 'Children's Online Privacy Protection Act'. *First Monday*.
18. Klimm, M. C., 2021. Design Systems for Micro Frontends-An Investigation into the Development of Framework-Agnostic Design Systems using Svelte *and* Tailwind CSS (Doctoral dissertation, Hochschulbibliothek der Technischen Hochschule Köln).
19. Aggarwal, S. and Verma, J., 2018. Comparative analysis of MEAN stack and MERN stack. International Journal of Recent Research Aspects, *5*(1), pp. 127–132.
20. Geewax, J. J. J., 2018. Google Cloud Platform in Action. Simon and Schuster.
21. Masinde, N., Bischoff, S. and Graffi, K., 2020, December. Capacity management protocol for a structured P2P-based online social network. In 2020 Seventh International Conference on Social Networks Analysis, Management and Security (SNAMS) (pp. 1–8). IEEE.

Computer Science Engineering and Emerging Technologies (ICCS-2022) – Prof (Dr.) Rajeev Sobti et al. (eds)
© 2024 Taylor & Francis Group, London, ISBN 978-1-032-52199-2

Chapter

22

Detailed Investigation of Influence of Internet of Things (IoT) and Big Data on Digital Transformation in Marketing

K. Arulrajan[1]
PSG Institute of Management, Peelamedu, Coimbatore

Roop Raj[2]
Lecturer in Economics, Education Department, Government of Haryana (India)

Lalit Mohan Pant[3]
Assistant Professor, Department of Psychology, Uttarakhand Open University, Haldwani, Nainital (Uttarakhand)

Ashutosh Kumar Bhatt[4]
Associate Professor, School of Computer Science and Information Technology, Uttarakhand Open University, Haldwani

Jeidy Panduro-Ramirez[5]
Professor, Universidad Tecnológica del Perú

José Luis Arias Gonzáles[6]
6Business Department, Pontifical Catholic University of Peru

Abstract: With the creation of novel business models based on the ideas, procedures, and resources of the digital environment, digitization blurs the distinctions between technology and management. The firms manage their digital transformation in relation to the Internet of Things and big data. Organizations now face enormous potential and considerable barriers as a result of the development of digital technology. The purpose is to bring out the current condition of corporate digitization in addition to existing theories given the increased awareness of big data and IoT. Cloud Platform, Big Data, and the Internet of Things all present potential for marketing to use technologies to change their tactics, notably in the use of "new service-oriented marketing strategies." Managers in marketing generally have the ability to update outdated procedures with new technology or improve the technical quality of services and goods. Businesses can obtain, analyze, and examine data and information, which enables them to create pertinent marketing plans. The roots of the current technological landscape and the drivers of the ensuing corporate shift are a collection of inventions. The Internet of Things technologies are essential for helping businesses increase the utilization of their machinery and develop service-based goods in manufacturing enterprises. The primary goal of this study is to examine how IoT and big data have affected the digital revolution in marketing.

Keywords: Internet of things, Big-data, Digital transformation

[1]arulrajan@psgim.ac.in, [2]rooprajgahlot@gmail.com, [3]lmpant33@gmail.com, [4]abhatt@uou.ac.in, [5]C21289@utp.edu.pe, [6]joseariasgon6@gmail.com

DOI: 10.1201/9781003405580-22

1. Introduction

Utilizing digital technology for development is referred to as digital transformation of new processes" and adaptation of current business, customer experiences, and culture for the requirements of the market" to satisfy the business shift. Digital transformation is also known as the reinvention of the digital age in companies. The level of digital transformation goes beyond the conventional job functions that include customer service, marketing, and sales. The way we think and the customer interaction are the beginning and end of digital transformation. By keeping the digital technologies to one side, we should have the ability to rethink how we do business and engage with clients during the transition from paper to spreadsheets and smart applications to manage our business. There is no requirement for building up the business processes and then modifying them for the small enterprises that we are starting up. The companies are future-proofed through digital transformation. Running a company in the 21st century is simply unsustainable in the digital transformation through handwritten ledgers and sticky notes. It is being adaptable, nimble, and ready for growth by knowing all the benefits of constructing, planning, and thinking in a digital way.

The digital revolution has an impact on corporate operations. To analyze the general changes brought on by digital technologies in the idea of marketing, its tools, and activities in small enterprises, as well as the influence of digital transformation on the operations of marketing in small and medium-sized businesses. The primary study question focuses on how marketing activities carried out by organizations nowadays develop. Analyses and concerns are supported by a critical literature assessment, an examination of empirical study findings, and the author's observations of the market. Analyses carried out have shown that, although they frequently fall under the category of traditional tools, firms covered by the study use digital technology in marketing. IT and digital tools have an impact on marketing as well, fostering client relationships and enhancing the value of each organization (Ziókowska, M. J., 2021).

In digital transformation, emerging technologies were propelled by business transformation and sorting. The program of digital transformation has greater potential for maximum growth and minimum savings than other initiatives of transformation. The changes in the fundamental functions of technologies within the organization are propelling the digital transformation. Technologies are now capable for longer runs, and the only support role that makes operations in business possible is support. The promotion of modern technologies, growth in sales, and enabling of new business models have even more potential to provide the organization with this competitive edge. The forces that drive the transformation are at different levels of raising the trends in technology. The most recognizable examples of digital transformation include big data and analytics, the Internet of Things, robotic process automation, mobility, cyber security, social media, blockchain, and cloud computing. Organizations and industries have major influences on this technology's usage. All the businesses are equipped with the potential for full digitization, alteration, and growth of the companies, which are very thankful for the advancement in technologies (Tang D., 2021).

Ecosystems for businesses are constantly changing. Businesses are progressively altering their business operations with cutting-edge digital technology. The time for debating and testing the effects of Industry 4.0 and digital transformation is over; now is the time for concrete initiatives. The effect of technologies in marketing that incorporate interoperability, digital actual frameworks, enormous information, and the Internet of Things on the execution of medium and little-estimated undertakings that have been recognized Interoperability, cyberphysical systems, and big data were found to have a considerable beneficial influence on improving business performance after employing multiple regression approaches, but the internet of things had a negligible impact. Additionally, it will support managers in their efforts to defend the expenditure of funds on the expansion of their companies' technological infrastructure. Finally, it will be useful for policymakers to design appropriate policies for growing human capital and improving its capacity for absorption (Mubarak et al., 2019).

2. Materials and Methods

2.1 Components of IOT

In business, the Internet of Things is considered the main key pillar of Industry 4.0 in enhancing and strengthening their competitiveness in the market and has a significant influence on the development of the modern economy. The perception layer, transmission layer, computational layer, and application layer are the four layers of IoT that make up the IoT architecture. Each layer has built-in security problems that are related to it. Each layer's components and purposes are shown in Fig. 22.1.

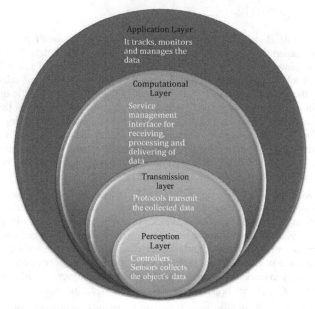

Fig. 22.1 Components of IoT in digital marketing (Tang D., 2021)

The insight layer, otherwise called the sensor layer, is responsible for distinguishing proof, gathering information, and following objects with the assistance of an assortment of innovations, including RFID labels, remote sensor organizations, and activators, which are utilized for checking and following the situation with the articles. The information gathered is then sent to the transmission layer.

The transmission layer acts as a conductor for data to go through the organization from the items to the cloud. This layer utilizes different conventions that incorporate low-power remote individual region organizations, which offer superb correspondence with insignificant energy use and self-association. Wi-Fi, 3G, and Zigbee are other remote organization innovations that can be utilized. Zigbee is a remote organization innovation that has the advantages of minimal expense, low energy utilization, negligible intricacy, unwavering quality, and security. The transmission layer and the application layer get proficient and secure administration from the process layer. This layer uses interface technologies to guarantee the effectiveness and security of the data transferred. Additionally, service management is in charge of functions including storage, exchange, and data gathering. The application layer, which comes last, is where data management takes place. The choice of the appropriate protocol for network management is crucial.

2.2 Big Data in Digital Transformation

The last decade has seen a rise in interest in big data analytics. There aren't numerous scholarly examinations in that frame of mind in the business sectors of ventures, in spite of the way that it is featured as a promising instrument for the B2B areas. While it is feasible to gather and investigate both purchaser information and machine-produced exchange information at the interorganizational level, current big data analytics place a greater emphasis on the marketing element of consumers. Therefore, it is necessary to focus more on stakeholder engagement and the components of big data analytics. As a result, this study explores and offers a conceptual framework for the digital transformation of industrial markets made possible by big data analytics. For identifying the collection of big data and its uses for creating value, it seeks out research publications that offer insights into diverse industrial settings (Wang, W. Y. C., & Wang, Y., 2020).

Data was assembled from organizations that had executed maintainable methodologies. 316 answers from Indian expert specialists are investigated using a cross-breed primary condition displaying counterfeit brain network strategy. Huge information investigations and supportability rehearsals are fundamentally impacted by the board and initiative style, state and national government strategy, provider coordination, inside business interaction, and client reconciliation, as per the consequences of a component examination. Also, the fake brain network model got the results of the underlying

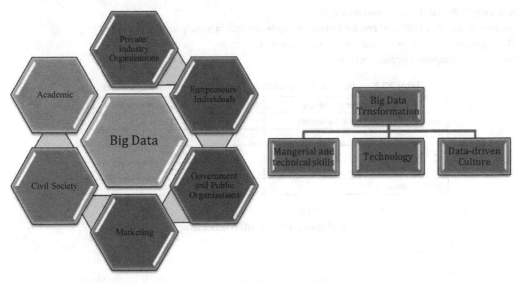

Fig. 22.2   Big Data transformation in digital marketing (Adusumalli, 2016)

condition displayed as information. The review's discoveries show that the two most critical indicators of large information investigation and maintainability rehearsal are the board and authority style and state and national government regulation. From the perspective of operations management, the results offer special insights into how manufacturing companies can enhance their performance in sustainable business. The study offers theoretical and practical insights into the challenges associated with using big data to implement sustainable practices in businesses in emerging economies (Raut et al., 2019).

3. Results and Discussion

Table 22.1   Value chain analysis influenced by IoT and Big data in digital transformation (Adusumalli, 2016)

S. No	Value Chains	Transformation
1	Vendors	Providers of software Providers of custom Software
2	Integration of System	Providers of professional service Integrators of system
3	Buyers	Banking and Financial institutes Industries and manufacturing plants Power and utility industries Construction companies Transportation and Logistics
4	Sales Report in Marketing	Maintenance and Software support

By reducing human intervention, the suggested framework is anticipated to have a major positive impact on warehouses and supply chains. Among the expected advantages is increased productivity.

- The protection of both commodities and workers.
- Cutting down on operation time.
- Minimizing accidents
- Reducing the number of employees.
- Increasing the picking and packing procedures' precision and dependability.

- Reducing theft, fraud, and counterfeiting
- Because of the accessibility of precise facts, assisting businesses in anticipate improvement.
- Making accurate decisions is facilitated by real-time data.
- Improving a company's overall success.

Table 22.2 Influence of IoT in Digital transformation (Adusumalli, 2016)

Components of Marketing	Influence of IoT in Marketing
Sensing and embedded components	82%
Connectivity	96%
IoT Cloud	95%
Analytics and Data Management	88%
User Interface	91%

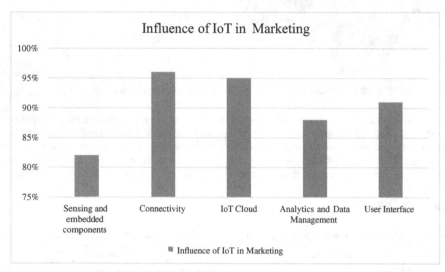

Fig. 22.3 Influence of IoT in Marketing (Adusumalli, 2016)

The most recent technological development, big data, has broad applications across practically all industries, including manufacturing. Although this technology presents commercial opportunities, several industries have not yet fully adopted it. The exploration concentrates on the half-and-half methodology for dynamic path and lab assessment of DEMATEL for versatile neurofussy surmising framework for ID and positioning of the huge variables affecting the reception of large information understudies for the creation of the effect of the enormous information reception in the organizations for assembling and execution. From a survey of the literature, this study identified the crucial adoption elements and divided them into three categories: technological, organizational, and environmental.

The five Vs—velocity, volume, variety, veracity, and value—characterize big data and how Hadoop and different arrangements are utilized to satisfy its needs, alongside circulated handling power. The review frames the abilities expected to assess large amounts of information, as well as the standards of data mining and how results are created. It also offers suggestions. Data scientists can be used by doctors to provide their patients with the greatest care possible, and by meteorologists to foresee the range of regional meteorological occurrences. Even the prediction of natural catastrophes like earthquakes and tornadoes can be done using data science. Data collection is a great place for firms to start when pursuing data science. As soon as they have the data, they can start assessing it. The following are a couple of instances of how people create information and how organizations like Netflix, Amazon, United Parcel Service (UPS), Google, and Apple utilize this information. At the point when an information science project is done, the eventual outcome ought to be utilized to inform critical leaders about new information and experiences found through the data analysis (Adusumalli, 2016).

In order to meet client needs, warehouses, which might hold thousands of products, should be used as efficiently as possible to ensure precise and quick performance in all activities. Since IoT can be utilized to screen different distribution center cycles progressively and can lessen manual obstructions, utilizing it in warehousing promises to have a major effect (Mostafa et al., 2019). In the examination, 15 tests in view of the impact of machining boundaries, including shaft speed, feed rate, and removing expansiveness, were conveyed related to the Box-Behnken architectural matrix. The use of the response surface technique in this study was made possible by its advantages over alternative methodologies, including the requirement for fewer tests to analyze the impacts of all the components and the ability to identify the best possible combination of all the variables. To wrap things up, a hereditary calculation was utilized to recognize the ideal interaction boundary setting that boosts the pace of content expulsion. 1.19 m was the best surface unpleasantness reaction esteem tracked down utilizing a single objective hereditary calculation (Panwar et al., 2021).

It might be difficult to use traditional drilling techniques to create small holes in various materials. However, these kinds of holes could be created using sophisticated machining techniques. Electrical discharge drilling is a type of advanced machining technique that has several advantages over other techniques. The discharge of electricity in the drilling of the alloy of titanium was carried out using well-planned orthogonal array L27 experiments (grade 5). The dielectric pressure, pulse off and on times, and discharge current are chosen as the experiment's input parameters for the process, while hole circularity and hole taper have been chosen as the experiment's output process characteristics. Utilizing the experimental data, the creation of multi-regression models withholds paper and holds circularity. The generated models' statistical analysis demonstrates their suitability and reliability, indicating that they can be utilized to accurately forecast certain quality features. Utilizing a MATLAB program with a genetic algorithm, these quality characteristics have been improved (Jain & Pandey, 2019). The objective functions of the regression model are taper and circularity, which are taken into consideration in genetic algorithm optimization. The results of the genetic algorithm's multi-objective optimization demonstrate improvements in both quality attributes (Jain & Pandey, 2017).

The focus of the current research is on employing electric discharge drilling to machine titanium grade 5 alloys. Through studies, the process response parameters known as hole taper and hole dilation have been computed. A brass electrode was used as a tool, and titanium alloy grade 5 was used as the workpiece during the trials. Utilizing gray relational analysis, the experimentally estimated process parameters have been improved. The major goal of this study is to choose the best input parameters to optimize hole circularity while minimizing hole taper and dilation (Jain et al., 2020).

4. Conclusion

Organizations now face both enormous potential and considerable barriers as a result of the development of digital technology. The motivation behind the review is the current state of corporate digitization and to add to the current hypotheses that have given rise to the expanded consciousness of the Internet of Things and big data. Big data, cloud platforms, and data analytics have the potential to change how businesses operate, particularly when it comes to the adoption of new service-oriented marketing techniques. Managers in marketing generally have the ability to update outdated procedures with new technology or improve the technical quality of goods or services. Businesses can obtain, analyze, and examine data and information, which enables them to create pertinent marketing plans. The roots of the current technological landscape and the drivers of the ensuing corporate shift are a collection of inventions. The "Internet of Things," in particular the "Industrial Internet of Things," is one of these technologies that is essential for helping businesses increase the utilization of their machinery and develop service-based goods in manufacturing enterprises. The prospects, challenges, and anticipated benefits of big data analytics (BD) have become more and more popular in theory and practice. Despite the fact that it has been constantly battling the obstacles preventing its acceptance, emerging economies in particular consider big data analytics to be of utmost importance.

REFERENCES

1. Ziółkowska, M. J. (2021). Digital transformation and marketing activities in small and medium-sized enterprises. Sustainability, 13(5), 2512.
2. Tang, D. (2021). What is digital transformation? EDPACS, 64(1), 9–13.
3. Mubarak, M. F., Shaikh, F. A., Mubarik, M., Samo, K. A., & Mastoi, S. (2019). The impact of digital transformation on business performance: A study of Pakistani SMEs. Engineering technology & applied science research, 9(6), 5056–5061.

4. Panwar, V., Sharma, D. K., Kumar, K. P., Jain, A., & Thakar, C. (2021). Experimental investigations and optimization of surface roughness in turning of en 36 alloy steel using response surface methodology and genetic algorithm. Materials Today: Proceedings, 46, 6474–6481.

5. Jain, A., & Pandey, A. K. (2019). Modeling and optimizing of different quality characteristics in electrical discharge drilling of titanium alloy (Grade-5) sheet. Materials Today: Proceedings, 18, 182–191.

6. Jain, A., & Pandey, A. K. (2017). Multiple quality optimizations in electrical discharge drilling of mild steel sheet. Materials Today: Proceedings, 4(8), 7252–7261.

7. Jain, A., Yadav, A. K., & Shrivastava, Y. (2020). Modelling and optimization of different quality characteristics in electric discharge drilling of titanium alloy sheet. Materials Today: Proceedings, 21, 1680–1684.

8. Mostafa, N., Hamdy, W., & Alawady, H. (2019). Impacts of internet of things on supply chains: a framework for warehousing. Social sciences, 8(3), 84.

9. Wang, W. Y. C., & Wang, Y. (2020). Analytics in the era of big data: The digital transformations and value creation in industrial marketing. Industrial Marketing Management, 86, 12–15.

10. Raut, R. D., Mangla, S. K., Narwane, V. S., Gardas, B. B., Priyadarshinee, P., & Narkhede, B. E. (2019). Linking big data analytics and operational sustainability practices for sustainable business management. Journal of cleaner production, 224, 10–24.

11. Adusumalli, H. P. (2016). Big Data as a Driving Tool of Digital Transformation. *ABC Journal of Advanced Research*, 5(2), 131–138.

Computer Science Engineering and Emerging Technologies (ICCS-2022) – Prof (Dr.) Rajeev Sobti et al. (eds)
© 2024 Taylor & Francis Group, London, ISBN 978-1-032-52199-2

Chapter **23**

Internet of Things (IoT)-based Smart Cities Help Achieving Sustainable Development Goals

Vipin Kumar*

Assistant Professor, Lovely Professional University

Abstract: The Internet of Things (IoT) network is a growing technology that helps monitor the environment and automate industrial processes. IoT will help collect data for the analysis and development of smart cities. IoT is a great tool for water and energy management, environmental monitoring, health, smart cities, smart manufacturing, and supply chain management. In 2015, the UNGA set 17 Sustainable Development Goals to guarantee everyone has access to quality education and a fair living standard. The Sustainable Development Goals (SDG) are a "shared framework for peace and prosperity for people and the planet." The new IoT paradigm can establish an ecosystem that uses networked devices efficiently, effectively, and safely to address global concerns and achieve goals. IoT can help achieve these SDGs. During the 7th International Telecommunication Union, there was universal support for adopting IoT to achieve sustainable development and deliver a brighter future for all people. This research identifies the IoT's relevance to the SDGs. This paper identifies how IoT can help SDGs. IoT creates smart cities with better infrastructure and fewer resources. In this research paper, we try to identify how smart cities help achieve SDGs by conserving resources, generating clean energy, and using it correctly. This study discusses the IoT's direct and indirect impacts on the SDGs.

Keywords: Internet of things, Sustainability development goals, Smart city, IoT networks

1. Introduction

The "Internet of Things" (IoT) is a worldwide network of linked electronic devices, software, and physical objects that gather and transmit data and instructions. In today's contemporary world, the Internet of Things enables a broad range of important day-to-day activities in business, academia, and human society (Chen et al., 2014). The UN Member States approved the 2030 Agenda for Sustainable Development in 2015 to ensure long-term peace and prosperity for current and future generations (Oliva-Maza et al., 2019). The 2030 Agenda for Sustainable Development, which focuses on 17 specific objectives, is an urgent call to action for rich and developing countries to collaborate in a global partnership. They recognize that we must concentrate on eradicating poverty and other forms of deprivation, enhancing health and education, reducing inequality, supporting economic growth, combating climate change, and conserving our forests and oceans. The SDGs reference disability and disabled people eleven times. Among the various SDGs that address the concerns of individuals with disabilities are inequality, accessible human settlements, growth, employment, education, and data monitoring. Even if the term "disabled" isn't in every goal, it's still important for developing and engaging people with disabilities with a graphic illustration of how each of the 17 SDGs addresses disability directly. The recently developed 2030 Agenda for Sustainable Development provides great hope to people with disabilities worldwide. Some of the SDGs are directly affected by technology, and IoT technology and industry can help achieve these goals.

*vipin.17730@lpu.co.in

DOI: 10.1201/9781003405580-23

1.1 IoT Applications

The Internet of Things (IoT) is a network of devices that provide data to a platform to allow communication and automated control. It is responsible for connecting physical equipment to digital interfaces. The top IoT applications are listed below.

Smart Homes

The most prominent use of the Internet of Things is the smart home. Sensors are used in intelligent house control and maintenance systems such as lighting, resource management, and security. A smart house is a smaller, self-contained version of a smart city. Natural language processing is used in an IoT-enabled smart home for contextual processing of voice requests. He has internet switches that provide electricity to the appliances hooked up to them. The technology uses occupancy to illuminate rooms and even plays customized music depending on who is in the room. His security system employs face recognition to alert the family to the identity of their guests (Marikyan et al., 2019).

Agriculture

The agricultural sector might gain a lot from the Internet of Things. By 2050, it's predicted that there will be 10 billion people on the planet. Governments thus give the development of agricultural systems priority. Due to this and climate change, farmers are integrating technology into their operations. Sensors provide data on the profiles of soil chemistry and fertilizers. The quality of a harvest is influenced by CO_2 levels, moisture, temperature, acidity level, and the availability of sufficient nutrients. An Internet of Things application called smart irrigation controls and efficiently utilizes water in agriculture. When the soil dries to a certain level, the IoT system only initiates the water flow. The supply is also turned off if a specific moisture level is reached (Farooq et al., 2020). This reduces waste brought on by errors made by people. RFID chips are used for livestock monitoring, which records an animal's vital signs, immunization history, and location.

Supply Chain Management

Supply chain management (SCM) is a method of expediting the flow of goods and services from the point of origin to the end of consumption (Manavalan & Jayakrishna, 2019). Fleet management, vendor contacts, inventory management, and scheduled maintenance were all part of it. Supply chain issues hit many businesses during the pandemic, most notably when they resulted in a global shutdown in early 2020. When operations became more distant, it was only logical for firms to consider implementing IoT into their SCM methods.

Healthcare

Patients, their loved ones, doctors, hospitals, healthcare providers, and insurers may all benefit from IoT applications in healthcare. Connected patient devices include fitness trackers like Fitbit and blood pressure and glucose monitors. Smart hygiene monitoring is obsolete due to Internet of Things-enabled monitoring technologies. IoT enables improvements in patient safety, hospital asset management (including pharmaceutical inventory control), environmental monitoring, humidity control, and temperature regulation in the healthcare sector (Aheleroff et al., 2020).

Smart Cities

The Internet of Things, often known as IoT, is a forward-thinking technological advancement with the promise of impacting our day-to-day lives. The Internet of Things may help a smart city save money and make life better for its citizens by, for example, simplifying infrastructure and maintenance activities so that they are more efficient.

Education

IoT in schools will make future education more connected and collaborative. IoT devices give students access to study materials and communication channels and enable instructors to monitor students' academic progress in real-time. A learning management system and other technologies are coupled to build an education application platform that provides a comprehensive, individualized education solution. The arrival of technology has drastically altered the educational landscape. The IoT alters contemporary education by making it more interactive and interesting. In addition, these technologies provide educators with more flexibility to personalize their students' educational experiences. The Internet of Things makes learning easier for students via play, which may be the finest part (Ramlowat & Pattanayak, 2019).

1.2 Sustainable Development Goals SDGs

In this research, we identify the role of IoT to achieve SDG. The 17 Sustainable Development Goals are a "common roadmap for peace and prosperity for people and the planet, today and in the future." The UNGA established the SDGs in 2015 to be accomplished by 2030. There is widespread agreement on the SDGs as a set of goals for the world. These exercises teach kids about global problems, including access to clean water and gender equality. The SDGs are a global call to action to boost economic growth while preserving natural resources. By 2030, the United Nations hopes to have achieved its Sustainable Development Goals (SDGs), which include ending poverty and inequality and safeguarding the planet. The four sustainability goals are: reducing poverty and hunger and improving health, which depends on steady economic growth (Nastic et al., 2015). These 17 goals are as follows:

Goal 1: No Poverty: The first goal of the SDGs is no poverty," which says that we have to remove poverty from the world in all its forms. There are many people in developing countries who are not capable of meeting their basic needs. We have to give them the opportunity to grow and raise awareness about a good life.

Goal 2: Zero Hunger: The second goal is also related to poor living conditions for people. Some people are not able to get food every day. We have to make efforts to provide food to every needy person and achieve zero hunger by 2030.

Goal 3: Good Health and Well-Being: The good health of human beings is very important, and healthcare facilities should be provided to everyone. Healthcare and infrastructure for good health are the third goal of the SDGs.

Goal 4: Quality Education: A quality education for every child should be provided, and all countries should ensure that every citizen in their country is educated. Good-quality education for all is one of the goals of sustainable development.

Goal 5: Gender Equality: Some social issues are also considered in the SDGs. The goal of gender equality requires equal weightage for male, female, or any other gender.

Goal 6: Clean Water and Sanitation: The problem of clean, drinkable water is also very big nowadays. Goal 6 is supposed to try to provide clean water to everyone.

Goal 7: Affordable and Clean Energy: Energy production must be clean and not pollute the environment. Efforts must be made to find sources of clean energy and stop doing harm to the environment.

Goal 8: Decent Work and Economic Growth: Economic growth of every country and the world

Goal 9: Industry, Innovation, and Infrastructure For a good nation, industry and infrastructure are musts for development. So, goal 9 is related to industry, infrastructure, and innovative development.

Goal 10: Reduced Inequality: Inequality among all humans must be removed in every form.

Goal 11: Sustainable Cities and Communities: Goal 11 ensures a good life for everyone. Good communities and cities must be developed for a good life.

Goal 12: Responsible Consumption and Production: As part of SDG 12, businesses, governments, universities, and consumers are all urged to take various measures to become more environmentally friendly. It foresees long-term production and consumption on the back of advanced technological capacity, resource efficiency, and reduced global waste.

Goal 13: Climate Action: Goal 13: Keep an eye on climate changes and ensure that no one is harming the climate. The environment must not be polluted in any form.

Goal 14: Life Below Water: The life of every living being is important for the ecological system of the earth, so life below water or on land must be taken care of.

Goal 15: Life on Land: Life on land is also important. Goal 15 is related to any form of life on land.

Goal 16: Peace and Justice Strong Institutions: For a good life on earth, justice and peace are required. Goal 16 is related to justice and peace.

Goal-17: Partnerships to achieve the Goal: All countries must work collaboratively to achieve the SDGs.

All 17 goals are given in Table 23.1.

Rest of the paper is structured as follows. Section 2 explain the characteristics and challenges of IoT networks. Section 3 describes the smart cities and their requirements. Section 4 explains direct and indirect support of IoT for SDGs. Section 5 finds the impacts of IoT on smart cities and Section 6 concludes the paper.

Table 23.1 The 17 sustainable development goals (SDGs) to transform our world

Goals S No.	Name	Description
Goal 1:	No Poverty	To Eradicating poverty
Goal 2:	Zero Hunger	To deal with hunger
Goal 3:	Good Health and Well-being	Healthcare infrastructure
Goal 4:	Quality Education	Same opportunity to all
Goal 5:	Gender Equality	Equality for all
Goal 6:	Clean Water and Sanitation	To deal with water problem
Goal 7:	Affordable and Clean Energy	Generate clean energy
Goal 8:	Decent Work and Economic Growth	Economic growth for all
Goal 9:	Industry, Innovation and Infrastructure	Innovative industry form
Goal 10:	Reduced Inequality	Same for all
Goal 11:	Sustainable Cities and Communities	Community developments
Goal 12:	Responsible Consumption and Production	Reduce consumption
Goal 13:	Climate Action	Urgent Action
Goal 14:	Life Below Water	Good environment for all
Goal 15:	Life on Land	Good environment for all
Goal 16:	Peace and Justice Strong Institutions	Justices for all
Goal 17:	Partnerships to achieve the Goal	Achieve goals

Source: Made by Author

2. Characteristics and Challenges of IoT Network

IoT networks are everywhere as they connect the various things in homes and buildings. IoT-based networks are used for controlling, monitoring, and collecting data. The devices in IoT networks are heterogeneous in terms of size, capability, and technology used. Many devices and sensors in these networks are very small and have limited computation power and memory. The biggest challenges in IoT networks are connectivity, heterogeneity, privacy, and the logical and physical security of data and devices. The security of IoT networks is also a big concern, and a lot of research is ongoing in this field. A user can be the week's link. Because humans are often the weakest link in cybersecurity, social engineering is very harmful and difficult to fight against (Mohanta et al., 2020). The simplest sort of social engineering attack is sending phishing emails intended to lure a victim in that fashion or installing a key logger on a victim's machine to steal credentials that might provide the attacker greater access. These sorts of assaults are possible even with the strongest cybersecurity measures simply because they prey on our flawed nature and the fact that we all make errors as humans. The main challenges associated with the implementation of the IoT are as follows: Inability to link all the data together and process it effectively. Incompetence in establishing the same technology standards to make all connected devices 'understand' each other; and inability to deal with security and data privacy threats. The main challenges of IoT networks are as follows:

2.1 IoT Security

IoT can be a vast network, and security is not only concerned with securing the data but also about the privacy of people and the trust of different devices. IoT security is the process of defending Internet-connected devices and the networks to which they are connected from threats and breaches. This is done by identifying, assessing, and monitoring risks and helping to patch any device. Additional steps include monitoring the probes for any recently recognized reconnaissance attacks. If hackers are researching you, there is a greater possibility of future attack attempts. Again, bring in outsourced teams to test and audit current security standings if you don't have the right team setup within.

2.2 Network Problem

Networks must be able to support growing demand as cellular connectivity is increasingly relied upon to power richer and more sophisticated IoT applications. As we've seen, numerous carriers are transitioning away from 2G and 3G networks in favours of LTE, which can support both sophisticated and less data-intensive applications.

2.3 High-Speed Connectivity

Many of the geographical areas where sustainability is most needed are less linked than other parts of the globe. Mobile network providers are always looking for new, creative ways to improve connections while lowering costs in rural locations. This is particularly crucial in regions with unequal access to resources (El-Sayed et al., 2008).

2.4 Mobility

The ability of people to obtain more information has never been greater as more of the world's population becomes connected. Mobile network operators have an unparalleled chance to connect with the almost 2.5 billion social media users globally as they attempt to achieve sustainable development objectives.

3. Smart-city Requirements and their Goals

A smart city's infrastructure must have sufficient water supply, consistent energy, sanitation, solid waste management, efficient urban mobility, public transit, cheap housing, especially for the poor, strong IT connections and digitization, and competent administration. It is an indefinitely inhabited area with well-defined administrative borders and a population that works mostly in non-agricultural occupations (Marikyan et al., 2019). Cities often have complex systems for housing, transportation, sanitation, utilities, land use, manufacturing, and communication. A smart city combines cutting-edge technology and data analysis to enhance the quality of life for its citizens, streamline municipal processes, and spur economic growth. Instead of how much technology is available, the value is in how it is used. To present a complete picture of the city, successful smart cities emphasize the integration of municipal infrastructure and applications (both new and old) into a unified system. The common goals of smart cities are as follows:

3.1 Good Governance

Governments foster enterprise, entrepreneurship, and technology-driven, innovative business models by enacting laws and regulations. Data privacy rules are an essential aspect of the city administration, and they serve a dual purpose of protecting citizens' rights and ensuring the smooth operation of government services. In contemporary India, a state that has transitioned from a rule-based to a welfare-oriented framework, SMART Governance incorporates simplicity, morality, accountability, responsibility, and transparency.

3.2 Law and Order

The social infrastructure, the physical infrastructure, the institutional infrastructure (including governance), and the economic infrastructure make up the four pillars of a smart city. The citizen is at the heart of each and every one of these tenets. The technique might revolve around improving the functioning of urban infrastructure. A contemporary city needs to be able to provide access to public data, electronic service delivery, 100 percent water waste treatment, water quality monitoring, and several other types of "smart" solutions (Angadi, 2019).

3.3 Infrastructure

According to one definition, smart infrastructure is "a cyber-physical system that enables integrated management of all elements it comprises through the use of a variety of technological tools that support data collection and analysis to meet efficiency, sustainability, productivity, and safety objectives." The infrastructure's productivity, efficiency, and safety may be improved to achieve these goals—modern infrastructure for waste management and sanitation. There is always access to power, along with an ample supply of water. By constructing a network of high-quality, well-connected roads, cities may achieve efficient urban transportation and public transit.

3.4 Social Life

A smart city will help its citizens decide everything from financial investments to lunch spots. By tracking foot traffic across the city, entrepreneurs may find new businesses like restaurants, retail stores, dry cleaners, etc. According to the study, our overall health is substantially impacted by elements that affect our everyday lives, including education, safe streets, and the availability of good food. These influence cities' liveability and economic vibrancy.

3.5 Health and Education

No matter where a city is situated, there is always a demand for medical services. The Internet of Things (IoT), artificial intelligence (AI), wearable devices and sensors, big data, business intelligence (BI), and several other technologies are used by smart healthcare to adapt to the requirements of the healthcare ecosystem intelligently. A "smart city" is often characterized by the widespread application of technological advances throughout the municipal infrastructure. For this discussion, the operation of smart cities needs to provide citizens with access to smart education. The schools that are available to our children in the future will look quite different from the ones that were available to us.

3.6 International Connectivity

Following are the results of a search for "international connection in the smart city" in images: Smart cities employ information and communication technology (ICT) to enhance operational efficiency, the quality of public services, citizen welfare, and information exchange. Information and communications technology (ICT) is used in a "smart city" to improve the efficacy, responsiveness, and interactivity of municipal services, as well as to reduce costs and resource consumption and to develop links between residents and local stakeholders.

3.7 Cultural and Sports

Smart cities and sports may share best practices for using sports to enhance urban development. Participate! Smart cities and sports networks. Creative enclaves and cultural zones make cities habitable. These actions will attract, retain, and develop India's creative talent. Creative clusters, often called "culture districts," are regions where art and cultural groups attract visitors. The local economy, cultural capacities, and identities benefited. Creative clusters include art and craft galleries, theatres, music venues, and dance and theatre venues to promote and profit from the city's culture.

4. IoT Support for SDGs

The IoT can potentially mitigate human-caused environmental degradation. IoT may assist organizations in being more sustainable by assisting in the management of water resources, the reduction of energy expenses, the streamlining of data collection on traffic patterns, and the reduction of gas consumption. Green IoT leads to a eco-friendlier and more sustainable environment for smart cities. Therefore, procedures and techniques for reducing environmental hazards, transportation waste, and resource usage must be addressed. The Internet of Things has the potential to drastically decrease industrial waste, which will aid in environmental preservation. It is a sensor-based system that analyses usable data to improve asset performance and facility management. Digital technologies, which are also used to analyse and monitor sustainability progress, optimize resource utilization, decrease greenhouse gas emissions, and reduce greenhouse gas emissions, have made a more circular economy possible (TARIQ et al., n.d.). However, digital technology also allows for creativity and cooperation.

4.1 Direct Support

Goal numbers 3, 4, 6, 7, 9, and 11 are directly related to technology, and the IoT can directly help achieve them at a faster pace. In the IoT, we have smart gadgets for patient monitoring and the health of humans. IoT can collect live data about the human body and send alerts. IoT also helps in education, teaching methods, knowledge, and awareness.

All the water treatment plant requirements for monitoring can be achieved using connected IoT devices, and monitoring and controlling can be done. In the same way, energy plants of any type can be highly maintained by IoT technology. The SDGs for direct IoT support are given in Table 23.2.

Table 23.2   Direct support of IoT

S No.	Goal name	IoT supports
Goal 3:	Good Health and Well-being	IoT provide Direct Support to Health Infrastructure and Healthcare
Goal 4:	Quality Education	Smart Education
Goal 6:	Clean Water and Sanitation	Water plat industry and IoT used
Goal 7:	Affordable and Clean Energy	IoT use in nucellar plant
Goal 9:	Industry, Innovation and Infrastructure	IoT used in industry infrastructure
Goal 11:	Sustainable Cities and Communities	Community developments IoT
Goal 12:	Responsible Consumption and Production	IoT automation and reduce combustions
Goal 13:	Climate Action	Awareness and urgent Action

Source: Made by Author

4.2 Indirect Support

Goals related to poverty, hunger, peace, and justice can be achieved when there are plenty of resources, good education, and awareness about human rights and responsibility. Information technology gives way to fast access to required information. Before IoT, a specific device like a desktop computer or laptop was required to fetch information, but with IoT, it becomes more efficient, easier to acquire, and faster. IoT speeds up information technology and gets rid of specific locations or specific devices. With the help of IoT, goals 5, 16, 17, and 10 can be archived more accurately. Life on land and below water can be saved and served if we have accurate information about them. IoT helps collect data about various species and make good policies for them. Hunger and poverty are also reduced by producing plenty of resources and sending them to the required places at an accurate time. IoT helps gather information about requirements and transportation. Other goals can be achieved by separating awareness from education, where the IoT directly helps. Indirect support for IoT in the SDGs is given in Table 23.3.

Table 23.3 Direct Support of IoT

S No.	Goal name	IoT supports
GOAL 1:	No Poverty	IoT to provide awareness
GOAL 2:	Zero Hunger	IoT techniques in agriculture field
GOAL 5:	Gender Equality	IoT to provide awareness
GOAL 8:	Decent Work and Economic Growth	Help in Industry development and
GOAL 10:	Reduced Inequality	IoT to provide awareness
GOAL 14:	Life Below Water	Water life monitoring
GOAL 15:	Life on Land	Wild life monitoring
GOAL 16:	Peace and Justice Strong Institutions	IoT use in governed
GOAL 17:	Partnerships to achieve the Goal	Awareness about SDGs

Source: Made by Author

5. Impact of IoT on Smart Cities

The cloud-based IoT solutions for Smart Cities are fitted with an open data platform. Small cities may work together to create a similar urban setting. Both small and big smart city systems are connected to and managed by a single cloud platform. Digital technology is used in "smart cities" to enhance the quality of life in general, as well as public safety, energy efficiency, and sustainability. They gather and analyse data in real-time using linked sensors, lights, and meters from the Internet of Things. According to the study, smart cities are energy-efficient, socially active, financially secure, business-focused, data-driven, and ecologically friendly (Ajay *et al.*, 2022). The research also showed that smart city efforts might help municipalities overcome obstacles and promote economic growth. They increased municipal utilities' efficiency and effective management of the city's lighting infrastructure. They have streamlined city traffic and enhanced the use and efficiency of public transportation. Applications for the Internet of Things (IoT) address many practical challenges, such as traffic congestion, municipal services, economic growth, citizen involvement, and public safety and security. IoT sensors are often used in the physical infrastructure of smart cities, such as streetlights, water meters, and traffic lights. To establish a comprehensive vision of the city, successful smart cities focus on combining municipal infrastructure and both new and old applications into a single, integrated system. Smart cities use the Internet of Things (IoT) devices like linked sensors, lighting, and meters to gather and analyse data. Cities use this data, among other things, to enhance their public utilities, infrastructure, and services (Chatterjee et al., 2018). What advantages may smart cities provide? To help city planners and inhabitants make better choices, a smart city may contextualize data sources such as vehicle mobility, energy use, and water distribution. Some major conclusions are as follows:

- A "smart city" is an urban region that is forward-thinking in terms of technology and employs a wide variety of electronic devices and sensors to gather certain data. IoT implements sensors and communication technology in almost everything and helps build up smart cities.
- The knowledge gathered from that data is used to manage assets, resources, and services successfully; that data is used to improve operations across the city.

- For proper operation of everything in urban cities, citizen information and monitoring are required, which can be archived with the help of IoT.
- Governance, law, and justice's policies can be implemented, and following the policies can be monitored and assured using IoT.
- Industry development, education, social life, and healthcare can be implemented with IoT in smart cities.

6. Conclusion

Although we have achieved progress over the last seven years, there is still work to be done, and the goals are now more vital than ever. We are avoiding starvation and poverty, which are excesses committed by violations. These Sustainable Development Goals, or SDGs, aim to provide solutions to challenges of such size that they may seem impossible. Still, with the help of IoT technology, these can be achieved. Appropriately utilizing technology will allow for accomplishing the SDGs. The Internet of Things makes it possible to build smart cities with improved infrastructure for living and a lifestyle that meets all of the needs for better infrastructure, education, and city traffic management. Smart cities may be established with the aid of the IoT. Both governance and mothering needed a significant amount of data and analysis. These things can be accomplished using IoT and other forms of technology, which helps to archive SDG. Some objectives, such as 4, 6, 7, and 9, are much more attainable than others since they are directly tied to greater control over the situation with technology. Using these technologies may indirectly accomplish the goals listed in 1, 2, and 3. The Internet of Things (IoT) has the potential to address some of the world's most important issues, including those related to the environment, the economy, and human lives.

REFERENCES

1. Aheleroff, S., Xu, X., Lu, Y., Aristizabal, M., Velásquez, J. P., Joa, B., & Valencia, Y. (2020). IoT-enabled smart appliances under industry 4.0: A case study. Advanced Engineering Informatics, 43, 10-43.
2. Angadi, R. (2019). Introduction to Smart City and Agricultural Revolution: Big Data and Internet of Things (IoT). In Smart Cities and Smart Spaces: Concepts, Methodologies, Tools, and Applications (pp. 135–176). IGI Global.
3. Chatterjee, S., Kar, A. K., & Gupta, M. P. (2018). Success of IoT in smart cities of India: An empirical analysis. Government Information Quarterly, 35(3), 349–361.
4. Chen, S., Xu, H., Liu, D., Hu, B., & Wang, H. (2014). A vision of IoT: Applications, challenges, and opportunities with china perspective. IEEE Internet of Things Journal, 1(4), 349–359.
5. El-Sayed, H., Mellouk, A., George, L., & Zeadally, S. (2008). Quality of service models for heterogeneous networks: overview and challenges. Annals of Telecommunications- Annales Des Télécommunications, 63(11), 639–668.
6. Farooq, M. S., Riaz, S., Abid, A., Umer, T., & Zikria, Y. bin. (2020). Role of IoT technology in agriculture: A systematic literature review. Electronics, 9(2), 319.
7. Manavalan, E., & Jayakrishna, K. (2019). A review of Internet of Things (IoT) embedded sustainable supply chain for industry 4.0 requirements. Computers & Industrial Engineering, 127, 925–953.
8. Marikyan, D., Papagiannidis, S., & Alamanos, E. (2019). A systematic review of the smart home literature: A user perspective. Technological Forecasting and Social Change, 138, 139–154.
9. Mohanta, B. K., Jena, D., Satapathy, U., & Patnaik, S. (2020). Survey on IoT security: Challenges and solution using machine learning, artificial intelligence and blockchain technology. Internet of Things, 11, 100227.
10. Nastic, S., Truong, H.-L., & Dustdar, S. (2015). SDG-Pro: a programming framework for software-defined IoT cloud gateways. Journal of Internet Services and Applications, 6(1), 1–17.
11. Oliva-Maza, L., Torres-Moreno, E., Villarroya-Gaudó, M., & Ayuso-Escuer, N. (2019). Using IoT for Sustainable Development Goals (SDG) in Education. Multidisciplinary Digital Publishing Institute Proceedings, 31(1), 1.
12. Ramlowat, D. D., & Pattanayak, B. K. (2019). Exploring the internet of things (IoT) in education: a review. Information Systems Design and Intelligent Applications, 245–255.
13. Rani, S., Maheswar, R., Kanagachidambaresan, G. R., & Jayarajan, P. (2020). Integration of WSN and IoT for smart cities. Springer.
14. Tariq, H., Abdaoui, A., Touati, F., Alhitmi, M. A. E., Doha, Q., Crescini, D., & Manouer, A. B. E. N. (n.d.). IoT/Edge Structural Health Monitoring System as a Life-Cycle Management tool for SDG-11 using Utility Computing Platform.

Computer Science Engineering and Emerging Technologies (ICCS-2022) – Prof (Dr.) Rajeev Sobti et al. (eds)
© 2024 Taylor & Francis Group, London, ISBN 978-1-032-52199-2

Chapter **24**

Logo Validation Using Unsupervised Machine Learning Technique—A Blockchain-based Approach

Aniruddha Prabhu B. P.[1]
Assistant Professor, Computer Science,
Graphic Era Hill University, Dehradun, Uttarakhand

Ojas Misra[2]
Associate Analyst, Digital and Emerging Technology,
Ernst & Young, Hyderabad, Telangana

Rakesh Dani[3]
Associate Professor, Hospitality Management,
Graphic Era Hill University, Dehradun, Uttarakhand

Abstract: Logo represents the organization. It is equally important as the CEO for the institution. It represents the creativity, motto and the organization itself. It plays a very important role. As the logo is unique to a system it is very important to make the process of registration faster. In this paper, we propose a blockchain-based technique of validating the logo of an organization. In this paper, we propose a new method of validating the logo.

Keywords: Logo, Blockchain, K-means clustering, Image hashing

1. Introduction

Once the logo is designed it should undergo several steps of validation, which include verifying whether the logo is previously used by some organization as the logo as the trademark is unique for that particular organization. The process of registering a logo is as follows firstly Search for the trade mark, Application presentation in front of registration attorney then Govt. processing.

Blockchain has attracted a lot of audience in the recent years. It has become a hot topic because of its exiting features like, openness, immutability, decentralized etc. It has this immutable and decentralized feature which helps one to create a new block whenever a new logo is registered. The new logo which came for registration undergoes a simple search for the existing logo. Once this process of validation is done the of registration completes by creating a new block which later added to the blockchain.

Our paper majorly concentrates on the second and the third step. The organization which is interested to register its new logo goes to the registration office, where the authority searches for the logo in the blockchain and confirms it is unique. Then this logo is added as a new block confirming registration[7][8].

---

[1]aniprabhubp@gmail.com, [2]misraojas@hotmail.com, [3]rakeshdani@geu.ac.in

DOI: 10.1201/9781003405580-24

2. Literature Review

2.1 Trademark

Trademark for any organization plays a very critical role in identifying and advertising the institution. They all mean to something that is inherited in the institution. The process of registering a trademark is a job of time. It has several steps which can be accounted as follows: i. Selecting the trademark. ii. Registering the trademark. iii. Govt. process.

The processes that are done by the govt. involves a lot of manual work and as a result it is very slow. But with blockchain it can be drastically reduced to as less as thirty minutes.

2.2 Blockchain

Blockchain has attracted a lot of crowds these days, starting from crypto systems, network security to healthcare and government agencies [5]. Blockchain are proven to be insensitive to any kind of faults and attacks including 51% attack.

Blockchain, powered with distributed, decentralized ledger system, makes it possible to create immutable records called blocks [4]. Every block that is created will have a unique hash and it is said that possibility of regenerating the same hash is nearly zero [4][5].

The present manual system of registration involves, selection, determination of class, attorney approval, filling the application, reviewing the application, examination of the trademark application, personal hearing before registering, publication and opposition, and registration and renewal. This can take anywhere from one to two months to 90 days depending on the class of trademark. There are 45 different classes of trademarks, in which 1 to 34 are for goods and rest for services. To register a logo one should decide, to which category does the organization belong and have to proceed further. But with the proposed blockchain-based system the process will reduce somewhere between 30 minutes to an hour.

2.3 Image Hash Generation

The main obstacle for the given problem is to generate the hash for each logo. We found a number of research papers that are given methodologies to generate hash for images. Ashwin Swaminathan et al [1] proposed a novel method for image hashing. The algorithm was insensitive to 10-degree rotation, 20% cropping and some of the filters. R. Venkatesan [2] pointed out that the hashing algorithm like MD5 and SHA are very sensitive for minute changes, a single digit can vary in a very broad sense. This can be an added advantage in validating a logo.

Qin, C et al [3] proposed a novel approach to generate the image hash, the process involves low pass filtering and anti-collision techniques, compression and quantization techniques finally these values used for hash generation.

3. Methodology and Model Specifications

3.1 K-Means Technique

The technique proposed in this paper concentrates on validating the logo. The validation is done only when the logo is unique. For this, the logo, the image has to be compared with all the images in the database, i.e., blockchain. The problem arises when the blockchain becomes really large and the process of comparing takes a lot of time. For that we have come up with a unique way of generating hash based on the image. So, whenever a new image comes in, if the image leads to generation of same hash, then the logo is already taken [9][10].

Now the task is to generate a hash using the image. So, we can take the pixel values and the region averages of the pixels and append the values together to get a unique hash. The appended value will be a large integer; this can be used to generate a hash. The hash is calculated using the MD5 hash generation technique. The below figure shows a general representation of the data flow through the system to create a new block. i.e., successful registration of a logo.

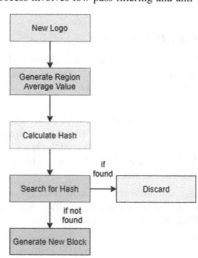

Fig. 24.1 Dataflow through the system

Source: Made by Author

Hash Generation

This involves 3 steps, Region clustering K-Means, Average calculation, calculating hash using MD5.

K-means Clustering

It is an iterative, unsupervised machine learning algorithm, which is an iterative clustering algorithm, separates the data points into 'k' predefined, non-overlapping clusters [6]. Where each datapoint belongs to single cluster. The objective function is given below.

$$J = \sum_{i=1}^{m} \sum_{k=1}^{K} w_{ik} \|x^i - \mu_k\|^2$$

We used k-means on images to generate a number of clusters. The cluster values are used to generate the hash values later.

Region Average Calculation

There will be randomly multiple values for a region. To avoid this confusion, we find out the average value for each region. Then these values are appended together to form a number with 32 digits. This 32-digit number will be given as input for the MD5 hash generator.

MD5 Hash Generation

It is a technique used to generate 128-bit hash values to the given text. The algorithm takes the region average value generated by the region average calculator, and generates a 128-bit unique hash.

3.2 Image Hash Method

This involves similar procedure. It uses image hash generation instead of k-means clustering and MD5 hash generation. Image hash is calculated and that hash is used as the unique hash for generating new blocks that specifies each logo. The flow chart is shown in Fig. 24.3.

4. Conclusion

The presented paper gives the implementation procedure for a new, faster and safer method of logo validation and registration technique. Further validations and uniqueness analysis can be done by blockchain miners who will get rewarded with the commission for validating a particular logo.

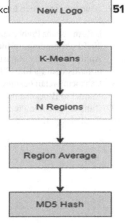

Fig. 24.2 Hash generation

Source: Made by Author

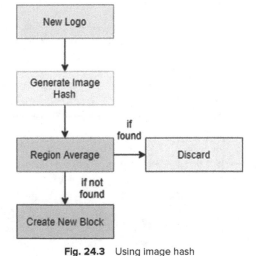

Fig. 24.3 Using image hash

Source: Made by Author

REFERENCES

1. Ashwin Swaminathan, Yinian Mao, and Min Wu, Robust and Secure Image Hashing, https://ieeexplore.ieee.org/abstract/document/1634363/
2. R. Venkatesan S. M. Koon, M. H. Jakubowski, P. Moulin, Robust image hashing, https://ieeexplore.ieee.org/abstract/document/899541/
3. Qin, C., Chen, X., Ye, D., Wang, J., & Sun, X. A novel image hashing scheme with perceptual robustness using block truncation coding.https://www.sciencedirect.com/scie nce/article/pii/S0020025516302857
4. Dinh, T. T. A., Liu, R., Zhang, M., Chen, G., Ooi, B. C., & Wang, J. (2018). Untangling Blockchain: A DataProcessing View of Blockchain Systems https://ieeexplore.ieee.org/abstract/document/8246573/
5. Wust, K., & Gervais, A. Do you Need a Blockchain? https://ieeexplore.ieee.org/abstract/document/8525392/
6. Krishna, K., & Narasimha Murty, M. Genetic K-means algorithmhttps://ieeexplore.ieee.org/abstract/document/764879/

7. B P, Aniruddha Prabhu and Das, Arup, Transforming Transactional Marketing of Retailers Using Blockchain Approach (February 25, 2019). Proceedings of International Conference on Sustainable Computing in Science, Technology and Management (SUSCOM), Amity University Rajasthan, Jaipur - India, February 26–28, 2019, Available at SSRN: https://ssrn.com/abstract=3350886 or http://dx.doi.org/10.2139/ssrn.3350886

8. Enhancing retail business and customer experience using blockchain approach B. P. Aniruddha Prabhu and Arup Das International Journal of Blockchains and Cryptocurrencies 2020 1: 3, 273–285

9. Clinical Outcome Prediction Using K-Nearest Neighbours Algorithm A. V. Aniruddha Prabhu B P IJSREM 5 (7), 4

10. Parallel Algorithm for Finding Top K High utility Itemset from Big Transaction Data AP B P IJEAST 2 (1), 113–115

Computer Science Engineering and Emerging Technologies (ICCS-2022) – Prof (Dr.) Rajeev Sobti et al. (eds)
© 2024 Taylor & Francis Group, London, ISBN 978-1-032-52199-2

Chapter **25**

Detailed Analysis of Machine Learning and Deep Learning Technologies for Web Security

Logeshwari Dhavamani[1]
Associate Professor, Department of Information Technology,
St. Joseph's College of Engineering Chennai

K. A. jayabalaji[2]
Assistant Professor, Department of Computer Science,
Sri Krishna Arts and Science College, Coimbatore Tamilnadu, India

Anupama Chadha[3]
Professor, Computer Applications, MRIIRS, Faridabad

Rahul Shyam[4]
Department of Computer Science and Engineering,
NSHM Institute of Engineering and Technology (MAKAUT)

Balaji Ramkumar Rajagopal[5]
Sr. Data Architect, Cognizant Technology solutions, Chennai, Tamil nadu, India

José Luis Arias Gonzáles[6]
Department of Business, Pontifical Catholic University of Peru

Abstract: The current world can be categorized as technologically advanced and digitally empowered. The rate of internet penetration is very high nowadays, which highly encourages the emergence of the web as well as digital life. Machine learning can be considered an effective branch of artificial intelligence that extensively focuses on the usage of data and algorithms to imitate the way humans learn and improve accuracy. The Web is transforming how people learn and work because of the unquestionable inside-out integration of online behavior with public action, but it also exposes us to more critical security risks. The best way to identify various organizational assaults, particularly assaults that haven't been observed recently, is a crucial point of interest that needs to be resolved urgently. Cybersecurity is a collection of technologies and processes designed to protect PCs, businesses, initiatives, and information from attacks and unauthorized access, alteration, or erasure. On the other hand, deep learning is a subset of machine learning that is primarily a neural network consisting of three or more layers. These networks attempt to stimulate the nature of the human brain and permit it to learn from a massive amount of data. Depending on the nature of those two technologies, they can be effectively used for web security.

Keywords: Machine learning, Deep learning, Web security, Technology

[1]logeshgd@gmail.com, [2]jayabalajika@skasc.ac.in, [3]anupamaluthra@gmail.com, [4]rahulshyam12@gmail.com, [5]balajiramkumar@gmail.com, [6]joseariasgon6@gmail.com

DOI: 10.1201/9781003405580-25

1. Introduction

The Internet is transforming how individuals are educated and employed as a result of the improved coordination of the Web and digital life; however, it also introduces people to more significant security risks. Network surveillance systems as well as application security systems combine to form a system for network protection. Firewalls, malware protection, and intrusion prevention systems are all features of these platforms (IDS). Unauthorized information activities, including usage, copying, manipulation, and removal, may be found, determined, and identified with the use of IDSs. Both internal and external invasions represent system vulnerabilities. For intrusion detection systems, there seem to be three basic categories of analysis tools: hybridized, anomaly-based, and misuse-based (also referred to as signature-based). Misuse-based testing procedures leverage the characteristics of attack patterns to search for those attacks. It is impossible to identify fresh (zero-day) threats with improper technology [1]. By examining the typical system or network activity, anomaly-based approaches can spot deviations from the standard. Furthermore, it is possible to specify the characteristics of abuse monitors using the data that anomaly-based approaches (new attacks) warn on. Since previously unknown system activities might be classified as abnormalities, the fundamental drawback of anomaly-based approaches is the possibility of significant false alarm frequencies. In anomalous detection techniques and hybridized intrusion detection systems, ML/DL techniques and early identification techniques indicate open issues and obstacles. This review discusses the use of ML and DL in multiple remote monitoring contexts and is not just focused on security solutions. Deep learning infiltration approaches are in the interest of researchers. On the NSL-KDD vulnerability scanning database, the researchers describe a full collection of machine-learning techniques; however, their analysis only uses a content-based filtering scenario [2]. In contrast, both exploitation detection and anomaly detection are addressed in this research. The formal definition of malicious URL identification as a machine-learning challenge is presented by specialists, who also classify and evaluate the accomplishments of works that handle the many aspects of this issue (e.g., design of feature representations and algorithms). They do not, meanwhile, describe the algorithm's fundamental specifics, in contrast to this study. Researchers concentrate on the use of machine learning techniques in intrusion detection [3]. In-depth descriptions are provided for algorithms including "decision trees, fuzzy logic, Bayesian networks, support vector machines, evolutionary computation, and fuzzy Infrastructures. Major ML/DL techniques like clustering, AI systems, and swarm intelligence are not mentioned, though. They concentrate on the detection of network intrusions in their article. In order to access a wired connection, an intruder must get past numerous operating systems and security protections or physically enter the network.

2. Literature Review

Current machine learning and deep learning methods, controlled by deep, convolutional, and recursive brain organizations, have grown quickly with the accessibility of expanded computational power and huge assortments of information and have been utilized in different prescient and scientific applications for business and consumer use, like self-driving vehicle frameworks, normal language partners and mediators, and others. These applications are ground-breaking, empowering genuinely brilliant frameworks and propelling the cutting edge in different regions. As talked about in Area I, the advancement of IoT and CPS empowers brilliant applications through the assortment, stockpiling, and examination of huge, circulated datasets. In this part, we center around the utilization of machine learning technologies for positive purposes in cyber security and CPS [4, 5].

2.1 Similarities and Differences in ML and DL

Automation, machine learning, natural language processing, and intelligent agents are all being studied in this field. Artificial intelligence (AI) is capable of simulating human awareness and thought. Although behaving like a human could be more intelligent than human intelligence, AI is not real ingenuity. A machine learning technique called DL is focused on the characterization of data understanding. An observational object, for instance, a picture, can be described in many different ways, such as a data vector for every pixel's intensity value or, in an even more abstract model, as a collection of vertices, an area with a certain geometry, or something similar. The learning of activities from cases is facilitated by the use of specialized depictions [6]. DL approaches have "supervised learning" and "unsupervised learning," much like classification techniques. Various learning paradigms have produced learning methods that are very dissimilar. The advantage of DL is the effective replacement of elements automatically using multilayer morphological operations and "unsupervised" or "semi-supervised" feature learning.

Deep learning and conventional machine learning contrast mostly in how well they function as the volume of information grows. Due to the fact that algorithms using deep learning need a significant amount of information to fully grasp the information, they do not operate similarly when the data volumes are minimal [7]. On the other hand, in this instance, the outcome will be greater whenever the conventional machine-learning method follows the specified principles.

Hardware Requirements

There are several matrix manipulations needed by the DL technique. The GPU is frequently used to effectively optimize matrix computations. Consequently, the equipment required for the DL to function effectively is the GPU. DL is more dependent on powerful computers with GPUs than typical machine-learning techniques are. Analysis of features Pattern pre-processing is the practice of incorporating subject expertise into a feature representation to simplify the information and provide trends that improve the performance of learning algorithms. The procedure for the techniques described takes some time and necessitates expertise [8]. In ML, the majority of a software's attributes need to be specified by a professional before being coded as a dataset. A key distinction among DL and other machine-learning techniques is the attempt to explicitly extract elevated characteristics from input. As a result, DL lessens the effort required to create a feature extraction technique for each issue.

3. Methodology

Research methods can be considered the effective strategies, techniques, and processes that are utilized for procuring data to analyze the inner information and create a better understanding. According to the current topic, a secondary qualitative data collection method has been used. As per the secondary data collection method, different journals, books, and peer-reviewed articles have been used, and information has been collected from those materials by correctly assessing the whole thing. Different tables and figures have also been added to this context depending on the information collected from those secondary resources. Thus, a clear finding has been established.

4. Analysis and Findings

4.1 Network Security Data Set

An investigation into the security of computer networks is grounded in data. In most cases, there are two methods for collecting information on computer network security: immediately and by leveraging an already-existing dataset. Immediate connection refers to the utilization of numerous techniques for directly obtaining the necessary cyberspace material, such as utilizing software applications like Wireshark or Win Dump to record network activity. For gathering short-term or modest volumes of data, this technique is extremely focused and appropriate; however, for protracted or huge quantities of data, acquisition time and warehousing costs will increase [9]. By swiftly accessing the different types of information needed for investigation, the utilization of current network security statistics can minimize the time spent on information gathering and improve the effectiveness of studies.

4.2 DARPA Intrusion Detection Data Sets

The Cyber Systems and Engineering Unit (previously the DARPA Intrusion Detection Assessment Division) at MIT Lincoln Laboratories collects and publishes "DARPA Intrusion Detection Large Datasets", which are directed by DARPA and AFRL/SNHS and are used to assess computerized intranet intrusion detection technologies.

A significant quantity of ambient traffic information and assault statistics is provided by the first dataset. Immediate distribution is possible from the webpage.

4.3 KDD Cup 99 Dataset

Among the most popular classification models is the KDD Cup 99 database, which is inspired by the DARPA 1998 database. There are 4,900,000 repeated assaults in this database. The 22 attacking variants are broken down into five broad sections: DoS ("Denial of Service attacks"), R2L ("Root to Local attacks"), U2R ("User to Root attack"), Probe ("Probing attacks"), and Ordinary. There is only the ground type with the identification "ordinary. The KDD Cup 99 instructional database contains a class identification and 41 pre-processing step characteristics for every document. Seven of the distinctive features of the 41 fixed feature characteristics are of the metaphorical kind; the remainder are ongoing.

As stated in Table 25.1, additional functionality comprises essential properties (numbers 1 through 10) as well as content-bbased (numbers 11 through 22) and traffic statistics (numbers 23 through 41). It is possible to give a more accurate conceptual underpinning for vulnerability scanning by using the testing set, which contains certain types of malicious code that vanish in the training dataset.

Table 25.1   Features of KDD cup 99 dataset [9]

No.	Features	Types	No.	Features	Types
1	Duration	Continuous	22	Is_guest_login	Symbolic
2	Protocol_type	Symbiolic	23	Count	Continuous
3	Service	Symbiolic	24	Srv_count	Continuous
4	Flag	Symbiolic	25	Serror_rate	Continuous
5	Sre_bytes	Continuous	26	Srv_serror_rate	Continuous
6	Dst_bytes	Continuous	27	Rerrror_rate	Continuous
7	Land	Symbolic	28	Srv_rerror_rate	Continuous
8	Wrong_fragment	Continuous	29	Same_srv_rate	Continuous
9	Urgent	Continuous	30	Diff_srv_rate	Continuous
10	Hot	Continuous	31	Drv_diff_host_rate	Continuous
11	Num_failed_logins	Continuous	32	Dst_host_count	Continuous
12	Logged_in	Symbolic	33	Dst_host_srv_count	Continuous
13	Num_compromised	Continuous	34	Dst_host_same_srv_rate	Continuous
14	Root_shell	Continuous	35	Dst_host_diff_srv_rate	Continuous
15	Su_attempted	Continuous	36	Dst_host_same_sre_port_rate	Continuous
16	Num_shells	Continuous	37	Dst_host_srv_diff_host_rate	Continuous
17	Num_access_files	Continuous	38	Dst_host_serror_rate	Continuous
18	Num_shells	Continuous	39	Dst_host_srv_serror_rate	Continuous
19	Num_access_flies	Continuous	40	Dst_host_rerror_rate	Continuous
20	Num_outbound_cmds	Continuous	41	Dst_host_srv_rerror_rate	Continuous
21	Is_host_login	Symbolic			

4.4 ADFA Dataset

The "Australian Defence Academy" (ADFA) released the ADFA statistical model, a collection of hosting layer intrusion detection systems data sources that are often utilized in the assessment of "intrusion detection systems" (IDs). Better approach functions in the database have indeed been identified and labeled for this kind of exploitation. The collection of data contains two OS versions that track the sequence of operating systems: "Linux (ADFA-LD)" and "Windows (ADFA-WD)". As seen in the image, ADFA-LD is designated according to the type of assault. User space on a Linux platform uses access to the kernel to generate mild interruptions, which allow programs running in kernel mode to carry out the necessary activities. Each process has a related system identifier. There are 5 distinct attack kinds in it and 2 normal types, which are shown in Table 25.1.

Support Vector Machine

Among all "machine-learning" techniques, "Support Vector Machine" (SVM) is among the most reliable and precise. "Support Vector Classification" (SVC) and "Support Vector Regression" (SVR) make up the majority of it. The idea of decision boundaries forms the foundation of the SVC. A collection of occurrences with different possible values is divided into two categories by a bounding box. Both binary and multi-class categorizations are supported by the SVC. The separating classifier, which establishes the ideal detachment in higher-dimensional space, is nearest to the support vector [10]. In the classifier, the places on the characteristic space's opposite side of the detachment higher-dimensional space as well as the translation input vectors placed there belong to different classes. The technique yields a strong classification performance for U2R and R2L assaults as well as a high predictive performance for "Denial of Service" (DoS) operations. On the NSL-KDD vulnerability scanning database, scholars offer a screening approach that relies on a "Support Vector Machine" (SVM) decoder to choose several intruder categorization jobs. The scheme yields 99% classification performance with 36 attribute values, 91% classification accuracy with just 3 different characteristics, and a 99% accuracy rate with all 41 attribute values. With an F1-score of 0.99, the technique performed satisfactorily on the training dataset. However, the efficiency is poorer in the testing set; the F1-score is just 0.77. Poor generality prevents it from reliably identifying unexpected networking breaches. "Support vector machine (SVM)" is a "classification algorithm" that may be used in storage systems for binary and multiclass in both sequential and non-linear scenarios. The cornerstone of SVM was the creation of a flat higher-dimensional space or a collection of flat separating hyperplanes. The smallest intervals between the two base classifiers for each classification are created by the hyperplanes, which separate specific regions of the high- or infinite-dimensional feature space [11, 12]. The basic goal of SVM is to address algorithmic forecasting problems. The goal of an SVM is to build a modeling approach from the testing process that prepares for testing data, which only needs a portion of the given dataset. SVM uses a sizable representative sample to achieve its goal of producing predictions with the maximum level of accuracy.

"Decision tree"

A "decision tree" is a tree data structure where each leaf uniquely identifies a classification and each intermediate node in the graph represents an analysis on a single property, so each branching reflects the test outcome. The "decision tree" is a prediction model within learning algorithms that depicts a mapping between object properties and object outcomes. Every leaf node in the tree correlates to the item's value that is indicated by the route from the parent node towards the tree structure, so each of the tree's nodes indicates a conceivable parameter value [13]. The "decision tree" has just one output; if you need a complicated output, use a separate ""decision tree"" to manage each output separately. The "decision tree" algorithms ID3, C4.5, and CART are often employed. As seen in Fig. 25.1, the "decision tree" uses training conditions to classify the data and improves detection performance by trying to incorporate techniques; however, it is not appropriate for detecting unidentified intrusions.

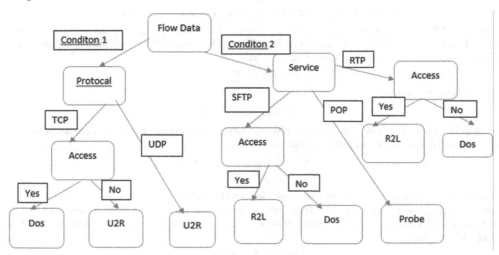

Fig. 25.1 Decision tree [14]

An example "decision tree"

Just on the NSL-KDD database, a different study employed C4.5 for intrusion detection. In this study, choosing characteristics and segmented levels are crucial concerns while creating "decision trees"; the technique is made to address each of these difficulties. The most pertinent features are picked using mutual information, and the segmented variables are set so that the classification is not biased toward the most prevalent values [14]. On the NSL-KDD dataset, 16 properties were chosen as features. The suggested "'decision tree' splitting (DTS)" technique may be applied to vulnerability scanning that is based on signatures. Therefore, this approach's accuracy is just 79.52%.

Recurrent Neural Networks

To analyze genetic sequences, a recursive neural network (RNN) is employed. The levels in the conventional model of neural networks are fully linked, and there is no relationship here between elements inside the layers. Data travels again from the hidden layer region to the activation function. There are several issues that this traditional neural network cannot resolve. The current output of a series is tied to the production that came before it, which is why an RNN is called a recursive neural network [15]. The network's ability to recall information from the previous instant and use it to determine the current outcome is the motivation behind utilizing it; the result of the input data as well as the most recent hidden layer result are included in the intake of the hidden units, which results in the connections seen between hidden units connecting. Any amount of sequence information in RNN could hypothetically be analyzed. To simplify things, it is frequently believed in practice that the present state is simply connected to the earlier states.

Researchers developed the dropout method, which uses exponentially unpredictable noise to randomize the hyperparameters for enhanced generalization. Further demonstrates that the prediction model may be randomized within the Bayesian network, allowing the model uncertainty to be represented as the variability of predictions. Researchers implement a dropout noise amplified by input in each layer after taking inspiration from this idea [20]. Researchers employ Gaussian noise and tweak it using a re-parameterization approach along with parameter estimation in a back-propagation way to gain improved fitness on the data. Researchers offer a volatility estimator to calculate model uncertainty for the prediction at inference time. Technically, observe that $\theta_j^l \sim q(1, \alpha_j^l)$ is the equivalent dropout

noise and x_j^l is the jth input in the lth layer. The result of this layer is then calculated as

$$y_i^l = \sigma \left(\sum_{j=1}^{J_l} W_{ij}^l \cdot \tilde{x}_j^l \right) \ , \ \tilde{x}_j^l = x_j^l \cdot \theta_j^l \tag{1}$$

where W^l is the weight vector, J_l is the intake vector, and $\alpha(.)$ is the perceptron. To maximise $\alpha = \alpha_j^l$ and $W = w^l$ is analogous to maximising the variational lower limit in the context of the Bayesian framework, as shown in (Eqn. 2), which strikes a balance across data probability and prior knowledge.

$$L(\alpha, W) = \sum (x, y) \in D \ p(y^L = y | x, \alpha, W) - KL(q(\ominus) \| p(\ominus)) \tag{2}$$

$K(q(\ominus) \| p(\ominus))$ and $\theta = \alpha_j^l$ is the Kullback-Leibler deviation from q to the prior p, and y^L is the modelling result. x is the input. Since there is no precedence for the prior of dropout noise in the domain of detecting attacks, researchers consider adopting the homogenous density on real value $\theta_j^l \sim p(\mathbb{R})$. Hence,

$$K(q(\ominus) \| p(\ominus)) = \sum_{i, j_2} \log(\alpha_j^l) \tag{3}$$

With the optimums obtained as:

$$\alpha^*, W^* = \arg \max L(\alpha, W) \tag{4}$$

The learned model's forecast is a random process that fits the dataset. Researchers offer an approximation for any input x to calculate the variation as model uncertainty as follows:

$$(\hat{x}) = \frac{\sum_{i=1}^N f(y^L(\ominus_i))}{N-1} \cdot \left(1 - \frac{\sum_{i=1}^N f(y^L(\ominus_i))}{N} \right) \tag{5}$$

The forecasting transfer function (.) yields the maximum's index (0,1) wherein $y^L(\ominus i)$ is the outcome predicated on the i-th sample for the dropout noise $\ominus$. $(\bar{y}^L)$(Eqn. 6) is a good option for questions pertaining to the projection itself. Additionally, researchers offer a quick replacement that is calculated as $(y^L(\Rightarrow [\ominus]))$, in which the system advances by setting the dropout noise as its average value.

$$(\bar{y}^L) = f \left(\tfrac{1}{N} \sum_{i=1}^N y^L (\ominus_i) \right) \tag{6}$$

Researchers utilise three criteria—detection rate, false alarm rate, and accuracy—to assess the efficacy of the technique for identifying Web assaults. To express the number of true positives, false positives, true negatives, and false negatives, correspondingly, they have used the terms TP, FP, TN, and FN in accordance with the conceptions frequently utilized in machine learning approaches. The percentage of identified anomalous inquiries that accounting for all abnormal responses is known as the detection accuracy (also known as the true positive rate). The ratio of the number of genuine normal inquiries that were mistakenly classified as abnormal to all legitimate normal requests is known as the false alarm rate (also known as false positive rate). A web attack detector should have high detection accuracy while also having a low false alarm rate. The percentage of queries that are accurately identified as normal or abnormal is known as the precision. The three criteria formulae are listed below.

$$Precision = \frac{TP}{TP + FP} \tag{7}$$

$$Recall = \frac{TP}{TP + FN} \tag{8}$$

$$Accuracy = \frac{TP + TN}{TP + FP + TN + FN} \tag{9}$$

$$F1\ Score = \frac{2 \cdot Recall \cdot Precision}{Recall + Precision} \tag{10}$$

5. Discussion and Future Direction

As demonstrated in Table 25.1, a substantial portion of academic research on intrusion detection has been conducted using deep learning and machine learning. Such research suggests several imbalances and some of the issues with this field of study, notably in the following regions: (i) The standard databases are rare, regardless of whether the same collection is utilised, and each institute uses a different technique of extraction procedure. (ii) The assessment measures are not consistent, many studies just evaluate the test's accuracy, and the outcome is biased. Furthermore, studies utilising multi-criteria assessment frequently use various metric configurations, making it impossible to evaluate the study findings between investigations [16].

6. Conclusion

Experts evaluate the progress made on ML and DL approaches for data security in this article. The paper emphasizes the three years before it as well as the far more current ML and DL approaches in the network monitoring field. Unfortunately, the ideal security testing method has not yet been discovered. The reviews of the different thoughts show that there are benefits and disadvantages to each approach for developing a system for intrusion detection. It might be difficult to decide which intrusion protection implementation and integration method to use. For the research and testing of platforms, anti-malware network datasets are essential. The ML and DL techniques cannot be employed in the absence of data sets; therefore, building such a collection is difficult and time-consuming. Furthermore, there are a number of problems with the current broadcast information, such as redundant content, inaccurate data, etc. These problems have severely limited the expansion of investigations in this sector.

The rapid alterations to network systems make it difficult to create and use DL and ML algorithms. Simulations need to be quickly and extensively trained as a consequence. Consequently, continuous learning and deep learning will be the focus of forthcoming studies in this field.

REFERENCES

1. Salloum, S.A., Alshurideh, M., Elnagar, A. and Shaalan, K., 2020, April. Machine learning and deep learning techniques for cybersecurity: a review. In *The International Conference on Artificial Intelligence and Computer Vision* (pp. 50–57). Springer, Cham.
2. Xin, Y., Kong, L., Liu, Z., Chen, Y., Li, Y., Zhu, H., Gao, M., Hou, H. and Wang, C., 2018. Machine learning and deep learning methods for cybersecurity. *Ieee access*, 6, pp. 35365–35381.
3. Liang, F., Hatcher, W.G., Liao, W., Gao, W. and Yu, W., 2019. Machine learning for security and the internet of things: the good, the bad, and the ugly. *IEEE Access*, 7, pp. 158126–158147.
4. Roopak, M., Tian, G.Y. and Chambers, J., 2019, January. Deep learning models for cyber security in IoT networks. In *2019 IEEE 9th annual computing and communication workshop and conference (CCWC)* (pp. 0452–0457). IEEE.
5. Dixit, P. and Silakari, S., 2021. Deep learning algorithms for cybersecurity applications: A technological and status review. *Computer Science Review*, 39, p.100317.
6. Sarker, I.H., Kayes, A.S.M., Badsha, S., Alqahtani, H., Watters, P. and Ng, A., 2020. Cybersecurity data science: an overview from machine learning perspective. *Journal of Big data*, 7(1), pp. 1–29.
7. Lv, Z., Qiao, L., Li, J. and Song, H., 2020. Deep-learning-enabled security issues in the internet of things. *IEEE Internet of Things Journal*, 8(12), pp. 9531–9538.

8. A. Jain, C. S. Kumar, Y. Shrivastava, (2021), "Fabrication and Machining of Fiber Matrix Composite through Electric Discharge Machining: A short review" Material Today Proceedings. https://doi.org/10.1016/j.matpr.2021.07.288

9. V. Panwar, D.K. Sharma, K.V.P.Kumar, A. Jain & C. Thakar, (2021), "Experimental Investigations And Optimization Of Surface Roughness In Turning Of EN 36 Alloy Steel Using Response Surface Methodology And Genetic Algorithm" Materials Today: Proceedings, https://Doi.Org/10.1016/J.Matpr.2021.03.642

10. Amanullah, M.A., Habeeb, R.A.A., Nasaruddin, F.H., Gani, A., Ahmed, E., Nainar, A.S.M., Akim, N.M. and Imran, M., 2020. Deep learning and big data technologies for IoT security. *Computer Communications*, *151*, pp. 495–517.

11. A. Jain, A. K. Pandey, (2019), "Multiple Quality Optimizations In Electrical Discharge Drilling Of Mild Steel Sheet" Material Today Proceedings, 8, 7252–7261. https://doi.org/10.1016/j.matpr.2017.07.054

12. A. Jain, A. K. Pandey, (2019), "Modeling And Optimizing Of Different Quality Characteristics In Electrical Discharge Drilling Of Titanium Alloy (Grade-5) Sheet" Material Today Proceedings, 18, 182–191. https://doi.org/10.1016/j.matpr.2019.06.292

13. A. Jain, A.K.Yadav & Y. Shrivastava (2019), "Modelling and Optimization of Different Quality Characteristics In Electric Discharge Drilling of Titanium Alloy Sheet" Material Today Proceedings, 21, 1680–1684. https://doi.org/10.1016/j.matpr.2019.12.010

14. Ghanem K, Aparicio-Navarro FJ, Kyriakopoulos KG, Lambotharan S, Chambers JA. Support vector machine for network intrusion and cyber-attack detection. Paper presented at: Proceedings of the Sensor Signal Processing for Defence Conference (SSPD). London, UK: IEEE; 2017: 1–5. doi:https://doi.org/10.1109/SSPD.2017.8233268..

15. A. Jain, A. K. Pandey, (2019), "Modeling And Optimizing Of Different Quality Characteristics In Electrical Discharge Drilling Of Titanium Alloy (Grade-5) Sheet" Material Today Proceedings, 18, 182–191. https://doi.org/10.1016/j.matpr.2019.06.292

16. V. Panwar, D.K. Sharma, K.V.P.Kumar, A. Jain & C. Thakar, (2021), "Experimental Investigations And Optimization Of Surface Roughness In Turning Of EN 36 Alloy Steel Using Response Surface Methodology And Genetic Algorithm" Materials Today: Proceedings, https://Doi.Org/10.1016/J.Matpr.2021.03.642

Computer Science Engineering and Emerging Technologies (ICCS-2022) – Prof (Dr.) Rajeev Sobti et al. (eds)
© 2024 Taylor & Francis Group, London, ISBN 978-1-032-52199-2

Chapter

26

A Detailed Investigation of Artificial Intelligence Applications in Cyber Security

Mukesh Madanan*

Lecturer-Department of Computer Science, Dhofar University, Oman

Abstract: In the modern world, safeguarding against cyberattacks has emerged as a crucial and urgent concern that includes safeguarding the computer system from potential dangers. The development of new prevention methods is necessary due to the increased cyber dangers brought on by technological development. The fundamental cause of the rise in cyberattacks against businesses is the growing reliance on digital media, which results in the storage of financial and individual data. Due to the fact that it not only results in economic damage but also generates the release of sensitive knowledge, it is therefore regarded as one of the most significant difficulties in the contemporary environment. "Artificial intelligence (AI)" is a useful tool for lessening the effects of cyberattacks. AI is the ability of machines to carry out human-like functions. When making decisions, such as when conducting medical diagnoses or drawing conclusions from experience, the knowledge of human specialists is incorporated. Moving in the right direction, AI enhances defence mechanisms, fosters privacy in cyberspace, and dramatically improves information security. Machine learning is now being used more frequently for malware analysis and network fault detection as a result of AI.

Keywords: Cyberattacks, Artificial intelligence (AI), Technology, Cybersecurity

1. Introduction

Cybersecurity lowers the possibility of losing crucial data, yet cyberattacks have proliferated and gotten stronger. A 2014 "Consumer News and Business Channel (CNBC)" research study estimated that cybercrimes cost the world economy $400 billion annually. The weakest link and primary cause of cybersecurity vulnerability is the human element. Automated technologies, including artificial intelligence (AI) implementations, are used in cyber security to solve this issue. Researchers have looked at cybersecurity alongside AI from a variety of angles. The use of AI is gaining popularity worldwide. Even in nations where there is little study in this area, it is well-liked. It is suggested that AI is a component of the fourth industrial transformation. It is used in a variety of industries, including disaster relief, medical, transportation, economics, administration, and business practices, combining an intelligent system with fuzzy rules to satisfy crucial data requirements for thwarting cyber-terrorist attacks [1]. To show how these strategies may be helpful, experts examine the developments achieved in the use of AI tools to combat cybercrime. To determine how safe a system is and identify its potential weaknesses, a cyber security audit of remote monitoring systems is necessitated. Since the mid-2000s, when cyberattacks started to rise, there has been excessive growth in cyber security. It is essential to use scientometric approaches to visually analyze the hotspots as well as emerging technologies in AI applications for cyber security [2].

The historical shifts in the field and the evolving trajectory of AI technologies in cyber security are also noted in this paper. It serves as a resource for research areas and applied advancements of AI technologies in cyber security in the near future. Sooner than later, as machine intelligence (MI) algorithms improve, people will begin to see more automated and

*mukesh@du.edu.om

DOI: 10.1201/9781003405580-26

increasingly sophisticated social engineering attacks. A wave of system intrusions, data thefts of personal information, and a pandemic-level spread of sophisticated PC viruses are expected to result from the rise of AI-powered cyberattacks. Funny enough, we want to use AI to defend against hacking that is enabled by AI [3]. However, this will likely lead to an AI arms race, the outcomes of which might be quite unsettling in the long run, especially when powerful governments become involved in the cyberwars. I'm looking at the intersection between cybersecurity and AI. Researchers are specifically looking at how people can protect AI frameworks from bad fictional characters as well as how experts can protect people from hostile or vengeful AI. This effort, which is part of a larger framework of AI security, aims to create extremely capable AI that is both advantageous and safe. Even nowadays, AI may be used to defend and attack cyber underpinnings as well as to increase the number of entry points for developers into a structure or the attacking area that they can target [4].

While many organizations are still using human efforts to complete internal security findings and combine them with external cybersecurity threats, cyber-aggressors are using automation technologies to launch attacks. These traditional methods might necessitate several weeks or months to identify disruptions, during which time attackers can take advantage of weaknesses to compromise systems and gather information. Proactive organizations are looking towards using AI in their routine cyber risk management activities to deal with these problems. According to the "Verizon Data Breach Report", more than 70% of attacks take advantage of vulnerabilities that have fixes available [5]. The discoveries show that programmers take advantage of flaws that are close to becoming conspicuously exposed in the meantime. These observations emphasize how important time is for remediation. In any event, it is not surprising that efforts to fix weaknesses are not keeping up with cyber adversaries given the shortage of security professionals and the overall challenge of handling huge informational collections in cybersecurity. Recent industry research shows that it typically takes organizations 146 days to fix fundamental vulnerabilities. This measure makes it quite clear that researchers need to reconsider how people currently approach large-scale company security [6]. The rise of cloud and mobile technologies, together with hyper-associated work settings, has sparked a chain reaction in terms of security threats. The vast quantities of connected devices feeding into networks provide cybercriminals with an ideal position, giving them many fresh access points to attack. Additionally, the protection at these admission points is generally insufficient. The most significant DDoS attack or mega-breach that made headlines and raised concerns prevents organizations from utilizing IoT [7]. However, the flexibility and computerization the IoT possesses suggest it isn't a flimsy trend. Businesses must look to recent developments, like AI, to successfully safeguard their customers as they expand internationally.

2. Literature Review

2.1 Potential Applications of AI in Cyber Security Applications

User Access Authentication

Criteria for access permission identification The platform must improve the administration of access control authorization, precisely identify all types of camouflage behaviors, and enable the identification of illicit or harmful items in its role as the first line of defense in cyber security. The system needs to make sure individuals are verified prior to going into activity. In addition, user information ought to be kept private to avoid additional risky situations like fraudulent user data acquisition.

Figure 26.1 demonstrates that one area of study in the existing authentication system focuses on enhancing the distinctiveness of the password recognition process in order to reduce the likelihood of other individuals passing for legitimate customers [8].

The problem in mode identification is to figure out how to match passwords and add additional selected features to assure the integrity of double verification. For instance, modern ATMs exclusively require PIN numbers to verify users' identities. The integrity of verification cannot be guaranteed by using this single method. Due to the drawbacks of one-time verification, multimodal authorization techniques have been studied. Scholars have employed Random Forest to accomplish this. In addition to performing credential verification in the credential authentication scheme, scholars are trained on the user's keyboards using a neural network and a few different keyboard layouts [9]. The user's typing skills, manner, key sequence, and other factors were among such patterns. Although less data was utilized in the simulation, scholars created a kernel function including both local and worldwide functionalities and developed a mobile communication network protection authentication mechanism relying on "Support Vector Regression" (SVR). Keystroke dynamics trend identification was achieved by using "one-class support vector machine" (one-Class SVM), and this trend has gained a lot of interest as a result of AI. To create a physiological verification system, scholars used "reinforcement learning", 'transfer learning", and "convolutional neural networks" (CNN). It was employed to fend against rogue edge assaults and was targeted at mobile cloud computing [10].

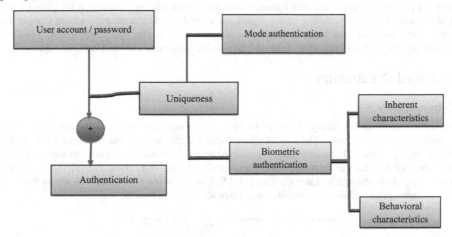

Fig. 26.1 Existing authentication system

Source: [10]

Cases of Biometric Authentication

"Biometric authentication" has drawn more attention than mode identification due to its distinctiveness, non-replicability, inheritance, and invariance. It was required to ascertain whether the opposing participant is an AI or a human operator in order to secure the networking security and safety of collaboration. Hence, the "reverse Turing test" was required (a group of problems that can be solved by humans but not by computers).

To stop individuals from brushing it off as a person after identifying whether it's a computer or a person, individuals must be verified. Currently, identification is mostly reliant on biological traits (like fingerprints, irises, etc.) and behavioral traits (like voice, movement, etc.), as well as the potent self-learning capabilities of AI that can effectively utilize them [11]. Scholars have presented a fingerprint identification approach that relies on sparse proximity in the area of fingerprint scanners. A fingerprint feature point identification approach utilizing artificial neural networks (ANN) and comparing the proximity among feature points was developed by scientists, and the learning rate was sped up using hardware. The paper omitted performance assessment, nevertheless.

The "Extreme Learning Machine" (ELM) with RBF kernel was based on modified "Histograms of Oriented Gradients" (HOG) descriptors. Despite removing characteristics, scholars are presented with an end-to-end identification system based on CNN. The framework for image recognition relies on CNN [12]. The triple-state regression model was enhanced, and the characteristics derived from the clear and fuzzy images were shared. To achieve contoured facial recognition software, an ANN that relies on local binary mode is employed. In order to recognize facial expressions, a hybrid genetic feature learning network is used. Several measurement approaches and the Scale Invariant Features Transform (SIFT) for the iris identification component A novel technique was put out by scholars to capture more iris characteristics using dilated convolution, and the model was tested using a variety of assessment techniques. For iris identification, scholars employed the Deep Convolutional Neural Network (DCNN). Scholars employed "genetic and evolutionary feature extraction technology", an additional method integrating AI and extraction and classification technology, to extract the pictures' most significant aspects (small sizes). "Multi-layer ELM", "multi-layer CNN", "fully CNN (FCN)", "transfer learning", and other techniques might be applied to obtain a classification from the viewpoint of the finger vein [13]. "Recurrent Neural Networks" (RNNs) have an essential function in the field of voice commands, according to scholars.

3. Research Methodology

Any academic study's approach can be thought of as its foundation. It includes a clear discussion grounded in logic as well as a methodical study of the various ways scholars have described gathering secondary and primary data. It can also serve as the strongest support for the entire study, serving as a guide for selecting the right methods and tools for enticing reliable information. In addition, a variety of methodological strategies are used to collect pertinent data in keeping with a certain research topic. In the current research approach, post-positivism has been utilized as the basis for a true logical examination of the study findings. Authentic books, significant journals, and research papers from Google Scholar were critically examined for this study, which used a secondary qualitative approach for data collection. As a result, it has been found that an econometric analysis can gather impressive knowledge from both relevant ideas and genuine realities.

4. Analysis and Discussion

4.1 AI in Cybersecurity

A DT is a guideline tree-structured binary classifier in which each branch depicts a possible outcome for a feature and each vertex (node) represents a feature. The root of a tree, located at the summit and including the best accuracy gain (discrepancies in entropy) across all characteristics, is employed to divide training examples into segments that are ideally balanced. The leaves are the nodes at the bottom. Every leaf stands for a different class. The DT follows the example that has to be classified top-down throughout categorization [14, 15]. The following is the information gain formula utilized in a DT to divide occurrences in the best way possible using a tree-structured approach:

$$\text{Gain}(P, Q) = \text{Entropy}(P) - \sum_{v \in D_Q} \frac{|P_v|}{|P|} \text{Entropy}(P_v) \tag{1}$$

$G(P, Q)$ represents the decrease in entropy that results from sorting P on feature Q. A top-down approach is used to choose the vertices, which are characteristics with enhanced information value obtained. In order to increase the buffer between the hyper-plane and the closest set of information, the hyper-plane is selected. Assume the hyper-plane, b, which was produced by N pieces of data, and in which (x_1, y_1) and (x_2, y_2), and $((w)$ are weights and (b) is biassed, correspondingly (x_n, y_n)

$$M = \frac{2}{|w|} \tag{2}$$

The Naive Bayes classifiers are a probabilistic-based supervised learning approach, calculates the probability of a class given all attribute values. The Bayes rule serves as the foundation for the Naive Bayes classifier, sometimes referred to as the forecasting model. This categorization calculates the prior distribution of a category, $p(b_{ja})$, given the prior probability of all classifications, or p, and the conditional dispersion of all features, or $p(a_{jb})$. The term "naive" is employed because every trait individually influences how likely a class is to exist:

$$(b|a) = \frac{p(a,b)}{p(a)} = \frac{p(a|b)p(b)}{p(a)} \tag{3}$$

where a and b are, respectively, the integral gain and the categorization matrix. The main advantage of the Naive Bayes classification algorithm is its ability to handle noisy training data without decreasing performance.

K-means segmentation, one of the unsupervised machine learning (ML) approaches, aims to locate specific groupings in the dataset given k as the number of cluster components. Clusters are built and used the shared characteristics of all the database's pieces of data. In order to determine the number of cluster centres, k, m data sets are initially employed. The nearest cluster centres are then identified employing Formula (4)'s Euclidean distances for each of the m pieces of data x_1, $x_2 \ldots \ldots . x_n$.

$$\text{distance} = \sum_{i=1}^{m}(x_i, \text{entroid } (x_i)) \tag{4}$$

Centroid (x_i) indicates the median whereby the x_i element of data relates. The defined as the distance from all the datasets assigned to those cluster centres is used to renew the cluster centres in the subsequent stages. The process repeats these steps until no further data may possibly modify any cluster centres. Minimize the distance among each centre and the related data elements inside a clustering is the goal. Clustering algorithms are widely used in the setting of AI, where categorising data has become a difficult task, to find patterns in the data or groups [16]. One of the problems with k-means clustering is that the k value must be chosen at the beginning. Since K-means clustering performs features matching calculations, it has been frequently used in surveillance systems. Artificial neural systems (ANNs) extremities (perceptron's) are patterned like the brain's neurons [17]. Processing elements, hidden units, and output units are the three levels of an ANN. There could be more than one hidden state, relying on the algorithmic framework. The conclusion is seen in the output layer after every tier has similarly communicated its signal to the hidden units and the next levels. Prior to the SVM's invention in 1990, ANNs were widely used. In the field of cybersecurity, "convolution," "feed-forward," and "recurrent neural networks" have all gained popularity. The ANN, called y, provides outputs for input data $(x_1, x_2 \ldots \ldots x_n)$, where throughout learning opportunity the required information is evaluated by a weight matrices $(w_1, w_2 \ldots \ldots w_n)$. During in the process of learning, the weights are adjusted to reduce the retraining losses, $E = Pn_i = 1$, that represent the discrepancy between the predicted output (d_i) and the ultimate effect (y_i) of the neuronal. This update employs back-propagation, a gradients approach, and repeated retraining till the role in accomplishing an inaccuracy that falls below its minimum threshold. The binary image is changed using the equation below:

$$w_{i,j} \leftarrow w_{i,j} + \Delta w_{i,j} \tag{5}$$

where $w_{i,j} = \eta \delta jxi$ When i is the inputs nodes and j is the hidden nodes.

The metrics used this to assess how well AI -based cybersecurity appears to be performing in this research project include "accuracy" (ACC), "precision" (p), "false alarm rate" (FAR), "true positive rate" (TPR), "false positive rate" (FPR), "selectivity", "receiver operating characteristics curve" (ROC), "area under the curve" (AUC), and "FF1 Score". These metrics can be computed using a clustering method or matrices representation of the classification results. The numbers of assaults and properly detected routine data are denoted, correspondingly, by the acronyms "True Positive" (TP) and "True Negative" (TN), False Positive" (FP) and "False Negative" (FN) show, correspondingly. the number of reports of assaults and unclassified data that were incorrectly classified. The percentage of forecasted categorised cases to all evaluated events is known as the "accurate classification rate" (ACC):

$$ACC = \frac{TP + TN}{TP + TN + FP + FN} \tag{1}$$

P is the ratio of correctly classified objects to all anticipated items.

$$p = \frac{TP}{TP + FP} \tag{2}$$

FAR is the ratio of things that were incorrectly classified as being in class C to all the other items.

$$FAR = \frac{FP}{TP + FN} \tag{3}$$

The TPR, which is also referred to by the names sensitivity, accuracy rate, probabilities of detection, and recall, calculates the percentage of items correctly classified as belonging to class C (attack or normal) compared to all the items in the sample.

$$TPR = \frac{TP}{TP + FN} \tag{4}$$

FPR refers for the ratio of falsely classified items (attack or normal) to all falsely classified objects in class C.

$$FPR = \frac{FP}{TP + FP} \tag{5}$$

Precision refers to the ratio of correctly recognised objects as pertaining to a subclass other than class C to all other objects. In relation to FPR, it is as follows:

TN

$$\text{Specificity} = 1 - FPR = \frac{TN}{TN + FP} \tag{6}$$

The ROC curve is obtained by plotting TPR across FPR. The location of a classification in the ROC space corresponds to how well it operates within a certain range. The ROC curve graphically illustrates the trade-off among categorization's benefits and drawbacks with respect to data dispersion. AUC represents the region below the ROC curve (values range between 0 and 1). It measures the degree of differentiation and assists in determining whether the framework likewise distinguishes between categories.

$$F_1 = \frac{2TP}{2TP + FP + FN} \tag{7}$$

4.2 Dangerous Behaviour Monitoring

The offensive techniques used by cybercriminals are continually evolving, along with emerging innovations like big data and cloud computing. Hackers are dedicated to locating "lethal spots" in the system and launching assaults on it at any moment, as a result of the fast development in storage capacity and the expansion of broadband internet. The initial intrusion detection devices were not able to adjust to the channel's features. Increased data flow also makes it easier to detect hacker activity, which has become crucial support for proactive safety precautions. Monitoring risky actions and their kinds instantaneously is necessary for achieving computer security with precise procedures. A condition of "emergency medical care" would otherwise arise, which would effectively safeguard the system but use a significant amount of resources. To do this, investigators have begun to enhance and develop on the basis of the original intrusion detection algorithms in order to render the intrusion prevention devices' current network needs as adaptable as feasible. A novel decentralized massive network anomalous behavior detection approach was identified by scholars. It reduced the dimensionality of the large-scale network traffic database and used dispersed DBN to find anomalous behaviors by combining deep feature extraction with "multi-layer integrated support vector machine" (SVM). The benefits of AI can significantly reduce a range of targeted attacks against the network [18]. With the arrival of the 5G period, several academics have been researching how 5G technologies might identify anomalies. For instance, academics have suggested an adaptable deep learning-based 5G network system for identifying anomalies. Two layers of deep neural networks were employed in this foundation: the first was concentrated on the technique of using the internet backbone for aggregation identification to easily search for unusual signs, and it primarily uses "Deep Neural Network" (DNN) for computation; the second was concentrated on the technique of using the network for aggregation identification to easily search for anomalous indications; The other method relied on the connection among the chronology and clinical manifestations to find connectivity abnormalities, and after doing so, it spoke immediately with the surveillance and diagnostic units. To effectively handle time-sseries data, the "Long Short-Term Memory" (LSTM) was created [19].

4.3 Maliciously Modified Model

Software that implements an AI model might be susceptible in various ways. These weaknesses might be the result of the model's structured design being designed in an illogical and negligent manner by the creator. They could result from difficulties with certain technologies, issues with specific high-level languages, or a vulnerability built into the system. Because it added a backdoor to the neural network, it performed terribly against the specific attacker's instance. These flaws also have the effect of making it so that the project's suggested responses are not always correct.

4.4 The Development of Human-in-the-loop

AI is being developed and put into practice, and neural networks in particular, in an effort to mimic brain activity. Its goal was to mimic human thinking processes by interconnecting neurons. Sadly, AI requires a lot of information to understand, as well as the capacity to reason, so the final version after training is difficult to comprehend. comprehend how it makes judgments. This work is still in its early stages, despite several attempts to identify an understanding of AI. Consequently, relying solely on these instruments without human involvement is far from sufficient to make efficient use of knowledge. Network capacity activities are prevented and detected in part by AI, but there are several unfavorable circumstances that can influence how AI makes decisions. The AI in this field is not meant to take over the job of security researchers but to support people [20]. As a result, it remains required for pertinent professionals to step in and utilize their best expertise to assess the existing network's shape. A new sort of AI called human-in-the-loop is currently being researched. The DARPA robotics challenge (DRC), created in 2017, was a physical manifestation of the concept of human-machine collaboration. DARPA unveiled the AI program KAIROS in January 2019 with the goal of developing a technology that could recognize occurrences and draw the public's attention. This government launched the ACE initiative in May to build combined human-machine aerial combat capacity. This new technology's development has started in the field of the military, which also reflects how important it is. An essential way to actualize the complementing benefits of humans and machines is the "person-in-the-loop" concept, which might integrate human knowledge with intelligent systems. A significant amount of information can be processed quickly by AI, and it has strong visual recognition abilities. It may, nonetheless, be unsettled and misjudge the brand-new circumstance. Humans are more adaptable than robots and therefore can make choices more quickly in the midst of topology changes, yet they also depend on technology for support. Cybersecurity has adopted participatory machine learning, which has been employed in AI. The capacity to discover program side-channel hazards, for instance, may be significantly improved by the employment of human-in-the-loop monitoring. Although attaining visualization was important, including this concept in spatial awareness also improved the program's dependability. Therefore, the capacity of the algorithms will also be enhanced by the employment of AI and "humans in the loop" in cyber security.

4.5 Machine Detection Module (MDM)

MDM serves the "leadership role" in HLCSM. MDM will convert the raw information into high-risk occurrences, which might also involve activities such as data cleansing and normalization. The extraction of characteristics from information is critical whenever the information is consistent. Along with other variables that have minimal association, the statistics include the crucial information of event type and location. In order to execute jobs rapidly as big data grows, it is vital to pick characteristics and minimize dimensionality. Following the extraction of features from the data, it is passed to the identification technique, which is a crucial link in MDM. The recognition rate won't be greater than necessary until the chosen approach satisfies the criteria. The "confidence level module" (CLM) will evaluate the operating conclusion after the identification outcome is supplied, and according to its value, it will evaluate if the final outcome is based on MDM. Two identification techniques are applied in MDM [20]. The current usage of a singular identification technique does not provide total trustworthiness of the output, as a result of which neural networks might introduce backdoors. As a consequence, knowledge and experience serve as the judgment foundation in MDM architecture, while two recognition techniques are employed to create the judgment outcomes concurrently. To improve the variety of judgment approaches, the judgment approaches employed for these two ways ought to be as dissimilar as feasible. The difficulty of elusion can be raised, as can the reliability of the outcome, by employing two classification models. CLM will manage both of the two generated outputs.

4.6 Manual Intervention Module (MIM)

MIM performs an "auxiliary role" in HLCSM. Whenever MDM produces disappointing results, MIM should indeed be provided with processing capability. The occurrence will be managed using experience after the security professionals have received the analysis of the collected data. The final decision regarding whether the activity is secure will be made by the safety experts without the involvement of MDM. Expanding MDM with the outcomes of MIM analysis is important due to the ambiguity in the categories of remote operations and in order to boost the processing capability of MDM. Data validation by professionals is also necessary after providing the final result. To fulfill the goal of growing MDM, new types of events are introduced to the knowledge base via extracting features [20].

4.7 Flow Chart of HLCSM

Figure 26.2 depicts the model's flow diagram in order to more effectively illustrate how well the components of the HLCSM relate to one another. The flow chart shows that following the judgment of the occurrence, certain follow-up work must be done, i.e., if it is an elevated occurrence, quarantined and other measures should indeed be undertaken; if it is a security occurrence, the activity must be stopped. A current network event defense framework will be created by doing this. The concept of "human-in-the-loop" is realized in HLASM. It is accomplished by MDM and MIM working together, as determined by LCM. According to this theory, AI will continue to cause problems despite its rapid advancement. Humans

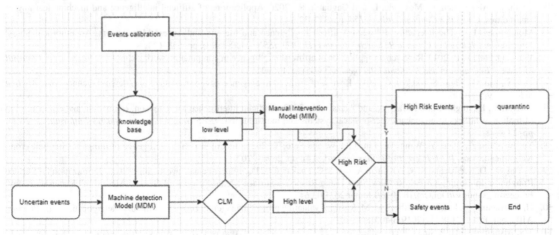

Fig. 26.2   Flow chart of HLCSM

Source: [20]

shouldn't be fully replaced by AI; rather, it should empower them. Since MDM handles the majority of the duties in this architecture, it is not necessary to employ a sizable number of security professionals. This can lower the cost of spending and manpower deployment. To more effectively withstand the quick shifts in the current distributed system, this activity requires security experts owing to the uniqueness of the utilized surroundings. More event types can be handled by MDM by growing the knowledge base. This enlargement method requires the use of MIM as an adjunct. The knowledge base must be modified to accommodate quick searches once it reaches a certain size. This model doesn't take this design into account. On the one hand, the issue of an inaccurate sole identification technique can be resolved by using two recognition systems. On the other hand, deploying too many classification methods won't put undue stress on the CLM unit [20].

The identification process is currently more complicated; thus, the local device requires additional processing capability. Additionally, adding to the stress on the device's functioning is the use of many processing algorithms simultaneously. However, even though cloud computing and other innovations might ease this load, it is not advised that the procedure instructions be conducted remotely in order to lessen vulnerability. The interim "translation" task is also crucial in order to achieve human-machine interaction. LCM assumes this duty and performs the function of human-computer interaction. Realizing the complementing benefits of both, which would be precisely the initial purpose of our approach, is the essence of human-machine interaction. A simulation has to have complete "communication" if it hopes to attain a high level of synchronization amongst them. A crucial connection that can't be established via human-machine contact is the confidence level's connection between human and machine interaction. The reciprocal collaboration between both the individual and the technology will be directly affected by the fulfillment of this relationship.

5. Conclusion

Since AI has promising importance for use in cyber security systems, it is crucial for the researchers and practitioners' communities to comprehend the situation as it is now and the difficulties that surround it. This research thus analysed studies concerning the use of AI in key areas of cyber security: user access authentication, monitoring of harmful conduct, and anomalous traffic identification. The study asserted the significance of "human-in-the-loop," offered a conceptual framework, and described how it may be used. It also described the research obstacles and possibilities. As a result, a further task will be to apply and assess the suggested conceptual framework in conjunction with an organization.

REFERENCES

1. Alhayani, B., Mohammed, H. J., Chaloob, I. Z. and Ahmed, J. S., 2021. Effectiveness of artificial intelligence techniques against cyber security risks apply of IT industry. *Materials Today: Proceedings.*
2. Khisamova, Z. I., Begishev, I. R. and Sidorenko, E. L., 2019. Artificial intelligence and problems of ensuring cyber security. *International Journal of Cyber Criminology, 13*(2), pp. 564–577.
3. Ullah, Z., Al-Turjman, F., Mostarda, L. and Gagliardi, R., 2020. Applications of artificial intelligence and machine learning in smart cities. *Computer Communications, 154*, pp. 313–323.
4. Mohammed, I.A., The Interaction Between Artificial Intelligence and Identity and Access Management: An Empirical Study. *International Journal of Creative Research Thoughts (IJCRT), ISSN, 2320*(2882), pp. 668–671.
5. Wang, Q. and Lu, P., 2019. Research on application of artificial intelligence in computer network technology. *International Journal of Pattern Recognition and Artificial Intelligence, 33*(05), p. 1959015.
6. Qiu, S., Liu, Q., Zhou, S. and Wu, C., 2019. Review of artificial intelligence adversarial attack and defense technologies. *Applied Sciences, 9*(5), p. 909.
7. Farivar, F., Haghighi, M.S., Jolfaei, A. and Alazab, M., 2019. Artificial intelligence for detection, estimation, and compensation of malicious attacks in nonlinear cyber-physical systems and industrial IoT. *IEEE transactions on industrial informatics, 16*(4), pp. 2716–2725.
8. Yu, K., Guo, Z., Shen, Y., Wang, W., Lin, J. C. W. and Sato, T., 2021. Secure artificial intelligence of things for implicit group recommendations. *IEEE Internet of Things Journal, 9*(4), pp. 2698–2707.
9. V. Panwar, D. K. Sharma, K. V. P. Kumar, A. Jain & C. Thakar, (2021), "Experimental Investigations And Optimization Of Surface Roughness In Turning Of EN 36 Alloy Steel Using Response Surface Methodology And Genetic Algorithm" Materials Today: Proceedings, https://Doi.Org/10.1016/J.Matpr.2021.03.642
10. H. J. Mohammed, I. A. M. Al-Jubori, M. M. Kasim, Evaluating project management criteria using fuzzy analytic hierarchy Process, AIP Conf. Proc., 2138 (1) (2019) 040018(1–6).
11. T.S. Alshammari, H. P. Singh, Preparedness of Saudi Arabia to Defend Against Cyber Crimes: An Assessment with Reference to Anti-Cyber Crime Law and GCI Index, Arch. Bus. Res., 6 (12) (2018).

12. A. Szychter, H. Ameur, A. Kung, H. Daussin, The Impact of Artificial Intelligence on Security: a Dual Perspective, Taylor & Francis Taylor & Francis Group http://taylorandfrancis. com, 2018.
13. A. Jain, A. K. Pandey, (2019), "Modeling And Optimizing Of Different Quality Characteristics In Electrical Discharge Drilling Of Titanium Alloy (Grade-5) Sheet" Material Today Proceedings, 18, 182–191. https://doi.org/10.1016/j.matpr.2019.06.292
14. A. Jain, A. K. Yadav & Y. Shrivastava (2019), "Modelling and Optimization of Different Quality Characteristics In Electric Discharge Drilling of Titanium Alloy Sheet" Material Today Proceedings, 21, 1680–1684. https://doi.org/10.1016/j.matpr.2019.12.010
15. H. J. Mohammed, M. M. Kasim, E. A. AL-Dahneem, A. K. Hamadi, An analytical survey on implementing best practices for introducing e-learning programs to students, J. Educ. Soc. Sci., 5 (2) (2016) 191–196.
16. A. Jain, A. K. Pandey, (2019), "Modeling And Optimizing Of Different Quality Characteristics In Electrical Discharge Drilling Of Titanium Alloy (Grade-5) Sheet" Material Today Proceedings, 18, 182–191. https://doi.org/10.1016/j.matpr.2019.06.292
17. A. Jain, A. K. Pandey, (2019), "Multiple Quality Optimizations In Electrical Discharge Drilling Of Mild Steel Sheet" Material Today Proceedings, 8, 7252–7261. https://doi.org/10.1016/j.matpr.2017.07.054
18. H. J. Mohammed, E. AL-dahneem, A. Hamadi, A comparative analysis for adopting an innovative pedagogical approach of flipped teaching for active classroom learning, J. Glob. Bus. Soc. Entrep., 3 (5) (2016) 86–94.
19. V. Panwar, D. K. Sharma, K. V. P. Kumar, A. Jain & C. Thakar, (2021), "Experimental Investigations And Optimization Of Surface Roughness In Turning Of EN 36 Alloy Steel Using Response Surface Methodology And Genetic Algorithm" Materials Today: Proceedings, https://Doi.Org/10.1016/J.Matpr.2021.03.642
20. A. Jain, C. S. Kumar, Y. Shrivastava, (2021), "Fabrication and Machining of Fiber Matrix Composite through Electric Discharge Machining: A short review" Material Today Proceedings. https://doi.org/10.1016/j.matpr.2021.07.288

Computer Science Engineering and Emerging Technologies (ICCS-2022) – Prof (Dr.) Rajeev Sobti et al. (eds)
© 2024 Taylor & Francis Group, London, ISBN 978-1-032-52199-2

Chapter

27

Use of Blockchain Technologies Against Cyber Security Threats and Increase IT Industry Security

Tejo Lakshmi Gudipalli[1]
Assistant Professor, Department of CSE,
KKR & KSR Institute of Technology and Sciences, Vinjanampadu, Guntur, Andhra Pradesh

Dipesh Uike[2]
Professor, Dr. Ambedkar Institute of Management Studies and Research

Gaikwad Anil Pandurang[3]
Assistant Professor, Department of MCA, JSPM's Jayawantrao Sawant College of Engineering,
(Savitribai Phule Pune University Maharashtra) S. No. 58, Indrayani Nagar, Handewadi Road, Hadapsar, Pune

Ripon Bhattacharjee[4]
Associate Professor, Department of Law, University of Engineering and Management, Kolkata, West Bengal

Nishakar Kankalla[5]
Associate Professor, ECE Department, St. Martin's Engineering College, JNTUH University

Firos A.[6]
Assistant Professor, Department of computer Science and Engineering Rajiv Gandhi University
(A Central University), Rono-Hills, Doimukh, Arunachal Pradesh, India

Abstract: This study looks into how blockchain technology is being used in business today and in the future, namely in the IT and cybersecurity sectors. Additionally, it links Blockchain's applications to contemporary concerns in the IT and cybersecurity industries. After reviewing the literature on topics like Big Data for the IT industry, the use of blockchain in economic freedom as well as cybersecurity, and its application in the financial IT sector employing record creation and as a method for detecting financial misbehaviour. In order to understand how the United States Government plans due to the relevance of cybersecurity advancement, it also examines the Department of Country Security's cybersecurity plan for the ensuing two years. It demonstrates how Blockchain has a variety of effects on auditing that will alter the profession. Additionally, it concludes that several aspects of cybersecurity and the IT sector, such as monitoring and fundamental IT industry approaches, should implement blockchain. Different IT industry innovations, such as artificial intelligence, the web of things, big data, and blockchain, have been the subject of research lately to see if they could produce significant breakthroughs. These developments open up new opportunities in the fields of supply chains and assembly. Blockchain is a technology that has gained a lot of attention and can improve the network environment for production and assembly.

Keywords: Hyperledger, Intellectual property (IP), Cybersecurity

[1]tejolakshmi.gudipalli@gmail.com, [2]dipeshuike@gmail.com, [3]anilgaikwad2@gmail.com, [4]bhattacharjeeripon99@gmail.com, [5]nishakarece@smec.ac.in, [6]firos.a@rgu.ac.in

DOI: 10.1201/9781003405580-27

1. Introduction

In the ongoing situation, it is important to comprehend blockchain and its incentive for the powerful execution of the IT industry. A few fields enjoy planned benefits for blockchain, such as monetary exchange applications in which blockchains can give belief. Government-issued currency and unfamiliar monetary rules are outlawed, and there may be a regulated stock exchange. The object itself and the distinctive proof component of its collection can also be related to various Blockchain applications in the IT sector. Information technology gives an update that the ability to perceive products with imperfections might be helpful. Here, blockchain will safeguard every one of the insights regarding an item: its sub-gatherings, parts, deals ways, and so forth. It decreases the cost and interference of recovery whenever it occurs in the production network. Cameras and sensors have gathered new data that might be used to create the Blockchain's organisation. It allows access to more details than a person could possibly gather in a short amount of time.

In the IT industry, a few components are not yet very much portrayed or completely perceived. This new innovation will guarantee that what's to come impacts of shrewd assembly arrangements are enhanced. The early deals encounters and the ongoing organizations have been taken in an extraordinary arrangement. It gives a comprehensive appropriation technique, executing and consolidating these arising advancements being advanced and upheld as assets to meet more extensive business objectives. Small and medium-sized businesses in particular might benefit from patent protection as a result of blockchain's potential to simplify, streamline, and eliminate middlemen in the patent process. This would encourage rivalry amongst businesses that have more difficulty obtaining permits. It will enable anyone to generate ecologically beneficial power energy using an unreservedly planned strategy.

Innovation on the planet has been changing at a remarkable rate. This is a pattern that will just go on at a rising rate in later years as extraordinary personalities keep on creating things to simplify daily existence and open it to everybody. While this pattern proceeds, changes will be wild in regular day-to-day existence as well as in the business world altogether (Nasir *et al.* 2020). Innovation has proactively ejected and has had the option to permit organizations to advance quickly to various degrees of profitability and competitiveness. Ongoing turns of events, for instance, man-made reasoning and AI have changed not just the business scene concerning creative items and advancements yet in addition affected decision-production as an opportunity for business pioneers to hoist attorneys to offer further to corporate systems and activities and blockchain innovations are upsetting the financial industry among others, for example, medical care, regulation, store network, and data innovation.

While these mechanical headways and explicitly blockchain innovations have permitted the bookkeeping calling to grow further and, on the way, to lay out blockchain- based bookkeeping rehearses as a potential future for business data frameworks, they likewise raised worries for the vast majority of various organizations in regards to general cybersecurity. Headways in the bookkeeping region have experienced the utilization of more particular bookkeeping programming and cloud-based frameworks. Firms' clients have additionally become more different mechanically (Liu *et al.* 2021). In any case, these headways have accompanied difficulties since the organization's cybersecurity plan presently should be so developed to attempt to keep away from a huge number of dollars and private/classified data misfortune due to cybersecurity information breaks.

2. Literature Review

Blockchain can be characterized as a decentralized, conveyed index driving shrewd agreements and allowing traceability, recording the board, robotization for the store network, instalment applications and other deals. Blockchain gives a record of practically continuous duplicates between an organization of colleagues and is constant. The cycle takes data that would have recently been put away in the Endeavor Asset Arranging of the organization. It presently makes it accessible in a conveyed organization of records across unique organizations. A few benefits of blockchain empower associations to comprehend their clients better, especially on the interesting side. Information examination and man-made reasoning have surely known instances of utilization. It can likewise arrive at an unreasonable impediment to mechanical viability; however, a few organizations take a stab at comfort. It works on the assurance and productivity of techniques and requires more endurance and versatility than sped-up monetary outcomes.

A blockchain is a digital, decentralized record that comprises blocks of exchanges between parties. Specialists characterize blockchain as a "disseminated data set of records, or public record of all exchanges or digital occasions that have been executed and divided between taking part parties" (Abd-Alrazaq *et al.* 2021). Blockchain has tremendous potential benefits for some businesses and has no central point of control. The innovation itself is independent of third parties. In 2008, blockchain became widely known, and over the following years, it gained popularity as a result of its efficiency and high level of security. This increased level of security is made possible by the fact that in order to modify anything on the blockchain, a majority of the exchanges in the ensuing blocks within the chain, all other things being equal, must agree to the change. Additionally, blockchains use complex math and innovative programming techniques that are generally challenging to control. This makes blockchain innovation engaging and fascinating because it makes the confirmation cycle simple that paces up the exchange interaction generally speaking. Globally, there are two main categories of blockchain bookkeeping: public blockchains, where any individual has access to the network and no organisation is required to participate in blockchain activities and exchanges; and private blockchains, which are more exclusive and complex types of bookkeeping and require permission from an outsider to attend gatherings (Ferrag *et al.* 2018). Confidential Blockchains might be framed by firms and associations working in a specific industry and may require validation. Analysts propose that private blockchain organizations can give dependable business programming answers for the development industry since the development industry works with sensitive information. One of the most well-known uses of blockchain is the utilization of blockchain in digital money, explicitly Bitcoin which uses a public blockchain type. Review papers and procedures archive the wide scope of functional applications because blockchain is something other than Bitcoin. While Bitcoin isn't the beginning stage for blockchain it ignited the substance of blockchain to the level that it is being used today. Blockchain, as an innovation all alone, is a more fascinating and significant development than that Bitcoin. Bitcoin is an application that causes sudden spikes in demand for the blockchain and also, and blockchain is utilized as the Hyperledger starting from the start of 2015. Hyperledger is an endeavour to put together a record that is based on blockchain innovation and is utilized to help all blockchain-based conveyed records. Hyperledger is intended for big business-level blockchain applications and presents part of the board administrations guaranteeing information security and trust among clients. The objective of the utilization of Hyperledger (or the Hyperledger project) is to help blockchain innovation and change and advance worldwide deals. The advancement of Blockchain can be ordered under the three surges of Blockchain. Blockchain 1.0 is the mainstream, which is where the vast majority would distinguish it as the most famous. It is comprised of for the most part, digital currencies, remembering Bitcoin for the capital business sectors. Models are Bitcoin, Litecoin, Ethereum, and so on. Blockchain 2.0 incorporates dispersion record arrangements and other base advances, like brilliant agreements and different conventions. Blockchain 3.0 can be viewed as the "future of the blockchain", meaning what else it might have the option to accomplish for us as a general public.

Blockchain has a few mechanical executions and consistently offers new applications. The utilization of blockchain innovation in the assembly area is picking up speed on a worldwide scale (Singh *et al.* 2022). Numerous new organizations are reading up on blockchain answers for the stock organization following and reviewing. Blockchain is at first just a solitary innovation that includes all electronic types of cash used to grasp future prerequisites. Huge improvements would occur in the web networks themselves after extra investigation. Development has consistently progressed, and the blockchain type has extended fundamentally. Subsequently, blockchain has essentially been utilized as a circulated record innovation; this innovation made a chain of information, assembled data, and endorsed it in a block. These blocks are analyzed and added to the exchange and data string alongside prior ones.

The maximum capacity of blockchain is expected to be delivered with a superior strategy for thought and an optimistic and fast approach. Market pioneers in the assembling business could utilize blockchain's inborn elements to determine issues that were already hindrances to specialized progression. This incorporates the inborn prosperity of blockchain innovation, the powerlessness to modify some prosperity before it has been approved and handled in a block, and decentralized work techniques to work with correspondence and responsibility (Ghiasi *et al.* 2021). On the blockchain network, clever agreements are placed close to the record. Brilliant agreements have several advantages since they allow business cycles to start as a result. By lowering exchange costs, accountability can be increased and decreased. There are information bases and conventional apps available that can also use blockchain to meet the majority of needs. Implementing blockchain innovations can be beneficial, especially if a few exchanges communicate with one another.

Blockchains could likewise facilitate casting a ballot, lessen extortion, and further develop administrative centre capabilities like buying. This spotlights future deals, information on the board, and how choices are made. Moreover, in each modern setting, organizations should monitor the manner in which parts work (Demirkan *et al.* 2020). Blockchain will provide the ability to track the actions and operations of any firm in these numerous situations. In order to ensure confidence and reduce extortion, organisations should also improve the start-to-finish management of the production network, integrating business logic and data from IoT sensors.

3. Methodology and Model Specifications

Research methodology is one of the strong backbones of a particular research study. It consists of a clear discussion based on systematic along with logical analysis in accordance with various methods utilised by researchers for procuring primary as well as secondary data. In this present research methodology, post-positivism philosophy has been utilised for exploring research findings in a reliable way. The importance of block chain technologies in mitigating cyber risks can be remarkably explored by this research philosophy. "Deductive research approach" can be considered as the next pillar that can be remarkably used in this research depending on creative scientific theories. On the other hand, "exploratory research design" has been extensively followed for efficiently addressing various consequences of topic background. As per the data collection method, a qualitative secondary method has been reflected, where authentic books, journals along with relevant research papers have been used from Google Scholar and other online resources. An empirical research analysis has been observed in the whole study by transparent logical analysis and using of real-life facts.

4. Empirical Results

A real store network based upon that blockchain is unusual since it is possible to reach consensus among all partners. Information will become a vital commodity in this trimming modern cycle of executives without the need for external guaranteeing professionals and the resulting development of confidence among clients and partners. There are instruments accessible to guarantee and additionally to lay out coordination processes between different industrial facilities. With a rising number of organizations, blockchain is utilized in different business sectors and industry areas (Javaid *et al.* 2021). Blockchain innovation further develops accountability and productivity across the store network. In pretty much every region, organizations utilize applications to coordinate and dissect material from the source, show validity and beginning, communicate forward surveys, and animate item improvement. As new information enters the creation organization, the data is refreshed inside the blockchain and adjusted.

Interest in blockchain applications is quickly filling different enterprises; the car industry is more disposed to present blockchain advances. In current assembling strategies, the store network will work in numerous ventures and numerous nations. This will make the creative way to deal with increased productivity and seek after individual occasions more perplexing (Fauziah *et al.* 2020). The connected pith of the IT industry makes protected digital plan information simple to share, further developing creation process consistency. Smart agreements complete pre-modified orders given that a progression of agreements recently arranged is conformed to. Blockchain empowers shrewd organizations to diminish high exchange costs and extensively accelerate the times required to circle back in the IT industry business.

In the IT industry, projects, PCs, and machines are regularly profoundly related. Insurance of complex modern organizations and working on actual access frameworks is the main concern in light of the fact that cyber-assault likewise compromises them. Distributable, complete, adaptable, and flexible network protection models utilizing solid public-key encryption conventions and data security hash calculations ought to replace the ordinary association separation and central consistency models (Zhang *et al.* 2019). Blockchain offers cutting-edge security and enables machine-to-machine and human-to-human verification, consistent sharing of information, the life cycle of administrators, access control consistency across devices, and self-supporting activities.

Hence, to lay out a strong hidden heading and component that can interface the entire stock framework from source to customer and then some, the blockchain can give a few sensible arrangements. It would allow for an extremely precise review of a product to be provided to the client. It provides businesses with a clear channel for correspondence or customer service. Direct interaction was not feasible until recently. Innovative strategies for steadfastness and robotized vouchers for executives are doable with blockchain (Panwar *et al.* 2021). A couple of this innovation's other fundamental execution fields are converse coordinated operations, ensuring control and item monitoring.

There are numerous administration associations, clinical consideration organizations, activities and transportation help projects, and schools. In a general blockchain, conceptualization zeroed in on improving these circles starting from the earliest stage and finishing each level basically in the IT business (Jain and Pandey, 2019). The particular sub-circles that finally help and back blockchain abilities to rehearse them all the more unambiguously for IT industry execution in different fields incorporate data assurance, solid thought, staying away from bogus cases, simplicity of record keeping, effective obtaining, financial practicality, further settled straightforwardness, etc.

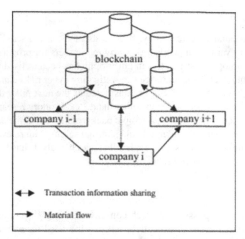

Fig. 27.1 System overview of block chain technology
Source: Jain and Pandey, 2019

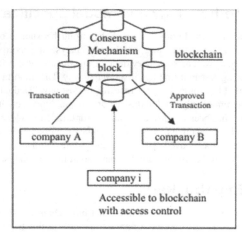

Fig. 27.2 Overview of the transaction process of block chain technology
Source: Panwar et al. 2021

According to the above picture, there are two basic pillars such as company and the block chain node. The scheme of information sharing is totally dependent on the IT companies, which serve as trusted third parties that can process as well as mediate any kind of electronic transaction (Jain *et al.* 2019). The main role of this trusted third party is to safeguards, validate as well as preserve transactions. The possible entities have been entrusted with effectively maintaining the block chain and a private protected data easily stored against incentives.

As per the above figure, company A has the motif to deliver the invoice to another company called company B. The transaction is completed online and it has been recorded purposefully. After completion of it, it has been broadcasted to each and every client in network. Those clients existing in the network approve the validity of the transaction and then the transaction is added to the chain that delivers a transparent along with indelible record of transactions. At last, the invoice is successfully moved from company A to B.

The blockchain is a remarkable development that has been carried out in various delineated spaces, including cash, property, the worldwide production network, casting a ballot, and energy stockpiling. This innovation can likewise be utilized to store different kinds of data and give a straightforwardly flowing record that is likewise safer than traditional informational indexes, notwithstanding safely and for all time putting away monetary exchanges. Additionally, it will help with acquiring intellectual property (IP) and creative interactive media products, such as digital books, music, photographs, and so on. Additionally, it can be used for the transfer of the asset in addition to the enlisting of a vehicle or piece of land. Through blockchain, the entire instalment framework is disorganised. Blockchain agreements use all data from digitally secure exchanges, and if the businesses agree to the agreements, the magnificent agreement will be automatically established. Blockchain is a potential innovation that outperforms the norm; it analyses data to produce evaluations and projections, solving problems in the IT sector. Customers can get to a significant stage of blockchain data. A representation awards admittance to a client by giving purchasers an approval structure. For example, the trading of information cultivates liability and consistently fabricates entrust and perseverance through associations with the client.

Blockchain can accelerate exchanging and increase the reasonability of new trading organizations. It is feasible to isolate merchant results and instalments straightforwardly from affirmed blockchain trades, which diminishes the requirement for testing and human affiliation. When blockchain is joined with IoT programming and sensors, items are cleverly and persistently spilt across the entire worth cycle, bringing about extraordinary openness and efficiency upgrades. Organizations utilize the accumulated resources of blockchain and IoT for transportation and arranged tasks. A complex agreement considers quick pick-ups, drops, or official activities about certified things in parts or portions.

The devotion to blockchain assists us in moving to a cutting-edge business worldview that is more reasonable, versatile, and zeroed in on the security of the IT area. Blockchain is, in this manner, a vital participant in the development of the area. By further eliminating the middleman, this invention allows businesses to assist others and profit more. Organizations can confirm and manage safe exchanges more easily thanks to blockchain technology. On a fundamental level, decisions can be made about managing judges, brokers, dealers, and other mediators. Also, these plans are in place smarter so that information can be altered and then understood and verified by anyone in the chain. It's possible for each and every computer in the digital organisation to see an exchange that is only active on one PC or hub.

With regard to blockchain wallets, the cycles of partner moves have become simpler thanks to blockchain. This invention has shown the potential to transform the ride-sharing industry and the state of public transportation. The inventory network and coordinated variables of the deck situation are upgraded by blockchain (Jain *et al.* 2021). This creation assists associations with monitoring all exchanges and cycles in decentralized blocks that reach out from creation to dealing, stockpiling, and transportation. Along these lines, the probability of mistakes, human blunders, and related uses would be decreased. Savvy arrangements are quickly arising inside blockchain associations as a position of help for the far and wide execution of blockchain, giving a framework to a pragmatic unthinking resource for blockchain exchange correspondence. Brilliant arrangements have made it conceivable to set up decisions that, in principle, will make trust-based biological systems.

5. Conclusion

Blockchain innovation can provide a device to facilitate openly visible and secure exchanges. In any case, because of the irreversible idea of exchanges on the blockchain, the beneficiary gets no discounts except if another exchange is given. Additionally, the regulations and guidelines encompassing the blockchain climate are not satisfactory, which can prompt disarray among purchasers. At long last, blockchain isn't quite as modest as certain individuals accept. The non-trifling activities cost and execution cost of blockchain frameworks ought to never be undervalued. Business process the executives.

Blockchain empowers proficient business process executives through savvy decreases by accumulating the control stream and business rationale of hierarchical business processes. Blockchain can likewise be utilized with brilliant agreements for the IT industry. These controls are empowered by triggers, and they act as an extension between the undertaking applications and the blockchain. A pilot investigation of the agreement with the board for a matrix administrator has uncovered that the data hole between different partners brings about less than ideal business execution. This makes solid contentions and an elevated degree of doubt among the related gatherings. A legitimate shrewd agreement execution for any solicitation for change or instalments would naturally set off an interaction stream in light of suitable endorsements accomplishing rate, trust and further developed business execution.

The method of exchange has considerably developed in the ongoing ten years because of the headway in innovation. The utilization of refined advancements like blockchain conventions or disseminated records in the IT area has outfitted the consideration of numerous monetary specialists, venture examiners, and technologists towards cryptos. Blockchain innovation has made business processes basic while keeping a safe record of exchanges. The monetary area is by all accounts its essential client because of its application in digital money, such as bitcoin, yet its use isn't limited to the monetary area. It can speed up change in various fields of our standard life. It advances digital instalment frameworks, facilitates shares issuance, and exchanges on decentralized digital trades to advance shrewd agreements, and constructs an immediate connection between parties without including a middle person.

REFERENCES

1. A. Jain, A. K. Pandey, (2019), "Modeling And Optimizing Of Different Quality Characteristics In Electrical Discharge Drilling Of Titanium Alloy (Grade-5) Sheet" Material Today Proceedings, 18, 182–191. https://doi.org/10.1016/j.matpr.2019.06.292
2. A. Jain, A. K. Pandey, (2019), "Modeling And Optimizing Of Different Quality Characteristics In Electrical Discharge Drilling Of Titanium Alloy (Grade-5) Sheet" Material Today Proceedings, 18, 182–191. https://doi.org/10.1016/j.matpr.2019.06.292
3. A. Jain, A. K. Pandey, (2019), "Multiple Quality Optimizations In Electrical Discharge Drilling Of Mild Steel Sheet" Material Today Proceedings, 8, 7252–7261. https://doi.org/10.1016/j.matpr.2017.07.054
4. A. Jain, A. K. Yadav & Y. Shrivastava (2019), "Modelling and Optimization of Different Quality Characteristics In Electric Discharge Drilling of Titanium Alloy Sheet" Material Today Proceedings, 21, 1680–1684. https://doi.org/10.1016/j.matpr.2019.12.010
5. A. Jain, C. S. Kumar, Y. Shrivastava, (2021), "Fabrication and Machining of Fiber Matrix Composite through Electric Discharge Machining: A short review" Material Today Proceedings. https://doi.org/10.1016/j.matpr.2021.07.288
6. Abd-Alrazaq, A. A., Alajlani, M., Alhuwail, D., Erbad, A., Giannicchi, A., Shah, Z., Hamdi, M. and Househ, M., 2021. Blockchain technologies to mitigate COVID-19 challenges: A scoping review. Computer methods and programs in biomedicine update, 1, p. 100001.

7. Demirkan, S., Demirkan, I. and McKee, A., 2020. Blockchain technology in the future of business cyber security and accounting. Journal of Management Analytics, 7(2), pp. 189–208.
8. Fauziah, Z., Latifah, H., Omar, X., Khoirunisa, A. and Millah, S., 2020. Application of Blockchain Technology in Smart Contracts: A Systematic Literature Review. Aptisi Transactions on Technopreneurship (ATT), 2(2), pp. 160–166.
9. Ferrag, M. A., Derdour, M., Mukherjee, M., Derhab, A., Maglaras, L. and Janicke, H., 2018. Blockchain technologies for the internet of things: Research issues and challenges. IEEE Internet of Things Journal, 6(2), pp. 2188–2204.
10. Ghiasi, M., Dehghani, M., Niknam, T., Kavousi-Fard, A., Siano, P. and Alhelou, H. H., 2021. Cyber-attack detection and cyber-security enhancement in smart DC- microgrid based on blockchain technology and Hilbert Huang transform. Ieee Access, 9, pp. 29429–29440.
11. Javaid, M., Haleem, A., Singh, R. P., Khan, S. and Suman, R., 2021. Blockchain technology applications for Industry 4.0: A literature-based review. Blockchain: Research and Applications, p. 100027.
12. Liu, W., Shao, X. F., Wu, C. H. and Qiao, P., 2021. A systematic literature review on applications of information and communication technologies and blockchain technologies for precision agriculture development. Journal of Cleaner Production, 298, p. 126763.
13. Nasir, A., Shaukat, K., Khan, K. I., Hameed, I. A., Alam, T. M. and Luo, S., 2020. What is core and what future holds for blockchain technologies and cryptocurrencies: A bibliometric analysis. IEEE Access, 9, pp. 989–1004.
14. Singh, J., Sajid, M., Gupta, S. K. and Haidri, R. A., 2022. Artificial Intelligence and Blockchain Technologies for Smart City. Intelligent Green Technologies for Sustainable Smart Cities, pp. 317–330.
15. V. Panwar, D. K. Sharma, K. V. P. Kumar, A. Jain & C. Thakar, (2021), "Experimental Investigations And Optimization Of Surface Roughness In Turning Of EN 36 Alloy Steel Using Response Surface Methodology And Genetic Algorithm" Materials Today: Proceedings, https://Doi.Org/10.1016/J.Matpr.2021.03.642
16. V. Panwar, D. K. Sharma, K. V. P. Kumar, A. Jain & C. Thakar, (2021), "Experimental Investigations And Optimization Of Surface Roughness In Turning Of EN 36 Alloy Steel Using Response Surface Methodology And Genetic Algorithm" Materials Today: Proceedings, https://Doi.Org/10.1016/J.Matpr.2021.03.642
17. Zhang, J., Thomas, C., FragaLamas, P. and Fernández-Caramés, T. M., 2019. Deploying blockchain technology in the supply chain. Computer security threats, p. 57.

Computer Science Engineering and Emerging Technologies (ICCS-2022) – Prof (Dr.) Rajeev Sobti et al. (eds)
© 2024 Taylor & Francis Group, London, ISBN 978-1-032-52199-2

Chapter 28

Examining Cyber Security Curricular Frameworks for Business Schools Using Artificial Intelligence

S. Durga[1]
Assistant Professor, K L Business School,
Koneru Lakshmaiah Education Foundation, K L University

K. Lakshmi Sujitha[2]
Student BBA, Koneru Lakshmaiah Education Foundation, K L University

V. Manusha[3]
Student BBA, Koneru Lakshmaiah Education Foundation, K L University

V. Narasimha[4]
Student BBA, Koneru Lakshmaiah Education Foundation, K L University

Kukatla Rajeshwar[5]
Assistant Professor, Electronics and Communication Engineering,
St. Martin's Engineering College Dhulapally, Kompally, Hyderabad 500014, JNTUH

Firos A.[6]
Assistant Professor, Department of Computer Science and Engineering Rajiv Gandhi University
(A Central University), Rono-Hills, Doimukh, Arunachal Pradesh, India

Abstract: Cybersecurity is becoming more and more crucial as society depends more and more on computers for essential tasks. Even recently, there have been assaults that crippled online education during the peak of COVID and placed the security of patient data at renowned hospitals at danger. Modern cybersecurity methods are increasingly using artificial intelligence approaches, particularly machine learning, due to the ongoing threat of privacy breaches and infrastructure damage. This is mainly because it has been challenging to incorporate AI and ML into cybersecurity curricula, and in many aspects, cybersecurity courses have lagged behind advancements in cybersecurity research. We suggest a novel technique to fill this void and incorporate AI and ML methodologies into the cybersecurity education curriculum. These results imply that for cybersecurity curricula to properly reflect improvements in the sector, AI and ML approaches should be examined in the future.

Keywords: Cybersecurity, Artificial intelligence, Machine learning

1. Introduction

Computers have become common place in daily life, raising concerns about cybersecurity. For example, current hacks and ransomware have highlighted the need for resilient software infrastructure in widely read literature, expanded curricula,

[1]sdurga1234@gmail.com, [2] , [3] , [4] , [5]kukatlarajeshwar@gmail.com, [6]firos.a@rgu.ac.in

DOI: 10.1201/9781003405580-28

and legislative decisions. Kaplan et al (2015). In response to complex and well-publicized cybersecurity issues, the US government launched projects with business titans to strengthen cybersecurity standards for the country. A number of public and private sector executives revealed their objectives to develop a trained cyber workforce. The expanding body of research in this field has led to the adoption of approaches and methodologies from other computer science specialties, particularly AI and, even more precisely, ML Klinger et al (2020).

In recent days, practitioners and researchers in cybersecurity have begun to rely heavily on AI and ML approaches. In order to create a skilled future workforce in the cybersecurity industry, it is crucial to incorporate AI into cybersecurity courses. Moreover, Kuzlu et al (2021) note that there are several reasons why combining AI with cybersecurity is difficult. First off, AI and cybersecurity are challenging fields of study that draw in a variety of learners. Second, within a limited number of credit hours, both cybersecurity and AI demand large contributions. Third, adding AI to cybersecurity demands lengthy coursework and curriculum design on top of a cybersecurity program that already has a lot of prerequisites. In reality, STEM degrees frequently have curricula that are so jam-packed that adding new subjects, like AI, might be difficult. Additionally, professors in cybersecurity and AI are not frequently cross-trained. Particularly, an expert in AI is hardly an expert in cybersecurity, and vice versa, according to Newaz et al (2019). Sadly, this leads to a small number of academics and practitioners who have received cross-training in the future cyber workforce.

Cybersecurity, like the majority of computer disciplines, depends on a number of computing sub-disciplines, including networking, systems, and infrastructure. A rising body of cybersecurity literature has extensively exploited AI techniques to address the difficult problems in cybersecurity (Abrishamchi et al 2017). Especially, cybersecurity has significantly depended on ML, a branch of AI that targets on automating the extraction of patterns and statistical relationships from data spanning sizable datasets that have been quantitatively quantified. Because machine learning mainly relies on mathematical approaches, it attracts those who already adhere to the accepted social standards in computer science, i.e., people who are particularly focused on highly technical, and mathematical topics (Acar et al 2020). As a result, ML alienates a sizable segment of the population that does not adhere to the dominant social standards in computer science. This article seeks to give higher education providers useful tools and approaches for creating effective cybersecurity programs.

2. Literature Review

Tao et al (2021): AI in the cybersecurity industry helps businesses monitor, identify, report, and combat cyber threats to maintain information confidentiality. Due to growing attention, advancements in information technology, improvements to intelligence and law enforcement systems, and growth in the volume of data gathered from multiple sources, the usage of reliable and enhanced cybersecurity measures has become essential across all organizations. The surge in the quantity and caliber of cyberattacks is motivating the development of cyber systems with AI capabilities. Because there are more big hacks happening globally, businesses are more aware of the necessity to protect their data. The motives behind these cybercriminals include political rivalry, rivalry-related moves made for financial gain or to damage the identities of others, international information theft, and radical non-secular cluster interests.

Qasim, & Kharbat (2020): Academics studying accounting have recently noted a rise in the use of technological innovations in the accounting field. These analyses merely show how these techniques are used in the field and potential areas for future study, omitting the requirement to enhance the accounting curriculum to keep up with technological advancements. This study adopts an integrated approach to curriculum development to account for the utilization of artificial intelligence, business data analytics, and blockchain technology in the accounting industry. We provide strategies for integrating these innovations into the accounting curriculum by focusing on the four primary design pillars of educational curricula. In order to educate graduates for the market and to secure their employability, academia should take into account how the current industry is using emerging innovations. In order to strike a balance between current accounting knowledge and information technology skills pertinent to the business, this study proposes significant modifications to the accounting curriculum.

Paranjape et al (2019): Along with the advancement of medical technology, there is an increasing call for reforming medical education. As medicine enters the era of artificial intelligence (AI), the volume of information needed to improve clinical decision-making will grow, boosting the necessity for proficient human-machine interaction. Technology like artificial intelligence (AI) is necessary as medical knowledge grows so that doctors can use it to perform medicine. Medical professionals need to be properly trained about this contemporary innovation's advantages for boosting the cost, quality, and accessibility of healthcare, in addition to its disadvantages, such as its lack of openness and accountability. The curriculum must seamlessly incorporate AI into every subject. In this study, we examined the state of medical education and put forth a proposal to modify the curriculum to include AI.

3. Methodology

In this part, we outline the process for developing cybersecurity study programmes for higher education, include examples of bachelor's and master's degree study plans, and offer suggestions for developing curriculum. These recommendations are meant to assist academic institutions in developing their own cybersecurity study programmes and to act as models for such actions. The outputs also include the SPARTA Curricula Designer Tool, a piece of software that allows institutions to create their own unique study programmes in cybersecurity and assess the viability of those programmes in light of the demands of various cybersecurity professional roles.

The identification of the topics required for curricula representing the actual KSA and their inclusion into programs that will be incorporated into study programs are tasks included in the curriculum design work. The results are good-practice curricula or suggestions for which courses should be included in study programs and how to divide them up into bachelor's and master's degree programs.

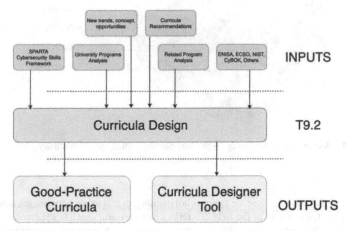

Fig. 28.1 Methodology for creating cybersecurity curricula (Hajny et al., 2021)

4. Results and Discussion

Table 28.1 lists the departments, institutions, and faculties that are primarily active in training cybersecurity. The overall number of providers does not directly correspond to the number of participating universities because some curricula are concurrently provided by various entities within the same university.

Table 28.1 Institutions of higher learning in Europe that conduct study programmes in cybersecurity (Hajny et al., 2021)

Study program	Faculty/Department/school of					Multi university
	Comp sci	Engineering	Social sci.	Mathematics	Others	
Bachelor	7	3	2	1	0	2
Master	32	9	3	6	3	4

The number of English study programmes, their ECTS credits, and average cost are displayed in Table 28.2. In actuality, the two bachelor's degrees in English are taught in the United Kingdom. Bachelor's courses are taught in the nation's primary language.

Table 28.2 Study programs features: Language, ECTS credits and cost in Europe (Hajny et al., 2021)

Study program	Language		ECTS					Average cost
	English	Others	210	180	120	90	60	
Bachelor	3	9	4	9				4632
Master (1 y.)	8	3		2		8	5	21954
Master (2 y.)	21	9		2	16			6774

4.1 Analysis of European Cybersecurity Bachelor Study Programs

The statistical studies for the European bachelor's and master's curricula are broken down by nation in Fig. 28.2 and then summarised. Here, it is evident that the computer science discipline is the primary foundation for cybersecurity bachelors, followed by security.

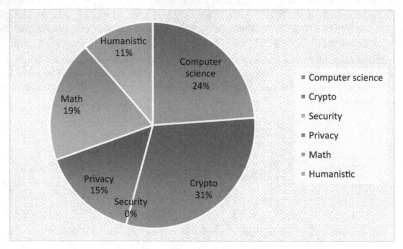

Fig. 28.2 Analysis of European cybersecurity bachelor study programs (Hajny et al., 2021)

5. Conclusion

In this post, we have put out a strategy to close the cybersecurity skills gap that exists between the demand from businesses and society and the supply of specialists in the field. To reflect new developments in cybersecurity, we intend to keep updating the SPARTA CSF in the future. There will be a number of new competencies introduced to reflect multidisciplinary elements as well. Additionally, we intend to expand the tools—and in particular, the Curriculum Designer—to support other Cybersecurity Skills methodology , including—when it's ready—the EU CSF. We also want to provide the capability to design expert training. These results show that in order to better reflect improvements in the sector and to take into account underrepresented groups, AI and ML approaches should be taken into consideration for future inclusion into cybersecurity curriculum.

REFERENCES

1. Klinger, J., Mateos-Garcia, J., & Stathoulopoulos, K. (2020). A narrowing of AI research?. *arXiv preprint arXiv:2009.10385*.
2. Kaplan, J. M., Bailey, T., O'Halloran, D., Marcus, A., & Rezek, C. (2015). *Beyond cybersecurity: protecting your digital business*. John Wiley & Sons.
3. Kuzlu, M., Fair, C., & Guler, O. (2021). Role of artificial intelligence in the Internet of Things (IoT) cybersecurity. *Discover Internet of things*, *1*(1), 1–14.
4. O'Leary, D. L. (2020). " Smart" Lawyering: Integrating Technology Competence into the Legal Practice Curriculum. *UNHL Rev.*, *19*, 197.
5. Abrishamchi, M. A. N., Abdullah, A. H., Cheok, A. D., & Bielawski, K. S. (2017, October). Side channel attacks on smart home systems: A short overview. In *IECON 2017-43rd Annual Conference of the IEEE Industrial Electronics Society* (pp. 8144-8149). IEEE.
6. Acar, A., Fereidooni, H., Abera, T., Sikder, A. K., Miettinen, M., Aksu, H., ... & Uluagac, S. (2020, July). Peek-a-boo: I see your smart home activities, even encrypted!. In *Proceedings of the 13th ACM Conference on Security and Privacy in Wireless and Mobile Networks* (pp. 207–218).
7. Newaz, A. I., Sikder, A. K., Rahman, M. A., & Uluagac, A. S. (2019, October). Healthguard: A machine learning-based security framework for smart healthcare systems. In *2019 Sixth International Conference on Social Networks Analysis, Management and Security (SNAMS)* (pp. 389–396). IEEE.

8. Tao, F., Akhtar, M. S., & Jiayuan, Z. (2021). The future of artificial intelligence in cybersecurity: a comprehensive survey. *EAI Endorsed Transactions on Creative Technologies*, *8*(28), e3–e3.
9. Qasim, A., & Kharbat, F. F. (2020). Blockchain technology, business data analytics, and artificial intelligence: Use in the accounting profession and ideas for inclusion into the accounting curriculum. *Journal of emerging technologies in accounting*, *17*(1), 107–117.
10. Paranjape, K., Schinkel, M., Panday, R. N., Car, J., & Nanayakkara, P. (2019). Introducing artificial intelligence training in medical education. *JMIR medical education*, *5*(2), e16048.
11. Hajny, J., Ricci, S., Piesarskas, E., Levillain, O., Galletta, L., & De Nicola, R. (2021). Framework, tools and good practices for cybersecurity curricula. IEEE Access, 9, 94723–94747.

Computer Science Engineering and Emerging Technologies (ICCS-2022) – Prof (Dr.) Rajeev Sobti et al. (eds)
© 2024 Taylor & Francis Group, London, ISBN 978-1-032-52199-2

Chapter

29

Weighted Ensemble Classification System for Prediction of Diabetes Mellitus

Gurbakash Phonsa[1]
Associate Professor, SCSE, Lovely Professional University

Sudhanshu Prakash Tiwari[2]
Associate Professor, SCSE, Lovely Professional University

Ravi Shanker[3]
Assistant Professor, SCSE, Lovely Professional University

Abstract: Diabetes mellitus (DM) is a debilitating condition classified by persistently elevated blood sugar levels that is quickly increasing in prevalence around the world. The body's failure to react could be to blame; perhaps neither of the pancreas is able to create enough insulin. We include both type 1 and type 2 diabetes in our research classification. In the worst-case scenario, organs crucial to our survival could be destroyed by diabetes mellitus if the disease is not treated and caught early. Researchers are using many different machine learning techniques on many different datasets in an effort to predict who may get diabetes mellitus. However, they are having a hard time getting closer to their goal of making the models more accurate.

Keywords: Machine learning, Classification, Feature selection, Ensemble, Diabetes mellitus

1. Introduction

Among the disorders that could endanger a person's life is diabetes, the most common cause of elevated blood sugar and diabetes mellitus. Diabetes mellitus encompasses both type 1 and type 2 forms of the disease. The pancreas produces insulin in type 2 diabetes, but either of them is not enough to meet the body's needs, or another reason may be that the cells in the body have become resistant to it, in contrast to type 1 diabetes, where the immune system decimates pancreatic cells that create insulin.

In our study, various machine learning algorithms are studied for categorizing and predicting diabetes. For this study, different datasets are being used, and various feature selection techniques are applied for better results. Vaishali R et al. (2017) used the algorithm in the pre-processing stage known as Goldberg's Genetic Algorithm, which made the results better than the previous ones. The use of Ensemble was necessary to achieve the high precision of the suggested model. Ensemble learning is a strategy that involves combining multiple separate classifiers into a single hybrid classifier to further enhance bias, variance, or better predictions. This is accomplished through the process of "ensemble learning." When compared to using only a single classifier, this method results in significantly better prediction performance using machine learning classifiers in the ensemble.

[1]gurbakash.15483@lpu.co.in, [2]sudhanshu.15813@lpu.co.in, [3]ravishanker@ lpu.co.in

DOI: 10.1201/9781003405580-29

2. Literature Review

Deepti Sisodia et al. (2018) and Han Wu et al. (2018) state that their prediction technique increases the probability of a more accurate diabetes detection approach for patients. The Pima Indian Diabetes Database (PIDD) served as the subject of the experiment. In this research, we present a method for predicting type 2 diabetes mellitus that is founded on data mining techniques. Heat rate variability signals (HRV), which are obtained from electrocardiogram (ECG) data, have been proposed by Swapna G et al. (2018) and Md. Faisal Faruque et al. (2019) as an approach for the categorization of diabetes signals that can be employed successfully to prevent the invasion prophecy of diabetes. evaluated the effectiveness of a number of machine learning methods. After that, the findings were evaluated, considering the relevant risk factors. Samrat Kumar Dey et al. (2018) created a web application based on higher prognosis accuracy with the assistance of various machine learning algorithms to improve the accuracy of the diagnosis.

Anjaneya L.H. et al. (2016) and Jasim et al. (2017) in the study have developed a new method by taking into consideration the frequency domain and the time domain aspects of EMG signals, and they employed a neural network. In this study, classification is done on the disease diagnosis by choosing the K nearest neighbor technique and assessing the method with an artificial neural network (ANN). In this study, Raid M. Khalil et al. (2017) attempted to predict depression using machine-learning techniques. Their report shows better accuracy when machine learning is applied to the assertion of depression in type 2 diabetic patients.

In their research, Francesco Mercaldo et al. (2017) and Roxana Mirshahvalad et al. (2017) present a novel approach capable of distinguishing between non-affected and diabetes-affected individuals using machine-learning algorithms, which were applied to eight features of the Pima Indian Diabetes Dataset. Anjli Negi et al. (2016) developed a novel way of keeping in mind the global character of type 2 diabetes. In this method, the proposed model is tested, trained, and validated on all different kinds of datasets. Aparimita Swain et al. (2016) and Vaishali R. et al. (2017) have proposed a method for categorization and employed a hybrid artificial neural network.

The study by Sidong Wei et al. (2018) and Abid Sarwar et al. (2014) gives an in-depth analysis of well-known machine learning methods, such as DNN and SVM, which are used in data pre-processing approaches to identify diabetes.

Table 29.1 Parametric based review analysis

Parameters used by papers	Papers using these parameters
Class variable, Insulin Serum, Skin thickness of triceps, Plasma Glucose Concentration,BMI, Pedigree function,Age,Count of Pregnancy, Blood Pressure	Deepti Sisodia et al, Han Wu et al, Samrat Kumar Dey et al, Ihsan Salman Jasim et al, Francesco `Mercaldo et al, Sidong Wei et al, J Pradeep et al, [1, 2, 5, 7, 9, 14, 16]
ECG of 20 people is used.	Swapna G et al. [3]
Age (Years), Sex, Weight (Kg's), Diet Nominal, Polyuria, Water Consumption, Excessive Thirst, Blood Pressure, Hyper Tension, Tiredness, Problem in Vision, Kidney Problem, Hearing Loss, Itchy Skin, Genetic, Diabetic.	Md. Faisal Faruque. [4]
Diabetes treatment, Body Mass Index, Number of co morbidity, Pill Burden, Number of Diabetic Complication, Physical Disability.	Raid M. Khalil et al. [8]
Age, Body Mass, Diastolic Blood Pressure (mm/Hg), Concentration (mg/dl), Suffering Diabetes, Diabetes Pedigree Function, Fasting Plasma Glucose	Aparimita Swain et al. [12]
Plasma glucose concentration (plas), BMI, Age, Diabetes pedigree function.	Vaishali R et al. [13]
Age, Family history, Weight, Sex , Drinking Smoking, Thirst, Frequency of Urination, Height, Fatigue.	AbidSarwar et al. [15]
Dataset was taken from the School of medicine, University of Virginia.	WeifengXu et al. [17]
How often the blood for sugar is checked? LDL Count? A1C checked? Recent SBP; How long you have been taking insulin? Recent DBP; No. of times you have seen a Dr. last year? How much A1C should be as per Dr? etc.	Adil Hussain et al. [18]
Pregnant, Glucose, Diastolic, Triceps, Insulin, BMI, Diabetes, Age, Test	Debadri Dutta et al. [20]
48 featues from dataset of King Fahad University Hospital, Khobar, Saudi Arabia were used.	Reem A. Alassaf et al. [24]

Source: Made by Author

Cross-validation was performed using the Pima Indian Diabetes Dataset to assess the validity of these strategies. J. Pradeep et al. (2015) and Weifeng Xu et al. (2017) present the comparison of algorithms of machine learning classifiers, which helps in diabetes prediction due to high blood sugar levels. They used the random forest methodology as the foundation for the model that was proposed in their study for the prediction of type 2 diabetes. This method trains the sample model using a number of different decision trees.

Adil Hussain et al.'s (2018) paper's goal is to forecast diabetes-related voting behavior. The probabilities of each model are given to the ensemble model, which then computes the unweighted average probability and generates a class label based on the average probability. ANNs and Bayesian networks were used in a comparative investigation by Berina Alic et al. (2017) and Debadri Dutta et al. (2018) to classify diabetes and cardiovascular disease. The article discusses the feature value of diabetes prediction using different sets of machine-learning algorithms. Deepika Verma et al. (2017) used data from the UCI machine learning repository to talk about two diseases: diabetes and breast cancer. On the WEKA interface, SMO, REP Tree, Naive Bayes, J48, and MCP were used for classification. Harleen Kaur et al. (2018) have used machine learning to create and study five different predictive models. RBF, linear kernel support machine (SVM-linear), ANN, KNN, and multi-factor dimensionality reduction (MDR) are the algorithms used in this study.

Piyush Samant et al. (2018) came up with a model to figure out how well soft computing techniques can be used to diagnose type 2 diabetes. A small group of 338 people was used to test the model. The study is based on infrared images of both eyes. R packages are used to make classifiers work. Reem A. Alassaf et al. (2018) came up with a plan for diagnosing diabetes mellitus ahead of time. Recursive feature elimination and correlation coefficient were used to pull out features, and four classification algorithms were analyzed based on classification for precision, accuracy, recall, and f-measure.

3. Proposed Methodology

To provide better prediction results in the prediction of diabetes mellitus. The pro-posed methodology has the following modules:

Data Collection: The PIMA India dataset has been used extensively in this study. The goal of the data set is to identify patients who may be at risk for developing diabetes.

Data Pre-Processing: Cleaning the dataset, removing any missing values, and removing duplicate values.

Feature Selection: A method that picks the most important features from the dataset and makes the results from the ensemble model more accurate. The benefits of using the feature selection are as follows:

1. reduce the over-fitting in the dataset;
2. when the right subset is chosen, the accuracy of the model can be improved;
3. reduce the complexity of the model; and
4. help the machine learning algorithm to train faster.

Classification using different classifiers: On the data set, numerous machine learning classifiers are utilized, and each classifier then delivers its own prediction based on the data set.

Construct Weighted Ensemble: Combining the different classifiers and finally assigning the weights to them according to the accuracy provided by each classifier.

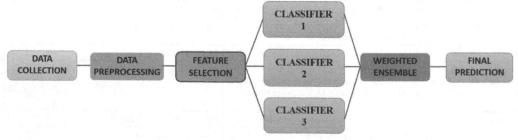

Fig. 29.1 Proposed Methodology

Source: Made by Author

4. Conclusion

Early diabetes diagnosis is crucial because it lowers the risk of developing major complications and keeps the patient healthy for the rest of their lives. Patients with diabetes are diagnosed using a various of machine learning algorithms, each of which has produced findings with varying degrees of accuracy. SVM, RF, Naive Bayes, decision trees, etc. are some of the most frequently used classifiers. Sometimes used alone, these classifiers are also combined for improved results.

REFERENCES

1. Sisodia, D. and Sisodia, D. S., 2018. Prediction of diabetes using classification algorithms. Procedia computer science, 132, pp. 1578–1585.
2. Wu, H., Yang, S., Huang, Z., He, J. and Wang, X., 2018. Type 2 diabetes mellitus prediction model based on data mining. Informatics in Medicine Unlocked, 10, pp. 100–107.
3. Swapna, G., Vinayakumar, R. and Soman, K. P., 2018. Diabetes detection using deep learning algorithms. ICT express, 4(4), pp. 243–246.
4. Faruque, M. F. and Sarker, I. H., 2019, February. Performance analysis of machine learning techniques to predict diabetes mellitus. In 2019 International Conference on Electrical, Computer and Communication Engineering (ECCE) (pp. 1–4). IEEE.
5. Dey, S. K., Hossain, A. and Rahman, M. M., 2018, December. Implementation of a web application to predict diabetes disease: an approach using machine learning algorithm. In 2018 21st international conference of computer and information technology (ICCIT) (pp. 1–5). IEEE.
6. Anjaneya, L. H. and Holi, M. S., 2016, May. Multilayer machine learning algorithm to classify diabetic type on knee dataset. In 2016 IEEE International Conference on Recent Trends in Electronics, Information & Communication Technology (RTEICT) (pp. 584–587). IEEE.
7. Jasim, I. S., Duru, A. D., Shaker, K., Abed, B. M. and Saleh, H. M., 2017, August. Evaluation and measuring classifiers of diabetes diseases. In 2017 International Conference on Engineering and Technology (ICET) (pp. 1–4). IEEE.
8. Khalil, R. M. and Al-Jumaily, A., 2017, November. Machine learning based prediction of depression among type 2 diabetic patients. In 2017 12th international conference on intelligent systems and knowledge engineering (ISKE) (pp. 1–5). IEEE.
9. Mercaldo, F., Nardone, V. and Santone, A., 2017. Diabetes mellitus affected patients classification and diagnosis through machine learning techniques. Procedia computer science, 112, pp. 2519–2528.
10. Mirshahvalad, R. and Zanjani, N. A., 2017, September. Diabetes prediction using ensemble perceptron algorithm. In 2017 9th International Conference on Computational Intelligence and Communication Networks (CICN) (pp. 190–194). IEEE.
11. Negi, A. and Jaiswal, V., 2016, December. A first attempt to develop a diabetes prediction method based on different global datasets. In 2016 Fourth International Conference on Parallel, Distributed and Grid Computing (PDGC) (pp. 237–241). IEEE.
12. Swain, A., Mohanty, S. N. and Das, A. C., 2016, March. Comparative risk analysis on prediction of diabetes mellitus using machine learning approach. In 2016 international conference on electrical, electronics, and optimization Techniques (ICEEOT) (pp. 3312–3317). IEEE.
13. Vaishali, R., Sasikala, R., Ramasubbareddy, S., Remya, S. and Nalluri, S., 2017, October. Genetic algorithm-based feature selection and MOE Fuzzy classification algorithm on Pima Indians Diabetes dataset. In 2017 international conference on computing networking and informatics (ICCNI) (pp. 1–5). IEEE.
14. Wei, S., Zhao, X. and Miao, C., 2018, February. A comprehensive exploration to the machine learning techniques for diabetes identification. In 2018 IEEE 4th World Forum on Internet of Things (WF-IoT) (pp. 291–295). IEEE.
15. Sarwar, A. and Sharma, V., 2014. Comparative analysis of machine learning techniques in prognosis of type II diabetes. AI & society, 29(1), pp. 123–129.
16. Kandhasamy, J. P. and Balamurali, S. J. P. C. S., 2015. Performance analysis of classifier models to predict diabetes mellitus. Procedia Computer Science, 47, pp. 45–51.
17. Xu, W., Zhang, J., Zhang, Q. and Wei, X., 2017, February. Risk prediction of type II diabetes based on random forest model. In 2017 Third International Conference on Advances in Electrical, Electronics, Information, Communication and Bio-Informatics (AEEICB) (pp. 382–386). IEEE.
18. Husain, A. and Khan, M.H., 2018, April. Early diabetes prediction using voting based ensemble learning. In International conference on advances in computing and data sciences (pp. 95–103). Springer, Singapore.
19. Alić, B., Gurbeta, L. and Badnjević, A., 2017, June. Machine learning techniques for classification of diabetes and cardiovascular diseases. In 2017 6th mediterranean conference on embedded computing (MECO) (pp. 1–4). IEEE.
20. Dutta, D., Paul, D. and Ghosh, P., 2018, November. Analysing feature importances for diabetes prediction using machine learning. In 2018 IEEE 9th Annual Information Technology, Electronics and Mobile Communication Conference (IEMCON) (pp. 924–928). IEEE.

21. Verma, D. and Mishra, N., 2017, December. Analysis and prediction of breast cancer and diabetes disease datasets using data mining classification techniques. In 2017 International Conference on Intelligent Sustainable Systems (ICISS) (pp. 533–538). IEEE.
22. Kaur, H. and Kumari, V., 2020. Predictive modelling and analytics for diabetes using a machine learning approach. Applied computing and informatics.
23. Samant, P. and Agarwal, R., 2018. Machine learning techniques for medical diagnosis of diabetes using iris images. Computer methods and programs in biomedicine, 157, pp.121–128.
24. Alassaf, R. A., Alsulaim, K. A., Alroomi, N. Y., Alsharif, N. S., Aljubeir, M. F., Olatunji, S. O., Alahmadi, A. Y., Imran, M., Alzahrani, R. A. and Alturayeif, N. S., 2018, April. Preemptive diagnosis of diabetes mellitus using machine learning. In 2018 21st Saudi Computer Society National Computer Conference (NCC) (pp. 1–5). IEEE.

Computer Science Engineering and Emerging Technologies (ICCS-2022) – Prof (Dr.) Rajeev Sobti et al. (eds)
© 2024 Taylor & Francis Group, London, ISBN 978-1-032-52199-2

Chapter **30**

Applications of Internet of Things (IoT) in Maintaining Privacy and Security of Smart Cities

Shahanawaj Ahamad[1]

Assistant Professor, Department of Information and Computer Sciences,
College of Computer Science and Engineering,
University of Hail, Hail City, Saudi Arabia

A. B. Mishra[2]

Associate Professor, International Institute of Management Studies, Pune

K. S. Raghuram[3]

Associate Professor, Department of Mechanical Engineering,
Vignan's Institute of Information Technology (A), Visakhapatnam, A. P., India

Mohit Tiwari[4]

4Assistant Professor, Department of Computer Science and Engineering,
Bharati Vidyapeeth's College of Engineering, Delhi A-4,
Rohtak Road, Paschim Vihar, Delhi

Y. Md. Riyazuddin[5]

Assistant Professor, Department of CSE, School of technology,
Gitam University Hyderabad

Joel Alanya-Beltran[6]

Universidad Tecnológica del Perú

Abstract: This study's main goal was to assess the impact of IoT adoption in smart cities. The goals were to determine how IoT was being used in smart cities and the approaches that were being employed. The third goal was to determine the value of IoT. For the gathering of secondary data, the qualitative approach was chosen. It has made it possible to compile secondary data from numerous internet articles. Google Scholar was also employed as a tool for the gathering of secondary data. It has made it possible to recognise the significance of IoT in smart cities, and the descriptive evaluation method was used to examine the data that was gathered. It has made it possible for us to understand the value and underlying technology of IoT applications in smart cities. Digital tools and technology are the primary focus of IoT applications in smart cities. IoT's cutting-edge technology can manage traffic and cut waste in urban areas. Municipalities are employing these technologies to concentrate on enhancing infrastructure. The population's lifestyles have undergone significant change as a result of numerous IoT-related aspects. Additionally, the gathering of secondary data and the descriptive method of analysis have helped us understand the significance of IoT technology in smart cities.

Keywords: IoT, Smart Cities, Privacy Security

[1]drshahwj@gmail.com, [2]amishra.iims@gmail.com, [3]hodmechanicals@gmail.com, [4]mohit.tiwari@bharatividyapeeth.edu, [5]rymd@gitam.edu, [6]C18121@utp.edu.pe

DOI: 10.1201/9781003405580-30

1. Introduction

Due to the cutting-edge innovation of the Internet of Things (IoT), cities have grown increasingly involved in an attempt to enhance the efficiency of emergency services' readiness, improve accuracy, reduce costs, develop infrastructure, and much more (IoT). The usage of IoT systems will lead to the emergence of more smart cities in the future (Arasteh et al., 2016). Cities are moving towards IoT technology primarily because it provides wireless connectivity. Expense is the primary factor in the choice to switch from wired to wireless systems (Qian et al., 2019). Landlines are costly to establish and maintain, and cellular data subscriptions are becoming more affordable (Al-Turjman (2018). As a result, new scenarios are now possible that were previously cost-prohibitive owing to wireless technology. Reliability is a crucial additional factor (Cvar et al., 2020). To maintain the communications network, service professionals must manually travel to the installation site, which is time-consuming and expensive.

IoT implementations can be remotely managed and monitored, thanks to wireless connections. Additionally, it enables administrators to apply firmware and security patch upgrades during the installation. It can send out automated alerts for all the problems and consume less energy overall (Muhammed et al., 2019). Additionally, IoT systems ensure the use of sensors to collect data and wireless devices to manage how a service is used (Ahmed & Rani, 2018). IoT application development is a rapidly expanding business. A group of industries, such as emergency services, sewage treatment, city lighting and transit, and others, can be grouped together as smart cities. Panwar et al (2021). Municipalities and smart cities that use wireless technology for lighting in order to conserve resources and money are common examples of IoT applications. This study's objective is to conduct a thorough examination of IoT usage in smart cities.

1.1 Research Objectives

The following are the objectives that were created based on the goal:

- To determine how IoT is being used in smart cities
- To assess the various deployment strategies for the Internet of Things
- To ascertain the techniques, the importance of the Internet of Things, and its uses.

1.2 Research Questions

The following questions have been developed for the study based on the goals:

- How do smart cities integrate the Internet of Things?
- What various techniques are applied during IoT deployment?
- What are the benefits of IoT technologies and how are they used in smart cities?

2. Literature Review

Witti & Konstantas (2018): Due to the widespread usage of smart devices, the Internet of Things has emerged as a key element of the smart city, helping to control power usage, offer real-time remote patient surveillance via smart homes, and predict the likelihood of traffic jams or air pollution before they happen. In order to enhance city life, the adoption of Internet of Things-enabled technology promises smart citizen management and governance Jain & Pandey (2019). Developing a smart city platform involves an adjusted architecture to secure citizen household data due to the issues with IOT-based devices, which are security and privacy issues in individual data collection. In this essay, we suggest a structure for the smart city's security and privacy protection.

Alsamhi et al (2019): Intelligent objects can routinely and cooperatively improve life quality, save lives, and serve as a responsible resource ecosystem in smart cities. Drones, robotics, artificial intelligence, and the Internet of Things (IoT) are needed to implement these cutting-edge collaborative innovations in order to boost the intellect of smart cities by enhancing connection, power efficiency, and service quality (QoS). Because of this, cooperative drones and IoT are essential to a variety of smart-city applications, including those that deal with communication, transit, agricultural sectors, security and safety, disaster mitigation, environmental conservation, service delivery, energy conservation, e-waste minimisation, weather forecasting, healthcare, etc. In order to improve the smartness of smart cities, a new study of prospective IoT and collaborative drone approaches and applications is presented in this study.

Talari et al (2017): Each smart city now has a variety of electronic gadgets thanks to the growth of smart metres, the Advanced Metering Infrastructure (AMI), and the Internet of Things (IoT). As a result, tools and technology help us become smarter and increase the usability and accessibility of a number of smart city features Jain et al (2020). The objective of the current article is to present a comprehensive overview of the idea of the smart city in addition to its various uses and benefits. Additionally, the majority of potential IoT technologies are described along with how they might be applied to various aspects of smart cities. Another insightful topic discussed in this article is how smart cities might be used to advance technologies in the future. While this is happening, various real-world examples from throughout the globe are presented, along with the main obstacles to its adoption.

Tragos et al (2014): In recent years, smart cities have been viewed as a viable way to leverage information and communication technologies to deliver effective services to inhabitants. With the most recent developments in the Internet of Things, a new age in the field of smart cities has developed, creating new prospects for the creation of effective and affordable applications intended to enhance urban Quality of Life Jain & Pandey (2017). Despite the fact that a lot of studies in these fields have been conducted and numerous commercial brands have been developed as a result, critical factors like accuracy, security, and privacy have not previously been seen to be highly relevant. With the citizen at the forefront, the recently created FP7-SmartCities-2013 project RERUM seeks to build on the advancements made in the field of the IoT in Smart Cities and establish a structure to improve the dependability and security of smart city applications.

Chakrabarty & Engels, (2016): For smart cities, researchers provide a secure Internet of Things (IoT) framework. IoT technology adoption on a large scale within a city has the potential of streamlining city operations and enhancing urban residents' quality of life. Mission-critical Smart City data that is collected from and transmitted over IoT networks must be protected against cyberattacks that could compromise city operations, collect personal information, and cause severe damage. For secure Smart Cities, we describe an architecture consisting of the Unified Registry, Black Network, Trusted SDN Controller, and Key Management System. These fundamental IoT-centric building pieces work together to create a safe Smart City that reduces cyberattacks that originate at IoT nodes themselves.

3. Research Methodology

The term "quantitative approach" refers to the gathering of numbers from diverse demographic categories within the study goal. In contrast to qualitative data, it is therefore more impartial and rational. Typically, structured questionnaires are used in the quantitative approach.

Depending on the objective of the investigation, the nature of the research questions, and the characteristics of the descriptive study, employing a quantitative data collection strategy utilising a questionnaire and a quantitative analytic approach utilising the SPSS software package.

A structured questionnaire is used to collect data, enabling researchers to reach a broad population quickly and effectively using the Bristol online survey tool. The questionnaire can also be simply coded and exported to SPSS for statistical analysis.

This research utilizes a statistical sampling method while taking into account the feasibility, research goal and issue, and also the population characteristics that are needed to be evaluated statistically. The study question's nature essentially consists of opinion variables, which track how participants in surveys feel about certain topics or what they consider to be true or false.

4. Results

4.1 Descriptive Statistics

The demographic variables are gender and age, which are numerated in Table 30.1.

Table 30.1 Descriptive statistics [15]

		Frequency	Percent	Valid percent	Cumulative percent
Gender	Male	57	31.6	31.6	31.6
	Female	33	25.8	25.8	98.9
	Total	90	98.9	98.9	

		Frequency	Percent	Valid percent	Cumulative percent
Age	18–25	16	14.2	14.2	14.2
	25–29	8	1.3	1.3	21.5
	30–35	21	21.7	21.7	15.8
	45–55	12	10.4	10.4	98.9
	Total	90	98.9	98.9	

4.2 Citizen Expectations for the Development of Smart Cities

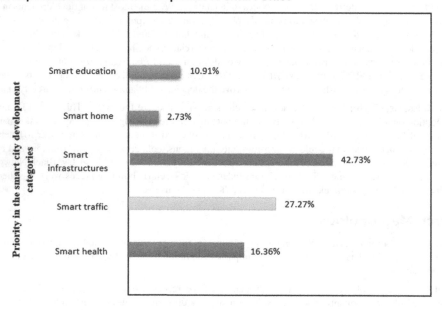

Fig. 30.1 Citizen expectations for the development of smart cities [15]

4.3 Cronbach's Alpha Test for Location and Financial Data Security and Privacy

Instead of assessing dependability, this study uses Cronbach's Alpha to assess consistency and predict the level of individual privacy preferences (see table 30.2 and 30.3)

Table 30.2 Cronbach's Alpha test [15]

	N	%
Valid	87	97.4
Excluded[a]	23	14.7
Total	90	98.9

4.4 Consistency of Statistics

Table 30.3 Consistency of statistics [15]

Cronbach's alpha	On the basis of standardised items, Cronbach's alpha	N of items
.442	.443	3

5. Discussion

The study's conclusions represent the views of the general public on these three IoT application service-related difficulties. First, for improved user experience, the scalability concern is anticipated to be handled in an integrated platform; Thirdly, privacy is the most important issue for Taiwanese citizens. Security knowledge needs to be raised in order to safeguard people from security vulnerabilities. Additionally, data controllers and processors must deal with different people's preferences for privacy. These three IoT issues and concerns are in line with the literature review, it can be inferred based on the study's findings. According to the study results, people's most pressing concern appears to be privacy. As a result, this dissertation suggests that IT firms implement privacy by design, using privacy-enhancing innovations to secure personal information and also setting a clear rule concerning how and when information will be gathered and analysed, demonstrating respect for user privacy preferences based on individual viewpoints. Transparency in personal privacy preferences is a technique to respect individual privacy and to win over people's confidence in the Internet of Things.

6. Conclusion

Through the growth of virtually endless creative application services, the IoT has the ability to significantly improve the societal and personal quality of life. As noted in the literature review and supported by the survey findings of this study, there are difficulties with it. In order to win users' acceptance and understand the benefits of IoT applications in the coming years, it is therefore extremely important to take into account other elements of IoT design scheme, like compatibility, information security, privacy, and regulations, in addition to simply putting in more attempt to create applications and services. Large-scale sensor implementations across numerous different heterogeneous networks worldwide were unavoidable in order to realise the full benefits of the IoT network. This presents a number of challenges, which include application compatibility /or interoperability, information security, and privacy concerns.

REFERENCES

1. Arasteh, H., Hosseinnezhad, V., Loia, V., Tommasetti, A., Troisi, O., Shafie-khah, M., & Siano, P. (2016, June). Iot-based smart cities: A survey. In *2016 IEEE 16th international conference on environment and electrical engineering (EEEIC)* (pp. 1–6). IEEE.
2. Qian, L. P., Wu, Y., Ji, B., Huang, L., & Tsang, D. H. (2019). HybridIoT: Integration of hierarchical multiple access and computation offloading for IoT-based smart cities. *IEEE network*, *33*(2), 6–13.
3. Al-Turjman, F. (2018). *Intelligence in IoT-enabled smart cities*. CRC Press.
4. Cvar, N., Trilar, J., Kos, A., Volk, M., & Stojmenova Duh, E. (2020). The use of IoT technology in smart cities and smart villages: similarities, differences, and future prospects. *Sensors*, *20*(14), 3897.
5. Muhammed, T., Mehmood, R., & Albeshri, A. (2017, November). Enabling reliable and resilient IoT based smart city applications. In *International conference on smart cities, infrastructure, technologies and applications* (pp. 169–184). Springer, Cham.
6. Ahmed, S. H., & Rani, S. (2018). A hybrid approach, Smart Street use case and future aspects for Internet of Things in smart cities. *Future Generation Computer Systems*, *79*, 941–951.
7. Witti, M., & Konstantas, D. (2018, December). A secure and privacy-preserving internet of things framework for smart city. In *Proceedings of the 6th International Conference on Information Technology: IoT and Smart City* (pp. 145–150).
8. Alsamhi, S. H., Ma, O., Ansari, M. S., & Almalki, F. A. (2019). Survey on collaborative smart drones and internet of things for improving smartness of smart cities. *Ieee Access*, *7*, 128125–128152.
9. Talari, S., Shafie-Khah, M., Siano, P., Loia, V., Tommasetti, A., & Catalão, J. P. (2017). A review of smart cities based on the internet of things concept. *Energies*, *10*(4), 421.
10. Tragos, E. Z., Angelakis, V., Fragkiadakis, A., Gundlegard, D., Nechifor, C. S., Oikonomou, G., ... & Gavras, A. (2014, March). Enabling reliable and secure IoT-based smart city applications. In *2014 IEEE International Conference on Pervasive Computing and Communication Workshops (PERCOM WORKSHOPS)* (pp. 111–116). IEEE.
11. Panwar, V., Sharma, D. K., Kumar, K. P., Jain, A., & Thakar, C. (2021). Experimental investigations and optimization of surface roughness in turning of en 36 alloy steel using response surface methodology and genetic algorithm. *Materials Today: Proceedings*, *46*, 6474–6481.
12. Jain, A., & Pandey, A. K. (2019). Modeling and optimizing of different quality characteristics in electrical discharge drilling of titanium alloy (Grade-5) sheet. *Materials Today: Proceedings*, *18*, 182–191.
13. Jain, A., & Pandey, A. K. (2017). Multiple quality optimizations in electrical discharge drilling of mild steel sheet. *Materials Today: Proceedings*, *4*(8), 7252–7261.
14. Jain, A., Yadav, A. K., & Shrivastava, Y. (2020). Modelling and optimization of different quality characteristics in electric discharge drilling of titanium alloy sheet. *Materials Today: Proceedings*, *21*, 1680–1684.
15. Tadili, J., & Fasly, H. (2019, October). Citizen participation in smart cities: A survey. In Proceedings of the 4th International Conference on Smart City Applications (pp. 1–6).

Computer Science Engineering and Emerging Technologies (ICCS-2022) – Prof (Dr.) Rajeev Sobti et al. (eds)
© 2024 Taylor & Francis Group, London, ISBN 978-1-032-52199-2

Chapter **31**

EMG Muscular Disorder Classification Using Motor Neuron Signals

Reema Jain[1]

PhD. Scholar, Department of Computer Application,
Lovely Professional University, Phagwara, Punjab, India

Vijay Kumar Garg[2]

Associate Professor, Department of Computer Science and Engineering,
Lovely Professional University, Phagwara, Punjab, India

Abstract: Electromyography (EMG) is a tool extensively used in practice to clinically analyze muscle-related disorders. In this study, we have analyzed the results of surface electromyography (sEMG) recordings of hand signals captured from both healthy and non-healthy patients to classify them using feature extraction, feature reduction, and classification using two-level classifiers, Support Vector Machines (SVM) and Feed Forward Backward Propagation Neural Network (FFBPNN). A comparison of results has been conducted on both the primary 59 data sets and the 2000 secondary data sets. The accuracy of 92.59% and 95.51% is achieved using real data sets and secondary data sets, respectively.

Keywords: Electromyography (EMG), Motor neuron, Support vector machine (SVM), Feed forward backward propagation neural network (FFBPNN)

1. Introduction

Electromyography (EMG) is an approach that has been widely used for evaluating the electrical signals to disclose vital data related to movement in muscles. The signals are recorded with varying parameters like amplitude and frequency. EMG-based applications have played a great role in the advancement of prosthetic devices in collaboration with human computers [1].

Healthcare systems are using EMG signals to diagnose the suffering of patients from muscle tiredness, aching, disorders, etc. In medical terminology, these identified health conditions are classified as myopathy and neuropathy. It is noticed that excess physical stress on the muscles and tissues also leads to a sensation of tiredness and deficiency within the muscles. In earlier days, EMG signals were extensively used in prosthetic grafts of human body parts, especially limbs, to examine their movements [2]. As a fact, EMG signals have wide applications, but getting a real prediction of muscle health conditions using these signals is a cumbersome and complex process. It requires great precision and proficiency.

The objective of this paper is to compare the results obtained from the training and classification using the multi-level architecture model, which is a computerized EMG model for categorizing normal and abnormal signals, of 59 primary data sets with the 2000 secondary data sets.

[1]reemarallan@gmail.com, [2]vijay.garg@lpu.co.in

DOI: 10.1201/9781003405580-31

2. Literature Review

The work on EMG signal pre-processing, row selection, transforming raw data, and classification of signal data to classify the signal data into normal and abnormal categories Scholars mainly focused on the extraction of features and classification of row EMG signal data using various methods. Following are a few techniques that offer improved outcomes with respect to EMG training and classification.

Too et al. (2019) have published an innovative application using binary particle swarm optimization (BPSO) for simplification of raw data extraction-related issues to categorize the EMG signals. The study gave the best results over various other methodologies, especially in the selection of the best parameters for analyzing signals. The study has achieved an accuracy of 85.20% [3].

Di Nardo et al. (2020) presented an approach related to binary classification for envisaging gait events by reading surface EMG signals. To achieve high performance in the system, a feed-forward neural network framework and EMG data have been executed. The average accuracy achieved is 96.1 1.9% [4].

Only and Mert (2020) have given a phasor-represented feature extraction (PRE) method, which was applied for the extraction of features out of the EMG signals. After using the PRE methodology, 71.17% accuracy has been achieved [5].

Badura et al. (2021) suggested one technique for evaluating pain-related problems. The authors executed the discrete wavelet transform (DWT) technique for feature extraction [6].

Karthick and Ramakrishnan (2021) presented a methodology to analyze muscle fatigue using EMG signals. For the extraction of features, authors implemented the geometric feature extraction method [7].

Jero and Bharathi (2021) suggested a method for grouping the various conditions of muscle fatigue by applying geometric extraction processes to surface EMG. Using geometric feature extraction and ANN, muscle fatigue can be identified.

However, the results of 86% accuracy show the need for better feature extraction techniques [8].

Bouhamdi Merzoug and Ouslim (2022), the study mainly described the impact of the application of the principal component analysis (PCA) technique on the sEMG data [9].

3. Methodology

3.1 Dataset Used

The dataset has been collected in real time by contacting hospitals and collecting the data manually. A mutual agreement with the hospital has been signed that declares that there will be no misuse of the data. The dataset is collected from the hospital under the guidance of a doctor. The image of the EMG machine used for data collection is shown in Fig. 31.1.

The online dataset used for the purpose of development and testing of the model is taken from the EMG repository website; the data includes 1000 records of pain EMG signal data and 1000 records of normal EMG signal data. The link to the website is https://www.kaggle.com/nccvector/electromyography-emg-dataset.

The EMG data set was acquired from 59 healthy and non-healthy patients. The signals are collected using non-invasive methods. Five electrodes are placed on the motor nerves of patients. The signals are recorded from the medial and ulnar nerves. For the medial nerve, electrodes are positioned on the wrist and elbow, and for the ulnar nerve, electrodes are applied on the wrist, below the elbow, and above the elbow sites. 59 signal data points are collected for the analysis of classification results. Table 31.1 depicts the sample data set collected, and Fig. 31.2 depicts the graphical representation of the same.

3.2 Proposed Methodology

The proposed work is shown in Fig. 31.3. The work has used the proposed method as mentioned by Jain and Garg for the classification of EMG signals. The method proposes the application of a nature-inspired algorithm, the Genetic Algorithm (GA), followed by a Support Vector Machine (SVM). Matlab has been used to simulate the model, and the classification accuracy attained was 92.4% for classes with no pain and 91.3% for classes with pain [9]. Furthermore, Jain and Garg proposed a multi-agent-based algorithm using SVM and FFBPNN, and a classification accuracy of 95.51 was observed

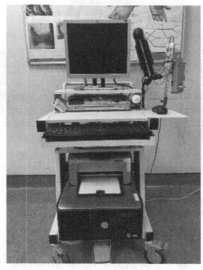
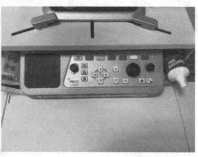

Fig. 31.1 EMG machine used for signal recording

Source: Author

Table 31.1 Motor neuron EMG signal data

Patient number	Median nerve		Ulnar nerve			Result (pain/normal)	Left/right arm
	Wrist	Elbow	Wrist	Below elbow	Above elbow		
1	6.10	6.00	7.00	6.90	7.00	Normal	L
2	5.50	5.20	2.70	2.80	2.60		L
3	9.00	9.00	6.90	6.90	7.00	Normal	L
4	8.00	7.80	4.80	5.00	4.80	Normal	L
5	7.20	7.10	4.00	4.00	3.80		L
6	9.20	11.10	8.30	2.30	4.40	Pain	L
7	8.00	8.00	7.00	7.30	7.40	Normal	L
8	5.30	5.00	4.80	4.40	4.60	Normal	L
9	2.60	2.40	5.00	5.00	4.90		R
10	4.80	4.50	7.60	7.70	7.70	Normal	R

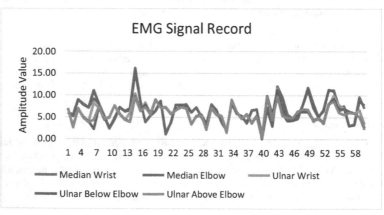

Fig. 31.2 Graphical representation of data

Source: Made by Author

using simulated data [12]. The present work focuses on using the aforesaid methods to test the results on real data collected from hospitals.

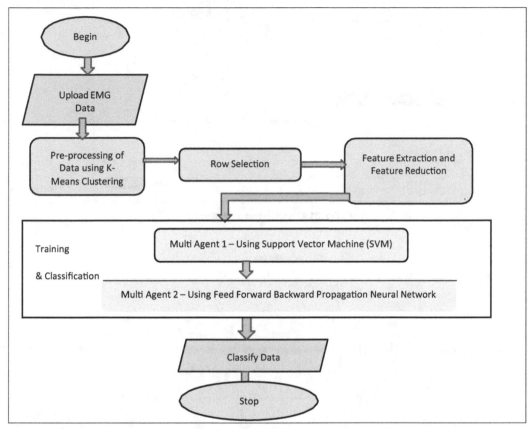

Fig. 31.3 Flowchart of Complete Process

Source: Made by Author

The EMG signal data is uploaded and segmented using the K-Means clustering algorithm. After that, pre-processing rows are selected and optimized using the genetic algorithm [11]. For the extraction of relevant features and further reduction of parameters in the model, the Hybrid Feature Extraction (HFE) method and the PCA method were applied, respectively [13]. The output after the GA step is shown in Fig. 31.4. The data is further normalized using the Critic Method. Training and classification of EMG signals using a multi-agent architecture using support vector machines (SVM) and feedforward backpropagation (FFBPNN) techniques The above-mentioned method returned the output of classified data sets.

The EMG signal data collected from the hospital is tested with the model. The 59 data sets were uploaded into the EMG model in MATLAB software. Fig. 31.4 shows the uploading of data.

The motor neuron dataset is uploaded in Matlab, and the signal data initially runs for pre-processing using the KMeans clustering algorithm. The output from the step is graphically presented in Fig. 31.5.

The GA process further refines the selection process by selecting the relevant rows for training and classification. Figures 31.6 and 31.7 depict the graphical and tabular representations of the output from the step, respectively.

The selected rows are further passed to a multi-level classification model. The output from SVM is passed to FFBPNN, and the model classifies the data into specified classes of pain and normal data. The result from the classifier is depicted in Figs 31.8 and 31.9. The parameters of the results are discussed in the following section.

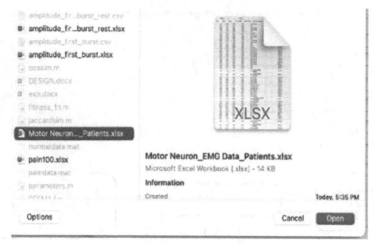

Fig. 31.4 Uploading to Matlab

Source: Made by Author

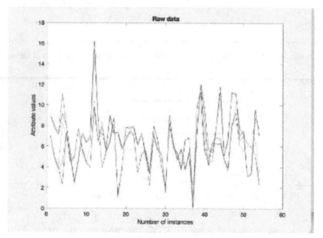

Fig. 31.5 Pre-processed data

Source: Made by Author

4. Comparison of Results

The EMG signal data classification of muscular disorders in pain and non-pain classes is evaluated by comparing the results of the repository dataset used in simulation rounds for model development [12] and testing with the real dataset collected from the hospital. The comparison parameters are the same in order to have an objective comparison of results. Table 31.2 demonstrates the parameters used for comparison.

Four parameters are considered for analyzing the performance of the proposed model for both cases, i.e., the first case using a real dataset and the second case using a repository dataset. The parameters used for analysis include precision, sensitivity, specificity, and accuracy.

4.1 Precision

One of the indicators that is used for calculating the efficiency of the model It quantifies the number of positive results from the model. The comparison of the precision values of both the real EMG dataset and the online repository dataset is given in Table 31.3.

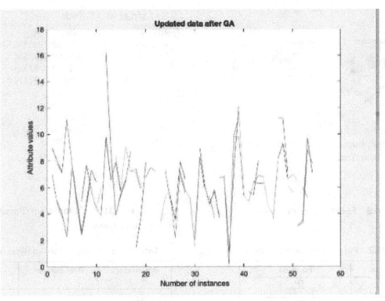

Fig. 31.6   Graphical Representation of GA Step

Source: Made by Author

54x6 double				
1	**2**	**3**	**4**	**5**
9	9	6.9000	6.9000	7
8	7.8000	4.8000	5	4.8000
7.2000	7.1000	4	4	3.8000
9.2000	11.1000	8.3000	2.3000	4.4000
8	8	7	7.3000	7.4000
5.3000	5	4.8000	4.4000	4.6000
2.6000	2.4000	5	5	4.9000
4.8000	4.5000	7.6000	7.7000	7.7000
7.3000	7.3000	5.6000	5.8000	5.7000
6.4000	6.3000	4.4000	4.5000	4.4000
7	6.6000	6	4	3.9000
16.2000	15.4000	10.4000	9.8000	9.6000
8.8000	8.7000	6.4000	6.6000	6.5000
3.9000	3.9000	8.4000	7.9000	7.3000
5.5000	5.4000	5.8000	5.7000	5.6000
6.6000	6.4000	9.1000	9	8.9000
8.8000	8.7000	7.2000	7.4000	7.2000
1.4000	1.1000	7.2000	7.3000	7.4000
3.8000	3.9000	5.7000	5.8000	5.9000
7.9000	7.8000	6.6000	6.8000	6.6000
7.7000	7.9000	7.3000	7.5000	7.4000
8	7.8000	7	7.2000	7.1000
6.2000	6.1000	3.4000	3.5000	3.5000
7.3000	7.3000	5.3000	5.3000	5.2000
5.3000	5	5.7000	5.6000	5.5000

Fig. 31.7   Output of GA Process

Source: Made by Author

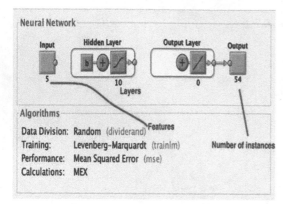

Fig. 31.8   FFBPNN Architecture

Source: Made by Author

Field ▲	Value
Accuracy	[92.5926;92.5926]
Precision	[0.9259;0.9259]
Recall	[0.9259;0.9259]
Fmeasure	[0.9259;0.9259]
TP	[25;25]
FP	[2;2]
FN	[2;2]
TN	[25;25]
Class	2x1 cell

1x1 **struct** with 9 fields

Fig. 31.9   Output from Classification

Source: Made by Author

Table 31.2   Parameters for evaluation

Parameters	Formula
Precision	$\dfrac{TP}{TP + FP}$
Sensitivity	$\dfrac{TP}{TP + FN}$
Specificity	$\dfrac{TN}{TN + FP}$
Accuracy	$\dfrac{TP + TN}{TP + TN + FP + FN}$

where TP = True Positive, TN = True Negative, FP = False Positive and FN = False Negative

Source: Made by Author

Table 31.3   Comparison Analysis of Accuracy

Parameters	Real dataset	Repository dataset
Precision	0.9259	0.931
Specificity	0.9259	0.9329
Sensitivity	0.9259	0.915
Accuracy	92.5926	95.51

Source: Made by Author

4.2 Sensitivity

This is another indicator that is used for calculating the performance of the model. It is also known as a recall or true positive rate calculator. The comparison of the sensitivity values of both the real EMG dataset and the online repository dataset is given in Table 31.3.

4.3 Specificity

The next indicator that is used for calculating the performance of the model is specificity. It is simply known as the "true negative rate." The comparison of the specificity values of both the real EMG dataset and the online repository dataset is given in Table 31.3.

4.4 Accuracy

The most important indicator that is used for calculating the performance of the model is accuracy. It actually calculates the fraction of predictions the model got right. The comparison of the accuracy values of both the real EMG dataset and the online repository dataset is given in Figure 31.10.

5. Conclusion

The rate of muscular-related problems has been escalating in recent years. Medical professionals have to face challenges

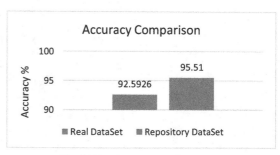

Fig. 31.10   Comparison of accuracy

Source: Made by Author

with the exponential rise in the number of muscular dysfunctions. The research work proposes to improve the accuracy of the identification of signals in relation to pain and normal class. The paper proposes to compare the results of the model achieved from the online dataset repository with the real dataset collected from the hospital. The comparative analysis of the outcomes reflects the efficiency of the proposed model. The results suggest practical applications of the model for the identification of EMG signals to classify EMG signal data into pain and normal classes. In the future, the model can be used for further classification into a higher number of classes, such as severe pain, moderate pain, and less severe pain.

REFERENCES

1. Jain, R., Garg, V. K. (2019). Review of electromyography signal with detection, decomposition, features and classifier theories. Int. J. Computer Sciences and Engineering, 7(5): 487–500.
2. Jain, R., Garg, V. K. (2021). Review of Emg signal classification approaches based on various feature domains. Matter: Int. J. Science and Technology, 6(3): 123–143.
3. Too, J., Abdullah, A. R., Mohd Saad, N. (2019). Hybrid binary particle swarm optimization differential evolution-based feature selection for EMG signals classification. Axioms, 8(3): 79.
4. Di Nardo, F., Morbidoni, G. C., Verdini, M. F., Fioretti, S. (2020). Intra-subject approach for gait-event prediction by neural network interpretation of EMG signals. Bio. Med. Engineering Online, 19(1): 1–20.
5. Only, F., Mert, A. (2020). Phasor represented EMG feature extraction against varying contraction level of prosthetic control. Bio. Med. Signal Processing and Control, 59: 101881.
6. Badura, A., Masłowska, A., Myśliwiec, A., Piętka, E. (2021). Multimodal signal analysis for pain recognition in physiotherapy using wavelet scattering transform. Sensors, 21(4): 1311.
7. Karthick P.A., Ramakrishnan, S. (2021). Muscle fatigue analysis in isometric contractions using geometric features of surface electromyography signals. Bio. Med. Signal Processing and Control, 68: 102603.
8. Jero, S. Edward et al. (2021). Muscle fatigue analysis in isometric contractions using geometric features of surface electromyography signals. Bio. Med. Signal Process. Control, 68: 102603.
9. Merzoug, B., Ouslim, M., Mostefai, L., Benouis, M. (2022). Evaluation of dimensionality reduction using PCA on EMG-based signal pattern classification. Engineering Proceedings. 14(1): 23.
10. Jain, R., Garg, V. K. (2020). EMG signal feature extraction, normalization and classification for pain and normal muscles using genetic algorithm and support vector machine. Rev. d'Intelligence Artif, 34(5): 653–661.
11. Jain, R., Garg, V. K. (2021). EMG classification using nature-inspired computing and neural architecture. 9th International Conference on Reliability, Infocom Technologies and Optimization (Trends and Future Directions) (ICRITO): 1–5, doi: 10.1109/ICRITO51393.2021.9596077.
12. Jain, R., Garg, V. K. (2022). An architecture of enhanced EMG signal classification based on multi-agent system. 3rd International Conference on Intelligent Engineering and Management (ICIEM): 664–674, doi: 10.1109/ICIEM54221.2022.9853167.
13. Jain, R., Garg, V. K. (2022). An efficient feature extraction technique and novel normalization method to improve EMG signal classification. 3rd International Conference on Intelligent Engineering and Management (ICIEM): 471–478, doi: 10.1109/ICIEM54221.2022.9853101.

Computer Science Engineering and Emerging Technologies (ICCS-2022) – Prof (Dr.) Rajeev Sobti et al. (eds)
© 2024 Taylor & Francis Group, London, ISBN 978-1-032-52199-2

Chapter

32

Role of IoT and Cloud in Smart Healthcare Monitoring System for Efficient Resource Utilization

Navneet Kumar Rajpoot[1], Prabhdeep Singh[2], Bhaskar Pant[3]
Department of Computer Science & Engineering,
Graphic Era Deemed to be University, Dehradun, India

Abstract: With the proliferation of IoT devices and cloud-based data processing solutions, cutting-edge smart, linked healthcare systems can be created. Intelligent healthcare systems analyse IoT-generated patient data to improve patient care quality and lower healthcare expenditures. The massive amount of data produced by the billions of IoT devices connected to the internet is a significant hurdle for these systems. The cloud computing infrastructure provides a potential answer by processing the huge volume of data and the numerous requests. When medical equipment is connected to the cloud, it will decrease both costs and response times in the smart healthcare system. The monitoring of vital signs and the detection and diagnosis of a wide range of ailments are only two examples of the applications and services made possible by IoT-connected devices. In this study, we discuss how the Internet of Things (IoT) can improve smart healthcare and identify some of the obstacles that need to be overcome.

Keywords: Cloud computing, Health monitoring, Internet of things (IoT), Smart healthcare

1. Introduction

In today's world, one's health is paramount. The old adage says something like, "Health is wealth," so it's vital that we use technology to improve our health. Hospitals have a social responsibility to provide on-time and sufficient services, including adequate infrastructure, resources, and personnel (such as pharmaceuticals, physicians, and nurses). A sophisticated healthcare system plays a crucial role in ensuring that patients receive high-quality care. By putting patients' access to high-quality medical treatment in the comfort of their own homes, smart healthcare systems have improved outcomes across the board. [4] In the past, patients and doctors had trouble getting in touch with one another during medical emergencies since there weren't enough doctors on call. However, the development of the Internet of Things (IoT) and more sophisticated means of communication have finally made this a reality. The Internet of Things (IoT) has made tremendous progress in recent years. Along with the explosion of biomedical data and the proliferation of "smart" healthcare communities, there has been a corresponding boom in "smart" healthcare technology. [1] Because of this, it is crucial to offer healthcare services that are both more efficient and less expensive. The use of technology in healthcare has the potential to both raise the standard of care provided to patients and lower overall expenses. With the help of this framework, doctors can remotely diagnose conditions, provide treatments, and monitor their patients' progress. By ensuring that patients receive prompt medical attention in the event of an emergency, the use of automation in healthcare monitoring systems has helped to save lives. Sensors, an Internet of Things gateway, and cloud-based storage are just some of the monitoring technologies available to collect, distribute, and analyse patient data. The Internet of Things (IoT) functions as a chain, with the primary duty of collecting data transmitted over the internet from smart devices. Using a healthcare app on a mobile device, patients

[1]shubham151515@gmail.com, [2]ssingh.prabhdeep@gmail.com, [3]bhaskar.pant@geu.ac.in

DOI: 10.1201/9781003405580-32

can gain access to their medical histories. Any digital healthcare solution that can function remotely, including components such as continuous health monitoring, emergency detection, and alarm capabilities, falls under the cover term "connected health." [2] By facilitating self-care and combining it with remote care, connected health aims to enhance the quality and efficiency of medical services. It has its beginnings in the modern era of telemedicine, when patients can receive information and advice about their health from a distance.

2. Smart Healthcare Goals

A functional smart healthcare system guarantees healthy living for inhabitants, which is especially important as the number of "smart cities" grows. Smart health care aims to assist users in maintaining a positive relationship with their health by keeping them informed about their condition. [12] Some medical emergencies can be handled by the patient themselves with the help of modern medical technology. Intelligent healthcare maximises the efficiency of existing facilities and equipment. It helps with patient remote monitoring and lowers treatment costs. [3] Figure 32.1 depicts an overview of an IoT-based, cloud-based fitness tracking system. An effective smart healthcare system must meet the following criteria:

   (i) Low power consumption
   (ii) Small form factor
  (iii) System reliability
  (iv) Quality of service
   (v) An enhanced user experience
  (vi) Increased efficiency
 (vii) Platform interoperability
(viii) Ease of deployment
  (ix) Widespread adoption
   (x) Continuous support
  (xi) Scalability
 (xii) Abundant connectivity

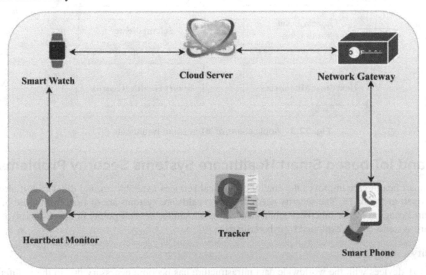

Fig. 32.1 Cloud-IoT based fitness tracking system [5]

3. Internet of Things for Smart Healthcare

The Internet of Things consists of pervasive networking, computation, and information sharing, as well as a background layer of artificial intelligence. [11] Regularly, the networked objects collect the data, analyse it, and then use it to trigger the necessary action, creating an intelligent system for analysis, planning, and decision-making. By allowing for remote access, the IoT serves as a bridge between the doctor and the patient, allowing the doctor to keep close tabs on the patient and offer virtual consultations. The Internet of Things (IoT) combines sensors, actuators, microcontrollers, computers, and the cloud to help get precise findings and make quality medical care affordable for everybody. [10] The identity, location, sensing, and communication capabilities afforded by the IoT are only a few of its many impressive features. There are many ways in which the Internet of Things might improve medical care [14].

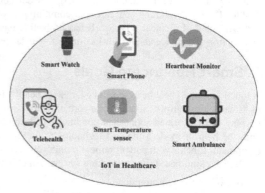

Fig. 32.2   IoT in smart healthcare [2]

3.1 The Use of the Internet of Things in Healthcare

Adults and patients can now live independently thanks to healthcare applications. During this time, IoT sensors are utilised to conduct health checks, re-evaluate previous assessments, and issue warnings when inappropriate behaviour is detected. If any more minor issues are found, the IoT device will notify the patient automatically.

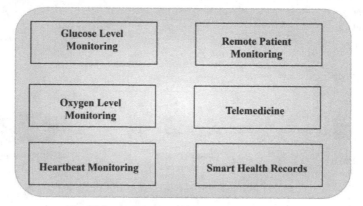

Fig. 32.3   Applications of IoT in smart healthcare [7]

4. Cloud and IoT-based Smart Healthcare Systems Security Problems

Even though smart health care improves the quality of medical services available around the world, it also leaves these systems more open to attack. [8] The security needs of smart healthcare systems are distinct from those of conventional security systems because of their inherent mobility and compact nature. Several points in the scalability architecture of smart healthcare systems can be exploited by cybercriminals. [9]

4.1 Scalability

Integration of IoT devices with the worldwide data infrastructure has become necessary due to the proliferation of such devices.

4.2 Limitations on Device Mobility and Power Consumption

Limitations on Device Mobility and Power Consumption Power is supplied via batteries. However, more efficient security techniques are required for mobility. [7]

4.3 Limitations on Memory

One of the biggest challenges with the storage and operation of IoT-based devices is the devices' typically meagre amounts of memory.

4.4 Multi-Protocol Network

To exchange data with one another, Internet of Things gadgets use a variety of network protocols through the local area network.

The following is a list of some additional security issues with smart health care.

(i)   Safeguarding the Privacy of Data
(ii) Integrity
(iii) Confidentiality
(iv) Confidentiality
(v)   Authentication
(vi) The ability to heal oneself
(vii) Privacy-Protected
(viii) Services Easily Accessible

5. Proposed Framework for IoT and Cloud-based Smart Healthcare

The foundation of our idea is the automation of the process by which patient data is collected via sensors attached to medical devices and transmitted to the cloud for storage, processing, and analysis by medical facilities. Figure 32.4 depicts the architecture of the proposed system, which consists of the cloud server layer, the hospital, the remote IoT-integrated medical nodes, and the distributed medical records collection.

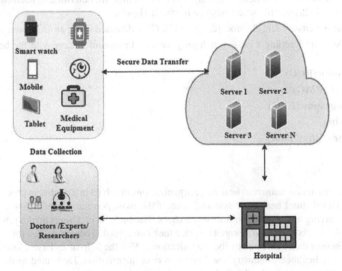

Fig. 32.4   Proposed framework for IoT & cloud-based smart healthcare [4]

5.1 Cloud Server Layer

The cloud makes possible healthcare technology, including electronic health records, mobile health apps, patient platforms, Internet of Things-connected gadgets, and big data analysis. Better choices are made as a result of its easy scalability and adaptability, as well as its collaborative features and security. [9] Cloud computing has the potential to improve healthcare by streamlining data administration and allowing for improved ERR monitoring. [4] Users make requests to the cloud server, which handles the data transfer and storage before sending the results back to the users.

5.2 Medical Facility

This layer serves as a data repository. Patient ID, name, disease history, and medications are just a handful of the many features used to keep track of each individual's health records. A smart healthcare system improves the quality of healthcare decisions by allowing for simple, scalable, and flexible collaboration among healthcare professionals. Clinical applications that support continuous therapy can be a great resource for doctors and healthcare teams. [5] Researchers have made it possible for doctors and nurses to access patient lab results.

5.3 Distributed Medical Data Collection

This layer works together with the hospital layer. As a precaution, sensitive patient information is dispersed across multiple nodes before being kept in the hospital layer.

5.4 Remote IoT-Integrated Medical Nodes

Nodes that are remotely connected to the Internet and used to monitor a patient's health can collect data on a wide range of vital signs and transmit that information to a central cloud storage system. The suggested health monitoring system collects information from all patient-attached wearables and medical sensors through the IoT device network [1]. The sensors keep track of vital signs like heart rate, cardiac output, and internal body temperature.

The following is a list of some of the sensors and wearable devices used in IoT-based smart health.

  (i) **Temperature Sensor:** One of its functions is as a thermometer.
 (ii) **Heart Rate Monitor:** When a finger is placed on the heart rate sensor, it provides a digital readout of the user's heart rate.
(iii) **Pulse Oximeter Sensor:** Pulse oximetry is a straightforward method for determining haemoglobin levels. Heart rate is typically expressed in hertz (HR) when using an oximeter (Bpm).
 (iv) **Heart Rate Monitor Sensor:** The electrocardiogram (ECG) is detected using an ECG sensor.
  (v) **Blood Pressure Sensor:** Keeping a close watch on your blood pressure is easy with the help of a blood pressure sensor.
 (vi) **Electrocardiography (ECG)**
(vii) **Electromyography (EMG)**
(viii) **Electroencephalography (EEG)**
 (ix) **Glucose Monitoring**
  (x) **Implantable Neural Stimulators**

6. Conclusion

Cloud computing makes it easier for numerous healthcare organizations involved in a treatment process to share information. The Internet of Things-based smart healthcare system is one of the most popular technologies, is expanding quickly all over the world, and is receiving major attention from researchers. The Internet of Things health revolution is here, and that means people may finally access high-quality care at a price they can afford. There is a need for efficient management of the massive amounts of sensor data generated by these applications. With the help of its base, cloud computing offers great potential for improving the healthcare industry's ability to process information. Dedicated to the patient, the presented framework can be utilised to manage cloud IoT devices and network data. You can use it to get around the problems and obstacles that plague conventional medical care. Sustainable solutions to the rising expense of healthcare have been identified as Internet of Things (IoT)-based smart health systems. This paper presents a comprehensive overview of the latest research tendencies, difficulties, and possibilities of smart health care. There has always been a significant market demand for needle-free, low-cost medical interventions. The new study is remarkable because it reduces latency and maximizes system performance. This work may enhance several facets of health care by making use of the cloud and various IoT technologies.

REFERENCES

1. lata Sahu, M., Atulkar, M. and Ahirwal, M. K., 2020, January. Comprehensive investigation on IoT based smart HealthCare system. In *2020 First International Conference on Power, Control and Computing Technologies (ICPC2T)* (pp. 325–330). IEEE.
2. Chang, V., Cao, Y., Li, T., Shi, Y. and Baudier, P., 2019, May. Smart healthcare and ethical issues. In *1st International Conference on Finance, Economics, Management and IT Business* (pp. 53–59). SciTePress.
3. Alekya, R., Boddeti, N. D., Monica, K. S., Prabha, R. and Venkatesh, V., 2020. IoT based smart healthcare monitoring systems: A literature review. *European Journal of Molecular & Clinical Medicine*, 7(11), p. 2020.
4. Kashani, M. H., Madanipour, M., Nikravan, M., Asghari, P. and Mahdipour, E., 2021. A systematic review of IoT in healthcare: Applications, techniques, and trends. *Journal of Network and Computer Applications*, *192*, p. 103164.
5. Reena, J. K. and Parameswari, R., 2019, February. A smart health care monitor system in IoT based human activities of daily living: a review. In *2019 International Conference on Machine Learning, Big Data, Cloud and Parallel Computing (COMITCon)* (pp. 446–448). IEEE.
6. Egala, B. S., Priyanka, S. and Pradhan, A. K., 2019, December. SHPI: smart healthcare system for patients in ICU using IoT. In *2019 IEEE International Conference on Advanced Networks and Telecommunications Systems (ANTS)* (pp. 1–6). IEEE.
7. Baucas, M. J., Spachos, P. and Gregori, S., 2021. Internet-of-Things devices and assistive technologies for health care: applications, challenges, and opportunities. *IEEE Signal Processing Magazine*, *38*(4), pp. 65–77.
8. Garg, N., Wazid, M., Das, A. K., Singh, D. P., Rodrigues, J. J. and Park, Y., 2020. BAKMP-IoMT: Design of blockchain enabled authenticated key management protocol for internet of medical things deployment. *IEEE Access*, *8*, pp. 95956–95977.
9. Garg, N., Obaidat, M. S., Wazid, M., Das, A. K. and Singh, D. P., 2021, June. SPCS-IoTEH: Secure Privacy-Preserving Communication Scheme for IoT-Enabled e-Health Applications. In *ICC 2021-IEEE International Conference on Communications* (pp. 1–6). IEEE.
10. Ojha, U. C., Singh, D. P., Choudhari, O. K., Gothi, D. and Singh, S., 2018. Correlation of severity of functional gastrointestinal disease symptoms with that of asthma and chronic obstructive pulmonary disease: a multicenter study. *International Journal of Applied and Basic Medical Research*, *8*(2), p. 83.
11. Islam, M. and Rahaman, A., 2020. Development of smart healthcare monitoring system in IoT environment. SN computer science, 1(3), pp. 1–11.
12. Naik, S. and Sudarshan, E., 2019. Smart healthcare monitoring system using raspberry Pi on IoT platform. ARPN Journal of Engineering and Applied Sciences, 14(4), pp. 872–876.
13. Yang, Z., Zhou, Q., Lei, L., Zheng, K. and Xiang, W., 2016. An IoT-cloud based wearable ECG monitoring system for smart healthcare. Journal of medical systems, 40(12), pp. 1–11.

Computer Science Engineering and Emerging Technologies (ICCS-2022) – Prof (Dr.) Rajeev Sobti et al. (eds)
© 2024 Taylor & Francis Group, London, ISBN 978-1-032-52199-2

Chapter **33**

Challenges Faced in Polygon Clipping Procedures and Visualization Technique in 3D Face Detection: A Comprehensive Review

Prabhjyot kaur Haryal[1]
Ph.D. Scholar Lovely Professional University

Punam Rattan[2]
Faculty School of Computer Application,
Lovely Professional University

Shilpa Sharma[3]
Faculty School of Computer Science and Engineering,
Lovely Professional University

Abstract: One of the most successful uses of image analysis, face recognition, has recently attracted a lot of attention. It is a result of the availability of workable technology, such as mobile solutions. Recent increases in interest in face recognition can be attributed to a number of factors, such as growing public security concerns, the necessity for identity verification in the digital age, face analysis and modelling approaches in multimedia data management, and computer entertainment. In this paper, we have reviewed processes that are involved in face recognition, covering key elements including facial detection, 3D image acquisition, alignment and feature extraction, the use of polygon clipping procedures, and visualization techniques in face detection.

Keywords: Face detection, 3D image acquisition, Polygon clipping, Visualization, Pattern recognition

1. Introduction

Since face recognition is regarded as a streamlined image analysis and pattern recognition application, it has attracted a lot of interest over the past three decades. [1] The performance of the current machine learning and recognition systems is constrained by the requirements placed on them by real-world applications, despite having attained a certain level of maturity. [2] The face is possibly the most prevalent and well-known biometric aspect of our daily life. Since the advent of photography, both public and private organizations have maintained facial images in various formats. These collections have been utilized as referential databases in forensic investigations to match and contrast a respondent's facial photos. [3] Additionally, it became simple to create facial photos on a daily basis because of the widespread usage of digital cameras and cellphones. [4] In comparison to other biometric modalities, such as the iris or fingerprint, the human face is not the most accurate modality because it can be affected by makeup, disguises, and lighting. It is also less precise than other modalities like the iris or fingerprint.

---

[1]prabhjyot.2019@gmail.com, [2]punamrattan@gmail.com, [3]Shilpa.sharma@lpu.co.in

DOI: 10.1201/9781003405580-33

1.1 Problem Statement

Inferring the 3D polygon images and structure of objects and scenes from one or more 2D photographs using the polygon clipping procedure and visualization techniques is the theory behind image-based 3D facial recognition. Numerous applications, including object identification, scene comprehension, 3D modelling and animation, etc., depend on solving this age-old, ill-posed problem. The topic of image-based 3D reconstruction is significant, and it serves as the foundation for many applications in fields including robotics, autonomous navigation, graphics, and entertainment.

1.2 Objectives

The core objectives on which the review paper is based are as follows:

1. To review 3D Image acquisition using Polygon Clipping Procedures and Visualization techniques.
2. To study various dataset of images and performance prediction parameters.

2. Review of Literature

Table 33.1 The literature review comprises of papers from 2017 till 2022

Author (Year)	Work/Analysis	Technique	Accuracy	Tool
[1]	Proposed a face recognition-based mobile automatic system	Contains different mobile applications for users.	89%	Andriod Mobile App
[2]	Proposed a system using fingerprinttemplate.	Fingerprint template.	90%	STC89C52 microcontroller, 12864 LCD, matrixkeyboard
[3]	Proposes a prototype based on Mifare1K and Raspberry Pi.	Mifare 1K and Raspberry Pi	78%	Andriod MobileApp
[4]	Implementation method of mobile phone attendance and positioning system.	attendance and positioning system based on campus network	95%	Andriod MobileApp
[5]	An automated system that can be used incrowded places.	algorithm detects faces inthe picture(s)	80%	Andriod MobileApp
[6]	Contributed an IoT-based system(IAAS).	An automatic attendancesystem	90%	Andriod MobileApp
[7]	Proposed an automated facialrecognition system.	Embedded devices andcombined with Cloud server.	77%	Andriod MobileApp
[8]	A mobile phone based lightweightattendance system.	Quick Response (QR) code	89%	Andriod MobileApp
[9]	A tool capable of tracking and recordingstudents' attendance.	Waterfall Model	92%	Andriod MobileApp
[10]	Three large scale scene sketch datasets.	Semantic Segmentation	95%	Feature fusion network architecture
[11]	Fully convolutional object detection.	FCOS architecture	79%	Anchor box
[12]	Deep-learning based image deblurringapproaches.	Image Deblurring	80%	CNN
[13]	An effective post processing refinementframework.	Image Segmentation	75%	BPR Framework
[14]	An illumination and contrast-invariantfeature.	Image Edges detection	80%	Multi-scale Phase Congruency
[15]	A multi task cascaded convolutionalneural network	Face Detection	85%	MTCNN
[16]	Splitting versions of augmentedLagrangian method.	Image Decomposition	92%	Numerical Algorithm using Lagrangian Method
[17]	Structured deep coupled metric learningframework (SDCML).	Structured RegionSegmentation	90%	SDCML Framework
[18]	Spatial feature interactions of images.	Fine-grained classification	95%	CFFN
[19]	Encode mesh connectivity usingLaplacian spectral analysis.	Laplacian PoolingNetwork	75%	3D Meshes
[20]	Novel neural network architecture for 3Ddata.	Semantic Segmentation	95%	3D SceneGraphs

Author (Year)	Work/Analysis	Technique	Accuracy	Tool
[21]	Discovering and fixing systematicdifferences from human vision.	Object Identification	82%	Computationalmodels
[22]	Review of Face Recognition System andits Applications	Computer Vision	90%	Holistic Matching, Feature-based andHybrid Methods
[23]	An end-to-end learning framework.	3D scene analysis	75%	SfSNet
[24]	It helps in significantly reducing the supervision level required for generic object counting.	Generic Object Counting	90%	RLC Framework
[25]	understanding the role of multiple visual localization paradigms.	Visual Localization	86%	Image Retrieval Techniques
[26]	Developed a tool capable of tracking andrecording data using the Waterfall Modelfor reference purposes.	Waterfall Model	92%	Andriod MobileApp
[27]	Benefits of a face detection system	Face Detection	89%	Andriod Mobile App

Source: Made by Author

3. Discussion

The findings of this paper demonstrate a significant increase in research in this field over the previous five years, particularly with the development of facial recognition, which has outperformed the most widely used computer vision techniques. In addition, numerous facial databases are also available for research and commercial purposes. Based on the above literature, the data sets, methods, and materials used are as follows.

3.1 Data Sets

The following available data sets will be helpful in developing new data set of 3D images.

Table 33.2   Data sets with description

S.No.	Data Sets	Description
1.	ScanNet[5], [7], [8], [9]	Annotated RGB-D video collection includes surface reconstructions, instance-level semantic segmentations, and 3D camera postures.
2.	Pix3D [6], [8]	It is a large-scale benchmark for different image-shape combinations with 2D and 3D alignment at the pixel level.
3.	Labeled Faces [11], [13], [17], [15], [16]	Labeled Faces is a public benchmark for face verification.
4.	ImageNet [12], [18], [19], [20]	ImageNet is an image database organized according to the WordNet hierarchy.
5.	CelebA-Dialog [10], [14]	CelebA-Dialog is a large-scale visual-language face dataset.

Source: Made by Author

3.2 Materials and Methods Used

Table 33.3   Various methods and materials used by researchers

Method	Materials Used
Classical face recognition algorithms [21], [22], [23]	Eigenface Method, Local Binary Patterns, Fisher face Technique
Artificial neural networks [24]	Convolutional Neural Network
Face descriptor-based methods [25]	Knowledge-based Technique
3D-based face recognition [26]	Iris recognition
Video-based recognition [27]	Feature extraction Technique

Source: Made by Author

3.3 Challenges

After analyzing papers, some challenges need to be acknowledged which are as follows:

- The authors have proposed a face recognition-based system needing no extra equipment but **the concept is not able to obtain the accuracy of data after filtration.**
- In this paper the authors have studied the implementation method of face recognition but are not able to define **the range of the total area is not mentioned.**
- A system is developed by researchers which **can be used only in Android devices.**
- A novel CNN architecture motivated by the popular architectures has been proposed **but they have missing data set.**
- The authors have developed a system which is **more prone to hacking or being misused by other physical attacks.**

3.4 Suggestions

1. **Training data issue.** The size of the publicly accessible datasets that contain both photos and their 3D annotations is sadly much smaller than the training datasets needed for tasks like classification and recognition.
2. **Generalization to unseen objects**. The majority of cutting-edge publications divide a dataset into three subsets for training, validation, and testing.
3. **Fine-scale 3D reconstruction**. Modern cutting-edge methods can retrieve the rough 3D structure of shapes.
4. **Specialized instance reconstruction**. In order to take advantage of domain-specific information, it is anticipated that class-specific knowledge modelling and deep learning-based 3D reconstruction would work together more in the future.
5. **Handling multiple objects in the presence of occlusions and cluttered backgrounds**. Modern methods mostly work with photos that just have one item in them. However, most photographs generally include a variety of things belonging to numerous groups.

4. Conclusion

The discipline of computer vision is still grappling with the problem of face recognition. Due to its numerous uses in numerous fields, it has drawn a lot of interest in recent years. Even though there is significant research being done in this area, facial recognition algorithms are still not ideally suited to function effectively in all real-world scenarios. There is still a lot of effort to be done in order to develop techniques that accurately represent how people recognize faces and best utilize the temporal evolution of a face's look for identification.

REFERENCES

1. Samet, R., & Tanriverdi, M. (2017). Face recognition-based mobile automatic classroom attendance management system. https://doi.org/10.1109/CW.2017.34
2. Zhan, H., Wang, Q., & Hu, Y. (2017). Fingerprint attendance machine design based on C51 single-chip microcomputer. https://doi.org/10.1109/ICCTEC.2017.00171
3. Bejo, A., Winata, R., & Kusumawardani, S. S. (2019, January 7). Prototyping of Class-Attendance System Using Mifare 1K Smart Card and Raspberry Pi 3. https://doi.org/10.1109/ISESD.2018.8605442
4. Xu, Z., Chen, P., Zhang, W., Liu, X., & Wu, H. (2019). Research on mobile phone attendance positioning system based on campus network. https://doi.org/10.1109/ICSGEA.2019.00094
5. Mery, D., Mackenney, I., & Villalobos, E. (2019). Student attendance system in crowded classrooms using a smartphone camera. https://doi.org/10.1109/WACV.2019.00096
6. Jeong, J. P., Kim, M., Lee, Y., & Lingga, P. (2020). IAAS: IoT-Based Automatic Attendance System with Photo Face Recognition in Smart Campus. https://doi.org/10.1109/ICTC49870.2020.9289276
7. Nguyen, D. D., Nguyen, X. H., Than, T. T., & Nguyen, M. S. (2021). Automated Attendance System in the Classroom Using Artificial Intelligence and Internet of Things Technology. https://doi.org/10.1109/NICS54270.2021.9700991
8. Chen, F., Li, J., & Wang, Z. (2021). A Mobile Computing Based Attendance System and Students' Attitude Study. https://doi.org/10.1109/TALE52509.2021.9678695
9. Acasamoso, D. M., Avila, E. C., & Vargas, S. (2021). Development and Acceptability of a Student Daily Attendance Monitoring System. https://doi.org/10.1109/HNICEM54116.2021.9731963

10. Ge, C., Sun, H., Song, Y. Z., Ma, Z., & Liao, J. (2022). Exploring Local Detail Perception for Scene Sketch Semantic Segmentation. https://doi.org/10.1109/TIP.2022.3142511

11. Tian, Z., Shen, C., Chen, H., & He, T. (2022). FCOS: A Simple and Strong Anchor-Free Object Detector. https://doi.org/10.1109/TPAMI.2020.3032166

12. Zhang, K., Ren, W., Luo, W., Lai, W. S., Stenger, B., Yang, M. H., & Li, H. (2022). Deep Image Deblurring: A Survey. https://doi.org/10.1007/s11263-022-01633-5

13. Hu, X., Tang, C., Chen, H., Li, X., Li, J., & Zhang, Z. (2022). Improving Image Segmentation with Boundary Patch Refinement. https://doi.org/10.1007/s11263-022-01662-0

14. Huang, J., Bai, B., & Yang, F. (2022). An effective salient edge detection method based on point flow with phase congruency. https://doi.org/10.1007/s11760-021-02048-4

15. Gu, M., Liu, X., & Feng, J. (2022). Classroom face detection algorithm based on improved MTCNN. https://doi.org/10.1007/s11760-021-02087-x

16. Xu, J., Shang, W., & Hao, Y. (2022). A new cartoon + texture image decomposition model based on the Sobolev space. https://doi.org/10.1007/s11760-021-02111-0

17. Fu, G., Zou, G., Gao, M., Wang, Z., & Liu, Z. (2022). Image matching based on a structured deep coupled metric learning framework. https://doi.org/10.1007/s11760-021-02120-z

18. Liao, K., Huang, G., Zheng, Y., Lin, G., & Cao, C. (2022). Coordinate feature fusion networks for fine-grained image classification. https://doi.org/10.1007/s11760-022-02291-3

19. Qiao, Y. L., Gao, L., Yang, J., Rosin, P. L., Lai, Y. K., & Chen, X. (2022). Learning on 3D Meshes with Laplacian Encoding and Pooling. https://doi.org/10.1109/TVCG.2020.3014449

20. Wald, J., Navab, N., & Tombari, F. (2022). Learning 3D Semantic Scene Graphs with Instance Embeddings. https://doi.org/10.1007/s11263-021-01546-9

21. Pramod, R. T., & Arun, S. P. (2022). Improving Machine Vision Using Human Perceptual Representations: The Case of Planar Reflection Symmetry for Object Classification. https://doi.org/10.1109/TPAMI.2020.3008107

22. Shahi, S., & Singh, B. (2022). Face Recognition System and its Applications.

23. Sengupta, S., Lichy, D., Kanazawa, A., Castillo, C. D., & Jacobs, D. W. (2022). SfSNet: Learning Shape, Reflectance and Illuminance of Faces in the Wild. https://doi.org/10.1109/TPAMI.2020.3046915

24. Cholakkal, H., Sun, G., Khan, S., Khan, F. S., Shao, L., & van Gool, L. (2022). Towards Partial Supervision for Generic Object Counting in Natural Scenes. https://doi.org/10.1109/TPAMI.2020.3021025

25. Humenberger, M., Cabon, Y., Pion, N., Weinzaepfel, P., Lee, D., Guérin, N., Sattler, T., & Csurka, G. (2022). Investigating the Role of Image Retrieval for Visual Localization: An Exhaustive Benchmark. https://doi.org/10.1007/s11263-022-01615-7

26. Acasamoso, D. M., Avila, E. C., & Vargas, S. (2021). Development and Acceptability of a Student Daily Attendance Monitoring System. https://doi.org/10.1109/HNICEM54116.2021.9731963

27. Chow, S. R., Josephng, P. S., Phan, K. Y., & Yeck, Y. P. (2021, September 24). JomAttendance: My face is the attendance. https://doi.org/10.1109/GUCON50781.2021.9573555

Computer Science Engineering and Emerging Technologies (ICCS-2022) – Prof (Dr.) Rajeev Sobti et al. (eds)
© *2024 Taylor & Francis Group, London, ISBN 978-1-032-52199-2*

Chapter

34

Use of IoT and Senso-based Big Data Applications to Develop Future Smart Sustainable Cities

K. K. Ramachandran[1]
Director/ Professor, Management/Commerce/International Business,
Dr. G R D College of Science, India

Jagadish R. M.[2]
Associate Professor, Department of CSE (AI&ML),
Vardhaman College of Engineering,Hyderabad, Telangana

G. Saravana Kumar[3]
Associate Professor, BMS-School of Commerce,
Jain (deemed to be) University, Bengaluru, Karnataka

Manik Deshmukh[4]
Associate professor, Sveris College of engineering,
Pandharpur, Maharashtra

Tanvi Jindal[5]
Assistant Professor, Chitkara Business School,
Chitkara University, Punjab, India

M. Kalyan Chakravarthi[6]
Senior Assistant Professor, School of Electronics Engineering,
VIT-AP University, Amaravathi, India

Abstract: The idea of smart and sustainable cities has continued to evolve as multiple technical, economic, and administrative barriers challenge their widespread implementation. A primary component of future smart and sustainable cities is the smart traffic system (STS). The requirements of smart traffic management systems (STMS) are not yet being met by traffic management and alarm systems. In order to offer a higher level of support for public traffic control, STS is highly costly and configurable. The idea of smart, sustainable cities was developed by the Internet of Things (IoT) and sensor-based big data applications, which were inspired by the explosive proliferation of linked heterogeneous systems. In order to improve services, this research suggests a low-cost real-time STS that employs traffic signals to update traffic information rapidly. Every 500 or 1000 meters, low-cost vehicles and detection sensors are embedded in the center of the road. Using the IoT, traffic data may be promptly collected and sent for processing. To do big data analysis, real-time broadcast data is supplied. A mobile program is developed as a user interface that provides an alternative technique of traffic control and enables users to look into the traffic densities in various areas.

Keywords: IoTs, Big data, Sensors, STMS, Smart sustainable cities

[1]dr.k.k.ramachandran@gmail.com, [2]rm.jagadish@gmail.com, [3]k.saravana@jainuniversity.ac.in, [4]mgdeshmukh@coe.sveri.ac.in, [5]anglebirth1990@gmail.com, [6]kalyanchakravarthi.m@vitap.ac.in

DOI: 10.1201/9781003405580-34

1. Introduction

Currently, cities are places of residence for more than 50% of the earth's population, and this number is steadily rising. Modern cities, particularly large cities, have issues in a number of sectors, including crowded transportation systems, energy consumption, water, climate change, etc., as urban settings grow more densely inhabited and more complicated [Cheng, B., et al., (2015)]. On the contrary, we observe that cities are more digitally advanced and interconnected than ever. As a result, the number of smart city programs and projects has increased recently [Ramu, S. P., et al., 2022].

Contemporary advancements in artificial intelligence (AI) and the internet of things (IoT) have contributed to this achievement by enabling the ongoing development of services like smart healthcare, transportation, and environmental control [Bokhari, S. A. A., and Myeong, S. (2022)]. There is no consensus agreement on how to define the term "smart cities," which has several different meanings. Nevertheless, there are requirements for smart cities, like the advancement of societal livelihoods through the use of disruptive innovations and societal, environmental, and economic sustainable growth [Esashika, D., et al., 2021].

Thus, understanding the need for service profiling to increase efficiency and perhaps bring about contemporary advancements in city administration is of the utmost necessity for urbanization. Few businesses now have IoT systems for live planning, monitoring, and collecting attributes of the urban process [Talebkhah, M., et al., 2021]. For example, broadband connections in Japan enable communication between individuals, individuals and objects, and objects and objects. Similar to this, South Korea's smart house allows residents to access items remotely. A safe and widespread U network is intended to help Singapore's next-generation I-Hub understand [Rathore, M. M., et al., (2015)]. So, the usage of IoT for smart networks leads to an increase in the number of things that are linked to one another, which produces an enormous quantity of diverse data, also known as big data. Cities would grow smarter by analyzing such data in accordance with user preferences and demands [Al Nuaimi, E., et al., (2015)].

Without taking into account the significance of big data development and management, the system under discussion only functions to a limited extent. In such a setting, data collection and analysis methods are typically challenging to implement. In order to improve city planning and growth, it is necessary to use smart technologies that can effectively collect data, do analyses, make judgments in the present, and anticipate the future. Thus, IoT and associated sensor-based big data technologies are unmistakably making inroads into various systems as well as areas of sustainable smart cities [Bibri, S. E., and Krogstie, J. (2017a)].

1.1 Scope of the Research

Applications for smart, sustainable cities in urban design and development are the initiatives taken by India and worldwide that have a significant influence on people's lives. This comprises the influence on the population with regard to health and welfare, pollution management, and other sustainable factors. Numerous initiatives involving the observation of cyclists, vehicles, and public parking spaces, among other things, are in progress that use sensor technologies to gather relevant data. It appears that several more applications have been discovered that make use of the IoT network for smart, sustainable cities to provide functions for the cities' pollution and security systems. The transportation system, nevertheless, is crucial to the growth of any metropolis. Even a nation can indeed advance quickly if its transportation infrastructure and citizen transit amenities are impressive. In addition to these and several other advantages, smarter transportation also helps citizens, promotes development, boosts the economy, and reduces pollution. There aren't many new study discoveries in the fields of smart sustainable cities as well as smart traffic systems (STS) in the most recent studies. Additionally, in this modern age where there are billions of items linked to the internet, millions of pieces of big data are produced. The analysis of many features of a smart, sustainable city is done using the sensor-based big data produced by the numerous IoT technologies.

It's important to note that the scope of the research is regarding the lack of investigation into creating comprehensive systems for smart and sustainable cities using IoT and sensor-based big data as a holistic urban advancement application, which serves as the foundation for the suggested empirical approach.

1.2 Research Objective

The aim of this investigation is to study utilization of IoT and sensor-based big data's to the development for the future sustainable smart cities with the objectives

- To develop comfortable driving model (CDM) for smart traffic management system (STMS) in India.

- To study the conceptual and technical deployment methods demonstrated how we can deploy sensors and system-provided interactivity.
- To study the process of practical implementation and experimental assessment of a system that monitors traffic conditions and updates users often.

1.3 Research Framework

This research includes five parts, including an introduction. In the following part two of the literature review, we explain the review of literature based on smart cities and its link with IoT, big data, and sustainability literature from 2015 to 2022. Section 3 describes the materials and methods utilized in this research. The outcomes are presented and discussed in Section 4; Section 5 ends with the key findings, their implications, and recommendations for theory as well as practice.

2. Review of Literature

2.1 Smart Sustainable Cities

As per Bibri, S. E., and Krogstie, J. (2017b), the concept of "smart sustainable cities," though it is not always utilized explicitly, refers to cities that are backed by the widespread and huge utilization of advanced ICT, which, in link with numerous urban platforms and contexts and how they interact with one another and are organized, respectively, facilitates the cities to regulate resources available securely, sustainably, and effectively to enhance social and economic results.

2.2 Sensing Regions and Sensor Types

As per Adams, D., et al. (2021), a broad range of sensors is used in big data analysis. A sensor can indeed be defined as a tool that recognizes or quantifies a physical characteristic or any other sort of information from the physical surroundings and then signals or responds to it in a certain manner. The following are some of the sensor types, among others, that can be commonly categorized based on the kind of energy they identify as signals: Location (GPS), sound (microphones), image (stereotype camera, infrared), temperature (thermometer), light sensors (photocells), etc.

2.3 The Connection Between Sensors, Big Data, and IoT

IoT implies that innovation in the sort of innumerable adjacent wirelessly linked sensing and processing systems will permeate urban areas and make common things smart by allowing them to connect with one another, with individuals and their things, and discover their contexts. Because of these distinguishing characteristics, the IoT involves intricate sensors and structures [Bibri, S. E. (2018)].

According to Bibri, S. E., and Krogstie, J. (2017c), a significant scientific and technical issue in the field of computational devices, generally, and in particular of big data analysis, is how to implement methods to preserve, combine, process, analyze, and handle the created data via scalable applications. This results from the different sensor collecting variables and their duration as to the data that is gathered and preserved. Despite the challenges in removing the barriers preventing the widespread acceptance of the IoT within smart, sustainable cities, the IoT has shown an exemplary capability to add a completely novel aspect to the usage and advancement of sustainable development throughout urban contexts by facilitating interaction and data exchange between the tangible and smart things utilized throughout urban settings in link with power and environmental structures.

In the coming years, surveillance, comprehension, analyzing, and assessing smart sustainable cities with regard to their operations and maintenance and preparing to enhance their involvement in the objective of ecologically sustainable development will be dominated by the center facilitating innovations of the IoT and thus sensor-based big data applications, notably digital sensor innovations, data processing portals, computing designs, and wireless communications systems [Bibri, S. E., & Krogstie, J. (2016)].

3. Materials and Method

3.1 Experimental Setup

For the general design of the research setup, there are 3 distinct parts. Figure 34.1 illustrates the deployment of technologies at the core level.

3.2 Internet of Thing (IoT) Component

The strategy is an entirely IoT-based automobile data collection system. With the newest features and automobile-detecting sensors, the Intel IoT kit In order to achieve the greatest outcomes, it is optimal to install the sensors very close together, at a distance of no more than one kilometer and a half. A minimum of ten sensors are interconnected, and they are all connected to the same Internet of Things kit. Each kit has a network connection, allowing them to share information online. It keeps an eye out for moving objects, transmitting updates to big data analytics and archives.

3.3 Big Data Analytics Component

It obtains the sensor data together using the sensor ID. Implement analytics activities by computing all the data. Numerous variables are taken into account while estimating each sensor's strength and adding or subtracting

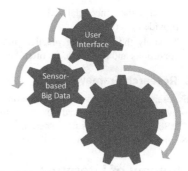

Fig. 34.1 Technology connections overflow on the technical end [14]

sensors for entering and exiting vehicles, as well as roadway capacity. Other aspects are taken into account when computing and analyzing a report, which must be prepared through an internet connection via a mobile application or web browser. Thus, several methodologies are employed in conjunction with cutting-edge real-time broadcast data analysis techniques.

3.4 User Interface Component

The most recent analytics and decision-making smart tools are provided for passengers in this section. Road capacity, vehicle presence, vehicle condition, and internet connection are all displayed. Users desire to access data in a variety of ways, such as through mobile applications, web browsers, devices with GPS enabled, etc. From the perspective of the user, very quick data processing and communication are to be accomplished via large data stream analysis. Real-time data flow computation is improved and accelerated, and then analytics are used.

3.5 Conceptual Implementation Process

The comfortable driving model (CDM) influences the portable model used for regenerations. It involves a traffic cell robot in which time and space are discretized into intervals of 1.5 m and 1 s, respectively.

A vehicle designated n's location and speed are determined by yn and vehn separately. The automobile before n is termed $n + 1$ when naming vehicles downstream. The first vehicles brake light t_{n+1} state is taken into account, together with the speed of the first automobile, to add expected repercussions

$$veh_{\text{speed}} = \min(veh_{n+v} d_{n+1}) \tag{1}$$

By calculating the compelling distance using equation 1

$$D_n^{eff} = \max(d_{\text{distance}} - veh_{\text{speed}}, 0) + d_n \tag{2}$$

Estimating the gap between the automobiles gn. Utilizing the following criteria, one can get each vehicle's priority computation and their speed computation.

If $(D_n(t + 1) > d_n^{eff} - g_n(t)$ and $g_n(t) > 0)$, then

$I(veh_n(t + 1) > veh_n(t))$ then:

$veh(t + 1) \leftarrow veh_n(t)$

$g_n(t + 1) \leftarrow \max(d_n^{eff} - veh_n(t + 1 > 0)$

Vehicle movement computation using the following formula

$$y(t + 1) \leftarrow y_n(t) + veh_n(t + 1) \tag{3}$$

Figure 34.2 depicts the real-time STMS process stream. It creates a simple activity computation that will be used in the motion paradigm. The areas of action are treated independently. We use information about the movement density of different roads at a certain moment.

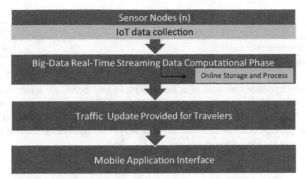

Fig. 34.2 Theoretical flow diagram of smart traffic management system for smart sustainable cities [15]

Based on the data we have, produced two yields. The total amount of time needed for one full rotation of the indication signals at any action point is known as the movement cycle (Tc). The activity cycle is considered as a component of the total vehicle motion thickness (TD) expressed as (4).

$$Tc = (TD) \tag{4}$$

The movement cycle lengthens as activity density increases. If there is higher mobility (such as during rush hour), this approach is linked for a longer cycle span so that extra automobiles can relax. The activity cycle is shortened if there is less motion so that automobiles don't have to wait in line for an extended period of time in indicator shifts. The 2nd variable is the time weighted component.

4. Result and Discussion

We take into account the displayed possibilities of the application when examining various possibilities. The first roadside vehicle movement detection sensors were implemented. Figure 34.3 from the Intel IoT board is linked and displays the vehicular density as well as the arrival rate of the automobiles. We take into account one road's accessibility to automobiles in terms of distance.

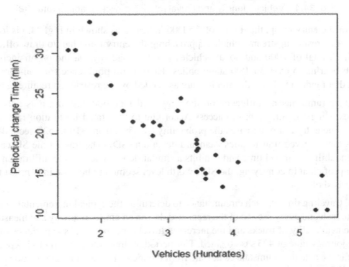

Fig. 34.3 Rate of periodic shift in the number of vehicles per each travel [16]

Table 34.1 Vehicle data set [17]

S. No	Factors	Data
1	Vehicle traffic per day	36,000
2	Additional Vehicle joining on-off incline	7000

We choose $m = 0.75$ for correspondence distances of at least 80 m. In any event, we select m = 1.5 for smaller distances because a clear observable path is likely to be present for small distances. We chose a dynamic roadway scenario with precise limit circumstances. A 12-km-long, 2-lane, thruway segment featuring an entry ramp and an exit ramp is being traveled by automobiles. This passage deals with a section of the A044 German Autobahn that runs involving two areas of the city. The selected throughway region geometry is shown in Fig. 34.4.

IoT Device Data sharing

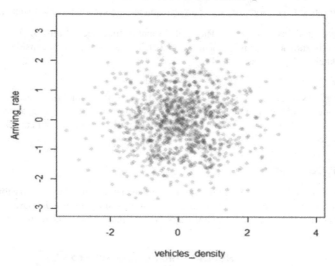

Fig. 34.4 Vehicle density and arrival rate IoT device enabling rates [18]

For all upstream signs of the entry ramp, the timing of the D06 indicator as shown in Fig. 34.5 is ideal: Around 7:15 AM, a breakdown occurred. As a result, upstream vehicles approaching the entry ramp had to draw off, resulting in a jammed upstream travel pattern. A total of 7000 additional vehicles join the roadway via the on-off-incline structure, bringing the daily traffic in each bearing to over 36, 000 automobiles. There is no preference for non-carrying automobiles, and automobiles are selected at random to leave the architecture as needed by the restriction requirements.

As a result, the departure ramp has no influence on the suggested methodology, but it is still necessary to partially account for automobiles using the entry ramp to access According to the stated infiltration rate, incoming automobiles are basically conveying The entry ramp increases the probability by 35%, from 819 to 527 seconds. Additionally, Figure 4's bottom bend shows the observed transit times' standard deviation (SD). The travel time SD can be understood as an assessment of the dependability of travel time and exhibits a similar dependence on the infiltration yield; with one out of four automobiles being proficient in conveying, the SD's worth level seemed to be 96 s, in contrast to and higher than 200 s while correspondence is shot.

We determined an ideal traveling time in each circumstance to determine the typical incremental time delay. To do this, we started an automobile at each and every second of the reenacted day on an empty roadway and measured the corresponding journey time. Given the availability of trucks and the increased travel time that trucks experience due to their lowered top speed, an ideal average journey time of 425 s is obtained. This period of time acts as a sort of viewpoint quality in Fig. 34.5, which highlights how far the actual circumstances deviate from the ideal state with no connections.

Average travel times for different penetration rates

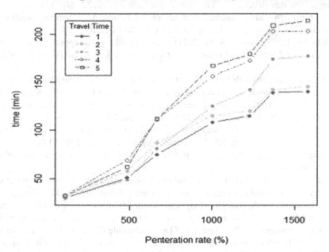

Fig. 34.5 Average travelling time with various travel time ranges for various penetration rates [20]

5. Conclusion

Smart and sustainable traffic management is one of the most significant concerns for the development of future smart and sustainable cities. So, our research suggested a low-cost real-time STMS to improve services by placing traffic indicators to instantly update the traffic information for the development of future smart, sustainable cities. Every 500 to 1000 meters, low-cost vehicle-detecting sensors are embedded in the center of the road. Rapid traffic information collection and transmission are made possible by the Internet of Things. Data provided via real-time broadcasting is used for sensor-based big data analytics. The analysis of traffic density and the provision of solutions using predictive analytics are covered in a number of analytical texts. To study the traffic density at different locations and offer a different method of controlling the traffic, a mobile application is created as the user interface. Additionally, in comparison to the current systems, our technique yields a better outcome.

The current technology just detects vehicles; vehicle types are not detected. Future work will focus on including more sophisticated sensors that can detect a vehicle's capacity type. The fundamental process of big data analytics applies a variety of cutting-edge techniques to make travel more adaptable.

REFERENCES

1. Cheng, B., Longo, S., Cirillo, F., Bauer, M., & Kovacs, E. (2015). Building a big data platform for smart cities: Experience and lessons from santander. In *2015 IEEE International Congress on Big Data* (pp. 592–599). IEEE. Doi:10.1109/BigDataCongress.2015.91
2. Ramu, S. P., Boopalan, P., Pham, Q. V., Maddikunta, P. K. R., Huynh-The, T., Alazab, M., ... &Gadekallu, T. R. (2022). Federated learning enabled digital twins for smart cities: Concepts, recent advances, and future directions. *Sustainable Cities and Society*, *79*, 103663. Doi:10.1016/j.scs.2021.103663
3. Bokhari, S. A. A., &Myeong, S. (2022). Use of artificial intelligence in smart cities for smart decision-making: A social innovation perspective. *Sustainability*, *14*(2), 620. Doi: 10.3390/su14020620
4. Esashika, D., Masiero, G., &Mauger, Y. (2021). An investigation into the elusive concept of smart cities: a systematic review and meta-synthesis. *Technology Analysis & Strategic Management*, *33*(8), 957–969. Doi:10.1080/09537325.2020.1856804
5. Talebkhah, M., Sali, A., Marjani, M., Gordan, M., Hashim, S. J., &Rokhani, F. Z. (2021). IoT and big data applications in smart cities: recent advances, challenges, and critical issues. *IEEE Access*, *9*, 55465–55484. Doi:10.1109/ACCESS.2021.3070905
6. Rathore, M. M., Ahmad, A., & Paul, A. (2016). IoT-based smart city development using big data analytical approach. In *2016 IEEE international conference on automatica (ICA-ACCA)* (pp. 1–8). IEEE. Doi:10.1109/ICA-ACCA.2016.7778510
7. Al Nuaimi, E., Al Neyadi, H., Mohamed, N., & Al-Jaroodi, J. (2015). Applications of big data to smart cities. *Journal of Internet Services and Applications*, *6*(1), 1–15. Doi:10.1186/s13174-015-0041-5

8. Bibri, S. E., &Krogstie, J. (2017a). ICT of the new wave of computing for sustainable urban forms: Their big data and context-aware augmented typologies and design concepts. *Sustainable cities and society, 32*, 449–474. Doi:10.1016/j.scs.2017.04.012

9. Bibri, S. E., &Krogstie, J. (2017b). Smart sustainable cities of the future: An extensive interdisciplinary literature review. *Sustainable cities and society, 31*, 183–212.Doi:doi.org/10.1016/j.scs.2017.02.016

10. Adams, D., Novak, A., Kliestik, T., &Potcovaru, A. M. (2021). Sensor-based big data applications and environmentally sustainable urban development in internet of things-enabled smart cities. *Geopolitics, History, and International Relations, 13*(1), 108–118. Doi: 10.22381/GHIR131202110.

11. Bibri, S. E. (2018). The IoT for smart sustainable cities of the future: An analytical framework for sensor-based big data applications for environmental sustainability. *Sustainable cities and society, 38*, 230–253. DOI: 10.1016/j.scs.2017.12.034

12. Bibri, S. E., & Krogstie, J. (2017c). The core enabling technologies of big data analytics and context-aware computing for smart sustainable cities: a review and synthesis. *Journal of Big Data, 4*(1), 1–50. DOI 10.1186/s40537-017-0091-6

13. Bibri, S. E., & Krogstie, J. (2016). On the social shaping dimensions of smart sustainable cities: A study in science, technology, and society. *Sustainable Cities and Society, 29*, 219–246. Doi:doi.org/10.1016/j.scs.2016.11.004

14. Aziz, F., Chalup, S. K., Juniper, J., Khan, J. Y.,&Yuce, M. R. (2019). Big data in iot systems. Internet of Things (IoT): Systems and Applications, 10, 9780429399084-2.

15. Rizwan, P., Suresh, K., & Babu, M. R. (2016, Real-time smart traffic management system for smart cities by using Internet of Things and big data. In 2016 international conference on emerging technological trends (ICETT) (pp. 1–7). IEEE.

16. Auer, M., Rehborn, H., & Bogenberger, K. Analysis of Dynamic Route Choice Behavior on German Freeway A8 Based on Large Scale Vehicle Fleet Data. In 6th Symposium of the European Association for Research in Transportation.

17. Auer, M., Rehborn, H., & Bogenberger, K. (2017Analysis of Dynamic Route Choice Behavior on German Freeway A8 Based on Large Scale Vehicle Fleet Data. In 6th Symposium of the European Association for Research in Transportation.

18. Auer, M., Rehborn, H., & Bogenberger, K. (2017). Empircal Analysis of Dynamic Route Choice Behavior on German Freeway A8 Based on Large Scale Vehicle Fleet Data. In 6th Symposium of the European Association for Research in Transportation.

19. Pojani, D., & Stead, D. (2015). Sustainable urban transport in the developing world: beyond mega cities. Sustainability, 7(6), 7784–7805.

Computer Science Engineering and Emerging Technologies (ICCS-2022) – Prof (Dr.) Rajeev Sobti et al. (eds)
© 2024 Taylor & Francis Group, London, ISBN 978-1-032-52199-2

Chapter

35

Dual-Level Encryption for Secure Communication

Nupur Kaushik[1]
Research Scholar, Department of Computer Science and Engineering,
Lovely Professional University, Phagwara, Punjab, India

Harwant Singh Arri[2], Dhiraj Kapila[3]
Associate Professor, Department of Computer Science and Engineering,
Lovely Professional University, Phagwara, Punjab, India

**Gobinda Karmakar[4], Siddharth Pansare[5],
Sahil Bhardwaj[6], Jayant Mehra[7]**
Research Scholar, Department of Computer Science and Engineering,
Lovely Professional University, Phagwara, Punjab, India

Abstract: Data is widely used in communication over the internet in today's society. As a result, internet users' primary worry is information security. The best approach is to utilize a cryptography method that encrypts data in a cipher, sends it over the internet, and then decrypts it back to the original data. The field of cryptography is concerned with the secure transmission of data.

The idea is to allow intended recipients of a communication to receive it correctly while preventing eavesdroppers from comprehending it. Cryptography is a set of techniques for scrambling or obscuring data so that it is only accessible to those who can restore it to its original state. Cryptography provides a solid, cost-effective foundation for keeping data classified and validating data integrity in today's computer systems. While traditional cryptography approaches like AES (encryption) and RSA (signing) function well on computers with sufficient processing power and memory, they don't scale well in an environment with embedded systems and sensor networks.

As a result, lightweight cryptography approaches are offered to overcome many of the problems associated with traditional cryptography. This study adds to the body of knowledge in the field of classical cryptography by proposing a new hybrid method of plaintext encryption. The encryption is done by first encrypting the plaintext with Vigenere Cipher and then using the ciphertext to encrypt the plaintext with Polybius Cipher.

Keywords: Encryption, Cryptography, Algorithm, Cipher

1. Introduction

Information Nowadays, science has progressed to the point where the overwhelming majority of people prefer to use the web as the primary method for delivering data from one end point to the next. Messages, conversations, and other forms of data distribution over the internet are among the options.

The sharing of information is astonishingly clear, fast, and accurate using the internet. However, one of the most significant concerns with it is the "security risk" it poses.

[1]nupurkaushiknk@gmail.com, [2]hs.arri@lpu.co.in, [3]dhiraj.23509@lpu.co.in, [4]gobindak2@gmail.com, [5]sidhu.pansare@gmail.com, [6]binny4166@gmail.com, [7]jayant46mehra@gmail.com

DOI: 10.1201/9781003405580-35

In this methodology, thinking about information security becomes second nature, as it is likely the most important factor to address during the information transfer process.

In the open framework, security is a significant thought, and cryptography assumes a fundamental part in such a manner. Cryptography is an old innovation that guarantees the security of data in an open environment. Regardless, cryptography's inspiration isn't just to provide requests yet. Moreover, to give deals with various hardships like data unwavering quality, affirmation, and non-repudiation. Cryptography is an expression that alludes to epitomizing and concocting ways that permit fundamental data and information to be passed on in a protected manner, with the main individual equipped for recuperating it being the cognizant recipient.

Cryptography is a technique for covering information and data through a correspondence channel using an orderly methodology and system. It takes the ability to keep information stowed away from inquisitive eyes. As development advances, the need for information security by means of correspondence turns out to be progressively more significant. Encryption is the most common way of changing plain text into ciphertext in a deliberate way. To change a plain message into a figure, the encryption system requires any modified encryption strategy and a key.

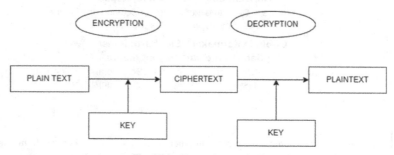

Fig. 35.1 Encryption method

2. Techniques Used for Cryptography

In today's world, cryptography is the process of converting an unencrypted plain text into a cipher text that can only be decrypted by the recipient of the text, and this process is referred to as encoding. Secret writing refers to the process of converting encrypted text to plain text.

3. Features of Cryptography

These are mentioned below.

Confidentiality: It involves keeping up with allowed limitations on data access and divulgence, as well as protections for individual security and exclusive information. Data may be gotten by the individual for whom it is planned, and no other person will approach it.

Those in the IT division, for instance, who don't consistently communicate with clients and possibilities, shouldn't approach client data. In the event that somebody doesn't need a particular kind of data to achieve their work, they shouldn't approach it.

Integrity: Integrity implies that the information or data in your framework is kept so that it can't be changed or erased by unapproved parties. This is a basic part of information: cleanliness, unwavering quality, and precision. Data can't be changed in that frame of mind during the progress among shippers and assumed recipients, with no expansion of data being recognized.

Non-repudiation: The sureness that somebody can't deny the authenticity of anything is known as non-renouncement. Non-disavowal is a lawful idea that is widely utilized in the field of data security and alludes to assistance that gives affirmation of information's starting point and uprightness.

Non-disavowal, at the end of the day, makes it entirely difficult to effectively question who/where a message came from, as well as its authenticity and uprightness. The maker/shipper of information|data|knowledge can't debate that the person expects to give data sooner or later.

Authentication: With regards to PC frameworks, verification alludes to the affirmation and approval of a client's personality. Prior to endeavoring to get to the information put away by an organization, a client should initially lay out their character and get approval to get to the information. A client should supply one-of-a kind sign-in accreditations.

4. Literature Survey

This study [5] discusses the importance of content protection in automated media for keeping currency, account passwords, messages, and secret words safe on the internet. It demonstrates the security as well as the pressure for information with the typical secret writing.

With the help of Polybius square, the age of the key has been traversed. The increase in the number of rounds will necessitate progressive machine speculation, which may make it uninteresting for the programmer to interrupt the system.

The shift cipher, often known as the Caesar cipher, is one of the simplest and most well-known old-style typeface secret writing systems. It's a type of substitution cipher in which each letter in the plaintext is replaced by a letter at a specific position down the alphabet.

With three shifts, for example, A would be replaced by D, B by E, and so on. A Caesar cipher's secret writing phase is frequently combined with larger and more intricate plans, such as the Vigenère cipher, and yet has gift day application within the ROT13 framework. The Caesar cipher is easily broken, just like all single letters and substitution ciphers, and offers little in the way of correspondence security [6].

In cryptography, a transposition cipher is a method of secret writing in which the positions of plaintext units are shifted by a standard framework or example, resulting in the ciphertext containing a stage of the plaintext. That is, near the end of the shifting procedure, the request for the units is changed. A bijective perform is used on the placements of the characters to code the Associate in Nursing mathematical function to rewrite.

The letters themselves are undamaged and unedited, implying that the impact is solely on their positions, resulting in their request being included in a message with many different themes. A geometrical style is used to create numerous transposition ciphers. [7] [8]

In [9], a modified variant of Vigenère's formula was projected, during which dispersion is given by adding an Associate in Nursing whimsical piece to each computer memory unit before the message is disorganized using Vigenere.

This strategy falls flat in the Kasiski assault to get the length of the key on the grounds that the artifact of the message has irregular bits. The basic drawback of this method is that the dimensions of the disorganized message are enlarged by around 56.

In [10], another technique for capital punishment, the Vigenere formula, was bestowed by naturally changing the cipher key once each secret writing step. During this technique, progressive keys were utilized that were dependent on the underlying key of the Associate in Nursing incentive throughout the secret writing method.

In [11], the adjustment of Vigenere cipher by irregular numbers, punctuation, and scientific pictures was introduced. In the projected technique, numbers, punctuation, and, what is more, scientific images were utilized for keys rather than characters to make it progressively laborious for animal power assault. It had been inferred that if irregular numbers square measure utilized for keying what is additional to unfold the vary, then simply ball-hawking individuals will acknowledge the message.

Another formula [12] was projected by combining Vigenere substitution cipher with stream cipher, during which recurrent bits of plaintext were systematically encrypted with the varied phase of the phrase or binary key.

The letters in odd locations were encoded with stream ciphers, and therefore the letters in even locations were encoded with Vigenere cipher. It had been inferred that the projected formula conceals the affiliation between cipher content and plain content, which makes cryptography much more difficult.

Tianfu [13] argues that the net is one of the foremost unsafe communication mediums because of its Brobdingnagian affiliation and public network. Data protection is an essential demand. At present, varied security algorithms are projected to realize security throughout communication.

Every one of them has a sure savvy reason and a sure unfortunate reason. To improve the strength of the mystery composition recipe, they projected a half-and-half model.

The projected model is a blend of AES and DES. Every calculation is a three-sided key method, and they're much more skilled for secret composition. A mix of AES and DES would give a strong degree of safety at the secret composition finish. A significant improvement in results is not set in stone with the proposed resolution.

Jakimoski et al. [14] investigated and assessed the main data security methods that are now acknowledged by distributed computing suppliers. They isolated them into four classifications in view of the security systems they provide: verification, secrecy, access for executives, and authorization.

That's what they infer, assuming all suggested techniques for confirmation, mystery, access control, and approval are considered. Distributed computing can be confided in as far as data security.

They focused on the security features that should be considered completely to guarantee legitimate information security in the cloud. They suggested significant security and safety measures for cloud information insurance that should be taken into mind.

5. Proposed Framework

Lightweight Cryptography as Ciphers is taken for thought for System. Two celebrated old-style figures square measure utilized for the framed imagine to do Combination of Cipher inside the System like

5.1 Vigenère Cipher

The Vigenère Cipher is a strategy for scrambling alphabetic text. It utilizes a straight-forward sort of polyalphabetic replacement. Any code that upholds replacement and utilizes various replacement letter sets is known as a polyalphabetic figure.

The underlying text's encoding is finished utilizing the Vigenère sq., or, on the other hand, Vigenère table. Accordingly, the code is less helpless against cryptographic letter frequencies. In 1585, Blaise First State Vigenère contrived what is currently known as the Vigenère figure. To encode messages, he created a table called the Vigenère sq.

Encryption:

The plaintext's essential letter, letter set S, is in succession, and the key, letter set L, is in a segment, and the mainly given letter of the source and collector side key, bringing about the result as D. Then, at that point, since E is a line and key I is a segment, the hybrid of the two lines as message by source and section as the key will bring about M. Different letters will be handled likewise, bringing about an encoded message. The modulus of 26 is duplicated by the plaintext (P) and key (K).

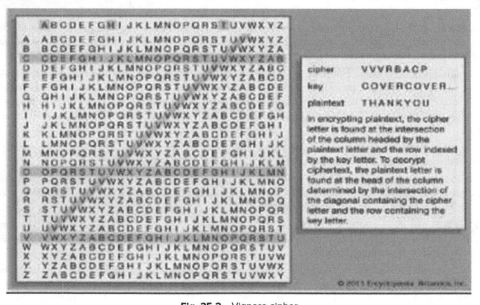

Fig. 35.2 Vignere cipher

Example:

Input: Plaintext: INDIAKey:

AYUSH

Output: ILXAH

	1	2	3	4	5
1	A	B	C	D	E
2	F	G	H	I,J	K
3	L	M	N	O	P
4	Q	R	S	T	U
5	V	W	X	Y	Z

Fig. 35.3 Polybius cipher

5.2 Polybius Square Cipher

A Polybius square is a spreadsheet that allows you to convert letters to numbers. To make the coding process a little easier, this table is randomized and sent to the recipient.

The letters 'I' and 'j' are quite often combined into one cell in order to fit the roman alphabet of the letter set within the 25 cells created by the table. Because the traditional Greek letter set contains 24 letters, there was initially no disadvantage. In the case of a language with a large number of alphabets, a larger table might be used [4].

Encryption:

Example:

The output code for D is 14 when it is placed in consecutive iterations and column 4; for O, it is 34 when it is arranged in row 3 and column 3. As a result, the message DOG was 14, 34, and 22 in the encrypted message.

Decryption: Polybius decryption involves an awareness of the grid and involves changing a pair of variables with the grid's matching letter.

Input: BUS Output:

124543

Example: 12 visualize for the first line and second column, resulting in the letter B; 45 visualize for the fourth line and fifth column, resulting in U; and so on. The decrypted message is returned as BUS. Presently, we'll consolidate the Vigenère and Polybius codes to make a crossover figureplot. This summation utilizes both alphabetic and polyalphabetic replacements, bringing about a plain message and an encoded message that are very convoluted, unstructured, unpretentious, and difficult to interrupt.

6. Methodology

The approach incorporates the Vigenère figure and the Polybius square cipher to preserve data. The Vigenère code will be utilized to make the ciphertext right away. The interaction will initiate with a key taken at random.

Near the end of the interaction, the accompanying ciphertext transforms into a code for the Polybius Square Cipher approach. The key is utilized to chip away at the plaintext message to make the last ciphertext. The last ciphertext will turn out to be progressively harder to break involving existing cryptanalysis strategies because of this procedure. For recovery of a message from the shipper, the recipient will decode the message

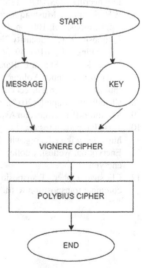

Fig. 35.4 Methodology

backward request. An item application will be composed to exhibit the suitability of the computation utilizing Python coding, and the ciphertext will be exposed to a few cryptanalysis procedures. The figure shows a flowchart exhibiting the hybrid algorithm.

We can see that the result is in NUMERICAL configuration, though the shipper sent in ALPHABETICAL organization. Indeed, even the Vigenere figure results in conveyed, muddled, and unformatted ALPHABETS, which is additionally secure, yet again passing that Vigenère yields are treated as Polybius info and afterward bring about mathematical organization, making it safer and more complex than the utilization of single ciphers.

We can see that the unravel result has shown up subsequent to switching to the most common way of going through the Polybius figure first and then the Vigenere figure.

Thus, we can perceive the encryption and decryption cycles of the hybrid code process stream. For the activity of the framework, a Python script for writing computer programs is composed anddead.

7. Conclusion and Future Enhancement

Cryptography is the most commonly used technique for the safety of information. Vigenere cipher is one of all the scientific discipline techniques that are viewed as least advanced and most vulnerable thanks to varied impediments. to overcome the impediments of the Vigenere cipher. We tend to be projected as an upgraded variant of the Combination of Polybius cipher, which is plenty secure against Kasiski and economic assaults. With the changed hybrid of each the Caesar Cipher and Vigenere Cipher, there's currently a high share of diffusion and confusion within the formula that generates them, making it a robust cipher and troublesome to interrupt. In spite of the fact that there are varied scientific discipline ways, this area still needs real thought in the analysis of networks for the development of information security. In the future, our purpose will be to convey approval of the projected approach through security and performance analysis.

REFERENCES

1. C. Sanchez-Avila and R. Sanchez-Reillo, "The Rijndael block cipher (AES proposal): a comparison with DES," in Security Technology, 2001 IEEE 35th International Carna-han Conference on, 2001, pp. 229–234

2. P. Gutmann—Cryptographic Security Architecture: Design and Verification‖Springer-Verlag,2004 V.Beal.(2009,Encryption. Available:Http://www.webopedia.com/TERM/E/ encryption.html

3. Q.-A. Kester, "A cryptosystem based on Vigenère cipher with varying key," International Journal of Advanced Research in Computer Engineering Technology (IJARCET), vol. 1, pp. pp: 108–113, 2012.q

4. C. Bhardwaj, "Modification of Vigenère Cipher by Random Numbers, Punctuations Mathematical Symbols," Journal of Computer Engineering (IOSRJCE) ISSN, pp. 2278–0661,2012.

5. F. H. S. Fairouz Mushtaq Sher Ali, "Enhancing Security of Vigenere Cipher by Stream Cipher," International Journal of Computer Applications, vol. 100, pp. 1–4, 2014

6. Jakimoski, Kire, "Security Techniques for Data Protection in Cloud Computing." International Journal of Grid and Distributed Computing 9.1 (2016): 49–56.

7. Puneet Kumar, Shashi B. Rana, Development of modified AES algorithm for data security, Optik - International Journal for Light and Electron Optics, Volume 127, Issue 4, 2016, Pages 2341–2345, ISSN 0030-4026, http://dx.doi.org/10.1016/j.ijleo.2015.11.188. (http://www.sciencedirect.com/science/article/pii/S0030402615018215)

8. Chaudhari, Swapnil. (2018). A Research Paper on New Hybrid Cryptography Algorithm.

9. M. Abror–Pengertian dan Aspek-Aspek Keamanan   Komputer, 2018. [Daring]. https://en.wikipedia.org/wiki/Vigen

10. Tersedia pada:https://www.ayoksinau.com/pengertian-dan-aspek-aspek-keamanankomputer-lengkap/. [Diakses: 01-Okt-2018]. https://en.wikipedia.org/wiki/Polybius-square

11. Encryption. Wellesley college Computer Science Department lecture note retrieved from: http://cs110.wellesley.edu/lectures/L18-encryption/

12. Classical cipher, Transposition ciphers, Retrieved from http://en.wikipedia.org/wiki/Classical-cipher Transposition ciphers, columnar transposition Retrieved from http://en.wikipedia.org/wiki/ Transposition-cipher

Computer Science Engineering and Emerging Technologies (ICCS-2022) – Prof (Dr.) Rajeev Sobti et al. (eds)
© *2024 Taylor & Francis Group, London, ISBN 978-1-032-52199-2*

A Detailed Investigation of Artificial Intelligence in Economic Growth and Development of Emerging Economies

Somanchi Hari Krishna[1]

Associate Professor, Department of Business Management, Vignana Bharathi Institute of Technology, Aushapur village Ghatkesar Mandal Malkangiri Medchal Dist, Telangana, India

Ayan Das Gupta[2]

WBES, Assistant Professor, Postgraduate Department of Geography, Chandernagore Government College, Hooghly, West Bengal, Chandernagore Government College affiliated to the University of Burdwan

Dipesh Uike[3]

Professor, Dr. Ambedkar Institute of Management Studies and Research

Christopher Raj D.[4]

Professor, Department of MBA,
Ballari Institute of Technology & Management, Ballari, Karnataka India

Venkanna Mood[5]

Associate Professor, ECE, St Martin's engineering college

Firos A.[6]

Assistant Professor, Department of computer Science and Engineering Rajiv Gandhi University
(A Central University), Rono-Hills, Doimukh, Arunachal Pradesh, India

Abstract: Presenting artificial intelligence in contemporary society generally creates one-of-a kind difficulties for humanity. The arising independence of AI holds the one-of-a-kind capability of the everlasting existence of robots, AI, and calculations, along with extraordinary monetary predominance, information capacity, and computational benefits. However, right up until now, it remains hazy what influence AI assuming control over the labor force will have on financial development.

Artificial intelligence can be characterized as the capacity of a machine to copy a smart human way of behaving or a specialist's capacity to accomplish objectives in a great many conditions. These definitions promptly bring out crucial monetary issues. For instance, what occurs assuming AI permits a consistently expanding number of assignments recently performed by humans to become robotized? Artificial intelligence might be sent to deliver labor and products, possibly affecting monetary development and pay shares. Be that as it may, AI may likewise change the interaction through which we make novel thoughts and advances, assisting with taking care of complicated issues and scaling innovative endeavors. In outrageous adaptations, a few eyewitnesses have contended that AI can turn out to be quickly self-improving, prompting singularities that highlight unbounded machine intelligence and unbounded monetary development in a limited time. Scientists give a detailed outline and discussion of the possibilities for a peculiarity from the point of view of financial matters.

Keywords: Robotization, Solubilisation, Natural language processing

[1]harikrishnasomanchi@gmail.com, [2]dasguptaayan11111@gmail.com, [3]dipeshuike@gmail.com, [4]christopherraj@bitm.edu.in, [5]venkannamoodece@smec.ac.in, [6]firos.a@rgu.ac.in

DOI: 10.1201/9781003405580-36

1. Introduction

The contemporary pattern of globalization is depicted as the dialling back of ordinary globalization of merchandise, administrations, and unfamiliar direct speculation streams, and simultaneously, we actually see human relocation and air travel, as well as information movement, proceeding to rise. Yet again, when America took a protectionist turn in its 2016 official political decision, they were first in detecting and following up on a contemporary identified, most clever overall pattern: individuals presently live in the time of globalization (Simon, 2019). Protectionism, exchange wars, arising economies' log jams, the diminishing of labour and product exchange, as well as a downturn in transnational speculation, are indications that the worldwide pattern of globalization has stopped. Joined Realm trailed behind the US official in deciding in favour of Brexit. Globalization has eased back in our present circumstances of 'globalization,' a term begat in 2015 by Adjiedj Bakas, who detected first that globalization has given way to another time of drowsiness. These market patterns of customary globalization easing back and rising AI-related ventures are proposed as the principal market disturbance following the huge scope of AI's entry into our contemporary economy. Development in the artificial age is then proposed to be estimated in light of two AI entrance intermediaries, the Worldwide Network File and The Condition of the Versatile Web Availability 2018 Record, which are viewed as profoundly essentially decidedly corresponding with the all-out inflow of transients and FDI inflow, filling in as proof that the as yet globalizing rising enterprises in the time of globalization are associated with AI (Sharma *et al.* 2022). Both lists are decidedly related to gross domestic product yield in getting sectional examinations around the world. To explain, assuming that the found impact is an indication of industrialization, the time series of overall information uncovers that web networks all over the planet are related to lower financial development from around 2000 until 2017.

A relapse plotting Web Network and Gross Domestic Product per capita as free factors to explain the dependent variable Gross Domestic Product Development frames that the impact of AI is a critical determinant of negative Gross Domestic Product Development possibilities for the years from 2000 until 2017. A board relapse plotting gross domestic product per capita and web network from the year 2000 to explain financial development combines the observation that AI-web availability is a critical determinant of negative development over the long haul for 161 nations of the world. The web network is related to financial development decline, though gross domestic product per capita has no critical connection with gross domestic product development. To cross-approve, the two discoveries hold for two distinct worldwide network estimations (Dhamija and Bag, 2020). The paper then examines a hypothetical contention of partitioning work parts into liquid, subsequently more adaptable (e.g., AI), and more earth, consequently more firm (e.g., human work), parts. The paper closes with a call for changing development hypotheses and coordinating AI parts into development hypotheses. AI entrance into monetary business sectors is demonstrated in the standard neoclassical development hypothesis by making an original record for addressing development in the artificial age, which contained gross domestic product per capita and AI entrance estimated by the intermediary of web access per cent per country (Peyravi *et al. 2020)*. Maps uncover the areas of the planet that include high gross domestic product per capita and AI networks. The conversation closes with a future point of view towards the law and financial matters of AI's entrance into our contemporary economies and society to aid an effective and sympathetic presentation of AI in our reality.

2. Literature Review

This pattern of polarisation between continuous polarisation of globalisation on information and individuals versus globalisation of conventional labour and products as well as money has been contended as the primary indication of AI entering financial creation and changing merchandise and administration exchange. Innovative and political variables could show a market disturbance that has proactively started and presently repeats globalisation versus solubilization happening in line with one another. The as-of-now depicted pattern of solubilization could simply be a trailblazer for the AI insurgency market interruption that is going to happen and make a world totally different from the one we know.

With the ringing of the AI insurgency, mechanical advancement is finishing creation and assembling nearer clients. In the Fourth Modern Upheaval, robots are supposed to turn out to be more productive and reasonable (Baryannis *et al. 2019)*. With that, ordinary globalisation rehearsals—for example, off-shoring assembly to modestly cost-conscious nations—will undoubtedly decline. Turning will carry back creation to where labour and products are really last consumed. The clearest model is energy and a forthcoming endeavour to decentralise the environmentally friendly power age. The sun-powered charger turns out to be more useful in the event that energy does not need to be put away yet can be imparted to your neighbour when not required.

One perspective on the most recent 150 years of financial advancement is that it is driven by computerization. The Modern Upheaval used steam and, afterwards, power to computerise numerous creation processes. Transfers, semiconductors, and semiconductors proceeded with this pattern (Zhang and Lu, 2021). Maybe artificial intelligence is the following period of this interaction as opposed to a discrete break. It could be a characteristic movement from autopilots, PC-controlled vehicle motors, and X-ray machines to self-driving vehicles and AI radiology reports. While up to this point robotization has mainly impacted daily schedules or low-talented errands, apparently AI may progressively computerise non-standard mental assignments performed by high-ability labourers. A benefit of this point of view is that it permits us to utilise verifiable experience to illuminate the conceivable future impacts of AI.

Presently, rescoring seems to be happening, in which homegrown innovation and upgraded creation are preferred over moving to destroy low-talented, low-paying regions. AI holds the possibility to duplicate human life yet live unceasingly (Chidepatil *et al.* 2020). Every minute of every day, working robots that can live interminably are supposed to turn into the drivers of industrialised economies and supplant most of the human labour force. 3D-printing procedures and nanotechnology that permit creation to begin at the sub-atomic or even nuclear level are encouraging rescoring as migrating creation locales from worldwide value chain locations that were fanned out during the brilliant long stretches of globalisation to where labour and products are consumed today. Turning of worldwide creation closer to where buyers seem positive considering environmental change and fossil fuel byproducts, yet evading low-gifted work in creating areas of the planet from creation for universally working multinationals may return a global turn of events.

So while organisations all over the planet included an off-shoring pattern during the brilliant period of globalisation, contemporary re-shoring and globalisation happen (Berente *et al.* 2021). Solubilization seems to fortify provincial exchange coalitions, particularly in Europe and Asia. Organizations give off the impression of zeroing in on their creations back where they serve their clients, and buyers have as of late gained significant interest in additional nearby items. There is an extended effect of mechanical improvement on global exchange. Robots are supposed to be more exact and work day in and day out while being less demanding than human specialists. A huge number of representatives in the East might lose their positions throughout the following couple of years, subbed by robots in the West. Likewise, propels in 3D printers may soon make it conceivable to substitute enormous production lines with a lot more modest ones, nearer to the shopper, where the assembling system is improved because of the propagation of models. New materials could be made close to the shopper to substitute for regular materials that should be moved from far-off mines and stores. Exchange joins inside territorial alliances might increment and blocks become more homogenous, both in Europe and Asia.

Very good quality creation has found the advantage of waking buyers up to the whole presentation and guaranteeing that corporate social obligation is lived all through the worth change. In addition, while organizations bring creation back into their nations for AI, untalented laborers miss out on the homegrown business sectors while abandoning markets that thrived due to reevaluating organizations. Reshoring implies that previously reevaluated undertakings are performed by AI in exceptionally gifted interconnected nations, with whom low-talented laborers in the creating scene currently should contend. The change to the new globalization has made the specialists in created markets lose bargaining power as they presently work in the creation stages that are generally defenseless against delocalization and robotization, while the Western world will confront a contest with AI in wage-deteriorating economies. A pattern that will, for example, pit a 5G computerized gadget in opposition to a low-gifted specialist in a barren place on earth with not even web access, which permits learning and efficiency gains (Adams-PrassL, 2019). Solubilization and, once again, shoring are subsequently expected to augment the gap between the rich and poor. AI entering our economies might prompt a pattern of re-shoring and, in this way, evade worldwide minimal expense creation destinations. The worldwide hole between AI-computerized center points and non-mechanized places on earth will hence expand in the years to come. So while re-shoring offers open doors for more sustainable creation considering environmental change, when we consider the natural effects of transporting merchandise all over the planet until they arrive at the end client, eventually, it additionally bears the gamble of limiting worldwide financial turn of events.

The first thought is that new AI innovations could permit the impersonation or learning of boondocks advances to become robotized. That is, machines would sort out in the blink of an eye how to impersonate boondocks advancements (Wirtz *et al.* 2019). Then, at that point, a main wellspring of disparity could become credit constraints, to the degree that those could keep more unfortunate nations or districts from obtaining hyper-genius machines, though created economies could manage the cost of such machines. Hence, one could envision a world in which best-in-class nations focus all their exploration exertion on growing new product offerings (i.e., on boondocks development), though more unfortunate nations would dedicate a positive and expanding part of their examination work to finding out about the new wilderness advancements as they can't manage the cost of comparing AI gadgets.

3. Methodology and Model Specifications

Research methodology is one of the key pillars of any kind of research study. It extensively delivers a clear discussion in a logical way about various types of methodological pillars. The main purpose of this research methodology is the collection of primary as well as secondary information from reliable sources. Appropriate techniques can be clearly identified based on those methodologies for extracting relevant information. Post-positivism research philosophy is one of the best pillars for extracting clear research findings in an appropriate way. Artificial intelligence reflects one of the most influential parts depending on the present competitive business perspectives, and it can be reliably used to gain economic stability. In the case of the research approach, a "deductive approach" has been taken, where innovative science-based concepts have been utilized to bring about productive results. As per the concept of research design, exploratory design can be more efficient for assessing different perspectives about the topic's background. The secondary qualitative data collection method has been used to procure reliable data from considerable resources such as important journals, books, research papers, and other areas. Empirical research analysis has been utilized in this present study to capture relevant ideas and findings about the importance of artificial intelligence in economic growth in a logical way.

4. Empirical Results

To explain if the presently identified globalization pattern is the principal indication of a market disturbance connected with AI entering markets, the observational examination highlights One-on-one studies show that the current polarization of globalization and globalization patterns is AI-market presentation driven. The review approves the globalization pattern, with a specific spotlight on demonstrating proof for as yet continuous globalization being associated with AI-driven development.

To unite the perception that there is a globalization pattern within customary globalization boundaries while globalization goes on in the AI domain, a connection study will be organized (Panwar *et al.*, 2021). As an intermediary for AI entering monetary business sectors, the web network, as estimated by the Worldwide Availability File, will be connected with the gross domestic product mainstays of farming, industry, and administration areas as gotten from the World Bank dataset on the gross domestic product of the year 2017, and a cross-approval check will be performed with the Condition of the Portable Web Network 2018 Record. This action ought to aid in understanding what gross domestic product areas AI is ascribed to. Further, the various parts of the globalization pattern will be connected in a related study to see whether globalization is an indication of AI entering markets and the development hypothesis not having the option to catch AI efficiency. A pattern of globalization going on in AI, including ventures and nations, will be featured by relating AI coordination with globalization signs of capital and work developments.

In the present economy, robots and calculations are assuming control over human dynamic errands and entering the labor force. Most of late, huge amounts of information have developed into a wellspring of significant resources, and states all over the planet are trying to burden abundance creation from data moves. This pattern presently provokes customary monetary hypotheses to catch the development in light of simply capital and work parts. Calculations, AI, and enormous information gains, in addition to the sharing economy, don't appear to be addressed precisely in ordinary development hypotheses about capital and work.

According to the above picture, it has been clearly explored that artificial intelligence comprises a broader application in various sectors, such as managing different solutions, technological interpretation, and other management solutions. All those things have a serious effect on strengthening the economic stability of an entire region. "Automated supply chain optimization,", infrastructural maintenance systems, price optimization, cost cutting, mitigating the effect of global warming, and remote surveillance are some of the important solutions that can be managed by AI (Jain *et al.* 2019). According to the technology part, machine learning, deep learning, computer vision, and "natural language processing" are some of the influential parts that can encourage and maintain significant economic stability. Effective management of the supply chain, statistical learning, detection of objects, recognition of patterns, and inventory management are some of the innovative steps of AI that remarkably help in the development of emerging economies.

Future exploration attempts may in this manner address disparity, drawing on the future vision that focal, judicious AI centres will outflank immature, far-off regions of the world considerably more in the computerised age. Globalization is projected to step back, rethink endeavours, and create AI centres in less associated regions (Jain and Pandey, 2019). The accompanying examination ought to be worried about the remarkably high split among gifted and untalented work and the

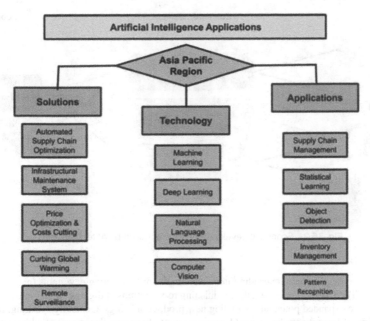

Fig. 36.1 Impact of AI in economic growth of Asia Pacific Region

Source: Jain and Pandey, 2019

redirection between AI centres and non-AI domains. Over the most recent forty years, the cost of talented work has taken off decisively compared with that of untalented work, despite a significant increase in the general stockpile of abilities. The idea of expertise predisposition in development speculations has presented the hypothetical chance that mechanical advancement helps just a sub-gathering of labourers, putting specialized change at the focal point of the pay circulation banter. Hierarchical changes have prompted AI innovations that diminish the expenses of correspondence, checking, and oversight inside the firm, which trigger a shift towards another hierarchical plan. The shift towards AI prompts an authoritative shift towards one-sided meritocracy. Endogenous specialized progress prompts monetary development, yet in addition, it produces wage imbalances among low- and high-talented labourers. The quicker specialized change builds the re-visitation of capacity and increments wage imbalances between and inside gatherings of high-talented and untalented labourers. Future examinations ought to coordinate a portion of the contemporary imbalance estimations, for example, the Palma proportion, the monetary turn of events, and abundance moves in contemporary development hypotheses and estimations. Wage disparity is just a single method for evaluating imbalance, yet to get a more extravagant image of disparity from AI, the future examination may likewise think about disparity in riches, well-being, status, and inside-group disparities. Understanding the connections between development and imbalance ought to likewise be put in the various settings of political, social, and verifiable conditions to determine deductions about a fruitful presentation of AI into the present labour force and society. At long last, more exploration is prescribed to show and amplify the original creation capability, including AI and data sharing, particularly considering G5 and the web of things, prompting further association and advantages from innovation. This large number of novel improvements might prompt a likely polarization between more proficient AI centres and low-expertise, low-work-cost regions that might be disregarded from monetary development because of an anticipated rescoring pattern combined with AI financial strength and uncommon innovation gains.

A guess is that, expecting the impact of AI on the extension and speed of impersonation, potential trend-setters might become hesitant to patent their developments, expecting that the exposure of new information in the patent would prompt straight impersonation. Proprietary innovations may then become the standard rather than licensing (Panwar *et al.* 2021). On the other hand, advancements would become like what monetary developments are today, that is to say, information creation with enormous organization impacts and with a very little degree of protection. At long last, with impersonational., getting the hang of being performed mainly by super machines in created economies organisation turn out to be (on the

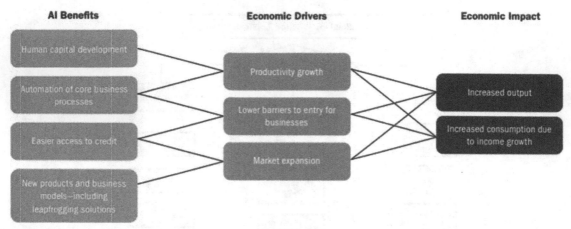

Fig. 36.2 Economic development accomplished by AI technologies

Source: Jain et al. 2021

whole) committed to item development, expanding item assortment, or concocting new items (new product offerings) to supplant existing items. Then, like never before, the diminishing re-visitations of digging further into a current line of items would be balanced by the expanded potential for finding new product offerings. Generally speaking, thoughts could turn out to be simpler to find, if by some stroke of good luck on account of the peculiar impact of AI on recombinant thought-based development.

According to the above picture, there are four extensive benefits of using AI: human capital development, easier credit access, new products and business models, and automation of key business processes. All those things effectively act as economic drivers, which include productivity growth, lowering barriers to entry into businesses, and new market expansion. Based on those things, output has been enhanced at a significant level, and consumption has also increased due to the higher growth of income.

As a piece of the exploration, artificial intelligence is connected to financial development, underscoring the creative elements of products and thoughts. Be that as it may, the development of artificial intelligence and its macroeconomic impacts will depend upon the possibly rich ways of behaving of firms. It is presented in one such view currently in the earlier area, where contemplations of imaginative obliteration give a motivationally arranged component that might be a significant impediment to singularities. This part is viewed as a firm motivating force and is conducted by and large as an additional framework for the AI research plan. Analyzed potential first-request issues that arise while presenting market structure, unearthly contrasts, and hierarchical contemplations inside firms.

5. Conclusion

Blockchain innovation can provide a device to help facilitate openly visible and secure exchanges. Existing work on rivalry and advancement driven development focuses on the presence of two checking impacts: from one perspective, a more serious item market contest actuates in a dead heat firm at the mechanical outskirts to enhance to get away from the contest; then again, the more extraordinary contest will, in general, deter firms behind the ongoing innovation boondocks to improve and consequently find wilderness firms. Which of these two impacts rules, thusly, depends on the level of rivalry in the economy and additionally upon how best-in-class the economy is. While the break-out impact will in general rule at low beginning degrees of rivalry and in further developed economies, the demoralization impact might overwhelm at more significant levels of rivalry or in less high-level economies.

In cutting-edge areas where firms benefit more from outside information, the previous impact of information dissemination will overwhelm, though in areas that don't depend a lot on outside information, the last option impact of rivalry or business taking will more often than not rule. Without a doubt, in more information-subordinate areas, firms see both their items and their imaginative capacities increase to a greater degree than the abilities of firms in areas that depend less on information from different areas. Hence, notwithstanding its immediate impacts on firms' development and creation capacities, its presentation and AI include an information dissemination impact that is increased by a sectored redistribution impact to the advantage of innovative areas that depend on additional information externalities from different fields and areas.

Not all associations are first adopters. As indicated by certain analysts, early movers will generally be enormous organizations that are carefully mature and more centred around AI-empowered development than just expensed investment funds. This view is shared by associations that have great information capacity and have an early advantage in becoming AI-prepared. It shocks no one subsequently that most IT organizations are now pioneers in the field, as they are in the field of enormous information. One of the fellow benefactors of Google, Larry Page, worked for his PhD on a web search research project under the management of T. Winograd, the main researcher on AI. Advanced local organizations have the absolute most critical and earliest interests in AI, giving experiments to possible profits from interests in AI.

REFERENCES

1. A. Jain, A. K. Pandey, (2019), "Modeling And Optimizing Of Different Quality Characteristics In Electrical Discharge Drilling Of Titanium Alloy (Grade-5) Sheet" Material Today Proceedings, 18, 182–191. https://doi.org/10.1016/j.matpr.2019.06.292
2. A. Jain, A. K. Pandey, (2019), "Modeling And Optimizing Of Different Quality Characteristics In Electrical Discharge Drilling Of Titanium Alloy (Grade-5) Sheet" Material Today Proceedings, 18, 182–191. https://doi.org/10.1016/j.matpr.2019.06.292
3. A. Jain, A. K. Pandey, (2019), "Multiple Quality Optimizations In Electrical Discharge Drilling Of Mild Steel Sheet" Material Today Proceedings, 8, 7252–7261. https://doi.org/10.1016/j.matpr.2017.07.054
4. A. Jain, A.K. Yadav & Y. Shrivastava (2019), "Modelling and Optimization of Different Quality Characteristics In Electric Discharge Drilling of Titanium Alloy Sheet" Material Today Proceedings, 21, 1680–1684. https://doi.org/10.1016/j.matpr.2019.12.010
5. A. Jain, C. S. Kumar, Y. Shrivastava, (2021), "Fabrication and Machining of Fiber Matrix Composite through Electric Discharge Machining: A short review" Material Today Proceedings. https://doi.org/10.1016/j.matpr.2021.07.288
6. Adams-Prassl, J., 2019. What if your boss was an algorithm? Economic Incentives, Legal Challenges, and the Rise of Artificial Intelligence at Work. Comp. Lab. L. & Pol'y J., 41, p. 123.
7. Baryannis, G., Validi, S., Dani, S. and Antoniou, G., 2019. Supply chain risk management and artificial intelligence: state of the art and future research directions. International Journal of Production Research, 57(7), pp. 2179–2202.
8. Berente, N., Gu, B., Recker, J. and Santhanam, R., 2021. Managing artificial intelligence. MIS quarterly, 45(3), pp. 1433–1450.
9. Chidepatil, A., Bindra, P., Kulkarni, D., Qazi, M., Kshirsagar, M. and Sankaran, K., 2020. From trash to cash: how blockchain and multi-sensor-driven artificial intelligence can transform circular economy of plastic waste?. Administrative Sciences, 10(2), p. 23.
10. Dhamija, P. and Bag, S., 2020. Role of artificial intelligence in operations environment: a review and bibliometric analysis. The TQM Journal.
11. Peyravi, B., Nekrošienė, J. and Lobanova, L., 2020. Revolutionised technologies for marketing: Theoretical review with focus on artificial intelligence. Verslas: Teorija ir praktika/Business: Theory and Practice, 21(2), pp. 827–834.
12. Sharma, M., Luthra, S., Joshi, S. and Kumar, A., 2022. Implementing challenges of artificial intelligence: Evidence from public manufacturing sector of an emerging economy. Government Information Quarterly, 39(4), p. 101624.
13. Simon, J.P., 2019. Artificial intelligence: scope, players, markets and geography. Digital Policy, Regulation and Governance, 21(3), pp. 208–237.
14. V. Panwar, D. K. Sharma, K. V. P. Kumar, A. Jain & C. Thakar, (2021), "Experimental Investigations And Optimization Of Surface Roughness In Turning Of EN 36 Alloy Steel Using Response Surface Methodology And Genetic Algorithm" Materials Today: Proceedings, https://Doi.Org/10.1016/J.Matpr.2021.03.642
15. V. Panwar, D. K. Sharma, K. V. P. Kumar, A. Jain & C. Thakar, (2021), "Experimental Investigations And Optimization Of Surface Roughness In Turning Of EN 36 Alloy Steel Using Response Surface Methodology And Genetic Algorithm" Materials Today: Proceedings, https://Doi.Org/10.1016/J.Matpr.2021.03.642
16. Wirtz, B. W., Weyerer, J. C. and Geyer, C., 2019. Artificial intelligence and the public sector—applications and challenges. International Journal of Public Administration, 42(7), pp. 596–615.
17. Zhang, C. and Lu, Y., 2021. Study on artificial intelligence: The state of the art and future prospects. Journal of Industrial Information Integration, 23, p. 100224.

Computer Science Engineering and Emerging Technologies (ICCS-2022) – Prof (Dr.) Rajeev Sobti et al. (eds)
© 2024 Taylor & Francis Group, London, ISBN 978-1-032-52199-2

Coal and Gangue Positioning and Classification Using Support Vector Machines

Prasoon Bisht[1]

Department of Mechatronics Engineering, Mohali, India

Gurmeet Singh[2], Harjot Singh Gill[3]

Department of Mechanical Engineering, Chandigarh University, Mohali, India

Abstract: Coal classification is mainly done by the manual screening method or by mechanical means. It cannot provide immediate production as it is very time-consuming. Coal and gangue sorting has gained attention recently. The first task of the robot is to classify whether the particle on the conveyor is coal or gangue. Computer vision and machine learning algorithms are being used for the recognition of coal and gangue and to apply them in a real-world scenario. This paper utilises support vector machines (SVM) for coal classification. The particle positioning and count were done correctly, and the accuracy of the SVM is 92% on the test set.

Keywords: SVM, Coal, Gangue, Connected components

1. Introduction

Manual and mechanical methods are mainly used for sorting coal and gangue. But these methods use a high cost of labour and energy, due to which environmental pollution and wastage of natural resources are caused [Li et al. 2020]. The automatic sorting of coal and gangue can provide a connection between the processing and production of coal [Liang et al. 2010]. X-rays and gamma rays are mainly used in equipment for the separation of coal and gangue particles. Coal and gangue are radioactive materials, and the radioactive material present in gangue is much greater than that of coal and can be ignored. Detectors for natural radiation were developed. It identifies the coal and gangue particles based on the reduction of the radiation passing through the samples [Zhang and Liu 2018]. The X-ray detects the coal and gangue particles based on the amount of radiation absorbed by the particles. Coals have a lower density as compared to gangue, so the amount of radiation absorbed by coal is much lower than that of gangue. The X-rays are collected by detectors and converted into digital signals. If the value of the digital signal is large, then the object through which the X-ray passed is coal; otherwise, it is gangue [Zhao and He 2013]. High-pressure valves and airflow are required for coal and gangue sorting by mechanical equipment. The limitations of these methods are the fast response of the system, the fact that ray detection should meet environmental standards, the moisture content, and the low precision of the execution part.

The coal-and-gangue sorting robot has gained attention in recent years. The primary task for the coal and gangue sorting robot is to recognise and position the coal and gangue perfectly. Many researchers have been trying to solve this problem through computer vision or image analysis and use these methods in real-life scenarios. The coal and gangue have different parameters for entropy, peak and mean grey scale, and contrast ratio. These results can be found by analysing texture level co-occurrence and the grey matrix [Li and Sun 2018].

[1]prasoon.bisht@gmail.com, [2]gurmeetsinghdec30@gmail.com, [3]harjot.gill@cumail.in

DOI: 10.1201/9781003405580-37

Many researchers have contributed in this field. By using image analysis, work has been done on methods for density fraction prediction [Zhang and Yang 2015] and ash content prediction [Zhang et al. 2014] of coarse coal. Particle size distribution (PSD) of coal using computer vision has been done on conveyors [Aldrich et al. 2010]. For the identification of different ores, a SVM model and a comprehensive model were established [Liu et al. 2019]. Many other coal and gangue identification models have been proposed, but they have high hardware requirements, complex algorithms, and long time consumption.

Many methods can be used for coal and gangue separation, but neural network-based classification, k-nearest neighbour-based classification, and SVM-based classification are the methods of choice for most researchers. The SVM algorithm performs better than a self-organising competitive neural network for coal identification and classification [Liang et al. 2010].

This paper studies the coal and gangue classification problem. Morphological processing and binarization of images are done to obtain clear and full target samples. The centre of mass is calculated to get the position information of the coal and gangue samples. SVM is used for the classification of coal and gangue.

2. Positioning of Coal and Gangue

2.1 Image Binarization

There is a need to remove noise from the image before performing any operation on it. For this purpose, we need a filter that does not affect the edges of the images. A well-known filter named the bilateral filter is used for this purpose. This filter not only removes noise from the image but also performs a smoothing operation on the image while preserving its edges. Bilateral filtering filters images on the basis of image intensity, colour, and spatial closeness and is a non-iterative process (Mkwelo et al., 2005; Tomasi and Manduchi, 1998).

To separate the object from the background, segmentation of the image is done. Imbinarize function, which uses Otsu's thresholding method for image segmentation.

2.2 Hole filling and Removing Objects from Background

Morphological operations are those that depend on shapes. A structuring element used in morphological operations is applied to the input image, and an output image of the same size is created. There are many morphological operations like erosion, dilation, opening, top-hat filtering, bottom-hat filtering, etc. (Suman Thapar and Shevani Garg, 2012). The morphological operation used for removing the holes or white pixels intensities is imfill. The Imfill function fills the holes in the background of the image. But we need to remove the holes inside the object, so we take a negative of the binarized image and then apply the imfill function. For removing connected components (objects) smaller than a certain value, area opening is done (Rani and Durgadevi, 2017; Thiele et al., 2013). The two parameters used in this function are the image and the numerical value. The numeric value determines the object having pixels less than the value and removes all those objects.

2.3 Solving Overlapping Problem

When there are multiple samples on the conveyor, one particle may overlap the other. Due to this, there is a small connection formed between the two samples in the binary image, and the objects are treated as one object, which causes a problem in the positioning of the samples. To solve this problem, erosion and dilation morphological operations are performed on the image. An erosion operation is performed on the image to separate the objects as erosion removes the pixels on the object boundaries. To get the image back to its original size, dilation is performed as it adds the pixels to the image boundaries (Suman Thapar and Shevani Garg, 2012).

2.4 Extracting the Centroid of the Samples and Counting the number of Samples

Before extracting the centroid of the samples, an erosion operation is performed on the object so that the overlapping problem can be fixed. For measuring the centroid of the samples, the regionprops function is used. The regionprops function returns the measurement of the properties of an object in a binary image (S. Mondal and J. Mukherjee, 2015). The illustration of the extraction of the centroid is shown in Fig. 37.1. The markers are shown by the red colour on the objects.

Fig. 37.1 Centroid detection of four objects (Bisht, Prasoon, 2022)

The bwconncomp function is used for counting the number of particles. This function counts all the connected components. The connected components that are connected form one sample object, and if two sample objects are very close or are counted as connected components, then these two sample objects are counted as one object (Marshall et al. 2018). To prevent this situation, we have used erosion to remove the boundary pixels of objects and area opening to remove particles less than a certain pixel value.

3. SVM Application on Coal and Gangue Recognition

3.1 Importing Images and Creating Training Set and Test Set

For importing images to the MATLAB workspace, the imageDatastore function is used, and subfolders are also included. Image Datastore supports various formats of images such as jpg, jpeg, tif, tiff, etc. Images in the image datastore are classified on the basis of the folder's name where they are stored, and the data is saved as an image data cache object. Image data is split into a training set and a test set with the help of the splitEachLabel function into ratios of 80% and 20%, respectively (Morankar et al. 2020).

3.2 Feature Extraction

Image samples of coal and gangue are taken from random sources. Gangue images contain images of shale and sandstone. Before extracting the features, all the images were converted to 128 x 128 pixels. Texture features, local binary pattern features, and gray scale features are calculated. Texture parameters are calculated with the gray-level co-occurrence matrix. The texture features include contrast, homogeneity, correlation, and energy (S. Mondal and J. Mukherjee, 2015). Tables 37.1 and 37.2 show the distribution range of gray-scale features and texture features, respectively.

Table 37.1 Range of gray scale features for coal and gangue (Bisht, Prasoon, 2022)

Features	Mean	Variance	Skewness	Kurtosis
Coal	12.768 - 19.35	243.01 - 10104	-2.6109 - 5.4884	1.4176 - 49.096
Gangue	16.131 - 238.56	200.04 - 7579.8	-2.0795 - 1.378	1.6426 - 12.95

Table 37.2 Range of texture features for coal and gangue (Bisht, Prasoon, 2022)

Features	Local binary pattern features	Contrast	Correlation	Energy	Homogeneity
Coal	1.3054 - 3.0804	0.013174 - 5.428	0.61658 - 0.99741	0.047157 - 0.80767	0.67657 - 0.99342
Gangue	2.7509 - 2.7509	0.027243 - 2.6938	0.28925 - 0.99107	0.028541 - 0.70854	0.58885 - 0.98785

3.3 Training the SVM Model

For the training of features with SVM, all the features were taken at once and trained. The Fitcsvm function is used for training the model. The parameters used for model classification are shown in Table 37.3.

Table 37.3   SVM Parameters and its options used (Bisht, Prasoon, 2022)

S.No.	Parameter	Parameter Option
1.	Kernal Function	Linear
2.	Standarization	True
3.	Hyperparamter Optimization	all

A graph between minimum observed objective and estimated minimum objective is drawn, and is shown in Fig. 37.2.

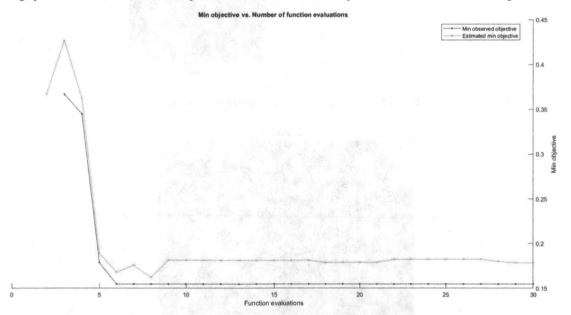

Fig. 37.2   A graph between minimum observed objective and estimated minimum objective (Bisht, Prasoon, 2022)

3.4 Cross-validation and Testing Accuracy on Test Set

Cross-validation of the model is done using the crossval function, taking the KFold value as 10. In our case, the KFold randomly partitions the data into 10 sets. For a given dataset, the cross-val function is used to evaluate the model and find the most favorable input parameters. According to random permutation, the training set data is reordered for each run of cross-validation (Annest et al. 2010). Then validation accuracy is calculated, which is found to be 85%.

After this, the SVM model is applied to the test set, which gives an accuracy of 92%. A chart of coal and gangue predictions for the test set is given in Fig. 37.3.

3.5 Testing of an Image

This image was taken at a local restaurant. After getting the results from the test set, the classifier was used to check the classifier. And we found that the classifier predicted the image correctly, as shown in Fig. 37.4. The results were displayed in such a manner that if the classifier detects the objects to be coal, then it will show the image by using the imshow function and display the title as coal.

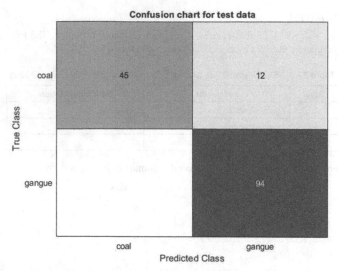

Fig. 37.3 Confusion chart of test set (Bisht, Prasoon, 2022)

Fig. 37.4 Test of coal classified correctly (Bisht, Prasoon, 2022)

4. Conclusion

The following conclusions can be drawn from the study:

1. Coal and gangue can be distinguished based on the above properties. More samples, quality of light, and images can increase the The following classification was made with 286 images of coal and 471 images of gangue. These were the randomly collected images, and the classification is 92% accurate on the test set.

2. For positioning the sample objects on the image, erosion performs very well. Small particles should be removed from the images by the area opening process, and the choice of removing the objects depends on the size chosen by the person. So, it provides sample objects larger than the size input on the computer.

3. When all the small sample objects have been removed, the number of objects in the image can be calculated by seeing the connected components. We get desirable results if erosion and the area opening process are done.

4. The performance of SVM in an imbalanced dataset is good. The correct classification of the minority class is challenging. So the datasets should be well balanced.

5. Acknowledgement

The authors gratefully acknowledge the Chandigarh University, Mohali, Punjab, for providing the support to complete the work.

REFERENCES

1. Li, M., Duan, Y., He, X. and Yang, M., 2020. Image positioning and identification method and system for coal and gangue sorting robot. *International Journal of Coal Preparation and Utilization*, pp. 1–19.
2. Liang, H., Cheng, H., Ma, T., Pang, Z. and Zhong, Y., 2010, August. Identification of coal and gangue by self-organizing competitive neural network and SVM. In *2010 Second International Conference on Intelligent Human-Machine Systems and Cybernetics* (Vol. 2, pp. 41–45). IEEE.
3. Zhang, N. and Liu, C., 2018. Radiation characteristics of natural gamma-ray from coal and gangue for recognition in top coal caving. *Scientific reports*, 8(1), pp. 1–9.
4. Zhao, Y.D. and He, X., 2013. Recognition of coal and gangue based on X-ray. In *Applied mechanics and materials* (Vol. 275, pp. 2350–2353). Trans Tech Publications Ltd.
5. Li, M. and Sun, K., 2018, August. An image recognition approach for coal and gangue used in pick-up robot. In *2018 IEEE International Conference on Real-time Computing and Robotics (RCAR)* (pp. 501–507). Ieee.
6. Zhang, Z. and Yang, J., 2015. The density fraction estimation of coarse coal by use of the kernel method and machine vision. *Energy Sources, Part A: Recovery, Utilization, and Environmental Effects*, 37(2), pp. 181–191.
7. Zhang, Z., Yang, J., Wang, Y., Dou, D. and Xia, W., 2014. Ash content prediction of coarse coal by image analysis and GA-SVM. *Powder Technology*, 268, pp. 429–435.
8. Aldrich, C., Jemwa, G. T., Van Dyk, J. C., Keyser, M. J. and Van Heerden, J. H. P., 2010. Online analysis of coal on a conveyor belt by use of machine vision and kernel methods. *International Journal of Coal Preparation and Utilization*, 30(6), pp. 331–348.
9. Liu, C., Li, M., Zhang, Y., Han, S. and Zhu, Y., 2019. An enhanced rock mineral recognition method integrating a deep learning model and clustering algorithm. *Minerals*, 9(9), p. 516.
10. Mkwelo, S.G., Nicolls, V. and De Jager, G., 2005. Watershed-based segmentation of rock scenes and proximity-based classification of watershed regions under uncontrolled lighting. *SAIEE Africa Research Journal*, 96(1), pp. 28–34.
11. Tomasi, C. and Manduchi, R., 1998, January. Bilateral filtering for gray and color images. In *Sixth international conference on computer vision (IEEE Cat. No. 98CH36271)* (pp. 839–846). IEEE.
12. Thapar, S. and Garg, S., 2012. Study and implementation of various morphology based image contrast enhancement techniques. *Int. J. Comput. Bus. Res*, 128, pp. 2229–6166.
13. Rani, A. Mercy, and R. Durgadevi. "Image Processing Techniques To Recognize Facial Emotions." *International Journal of Engineering and Advanced Technology (IJEAT)* 6, no. 6 (2017).
14. Thiele, Simon, Tobias Fürstenhaupt, Dustin Banham, Tobias Hutzenlaub, Viola Birss, Christoph Ziegler, and Roland Zengerle. "Multiscale tomography of nanoporous carbon-supported noble metal catalyst layers." *Journal of Power Sources* 228 (2013): 185–192.
15. Mondal, Satyajit, and Joydeep Mukherjee. "Image similarity measurement using region props, color and texture: an approach." *International Journal of Computer Applications* 121, no. 22 (2015).
16. Marshall, Lauren, Adam Schroeder, and Brian Trease. "Comparing fish-inspired Ram filters for collection of harmful algae." In *ASME International Mechanical Engineering Congress and Exposition*, vol. 52101, p. V007T09A093. American Society of Mechanical Engineers, 2018.
17. Morankar, Devendra, Deepak M. Shinde, and Suvidya R. Pawar. "Identification of pests and diseases using alex-net." *SSRN Electronic Journal* 7, no. 4 (2020): 53–61.
18. Annest, Amalia, Roger E. Bumgarner, Adrian E. Raftery, and Ka Yee Yeung. "The iterative bayesian model averaging algorithm for survival analysis: an improved method for gene selection and survival analysis on microarray data." (2010).

Computer Science Engineering and Emerging Technologies (ICCS-2022) – Prof (Dr.) Rajeev Sobti et al. (eds)
© 2024 Taylor & Francis Group, London, ISBN 978-1-032-52199-2

Chapter **38**

IoT and Its Escalating Security Needs

Siddharth Pansare[1]
Research Scholar, Department of Computer Science and Engineering,
Lovely Professional University, Phagwara, Punjab, India

Harwant Singh Arri[2]
Associate Professor, Department of Computer Science and Engineering,
Lovely Professional University, Phagwara, Punjab, India

**Nupur Kaushik[3], Nancy Sharma[4], Gobinda Karmarkar[5],
Sahil Bhardwaj[6], Jithin Govind[7], Jayant Mehra[8]**
Research Scholar, Department of Computer Science and Engineering,
Lovely Professional University, Phagwara, Punjab, India

Dhiraj Kapila[9]
Associate Professor, Department of Computer Science and Engineering,
Lovely Professional University, Phagwara, Punjab, India

Abstract: The Internet of Things (IoT) has created a world of limitless opportunities for applications across many facets of society, but it also comes with a number of difficulties. Security and privacy are two such issues. The IoT has grown significantly in importance and concern recently, and as a result, especially with the broad use and acceptance of projects and applications of the IoT in several fields, concern about IoT security has also expanded significantly. IoT devices are more vulnerable to attacks and security issues. There is a dearth of suitable security solutions for devices and applications of the IoT because of their limitations, including those related to space, power, memory, etc. The manufacturers are still unable to come up with a suitable fix, despite the fact that there are several vulnerabilities. This paper provides a landscape overview of IoT security with the goal of highlighting the demand for secure IoT-related products and applications.

Keywords: IoT, IoT security, Blockchain in IoT, Threats in IoT, Blockchain security

1. Introduction

At the Massachusetts Institute of Technology, a technologist named Kevin Ashton popularized the Internet of Things concept for the first time in 1999. According to Kevin Ashton, the Internet of Things and its effects on our environments will eventually allow gadgets and systems to know everything about things that are connected, so that everything may be monitored and recorded, and so that the cosmos and humanity can greatly benefit from such data [1]. IoT is defined as "a cyber-physical ecosystem of interconnected sensors and actuators that enable decision-making" [2]. Numerous organizations and academic institutions have worked to try to offer a uniform definition for IoT over time and as a result of its dynamic nature. John Romkey established the first toaster-internet connection in 1990. A year later, some University of Cambridge students conducted a webcam report on coffee. They had the bright notion to use the first web camera prototype to keep an eye on how much coffee was left in the coffee maker at the computer lab. They achieved this by setting the web

---
[1]sidhu.pansare@gmail.com, [2]hs.arri@lpu.co.in, [3]nupurkaushiknk@gmail.com, [4]nancysharma2177@gmail.com, [5]gobindak2@gmail.com,
[6]binny4166@gmail.com, [7]jithingovindkanayi001@gmail.com, [8]jayant46mehra@gmail.com, [9]dhiraj.23509@lpu.co.in

DOI: 10.1201/9781003405580-38

camera to capture pictures of the coffee maker three times every minute. So that everyone could see if there was coffee available, the photographs were then shared on nearby computers. In the Institute of Electrical and Electronics Engineers (IEEE)'s 2014 IEEE "Internet of Things" special report, the word "Internet of Things" was described as *"a network of items—each embedded with sensors—which are connected to the Internet"* [4]. The number of industries using IoT applications is growing, and as a result, more IoT devices and apps will be developed.

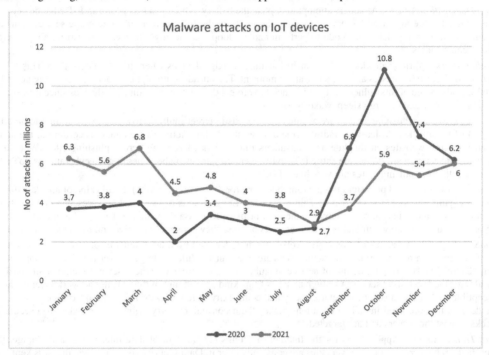

Fig. 38.1 Malware attacks on IoT devices (Siddharth Pansare)

2. Threats in IoT

IoT technology gives our devices the ability to do more for us and make our lives more efficient. However, IoT is also a relatively new technology, which means there are key security threats to be aware of. The most important threats to security that can be confronted at various levels of the IoT are:

- *Capturing of Node:* Numerous nodes that require less power, including actuators and some sensors, are used in IoT products. These nodes are open to several attacks from the opposition. Attackers can attempt to seize control of the node or swap it out for a rogue node in the IoT system. The new node may seem to be a component of the system, but it is actually under the control of the attacker. This could result in the security of the entire IoT application being compromised [5].

- *Injection of Code Attack:* The intruder inserts a malicious code into the memory of the node to carry out the attack. The software or firmware of IoT nodes is typically revised over the air, which provides a conduit for attackers to introduce malicious code. The attackers may try to access the entire IoT system or impose nodes for performing unwanted operations using such malicious code.

- *Injection of Bogus Data Attack:* After seizing the node, the attacker can utilise it to introduce false data into the IoT system. This could produce inaccurate findings and cause the IoT application to malfunction. This technique could be used by the attacker to launch a DDoS assault.

- *Channel Attacks:* Other than the attacks that happen directly on the nodes, a number of side channel attacks may cause the leakage of private information. Processor microarchitectures, electromagnetic emission, and power consumption make sensitive data accessible to enemies. Attacks on the side channels could be electromagnetic, laser, timing, or power consumption-based. While implementing the cryptography modules, modern chips take care of different safeguards to stop these side-channel attacks.

- *Interference and Eavesdropping:* Applications of IoT often include a range of nodes placed in spaces that are open. These applications are therefore vulnerable to eavesdroppers. Intruders may eavesdrop on and intercept data while it is being transmitted or authenticated [6].

- *Sleep Deprivation Attacks:* Attackers attempt to deplete the battery, which has less power in IoT edge devices, in this type of attack. Due to a dead battery, this causes the nodes in the IoT application to deny the service. This can be accomplished by using malicious code to perform endless loops on the edge devices or by artificially raising their power requirements.

- *Booting Attacks:* Various attacks can be launched against the edge devices when they are booting up. This is because the built-in security processes are not active at the moment. The intruders attempt to attack the restarting node devices by taking advantage of this vulnerability. It is crucial to protect the boot process on edge devices since they frequently run on low power and undergo sleep–wake cycles.

- *Attack of Phishing:* Phishing attacks are assaults that can easily target multiple IoT gadgets with little to no effort on the part of the attacker. At least a handful of the devices should fall victim to the attack, according to the attackers. When browsing websites on the Internet, consumers run the risk of running across phishing sites. When a user's password and account are stolen, the entire IoT environment they are using becomes open to cyberattacks. IoT network layer assaults from phishing sites are very likely [7].

- *Access Attack:* Advanced persistent threat is another name for access attack (APT). In this kind of attack, a third party or enemy gains access to the Internet of Things network. Long periods of the attacker's presence in the network go unnoticed. Instead of harming the network, the goal or motive of assault of this sort is to take important data. IoT applications are extremely vulnerable to such assaults because they constantly receive and transport vital data.

- *DDoS/DoS Attack:* An attack of this kind involves the intruder sending a large number of unwanted requests to the target servers. As a result, services for actual users are interrupted while the target server is rendered inoperable. The term "DDoS," or "distributed denial of service assault," refers to an attack where several methods are used by the intruder to flood the target server. Although attacks of this kind are not rare in the IoT, the network layer of the IoT is susceptible to them because of the heterogeneity and complexity of IoT networks. The weak configuration of several IoT devices that are used in IoT applications makes them convenient entry points for intruders to execute DDoS attacks against the servers that are targeted.

- *Data Transit Attacks:* Applications for the Internet of Things handle a lot of data interchange and storage. Data is important, so hackers and other adversaries are constantly after it. Data security risks exist whether it is kept on local servers or in the cloud, but moving data from one place to another makes it much more vulnerable to cyberattacks. Data transfer between actuators, sensors, and other parts in IoT applications is tremendous. IoT applications are vulnerable to data breaches since numerous connection technologies are present in these data flows.

- *Routing Attacks:* Malicious nodes in the application of IoT might attempt to change the transmitting pathways during the transit of data in such attacks. There is a type of routing assault known as a "sinkhole attack," which entices nodes to route traffic down a fictitious shortest path by advertising it. Another assault that poses a severe security risk is a wormhole attack, especially when paired with sinkhole attacks. The creation of a link for fast data transfer takes place in the warm hole. In order to get beyond the fundamental security procedures in an IoT application, an attacker can try to establish a warm hole between a device that is connected to the internet and the device that is compromised.

- *Man in the Middle Attack:* MQTT, which essentially serves as a substitute, is used by the MQTT communications protocol to implement the subscribe-publish paradigm of interaction between the subscribers that are present and the clients. Messages can be transmitted without knowing their destination thanks to the decoupling of the publishing and subscribing clients. The attacker can have total command over all communication without the clients' knowledge if he or she can take over the MQTT and behave as a man in the middle.

- *SQL Injection Attack:* SQL injection (SQLi) attacks can also affect middleware. Attackers can insert dangerous SQL statements into software during such attacks. The attackers can then get any user's sensitive information and even change database records [9]. In their OWASP Major 10 2022 document, the Open Web Application Security Project (OWASP) identified SQLi as one of the leading dangers to the security of the web.

- *Attack on Signature Wrapping:* Signatures of XML are applied in the middleware's net services. By taking advantage of SOAP flaws, the attacker can execute commands or modify eavesdropped messages in an attack of signature wrapping, which compromises the signature algorithm (Simple Object Access Protocol).

- *Injection of Malware in Cloud:* In the case of cloud malware injection, the intruder has the option of taking over, inserting malicious code, or inserting a virtual machine. By making an effort to construct a virtual machine or component of a malicious service, the attacker poses as a legitimate service. By doing so, the attacker can gain access to the victim's requests for services to collect data that is very important and can be altered depending on the situation.
- *Flooding Assault in the Cloud:* This attack degrades service quality and functions virtually identically to a DoS attack in the cloud (QoS). Intruders repeatedly make requests to a server in order to exhaust cloud resources. Due to the increased workload on the servers that are present in the cloud, these attacks have a significant impact on these systems.
- *Secure On-boarding:* Protecting encryption keys is essential as sensors or devices are added to an IoT system. All keys pass through gateways, which serve as a mediator between managing services and newly added devices. Particularly during the on-boarding process, the gateways are vulnerable to man-in-the middle attacks and eavesdropping to obtain the keys, which are encrypted.
- *Extra Interfaces:* A crucial technique that must be kept in mind when deploying IoT devices is reducing the attack surface. An IoT gateway maker should only use the essential interfaces and protocols. To prevent backdoor authentication or data breaches, several services and functionalities should be blocked for end users.

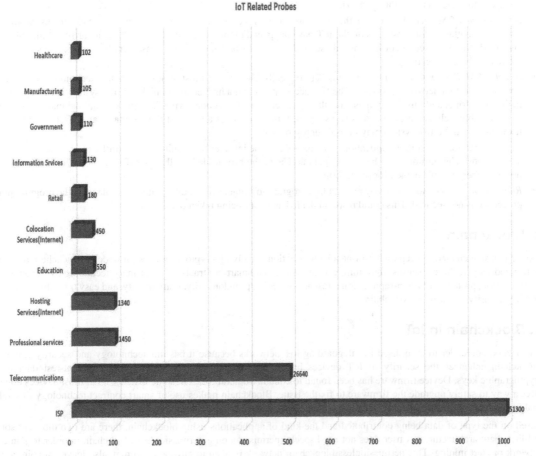

Fig. 38.2 Top Sectors Generating IoT-related probes (Siddharth Pansare)

- *End to End Encryption:* To guarantee data confidentiality, true end-to-end application layer security is necessary. The application shouldn't allow anyone else to decipher the encrypted communications outside of the specific receiver. Although the protocols of Zwave and Zigbee enable encryption, this is not end-to-end encryption, as the gateways must decrypt and re-encrypt the messages to transform the data from one protocol to another. The data is vulnerable to data breaches because of this decryption at the entry point of the device.

- *Firmware updates:* The majority of Internet of Things (IoT) gadgets are constrained by resources, so they lack the user interface and processing power necessary to obtain and install firmware upgrades. The firmware upgrades are often downloaded and applied through gateways. For a secure update of firmware, the old and latest versions of the firmware should be noted, and the signature's authenticity should be examined.

- *Data Theft:* A lot of sensitive and confidential data is used in IoT applications. In IoT applications, there is a lot of data movement, which makes it even more vulnerable to assaults than data at rest. If Internet of Things applications are susceptible to data theft threats, users will be hesitant to register their sensitive data on these applications. Some of the strategies and protocols being utilised to protect IoT applications against data thefts include data encryption, data isolation, user and network authentication, privacy management, etc.

- *Access Control Attacks:* Only authorized individuals or processes are permitted access to the data or account, thanks to access control. Since the entire IoT application becomes exposed to attacks once access is compromised, attacks on access control are a crucial threat in IoT.

- *Interruption of Service Attacks:* In the literature, these kinds of attacks are known as DDoS attacks or illegal interruption attacks. Such assaults on the IoT have happened on numerous occasions. By using artificial intelligence and overloading the servers or network, these kinds of attacks prevent genuine consumers from using the services of the IoT and its applications.

- *Attack of Malicious Code Injection:* Attackers typically choose the most simple or easiest technique they can to obtain access to a network or system. The first access point that a hacker would pick is if the system is susceptible to malicious scripts and misdirection as a result of poor checks of the code. Typically, attackers upload malicious script to a reputable website via XSS (cross-site scripting). In the event of a successful XSS attack, an IoT account may be taken over, and the IoT system may become unresponsive.

- *Sniffing Attacks:* The sniffer applications may be used by the intruder for monitoring the traffic on the network in IoT applications. The intruder may be able to gain access to the private data of the user if there aren't enough security protocols being implemented for prevention.

- *Reprogram Attacks:* Attackers may attempt to reprogram IoT objects from different remote places if the programming procedure is not secured. This could result in the IoT network being taken over.

3. Blockchain

Blockchain was created to keep track of financial transactions involving cryptocurrencies (or nodes). Blockchain uses the distributed ledger, the consensus algorithm, cryptography, and smart contracts as its primary technologies. Absence of centralization, protection by non-repudiation, presence of clarity, pseudonymity, immutability, and easy traceability are the primary security features of blockchain.

4. Blockchain in IoT

It is a good contender to be utilised in safeguarding IoT networks because it has this technology and security features. Blockchain enhances the security of IoT devices by digitally signing and encrypting stored and at-rest data with cryptographic keys. Device firmware has been found to contain vulnerabilities in some instances, but most devices do not offer a way to safely upgrade the firmware to fix the issue. Blockchain makes use of smart contract technology to safely enable automatic firmware updates that can close any flaws discovered in IoT devices.

Based on the type of data being contributed and the kind of applications using blockchain, there are two different sorts of blockchain architectures. A user does not need special permission on a permissionless blockchain in order to join the network or start mining. This permissionless blockchain network is open to anyone, who may also leave. Bitcoin is the ideal illustration of a permissionless blockchain. Although the transaction throughput is not very great, a large number of nodes can be supported by permission-less blockchains.

The permissioned blockchains, on the other hand, include a set of guidelines for participation in the blockchain network. The blocks can only be added to the chain after being validated by the miners, who are also the authorised parties. Hyperledger and the Ripple blockchain are two prominent examples of permissioned blockchain. Compared to permissionless blockchains, the permissioned blockchain approach increases the overall throughput of transactions.

5. Benefits of Using the Blockchain in IoT

There are many benefits of using blockchain in order to secure the IoT devices and its data. The key benefits of using blockchain for IoT applications are:

- *Blockchain let us keep the storage of IoT device data:* Applications for the Internet of Things (IoT) use a wide range of interconnected devices. Other gadgets are connected to and in control of these devices as well. The use of IoT apps from any location is made possible by this setup's additional connection to the cloud. Blockchain is a potential method for storing data and guarding against its exploitation because of the wide space for data flow it provides. Blockchain can serve as an appropriate option to store and transport data, regardless of the layer in an IoT application.

- *Secure data storage made possible by the distributed structure of the blockchain:* Due to the distributed nature of the blockchain design, it can minimise the possibility of having a failure of single point, which is a problem for many cloud-based IoT systems. Regardless of the distance between the devices, it is simple and secure to store the data they produce on the blockchain [11].

- *Employing the hash key for data encryption, which is validated by miners:* Blockchain allows for the storage of the hash key at 256 bits, not the actual data itself. The key used in hashing can be associated with the original and genuine data, and the actual data can be kept on the cloud. The data's hash will change if the data changes in any way. The information is now private and protected. Since the hash values are the only values that are stored in the chain, the size of the data will not have an impact on the size of the blockchain. Using the hash of the data, only the parties that are authenticated and those who are permitted to use that data can be allowed to access the data that is present on the cloud. Blockchain technology decreases the likelihood of storing faulty data on devices because all the sets of data that are kept on it are correctly checked by various miners that are present on the network.

- *Prevention of data from getting lost and as well as from spoofing attacks:* Spoofing attacks on applications of the IoT involve the introduction of a new adversary node into the IoT network, which begins acting like it is a component of the original network. The intruder can quickly inject the data, observe the data, or capture the data into the network using spoofing. Blockchain offers a possible defence against these threats. Each genuine user or the IoT gadget is recorded on the blockchain and without the aid of central brokers or certification authority, devices may quickly identify and authenticate one another. IoT devices carry a risk of data loss due to their low power nature [12].

- *Blockchain to restrict unauthorized access:* A number of Internet of Things applications require regular connections between various nodes. Since public and private keys are used for communication in blockchain, only the person who is authenticated can have access to the data. The data is encrypted with keys, so even if the undesired person is able to view it, the contents will be incomprehensible. As a result, the blockchain data format aims to address the many security problems that IoT applications encounter.

- *Blockchain's proxy-based architecture for devices with limited resources:* Although blockchain offers numerous security characteristics for a distributed system, resource limitations provide a unique difficulty for the IoT. IoT devices are unable to store huge ledgers due to their severe resource limitations. To make the usage of blockchain in IoT easier, numerous efforts have been made in this area. One of the possible approaches for enabling IoT gadgets for the usage of blockchain is proxy based architecture. To save the resources in an encrypted format, the installation of proxy servers on the network can be done. The client can download the encrypted resources from the proxy servers [13].

- *Centralised cloud servers can be removed:* Because blockchain finally gets rid of centralised servers that are present in the cloud and makes peer-to-peer networks, it can increase the security of IoT devices. Data thieves focus primarily on centralised cloud servers. The sharing of data will be done between all network nodes using blockchain, and its encryption will take place with a cryptographic hash function.

6. Conclusion

IoT has unlocked a world of limitless opportunities for applications across various societal areas, but it also faces numerous obstacles. Security and privacy are two such issues. Due to their limitations, the security of IoT devices is compromised, and they are vulnerable to risks and assaults. For IoT applications, there is a shortage of appropriate security solutions, and because of this, the world of safely linked things takes a transition to the network of insecure things. We discussed the current state of IoT security in this review article, as well as the solutions that must be implemented to convince users that the reputation of IoT is not just about offering inexpensive devices; it is also important to offer the best security solutions on the market and also address privacy concerns and threats to security. All users, including IoT developers and security administrators, must be informed of IoT security issues if they are to be kept secure. The developer's responsibility is to make sure that security is prioritized throughout the creation of the hardware or software. We illustrated one of the most significant developing technologies, blockchain, how it affects security when used in the IoT, and suggested strategies to reduce these risks. This review can provide researchers and scholars with fresh ideas for the field.

REFERENCES

1. K. Ashton (2009). "That 'Internet of Things' Thing", vol. 22, no. 7, pp. 99–114.
2. European Union Agency for Network and Information Security (ENSIA) 2017. "Baseline security recommendations for IoT".
3. IETF.org , "The Internet of Things".
4. ITU-T (2018). "Internet of Things Global Standards Initiative" Recommendation ITU-T Y.2060 (06/2012))
5. S. Kumar, S. Sahoo, A. Mahapatra, A. K. Swain and K. K. Mahapatra (2017). "Security enhancements to system on chip devices for IoT perception layer", *Proc. IEEE Int. Symp. Nanoelectron. Inf. Syst. (iNIS)*, pp. 151–156.
6. C.-H. Liao, H.-H. Shuai and L.-C. Wang (2018). "Eavesdropping prevention for heterogeneous Internet of Things systems", *Proc. 15th IEEE Annu. Consum. Commun. Netw. Conf. (CCNC)*, pp. 1–2.
7. Phishing Activity Trends Report, Sep. 2022.
8. C. Li and C. Chen (2011). "A multi-stage control method application in the fight against phishing attacks", *Proc. 26th Comput. Secur. Acad. Commun. Across Country*, pp. 145.
9. R. Dorai and V. Kannan (2011), "SQL injection-database attack revolution and prevention", J. Int. Commercial Law Technol., vol. 6, no. 4, pp. 224.
10. H. Dai, Z. Zheng, Y. Zhang (2019). Blockchain for Internet of Things: a survey, IEEE Internet Things J. vol. 6, no. 5, pp. 8076–8094.
11. T. T. A. Dinh, R. Liu, M. Zhang, G. Chen, B. C. Ooi and J. Wang (2018). "Untangling blockchain: A data processing view of blockchain systems", *IEEE Trans. Knowl. Data Eng.*, vol. 30, no. 7, pp. 13661385.
12. B. Dickson (2019). How Blockchain Can Change the Future of IoT
13. O. Alphand, M. Amoretti, T. Claeys, S. Dall'Asta, A. Duda, G. Ferrari, et al. (2018). "IoTchain: A blockchain security architecture for the Internet of Things", *Proc. IEEE Wireless Commun. Netw. Conf. (WCNC)*, vol, 45, no. 3, pp. 1–6.
14. N. Kshetri (2017), "Can Blockchain Strengthen the Internet of Things?," in IT Professional, vol. 19, no. 4, pp. 68–72.

Computer Science Engineering and Emerging Technologies (ICCS-2022) – Prof (Dr.) Rajeev Sobti et al. (eds)
© 2024 Taylor & Francis Group, London, ISBN 978-1-032-52199-2

Chapter **39**

Empirical Analysis of Machine Learning (Ml) for Big Data and its Applications Using CNN

D. Lakshmi Padmaja[1]
Associate Professor, Department of IT, Anurag University

Imran Qureshi[2]
Lecturer, Department of Information Technology,
University of Technology and Applied Science-AlMusanna, Sultanate of Oman.

Sudha Rajesh[3]
Assistant Professor, Department of Computational Intelligence,
College of Engineering and Technology, School of Computing, SRMIST, Kattankulathur, Chennai

M. K. Sharma[4]
Professor, Department of Mathematics,
Chaudhary Charan Singh University, Meerut, Uttar Pradesh, India

Ravi Kumar Sanapala[5]
Associate Professor, Department of Electronics and Communication Engineering,
St Martin's Engineering College, Dhulapally, Secunderabad

Firos A.[6]
Assistant Professor, Department of computer Science and Engineering Rajiv Gandhi University
(A Central University), Rono-Hills, Doimukh, Arunachal Pradesh, India

Abstract: Due to its abilities to extract features and classify data, machine learning has ignited a lot of interest in the big data analytics space. In the past, researchers classified large amounts of data using machine learning algorithms; researchers found machine learning methods for feature extraction via the use of algorithms. The accuracy and precision of big data analytics are studied in this study using the "Convolutional Neural Network" method, or CNN. The efficiency of this neural network has been studied in detail to understand the effects of hidden layers and nodes. The other two approaches chosen are "Long Short-term Memory" or LSTM and "Multilayer Perception" or MLP. Additionally, CNN is compared to other approaches to determine whether it is outperforming the other algorithms or not. The CNN-based system can detect and classify instance connections in framework logs with high exactness, rather than other existing measurable strategies or regular rule-based ML (machine learning) approaches. The CNN, MLP, and LSTM dependencies were the variables. According to research, CNN has an accuracy rate of 99.9% in big data analytics, compared to less than 98% for other classifiers. On CNN's accuracy, the concealed nodes have a very good effect.

Keywords: Machine learning, Big data, CNN

[1]lakshmipadmajait@anurag.edu.in, [2]imran@act.edu.om, [3]drsudharajesh84@gmail.com, [4]drmukeshsharma@gmail.com, [5]sravikumarece@smec.ac.in, [6]firos.a@rgu.ac.in

DOI: 10.1201/9781003405580-39

1. Introduction

Along with the accelerated expansion of large data sizes, big data systems play a growingly significant role. The equal figuring systems have all been widely used in true applications. These large information frameworks make gigantic logs as they dissect a few informational indexes lined up on conveyed record frameworks. These logs can be utilized to separate crucial information for execution tuning and abnormality identification to look at issues in enormous information frameworks and upgrade their exhibition. However, it can be very difficult to analyse these logs. For instance, sometimes require lengthy execution times, which results in enormous log volume generation (Ghassemi et al., 2020). Additionally, each system could use a different logging framework, such as log4j or self4j (Çınar, A., and Tuncer, S. A. 2021), leading to a variety of log formats. Additionally, some unanticipated events that occur while the programme is running could significantly reduce performance or even result in failures (Lu et al., 2018). Even for system professionals, it can be challenging to manually identify certain circumstances. As big data analytics technology has advanced, more focus has been placed on disease prediction from this perspective. Various studies have been conducted using automatic characteristic selection from a large number of data to increase the accuracy of risk classification (Jang et al., 2019), as opposed to manually selecting characteristics. However, the majority of that previous work was considered structured data. Convolutional neural networks (CNNs) have already gained a lot of attention and produced excellent results when used to automatically extract text characteristics from unstructured input, for instance (Allagi, S., and Rachh, R. 2019). To our knowledge, CNN hasn't handled any Chinese medical text data in any of their prior work, though. In addition, there are significant differences between disorders in different geographic areas, mostly due to the variations in environment and way of life.

Laboratory workers are becoming more and more interested in the hot issues of artificial intelligence (AI) and ML, in particular (Coccia 2020), (Ghassemi et al., 2020). The hypothesis and formation of PC frameworks to complete muddled exercises take part in customary human knowledge, for example, navigation, visual discernment, discourse acknowledgment, and language interpretation, is implied by the exceptionally wide expression "man-made reasoning" (computer-based intelligence). PCs can gain information without being unequivocally instructed thanks to the study of programming known as AI (ML) (Ghassemi et al., 2020). Albeit this word was first utilized for quite a while, potential was not completely acknowledged until the 1980s due to an absence of PC power, sufficient information and capacity, and viable applications. The accessibility of strong and more affordable PCs, the downpour of data delivered by an additional information driven society, and the far reaching availability of open source instruments, (for example, creation prepared Python systems like Scikit-Learn, TensorFlow, and Keras) are contributing elements to the momentum of ML penetration in practically every industry under the sun (like business, exploration, and medical care). Clinical research facilities are becoming successful makers of immense and convoluted datasets simultaneously on account of lab robotization. A couple of ML-based business items are currently accessible in the clinical research facility, notwithstanding the way that ML models, especially profound learning models, flourish within the sight of tremendous measures of information. A few elements, including the kind of management, whether the calculation can advance continuously from an underlying stream of information (bunch versus internet learning), and how they sum up (example based versus model-based learning), can be used to group ML models into broad categories (Coccia 2020).

2. Literature Review

2.1 Unsupervised Learning vs. Supervised

In view of the amount and kind of management the models get during preparation, four huge sorts can be recognized: directed, unaided, semisupervised, and support learning. In regulated learning, information tests are anticipated utilizing information on the expected arrangements and they are marked to prepare information. Relapse and arrangement are the two principal uses of them. Straight relapse, strategic relapse, K-closest neighbors (KNN), support vector machines (SVM), choice trees (DTs), irregular woodlands (RFs), and regulated brain networks are probably the main administered calculations. Preparing information is left unlabeled in solo learning (Ghassemi et al., 2020). To put it another way, perceptions are sorted with next to no earlier information on the information test. Head part investigation (PCA), portion PCA, locally direct implanting, t-appropriated stochastic neighbor installing, oddity identification and curiosity recognition (one-class SVM, disconnection woodland), and affiliation rule learning are instances of unaided calculations that can be utilized for bunching, perception, and dimensionality decrease (for example, a priori, eclat). A few models, in any case, can utilize semi-directed figuring out how to manage to some extent marked preparing information. At last, in support learning, a specialist (i.e., the learning framework) realizes what activities to perform to expand the combined prize or to streamline the result of a procedure (i.e., a strategy) (Coccia 2020). In learning games like Go, chess, or even poker, or in circumstances where the result is persistent as opposed to parallel (for example, right or wrong), this situation is like the way in which individuals figure out how to ride a bicycle.

2.2 Learning in Batches and Online

The model of ML is built utilizing the whole dataset when batch learning is used. Once the training is complete, the algorithm's weights are fixed and it can be utilised in a production environment to analyse new data. The weights in the algorithm are unaffected by the new knowledge learned during production; therefore, the framework isn't learning at this point. Such frameworks have the advantages of being reliable and stable, and it is simple to test their accuracy and performance beforehand. To update the system with new information, notwithstanding, it should be prepared without any preparation utilizing both the old and new information tests on the grounds that the framework can't adjust to new data. As a result, the method often demands a lot of computing resources and can be time-consuming. Online learning is another option, where the model is refreshed by adding individual information or little clusters of information. The method is appropriate for handling a continuous data flow because each learning step is relatively quick and affordable. The system's volatility and difficulty to verify its efficacy and effectiveness are drawbacks because the algorithm is always changing, which causes issues with licencing (Ghassemi et al., 2020).

2.3 Model-based Learning Versus Instance-based Learning

In example-based learning, the calculation retains the preparation information tests and sums up to groundbreaking perceptions by looking at the noticed information tests to the learned data samples using a similarity metric. Instead of creating a broad internal model, the algorithm saves specific training data instances. Predicting new data samples using a model created from a group of examples is how model-based learning achieves generalisation to new data samples (Ghassemi et al., 2020).

2.4 Detection Methods

Machine learning is becoming increasingly used in many industries nowadays, particularly computer vision. It can also be useful for log analysis. A unique sort of RNN (recurrent neural network) that is popular in the Regular Language Handling (NLP) field is the long transient memory (LSTM) organization. A procedure named Deeplog is proposed by Yuan et al. (2020) that involves LSTM as its preparation model to track down peculiarities in the log execution path. An unsupervised RNN with the goal of finding relationships hidden in system logs is presented by Zebari et al. (2020). They suggest a straightforward CNN model for categorising distributed word embeddings in the NLP space.

CNN has been extensively used in computer vision applications, including Google Net, Alex Net (Çınar, A., and Tuncer, S. A. 2021), and other specialised tasks. Deep Resnet (Lu et al., 2020) has more recently accomplished performance on picture classification challenges that is on par with human recognition. Text analysis also makes use of CNN. Additionally, it demonstrates that discrete embeddings can use the CNN model to obtain excellent accuracy. Different CNN models are now being employed for text classification. CNNs enable for the programmed learning of space explicit highlights, though standard ML approaches for taking care of picture acknowledgment issues vigorously depend on the element extraction procedure (Zebari et al., 2020). An ordinary some few layer of convolutional, a pooling layer, and a few additional convolutional layers, one pooling layer and so on make up the CNN architecture, shown in Fig. 39.1.

3. Empirical Methodology

3.1 CNN-based Model

Convolutional neural networks (CNN) have been offered as a solution to the overfitting problems in conventional neural networks by capturing local semantic information rather than global information. Convolution, which is the fundamental technique used in convolutional layers, pulls features from nearby receptive fields onto feature maps from the prior layer, as shown in Fig. 39.1. A nonlinear transformation is carried out using an activation function, such as the sigmoid, Rectified Linear Units (ReLU), and Tanh. According to Equation 1, the value of a unit at a place follows (m, n) in the feature map j^{th} of layer i^{th} can be indicated as $v_{ij}^{m,n}$ (Jang et al., 2019).

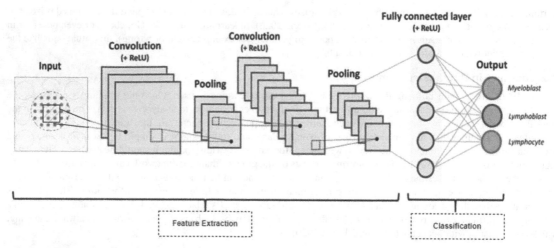

Fig. 39.1 A basic convolutional neural network (CNN) design is shown, consisting of an input, layer of convolution and pooling layers for include extraction, completely associated layers, and a result layer for order in the end. An activation layer, usually a ReLU layer, follows each convolutional layer in general [11]

$$v_{ij}^{m,n} = \sigma \left(b_{ij} + \sum_{N} \sum_{p=0}^{P_{i-1}} \sum_{q=0}^{Q_{i-1}} w_{ij(i-1)N}^{pq(x+p)(y+q)} \right) \tag{1}$$

where w_{ij}^{pq} is the parameter value, P_i is the kernel's height and Q_i is its width, and b_{ij} stands for the feature map's bias function. N Records over the assortment of element maps in the $(i\text{-}1)^{th}$ layer.

As previously indicated (Allagi, S., and Rachh, R. 2019), initial proposal for a straightforward and successful CNN model for sentence grouping utilizing non-static and static channels is based on word2vec (Jang et al., 2019) and vanilla CNN, and the researchers achieve outstanding outcomes in natural language processing. Because log files are a particular type of text, log examination can acquire from the headways made in NLP procedures. Be that as it may, log investigation is different from standard NLP. In natural language contexts, such a lengthy statement with complicated structures, the long span relationship is frequently present. However, logs only hold a minimal number of log keys. In addition, while NLP aims to categorise phrases into several groups, anomaly detection looks for unexpected execution paths (sequence of keys in the log), which is a categorization in binary.

We developed a trainable matrix, that is 30 × 129 codebook, in the embedding layer to convert each log key in a meeting into a vector. The log key 5 in the meeting bunch 5 5 12... 25 25 will, for example, be encoded as 0.6421, 0.7262, and 0.9567 during the implanting system, and the whole meeting will be encoded as a framework.

This implanting procedure is known as keylog2vec. Each log key will create log embeddings in light of the 30 × 129 codebook, in contrast to word embeddings that employ words as a fine-grained unit, such as word2vec. A trainable layer that uses gradient descent during neural network training is the logkey2vec. The codebook is utilised to provide a more thorough mapping of 1D vector to 2D matrix as CNN input, enhancing the relationships concealed behind logs (Allagi, S., and Rachh, R. 2019).

Convolutional layers are the next stage of CNN, which simultaneously applies three one-layer convolutions (filters) to the embedded log vectors. As indicated in Eq. 1, where P = 4, 5, 6, and Q = 129, we employed 3 layers of convolution in the training of CNN after the encrypting layer, each with a size of 4 × 129, 5 × 129, and 6 × 129, respectively. Leaky Rectified Linear Unit (leaky ReLU or LReLU), depicted in Equation 2, serves as the activation function because it prevents overfitting and resolves the dead ReLU problem by setting the initial component of the ReLU to non-zero (an unobtrusive positive inclination). On account of the dead ReLU issue, a portion of the organization's neurons might in all likelihood never fire, implying that the boundaries won't ever be changed. There are two factors that contribute to dead ReLU. The first is mistaken boundary introduction, and the second is a high learning rate setting that could bring about inordinate boundary refreshing. A maximum pooling layer is then applied to connect the results of the convolutional layers after three unmistakable convolutional methods. Defective ReLU, then again, will give a useful update after every cycle on the grounds that the slope in its spaces won't be all 0. By eliminating the feebly related elements and saving the most grounded related highlights for the accompanying layer, the maximum pooling layer can likewise effectively diminish overfitting. To abstain from over-fitting, a dropout capability is likewise utilized as a regularization in the second-to-last layer. In the output layer, a softmax function is inserted last. In Equation 3, the softmax function is displayed (Allagi, S., and Rachh, R. 2019).

$$(x) \begin{cases} x \text{ if } x \geq 0 \\ 0.1x \text{ if } x < 0 \end{cases} \tag{2}$$

where x stands for the input before to the activator.

$$S_i = \frac{e^{a_i}}{\sum_{k=1}^{T} e^{a_k}} \tag{3}$$

With $T = 2$ in our implementation, $I = 1$ to 2, and a_i specifies the ith number of input.

3.2 Model Based on MLP

According to our empirical investigation, parameter tweaking for LSTM is highly difficult due to the gradient vanish/ exploding concerns that are present in recurrent neural networks like LSTM. It is also problematic to prepare such a complex exemplary since of these issues. As a result, anomaly detection may become less accurate. We therefore chose to utilise a straightforward network with easily modifiable limits as the benchmark to contrast with CNN in order to demonstrate its effectiveness. So, as a starting point, we create a Multilayer Perceptron (MLP) and train it using logkey2vec of HDFS data. A type of fundamental feed-forward artificial neural network is the MLP. There are three parts to it: the output-layer, hidden-layers, and input-layer. Each buried layer has a nonlinear function that activates it. Updates to the weights of MLP are frequently made using BP. The complexity of models can be increased or decreased by using many hidden layers. The objective function may determine a distinct output layer. It utilizes the equivalent codebook and input installing stage as CNN's logkey2vec to scramble vectors. The boundaries of the MLP model for each layer are as follows: the secret layers are three completely associated (FC) layers with practically no convolutional layers, and there are 130, 66, and 34 MLP stowed away neurons for each FC layer, correspondingly. LReLU is likewise used as the MLP's enactment capability, following the CNN model. A normal pooling layer adds the result of the FC layer to a vector (Lu et al., 2018).

3.3 Experiments

TensorFlow is used to implement our CNN-based strategy [45]. Using HDFS log, a popular benchmark dataset utilised by other methodologies (Du et al., 2017; Lu et al., 2018), we evaluate the performance of proposed methodology with existing techniques for profound learning in log-based peculiarity identification. The HDFS log is a dataset produced by an experiment that was run on Amazon EC2 for more than 250 days. The data was initially released by (Lu et al., 2018), and anomaly detection methods like SVM, LSTM, logistic, and PCA were used to evaluate it. 1,58 GB worth of log entries total 11,189,994 in the raw log file. Additionally, HDFS log has 30 distinct log keys and records the statuses of each HDFS block at the moment a job is being executed. Additionally, the session windows are always used to parse the raw data, and each line contains a distinct blockId and associated log keys in the organization of the parsed. We use the same ground truth data as Du et al. (2017) that has been processed and tagged. The normal training (4,685 sessions of parsed), the usual testing set (564,386 sessions of parsed), the aberrant training (1,658 sessions of parsed), and the unusual testing set are all included (14,290 sessions of parsed).

4. Results and Discussion

4.2 Accuracy Check

On HDFS logs, we assess CNN using the proposed baseline models of MLP and LSTM. We used the normal training set from Du et al. (2017) and selected 1% of the strange testing informational index as the unusual preparation set because CNN and MLP are both supervised techniques and both require first training and then testing. Here, the normal testing set and the remaining 99% abnormal testing set merge to form the entire testing set. These models are assessed using the metrics below: The number of genuine anomalies that our method accurately identified as such is referred to as true positive (TP). The regular cases that have been appropriately identified as regular cases are represented by true negative

(TN). False positive (FP) scenarios show typical situations that are mistakenly labelled as abnormalities. The unusual cases of log that are mistakenly classified as normal are represented by false negatives (FN). We determine the F1-measure, Recall, accuracy, and Precision (P) for each examined technique based on the four criteria. Equation 4, which indicates the percentage of reported abnormalities that were accurately recognised, is used to compute precision. Equation 5, which displays the discovered true anomalies as well as the actual abnormalities, calculates recall. Equation 6, which reflects the average of harmonic P and recall, calculates the F1-measure.

Table 39.1 On HDFS log comparison with different models [12]

Model	Precision	% of Accuracy	Recall	F1 score
CNN	98.2	99.8	99.3	98.5
MLP	97.8	98	97.9	97
LSTM	95	87	95	96

$$P = \frac{TP}{TP + FP} \qquad (4)$$

$$\text{Recall} = \frac{TP}{TP + FN} \qquad (5)$$

$$F1 \text{ score} = \frac{2P.\text{Recall}}{(P + \text{Recall})} \qquad (6)$$

We include all the assessment measurement discoveries in Table 1 to assess the precision of our CNN model with LSTM and our MLP gauge model. Our CNN outperforms the other two models across the board.

Even though MLP and CNN both eventually reach high precision and accuracy, MLP begins with lesser exactness and gradually increases to high accuracy over the course of 86 epochs. Compared to MLP, the CNN model's curve is substantially more stable. Additionally, MLP converges in 100 epochs, but CNN could combine with high accuracy after a couple of eons. CNN's review is generally 0.9 toward the beginning, which is considerably more noteworthy than MLP's review, though MLP's review begins at 0 and combines to 97.9 in 21 eons. CNN might achieve a high level of accuracy in a short period of time, whereas MLP does not converge until 92 epochs. The MLP model on the training of HDFS logs converges slowly and takes longer than the CNN model, according to all evaluation criteria. We create an additional try-out by removing the implanting layer from the model of MLP in order to assess whether the embedding layer may have an impact on accuracy. We got results with exactness of 0.998, accuracy of 0.9822, review of 0.96054, and F1-proportion of 0.971736 after the MLP model trains with a progression of log key vectors straightforwardly without inserting steps. It illustrates that the embedding process could make a significant change in the effectiveness of MLP for HDFS log classification when compared to the findings provided in Table 1. The implanting layer utilizes a codebook to change over vectors into frameworks, and this strategy could learn the inside and out of the log's semantic portrayal.

4.3 CNN and MLP

The CNN and MLP models exhibit varied levels of accuracy on HDFS log data for two distinct reasons. First, a CNN network uses a 2-dimensional convolution operation to learn weights that account for both the connection between longitudinal sections in logs and the relationship between flat implanting codes. All the more explicitly, the MLP approach is speedy and simple to utilize, yet the preparation cycle doesn't consolidate setting data. Second, by using a few channels, our CNN can data mine more relationships in log settings. Each line of parsed information after input implanting has a place with a particular identifier bunch and is comprised of identifiers related to log occasions in an arranged request. The parsed information explicitly shows a separated execution course with better co-relationship, every identifier having a dense and succinct design, and each log being set in a huge setting, (Lu et al., 2018).

4.4 CNN and LSTM

A model for text classification known as LSTMs is efficient and outperforms other methods. In general, LSTM can continually roll up each cell for the calculation of the following cell while storing context information in each cell. The outputs of the prior cell and the present cell are used to calculate the input. LSTM can therefore generate long-range data in a log implementation route. The performance of the LSTM in log-based anomaly detection, however, may be impacted by a number of factors. First off, unlike NLP, where text files have a similar structure to system logs, log analysis has quite distinct requirements. Second, word separation based on word2vec is necessary for NLP, and log separation is used in log analysis. Thirdly, as was already established, log entries are related to one another in a short sequence. A log entry may not be associated with a log entry far away since each extracted execution route from a log is made up of numerous log entries (log keys) (Lu et al., 2018).

5. Conclusion and Future Scope

In order to identify anomalies from system logs, this research introduces a novel neural network-based methodology. Different filters are used to build a CNN-based method for convoluting with embedded log vectors. A group of log entries' total length is equal to the width of the filter. The maximum value is picked up via max-overtime pooling. Additionally, numerous convolutional layers are used in the computation. After that, a completely linked layer-softmax is added to generate the results for the distribution of probability. As well as put into practise the model based on MLP with 3 hidden layers and no convolutional kernels. Our test results show that, when applied to big data system logs, the CNN-based technique outperforms MLP and LSTM in terms of detection accuracy as well as speed. Furthermore, the CNN model is a universal approach that requires no framework or specific application information and can parse logs directly. More sophisticated system logs will be taken into consideration for testing sets and training in the upcoming development. Additionally, we intend to create an automatic log analyser that may make use of deep learning techniques to find abnormalities and divide root causes into various categories.

REFERENCES

1. Lu, S., Wei, X., Li, Y., & Wang, L. (2018, August). Detecting anomaly in big data system logs using convolutional neural network. In *2018 IEEE 16th Intl Conf on Dependable, Autonomic and Secure Computing, 16th Intl Conf on Pervasive Intelligence and Computing, 4th Intl Conf on Big Data Intelligence and Computing and Cyber Science and Technology Congress (DASC/PiCom/DataCom/CyberSciTech)* (pp. 151–158). IEEE.
2. Du, M., Li, F., Zheng, G., & Srikumar, V. (2017, October). Deeplog: Anomaly detection and diagnosis from system logs through deep learning. In *Proceedings of the 2017 ACM SIGSAC conference on computer and communications security* (pp. 1285–1298).
3. Allagi, S., & Rachh, R. (2019, March). Analysis of Network log data using Machine Learning. In *2019 IEEE 5th International Conference for Convergence in Technology (I2CT)* (pp. 1–3). IEEE.
4. Jang, B., Kim, I., & Kim, J. W. (2019). Word2vec convolutional neural networks for classification of news articles and tweets. *PloS one, 14*(8), e0220976.
5. Çınar, A., & Tuncer, S. A. (2021). Classification of lymphocytes, monocytes, eosinophils, and neutrophils on white blood cells using hybrid Alexnet-GoogleNet-SVM. *SN Applied Sciences, 3*(4), 1–11.
6. Zebari, R., Abdulazeez, A., Zeebaree, D., Zebari, D., & Saeed, J. (2020). A comprehensive review of dimensionality reduction techniques for feature selection and feature extraction. *Journal of Applied Science and Technology Trends, 1*(2), 56–70.
7. Lu, Y., Ma, C., Lu, Y., Lu, J., & Ying, L. (2020, November). A mean field analysis of deep resnet and beyond: Towards provably optimization via overparameterization from depth. In *International Conference on Machine Learning* (pp. 6426–6436). PMLR.
8. Yuan, Y., Adhatarao, S. S., Lin, M., Yuan, Y., Liu, Z., & Fu, X. (2020, July). Ada: Adaptive deep log anomaly detector. In *IEEE INFOCOM 2020-IEEE Conference on Computer Communications* (pp. 2449–2458). IEEE.
9. Coccia, M. (2020). Deep learning technology for improving cancer care in society: New directions in cancer imaging driven by artificial intelligence. *Technology in Society, 60*, 101198.
10. Ghassemi, M., Naumann, T., Schulam, P., Beam, A. L., Chen, I. Y., & Ranganath, R. (2020). A review of challenges and opportunities in machine learning for health. *AMIA Summits on Translational Science Proceedings, 2020*, 191.
11. Samat, N. A., Salleh, M. N. M., & Ali, H. (2020). The comparison of pooling functions in convolutional neural network for sentiment analysis task. In Recent Advances on Soft Computing and Data Mining: Proceedings of the Fourth International Conference on Soft Computing and Data Mining (SCDM 2020), Melaka, Malaysia, January 22–23, 2020 (pp. 202–210). Springer International Publishing.
12. Jang B, Kim I, Kim JW (2019) Word2vec convolutional neural networks for classification of news articles and tweets. PLoS ONE 14(8): e0220976.

Computer Science Engineering and Emerging Technologies (ICCS-2022) – Prof (Dr.) Rajeev Sobti et al. (eds)
© *2024 Taylor & Francis Group, London, ISBN 978-1-032-52199-2*

Chapter **40**

Applications of Optical Networking in Enhancing 5G Communications in Smart Cities

S. K. UmaMaheswaran[1]
Professor, Department of Mathematics,
Sri Sai Ram Engineering College, Chennai, T.N. India

Sunil S. Chavan[2]
Principal, Smt. Indira Gandhi College of engineering,
Navi Mumbai, University of Mumbai

Prabhakara Rao Kapula[3]
Professor, Department of ECE, B V Raju Institute of Technology,
Narsapur, Telangana

A. Suneetha[4]
Assistant Professor, Department of MCA,
Sree Vidyanikethan Institute of Management Tirupati

Prakash Pareek[5]
Associate Professor, Department of ECE,
Vishnu Institute of Technology, Bhimavaram, A.P. India

Rachit Garg[6]
School of Computer Science and Engineering,
Lovely Professional University

Abstract: 5G is a game-changing improvement to the mobile communication infrastructure that will have far-reaching positive effects on humanity. The most promising answer to meeting the growing capacity and mobility needs of the next generation of 5G networks while keeping costs down is found in systems that combine optical and wireless components. To make the 5G communications network a reality, a variety of optical technologies have been implemented. This article has gone over the significance of the 5G network and the difficulties that come with the 5G communication system. In addition, this study discusses a variety of optical access techniques that have been invented to overcome obstacles in 5G communication. The proliferation of wireless communications advances implies that the worldwide market must take into account the impact that 5G will have on the planet, society, or economy before implementing it on a large scale. The importance of this lies in the fact that it allows potential threats to be identified and mitigated. The technology behind 5G communications infrastructure will undoubtedly alter the way mobile devices are employed and the capabilities they provide. The evolution of technology will also affect how it interacts with its surroundings. A huge number of devices will be able to be produced and used as a result of the paradigm shift from radio waves to mm waves, and the new function of tiny cells.

Keywords: Optical networking, 5G communications, Infrastructure, Smart cities

---

[1]umamaheswaran.maths@sairam.edu.in, [2]chavan_s_s@hotmail.com, [3]prabhakar.kapula@bvrit.ac.in, [4]suneetha.jkccs@gmail.com, [5]prakash.p@vishnu.edu.in, [6]gargrachit@gmail.com

DOI: 10.1201/9781003405580-40

1. Introduction

In the future, data traffic will rise at a pace of over 50% annually per subscriber due to the ever-increasing number of customers and the corresponding need for a high data rate. This need for a high rate of information will only increase as more and more cutting-edge technologies like the Internet of Things (IoT) and virtual reality, enter the market. The increased data rates and advanced connectivity that the 5G network promises are precisely why it was developed. To meet the need for high speed as well as capacity, 5G networks will include a variety of optical technologies and ideas such as radio over fiber (RoF) systems, passive optical networks (PON), optical millimeter-wave bridges (OMWB), light-field communications (LiFi), etc. Today's 4G networks are limited in their ability to improve data rates and transfer speeds due mostly to constraints in transmission capacity. 5G networks have been able to circumvent this issue by using several different methods. The use of optical methods is a key idea since it allows for wide bandwidth and speeds in the gigabit range. Many obstacles must be overcome to bring about 5G communication networks. These include an ever-increasing number of connections, a massive data volume, an increase in capacity without an increase in cost, a rapid and flexible provision of architecture, reduced latency (1 MMS) fast data transmission, densification of networks, a reduction in cell size, and so on.

Due to the massive bandwidth available in the optical spectrum and cost-effectiveness, optical network technologies have recently emerged as a possible potential solution to alleviate many challenges experienced in 5G communication networks. Optical networking is being used to facilitate the development of photonic-based systems for 5G. LiFi or optical cameras communication (OCC) was developed as a 2 alternative for Wi-Fi, free space optical communication approaches for long haul communication, and several methods have been suggested to bridge optical frequencies to millimeter waves, which play a key role in 5G networking. Because of their wide bandwidth availability, cheap cost, and simplicity of development, free space optical (FSO) communications systems, which utilize the visible and ultraviolet bands of the electromagnetic spectrum for data transmission, are also playing major roles in various parts of 5G networks. FSO is beneficial in 5G indoor communication networks because of its range-dependent signal attenuation, absorption, and loss, unlike fiber-based solutions. FSO technologies such as Light Fidelity (LiFi) and optical camera communication technology are useful for short-range communication on the 5G network at a high data rate and low cost [8]. The biggest obstacle for the 5G network is making sure we can get the data we need, when we require it, in the format that needs it. The use of optical or communication connectivity is crucial to doing this. However, in areas where it is installed, optical fiber delivers enormous bandwidth, which is crucial for meeting the speed and capacity demands of a 5G network. Incorporating wireless and optical networks into a single infrastructure is termed a radio over fiber (RoF) network, and it's an intriguing method for maximizing the benefits of both types of infrastructure. It seems that RoF increases cell coverage, and it also necessitates the modulation of light using radio information for optical communication. There is no need for digital-to-analogy conversion (DAC), making it a low-latency option, as well as the bandwidth it provides is far higher than that of competing systems.

The rest of the paper is structured as follows. Section 2 reviews the extant literature. Section 3 describes the sample and variables. Section 4 explains the research methodology. Section 5 discusses the empirical findings. Section 6 summarizes the paper.

Among the most important technologies allowing for the development of 5G networks is optical millimeter-wave technology. One of the most promising ideas is to make use of the millimeter wave frequency spectrum (30 GHz to 300 GHz), which provides a wide range of frequencies and speeds in the gigabit range (Gbps). Millimeter-wave communication systems face a significant hurdle in the creation of high-quality carrier signals at millimeter-wave frequencies. Common electrical oscillators may be used to produce signals in the megahertz region, and the idea of frequency multiplication can then be utilized to produce a signal with twice the original frequency. Nevertheless, the phase noise grows by 6 dB for every doubling of frequency, making it not only challenging but also expensive to manufacture low-phase-noise millimeter waves using electronic components. Optical millimetre wave networking is being used for 5G with the development of a photonic-based MMW generation technology. To connect optical waves into millimeter waves, which are crucial in mm-wave networking, many strategies have been suggested.

2. Literature Review

2.1 5G Networking

The following are some of the most vital services that 5G will presumably provide to humans. Extreme broadband internet communication: This infrastructure will allow for improvements in human-to-human or human-to-machine communication via the use of ultra-high-definition video, video calling, plus fixed wireless services that include augmented or virtual reality. In addition, M2M interactions, such as video surveillance and cloud computing on the go, are becoming the norm. Massive scale communication: 5G provides massive scale communication through wearable gadgets, social networking, connected residences with health monitoring, car to infrastructure, etc. industrial automation. To enhance the safety of the public, remote medical monitoring, and vehicle-to-pedestrian and automotive communication, 5G is aiming to provide ultra-reliable minimal services.

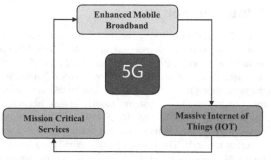

Fig. 40.1 5G Networking (Chang et al., 2020)

The installation of 5G data transmission faces a number of challenges, chief among them those related to the Internet of Things and the ever-increasing number of connections. Despite the fact that IoT is expected to cause a significant rise in the total number of devices connected to the network, it is still seen as a major and promising component in 5G data transfer. The proliferation of devices portends a greater need for overall data storage and a more robust infrastructure to manage a vastly expanding set of devices. Current 3Gpp-based networks control plane will not be able to handle the increased number of connections burden, thus network infrastructure control for a growing number of links there in 5G communications network must be designed.

Massive data transfer: 5G is expected to make high-definition ultra-high-definition (UHD) video possible, along with virtual reality and wearable devices. This indicates that the number of documents that need to be managed will expand by 25–50 percent annually. Data use is predicted to increase tenfold, from 2.5 exabytes per month now to 25 exabytes per month by 2020, if 5G communication technology is implemented. A major challenge for a 5G communication network, then, would be its limited storage space for data.

In today's world, customers not only want to use more data, but they also really want to spend more money on their bills than they have in the past. One of the key challenges in increasing data capacity without increasing the cost of operation is the development of a 5G communications network, which means that users will have to pay more for their increased data capacity than originally anticipated. Both the big cell and the tiny cell concepts are being considered to be utilized in the 5G system as potential solutions to this issue.

The construction of a rapid and malleable architecture for a 5G transmission medium is challenging. The concept of a cloud-based radio access network (c-RAN) is gaining traction, and it will likely be included in a 5G communication system. Scalability, cost-effectiveness, adaptability, and reconfigurability may all be improved by the centralized processing unit.

2.2 High-potential Frequency Ranges for Fifth-generation Wireless Networks

In the millimeter wave band, the wavelengths are between 1 mm and 10 mm, while the frequencies are between 300 GHz and 30 GHz. Components for this band may be smaller and more compact compared to a microwave system, which has piqued the curiosity of modern researchers. Additionally, the vast unlicensed bandwidth availability is helpful for its application in 5G for large data speeds. Despite its usefulness, the mm-wave band is plagued by severe drawbacks during propagation in free space, including a high attenuation loss and an inability to penetrate any obstructions in its path.

The optical spectrum covers wavelengths from 390 nm to 750 nm. That band is a prospective wave band of 5G communication because of the large amount of available bandwidth, which will allow for higher data rates and storage capacities. The importance of the newly designed photonic mm-wave transceiver, which acts as a bridge between photonic & mm-wave techniques, cannot be overstated in the context of a 5G system.

2.3 Software-Defined Flexibility in Flexible Grid Optics Networks for 5G

The dynamic or variable/flexible bandwidth needs of the 5G network may be met by the flex grid optical communication system, which has now been developed as a potential network solution for the 5G communications network. For optimal resource utilization and throughput enhancement in a 5G network, flexible bandwidth distribution is required to accommodate the time-varying and application-specific nature of data traffic. Optical networking holds enormous potential for meeting this expected need. In 5G, a flexible grid optically network allows for elastic optical spectral efficiency for multiple-rate traffic, as well as transparent overall low-latency interconnection provisioning. Sliceable bandwidth variable transmitters, bandwidth wavelength-dependent cross-connections, optical splits, or broadband variable wavelengths choose switches are some of the most important optical technologies that make flexible grid networks possible.

3. Data and Variables

3.1 Study Period and Sample

Complex communication infrastructure needs the integration of a wide range of new technologies to support a wide range of potential future uses. Some believe that 5G wireless as well as optical technology integration is necessary to achieve this aim. The impending concept of a smart metropolis becomes viable thanks to 5G communications technology and cell densification, garnering a lot of interest from the scientific community owing to its potential to enhance and modernize people's daily lives. The transfer of massive amounts of data is essential to the notion of a "smart city," which is intended to assist everything from power grids to traffic control. Without the combination of optical as well as wireless technologies, it is not possible to create smart cities with a communication infrastructure that really can meet demanding network needs. This paper's goal is to provide readers with an introduction to the state of the art in optical networking, specifically as it relates to the provision of 5G transportation systems and their potential uses in the interconnection of a vast array of devices in the next smart city architectures. Questions about how wireless or optical could coexist to deliver sophisticated potential opportunities, like the smart city idea, are raised by the incorporation of optical technology in 5G core networking. The most pressing concerns in this area will be addressed in this study.

3.2 Multi-dimensional 5G/6G Telecommunications for Facilitating Environmentally Responsible Smart Cities

To achieve sustainable growth in many different domains, 5G/6G communication networks are essential facilitators of the Internet of Things. Existing mobile networks do not have the resources to meet the connectivity and coverage requirements of a sustainable community in the areas of energy, the ocean, freshwater, and climate. Therefore, a multifunctional communication network that can integrate terrestrial or non-terrestrial communications infrastructure is necessary to allow sustainable IoT applications. The five levels of a communication network that might facilitate this consolidation: space, aviation, ground, subterranean, and undersea. Following is an examination of the five tiers of communications infrastructure: ground, orbital, aerial, subterranean, and subterranean.

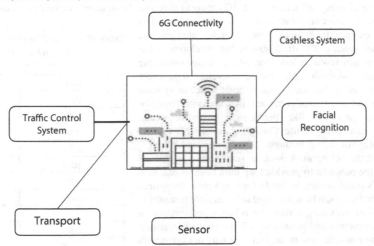

Fig. 40.2 5G/6G Telecommunications For Facilitating Environmentally Responsible Smart Cities (Dong et al., 2017)

3.3 Independent Variable

With the use of SDN and NFV, 5G networking will be used to link machine parks, and promote industrial, and industrial locations, opening up new opportunities for automation, flexibility, and innovative applications. The term "smart manufacturing" refers to the usage of internet-connected machines for production supervision. Smart manufacturing seeks to improve output by making better use of data analytics and robotics to streamline processes (SDG 9 – innovation and infrastructure, SDG11 – sustainable cities) Industry 4.0 and the Internet of Things (IoT) have many uses, but one of them is smart manufacturing (IIoT). Sensors are installed in machinery as part of the implementation process to collect data and information on the machines' performance and operational state. Data used to be stored in databases that are only accessible from inside a single device, and this information was only used to investigate post-mortem equipment failures. Currently, engineers may verify the warning flags for certain components of a machine by evaluating the data transmitted from all of the machines in a facility. Because of this, preventative maintenance may be used to keep machines from breaking down unexpectedly. Additionally, engineers may utilize the data trends to identify bottlenecks in production or resource use. Data engineers and researchers may also use the data to simulate different activities to determine the most efficient and adaptable course of action.

4. Methodology and Model Specifications

The sustainability of 5G network systems and intelligent cities may be evaluated using several different metrics. These indicators are organized according to the three main tenets of sustainability (environmental, social, & economic). Energy efficiency, electricity consumption, emissions of carbon dioxide (CO_2), and pollution are only a few of the sub-indicators that make up the environmental indicator. Human development, safety, and security are examples of social indicators, whereas cost and spectrum efficiency are examples of economic indicators. Table 2 displays the most important sources together with the sustainability performance and sub-indicators covered in each source. The terms "5G and Sustainability," "5G or Green Communication," and "Smart Cities and Sustainability" were searched in the title, abstract, and keywords of publications published between 2010 and 2021 and accessible in December 2021 as part of the systematic review. The organized macroscopic review was performed using Scopus with the chosen keyword combination. Based on our findings, we can see that 42% of respondents are interested in environmental indicators as a means to build eco-friendly, long-lasting 5G networks. Nonetheless, many research efforts are concentrated on economic (37%) and social (21%). The review was condensed to indicate the percentage of sub-indicators that were looked for in each publication, revealing the proportion of papers that concentrate on several sustainability performances. Studies evaluating the impact of 5G networks as well as smart cities on the environment overwhelmingly focused on energy efficiency (20%), accompanied by energy consumption (17%), expense (15%), spectrum efficiency (11%), public health (9%) and carbon footprint (9%) and finally security (7%), pollution (6%), as well as safety (6%). As a result, 5G networks play a vital role in promoting environmental responsibility in smart cities. Many sustainability indicators have been addressed in studies, but a true essence in defining how firm-level changes and technological advancements could affect sustainable development has been lacking. Not enough research has gone into creating sustainable development indicator systems that include several stakeholder perspectives. Too little effort has been made to build indicator systems for evaluating how broad adoption of communications infrastructure like 5G/6G affects core problems like public safety, environmental sustainability, health, and quality of life. Concerns have also been raised regarding the viability of using business practice indicators in the specified domains of the 5G network, such as smart cities, to oversee initiatives that have the potential to provide long-term benefits and help achieve the network's smart sustainable goals. One such indicator system is business-practice indicators, which may lead to financially sustainable investment decisions by providing context for network performance in communication infrastructure and smart cities. Some of the preexisting approaches taken into consideration in the literature may not agree with the authors' perspectives on the indicators for sustainable building in 5G networks. Indicators addressing stakeholder problems and company

Table 40.1 Investment prediction for 5G technology installation in smart cities (Rafel & Maes, 2022)

Years	$ millions
2019	1800
2020	1900
2021	1920
2022	1960
2023	2000
2024	2010
2025	2020
2026	2050
2027	2060
2028	2065
2029	2070

strategy directives within smart-based technologies have been employed in previous research aimed at addressing sustainable development concerns. Publications are more inclined to emphasize "off-the-shelf" indicators. Several indicators are combined using "bottom-up"–"community scoped"–techniques to evaluate "top-down"–"expert produced"–approaches in order to harmonize and manage difficulties in sustainable development.

5. Empirical Results

5.1 It's Optical Networks That will Power the Next Generation of the Internet

Optical networking is fundamental to the Future Internet since it will serve as its primary backbone's physical infrastructure. Recent advancements have allowed for a far bigger capacity to be supported, resulting in a significantly improved quality of service/experience for end-users. In addition, advances in optical networking make it easier to simplify IP-layer activities, which in turn decreases connection latency and operational costs. Insights gained from new study areas in optical networking can help the Future Internet develop even further.

Internet communication is supported by optical networks. The bandwidth of optical networks must increase as Internet traffic grows rapidly due to the increasing number of services and applications. The backbone of the Internet is expanding to accommodate the increasing data needs of the modern world. Fiber-optic technology is used to achieve the current top speeds (100Gbps, 200Gbps, 400Gbps, etc.). Commonly used for Internet backbones are fiber optic trunk lines. With the trunk line's many fiber optic cables working in tandem, data transfer rates and capacity are greatly increased. Optical carrier, or OC, designations are used to categorize different types of fiber optic cables. The maximum data rates for different OC lines are as follows: OC-48, 2.5 Gbps; OC-192, 9.953 Gbps; OC-768, 39.813 Gbps.

Table 40.2 Comparision of 5G networking with 3G and 4G networking speed (Song et al., 2018)

Network type	Average downloadspeeds	Peak downloadspeeds	Theoretical maximum download speeds
3G	9.4Mbps	~20Mbps	58Mbps
4G	45.4Mbps	95+Mbps	400Mbps
5G	95Mbps-330Mbps	796Mbps+	10-60Gbps

6. Conclusion

The study states that Developers of 5G networks must thus do a sustainability assessment, which takes into account the social, ecological, and economic effects of the network. Energy harvesting, alternative energy resources, green 5G technologies, enormous IoT sensors, smart meters, and life cycle assessment are only a few of the approaches used to accomplish the sustainability indicators discussed in this article (LCA). The use of Internet of Things sensors is a key strategy for ensuring the long-term viability of 5G networks. The topic of environmental, economic, and social sustainability in 5G networks was examined. They emphasized the various uses of Internet of Things sensors, including water conservation in cities (SDG 6: clean sanitation and sanitation), urban planning, traffic management, and air quality monitoring (SDG 13 – climate action). Increased uses for the Internet of Things sensors include ag apps that provide farmers access to data that may guide their choices (SDG 15 – life on land). Energy efficiency is a key indicator for gauging sustainability in 5G network systems, and its improvement was the focus of the research presented. Deploying smart meters to track energy use may help optimize consumption, save costs (SDG 8: economic development), and boost efficiency. In addition, the researchers analyzed and predicted the path loss for all these networks to guarantee efficient and steady communications of the Smart sensors networks as well as to overcome the difficulties of running the IoT networks in highly complex environments. Therefore, IoT networks are better able to adapt to their surroundings.

REFERENCES

1. Optical networks for 5G and beyond. (n.d.). Retrieved October 20, 2022, from http://www.eitc.org/research-opportunities/future-internet-and-optical-quantum-communications/optical-and-quantum-communications-and-the-quantum-technology/optical-networks-for-5g-and-beyond

2. An optical wireless communication based 5G architecture to enable Smart City Applications. (n.d.). Retrieved October 20, 2022, from https://ieeexplore.ieee.org/document/8473657/

3. Dong, P., Zheng, T., Yu, S., Zhang, H., & Yan, X. (2017). Enhancing vehicular communication using 5G-enabled Smart Collaborative Networking. IEEE Wireless Communications, 24(6), 72–79. doi:10.1109/mwc.2017.1600375

4. Simeonidou, D. E. (2017). Co-ordinated fiber and 5G Technologies Transforming Smart Cities. Optical Fiber Communication Conference. doi:10.1364/ofc.2017.w4c.1

5. Authors index. (2019). 2019 International Conference on Smart Applications, Communications and Networking (SmartNets). doi:10.1109/smartnets48225.2019.9069782

6. Chatterjee, S., Kar, A., & Gupta, M. (2019). Critical success factors to establish 5G network in Smart Cities. Smart Cities and Smart Spaces, 386–410. doi: 10.4018/978-1-5225-7030-1.ch017

7. Tzanakaki, A., Anastasopoulos, M. P., & Simeonidou, D. (2017). Optical networking: An important enabler for 5G. 2017 European Conference on Optical Communication (ECOC). doi: 10.1109/ecoc.2017.8345855

8. Liu, X., & Effenberger, F. (2017). Evolution of mobile fronthaul towards 5G Wireless and its impact on time-sensitive optical networking. Optical Fiber Communication Conference. doi: 10.1364/ofc.2017.w4c.4

9. Song, S., Liu, Y., Guo, L., & Song, Q. (2018). Optimized relaying and scheduling in Cooperative Free Space Optical Fronthaul/backhaul of 5G. Optical Switching and Networking, 30, 62–70. doi:10.1016/j.osn.2018.06.004 Iovanna, P. (2019). Optical networking for 5G XHAUL and service convergence: Transmission, switching and Control Enabling Technologies. 45th European Conference on Optical Communication (ECOC 2019). doi: 10.1049/cp.2019.0748

10. Rafel, A., & Maes, J. (2022). Comparing optical transport technologies for x-hauling 5G small cells in the sub-6 GHz. Journal of Optical Communications and Networking, 14(4), 204. doi: 10.1364/jocn.447057

11. Tomkos, I., Effenberger, F., & Rhee, J. K. (2016). Introduction to the special issue on optical networking for 5G Mobile and Wireless Communications. Journal of Optical Communications and Networking, 8(12). doi: 10.1364/jocn.8.00fgm1

12. Carrozzo, G. (2020). 5G enabling technologies and Autonomic Networking. Wiley 5G Ref, 1–23. doi: 10.1002/9781119471509.w5gref133

13. Chang, G., Xu, M., & Lu, F. (2020). Optical networking for 5G and fiber-wireless convergence. Springer Handbook of Optical Networks, 1031–1056. doi: 10.1007/978-3-030-16250-4_33

14. Katsaros, K., & Dianati, M. (2016). A Conceptual 5G vehicular networking architecture. 5G Mobile Communications, 595–623. doi: 10.1007/978-3-319-34208-5_22

15. Tzanakaki, A., Anastasopoulos, M. P., & Simeonidou, D. (2018). Converged Optical, wireless, and Data Center network infrastructures for 5G services. Journal of Optical Communications and Networking, 11(2). doi: 10.1364/jocn.11.00a111

Computer Science Engineering and Emerging Technologies (ICCS-2022) – Prof (Dr.) Rajeev Sobti et al. (eds)
© 2024 Taylor & Francis Group, London, ISBN 978-1-032-52199-2

Chapter **41**

Role of Image Segmentation and Feature Extraction Methods in Cotton Plant Disease Detection

Sandhya N. Dhage[1]

Research Scholar, Computer Science & Engineering,
Lovely Professional University Phagwara, Punjab, India

Vijay Kumar Garg[2]

Associate Professor, Computer Science & Engineering,
Lovely Professional University Phagwara, Punjab, India

Abstract: Plant diseases can be detected and classified using traditional machine learning algorithms which require pre-processing the cotton plant diseased images, segmenting the image, and extracting the colour and texture features from diseased affected regions. In this study, we tried to analyze different image segmentation and feature extraction methods on the dataset of fungal diseases of cotton plants. Segmentation is performed on cotton diseased images by applying K-means clustering, Fuzzy C means clustering, Ostu thresholding, and the influence of these methods is evaluated based on the performance of ML classifier. Colour features from the diseased affected region are extracted using colour histogram and colour moment techniques. Texture features are extracted using Grey level co-occurance matrix and local binary pattern which are used for the classification of fungal disease images using SVM, KNN, and CNN classifiers. Comparative analysis of colour and texture feature extraction methods is performed based on the classification accuracy of three different classifiers. Detection and classification are carried out using SVM and KNN. Classification accuracies of 88% and 70% were obtained using SVM and KNN classifiers.

Keywords: Color feature, Texture feature, Segmentation

1. Introduction

Damage caused by different fungal diseases in cotton plants based on natural conditions causes economic loss to the agriculture sector. Continuous monitoring by farmers with the naked eye for disease detection is a time-consuming task. Also, manual disease detection and classification is a challenging task that requires expertise skills. So the main goal of this research is the automatic identification and classification of cotton plant fungal disease using techniques of image processing and machine learning algorithms which help the farmers to decrease the production loss of cotton plants.

Cotton-diseased leaf images can be detected and classified using image processing methods followed by classification methods. In the given approach, the image is acquired through a digital camera which is preprocessed using image enhancement and histogram equalization techniques. Preprocessed image is segmented using k-means clustering algorithm for segmenting affected areas. On the segmented image, feature extraction is carried out by applying colour and texture feature extraction methods. Statistical features are calculated using colour histogram, colour moment, grey level co-

[1]dsand8@gmail.com, [2]vijay.garg@lpu.co.in

DOI: 10.1201/9781003405580-41

occurance matrix, and local binary pattern. Classification is performed on the extracted colour and texture features by implementing SVM, KNN, CNN, and classification accuracy is measured. The processing stages are as follows:

1. Image acquisition
2. Preprocessing the image using contrast enhancement
3. Histogram equalization
4. K-means clustering for segmenting image
5. Computing features using feature extraction methods
6. Classification using SVM, KNN, CNN
7. Statistical feature analysis

2. Feature Extraction

Image data is converted into a set of features using feature extraction for the purpose of dimensionality reduction that can differentiate one image from others. Detection and Classification of cotton crop diseases are performed on the most important and relevant features using different machine learning algorithms. The feature specifies the countable property of the image and is classified as low-level features and high-level features. Different types of feature extraction methods are categorized as Color feature extraction, texture feature extraction, and shape feature extraction. For Plant diseased image detection, colour and texture features are mostly considered.

2.1 Colour Feature Extraction

Colour is the most prominent feature of the image and has the combination of different variances defined in specific colour spaces or models. Suitable colour space followed by a feature descriptor is required to extract the colour features from the leaf image. A variety of colour spaces have been considered in different research such as RGB, CMYK, CMY, HSI, YCbCr, and HSV. After the identification of colour space, colour features are extracted from the images or regions. Colour moments and histograms, and colour coherence vectors are colour feature extraction methods. The most widely used system is RGB colour space used for representing colour images which is followed by the most widely used colour histogram descriptor. Colour moments are the simplest feature descriptor among all feature extraction methods.

Color Histogram

Colour histogram is simple to implement and a fast method to extract features from RGB colour spaces. A colour histogram is used to count the frequency of pixels within a given image that are the same colour. In RGB colour space, each pixel in any digital image is represented by three relevant values such as red value, blue value, and green value which determine its colour. A histogram specifies how many pixels of each colour are of the same intensity in the image.

The definition of the colour histogram H for an image is as follows: H={H[1], H[2]....H[i], H[n]}

Where the colour, number of bins, and number of pixels in the colour histogram are represented by I, n, and h[i]

The colour histogram H' is normalized as:

$$h'[i] = \frac{h[i]}{XY} \tag{1}$$

Histogram is described by center moment to reduce the feature vector dimension. Six statistical features of colour images are extracted by calculating the Mean and standard deviation of all three colour channels in RGB colour space.

Moment 1: Mean(μ_i): It specifies the average colour value of the image and is defined by:

$$\sum_{j=1}^{N} Pij \tag{2}$$

Moment 2: Standard Deviation(σ_i): It specifies the square root of the variance of the distribution and is defined by:

$$\frac{1}{N}\sum_{j=1}^{N}(Pij - Ei)2 \tag{3}$$

Colour Moment

Calculation of Color moments for diseased leaf image is executed as following steps:

- The RGB images are preprocessed.
- The RGB component is converted into HSV Component.
- Histogram equalization is performed for three components
- Calculate the colour moment for the three components' histogram
- Steps 1 & 4 are executed for all images.

From equalized histograms of RGB images, M1-Mean, M2-Varience & M3-Skewness moments are computed. Hence a total of 9 moment features are obtained for a single leaf. Colour moment steps are applied for all the images.

2.2 Texture Feature Extraction

For the characterization of an image, texture can be used as a very interesting image feature. Texture patterns over a region are characterized by the repetition of a pattern in a region. The elements of patterns in an image are called textons. Properties of textons such as size, shape, colour, and orientation of the textons can change over the region. The degree of variation in textons gives the difference between two textures of the texton. GLCM and LBP are texture feature extraction methods.

Gray Level Co-occurrence Matrix

The spatial relationship of pixels is indicated in GLCM. The co-occurrence of grey values i and j of pixels is counted by co-occurrence matrixC(i,j) when distance d is given.

The co-occurrence matrix is defined as:

$$C(i, j) = \text{cord} \begin{cases} ((x1, y1), (x2, y2)) \in (XY) \times ((DY) \\ \quad \text{for } f(x1, y1) = i, f(x2, y2) = j \\ (x2, y2) = (x1, y1) + (d\cos\theta, d\sin\theta); \\ \quad \text{for } 0 < i, j < N \end{cases} \tag{4}$$

where, d is a distance well-defined in polar coordinates(d,θ) with discrete length and orientation. 0°,45°, 90°,135°, 180°, 225°,270° and 315° are values of θ

cord {.} is elements belonging to the set.

Various statistical features including energy, inertia, correlation, and entropy are extracted from the co-occurrence matrix to reduce the dimensionality of the feature set. The definition of the texture features are as follows

$$\text{Inertia} = \sum_i \sum_j (i - j)^2 \, c(i, j) \tag{5}$$

Inertia is also known as variance and Contrast. The local variations in the grey-level co-occurrence matrix are measured by inertia.

$$\text{Correlation} = \frac{\sum_i \sum_j (i - \mu_i)(j - \mu_j)c(i, j)}{\sigma_i \sigma_j} \tag{6}$$

The joint probability occurrence of the specified pixel pairs is given by correlation.

$$\text{Energy} = \sum_i \sum_j c(i, j)^2 \tag{7}$$

Energy measures the sum of squared elements in the grey-level co-occurrence matrix.

$$\text{Homogeneity} = \sum_{i, j} \frac{c(i, j)}{1 + |i - j|} \tag{8}$$

It measures the closeness of the distribution of elements in the grey-level co-occurrence matrix to the diagonal of the GLCM grey-level co-occurrence matrix diagonal.

$$\mu_i = \sum_i i \sum_i c(i, j)$$

$$\mu_j = \sum_i j \sum_i c(i, j)$$

$$\sigma_i = \sum_i (i - \mu_i)^2 \sum_j c(i, j)$$

$$\sigma_j = \sum_i (j - \mu_j)^2 \sum_j c(i, j) \tag{9}$$

Local Binary Pattern

Statistical texture analysis is done by the unified approach of local binary patterns. Eight neighbouring pixels for one grey scale pixel are considered and the values of these pixels are operated by the value of the central pixel which is considered as the threshold. For each neighbouring pixel, if the pixel value is greater than the value of the central pixel, the value is set to one otherwise the value of the pixel is set to zero. The values are multiplied by weights. The final LBP code of the central pixel is obtained by summing up the values.

If the radius of the neighbourhood and total number of neighbours is given by R and N is then the LBP code is given by

$$LBP_{N,R} = \sum_{n=0}^{n-1} s(v_n - v_c) 2^n$$

$$s(x) = \begin{cases} 1, x \geq 0 \\ 0, x < 0 \end{cases} \tag{10}$$

Once the LBP code of each pixel is computed, the Texture image is represented using a histogram.

$$H(k) = \sum_{i=1}^{I} \sum_{j=1}^{J} f(LBP_{N,R}(i, j), k), k \in [0, K]$$

$$f(x, y) = \begin{cases} 1, & x = y \\ 0, & \text{otherwise} \end{cases} \tag{11}$$

3. Experimental Results

Different image segmentation and feature extraction methods are carried out on diseased leaf images of cotton plants in PYTHON. For experimentation 139 different leaves of the cotton affected by Alternaria leaf spot, Cercospora leaf spot and Verticilium wilt are used. The diseased leaves images of three different types of the diseased cotton plant and their histogram is as shown in Fig. 41.1.

Colour features and texture features are obtained from the colour histogram, colour moment, gray level co-occurrence matrix, and local binary pattern of each diseased leaf image. Statistical features of the colour moment for three diseases are calculated which are tabulated in Tables 41.1, 41.2, and 41.3.

Local Binary pattern method is applied on each diseased leaf image for extraction of texture features which is shown in Fig. 41.2.

On three diseased images of cotton plants, various segmentation methods such as K-means clustering, Fuzzy C-means and Ostu thresholding are implemented to find affected regions of diseased leaf images of cotton plants for useful feature extraction. Segmented images of Alternaria leaf spot, Cercospora leaf spot, and Verticilium wilt after applying three segmentation methods are shown in Fig. 41.3 respectively.

Colour moment feature extraction method is applied on segmented images obtained from Fuzzy c-means, K-means, Ostu thresholding, and statistical features are extracted from each diseased image which is given in Table 41.4.

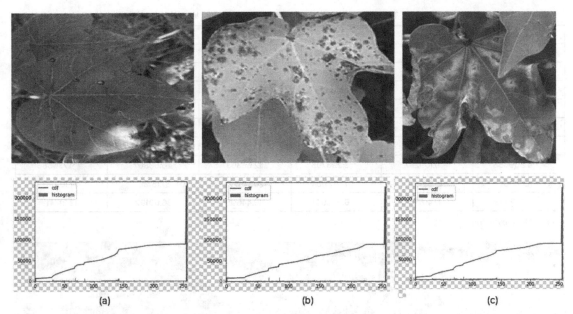

Fig. 41.1   (a) Original image and histogram of Cecospora leaf spot, (b) Original image and histogram of Alternaria Leaf Spot, (c) Original image and histogram of Verticillium Wilt

Source: Made by Author

Table 41.1   Statistical features of Alternaria Leaf Spot

mean_r	mean_g	mean_b	stddev_r	stddev_g	stddev_b
38.27209	46.67687	29.82419	56.52312	66.15395	45.39837
49.76305	57.94777	42.71746	72.9563	82.84263	63.62568
38.24926	51.78702	41.40701	62.44662	83.56118	67.76268
30.97888	39.12883	27.61596	52.65602	64.1568	46.2263
25.22647	28.36478	17.58485	48.91729	52.24468	34.38717
43.67645	47.7087	22.76728	69.79742	75.86529	36.81394
38.11489	42.15232	27.64522	64.40468	70.49953	47.01237
49.82946	47.87724	26.66025	83.78996	80.01781	45.49295

Source: Made by Author

Table 41.2   Statistical Features of Cercospora Leaf Spot

mean_r	mean_g	mean_b	stddev_r	stddev_g	stddev_b
44.15108	59.27119	43.36848	68.32238	90.81402	67.49426
26.92621	29.21518	23.54072	58.43324	63.45676	51.39209
39.21877	46.46783	35.51978	70.28066	83.75623	65.05229
24.50646	29.33701	24.39804	44.29126	52.93627	44.17465
31.35315	43.33861	33.51129	53.33353	72.34062	57.20669
45.13103	42.34295	29.00673	66.64606	66.11119	43.2546
33.71106	41.02093	28.39788	66.15062	80.3583	57.13607

Source: Made by Author

Table 41.3   Statistical features of Verticilium Wilt

mean_r	mean_g	mean_b	stddev_r	stddev_g	stddev_b
11.90822	20.09579	11.37818	29.42101	48.6393	28.2303
7.911105	13.1659	5.047446	20.324	33.64268	13.06688
5.498746	11.85484	3.915196	14.50009	30.91041	10.39175
5.951083	13.62097	3.698929	15.30901	34.28533	9.477162
5.361015	11.04286	3.239495	15.09131	30.69323	9.405089
5.54243	13.73354	4.226828	13.53532	33.11501	10.28967
4.309558	9.109287	3.296795	12.68363	26.58867	9.735666
11.08981	19.82724	7.538604	20.94172	37.15186	14.19214
7.722238	17.40715	6.266051	16.44695	36.60192	13.31741

Source: Made by Author

(a)   (b)   (c)

Fig. 41.2   (a) LBP of Alternaria Leaf Spot (b) LBP of Verticillium Wilt (c) LBP of Cercospora Leaf spot
Source: Made by Author

Fig. 41.3 (a) Original images (b) Fuzzy C-means segmented images (c) K-means segmented images (d) Ostu Thresholding segmented images

Source: Made by Author

Table 41.4 Comparison of statistical features of colour moment

	mean_r	mean_g	mean_b	stddev_r	stddev_g	stddev_b
Alternaria k means	44.1510	59.2711	43.3684	68.3223	90.8140	67.4942
Alternaria Fuzzy c	36.5807	57.8181	33.9453	57.6159	89.4002	48.2299
Cercospora k means	11.9082	20.0957	11.3781	29.4210	48.6393	28.2303
Cercospora Fuzzy C	21.5581	30.9246	40.5415	29.8226	63.3791	54.3368
VT K means	38.2720	46.6768	29.8241	56.5231	66.1539	45.3983
VT Fuzzy C means	27.29381	50.40065	41.02402	41.83096	79.45035	55.29638

Source: Made by Author

After image segmentation and feature extraction implementation, classification is carried out on extracted features of three diseased leaf images using SVM and KNN, and performance accuracy is analyzed for three segmentation methods which are shown in Table 41.5.

Table 41.5 Performance accuracy of segmentation methods

	K-means	Fuzzy C-means	Ostu thresholding
SVM	0.62	0.57	0.88
KNN	0.70	0.71	0.70

Source: Made by Author

4. Conclusion

It is concluded that image segmentation and feature extraction methods are applied on cotton plant fungal diseased leaf images for the analysis of various features and parameters used in disease detection and classification approach. Colour and texture feature extraction methods play a vital role in the detection and classification of diseased images. It is found that SVM gives more accuracy than KNN when the image is segmented using the Ostu thresholding method.

REFERENCES

1. Patil J. K., Raj kumar,"feature extraction of diseased leaf images", journal of signal and image processing issn: 0976-8882 & e-issn: 0976-8890, volume 3, issue 1, 2012, pp. 60–63.
2. Umapathy Eaganathan , Dr. S. Prasanna , Dr. Sripriya ," Various Approaches of color feature extraction on leaf diseases under imge processing:a survey", International Journal of Engineering & Technology, 7 (2.33) (2018) 712–717
3. Laleh Armi, Shervan Fekri-Ershad," texture image analysis and texture classification methods—a review", Journal of Image Processing and Pattern Recognition Vol. 2, No.1, pp. 1–29, 2019
4. Ch. Usha Kumari, N. Arun Vignesh, Asisa Kumar Panigrahy, L. Ramya, T. Padma, "Fungal Disease in Cotton Leaf Detection and Classification using Neural Networks and Support Vector Machine", International Journal of Innovative Technology and Exploring Engineering (IJITEE) ISSN: 2278–3075, Volume-8 Issue-10, August 2019
5. H. Al-Hiary, S. Bani-Ahmad, M. Reyalat, M. Braik and Z. ALRahamneh, "Fast and Accurate Detection and Classification of Plant Diseases", International Journal of Computer Applications (0975–8887)Volume 17– No.1, March 2011
6. Anne Humeau-heurtier, "Texture Feature Extraction Methods: A Survey", IEEE, volume 7, 2019
7. A. Sabah Afroze, M. Parisa Beham, R. Tamilselvi, S. M. Seeni Mohamed Aliar Maraikkayar, K. Rajakumar, " Cotton Leaf Disease Detection Using Texture and Gradient Features", International Journal of Engineering and Advanced Technology (IJEAT) ISSN: 2249–8958, Volume-9 Issue-1, October 2019
8. M. Bala Naga Bhushanamu, M. Purnachandra Rao, K. Samatha, "Plant Curl Disease Detection And Classification Using Active Contour And Fourier Descriptor", European Journal of Molecular & Clinical Medicine ISSN 2515–8260 Volume 07, Issue 05, 2020
9. Hidayat ur Rahman, Nadeem Jabbar Ch, SanaUllah Manzoor, Fahad Najeeb, Muhammad Yasir Siddique,Rafaqat Alam Khan, "A comparative analysis of machine learning approaches for plant disease identification", Advancements in Life Sciences ,August 2017, Volume 4 , Issue 4 120
10. Vijay S.Bhong, B.V.Pawar, "Study and Analysis of Cotton Leaf Disease Detection Using Image Processing", International Journal of Advanced Research in Science, Engineering and Technology, Vol. 3, Issue 2 , February 2016

Computer Science Engineering and Emerging Technologies (ICCS-2022) – Prof (Dr.) Rajeev Sobti et al. (eds)
© 2024 Taylor & Francis Group, London, ISBN 978-1-032-52199-2

Chapter **42**

An Approach to Reconstruct Cervical Spondylosis MRI Image Using Generative Adversarial Networks

Robin Kumar[1]
Computer Science Engineering.
LPU lovely professional university, Punjab, India

Rahul Malik[2]
Assistant Professor, Computer science engineering.
LPU lovely professional university, Punjab, India

Abstract: Medical imaging is the field that comes in pace with the GANs' ability to generate the image. GANs have been used in the medical field to generate an image in reconstruction and classification. In this paper, we have designed an approach to reconstruct cervical spondylosis MRI images from noisy MRI images. Cervical spondylosis is an age-related problem that causes neck pain. In this approach, we follow the footprint of the image-to-image translation with the paired dataset. The collection of the dataset is performed using a manual way by taking samples from diagnostic centers. The process of acquiring an MRI is a time-consuming process and the MRI image may contain noise-like movement artifacts and objects. The implementation was performed using a dataset on colab. This approach shows good results and generates good MRI images.

Keywords: GANs, MRI, CNN, Reconstruction, Deep learning

1. Introduction

Artificial intelligence (AI) advancements in recent years, notably in deep learning, have made it possible to apply technology to the interpretation of medical images. Machine learning advances create new opportunities and provide a platform for academics to apply their knowledge. Bengio et al. (2017) introduced deep learning for computer vision. Kumar and Malik (2021) began applying deep learning in medical imaging because of its vulnerability and usefulness. Machine learning is a sub-section of deep learning that mimics how people acquire knowledge (Alzubaidi et al., 2021). Convolution neural networks (CNNs), a form of learning algorithm, have demonstrated astounding efficiency, for instance, in the classification of lesions on medical images. In addition to CNN, there are several more deep-learning algorithms that are implemented in the same manner (Litjens et al., 2017). Deep learning provides the possibility for image interpretation, classification, feature detection, segmentation, registration, and other medical imaging applications such as neuro, optical, respiratory, diagnostic imaging, uterine cancer, cardiovascular, abdominal, and musculoskeletal imaging. In many Computer Vision and Medical Image Analysis applications, Deep Learning is currently the best in class but it requires a big annotated data set. In addition to CNN, Generative adversarial networks are also employed. Ian Goodfellow pioneered the use of GANs, which have resulted in exceptionally realistic images. GANs have been used in medical imaging for the reconstruction of compressed sensing MRI, reconstruction of MRI Super-Resolution of a brain MRI, Vertebrae Labeling, reconstruction of

[1]robin12370@gmail.com, [2]rahul.23360@lpu.co.in

DOI: 10.1201/9781003405580-42

Low Dose CT Images of the abdomen using GANs, CT to MRI image synthesis using Generative adversarial network, and PET image creation from CT images. In another work, GANs were utilized to generate CT scans using magnetic resonance (MR) pictures. MRI and CT pictures are essential in the treatment of cervical Spondylosis spine illnesses Figure 42.1 (Binder AI 2007). Cervical spondylosis, a chronic degenerative condition of the cervical spine, affects the vertebral bodies and intervertebral discs of the neck. The neck's spinal discs suffer from wear and strain due to these age-related issues. The most frequent cause of increasing spinal cord and nerve root compression is chronic cervical degeneration. Two-thirds of the population is affected by this issue, which is highly frequent. CS has a real impact on people's physical and mental health.

Particularly fast and precise methods for examining skeletal bones include CT scans. However, it might be challenging to distinguish between soft tissues. On the other hand, MR scans are helpful for examining soft tissues but are frequently contraindicated, such as in individuals who have pacemakers or claustrophobia. Furthermore, MRI is a diagnostic imaging technique that is often utilized in a range of clinical contexts. MRI can provide quantitative, reproducible tissue measurements as well as structural, anatomical, and functional information. The prolonged acquisition duration is one of MRI's major drawbacks, though. MRI has a sluggish collection speed by definition since data samples are acquired in k-space rather than image space. Movement artifacts in MRI degrade image quality and might cause misinterpretation, especially in low signal-to-noise scans (SNRs). Foreign bodies in the patient's body and artifacts in magnetic resonance imaging might result in pathology being misdiagnosed or lowering the quality of investigations. The goal of this research was to use GANs to create noise-free spine MR images. The similarities between created and actual MR images were statistically and subjectively assessed to determine the method's usefulness in medical therapy.

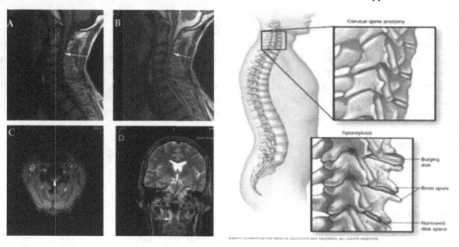

Fig. 42.1 Cervical Spondylosis image (Binder AI, 2007)

2. Generative Adversarial Networks

Ian Goodfellow and colleagues introduced GANs in 2014. GANs' ongoing growth process enables researchers to conduct fresh studies. An intriguing idea behind GAN is the utilization of an adversarial training method. This idea has become one of the most significant and fascinating machine learning architectures (ML). Generator and discriminator models for GANs are simultaneously trained using an adversarial methodology (Kumar and Malik, 2021). As an input, Generator is a neural network that converts random noise into a sample from the model distribution. The discriminator is a neural network that differentiates output data points (fake) from training data samples (real) (Xin et al. 2019), gradient-based approaches are widely used in the training. The basic GANs model is shown in Fig. 42.2. The use of a creative trade-off between the generator and discriminator allows GAN, an autonomous optimization solution approach, to develop the projected model while also extracting features. GANs are commonly used to tackle image-related challenges, such as transforming low-resolution images from other datasets into high-resolution images or solving image-to-image translation problems.

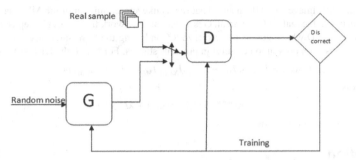

Fig. 42.2 Basic GAN model (Kumar and Malik, 2021)

3. Data and Data Preprocessing

For data collecting, we used a manual procedure. From the Jammu health care diagnostics center, we have gathered data on 100 patients, with each data set consisting of a distinct orientation. From diagnostic facilities, we gathered images from both clean and noisy MRIs. Each patient who underwent a cervical spine scan had an MRI recorded. The MR scan was obtained using the MR scanner. The examination of degenerative diseases has been covered. Magnetic resonance T2 MRI cervical spine sagittal anatomy images were gathered from the MR images. There was just one kind of MR sequence used. Figure 42.3 shows the collected sagittal cervical spine image. In total, we have 570 images. To ensure effective training, we improved the instructional visuals. The pictures were all changed to 256-grayscale. Cropping was done on both the real noisy and normal MRI scans. To further demonstrate the generalizability of the deep learning model, we employed structural MRI data from the cervical spine. Data from a diagnostic lab was gathered. 100 participants' worth of data was obtained from the MRI scanner's name. The picture is 556*321 pixels in size. The

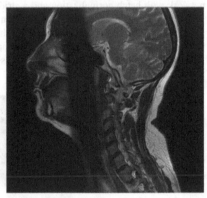

Fig. 42.3 Sagittal MRI image (Binder AI 2007)

data set is divided into training, validation, evaluation, and test datasets for experimental purposes. No subjects or image patches appear twice in different subgroups. Training data is the information used to train a model to predict the outcome that your model is supposed to do. A validation dataset is a set of data from your model's training that is used to test model competency while altering hyperparameters. To avoid customizing the model to the test set data, the test data set is utilized for the final performance evaluation.

4. Materials and Methods

4.1 Reconstruction of Noise MRI Image

According various research GAN can generate image using paired data such as image to image. Likewise, MRI can be generated using noisy MRI. Let G be the Generator so via mapping

$$(G: NMR, MR)$$

Let D be the adversarial trained discriminator network, which is used to recognize the generators produced image as efficiently as feasible, and tell G to make realistic MRI. The networks are subjected to adversarial losses. As an example, the goal may be stated as follows:

$$MRGAN (G, D) = EI_{NMR, MR} - P_{data} (I_{NMR}, I_{MR}) [\log D (I_{NMR}, I_{MR})] + EI_{NMR} \sim P_{data (NMR)}$$
$$[\log (1 - D (I_{NMR}, G(I_{NMR})))]$$

G attempts to convert an NMR image to a MR image. That seems like something out of the MR image. The discriminator D seeks to distinguish between the real and the unreal. G is a generator network that seeks to keep costs as low as possible. Same goal versus an opponent D whose goal is to maximize it Combining the adversarial loss with a more conventional loss, such as L1 distance, has been proven to be useful in previous studies. For the G, the L1 loss term was:

$$L_{L1}(G) = EI_{NMR}, I_{MR} \sim P_{data} (I_{NMR}, I_{MR}) [\|I_{MR}\text{-}G(I_{NMR})\|1]$$

The overall objective was:

$$G = arg_G^{min\ max} D\ L^L_{GAN} (G,D) + \lambda L_{L1}(G)$$

λ control adversarial loss and voxel-wise loss.

5. Implementation

For the reconstruction of the medical image, we follow the process of (Isola et al., 2017) image-to-image translation using GAN in this we have two network generators and discriminators which are competing with each other to give good results. In this network, we have a generator that consists of down-sampling and up-sampling. Downsampling is a 2D Convolution network with batch normalization and a stride of two. In this, we have leakyrelu activation function. In upsampling, we set dropout to false and used 2D Convolution transpose with relu activation function. In down sampling and up sampling, we have a stack of operations that perform the sampling from 256*256 image size. Discriminators take two inputs one is the input image and the other is the target image, which is a 2D Convolution network. This network removes the padding from the input image. This network performs batch normalization and uses the leakyrelu activation function. Some of the initial results are shown in Fig. 42.4.

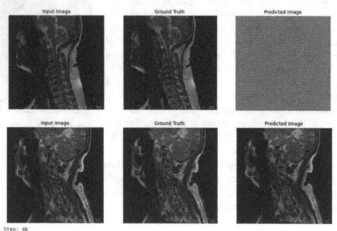

Fig. 42.4 Generated images results

Source: Made by Author

6. Conclusion

GAN is an artificial intelligence technique in which two networks play with each other to give results. Since its origin, it has been applied to a wide range of applications. Some of the applications are image super-resolution and image reconstruction. In this paper, we have used GANs for the reconstruction of the medical image of Cervical Spondylosis MRI and demonstrate that reconstruction can be done using the paired dataset approach. This approach uses image-to-image translation in which good MRIs are generated from noisy MRIs. This study was the first to create a cervical spine MRI from noisy MRI data using GANs. The reconstructive MRI was completed rather successfully despite the small dataset. A novel AI paradigm in medical imaging is the use of GANs to reconstruct pictures. Clinical applications will be aided by more studies employing massive data sets, various disorders, and different MR sequences.

REFERENCES

1. Lee J. H., Han I. H., Kim D. H., Yu S., Lee I. S., Song Y. S., Joo S., Jin C. B., Kim H. Spine Computed Tomography to Magnetic Resonance Image Synthesis Using Generative Adversarial Networks: A Preliminary Study. J Korean Neurosurg Soc. 2020 May; 63(3): 386–396. doi: 10.3340/jkns.2019.0084. Epub 2020 Jan 14. PMID: 31931556; PMCID: PMC7218205.
2. Binder A. I., Cervical spondylosis and neck pain. BMJ. 2007 Mar 10; 334(7592): 527–31. doi: 10.1136/bmj.39127.608299.80. PMID: 17347239; PMCID: PMC1819511.
3. R. Kumar and R. Malik, "A Review on Generative Adversarial Networks used for Image Reconstruction in Medical imaging," 2021 9th International Conference on Reliability, Infocom Technologies and Optimization (Trends and Future Directions) (ICRITO), 2021, pp. 1–5, doi: 10.1109/ICRITO51393.2021.9596487.
4. S. Goudarzi, A. Asif and H. Rivaz, "High Frequency Ultrasound Image Recovery Using Tight Frame Generative Adversarial Networks," 2020 42nd Annual International Conference of the IEEE Engineering in Medicine & Biology Society (EMBC), 2020, pp. 2035–2038, doi: 10.1109/EMBC44109.2020.9176101.
5. Bengio, Y., Goodfellow, I., & Courville, A. (2017). *Deep learning* (Vol. 1). Cambridge, MA, USA: MIT press.
6. Alzubaidi, L., Zhang, J., Humaidi, A. J., Duan, Y., Santamaría, J., Fadhel, M. A., & Farhan, L. (2021). Review of deep learning: concepts, CNN architectures, challenges, applications, future directions. *Journal of Big Data*, 8(1), 1–74. https://doi.org/10.1186/s40537-021-00444-8
7. P. Isola, J. Y. Zhu, T. Zhou and A. A. Efros, "Image-to-Image Translation with Conditional Adversarial Networks," 2017 IEEE Conference on Computer Vision and Pattern Recognition (CVPR), 2017, pp. 5967–5976, doi: 10.1109/CVPR.2017.632.

Computer Science Engineering and Emerging Technologies (ICCS-2022) – Prof (Dr.) Rajeev Sobti et al. (eds)
© 2024 Taylor & Francis Group, London, ISBN 978-1-032-52199-2

Chapter

43

Collective Intelligence in Digital Marketing and Business Decision-making Through Artificial Swarm Intelligence

M. Sivakoti Reddy[1]
Associate Professor, Department of Management Studies,
VFSTR Deemed to be University, Vadlamudi, Guntur, Andhra Pradesh, India

Suraj Chandrakant Kamble[2]
Associate Professor, DES's Institute of Management Development and Research (IMDR®),
DES Campus, Agharkar Rd, Deccan Gymkhana, Pune, Maharashtra

Shikha Salil Jain[3]
Director, DES's Institute of Management Development and Research (IMDR®),
DES Campus, Agharkar Rd, Deccan Gymkhana, Pune, Maharashtra

Archana Saxena[4]
Associate Professor, Uttaranchal University (UIM) Arcadia Grand,
Dehradoon, Uttarakhand

Jeidy Panduro-Ramirez[5]
Professor, Universidad Tecnológica Del Perú

José Luis Arias Gonzáles[6]
Business Department, Pontifical Catholic University of Peru

Abstract: Artificial swarm intelligence effectively connects specific human groups into different kinds of emergent systems operated by AI algorithms. It can be remarkably useful for getting a situational overview, searching for different objects, monitoring the productive environment, and establishing communication networks. AI enables marketers to personalize communications on an individual level. This definite technology works through the prediction of customer behavior depending on the intelligence achieved from previous interactions. In accordance with this, the current business environment is creatively progressing, technologically advanced, digitally empowered, immensely flexible, and forward-moving. Due to this reason, a competitive business environment has been observed throughout the entire world. Globalization also encourages this competitive business world. Based on those reasons, it is important to implement AI in the fields of business decision-making and digital marketing. It is also necessary to identify significant customer segments, their product preferences, current demand, and valuable feedback. On the other hand, collective intelligence refers to a group of intelligence that emerges from collective efforts, efficient collaboration, and competition among various individuals.

Keywords: Customer segment, Product preference, Conjecture framework

[1]shiva.manukonda@gmail.com, [2]suraj.kamble03@gmail.com, [3]shikhasalil@gmail.com, [4]Dr12archana@gmail.com, [5]C21289@utp.edu.pe, [6]joseariasgon6@gmail.com

DOI: 10.1201/9781003405580-43

1. Introduction

The world we live in today is quite similar to the Wonderland portrayed in the well-known books by some well-known researchers, also known by his pen name, Lewis Carroll. Innovations in artificial intelligence have made self-driving cars, intelligent speakers, and image recognition conceivable, defined as "a framework's capacity to interpret outside information accurately, to gain from such information, and to utilize those learnings to accomplish explicit objectives and errands through adaptable transformation." Man-made intelligence was established as a field of study in the 1950s, but it remained undefined logically and of limited practical importance for more than 50 years. Huge amounts of information have now become a topic of conversation in society and industry because of advancements in computing power. Artificial intelligence has empowered organizations to understand clients remarkably, and countless organizations are soliciting to embrace artificial intelligence to further develop their business practices (Saura *et al.,* 2021). Digital marketing has added to achieving admission to them; also, the Crown pandemic has provoked various clients to manage banks and include them in financial administrations because of the burden of check-in time and the total and semi-complete terminations of numerous areas. This may lead to a shift in social perceptions of banks, according to a few industry analysts, including financial specialists. Artificial intelligence and internet marketing for financial services are used to create innovative, popular services and products that go above and beyond what customers expect. However, the incorporation of artificial intelligence into internet advertising could have other negative effects, such as predisposition and increasing social and financial vulnerability, that prevent the achievement of the stated benefits.

Associations need to use sound judgment, and the high speed of business frequently demands that decisions are made rapidly and precisely. However, this is increasingly challenging in a dispersed and information-soaked work environment. Man-made intelligence was established in the 1950s as a field of study. In order to improve decision-making, many organizations have turned to digital innovations, including user-ggenerated content, business analytics frameworks, and publicly accessible stages. Particularly large swarms stood out sufficiently to be observed for providing information and making choices (Mogaji *et al.* 2020). In fact, research shows that inventions allowing swaths of people to independently make judgments might help people avoid corrupt social forces. However, because they are still sensitive to social pressure, swarms do have limitations. Because communication moves that can skew the judgments made by swarms (Dumitriu and Popescu, 2020). While these developments can provide crucial insights, constant information, and conjectures, in many cases, people working in bunches use this information to settle on a choice. Indeed, bunches are frequently defined as information processing elements that simply decide; in any event, gatherings might not arrive at an agreement or neglect to sufficiently perform.

2. Literature Review

Digital marketing strategies are being rapidly changed by artificial intelligence. While the existing material significantly covers man-made intelligence affiliations that exacerbate problems for customers who lack financial resources, there is less research on man-made intelligence linkages that typically help firms and clients (Aladayleh, 2020). These clients have confined their permission to financial structures, administrations, or advances. This study illustrates the challenges faced by firms as they attempt to incorporate PC-based information into the digital marketing of their payrolls in order to solve this lack of research. Moreover, AI-enabled digital marketing is still not typically as straightforward as gathering enormous data and making sense of estimates; the technology may not be certain to help companies target their customers more precisely. In order to provide the best possible customer experience and fulfill our responsibility to financial administration providers, this paper examines the relationships between artificial intelligence, digital marketing, and economic governments that are equivalent to providing powerless clients with services. It does so by highlighting significant effects on the information that is collected, processed, and transported (Rabby *et al.,* 2021). It is essential for the successful design of artificial intelligence to comprehend moral implications as well as informational and modeling challenges. In order to help understand the temperamental conditions faced by powerless clients and how they can all the more effectively be reached at whatever point, this study provides a framework based on conjecture for corporate accounting providers, duplicated intelligence fashioners, promoters, decision makers, and academics.

Second, the essays in this exceptional edition dissect how simulated intelligence alters how businesses operate internally, specifically general processes and correspondence decision-making (Duan *et al.* 2019). Researchers developed a construction to clarify when final decisions should be made entirely by computer-based intelligence, in combination (either using machine intelligence as a contribution to rational decision-making or using individual decisions as an input to AI-ppowered structures), or collectively. The decision-making space's expressions, the size of the elective set, the speed at which decisions are made, as well as the requirements for interpretability and replication, all influence the direction in which a decision should be taken.

Customary marketing strategies are not practical at this point in the new business climate. A few organizations are increasingly examining more compelling innovations (Shrestha *et al.* 2019). Digital marketing likewise intends to adjust innovation to fulfill clients and partners, as well as combine digital marketing hypotheses with the genuine act of marketing. The quick spread of the Internet and the increasing utilization of cell phones have supported the fast development of simulated intelligence (Tariq *et al.*, 2022). Client gatherings and business organizations have profited from it by changing the conventional deal process and interacting with individual clients through different touch points.

Simulated intelligence processes information, pursues better choices, and eliminates predispositions in making decisions. The collection of diverse sorts of huge information through quick-sensing robots for chatting in web-based entertainment, email, sites, and notices in enormous volumes and in a fast and efficient way has increased the force of computer-based intelligence. Artificial intelligence-empowered frameworks can likewise distinguish characteristics, feelings, or feelings from text-based and unstructured information, as well as non-verbal information like pictures and regular language understanding and processing, for instance, in client interaction with brands. Computer-based intelligence uses a wide range of information to make informed choices that add value. Besides, there are artificial intelligence frameworks that can uphold the examination of sound information, as they gather and dissect voice remarks and convert them into meaningful information that advertisers use in basic frameworks like client relationship and executive frameworks (Sourdin, 2018). It is likewise conceivable to gather information and distinguish designs from many sources, like the web, versatile stages, and customary or virtual entertainment, and perform a proper examination that aids in understanding client patterns, predicting their ways of behaving, and building long-haul associations with clients. Artificial intelligence advances can assist advertisers in developing client division techniques and targeting individuals and gatherings through customized messaging. Artificial intelligence frameworks can advance by processing large amounts of information since all areas of human learning can be completed by machines. In addition, there are cross-breed frameworks that combine human intelligence and machine intelligence. Nearly three factors contribute to the significance of swarm.ai in this survey. The dynamics of a complicated, flexible system—the kind of design that swarm.ai engages in—are where total intelligence first arises. At the most fundamental level, it gives people the authority to act as a reliable system that reacts to environmental changes. At the miniature scale, it provides people with the same amount of time and purpose in accordance with the direction and size of the graphic magnet and the advancement of the puck (James, 2020). Swarm.ai, on the other hand, may provide a more precise range of level creations, including gathering social insight. The dependency on successfully implementing a collection level by combining data gathered at the individual scale is a common barrier to gathering-level investigation. This is dangerous because evaluation operates at the interpersonal level and is therefore inadequate to identify the underlying interest-gathering patterns (Jarrahi, 2018). The design of swarm.ai circumvents this limit by allowing many people to collaborate on a short answer as a holistic structure that takes everything into account. The response takes into account all of the gathering techniques used throughout the gathering. Swarm.ai's design offers a compelling balance between perceptibility and mystery that helps reduce social influence tendencies. (Jarek and Mazurek, 2019) Pack members can express their opinions clearly by moving the puck, but their personalities remain enigmatic. Finally, swarm.ai makes use of people's urge to be alert to subtle, meaningful messages (León-Castro *et al.*, 2021). The graphical puck's development emphasizes the understated indicators that express the group's intention. When you consider that no incredibly important information is being delivered, this becomes significant. People each have unique perspectives, experiences, sentiments, and information that might make it difficult to interact with others. Many people can return to their implicit information when making a final decision by moving the puck.

3. Methodology and Model Specifications

Research methodology is the backbone of a research study. It consists of a clear discussion based on systematic and logical analysis in accordance with the different methods mentioned by researchers for procuring primary as well as secondary data. It also acts as one of the most efficient pillars for the entire study to detect authentic techniques as well as different tools for collecting reliable information. Various types of methodological tools have also been used to procure the most reliable information related to a particular research topic. In this present methodology, "post-positivism research philosophy" has been utilized for exploring research findings in a logical way. The "deductive research approach" is mostly applied in this present research due to the emergence of creative scientific theories. It is essential to rely on diverse theories about artificial intelligence and the effects of AI in digital marketing. An empirical research methodology has been followed in this area, which comprises different kinds of mathematical expressions and logical factors. A secondary qualitative data collection method has been used for this study, and authentic journals, books, and research papers have been extensively analyzed on Google Scholar.

4. Empirical Results

$$f'(x) = \lim_{\Delta x \to 0} \frac{(x + \Delta x) - x}{\Delta x}$$

The above formula reflects the visualization technique of artificial intelligence, and in a truly gradient-based approach, one can calculate the gradient of each and every input relative to an output. A small change in input data leads to an outcome change, and it can be visualized easily.

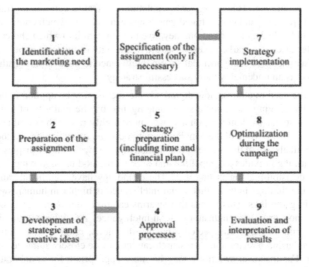

Fig. 43.1   Evaluation and implementation process of digital marketing strategies

Source: Elia et al. 2020

The above picture depicts a clear digital marketing strategy where the first step is the detection of a special marketing need and the second is the preparation of the assignment. The development of creative ideas as well as strategies is the third step, which is followed by process approval. A definite financial plan and time frame have also been established for the preparation of a clear strategy. It is required to specify the assignment and implementation of important strategies. The optimization process during campaigning as well as the evaluation and interpretation of results occurred at the last stage.

According to the above figure, a clear process map has been depicted where four important pillars have been clearly observed. Management support and leadership are two of the first steps, followed by an innovation culture. Those two things are interrelated with each other in devising a new process. On the other hand, a correct technical infrastructure has been established, such as artificial intelligence, to purposefully analyze various kinds of relevant datasets. At last, analytical focus has occurred to adopt AI in digital marketing.

Fig. 43.2   Process map of digital marketing

Source: Lies, 2019

5. Conclusion

Artificial Swarm Intelligence is a special and strong technique for tapping the information, shrewdness, intuition, and insights of human populations, enabling upgraded answers to quickly arise. While many are enticed to contrast the cycle with customary surveys, studies, and center gatherings, the relationship is shaky in the best-case scenario. Indeed, these strategies gather input from human members, yet surveys, overviews, and center gatherings treat individuals as "respondents"—for example, as a wellspring of confined information points that are added to a growing dataset. Since such strategies are measurable, their legitimacy depends entirely on basic factual tests. And still, at the end of the day, a measurably critical survey doesn't imply that the survey is providing specialists with exact insights; it simply implies that repeating the survey on a comparable populace will yield similar responses, precise or not. Artificial Swarm Intelligence frameworks, then again, treat individuals as "members" and errand them with being dynamic "information processors" instead of uninvolved data of interest. This empowers populations to frame continuous frameworks that meet ideal arrangements. While surveys, reviews, and concentrated gatherings can indicate which choice among a bunch of choices may be generally famous to individuals, in segregation, they give little insight into which choices the populace would best concur upon "in the wild." Because most marketing exercises are tied in with influencing populations in certifiable settings, not polling individuals in disconnection, using artificial swarm intelligence to uncover how gatherings are probably going to unite as regular frameworks is an undeniably more successful strategy.

This study was justified by the need to address how digital advancements may be applied to enhance group intelligence overall. We monitored this by gauging the group's social intelligence by the majority of votes and human swarming. The findings demonstrate that social wisdom was, on average, more highly rated when evaluated as a swarm than when evaluated individually or by a larger portion of the population, with both the swarm grade and the individual grade earning in the 94th percentile of individuals. All of this suggests that human swarms occasionally display greater overall knowledge than gatherings. Human swarming provides a compelling and original method through which affiliations could influence the caliber and velocity of decision-making in this way. These findings have significant ramifications for theory and application. Most crucially, the findings indicate that social intelligence is higher in human swarms working together as a stable structure than it is in gatherings. This means that swarms can do better on a variety of tasks and judgments, as cordial understanding is the most prominent indicator of total intelligence. This interpretation is supported by numerous effective uses of human swarms to make unexpectedly precise decisions, ranging from anticipating the outcomes of athletic events to the financial business sector. Future research can look more closely at the decisions and tasks that human swarming is best suited for. For instance, swarming may be more appropriate for collaborative thinking even though swarm-based organizations frequently predominate in distinct thinking. An alternative interpretation of the findings is that a swarm, as opposed to a complete, more accurately assesses pack social insight. This view is accordingly intriguing and has prospective repercussions for the evaluation of staggered improvements such as groups, significant level subunits, and complete affiliations.

REFERENCES

1. Aladayleh, K., 2020. A framework for integration of artificial intelligence into digital marketing in Jordanian commercial banks. Journal of Innovations in Digital Marketing, 1(1), pp. 32–39.
2. Duan, Y., Edwards, J. S. and Dwivedi, Y. K., 2019. Artificial intelligence for decision making in the era of Big Data–evolution, challenges and research agenda. International journal of information management, 48, pp. 63–71.
3. Dumitriu, D. and Popescu, M. A. M., 2020. Artificial intelligence solutions for digital marketing. Procedia Manufacturing, 46, pp. 630–636.
4. Elia, G., Margherita, A. and Passiante, G., 2020. Digital entrepreneurship ecosystem: How digital technologies and collective intelligence are reshaping the entrepreneurial process. Technological Forecasting and Social Change, 150, p. 119791.
5. James, L., 2020. Identifying the effect of Digital Marketing channels on the growth of SME in South Asia: A Case Study on Faheem Haydar Dealzmag.
6. Jarek, K. and Mazurek, G., 2019. Marketing and artificial intelligence. Central European Business Review, 8(2), p. 46.
7. Jarrahi, M.H., 2018. Artificial intelligence and the future of work: Human-AI symbiosis in organizational decision making. Business horizons, 61(4), pp. 577–586. León-Castro, M., Rodríguez-Insuasti, H., Montalván-Burbano, N. and Victor, J. A., 2021. Bibliometrics and Science Mapping of Digital Marketing. In Marketing and Smart Technologies (pp. 95-107). Springer, Singapore.
8. Lies, J., 2019. Marketing intelligence and big data: Digital marketing techniques on their way to becoming social engineering techniques in marketing.

9. Mogaji, E., Soetan, T. O. and Kieu, T. A., 2020. The implications of artificial intelligence on the digital marketing of financial services to vulnerable customers. Australasian Marketing Journal, pp.j-ausmj.
10. Rabby, F., Chimhundu, R. and Hassan, R., 2021. Artificial intelligence in digital marketing influences consumer behaviour: A review and theoretical foundation for future research. Academy of Marketing Studies Journal, 25(5), pp. 1–7.
11. Saura, J. R., Ribeiro-Soriano, D. and Palacios-Marqués, D., 2021. Setting B2B digital marketing in artificial intelligence-based CRMs: A review and directions for future research. Industrial Marketing Management, 98, pp. 161–178.
12. Shrestha, Y. R., Ben-Menahem, S. M. and Von Krogh, G., 2019. Organizational decision-making structures in the age of artificial intelligence. California Management Review, 61(4), pp. 66–83.
13. Sourdin, T., 2018. Judge v Robot?: Artificial intelligence and judicial decision-making. University of New South Wales Law Journal, The, 41(4), pp. 1114–1133.
14. Tariq, E., Alshurideh, M., Akour, I. and Al-Hawary, S., 2022. The effect of digital marketing capabilities on organizational ambidexterity of the information technology sector. International Journal of Data and Network Science, 6(2), pp. 401–408.

Computer Science Engineering and Emerging Technologies (ICCS-2022) – Prof (Dr.) Rajeev Sobti et al. (eds)
© 2024 Taylor & Francis Group, London, ISBN 978-1-032-52199-2

Chapter

44

The Advancement of Using Internet of Things in Blockchain Applications for Creating Sustainable Environment in the Real Word Scenario

Hashem Ali Almashaqbeh[1]
Assistant Professor, Istanbul Galata University, Istanbul, Turkey

K. K. Ramachandran[2]
Director/ Professor, Management/Commerce/International Business,
Dr. G R D College of Science, India

Shyam Sunder. T.[3]
Assistant Professor, Aurora's PG College (MBA), Ramanthapur

Shouvik Kumar Guha[4]
Assistant Professor (Senior Scale),
The West Bengal National University of Juridical Sciences

Mahabub Basha S.[5]
Assistant Professor, Department of Commerce,
International Institute of Business Studies, Bangalore

M. Z. M. Nomani[6]
Professor, Faculty of Law Aligarh Muslim University,
Aligarh-202001(U.P./India)

Abstract: The potential and advantages of Internet of Things (IoT) technology are increasingly being applied in sustainable environment to enhance the longevity of resources using sensors and devices. Despite the IoT's limitless possibilities, its centralized server/client approach makes it difficult to implement in the real world. For instance, the excessive quantity of IoT gadgets in the network can cause scalability and security difficulties. All gadgets should be connected to and verified by the server in the server/client model, making a solitary failure point. Thus, moving the IoT framework to a decentralized methodology may be the finest action-plan. Blockchain is one of the most notable decentralization innovations. The Blockchain is a potent technology that decentralizes administration and computation processes, which can address many IoT problems, particularly security. This article presents an overview of the blockchain and IoT integration while emphasizing advantages and obstacles. For a sustainable environment, the Particle Swarm Optimization (PSO) algorithms and Bees Algorithm (BA) performance is examined. The convergence rate was used to analyse the algorithms. The findings demonstrated that whereas BA initially discovered superior fitness values and was faster, the PSO method gradually converging to higher upsides of goal capabilities. Additionally, the PSO was less sophisticated than BA. As a result, the PSO algorithm produced improved results for the implementation of IoT-based sensor networks.

Keywords: IoT, Blockchain, Sustainable environment, BA optimization, PSO

[1]hashem61994@gmail.com, [2]dr.k.k.ramachandran@gmail.com, [3]shyamtumma19@gmail.com, [4]shouvikkumarguha@gmail.com,
[5]shaiks86@gmail.com, [6]zafarnomani@rediffmail.com

DOI: 10.1201/9781003405580-44

1. Introduction

The environment is a vital resource that directly affects sociopolitical and economic factors in every element of how cities and communities are administered on a daily basis. Rapid urbanization, projected population growth, and climate change brought on by unpredictable weather patterns around the world all call for effective methods of protecting, utilizing, and managing the environment's finite resources [1], especially in developing economies like the African continent [2].

The Internet of Things has significantly altered how people interact with one another and the environment and offers us a better means of comprehending what is occurring around us. Our infrastructure and cities are becoming smarter thanks in large part to IoT. In only two years, in 2020, Cisco Internet Business Solutions Group (IBSG) predicts that there will be 50 billion connected IoT devices, and ARM, a software and semiconductor design company, predicts that there will be 1 trillion connected IoT devices by 2035. Despite all the benefits it offers, IoT technology raises a number of concerns, including the security and privacy of the data that these massive sensors are constantly producing [3], the heterogeneity of the gadgets, adaptability, power productivity, and interoperability, as well as the standardization of protocols for network communication [4]. Many scholars have suggested various approaches to addressing these IoT problems for the Industrial Internet of Things, and real-time IoT Industry application scenario (IIoT) [5]. Since of the decentralized geography of IoT gadgets, which are continually helpless against physical and digital assaults due to the secret information produced and conveyed by these shrewd and asset compelled gadgets, there are as yet open inquiries and difficulties, especially with security and protection [6].

The Climate Change and Innovation Bureau (CCIB) of Canada regarding health received recommendations from the University of Waterloo regarding the potential for incorporating cutting-edge technologies in the planning phase and innovation of pan-Canadian tracking and activities of surveillance related to health, environmental effects and the sustainable development system [7]. One of these efforts is combining data from many ecosystems of environmental and health data so that researchers, policymakers, and health officials can use analytical services to extract insights from the information giving an incorporated location for the analysis of health, processing, environmental data and storage [8]; operationalizing the use of this data within the abovementioned offices and locally. Several emerging innovations, including processing systems and cloud storage, artificial intelligence (AI), internet of things (IoT) including data science, machine learning (ML), mobile health, blockchain, Ambient assisted living, wearables, and others, may help with the execution of these activities. These disruptive technologies are widely used in many Big Data-related fields, like flu reconnaissance and air quality checking, so they have a strong chance of assisting the development of the pan-Canadian surveillance system in the future [9]. This research arrives at a key moment. We must adjust to the demands of our healthcare systems as a result of the rapid changes in our climate, which have an effect on human health and wellbeing. Climate change is "the greatest health threat of the 21st century," and it is a huge task that calls for creative solutions [10].

Including blockchain in IoT will offer several benefits. The blockchain's decentralized organization structure will be capable of handling the processing of billions of the exchange of payments between IoT devices, which greatly cut down on the price of installing and keeping up massive centralized data centers, as well as spread out the requirements for storage and computation networks made up of billions of devices [11]. Aside from that Utilizing blockchain technology will get rid of the centralized system's single point of failure IoT edifice. Additionally, incorporating blockchain IoT will enable peer-to-peer messaging and file sharing distributed and independent IoT coordination devices without a centralized server-client model [12].

1.1 Objectives

1. To examine the effects of combining blockchain usage a sustainable environment management system, and IoT technology.
2. To give some examples of current and potential applications for such technology in the field of environmentally sustainable practices.
3. To analyze the performance of Particle Swarm optimization (PSO) and Bee algorithm (BA) for environment.

2. Related Studies

2.1 Advances in Blockchain Technology

Blockchain is an open-source distributed ledger that promotes trust between parties thanks to cryptography tools. The idea of transactions is the foundation of the technology. In today's world, when a user performs a transaction, it is typically handled by an outsider, for example, insurance agency, bank, and a government. The amount of security that blockchain provides is what makes using it in healthcare so intriguing. At the point when a client manages an exchange in the Blockchain organization, the exchange is time-stepped, checked by the partaking hubs, and "fixed" in a block with different exchanges. The name "blockchain" refers to the addition of this block to a previous chain of blocks [13].

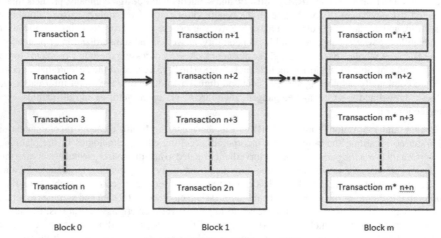

Fig. 44.1 Blockchain Structure [31]

An agreement technique adds the exchange across all organization members. Different agreement processes come in many structures. Agreement with regards to the Bitcoin Blockchain depends on a strategy known as Proof of Work (PoW), which involves contest between the organization's upkeep hubs. Each hub tries to decide an irregular number, or "nonce," that settle a numerical problem before some other hub. The best way to decide the nonce is to figure a number and check whether your supposition is precise. The victor hub involves the nonce as a cryptographic key to seal the block and add it to the Blockchain whenever it has been found [14].

Smart Contracts

The generation of smart contracts is becoming possible because to the advancement of technology and the emergence of new Blockchains like Ethereum. Smart contracts are contract clauses that are guaranteed to be fulfilled by software by being incorporated into the programme. Although smart contract applications are still in the early phases of development, they can be applied in numerous ways in the context of environment management and healthcare. For instance, they can be used to codify the provisions of the insurance plans so that health insurance claims can be settled continuously [15]. Another model is to systematize assent terms in wellbeing concentrates with the end goal that a member is naturally enlisted after assent is gotten (and eliminated assuming assent is disavowed), or a member is given a legitimate parental figure or watchman assuming agree should be conceded for their sake. This model additionally shows how, in principle, delegate outsiders' effect may be decreased or killed. The reconciliation of IoT and brilliant agreements can prompt more prominent computerization (or, in the previously mentioned situations, more noteworthy effectiveness and patient (or member) independence, all while safeguarding individual information). Whether Blockchain is the ideal answer is another thing to take into account. While there are in this case, technologies that are similar to smart contracts, there are a number of obstacles to their adoption, such as costs that are frequently raised by intermediaries (for instance, in 2016, it was estimated that the fees for using a credit card were 5.5 times higher than those for using Bitcoin) [13].

Blockchain in the Environment

Similar to how it does in healthcare, blockchain technology can assist in resolving interoperability and data sharing concerns, resulting in greater information for decision-making and resource efficiency. The technology can also be used to address urgent environmental issues like energy, natural disasters, air pollution, declining ocean health, and climate change, among others. For illustration, we can use the tracking of the medicine store network with food items. Utilizing blockchain innovation to follow food can improve customers to make environmentally beneficial decisions by providing transparency into the entire production process. Organizations like IBM are as of now in the beginning stages of coordinating blockchain-controlled food production network arrangements. Another model is the observing of fish provenance or imperiled species possible use [16].

The potential of blockchain to support peer-to-peer trade has received a lot of attention. In environmental settings, this might lead to the development of peer-to-peer energy-trading platforms where users can exchange energy. Additionally, it could upgrade the general energy market and be a problematic innovation in regions that experience power deficiencies. Both new business sectors and the value of assets that are right now wasted could be expanded by the innovation. By paying clients who gather recyclables with cryptographic tokens, there are drives to advance association in reusing projects and exercises tokens that can be utilized to purchase or trade different items or administrations. Along these lines, a Blockchain-based carbon use global positioning framework with notoriety and prize frameworks could boost individuals and organizations to decrease their carbon impressions while likewise upgrading auditability and administrative consistence using ecological regulations and arrangements [17].

Blockchain's resilience can aid with natural disasters, and its connection with IoT sensors can bring about more straightforward, viable, and secure checking of factors like air and water contamination [18]. These are only a few of the blockchain's potential uses in the environmental industry. It is crucial to remember that relying solely on IoT and AI technologies; Blockchain does not constitute a comprehensive solution in the majority of these scenarios. Smart metres and other sensors are required, for example, in automated energy markets. IoT utilisation has potential for advancement one of the difficulties presented by blockchain. The entry of these data must be trustworthy and correct despite giving an unchangeable track of information. IoT devices are used to automate inputs to reduce errors and improve data reliability. But in this situation, it's critical to understand the importance of security in relation to IoT gadgets since they might defenseless to hack. Notwithstanding the issue of guaranteeing precise data sources, a few doubters of the innovation battle that bitcoin and blockchain in everyday utilize a lot of energy during calculations and are in this way not environmentally well disposed. Blockchain is as yet growing, however, and the carbon impression of innovation can be decreased with the utilization of new strategies and agreement building processes. Most of experts know about the benefits and undiscovered latent that blockchain innovation might bring to the natural area, especially when incorporated with IoT, computer-based intelligence, and other state-of-the-art advances [19].

2.2 Advances in Internet of Things (IoT)

IoT is becoming more prevalent in a variety of fields, such as environmental monitoring and health, as stated by Ziegler [20]. This part gives setting to a portion of the forthcoming information sources (Far off Quiet Checking, Encompassing Helped Living — AAL), portraying current purposes of IoT innovation inside these fields that could be taken into account while determining the scope and creating the system include RPM, public health, environmental monitoring, and surveillance.

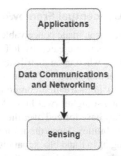

Fig. 44.2 Functional architecture of IoT [32]

IoT in Environment

Health is directly impacted by outrageous climate related occasions welcomed on by an evolving environment, like sudden temperature variances, woods fires, and quantities of precipitation that cause flooding. For instance, as heat waves occur more frequently, especially in urban areas, heat-related health problems including death, particularly among the elderly, will become more common. Since people depend on their ecosystem, these changes have a direct impact on human health [21], counting the expanded spread and sickness transmission and air poisons. IoT environment monitoring could advance our knowledge of how these factors interact and pave the way for viable remedies to reduce unfavourable effects. IoT devices are currently used in the environment to map spatiotemporal data, such as travel times and pollution sources, and using data crowd sourced from people or acquired from sensors for epidemiological surveillance. Sensors for measuring air quality are primarily utilized for personal monitoring and outdoor and/or interior monitoring. Through the utilization of the Global Positioning System (GPS), wearable sensors may quantify individual exposure to various contaminants, and this information can then be utilized to estimate the geographical appropriation of air contaminations in various microenvironments [22].

IoT advances can follow and make ongoing guides of water contamination, hazardous radiation, public health, noise levels, and temperature and in addition to air pollution [23]. For water checking, sensors that action water levels could give individuals advance notice of water disasters like flood the window of opportunity for evacuation or pre-event planning. Similar to this, early identification provided by radiological risk monitoring aids in minimizing or eliminating the effects of radioactive element releases [24]. Sensors that could estimate the relative humidity and temperature of the air could potentially be useful.

Identify and control the spread of fungi illnesses in crop fields, which are pivotal for supplying the people with food [25]. These IoT arrangements could assist emergency the executives by observing emergencies with preferring quakes, floods, and radiation levels; organizing catastrophe help tasks; giving help from outside calamity zones; and illuminating and refreshing individuals as essential when combined with publicly supported maps comprehends the emergencies [26]. Albeit these guides are not IoT merchandise without anyone else, their blend with sensors that track factors continuously may bring about frameworks that might offer early discovery and admonitions of cataclysmic events [27]. Concerns about the accuracy and dependability of the data collected and monitored by consumer-level technology are one of the difficulties in deploying IoT technologies in environmental applications. The quality and accuracy of the data are also issues.

Issues with IoT Technology Use

Lack of trustworthy duration and coordination in IoT development and deployment prevents technology to be able of best worldwide practices, harmonization, and normalization. Nations would be passed on in obscurity without a planned work to track down prescribed procedures and spread them to all countries to coordinate the new innovation into their public observation programmes, and must independently evaluate and test various approaches. As a result of technological developments, more datasets are now available in a variety of settings (e.g., environmental, insurance, and clinical). The data must be arranged into standard forms that statisticians, public health authorities, and other stakeholders may use in order to find examples and connections among these different information types. This makes it worse. The lack of interoperability in many systems makes it problematic because those systems are governed by regulations and laws that frequently encompass various data collecting, storage, and sharing procedures as well as various perspectives on privacy and security [28].

3. Methodology

3.1 Conceptual Framework for Blockchain and IoT

IoT has been made conceivable by distributed computing, which considers the constant filing, handling, and investigation of information created by IoT detecting gadgets. The suspicion of good Web availability, high transfer speed, and low idleness, whereupon distributed computing ideas have been worked, as well as the extended expansion of IoT gadgets to arrive at more than 50 billion soon, imply that this cloud-focused structural game plan will never again be ideally possible. Partners in distributed computing have additionally authentically communicated stresses over different issues including trust and straightforwardness. Most of these natural issues with distributed computing actually exist, regardless of the way that they have formed over the long run into new and integral thoughts like edge, haze, land, and populace figuring to work on its abilities. Since the information will remain changeless and appendable in a worldwide conveyed open record, the joining of IoT and blockchain is a promising cooperative energy that could build the capability of IoT by offering security, trust, devotion, and mystery in data sharing. A portion of the benefits that the combination of blockchain-IoT guarantees are decentralization, versatility, dependable hub distinguishing proof, independence, unwavering quality, security, and safeguarded firmware organization into gadgets. We suggested a half and half methodology combination proposed in for coordinating blockchain and the Web of Things into reasonable climate the executives, where distributed computing and its progressing new ideas like edge, haze, and land registering could be integrated into the plan to assume a reciprocal part, as portrayed in Fig. 44.3.

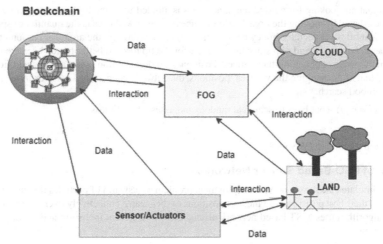

Fig. 44.3 Integration of hybrid blockchain with IoT in concept [33]

3.2 Deployment of BA-Based Sensor Networks

In order to maximise coverage and longevity, the BA algorithms simulate bees' foraging patterns to select the ideal positions for sensor nodes throughout the network. The BA has three different types of bees, including employed bees (tasked with finding food sources), spectator bees (observing the employed bee's dance), and scout bees (randomly looking for new food sources) [66].

Make a bee settlement by creating an underlying irregular populace with p employed bees. Every bee, which represents a solitary sensor organization, is delivered by UDG utilizing n vertices set indiscriminately areas. In the WSN, every vertex subs for a sensor hub or asset. In the graph, there are no connections between the vertices that are outside the sensors' communication range. As long as and only if, the adjacency matrix (G) is used to examine the connectedness of the randomly produced network

$$Y = G + G^2 \ldots + G^{n-1} \neq 0 \tag{1}$$

$$G = \{ xi \} \times n\ i = 1, \ldots, n;\ j = 1, \ldots, n \tag{2}$$

The places of specific vertices are modified until the associated UDG diagram is gotten if the pseudorandom graph is not connected. To accomplish this, the connected graph components must first be identified, and then the locations of the vertices of a part with the fewest vertices must be moved toward the closest component.

Step 1: Use the generated UDG to build MST using the Kruskal algorithm and the sensor node distances as edge weights.

Step 2: Assess the hired bees from the starting population's fitness function in accordance with Equation (2).

Step 3: $t = 0$. The subsequent stages are carried out until $(t < N_{iteration})$ t is not exactly the quantity of ages.

Step 4: Pick the m bees that have greater fitness esteem (fi) as the better bees.

Step 5: From the m selected bees, choose e elite bees.

Step 6: Select onlooker honey bees to look about each picked first class and (m-e) better honey bee and survey their wellness. To do this, the sweep and size of the local quest for each kind of chosen honey bee.

The local pursuit distance exhibits the number of the honey bee's vertices are dependent upon inconsistent change inside the detecting range. To put it another way, the looking through distance in the sending of the sensor network is a worth that lays out the greatest number of sensors that can be altered depending on the type of bees. As a result, at this stage, the bee's neighborhood search involves randomly changing the position of a random number of vertices, as seen below:

$$x_i = x_i \pm \text{Rand}\,(0, d) \tag{3}$$

$$y_i = y_i \pm \text{Rand}\,(0, d) \tag{4}$$

The amount of bees that are looking for around the honey bees is alluded to as the looking through size. The quantity of extra bees that can be created by moving the organization vertices of the picked bees is the quantity of spectator bees in the WSN sending. The quantities of spectator honey bees dispatched to look through the area from around tip top and further developed bees, separately, are nep and nbp since the numbers for the tip top and better honey bees are unique. It ought to be referenced that in the wake of changing the vertices' positions, the organization association is additionally analyzed. It should be mentioned that after changing the vertices' positions, the network connection is also examined. Choose the ideal bee for neighborhood search.

Step 4.5: Distribute ($s = n\,m$) scout bees to search at random and assess their fitness.

Step 4.6: $t = t + 1$

Step 5: Identify the top global bee (WSN).

3.3 Deployment of PSO-Based Sensor Networks

The PSO algorithm simulates the sensor network deployment problem as a swarm of particles that move through the space of search and improve their best positions and the best positions of the swarm collectively over generations to find the best solution [29]. This algorithm uses MST-based network arrangement to augment inclusion and lifetime. The algorithm is described in detail below.

Step 1: Create an initial random population of p particles, which stand for sensor networks. The BA step is exactly the same as this one. The place of the assets is treated as the place of every molecule in this calculation.

Step 2: Produce an MST graph akin to BA step 2.

Step 3: $t = 0$. The subsequent stages are carried out until t is < the generations number ($t < N_{iteration}$).

Step 3.1: Fitness functions calculated in accordance with Equation in (2).

Step 3.2: Define the swarm's global best particle (gbest), which has the highest fitness value, as well as the best positions for each particle (pbest). The initial pbest is taken into account as the particle's position for the first iteration.

Step 3.3: Update each particle's velocity vector. Each particle's velocity is given by the vector $2n + 1$. The x and y velocities of the network vertices are represented in this vector by the odd and even elements, respectively. The first distance matrix D is defined using an $n \times n'$ matrix as follows to determine velocity.

Second, the minimum distance is represented by computing the littlest component in every network column. Third, it is computed how much each vertex of the pest (or gbest) particle differs from the chosen vertex in terms of x and y. For the gbest and pbest particles independently, the velocity vector is determined. Equation is used to compute the total velocity in the end (5).

$$\vec{V_i} = \overrightarrow{\omega\,V_i} + C_1 \to \overrightarrow{\varphi_{1i}} \overrightarrow{\text{dpbest}} + \to \overrightarrow{C_{2\varphi 2i}} \overrightarrow{\text{dgbest}} \tag{5}$$

where C_1 and C_2 are acceleration coefficient and constant parameters, w is the inertia weight, and φ_1 and φ_2 are randomly chosen parameters that are applied to the particles in each step. If a particle's velocity is measured at a distance greater than 200 metres, into 0.1. It would be mentioned that the initial velocity = 0.

Step 3.4: Update each particle's location vector. Each particle's position vector is restored involving its speed vector as displayed beneath.

Step 3.5: $t = t + 1$

$$[x_1 y_1 \ldots x_n\,y_n] = [x_1 y_1 \ldots x_n\,y\,] + \vec{Vi} \tag{6}$$

Step 4: Best global bee (WSN) find.

4. Outcomes and Discussions

4.1 Performance Analysis of BA and PSO

The POS and BA algorithms are constructed and are mentioned in this division in order to assess the sensor network deployment. Finding the best locations for the sensor nodes in these situations to maximize coverage and longevity is very difficult. Today, the primary priority for sustainable development is to monitor water contamination or the condition of water resources. Wireless sensor network (WSN) is an appropriate answer to the problem. It is fundamental to convey WSN with the least no. of sensors and expand inclusion because of the significant expense of arrangement and change of battery sensors in the water resource, particularly for submerged asset. Another example is keeping an eye on a hospital wheelchair. In a hospital, there are only so many wheelchairs available, therefore it's crucial to keep an eye on this equipment. Hospitals are sensitive environments, making it impossible to construct (position and change the sensor nodes) at any time or location without causing pollution. Therefore, it's crucial to determine the coverage and longevity of the network as well as the best locations for the sensors when deploying WSN for monitoring medical equipment. The significance of GIS-based optimization techniques for WSN deployment is demonstrated by instances.

For these instances, a 1000 m × 1000 m rectangle is used to replicate the experiment area, where a set number of sensor nodes must be deployed. The same parameters were taken into account for both algorithms and all sensor hubs in this analysis investigation. Additionally, the objective function's (Equation 2) parameters are identical for both algorithms: $\alpha = 0.6; \beta = 0.4$. The region of the recreated area, or 106 m^2, is utilized as the worth of CR in this mathematical examination.

$$n = 20, \text{Rc} = 200 \text{ m}, \qquad E = 5 \text{ J, Rs } 300 \text{ m, and}$$

$$\text{Eelec } 50 \text{ nJ/bit}, \qquad \text{amp } 100 \text{ pJ/bit};$$

Algorithm plan for WSN organization in wellbeing and natural applications is a key stage in the utilization of developmental calculations. A significant kind of algorithm configuration is boundary alignment, which considers factors like populace size and the quantity of emphases expected to choose the proper boundary values. The boundary tuning method is one of the ways for boundary alignment [30]. In this strategy, the boundary values are chosen in the introduction stage and stay consistent while the calculation is running. To adjust the boundaries, two calculations were executed with different boundary values in the mimicked locale. The quantity of emphases, employed honey bees, better honey bees, world class honey bees, observer honey bees, and neighborhood search are the BA boundaries that should be set. It is important to align the PSO calculation's emphasis and molecule considers well as the inactivity weight, speed increase component, and steady boundary. Tables 44.1 and 44.2 display the discoveries of the utilization of the PSO and BA calculations with various qualities.

Table 44.1 Trial and error procedure for calibrating the BA parameters [34]

No. of Run	No. of Iterations	e	m	p	s	dbp	dep	nbp	nep	Value of Fitness
1	20	10	35	100	55	5	5	5	5	0.711
2	20	10	35	100	55	5	5	5	12	0.716
3	20	10	35	100	55	5	5	5	20	0.722
4	20	10	35	100	55	5	5	12	12	0.715
5	20	10	35	100	55	5	5	20	12	0.743
6	20	10	35	100	55	5	5	20	12	0.744
7	20	10	35	100	55	5	10	20	12	0.745
8	20	10	35	100	55	5	12	20	12	0.72
9	20	10	35	100	55	10	20	20	12	0.701
10	20	10	35	100	55	12	12	20	12	0.721
11	20	10	35	100	55	10	10	20	12	0.717
12	20	5	40	100	55	5	10	20	12	0.728
13	20	15	30	100	55	5	10	20	12	0.695
14	20	10	40	100	55	5	10	20	12	0.699
15	20	5	17	50	28	5	10	20	12	0.717
16	20	5	20	50	25	5	10	20	12	0.731
17	20	10	35	100	55	5	10	20	12	0.714
18	50	10	35	100	55	5	10	20	12	0.735
19	70	10	35	100	55	5	10	20	12	0.742
20	100	10	35	100	55	5	10	20	12	0.765 (best)

4.2 Rate of Convergence

Combination rate (Convergence) is one of the vital elements in deciding whether a meta-heuristic calculation is reasonable. This model was decided to assess the adequacy of the two calculations for the execution of an IoT-based network. The places of the sensors were arbitrarily different (equations (3) and (4)) in every emphasis of the BA and PSO calculations while considering the availability requirement and making the MST chart between the sensor hubs. The wellness esteem was then determined by processing the organization inclusion and lifetime. The best wellness esteem that could be acquired inside the populace size of the calculations is the worldwide wellness of every cycle. In 100 cycles of the BA calculation, the worldwide wellness expanded from 0.695 to 0.765, however in 70 emphases of the PSO technique, it diminished from 0.695 to 0.885 (in the best emphasis). The Table shows that the two calculations have a higher pace of union in the underlying emphases and resulting runs. When the worldwide wellness is found, the assembly rate is dialed back and done without a hitch. Notwithstanding, on the grounds that the BA calculation utilizes neighborhood looking through around prevalent and tip top honey bees by observer honey bees, it meets quicker than the PSO technique in the initial ten cycles. As a general rule, PSO's pace of union is smoother than BA's over all cycles. The initial 30 cycles of the PSO calculation bring about union. The particles might have changed fairly with every emphasis, which could be the reason for this issue. Also, this issue exhibits that the PSO strategy performs better compared to BA while managing neighborhood ideal states.

Table 44.2 Trial and error method for calibrating the PSO parameters [35]

No. of Run	No. of Iterations	c1	c2	p	ω	Value of Fitness
1	20	0.5	0.3	100	0.3	0.731
2	20	1.5	0.3	100	0.3	0.736
3	20	2	0.3	100	0.3	0.732
4	20	4	0.3	100	0.3	0.735
5	20	4	1.5	100	0.3	0.763
6	20	4	2	100	0.3	0.764
7	20	4	4	100	0.3	0.765
8	20	2	2	100	0.3	0.752
9	20	2.5	2	100	0.8	0.761
10	20	2	2	100	0.5	0.761
11	20	2	2	100	0.3	0.767
12	20	2	2	100	0.3	0.773
13	20	2	2	100	0.3	0.781
14	20	2	2	100	0.3	0.785
15	20	2	2	100	0.3	0.783
16	20	2	2	100	0.3	0.788
17	20	2	2	100	0.3	0.787
18	30	2	2	100	0.3	0.802
19	50	2	2	100	0.3	0.846
20	70	2	2	100	0.3	**0.885 (best)**

In all the other terms, the PSO converges to considerably higher upsides of the fitness capability in the ensuing emphases than it does in the initial 20 cycles, and the best wellness esteem found by the PSO strategy in the coordination is around 70, which was not found by BA. These discoveries propose that the PSO calculation beat BA as far as the compromise between network inclusion and life span by 5% or so overall.

5. Conclusion

The adaptive optimization algorithms BA and PSO, as well as others, aid in determining the best locations for sensors in wireless networks. Because PSO algorithms are less sophisticated, have a higher rate of convergence than BA, and perform well in terms of repeatability, they aid decision-makers in the health and environmental domains in managing the deployment of wireless networks in respective settings. The persistence of the problem in deployment is what accounts for PSO's improved performance. The PSO technique is appropriate for continuous optimization issues, according to the research. Since the sensors can be found everywhere in the area. Additionally, PSO can optimize the topology of the network and the situation of the sensors while amplifying the compromise among lifetime and inclusion. Additionally, because it is feasible to deliver omnipresent health and environmental services at any point and everywhere with a maximum level of coverage and lifetime, this algorithm aids in the development of IoT-based systems and smart cities.

REFERENCES

1. Ryder, G. (2018). How ICTs can ensure the sustainable management of water and sanitation. Available: https://news.itu.int/icts-ensure-sustainable-management-water-sanitation/.
2. UN.(2015). Sustainable development goals: 17 Goals to transform our world. Available: https://www.un.org/sustainabledevelopment/.
3. Atlam, H. F., Alenezi, A., Alassafi, M. O., & Wills, G. B. (2018). Blockchain with internet of things: Benefits, challenges, and future directions. International Journal of Intelligent Systems and Applications, 9(6), 40–48. https://doi.org/10.5815/ijisa.2018.06.05.
4. Robles, T., Alcarria, R., Martin, D., Navarro, M., Calero, R., Iglesias, S., & Lopez, M. (2014). An IoT based reference architecture for smart water management processes. Journal of Wireless Mobile Networks, Ubiquitous Computing, and Dependable Applications, 6(1), 4–23.
5. Al-Turjman, F., & Alturjman, S. (2018). Context-sensitive access in industrial internet of things (IIoT) healthcare applications. IEEE Transactions on Industrial Informatics, 14(6), 2736– 2744.
6. Dorri, A., Kanhere, S. S., & Jurdak, R. (2016). Blockchain in internet of things: Challenges and solutions. Available: http://arxiv.org/abs/1608.05187. Accessed 25 August 2018.
7. M. Bublitz, F., Oetomo, A., S. Sahu, K., Kuang, A., X. Fadrique, L., E. Velmovitsky, P., ... & P. Morita, P. (2019). Disruptive technologies for environment and health research: an overview of artificial intelligence, blockchain, and internet of things. *International journal of environmental research and public health*, *16*(20), 3847.
8. Oetomo, A.; Kuang, A.; Fadrique, L.; Sahu, K. S.; Nobrega, R. M.; Velmovitsky, P. E.; Bublitz, F. M.; Morita, P. P.(2019) "Emerging Technologies for Climate Change and Health Research"; Technical Report; Health Canada: Ottawa, ON, Canada, 2019.
9. Santillana, M., Nguyen, A. T., Louie, T., Zink, A., Gray, J., Sung, I., & Brownstein, J. S. (2016). Cloud-based electronic health records for real-time, region-specific influenza surveillance. *Scientific reports*, *6*(1), 1-8.
10. Costello, A., Abbas, M., Allen, A., Ball, S., Bell, S., Bellamy, R., & Patterson, C. (2009). Managing the health effects of climate change: lancet and University College London Institute for Global Health Commission. *The lancet*, *373*(9676), 1693-1733.
11. The Intergovernmental Panel on Climate Change. Global Warming of 1.5 C; The Intergovernmental Panel on Climate Change: Geneva, Switzerland, 2017.
12. Banafa, A. (2017). IoT and blockchain convergence: benefits and challenges. *IEEE Internet of Things*, *9*.
13. Urban, M. C.; Pineda, D. (2019) Inside the Black Blocks: A Policymaker's Introduction to Blockchain, Distributed Ledger Technology and the "Internet of Value".
14. Shehryar Hasan. (2019) "We're not PoW or PoS Fans"—Co-founder of Geeq Discusses Consensus Protocols. Available online: https://blockpublisher.com/were-not-pow-or-pos-fans-co-founderof-geeq-discusses-consensus-protocols.
15. Smith, B. Dokchain (2017) Intelligent Automation in Healthcare Transaction Processing. PokitDok.
16. Armonk, N. (2018) IBM Food Trust Expands Blockchain Network to Foster a Safer, More Transparent and Efficient Global Food System. Available online: https://newsroom.ibm.com/2018-10-08-IBM-Food-TrustExpands-Blockchain-Network-to-Foster-a-Safer-More-Transparent-and-Efficient-Global-Food-System-1 (accessed on 12 March 2019).
17. World Economic Forum. (2018) Building Block(chain)s for a Better Planet; World Economic Forum: Geneva, Switzerland.
18. Gilliland, M.; Ivanova, E.(2017) 7 Ways The Blockchain Can Save The Environment and Stop Climate Change. Future Thinkers. Available online: https://futurethinkers.org/blockchain-environment-climatechange/.
19. Kite-Powell, J.(2018) Can Blockchain Technology Save The Environment?. Available online: https://www.forbes.com/sites/jenniferhicks/2018/12/01/can-blockchain-technology-save-theenvironment/#121bceb3233b.
20. Ziegler, S.; Nikoletsea, S.; Krco, S.; Rolim, J.; Fernandes, J. (2015) Internet of Things and crowd sourcing—A paradigm change for the research on the Internet of Things. In Proceedings of the 2015 IEEE 2nd World Forum on Internet of Things (WF-IoT), Milan, Italy, pp. 395–399.
21. Haines, A.; Kovats, R.; Campbell-Lendrum, D.; Corvalan, C. (2006) Climate change and human health: Impacts, vulnerability and public health. Public Health 2006, 120, 585–596.
22. Morawska, L.; Thai, P. K.; Liu, X.; Asumadu-Sakyi, A.; Ayoko, G.; Bartonova, A.; Bedini, A.; Chai, F.; Christensen, B.; Dunbabin, M.; et al. (2018) Applications of low-cost sensing technologies for air quality monitoring and exposure assessment: How far have they gone? Environ. Int., 116, 286–299.

23. Talavera, J. M.; Tobón, L. E.; Gómez, J. A.; Culman, M. A.; Aranda, J. M.; Parra, D. T.; Quiroz, L. A.; Hoyos, A.; Garreta, L. E. (2017) Review of IoT applications in agro-industrial and environmental fields. Comput. Electron. Agric. 2017, 142, 283–297.

24. Tocchi, A.; Roca, V.; Angrisani, L.; Bonavolonta, F.; Moriello, R.S.L.(May 2017) First step towards an IoT implementation of a wireless sensors network for environmental radiation monitoring. In Proceedings of the 2017 IEEE International Instrumentation and Measurement Technology Conference (I2MTC), Turin, Italy, 22–25; pp. 1–6.

25. Truong, T.; Dinh, A.; Wahid, K.(2017) An IoT environmental data collection system for fungal detection in crop fields. In Proceedings of the 2017 IEEE 30th Canadian Conference on Electrical and Computer Engineering (CCECE), Windsor, ON, Canada, pp. 1–4.

26. Kamel Boulos, M. N.; Resch, B.; Crowley, D. N.; Breslin, J. G.; Sohn, G.; Burtner, R.; Pike, W. A.; Jezierski, E.; Chuang, K. Y. (2011) Crowdsourcing, citizen sensing and sensor web technologies for public and environmental health surveillance and crisis management: Trends, OGC standards and application examples. Int. J. Health Geogr. 2011, 10, 67.

27. Kohler, M. D.; Heaton, T. H.; Cheng, M. H. (2013) The community seismic network and quake-catcher network: Enabling structural health monitoring through instrumentation by community participants. Int. Soc. Opt. Photonics, 86923X.

28. Savel, T. G., Foldy, S., & Centers for Disease Control and Prevention. (2012). The role of public health informatics in enhancing public health surveillance. *MMWR Surveill Summ*, *61*(2), 20–24.

29. Panda, S. (2018). Performance improvement of clustered wireless sensor networks using swarm based algorithm. *Wireless Personal Communications*, *103*(3), 2657–2678.

30. Eiben, A. E., & Smit, S. K. (2011). Parameter tuning for configuring and analyzing evolutionary algorithms. *Swarm and Evolutionary Computation*, *1*(1), 19–31.

31. Ma, Z., Huang, W., Bi, W., Gao, H., & Wang, Z.(2018). A master-slave blockchain paradigm and application in digital rights management. China Communications, 15(8), 174–188.

32. Abbasi, M., Yaghmaee, M. H., & Rahnama, F. (2019,April). Internet of Things in agriculture: A survey. In 2019 3rd International Conference on Internet of Things and Applications (IoT) (pp. 1–12). IEEE.

33. Nartey, C., Tchao, E. T., Gadze, J. D., Keelson, E., Klogo, G. S., Kommey, B., & Diawuo, K. (2021). On blockchain and IoT integration platforms: current implementation challenges and future perspectives. Wireless Communications and Mobile Computing, 2021, 1–25.

34. Chen, P. Y. (2017). Effects of microparameters on macroparameters of flat-jointed bonded-particle materials and suggestions on trial-and-error method. Geotechnical and Geological Engineering, 35, 663–677.

35. Hosseiny, H. (2022). Implementation of heuristic search algorithms in the calibration of a river hydraulic model. Environmental Modelling & Software, 157, 105537.

Computer Science Engineering and Emerging Technologies (ICCS-2022) – Prof (Dr.) Rajeev Sobti et al. (eds)
© 2024 Taylor & Francis Group, London, ISBN 978-1-032-52199-2

Chapter · **45**

The Recent Advancements in Security, Privacy and Trust in Mobile and Wireless Communication in the Emerging Economies

David Boohene[1]
Lecturer, Entrepreneurship and Business Sciences,
University of Energy and Natural Resources, Ghana, Sunyani, Bono Region

Thomas Felix K[2]
Assistant Professor, Agricultural Development and Rural Transformation Centre (ADRTC),
Institute for Social and Economic Change, Bengaluru, India

A. Sai Manideep[3]
Assistant professor, Department of Management Studies,
Vignan's Foundation for Science Technology and Research, Guntur, Andhra Pradesh

Pralay Ganguly[4]
Professor, Tourism and hospitality management,
MAKAUT (NSHM Knowledge Campus), Durgapur, W.B

Shouvik Kumar Guha[5]
Assistant Professor (Senior Scale),
The West Bengal National University of Juridical Sciences

P. Naveen Kumar[6]
Department of Agricultural Economics, Amrita School of Agricultural Sciences,
Amrita Vishwa Vidyapeetham University, Coimbatore, India

Abstract: In comparison to wired telecom, the mobile telecommunications industry's explosive expansion has been impacting massive technology diffusion by providing cheaper access costs, potency, and amenity-based interaction. In contrast to normal issues of incapabilities caused by monopolies in wired systems, as cellular phone contests increased globally, enable network operators proposed significantly better services in the areas of informatics, data processing, and interaction. While there are many ways to harness the rise of mobile devices to boost users' productivity, there are also many reasons to be concerned about the confidentiality and safety of personal information managed by these systems. The implementation of technology based on the sense-and-respond model is thought to be an efficient way to accomplish these goals.

Keywords: Security issues, Privacy, Mobile communication

[1]david.boohene@uenr.edu.gh, [2]thomas@isec.ac.in, [3]sn8820@gmail.com, [4]pralay.ganguly@gmail.com, [5]shouvikkumarguha@gmail.com,
[6]p_naveenkumar@cb.amrita.edu

DOI: 10.1201/9781003405580-45

1. Introduction

ICT (information and communication technology) is becoming more and more important in business. The significance of ICT has increased due to both the cutting-edge advancements in wireless communication technology and the companies' propensity to contact their clients through mobile services (Ozer et al., 2013). The fusion of diverse technologies, notably networking, decorum, mobile interaction devices and the Internet, enables mobile communication networks (Pierre, 2001). The concerns of compromising the confidentiality and safety of mobile users through the usage of third-party downloading "apps" are rising as smart phone benefits leverage this convergent technique (Mylonas et al., 2013).

The advancement of what is referred to as the universal and ubiquitous computing paradigm on the Internet has been made possible by these wireless systems, as well as the continuous growth of cutting-edge mobile technology and the related web services. Mobile computing and ubiquitous networking can provide recognizing and tracking capacity to smart homes with identity, personalisation, and other systems for intelligent assembly, among other things. It permits using e-mail, fax, audio and video apps while walking on the sidewalk, driving, and flying (see Fig. 45.1).

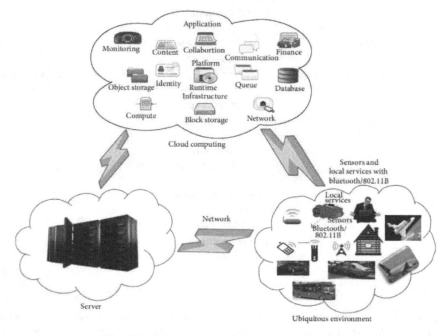

Fig. 45.1 A model for ubiquitous mobile services [22]

Siege, exploration, and assistance consumption from a variety of service and content providers are all made possible by ubiquitous services, allowing users to do so conveniently while on the go. Although it provides many beneficial functional capabilities and advantages, the ubiquitous mobile environment also sadly introduces new and distinct security threats or concerns (2007).

Risk is the likelihood that an issue will arise when a danger is activated by a vulnerability. Threats are strongly correlated with asset attributes, while vulnerabilities are pertinent to security controls (Rabai et al., 2013). Varying conceptions of vulnerability include the inclusion of race and poverty as key determinants, as well as demographic features, interpersonal interactions, access to resources, and the accessibility of assistance. Information technology resources linked to business assets are known as information security assets. Any piece of information with value is referred to as an asset. It encompasses both material and immaterial assets. Assets, threats, and vulnerabilities are taken into account when estimating the loss of resources in a firm caused by cyber security incidents, and the following formula could be used to estimate the risk of an information system's resources: risk is equal to threat, vulnerability, and impact (Rabai et al., 2013).

Various viewpoints can be used to manage the risks and/or issues associated with mobile security.

These viewpoints are covered in the following sections.

1.1 Research Aim

- To make clear and definite inference about the nature of technical evolution and how such assumptions might lead to security concerns,
- To address managerial and technological views on security concerns, and
- To display them using a methodology-focused taxonomy.

2. Literature Review

Mazurczyk et al. (2020): It is anticipated that 5G communications will provide apparently more data bandwidth and greatly enhanced networking ability, culminating in services like massive content broadcasting, teleconferencing, AR, congested area connectivity, smart social contacts, smart buildings, and cities, etc. with unwavering user experiences. Since 5G systems are driving numerous new requirements for various network capabilities, they are currently the focus of interest for academics, industry, and governments worldwide.

Feng et al. (2017): Mobile crowdsourcing (MCS) has become a useful technique for data collection and interpretation as a result of the prevalence of sensor-rich mobile devices. MCS has various benefits over conventional wireless sensor networking, including mobility, scalability, affordability, and human intelligence. MCS still has a lot of issues to work through in regards to security, privacy, and trust, though. The essay explores potential remedies while providing a survey of these difficulties. We examine the characteristics of MCS, pinpoint security risks, and list fundamental needs for a reliable, secure, and secure MCS system. In addition, we evaluate current solutions in light of these demands and contrast their benefits and drawbacks. Finally, we identify any outstanding problems and suggest some lines of further investigation.

Sharma et al. (2020): The emphasis has evolved from simple IoT to smart, linked, and mobile IoT systems as a result of advancements in wireless infrastructure. M-IoT and platforms can provide low intricacy, low-cost, and economical machines, and even crowdsourcing. These gadgets can all be categorized under the umbrella term "M-IoT." Even if there has been a significant positive influence on applications, security, privacy, and trust remain the top issues for such networks, and inadequate implementation of these criteria poses inconsequential risks to M-IoT platforms and devices. Understanding the variety of results that are available to provide a safe and reliable method is crucial.

Kyriazanos et al. (2008): The authors of this research propose a major entity security, confidentiality, and integrity manager in a cross-layer system security platform that handles the following issues: a) the specified prerequisites taking into consideration the various application spaces and their circumstances; b) the varied node abilities that are a distinctive feature of wireless sensor networks; and c) the alteration of the user's context and priorities in circumstances where the end user is heavily occupied. The framework guarantees secure interactions and offers adaptation and flexibility because it is context-aware. To better clarify the functionality of the building pieces making up the streamlined architecture and their relationships, which are also shown through a number of communication charts, the result is offered along with an instance of a medical care case.

Ni et al. (2020): In order to efficiently provide service environments and cloud-storage capacities at the edge of networks, mobile edge caching is a viable solution for mobile networks. Edge caching, however, is exposed to several risks related to security and privacy concerns. The concept is initially described, after which we discuss the major issues surrounding why, where, what, and how to cache. Then, we look at possible cyberthreats such as cache poisoning, pollution, side-channel, and deception assaults, which raise serious issues with mobile users' privacy, security, and confidence in the placement, delivery, and use of content, respectively.

Sicari et al. (2020): This research conducted a thorough analysis of the state-of-the-art for 5G-specific security and privacy measures. Data reliability, access control, non-repudiation, integrity, privacy, policy enforcement are some of the criteria that are covered in further depth. The article also attempts to provide light on future study avenues leading to the development of safe and privacy-conscious 5G systems. In order to do this, the function of developing concepts like Internet of Things, fog computing, and blockchain is examined.

Yarali et al. (2017): This section's major goals are to identify potential risks to 5G mobile communications systems and to examine potential countermeasures that might be used to protect against those attacks. At the beginning of the deployment phase, the architecture of the 5G networks needs to be carefully examined in light of the extensive M2M and D2D connections as well as the new services and applications. Since this new era of mobile communication is intended to combine and connect numerous industries, including the power grid, health, logistics, and production, the switch from 4G to 5G represents more than just a quantitative transformation. Cryptographic methods and other novel security concepts for identity management, cloud, radio access, and infrastructure must be taken into account in order to combat such threats in 5G.

3. Research Methodology

A literature review of security viewpoints has been done to evaluate security awareness in a mobile interaction context. As a result of the demand for an integrated and comprehensive solution framework, security and privacy management provide difficulties for the field of mobile security. The supply chain management paradigm and the security taxonomy are therefore thought to work together to create a thorough knowledge map of pertinent items and problems. Second, risk management in the context of mobile security looks for skills for actual analysis. The choice of an appropriate management method becomes essential to carry out the risk assessment-based performance management in order to properly characterise and display such artefacts and challenges (Li et al., 2009).

Edge platforms are a critical element for the network operator in the ubiquitous computing setting in order to detect and react to the client's quickly shifting needs and offer novel solutions in response. By integrating service platforms with machine settings, network operators and device makers are impacting one another to achieve expanded operational efficiencies (Fellenstein et al., 2005). Since the cloud has the ability to reduce the dispute that emerges during interior laws and regulations while aiming to provide a cogent framework for governance, risk assessment, and conformity, it is crucial to securely integrate the cloud in the edge processes. Infrastructure-as-a-Service, Platform-as-a-Service, and Software-as-a-Service are the 3 distinct models that cloud computing intrinsically mixes. Furthermore, it can also be recommended that the cloud computing stacks include a layer for business process management. In order to comply with government legislation and better comprehend service theft, it develops a one-stop accessible platform for operators so they can give their users who are participating in service delivery clear data in a fair manner.

The strategic sense-and-respond paradigm serves as the foundation for the development and proposed application of the CRASP management approach. By adding both the consumer and provider viewpoints to the general business design proposed by Donovang-Kuhlisch, may also be applied to security in the form of CRASP method (2006). In order to provide the desired qualities, like security, flexibility, and cost-effectiveness, the CRASP management methodology was adopted (Andrade, 2011). The concept of providing IT systems with a greater comprehension of the syntax of what can be viewed underlies the trend toward this sense-and-respond technology (see Fig. 45.2).

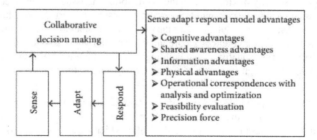

Fig. 45.2 Generic business strategy using the sense–adapt–respond paradigm [22]

By utilising the cutting-edge technology for enduring mobile business growth, the CRASP management approach gives a way to promote innovation and company expansion. Mobile devices of today can no longer be considered to be simple phones. It has gone through a number of stages of development to become a visual version of oneself in the virtual environment, notably working as a medium of communication, a software architecture, and a sense-and-respond framework. The way business is conducted has altered as a result of mobile devices' ability to manage digital information.

3.1 Viewpoints on Controlling Potential Threats in Mobile Services

The popularity of mobile services is fueled by an expanding desire for portability as well as technological possibilities to increase interactivity and expedite corporate activities. In the mobile industry, wireless data security is a crucial concern.

Offering a unified viewpoint may result in security and performance problems (Alanen & Autio 2003). The supply and the demand sides of the economy can both influence the mobile business services industry. However, by using the CRASP approach and taking into account the cloud computing concept for an effective way of executing mobile business service provisioning (Alsudairy & Vasishta 2014), the subsequent categorization of agile-based viewpoints is taken into account in the scenario. As a result, the existing system chooses to function as a hybrid approach that is both CRASP methodology- and demand-based. Implementing this framework enables cost savings for both consumers and providers in a way that ensures the security of the user's information and applications.

Security is a complex idea that is difficult to quantify. Privacy, consistency, and reliability are the three primary security goals that must be maintained in this context (Kim & Moskowitz 2010).

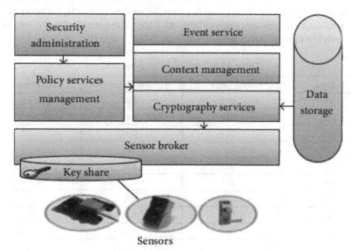

Fig. 45.3 A security viewpoint on sensor insights in mobile system design [22]

We conducted empirical research using information from the self-survey questionnaire to validate our research model. To evaluate the gathered data and the research model, we used SEM. SEM is a statistical approach that combines path analysis with factor analysis. Confirmatory factor analysis is used in the first phase to analyse the measurement model, and structural links between the latent constructs are tested in the second step. However, the former is a requirement for the latter because it is only logical to calculate the structural model when the measurement model shows indications of validity and dependability.

Research Hypothesis

H1: Users' trust would negatively affect how risky using mobile phones is viewed.

H2: The user's perception of danger is significantly associated with threat risk toward utilising a mobile phone.

H3: The user's perception of danger is significantly associated with security risk when using a mobile phone.

H4: The user's perception of danger is significantly associated with privacy risk when using a mobile phone.

4. Results and Discussion

Table 45.1 Reliability and validity through CFA [23]

		CR	AVE	MSV	MaxR(H)	1	2	3	4
1	UTrust	.789	.624	.895	.971				
2	TRisk	0.846	0.731	0.783	0.769	0.863			
3	SRisk	0.968	0.842	0.749	0.953	0.860	0.794		
4	PRisk	0.871	0.776	0.848	0.831	0.849	0.749	0.981	

Note: UTrust – User trust; TRisk – Threat Risk; SRisk – Security risk; PRisk – Privacy risk

The convergent validity of the scales was evaluated when estimating the AVE, which estimates the fraction of the variance of the measurement items that may be allocated by the components underlying the standard errors. Table 45.1 shows that all of the AVEs fall within the range of 0.789 to .968, above the cut-off value of 0.5 and meeting the requirements for convergent validity.

In order to evaluate the discriminant validity, we also considered how a latent construct differed from other constructs. This was confirmed by comparing the square root of AVE to each inter-factor association. The results supported Hair et al. (2006)'s contention that our constructs had discriminant validity in all aspects, with the square root of AVE being found to be larger than the off-diagonal elements in the pertinent rows and columns. Furthermore, as shown in Table 45.1, MSVs is smaller than the average variance (AVEs).

The structural model specifies the emergent connections between the model constructs. Path coefficients and R^2 values are measured as part of the structural model's assessment. Table 45.2 shows the standardised routes in the structural model along with a number of model fit indices. All of the different indices fell inside their assigned ranges.

Table 45.2 Statistical analysis [23]

Indices	CFA Value	SEM Value	Thresholds
X^2	.985	.698	Pval < 0.01
$X^2_{/DF}$	.848	.859	1 > x2
RMS	.659	.935	> .07
GFI	1075.79	10.87	< .03
AGFI	.915	.709	> .04
NFI	.784	.680	< .98
CFI	.689	.915	
TLI	.954	.832	.78
RMSEA	.047	.036	< 0.05 good fit

5. Conclusion

Synthetic indicators provide a fairly accurate and consistent picture of how each country compares to others in terms of creative activity. The most important divergences can be linked to various approaches to research and administration, or to differing interpretations of technological advancement. Regardless of the fact that there are only very few substantial explanatory outliers in the main body of the text, the suggested convergent technique and the preliminary outline of this manuscript are thought to help in the recognition and fabrication of an interconnected conceptual perspective of security risk elements through abstraction, which in turn leads to assessing security risk performance management. It is important to underline that this method is being used to draw attention to and concentrate on the existence of the natural connection between the macrolevel and microlevel contemplation. Mobile services provide macrolevel generalizations, whereas microlevel notations are represented by security threats associated with the use of cutting-edge technology. It is thought that developing and visually displaying this innate connection is key to improving security risk management. To demonstrate or integrate the intuitive grasp of the modality for quicker verifications and to endorse the appropriate responses in the future in order to prevent the possible risk of threats and attacks right at the gatekeeping framework level itself, a kind of sensor theme plan of the sensortic input specifically founded from arbitrary recognition is used by the visual field to construct the interaction between the embedded sensors.

As a result, the integrated data security gatekeeper is a crucial part of managing security, and it is the barrier through which all crucially transferred data passes. It allows the system to impose both integrity and confidentiality guarantees. In order to prevent tampering, the gatekeeper must be responsible for securely storing all cryptographic data and carrying out cryptographic functions, including signing and confirming alerts.

6. Implications

Policymakers and regulators must examine the types of security flaws related to the cloud storage of sensitive data. First and foremost, they should be able to identify the types of sensitive government data that must be segmented according to confidentiality, anonymity, and invisibility; or else, when mobile users attempt to obtain such vital and confidential material using their cell phones and Google apps-type applications, there is a risk that government data will end up on computer servers in other countries and/or involve parties that are outside the legal authority of national courts. Royal Couple (2012). WPA2 is a wireless network security protocol based on the IEEE 802.11i standard. WPA-2 implements the NIST (USA) FIPS 140- 2 compliant AES encryption algorithm and 802.1x-based identification to provide government-grade security.

REFERENCES

1. Mazurczyk, W., Bisson, P., Jover, R. P., Nakao, K., & Cabaj, K. (2020). Challenges and novel solutions for 5G network security, privacy and trust. *IEEE Wireless Communications*, 27(4), 6–7.
2. Feng, W., Yan, Z., Zhang, H., Zeng, K., Xiao, Y., & Hou, Y. T. (2017). A survey on security, privacy, and trust in mobile crowdsourcing. *IEEE Internet of Things Journal*, 5(4), 2971–2992.
3. Sharma, V., You, I., Andersson, K., Palmieri, F., Rehmani, M. H., & Lim, J. (2020). Security, privacy and trust for smart mobile-Internet of Things (M-IoT): A survey. *IEEE access*, 8, 167123–167163.
4. Kyriazanos, D. M., Prasad, N. R., & Patrikakis, C. Z. (2008, September). A security, privacy and trust architecture for wireless sensor networks. In *2008 50th International Symposium ELMAR* (Vol. 2, pp. 523–529). IEEE.
5. Ni, J., Zhang, K., & Vasilakos, A. V. (2020). Security and privacy for mobile edge caching: Challenges and solutions. *IEEE Wireless Communications*, 28(3), 77–83.
6. Özer, A., Argan, M. T., & Argan, M. (2013). The effect of mobile service quality dimensions on customer satisfaction. *Procedia-Social and Behavioral Sciences*, 99, 428–438.
7. Pierre, S. (2001). Mobile computing and ubiquitous networking: concepts, technologies and challenges. *Telematics and Informatics*, 18(2-3), 109–131.
8. Mylonas, A., Kastania, A., & Gritzalis, D. (2013). Delegate the smartphone user? Security awareness in smartphone platforms. *Computers & Security*, 34, 47–66.
9. Leung, A., Sheng, Y., & Cruickshank, H. (2007). The security challenges for mobile ubiquitous services. *Information Security Technical Report*, 12(3), 162–171.
10. Rabai, L. B. A., Jouini, M., Aissa, A. B., & Mili, A. (2013). A cybersecurity model in cloud computing environments. *Journal of King Saud University-Computer and Information Sciences*, 25(1), 63–75.
11. Li, X., Chandra, C., & Shiau, J. Y. (2009). Developing taxonomy and model for security centric supply chain management. *International journal of manufacturing technology and management*, 17(1), 184.
12. Donovang-Kuhlisch, M. (2006, September). Security and privacy within an intelligent sensor grid. In *11th International Commands and Control Research and Technology Symposium. September* (pp. 26–28).
13. Andrade, A. (2011). *Strong mobile authentication in single sign-on systems* (Master's thesis).
14. Hair, J. F., Black, W. C., & Babin, B. J. (2006). Anderson, R. E., & Tatham, R. L. Multivariate data analysis.
15. King, N. J., & Raja, V. T. (2012). Protecting the privacy and security of sensitive customer data in the cloud. *Computer Law & Security Review*, 28(3), 308–319.
16. Alsudairy, M. A. T., & Vasista, T. G. K. (2014, May). CRASP—a strategic methodology perspective for sustainable value chain management. In Proceedings of the 23rd IBIMA Conference.
17. Alanen, J., & Autio, E. (2003). Mobile business services: A strategic perspective. In *Mobile commerce: technology, theory and applications* (pp. 162-184). IGI Global.
18. Kim, A., & Moskowitz, I. S. (2010). *Incentivized cloud computing: a principal agent solution to the cloud computing dilemma*. Naval Research Lab Washington DC Information Technology Div.
19. Fellenstein, C., Joseph, J., Lim, D., & D'orsay, J. C. (2005). On-Demand Business: Network Challenges in a Global Pervasive Ecosystem. *Mobile, Wireless, and Sensor Networks: Technology, Applications, and Future Directions*, 381–408.
20. Sicari, S., Rizzardi, A., & Coen-Porisini, A. (2020). 5G in the internet of things era: an overview on security and privacy challenges. *Computer Networks*, 179, 107345.
21. Yarali, A., Yedla, R., Almalki, S., Covey, K., & Almohana, M. (2017). Security, Privacy & Trust in 5G Wireless Mobile Communications. In *5G mobile: From research and innovations to deployment aspects* (pp. 147-162). Nova Science Publishers, Inc.
22. https://www.researchgate.net/publication/282239909/figure/fig3/AS:325630408314883@1454647747991/A-mobile-ubiquitous-services-scenario-5.png Al Sudiary, M. A. T. (2015). Perspectives of mangi mobile service security risks
23. Othman, N. B., Hussein, H. B., Salleh, S. B. M., & Wahid, H. B. A. (2014). Resilience scale: Exploration of items validity and reliability (first-order cfa model). In The 2014 WEI International Academic Conference Proceedings. Bali, Indonesia. The West EastInstitute (Vol. 24, pp. 24–33).

Computer Science Engineering and Emerging Technologies (ICCS-2022) – Prof (Dr.) Rajeev Sobti et al. (eds)
© 2024 Taylor & Francis Group, London, ISBN 978-1-032-52199-2

Chapter

46

Intelligent Computing Techniques for The House Price Prediction Model: A Review

Sumit Kumar[1]

Research Scholar, School of Computer Science and Engineering,
Lovely Professional University Phagwara, Punjab, India

Vijay Kumar Garg[2]

Associate Professor, School of Computer Science and Engineering,
Lovely Professional University Phagwara, Punjab, India

Abstract: Well-known approaches for predicting home prices include intelligent computing techniques and knowledge-based systems. This essay is based on a survey of several artificial intelligence techniques for predicting home prices. The primary focus is on examining the vicinity of the outdoor playground at the college, the hospital, and the school. The most popular research-related technology is based on intelligent computing methods, including ML, SVR, SVM, RF, k-nearest neighbors, and flask framework knowledge-based. Various techniques and its implementation has been discussed in this review in regards to their benefits and drawbacks.

Keywords: Decision tree regression, Machine learning, ANN, K-NN, SVR, SVM, RF, Other intelligent technologies

1. Introduction

Today, the house is a needful asset to human life along with the house. Human needs some other such as food, water, and others. These days house demand increases more. People need houses. They always find the best house for them. Humans are starting their investment in house and properties. People want to house them and their families. Prediction models and machine learning models may both be used to anticipate home prices. ML models include LR, ANN, SVR, and RFM. With the help of these models, humans can easily find out the best houses according to location or other assets. Humans can easily find knowledge and information about homes and budgets for their homes. According to the analysis, Machine learning models are used to forecast and influence the factors that impact home values. This review paper is on the prediction of house prices according to the model of ML and analyzing assets primarily used and that effect house prices. In this paper, we are applying the ML Model to attributes such as area, location, market, road, hospital, and others. In this paper, we are discussing of ML Model used in previous studies to predict house prices.

ML plays a very crucial role in this field. Intelligent computing techniques such as K-NN, Linear Regression, SVR, SVM, Random-forest, flask framework, etc. With the help of these techniques, we can find the knowledge of house prices and predict a particular area according to accuracy. Various housing issues were examined by (Quang Truong, Minh Nguyen, Hy Dang, and Bo Mei 2019). prices prediction [1] with the help of machine learning techniques. They found the RSMLE is 0.14969.(Hujia Yu and Jiafu Wu 2016) applied the technique of Real estate price prediction using the SVR-based forecasting approach: SVM was effectively used for classification, clustering, and forecasting In paper [3]

[1]sk1761993@gmail.com, [2]vijay.garg@lpu.co.in

DOI: 10.1201/9781003405580-46

The experimental results and calculations of the Mean Absolute Error, Root Mean Squared Error, and Mean Absolute Percentage Error were washed impetus for using this strategy, and the SVR approach was a crucial tool for predicting real estate values. The paper may be expanded by predicting house resale value using the aforementioned methods. The author found Gradient Boosting Regression with an accuracy score of 91.77%. (M. Vani Pujitha 2019). For multi-linearity or interactions explanatory factors, the hedonic pricing model in property evaluation may be limited in its ability to predict prices accurately. The comprehensive examination of the hybrid PSO-Bagging-ANNs model was indicated by all three models. In terms of R (0.970), RMSE (3,390,016 NTD), MAE (2,273,866 NTD), and MAPE (11.59%), the bagging-ANNs model beat the control. (Chou, J.S., Troung, D.N., and Fleshman, D.B. 2022). In Paper [4] (Dr. M. Thamarai 2020) used a machine learning tool utilized in the work is Scikit-Learn. Users of this work can anticipate both the price and the supply of dwellings in the city. Two methods of Home price predictions were made using DTR and MLR. In paper [5] through the use of linear regression and particle swarm optimization techniques, the study's prediction of housing prices has been put to the test in many different ways. The best settings produced the lowest prediction error: Taufiq et. al. used a model of 1800 particles, 700 iterations, and inertia weights of 0.4 and 0.8 (RMSE) of 14.186 IDR.). This paper utilizes a neural network [7] to estimate housing price predictions. The public and decision-makers are very concerned about house price forecasts. As the housing market in China is increasing quickly, we focused on the topic in the current study utilizing data on monthly home prices from 89 major Chinese cities from June 2010 through May 2019. (Wei and Cao, 2017; Xu, 2018a; 2018c). For many decision-makers, the ability to apply our empirical technique for housing price forecasts in other Chinese cities or other countries or areas is crucial Brandt and Bessler, 1983 (Xiaojie Xu and Yun Zhang 2021). The paper [15] uses some machine-learning techniques to build a geographic model for Beijing housing costs based on a significant collection of house attributes acquired from Lianjia, Co. Six machine learning algorithms—XGboost, bagging, boosting, lasso, Ridge, and Random Forest—as well as the traditional linear regression model and two ensembles, are specifically examined (boosting plus ridge and bagging plus ridge.) The findings demonstrated the limitations of the traditional linear regression approach or the Hedonic model in managing the nonlinearity of real estate prices and attributes. (Yan, Z. and Zong, L.)

2. Objectives and Scope of the Study

To study what the technologies implemented and to find out the research gap present. After doing the research, we can fill the research gap which is created by multiple states' house prices predicted and can find the best house in different states according to the prices, location, and area. This technology can help people who are looking for the best house for them. They can easily find the best house and check the prices of the house according to the location and state. We can find the house in the future according to the best location.

3. Background Knowledge

3.1 Machine Learning

ML is the artificial tool for using the prediction of the model. In computer science, ML is the trending technology. To analyze data, we can use ML technology. Machine Learning gives you the idea to implement the thing everywhere. A human can understand raw data for analysis with the help of ML. ML is a branch of Artificial Intelligent. Human Can easily understand the concept of ML algorithms and detect the data. Type of ML is Supervised Learning and Unsupervised Learning. We use labeled data to work on supervised learning. We use unlabeled data for performing unsupervised learning.

3.2 Linear Regression

The most widely used ML algorithm is LR. This statistical approach is employed in predictive analysis. For actual values or numerical values like prices, sales, ages, etc., it makes predictions. It displays how the dependent and independent y variables are related. The link between the dependent variable's value and the independent variable is demonstrated through linear regression

3.3 Support Vector Machine

Support The algorithm for supervised learning is vector regression. Discrete values can be predicted using it. It adheres to the SVM algorithm's basic principles. For the finest fit line, it is utilized. Support Vector Machine Algorithm work for the best hyperplane line which works on the maximum number of points in this algorithm, output comes from the real number which can-not predicts easily. Because of the real number output, it can be infinite possibilities. In this diagram fit line is the hyperplane line. It is used for the maximum number of points. It tries to hold the best fil line maximum number point. The support Vector Machine Algorithm does not fit a large amount of data.

3.4 Decision Tree Regression

The decision tree regression model examines the tree's characteristics and alters them into a structure that may be used to forecast the outcome of the continuous meaningful output. It has root nodes, inner nodes, and leaf nodes as its three different node kinds. The maximum depth and minimum depth of the graph are learning the decision tree regression model. It performs maximum operations and data analysis.

3.5 Support Vector Regression

The algorithm for supervised learning is support vector regression. Discrete values can be predicted using it. It adheres to the SVM algorithm's basic principles. For the finest fit line, it is utilized. Support Vector Machine Algorithm works for the best hyperplane line which works on the maximum number of points in this algorithm, output comes from the real number which can-not predicts easily.

Because of the real number output, it can be infinite possibilities. In this diagram fit line is the hyperplane line. It is used for the maximum number of points. It tries to hold the best fil line maximum number point. The support Vector Machine Algorithm does not fit a large amount of data

4. Literature Review

Better machine learning was used by Truong et. al. to examine various home price estimate algorithms in this study [1]. This study looks at several house price forecasting techniques. Three distinct machine learning strategies—The performance of three ML algorithms - RF, XGBoost, LightGBM - and two others - HR and Stacked Generalisation Regression - are compared and examined. Since the data set has to be adjusted numerous times, it takes a while to complete. Stacked Generalisation and Hybrid Regression compared to the three classical ML techniques Both the training dataset and the test dataset showed the potential of regression without the need for complex implementation or optimization. HR can be considered the model for the training set when the RSMLE is 0.14969, as Random Forest is shown to overfit.

The authors of this paper, Nor Hasbiah Ubaidullah, Ismail Ibrahim, Shuzlina Abdul Rahman, nor Hamizah Zulkifley [2], have studied and examined current studies on the major variables affecting home prices as well as the data mining techniques used to anticipate home values. The characteristics employed by past studies to estimate a property price using various prediction algorithms were the subject of this study. The survey's results together show the capability to predict home prices, using SVR, ANN, and XGBoost. These models, which significantly raise housing prices, were developed using a range of input factors. The ultimate objective of research was assisting other academics in developing a useful model that can accurately predict home prices.

The comparison authors of this paper, Madhuri et. al. primarily focuses on different ML techniques for house price prediction analysis, such as MLR, ridge regression, LASSO regression, ENR, ADA, BR, and gradient boosting [3]. The results of the above experiment show that the gradient boosting strategy has a high accuracy value compared to all other property price estimation algorithms. The accuracy value of the algorithm is calculated using the MS Error and RMS Error. After contrasting all available techniques, the author has found Gradient Boosting Regression with an accuracy score of 91.77%.

Thamarai et. al. [4] used machine learning-based housing price forecast algorithm. The simplest ML techniques - decision tree classifier, DTR, and MLR - are used in this article. Users of this work can predict the cost and availability of housing in the city. Two techniques - DTR and MLR - were used to predict housing prices.

Taufiq et. al. created the home price projection model for this study [5]. with the application of particle swarm checking and LR methods. Kelurahan Karang Besuki, Tunggulwulung, Lowokwaru, Puncak Trikora, Sumbersari, Dinoyo, and Manggar are some of the sites that are replicated. The M-1 parameter is the best choice for the most accurate prediction, as shown by results of particle, iteration, and inertial weight tests. M-1 reflects the Karang Besuki area. The error prediction numbers are still high for the alternative model.

Gao et. al. study focuses on location-centered housing price prediction [6]. The usage of MTL for the issue of predicting property prices has been thoroughly researched by the author of this study. Depending on different dwelling features, they came up with two different types of task-building methods. Three broad MTL-based approaches were used, each with a different regularisation. Through using extensive experimental research, we first showed how MTL-based modeling can significantly improve overall home price performance forecasting. We have shown how the MTL formulation for the issue of housing price prediction benefits from the variety of task descriptions.

The authors of this article, Xu et. al. [7], suggested utilizing neural networks to estimate housing price predictions. To develop perspectives on housing price trends and conduct policy research, the models can be employed alone or in conjunction with basic forecasting techniques (Wei and Cao, 2017; Xu, 2018a; 2018c). For many decision-makers, the ability to apply our empirical technique for housing price forecasts in other Chinese cities or other countries or areas is crucial (Brandt and Bessler, 1983).

The housing price projection model for this article was developed by Imran et. al. [8]. using the eleven algorithms for machine learning. The data collected in this study is used to generate the first scientific home dataset for the Pakistani housing market. Deep learning neural network methods and machine learning support vector regression were used to get the price that was the closest to the exchange rate. The accuracy of the different algorithms is compared and the best method is selected.

Huang et. al. [9] created a trustworthy model for house prediction. The sting of home prices using a network of spatial transformers, heterogeneous data, Google satellite map, and a shared self-attention mechanism. The proposed model outperforms competing models in all experiments, due to the advantages of these tactics.

Using linear regression and particle swarm optimization, Taufiq et. al. [10] carried out several tests to predict house prices. To forecast home values, the algorithm divides the NJOP data of 9 properties into 7 models, each of which represents a distinct region. Future research will concentrate on using more data and reducing error prediction values to provide better outcomes by appl. ng a variety of approaches that match the time-series data.

Varma et. al. [11] developed a technique to give a correct forecast of property prices. System makes extensive use of Boosted Regression, Forest Regression, and Linear Regression. The effectiveness of the algorithm has increased significantly with the use of neural networks. The addition of larger cities to the database will allow our clients to look at more properties, get more precise information, and eventually arrive at the correct assessment, which might be a huge boost in the future.

The Phan et. al. [12] study searches for useful techniques for forecasting housing values. It also provides details regarding the Melbourne property market. The first processing and creation of a clean dataset ready for analysis from the raw data. The data is then modified and reduced using stepwise and PCA techniques. The usage and assessment of many tactics lead to the optimal solution.

This study looks for useful examples. Xu et. al. [13] now have access to a variety of data sources and affordable analysis methods thanks to the big data era. By utilizing crawler technology, we can fully leverage Internet resources to compile a range of used housing statistics in China's top cities. We discovered that a drop in the cost of second-hand homes is associated with an increase in longitude. We converted the text from the description of the secondhand house into a text matrix using the natural language analysis approach so that it could be used as a data type for modeling. The word vectors were included in the regression. Using a model, supporting systems, and other elements, we can statistically study salespeople's thinking. Then, an empirical study on second-hand real estate data in China's first-tier cities shows that ML models perform better than basic models such as RF, AdaBoost, GBDT, LightGBM, and XGBoost and meta-models like BPNN in fitting and forecasting traditional multiple linear regression. The assessment quality is significantly improved by the stacking model's superior performance, which also supports the market for used houses' long-term, healthy growth of the data utilized in the modeling process.

Real estate is one of a family's most valuable investment assets, according to Chou et. al. [14]. In their initial incarnations, four ML techniques - specifically ANN, SVR, CART, and LR - were used. The results showed that among the basic and ensemble models, the ANNs and the bagging ANN gave the best predictive performance. The PSO-Bagging-ANNs hybrid model was then used to compare the ANN with Bagging ANN. The PSO-Bagging-ANNs model outperformed the control in terms of R (0.970), RMSE (3,390,016 NTD), MAE (2,273,866 NTD), and MAPE (11.59%), as revealed by the thorough analysis of all three models. Comparison of the recommended PSObagging ANNs to other models that had been published before demonstrated their exceptional prediction performance neighborhood views and building orientation are crucial elements in predicting housing costs.

Yan et. al. [15] use some machine learning techniques to build a geographic model for housing costs in Beijing built utilising a significant amount of data on dwelling characteristics gathered by Lianjia, Co. Six ML algorithms - XGboost, Bagging, Boosting, Lasso, Ridge, and RF - as well as the traditional linear regression model and two ensembles, are specifically addressed (Boosting and Ridge and Bagging and Ridge). For a comprehensive study, the effectiveness of different approaches is tested. Despite a small error, the results have shown that XGBoost performs better than other machine learning models, as evidenced by its high performance in tuning and prediction. Second, a performance comparison of different ML techniques, including SVMs and ANNs. In this review paper, they check the prices of houses by area and location, nearby shops, schools, colleges, outdoor facilities, parks, shopping malls, and police stations, hospitals.

S. No.	Literature Survey Summary		
	Author	Algorithm Used	Accuracy
1.	Truong et. al. (2019)	Random Forest, XGBoost, and LightGBM	92.23%
2.	Zulkifley et. al. (2020)	SVR, ANN, and XGBoost	—
3.	Madhuri et. al. (2019)	Such as multiple linear regression, LASSO regression, ridge regression, elastic net regression, and	91.77%
4.	Thamarai et. al. (2020)	Multiple linear regression, choice tree regression, and decision tree classifier	—
5.	Alfiyatin et. al.	Particle swarm optimization and linear regression forecast models	—
6.	Gao et. al. (2022)	MTL Model	82%
7.	Gao et. al. (2021)	Single-neuron network model	—
8.	Imran et. al. (2021)	Deep learning neural network methods and machine learning support vector regression	90.76%
9.	Wang et. al.	Machine learning and Deep Learning	—
10.	Alfiyatin et. al. (2017)	Linear Regression	
11.	Varma et. al. (2018)	Boosted regression, forest regression, and linear regression	84%
12.	Phan et. al. (2018)	PCA technique and SVM Model	—
13	L. Xu et. al. (2021)	Base models RF, AdaBoost, GBDT, LightGBM, and XGBoost, as well as meta-models BPNN	87.93%
14.	Fleshman et. al. (2022)	ANNs, SVR, CART, and LR	90.46%

5. Conclusion

In this paper, we have given an overview of the various technologies for smart computing. From this review work, we can see that many researchers have used the combined technology ANN-KNN, SVM-SVR, and Linear Regression-Random Forest and found the best accuracy using the combination of technologies. These technologies are applied to the house These technologies can be used to build price prediction models and measure their accuracy. We found that Support Vector Machines (SVM), ANN and KNN are the most commonly used algorithms for this topic.

REFERENCES

1. Housing Price Prediction using Improved Machine Learning Techniques: A 2019 International Conference on Identification, Information and Knowledge in the Internet of Things paper by Quang Truong, Minh Nguyen, Hy Dang, and Bo Mei (IIKI2019))
2. I. J. Modern Education and Computer Science, 2020, Nor Hamizah Zulkifley, Shuzlina Abdul Rahman, Nor Hasbiah Ubaidullah, and Ismail Ibrahim, "House Price Prediction Using a Machine Learning Model: A Survey of Literature."
3. House Price Prediction Using Regression Techniques: A Comparative Study—IEEE 6th International Conference on Smart Structures and Systems, CH. Raga Madhuri, Anuradha G, and M. Vani Pujitha ICSSS 2019
4. House Price Prediction Modeling Using Machine Learning by Drs. M. Thamarai and S. P. Malarvizhi - I.J. Information Engineering and Electronic Business, 2020
5. International Journal of Advanced Computer Science and Applications paper by Adyen Nur Alfiyatin, Hilman Taufiq, Ruth Ema Febrita, and Wayan Firdaus Mahmudy titled "Modeling House Price Prediction Using Regression Analysis and Particle Swarm Optimization"

6. Location-Centered House Price Prediction: A Multi-Task Learning Approach by Guanglian Gao, Zhifeng Bao, Jie Cao, A. K. Qin, and Timos Sellis is published in ACM Transactions on Intelligent Systems and Technology, Vol. 13, No. 2, Article 32. Date of publication: January 2022

7. House price predictions using neural networks by Xiaojie Xu and Yun Zhang were published in Intelligent Systems with Applications in 2021.

8. Waqar, M., Imran, I., and Zaman, A., 2021. Using machine learning algorithms to anticipate home prices: the instance of housing data in Islamabad. pp. 11–23 in Soft Computing and Machine Intelligence, 1(1).

9. A study from 2021 by Wang, P.Y., Chen, C.T., Su, J.W., Wang, T.Y., and Huang, S.H. A combined self-attention mechanism and heterogeneous data analysis are both used in the deep learning model for predicting home prices. IEEE Access, 9, pages 55244–55259

10. A. N. Alfiyatin, R. E. Febrita, H. Taufiq, and W.F. Mahmudy, 2017. Case study: Malang, East Java, Indonesia, modeling the forecast of housing prices using regression analysis and particle swarm optimization. Advanced Computer Science and Applications International Journal, 8 (10).

11. A. Varma, A. Sarma, S. Doshi, and R. Nair, April 2018. using neural networks and machine learning to anticipate home prices. 2018 saw the second iteration of the international conference on creative computing and communication technologies (ICICCT) (pp. 1936–1939). IEEE.

12. T. D. Phan, December 2018. Machine learning algorithms used to anticipate housing prices: The case of Melbourne, Australia. An international conference on data engineering and machine learning was held in 2018. (pp. 35–42). IEEE.

13. L. Xu and Z. Li, 2021. a new machine learning-based evaluation methodology for second-hand housing costs in China's top cities. 617–637 in Computational Economics, 57(2).

14. Fleshman, D.B., Truong, D.N., and Chou, J.S. 2022 For preliminary real estate price predictions, compare machine learning methods. Pages. 1–36 in Journal of Housing and the Built Environment.

15. 2020, July. Yan, Z., and Zong, L. Using machine learning methods, Beijing home prices may be predicted spatially. In Proceedings of the 2020 3rd International Conference on Big Data and Artificial Intelligence and 2020 4th High-Performance Computing and Cluster Technologies Conference (pp. 64–71).

Computer Science Engineering and Emerging Technologies (ICCS-2022) – Prof (Dr.) Rajeev Sobti et al. (eds)
© *2024 Taylor & Francis Group, London, ISBN 978-1-032-52199-2*

Chapter **47**

An Empirical Evaluation of Machine Learning Image Augmentation Models from a Pragmatic Perspective

Dipen Saini[1], Rahul Malik[2]

School of Computer Science and Engineering, Lovely Professional University, Punjab, India

Abstract: The process of designing models for image augmentation involves multiple domains of work, including the selection of augmentation operations, the pre-processing of images for augmentation, the selection of features that will lead to effective augmentation, and the application of augmentation operators to images. Researchers have suggested a wide variety of methods that are based on machine learning and bio-inspiration, and each of these methods has a distinct set of dependencies and configurations, both within and outside of the system. Methods such as the Genetic Algorithm (GA) are highly generic but offer only moderate levels of efficiency. This is in contrast to ensemble methods, which are reconfigured at the application level and have higher levels of both complexity and accuracy. Because of this, it can be difficult for researchers and system designers to select the most appropriate augmentation Models for the context-specific deployments they are working on. As a consequence of this, they frequently validate several models in order to ensure that they work with their use cases. This contributes to the overall delay and expense of the deployments that are being supported. This text offers a comprehensive analysis of the existing machine learning image augmentation models in order to address these issues. Specifically, it examines these models in terms of their contextual nuances, functionality-specific benefits, deployment-specific drawbacks, internal and external reconfiguration needs, and application-specific future scopes. In light of the information presented here, readers will be able to zero in on the appropriate function models for their particular use cases. In addition to that, this piece of writing compares and contrasts the qualitative performance metrics of the models, such as the models' levels of accuracy and precision, as well as their computational complexity, deployment costs, and scalability capacities. Readers will be able to select the most appropriate models for the performance requirements of their individual use cases with the assistance of these comparisons.

Keywords: Image, Augmentation, Machine, Learning, Convolutional, Bioinspired, Accuracy, Precision, Complexity

1. Introduction

Convolutional neural networks (CNNs) have risen to popularity as the most effective method for classifying images. CNN's existing models still have significant issues. It's typical for datasets to lack training samples or have an uneven class composition (Takahashi, et al., 2019). Creating a large collection of images requires time and resources. Numerous data augmentation strategies have been presented. Using generative adversarial networks (Shen,et al., 2022) to randomly crop, flip, delete, and enhance images. Data augmentation techniques move, rotate, or resize data. Despite varying lighting and exposure conditions, the brightness and contrast of the final image remain unaffected. Since digital cameras employ an imaging process, many image augmentation techniques raise the image's brightness or contrast.

Numerous deep-learning models have been developed (Shang et al., 2022). Also improving are training methods (Zhang et al., 2020). The idea of deep learning has various unanswered problems. Interpretation issues may impede the development

[1]er.dipensaini@gmail.com, [2]rahul.23360@lpu.co.in

DOI: 10.1201/9781003405580-47

of deep learning models. Scientists are required to generalize and optimize. Despite vast volumes of data, Deep CNNs cannot transfer their performance from the known training set to the unknown test data. Caused by overfitting. Larger models compare more favourably (Wang et al., 2022), but in practice, precision overcomes velocity. Both expressive feature extraction and implicit data mining are impacted by image noise. Its use in medical diagnostics (Chen et al., 2022) and autonomous driving systems (Du et al., 2022) is constrained by the lack of training data and the necessity for real-time performance.

Data augmentation, such as horizontal flipping, random cropping, size modification, and noise disruption, may aid deep CNNs in avoiding overfitting. Increasing the number, quality, and variety of the dataset may improve model performance. Sample pairing, which produces a new image from the original by superimposing a random image from the training set, is a simple yet effective method for enhancing data for image classification. Their unique nature precludes their general use. Smart and neural augmentations minimize network error and teach neural networks to synthesize new samples. Generative Adversarial Networks have enabled the study of data augmentation (GANs). A number of studies indicate that training deep CNNs using adversarial GAN samples may enhance activation function and generalization. GANs educate and converge slowly. In experiments on data augmentation, researchers used underlying networks to rotate, flip, resize, and add random noise to images. Lengthening the test increases segmentation precision and assesses the uncertainty of the outcome. Several data augmentation techniques have been developed by deep learning, but current research focuses on how to employ them effectively. In order to prevent incorrect augmentations, sounds are added to implicitly enhanced samples. These tactics may increase the applicability of the model, while it is unclear how noise affects the decision boundary. Data augmentation helps approximate the input spaces of the actual world. A larger input space may enhance the local or global minimum of the model. Since deep CNNs continue to "overfit," the effect of data augmentations on optimization and generalization must be re-evaluated. These models may be improved using machine learning techniques, which are explained in the next section.

2. In-depth Review of Image Augmentation Models

A wide variety of machine-learning-based techniques are proposed for the augmentation of images, and each of them vary in terms of their quantitative performance measures, and qualitative characteristics. Deep convolutional neural networks (CNNs) have shown promising results when processing images (Takahashi, et al., 2019). Their eloquence might come out as being too exact. Existing data sets may be improved using techniques for data augmentation without the introduction of unintended bias. Modern CNN designs with more parameters make it useless to apply traditional data augmentation techniques.

Table 47.1 Literature survey

Sr. No	Authors	Model	Findings
1	Takahashi, et al., 2019	RI CAP	The merging of image class labels in RICAP is advantageous for soft labels. The authors of the paper evaluated and compared RICAP with contemporary CNNs (such as shake-shake regularization).
2	Shen, et al., 2022	Cut Mix	The initial step is to locate buildings using a U-Net. In the second step's evaluation of the building's damage, the weights from the network from the preceding stage are applied. In the next step, images captured before and after a disaster are delivered independently into a two-branch multiscale U-Net. The CutMix data augmentation tool is useful when working with challenging issues.
3	Xu, et al., 2020	GAN	EF-GANs integrate geometry modification techniques with GANs to enhance EM images. First, researchers broaden the color palette of the source photos since an EM image's color has no influence on the identification assigned to it. Second, researchers train an EF-GAN to generate fresh EM images using better images.
4	Zhu, et at., 2020	SA GAN	First, a better Self-Attention Generative Adversarial Network generates brand-new X-ray images of limited goods (SAGAN). Then, researchers demonstrate how to use a technique based on Cycle GAN to transform common images into X-rays.
5	Yamashita, et al., 2021	RST	A data augmentation method that generates domain-independent visual representations by using random style transfer (RST) from non-medical style sources like paintings may be beneficial for computational pathology.

Sr. No	Authors	Model	Findings
6	Kim, et al., 2021	LA CNN	a brand-new data augmentation technique called Local Augment (LA) is presented. LA alters the local bias attribute to produce distinctive augmented images and increase the network's augmentation effectiveness
7	Shang, et al., 2022	ITSA MMP	ITSA starts by gradually accumulating data while using a spatial-spectral grouping technique (SRCS). High-quality additions to a sample pool are found using the Box-plot for Representative Sample Selection (BPRSS) method (ASS).
8	Zhang, et al., 2020	Big Aug	The findings demonstrate that BigAug outperforms "shallower" stacked, BigAug's performance on an unknown domain exceeds "deeper" stacked when trained on relatively small datasets, and BigAug outperforms conventional augmentation when trained on relatively large datasets.
9	Nesteruk, et al., 2022	XAug	Researchers examine Xtreme Augment (XAug), an automated technique for cataloguing and improving enormous collections of photographs.
10	Wang, et al., 2022	SCNN	Introduces CutMix, a technique for Siamese CNN (SCNN) that allows pairings of data from the same or different classes to be added to training datasets. New training samples may be produced by adding fresh data to an already existing collection.
11	Chen, et al., 2022	PNet	Prototypical networks (P-Nets) are a potent few-shot learning technique for identifying species in forests. Due to a paucity of training data, overfitting still affects few-shot classifiers, which makes it difficult to train correct models.
14	Kim, et al., 2021	UNet	This paper proposes a data augmentation strategy for visual surveillance to enhance performance while maintaining their current network. In deep learning data augmentation methods, object recognition and image categorization are ubiquitous.
13	Pan, et al., 2020	SSFA	Researchers present a self-supervised feature augmentation (SSFA) network in this paper that can use sampled photographs as inputs and produce features that are similar to those in upscaled images.
14	Chen, et al., 2022	IAug	Researchers propose Instance-level change Augmentation (IAug) as a technique for using generative adversarial training to create bitemporal images that involve changes involving numerous structures. Building computer models are composited onto image backgrounds by IAug.
15	Nalepa, et al., 2022	DNN	The authors recommend augmenting hyperspectral data during deep network inference's test phase. The authors of the research suggest two ways to enhance training and exams.
16	Luo, et al., 2021	Deep Lab	This model is capable of picking up on subtle changes in subpixel-level remote sensing images. The generalization skills of the network are assessed using the satellite change detection datasets from Landsat 8, Google Earth, and Onera
17	Xia, et al., 2021	MDCF	Researchers develop a straightforward Random Erasing approach to improve cloud/snow identification.

3. Statistical Analysis and Comparison

According to the assessment, it can be shown that the functionality and deployment capabilities of the current models vary greatly. A comparison of the studied models' levels of accuracy (A), precision (P), delay (D), computational complexity (CC), and scalability (S) is included in this section. Researchers assess accuracy and precision levels directly, while latency, computing complexity, and scalability values are approximated using fuzzy ranges of Low (L), Medium (M), High (H), and Very High (VH), depending on their performance characteristics. Using this approach, Table 47.1's comparison is as follows.

Table 47.2 Comparison of various models

Model	A	P	D	CC	S
RI CAP (Takahashi, et al., 2019)	97.3	88.7	M	L	H
Cut Mix (Shen, et al., 2022)	97.8	91.7	H	M	VH
GAN (Xu, et al., 2020)	98.5	89.4	VH	H	VH
SA GAN (Zhu, et at., 2020)	93.8	89.6	VH	H	VH

Model	A	P	D	CC	S
RST (Yamashita, et al., 2021)	98.9	92.1	L	L	H
LA CNN (Kim, et al., 2021)	99.1	91	H	H	H
ITSA MMP (Shang,et al., 2022)	76.5	66	M	H	M
Big Aug (Zhang, et al., 2020)	65.4	72.7	H	M	H
XAug (Nesteruk,et al., 2022)	91	84.4	M	L	VH
SCNN (Wang, et al., 2022)	90.4	88.2	H	H	H
PNet (Chen, et al., 2022)	99.2	92	L	M	VH
UNet (Kim,et al., 2021)	89.4	82.3	H	VH	H
SSFA (Pan, et al.,2020)	87.5	87	M	H	M
IAug (Chen, et al., 2022)	99.5	92.1	L	L	VH
DNN (Nalepa, et al., 2022)	98.6	89.5	H	H	H
Deep Lab (Luo,et al., 2021)	95.1	88.4	H	H	M
MDCF (Xia, et al., 2021)	97.2	90.7	VH	M	H

4. Conclusion

This piece of writing examined a broad range of different augmentation models and compared them in terms of the statistical parameter sets that they used. IAug (Chen,et al.,2022), PNet(Chen,et al., 2022), LA CNN(Kim,et al.,2021), RST(Yamashita,et al.,2021), DNN (Nalepa,et al.,2022), GAN(Xu,et al.,2020), and ENC DEC (Du,et al.,2022) were shown to exhibit high accuracy based on this comparison, and as a result, they may be used for high-performance augmentations. While RST (Yamashita,et al.,2021), IAug (Chen,et al.,2022), PNet (Chen,et al., 2022), Cut Mix (Shen,et al.,2022), LA CNN (Kim,et al.,2021), MDCF (Xia,et al.,2021), and Det DSCI (Pérez-Hernández,et al.,2021) are all capable of achieving better accuracy, Cut Mix (Shen,et al.,2022), LA CNN (Kim,et al.,2021), MDCF (Xia,et al.,2021) may be employed for augmentation situations that demand higher consistency levels. The models that are proposed in RST (Yamashita,et al.,2021), PNet (Chen,et al., 2022), and IAug(Chen,et al.,2022) have a low delay, and the models that are proposed in RI CAP(Takahashi, et al., 2019), NST (Xiao,et al.,2021), RST (Yamashita,et al.,2021), XAug (Nesteruk,et al.,2022), and IAug (Chen,et al.,2022) have a lower complexity. These models are useful for high-speed scenarios in which there is limited computational capacity available, which enhances their levels of scalability. While Cut Mix(Shen,et al.,2022), GAN (Xu,et al.,2020), SA GAN (Zhu,et at.,2020), XAug(Nesteruk,et al.,2022), PNet (Chen,et al., 2022), and IAug (Chen,et al.,2022) demonstrate improved scalability, which makes them applicable for use cases involving several domains. In future, these models must be validated for large-scale applications and can be improved via the integration of bioinspired computing models for parameter optimizations. This performance can also be improved via the use of hybrid deep learning techniques like Auto Encoders, Gated Recurrent Units, Q-Learning, etc. which assist in continuous optimizations for different image sets, and multiple application scenarios.

REFERENCES

1. Chen, H., Li, W. and Shi, Z. (2022). Adversarial Instance Augmentation for Building Change Detection in Remote Sensing Images. *IEEE Transactions on Geoscience and Remote Sensing*, 60, pp. 1–16. doi: 10.1109/tgrs.2021.3066802.
2. Chen, L., Wei, Y., Yao, Z., Chen, E. and Zhang, X. (2022). Data Augmentation in Prototypical Networks for Forest Tree Species Classification Using Airborne Hyperspectral Images. *IEEE Transactions on Geoscience and Remote Sensing*, 60, pp. 1–16. doi:10.1109/tgrs.2022.3168054.
3. Kim, J. Y. and Ha, J. E. (2021). Spatio-Temporal Data Augmentation for Visual Surveillance. *IEEE Access*, 9, pp. 165014–165033. doi:10.1109/access.2021.3135505.
4. Kim, Y., Uddin, A. F. M. S. and Bae, S. H. (2021). Local Augment: Utilizing Local Bias Property of Convolutional Neural Networks for Data Augmentation. *IEEE Access*, 9, pp. 15191–15199. doi:10.1109/access.2021.3050758.
5. Nalepa, J., Myller, M. and Kawulok, M. (2020). Training- and Test-Time Data Augmentation for Hyperspectral Image Segmentation. *IEEE Geoscience and Remote Sensing Letters*, 17(2), pp. 292–296. doi:10.1109/lgrs.2019.2921011.

6. Nesteruk, S., Illarionova, S., Akhtyamov, T., Shadrin, D., Somov, A., Pukalchik, M. and Oseledets, I. (2022). XtremeAugment: Getting More from Your Data Through Combination of Image Collection and Image Augmentation. *IEEE Access*, 10, pp. 24010–24028. doi:10.1109/access.2022.3154709.

7. Pan, X., Tang, F., Dong, W., Gu, Y., Song, Z., Meng, Y., Xu, P., Deussen, O. and Xu, C. (2020). Self-Supervised Feature Augmentation for Large Image Object Detection. *IEEE Transactions on Image Processing*, 29, pp. 6745–6758. doi:10.1109/tip.2020.2993403.

8. Shang, X., Han, S. and Song, M. (2022). Iterative Spatial-Spectral Training Sample Augmentation for Effective Hyperspectral Image Classification. *IEEE Geoscience and Remote Sensing Letters*, 19, pp. 1–5. doi:10.1109/lgrs.2021.3131373.

9. Shen, Y., Zhu, S., Yang, T., Chen, C., Pan, D., Chen, J., Xiao, L. and Du, Q. (2022). BDANet: Multiscale Convolutional Neural Network with Cross-Directional Attention for Building Damage Assessment From Satellite Images. *IEEE Transactions on Geoscience and Remote Sensing*, 60, pp. 1–14. doi:10.1109/tgrs.2021.3080580.

10. Takahashi, R., Matsubara, T. and Uehara, K. (2019). Data Augmentation using Random Image Cropping and Patching for Deep CNNs. *IEEE Transactions on Circuits and Systems for Video Technology*, pp. 1–1. doi: 10.1109/tcsvt.2019.2935128.

11. Wang, W., Chen, Y., He, X. and Li, Z. (2022). Soft Augmentation-Based Siamese CNN for Hyperspectral Image Classification with Limited Training Samples. *IEEE Geoscience and Remote Sensing Letters*, 19, pp. 1–5. doi: 10.1109/lgrs.2021.3103180.

12. Xia, M., Wang, Z., Han, F. and Kang, Y. (2021). Enhanced Multi-Dimensional and Multi-Grained Cascade Forest for Cloud/ Snow Recognition Using Multispectral Satellite Remote Sensing Imagery. *IEEE Access*, 9, pp. 131072–131086. doi: 10.1109/access.2021.3114185.

13. Xie, J., Yu, F., Wang, H. and Zheng, H. (2022). Class Activation Map-Based Data Augmentation for Satellite Smoke Scene Detection. *IEEE Geoscience and Remote Sensing Letters*, 19, pp. 1–5. doi: 10.1109/lgrs.2022.3179013.

14. Xu, H., Li, C., Rahaman, M. M., Yao, Y., Li, Z., Zhang, J., Kulwa, F., Zhao, X., Qi, S. and Teng, Y. (2020). An Enhanced Framework of Generative Adversarial Networks (EF-GANs) for Environmental Microorganism Image Augmentation with Limited Rotation-Invariant Training Data. *IEEE Access*, 8, pp. 187455–187469. doi: 10.1109/access.2020.3031059.

15. Yamashita, R., Long, J., Banda, S., Shen, J. and Rubin, D.L. (2021). Learning Domain-Agnostic Visual Representation for Computational Pathology Using Medically Irrelevant Style Transfer Augmentation. *IEEE Transactions on Medical Imaging*, 40(12), pp. 3945–3954. doi: 10.1109/tmi.2021.3101985.

16. Zhang, L., Wang, X., Yang, D., Sanford, T., Harmon, S., Turkbey, B., Wood, B. J., Roth, H., Myronenko, A., Xu, D. and Xu, Z. (2020). Generalizing Deep Learning for Medical Image Segmentation to Unseen Domains via Deep Stacked Transformation. *IEEE Transactions on Medical Imaging*, 39(7), pp. 2531–2540. doi: 10.1109/tmi.2020.2973595.

17. Zhu, Y., Zhang, Y., Zhang, H., Yang, J. and Zhao, Z. (2020). Data Augmentation of X-Ray Images in Baggage Inspection Based on Generative Adversarial Networks. *IEEE Access*, 8, pp. 86536–86544. doi: 10.1109/access.2020.2992861.

Computer Science Engineering and Emerging Technologies (ICCS-2022) – Prof (Dr.) Rajeev Sobti et al. (eds)
© 2024 Taylor & Francis Group, London, ISBN 978-1-032-52199-2

Chapter

48

Wireless Network Security: Requirements, Attacks, Vulnerabilities, Security Solutions

Nancy Sharma[1]
Research Scholar, Department of Computer Science and Engineering,
Lovely Professional University, Phagwara, Punjab, India

Harwant Singh Arri[2]
Associate Professor, Department of Computer Science and Engineering,
Lovely Professional University, Phagwara, Punjab, India

Dhiraj Kapila[3]
Associate Professor, Department of Computer Science and Engineering,
Lovely Professional University, Phagwara, Punjab, India

**Gobinda Karmakar[4], Siddharth Pansare[5], Jithin Govind[6],
Sahil Bhardwaj[7], Nupur Kaushik[8], Jayant Mehra[9]**
Research Scholar, Department of Computer Science and Engineering,
Lovely Professional University, Phagwara, Punjab, India

Abstract: The wireless air interface is open and available to both legitimate and unauthorized users due to the broadcast nature of radio propagation. With a wired network, communicating devices are physically connected by wires, making it possible for a node without a direct association to access the network for evil purposes. Due to the open communication environment, hostile attacks, such as active jamming and passive eavesdropping for data interception, are more likely to target wireless signals than cable communications.

By removing the barrier of a physical network, a wireless network is used to connect various wired organisational structures and to provide connectivity within the organisation for employees to move around freely. Because WLANs are directly connected to the main network of the organisation, maintaining WLAN security is essential for that organisation. In this work, the author has explained about the security requirements of wireless networks, including their authenticity, confidentiality, integrity and availability, wireless network attack, different types of attacks/threats, and their associated solutions. The author concluded by talking about ongoing research towards creating a wireless network that is secure and safe for data transit.

The security of wireless networks is crucial given their rising popularity. The authors outline the security options for WLANs in this study. Wired Equivalent Privacy, Wi-Fi Protected Access, and 802.11i are these security measures (WPA2).

Keywords: Wireless network, Attacks, Wireless security, Encryption, Decryption, Access point, Wired equivalent privacy

[1]nancysharma2177@gmail.com, [2]hs.arri@lpu.co.in, [3]dhiraj.23509@lpu.co.in, [4]gobindak2@gmail.com, [5]sidhu.pansare@gmail.com,
[6]jithingovindkanayi001@gmail.com, [7]binny4166@gmail.com, [8]nupurkaushiknk@gmail.com, [9]jayant46mehra@gmail.com

DOI: 10.1201/9781003405580-48

1. Introduction

Today, the Internet has evolved into a need for everyday life and is utilized for more than just amusement. It also provides facilities to do ordinary tasks like money transfers, bill payments, academic research, learning perspectives, business trade, press coverage, etc. Leonard Kleinrock proposed the ARPANET (Advanced Research Project Agency Network) in his research titled "Information Flow in Large Communication Nets" in 1961[1]. Data is sent from one node to another using the term "packet," which was first used in 1965. TCP/IP was created in 1978 by Bob Kahn with the intention of transferring data between different forms. Up to 2Mbps can be sent at the first generation of the 802.11 WiFi standards. A higher level of security provides greater protection, and WAP3 added WIFI encryption in 2018. Computer networks have two basic types: wired networks and wireless networks, and their primary function is resource exchange.[1]

WEP is the standard WLAN security method. In order to offer wireless security, the WEP encryption algorithm and the 802.1 lb standard were created in 1999. It uses the RSA Data Security RC4 (Rivest Cipher 4) algorithm. But after cryptanalysts discovered a number of significant flaws, Wi-Fi Protected Access and the entire IEEE 802.11i standard replaced WEP in 2003 and 2004, respectively. WEP still offers a basic amount of security despite the significant security issues.

In this author, has looked into the many real-time vulnerabilities and bypassing techniques for WLAN security systems.

2. Security Requirements of Wireless Network

Information is exchanged among authorized users in wireless networks, however, due to the wireless medium's broadcast nature, this method is prone to various cyber threats. The security standards for wireless networks are established in order to safeguard wireless communications from wireless assaults such as node compromise attacks, denial of service attacks, data forgery attacks, and eavesdropping attacks. In general, secure wireless communications should meet the criteria for availability, confidentiality, and integrity, as explained in the following.[2]

2.1 Confidentiality

Confidentiality refers to preventing the disclosure of information to unauthorized parties and limiting access to the data to intended users alone. In the case of symmetric key encryption, the source node first uses an encryption algorithm to encrypt the original data with the help of a secret key that is only shared with the intended destination. The destination then uses the secret key to decrypt the received cypher text after receiving the encrypted plaintext (cypher text) from the source.

2.2 Integrity

The information transferred via a wireless network should maintain its accuracy and dependability over its entire life cycle, accurately reflecting the information's source without being fabricated or modified by unauthorized users. So-called insider attacks, such as node compromise attacks, may damage the data integrity.

2.3 Availability

If a wireless connection is available, it means that registered persons can seek access to it whenever they want from wherever. The registered persons will be unable to access the wireless network as a result of the denial of service, which is a violation of availability and leads to an unacceptable customer experience.[2]

3. Wireless Network Attacks

3.1 Accidental Association

Unauthorized access to corporate wireless and wired networks may result from a variety of techniques and purposes. "Accidental association" is a term used to describe one of these techniques. The user may not even be aware that this has happened when they turn on a computer and it connects to a wireless access point from a nearby company's overlapping network. However, there has been a security breach because confidential firm information was made public, and now there may be a connection between the two businesses. If the laptop is also connected to a wired network, this is especially true.

3.2 Man-in-the-middle-attack

A computer that is configured as a soft AP is lured into being accessed by computers by a man-in-the-middle attacker. After completing this, the hacker uses another wireless card to connect to a real access point, providing a constant flow of traffic from the transparent hacking machine to the real network. After then, the hacker can examine the traffic. A "de-authentication attack" is one sort of man-in-the-middle attack that takes the use of security flaws in challenge and handshake protocols. The cracker's soft AP is forced to re-establish contact with AP-connected machines as a result of this attack.

3.3 Denial of Service Attack

When an attacker repeatedly floods a targeted Access Point or network with fake requests, prematurely successful connection messages, failure messages, and/or other commands, it is known as a Denial-of-Service (DoS) assault. These prevent legitimate users from connecting to the network and may even bring it to a halt. These attacks make use of exploits for protocols like the Extensible Authentication Protocol (EAP).

3.4 Network Injection

A cracker can exploit access points that are open to broadcasting network traffic, such as "Spanning Tree" (802.1D), OSPF, RIP, and HSRP, in a network injection attack. The cracker injects fake commands to reconfigure the networking system that have an impact on routers, switches, and intelligent hubs. This can bring down an entire network, necessitating a reboot or possibly a reprogramming of all networking devices with intelligence.

3.5 Identity Theft (MAC Spoofing)

When a cracker is able to monitor network traffic and determine the MAC address of a computer with network privileges, identity theft takes place. Most wireless networks include some form of MAC filtering, which restricts access to the network to only those machines with specified MAC IDs that have been granted permission. There are numerous programs with network "sniffing" capabilities, though. The cracker can easily get around that obstacle if they combine these programs with other software that enables a machine to pretend to have any MAC address, they want.[3]

4. Wireless Network Vulnerabilities

The following are some typical flaws in wireless networks:

1. End users aren't security specialist thus they might not be aware of the dangers that wireless LANs poses.
2. Nearly all access points with default setups do not have WEP security activated.
3. The majority of consumers leave the default access point key that comes pre-programmed in all of the vendors product alone.
4. Wireless access points that use WEP can be readily cracked.[4]

5. Wireless LAN Security

5.1 Wired Equivalent Privacy (WEP)

The cryptography process WEP was created by an IEEE participant batch. The purpose of this algorithm is to provide secure radio connections involving several WLAN end users. WEP uses the RC4 encryption technique and has two key sizes: 40-bit and 104 bits. Each key size also has an initialization vector (IV) of 24 bits, which is broadcast directly. The cypher text is retrieved at the receiver side by XORing the plaintext with the key stream produced by the RC4 KSA and PRGA processes. The identical key is used at the receiver side to complete these procedures in reverse. Data integrity is ensured by WEP using the CRC-32 algorithm.[5]

5.2 Wi-fi Protected Access (WPA)

In the near term, WPA has been designed as a bridge between 802.11i, the use of a second-generation network security to ensure a more reliable connection. In this case, the Temporal Key Integrity Protocol [5] has been created as a fix for WEP. TKIP uses the RC4 method as well but with some significant changes. Keys are dynamically changed during communication, and a much larger IV (48-bit) is employed. On every session, a key mixing feature is utilized for various keys. During transmission, a novel process named Michael is utilized as the message integrity code to ensure data integrity (MIC). Shortly, TKIP offers message integrity checking, per-packet key mixing, and a re-keying method.

WPA does a fantastic job of fixing the issues with WEP. It fixed practically all security issues that WEP either overlooked or manufactured with just a software upgrade. WPA, however, also brought about fresh issues:

1. If an attacker could get past multiple additional layers of defence, one weakness permitted the attacker to launch a denial-of-service assault.
2. The process by which WPA initializes its encryption system has a second issue. Therefore, breaking WPA is really simpler than breaking WEP.[5]

5.3 802.11i

802.11i is the long-term remedy created by Task Group I (TGi) for wireless networks (also called WPA2). In 2004, it was approved as a standard. 802.11i encrypts network communication using Counter Mode with CBC-MAC Protocol, not RC4 like WEP or WPA. The Advanced Encryption Standard is the cryptography process used by CCMP. WPA but not WEP are backwards compatible with 802.11i.[5]

6. Security Solutions for Wireless Network

The following strategies are advised to reduce the security risks associated with wireless networks in order to deal with the above mention security threats/attacks.[4]

6.1 Educating and Training Users

Teaching users how to secure a network is the first step in wireless network security. End users frequently fail to implement security, which creates a number of openings for attackers. It is quite possible to lower security risks if users are well informed on wireless tool configuration/settings and how to secure their respective networks.[4]

6.2 Auditing Wireless Network

It is an effective method for securing wireless networks. To learn about the activity on the network, the user should scan it with a network scanner. On the internet, you may find a number of free network scanning programs like NetStumbler and Kismet.[4]

6.3 When Not in Use, Turn Off AP

We can reduce the amount of time that a wireless network router or access point is vulnerable to hacking if the user switches it off when not using it.[4]

6.4 Alter the Router's Default Password

Every wireless router/access point manufacturer sets a default user name and password. If the user does not alter it, it will be relatively easy for the attacker to access the access point by scanning it and using the default username and password. Therefore, it is strongly advised that the user change their default login and password as soon as possible.[4]

6.5 Change the SSID

Every wireless device has a default ID, which makes it simple for attackers to locate access points by typing in the default ID.

The SSID used by all connected wireless devices is the same. If a user doesn't alter the default SSID, the password is likely to be left alone as well. Additionally, it's recommended to change your SSID no later than 30 days from now.[4]

6.6 Turn Off SSID Broadcasting

The access point displays its existence in the environment in which it is operating using the SSID broadcasting approach. It is very difficult for the attacker to scan the network by turning off the SSID broadcasting function. Therefore, if your router supports it, it's advised that you disable this feature.[4]

7. Conclusion

There are many chances to boost productivity and save costs with wireless networking. Additionally, it changes the entire computer security risk profile of a company. However, it is difficult to completely remove all hazards related to wireless networking, a fair level of overall security can be attained by using a methodical approach to risk assessment and management. In this review, the author has examined security threats and issues that are utilized to compromise client data and render networks unreliable.

The confidentiality, integrity, and availability of wireless transmissions are all protected in this study against malicious attacks via an overview of wireless security challenges and defence techniques.

Wireless technologies are quickly becoming the most widely used technology in the world; as a result, they need to be effectively protected to avoid the misuse of private information. We provided a quick review of them in this paper, concentrating on the three primary security protocols WEP, WPA, and WPA2. The authors study revealed that contrary to popular opinion that WPA/WPA2 security measures are now challenging for a stranger to penetrate, any wireless connection could be susceptible to effective hacking attempts if it is not properly aligned up and defended.

REFERENCES

1. R. Nazir, A. A. laghari, K. Kumar, S. David, and M. Ali, "Survey on Wireless Network Security," Archives of Computational Methods in Engineering, vol. 29, no. 3. Springer Science and Business Media B.V., pp. 1591–1610, May 01, 2022. doi: 10.1007/s11831-021-09631-5.
2. Y. Zou, J. Zhu, X. Wang, and L. Hanzo, "A Survey on Wireless Security: Technical Challenges, Recent Advances, and Future Trends," Proceedings of the IEEE, vol. 104, no. 9. Institute of Electrical and Electronics Engineers Inc., pp. 1727–1765, Sep. 01, 2016. doi: 10.1109/JPROC.2016.2558521.
3. M. K. Choi, R. J. Robles, C. H. Hong, and T.-H. Kim, "Wireless Network Security: Vulnerabilities, Threats and Countermeasures," 2008.
4. "WIRELESSSECURITYANDTHREATS".
5. V. Kumkar, A. Tiwari, P. Tiwari, A. Gupta, and S. Shrawne, "Vulnerabilities of Wireless Security protocols (WEP and WPA2)," 2012.

Computer Science Engineering and Emerging Technologies (ICCS-2022) – Prof (Dr.) Rajeev Sobti et al. (eds)
© 2024 Taylor & Francis Group, London, ISBN 978-1-032-52199-2

Chapter **49**

A Systematic Literature Review on Various Methodologies Used from Time to Time for Predicting Rainfall

Deepa Sharma[1]

Phd Scholar, School of Computer Science & Engineering,
Lovely Professional University, Phagwara, Punjab India

Punam Rattan[2], Shilpa Sharma[3]

Associate Professor, School of Computer Science & Engineering,
Lovely Professional University, Phagwara, Punjab India

Abstract: The maintenance of life on Earth depends in large part on rainfall. A great deal of flora and wildlife are lost as a result of several natural disasters like landslides and floods caused by excessive rainfall. In addition to this, severe rainstorms can ruin a nation's economy. If there were a reliable way to anticipate rainfall, these losses might be prevented. Due to the consequences of rain, rainfall forecasting is one of the most difficult issues. It might be useful in preventing natural disasters. Traditional models like ARIMA that relied on statistical techniques don't accurately estimate when it will rain. But now that artificial neural networks (ANN) have been developed, prediction models are based on them and produce results that are more accurate. This article focuses on many rainfall prediction models that use deep learning algorithms like Convolutional Neural Networks (CNN) and Long Short Term Memory (LSTM) as well as machine learning techniques like Random Forest (RF), Support Vector Machines (SVM), and Decision Trees (DT).

Keywords: ANN, RF, SVM, DT, CNN, LSTM

1. Introduction

The existence of plants and creatures on our planet depends heavily on rainfall. Rainfall provides life-sustaining fresh water for all living creatures. Droughts are caused by a lack of water owing to little or no rain, whereas floods and landslides are caused by an abundance of rain. Both circumstances are awful for the people involved. Rainfall is also crucial for a country's agriculture. As a result, it has an impact on a nation's economy that is dependent on agricultural production. The process of calculating or estimating future rainfall is known as rainfall forecasting. It can assist governments in formulating a variety of measures to prevent the destruction caused by floods or to efficiently utilise water during droughts. So, in order to develop a trustworthy method for prediction with greater accuracy, rainfall prediction has turned into a research area. Theil's Regression (T.O.Olatayo & Taiwo, 2014), Fuzzy Time Series (FST) Model and "Auto Regressive Integrated Moving Average" (ARIMA) are examples of classical approaches.

Extreme precipitation due to high moisture content in the atmosphere leads to various natural disasters like floods, mud puddles, landslides etc. An early prediction of rainfall can help in minimizing the losses accompanying these disasters. Precipitation forecasts in the future can be made with the help of data mining techniques applied to historical precipitation records. The quality of historical data utilised to train a rainfall forecast model determines its accuracy. Using time series rainfall data, (Sarma& Mishra, 2022) employed a number of Data Mining Techniques, including "DECISION TREES",

---

[1]apdeepasharma@gmail.com, [2]punam.26558@lpu.co.in, [3]shilpa.sharma@lpu.co.in

DOI: 10.1201/9781003405580-49

"ARTIFICIAL NEURAL NETWORKS" (*ANN*), "NAIVE BAYES", "SUPPORT VECTOR MACHINES" (*SVM*), "FUZZY LOGIC", and various "Rule Based Techniques", which include Memory-based Reasoning Techniques, and "GENETIC ALGORITHMS", to extract previously hidden insights (Mohd et al., 2018). Authors (Kaliyaperumal et al., 2021) compared various data mining classifiers techniques viz Decision Tree, Multi-linear regression, "K NEAREST NEIGHBOUR", "SUPPORT VECTOR MACHINE", "ARTIFICIAL NEURAL NETWORK" AND "RANDOM FOREST". Other Researchers ((Sheikh et al., 2016) compared Naïve Bayes & C4.5 Decision Tree Algorithms over dataset for a period of 2 years. (Sarkar et al., 2022) in their paper tested various ensemble methods for forecasting short-term electric load in Nagaland. To handle the issue of disproportion of data they used synthetic minority over-sampling technique for regression (SMOTE-R). Out of the different techniques used by them, they found Random Forest to give precise results. An accurate prediction of rainfall can be helpful in number of societal and governmental benefits. It can help in forecasting many disasters that accompany heavy rainfalls such as floods, flash floods, landslides, mud puddles etc. in a particular region. An early warning system can be developed if an accurate prediction can be done. An early prediction also helps in developing better infrastructure for Rain Water Harvesting so that the same can be used in dry seasons.

This study deals with studying different prediction models developed for rainfall prediction using various "Machine And Deep Learning Algorithms". This research aims to identify the optimal design and technique for creating a model that outperforms its predecessors across a range of performance measures. The rest of the paper is divided into Literature Review, Discussions, Challenges and Conclusion & Future scope.

2. Literature Review

The present study covers published research paper from year 2017 to 2022 searched from Google Scholar. The literature review has been categorically divided as discussed below:

On the Basis of Neural Network

Different rainfall prediction models using neural networks like TDNN, CNN, LSTM, BiLSTM, stacking ensemble learning model were developed by different researchers and on comparison with various other traditional models like ARIMA etc., the proposed models were found to be performing better based on the values of various performance metrics used. The latest methods used for prediction is using LSTM networks and learning techniques. Also, these different models need to be compared so that the best one can be chosen.

Table 49.1 summarizes different types of models, the basic neural networks they use, and other models, along with a comparison between them since 2017.

Table 49.1 Different Prediction Models and their comparison

Authors	Model Name/ Neural Network Used	Comparison done	Dataset / Images	Accuracy/ Performance Metrics	Parameters
(Sulaiman & Wahab, 2017)	Time Division Neural Network TDNN (ANN)	ARIMA	50 years from 1965 to 2015	- RMSE, R^2	Rainfall
(Haidar & Verma, 2018)	Deep Convolutional Network (CNN)	ACCESS MLP	January 1908 to December 2012	- RMSE, PEARSON COEFFICIENT (r), NASH SUTTCLIFF COEFFICIENT	Rainfall, Max Temperature, Min Temperature, Nino 1.2, Nino 3.0, Nino 3.4, Nino 4.0, Dipole Mode Index, INTERDECADAL PACIFIC OSCILLATION (IPO), SOUTHERN OSCILLATION INDEX (SOI), Tripole Mode Index (TPI), North Pacific Index (NPI), North Atlantic Oscillation (NAO) AND Pacific Decadal Oscillation (PDO)
(Xiang et al., 2018)	E-SVR-ANN Model (ANN)			- R, MAE, RMSE	Rainfall
(Poornima & Pushpalatha, 2019)	Intensified LSTM Model (RNN)	LSTM Holt-Winters Extreme Learning Machine	1980–2013	88% RMSE, Accuracy, No of Epochs, Loss, Learning Rate	Maximum Temperature, Minimum Temperature, Maximum Relative Humidity, Minimum Relative Humidity, Wind Speed, Sunshine And Evapotranspiration

Authors	Model Name/ Neural Network Used	Comparis on done	Dataset / Images	Accuracy/ Performance Metrics	Parameters
(Abdul-Kader et al., 2020)	MLP based on Particle Swarm Optimization (FFNN)	MLP	2009	- RMSE	LOW TEMPERATURE, HIGH TEMPERATURE, HUMIDITY, AND WIND SPEED
(Chhetri et al., 2020)	BLSTM-GRU Model (RNN)	MLP LSTM BLSTM	1997–2017	- MSE, RMSE, R^2 Correlation	tmax, tmin, relative_humidity, wind_speed, and wind_direction, sunshine hours and rainfall amount
(Haq et al., 2021)	LSTM RNN		December 2014– August 2019	- MAAPE	EL Nino and IOD
(Zhang et al., 2021)	High Altitude Combined Rainfall Forecast Model Temporal CNN	ARIMA MLP ECMWF JMA BPNN SVM LSTM	2015–2017	- Threat Rating (TS), MEAN SQUARE ERROR (MSE) and MEAN ABSOLUTE ERROR (MAE)	SURFACE WIND DIRECTION SURFACE PRESSURE, 3-H VOLTAGE TRANSFORMATION ON THE GROUND GROUND TEMPERATURE, GROUND DEW POINT TEMPERATURE, 200-1000HPA TEMPERATURE, 200-1000hpa temperature, DEW POINT DIFFERENCE, WIND DIRECTION 200-1000HPA, 200-1000HPA WIND SPEED
(Peng et al., 2022)	Hyperparameter Optimization DNN Model DNN	MLP BPNN SVM RF	1957–2018	- MSE, RMSE, MAE, R^2	Precipitation
(Endalie et al., 2022)	LSTM RNN	ARIMA MLP SVM	1985–2017	- RMSE, NORMALIZED ROOT MEAN SQUARED ERROR, NSE, MEAN ABSOLUTE ERROR, MAPE AND R^2	Maximum Temperature, Minimum Temperature, Relative Humidity, Solar Radiation, Wind Speed And Precipitation
(Liu et al., 2022)	SVM-BiLSTM LSTM	LSTM, BiLSTM SVM-LSTM	1981–2020	- MEAN SQUARE ERROR, NASH–SUTCLIFFE EFFICIENCY COEFFICIENT AND MEAN ABSOLUTE ERROR	Daily rainfall data
(Gu et al., 2022)	Ensemble learning Stacking Model KNN, XGB, SVR, ANN		1961–2019	- RMSE, MAE, R^2	Nino 3.4, Southern Oscillation Index (SOI), Southern Hemisphere Annular Mode Index (SAMI), Western Pacific Subtropic High Intensity (WPSH), Sea Level Pressure (SLP), Meridional Wind(V-WIND(1)) AND (V-WIND(2)), Monthly Mean Air Temperature, Monthly Maximum Air Temperature, Monthly Minimum Air Temperature, Monthly Mean Air Pressure, Monthly Mean Vapor Pressure, Relative Humidity, Sunshine Duration
(Chandra Mouli et al., 2022)	Ensemble Model RNN-LSTM, Bi-LSTM, CNN		2015–2021	- RMSE, MAE, MSE	Rainfall, Relative Humidity, Temperature

Source: Made by Author

On the basis of comparisons done between different machine learning algorithms

This category deals with finding the best learning algorithm when implemented over same model based on various performance metrics used. Extreme Gradient Boosting Technique gave most promising results. In one paper, Naïve Bayes Classifier algorithm gave an accuracy of 95.91% accuracy in classifying rainfall categorically.

Table 49.2 provides a summary of the research that was done to find the best machine learning algorithms and techniques by comparing several algorithms used.

Table 49.2 Different Techniques/Algorithms Used by Researchers

Author	Algorithm Used	Best
(Mishra & Sharma, 2018)	LMBP and BRBP backpropagation algorithms on NARX recurrent network	LMBP (2 cases) BRBP (1 case)
(Sharma et al., 2018)	Random Forest, Naïve Bayes, MLP & SMO	Random Forest
(Abdul-Kader et al., 2020)	Levenberg Marquardt Backpropagation Algorithm & PSO	Particle Swarm Optimization
(Muchamad Taufiq Anwar et al., 2020)	Decision Tree, J48	J48
(Sethupathi M et al., 2021)	Random Forest, Logistic Regression	Logistic Regression
(Azmi et al., 2021)	Naïve Bayes algorithm	NBC gives an accuracy of 95.91% in classifying the rainfall categorically
(M. T. Anwar et al., 2021)	XG Boost Technique	
(Liyew & Melese, 2021)	MLR, Random Forest, XGBoost	XGBoost

Source: Made by Author

On the basis of Comparisons between models

In this category different models were compared by different authors and based upon the performance metrics the best one is found out. LSTM-based models were giving better results when compared with the RF-based model, ANN. Among various other variations of LSTM based model, the BiLSTM model was found to be performing better than the LSTM model.

Table 49.3 gives a comparative analysis of different models developed by different researchers and other models and finds the best one based on some performance metrics.

Table 49.3 Comparison between different models developed with different machine learning/ deep learning algorithms

Author	Comparison Done Between					Best One	Performance Metrics Used
	I	II	III	IV	V		
(Velasco et al., 2019)	MLNPP with 50 hidden neurons and SCG-Tangent	MLNPP with 100 hidden neurons and SCG-Sigmoid	-	-	-	MLNPP with 50 hidden neurons and SCG-Tangent Activation Function	MAE, RMSE
(Pham et al., 2020)	PSOANFIS	ANN	SVM	-	-	SVM	R, MAE, POD, CSI, FAR, Robustness analysis
(Ridwan et al., 2021)	BDTR	DFR	NNR	BLR	-	BDTR	MAE, RMSE, RAE, RSE, R2
(Kanchan, 2021)	ANN	RNN	LSTM	-	-	LSTM	MAPE, RMSE
(Anochi et al., 2021)	BAM (Brazilian Global Atmospheric Model)	NN-TensorFlow	NN-MPCA	-	-	Summer, Autumn & Winter Spring	RMSE COV-Covariance ME-Mean Error

Author	Comparison Done Between					Best One	Performance Metrics Used
	I	II	III	IV	V		
(Barrera-Animas et al., 2022)	LSTM based Model	Stacked LSTM-based Model	Bidirectional LSTM based Model	XGBoost based Model	Ensembl e Model	BiLSTM and Stacked LSTM based Model and based Model	Loss, RMSE, RMSEL
(Chen et al., 2022)	LSTM based model	RF Based Model	-	-	-	LSTM based model	RMSE, RSR, LMI, R2, NSE, Taylor & Violin Diagrams

Source: Made by Author

3. Discussions

Parameters, machine learning methods, tools, and performance indicators used by scientists for rain forecasting are all discussed in this section.

Parameters used in rainfall prediction

Different authors have used different parameters in their studies for training the model. Most commonly used parameters were Rainfall in mm, Minimum Temperature, Maximum Temperature, Humidity and Solar Radiation.

Figure 49.1 shows the number of researchers using different parameters for rainfall prediction

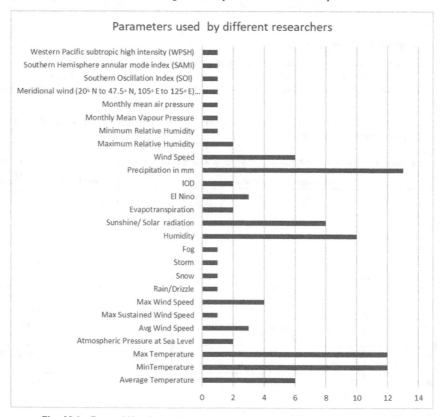

Fig. 49.1 Figure 1 Number of times a parameter is used by different researchers

Source: Made by Author

Machine/deep learning algorithms

Various researchers have used different learning algorithms in their research work. Some of them are CNN, LSTM, BiLSTM, MLP (Deep Learning Algorithms) that are giving better results than many other Machine Learning Algorithms like 'LMBP', 'BRBP', 'SVM', 'RF', 'Naïve Bayes' etc.

Table 49.4 shows the various learning algorithms used by different researchers.

Table 49.4   Different techniques/Algorithms Used by researchers

Author (Year)	Technique/Algorithm Used
(Sulaiman & Wahab, 2017)	TDNN
(Haidar & Verma, 2018)	Adam Optimiser, Stochastic Gradient Boosting, RMS Prop
(Mishra & Sharma, 2018)	LMBP and BRBP backpropagation algorithms
(Xiang et al., 2018)	"Ensemble Empirical Mode Decomposition (EEMD)", SVR, ANN
(Sharma et al., 2018)	Random Forest, Naïve Bayes, MLP & SMO
(Velasco et al., 2019)	MLPNN SCG-Tangent model
(Poornima & Pushpalatha, 2019)	LSTM
(Abdul-Kader et al., 2020)	Levenberg Marquardt Backpropagation Algorithm & PSO
(Pham et al., 2020)	PSO, ANN, SVM, Fuzzy Inference
(Chhetri et al., 2020)	Bi-directional Long-Short-Term Memory (BLSTM), Gated Recurrent Unit (GRU)
(Muchamad Taufiq Anwar et al., 2020)	Decision Tree, J48
(Zhang et al., 2021)	K-Means Clustering, Principal Component Analysis, CNN
(Sethupathi M et al., 2021)	Random Forest, Logistic Regression
(Azmi et al., 2021)	Naïve Bayes algorithm
(M. T. Anwar et al., 2021)	XG Boost Technique
(Haq et al., 2021)	LSTM
(Ridwan et al., 2021)	DBTR, DFR, NNR and BLR, LogNormal, Z Score and Min Max Normalisation techniques
(Liyew & Melese, 2021)	MLR, RF, XGBoost
(Anochi et al., 2021)	MLP, MPCA
(Peng et al., 2022)	Gene Expression Programming
(Endalie et al., 2022)	LSTM
(Liu et al., 2022)	SVM, GA, SW, Zero Sum Game, Discrete Wavelet Transformation, K-Means Clustering Algorithm, Adaptive Moment Estimation
(Barrera-Animas et al., 2022)	LSTM, XGBoost, "Gradient Booster Regressor", "Linear Support Vector Regression", "Extra Trees Regressor", Correlation Matrix
(Chen et al., 2022)	LSTM, RF
(Gu et al., 2022)	SVR, XGB, ANN, KNN, Stacking Ensemble Learning

Source: Made by Author

Tools used in rainfall prediction model by various researchers

Various tools like Python, Keras, Kaggle, Encog 3.3.0, PyCharm, Anaconda Framework have been used by researchers to train, test and validate their models.

Table 49.5 shows tools used by different researchers.

Table 49.5   Summary of different tools used by the researchers

Author (Year)	Tools
(Haidar & Verma, 2018)	Keras on Tensorflow Framework
(Mishra & Sharma, 2018)	MATLAB R2013

Author (Year)	Tools
(Velasco et al., 2019)	Encog 3.3.0 framework that runs on JAVA and .net
(Poornima & Pushpalatha, 2019)	Keras, Tensorflow Framework
(Chhetri et al., 2020)	Python Jupyter Notebook in Keras, Tensorflow at backend
(Zhang et al., 2021)	PyCharm Platform
(Sethupathi M et al., 2021)	Anaconda Framework, Python
(Kanchan, 2021)	Keras
(Peng et al., 2022)	"Scikit-learn and Keras", Hyperas ("Bayes Search", "Grid Search", "Randomized Search"), Chocolate (Quasi Random Search method)
(Barrera-Animas et al., 2022)	Auto ML, TPot Tool
(Chen et al., 2022)	Mathematica 21

Source: Made by Author

Performance metrics used by different researchers

Different academics employ different metrics for evaluating the performance of the model. Researchers have used various kinds of Performance Metrics such as "Root Mean Square Error" RMSE, "Linear Correlation Coefficient" R, "Coefficient of Determination" R2, "Pearson Coefficient" (r), "Nash Suttcliff coefficient" (NSE), "Accuracy", "Number of Epochs", "Loss", "Learning Rate", "Mean Absolute Error" (MAE), "Mean Square Error " (MSE)," Normalized Root Mean Squared Error" (NRMSE), MAPE, MAAPE, Covariance, Mean Error.

Table 49.6 gives the details of performance metrics used by various researchers.

Table 49.6   Performance metrics used by different researchers

Authors	Performance Metrics
(Sulaiman & Wahab, 2017)	RMSE, R^2
(Haidar & Verma, 2018)	RMSE, Pearson Coefficient (r), Nash Suttcliff coefficient
(Xiang et al., 2018)	R, MAE, RMSE
(Poornima & Pushpalatha, 2019)	RMSE, ACCURACY, NO OF EPOCHS, LOSS, LEARNING RATE
(Abdul-Kader et al., 2020)	RMSE
(Chhetri et al., 2020)	MSE, RMSE, R^2 Correlation
(Haq et al., 2021)	MAAPE
(Zhang et al., 2021)	Threat Rating (TS), Mean Absolute Error (MAE) and Mean Square Error (MSE)
(Anochi et al., 2021)	RMSE, COV, ME
(Peng et al., 2022)	MSE, RMSE, MAE, R^2
(Endalie et al., 2022)	rmse, normalized root mean squared error (nrmse), nse, Mean Absolute Error, mape AND r^2 METRICS
(Liu et al., 2022)	mean square error (mse), nash–sutcliffe efficiency coefficient (nse) and mean absolute error (mae)
(Gu et al., 2022)	RMSE, MAE, R^2

Source: Made by Author

4. Challenges

After the literature survey, the following challenges needed to be solved for the development of a model predicting more accurate results.

1. To find the most relevant parameters affecting rainfall.
2. To find the best architecture and learning algorithm to be used for creating the rainfall prediction model.
3. To incorporate the use of Sensor data for real-time prediction of rainfall.
4. To use ensemble learning techniques for more accurate predictions.

5. To develop a method of incorporating other features like regional and meteorological parameters affecting rainfall in a particular area.

5. Conclusion and Future Work

Because Deep Learning techniques are better at solving many problems than Machine Learning techniques, the goal of this study is to compare the best models that have been made so far for predicting rain over a region. The model can then be enhanced further for more accurate results in future.

REFERENCES

1. Abdul-Kader, H., Abd-Elsalam, M., & Mohamed, M. (2020). Hybrid Machine Learning Model for Rainfall Forecasting. Journal of Intelligent Systems and Internet of Things, 1(1), 5–12. https://doi.org/10.54216/jisiot.010101
2. Anwar, M. T., Winarno, E., Hadikurniawati, W., & Novita, M. (2021). Rainfall prediction using Extreme Gradient Boosting. Journal of Physics: Conference Series, 1869(1). https://doi.org/10.1088/1742-6596/1869/1/012078
3. Anwar, Muchamad Taufiq, Nugrohadi, S., Tantriyati, V., & Windarni, V. A. (2020). Rain Prediction Using Rule-Based Machine Learning Approach. Advance Sustainable Science, Engineering and Technology, 2(1), 1–6. https://doi.org/10.26877/asset.v2i1.6019
4. Azmi, A. U., Hadi, A. F., Anggraeni, D., & Riski, A. (2021). Naive bayes methods for rainfall prediction classification in Banyuwangi. Journal of Physics: Conference Series, 1872(1). https://doi.org/10.1088/1742-6596/1872/1/012028
5. Budiman, H., & Naparin, H. (2021). Research Article RAINFALL PREDICTION USING BACKPROPAGATION NEURAL NETWORK. 2(1), 22–29.
6. Chhetri, M., Kumar, S., Roy, P. P., & Kim, B. G. (2020). Deep BLSTM-GRU model for monthly rainfall prediction: A case study of Simtokha, Bhutan. Remote Sensing, 12(19), 1–13. https://doi.org/10.3390/rs12193174
7. Haidar, A., & Verma, B. (2018). Monthly Rainfall Forecasting Using One-Dimensional Deep Convolutional Neural Network. IEEE Access, 6, 69053–69063. https://doi.org/10.1109/ACCESS.2018.2880044
8. Haq, D. Z., Rini Novitasari, D. C., Hamid, A., Ulinnuha, N., Arnita, Farida, Y., Nugraheni, R. D., Nariswari, R., Ilham, Rohayani, H., Pramulya, R., & Widjayanto, A. (2021). Long Short-Term Memory Algorithm for Rainfall Prediction Based on El-Nino and IOD Data. Procedia Computer Science, 179(2019), 829–837. https://doi.org/10.1016/j.procs.2021.01.071
9. Mishra, S. K., & Sharma, N. (2018). Rainfall Forecasting Using Backpropagation Neural Network. Studies in Computational Intelligence, 713, 277–288. https://doi.org/10.1007/978-981-10-4555-4_19
10. Pham, B. T., Le, L. M., Le, T. T., Bui, K. T. T., Ly, H. B., & Prakash, I. (2020). Development of advanced artificial intelligence models for daily rainfall prediction. Atmospheric Research, 237, 104845. https://doi.org/10.1016/j.atmosres.2020.104845
11. Poornima, S., & Pushpalatha, M. (2019). Prediction of rainfall using intensified LSTM based recurrent Neural Network with Weighted Linear Units. Atmosphere, 10(11). https://doi.org/10.3390/atmos10110668
12. Sethupathi M, G., Ganesh, Y. S., & Ali, M. M. (2021). Efficient Rainfall Prediction and Analysis using Machine Learning Techniques. Turkish Journal of Computer and Mathematics Education, 12(6), 3467–3474.
13. Sharma, A. K., Chaurasia, S., & Srivastava, D. K. (2018). Supervised Rainfall Learning Model Using Machine Learning Algorithms. Advances in Intelligent Systems and Computing, 723, 275–283. https://doi.org/10.1007/978-3-319-74690-6_27 Sulaiman, J., & Wahab, S. H. (2017). Heavy rainfall forecasting model using artificial neural network for flood prone area. Lecture Notes in Electrical Engineering, 449, 68–76. https://doi.org/10.1007/978-981-10-6451-7_9
14. T. O. Olatayo, & Taiwo, A. I. (2014). Statistical Modelling and Prediction of Rainfall Time Series Data. Global Journal of Comuter Science and Technology:, 14(1), 1–10. http://computerresearch.org/index.php/computer/article/view/58
15. Velasco, L. C. P., Serquiña, R. P., Abdul Zamad, M. S. A., Juanico, B. F., & Lomocso, J. C. (2019). Week-ahead rainfall forecasting using multilayer perceptron neural network. Procedia Computer Science, 161, 386–397. https://doi.org/10.1016/j.procs.2019.11.137
16. Xiang, Y., Gou, L., He, L., Xia, S., & Wang, W. (2018). A SVR–ANN combined model based on ensemble EMD for rainfall prediction. Applied Soft Computing Journal, 73, 874–883. https://doi.org/10.1016/j.asoc.2018.09.018
17. Zhang, P., Cao, W., & Li, W. (2021). Surface and high-altitude combined rainfall forecasting using convolutional neural network. Peer-to-Peer Networking and Applications, 14(3), 1765–1777. https://doi.org/10.1007/s12083-020-00938-x
18. Zhang, X., & Wang, T. (2022). A Novel Integrated Learning Model for Rainfall Prediction CEEMD-FCMSE -Stacking. Research Square.

Computer Science Engineering and Emerging Technologies (ICCS-2022) – Prof (Dr.) Rajeev Sobti et al. (eds)
© 2024 Taylor & Francis Group, London, ISBN 978-1-032-52199-2

Chapter **50**

Recent Advances in Optical Networks and Their Implications for 5G and Beyond Communications

Ramapati Mishra[1]
Director, Institute of Engineering and Technology,
Dr. RML Avadh University, Ayodhya

Sachin Kumar[2]
SDE BSNL

Pedada Sujata[3]
Assistant Professor, ECE,
Lendi Institute of Engineering and Technology, Jonnada, Vizianagaram

R. Swaminathan[4]
Associate Professor, Department of Electrical, Electronics and Communication Engineering,
Galgotias University, Greater Noida, Uttar Pradesh

Yashpal Singh[5]
Professor, Department of Computer Science and Engineering,
Jain Deemed to be University, Bengaluru, Karnataka, India

Joel Alanya-Beltran[6]
Universidad Tecnológica Del Perú

Abstract: 5G and beyond 5G wireless connections have become necessary because of the unprecedentedly rapid expansion of high-speed multimedia services and the variety of applications brought on by the widespread connectivity of IoT devices. Consequently, the vast future data rate needs cannot be met by the current RF ranges of the electromagnetic spectrum. Due to the usage of developmental data devices that include laptops and smart phones, data traffic on mobile devices has significantly increased. Designers and experts were inspired to create the most network-effective architectures as the output. The researcher examined the technology that can enable eventual fifth-generation (5G) networks to achieve speeds of several Gbps. They look at the various issues, questions, and challenges that come up during the research and design phases and come to the conclusion that the network paradigm must be drastically altered in order to accommodate the anticipated high traffic demands and low latency requirements resulting from the internet of things and machine-to-machine communications. Smart devices will also need to be changed or modified in order to support the 5G revolution since the millimeter-wave signal is fundamentally incompatible with their frequency. This means that a considerable change in architecture and network nodes will be necessary. Higher internet speeds, more dependable networks, and more apps will be part of this transformation, though.

Keywords: 5G, Optical networks, IoT

[1]director.rpm@gmail.com, [2]id-sachintyagi@bsnl.co.in, [3]sujatavadisa@gmail.com, [4]r.swaminathan@galgotiasuniversity.edu.in, [5]yashpalsingh009@gmail.com, [6]C18121@utp.edu.pe

DOI: 10.1201/9781003405580-50

1. Introduction

Transmission of ultra-large capacity that had become the rigorous need up to the networks of optical core due to the quick growth of future technologies in 5G Light pulses are used to transfer data signals over optical fibers. Thus, optical signal transmission relies on optical networks. The need for an optical network is also being questioned given the existence of alternative communication networks. The answer to this issue largely depends on how simple it is to deliver a signal using light pulses. Since fiber cable has a cheap cost of manufacture, transmission over it is a simpler operation. A fiber cable also enables more information transport capacity and longer transmission distances than conventional connections. As a result of the utilization of fiber cables, the optical network is a crucial component of the communication network. Rak, J., Giro-Silva, R., Gomes, T., et al. (2021), highlighted In today's culture, communication networks are essential infrastructures that offer end users a variety of basic network services, such as smart grid management, e-banking and e-government services, and remote working. Due to their large capacity and extended transmission range, optical networks have served as the main communication infrastructure for a number of decades. However, a wide range of potential catastrophic events that might result in the simultaneous collapse of several network components endanger their proper operation.

The internet of things, virtual reality, and other high-data-rate developing applications have experienced exponential development, which has caused massive amounts of traffic in 5G and beyond communication infrastructures. The passive optical network (PON), which combines optical and wireless technologies, is gaining popularity. The rigorous delay constraints of PON networks are maintained by this conjugation. The relationship between several delay performance characteristics, such as the quantity of optical network units, the quantity of time slots, the throughput, and the bandwidth in a PON system, is examined by Rawshan, F., Hossen, M., & Islam, M. R. (2021). In order to meet end-user needs, the web services should be able to provide an acceptable degree of latency and more capacity. End-to-end (E2E) latency is a crucial factor in 5GB communications networks for meeting user QoS requirements. Before analyzing the options for transport technology, it is important to understand the major needs of 5G and the way it will impact the architecture of the transport network. PON comes out as a strong choice among the competing technologies due to its architecture of multi-points for the effective use of the resources of fiber. It was then deployed widely to access static services globally. The PON market has grown quickly since its launch in the late 1990s to presently support almost 100 million broadband customers globally. Before analyzing the options for technology, it is important to understand the major needs of 5G and how it will impact the architecture of the transport network. PON comes out as a strong choice among the competing technologies due to its architecture of point-to-multipoint for effective use of fiber resources and its widespread deployment for static access services globally. The PON market has grown quickly since its launch in the late 1990s to presently support almost 100 million broadband customers globally. Key 5G wireless transport standards are covered, followed by a discussion of technologies for optical access as well as ongoing developmental standards. Therefore, some cutting-edge PON technologies are highlighted by Wey, J. S., and Zhang, J. (2018).

Many technologies are already being considered for a forthcoming wireless system through wireless research activities. The future 5G environment's focus will be on requirements for fast data and low latency. The current 5G network cannot just be modified or evolved to meet the extremely high data throughput and extremely low latency requirements of 6G and beyond. As a result, research must concentrate on technologies that would significantly affect system performance. To achieve this, drastic modifications will be made to the base station, component, and network levels. The V.Panwar, D.K. Sharma, K. V. P. Kumar et al. (2021) study covers a variety of topics related to wireless network optimization and design, including physical layer research, network administration, and channel measurements, modeling, and estimation.

2. Literature Review

The development of fifth-generation (5G) and beyond communication networks is expected to offer services with excellent quality of experience, huge connections, an ultrahigh data rate, ultralow latency, significantly better security, and extremely low energy usage. Compared to legacy systems, 5G and beyond communication technologies are anticipated to be both more sophisticated and more complicated, according to Chowdhury, M. Z., and Cano (2019). Many technological challenges need to be tackled in order for the heterogeneous networks to fully converge.

New difficult technological paths are emerging on a long investigation scope, heading beyond 5G or 6G communications, which promise to transform the user network experience. The future service needs are anticipated to be further aggravated in regards to capacity, latency, reconfigurability, dependability, and security, even if this is just a vision and the precise descriptions of the novel services have not yet been determined. Therefore, it is not possible to simply scale up the current manner of operation in optical networks. There will need to be a redesign that incorporates new optical networks with built-in security, sub-linear bandwidth scalability costs, extremely low latency, and reconfigurability (Tornatore, M., Wong, E., Zhu, Z., et al., 2021). To determine the relationship among performances and machining parameters, regression analysis is typically performed. In A. Jain's and A. K. Pandey's (2019) work, a mathematical model was created between the experimentally collected data using linear regression analysis.

Optical networks, which serve as the foundation for 5G and future communications, can provide a low-cost option for quantum key distribution implementation by exploiting the available fiber resources. Particularly, QKD measurement-device independence demonstrates its capacity to increase the distance of security using an unreliable relay. The untrusted relay clearly provides stronger security compared to the trustworthy relay because it doesn't rely on any measurement assumptions and even permits access by an eavesdropper. According to Cao, Y., Zhao, Y., Li, J., et al. (2021), it is anticipated that it will be paired with trustworthy relay by QKD deployment on a large scale since it could not be extended to QKD indefinite distance like trusted relay can. A novel network architecture based on hybrid untrusted and trusted relays across QKD is presented, with a backbone of optical backbone, untrusted relay, and architectural nodes of the trusted relay of the network. Models for the associated networks, costs, and security are created.

It would be wise to investigate future research directions for novel multiplexing techniques that significantly increase fiber transmission capacity. Space division multiplexing, which has become a research hotspot, is the major method to improve optical fiber communication capacity in the future due to the limitations of single fiber transmission. SDM, however, also introduces some fresh issues, such as sophisticated crosstalk evaluation and the creation of multi-dimensional resource pieces, leading to more intricate and varied characteristics impacting service transmission. As per Yao, Q., Yang, H., Yan, et al. (2020), the service quality cannot be adequately assured if the effects of several parameters cannot be thoroughly assessed. In light of this, we suggest a routing and resource allocation (RRA) system for multi-core fiber-core optical networks that relies on self-organizing feature maps (SOM).

Open Space Optics (FSO) is an optical communication method that uses light transmission to wirelessly send data through free spaces like the air, vacuum, or astronomical space. High data speeds of up to 2.5 Gbps are available at distances of 100 m to a few kilometers using FSO communication, and it has the opportunity to replace conventional communication methods in a number of applications. Although it offers benefits like unlicensed spectrum and large bandwidth, issues like interference and atmospheric turbulence have restricted its widespread adoption. Researchers have suggested modulation methods, coding schemes, diversity, hybrid systems, and physical deployment of hardware to overcome many of these problems, according to Zafar, S., and Khalid, H. (2021).

3. Methodology and Model Specifications

The convergence of the diverse wireless technologies has come to be recognized as one of the essential options for achieving the objectives of 5G and beyond in communication networks. This requires the convergence of optical and RF wireless communication technologies in addition to radio frequency (RF) technologies. Possible future high-capacity optical wireless communication (OWC) networks are being developed, and the optical spectrum is being viewed as a potential option. It provides special benefits, including a sizable unregulated optical spectrum and built-in security. Consequently, it is projected that future networks will employ a multitier RF and optical design. According to Chowdhury, Shahjalal, M., Hasan, M. K., et al. (2019), high capacity, enormous connection, high security, low latency, reduced energy usage, a high level of experience, and dependable connectivity are a few of the few significant and widespread challenges connected to the quality of service of communication systems in 5G and 6G. In terms of these concerns, 6G communication will undoubtedly perform several times better than 5G communication. A key component of 5G and beyond will also be the Internet of Things, built on the tactile internet. A. Jain and A. K. Pandey's (2019) generated models' statistical analysis demonstrated their suitability and reliability, indicating that they may be utilized to accurately forecast certain quality features. The genetic algorithm tool has been used to maximize these quality attributes (Jain A., Yadav A.K., & Shrivastava Y., 2019).

RF is now a popular technology for a variety of wireless connectivity applications. There are a number of restrictions for RF-based wireless communication, including a small spectrum, significant interference, and rigorous regulation. The need for 5GB and IoT networks cannot be met by any other wireless communication technology except those based on radio frequency. As a result, scientists are working hard to identify a new spectrum that will satisfy the ever-expanding demands. For the development of 5GB, a very wide optical band is seen as a potential approach. The average transmission speed of the 5G wireless communication networks is predicted to be 1 Gbps, with a peak rate of 10 Gbps. As a result, tens of Gbps to Tbps data rates per device will subsequently be supported by 6G.

4. Results and Discussions

To achieve a thousand-fold increase in capacity on 5GB networks, substantially greater bandwidth is required. The optical spectrum offers this greater bandwidth. The electromagnetic spectrum's radiofrequency and optical frequencies are listed in Table 50.1. The optical bandwidth is extremely high by a wide margin. But today, just a small section of the optical spectrum—parts of the visible, near-infrared, and middle ultraviolet—is employed. The utilization of the optical spectrum component will be expanded in the future, along with improvements to its effectiveness.

Table 50.1   Optical and RF [15]

	Category	Frequency-Range
RF	Low-to-extremely-high frequency	4 kHz to 40 GHz
Optical	IR	101–214.4 THz
	VL	506.6–525.3 THz
	UV	2.458–2.478 PHz

5. Conclusion

In order to bridge the distance between the optical fiber infrastructure and the end users, systems have received attention because they offer an effective solution to the bottlenecks of the last mile problem. The development of links and significant investments in fiber backbone are being made by telecom operators in order to make the most of the current configuration. This development at the network boundary, where end users may quickly connect with high-speed systems, is also significant. In situations where underground optical fiber communication is expensive and/or impractical, these methods can be a potential option. To fulfill the ever-increasing higher data rate requirements in future-generation communication networks, it is crucial to create ubiquitous and effective wireless systems for a variety of transmission connections. Communication has been recognized as a promising option for next-generation optical networking due to its radio-frequency (RF) counterparts' limited spectrum availability. That the communication can support the enormous traffic demand brought on by IoT/IoE devices and next-generation cellular communications networks.

REFERENCES

1. Cao, Y., Zhao, Y., Li, J., Lin, R., Zhang, J., & Chen, J. (2021). Hybrid trusted/untrusted relay-based quantum key distribution over optical backbone networks. IEEE Journal on Selected Areas in Communications, 39(9), 2701–2718.
2. Chowdhury, M. Z., & Cano, J. C. Convergence of Heterogeneous Wireless Networks for 5G-and-Beyond Communications: Applications, Architecture, and Resource Management.
3. Chowdhury, M. Z., Shahjalal, M., Hasan, M. K., & Jang, Y. M. (2019). The role of optical wireless communication technologies in 5G/6G and IoT solutions: Prospects, directions, and challenges. Applied Sciences, 9(20), 4367.
4. Jahid, A., Alsharif, M. H., & Hall, T. J. (2022). A contemporary survey on free space optical communication: Potentials, technical challenges, recent advances and research direction. Journal of Network and Computer Applications, 103311.
5. Jain, A., & Pandey, A. K. (2017). Multiple quality optimizations in electrical discharge drilling of mild steel sheet. Materials Today: Proceedings, 4(8), 7252–7261.
6. Jain, A., & Pandey, A. K. (2019). Modeling and optimizing of different quality characteristics in electrical discharge drilling of titanium alloy (Grade-5) sheet. Materials Today: Proceedings, 18, 182–191.
7. Jain, A., Yadav, A. K., & Shrivastava, Y. (2020). Modelling and optimization of different quality characteristics in electric discharge drilling of titanium alloy sheet. Materials Today: Proceedings, 21, 1680–1684.
8. Panwar, V., Sharma, D. K., Kumar, K. P., Jain, A., & Thakar, C. (2021). Experimental investigations and optimization of surface roughness in turning of en 36 alloy steel using response surface methodology and genetic algorithm. Materials Today: Proceedings, 46, 6474–6481.
9. Rak, J., Girão-Silva, R., Gomes, T., Ellinas, G., Kantarci, B., & Tornatore, M. (2021). Disaster resilience of optical networks: State of the art, challenges, and opportunities. Optical Switching and Networking, 42, 100619.
10. Rawshan, F., Hossen, M., & Islam, M. R. (2021, October). Delay Performance Optimization in Passive Optical Network. In 2021 International Conference on Information and Communication Technology Convergence (ICTC) (pp. 551–554). IEEE.
11. Tornatore, M., Wong, E., Zhu, Z., Casellas, R., Bathula, B. G., & Wosinska, L. (2021). Guest Editorial Latest Advances in Optical Networks for 5G Communications and Beyond. IEEE Journal on Selected Areas in Communications, 39(9), 2667–2671.
12. Wey, J. S., & Zhang, J. (2018). Passive optical networks for 5G transport: technology and standards. Journal of Lightwave Technology, 37(12), 2830–2837.
13. Yao, Q., Yang, H., Yan, B., Bao, B., Yu, A., & Zhang, J. (2020, June). Routing and resource allocation leveraging self-organizing feature maps in multi-core optical networks against 5G and beyond. In 2020 International Wireless Communications and Mobile Computing (IWCMC) (pp. 857–860). IEEE.
14. Zafar, S., & Khalid, H. (2021). Free space optical networks: applications, challenges and research directions. Wireless Personal Communications, 121(1), 429–457.
15. Dhury, M. Z., Shahjalal, M., Hasan, M. K.,&Jang, Y. M. (2019). The role of optical wireless communication technologies in 5G/6G and IoT solutions: Prospects, directions, and challenges. Applied Sciences, 9(20), 4367.

Computer Science Engineering and Emerging Technologies (ICCS-2022) – Prof (Dr.) Rajeev Sobti et al. (eds)
© 2024 Taylor & Francis Group, London, ISBN 978-1-032-52199-2

Chapter **51**

Depression Detection Using Artificial Intelligence: A Review

Vishnu Kant Pandey[1]

Research Scholar, School of Computer Science and Engineering,
Lovely Professional University Phagwara, Punjab, India

Vijay Kumar Garg[2]

Associate Professor, School of Computer Science and Engineering,
Lovely Professional University Phagwara, Punjab, India

Abstract: Depression is a common mental disorder that causes feelings of sadness, anger, and disinterest. According to the World Health Organization, more than 5% of adults suffer from depression, which is one of the major contributors to suicide globally. Previously, a lot of studies had been done to detect depression. The most common studies used by many researchers are based on artificial intelligence techniques such as machine learning and deep learning, or on data mining and other visual indicator-based methods. In this paper, we did a comparative analysis of previously published studies on those methods, such as support vector machine (SVM), Bayesian network (BN), random forest (RF), K nearest neighbor (KNN), long short-term memory network (LSMT), and convolution neural network (CNN), and analyzed their respective accuracy and results.

Keywords: Depression detection, SVM, RF, BN, CNN, KNN, LSMT, Artificial intelligence

1. Introduction

Depression is a common mental disorder that has a major effect on how a person feels and acts and makes them sad and aggressive. According to the World Health Organization, nearly 280 million people suffer from depression. The WHO describes it as one of the most painful disorders. A person suffering from depression may feel anything from sad and unhappy to guilty and worthless, depending on the severity of the disorder. Even though it is a treatable disorder, nearly two-thirds of people do not get any treatment, and sometimes it translates into self-harm. Even in those cases where people get treatment, it is really difficult to detect and treat in one session. It generally takes 15 days and more than one session to receive an appropriate treatment.

According to the recent statistics of the National Crime Records Bureau, the suicide rate in India has gone up to 12% in 2021 from 9.9% in 2017. The majority of this increase came after the outbreak of COVID-19, which made people stay at home for a longer duration of time, which resulted in an increased rate of depression.

2. Artificial Intelligence Techniques

Artificial intelligence (AI) is a field that aims to create algorithms and computer models in such a way that machines can perform tasks with human intelligence or better. AI performance can range from simple image and speech recognition

*Vishnujnp45@gmail.com, [2]vijay.garg@lpu.co.in

DOI: 10.1201/9781003405580-51

to highly critical decision-making in medical and business fields. Here we took some well-known artificial intelligence techniques and compared models developed in them to detect depression.

2.1 Support Vector Machine

The support vector machine (SVM) algorithm finds the maximum margin in the N-dimension to create an optimal hyperplane to separate two classes of data. This supervised algorithm can be used in both classification and regression of data on the basis of hyperplane. Here, we compared some of the models developed on the basis of SVM to find out their performance on the basis of accuracy. In the following model, social media posts and comments are used as primary data sets to find out the prevalence of depression among users.

Table 51.1   SVM research papers and accuracy

Author	Model	Dataset	Accuracy
Bohang chen et al [12]	Hyperplane maximumseparation	Twitter	74.18
Li et al [11]	Universal sentenceencoder	Twitter	87
Fatima et al [15]	Input classificationalgorithm	LiveJournal	80
Islam et al [3]	Emotional, linguistic andtemporal informationprocessing	Facebook	73
Gamon et al [9]	Egocentric social behaviour by graphicalanalysis	Twitter	71.2
Shatte et al [10]	Fathers' behaviour andtopic analysis	Reddit	66
Priyanka et al [13]	Feature extraction	Twitter	79.7

Source: Made by Author

2.2 Bayesian Network

A Bayesian network is a probability-based graphical model that consists of nodes and edges, where nodes denote probability and nodes are random variables due to this node and edge formation. Bayesian networks are also called Bayes nets or belief networks. In this study, we took five models based on Bayesian networks and compared their ability to detect depression in publicly available databases. These databases may have textual or descriptive types. Here, textual features describe the dataset used in the study as texts, words, sentences, or n-grams. And the descriptive feature shows that in this database, the information of the users is taken into account, such as age, gender, profession, education, and income level.

Table 51.2   Bayesian models and accuracy

Author	Accuracy	Dataset	Feature type	Year
Priya et al [4]	85.5	DASS-21	Descriptive	2020
Neesha et al [5]	95.7	Onlinesurvey	Descriptive	2020
Alsagri HS et al [6]	82.7	Twitter	Textual	2020
Hassan AU et al [8]	91	Twitter	Textual	2017
Shen G et al [7]	85	Twitter	Descriptive	2017
Chen B et al [12]	78	Twitter	Textual	2018
Tao x et al [14]	76.6	Facebook	Descriptive	2019

Source: Made by Author

2.3 Random Forest

Each random forest has multiple trees. Each tree samples data from the dataset. Then each node has its own subset of features on the basis of which it spits out and averages out to control overfitting and improve accuracy. Fatima [15] has developed a model on the basis of splitting data into positive and negative emotions on a first-person basis, which gives an accuracy of 89.8%. [21] is another model where 89% accuracy was achieved.

2.4 K Nearest Neighbour

K nearest neighbor (KNN) calculates the distance from existing data to new data and puts it into the category that has the minimum distance from it. KNN can be used for both classification and regression. In [19], it was used as a classification method to analyze extremist affiliations and gave an accuracy of 72%. In another study, [18] was used to classify Twitter posts using the lexicon dictionary and performed with an accuracy of 73%.

2.5 Convolutional Neural Network

A convolutional neural network (CNN) is a class of artificial neural networks that have an extra layer called convolutional, which enables them to perform better with audio signals and visual imagery. In [2], it worked on a dataset combined with tweets and images and gave an accuracy of 88.4%, and in the case of textual data [1] only based on Reddit posts, it gave an accuracy of 75.13%.

2.6 Long Short-term Memory Network

Long short-term memory network (LSMT) is a special kind of recurring neural network (RNN). LSMT takes care of the long-term dependencies of the network to handle the vanishing gradient problem of RNN. In [23] and [22], they used modules in which RNN formed a chain of repeating modules, and it has an accuracy of 85% and 71.17%.

3. Result and Discussion

In this study, an attempt was made to study various techniques individually, examine their stand-alone models, and analyze them on the basis of their accuracy. In this study, we compared SVM, Bayesian network, random forest, KNN, CNN, and LSMT techniques. In the process of reviewing these papers for each of these techniques, we took multiple parameters into account: datasets, data features, and accuracy.

In Fig. 51.1, we can see more than half of the authors took textual features into consideration, such as texts, words, sentences, or n-grams. And nearly one third of them used descriptive features such as age, gender, profession, education, and income level of the users, while the rest of the authors used visual data like images and videos. Figure 51.2 shows the source of the data. As per the figure, we can see that Twitter posts and tweets were used to acquire data by 8 researchers, Reddit was used by 3, online surveys and Facebook were used by 2, and DASS and LiveJournal were used by one each.

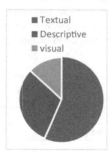

Fig. 51.1 Data Feature

Source: Made by Author

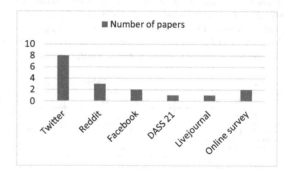

Fig. 51.2 Datasets

Source: Made by Author

In Fig. 51.3, we compare the accuracy ranges of the various different techniques. Even though SVM has a model with a minimum accuracy of 66, it also has one of its models with an accuracy of 87 percent, which shows it has improved a lot in recent years. The KNN model with the most accuracy has 73 percent accuracy, which makes it the least efficient technique, and BN has a model with 95.7 percent accuracy, which makes it the most efficient technique among all the analyzed models.

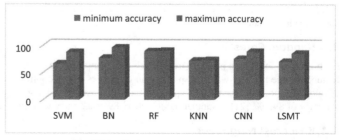

Fig. 51.3 Techniques and accuracy ranges

Source: Made by Author

4. Conclusion

In this paper, we wanted to summarize the brief scenario of the development going on in various standalone artificial techniques for the detection of depressive disorders. We analyzed 20 papers covering depression detection from various inputs, such as text from social media platforms and visual imagery. We used six standalone approaches used in the field of artificial intelligence. These six techniques are support vector machines, Bayesian networks, random forests, K nearest neighbors, convolutional neural networks, and long-short-term memory networks. Out of these six techniques, CNN is most widely used in machine learning approaches, and LSMT is used in combined techniques of deep learning. Our study will provide a basic understanding of problem solving in other related medical domains.

REFERENCES

1. Kim J, Lee J, Park E, Han J (2020) A deep learning model for detecting mental illness from user content on social media. Scientific reports 10 (1): 11846–11846.
2. Srimadhur N S, Lalitha S (2020) An End-to-End Model for Detection and Assessment of Depression Levels using Speech. Procedia Computer Science 171: 12–21
3. Islam M R, Kabir M A, Ahmed A, Kamal A R M, Wang H, Ulhaq A. Depression detection from social network data using machine learning techniques. Health Inf Sci Syst 2018
4. Priya A, Garg S, Tigga N P (2020) Predicting anxiety, depression and stress in modern life using machine learning algorithms. Procedia Computer Science 167: 1258–1267
5. Jothi N, Husain W, Rashid N A (2020) Predicting generalized anxiety disorder among women using Shapley value. J Infect Public Health 14 (1): 103–108.
6. Alsagri H S, Ykhlef M (2020) Machine Learning-Based Approach for Depression Detection in Twitter Using Content and Activity Features. IEICE Transactions on Information and Systems E103.D (8): 1825–1832.
7. Shen G, Jia J, Nie L, Feng F, Zhang C, Hu T, Chua T-S, Zhu W Depression detection via harvesting social media: A multimodal dictionary learning solution In: Proceedings of the Twenty-Sixth International Joint Conference on Artificial Intelligence, Melbourne, Australia, 19–25 August 2017.
8. Hassan A U, Hussain J, Hussain M, Sadiq M, Lee S Sentiment analysis of social networking sites (SNS) data using machine learning approach for the measurement of depression. In: Proceedings of 2017 International Conference on Information and Communication Technology Convergence (ICTC), Jeju, South Korea, 18–20 Oct. 2017
9. De Choudhury M, Gamon M, Counts S, Horvitz E. Predicting depression via social media. : AAAI; 2013 Jul 10 Presented at: the Seventh International AAAI Conference on Weblogs and Social Media; July 8–11, 2013
10. Shatte A B R, Hutchinson D M, Fuller-Tyszkiewicz M, Teague S J. Social Media Markers to Identify Fathers at Risk of Postpartum Depression: A Machine Learning Approach. Cyberpsychol Behav Soc Netw 2020
11. Li D, Chaudhary H, Zhang Z. Modeling Spatiotemporal Pattern of Depressive Symptoms Caused by COVID-19 Using Social Media Data Mining. Int J Environ Res Public Health 2020 Jul 10; 17(14): 1–23
12. Chen B, Cheng L, Chen R, Huang Q, Phoebe Chen Y-P. Deep neural networks for multiclass sentiment classifcation. In: IEEE 20th International Conference on high performance computing and communications, IEEE 16th International Conference on Smart City, IEEE 4th International Conference on Data Science and Systems 2018; pp. 854–59.
13. Arora P, Arora P. Mining Twitter data for depression detection. In: IEEE International Conference on signal processing and communication (ICSC), 2019
14. Tao X, Dharmalingam R, Zhang J, Zhou X, Li L, Gururajan R. Twitter analysis for depression on social networks based on sentiment and stress. In: 6th International Conference on behavioral, economic and socio-cultural computing, 2019
15. Fatima I, Mukhtar H, Ahmad H F, Rajpoot K. Analysis of user-generated content from online social communities to characterise and predict depression degree. Journal of Information Science 2017
16. Katchapakirin K, Wongpatikaseree K, Yomaboot P, Kaewpitakkun Y. Facebook social media for depression detection in the Thai community. In: 15th International Joint Conference on computer science and software engineering (JCSSE), 2018;
17. Han Y, Liu M, Jing W. Aspect-level drug reviews sentiment analysis based on double BiGRU and knowledge transfer. IEEE Access. 2020
18. Gaikwad G, Joshi DeJ. Multiclass mood classifcation on twitter using lexicon dictionary and machine learning algorithms. In: International Conference on inventive computation technologies (ICICT) 2016
19. Ahmad S, Asghar M Z, Alotaibi F M, Awan I. Detection and classifcation of social media-based extremist afliations using sentiment analysis techniques. Human Centric Comput Inf Sci. 2019; 24: 1–23
20. Sobin C, Sackeim H A. Psychomotor symptoms of depression. American Journal of Psychiatry. 1997 Jan 1; 154(1): 4–17.
21. Filho E M S, Veiga Rey H C, Frajtag R M, Arrowsmith Cook D M, Dalbonio de Carvalho LN, Pinho Ribeiro AL, Amaral J (2021) Can machine learning be useful as a screening tool for depression in primary care? J Psychiatr Res 132
22. Han Y, Liu M, Jing W. Aspect-level drug reviews sentiment analysis based on double BiGRU and knowledge transfer. IEEE Access. 2020
23. Katchapakirin K, Wongpatikaseree K, Yomaboot P, Kaewpitakkun Y. Facebook social media for depression detection in the Thai community.

Computer Science Engineering and Emerging Technologies (ICCS-2022) – Prof (Dr.) Rajeev Sobti et al. (eds)
© 2024 Taylor & Francis Group, London, ISBN 978-1-032-52199-2

Chapter

52

A Review for Weather Forecasting and Photovoltaic Load Forecasting Systems

Dora Praveen Kumar[1]

Student, Computer Science and Engineering,
Lovely Professional University, Phagwara, India

Navjot Kaur[2]

Assistant professor, Computer Science and Engineering,
Lovely Professional University, Phagwara, India

Abstract: This study primarily focuses on the transition from non-renewable energy sources to renewable resources. For countries to be self-sufficient, they are switching to solar, wind, tidal, and hydroelectric power plants; this change is being driven by the non-renewable resource dominating countries' targeting the fuel resources and the regulation of their prices, along with the rapid replenishment forcing everyone to turn to an alternative form of energy and to save the planet's ecological balance and reduce global warming. In this paper, the literature on PV load forecasting and weather forecasting with a focus on solar power was examined. As the parameters list varies depending on the geographic location for load forecasting, we will discuss and conclude the methodologies they used and the variables they discussed for implementation. We included weather forecasting because the PV panel is mostly dependent on the weather as it only functions on solar irradiance and if this irradiance is hampered by rain, snow, or panel shedding, its efficiency goes down. We even detailed the dataset that they used, the research gaps, and the potential areas for future study that future researchers could pursue to increase the productivity and output efficiency of PV panels.

Keywords: Weather forecasting, Global solar radiation, Solar energy, Modelling, Meteorological variables, Machine learning, Deep learning, Photovoltaic solar power estimation

1. Introduction

This study examines the facts regarding how the PV panels' load output is influenced by the constantly changing, adverse weather, which has a direct bearing on the solar panel's power output. Since the world is running out of non-renewable resources like coal and petroleum on which we have relied for hundreds of years without considering the rate of depletion there will come a time when we must turn to another source of energy that we can rely upon for following several centuries without affecting or polluting the environment.

Earlier, there used to be a pattern in weather change, with summers, rains, and cold winters occurring for a period that was similar for a few decades. Now, however, there is no such pattern. It may rain between summers or winters; the temperature in summers is rising to an intolerable limit; and if our algorithms found a pattern in this rapidly changing climate, then we will be able to predict the future if there is another prophecy for an adverse climatic condition such as rain, hail, snow or dust storm, then we will be able to compensate for it beforehand.

[1]kumardorapraveen@gmail.com, [2]navjot.23838@lpu.co.in

DOI: 10.1201/9781003405580-52

The PV panels' efficiency reaches its maximum only when the irradiance approaches the irradiance level. If the irradiance is lower, they still function fine; it's only the coherence that falls. Since there is no sun to receive solar radiation during the night, the irradiance is at its lowest, or we may say; zero.

1.1 Weather Forecasting

Weather forecasting foretells the aeronautical conditions for a certain place and time stretch using science and technology. Individuals have been trying forecasting the climatic conditions offhandedly for millennia and methodically since the seventeenth centennial. Weather prognostication, which was formerly done with hardware paying major attention to changes in contemporary weather patterns, barometric pressure, and sky condition, i.e., cloud coverage, is now automated using complex math put in computer-based algorithms to take a variety of atmospheric attributes into account. Climatic procrastination is created by accumulating accurate data on a location and using meteorology to foresee how the weather will act in future. Human response is also essential in order to pick the foremost prediction algorithm on which forecast to rely on. With a $17 billion market and 51,875 job opportunities, the weather forecasting service business is a massive industry within the United States. The industry's average profit margin outpaces the annual investment made in it by more than 6% among the 45,255 active businesses.

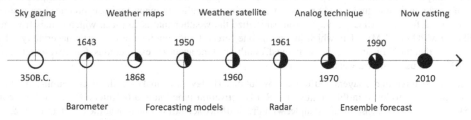

Fig. 52.1 Evolution of weather forecasting with time [31]

Source: Dora Praveen Kumar

Modern machine learning and deep learning models are using the timeline as the most crucial parameter for the prognostication of weather. They consider a span of hours, days, weeks, and more for guessing the subsequent weather. The following are the models depending on horizons:

1. Now Forecasting (3-4 hrs.)
2. Short-Range Forecasting (1-2 days)
3. Medium-Range Forecasting (3-4 days, 2 weeks)
4. Long-Range Forecasting (> 4 weeks)
5. Hazardous Weather Forecasting

1.2 Photovoltaic Power Forecasting

PV power forecasting in simple terms is solar power divination, in order to lessen the effects of solar intermittency, it is a process of gathering traits and statistics to infer solar power output over a range of time periods. For effective grid management and power trading, solar power projections are employed. As significant obstacles to the use of solar energy, such as the high cost of materials and poor conversion efficiency, continue to disappear, difficulties with erratic operation and dependability have gained prominence. Solar forecasting has often been used to successfully solve and reduce the intermittency problem.

The path of the Sun, the state of the atmosphere, light scattering, and the features of the solar energy plant are all common pieces of information utilized in solar power forecasts. The output of the panel is calculated by the formula

$$A \times \beta \times 75\% = \text{daily watt-hours} \qquad (1)$$

In Equation (1) A is the average number of hours of sunlight, β which is solar collectors watts. There are now 4 produced cell types that are extensively used:

1. Monocrystalline solar cells
2. Polycrystalline solar cells
3. Passivated Emitter and Rear Cell (PERC)

4. Thin-film solar cells
   (a) Cadmium telluride (CdTe)
   (b) AmorphousSilicon (a-Si).

2. Literature Review

Weather forecast and PV power has been the subject of a substantial amount of research employing a variety of methodologies. There have been several study efforts designed on the topic of foretelling by a variety of researchers with numerous ML and DL algorithms and modern high-class equipment.

Let's discuss the preliminary investigations conducted by scientists across the world who have used a wide variety of methods.

2.1 Weather Forecasting Literature Review

A stochastic weather forewarning error-model was implemented in paper "Weather forecast error modelling and performance analysis of automatic greenhouse climate control" published in 2021 by Wouter J.P. Kuijpers to expand the capability of producing conjecture based on a set of determining weather to many forecasts produced on a single set of rhythmic condition for the RMPC technique. You can utilize the weather that is foreseen which comes from a weather service, like CEMPC or CEMPC KF, which just needs one forecast and ignores the forecast's uncertainty. The study's shortcoming was that the Kalman filter they employed, didn't meet the accuracy expectations. Future research would focus on putting RHOC to use with real weather forecasts.

Ibrahim Gada used three dense layers and three convolutions 1D layers to make up the deep learning model, each of which is configured as follows: In this context, the ReLU activation function and 64 filters of length 3 are considered. We used 512 neurons in the dense layer example, with the SoftMax activation function at the resultant layer & the ReLU activation method in the inner levels. Furthermore, the loss is calculated using categorical cross-entropy. We considered the classification and regression tasks' accuracy and R2 scores, as well as the Adam optimizer, to examine the execution of the suggested models. The conduction of the KNN algorithm, random forest, and XGBoost models, on the other hand, typically outperformed other models for weather prognosis in the learning stage, albeit their interpretation considerably dropped in the testing stage, indicating some degree of overfitting. Linear regression performs well for the prediction task during the testing phase. The k-Neighbour's model had low performance, but the prediction error might be reduced by utilizing a lot of data during training.

Lingaraju Naveen, Hosaagrahara Savalegowda Mohan for data training, the system used a linear regression technique. Information for pedagogy was gathered through the UCI data repository, 'data.gov.in', and 'ncdc.noaa.gov'. The suggested IoT-based weather station provided a data set. Data from September 1, 2021, to September 30, 2021, were given by the dataset. Results indicate that, with 90.5% accuracy, the test with 7 secret layers was more accurate than the tests with 5, 6, 8, 9, and 10 hidden levels. Tests using hidden layer numbers 7, and 10 were more accurate than tests using hidden layer numbers 5, 6, 8, and 9 (87.2%). The test with 8 secret layers had an accuracy of 68.2%, which was higher than the tests with 5, 6, 7, 9, and 10 hidden levels. The test with 5 secret layers had an accuracy of 89.6%, which was higher than the tests with 6, 7, 8, 9, and 10 hidden levels. The test with 9 secret layers had an accuracy of 90.5%, which was higher than the tests with 5, 6, 7, 8, and 10 hidden levels.

2.2 PV Power Forecasting Literature Review

The main thing that researchers play with, while making a model for forecasting is parameter list and hybrid models or modern deep learning models along with accuracy improvement. Below are a few methods that people have tried and tested.

Sonia Leva and team used data from a Monocrystalline Photovoltaic cell during study at SolarTechLab in Milano and the model they propose is a Physical Hybrid Artificial neural network with the first layer comprising 12 neurons and second layer with 5 which helped in decreasing the computational part. Karimatun Nisa, Berhane Darsene Dimd, and Vrettos all have used (ANN) Artificial neural network with the SARIMA model, Levenberg-Marquardt method, or LSTM and the accuracies improved by MSE 0.18 and 33% more than just the ANN alone. This approach was mainly focused on a timeline of short-term and now forecasting 1-24 hours.

In the study "Spatio-Temporal Graph Neural Networks for Multi-Site PV Power Forecasting," two brand-new graph neural network models- The graph-convolutional transformer (GCTrafo) and graph-convolutional long short-term memory (GCLSTM) models graph neural network algorithms which were employed deterministic multi-site PV were foreseen. The two data sets used to assess the suggested methodologies were scattered across Switzerland and included constructive data from 304 real-time PV systems and replicated production of 1000 PV machines. On the synthetic dataset, the average NRMSE error was 8.3% (GCLSTM) & 8.4% (GCTrafo), whereas the average error on the actual dataset was 12.6% (GCLSTM) & 13.6% (GCTrafo)., they exceed state-of-the-art approaches. Both architectures are interesting for grid management implementation with a greater number of nodes since they were scaled to 1000 nodes using a single GPU and can support more nodes utilizing multi-GPU computation.

In this paper by Shree Krishna Acharya titled "Day-Ahead Forecasting for Small-Scale Photovoltaic Power Based on Similar Day Detection with Selective Weather Variables," they tested a model they had developed using hourly recorded data for a year from a 1 MW PV installation in Goheung, Korea (January 2015 to December 2015). The model performed primary selection using pwv and secondary selection using swv, and then used LSTM to forecast.

3. Tabular Comparison and Findings

After reviewing all the papers thoroughly and aligning them in a tabular format, we analysed the data and inferred that mostly 'Machine Learning Algorithms' were used before, and in recent times, we are resorting to more hybrid models and deep learning models. This is because, these models have a much better training and learning curve as compared to state-of-art methods and it even learns the drastic changes in adverse conditions. Below is a word cloud of all the keywords mentioned in the papers we listed.

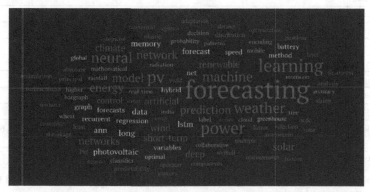

Fig. 52.2 Word cloud of all keywords mentioned in papers listed [32]

Source: Dora Praveen Kumar

From Fig. 52.2. it's quite evident that the neural network model i.e., ANN is used rigorously by researchers and is now targeting short-term forecasting.

Below is Table 52.1. listing all the research gaps and future works which would be helpful for future investigation topic selection.

Table 52.1 Research gaps and future scopes

	Details
1	Modern Deep-learning models must replace just conventional machine-learning models to adapt to datasets and make predictions more effectively.
2	For the prediction model to be more stable, we need to research PV power forecasts under harsh weather conditions.
3	In three types of weather, including snow, rain & fog, the short-term photovoltaic load is excluded, which was projected by researchers to be taken into account.
4	The HDNN model & dispatching method may be combined to duplicate transactive energy scenes for PV power forecasting.
5	The impact of various meteorological factors, like wind, on the cooling of solar modules, the removal of potential fine foreign particles like dust depositions in rains, etc., may be researched.

	Details
6	If ensemble predictions for weather forecasting were accessible, the stochastic weather forecast error model and related premises would no longer be necessary. A future step would thus be to apply RHOC to real weather forecasts.
7	Where radiation data is lacking, a mathematical model employing trigonometric functions can be used to approximate solar radiation.
8	A fascinating undertaking in the future would be to generate predictions using a stockpile ensemble learning AI model. It involves combining the results of many regression algorithms on the same dataset.
9	The resilience and adaptation of models to incomplete datasets, which is critical for autoregressive models, is another area of research.
10	The suggested deterministic multi-site PV forecasting models, the graph-convolutional transformer (GCTrafo) and the graph-convolutional long-short-term memory (GCLSTM), may be transformed into probabilistic models by adding noise to the deterministic model to produce a generator in a similar fashion. This generator should be given training using a suitable classifier as a determiner in an adversary setting in order to provide a probabilistic forecast.

Source: Dora Praveen Kumar

Table 52.2 lists all the publicly available datasets and the physical plant location from where data is acquired and collaborated.

Table 52.2 Datasets used by researchers

	Datasets
1	Welcome - KNMI Data Platform - KNMI Data Platform
2	Meteorological data
3	https://www.seinfra.ce.gov.br/ http://sonda.ccst.inpe.br/
4	Indian Monsoon Data Assimilation and Analysis (IMDAA) (1980–2018)
5	NCDC meteorological data
6	Advancing Earth and Space Science (agu.org)
7	https://github.com/pangeo-data/WeatherBench
8	Monocrystalline PV plant under experimentation at SolarTechLab, Politecnico, Italy.
9	Department of Electric Power Engineering, Norwegian
10	Physical plants in Bangladesh, Korea, Netherlands, Uruguay, Switzerland, Arlington, Thailand, Queensland, Norway, Milano, India, Canberra

Source: Dora Praveen Kumar

Below is the description of all the deep-learning models, machine-learning models, classifiers, and hybrid models, that were used during the experimental analysis.

Table 52.3 ML, Hybrid, and DL models

	Model description
1	Stochastic model
2	Cosine wave model, Sine wave model, Sine and Cosine wave model
3	MERRA-2 reanalysis, Holt-Winter model, ANN's & hybrid(nnetar-stlm-tbats functions) algorithm
4	5 AI models namely Multilayer Perceptron (MLP), Multiple Linear Regression (MLR), K-Nearest Neighbor's (KNN), Convolutional Neural Networks (CNN), and Multiple Polynomial Regression (MPR) were examined using associative and non-associative algorithms
5	The classifiers used for research were: Logistic Regression, Decision Tree Classifier, Linear Regression, Neighbors Classifier, Random Forest Classifier, Gaussian Naive Bayes, Classifier (Gaussian NB), Multilayer perceptron (MLP), KMeans clustering, and Support Vector Classifier (SVC)
6	principal component analysis (PCA), stepwise multiple linear regression (SMLR), combined with artificial neural network (ANN) and in amalgamation with PCA, (ENET) elastic net, and (LASSO) least absolute shrinkage and selection operator methods.
7	SVM, Logistic regression, Linear regression, KNN, Linear discriminant analysis, Deep learning, GaussianNB, AdaBoost, Randomforest, XG-Boost, MLP, and Decisiontree(CART)

	Model description
8	(RNN) recurrent neural networks (including Elman, long-short term memory, gated recurrent units, and bidirectional networks), feed-forward network, and convolutional neural networks(CNN)
9	The physical Clear Sky Solar Radiation (CSRM) method is hybridised with a multilayer perceptron (MLP) that has 12 neurons in the first hidden neurons and 5 in the second, as well as an extra input. This PHANN technique (Physical Hybrid Artificial Neural Network)
10	Artificial neural network (ANN)-based seasonal auto-regressive integrated moving average (SARIMA) framework with periodic least squares problem-based weighted elements
11	The lost data are recovered using a super-resolution perception convolutional neural network (SRPCNN), and the recoverable data is utilized in conjunction with a stochastic configuration network (SCN) to anticipate PV generation.
12	Holt-Winters method
13	multilayer perceptron's, encoder-decoder LSTM-RNNs, and long short-term memory recurrent neural networks
14	The graph-convolutional transformer (GCTrafo) and graph-convolutional long short-term memory (GCLSTM) designs are two new graphing neural network models for probabilistic multi-site PV forecasting.
15	ANN with training algorithm that used Levenberg-Marquardt (LM) Algorithm
16	Batch lstm, online lstm

Source: Dora Praveen Kumar

4. Conclusion and Future Scope

There are multitudinous approaches, criteria, situations, etc. in the implementation technologies that can forecast the weather and the output of solar panels. Since the PV plant's prediction is strongly influenced by the atmosphere, climate, azimuthal angle, irradiance, and whether—all of which vary depending on the location—selecting a single standard model for all the plants is both impossible and not advised. Alternatively, it is necessary to conduct comprehensive research and experiments to find the best model and parameters.

For enhanced learning and predictions, contemporary researchers should attempt to apply more hybrid models or deep learning models. Since it is not often addressed, researchers should focus on rain, snow, and fog for short-term PV power forecasts in a forthcoming study, it is recommended to use trigonometric functions to create mathematical models that approximate sun radiation for locations with low irradiance. To determine how well the model works in real-world circumstances, training should be conducted using a bigger dataset including data on unfavorable weather conditions.

The issue of panel shedding, which is a serious issue that is impeding productivity even when the irradiance is high in an area, needs special attention with both a computer model and physical hardware. Panel work's productivity is adversely affected by rain or any unfavourable conditions, but this shedding further reduces productivity even when the irradiance is high in an area.

REFERENCES

1. Brockman, P., French, D. and Tamm, C. (2014). REIT organizational structure, institutional ownership, and stock performance. J. Real Estate Portf. Manag. 20(1): 21–36.
2. Meenal, R., Selvakumar, A. I., & Rajasekaran, E. (2019). Review on mathematical models for the prediction of Solar radiation. Indonesian Journal of Electrical Engineering and Computer Science, 15(1), 54–59.
3. Ferreira, M., Santos, A., & Lucio, P. (2019). Short-term forecast of wind speed through mathematical models. Energy Reports, 5, 1172–1184.
4. Fowdur, T. P., & Ibn, R. M. N. U. D. (2022). A real-time collaborative machine learning based weather forecasting system with multiple predictor locations. *Array*, *14*, 100153.
5. Neal, R., Guentchev, G., Arulalan, T., Robbins, J., Crocker, R., Mitra, A., & Jayakumar, A. (2022). The application of predefined weather patterns over India within probabilistic medium-range forecasting tools for high-impact weather. *Meteorological Applications*, *29*(3), e2083.
6. Mondal, S. K., Chakraborty, R., Choudhury, S., Roy, B., Podder, S., Dey, P., & Ghosh, A. (2022). Weather Forecasting System. *AJEC*.
7. Aravind, K., Vashisth, A., Krishanan, P., & Das, B. (2022). Wheat yield prediction based on weather parameters using multiple linear, neural network and penalised regression models. *Journal of Agrometeorology*, *24*(1), 18–25.

8. Bahrami, A., Teimourian, A., Okoye, C. O., & Khosravi, N. (2019). Assessing the feasibility of wind energy as a power source in Turkmenistan; a major opportunity for Central Asia's energy market. *Energy*, *183*, 415–427.

9. Gad, I., & Hosahalli, D. (2022). A comparative study of prediction and classification models on NCDC weather data. *International Journal of Computers and Applications*, *44*(5), 414–425.

10. Duan, W., Feng, R., Yang, L., & Jiang, L. (2022). A New Approach to Data Assimilation for Numerical Weather Forecasting and Climate Prediction. Journal of Applied Analysis & Computation, 12(3), 1007–1021.

11. Torres, J. F., Hadjout, D., Sebaa, A., Martínez-Álvarez, F., & Troncoso, A. (2021). Deep learning for time series forecasting: a survey. Big Data, 9(1), 3–21.

12. Naveen, L., & Mohan, H. S. (2022). A novel weather parameters prediction scheme and their effects on crops. International Journal of Electrical & Computer Engineering (2088-8708), 12(1).

13. Najib, F., & Mustika, I. W. (2022, June). Weather Forecasting Using Artificial Neural Network for Rice Farming in Delanggu Village. In IOP Conference Series: Earth and Environmental Science (Vol. 1030, No. 1, p. 012002). IOP Publishing.

14. Bochenek, B., & Ustrnul, Z. (2022). Machine learning in weather prediction and climate analyses—Applications and perspectives. Atmosphere, 13(2), 180.

15. Rittler, N., Graziani, C., Wang, J., & Kotamarthi, R. (2022). A Deep Learning Approach to Probabilistic Forecasting of Weather. arXiv preprint arXiv:2203.12529.

16. Sharma, R., & Singh, D. (2018). A review of wind power and wind speed forecasting. Journal of Engineering Research and Application, 8(7), 1–9.

17. Garg, S., Rasp, S., & Thuerey, N. (2022). WeatherBench Probability: A benchmark dataset for probabilistic medium-range weather forecasting along with deep learning baseline models. arXiv preprint arXiv:2205.00865.

18. Leva, S., Mussetta, M., Nespoli, A., & Ogliari, E. (2019, June). PV power forecasting improvement by means of a selective ensemble approach. In 2019 IEEE Milan PowerTech (pp. 1–5). IEEE.

19. Vrettos, E., & Gehbauer, C. (2019, June). A Hybrid approach for short-term PV power forecasting in predictive control applications. In 2019 IEEE Milan PowerTech (pp. 1–6). IEEE.

20. Hossain, M. S., & Mahmood, H. (2020). Short-term photovoltaic power forecasting using an LSTM neural network and synthetic weather forecast. Ieee Access, 8, 172524–172533.

21. Liu, W., Ren, C., & Xu, Y. (2020). PV Generation Forecasting With Missing Input Data: A Super-Resolution Perception Approach. IEEE Transactions on Sustainable Energy, 12(2), 1493–1496.

22. Keerthisinghe, C., Mickelson, E., Kirschen, D. S., Shih, N., & Gibson, S. (2020). Improved PV Forecasts for Capacity Firming. IEEE Access, 8, 152173–152182.

23. Simeunović, J., Schubnel, B., Alet, P. J., & Carrillo, R. E. (2021). Spatio-temporal graph neural networks for multi-site PV power forecasting. IEEE Transactions on Sustainable Energy, 13(2), 1210–1220.

24. Mahendra, L., Eko, H., & Farid, I. W. (2021, December). PV Power Forecast Based on Artificial Neural Network at Indonesia Shopping Mall PV Rooftop. In 2021 International Conference on Advanced Mechatronics, Intelligent Manufacture and Industrial Automation (ICAMIMIA) (pp. 335–338). IEEE.

25. Theocharides, S., Alonso-Suarez, R., Giacosa, G., Makrides, G., Theristis, M., & Georghiou, G. E. (2019, June). Intra-hour forecasting for a 50 MW photovoltaic system in uruguay: Baseline approach. In 2019 IEEE 46th Photovoltaic Specialists Conference (PVSC) (pp. 1632–1636). IEEE.

26. Razavi, S. E., Arefi, A., Ledwich, G., Nourbakhsh, G., Smith, D. B., & Minakshi, M. (2020). From load to net energy forecasting: Short-term residential forecasting for the blend of load and PV behind the meter. IEEE Access, 8, 224343–224353.

27. AlSkaif, T., Dev, S., Visser, L., Hossari, M., & van Sark, W. (2020). A systematic analysis of meteorological variables for PV output power estimation. Renewable Energy, 153, 12–22.

28. A. Singh, D. P. Kumar, K. Shivaprasad, M. Mohit and A. Wadhawan, "Vehicle Detection And Accident Prediction In Sand/Dust Storms," 2021 International Conference on Computing Sciences (ICCS), 2021, pp. 107–111, doi: 10.1109/ICCS54944.2021.00029.

29. https://gargicollege.in/wp-content/uploads/2020/03/weather_forecast.pdf

30. https://www.ibisworld.com/industry-statistics/market-size/weather-forecasting-services-united-states/

31. https://commons.wikimedia.org/wiki/File:Cloud_cover_in_oktas_ptbr.svg

Computer Science Engineering and Emerging Technologies (ICCS-2022) – Prof (Dr.) Rajeev Sobti et al. (eds)
© 2024 Taylor & Francis Group, London, ISBN 978-1-032-52199-2

Chapter **53**

Image Enhancement Using Morphological Techniques

Navjot Kaur[1]
Research Scholar, Bhagwant University, Ajmer,
Assistant Professor at Lovely Professional University, Punjab

Kalpana Sharma[2]
Assistant Professor, Bhagwant University, Ajmer

Anuj Jain[3]
Professor, Lovely Professional University, Punjab

Someet Singh[4]
Associate Professor, Lovely Professional University, Punjab

Balwinder Kaur Dhaliwal[5]
Assistant Professor, Lovely Professional University, Punjab

Abstract: The proposed paper presents morphological techniques for the enhancement of images with poor contrast. The proposed method detects the background in low-contrast images. Image background analysis is used to extract image background information, and open and close operations are used to define multi-background grey-scale images. In the proposed paper the method to improve the image contrast and remove the noise is proposed by applying morphological operations. Mathematical morphology techniques are also more useful for identifying objects or defects than image processing convolution processes because morphological operators are directly related to image structure.

Keywords: Image background analysis, Morphology, Erosion, Dilation

1. Introduction

Morphology alludes to a gathering of image-handling techniques that work with images relying upon their structures. Morphological activities apply an organizing component to an image and produce a comparable output image. The worth of every pixel in the result is still up in the air by contrasting the coordinating pixel in the image with its neighbors in a morphological operation. During the image enhancement process, images are improved so the outcomes are more appropriate for image analysis to be conducted. Image processing is generally employed in the image to improve the efficacy of the image data. The image has an eight-bit dynamic range that is, there are 2^8 grey levels in the image, thus the grey levels will range from 0–255, with zero referring to black and 255 referring to white. Color images typically consist of arrays of integers that represent the red, green, and blue images, which are merged to produce the complete color spectrum.

[1]navjot.20506@lpu.co.in, [2]kalpanasharma56@gmail.com, [3]anuj.22631@lpu.co.in, [4]someet.17380@lpu.co.in, [5]balwinder.25673@lpu.co.in

DOI: 10.1201/9781003405580-53

1.1 Image Color Enhancement

By expanding the brightness distinction between objects and their background, contrast enhancements affect the discernible quality of objects in the scene. Contrast enhancements are usually performed in two steps: contrast stretching and tonal enhancement, although they can be performed simultaneously. Tonal enhancement improves the brightness differences in the dark, grey, or bright regions based on the brightness variances in the supplementary areas.

1.2 Morphology for Image Contrast Enhancement

The average pixel intensity across all pixels in an image is called average intensity. To calculate the average intensity, integrated intensity is divided by total object pixels, or multiply the average intensity by total object pixels.

$$\text{Average intensity} = \frac{\text{integrated intensity}}{\text{Object Area in Pixels}} \tag{1}$$

$$\text{Object Area in Pixels} = \frac{\text{Object Area in } \mu m^2}{\left(\frac{\text{Image Calibration in } \mu m}{\text{pixel}}\right)^2} \tag{2}$$

Image contract is the difference in high and low-intensity values in an image. Standard strategies for correcting the weak contrast of a degraded image include histogram equalization and histogram stretching. The goal of foreground detection is to detect changes in image sequences. Background subtraction aims to isolate the foreground image for further processing. Foreground detection distinguishes the foreground from the background by detecting changes in the foreground. It's a set of approaches for analyzing real-time video sequences captured by a stationary camera.

2. Methodology

Before analyzing an image, improve it as a preprocessing step. To make it easier to recognize foreground items, transform the image to a binary image. evaluate the objects in the image and produce statistics for all of them. To convert a RGB image to a grey scale image, a weighted method is applied. To find weights, this method uses red, green and blue as per the wavelength. *gscale refers to* grey scale.

$$gscale = 0.299R + 0.587G + 0.114B \tag{3}$$

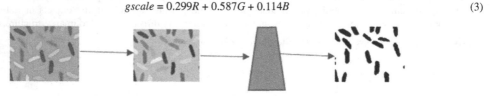

Fig. 53.1 Conversion of RGB to greyscale and binary image

Source: Made by Author

A method is presented for anticipating the shape by defining morphological operations and an appropriate structuring element that provides picture boundary points and decreases object identification time by providing morphological operations and a suitable structuring element.

2.1 General Work Flow

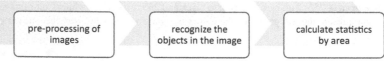

Fig. 53.2 General work from of the proposed work

Source: Made by Author

2.2 Flow Chart

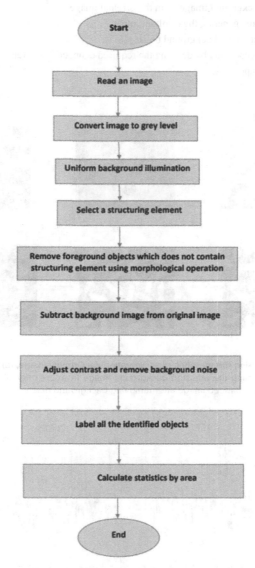

Fig. 53.3   Flow chart of the proposed work

Source: Made by Author

2.3 Pseudo Code

1. Main function
   (a) Input an RGB image
   (b) Convert RGB image to GreyScale image
   (c) Define a suitable structuring element
       (i) Apply structuring element to an image

2. Background Subtraction
   (i) Function to subtract background image from the original image
3. Adjust the image contract and generate the resultant image
4. Generate the image after removing background noise
5. Locate all the connected components by defining the required connectivity value.
6. Visualize all connected components.

3. Results

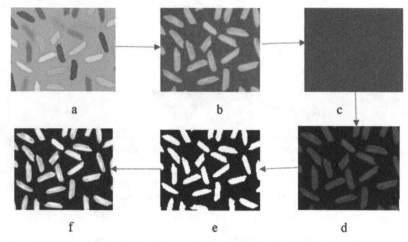

Fig. 53.4 Image enhancement using the morphological operation. (a) Original image, (b) Greyscale image (c) Background image, (d) After subtracting the adjusted background image from the original image (e) Processed image after increasing contrast, (f) Enhanced image after removing background noise

Source: Made by Author

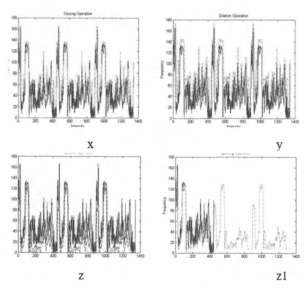

Fig. 53.5 (x) Closing operation, (y) Dilation operation (z) Erosion operation, (z1) Opening operation

Source: Made by Author

3.1 Statistics by Area

Calculate the area of each image object. To achieve this, regionprops () is used.

Table 53.1 Area per object

Object	Area	Centroid
1	1	24
2	134	34
3	122	62
4	154	140
5	84	171
6	196	200
7	134	164
8	176	96

Source: Made by Author

3.2 Object vs. Object Area

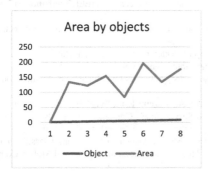

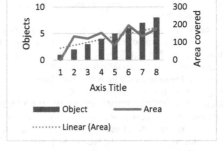

Fig. 53.6 Area covered by objects

Source: Made by Author

Fig. 53.7 Area per object type

Source: Made by Author

Figure 53.4 depicts that as the number of objects increases, the area covered by the objects also increases.

4. Conclusion

A morphological-based approach is proposed for enhancing the image. Those objects that do not contain defined structuring elements are removed from the original image. The image contrast is adjusted after subtracting the background image. Later all the objects are labeled and area per image statistics are computed. The type of structuring element used affects the identification time for recognizing overlapped items in any image when any morphological operation is applied to the image for object recognition. Conclusions may be drawn from the results, which suggest that applying erosion with a line-shaped structuring element improves identification time and reduces elapsed time, even if the choice of structuring element relies on the type of images to be identified.

REFERENCES

1. Sujatha V., "A Genetic Algorithm Based on Fog Intensity Detection method for Driver Safety", International Journal Of Advanced Engineering Sciences And Technologies, Vol No.5, Issue No. 2, 261–268, 2011.
2. Pavlic M., Belzner H., Rigoll G., Ili S., "Image based fog detection in vehicles", IEEE, 2011.
3. Pavlic M., Belzner H., Rigoll G., Ili S., "Image based fog detection in vehicles", Intelligent Vehicles Symposium Alcalá de Henares, SCI indexed, 2012.

4. Dong Z., Wu Y., Pei M, Jia Y., "Vehicle type classification using a semisupervised convolutional neural network", IEEE Transactions on Intelligent Transportation Systems, vol. 16, no. 4, pp. 2247–2256, SCI Indexed 2015.

5. Fu H., Ma H., Liu Y., Lu D., "A vehicle classification system based on hierarchical multi-SVMs in crowded traffic scenes," Neurocomputing, vol. 211, pp. 182–190, SCI indexed, 2016.

6. Singh R., Singh S., Kaur N., "A Review: Techniques of Vehicle Detection in Fog", Indian Journal of Science and Technology, Zoological Record, Vol 9(45),DOI:10.17485/ijst/2016/ v9i45/106793,2016.

7. Zhuo L., Jiang L., Zhu Z., Li J., Zhang J., Long H., "Vehicle classification for large-scale traffic surveillance videos using convolutional neural networks", Machine Vision and Applications, SCI, vol. 28, no. 7, pp. 793–802, 2017.

8. Murugan V., Kumar V. R, "Automatic moving vehicle detection and classification based on artificial neural fuzzy inference system," Wireless Personal Communications ,SCI, Springer, vol. 100, no. 3, pp. 745–766, 2018.

9. Chowdhury P. N., Ray T. C., "A Vehicle Detection Technique for Traffic Management using Image Processing", International Conference on Computer, Communication, Chemical, Material and Electronic Engineering (IC4ME2),SCI, 2018.

10. liu W., Luo Z., Li S.," Improving deep ensemble vehicle classification by using selected adversarial samples", Knowledge-Based Systems, vol. 160, pp. 167–175, SCI, 2018.

11. Wang X., Zhang W., Wu X., Xiao L., Qian Y., Fang Z., "Real-time vehicle type classification with deep convolutional neural networks", Journal of Real-Time Image Processing, vol. 16, no. 1, pp. 5–14, SCI, 2019.

12. Jyothi R. A., Babu R. K., Bachu S., "Moving Object Detection Using the Genetic Algorithm for Real Times Transportation", International Journal of Engineering and Advanced Technology (IJEAT), Volume-8, Issue-6,2019.

13. Chandrika R. R., Ganesh G. N. S., Raghunath K. M. K, "Vehicle Detection and Classification using Image processing", IEEE Xplore, SCI, 2020.

14. Kalyan S. S., Pratyusha V., Nishitha N., Ramesh T. K., "Vehicle Detection Using Image Processing", IEEE International Conference for Innovation in Technology, SCI, 2020.

15. Shyamala A., "Certain investigations on moving Vehicle detection and classification Using soft computing techniques", shodhganga, 2020.

16. Şentaş A., Tashiev İ., Küçükayvaz F., "Performance evaluation of support vector machine and convolutional neural network algorithms in real-time vehicle type and color classification", Evolutionary Intelligence, vol. 13, no. 1, pp. 83–91, SCI,2020.

17. Hedeya M. A., Eid A. H., Abdel-Kadar R. F., "A super learner ensemble of deep networks for vehicle-type classification", IEEE Access, vol. 8, pp. 98266–98280, SCI, 2020.

18. Zahra G., Imran M., Qahtani A. M., Alsufyani A., Almutiry O., Mahmood A. Alazemi F. E., "Visibility Enhancement of Scene Images Degraded by Foggy Weather Condition: An Application to Video Surveillance", Computers, Materials & Continua Tech Science Press, DOI:10.32604/cmc.2021.017454, SCI, 2021.

19. Jagannathan P., Kumar S. R., Frnda J., Divakarachari P. V., Subramani P., "Moving Vehicle Detection and Classification Using Gaussian Mixture Model and Ensemble Deep Learning Technique" Hindawi Wireless Communications and Mobile Computing, https://doi.org/10.1155/2021/5590894, SCI 2021.

20. Miclea R. C., Ungureanu V. I., Sandru F. D., Silea I., "Visibility Enhancement and Fog Detection: Solutions Presented in Recent Scientific Papers with Potential for Application to Mobile Systems", Sensors,21, 3370, https://doi.org/10.3390/s21103370, SCI, 2021.

Computer Science Engineering and Emerging Technologies (ICCS-2022) – Prof (Dr.) Rajeev Sobti et al. (eds)
© 2024 Taylor & Francis Group, London, ISBN 978-1-032-52199-2

Chapter 54

Efficient Novel Cryptographic Algorithm to Improve Security: A Review

Innam Ul Haq[1]
Student, School of Computer Science And Engineering,
Lovely Professional University, Punjab, India

Richa Jain[2]
Assistant Professor, School of Computer Science And Engineering,
Lovely Professional University, Punjab, India

Abstract: Cryptography plays a very important role in securing the information which is confidential. It ensures that the data or information being transmitted is in its original form and away from the unauthorized access. For securing the organization database and information, certain cryptographic techniques are already developed and being used, which include AES, DES, Blowfish, Hill Cipher, Vernam Cipher, etc. In this paper, we focus on all the existing ciphers and cryptographic techniques and compare them to measure the level of accuracy, security and throughput. Then, we will be developing a new hybrid algorithm using the combination of calculations that are existing in already generated ones, which will be trying to overcome the weaknesses of the previous existing ones which mainly is the time taken.

Keywords: Plain text, Security, Cipher text, Encryption, Decryption, Cryptography

1. Introduction

Cryptography is derived from two Greek words which means "secret" or "hidden". It is the method of protecting the data or information by encrypting or encoding it into non-readable format. It is the method of exchanging of the data in the form which is only intended for particular authorized user who can read and process it (AbdElminaam and Diaa Salama, 2018).

Internet has nowadays become a very essential part of every communication that is going all over the world using messaging, mailing, internet banking, web surfing, transactions and many more. (Goyal, Tarun Kumar, Vineet Sahula, and Deepak Kumawat, 2022). So as the use of online interactions and communications has drastically increased so is the security being compromised by the attackers. (Nilesh, Dudhatra, and Malti Nagle, 2014). In this case, if we want to make sure that our information is secure and is in safe hands, then there comes the use of cryptography which ensures that the information that is processed over the internet is not compromised by any unauthorized person.

Security has become the main issue in every organization and it can be achieved through these categories (AbdElminaam And Diaa Salama, 2018).

- *Authorization:* It means that only the intended user or authorized is allowed to have access to particular information. None other than that person is allowed to view the information.

[1]Innamulhaq01@gmail.com, [2]richa.17688@lpu.co.in

DOI: 10.1201/9781003405580-54

- *Authentication:* It is the process of verifying the user or receiver whether the person who is receiving the information is the appropriate person or not.
- *Integrity:* It checks whether the data that is sent over a network doesn't have any alteration or changes in its way to receiver, and the data is still same or not.
- *Availability:* It is the process of protecting the proper functionality of the organization and making ensure that the data and services are fully available at any point of time.
- *Confidentiality:* It is the process of protecting the information from any kind of unauthorized disclosure.

To secure the communication there is a proper process of cryptography (Sharma, Neha, 2017) which is shown in Fig. 54.1 and explained below:

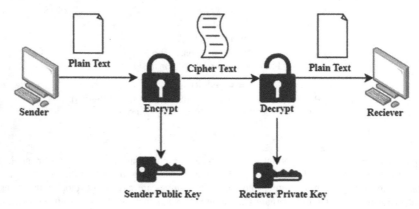

Fig. 54.1 Cryptography process (AbdElminaam, Diaa Salama, 2018)

When a sender sends the message it is in human readable form called Plain Text. Then we use encryption method to hide actual data and is converted into non-human readable form called Cipher Text. When receiver wants to see the data he needs to decrypt it using same method to turn Cipher Text to Plain Text

In this particular paper, we will be reviewing constantly used techniques or algorithms and compare different model of approaches to understand the best-fit technique with better accuracy.

2. Related Work

As of now, the internet has been executed in the market for a long time now. So till now there are various communications and large number of information is being transferred online. For the security of all that data and information of individual persons and as well as for organizations, there have been already few developed strategies that focus on the security enhancements. (Mitali, Vijay Kumar, and Arvind Sharma, 2014)

The proper hierarchy of the cryptography is shown in Fig. 54.2 in which we get an overview of all the techniques and the root of them under which the particular algorithm falls.

These developed techniques differ from each other on the basis of key, length of inputs and output and many more. Some of the major techniques related to our area of interest are reviewed below (Acharya, Kritika, Manisha Sajwan, and Sanjay Bhargava 2013) and shown in Fig. 54.2:

- **AES:** It is a block cipher with different key lengths of 128 bits, 192 bits or 256 bits. It uses rounds of 10, 12 or 14 which id dependent on the key size for the encryption of data. Dictionary attack can rack it.(Sharma, Dilip Kumar, 2022).
- **DES**: This uses 64 bits of plain text for encryption with 56 bits of key size. It is a block cipher and due to its small and fixed size of key it would be easier for an attacker to compromise the data.

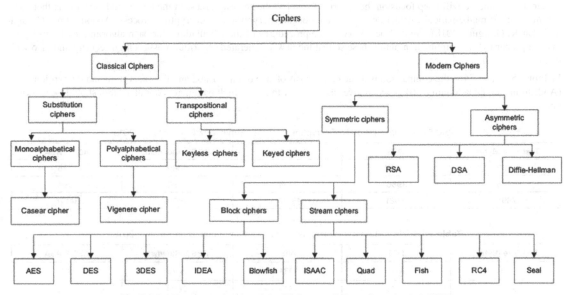

Fig. 54.2 Cryptography Hierarchy (Mohammad, Omar Farook, et al, 2017)

- **Vignere Cipher:** It is the process of encrypting the alphabetical text using string of Caesar Cipher based on letters of keyword (Soofi, Aized Amin, Irfan Riaz, and Umair Rasheed, 2016).
- **Caesar Cipher**: This encryption is done by rearranging the alphabets of plain which is easy for attacker to guess (D. Gautam, C. Agrawal, P. Sharma, M. Mehta and P. Saini, 2018).

These were some of the already developed encryption algorithms which are being used in the field of securing the communications and the data exchange between the individuals and the networks (Bernstein, Daniel J, 2020). There are some other algorithms like Hill cipher, Vernam Cipher, RSA, Deffie Hellman which we will also observe before creating our new algorithm. But still the process which is secure takes more time, so we try to fill this gap and make an algorithm which will be secure as well as less time-consuming.

In Charru, P. Singh, and Shaveta Rani (2014). they have studied the AES algorithm, and to improve their security, they have proposed a model of doing so by adding XOR operation to the existing algorithm. It has helped them to strengthen the security as they have shown that the number of decryption steps will be increased. So the time taken by the attacker to compromise the data will be more as compared to previous simple AES algorithm.

3. Comparative Analysis and Proposed Work

As shown in Table 54.1, we have compared the working of some cryptographic algorithms (Ali, Khalid, 2020), which are currently in use. Performance factors of these cryptographic algorithms have been compared. As we can interpret from the table that each of the algorithm possess different key sizes and there are differences in the speed as well. Some algorithms which are very fast are accurate but the security they provide is not secure enough.

Table 54.1 Comparison of algorithms (Acharya, Kritika, Manisha Sajwan, and Sanjay Bhargava, 2013)

Algorithm	Size Of Key	Speed	Speed depend on key	Security
AES	128,192,256 bits	Moderate	yes	Secure
DES	56 bits	Slow	Yes	Insecure
3DES	112 or 168 bits	Very Slow	No	Less Secure
BlowFish	32 To 448 bits	Moderate	No	Believed to be secure
RSA	1024 Bits	Fast	Yes	Secure

In our Algorithm, we will keep focus on the security as well as the security areas. In the above said algorithms there are certain types of mathematical calculations being done for the encryption and decryption process (Abood, Omar G., and Shawkat K. Guirguis, 2018). We will be observing the procedures of the calculations for each algorithm and will try to make a proper hybrid combination out of these so that the newly generated algorithm possess high security and also will be faster in speed.

In Tables 54.2 and 54.3, the comparison is made on the basis of size of cipher text and the encryption and decryption time (AbdElminaam, Diaa Salama, 2018) which gives us overview that on which parameters our algorithm should be working upon.

Table 54.2 Time Taken By Encryption (ms) (AbdElminaam, Diaa Salama, 2018)

Text Size (Bytes)	DES	AES	AES & Blowfish	AES & RSA
112	2070	2073	4389	4876
2305	3986	3994	5883	5994
7894	14981	15107	33900	34101

Table 54.3 Time Taken By Decryption (ms) (AbdElminaam, Diaa Salama, 2018)

Text Size (Bytes)	DES	AES	AES & Blowfish	AES & RSA
112	1034	1034	3278	3497
2305	1675	1675	2634	3012
7894	1535	1535	12641	13501

Apart from the modern ciphers our focus will also be on the classical ciphers which include Ceaser, Vignere, Hill (Qasem, Mais Haj, and Mohammad Qatawneh, 2018), Vernam Cipher, Play fair cipher etc. In these ciphers many types of substitutions, Transpositions and permutations are being done to make the cipher strong and secure. We will observe these classical cryptography techniques (Gorbenko, Ivan, 2017) also so we can use any substitution method or any other operations done by these ciphers in our algorithm where it fits properly and add to the value of our algorithm's security and throughput.

4. Conclusion

In this paper we reviewed algorithms and some work which we will be focusing in our project. We saw already done work and we need to overcome the issues that are present in them. We compared the algorithms to get an overview about the security capabilities and the supposed weaknesses. Our goal is to make new algorithm which will be more secure with high throughput. We will try to improve the performance by using simple calculations.

In future, we will be trying to modify it if any such need occurs because nowadays more attacks are being performed. So for that if such condition arises, we will be trying to add more complexity to our algorithm.

REFERENCES

1. Charru, P. Singh, and Shaveta Rani. "Improved Cryptography Algorithm to Enhanced Data Security." *International Journal for Research in Applied Science and Engineering Technology (IJR ASET)* 2.IX (2014).
2. Hasan, Mohammad Kamrul, et al. "Lightweight cryptographic algorithms for guessing attack protection in complex internet of things applications." *Complexity* 2021 (2021).
3. Bernstein, Daniel J. "Cryptographic competitions." *Cryptology ePrint Archive* (2020).
4. Mousavi, Seyyed Keyvan, et al. "Improving the security of internet of things using cryptographic algorithms: a case of smart irrigation systems." *Journal of Ambient Intelligence and Humanized Computing* 12.2 (2021): 2033–2051.
5. Nilesh, Dudhatra, and Malti Nagle. "The new cryptography algorithm with high throughput." *2014 International Conference on Computer Communication and Informatics*. IEEE, 2014.
6. AbdElminaam, Diaa Salama. "Improving the security of cloud computing by building new hybrid cryptography algorithms." *International Journal of Electronics and Information Engineering* 8.1 (2018): 40–48.

7. Sharma, Neha. "A Review of Information Security using Cryptography Technique." *International Journal of Advanced Research in Computer Science* 8.4 (2017).
8. Mitali, Vijay Kumar, and Arvind Sharma. "A survey on various cryptography techniques." *International Journal of Emerging Trends & Technology in Computer Science (IJETTCS)* 3.4 (2014): 307–312.
9. Acharya, Kritika, Manisha Sajwan, and Sanjay Bhargava. "Analysis of cryptographic algorithms for network security." *International Journal of Computer Applications Technology and Research* 3.2 (2013): 130–135.
10. Sharma, Dilip Kumar, et al. "A review on various cryptographic techniques & algorithms." *Materials Today: Proceedings* 51 (2022): 104–109.
11. Soofi, Aized Amin, Irfan Riaz, and Umair Rasheed. "An enhanced vigenere cipher for data security." *Int. J. Sci. Technol. Res* 5.3 (2016): 141–145.
12. D. Gautam, C. Agrawal, P. Sharma, M. Mehta and P. Saini, "An Enhanced Cipher Technique Using Vigenere and Modified Caesar Cipher," 2018 2nd International Conference on Trends in Electronics and Informatics (ICOEI), 2018, pp. 1–9, doi: 10.1109/ICOEI.2018.8553910.
13. Qasem, Mais Haj, and Mohammad Qatawneh. "Parallel Hill Cipher Encryption Algorithm." *International Journal of Computer Applications* 179.19 (2018): 16–2
14. Gorbenko, Ivan, et al. "The research of modern stream ciphers." *2017 4th International Scientific-Practical Conference Problems of Infocommunications. Science and Technology (PIC S&T)*. IEEE, 2017.
15. Ali, Khalid, et al. "Performance of cryptographic algorithms based on time complexity." *2020 3rd International Conference on Computing, Mathematics and Engineering Technologies (iCoMET)*. IEEE, 2020.
16. Goyal, Tarun Kumar, Vineet Sahula, and Deepak Kumawat. "Energy efficient lightweight cryptography algorithms for IoT devices." *IETE Journal of Research* 68.3 (2022): 1722–1735.
17. Abood, Omar G., and Shawkat K. Guirguis. "A survey on cryptography algorithms." *International Journal of Scientific and Research Publications* 8.7 (2018): 495–516
18. Mohammad, Omar Farook, et al. "A survey and analysis of the image encryption methods." *International Journal of Applied Engineering Research* 12.23 (2017): 13265–13280.

Computer Science Engineering and Emerging Technologies (ICCS-2022) – Prof (Dr.) Rajeev Sobti et al. (eds)
© 2024 Taylor & Francis Group, London, ISBN 978-1-032-52199-2

Chapter

55

A Study on Blockchain Technology for the Future E-Voting Systems

Pyla Uma[1]

Research Scholar, Dept. of CSE, GITAM School of Technology, GITAM University (Deemed to be), Visakhapatnam, Andhra Pradesh, India

P. V. Lakshmi[2]

Professor, Dept. of CSE, GITAM School of Technology, GITAM University (Deemed to be), Visakhapatnam, Andhra Pradesh, India

Abstract: Due to the large population in places like India, traditional voting systems done in physical mode have many disadvantages like manipulation, security issues, transparency, and privacy issues. So, countries like India need to modernize their voting systems from traditional voting to electronic voting (e-voting). E-voting is an election system that uses electronic means to allow voters to cast votes with privacy, ballot security, and integrity. The e-voting systems use computers connected to the internet. The use of these technologies enables the government to successfully deal with the requirements associated with security, accuracy, scalability, auditability, cost-effectiveness, and sustainability. Based on the new technologies in voting, one recent technology that has attracted many is block chain technology. A block chain is a distributed digital ledger. This ledger is never stored but rather exists on the chain linked to data blocks or nodes connected to each other using encryption and hashing techniques, which makes voting secure. The current trends in block chain technology analysis are being discussed in this paper, highlighting the issues and challenges raised so far in the community regarding the privacy and security of the voter and the vote without putting complete trust in the third-party system.

Keywords: Blockchain, e-voting, Security, Hashing

1. Introduction

In democratic societies like India, the right to vote is the basis for representing the "empowerment" of each being. Initially, voting in India was done using paper ballots and manual counting, where the process is expensive and the result of the vote is counted for ever. To manipulate and tamper with the results is simple. And, also, elderly and disabled persons cannot move to the polling station to vote. Due to this, the problems of voting done using paper ballots are solved with the help of information systems.

Information systems are applied in a wide variety of applications in different fields, and research about them focuses on the implementation and deployment of the system processes that allow them to meet their non-functional and functional requirements. Also, information systems provide some specialized properties. One such property or application is electronic voting. While electronic voting systems, where voting is done via the internet and is known ase-voting," can acquire a certain legitimacy, they can also improve the security and efficiency of voting processes. In electronic voting systems, features like no-receipt, justice, data reliability, voter anonymity, robustness, and verifiability are included. The currently used systems do not meet all the requirements. The e-voting may cause concern about security risks posed by third parties

[1]upyla@gitam.in, [2]vpanga@gitam.edu

DOI: 10.1201/9781003405580-55

to the government. The use of electronic voting systems, being a centralized architecture, has the limitation of keeping and administering voting records since functions are incorporated into a single subsystem. Hence, a new decentralized technology named Blockchain can be designed as a base for electronic voting systems. "Block chain is a decentralized digital ledger in a peer-to-peer network," which means it allows data or transactions to be accessible to other peers directly without passing intermediaries.

1.1 Block Chain

Blockchain is a distributed ledger that allows peer-to-peer interaction among computer systems for exchanging information in the form of transactions and values in a decentralized manner. Also, a blockchain eases the process of tracking the values and records the information in a functional network. Any value can be traced and recorded virtually on a blockchain network, thereby reducing uncertainty and costs. Once the transaction is done, a block is created and recorded in the blockchain, making it impossible to hack, cheat, or change the information on the system.

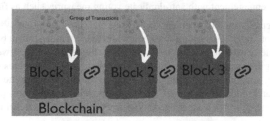

Fig. 55.1 Blocks chained together

Source: https://www.c-sharpcorner.com/article/blockchain-and-its-structure-an-introduction/

The block is created when a transaction is validated by a node, and then information is recorded. The block in a blockchain is composed of a header and a body, where the header part contains the "hash" of the prior block, a nonce value, a time stamp, and the "Merkle root". The hash value is generated by using hash functions like "SHA256". "A hash is a mathematical function that converts an input of arbitrary length into an encrypted output of a fixed length". Using the "hash" values by storing them forms a chain of blocks, and even tampering with the previous block can be easily traced. Nonce is used for block generation and by the miners. The creation time of the block is recorded in the timestamp. The "Merkle root" which is stored in the block body, is the root hash of a "Merkle tree". Any small change in the transaction completely generates a different merkle root that simplifies the verification of all transactions by simply using the "Merkle root".

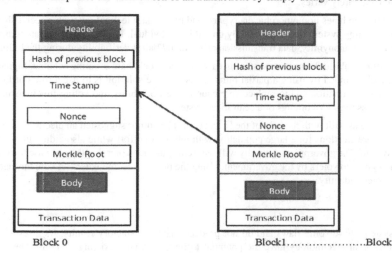

Fig. 55.2 The structure of a block in blockchain

Source: https://www.researchgate.net/figure/The-structure-of-a-Blockchain-A-block-is-composed-of-a-header-and-a-body-where-a-header_fig1_337306138 Basing on this figure Author defined the structure of a block in blockchain in his own words in the design of figure

2. Related Works

[13]: Proposed a system for using block chain in electronic voting systems. And discussed the unique characteristics of blockchain, such as consistency and architecture, as well as how block chain ensures election transparency by storing all details or messages in the Ethereum blockchain and how it protects each voter's privacy with the greatest security and an efficient sign-up process. This system also includes voter identification numbers, including individual Andhra Pradesh numbers, as well as related data. Instead of a single data point, this system will use multi-factor authentication to verify voters and a blockchain database, including their OTP, PIN, and voter identification number.

[4]: This voting application system was developed in this natural and true environment by taking some specific requirements such as privacy, convenience, eligibility, verifiability, and no-receipt into account. The system is assembled using an open, friendly administrator interface to facilitate services like the administration of individual voters, constituencies, and candidates for each constituency. The proposed system, designed with a web-based user interface, aims to achieve secure digital voting and facilitate user engagement with anti-duplicate voting measures such as finger printing.

[10]: The proposed system discusses the development and representation of a voting system called ElectionBlock that works on a centralized network of nodes. This voting system provides its own independent block chain network to maintain integrity, incorporates a biometric scanner for user security, and shows the relationship between registered and unregistered voters. The outcome shows that the system has the possibility of handling large volumes of votes from multiple servers while maintaining performance, security, and data integrity. The advantage of using the ElectionBlock platform is the simple interface, transparency, and reduced voter fraud. The limitations addressed in this paper are that Election Block is designed to be a practical implementation of a centralized and permission-based blockchain system but not an open-source solution.

[12]: The proposed system describes the design of a decentralized e-voting system with the capability to improve cost-efficiency, security, and transparency. Using the Hyperledger Fabric platform for blockchain networks and smart contracts, the e-voting system was implemented and used to cast votes. And then are recorded immutably, providing voters with trust and anonymity in the election process. The SHA-256 algorithm was used to encrypt the data contained within the various blocks, and to guarantee the immutability of votes, the blocks were also chained using hashes.

[5]: The proposed solution employs blockchain technology to ensure the interest and transparency of all voting links. To keep all users' identity data and poll data separate, a data security separator is set. As a result, while voting, the link between the polls and the voter's is broken, and the user's privacy is protected from leakage. In comparison to voting schemes done using traditional methods, this scheme guarantees that all voting results are open, exact, and verifiable, and poll data is unspecified and rarely varies.

[8]: The proposed system combines homomorphic encryption and blockchain technology with a secret sharing scheme to create a decentralized e-voting system that does not rely on a third individual. It ensures a transparent and public voting scheme while guarding voter anonymity, data transmission privacy, and ballot verifiability during the billing phase.

[7]: The suggested SM9 partial blind signature system is based on the blockchain e-voting scheme. Signature denial and tracking can be effectively avoided by using a partial blind signature. The solution is to use a true third party to prevent attackers from modifying information and to replace vote counting responsibility and voting functions using blockchain mechanisms, which address the shortcomings of a centralized system.

[9]: The proposed system was built with the help of the blockchain. The author suggested an electronic voting system that ensures efficient and secure elections for a large population with minimum effort while also aiding in the development of trust in the electoral system. The government authority will issue coins to each voter that they can use to vote, and a private and public key are also given to voters by the government. Using the private key, the voter can vote through their account, which will check the voter's identity.

3. Conclusion

The current voting systems have some flaws and do not produce many satisfactory results. As a result, modern voting systems based on block chain technology have the potential to improve many existing systems. The major advantage of setting up voting systems on a block chain is the quality of transparency provided by the block chain. As part of the literature survey a total of eight research papers are surveyed and the methodologies used in them are presented

In various block-chain-based voting systems. Based on the analysis, block chain can provide solutions to the majority of existing election problems.

REFERENCES

1. Patricia Baudier , Galina Kondra, Chantal Ammi, and Eric Seulliet, "Peace engineering: The contribution of blockchain systems to the e-voting process," Technological Forecasting & Social Change. Oct. 14, 2020. https://doi.org/10.1016/j.techfore.2020.1 20397.
2. Jun huang and debiao he, mohammads. obaidat, pandi vijayakumar, min luo, and kim-kwang raymond choo, "The Application of the Blockchain Technology in Voting Systems: A Review," ACM Computing Surveys. Apr, 2021. https://doi.org/10.1145/3439725.
3. Kamran, Muhammad Hammad Nasir, Muhammad Imran, and Joon-Sung Yang, "Study on E-Voting Systems: A Blockchain Based Approach," IEEE International Conference on Consumer Electronics-Asia (ICCE-Asia). 2021. doi: 10.1109/ICCE-Asia53811.2021.9641914.
4. Kashif Mehboob Khan, Junaid Arshad, and Muhammad Mubashir Khan, "Secure Digital Voting System based on Blockchain Technology," CORE.
5. Guan Zhongxu, Zhai Jianhong, Xu Qian Faculty of Computing, Shi Jiyuan, and Zhang Jingrun, "A Blockchain Voting Scheme Based on Data Security Separation," IEEE International Conference on Electronic Technology, Communication and Information (ICETCI) l. 0 0, 2021. DOI: 10.1109/ICETCI53161.2021.9563532.
6. Nugraha Wiguna Tiera, Adhitya Bhawiyuga, and Achmad Basuki, "An Ethereum Based Distributed Application for Ensuring the Integrity of Stored E-Voting Data," Association for Computing Machinery. Sep. 13, 2021. https://doi.org/10.1145/347964 5.3479706.
7. Dongqing Yin, Mingshu Zhang, and Bin Wei, "Blockchain E-voting Scheme Based on SM9 Partial Blind Signature," International Conference on Computer Information Science and Artificial Intelligence (CISAI) l. 2021. DOI: 10.1109/CI-SAI54367.2021.00201.
8. Raylin Tso, Chien-Ming Chen, and mu-en wu, "Decentralized E-Voting Systems Based on the Blockchain Technology," springer, Sep. 2018, doi: 10.1007/978-981-10-7605-3_50.
9. Hrithvick Rao Rewatkar, Devansh Agarwal, Anmol Khandelwal, and Subho Upadhyay, "Decentralized Voting Application Using Blockchain," 10th IEEE International Conference on Communication Systems and Network Technologies. 2021. DOI: 10.1109/CSNT.2021.129.
10. Blockchain and Fingerprint Authentication Mohamed Ibrahim, Kajan Ravindran, Hyon Lee, Omair Farooqui, and Qusay H. Mahmoud, "ElectionBlock: An Electronic Voting System using Blockchain and Fingerprint Authentication," IEEE 18th International Conference on Software Architecture Companion (ICSA-C). DOI: 10.1109/ICSA-C52384.2021.00033.
11. Noor Mohammedali and Ali Al-Sherbaz, "Election System Based on Blockchain Technology," International Journal of Computer Science and Information Technology. Oct, 2019. DOI: 10.5121/ijcsit.2019.11502.
12. Javier Díaz-Santiso and Paula Fraga-Lamas, "E-Voting System Using Hyper-ledger Fabric Blockchain and Smart Contracts," Engineering Proceedings. Sep. 30, 2021. https://doi.org/10.3390/ engproc2021007011.
13. Govinda H. S., Yogesh Chandrakant, Girish D. S., Lokesh S., Ravikiran, and Jayasri B. S., "Implementation of Election System Using Blockchain Technology," International Conference on Innovative Computing, Intelligent Communication and Smart ElectricalSystems (ICSES) l. 2021. DOI: 10.1109/ICSES52305.2021.9633828.
14. patrick mccorry, maryam mehrnezhad, ehsan toreini, sia-mak f. shahandashti, and feng hao, "On Secure E-Voting over Blockchain," ACM. Oct, 2021. https://doi.org/10.1145/3461461.
15. Mohit Kumar, "Securing the E-voting system through blockchain using the concept of proof of work," International Conference on Technological Advancements and Innovations (ICTAI). 2021. DOI: 10.1109/ICTAI53825.2021.9673389.

Computer Science Engineering and Emerging Technologies (ICCS-2022) – Prof (Dr.) Rajeev Sobti et al. (eds)
© 2024 Taylor & Francis Group, London, ISBN 978-1-032-52199-2

Chapter **56**

Implementation of Waste Management, Renewable Energy and Green Buildings in Smart Cities for Quality Life

K. K. Ramachandran*

Director/Professor, Management/Commerce/International Business,
DR G R D College of Science, India

Abstract: Indeed, sustainable development has a global reach, but effective policy measures must be meso-oriented, for instance, by focusing on certain economic sectors and areas. For the purpose of evaluating sustainability in an organizational environment, a spatial or urban perspective is unquestionably necessary. Green construction, the intelligent building industry, and high-quality development are currently dealing with a number of new opportunities and problems. It is difficult to properly specify all the practical ways that municipal operators might improve their city's services. Citizens will, however, unquestionably gain from the adoption of IoT-focused solutions in the urban setting in which they live and which they help to enhance through their activities. This study looks at several facets of the growth of smart cities, offers new workable indicators connected to green buildings and electronic vehicles in developing smart cities, and discusses current obstacles to the growth of smart cities as well as ways to get beyond them. The findings show the importance of feasible and doable policies in the development of smart cities, including the development of zero-energy, attention to design parameters, implementation of useful indicators for GBs and EVs, strategies to lower the cost of EV production while maintaining high standards of quality, load management, and successfully integrating EVs into the electrical grid.

Keywords: Smart city, Waste management, Renewable energy, Green building, Sustainable building, Smart infrastructure.

1. Introduction

Smart technology can play a significant role in solving today's major population problems and laying the groundwork for a green future. A clever strategy offers the chance to integrate information, which is essential to addressing the major issues facing modern civilizations. Smart cities are effective and responsive thanks to IoT and big data, two closely connected and growing technological frameworks. Smart cities can now be created since technology is advanced enough. However, a smart city's digital technologies translate into improved public services for residents and enhanced resource utilisation while decreasing environmental consequences. [1] A growing number of cities around the world are focusing their development strategies on smart policies that promote sustainable mobility, energy-efficient building upgrades, an increase in the production of energy from renewable sources, better waste management practises, and the implementation of infrastructures. One of the behaviours that threatens the local ecosystem the most frequently is the discharge of untreated wastewater. Furthermore, maintaining access to clean water sources is becoming a bigger concern for both urban and rural areas. The construction of green buildings is currently gaining popularity, which reflects the importance of designing constructed environments that are ecologically friendly [2]. Today's key challenges are ensuring the balanced economic growth of society and reducing the impacts of global warming. It is essential for all engaged engineering professionals to

*dr.k.k.ramachandran@gmail.com

DOI: 10.1201/9781003405580-56

work closely together to develop multidisciplinary synergies and solve difficult engineering issues [3, 4]. Many international sectors, including policymakers and developers, are paying more attention to the growing debate over sustainable development as it relates to advanced sustainable cities and the effects of sustainability on urban transformation.

In this sense, renewable energy plays a wonderful and crucial role in ensuring inhabitants' comfort and wellbeing. [5, 6] suggested linking the necessary structure, the ability to retain information, the public programmes, and the commercial infrastructure to exploit the intellectual capabilities of the smart city. Despite the advantages of smart cities, there are numerous obstacles in the way of their development, making the execution of suitable laws and planning essential to their success. [7] Smart cities must also carefully manage their urban resources, including providing adequate electricity, transportation, and construction infrastructure.

The subsequent actions centered on increasing water management and energy efficiency, developing environmentally friendly structures, and reducing waste. Additional topics included the enhancement of consumption optimization and, green building, and the encouragement of the development of renewable energy sources.

2. Literature Review

Waste Management System

In light of this complex circumstance, a multilayer IoT-based digital infrastructure support and maintenance architecture is provided by [8], and the performance of the suggested solution is assessed using the problem of waste management as a case study. Research showed that the design is capable of managing up to 3902 waste bins at once, proving the principle behind it. These bins can accurately segregate organic and recyclable garbage in both outdoor and indoor settings, and they have quick reaction times, which gives system users a positive user experience. The fast expansion of urban populations owing to migration and unplanned urbanization's impact on the characteristics of urban garbage have been major concerns for government municipalities in metropolitan areas as they attempt to create an efficient solid waste management strategy. Understanding the amounts, types, and current waste management techniques is necessary to design a brief SWM plan that adheres to the goals of government efforts. The field studies to evaluate SWM systems in accordance with waste management regulations were published in [9], together with a summary of the current waste management operations, financial and institutional demographics, and six selected Indian smart cities.

Municipal solid waste management, a critical component of SCs in contemporary society, has a number of costs that must be cut. Two sub-models are taken into consideration in this work to address this issue. The first sub-model routes the fleet among waste generation and separation facilities using the vehicle routing problem (VRP). The sub-model is designed to distribute resources from facilities for separation to a collection of plants for resource recovery or landfill centers. The stochastic optimization model has been addressed using chance-constrained programming. The most effective solution is determined using four metaheuristic algorithms. Additionally, the effectiveness of the suggested algorithms is assessed. Finally, sensitivity studies and a variety of scenarios have been devised to assess how tightly the suggested problem may be defined. Findings [10] demonstrated the ideal amount of automobiles that can support administrators and decision-makers in a range of constrained situations.

Renewable Energy System

The energy system is one of the key elements of a smart city and is crucial to the transition to a sustainable urban lifestyle. It has been shown [11] that using renewable energy sources significantly contributes to lowering pollutant emissions and improving the quality of the environment in which people live. As a result, it is thought that developing energy systems using renewable and clean criteria is a sustainable answer for smart cities. In fact, the quick and deep adoption of renewable energy-based technology has been seen to fit extremely well into a smart city of a variety of sizes, providing a stable foundation for a contemporary civilization with a low-carbon economy. A public library building's energy system has to be retrofitted, and new technology solutions are used to increase the energy efficiency of public lighting. LEDs are two new energy models that leverage the utilization of renewable energy as a power source, as described by [12]. They are also new techniques of control and management. The growth of energy generation based on renewable energies, such as biomass and sunshine, as well as the ideas of smart cities (SC) and the Internet of Things (IoT), may all be communicated through either or both. By using the most recent tools and procedures, which encourage more effective management, these two suggestions aim to increase energy-efficient behaviors while minimizing energy waste.

Investments in renewable energy sources (RES), which are now a prominent route in urban development, are one embodiment of the smart city idea. Therefore, it seems relevant to investigate how Polish cities are addressing this issue and if they are incorporating the installation of RES facilities into their development plans. This objective is accomplished on two levels: theoretically and practically. [13] has demonstrated the significance of renewable energy installations in Polish cities' development plans, particularly in those that seek to be dubbed smart cities. Additionally, it is demonstrated that solar-powered RES facilities are the most common. An integral part of the smart city is the integrated renewable energy system. Power grid and demand-related problems can be resolved by incorporating accessible sources of renewable energy. Their right size is required to accommodate IRES in the future in order to maintain a steady condition of energy supply and demand. As indicated by several writers, alternative algorithms were required to construct the renewable energy integrated plan in order to handle technological, economic, and sizing issues. On the basis of IRES, [14] gave an extensive assessment of subjects pertaining to power production for smart cities. The integration of various energy sources, the use of micro-grids for integration, and techniques for scaling IRES utilizing software and AI algorithms are all covered in detail.

Green Buildings

People's significant social characteristics in a smart city cannot be overlooked. Residents of a smart city contribute to its co-creation, start projects, and are creative in addition to being its beneficiaries. [15] proposed intelligent sustainable buildings as one of the technical infrastructure elements of the smart city and examined the traits of smart sustainable buildings (SSB) and the potential for their growth. A SWOT matrix was created with this objective in mind. Using the DEMATEL approach, a cause-and-effect analysis was performed on the variables in this matrix to determine their correlations. The analysis's findings enabled us to investigate the social side, or the influence of ecological, innovative architectural designers and users on such structures' growth and the potential for their innovative and creative usage in urban settings. Cryptocurrency and building information management have huge potential to improve the performance of building projects, according to research to date. On the other hand, nothing is known about how BIM and blockchain might help with environmentally friendly building design. As a result, in the framework of CIM/Smart Cities, [16] investigated the possible effects of the merging of BIM and cryptocurrency in a smart city setting on increasing the sustainability of buildings. The study searches the Web of Science (WoS) database for relevant publications using keywords and then utilizes the VOSviewer to graphically assess the linkages among blockchain, BIM, and sustainable construction within the framework of smart cities and CIM, which is done through data analysis accompanied by micro-scheme analysis.

All methods connected to public involvement, such as decision-making, public and social services, transparent government, and political tactics and viewpoints, are included in this area. To enable their development and expansion, sustainable cities require a human resource that is both legitimate and well qualified. [17] As a result, it is important to take into account the following factors: degree of qualification, aptitude for lifelong learning, socioeconomic and cultural diversity, adaptability, inventiveness, cosmopolitanism, and involvement in public life. The use of the accumulated data to infer the operation of Santander's city government and provide users with new features and services while more effectively managing the city's resources is made possible by all of this consumption of data-gaining technologies and communication platforms.

3. Methodology

Intelligent garbage collection system using smart containers that can measure numerous characteristics to help plan the best path for collection. The AI-based smart garbage bin Bin-e was created for public spaces to make recycling easier. Figure 56.1 illustrates easy trash management; it automatically classifies and compresses the garbage, regulates the fill level, and processes data. The use of wireless sensor networks has led to the development of several smart sensors. The cluster members will be quite close to one another because there are many nodes placed densely. Therefore, multi-hop communication that uses less power is favored in WSN. Every bin has nodes known as Wireless Monitoring Units, and each one has a sensor that detects the level of the bins when they are empty and sends the information to the WAPU. The WAPU collects data from the WMUs and transmits it to the centralized monitoring station, where an application is used to track the levels of the bins.

In these densely populated cities and emerging urban regions, society must face new problems if it is to reduce its use of fossil fuels, support renewable energy sources, and lower CO_2 emissions. Modern smart cities are said to require this efficient waste management or disposal system. IoT implementation is possible in both MSC and IS, producing a fully developed proposal for the next operations. To improve the technology employed in waste management systems' excellent service quality, special techniques can be implemented. For effective trash management, inspection systems and intelligent systems use IoT components, including sensors, detectors, and actuators.

Fig. 56.1 Smart garbage bin

Source: https://www.bine.world/assets/images/photo_homepage_block_01.png

For efficient waste disposal in smart cities, [18] suggests a sophisticated IS. The suggested method is an automated alert-based garbage collection or smart bin system, and it is intended to inform the appropriate authorities, such as a corporate or municipal waste disposal team, efficiently monitor the entire garbage disposal process with this.

Given that traditional fossil fuels will become increasingly scarce in the near future, along with their ecological drawbacks, new smart grids have shown the ability to combine non-renewable and renewable energy sources, reducing environmental issues and maximizing operational costs. supplying a mix of renewable and non-renewable energy sources that are dependable and sustainable.

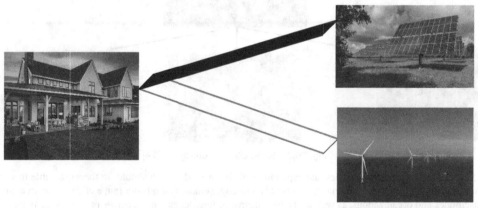

Fig. 56.2 Smart renewable energy [23]

Intelligent energy systems are used to produce and distribute energy, minimizing certain major issues, including long-distance transportation's energy losses and associated costs. Intelligent load and building automation [19], which increases energy efficiency, safety, and comfort on both a home and industrial scale, is the cause of this. Increasing energy efficiency in well-run cities is a direct method to meet challenging environmental objectives. Although the use of solar and other RES is expanding quickly, they still primarily provide off-take energy and have not yet been fully incorporated into grid operations or significantly boosted the resilience of electric and urban systems. Fig. 2 shows a significant and multifaceted endeavor: it is essential to use RES as a completely interconnected grid operational asset and as a resource to improve security, dependability, and resilience. It is crucial to improve utility forecasting skills in terms of both assets and organizations utilization, accessibility, and usefulness before, during, and after a big disaster [20]. The challenge depends on many intricate and frequently illogical relationships between factors.

Green buildings have a large impact on a building's annual energy efficiency and CO_2 emissions reduction, and these positive benefits will rapidly develop due to population growth and rural-to-urban migration. Consequently, introducing GBs is one of the best ways to minimize energy usage and CO2 emissions. The installation of solar panels by GBs to supply the necessary electricity and use natural resources in metropolitan areas might lessen the adverse effects of climate change. Maintaining indoor environmental quality and lowering health risks are the key goals. Throughout a building's lifecycle, green building practices use methods that are resource- and ecologically-conscious. from creation to operation, upkeep, remodeling, and destruction.

On the one hand, fossil fuels account for around 95% of the world's energy sources, whereas conventional resources barely make up 3% [21]. Because non-traditional energy sources are expected to diminish quickly in the future, conventional energy sources will serve as the primary source of energy supply. Therefore, for architectural system integration and assessment in green BIM, explicit, precise information is required.

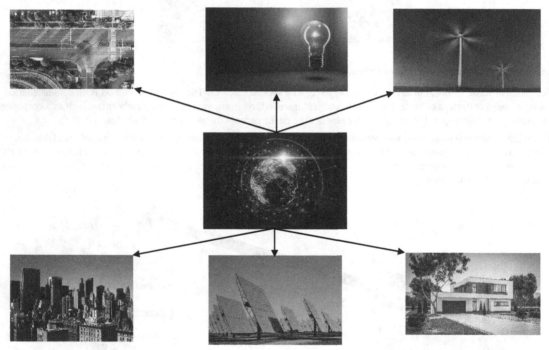

Fig. 56.3 Smart cities for quality life [24]

Figure 56.3 demonstrates the techniques and capabilities of Green BIM, which should, in theory, be able to significantly enhance both design procedures and final products [22]. The engagement of a broader range of design team members from other disciplines and organizations, as well as the high degree of interdependencies across processes, activities, and tasks, are two major obstacles to green BIM.

4. Results and Discussions

To enable sustainable development and expansion, sustainable cities require a human resource that is both legitimate and well qualified. As a result, it is important to take into account the following factors: degree of qualification, aptitude for lifelong learning, socioeconomic and cultural diversity, adaptability, inventiveness, cosmopolitanism, and involvement in public life. The government has set out to improve air quality, protect water resources, increase clean energy, carry out green growth strategies, and further improve the quality of life for its people. The Municipality and Planning Department faced more obstacles as a result of the industrial revolution, which also improved society's wellbeing, lifestyle, and population of the region.

4.1 Discussion

In order to assure welfare and happiness and to turn into a sustainable city with its residents living beautiful, pleasant lives, municipal sustainability performance was improved to include sustainability into all operations, but much work still must be done in regard to the physical infrastructure. Below, Fig. 56.4 shows an effective way to organize a smart city management system.

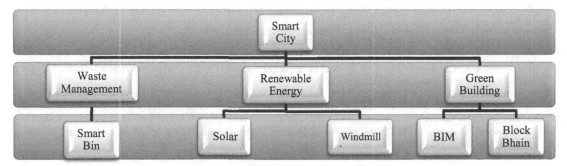

Fig. 56.4 Organization—Area of application [25]

Development of Smart Cities is Hampered by Current Barriers

Electric vehicle adoption, increased use of renewable energy, CO_2 emissions reduction, development of GBs, energy efficiency, greater use of renewable energy, energy management via smart meters, particularly for buildings, inexpensive energy, improved IT networks, and expansion of green space are all results of policies. As a result, the barriers are analytical and address the primary difficulties in this manner.

Important Role of Policy in the Formation of Smart Cities

Policymakers should take stakeholder expectations into account when making decisions in order to successfully execute policies and prevent public opposition, as active engagement is a crucial component of success.

Identifying Obstacles and Discovering Quick fixes

In order to promote SC, international and regional governments can benefit from identifying the key challenges as indicated above. Therefore, by taking these obstacles into account, policymakers will be able to identify the best solutions for them, which will hasten the development of smart cities. As a group, these obstacles encompass both minor and major problems that policymakers want to resolve in the development of SC.

REFERENCE

1. Casini, M. (2017, August). Green technology for smart cities. In IOP Conference series: earth and environmental science (Vol. 83, No. 1, p. 012014). IOP Publishing.
2. Rashidi, H., GhaffarianHoseini, A., GhaffarianHoseini, A., Sulaiman, N. M. N., Tookey, J., & Hashim, N. A. (2015). Application of wastewater treatment in sustainable design of green built environments: A review. Renewable and Sustainable Energy Reviews, 49, 845–856.
3. Nižetić, S., Djilali, N., Papadopoulos, A., & Rodrigues, J. J. (2019). Smart technologies for promotion of energy efficiency, utilization of sustainable resources and waste management. Journal of cleaner production, 231, 565–591.
4. Santa, S. L. B., Ribeiro, J. M. P., Mazon, G., Schneider, J., Barcelos, R. L., & de Andrade, J. B. S. O. (2020). A Green Airport model: Proposition based on social and environmental management systems. Sustainable Cities and Society, 59, 102160.
5. Alhosani, K. M., Kaied, Y. O., & Darwish, A. S. K. (2021). Ajman an environmentally friendly city with its quality of life: review of sustainability challenges and achievements by Ajman Municipality and Planning Department. Renewable Energy and Environmental Sustainability, 6, 12.
6. Mohanty, S. P., Choppali, U., & Kougianos, E. (2016). Everything you wanted to know about smart cities: The Internet of things is the backbone. IEEE Consumer Electronics Magazine, 5(3), 60–70.
7. Razmjoo, A., Gandomi, A. H., Pazhoohesh, M., Mirjalili, S., & Rezaei, M. (2022). The key role of clean energy and technology in smart cities development. Energy Strategy Reviews, 44, 100943.

8. Marques, P., Manfroi, D., Deitos, E., Cegoni, J., Castilhos, R., Rochol, J., ... & Kunst, R. (2019). An IoT-based smart cities infrastructure architecture applied to a waste management scenario. Ad Hoc Networks, 87, 200–208.

9. Akbarpour, N., Salehi-Amiri, A., Hajiaghaei-Keshteli, M., & Oliva, D. (2021). An innovative waste management system in a smart city under stochastic optimization using vehicle routing problem. Soft Computing, 25(8), 6707–6727.

10. Anagnostopoulos, T., Zaslavsky, A., Sosunova, I., Fedchenkov, P., Medvedev, A., Ntalianis, K., ... & Khoruznikov, S. (2018). A stochastic multi-agent system for Internet of Things-enabled waste management in smart cities. Waste Management & Research, 36(11), 1113–1121.

11. Hoang, A. T., & Nguyen, X. P. (2021). Integrating renewable sources into energy system for smart city as a sagacious strategy towards clean and sustainable process. Journal of Cleaner Production, 305, 127161.

12. Galvão, J. R., Moreira, L. M., Ascenso, R. M., & Leitão, S. A. (2015, September). Energy systems models for efficiency towards Smart Cities. In IEEE EUROCON 2015-International Conference on Computer as a Tool (EUROCON) (pp. 1–6). IEEE.

13. Lewandowska, A., Chodkowska-Miszczuk, J., Rogatka, K., & Starczewski, T. (2020). Smart energy in a smart city: Utopia or reality? evidence from Poland. Energies, 13(21), 5795.

14. Kanase-Patil, A. B., Kaldate, A. P., Lokhande, S. D., Panchal, H., Suresh, M., & Priya, V. (2020). A review of artificial intelligence-based optimization techniques for the sizing of integrated renewable energy systems in smart cities. Environmental technology reviews, 9(1), 111–136.

15. Radziejowska, A., & Sobotka, B. (2021). Analysis of the social aspect of smart cities development for the example of smart sustainable buildings. Energies, 14(14), 4330.

16. Liu, Z., Chi, Z., Osmani, M., & Demian, P. (2021). Blockchain and building information management (BIM) for sustainable building development within the context of smart cities. Sustainability, 13(4), 2090.

17. Pellicer, S., Santa, G., Bleda, A. L., Maestre, R., Jara, A. J., & Skarmeta, A. G. (2013, July). A global perspective of smart cities: A survey. In 2013 Seventh International Conference on Innovative Mobile and Internet Services in Ubiquitous Computing (pp. 439–444). IEEE.

18. Ramson, S. J., & Moni, D. J. (2017). Wireless sensor networks based smart bin. Computers & Electrical Engineering, 64, 337–353.

19. Farmanbar, M., Parham, K., Arild, Ø., & Rong, C. (2019). A widespread review of smart grids towards smart cities. Energies, 12(23), 4484.

20. Konstantinou, C. (2021). Toward a secure and resilient all-renewable energy grid for smart cities. IEEE Consumer Electronics Magazine, 11(1), 33–41.

21. Gandhi, R., Pitroda, J., & Bhatt, B. A Review on Green Building Based Smart City for the Next Millennium.

22. Liu, Z., Jiang, L., Osmani, M., & Demian, P. (2019). Building information management (BIM) and blockchain (BC) for sustainable building design information management framework. Electronics, 8(7), 724.

23. https://www.vecteezy.com/vector-art/17038336-the-house-is-powered-by-renewable-energy-sources-green-energy-solar-panels-produce-electricity-vector-illustration

24. Silva, B. N., Khan, M., & Han, K. (2020). Futuristic sustainable energy management in smart environments: A review of peak loads having and demand response strategies, challenges, and opportunities. Sustainability, 12(14), 5561.

25. Casini, M. (2017, August). Green technology for smart cities. In IOP Conference series: earth and environmental science (Vol. 83, No. 1, p. 012014). IOP Publishing.

Computer Science Engineering and Emerging Technologies (ICCS-2022) – Prof (Dr.) Rajeev Sobti et al. (eds)
© 2024 Taylor & Francis Group, London, ISBN 978-1-032-52199-2

Chapter **57**

A Review—Rice Plant Disease Detection Using Machine Learning Algorithms

Manoj Kumar Ahirwar[1]

Department of Computer Science and Engineering,
Lovely Professional University, Punjab

Tejinder Thind[2]

Assistant professor, Department of Computer Science and Engineering,
Lovely, Professional University, Punjab

Abstract: A rise in crop production is necessary to support an increase in the human population. Plant disease is the major reason behind the reduction in quality and quantity of crops. It also has an impact on farmers' incomes, as many farmers today commit suicide as a result of bad fortune. Identifying the plant disease in its early stages is the key to stopping the loss to farmers and maintaining the quality of the crop. In general, plant diseases are identified with the naked eye and appropriate pesticides are used, but this process is very time-consuming and also requires a lot of experience. Rice crop production dominates overall production and consumption around the world. Due to diseases in the plants, it stops the production of the crop and is also a major threat to food security. This problem in the agriculture sector can be minimized with the help of various machine learning algorithms and image processing techniques. The leaves are the most affected part of the rice plant, so with the help of image processing and the classifier, we can detect the disease in its early stages, prevent the loss of farmers, and even save the reduction in crop. Support Vector Machine (SVM), Probabilistic Neural Network (PNN), and Artificial Neural Network (ANN) are the various classification techniques used in agriculture applications.

Keywords: Rice plant disease, Image processing, Support vector machine, Segmentation, Supervised learning

1. Introduction

India is an industrialized economy where 70% of people work in agriculture. The agriculture sector is the backbone of our country. India is the world's second-largest producer of rice and the world's largest exporter of rice, but in recent years, diseases in the rice plant have reduced the quantity of production. The major problem is that there is no continuous monitoring of the plants, and some of the farmers even don't know about the diseases. Rice is a major food crop in Asian countries. Plant diseases, both directly and indirectly, cause certain environmental harms. As these diseases spread around the globe, they harm a plant's ability to function as a whole and harm the economy by drastically reducing the amount of food grown. Vegetation is impacted by several bacterial and fungi-related illnesses. Brown spot, NBSD leaf blast, and sheath blight are the three different diseases that affect rice plants in different ways. The destruction caused by the blast demonstrates the severity and magnitude of the illness. Brown spot, another prominent rice disease, is caused by Bypolaris oryza, a fungus that is constantly present during the growth season. Brown areas typically worsen. When rice is cultivated on soils low in silicon. In Asia, 10 to 15 percent of the yield is lost to rice illnesses.

[1]manojsinghrana467@gmail.com, [2]tejinder.15312@lpu.co,in

DOI: 10.1201/9781003405580-57

A specialist in agriculture has recently supported manually the analysis and monitoring of plant diseases, which takes more work and processing time [9]. Farmers can have trouble identifying the infections, which results in crop loss. Processing the photos of "seemingly" sick leaves that have been acquired by an automated system is one of the best solutions for farmers. To find illnesses, one looks at the plant leaf that displays the symptoms. The automated technology enables farmers to quickly detect infections. The failure of certain plants to yield was caused by slow disease detection. Early illness detection is therefore crucial. The paddy fields are seen in the pictures. The diseased leaf segments in those photos were then segmented during preprocessing. The characteristics are then extracted from the segmented pictures, and ultimately, the illnesses are classified using ML algorithms. The effectiveness of such a system depends on how well it executes the ML and image processing tasks.

2. Literature Review

Lawrence C. Ngugi (2021): The writers of this article have thoroughly analyzed previous studies. Employing IPTs, the outcomes of plant disease detection are summarized here. There are several designs reported in recent literature that have been assessed depending on how well they do, based on the writers, classifiers taught with shallow Deep learning has taken on the role of handcrafted features. As the authors have highlighted, algorithms Deep learning strategies, if adequate, may correctly identify pathogens and diseases. Data for training is accessible, methods such as data augmentation as well as the use of transfer learning to improve categorization exactness.

Using incremental back propagation neural networks with CFS, R. K. Samanta et al. (2012) developed an autonomous classification method for spotting tea insect infestations. There are obvious benefits to limiting the feature set as long as the performance of the intelligent system is not affected. We employ CFS for feature reduction. The original and reduced feature sets were then classified using an incremental back propagation learning neural network (IBPLN). The authors compare the two outcomes. In this study, it was shown how to use CFS to minimize the feature vector and how to use CFS+IBPLN to address various classification problems.

Prakanshu Srivastava (2021) The productivity of the nation's agriculture sector may suffer as a result of insect infestations. The majority of the time, farmers and other experts keep a tight check on the plants to hunt for illness. Contrarily, this approach is time-consuming, costly, and erroneous. Results from autodetection methods based on image processing are quick and accurate. This paper suggests a novel method for building a disease detection model based on leaf image classification using deep convolutional neural networks.

3. Image Processing Technique

Image processing is the techniques to remove the background noise from the image.

There are five steps in the image processing techniques

3.1 Image Acquisition

Image acquisition in the sense of image processing is essentially the action of obtaining a visual from a source, frequently one that is hardware-based, in order to pass it via the following processes: Since processing is difficult without an image, picture acquisition is always the first step in the workflow sequence for image processing.

Because the resulting image is fully unedited and is the result of whatever instrument was used to make it, it might be vital in particular fields to maintain a continuous standard from which to operate. One of the ultimate aims of this approach is to have an input source that runs within such precise and regulated parameters that the same image can, if required, be nearly precisely duplicated under the same circumstances, making it simpler to identify and remove anomalous variables. Depending on the industry, the initial configuration and ongoing maintenance of the gear used to collect the images might have a significant influence on image acquisition and processing. The hardware itself might range from a small desktop scanner to a huge optical telescope. Visual artifacts may result from improperly configured and aligned hardware, which will make image processing more challenging. Inadequately configured hardware may also produce photos of such poor quality that they cannot be saved despite intensive processing. All of these components are essential to some fields, such as comparative image processing, which seeks particular variations among picture collections.

3.2 Image Segmentation

A key element of computer vision is image segmentation. An image is split into numerous sections based on the characteristics of its pixels in order to detect objects or borders, which simplifies and improves analysis. Only two of the numerous industries that segmentation affects are the movie industry and the medical field. The software that runs green screens might employ image segmentation to crop off the front and place it on a backdrop for situations that cannot be shot or would be dangerous to capture in real life. Image segmentation is also used to classify terrain in satellite photographs, such as oil reserves, and to identify objects in a sequence of pictures. Medical uses of segmentation include the measurement of bone and tissue, the detection of dubious formations to aid radiologists, and the recognition of injured muscle.

3.3 Pre-processing

Before creating a model, the majority of machine learning engineers spend a lot of time and effort on data pre-processing, commonly referred to as data purification. Data pre-processing includes, among other things, the detection of outliers, fixing missing numbers, and eliminating undesirable or noisy data.

Similar to this, "image pre-processing" describes operations carried out on images at their most fundamental level of abstraction. These procedures actually lessen the amount of information that is present in the picture when measured by entropy. Preprocessing is done to improve some aspects of an image that are crucial for later processing and analysis jobs or to lessen undesirable distortions in the image files.

3.4 Feature Extraction

Feature extraction is part of the dimensionality reduction process, which reduces the size and complexity of a beginning collection of raw data into manageable chunks. It requires a lot of processing resources to process these variables. By selecting and merging variables into features, feature extraction assists in extracting the best feature from such enormous data sets to efficiently minimize the amount of data. These features properly and distinctively describe the actual data set while being straightforward to utilize.

4. Classification Techniques

4.1 Convolutional Neural Networks (CNN)

Convolutional neural networks are a type of multi-layer neural network that is meant to identify visual patterns directly from pixel pictures with little pre-processing. In artificial neural networks, it is a unique architecture. To attain state-of-the-art outcomes in computer vision challenges, convolutional neural networks employ some of the properties of the visual cortex. Two very basic components—convolutional layers and pooling layers—make up convolutional neural networks. Despite being straightforward, there are practically endless combinations of how to construct these layers for a specific computer vision issue. Convolutional and pooling layers, for example, are among the better understood components of a convolutional neural network.

4.2 Artificial Neural Networks (ANN)

A unique class of machine learning algorithms called artificial neural networks is based on how the human brain functions. That is, the ANN is able to learn from the data in a manner similar to how the neurons in our nervous system are able to learn from previous data and produce answers in the form of predictions or classifications. These artificial neural networks are used for a wide range of activities, including image identification, speech recognition, machine translation, and medical diagnosis. The ability of ANN to learn from example data sets is a key benefit. The most frequent application of ANN is as a rough approximation of a random function. These kinds of technologies enable one to specify the distribution's solutions in a cost-effective manner. Instead of using the complete dataset, ANN is also capable of using a sample of the data to get the end result. Because of their sophisticated forecasting skills, ANNs may be used to improve current data analysis methods.

4.3 Random Forest

For both classification and regression, the Random Forest supervised learning method is used. The random forest method generates decision trees on samples of data, receives predictions from each one, and then votes to decide which is the best response. A forest is made up of trees, and more trees equal a more robust forest. The ensemble approach, which is better than a single decision tree, reduces overfitting since it averages the outcomes. The random forest is a categorization method composed of several decision trees. By using feature randomization and bagging while creating each individual tree, it seeks to create an uncorrelated forest of trees whose forecast by the committee is more precise.

5. Conclusion

The numerous image processing and machine learning techniques used in the identification and categorization of plant diseases are discussed in this review study. Each method of image processing has been explored in depth. Different categorization methods have been compared and discussed in detail. Researchers should use the aforementioned review to apply a few new algorithms and gain methodological knowledge to provide better results. Methods for detection and classification might be improved by combining hitherto untried processing, selection, and training techniques. Farmers may provide instant responses by creating mobile applications. Websites may need to offer online treatments for plant diseases.

REFERENCES

1. T. Rumpf, A. K. Mahlein, U. Steiner, E. C. Oerke, H. W. Dehne, L. Pumer, "Early detection and classification of plant disease with support vector machines based on hyperspectral refelcetance," Computers and Electronics in Agriculture, vol. 74, pp. 91–99, 2010.
2. Haiguang Wang, Guanlin Li, Zhanhong Ma, Xiaolong Li, "Image Recognition of Plant Diseases Based on Backpropagation Networks", 5th International Congress on Image and Signal Processing (CISP 2012) 2012.
3. Sujeet Varshney and Tarun Dalal, "A novel approach for the detection of plant diseases", IJCSMC, vol. 5, no. 7, pp. 44–54, 2016.
4. Arivazhagan S and Ligi S V, "Mango leaf diseases identification using Convolutional Neural Network", International Journal of Pure and Applied Mathematics, vol. 120, no. 6, pp. 11067–11079, 2018.
5. Pinki, "Content based Paddy Leaf Disease Recognition and Remedy Prediction using Support Vector Machine," pp. 22–24, 2017.
6. Phadikar S, Sil J and KumarDas A, "Region identification of infected rice images using the concept of Fermi energy", Advances in Computing and Information Technology, pp. 805–811, 2013.
7. Jitesh Shah P, Harshadkumar B Prajapati and Vipul K Dabhi, "A survey on detection and classification of rice plant diseases", In IEEE International Conference on Current Trends in Advanced Computing, pp. 1–8, 2016.
8. Md . Mursalin and Md . Motaher Hossain et. Al, "Performance Analysis among Different Classifier Including Naive Bayes, Support Vector Machine and C4.5 for Automatic Weeds Classification", Global Journal of Computer Science and Technology Graphics Vision, Volume 13 Issue 3 Version 1.0 Year 2013.
9. Lumini, A., Nanni, L., 2019. "Deep learning and transfer learning features for plankton classification,"Ecol. Inform. 51, 33–43.
10. Y. Lu, S. Yi,N.Zeng,Y. Liu, and Y. Zhang, "Identification of Rice Diseases Using Deep Convolutional Neural Networks," Neurocomputing, 267, pp. 378–384,2017.
11. Vanitha V, "Rice disease detection using deep learning", International Journal of Recent Technology and Engineering, vol. 7, pp. 2277–3878, no. 5S3, 2019.
12. Hemanta Kalita, Shikhar Kr Sarma and Ridip Dev Choudhury, "Expert system for diagnosis of diseases of rice plants: prototype design and implementation", International Conference on Automatic Control and Dynamic Optimization Techniques, pp. 723–730, 2016.
13. R. Sharma, S. Das, M. K. Gourisaria, S. S. Rautaray, and M. Pandey, "A Model for Prediction of Paddy Crop Disease Using CNN," in Progress in Computing, Analytics and Networking, 2020, pp. 533–543, doi: 10.1007/978-981-15-2414-1.

Computer Science Engineering and Emerging Technologies (ICCS-2022) – Prof (Dr.) Rajeev Sobti et al. (eds)
© 2024 Taylor & Francis Group, London, ISBN 978-1-032-52199-2

Chapter **58**

Enhancement of Key Management System in Cloud Environment

Shahnawaz Ahmad[1], Shabana Mehfuz[2]
Department of Electrical Engineering,
Jamia Millia Islamia (A Central University), New Delhi, India
Javed Beg[3]
Oracle, Noida, India

Abstract: The significance of the cloud environment is because of its infinite provision of services like servers, storage systems, and sharing. Data security is an important concern in collective data sharing. As the data is stored and handled through semi-trusted third-party cloud providers, the necessity of safety for the outsourced information has significantly increased in the cloud environment. In a traditional protection paradigm, the whole file is immediately encrypted utilizing the secret key; nevertheless, this approach cannot be utilized in a cloud environment for group mechanisms because of difficulty with key distribution. An effective hierarchical group key management system (KMS) for a cloud environment is suggested in this study. The Key Distribution Server (KDS), which executes cryptography key functions for protecting the data stored in the cloud, is the foundation of the developed framework. Additionally, for scaling, this system maintains the hierarchical tree using the logical key hierarchy (LKH) method. The private data supplied by the KDS server and the members' private data are combined to create the group key. The suggested KMS is more effective and considerably better suited for a cloud environment, according to a quantitative study of the system.

Keywords: Key management system, Cloud environment, Key distribution server, Cryptographic keys

1. Introduction

A cloud-based storage environment has received a lot of interest in recent years from both academics and businesses. Because of its protracted list of advantages, which includes access freedom and a lack of local data administration, it may be extensively employed in multiple Internet-based business programs (such as Apple iCloud) [Li, J., et al. (2016)]. Currently, a growing proportion of people and businesses choose to outsource their information to faraway clouds in order to avoid having to upgrade their local data handling resources or systems. Nevertheless, one of the biggest barriers preventing Internet users from embracing cloud storage environment services generally may be their concern about security breaches involving outsourced data [Li, W., et al. (2015)].

Key management systems (KMSs) are among the most effective and well-liked methods of ensuring security. In a cryptosystem, managing cryptographic keys is known as key management. A trustworthy KMS enhances organizational security and helps businesses comply with compliance and data management regulations. Encryption and decryption are the two basic parts of cryptography. Plaintext is changed by encryption into a cipher that has to be broken open in order

[1]Shahnawaz98976@gmail.com

DOI: 10.1201/9781003405580-58

for the information to be made clear. One key is used to encrypt the information, while another key is used to decode it [Oruganti, R., & Churi, P. (2022)].

Outsourced information may be required to be subsequently shared with others in numerous practical scenarios [Ning, J., et al., (2016)]. Alice, a Dropbox user, may send her buddies pictures. Without employing data encryption, Alice must first create a link for sharing and then distribute it to others in order to share the images. The sharing url may be exposed at the Dropbox administrative level; for example, an admin may view the link, even though it guarantees a certain degree of access restriction for unauthorized users, for example, those who are not Alice's buddies. In order to protect privacy and the security of data, it is typically advised to encrypt the information before uploading it to the cloud because the cloud, which is installed on an open platform, cannot be entirely trusted. One of the appropriate alternatives is to explicitly utilize an encryption approach (such as AES) on the data that is outsourced prior to uploading it in the cloud, ensuring that only the authorized cloud user (containing a legitimate decryption key) may access the information via a legitimate decryption method [Preetha, V., and Soms, N. (2022)]. The fundamental technique that was previously used was to preserve and retrieve information into and out of cloud memory using cryptographic processes of decryption and encryption. The key update and key distribution procedures, which are the most significant issues, are not addressed by this fundamental technique. An important aspect of ensuring the security of collective data exchange is key distribution [Indu, I., et al., (2016)].

1.1 Research Statement

A recent study found that 94% of businesses anticipate having more than 50% of their operations in the cloud environment, and that the Internet of Things (IOTs) would expand quickly as a result of the widespread use of communication technologies. In the systems of cloud data centers, traffic has grown tremendously due to the quick growth of programs. These strategies, which are now in their infancy, have garnered a lot of interest as a means of lowering capital expenditure and raising system effectiveness. It keeps user data on a huge virtual memory system made up of several servers connected by a network. Although there are numerous advantages to storing data at remote sites, there is always a chance that the confidential data may be changed, leaked, or replaced. Since every user anticipates that every text they send via a computer will be secure, legitimate, and trustworthy, IoT cybersecurity is a matter of concern since it serves as a source of information for the IoT system, protecting its networks as well as hardware. Verifying the eligibility of customers, flaws within the company, malware assaults, external connections to the networks of the business, a shortage of experienced security personnel, and numerous other challenges are among the key security concerns. Data holders seek cloud server environments with a higher degree of security and the provision of appropriate security measures in order to mitigate these dangers. Certain efficient techniques and useful security algorithms are capable of delivering this security.

We thus seek to safeguard the cloud environment and enhance security using KMSs in order to enable the reliable usage of cloud servers.

1.2 Research Objective

This research aims to investigate the enhancement of KMS in cloud environment with the following objectives:

- To propose the cloud model system.
- To develop a productive hierarchical group KMS for cloud-based safe data sharing.
- To perform key management tasks including key generation, re-keying, and other tasks using key distribution server (KDS).

1.3 Research Framework

This research includes five parts, including an introduction. In the following part two of the literature review, we explain the different types of KMS and other related works between 2015 and 2022. Section 3 describes the materials and methods utilized in this research. The outcomes are presented and discussed in Section 4; Section 5 ends with the key findings, their implications, and recommendations for theory as well as practice.

2. Review of Literature

As per Abualghanam, O. R. I. E. B., et al. (2019), there are numerous methods that may be used to distribute keys in groups, including (1) centralized KMS, in which the whole group is under the control of a single entity, and (2) distributed KMS, in which no one entity is accountable for key production. (3) Decentralized KMS, where the unit is split into numerous sub-groups and managed by the administrators of the sub-group individuals. In this method, each individual group member contributes to the development of the group key, which is performed by themselves. According to Pasupulati, R. P., and Shropshire, J. (2016), the idea behind the LKH protocol serves as the foundation for centralized KMS. A trustworthy server, such as Key Distribution Center (KDC), will keep a hierarchical tree layout in this case. Each user of the group will receive a copy of the group key, and they are familiar with all of the keys. In decentralized KMS, the group is fragmented into several tiny groups. Each subgroup is under the management of an intermediary key server to combat the issue of a single source of breakdown. Data encryption with a symmetrical key is the owner's responsibility. In this approach, the key and the encrypted data are posted to the cloud. The encryption key is then subsequently re-encrypted on the cloud, whereby the customer's private key may then be used to decode. The suggested scheme's key pair is not based on credentials. A key pair containing a public key as well as a private key is produced depending on the customer's identification. The CL-PRE method is centered on BDH as well as a bilinear duo, which adds computational complexity to the system. The proxy is used as a trustworthy entity for calculation during key generation as well as data accessibility activities.

In addition to proposing a novel multicast batch rekeying method that constantly reallocates the tree to preserve equitable endpoints, Srinadh, V., and Nageswara Rao, P. V. (2021) also established a straightforward but effective highlighting batch rekeying algorithm that upgrades the hierarchy tree layout when there is an alteration in the group identity.

The research of Zhang, Y., et al. (2020) provides insight into attribute-based encryption (ABE). In this case, the properties are connected to the data and utilized for encryption. They suggested an important, policy-oriented ABE. In this system, the data and characteristics are connected through private keys. They suggested an access control system in which identity-based open-key cryptography is used to govern files.

An accessibility control technique for cloud environments was introduced by Niu, S., et al. (2015). The suggested method enables portable devices to safely use cloud computing assets and outsources encryption and decryption tasks. Furthermore, there is no requirement to be concerned about the private key or the contents of the data being revealed. Before sharing a work in the cloud, one common strategy is to perform encryption of the whole file utilizing a private key and then distribute it to all group users. The two most crucial security aspects to take into account, together with access control, are identification and privacy. To fulfill the safety objective, present approaches employ capability lists and access control lists (ACLs) combined over encryption.

3. Materials and Method

3.1 Proposed Cloud System Model

Figure 58.1 depicts the model of the system for the suggested system, which allows users of the group to join or depart at any moment. The Data Owner (DO) in this scenario will be in charge of carrying out system setup, which involves giving users accessibility control rules, creating group keys, etc., and uploading the encrypted dataset to the cloud servers. This model's different components include the cloud server (CS), the DO, the group members (GM), and the key distribution server (KDS), a dependable server for safe data exchange in a cloud environment. The users' shared data is secured by a cryptography key. Every time a user of the group leaves or joins, KDS changes the group key.

In this network structure, users of the group who are simultaneously online and offline are taken into account. Whenever the offline users reconnect, the key has to be synced with them. By guaranteeing that the user who quits the group won't have any privileges for accessing data in the group, forward secrecy is established. By enabling the new member to view just the most recent data transfer and not the earlier one, backward secrecy is achieved. To ensure forward secrecy, the suggested system uses an accessibility management policy approach that prevents the data from being accessed by departing members.

3.2 Conceptual Framework of KMS

The goal of the suggested key management system is to securely distribute a symmetrical key to each user in the group. To guarantee the confidentiality of the group's contents, a fresh secret group key must be established and disseminated whenever a user joins or leaves the group. The suggested protocol maintains groups using the LKH method's mechanism. The group is preserved as a structure of hierarchical trees in the suggested approach in Fig. 58.2.

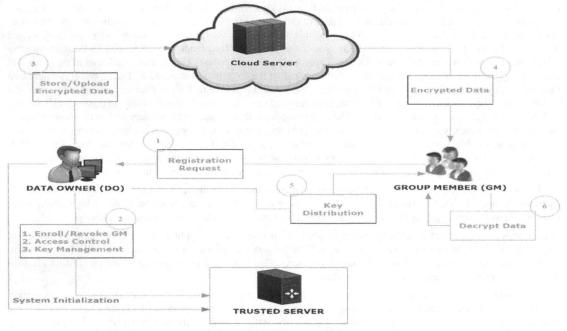

Fig. 58.1 Model of the suggested system

Source: Made by Author

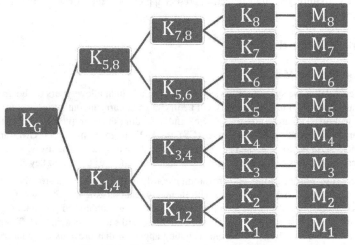

Fig. 58.2 Hierarchy tree of proposed LKH

Source: Made by Author

3.3 Experiment Setup

For encrypting and decrypting, the group key is represented by the key KG. In contrast to the key nodes in the route, which are K1,2, K1,4, as well as the group key KG, the M1 and M2 members possess the K1 and K2 keys, respectively. The other members each possess a unique collection of keys. The unit key in the suggested approach is only accessible by the DO. For cloud file accessibility, the DO provides the group key to the user's of the group. The suggested system employs the RSA algorithm to ensure that the cloud server, DO, as well as group members may communicate securely.

The suggested system makes use of the marking algorithm to enable batch rekeying in an attempt to address the problems that are currently present in rekeying. For each join and leave demand in this system, the key tree is enhanced and a fresh rekey sub-tree is created. The KDS substitutes for the departures by joining if there are more new members than leaving members. Where the requirements are met, re-keying may be done in a variety of ways, including more joins, more leaves, and batch re-keying algorithms when the join and leave counts are equivalent.

4. Result and Discussion

The suggested method is implemented using frameworks from Amazon EC2 as well as S3. Instances of virtual servers running multiple operational systems, like Windows/Linux, can be started on Amazon data centers as well as accessible using Amazon EC2. An online service used for retrieving and storing data is Amazon S3. For the suggested system, we took into account the DO, GM, KDS, and CS modules. The Data Owner runs the DO unit to carry out group leader tasks like startup, GM administration, and file setup for assigning users of the group accessibility control rights. Just the GM with permission to do so can use the GM unit to communicate with the KDS and CS modules and download the outsourced information. The most reliable unit for key management and generation is KDS. The KDS unit is maintained by DO for the group's key functions. The cloud providers utilize the CS unit, which is based on Amazon EC2, to maintain and access information from Amazon S3. For the CS unit, we utilized a tiny Amazon EC2 setup. The instance model selected for the investigation offers 1 virtual core, 2 GB of memory, and 1 EC2 computing unit. A 2007 Xeon processor with a clock speed of 1.0–1.2 GHz is provided by one ECU. A workstation PC with Windows 7 featuring the KDS unit is equipped with an Intel Core (TM) i3 CPU operating at 3.3 GHz with 8 GB of RAM.

The user-server cloud deployment method was established in the cloud environment in order to examine the functionality of the suggested method. Java and the Netbeans IDE were utilized to execute the suggested KMS. Prior to outsourcing to the cloud, the key generation operation was carried out in the KDS unit and evaluated using a Java program. The open and private keys are created by the GM and DO using the RSA method. The DO interacts with the KDS unit to preserve and operate the KDS server, where the group key of the hierarchical tree is produced and saved.

Table 58.1 Outcomes of computation-related overhead time

Size of thegroup	Key server		Node member		Overall Time
	Join	Leave	Join	Leave	
2	0.0083	0.0031	0.0054	0.0016	0.0184
4	0.02	0.021	0.011	0.0031	0.0501
18	0.03	0.05	0.016	0.0087	0.1007
16	0.074	0.07	0.021	0.015	0.177
32	0.127	0.091	0.027	0.021	0.266
64	0.179	0.111	0.032	0.027	0.349

Source: Made by Author

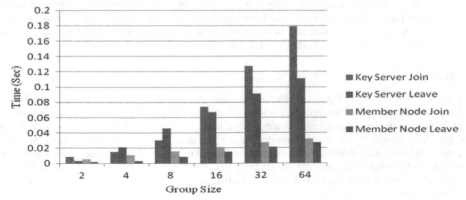

Fig. 58.3 Graphical representation of computation-related overhead time

Source: Made by Author

Table 58.2 Outcomes of duration of time for file upload and download in cloud

Size of File (MB)	Cloud Environment	
	Download(s)	Upload(s)
0.5	1.08	1.01
1	1.49	1.42
2	1.93	1.86
5	3.31	3.25
10	6.57	6.54
20	7.46	7.41
50	10.47	10.21
100	14.78	14.23

Source: Made by Author

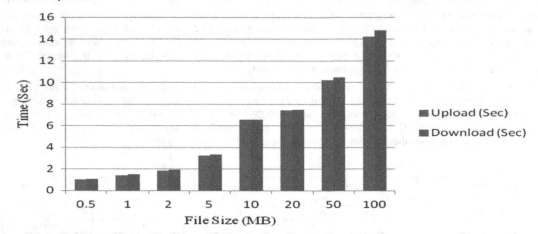

Fig. 58.4 Graphical Representation of duration of time for file upload and download in cloud

Source: Made by Author

We assessed the KDS Server as well as the computation overhead time of node members, which takes into account generation of keys, distribution, and decryption and encryption throughout join and leave operations. The computational overhead time, which is estimated before the DO uploads the encrypted document to the cloud servers, is shown in Table 58.1 and Fig. 58.3. The results of our evaluation of the cloud servers' uploading and downloading times are shown in Table 58.2 as well as Fig. 58.4. The time is measured from the beginning of the file uploading process until the moment when the cloud server has received the entire file. In an identical vein, the interval between making a demand for a file's downloading and after it has finished downloading is taken into account.

5. Conclusion

The suggested research demonstrates that it is a robust and effective protocol for group interaction in a cloud environment. Whenever a user of the group quits, this procedure is more effective at lowering complication, and this system employs inverted data to enhance the key in an effective manner when a leave action is performed. The users of the group can compute the key independently by utilizing the inverted value rather than relying on the DO to do so. As a result, each user of the group will keep the inverted value of the remaining users of the group. All the parties participating in this KMS communicate with one another using open and private key pairs. When a user quits the system, the fresh group key is multi-cast to the other users of the group as well as the user's inverted data. The following are a few of the achievements achieved in this program:

This method has a minimal computational cost in the re-keying technique as compared to the earlier described method of LKH during departure activity. The DO is not required to produce the group key while leaving operating conditions. The keys are sent through multicast to the users of the group, and the text size sent during the departure operation is reduced. Data is distributed among the users of the group by taking into account the access privileges supplied by the DO if there is a dynamic shift in the membership. The ACL is prepared by the cloud server in order to validate the user's access privileges. The suggested technique achieves forward and reverse secrecy.

REFERENCE

1. Li, J., Lin, X., Zhang, Y., & Han, J. (2016). KSF-OABE: Outsourced attribute-based encryption with keyword search function for cloud storage. *IEEE Transactions on Services Computing*, *10*(5), 715–725. DOI:10.1109/TSC.2016.2542813.
2. Li, W., Xue, K., Xue, Y., & Hong, J. (2015). TMACS: A robust and verifiable threshold multi-authority access control system in public cloud storage. *IEEE Transactions on parallel and distributed systems*, *27*(5), 1484–1496. DOI:10.1109/TPDS.2015.2448095
3. Oruganti, R., & Churi, P. (2022). Systematic Survey on Cryptographic Methods Used for Key Management in Cloud Computing. In *International Conference on Innovative Computing and Communications* (pp. 445–460). Springer, Singapore. DOI: 10.1007/978-981-16-2597-8_38
4. Ning, J., Cao, Z., Dong, X., & Wei, L. (2016). White-box traceable CP-ABE for cloud storage service: how to catch people leaking their access credentials effectively. *IEEE Transactions on Dependable and Secure Computing*, *15*(5), 883–897. DOI: 10.1109/TDSC.2016.2608343
5. Preetha, V., & Soms, N. (2022). An Effective Hierarchical Key Management System Using Elliptic Curve Cryptography And Session Key Establishment On Cloud. *IJRAR-International Journal of Research and Analytical Reviews (IJRAR)*, *9*(2), 263–267. http://www.ijrar.org/IJRAR1COP046
6. Indu, I., Anand, P. R., & Shaji, S. P. (2016). Secure file sharing mechanism and key management for mobile cloud computing environment. *Indian Journal of Science and Technology*, *9*(48), 1–8. DOI:10.17485/ijst/2016/v9i48/89496.
7. Abualghanam, O. R. I. E. B., Qatawneh, M. O. H. A. M. M. A. D., & Almobaideen, W. E. S. A. M. (2019). A survey of key distribution in the context of the internet of things. *Journal of Theoretical and Applied Information Technology*, *97*(22), 3217–3241. http://www.jatit.org/volumes/Vol97No22/6Vol97No22.pdf.
8. Pasupulati, R. P., & Shropshire, J. (2016). Analysis of centralized and decentralized cloud architectures. In *SoutheastCon 2016* (pp. 1–7). IEEE. DOI:10.1109/SECON.2016.7506680
9. Srinadh, V., & Nageswara Rao, P. V. (2021). Dynamic and Collaborative Group Key Generation with Quadtree-Based Queue-Batch Algorithm. In *Communication Software and Networks* (pp. 379–391). Springer, Singapore. DOI: 10.1007/978-981-15-5397-4_39
10. Zhang, Y., Deng, R. H., Xu, S., Sun, J., Li, Q., & Zheng, D. (2020). Attribute-based encryption for cloud computing access control: A survey. *ACM Computing Surveys (CSUR)*, *53*(4), 1–41. DOI: 10.1145/3398036
11. Niu, S., Tu, S., & Huang, Y. (2015). An effective and secure access control system scheme in the cloud. *Chinese Journal of Electronics*, *24*(3), 524–528. DOI:10.1049/cje.2015.07.015
12. Ahmad, S., Mehfuz, S. & Beg, J. Hybrid cryptographic approach to enhance the mode of key management system in cloud environment. J Supercomput (2022). https://doi.org/10.1007/s11227-022-04964-9
13. Ahmad, S., Mehfuz, S., Mebarek-Oudina, F. et al. RSM analysis-based cloud access security broker: a systematic literature review. Cluster Comput 25, 3733–3763 (2022). https://doi.org/10.1007/s10586-022-03598-z.
14. Shahnawaz Ahmad, Iman Shakeel, Shabana Mehfuz, Javed Ahmad, "Deep learning models for cloud, edge, fog, and IoT computing paradigms: Survey, recent advances, and future directions", Computer Science Review, Volume 49, 2023, 100568, ISSN 1574-0137, https://doi.org/10.1016/j.cosrev.2023.100568.
15. Shahnawaz Ahmad, Shabana Mehfuz, Javed Beg, "An efficient and secure key management with the extended convolutional neural network for intrusion detection in cloud storage", Concurrency and Computational Practice and Experience, 2023, https://doi.org/10.1002/cpe.7806.

Computer Science Engineering and Emerging Technologies (ICCS-2022) – Prof (Dr.) Rajeev Sobti et al. (eds)
© 2024 Taylor & Francis Group, London, ISBN 978-1-032-52199-2

Chapter **59**

A Comparative Study of Load Balancing Algorithms in Cloud Computing

Nahita Pathania[1], Balraj Singh[2]

School of Computer Science & Engineering, Lovely Professional University, India

Abstract: Cloud computing has gained more popularity during the lockdown period due to the increased demand for online resources. The major challenge is balancing the load in the data centers. To reduce response time and maximize resource efficiency, the dynamically changing requirements of the users should be taken into account and implemented on heterogeneous nodes rather than homogeneous nodes. This paper tried to represent the numerous load-balancing approaches that have been proposed in recent times. A summary of several LB approaches grounded on many parameters and their performance has been presented. Moreover, the explanation of performance metrics that are used for validating the anticipated schemes has been discussed.

Keywords: Load balancing, Cloud computing, Virtual machines

1. Introduction

Cloud computing is an online utility that enables on-demand access to a shared pool of computer resources. Cloud computing progresses to offer anything as a service. Cloud computing's basic characteristics include on-demand self-service, widespread network connectivity, resource pooling, quick elasticity, and measured service (Thakur, A., & Goraya, M. S. ,2017). The "pay-as-you-go" pricing model used by cloud service providers allows customers to only pay for the resources and services according to their usage (Afzal, S., & Kavitha, G. 2019). It allows users to concentrate on their main goals rather than worrying about the requirements for their computing infrastructure. Nowadays, every company is offering cloud facilities and some of the great players in this field are Amazon, Google, Microsoft, etc. (Ramezani, F., et al. 2020). The CC offers the following service models—namely SaaS, PaaS, and IaaS and the four deployment models, which are categorized as private, public, community, and hybrid clouds.

A CC model is effective if its resources are used as efficiently as possible, and this kind of effective utilization can be attained by implementing and maintaining adequate management of cloud resources. Massive data centers ,which are houses of extensive computing resources, have been implemented at the back end of cloud services to offer consumers streamlined computer services. However, owing to the incessant demand for services, maintaining the proper utilization of resources has become one of the major concerns (Batra, S., & Singh, A., 2021). This may lead to a dearth of resources. Therefore, in order to have effective resource usage, the allocation must be proper, i.e., no resource must be underloaded or overloaded. Overloading of resources lowers the quality of the service in a contrast to resource underloading, which wastes resources (Mishra, S. K., Sahoo, B., & Parida, P. P., 2020).

Balancing the load is considered one of the major concerns these days due to the increased demand for resources during the lockdown. The mismanagement of load can be taken care of by seamlessly managing the load, and this is possible with

---

[1]nahita.19372@lpu.co.in, [2]balraj.13075@lpu.co.in

DOI: 10.1201/9781003405580-59

the help of efficient load-balancing algorithms. LB can be either static or dynamic (Batra, S., et al. 2022 and Ala'Anzy, et al.2019). Static load balancing evenly distributes the traffic load across the servers. An algorithm with prior knowledge of the system's resources and task needs performs this. The static LB algorithm plans tasks to be executed by the virtual machine at compile time. Static algorithms need prior knowledge about the resources, but they do not need to know the current status of the system (Shahid, M. A. et al., 2020). On the other hand, in dynamic load balancing, the current behaviour of the system is taken into consideration; therefore, it has the ability to tackle unpredictable loads (Hota, A., Mohapatra, S., & Mohanty, S., 2019) Fig. 59.1 represents the architecture for load balancing.

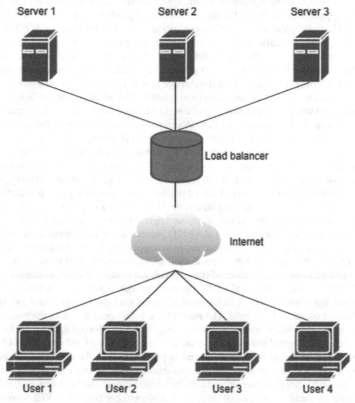

Fig. 59.1 Architecture of Load Balancing

Source: Made by Author

2. Literature Review

Arif Ullah et al. (2022) presented an LB approach using the modified Bat algorithm for distributing the tasks. The author did modifications to the search process and fitness function value. The different parameters that have been considered to measure the performance of the system are makespan, processing time, throughput, and degree of imbalance. The proposed algorithm proves to be better as compared to the RR, ABC, BAT, and GA algorithms, thus enhancing the accuracy and efficiency of cloud data centers. Simin Abedi et al. (2022) proposed a technique known as IFA for Dynamic Resource Allocation, which not only manages the load between VMs but also lessens the completion time with the help of a suitable choice of objectives in the objective value. The initial population is created by assigning priority to the tasks and the priority is decided based on the fuzzy technique. The proposed technique shows an improvement in the makespan over alike methods owing to the advantage of the firefly and fuzzy technique. Jing He (2022) proposed a technique in which the ACO algorithm is modified and runs in the controller. The controller is basically responsible for the load distribution and it performs some calculations in link to the smallest load and accordingly, the data is forwarded. In the proposed algorithm response time is 30% better than the other algorithms ultimately leading to a better-optimized effect. SeyedSalar Sefati et al. (2022) proposed a newer version of GWO in order to improve the response time and cost that has been spent in search of resources. The new approach first identifies whether the nodes are busy or unemployed and then based on that calculates the fitness and threshold. It has been found that this novel technique is found to provide better results as compared to ABC, PSO, and GA algorithms. Kruekaew, B., & Kimpan, W(2022) designed an approach by combining the ABC algorithm with the Q-learning Algorithm which helps in improving the working speed of the ABC. With the help of the proposed technique, the authors are able to make effective resource utilization and enhance the scheduling process. The proposed method has been compared with existing algorithms and the approach has been implemented using different datasets. The results indicate that this approach outperforms the already existing algorithms in terms of DOI, throughput, makespan, and resource utilization. Mangalampalli, S et al. (2022) perform the task scheduling using CSO. The tasks were scheduled based on their priorities and VMs were also sorted according to the priorities so that appropriate mapping of tasks can be done. The proposed approach was implemented using the cloudsim tool and the results were compared with PSO and CS algorithms, and it has been found to be better in terms of power cost, migration time, energy consumption, and makespan. Purshottam J. Assudani et al. (2021) proposed a hybrid technique in which the PSO has been modified with GA. The main idea is to minimize the chances to get into the minimum local solution. The advantage of GA is it helps improve the search space ultimately providing a variety of populations. This novel technique outperforms as compared to other techniques in terms of makespan, utilization of resources, and execution time. G. Annie Poornima Princess et al. (2021) presented a technique that is a combination of Pigeon Inspired and Harries Hawk Optimization to ensure the proper utilization of responses and response time. The features of both these algorithms have been extracted and the performance of the algorithm has been tested on the varied number of tasks and proves that load among the VMs is managed in less time as compared to HHO, SMA, ACO, and HBO. Dalia Abdulkareem Shafiq et al. (2021) presented an improved Load balancing approach that takes into consideration the priority of virtual machines and aims to improve the allotment of resources. The author focuses on the length of the task and the deadline is decided for every task to reduce SLA violations. The results prove that this technique is better than the existing dynamic approaches that are used to balance the load. Moreover, resource utilization is also improved. Xueliang Fu et al. (2021) presented a hybrid technique based on PSO and PGA. In this technique, the mechanism of GA is used to increase the search space and for the PSO, the feedback mechanism of the experience of the flight feedback ensures that the particle shall move in the direction of the best solution. The results of the algorithm proposed proved to be better in terms of convergence and completion time as compared to the PSO and GA. Jianguo Zheng et al. (2021) presented a hybrid MO BAT algorithm in which modifications have been done to improve the searching capability of the algorithm globally. This has been achieved with the help of a back-propagation algorithm and a random walk is performed based on levy flight. The results have been compared with the multi-objective ACO, PSO, GA, and CS algorithms and improvement has been observed in terms of DI, throughput, and Makespantime. Shridhar G. Domanal et al. (2017) presented a hybrid technique based on known as Modified CSO+ Modified PSO. The modifications in PSO have been done based on the global best value and in modified CSO, the seeking mode is used rather than the tracing mode. The CSO has been used to improve the management of resources and PSO is used for scheduling purposes. The results of the proposed technique have been proved to be better as compared to ACO, exact Algorithm, RR, and MPSO. Table 59.1 represents the comparative analysis of the reviewed algorithms and Table 59.2 represents the performance metrics that have been used by numerous authors.

Table 59.1 Comparative Analysis of Reviewed algorithms

Author	Algorithm/Technique	Tool Used	Performance
Arif Ullah et al.	Modified BAT	Cloudsim	Reduction of time consumptionis improved by 1.78%
Simin Abedi et al.	Improved Firefly Algorithm - Dynamic Resource Allocation (IFA-DSA)	MATLAB	Improvement in Makespan by3%.
Jing He	Modified ACO	Not Specified	Improvement in response timeby 30%
Purshottam J. Assudaniet al.	IPSOGA	Cloudsim	Less execution time, makespan.
SeyedSalar Sefati et al.	New version of GWO	Cloudsim	Less makespan and responsetime
Kruekaew et al.	MOABCQ	Cloudsim	Reduction in makespan, DOI,increase in throughput and resource utilization

Author	Algorithm/Technique	Tool Used	Performance
Mangalampalli, S et al.	Scheduling using CAT	Cloudsim	Improvement in Makespan, energy consumption, migration time, and total power cost.
G. Annie PoornimaPrincess et al.	HHO-PIO	Cloudsim	97% improvement in efficiency
Dalia AbdulkareemShafiq et al.	Improved LBA	Cloudsim	Less execution time, makespan, and improved resource utilization.
Xueliang Fu et al.	PSO_PGA	Cloudsim	Higher convergence Rate and improved completion time.
Jianguo Zheng et al.	Hybrid multi-objective batalgorithm	MATLAB	Improved DI, throughput, and makespan time.
Shridhar G. Domanal etal.	Modified PSO + Modified CSO	Pysim	Appropriate utilization of resources, less response time, and reliability.

Source: Made by Author

Table 59.2   Summary of Performance Metrics

Reference	Algorithm	A	B	C	D	E	F	G	H	I
Arif Ullah et al.	Modified BAT	✓	✓	×	×	✓	×	×	×	✓
Simin Abedi et al.	IFA-DSA	✓	×	×	×	×	×	×	✓	✓
Jing He	Modified ACO	×	×	✓	×	×	×	×	×	×
Purshottam J. Assudaniet al.	IPSOGA	✓	×	×	✓	×	×	✓	×	×
SeyedSalar Sefati et al.	New version of GWO	✓	×	✓	×	×	×	×	×	×
Kruekaew et al.	MOABCQ	✓	✓	×	×	✓	×	✓	×	×
Mangalampalli, S et al.	Scheduling usingCAT	✓	×	×	×	×	✓	×	✓	×
G. Annie PoornimaPrincess et al.	HHO-PIO	✓	✓	×	✓	×	×	×	×	×
Dalia AbdulkareemShafiq et al.	Improved LBA	✓	×	×	✓	×	×	✓	×	×
Xueliang Fu et al.	PSO_PGA	✓	×	×	✓	×	×	×	×	×
Jianguo Zheng et al.	Hybrid multi-objective bat algorithm	✓	✓	×	×	✓	×	×	×	×
Shridhar G. Domanal etal.	Modified PSO + Modified CSO	×	×	✓	×	×	×	✓	×	×

Note: A-Makespan, B-Throughput, C-Response Time, D-Execution Time, E-Degree of Imbalance, F-Energy Conservation, G-Resource Utilization, H-Migration Time, I-Processing Time (✓-Considered, ×-Not Considered)
Source: Made by Author

3. Research Gaps

The research work is intended to encounter the below-mentioned research gaps.

- Maintaining a deterministic approach to ensure load balancing when tasks carry the load of varying computational complexities.
- Maintaining the elasticity and optimality of cloud computing by enhancing resource provisioning and resource allocation in an operational environment.
- Concentrating on the factors causing load unbalancing in a cloud environment.
- Task scheduling has been considered an NP-hard problem for which identification of an optimized solution in polynomial time is a challenging task, so there is a need to use optimization techniques for finding the closest solution that is nearer to a fully optimized solution.
- To optimize the utilization of virtual machines responsible for managing the available resources in the cloud.

4. Conclusion

In this paper, a brief overview of load-balancing algorithms is presented. After the analysis, it has been found that metaheuristic optimization techniques are widely used to optimize the resources in the cloud computing environment. Other than metaheuristic approaches, numerous traditional algorithms have been used to balance the load. Resource utilization is one of the major concerns due to the exponential growth of the load on cloud servers; therefore, a technique can be designed to improve the performance of the cloud servers.

REFERENCES

1. Thakur, A., & Goraya, M. S. (2017). A taxonomic survey on load balancing in cloud. Journal of Network and Computer Applications, 98, 43–57.
2. Afzal, S., & Kavitha, G. (2019). Load balancing in cloud computing–A hierarchical taxonomical classification. Journal of Cloud Computing, 8(1), 22.
3. Ramezani, F., Naderpour, M., Taheri, J., Romanous, J., & Zomaya, A. Y. (2020). Task Scheduling in Cloud Environments: A Survey of Population-Based Evolutionary Algorithms. Evolutionary Computation in Scheduling, 213–255.
4. Batra, S., & Singh, A. (2021, November). An Overview of Task Scheduling Approaches in Fog Computing Environment. In 2021 Fifth International Conference on I-SMAC (IoT in Social, Mobile, Analytics and Cloud)(I- SMAC) (pp. 701–707). IEEE.
5. Mishra, S. K., Sahoo, B., & Parida, P. P. (2020). Load balancing in cloud computing: a big picture. Journal of King Saud University-Computer and Information Sciences, 32(2), 149–158.
6. Batra, S., Anand, D., & Singh, A. (2022, April). A Brief Overview of Load Balancing Techniques in Fog Computing Environment. In 2022 6th International Conference on Trends in Electronics and Informatics (ICOEI) (pp. 886–891). IEEE.
7. Kruekaew, B., & Kimpan, W. (2022). Multi-Objective Task Scheduling Optimization for Load Balancing in Cloud Computing Environment Using Hybrid Artificial Bee Colony Algorithm With Reinforcement Learning. IEEE Access, 10, 17803–17818.
8. Mangalampalli, S., Swain, S. K., & Mangalampalli, V. K. (2022). Multi Objective Task Scheduling in Cloud Computing Using Cat Swarm Optimization Algorithm. Arabian Journal for Science and Engineering, 47(2), 1821–1830.
9. Ala'Anzy, M., & Othman, M. (2019). Load balancing and server consolidation in cloud computing environments: a meta-study. IEEE Access, 7, 141868–141887.
10. Shahid, M. A., Islam, N., Alam, M. M., Su'ud, M. M., & Musa, S. (2020). A Comprehensive Study of Load Balancing Approaches in the Cloud Computing Environment and a Novel Fault Tolerance Approach. IEEE Access, 8, 130500–130526.
11. Hota, A., Mohapatra, S., & Mohanty, S. (2019). Survey of different load balancing approach-based algorithms in cloud computing: a comprehensive review. In Computational intelligence in data mining (pp. 99–110). Springer, Singapore.
12. Ullah, A., & Chakir, A. (2022). Improvement for tasks allocation system in VM for cloud datacenter using modified bat algorithm. Multimedia Tools and Applications, 1–15.
13. Abedi, S., Ghobaei-Arani, M., Khorami, E., & Mojarad, M. (2022). Dynamic Resource Allocation Using Improved Firefly Optimization Algorithm in Cloud Environment. Applied Artificial Intelligence, 1–27.
14. He, J. (2022). Cloud Computing Load Balancing Mechanism Taking into Account Load Balancing Ant Colony Optimization Algorithm. Computational Intelligence and Neuroscience, 2022.
15. Assudani, P. J., & Balakrishnan, P. (2021). An efficient approach for load balancing of VMs in cloud environment. Applied Nanoscience, 1–14.
16. Sefati, S., Mousavinasab, M., & Zareh Farkhady, R. (2022). Load balancing in cloud computing environment using the Grey wolf optimization algorithm based on the reliability: performance evaluation. The Journal of Supercomputing, 78(1), 18–42.
17. Annie Poornima Princess, G., & Radhamani, A. S. (2021). A hybrid meta-heuristic for optimal load balancing in cloud computing. Journal of Grid Computing, 19(2), 1–22.
18. Shafiq, D. A., Jhanjhi, N. Z., Abdullah, A., & Alzain, M. A. (2021). A load balancing algorithm for the data centres to optimize cloud computing applications. IEEE Access, 9, 41731–41744.
19. Fu, X., Sun, Y., Wang, H., & Li, H. (2021). Task scheduling of cloud computing based on hybrid particle swarm algorithm and genetic algorithm. Cluster Computing, 1–10.
20. Zheng, J., & Wang, Y. (2021). A hybrid multi-objective bat algorithm for solving cloud computing resource scheduling problems. Sustainability, 13(14), 7933.
21. Domanal, S. G., Guddeti, R. M. R., & Buyya, R. (2017). A hybrid bio-inspired algorithm for scheduling and resource management in cloud environment. IEEE transactions on services computing, 13(1), 3–15.

Computer Science Engineering and Emerging Technologies (ICCS-2022) – Prof (Dr.) Rajeev Sobti et al. (eds)
© 2024 Taylor & Francis Group, London, ISBN 978-1-032-52199-2

Chapter **60**

Examining How Human Perceptions and Abilities are Used in Cryptography

Jithin Govind[1]
Research Scholar, Department of Computer Science and Engineering,
Lovely Professional University, Phagwara, Punjab, India

Dhiraj Kapila[2]
Assistant Professor, Department of Computer Science and Engineering,
Lovely Professional University, Phagwara, Punjab, India

Harwant Singh Arri[3]
Associate Professor, Department of Computer Science and Engineering,
Lovely Professional University, Phagwara, Punjab, India

Nupur Kaushik[4], Gobinda Karmakar[5], Nancy Sharma[6],
Siddhart Pansare[7], Sahil Bhardwaj[8], Jayant Mehra[9]
Research Scholar, Department of Computer Science and Engineering,
Lovely Professional University, Phagwara, Punjab, India

Abstract: In the digital age, cryptography is essential for building trust and enabling services. At the moment, cryptography is implemented using mathematical operations and presented in ways that are difficult for humans to understand. As a result, when it comes to creating confidence and security in the digital world, contact between users and machines is becoming more prevalent in various domains. However, cryptography has not truly benefited from such development, becoming less smooth and user-friendly. That is In this work, we evaluate the prior studies on applying human senses and skills to cryptography. We outline the state of trt today and give the most pertinent methods that are currently available. Aside from that We suggest a number of subjects and issues that must be resolved in order to construct encryption that is easier for people to obtain. These include practical applications of current techniques, using a larger variety of human senses, and developing the theoretical underpinnings for this novel method of encryption.

Keywords: Human perception, Cryptography, Computer-aided systems, CPA and CCA

1. Introduction

Modern communication protocols depend heavily on cryptography, which is also a crucial component of many digital services. Public key cryptography and digital signatures are two examples of recent cryptography advancements (e.g., [1]), to name a few: homomorphic encryption [2], safe multi-party computation [3], and secure and efficient encryption techniques (like AES). These are used every day by billions of people. as a variety of digital services, including messaging,

[1]jithingovindkanayi001@gmail.com, [2]dhiraj.23509@lpu.co.in, [3]hs.arri@lpu.co.in, [4]nupurkaushiknk@gmail.com, [5]gobindak2@gmail.com,
[6]nancysharma2177@gmail.com, [7]sidhu.pansare@gmail.com, [8]binny4166@gmail.com, [9]jayant46mehra@gmail.com

DOI: 10.1201/9781003405580-60

online buying and banking, using the cloud, etc. The foundation of modern cryptography is verifiable security. This signifies that there is a specific cryptographic protocol or primitive for a given security objective that should be made clear, along with any associated threats. Models) and a demonstration (often through reduction) of how the proposed system accomplishes these objectives and on what grounds. Although there is considerable opposition to this strategy, it is commonly regarded as one of the finest assurances, for instance [4, 5], of cryptosystem (theoretical) security. Of course, the actual implementations may include a number of weaknesses that might be exploited, such as and do so. Nonetheless, without a security, significantly less evidence would exist regarding the security, even though the implementation might make mistakes that the original threat model did not consider, such as side timing and power consumption channels.

Despite these developments and the advantages acquired, there remains one area of cryptography that is not well covered and for which there are no complete answers. The prevailing paradigm systems' human users tend to be neglected in favour of verifiable security out of consideration and to create security models based on the universal client-server communication model. This design is in machine-to-machine communications, of course, but it is insufficient to describe the human aspect that the system's user brings. The structure of this essay is as follows: The work that has already been done on the subject of cryptography using human senses and skills is presented and summarized in the next part. In the third segment, we discuss our suggestions for solving this issue and potential solutions. Researching locations might result in better solutions. After this, the paper presents our research's findings and conclusions.

2. Previous Work

There hasn't been a lot of prior research specifically addressing the issue of cryptography for human senses. The usefulness of security mechanisms has been examined in a variety of ways, and noteworthy recommendations on particular topics, such as authentication, have also been made. Where user-friendliness has received some attention and some results have been obtained. On the other hand, the issue of human senses and cryptography is resolved by not being accessible. Additionally, there is a striking absence of theoretical investigation on this subject.

2.1 Visual Cryptography

One of the few solutions to the issue of cryptography for the human senses is visual cryptography. The original concept from [6] demonstrates how to create a picture's visual encryption. (in black and white) that are easily decipherable by simply looking at the shares. The technique is based on the secret sharing technique. An image can be encrypted into two or more different versions using [7] shares. Machine calculations are needed for this. When analyzing the message, the various shares must be suitably aligned. The user can view the hidden image after it displays, without any assistance from computation.

2.2 Visualizable Encryption

The Eye Decrypt system is described in [9] by the authors as a way to use augmented reality (AR) to address some of the problems associated with untrusted terminals and shoulder surfing. The formalization of visualizable encryption is the more fascinating aspect of the research. Various solutions to this issue have been put forth in the past. This broadens the use of the standard CPA (selected plaintext attack) and CCA (chosen ciphertext attack) adversarial models and associated security games to systems that also take into account users' behavior and interactions with various gadgets. They can demonstrate that by combining safe hash and MAC functions with the corresponding standard encryption schemes, it is possible to create CPA- and CCA-secure, visualizable encryption methods.

2.3 Hash Visualization

The authors introduce the concept of hash visualization in [10]. Their argument is that human users are inferior at comparing nonsensical texts, such as hexadecimal hash values, yet more adept at spotting discrepancies in images. They suggest that they use Random Art as their visual hashing algorithm scheme. They also provide a formal framework to assess and offer Despite having security proofs for hash visualization systems, the Random Art construction cannot, sadly, be shown to be secure in this context.

2.4 Computer-aided Security Schemes

The use of computer-aided systems, in which the user inputs some of the secret data and the input terminal adds on, is one way to assist human users. This was done with the use of force and some outside data (a hint). This idea was put forward in, and the authors show the potential for symmetric and asymmetric encryption as a technique of user authentication using computer-aided security measures.

2.5 Authentication of Users, Devices and Computations

There has been a significant amount of effort put into various authentication techniques with human-verifiable results. The objective of these methods is to make it simple for human users to check the authentication outcome (such as device pairing). The methods range from physical activities like bumping the phones together to visual comparisons of various variables in the devices to be validated. This paper presents an analysis of several of these methods. On visual clues like barcodes or light, many human-verifiable authentication systems are based. These give users the chance to visually verify that the authentication was carried out correctly and that there are no intruders interfering. It is effective to check using this kind of visual feedback. Of course, consumers can examine the outcome of an authentication in other ways than only with their eyes. Other comparison techniques include sound, device shaking, proximity to other devices, and combinations like those shown in All of these are intended to give users a way to confirm that the authentication process has been completed correctly or to ensure that the authentication cannot be carried out without the user's permission.

There are other additional areas as well where answers to specific issues with human capacities and authentication have been addressed. A way to authenticate potentially untrustworthy terminals for human users is provided and is utilized to access various distant services. In order to accomplish this attribute for various threat models, the study describes two distinct techniques. The authors of [11] present a technique for utilizing visual memory schemas for user authentication and digital rights management. Additionally, there have been suggestions for a technique for human message authentication [13] as well as a mechanism to authenticate pervasive devices using human protocols [12].

3. Cryptography for Human Senses and Capabilities

We suggest various areas for more research in order to reach new levels for cryptography for human senses and certain applications for users. To truly push encryption in the direction of being more user-friendly, these may and should all be addressed simultaneously.

3.1 Extending and Applying Visual Cryptography

Applying and enhancing the existing visual cryptography techniques would, in our opinion, be the new study area's easiest to exploit. Some work has already been done in this direction, for instance, by [8]. Although applications for the more sophisticated techniques have not yet been reported, they may do so in the future for suitable AR applications, for instance.

The ability to visualize encryption could also be expanded to include public-key cryptography, authenticated encryption, digital signatures, etc. This would also require new definitions and theories for such systems. For this reason, it is undoubtedly a harder and more long-term attempt.

The fundamental drawback of visual cryptography (and visualizable encryption) is that it necessitates a level of visual aptitude that not all people possess. For instance, according to the WHO (World Health Organization), around 250 million people have vision impairment. Of these, 36 million or so are completely blind. Thus, if only visual or visualizable cryptography were accessible, a considerable number of people (especially elderly people) would be excluded from the advantages of human cryptography. It's interesting to notice that most websites currently use a button to play the visual challenge for CAPTCHA security questions.

3.2 Beyond Symmetric Cryptography

Advances in the capabilities of the cryptographic systems that are conceivable to actualize with human senses are required to truly shift the paradigm of human-friendly cryptographic systems. Visual cryptography, for instance, provides "only" perfect secrecy, which has been found to be insufficient for the majority of contemporary cryptographic requirements and is being superseded by systems that provide CPA or CCA security. Most critically, data cannot be authenticated when there is full confidentiality. For symmetric encryption systems, authenticated encryption with related data is currently the chosen standard. A secure block cipher and an appropriate mode of operation can accomplish this. Visualizable encryption gives the theoretical underpinnings for such an approach, although the method of [9] does not fully implement these.

It would be crucial to have these capabilities for human cryptography because public-key cryptography has been a crucial enabler for many digital services. There is currently no theory-based or application-based research in this area. Both conventional and post-quantum public key systems are based on complex mathematics that cannot be applied to the human senses. It's an intriguing research question and a critical step in developing cryptography for human senses and abilities to find alternatives for these fundamental components.

3.3 Encryption with Human Senses and Abilities

The possibility of also encrypting (and signing) using human senses and skills should not be discounted as a research challenge, even though it may be argued that decryption and verification with human senses are more crucial. All currently in use systems operate under the presumption that a computer performs cryptography's encryption function. Human senses are only used for verification or decryption. It would obviously be necessary to be able to encrypt data without the aid of computers in order to build a completely functional system for human cryptography. In the past, handwritten signatures were frequently used for authentication.

4. Discussion

What are the advantages of humans over computers and other technologies, and how can this be achieved before cryptography for human senses becomes a reality? When such benefits are discovered, research should be done on how they might be used in cryptography as well as how to scale them globally and make them function via digital media.

We suggest a paradigm shift away from defining security goals in a way that results in cryptographic systems only usable by computers and other machines and in the direction of more user-friendly cryptography. We contend that it ought to be possible to develop cryptographic protocols and primitives that are accessible to human senses, human brains, and "computer power," have meaningful security goals, and have provable security under reasonable assumptions. The system should take the capabilities of the human user into account.

User discomfort is another defense against cryptography for the human senses. It is natural that a typical user would not want to get engaged in cryptography because the current paradigm relies on complex mathematics and things seem to work. In order for the convenience of use to outweigh the unpleasantness of participation, it is crucial that cryptography be usable by the human senses. Furthermore, the human user has no position in the trust chain given the level of encryption today, and we are unable to even provide them the opportunity to participate without more study.

The limitations of various senses and how well humans comprehend various visual, aural, and tactile sensory data have already been discussed. The common necessity of correctness in cryptosystems presents a hurdle to the theoretical development of cryptography for human senses. Correctness requires that we have $D(E(m)) = m$ for each message m, encryption function E, and decryption function D.

However, due to our propensity for sensory perception errors, it may not be possible to develop cryptography that adheres to the standard criterion of accuracy. A probabilistic notion of accuracy might be useful, but it begs the question of what happens if human recognition is unsuccessful: what is the result of $D(E(m))$? Will this present a potential side channel for enemies or a chance for denial-of-service assaults of this kind?

The key generation and other randomness required for modern cryptography to work present another problem. Entropy is present in natural sources, but it is difficult for people to use it without the aid of technology. On the other side, will there be sufficient entropy to guarantee secure encryption if only human participants in the cryptographic procedures are used?

Entropy from biometrics can be used, and there are ways to uniformly distribute it as required by cryptographic protocols, such as by using fuzzy extractors [14]. But using human senses to extract information in this way is impossible. The fact that people choose lousy passwords for user authentication is one example of how poorly humans tend to generate randomness.

5. Conclusion

In this study, we assessed the state-of-the-art in human senses cryptography.

Such encryption is largely based on the already thoroughly researched ideas of visual and visualizable cryptography. As a result, there aren't many techniques that make use of human abilities and other senses. More study is required in both implementations and theoretical underpinnings in order to construct a wider variety of capabilities (such as message authentication) and achieve more complex security goals.

In order to develop new cryptography methods for human senses, it is also necessary to consider the potential of senses other than vision. We are confident that research in this area will yield better and more human-friendly cryptographic methods that are more accessible with human capabilities. This will then result in better building blocks for trust in our increasingly linked and digital world.

REFERENCES

1. S. Goldwasser, S. Micali, R. L. Rivest, A digital signature scheme secure against adaptive chosen-message attacks, SIAM J. Comput. 17 (2) (1988) 281–308.
2. C. Gentry, A Fully Homomorphic Encryption Scheme (Ph.D. thesis), Stanford University, 2009.
3. A. C. Yao, Protocols for secure computations, in: Foundations of Computer Science, 1982. SFCS'08. 23rd Annual Symposium on, IEEE, 1982, pp. 160–164.
4. N. Koblitz, A.J. Menezes, Another look at "provable security", J. Cryptol. 20 (1) (2007) 3–37.
5. N. Koblitz, A. Menezes, Another look at security definitions, Adv. Math. Commun. 7 (1) (2013) 1–38.
6. M. Naor, A. Shamir, Visual cryptography, in: Advances in Cryptology, EUROCRYPT'94, Springer, 1995, pp. 1–12
7. A. Shamir, How to share a secret, Commun. ACM 22 (11) (1979) 612–613.
8. Y. -W. Chow, W. Susilo, M. H. Au, A. M. Barmawi, A visual one-time password authentication scheme using mobile devices, in: International Conference on Information and Communications Security, Springer, 2014, pp. 243–257.
9. A. G. Forte, J. A. Garay, T. Jim, Y. Vahlis, EyeDecrypt—Private interactions in plain sight, in: International Conference on Security and Cryptography for Networks, Springer, 2014, pp. 255–276.
10. A. Perrig, D. Song, Hash visualization: A new technique to improve real world security, in: International Workshop on Cryptographic Techniques and E-Commerce, 1999, pp. 131–138.
11. M. Nishigaki, T. Yamamoto, Making use of human visual capability to improve information security, in: Availability, Reliability and Security, 2009. ARES'09. International Conference on, IEEE, 2009, pp. 990–994.
12. A. Juels, S. A. Weis, Authenticating pervasive devices with human proto cols, in: Annual International Cryptology Conference, Springer, 2005, pp. 293–308.
13. J. King, A. Dos Santos, A user-friendly approach to human authentication of messages, in: International Conference on Financial Cryptography and Data Security, Springer, 2005, pp. 225– 239.
14. Y. Dodis, R. Ostrovsky, L. Reyzin, A. Smith, Fuzzy extractors: How to generate strong keys from biometrics and other noisy data, SIAM J. Comput. 38 (1) (2008) 97–139.

Computer Science Engineering and Emerging Technologies (ICCS-2022) – Prof (Dr.) Rajeev Sobti et al. (eds)
© 2024 Taylor & Francis Group, London, ISBN 978-1-032-52199-2

Chapter

61

Online Cab Booking System Uber Clone Using Next JS

Abhishek[1], Aditya Gautam[2]
Student, Chandigarh University, Mohali, India

Aparna[3]
Assistant Professor, Chandigarh University, Mohali, India

Abstract: The transportation industry is one of the most popular sectors in terms of technology because customers want to minimize the amount of time and effort spent satisfying their needs. Many customers stay for a while somewhere different than where they live and desire to get a car for their daily needs, which will be very useful when it comes to booking cars for users from anywhere in the world. A fully integrated online system has been created. By automating the manual processes, it makes them more efficient and effective. This automated method will allow customers to fill in specific details according to their needs, which include pick-up and drop-off locations and the type of car they prefer. This system will be very easy to use and user-friendly, making car bookings easy for the customer.

Keywords: Technology, Booking system, Automates, Efficiently, Effectively, User-friendly

1. Introduction

Transport services over the past decade have undergone major changes, especially in urban areas. Cabs have become an important means of transportation among various alternatives in major cities and towns in India and are growing steadily with the support of technology. Surveys show that 65% of people use online cab booking services. That means cab resources are in high demand today. The much-needed cab booking app also shows us the estimated cost before booking a ride. As opposed to traditional methods such as cars and the local bus service, the company offers a wide range of vehicle choices for customers to choose from. Due to its door-to-door service advantage, it gained popularity, and now customers can book cabs using their mobile phones with just one click at competitive prices. Taking advantage of these app-based services has become extremely popular in countries with dense populations, such as India, where parking can be a major problem due to a shortage of space and overcrowded public transport during peak hours. The cab would be without passengers 30% of the time before these app-based cab services were introduced. The companies in charge of these aggregated cab services in particular do not own cars but are tied to drivers who use local resources who agree to register with the organization, and the organization simply acts as a liaison between drivers and customers by charging the commission only for their "doing the same" services at a time to improve the cab application. These in-app services require an easy-to-navigate app that requires good Android or iOS upgrade skills. Also, a very powerful and secure cloud architecture is easily scalable because many users will use it, which is why cloud infrastructure really needs to support thousands of connections as well as a well-functioning, well-constructed website. In India, there are numerous apps that provide such services, such as Ola, Uber, etc. These companies provide commercial services. However, there are some cab booking apps that aim to clear traffic jams, such as those offering fast rides. Cab booking apps reduce carbon emissions on a daily basis and improve society in

[1]abhiahlawat02@gmail.com, [2]adityagautam765@gmail.com, [3]jindalaparna124@gmail.com

DOI: 10.1201/9781003405580-61

a positive way. However, the question arises as to whether the person will use carpooling or will choose to go it alone out of concern for their privacy. How important is price to the customer? Do people decide what to do every day based on the atmosphere in their neighborhood? Not only for customer service trips, but businesses also choose cab booking apps so that their business can grow faster than others.

1.1 Problem Formation

Taxis or lifts are not as easy to hail at midnight, and they are more expensive than you might think. There should always be a vehicle available, no matter where you are. An important objective of the application is to create jobs for drivers and provide them with a dependable income. All decisions it makes are centred around the customer.

The next chapters of the paper will follow the basic things like:

(i) Literature Review

   In this section the works which are previously done on the subject are described and a brief description of them is given.

(ii) Problem Design

   In this section the flowcharts related to the problem statement are described and how the application works.

(iii) Objective

   In this section the main objective of the application is written.

(iv) Methodologies Used

   In this section of the paper, the technologies that are used in the making of the application are described.

(v) Result and Discussion

   In this section, the outcomes of the applications with respect to both users and the drivers are described.

(vi) Conclusions and Future Scope

   In this section of the paper, the final outcomes and the modifications that can be done in the future are discussed.

2. Literature Review

In 2008, Ekiz et al. [1] gave their observation that as international tourism grows and quality assurance and improvement models and measures become more popular, booking car services are likely to become better in the future than in the past. Studies that report empirical findings regarding the role and importance of these services in the tourism phenomenon are very few in number. In most of these studies, the focus is on the surface parts of the service industry such as banks, hotels, insurance, with limited attention to the demand factors of international tourists. In spite of this, it would not be exaggerated to suggest that a destination's success depends completely on its core and sub industries. A scale to measure the service quality perceptions of tourists was developed by this study as a conceptual and methodological advancement in the literature on service quality and rent-a-car businesses.

Then, in 2011, researchers Waspodo et. al. [2] concluded the following three points in their studies:

(a) Through a web-based car rental management information system, rental history data transmission could be made more efficient. The time difference between using a web application and not using one is reduced to seconds. Upon completion of the verification process, the delivery took about three hours by transport to the head office and was not immediately shipped.

(b) The paper procurement method for charging rental history is efficient, and there is no transportation cost involved in delivering rental history data. In addition, the web application keeps the data neat and keeps track of car rental costs, avoiding overspending.

(c) The consolidation of data into a computerized database will ease the data storage, retrieval, and reporting process for a company, where all data is arranged neatly, makes sure data is protected, and will not be lost or smeared.

During the research for the Online Car Rental System in 2015, Tuhin et al. [3] wrote that unlike the past, when car rental businesses were restricted to a physical location for all activities, car rental businesses have a new goodie to offer. Even though physical locations have not been completely eliminated, the internet has reshaped the nature of how functions are accomplished. The customer can now reserve or rent vehicles online, and the car can be delivered to the customer's door once they have become a registered member, or they can pick the vehicle up at the office. With web-based car rental software, both customers and car rental companies are able to manage the business more efficiently and effectively, ensuring customer satisfaction.

In 2017, Osman et al. [4], during their study of the use of SMS and web-based technology for online car rental, introduced specific information on user technology to build and integrate a web-based SMS technology system to improve the services provided by car rental services. This app has enabled employees to notify customers via SMS system by sending a reliable message to inform customers about the booking status and availability of vehicles. Thus, the system provides an easy way to notify them through their cell phones, which is a normal communication method these days.

Then in 2018, Gao [5] reported in the context of China that, against the background of the rise of the sharing economy in China, shared cars have made a vigorous development. Shared cars improve the efficiency of the use of vehicle resources, alleviate urban traffic pressure, facilitate the travel choices of consumers, and help enterprises get a lot of investment. At the same time, the development of shared cars also faces a series of difficulties and challenges, such as inadequate government support, larger operating costs, higher operating risk, inconvenient parking, immature user habits, etc. This paper summarizes the development situation, business models, stakeholder relations, and other issues of shared cars in China. On this basis, this paper puts forward countermeasures and suggestions to promote the development of shared cars, such as perfecting laws and regulations, building a credit system, improving operating models, expanding profit patterns, strengthening the cooperation of the stakeholders, etc.

In 2019, four researchers, Sarkar et al. [6], in their study of the automotive rental system in Maharashtra, concluded that using their app, users could book any car of their choice as a matter of time or with an unselected driver. The system consists of three applications. There is one application for the user, one for the administrator, and one for the driver, which allows the user to choose a variety of vehicles and determine the point of departure and destination. Additionally, it offers payment options. Drivers have the option of accepting or rejecting requests made by administrators.

In 2020, Mon et al. [7] created the app and concluded that it is secure and can be used to rent a car based on what the customer requests. The app ensures that its content can only be accessed if you are logged in. A user can also look at rental cars available and pay for a rented car using a credit card through the app, so they don't have to go to the rental company to see what rental car they want to hire instead. With the Mobile Car Rental program, users can browse the car rental list at any time, select a car, and make a payment. Furthermore, the app also allows the administrator to edit and delete any vehicle information at any time when adding, editing or removing it. Customers can view car rental details in their app and in their e-mail, which has allowed them to trust the Car Rental System.

In 2020, during the conference series *Journal of Physics*, Azila et al. [8] talked about their research and concluded that a car booking system is proposed for users to assist them in the process. A computerized database will also assist AMCT Enterprise in managing their customers' personal information and bookings properly. Their system features customization features that allow them to add-on features for customer satisfaction. Hopefully, the system's development will satisfy all of the stakeholders' requirements and be implemented successfully in terms of functionality and usability.

In August 2020, Nasr et al. [9] were working on a GPS-based car rental and web-based system and proposed using servers supported by car rental agencies to improve tracking and tracing after customer hire on the car rental web-based system. Tracking and tracing the car at anytime and anywhere is possible with GPS in a web-based rental car system. Finally, in July 2021, Thakur [10], a student at the University of Mumbai, found that the industry had evolved from the previous practice, when all car-related activities were confined to the visible area. In spite of the fact that the physical environment hasn't been totally eradicated, the internet has changed how jobs are done as well as the nature of these jobs. With online booking and renting, customers can pick up the cars from either the office or their home if they are registered members.

3. Problem Design

In this flow chart (Fig. 61.1), the basic flow of the application is described, like how the user will enter the application and what will the further processes after that.

In this use case diagram (Fig. 61.2), the basic models of connection of User with the Server is described like the payments, cost estimation, etc.

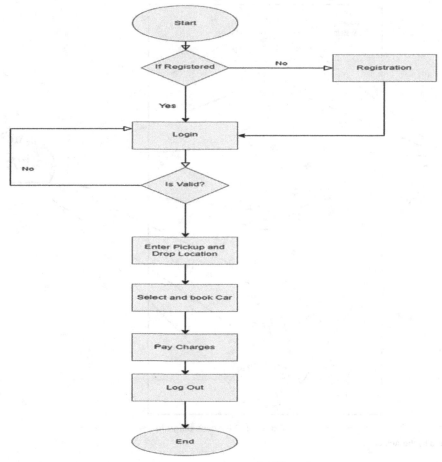

Fig. 61.1 Flow chart for the website

Source: Created by the Author

In this data flow diagram (Fig. 61.3), the basic flow of Login, Signup and email verification is displayed.

In this image (Fig. 61.4), the working of the whole application is described using a data flow diagram, specifically regarding the registration, booking and the payments on the application.

4. Objective

To make an online cab booking system for users to use at different places.

5. Methodology and Model Specifications

1. **Figma [11]:** Figma is used in the project because it allows group members to work on the project at the same time and to see what is being designed in real time. Figma can be used in any browser and on any OS. Figma has the functionality to save the project status offline in saved files. And its cloud nature makes it simple, and Figma is very fast and frictionless for every user, and Figma has slack integration. Micro-interactions, animations, and prototypes can be easily created directly in Figma without switching tools. Live Figma designs or prototypes can be easily imbibed anywhere.

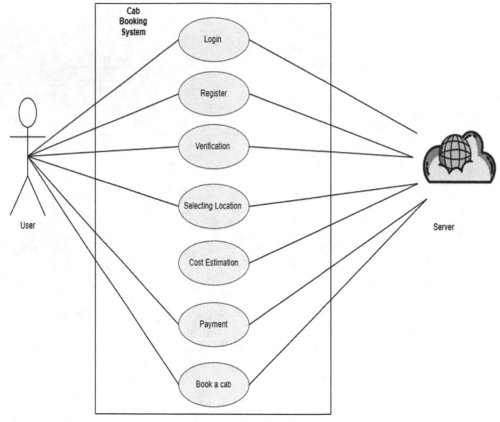

Fig. 61.2 Use case diagram

Source: Created by the Author

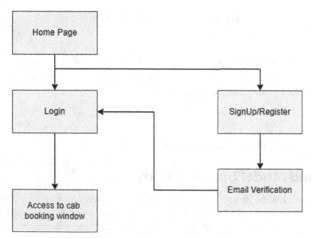

Fig. 61.3 Level 0 DFD for LOGIN

Source: Created by the Author

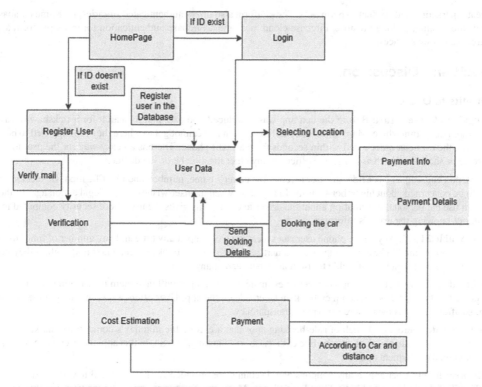

Fig. 61.4 Level 1 DFD for the website

Source: Created by the Author

2. **Next JS [12]:** Next JS is used in the project because it uses data-fetching APIs that enable pre-rendering. It also provides a better experience than the other tools. It gives functionality like single-page rendering, server-side rendering, automatic routing, automatic code splitting, hot module replacement, etc. In Next JS, we don't need to worry about extra tools and bundlers because everything is included within its initial configuration. Using server-side rendering provides search engines with a searchable, indexable, and crawlable web page out-of-the-box, which is very To view the content of the page, no JavaScript is required on the client side. As well as being faster than React, Next JS is also easier to use.

3. **Tailwind CSS [13]:** In this project, Tailwind CSS is used because there is no faster framework than Tailwind when it comes to styling HTML. As a result of this, members can easily create good-looking layouts by styling elements. Another reason for using Tailwind is that it offers thousands of builds in classes that are easy to access, and we do not have to create designs from scratch or download them. A number of small utilities are also created by Tailwind CSS, allowing existing classes to be easily integrated directly into HTML code. There are additional features that Tailwind CSS offers, such as control over styling, a faster CSS styling process, responsiveness, and security.

4. **Mapbox [14]:** Mapbox is used in the project because the standardized data flow is very easy and the map will load much faster than Google Maps due to custom tile generation. Using this customization of the map makes accessing the data very easy, and Mapbox provides beautiful base maps that can be easily modified by the programmer. Mapbox is also very interactive, and it can load large amounts of data very easily.

5. **Firebase (v9) [15]:** Firebase is used in the project because it enables it to develop the app easily and efficiently by giving great control over the project by optimizing the project bundle size by stripping away features that are not needed and also tailoring the dependencies for the project. It basically customizes the app size and allows you to import only those artifacts that the app We can also use Firebase to track analytics, report and fix app crashes, and

create marketing and product experiments. The platform also offers authenticated libraries, real-time databases, fast and safe hosting, a cloud firestore, Firebase cloud messaging, Firebase authentication for cross-platform apps, and Firebase testing services.

6. Result and Discussion

6.1 Benefits to Users

Not Struggle to Chase a Taxi: Before the taxi app was introduced, the user had to search for a rickshaw or taxi at the market before going somewhere. Many times, they fail to get both and cannot get to where they are supposed to be on time. With the app, the user can order a taxi within seconds from a smart phone. There is an easy way for the user to get a taxi anywhere he or she wants, such as home, the office, or any other location he or she decides.

Security: Upon booking an Uber ride, the user receives the driver's name, number, and identification. Hence, the user does not have to be concerned about his or her security. In any case, when the user wishes to take legal action against the driver, the user can use the personal information about the driver to do so. This gives the user more security compared to getting a taxi without knowing the driver's information.

Service Available 24 × 7: Any smart-phone user can access the Uber app at any time and any number of times through the app because it is designed to be accessible on any smart-phone. Users can book and get a taxi mid-night if they need one. It is one of Uber's best benefits to be able to use it anywhere and at any time.

Pricing Lucidity: If the user of the app can get an estimate of how long it will take them to reach their destination and a total distance for their Uber ride when they book an Uber ride on the app. Uber offers a ride fare before the user makes a booking, so after the trip is over, there is no price transparency.

Flexible Payment: There are a bunch of ride-booking apps that are available in today's competitive market. Most of the applications offer multiple payment options like cash, cards, net banking, etc. So, in this app, the user can pay the ride fare as per their choice of payment option.

Cost-effective: In this Uber app, many coupons and discounts are provided for both old and new users so that they can efficiently utilize their money and have a good experience. Many taxi options are given, so the user can choose his or her ride according to their budget.

6.2 Benefits to Drivers

Discover Passenger: In the case of a shuttle driver, the driver is responsible for finding passengers on his or her own. In contrast, if the user is using an Uber cab, a driver request will be sent to his or her smart phone. Consequently, the driver doesn't need to look for other passengers, is able to respond to ride requests quickly, and is able to manage their journey requests easily and efficiently.

Identify User Profile: Drivers can view the name, rating, and feedback provided by other drivers when they receive a new ride request for a specific route. Drivers can reject ride requests from users if they receive negative reviews when they request a new ride. A feature like this gives the drivers an easy way to recognize their past riders based on their profiles.

Eliminate Price Bargaining: During ride booking, the user receives a base fare, so he or she is not obligated to bargain the ride fare. Users can only book the ride if it's within their budget; otherwise, they will have to choose from other options available in the app.

7. Conclusion and Future Scope

An online car booking website has been developed. This website facilitates the booking of any car the user desires, depending on the occasion. Additionally, the user can use a credit or debit card to make payments through a payment gateway. Through the app, users can choose between a variety of cars, pick-up locations, and destinations. A variety of payment options are included as well.

A future version of the app could be developed for Android and iOS. There is also the possibility of using machine learning. By analyzing user behavior patterns and search requests, machine learning algorithms can provide better recommendations. Additionally, it is possible to optimize the search process by utilizing machine learning in the application. It will make searching easier and more intuitive for users if voice search, spelling corrections, and suggestions are added.

REFERENCES

1. Ekiz, E. H. and Bavik, A. "Scale Development Process: Service Quality in Car Rental Services." The Electronic Journal of Business Research Methods Volume 6 Issue 2 2008, pp. 133–146.
2. B. Waspodo, Q. Aini and Syamsuri: "Development of Car Rental Management Information System" Proceedings of the 1st International Conference on Information Systems for Business Competitiveness (ICISBC) 2011
3. S. Arefin (ID No-01, 51D) D. Sree Rajib Kumar (ID No-05, 51D) Ariful Hossain Tuhin (ID No-29, 51D): "Software Requirements Specification for Online Car Rental System", 2015
4. M. Nizam Osman et. al.: "Online car rental system using web-based and SMS technology CRINN, Vol 2, Oct 2017
5. H. Gao: "Research on development problems of shared cars in China" 4th International Conference on Economics, Management, Law and Education (EMLE 2018)
6. J. Sarkar, Y. Khode, S. Jadhav, Prof. A. Laddha: "Car Rental System for Maharashtra (Android app)" IJRTI | Volume 4, Issue 5 | ISSN:2456-3315,2019
7. C. Su Mon et al: "A Prototype of a Mobile Car Rental System" J. Phys.: Conf. Ser. 152903202,2020
8. N. Azila Awang Abu Bakar and M. Fakrurrazi Yuspani: "Initial stage in developing an online car rental system (OCRS) using customization business model"
9. J. Phys.: Conf. Ser. 1529 02203,2020 [9] O. A. Nasr: "CAR RENTAL AND TRACKING WEB-BASED SYSTEM USING GPS" International Journal of Information System and Computer Science,2020
10. A. Thakur: "Car Rental System" International Journal for Research in Applied Science & Engineering Technology (IJRAS),2021
11. "Figma." https://www.figma.com/developers.
12. "Getting Started | Next.js." https://nextjs.org/docs.
13. "Installation: Tailwind CLI - Tailwind CSS." https://tailwindcss.com/docs/installation.
14. "Firebase" https://firebase.google.com/docs
15. "Documentation | Mapbox." https://docs.mapbox.com/

Computer Science Engineering and Emerging Technologies (ICCS-2022) – Prof (Dr.) Rajeev Sobti et al. (eds)
© *2024 Taylor & Francis Group, London, ISBN 978-1-032-52199-2*

Chapter | **62**

Contemporary Software Cloning Detection Methods: Meta-Analyses

Chavi Ralhan[1]
Research scholar & Assistant Professor LPU,
Jalandhar-Delhi, G.T. Road, Phagwara, Punjab, India

Navneet Malik[2]
Associate Professor LPU,
Jalandhar-Delhi, G.T. Road, Phagwara, Punjab, India

Abstract: This study examines numerous open-source clone detection studies. Code tokens feed most ML and DL algorithms. Duplicate code algorithms have nine categories (XX). Lexical tokens first. Distance-based clone detection follows. Third, tree-based and semantic clone detection Researchers combine detection approaches to generate the sixth category. This study shows that academics employ machine learning and deep learning to find textual clones. Unsupervised and supervised machine learning can find clones. K-means and DBScan are popular machine learning approaches. Naive Bayes, Decision Tree, SVM, and others are prominent supervised algorithms. Datamining. Subgraph and FP-growth find code. Applications find duplicate codes. Visual Studio or GitHub apps Clone detection checks for vulnerability, licensing, and security in several apps. Code rearrangement and analysis tools find duplicate code chunks. Academically and commercially, it's underdeveloped. Analysis The largest code repository has duplicate Java, C++, C, Python, and JavaScript code, and most non-focked projects have borrowed files from other projects (inter-project level analysis). Some researchers want faster, smaller clone-detecting technologies.

Keywords: Clone detection, Deduplication

1. Introduction

The clone detection industry identifies four categories of software clones. All clone detection algorithms attempt to detect these four categories with variable capacities and accuracy [1], [2]. Few authors classify clones by their activity or passive presence in projects. Active projects continue to grow and duplicate code, while inactive ones are correcting and maturing. Packagers create passive clones. After code optimisation and quality testing, the project is maturing as libraries are added. As per definitions given in the current literature, clones of type I are described as fragments of code that are identical duplicates of one another. However, there might be differences in layout, spacing, and comments. Clone Type II is referred to as "code fragments (C.F.) that are identical in syntax. Types, identifiers, whitespace, literals, layout, and comments may differ. The type is defined as a C.F. that resulted from statement modifications, additions, or deletions. Types, identifiers, whitespace, literals, layout, and comments may differ, and the last is functionally defined as C.Fs that are functionally equivalent but have distinct syntax structures. These kinds of clones are evaluated based on semantic criteria. However, "clone" is the word for all sorts of duplicate software; therefore, cloning is a broad term. Clone identification has three aspects [1, 3]. "Detection" checks a file's source code and software application version. A file is a clone if its content,

[1]chaviralhan@gmail.com, [2]subhash.14335@lpu.co.in

DOI: 10.1201/9781003405580-62

timing, functionality, operation, and behaviour are almost identical to those of the original application. Correcting clones, errors, and low-quality code is the second step. This prevents malicious malware from creating entire software copies. The third stage, "auditing," involves searching the software for clones that may increase maintenance costs, problem propagation, refactoring, and decoupling. [4], [5]. All three are related. There are several prevalent industry procedures and philosophies. Searching by software application and file path is easiest. Detecting cloning means discovering all or some software or apps that use files from their original source. These instruments are usually rated on detection rate and time. There are several approaches to calculate the detection rate (DR) and time spent recognising cloned files. Timeline matching is another way. By comparing time series data, clone detection software may determine if any programme files are copies and if their contents match the original.

Hashing techniques can also be used to compare file sections. These hash functions map one-to-one elements $f(x1) \rightarrow f(y1)$ and produce "collision-free" output [5], [6]. Lookup tables use injective functions. Clone detection techniques use lookup tables [7]. Secure hash functions prevent file collisions [8]. These secure hashing methods are typically used to detect fakes and fraud. These methods include static and dynamic hash functions. Static hash functions are like "any" hash functions because they return a few bytes regardless of content. Data generates static hashes without previous outputs. Dynamic hashes require pre-existing data. GNU unrad and Unix canonical hashes are static hash algorithms. Comparing "content," size, and resource utilisation can help identify similar programming code or files. In this scenario, the code must be checked to see if it is from the same release series as the programme [9], [10].

CCD aids in code simplicity, maintainability, and plagiarism. It detects malware and reports flaws. This research aims to show what's significant in this field to those who matter. The purpose is to document strategies to improve clone detection (gap analysis) for future researchers. After this introduction, the study reviews 2013–2022 research. This area has few publications [see Fig. 62.1], and producing high-quality software nowadays requires a lot of attention.

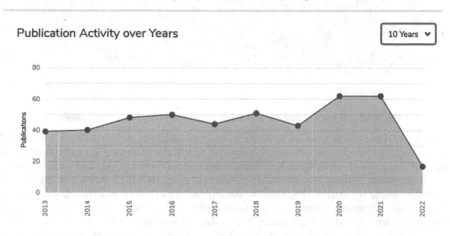

Fig. 62.1 Publications in the duplicate code detection domain. [wizdon.ai]

2. Methodology of Literature Survey

Mendeley, Researchgate, Microsoft Academic, and Google Scholar were used to find high-quality peer-reviewed reviews, technical reports, and research articles on duplicate code detection, clone detection, etc. Wizdom.ai was used for bibliographies. Github, Gitlab, and SourceForge were examined. A total of 220 papers from 2012–2022 were chosen. The publications' cited articles were also assessed. Several semantic networks were built to include interlinked, correlated, and cross-linked work in each context of the notion under evaluation for the review structure.

3. A Literature Survey

Previous polls suggest that most queries have compared ready-to-use clone detection techniques or software. These surveys show that ready-to-use clone detection solutions are not clear winners. This study also revealed that fresh software versions are released periodically. This changes their cost–benefit ratio. Thus, a new survey is required. Second, modern authors on clone detection algorithms show that syntactical and token-based analysis are the most common methods. The most frequent approaches for finding clones are the Abstract Syntax Tree (A.S.T.) and its modifications [11], programme code graph dependence (P.C.G.D.) [12]–[14], and those stated in the introduction. Most algorithms start with code preparation. Remove comments, white lines, and special characters before processing the target code. The algorithm then finds "single unit" chunks. It then checks all units for clones. The programme collects and eliminates tokens to create a clone pair. Finally, rate the clone map by similarity. The "Code Once, Use Many Times" (C.O.U.M.T.) philosophy is a common reason for cloning [15–18]. The software industry's best practise manual recommends reusing code. Resource-wise, this favours the industry. Most individuals copy and paste, use templates, or copy existing code. Other reasons for copying and pasting code include when the coder wants to accomplish things the same way, when he or she is under pressure to work quickly, or when there is a favourable cost-benefit ratio. To prevent code duplicate propagation, just 140 patents have been filed in the recent decade (see Fig. 62.2).

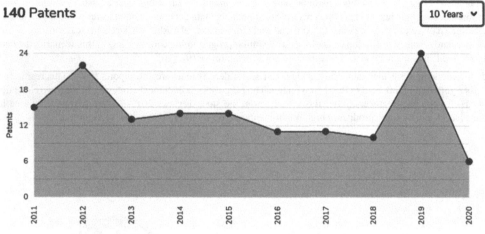

Fig. 62.2 Number of patents filed in last deceased in duplicate code detection

Many studies have found that new software versions, due to business situations, shorten the clone's lifespan. Copy-pasted code decreases as the project progresses. However, "copy-paste" code is more common in small software modules than in the full package. Of course, open source projects have many clones, and time-series analysis and natural language processing algorithms like Bidirectional Encoder Representations from Transformers (B.E.R.T.) may follow their evolution [1], [4]. Researchers say that cloning is inevitable [19]. Thus, the company must teach clone avoidance from the outset (preventive measures). Some academics suggest optimising and refactoring the code before clone removal to improve code quality. Problem mining detects harmful code [20–22]. Researchers evaluate clone detection systems using several metrics. Recall, precision, accuracy, and confidence. Modern researchers illustrate cloning scenarios using Hasse diagrams, scatter plots, polymetric views, and graphs. To increase software quality, the industry focuses on complete or exact, partial, grabbed, or near-miss, structurally, semantically, and function-based clones. Some researchers compare code text, according to previous studies. The researcher uses distance measuring measures including cosine similarity, euclidean distance, and others to analyse the code's tokens and create a reliable clone detection system. Text-based clone analysis has more false positives [23]. It cannot detect context and code changes linked to variables and code blocks. Understanding the differences and similarities between the various strategies can make them trustworthy beyond string matching with hashes, sub-trees, etc.

From the tabular summary of the tools, algorithms, and approaches, it is clear that with time, the field of clone detection is moving into the realm of deep learning paradigms. Many of the clone detection algorithms leverage attention networks for building code detection systems. Most of these algorithms are able to detect the main three types of clones (*1 = exact clone, 2 = renamed clones, and 3 = near-miss clones*).

4. How the Evaluation of Clone Detection Algorithms is Done

Evaluation of the clone detection algorithms is essential for their industrial acceptance. Since the aim of clone detection methods is not only to discover clones but also to aid in restructuring and maintaining code, the performance or benchmarking of the code cloning detection system cannot be neglected. The measures currently employed [3], [4], [39], [55]–[57] in this context are shown in Table 62.1.

Table 62.1 The metrics measures currently employed

S. No	Metric	Description
1	Scalability	How large a subject system or collection of source code a clone detector can execute with limited compute resources without crashing or needing excessive execution time.
2	Complexity	The algorithm's difficulty is determined by the amount of space (memory) required for its execution and the number of loops (iterations) required to finish the task. The sum of memory (space) and the number of loops competes with the complexity definition.
3	Time Analysis	Specifies a restricted set of processing resources, the amount of time a clone detector needs to find clones inside a given subject system or source code collection.
4	Accuracy	In the case of machine, deep, and attention learning algorithms, the definition is the fraction of predictions the CCD code clone detection model got right and the validation of the model.
6	Recall	The percentage of real clone pairs inside a software system that can be detected by a clone detector.
7	Precision	The proportion of clones discovered by a clone detector that are authentic clones as opposed to false positives.
8	The Degree of Difficulty	If the code clone detection system can identify all four types of code fragments, then its difficulty score is equal to four, and so on.

Source: Made by Author

The knowledge of code cloning systems supplied earlier allows us to comprehend code clone detection methods and their business applications. Algorithms and commercial tools that identify plagiarism rather than code in many languages were found. Comparing the two research areas revealed this. Because of this, some work on this subject focuses on text duplicate detection, while others focus on visual content in context. Finding duplicate text in files inspired code cloning approaches. Machine and deep learning algorithms usually use tokens from the source code as input. Nine categories define code copy detection. Lexical analysis and token-to-token comparison are the first. Distance-metric-based clone detection approaches are the second. Modern academics also cite tree-based approaches and semantic algorithms for clone detection. Some articles use combinational or hybrid detection methods. This study shows that while many researchers use machine learning and deep learning algorithms to detect plagiarism in text, others use them to detect duplicate code or clones. All clones have been detected using supervised and unsupervised machine learning. K-means, DBScan, and other clustering techniques are popular here. Naive Bayes, Decision Tree, SVM, and others are popular supervised machine learning algorithms. Data mining belongs here. FP-growth and subgraphs help construct code detection systems. VS and Github have a lot of commercial applications that detect duplicate code. Many projects utilise clone detection algorithms or tools for vulnerability, licencing violations, and security checks. Refactoring and best coding practises can detect redundant code blocks. Comparatively, this field has little academic and economic activity. Project-Level Scan Analysis demonstrates that the world's largest code repository contains Java, C++, C, Python, and JavaScript code that is duplicated in a non-trivial manner and that most (non-focked) projects have created files from other projects when inter-project analysis is done. Some researchers benchmark and enhance clone detection systems' speed and hardware size. Software development design approaches evolve often, so tools and procedures must be more flexible. All clone detection techniques need flexible representations (embeddings). Current researchers have not used "Embedding Hub" or other multi-embedding database management solutions.

5. Conclusion

This report analyses most open-source projects based on many studies. Code tokens feed most machine learning and deep learning algorithms. Six categories of methods detect duplicate code or cloning. Lexical analysis first. Distance-based clone detection. Modern clone detection approaches include semantic algorithms and tree-based systems. Articles use hybrid detection methods. This study shows that academics use machine learning and deep learning to detect code clones and literary plagiarism. Machine learning techniques identify clones. K-Means and DBScan are popular clustering techniques. Naive Bayes, Decision Tree, SVM, and others are popular supervised machine learning algorithms. Mine data here. FP-growth and Subgraph facilitate code-locating system development. Many applications find duplicate codes. Visual Studio and GitHub contain these apps. Several projects use clone detection to evaluate licencing, security, and vulnerability. Code rearrangement and best practises applications find duplicate code blocks. This theme is underdeveloped academically and commercially. Evaluation: The largest code repository in the world has duplicate Java, C++, C, Python, and JavaScript code, and most non-focked projects have borrowed files from other projects (inter-project level analysis). Some researchers want to speed up and shrink clone detecting systems.

REFERENCES

1. L. Muxin, "Research on Code Plagiarism Detection Based on Code Clone Detection Technologies," Apr. 2021.
2. A. Schafer, W. Amme, and T. S. Heinze, "Stubber: Compiling Source Code into Bytecode without Dependencies for Java Code Clone Detection," Oct. 2021.
3. G. Shobha, A. Rana, V. Kansal, and S. Tanwar, "Comparison between Code Clone Detection and Model Clone Detection," Sep. 2021.
4. A. Walker, T. Cerny, and E. Song, "Open-source tools and benchmarks for code-clone detection: past, present, and future trends," ACM SIGAPP Applied Computing Review, vol. 19, no. 4. The Association for Computing Machinery (ACM), pp. 28–39, Jan. 28, 2020.
5. R. Sharma and B. Kaur, "A Survey on Trending Algorithms for Software Code Clone Detection," International Journal of Computer Applications, vol. 170, no. 5. Foundation of Computer Science, pp. 8–14, Jul. 17, 2017.
6. P. Sowmya and M. Chatterjee, "Detection of Fake and Clone accounts in Twitter using Classification and Distance Measure Algorithms," Jul. 2020.
7. D. K. Kim, "Enhancing code clone detection using control flow graphs," International Journal of Electrical and Computer Engineering (IJECE), vol. 9, no. 5. Institute of Advanced Engineering and Science, Oct. 01, 2019.
8. B. Bowman and H. H. Huang, "VGRAPH: A Robust Vulnerable Code Clone Detection System Using Code Property Triplets," Sep. 2020.
9. Z. S. OTHMAN and M. KAYA, "Refactoring Code Clone Detection," Jun. 2019.
10. A. A. Elkhail, J. Svacina, and T. Cerny, "Intelligent token-based code clone detection system for large scale source code," Sep. 2019.
11. D. Fu, Y. Xu, H. Yu, and B. Yang, "WASTK: A Weighted Abstract Syntax Tree Kernel Method for Source Code Plagiarism Detection," Scientific Programming, vol. 2017. Hindawi Publishing Corporation, pp. 1–8, Jan. 01, 2017.
12. H. Cheers and Y. Lin, "A Novel Graph-Based Program Representation for Java Code Plagiarism Detection," Jan. 2020.
13. Z. Haojie, L. Yujun, L. Yiwei, and Z. Nanxin, "Vulmg: A Static Detection Solution For Source Code Vulnerabilities Based On Code Property Graph and Graph Attention Network," Dec. 2021.
14. B. Pathik* and M. Sharma, "Detection of Syntax Similarity of Source Code using a Graph based Hybrid Technique," International Journal of Innovative Technology and Exploring Engineering, vol. 9, no. 4. Blue Eyes Intelligence Engineering and Sciences Engineering and Sciences Publication - BEIESP, pp. 1301–1305, Jan. 30, 2020.
15. Z. Guan, X. Wang, W. Xin, and J. Wang, "Code Property Graph-Based Vulnerability Dataset Generation for Source Code Detection," 2020, pp. 584–591.
16. Y. Bai, L. Zhang, and S. Yan, "Automatic Generation of Code Comments Based on Comment Reuse and Program Parsing," Nov. 2019.
17. T. Diamantopoulos, A. Noutsos, and A. Symeonidis, "DP-CORE: A Design Pattern Detection Tool for Code Reuse," Jan. 2016.
18. Q. Xin and S. Reiss, "Better Code Search and Reuse for Better Program Repair," May 2019.
19. T. A. D. Henderson and A. Podgurski, "Rethinking dependence clones," Feb. 2017.
20. Y. Yang, Y. Zhao, and X. Liu, "The algorithm of malicious code detection based on data mining," Jan. 2017.
21. B. Thuraisingham, "Data Mining for Malicious Code Detection and Security Applications," Jan. 2009.
22. B. Thuraisingham, "Data Mining for Malicious Code Detection and Security Applications," Sep. 2011.
23. K. Inoue, "Introduction to Code Clone Analysis," 2021, pp. 3–27.
24. A. Selamat and N. Wahi, "Code Clone Detection Using String Based Tree Matching Technique," 2010.
25. K. E. Rajakumari, "Comparison of Token-Based Code Clone Method with Pattern Mining Technique and Traditional String Matching Algorithms In-terms of Software Reuse," Feb. 2019.
26. S. Ducasse, O. Nierstrasz, and M. Rieger, "On the effectiveness of clone detection by string matching," Journal of Software Evolution and Process, vol. 18, no. 1. Wiley, pp. 37–58, Jan. 01, 2006.

27. R. Koschke, "Large-scale inter-system clone detection using suffix trees and hashing: LARGE-SCALE INTER-SYSTEM CLONE DETECTION," Journal of Software Evolution and Process, vol. 26, no. 8. Wiley, pp. 747–769, Feb. 10, 2013.

28. Roopam and G. Singh, "To enhance the code clone detection algorithm by using hybrid approach for detection of code clones," Jun. 2017.

29. Y.-Y. Zhang and M. Li, "Find Me if You Can: Deep Software Clone Detection by Exploiting the Contest between the Plagiarist and the Detector," Proceedings of the AAAI Conference on Artificial Intelligence, vol. 33. Association for the Advancement of Artificial Intelligence, pp. 5813–5820, Jul. 17, 2019.

30. H. Xue, G. Venkataramani, and T. Lan, "Clone-hunter: accelerated bound checks elimination via binary code clone detection," Jun. 2018.

31. X. Ji, L. Liu, and J. Zhu, "Code Clone Detection with Hierarchical Attentive Graph Embedding," International Journal of Software Engineering and Knowledge Engineering, vol. 31, no. 06. World Scientific Publishing, pp. 837–861, Jun. 01, 2021.

32. Y. Zou, B. Ban, Y. Xue, and Y. Xu, "CCGraph: a PDG-based code clone detector with approximate graph matching," Dec. 2020.

33. M. A. Nishi and K. Damevski, "Scalable code clone detection and search based on adaptive prefix filtering," Journal of Systems and Software, vol. 137. Elsevier, pp. 130–142, Mar. 01, 2018.

34. J. Lee, J. Jeong, and H. In, "Code clone detection technique of android layout codes using view attribute filtering," Contemporary Engineering Sciences, vol. 9. Hikari, pp. 571–577, Jan. 01, 2016.

35. S. B. Ankali, R. S. at V.-R. & F. India,591201 Dept. of CSE, KLE College of Engineering &. Technology, Chikodi, and L. Parthiban, "Detection and Classification of Cross-language Code Clone Types by Filtering the Nodes of ANTLR-generated Parse Tree," International Journal of Intelligent Systems and Applications, vol. 13, no. 3. MECS Publisher, pp. 43–65, Jun. 08, 2021.

36. A. El-Matarawy, M. El-Ramly, and R. Bahgat, "Code Clone Detection using Sequential Pattern Mining," International Journal of Computer Applications, vol. 127, no. 2. Foundation of Computer Science, pp. 10–18, Oct. 15, 2015.

37. A. El-Matarawy, M. El-Ramly, and R. Bahgat, "Parallel and Distributed Code Clone Detection using Sequential Pattern Mining," International Journal of Computer Applications, vol. 62, no. 10. Foundation of Computer Science, pp. 25–31, Jan. 18, 2013.

38. S. K. Abd-El-Hafiz, "A Metrics-Based Data Mining Approach for Software Clone Detection," Jul. 2012.

39. A. Kaur, S. Sharma, and M. Saini, "Code Clone Detection Using Machine Learning Techniques: A Systematic Literature Review," International Journal of Open Source Software and Processes, vol. 11, no. 2. IGI Publishing, pp. 49–75, Apr. 01, 2020.

40. Y. He, W. Wang, H. Sun, and Y. Zhang, "Vul-Mirror: A Few-Shot Learning Method for Discovering Vulnerable Code Clone," ICST Transactions on Security and Safety, vol. 7, no. 23. European Alliance, Jun. 30, 2020.

41. S. Jadon, "Code clones detection using machine learning technique: Support vector machine," Apr. 2016.

42. A. Kaur, S. Jain, and S. Goel, "A Support Vector Machine Based Approach for Code Smell Detection," Dec. 2017.

43. M. Duracik, E. Krsak, and P. Hrkut, "Scalable Source Code Plagiarism Detection Using Source Code Vectors Clustering," Nov. 2018.

44. A. Jadalla and A. Elnagar, "PDE4Java: Plagiarism Detection Engine for Java source code: a clustering approach," International Journal of Business Intelligence and Data Mining, vol. 3, no. 2. Inderscience Publishers, Jan. 01, 2008.

45. T. Ohmann and I. Rahal, "Efficient clustering-based source code plagiarism detection using PIY," Knowledge and Information Systems, vol. 43, no. 2. Springer Nature, pp. 445–472, Mar. 22, 2014.

46. L. Li, H. Feng, N. Meng, and B. Ryder, "CCLearner: Clone Detection via Deep Learning," 2021, pp. 75–89.

47. G. Zhao and J. Huang, "DeepSim: deep learning code functional similarity," Oct. 2018.

48. V. Saini, F. Farmahinifarahani, H. Sajnani, and C. Lopes, "Oreo: Scaling Clone Detection Beyond Near-Miss Clones," 2021, pp. 63–74.

49. A. Sheneamer, "CCDLC Detection Framework-Combining Clustering with Deep Learning Classification for Semantic Clones," Dec. 2018.

50. V. Saini, F. Farmahinifarahani, Y. Lu, P. Baldi, and C. V. Lopes, "Oreo: detection of clones in the twilight zone," Oct. 2018.

51. Y. Meng and L. Liu, "A Deep Learning Approach for a Source Code Detection Model Using Self-Attention," Complexity, vol. 2020. Hindawi Publishing Corporation, pp. 1–15, Sep. 16, 2020.

52. W. Hua, Y. Sui, Y. Wan, G. Liu, and G. Xu, "FCCA: Hybrid Code Representation for Functional Clone Detection Using Attention Networks," IEEE Transactions on Reliability, vol. 70, no. 1. IEEE, pp. 304–318, Mar. 01, 2021.

53. M. M. Draz, M. S. Farhan, S. N. Abdulkader, and M. G. Gafar, "Code Smell Detection Using Whale Optimization Algorithm," Computers Materials & Continua, vol. 68, no. 2. Tech Science Press, pp. 1919–1935, Jan. 01, 2021.

54. "Design and Analysis of Improvised Genetic Algorithm with Particle Swarm Optimization for Code Smell Detection," International Journal of Innovative Technology and Exploring Engineering, vol. 9, no. 1. Blue Eyes Intelligence Engineering and Sciences Engineering and Sciences Publication - BEIESP, pp. 5327–5330, Nov. 10, 2019.

55. S. Bellon, R. Koschke, G. Antoniol, J. Krinke, and E. Merlo, "Comparison and Evaluation of Clone Detection Tools," IEEE Transactions on Software Engineering, vol. 33, no. 9. IEEE, pp. 577–591, Sep. 01, 2007.

56. C. K. Roy, J. R. Cordy, and R. Koschke, "Comparison and evaluation of code clone detection techniques and tools: A qualitative approach," Science of Computer Programming, vol. 74, no. 7. Elsevier, pp. 470–495, May 01, 2009.

57. H. Kaur and R. Maini, "Performance Evaluation and Comparative Analysis of Code-Clone-Detection Techniques and Tools," International Journal of Software Engineering and Its Applications, vol. 11, no. 3. Global Vision Press, pp. 31–50, Mar. 31, 2017.

Computer Science Engineering and Emerging Technologies (ICCS-2022) – Prof (Dr.) Rajeev Sobti et al. (eds)
© 2024 Taylor & Francis Group, London, ISBN 978-1-032-52199-2

Chapter

63

Deep Learning for Aquatic Object Recognition in Seafloor

Vivek Veeraiah[1]
Department of R & D Computer Science,
Adichunchanagiri University, Mandya, Karnataka, India

Shahanawaj Ahamad[2]
College of Computer Science and Engineering,
University of Hail, Hail City, Saudi Arabia

Dharmesh Dhabliya[3]
Department of Information Technology,
Vishwakarma Institute of Information Technology, Pune, Maharashtra, India

Vinod D. Rajput[4]
Department of Computer Science,
SAM Global University, Bhopal, Madhya Pradesh, India

Subodihini Gupta[5]
Department Computer Science,
SAM Global University, Bhopal, Madhya Pradesh, India

Kajal Jaisinghani[6]
Department of Computer Science,
B. K. Birla College (Autonomous), Kalyan, Maharashtra, India

Ankur Gupta[7]
Department of Computer Science and Engineering,
Vaish College of Engineering, Rohtak, Haryana, India

Abstract: The use of deep learning has lately seen great success in the categorization and object recognition of digital images. They are thus quickly garnering recognition and interest from the computer vision research fraternity. The gathering of digital pictures due to the monitoring of undersea ecology, especially seaweed grasslands, has significantly increased. Due to the increase in picture data, deep neural network-based classifiers are now required for automated detection and classification. The application of deep learning to the interpretation of underwater photography in the recent past is comprehensively described in this study. The characteristics and deep learning architectures employed are emphasized, and the analytical methodologies are grouped according to the object of detection. The investigation of digital images of the seafloor utilizing deep neural networks has significant potential for automation, particularly in the discovery and tracking of seaweed.

Keywords: Object detection, Deep learning, Convolutional architecture, Underwater, Seagrass, Neural networks

[1]Vivek@EdVista.in, [2]drshahwj@gmail.com, [3]dharmesh.dhabliya@viit.ac.in, [4]vinodrajput1976@gmail.com, [5]kajaljaisinghani1234@gmail.com, [6]kajaljaisinghani5@gmail.com, [7]ankurdujana@gmail.com

DOI: 10.1201/9781003405580-63

1. Introduction

With 97% of the world's water contained in them, the seas are the soul of nature. They generate the majority of the oxygen and remove the majority of the carbon from our atmosphere. Critical marine habitats must be preserved if these and other ocean ecosystem services are to be preserved. Seaweed meadows and coral islands are significant examples of these because they are essential for seawater food chains, territory supply, and nourishment cycling. For instance, removing oceanic species such as seaweeds by dredging might result in their burial and therefore lessen the amount of light required for photosynthesis. As a result of tourism, shipping, urbanization, and human activity, 26% of the world's coral reefs were damaged or endangered by 2018. Deep learning, the most advanced machine learning technique, offers numerous, perhaps unheard-of, options to address this problem. Until now, typical classification methods have used low-level, manually created characteristics. Local Binary Patterns (LBP) are utilized in classifying faces, while Scale Invariant Feature Transform (Bhattacharya, A. et al. 2021) and manually created features like the Histogram of Oriented Gradients are often used in recognizing features and objects. Additionally, when the number of training data rises, traditional machine learning algorithms like SVM (Dushyant et al., 2022), LDA, PCA, and others rapidly become saturated. To solve these shortcomings, Hegde et al. (2021) proposed using DNNs for learning features. Deep learning (DL) (Gupta, A. et al., 2022) alters input data via additional layers than shallow learning algorithms to make sense of words, pictures, sounds, etc.

2. Detecting Marine Objects Underwater

This section discusses the entire popular machine learning approaches, mainly those that use DNNs for object identification, classification, and the analysis of digital marine data. The methods are categorized into groups depending on the target of the detection.

2.1 Fish Detection and Classification Using Deep Learning

Prior to 2018, there were relatively few efforts to include deep learning in fish detection. Yang et al. (2021) classified shape features using Haar classifiers. The characteristics were modeled using principal component analysis (PCA). Large amounts of underwater footage cannot be processed using any of these approaches. They efficiently and correctly detected fish using a Fast R-CNN. Additionally, they created a clean fish dataset, a subset of the ImageCLEF training and test dataset (Pramanik, S. et al., 2022), with 24272 pictures divided into 12 classes. The results of their experiment indicated that performance was improved with a greater maximum a posteriori estimate. They achieved average accuracy gains of 9.4% over DPM. Table 63.1 compares the effectiveness of their method for fish identification to several other methods that use non-DL techniques.

Table 63.1 Contrast of fish detection accuracy

Technique	Accuracy (%)
LSTM	78.28
GAN	80.36
Kernel SVM	85.71
RBFN	88.94
Deep Belief Network	91.72
Deep CNN	97.21

Source: Made by Author

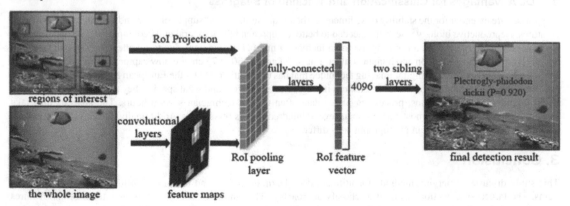

Fig. 63.1 Fast R-CNN-based fish detection and identification architecture

Source: Made by Author

For assessing the performance of deep learning, Knausgård et al. (2021) used the Fish4Knowledge project's Ground-Truth dataset

2.2 DL for Classification of Plankton

Because plankton are usually the base of aquatic food webs, they are widely used as indicators of the health of ecosystems. For the extent of large-scale investigations, conventional plankton monitoring and measuring technologies are insufficient. In association with the Great Lakes Maritime Academy at Northwestern University, a data science competition was launched in 2015 for categorizing photos of plankton. Although it is often believed that massive datasets are necessary for deep learning algorithms, in this instance the classification accuracy was 81.52% with around 30000 samples for 121 classes, some of which had less than 20 examples overall. The heap of convolutional layers was enforced and catered into a heap of dense layers, and at the top, the feature maps were pooled together, allowing the network to utilize the same feature extraction process for examining the input from multiple viewpoints.

2.3 DL for Classification of Coral

Depending on the change in class, corals may have a variety of colors, sizes, shapes, and textures. Furthermore, the border distinctions are hazy and organic. Additionally, water flow, algae blooms, and plankton quantity may alter the water's mud content and the amount of light available, which can alter the hue of the picture. Conventional annotation methods, such as picture labeling and complete segmentation, are ineffective in these situations. Hazgui et al. (2022) used the LBP for texture and the Normalized Chromaticity Coordinate for color. For classification purposes, they employed a 3-layer backpropagation NN. But Ganesan et al.'s (2022) introduction of the Moorea Labeled Corals (MLC) collection was the first to handle self-operated comment on a broad scale for coral reef survey images (Jayasingh, R. et al., 2022). They devised a strategy that outperformed conventional ones by using descriptors of color and texture at different scales.

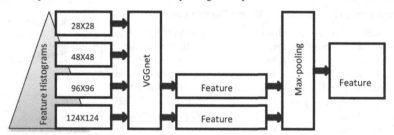

Fig. 63.2   Local-SPP-dependent feature extraction method for coral classification from the VGGNet

Source: Made by Author

2.4 DL Advantages for Classification and Tracking of Seagrass

Sea grasses are essential for the stability of sediment, carbon sequestration, and supply of food and habitat for large marine creatures. Reproductive biology research is needed to better comprehend the temporal and geographical patterns in species composition. It is crucial to monitor seagrass in an increasing number of locations due to its phenology, abundance, and the effects of commercialization and human contact. Images of around 60 to 75 cm are now captured from a digital camera every 4 sec as part of a typical digital imaging technique that has been authorized by the European Maritime Safety Agency (EMSA) (Fig. 63.3). A human operator determines if seagrasses are present and what species they are. For a single transect of 50 m and with 25–50 photos, processing image data often takes a technician several hours. The analysis may take many days to complete since most surveys span several hundred meters of seafloor. Additionally, the capacity of various specialists to identify seagrass in photographs may differ.

3. Conclusion

This study discusses emerging methods for utilizing deep learning to find and categorize different underwater marine items. The targets of detection are used to classify approaches. The employed deep learning architectures and features are compiled. In order to concentrate on the potential of future research depending on DNN technology, it is required to emphasize all the major methods of marine data analytics in a complete study. Deep learning has been used more often

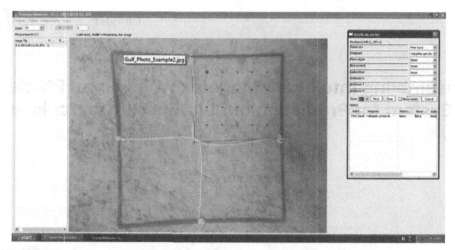

Fig. 63.3 Shows a snapshot of the Transect Measure programme, which is used to examine seagrass

Source: Made by Author

to identify and classify coral, but little research has been done on seagrass, despite its importance to maritime ecology. Combining information based on color and texture may significantly improve the efficiency, accuracy, and resilience of any detection and classification method. For the identification and classification of seagrass, the assembly of hand-crafted features and NNs may supply superior outcomes. As a result, there is a chance to create a deep learning method that is efficient and effective for using underwater seagrass pictures, and this will be the main goal of our future study.

REFERENCES

1. Bhattacharya, A., Ghosal, A., Obaid, A. J, Krit, S., Shukla, V. K., Mandal, K. and Pramanik, S. (2021). Unsupervised Summarization Approach with Computational Statistics of Microblog Data, in Methodologies and Applications of Computational Statistics for Machine Learning, D. Samanta, R. R. Althar, S. Pramanik and S. Dutta, Eds, IGI Global, pp. 23–37, DOI: 10.4018/978-1-7998-7701-1.ch002

2. Dushyant, K., Muskan, G., Gupta, A. and Pramanik, S. (2022). Utilizing Machine Learning and Deep Learning in Cyber security: An Innovative Approach", in Cyber security and Digital Forensics, M. M. Ghonge, S. Pramanik, R. Mangrulkar,D. N. Le, Eds, Wiley, https://doi.org/10.1002/9781119795667.ch12

3. Ganesan, A., Santhanam, S.M. (2022). Fractal adaptive weight synthesized–local directional pattern–based image classification using enhanced tree seed algorithm. Environ Sci Pollut Res 29, 77462–77481, https://doi.org/10.1007/s11356-022-20265-3

4. Gupta, A., Verma, A. and Pramanik, S. (2022). Security Aspects in Advanced Image Processing Techniques for COVID-19, in An Interdisciplinary Approach to Modern Network Security, S. Pramanik, A. Sharma, S. Bhatia and D. N. Le, Eds, CRC Press.

5. Hazgui, M., Ghazouani, H. & Barhoumi, W. (2022). Genetic programming-based fusion of HOG and LBP features for fully automated texture classification. Vis Comput 38, 457–476, https://doi.org/10.1007/s00371-020-02028-8

6. Hegde, R., Patel, S., Naik, R.G., Nayak, S.N., Shivaprakasha, K.S., Bhandarkar, R. (2021). Underwater Marine Life and Plastic Waste Detection Using Deep Learning and Raspberry Pi. In: Kalya, S., Kulkarni, M., Shivaprakasha, K.S. (eds) Advances in VLSI, Signal Processing, Power Electronics, IoT, Communication and Embedded Systems. Lecture Notes in Electrical Engineering, vol 752. Springer, Singapore. https://doi.org/10.1007/978-981-16-0443-0_22

7. Jayasingh, R., Kumar, J., Telagathoti, D. B., Sagayam, K. M. and Pramanik, S. (2022). Speckle noise removal by SORAMA segmentation in Digital Image Processing to facilitate precise robotic surgery, International Journal of Reliable and Quality E-Healthcare, vol. 11, issue 1, DOI: 10.4018/IJRQEH.295083.

8. Knausgård, K.M., Wiklund, A., Sørdalen, T.K. et al. (2022). Temperate fish detection and classification: a deep learning based approach. Appl Intell 52, 6988– 7001 https://doi.org/10.1007/s10489-020-02154-9

9. Pramanik, S. (2022). Carpooling Solutions using Machine Learning Tools, in Handbook of Research on Evolving Designs and Innovation in ICT and Intelligent Systems for Real-World Applications, K. K. Sarma, N. Saikia and M. Sharma, IGI Global, DOI: 10.4018/978-1-7998-9795-8.ch002.

10. Yang, L., Liu, Y., Yu, H. et al. (2021). Computer Vision Models in Intelligent Aquaculture with Emphasis on Fish Detection and Behavior Analysis: A Review. Arch Computat Methods Eng 28, 2785–2816. https://doi.org/10.1007/s11831-020-09486-2

Computer Science Engineering and Emerging Technologies (ICCS-2022) – Prof (Dr.) Rajeev Sobti et al. (eds)
© 2024 Taylor & Francis Group, London, ISBN 978-1-032-52199-2

Chapter **64**

Ensembling Intelligent Models to Design an Efficient System for Prediction of Pulmonary Tuberculosis

Abdul Karim Siddiqui[1]
School of Computer Science & Applications, LPU-Punjab, India
Vijay Kumar Garg[2]
School of Computer Science & Engineering, LPU-Punjab, India

Abstract: Tuberculosis, as a contagious pulmonary disorder, may spread easily from an infected person to a non-infected person. The Microbiologically Confirmed Pulmonary TB Survey done from 2019–2021 in a population aged $\geq$ 15 years shows Delhi with 534 per lakh at the top among the high prevalence 20 states of India. The gravity of incidences and the increasing mortality rate in tuberculosis indicate limited progress in technological advancements in AI-based diagnosis systems. The prediction of pulmonary tuberculosis through preprocessing of image inputs is proposed here with reliable intelligent techniques. DL needs huge training on high-quality data samples. Normally, chest X-rays have low contrast. So three image enhancement methods are applied in image preprocessing: UM, HEF, and CLAHE. An ensembling model using deep learning networks and machine learning algorithms may reduce heavy computational work. The pivotal features gained from the deep neural networks will then be grouped and processed into the classifiers. The machine learning algorithms will predict positive and negative pulmonary tuberculosis cases. The proposed model will undergo n-fold cross-validation, and furthermore, its accuracy will be evaluated.

Keywords: Pulmonary Tuberculosis, TB, Deep convolutional networks, AI in TB

1. Introduction

Slowing down of TB diagnosis and lack of improved interpretation during the Covid period has impacted the increase in TB mortality. The worldwide pandemic situation has turned back the direction of assistance in availing urgent TB predictions and prevention campaigns. Among all the major nations that accounted for 93% of this drop-down in newly, TB diagnosed are—India, Indonesia, and the Philippines. Worsening trends suggest that the negative impacts on TB mortality will remain to continue in 2022 [WHO]. Kwan et al-HIV infected person has more chance to become sick with tuberculosis. HIV weakens the immune system to fight against Mycobacterium. Sutter et al.-TB is carried in droplet nuclei of airborne particles. It is spread by the patient with pulmonary or laryngeal TB coughs or sneezing or even shouting.

Global trends 2000–2020 in the estimated number of TB deaths (Fig. 64.1(a)) and the mortality rate (b)

Parsons et al.: The two conventional methods that are widely used to diagnose pulmonary TB are Chest X-ray and Sputum Smear Microscopy. Roy et al. found that chest radiography is a cost-effective way to diagnose TB. TB Manifestations in the lungs, such as consolidation infiltrates and cavitations, are identified through image screening.

---

[1]abdul.41900407@lpu.in, [2]vijay.garg@lpu.co.in

DOI: 10.1201/9781003405580-64

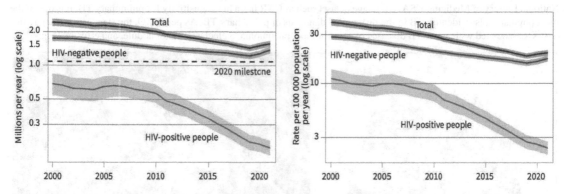

Fig. 64.1 (a) Estimated TB deaths (b) Mortality rate

Source: WHO Global TB Report

Deep learning is an extension of a neural network that employs multiple layers. The nodes of a layer receive signals, process them, and transmit them to the nodes of the next layer. Training with a large number of data inputs, viz., clinical, microbiological, and image inputs such as X-ray, with efficient deep learning models may lead to a more reliable TB diagnostic system. Many researchers have shown greater efficiency in DL using machine learning algorithms.

2. Related Work and Eesearch Gap

Earlier work done in diagnosing pulmonary tuberculosis is analyzed here. Khan et al. developed an approach based on an ANN for the prediction of TB. The data incorporated were based on geographical location, personal values, and clinical values. Qin et al. conducted retroactive tests of three DL systems—CAD4TB, Lunit INSIGHT, and qXR—on chest images. Pasa et al. presented a neural network system for tuberculosis diagnosis and discussed the findings of the training sets using saliency maps and Gradient-weighted CAMs. Huerta et al. presented a segmentation algorithm to detect AFB in smear bacilloscopy using Ziehl-Neelsen (ZN) staining. A Bayesian classifier on a GMM was used, and the result was validated by the Jaccard index. Shih et al. hypothesized a predictive model for the prevalence of pulmonary TB in Human Immunodeficiency virus-negative or unknown victims using multivariable logistic regression. Garnier et al. trained and evaluated a CNN to interpret MODS cultures' digital images. Rahman et al. used deep CNNs and validated the classification of TB and non-TB through the segmentation of X-ray images. Eui Jin Hwang et al. proposed a DLAD algorithm with a DCNN having 27 layers and 12 residual connections. The samples for Chest Radiographs were received from TB Patients who were suspected of active pulmonary TB and had gone through either Mycobacterium culture or polymerase chain reaction tests. Paras Lakhani et al. used classifiers AlexNet and GoogleNet to evaluate the efficacy of DCNNs on TB chest radiographs. As for the pre-trained models' process, the radiographs' size may be reduced to an acceptable range for individual models, which may cause some information loss.

In general, a deep convolutional network demands large computational resources. Also, it uses the equivalent data sets for testing and training the system model. It is, therefore, probably a biased result that may come from a particular set of data. Image datasets may result in less accurate and varied manifestations of TB X-ray images. This may cause an undiagnosed challenge in TB detection models.

3. Materials and Methodology

3.1 Dataset Description

Training the system for the prediction of pulmonary tuberculosis requires an adequate number of datasets. Chest X-ray images are considered inexpensive inputs in image data. Getting a resourceful and reliable dataset is important. Hamdard Institute of Medical Sciences and Research—New Delhi runs a DMC center under the RNTCP program to diagnose and treat Tuberculosis patients. The online dataset was collected from the Montgomery County CXR Set, the Shenzhen Hospital CXR Set, and the NIAID TB dataset. It contained more than 3000 TB-positive chest X-ray images listed on the

National Library of Medicine-USA. An image dataset such as CXR has a high sensitivity for pulmonary TB. It is one of the most popular tools to identify TB in the differential diagnosis of pulmonary TB. As per WHO, the standard characteristics of CXR associated with active TB disease cover infiltration, pneumonia, atelectasis, mass, nodule, and effusion [Fig. 64.2].

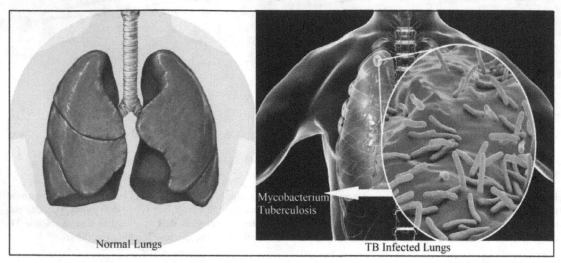

Fig. 64.2 Normal and TB-infected lungs

Source: www.uab.edu

3.2 Preprocessing

Preprocessing is a key task in biomedical imaging transformations. We need to extract the region of interest also called ROI from the chest X-ray and then preprocess it until better image features come for subsequent processing. Images are stored as matrices or digital imaging. The digital grayscale image has a pixel value ranging [0, 255].

1. **Unsharp Masking**: Using a blurred or unsharpened image to make a mask is called unsharp masking.

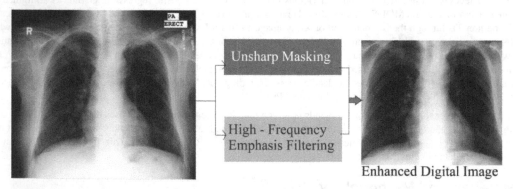

Fig. 64.3 Sharpening of X-Ray Images

Source: Made by Author

2. **HEF:** HEF filters images by sharpening it. It is a 2-D Fourier filtering involves 5 steps (See Fig. 64.4)

3. **CLAHE:** CLAHE is a variant of adaptive histogram equalization. CLAHE overcomes over-amplifying noise by limiting the amplification. It distributes light values fairly on the image and balances the visibility of edges and local contrast. Every central pixel is transformed by the derivative of the transformation function. Adjacent pixels

are adjusted using the contrast feature. Final pixels produce proportionality with the neighboring pixels and hence improved image is gained through contrast-limited adaptive histogram equalization.

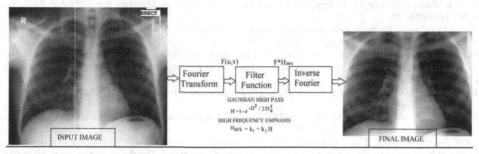

Fig. 64.4 Fourier-domain filtering to apply HFE filter

Source: Made by Author

3.3 The Overall Architecture of the Proposed System

CNNs are a kind of Deep Neural Network that can distinguish and organize pure features from images. That is why they are widely used for analyzing clinical images where quick diagnosis matters. A pulmonary X-ray image is the input of a network backend, which can be a set of existing architectures such as ResNet-50, VGG16, VGG19, DenseNet-121, and Inception Resnet. The proposed model extracts the region of interest (ROI) from available datasets. Preprocessing, as described above, may be done by sharpening the input image, emphasis filtering, and image contrasting to improve the quality. Pivotal features are then extracted by different deep-learning techniques. The features of pre-trained networks are further pooled together for next-level machine learning classifications. On n-fold cross-validation, the problem of over-fitting can be reduced. Various classifiers—SVM, k-NN, and Ensemble classifiers—are primarily applicable.

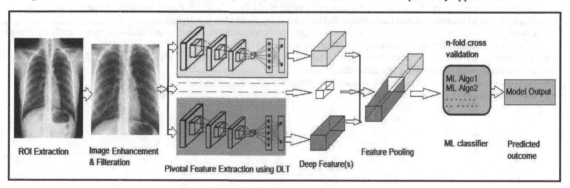

Fig. 64.5 Proposed ensembled model for Pulmonary TB prediction

Source: Made by Author

4. Conclusion

In previous studies, it was observed that pulmonary tuberculosis prediction is not confined to examining X-rays alone. Mixed data set inputs such as patient history and lab investigations may be helpful in the final analysis. An interpretable model containing clinical and image data inputs would make it a more efficient model to predict pulmonary tuberculosis. On the other hand, we may advance the performance of the proposed system by ensemble learning with different classification algorithms such as SVM, random forests, k-nearest neighbors, etc. on pivotal feature extraction using deep learning techniques.

REFERENCES

1. Kwan C. K., Ernst J. D.. HIV and tuberculosis: a deadly human syndemic. Clin Microbiol Rev. 2011 Apr; 24(2): 351–76. doi: 10.1128/CMR.00042-10.
2. Sutter, Charles Clyde. "Contagious Diseases: Their Modes of Transmission." The American Journal of Nursing, vol. 14, no. 7, 1914, pp. 508–12. JSTOR, https://doi.org/10.2307/3404005.
3. L. M. Parsons, Á. Somoskövi, C. Gutierrez, E. Lee, C. N. Paramasivan, A. Abimiku, S. Spector, G. Roscigno, and J. Nkengasong, "Laboratory diagnosis of tuberculosis in resource-poor countries: Challenges and opportunities," Clin. Microbiol. Rev.doi: 10.1128/Cmr.00059-10.
4. M. Roy and S. Ellis, ``Radiological diagnosis and follow-up of pulmonary tuberculosis," Postgraduate Med. J., vol. 86, no. 1021. doi: 10.1136/pgmj.2009.084418.
5. Khan MT, Kaushik AC, Ji L, Malik SI, Ali S, Wei DQ. Artificial Neural Networks for Prediction of Tuberculosis Disease. Front Microbiol. 2019. doi: 10.3389/fmicb.2019.00395.
6. Qin, Z.Z., Sander, M.S., Rai, B. et al. Using artificial intelligence to read chest radiographs for tuberculosis detection: A multi-site evaluation of the diagnostic accuracy of three deep learning systems. Sci Rep 9, 15000 (2019). https://doi.org/10.1038/s41598-019-51503-3
7. F. Pasa,V. Golkov, F. Pfeiffer, D. Cremers, and D. Pfeiffer. Efficient deep network architectures for fast chest X-ray tuberculosis screening and visualization. Sci. Rep.
8. Díaz-Huerta J. L., Téllez-Anguiano AdC, Fraga-Aguilar M., Gutiérrez-Gnecchi J. A., Arellano-Calderón S. (2019) Image processing for AFB segmentation in bacilloscopies of pulmonary tuberculosis diagnosis. PLoS ONE 14(7): e0218861. https://doi.org/10.1371/journal.pone.021886
9. Shih, Y. J., Ayles, H., Lönnroth, K. et al. Development and validation of a prediction model for active tuberculosis case finding among HIV-negative/unknown populations. Sci Rep 9, 6143 (2019). https://doi.org/10.1038/s41598-019-42372-x
10. Lopez-Garnier, Santiago et al. "Automatic diagnostics of tuberculosis using convolutional neural networks analysis of MODS digital images." PLoS ONE 14 (2019): n. pag.
11. T. Rahman et al., "Reliable Tuberculosis Detection Using Chest X-Ray With Deep Learning, Segmentation and Visualization," in IEEE Access, vol. 8, pp. 191586-191601, 2020, doi: 10.1109/ACCESS.2020.3031384.
12. Hwang EJ, Park S, Jin KN, Kim JI, Choi SY, Lee JH, Goo JM, Aum J, Yim JJ, Cohen JG, Ferretti GR, Park CM; DLAD Development and Evaluation Group. Development and Validation of a Deep Learning-Based Automated Detection Algorithm for Major Thoracic Diseases on Chest Radiographs. JAMA Netw Open. 2019 Mar 1; 2(3): e191095.
13. Lakhani P, Sundaram B. Deep Learning at Chest Radiography: Automated Classification of Pulmonary Tuberculosis by Using Convolutional Neural Networks. Radiology. 2017 Aug;284(2): 574–582.
14. A. Narin, C. Kaya, and Z. Pamuk, "Automatic detection of coronavirus disease (COVID-19) using X-ray images and deep convolutional neural networks," 2020, arXiv:2003.10849.
15. https://www.who.int/publications-detail-redirect/9789240037021
16. https://tbcindia.gov.in/showfile.php?lid=3659

Computer Science Engineering and Emerging Technologies (ICCS-2022) – Prof (Dr.) Rajeev Sobti et al. (eds)
© 2024 Taylor & Francis Group, London, ISBN 978-1-032-52199-2

Chapter **65**

Evaluation of Machine Learning Classifiers for Multiple Disease Prediction

Richa Jain[1], Devendran V.[2], Parminder Singh[3]
School of Computer Science & Engineering,
Lovely Professional University, India

Ritika[4]
Computer Science & Engineering,
DAV Institute of Engineering & Technology, India

Abstract: Data is developed, processed, and stored at breakneck speed through multiple frames. Data mining has a huge effect on healthcare services due to the rapid growth of electronic health records. Predicting diseases accurately is a challenging task. To identify diseases, there are many machine learning and deep learning categorization methods that work accurately. This paper compares and contrasts nine distinct classification strategies including Random Forest, Naïve Bayes, SGD, Logistic Regression, MLP, Decision Tree, Gradient Boosting, KNN, and Adaboost on a multi-disease dataset which comprises 41 different diseases by taking 132 symptoms into account. The different techniques are compared based on four different parameters—Accuracy, Recall, F1-score, and Precision. It is noticed based on the performance assessments that MLP outperformed all other base classifiers by achieving an accuracy of 93.65%.

Keywords: Data mining, Machine learning, Disease Prediction

1. Introduction

Since the 20th century, as a consequence of the drastic changes observed in the environmental conditions and the living habits of people, the human body is more prone to diseases. According to the World health organization (WHO), it is proposed that more than 23.6 million people would be dead by 2030 due to such chronic diseases [1].

The Prediction of the action-reaction mechanism of the human body is an emerging aspect in the modern world and the healthcare and medical field. Diagnosis of disease in the healthcare domain is a very tedious and difficult task [2]. This is a major problem in the medical as well as healthcare field. Currently, the methods for illness prediction are mostly based on a thorough study of the patient's medical history, the disease's symptoms, and a physical examination by the doctor. [4]. The computer can be made more intelligent with the help of AI. Machine learning, a subfield of AI is also used for performing different research tasks [3]. Machine Learning techniques are used for the prediction of diseases at an earlier stage. The techniques check the data set that comprises data of many different patients suffering from various diseases [2]. The healthcare industry will benefit greatly from data mining because it will enable health systems to use data and analytics regularly to recognize vulnerabilities and best practices to deliver adequate services at a low cost. It is significant to inspect and cultivate novel data mining methods for the efficient analysis of biotic information.

[1]richa.17688@lpu.co.in, [2]devendran.22735@lpu.co.in, [3]parminder.16479@lpu.co.in, [4]ritikamalhotra2014@gmail.com

DOI: 10.1201/9781003405580-65

A significant part of data analysis and prediction is played by machine learning and hence it is used in almost every field (medical, technical, healthcare, etc.). Without even knowing about the machine learning techniques, we are utilizing them daily [3]. Due to an increase in population each year, medical data is growing tremendously, so using and processing big data is a very critical task. Data mining acts like a boon here and provides various methods to classify the data for the prediction of diseases accurately [5].

This paper presents the comparison of various standard classifiers performed on a multi-disease dataset. The dataset is preprocessed and then 9 different classifiers as represented in Fig. 65.1 are implemented on the processed dataset and the top performed classifiers based on the results are selected. The detailed discussion is further done in the methodology section.

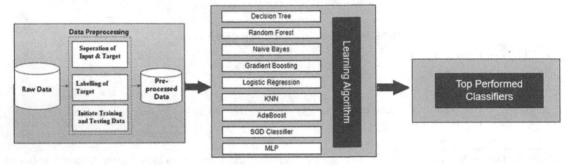

Fig. 65.1 Proposed methodology

Source: Made by Author

2. Literature Review

Shamrat et al. [1] evaluated different classifiers for the prediction of breast cancer disease. The authors have used six machine learning algorithms SVM, KNN, LR, Naïve Bayes (NB), DT, and Random Forest (RF). The performance measures used were accuracy, sensitivity, f1 measure, and specificity. SVM outperformed the other six classifiers employed for the study of breast cancer, with an accuracy of 97.07%.

Dahiwade et al. [3] have proposed a general disease detection model considering Convolutional KNN and CNN machine learning algorithm. The authors analyzed records of the patient's living habits and his checkup data to predict the disease accuracy. The accuracy of CNN algorithm for general disease prediction came out to be 84.5%, which was more than KNN algorithm.

Akbar et al. [7] presented an efficient machine-learning model to analyze the prediction of a chronic disease called Asthma. This paper has classified asthma based on its severity: asthma that flares up intermittently, mildly, moderately, or severely. They have made use of four machine learning algorithms which are Decision tree, Random tree, Random Forest ad Naïve Bayes. The authors examined that the Naïve Bayes algorithm performed with the largest accuracy 98.75%.

Faisal et al. [8] used machine learning classifiers like MLP, Gradient Boosted Tree, Naïve Bayes, Neural Network, SVM, and DT for the prediction of lung cancer. Majority Voting Based and Random Forest ensembles have been utilized for analyzing the outcomes of ensemble methods. After performing the research experiment it was observed that the Majority Voting ensemble method surpassed all other classifiers but the performance of the Gradient Boosted Tree attained the utmost precision with an accuracy of 90%.

Mir et al. [9] is this paper used the WEKA for the prediction of Diabetes. With the help of WEKA, they implied Naïve Bayes, Random Forest, Simple CART algorithm, and Support Vector Machine for the diagnosis of diabetes. The accuracy value, testing time, and training time have been used as a measure to compare the four classifiers. According to the results obtained from the experiments, SVM has the highest classification accuracy followed by Random Forest, Naïve Bayes, and Simple CART algorithm.

Kumar et al. [10] proposed a method using machine learning classifiers to predict Cardio Vascular Disease (CVD). In their work, the authors have used classifiers such as Random Forest, Decision Tree, SVM, K-nearest neighbor, and Logistic

Regression have been used to detect CVD at an earlier stage. Out of all the classifiers, the Random Forest ML classifier attained the highest accuracy bearing an ROC AUC score of 0.8675.

Rahman et al. [11] have analyzed the diagnosis of diseases concerning with liver. Since the prediction of this disease is very costly so the authors proposed a model to make liver disease detection cost-efficient. Six machine learning algorithms have been used which were KNN, SVM, Random Forest, Naïve Bayes, Decision Tree, and Logistic Regression. The algorithms have been applied to clinical data sets. From all the six classifiers used, Logistic regression was performed with a precision value of 75%. The performance of the Naïve Bayes algorithm has the least precision value.

Kruthika et al. [12] have researched on prediction of Alzheimer's. A multistage approach based on machine learning classifiers has been used by the authors. By merging an automated image classification system and a radiologist's expert knowledge, the author's primary goal was to improve the accuracy of disease diagnosis and prediction. The researchers used KNN, SVM, and Naïve Bayes classifier for analyzing Alzheimer's efficiently.

3. Methodology

The suggested methodology begins with data selection which is then followed by pre-processing. After that, the dataset is used to train and test the chosen base classifiers. The outcomes are calculated and assessed to determine the best classifier that can aid in more precise disease prediction. An overview of the methodology is presented using the flow diagram as shown in Fig. 65.2.

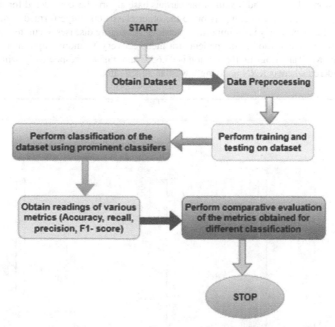

Fig. 65.2 Overview of methodology

Source: Made by Author

3.1 Description of the Dataset

The dataset is obtained from the source: kaushil268/disease-prediction-using-machine-learning [19]. The dataset comprises multiple attributes specifying the symptoms of a particular disease. The dataset contains class labels of 41 different diseases by taking 132 symptoms into account. The dataset contains 4920 instances of various persons. Diseases considered for the research are as follows:

Fungal infection, common cold, malaria, vertigo, allergy, pneumonia, chicken pox, urinary tract infection, gerd, piles, dengue, psoriasis, chronic cholestasis, heart attack, typhoid, impetigo, drug reaction, varicose, hepatitis A, B, C, D and

E, migraine, peptic ulcer disease, hypothyroidism, cervical spondylosis, AIDS, hyperthyroidism, paralysis, diabetes, hypoglycemia, jaundice, gastroenteritis, osteoarthritis, alcoholic hepatitis, bronchial asthma, arthritis, tuberculosis, and hypertension.

3.2 Data Preprocessing

The dataset taken for research is clean; there are no null values, and all of the characteristics are made up of 0's and 1's and only the prognosis column is in string format and is encoded to numerical form using a label encoder.

After the pre-processing stage training and testing of the dataset is performed and we conducted the classification using different machine learning classifiers to witness the change in the readings of performance evaluation metrics like accuracy, F1-Score, Recall, and Precision. For the Performance analysis of various classifiers, the test train ratio considered is 80:20. The various classifiers compared for analyzing the exactness in the prediction of disease are Gradient Boosting, Random Forest, Naïve Bayes, Decision Tree, Logistic Regression, KNN, AdaBoost, SGD classifier and MLP.

4. Results and Discussion

To assess the effectiveness of several classifiers on the multi-disease dataset, four different performance evaluation metrics including Accuracy, F1-Score, Recall, and Precision are considered.

Figure 65.3 depicts the graphical representation of the comparative analysis of the different performance indicators including accuracy, precision, F1-score, and Recall of the various base algorithms considered for the research. The results show that MLP and Logistic regression in comparison to the other classifiers outperformed better in terms of accuracy and other metrics as well. Since accuracy is an important metric in predicting diseases accurately and which further helps in providing the right care and medication to the patients for their recovery, so more emphasis is given to accuracy. The accuracy achieved through MLP and Logistic Regression is 93.65% and 93.54%, respectively, which is the highest among all other classifiers considered whereas KNN is giving lowest accuracy rate.

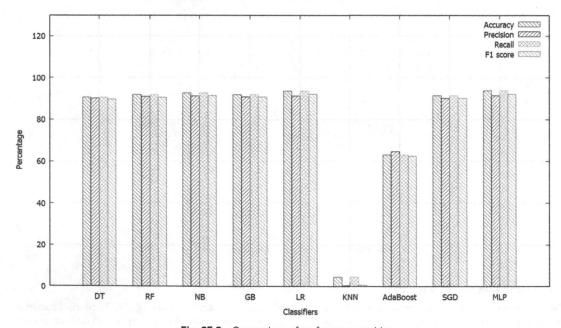

Fig. 65.3 Comparison of performance metrics

Source: Made by Author

5. Conclusion and Future Work

The evaluation of machine learning classifiers for multiple disease identification is the main objective of this study. Various classifiers are evaluated for this purpose, including Decision tree, Random forest, Naive Bayes, Gradient Boosting, Logistic Regression, KNN, Adaboost, SGD, and MLP. It has been noted that MLP outperformed all other base classifiers by providing an accuracy of 93.65%. In the future, we intend to assess multiple diseases using ensemble techniques like stacking, majority voting, bagging, and boosting.

REFERENCES

1. Shamrat, F. J. M., Raihan, M. A., Rahman, A. S., Mahmud, I. and Akter, R., 2020. An analysis of breast disease prediction using machine learning approaches. *International Journal of Scientific & Technology Research*, 9(02), pp. 2450–2455.
2. Dahiwade, D., Patle, G. and Meshram, E., 2019, March. Designing disease prediction model using machine learning approach. In *2019 3rd International Conference on Computing Methodologies and Communication (ICCMC)* (pp. 1211–1215). IEEE.
3. Reddy, K. V. V., Elamvazuthi, I., Aziz, A. A., Paramasivam, S., Chua, H. N. and Pranavanand, S., 2021. Heart disease risk prediction using machine learning classifiers with attribute evaluators. *Applied Sciences*, *11*(18), p. 8352.
4. Djerioui, M., Brik, Y., Ladjal, M. and Attallah, B., 2020, September. Heart Disease prediction using MLP and LSTM models. In *2020 International Conference on Electrical Engineering (ICEE)* (pp. 1–5). IEEE.
5. Hasan, M. K., Alam, M. A., Das, D., Hossain, E. and Hasan, M., 2020. Diabetes prediction using ensembling of different machine learning classifiers. *IEEE Access*, 8, pp. 76516–76531.
6. Akbar, W., Wu, W. P., Faheem, M., Saleem, M. A., GOLILARZ, N.A. and Haq, A. U., 2019, December. Machine learning classifiers for asthma disease prediction: a practical illustration. In *2019 16th International Computer Conference on Wavelet Active Media Technology and Information Processing* (pp. 143–148). IEEE.
7. Mir, A. and Dhage, S. N., 2018, August. Diabetes disease prediction using machine learning on big data of healthcare. In *2018 fourth international conference on computing communication control and automation (ICCUBEA)* (pp. 1–6). IEEE.
8. Kumar, N. K., Sindhu, G. S., Prashanthi, D. K. and Sulthana, A. S., 2020, March. Analysis and prediction of cardio vascular disease using machine learning classifiers. In *2020 6th International Conference on Advanced Computing and Communication Systems (ICACCS)* (pp. 15–21). IEEE..
9. Kruthika, K. R., Maheshappa, H. D. and Alzheimer's disease Neuroimaging Initiative, 2019. Multistage classifier-based approach for Alzheimer's disease prediction and retrieval. *Informatics in Medicine Unlocked*, *14*, pp. 34–42.
10. Patra, R., 2020, March. Prediction of lung cancer using machine learning classifier. In *International Conference on Computing Science, Communication and Security* (pp. 132–142). Springer, Singapore.
11. Jamkhandikar, D. and Priya, N., 2020. Thyroid Disease Prediction Using Feature Selection and Machine Learning Classifiers. *The International Journal of analytical and experimental modal analysi*s, ISSN, (0886-9367).
12. Darvishi, S., Hamidi, O. and Poorolajal, J., 2021. Prediction of Multiple sclerosis disease using machine learning classifiers: a comparative study. Journal of preventive medicine and hygiene, 62(1), p. E192.
13. Disease Dataset: https://www.kaggle.com/kaushil268/disease-prediction-using-machine-learning
14. Alanazi, R., 2022. Identification and prediction of chronic diseases using machine learning approach. Journal of Healthcare Engineering, 2022.

Computer Science Engineering and Emerging Technologies (ICCS-2022) – Prof (Dr.) Rajeev Sobti et al. (eds)
© 2024 Taylor & Francis Group, London, ISBN 978-1-032-52199-2

Chapter

66

Machine Learning-based Approaches to Biosignal Processing

Mohammad Asif Ikbal[1], Suverna Sengar[2]

Assistant Professor, School of Electronics & Electrical Engineering,
Lovely Professional University, Punjab

Abstract: The main aim of this paper is to incorporate the leading Machine Learning (ML) and Artificial Intelligence (AI) tools for processing biosignals. A proper processing of the biosignals and their effective analysis may provide a lead for faster and more effective diagnostics of life-threatening diseases. Researchers from across the globe have already contributed in this field, and numerous approaches have been suggested considering the importance and severity of the issue. In science, while traditional signal processing methods are simple and economical, the adaptation of Machine learning-based processing methods is not getting the desired acceptance and implementation at ground level. The purpose of this work is to bring that threshold between them so that the effectiveness of the Machine learning-based modules can be adopted without any compromise. In the proposed work, some changes are suggested to the existing ML-based adaptive algorithm by incorporating global optimization techniques. This will improve the effectiveness and flexibility of ML-based algorithms and make them more adaptable to nonstationary environments.

Keywords: Machine learning, LMS, ECG, Filtering

1. Introduction

A proper understanding of the cause of disease, precautions against those causes, and effective treatment of the disease are equally important. Figure 66.1 represents the data on the cause of deaths in an age group from 15 to 49 years in the year 2019 (Hannah Ritchie, 2018). The above data clearly depicts that the leading cause of death has been cardiovascular disease (CVD). As per an estimation, around 17.9 million people died from CVDs in 2019, which represents 32% of all global deaths (Cardiovascular diseases (CVDs), 2021). This static is really frightening, and all the required efforts must be made in order to suppress this figure. Considering the recent advancement of technologies and applications of machine learning (ML) in various fields and its popularity, it is quite encouraging and justified to adopt these approaches to remedy the above-mentioned concern. The signals generated because of certain electromechanical activities in the human body are characterise as biomedical signals, these are electrical in nature.

Quantitative data from these signals provides vital information regarding the health of a human being. Some of the important characterizations of the signals generated by the human body are electrooculogram (EOG), electrocardiogram (ECG), electromyogram (EMG), electroencephalogram (EEG), and electroretinogram (ERG) (Patel, 2021). In order to use these signals efficiently, care must be taken at every stage of processing and analyzing them, as they are in the range of millivolts (J. L. A. de Melo), and any possible occurrence of noise must be omitted. The process of analyzing these signals for useful information and making efficient use of them is known as signal processing. In this process, one needs to

[1]asif.22797@lpu.co.in, [2]suverna.22490@lpu.co.in

DOI: 10.1201/9781003405580-66

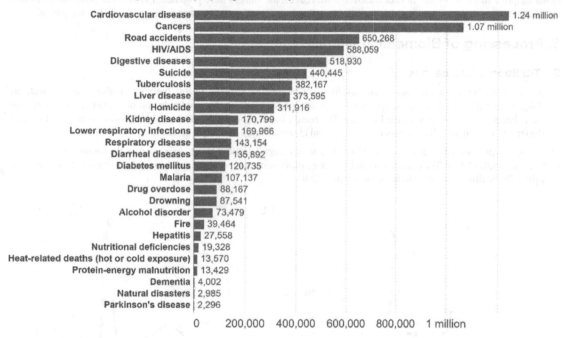

Causes of deaths for 15 to 49 year olds, World, 2019

Annual number of deaths – by cause – for people aged 15 to 49 years old.

Cardiovascular disease	1.24 million
Cancers	1.07 million
Road accidents	650,268
HIV/AIDS	588,059
Digestive diseases	518,930
Suicide	440,445
Tuberculosis	382,167
Liver disease	373,595
Homicide	311,916
Kidney disease	170,799
Lower respiratory infections	169,966
Respiratory disease	143,154
Diarrheal diseases	135,892
Diabetes mellitus	120,735
Malaria	107,137
Drug overdose	88,167
Drowning	87,541
Alcohol disorder	73,479
Fire	39,464
Hepatitis	27,558
Nutritional deficiencies	19,328
Heat-related deaths (hot or cold exposure)	13,570
Protein-energy malnutrition	13,429
Dementia	4,002
Natural disasters	2,985
Parkinson's disease	2,296

Source: IHME, Global Burden of Disease (2019)   OurWorldInData.org/causes-of-death • CC BY

Fig. 66.1   Major cause of deaths

filter the information, classify the signals, and perform feature extraction by using various engineering tools, algorithms, and formulae. Traditionally, these signals were examined with the help of software, and real-time data was provided to healthcare professionals to help them understand the health of patients. With the help of ML-based approaches, the effectiveness of this process can be improved, and more accurate measures and decisions can be made with the help of the latest ML tools. This will eliminate the traditional educated guesswork of health-care professionals.

ML and AI are branches of computer science and engineering that tend to effectively utilize the intelligent behavior of computers. It allows the computers to represent and manipulate the data for efficient use with the help of various algorithms and tools (Wasimuddin, Muhammad, et al., 2020). ML can be basically understood as the optimization of certain performance criteria with the help of computer programming by making use of past experience or example data. The proper selection of an optimization criterion is important, and that can be accuracy provided by a predictive model in the case of modeling problems, or the value of an evaluation or fitness function can be an effective optimization criterion in optimization problems (Larranaga, Pedro, et al., 2006).

The rest of the literature is organized as follows: Section 2 represents some of the important literature studied for developing the required understanding for the articulation of this literature. Section 3 describes the important concepts regarding biomedical signals and the proposed model. Section 4 summarizes the paper with a conclusion and future scope.

2. Literature Review

Some important literatures reviewed by the authors are mentioned in this section.

N.V. Thakor (1991) has developed various structures of an adaptive filter to suppress the noise in an ECG signal. In Eltrass, Ahmed S. (2022), a new multi-stage cascade system for ECG denoising and artifact removal was proposed. In R. Qureshi

(2017), the authors have represented various filtering algorithms for the removal of noise in the ECG along with their weight update equation. In C. Venkatesan (2018), the Gaussian noise is eliminated from the ECG signal using a DENLMS-based adaptive filter algorithm. In Ganatra, Miloni M. (2022), the authors have proposed a systematic design of an FPGA for variable step-size noise removal that provides an efficient trade-off between error tracking and fast convergence.

3. Processing of Biomedical Signals

3.1 Traditional Approaches

As discussed earlier, there are various classifications of biomedical signals. In this literature, authors have considered ECG signals for their analysis and discussion, which is actually a plot of the amplitude and time intervals generated by the heart because of some bioelectrical activity. The reason for the generation of these signals is the depolarization and repolarization of cardiac cells presents in ventricles and atriums (Salari, Nader, et al, 2022).

Figure 66.2 represents one cardiac cycle of an ECG signal from a healthy heart. As shown in the image, it has certain parts named PQRST (U). These parts and their accurate measurement are instrumental in fetching important information regarding the health of a heart (Diker, Aykut, et al., 2020).

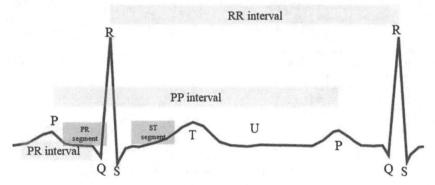

Fig. 66.2   One cycle of an ECG signal

Source: Made by Author

The ECG signal got contaminated with various kinds of noise and error signals during the process of measurement. Once measured, the data is processed to extract meaningful information from the signal. Figure 66.3 represents all the processes involved, from the measurement of signals to the final implementation of the results obtained.

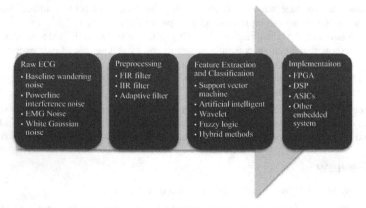

Fig. 66.3   Process of ECG signal processing

Source: Made by Author

3.2 ML based Approaches

In order to collect the required information from the ECG signals, the noise components must be adequately suppressed, and the important information signals must be recovered or improved. Generally, the ECG signals range between 0.5 and 100 Hz, but most of the important information-carrying signals lie in the range of 5-35 Hz with an amplitude range of 1-2 mV (J. Zhang, B., 2019), which is actually similar to a weak physiological signal of low frequency. The process of measuring the ECG signals is simple and can be measured easily with the help of electrodes and electrolyte gel. But this process is equally vulnerable and requires extra precaution; otherwise, signals can be contaminated easily.

A proper procedure must be adopted for extracting useful information from the received signal. This can be done by selecting an appropriate filter with fixed coefficients, but this is only suitable and applicable for signals with fixed internal parameters. On the other hand, ECG signals are time-varying in a non-stationary environment. Some solutions are proposed with the adaptation of an ML-based adaptive algorithm for filtering the ECG signals in a nonstationary environment (Sharma, Yojana, 2022; Yigzaw, Tsion, 2021).

An adaptive filter algorithm can automatically update the coefficient in the time-varying environment. One simple configuration of existing adaptive filter algorithm is shown in Fig. 66.4.

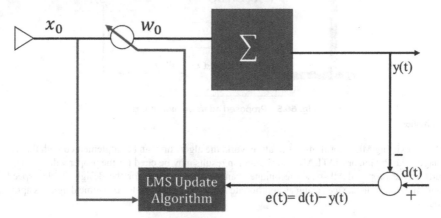

Fig. 66.4 Existing adaptive algorithms

Source: Made by Author

The error signal e(t) is calculated as a difference of the input signal y(t) and noise signal d(t) and accordingly the filter coefficients are updated using various ML-based algorithm to minimize the error signal.

3.3 Proposed Model

The above-discussed model has its limitations and will be inefficient in cases where the nature of ECG signals contains a multi-model error surface. One possible solution to this problem is the incorporation of global optimization techniques like Particle Swarm Optimization (PSO) and Ant Colony Optimization (ACO) for effective optimization of the step size for the Lease Mean Square (LMS) algorithm, as proposed in this literature. The proposed model is shown in Fig. 66.5. In this model, the authors have proposed that for calculating the filter coefficients more adequately, the step size for the LMS algorithm must be optimized with the help of ACO or PSO, and then the optimized step size is used for finding the most appropriate filter coefficients. This will make it capable of finding the filter coefficients even for signals with a multi-model error surface.

4. Conclusion and Future Scope

In this study, authors have discussed various ML-based algorithms and their applications in biomedical signal processing. In the first part of the literature, the importance and need of ML-based techniques for biomedical signals are discussed, and in the later part, the authors have discussed some LMS-based ML algorithms. The limitations of existing models are also explained in the last part of the literature, and their possible solution is proposed by incorporating global optimization

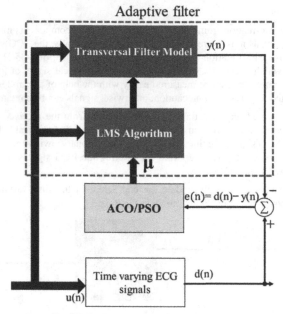

Fig. 66.5 Proposed adaptive algorithms

Source: Made by Author

techniques into the existing ML algorithms. As a future work, the algorithm can be implemented with the help of machine learning languages like Python or MATLAB, and simulation results may be cited for the proper validation of the proposed algorithm. Further, the proposed ML-based techniques can be implemented for the design of high-speed, low-power, economical, and more accurate devices using an appropriate embedded platform for real-time diagnosis applications in the field of biomedicine.

REFERENCES

1. C. Venkatesan, P. Karthigaikumar, R. Varatharajan, FPGA implementation of modified error normalized LMS adaptive filter for ECG noise removal, Clust. Comput. (2018) 1_9. Cardiovascular diseases (CVDs), 11 June 2021, accessed on 20 July 2022,https://www.who.int/news-room/fact-sheets/detail/cardiovascular-diseases-(cvds)
2. Diker, Aykut, et al. "A novel ECG signal classification method using DEA-ELM." Medical hypotheses 136 (2020): 109515.
3. Eltrass, Ahmed S. "Novel cascade filter design of improved sparse low-rank matrix estimation and kernel adaptive filtering for ECG denoising and artifacts cancellation." Biomedical Signal Processing and Control 77 (2022): 103750.
4. Ganatra, Miloni M., and Chandresh H. Vithalani. "FPGA Design of a Variable Step-Size Variable Tap Length Denlms Filter with Hybrid Systolic-Folding Structure and Compressor-Based Booth Multiplier for Noise Reduction in Ecg Signal." Circuits, Systems, and Signal Processing 41.6 (2022): 3592–3622.
5. Hannah Ritchie, Fiona Spooner and Max Roser (2018) - "Causes of death". Published online at OurWorldInData.org. Retrieved from: 'https://ourworldindata.org/causes-of-death' [Online Resource]
6. J. L. A. de Melo, F. Querido, N. Paulino and J. Goes, "A 0.4-V 410-nW opamp-less continuous-time ΣΔ modulator for biomedical applications," 2014 IEEE International Symposium on Circuits and Systems (ISCAS), 2014, pp. 1340–1343, doi: 10.1109/ISCAS.2014.6865391.
7. J. Zhang, B. Li, K. Xiang, X. Shi, Method of diagnosing heart disease based on deep learning ECG signal. (2019).
8. Larranaga, Pedro, et al. "Machine learning in bioinformatics." Briefings in bioinformatics 7.1 (2006): 86–112.
9. N.V. Thakor, Y.-S. Zhu, Applications of adaptive filtering to ECG analysis: noise cancellation and arrhythmia detection, IEEE Trans. Biomed. Eng. 38 (8) (1991) 785794.
10. Patel, Vandana, and Ankit K. Shah. "Machine learning for biomedical signal processing." Machine Learning and the Internet of Medical Things in Healthcare. Academic Press, 2021. 47–66.

11. R. Qureshi, M. Uzair, K. Khurshid, Multistage adaptive filter for ECG signal processing, Proc. 2017 Int. Conf. Commun. Comput. Digit. Syst. C-CODE 2017, (2017) pp. 363–368.

12. Salari, Nader, et al. "Detection of sleep apnea using Machine learning algorithms based on ECG Signals: A comprehensive systematic review." Expert Systems with Applications 187 (2022): 115950.

13. Sharma, Yojana, Shashwati Ray, and Om Prakash Yadav. "Applications of Machine Learning Algorithms in Fetal ECG Enhancement for E-Healthcare." Intelligent Interactive Multimedia Systems for E-Healthcare Applications. Apple Academic Press, 2022. 199–222.

14. Wasimuddin, Muhammad, et al. "Stages-based ECG signal analysis from traditional signal processing to machine learning approaches: A survey." IEEE Access 8 (2020): 177782–177803.

15. Yigzaw, Tsion, Fikreselam Gared, and Amare Kassaw. "Performance Analysis of Adaptive Filter and Machine Learning Algorithms for Heart Rate Estimation Using PPG Signal." 2021 International Conference on Information and Communication Technology for Development for Africa (ICT4DA). IEEE, 2021.

Computer Science Engineering and Emerging Technologies (ICCS-2022) – Prof (Dr.) Rajeev Sobti et al. (eds)
© 2024 Taylor & Francis Group, London, ISBN 978-1-032-52199-2

Chapter **67**

A Neoteric Review of Story Point Estimation in Agile-Scrum Projects Using Machine and Deep Learning Algorithms

Shivali Chopra[1], Arun Malik[2]

Lovely Professional University, Phagwara, India

Abstract: In recent years, machine and deep learning approaches have become increasingly popular for assisting with software effort estimation, and many organizations are beginning to implement this practice in their projects. In this paper, we have articulated various research questions and reviewed the most recent studies in the field of scrum estimation. The review's most striking finding is that moving from waterfall to agile software development necessitates switching from a traditional to a continuous estimation approach. Due to various people and project-related factors, it's clear that there is no "one size fits all" strategy for making estimates. Recent advancements in estimation models include "end-to-end trainable" and "Explainable AI-driven estimation. The transition from point-based estimation to category-based estimation has also been seen in practice, and software development estimation is not intended to anticipate how long a task will take but rather its complexity.

Keywords: Story point estimation, Agile, Scrum, Machine learning, Deep learning

1. Introduction

According to the International Society of Parametric Analysis (ISPA) (Arora, Verma, and Kavita 2018), incorrect effort estimation leads to the failure of nearly 67 percent of software projects. It becomes even more challenging when it comes to estimation in an agile environment. A state-of-the-art report by CollabNet Version One (CollabNet 2018) reveals scrum as the most widely used agile methodology framework and Story Points as the most widely used metric of estimation. Numerous attempts have been made by researchers to improve estimation accuracy, ranging from improvements in traditional to machine learning-assisted estimation techniques. Although a slight improvement has been observed and reported in the related literature, it lacks practicality and real-world implementation due to the "black box" nature of the developed software. We have seen only one study where authors have developed a system with an explainable AI (Fu and Tantithamthavorn, 2022). In spite of many distinct contributions, present estimation techniques are still not able to incorporate the essence of continuous development. Chopra and Malik (2021) have proposed a deep learning-inspired continuous estimation framework, which is the foundational step in this direction. To the best of our knowledge, there is currently no review that focuses on the use of machine learning and deep learning-assisted estimation techniques in Agile-Scrum projects. The sections of this paper are as follows: Section 2 presents relevant work. Section 3 outlines the research questions, and Section 4 describes the conclusion and future possibilities.

[1]shivali.19259@lpu.co.in, [2]arun.17442@lpu.co.in

DOI: 10.1201/9781003405580-67

2. Related Work

A concise knowledge of effort and schedule estimates is critical to project success or failure. Although many traditional techniques are used to estimate effort for agile software projects, the majority of them result in inaccurate estimates. Tawosi, Moussa, and Sarro (2022) extended the work of Deep-SE with a larger dataset of 31,960 user stories extracted from 29 open source projects. The authors claimed that an augmented dataset has no major impact on improving the accuracy of the estimation. (Phan and Jannesari 2022) estimated the story points of a scrum project using a text-level Graph Neural Network (TL-GNN). The authors claimed an accuracy rate of 80% for story point classification. Many techniques were outperformed, like TF-IDF. Fu and Tantithamthavorn (2022) developed an agile story point estimation approach by using transformers. They have also carried out comparisons and addressed various challenges in story point estimation. The authors have substantially improved the estimation accuracy percentage and outperformed the Deep-SE (Choetkiertikul et al. 2019) approach from 6 percent to 47 percent. Raharjana, Siahaan, and Fatichah (2021) presented a systematic literature review of user stories and natural language processing. The authors identified 718 papers from 2009 to 2020 and concluded a review of 38 studies. The various NLP techniques used in user stories are presented in this paper. Kasem, Mahar, and Saad (2022) proposed a story point-based machine learning classifier to classify the issues based on the different levels of complexity. The model's accuracy is then evaluated on a test set of issue reports created from the agile project, and it has been found that various metrics like F score, precision, and recall have been used to compare it to other classifiers. The user story, which is part of the issue's metadata (the title and description), is one piece of information that can be used by intelligent task-level effort estimation approaches. Predicting the difficulty of a task in SP by analyzing features retrieved from user stories has been the subject of numerous research proposals for nearly a decade (Tawosi, Moussa, and Sarro, 2022; Arora et al., 2022; Arora, Verma, and Chopra, 2020; Arora et al., 2021). These studies generally argue that their approach may serve as a helpful tool for expert estimators on agile teams when making estimates. More than 15 features, such as priority, size, and complexity of the user story, were proposed by Abrahamsson et al. (2011) for use in training a prediction model. They used regression models, neural networks (NN), and support vector machines (SVM) to develop estimation models for two industrial case studies. When compared to its competitors, SVM consistently produces the best results. Five years later, Porru et al. (2016) proposed categorizing user stories into story point classes. Their method takes features from more than 4000 user story descriptions from eight open-source projects that were written in Jira issue reports. (Marapelli, Carie, and Islam 2020) (2020) proposed a bidirectional LSTM and CNN to estimate the story points of various open source projects. The proposed model gives an accuracy of 74.2 percent in a popular dataset named "Bamboo." The authors have not presented the efficacy of the proposed algorithm with any other dataset. Scott and Pfahl (2018) estimated story points using SVM in 2018 by combining developer-related data with features taken from 4,142 user stories from eight open-source projects. Simultaneously, Soares (2018) proposed using multiple NLP techniques with auto-encoder neural networks to classify user stories based on semantic differences in their titles in order to assess their effort in terms of (Abadeer and Sabetzadeh 2021) assessed the effectiveness of Deep-SE for SP prediction using a commercial dataset of 4,727 user stories obtained from a healthcare data science business. We have created research questions and recorded many unique observations, like state-of-the-art story point estimation algorithms, datasets used for estimation, metrics used, baselines, and future research directions.

3. Research Questions

RQ1: What are the various text classification techniques in context to story point classification in scrum using machine learning?

The various machine learning techniques are Naïve Bayes classifier, Support Vector Classifier (SVC), Linear Classifier aka Logistic Regression, Bagging Models (e. g. Random Forest), Boosting Models (XGB (eXtreme Gradient Boosting), SGB (Stochastic GB), CatBoost (Categorical Boosting), AdaBoost (Adaptive Boosting), Facebook fastText classifier. The following NLP techniques are used for text representation/preprocessing. Bag-of-words, TF-IDF (Term Frequency-Inverse Document Frequency), Word2Vec, Doc2Vec, GloVE and Seq2Seq (*Source: Author's compilation*)

RQ2: What are the text classification techniques using deep learning in context to story point classification in scrum?

The various deep learning techniques are Multilayer Perceptron (MLPANN), GRU (Gated Recurrent Unit), LSTM (Long Short-Term Memory), RHWN (Recurrent Highway Neural Network), RNN (Recurrent Neural Network), Stacked Auto encoders, Deep Belief Network-Restricted Boltzmann Machine (DBN-RBM), CNN (Convolutional Neural Network),

CNN-LSTM, Recurrent CNN (Marapelli, Carie, and Islam 2020), GAN (Generative Adversarial Network) (Morais 2021), and HAN (Hierarchical Attention Network) (Kassem, Mahar, and Saad 2022)

RQ3: What is the accuracy of the state-of-the-art text classification techniques using traditional and machine/deep learning in context to story point classification in scrum? Table 67.1 is showing the accuracy matrix. The various metrics are MAE (Mean Absolute Error) and SA (Standardized Accuracy)

Table 67.1 Accuracy matrix

Techniques used	Dataset used	MAE	SA
DEEP-SE (Choetkiertikul et al. 2019)	16 projects	0.81	57.8
LSTM+RF (Choetkiertikul et al. 2019)	16 projects	0.94	52.2
LSTM+SVM	16 projects	0.92	51.8
LSTM+ATLM	16 projects	1.04	46.5
LSTM+LR	16 projects	1.02	47.3
BOW+RF	16 projects	0.94	52
D2V+RF	16 projects	0.95	51.5
Mean	16 projects	1.45	18.1
Median	16 projects	1.36	22.2
SVM	9 projects	NA	0.64
Naïve Bayes	9 projects	NA	0.44
KNN	9 projects	NA	0.36
Decision trees	9 projects	NA	0.23
DEEP-SE (Tawosi 2022)	29 projects	NA	58
Text level GNN (Phan 2022)	16 projects	NA	80
LSTM+CNN (Marapelli 2020)	Bamboo dataset	NA	74.2
ZeroR classifier	9 projects	NA	0.34
GPT2SP (Fu and Tantithamthavorn 2022)	16 projects	NA	0.7*
HAN (Kassem, Mahar, and Saad 2022)	7 projects	NA	.87

Source: Author's compilation) NA: Not Available, *- GPT2SP outperformed DEEP-SE by 0.06-0.47.

RQ4: What are the pros and cons of deep learning techniques in context to story point classification? Table 67.2 mentions the pros and cons.

Table 67.2 Deep learning techniques pros and cons

Algorithms	Pros	Cons
Multilayer Perceptron (MLPANN)	Fast to train and Simple to implement	Efficient for simple problems. Easily fail in convergence
Gated recurrent unit	Better than LSTM as they fix the vanishing gradient problem	High computing complexity and memory requirement
LSTM (Long Short-Term Memory)	Can model long-term dependencies	Vanishing gradient problem
RHWN (Recurrent Highway Neural Network)	Highly accurate sequence prediction	Over fit for problems having low depth
RNN(Recurrent Neural Network)	Can memorize sequential data	Affected by vanishing gradient problem
Stacked Auto encoders	Efficient in learning compact representation of data	Low interpretability
CNN(Convolutional Neural Network)	Very efficient for short text classification	Need large amount of data to provide good accuracy
CNN-LSTM	Can trained on spatial data	Ineffective for short text classification
Recurrent CNN	Efficient for long text classification	Ineffective for short text classification

Source: Author's compilation

3. Conclusion

Estimation is an inevitable activity in project management. Agile-Scrum estimation using machine or deep learning techniques will assist project managers in making accurate decisions quickly. It will never replace the traditional estimation techniques; instead, it will participate in the decision-making process.

REFERENCES

1. Abadeer, Macarious, and Mehrdad Sabetzadeh. 2021. "Machine Learning-Based Estimation of Story Points in Agile Development : Industrial Experience and Lessons Learned." In *29th International Requirements Engineering Conference Workshops*, 106–15. IEEE.
2. Abrahamsson, Pekka, Ilenia Fronza, Raimund Moser, Jelena Vlasenko, and Witold Pedrycz. 2011. "Predicting Development Effort from User Stories." In *International Symposium on Empirical Software Engineering and Measurement*, 400–403.
3. Arora, Mohit, Abhishek Sharma, Sapna Katoch, Mehul Malviya, and Shivali Chopra. 2021. "A State of the Art Regressor Model's Comparison for Effort Estimation of Agile Software." *2nd International Conference on Intelligent Engineering and Management (ICIEM)*, 211–15.
4. Arora, Mohit, Sahil Verma, and Shivali Chopra. 2020. "A Systematic Literature Review of Machine Learning Estimation Approaches in Scrum Projects." In *Cognitive Informatics and Soft Computing*, 573–86.
5. Arora, Mohit, Sahil Verma, and Kavita. 2018. "An Efficient Effort and Cost Estimation Framework for Scrum Based Projects." *International Journal of Engineering and Technology* 7 (4.12): 52–57.
6. Arora, Mohit, Sahil Verma, Kavita, Marcin Wozniak, Jana Shafi, and Muhammad Fazal Ijaz. 2022. "An Efficient ANFIS-EEBAT Approach to Estimate Effort of Scrum Projects." *Scientific Reports* 12 (1). Nature Publishing Group UK: 1–14.
7. Choetkiertikul, Morakot, Hoa Khanh Dam, Truyen Tran, Trang Thi Minh Pham, Aditya Ghose, and Tim Menzies. 2019. "A Deep Learning Model for Estimating Story Points." *IEEE Transactions on Software Engineering* 45 (7): 637–56.
8. Chopra, Shivali, and Arun Malik. 2021. "Deep Learning Inspired Continuous Estimation Framework for Scrum Projects." *Intelligent Circuits and Systems*, 609–13.
9. CollabNet. 2018. "The 12th Annual State of Agile Report." *Version One*. https://www.versionone.com/about/press-releases/12th-annual-state-of-agile-survey-open/.
10. Fu, Michael, and Chakkrit Tantithamthavorn. 2022. "GPT2SP: A Transformer-Based Agile Story Point Estimation Approach." *IEEE Transactions on Software Engineering*, no. March
11. Kassem, Haithem, Khaled Mahar, and Amani Saad. 2022. "Software Effort Estimation Using Hierarchical Attention Neural Network." *Journal of Theoretical and Applied Information Technology* 100 (18): 5308–22.
12. Marapelli, Bhaskar, Anil Carie, and Sardar M.N. Islam. 2020. "RNN-CNN MODEL: A Bi-Directional Long Short-Term Memory Deep Learning Network for Story Point Estimation." *CITISIA 2020 - IEEE Conference on Innovative Technologies in Intelligent Systems and Industrial Applications, Proceedings*.
13. Morais, Rene Avalloni de. 2021. "Deep Learning Based Models for Software Effort Estimation Using Story Points in Agile Environments." *Concordia University of Edmonton*.
14. Phan, Hung, and Ali Jannesari. 2022. "Story Point Effort Estimation by Text Level Graph Neural Network." http://arxiv.org/abs/2203.03062.
15. Porru, Simone, Alessandro Murgia, Serge Demeyer, Michele Marchesi, and Roberto Tonelli. 2016. "Estimating Story Points from Issue Reports." In *Proceedings of the The 12th International Conference on Predictive Models and Data Analytics in Software Engineering*, 1–10.
16. Raharjana, Indra Kharisma, Daniel Siahaan, and Chastine Fatichah. 2021. "User Stories and Natural Language Processing: A Systematic Literature Review." *IEEE Access* 9: 53811–26.
17. Scott, Ezequiel, and Dietmar Pfahl. 2018. "Using Developers ' Features to Estimate Story Points." In *International Conference on the Software and Systems Process*, 106–10.
18. Soares, Rodrigo G.F. 2018. "Effort Estimation via Text Classification and Autoencoders." In *International Joint Conference on Neural Networks (IJCNN)*, 2018-July:1–8.
19. Tawosi, Vali, Rebecca Moussa, and Federica Sarro. 2022. "Deep Learning for Agile Effort Estimation Have We Solved the Problem Yet?," 1–17.

Computer Science Engineering and Emerging Technologies (ICCS-2022) – Prof (Dr.) Rajeev Sobti et al. (eds)
© *2024 Taylor & Francis Group, London, ISBN 978-1-032-52199-2*

Chapter **68**

Image-Based Dragonfly Classification Using Capsule Networks

Aniruddha Prabhu B. P.[1]
Assistant Professor, Computer Science,
Graphic Era Hill University, Dehradun, Uttarakhand

Ojas Misra[2]
Associate Analyst, Digital and Emerging Technology,
Ernst & Young, Hyderabad, Telangana

Rakesh Dani[3]
Associate Professor, Hospitality Management,
Graphic Era Hill University, Dehradun, Uttarakhand

Abstract: Deep learning plays a virtuoso role in automated image classification and identification systems. A powerful technique called Capsule Neural networks is known for its high precision outputs in identifying objects that require accounting for angle and position. Dragonflies are popularly known for keeping our ecosystem clean and hygienic, so in this paper, image-based identification of dragonflies is studied by taking 2280 images of 15 different species as an example. It's simple to identify these flies with our naked eyes, but due to the diversity and similarity they share, it gets more and more difficult to differentiate them. We used the capsule neural network technique, which showed higher accuracy for 75 epochs of training and achieved good identification accuracy in practical applications.

Keywords: Deep learning, Capsule neural network, Insects and dragonflies

1. Introduction

Hexapod invertebrates, commonly known as insects, are one of the most enormous groups that fall within the arthropod phylum. 'Insects' or 'Insecta' is synonymous with the term Ectognatha. A study says that in the animal kingdom, 90% of them are in fact insects.

They are among the most diverse groups of animals. Insects are classified into two sub-groups: Pterygota (winged insects) and Apterygota (wingless insects). There are various ways in which insects interact with one another. For instance, female moths secrete a substance called pheromones, which the male moths can sense from a great distance. Some insects are also known for spreading diseases through feeding on leaves, sap, wood, and fruits. The life cycle of several plant species that bloom is supported by insects that act as pollinators. A wide variety of insects act as predators that are ecologically beneficial, with some contributing directly, like silkworms and honeybees. Odonata is one of the ancient orders of insects, which includes a few of the most ancient and appealing insects to ever exist on Earth. Some are believed to be the largest invertebrates that fly.

[1]aniprabhubp@gmail.com, [2]misraojas@hotmail.com, [3]rakeshdani@geu.ac.in

DOI: 10.1201/9781003405580-68

Based on morphology, Odonates are classified into three groups: Zygoptera (damselflies), Anisoptera (dragonflies), and Anisozygoptera (remnant group constituted from two species). Odonates and their ancestors come from one of the oldest winged insect groups. At first glance, both dragonflies and damselflies look alike since they are closely related to one another. They are predatory at adult as well as aquatic nymphal stages. Dragonflies wings are held horizontally, both while flying and resting, mainly due to their strong and heavy body structure, whereas damselflies have weak and slender bodies. Generally, most of the species have their eyes at the sides of the head separated and their wings folded over their abdomen while stationary. Dragonflies have hindwings that broaden out towards the base, whereas damselflies' wings are of the same shape and size throughout; as their wings connect to the main body, they become narrower.

The compound eyes of dragonflies are larger than those of damselflies. Dragonflies' eyes extend from the sides, wrapping towards the front face, which takes up most of the head, but damselflies have a proper gap between both eyes. Odonates play a vital role in the wetland ecosystem as predators at either of their life stages. At the adult stage, they tend to feed on blackflies, mosquitoes, and other parasitic flies, acting as crucial bio-control organisms for these deleterious insects and diminishing the spread of diseases. Some species of odonates inhabiting agro-ecosystems act as pest population controllers [2].

Dragonflies serve as ecological indicators. The inhabitation of dragonflies indicates freshwater in the surroundings. India is well known for having as many as 500 studied species, with Odonata being the most ancient order. It is believed that the species appeared about 250 million years ago in the Carboniferous Era, when there were giant dragonflies with wingspans up to 1.5 m due to an abundance of atmospheric oxygen levels between 30% and 50% higher than current levels, which led to high oxygen toxicity in the body. As time moved on, the size of the dragonflies reduced due to reduced oxygen levels in the environment, which led to low oxygen toxicity in the body [2, 3].

2. Literature Review

In 686 genera of odonates, globally, 6256 species are found. Dragonflies are among the most enticing creatures on earth [1]. Dragonflies can be identified with the naked eye, but classifying them among their species and families is a difficult task because of the supernumerary similarity of their appearance in the marked species. Though the classification of dragonflies for the identification of species is a challenge, it in turn helps the Ecologist and Taxonomist in the conservation of species. F.A. Faria Et Al. proposed a robotic system for identifying fruit flies [4]. In his proposed system, wings and aculei are considered key features for identification. The author used three distinct approaches for the purpose: SVM for wings, SVM for aculei, and a connected model, which gave them a proper understanding of the classification of these fruit flies.

Jiangning Wang Et Al. showcased an automatic system that identifies images of insects with a level of order [5]. The proposed System uses SVMs, a risk-minimizing classification technique, to extract features from the dataset during the training process. They considered major classification features like shape, size, patterns, and structure of the body. The system recommended by both F.A. Faria et al. and Jiangning Wang et al. used the K-Fold cross-validation technique to consider the best output, which in turn gave an optimal result. Ankang Xue et al. implemented a system for automatic identification of butterflies [6]. In their proposed system, they used to weigh based on the KNN (K-nearest Neighbor) and the GLCM (Gray-Level Co-occurrence Matrix) for classification.

In GLCM methodology, an image is first transformed into a grayscale, dividing the grayscale into several blocks that will be given as input for the classifier. The weight-based KNN classified efficiently for fewer species, but for a greater number of species, the efficiency dropped to 80. P.J.D. Weeks Et Al. proposed Automating the system to identify insects [7]. In his recommended system, a semi-automated technique is used to identify individuals belonging to five closely related species based on the differences in wing patterns. Gaussian smoothing highlighted the features better than other techniques; hence, Gaussian smoothing gave higher accuracy.

P. J. D. Weeks Et Al. did it after inspecting shortcomings of the prototype system [8]. The proposed system first digitizes the image and converts it to a vector by using the DAISY technique. which was then subjected to principal component analysis. The PCA has a set of eigenfunctions that describe the variations accurately. The system uses Kendal's t statistics to compare the original and reconstructed images. P.J.D. Weeks et al. found that both the proposed systems gave 84% and 86% accuracy, respectively. Chenglu Wen Et Al. developed an image-based orchard insect automated identification system.

Classification Method [9]. The proposed system uses both local and global features to classify orchard insects. They have used GLCM texture features for insect identification and classification. 85.3% correct rate of accuracy was obtained for global feature-based classification and 74.7% accuracy for local feature-based classification, whereas the combined model yielded 86.6% correct classification. Faith Praise Fina Et Al. proposed Automatic Plant Pest Detection and Recognition using K-Means Clustering [10]. In their work, the authors used K-means clustering as a classifier and correspondence filters. Correspondence filters being constructed from different angular rotations of the k-means output clusters aid in their recognition owing to the feature of distortion invariance they exhibit. This system has high accuracy. The result was successful in the exact detection and identification of plant pests with numerous sizes, shapes, orientations, and positions using efficient computing algorithms.

P. J. D. Weeks Et Al. proposed Automated Identification of Copepods using Digital Image Processing and an artificial neural network [8]. The recommended system exhibits the usage of classical digital image processing techniques such as edge detection, rotation of ROI, and removal of noise with ANNs as classifiers for the classification of copepods. ANNs flaunting a great generalization on the input feature vectors are used to classify and generalize on the selected feature vector after the pre-processing. The authors have published a result of 97.3% on 240 samples after 137 epochs.

Evaluation of the network output layer is done using MSE and confusion matrices. As we have examined many papers, there is no specified paper released on dragonfly species. This intended us to select a dragonfly species as our challenge. As per the research, dragonfly species are widespread in the world. So, we are proposing a system that classifies and identifies dragonfly species using a capsule neural network.

3. Data and Variables

The Major task is collecting the required datasets. Most of the Datasets have been collected through web scraping; thanks to the Python Selenium tool, we collected 2280 images of 15 dragonfly species illustrated in Fig. 68.1. The images gathered in the datasets are of different sizes. The entire dataset is resized to 256 × 256, keeping the aspect ratio unchanged. We collected the images of individuals of the coral-tailed cloud wing, black stream glider, ground skimmer, blue marsh awk, common picture wing, crimson-tailed marsh hawk, crimson marsh glider, ditch jewel, fulvous forest skimmer, pied paddy skimmer, scarlet skimmer, trumpet tail, and wandering glider, which belong to the family Libellulidae, and the common club tail, which belongs to the family Gomphaceae. Dragonfly species look similar to one another. It is difficult to differentiate among the species. The common picture wing is different among all species in appearance. Trumpet tail, Club tail,

The ground skimmer is similar in color and body shape. Coral-tailed cloud wing, Wandering glider, scarlet skimmer, and Crimson-tailed Marsh Hawk, Crimson Marsh, and Scarlet Skimmer are similar in their body color.

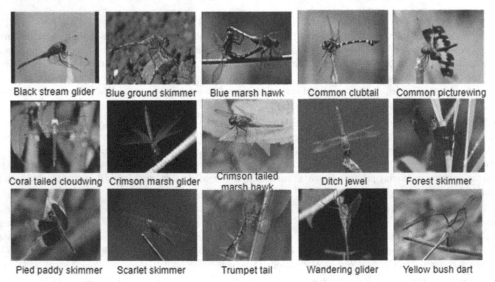

Black stream glider	Blue ground skimmer	Blue marsh hawk	Common clubtail	Common picturewing
Coral tailed cloudwing	Crimson marsh glider	Crimson tailed marsh hawk	Ditch jewel	Forest skimmer
Pied paddy skimmer	Scarlet skimmer	Trumpet tail	Wandering glider	Yellow bush dart

Fig. 68.1 Few images from dataset

Source: Google Image, 2000-2021: online

4. Methodology and Model Specifications

Capsules are the building blocks of capsule networks. Each capsule is a combination of layers within a layer of the neural network. Each capsule tends to identify a feature. During the process of identifying or classifying a dragonfly, it not only captures the presence of features like wing pattern or color but also takes into account how the parameters are organized. This means the network only identifies the dragonflies that have the features in the correct order.

The capsule aims to do inverse image rendering, which results in considering the initialization parameters like angle, scale, and position by analyzing the given image with a given training sample.

4.1 Working of Capsule Networks

First, the input image matrices are multiplied with weight metrics, which define the contiguous relationship between a few lower- and higher-level features. Via the dynamic routing technique, parents are selected by these capsules. The lower capsule that sends the data to the dominant capsule is called the parent capsule. The parent capsule proceeds with routing based on expectation maximization, mixture model usage, and the dot product. The capsule whose dot product is highest among others is selected as a parent.

Encoder Network: It takes the image as input and converts it into a vector that contains all initialization parameters. The encoder consists of a primary convolution layer that detects basic image features like color. Followed by a primary cap layer that combines the features extracted by the convolution layer. A digitCaps layer that contains all initialization parameters.

Decoder Network: It decodes a 16-dimension vector obtained from the digitCap layer across an image. The image is recreated successfully without any loss of pixels with the help of the decoder.

4.2 Functions of Capsule Net

There are various ways to implement capsules. One of the successful techniques is to squash the short vectors into zero and long vectors to one. This can be implemented using the equation below.

$$\mathbf{v}_j = \frac{\|\mathbf{s}_j\|^2}{1 + \|\mathbf{s}_j\|^2} \frac{\mathbf{s}_j}{\|\mathbf{s}_j\|}$$

The first layer of the capsule is calculated by the weighted sum of the input vectors. Which can be calculated as shown below.

$$\mathbf{s}_j = \sum c_{ij} \hat{\mathbf{u}}_{jli}, \quad \hat{\mathbf{u}}_{jli} = \mathbf{W}_{ij} \mathbf{u}_i$$

The new vector that formed, as a result, will be fed as input to the following layers in Fig. 68.2.

The proposed dragonfly classifier/identifier takes ($256 \times 256 \times 3$) images as inputs and converts them into a vector of 196608 lengths. It falls through a 9×9 convolution layer, and it falls through the primary capsule, which gives the metrics to be identified and forms the preliminary capsules that constitute the network.

The initial capsule is combined with the number of capsule layers that perform classification. These classification results are decoded by the decoder network. Which consists of three sequential dense layers followed by a reconstruction layer to give a SoftMax output.

5. Conclusion

The Dataset contained 2391 images of 16 classes, which are divided into 1921 training and 470 validation and testing partitions. The images are resized to 256×256 without alteringhe aaspect ratio.

A learning rate of 0.001 was obtained by training for 50 epochs i.e., present in Fig. 68.3. The model was evaluated for 98% Training accuracy and showed 84% Validation accuracy.

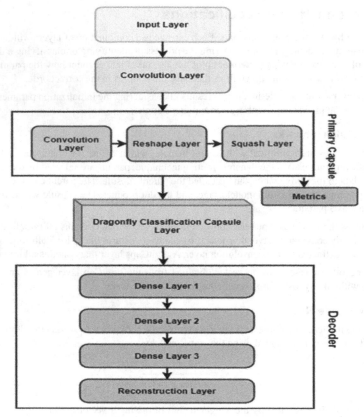

Fig. 68.2 System architecture

Source: Authors

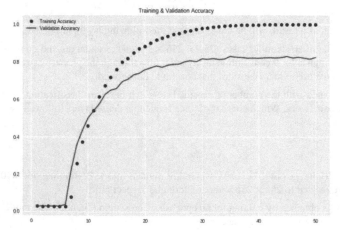

Fig. 68.3 Training & validation accuracy

Source: Authors

Loss occurred in the model drastically decreased for 20 epochs and gradually dropped for next 30 epochs as present in Fig. 68.4.

Training & Validation loss

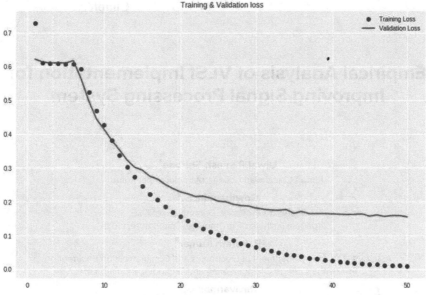

● Training Loss
— Validation Loss

Fig. 68.4 Training & validation loss

Source: Authors

Therefore, in our paper, we have presented an alternative approach for classifying and identifying dragonflies using capsule neural networks and achieved an accuracy of 92.35%.

The major setbacks for the process were interspecies similarity and intraspecies dissimilarity. These made the model work poorly under some circumcisions. The multi-label-class classification can be implemented to improve the system's robustness.

REFERENCES

1. Subramanian, K. A. (2018). Dragonflies and Damselflies of India-A field Guide. Project Lifescape.
2. Evolution and Ancestors. Retrieved August 1, 2006, from Dragonflies—Living Fossils Web site: http://skurvits.tripod.com/dragonflieslivingfossils/index.html
3. M. Macedo Leonardo, S. Avila, R. A. Zucchi and F. A. Faria, "Mid-level Image Representation for Fruit Fly Identification (Diptera: Tephritidae)," 2017 IEEE 13th International Conference on e-Science (e-Science), Auckland, 2017, pp. 202–209, doi: 10.1109/eScience.2017.33.
4. Wang, J., Lin, C., Ji, L., & Liang, A. (2012). A new automatic identification system of insect images at the order level. Knowledge-Based Systems, 33, 102–110. doi: 10.1016/j.knosys.2012.03.014
5. Xue, A., Li, F., & Xiong, Y. (2018). Automatic Identification of Butterfly Species Based on Gray-Level Co-occurrence Matrix Features of Image Block. Journal of Shanghai Jiaotong University (Science). doi: 10.1007/s12204-018-2013-y
6. Weeks, P. J. D., Gauld, I. D., Gaston, K. J., & O'Neill, M. A. (1997). Automating the identification of insects: a new solution to an old problem. Bulletin of Entomological Research, 87(02), 203. doi: 10.1017/s000748530002736x
7. Weeks, P. J., O'Neill, M., Gaston, K., & Gauld, I. . (1999). Species–identification of wasps using principal component associative memories. Image and Vision Computing, 17(12), 861–866. doi: 10.1016/s0262-8856(98)00161-9
8. Wen, C., & Guyer, D. (2012). Image-based orchard insect automated identification and classification method. Computers and Electronics in Agriculture, 89, 110–115. doi: 10.1016/j.compag.2012.08.008
9. Faithpraise, Fina & Birch, Phil & Young, Rupert & Obu, Joseph & Faithpraise, Bassey & Chatwin, Chris. (2013). Automatic plant pest detection & recognition using k-means clustering algorithm & correspondence filters. International Journal of Advanced Biotechnology and Research. 4. 1052–1062.
10. Jagadeeshan, Manoj Balaji & Sharma, Ganesh. (2019). Recognition of Off-line Kannada Handwritten Characters by Deep Learning using Capsule Network. 10.35940/ijeat.F8726.088619.

Computer Science Engineering and Emerging Technologies (ICCS-2022) – Prof (Dr.) Rajeev Sobti et al. (eds)
© 2024 Taylor & Francis Group, London, ISBN 978-1-032-52199-2

Chapter **69**

Empirical Analysis of VLSI Implementation for Improving Signal Processing System

Ujwal Ramesh Shirode[1]
Pimpri Chinchwad College of Engineering, Pune

Gowtham M. S.[2]
Associate Professor, Department of ECE,
Karpagam Institute of Technology, Coimbatore, India

R. Sarath Kumar[3]
Assistant Professor, Department of Electronics and Communication Engineering,
Sri Krishna College Of Engineering and Technology, Coimbatore

Ravivarman G.[4]
Assistant professor, Department of EEE,
Karpagam academy of higher education, Coimbatore, Tamilnadu

S. Srinivasulu Raju[5]
Assistant Professor, Department of Electronics and Instrumentation Engineering,
VR Siddhartha Engineering College, Vijayawada

Prabin Kumar Bera[6]
Research Scholar, Department of ECE, N. I. T. Durgapur, West Bengal

Abstract: The study of VLSI signal processing focuses on the development of signal processing algorithms for use in very large-scale integrated (VLSI) hardware, such as customizable digital signal processors, including dedicated signal processors. This chapter provides a broad overview of recent advancements in the subject, including topics such as algorithm design, architectural evolution, and design process. The hardware implementation of digital signal processing algorithms and their synthesis are also highlighted. Certain digital signal processing (DSP) algorithm implementations are made up of both software and hardware. A suitable illustration of a DSP algorithm is an n-level stacked Do-loop, a recurrence equation, or a data flow graph (DFG). Then, one of the representations is used to create a hardware implementation. In addition to how the algorithm is represented, the hardware design is heavily influenced by the input and output signals' sample rates. A certain algorithm's processes and data may be distributed to the proper execution units at the proper times due to hardware limitations, provided the algorithm's precedence and semantics are preserved. For a process that produces the greatest amount, like image or video processing, the synthesis of either a network system of processing units (PEs) or a hybrid architecture is thoroughly investigated. After some time has passed, the technology and tools used in a certain architecture's implementation are analyzed.

Keywords: DSP, VLSI, Silicon validation, ICs, RF communication, FPGA, Parallelism, Reconfigurability

[1]ujwalshirode@gmail.com, [2]gowtham.ece@karpagamtech.ac.in, [3]sarathkumar@skcet.ac.in, [4]ravivarman.govindarajulu@kahedu.edu.in, [5]srinu85raju@gmail.com, [6]prabinbera@gmail.com

DOI: 10.1201/9781003405580-69

1. Introduction

Digital signal processing applications have been extending the capabilities of computers since their inception, especially in terms of their capacity to do computations in real time. Although the signals that signal processing systems analyze may include media-driven video, audio, and speech waveforms as well as specialized sonar and radar data, most of the calculations performed by these systems have typically shown similar fundamental computational features. Despite the fact that the signals they analyze show this, DSP algorithms are particularly suited for hardware implementation since many DSP functions have intrinsic data parallelism. They may make use of the growing capabilities of VLSI technology in this way. Recent advancements in multimedia computing and high-speed wired and wireless connections have directly contributed to a huge increase in DSP productivity. These modifications have resulted in a greater focus being put on the investigation and creation of innovative arithmetic-intensive circuit implementations. Although programmable digital signal processors (PDSPs) and application-specific integrated circuits (ASICs) remain the most common options available on the market for many DSP applications, new system implementations are being created every day. These platforms are rapidly expanding as a consequence of Moore's Law, which keeps increasing the logic capacity of programmable devices, and as advanced automated design methodologies become more accessible. They combine the functional efficiency of hardware with the programmability of software. New research and commercial initiatives have been started as a result of the introduction of new applications to help with power optimization, cost reduction, and improved run-time performance. New research and business endeavors have made these endeavors viable. Two key computational factors that are constant with most DSP operations are real-time performance within the confines of the target system's operating settings and, in most situations, the need to adapt to new data sets and varied computing environments. Although digital signal processors have a wide variety of potential applications, their computational characteristics remain constant. The development of application- and domain-specific chipsets, which are used in anything from low-cost embedded radio components to specialized ground-based radar centers, has been driven by the need for optimal performance.

2. Literature Review

2.1 Evolution of Hardware of Digital Signal Processing

The term "digital signal processing," abbreviated as "DSP," refers to the performance of signal processing using digital methods with the assistance of digital hardware and/or some sort of computer equipment. Even if analog processing of signals is possible, digital processing of signals is often preferred for several reasons. These reasons include: The digital procedure has two significant drawbacks, which are as follows: It is far more difficult than the analog method because computers can only process numbers with a limited level of detail. The "potentially unlimited resolution" of the analog signal is thus rendered unusable as a result. There must be some positive side effects that come along with the digital process, and sure enough, there are. To begin, the signal is guaranteed to remain unchanging after it has been reduced to numerical form. It is feasible to store, transmit, and reproduce numbers without any corruption by using methods like error detection and repair. Moreover, this is also achievable. As a result, the accuracy of the twenty-first generation of recordings is equivalent to that of the first generation. This chapter helps us learn both the theory behind DSP as well as the practical information required to comprehend how a DSP system functions.

Design considerations for DSP system implementation often include a delicate balancing act between these three system objectives. Consequently, many other kinds of DSP-specific hardware implementations and accompanying design tools have been created, such as those for associative processing, bit-serial processing, online arithmetic, and systolic processing. These foundational methods have progressed to satisfy the demands of application designers as implementation tools have become more accessible. To evaluate the quality of different DSP implementations, many cost indicators are shown in the table above. Since DSP systems often have rigorous real-time limitations, performance has virtually always been the most important system requirement. However, the cost has become more important over the last three decades as DSP has shifted from largely military and scientific uses to a wide variety of inexpensive consumer applications. As digital signal processing (DSP) methods have grown increasingly integrated into mobile, battery-operated devices like cell phones, CD players, and laptops over the last decade, energy consumption has emerged as an essential metric. Finally, flexibility has proven to be an important difference in DSP implementations by allowing for modifications to the system's functionality at several stages of the design process. Results of these cost trade-offs in four fundamental implementation options These options include reconfigurable hardware, general-purpose microprocessors, programmable digital signal processors

(PDSPs), application-specific integrated circuits (ASICs), and ASICs. Each implementation technique has different trade-offs in terms of performance, cost, power, and flexibility. The optimal solution may be chosen based on the end-use case.

2.2 The Concept of Parallelism and Time-Multiplexing

Several distinct architectural designs that each have their use throughput and latency may be mapped onto a single algorithm via the use of parallelism and time multiplexing. Architectural transformations such as data-stream interleaving, loop retiming, and folding may let more intricate activities, such as feedback loops, be carried out either in parallel or in serial fashion. This is possible because of the flexibility of these techniques.

Multiplexing in time and parallel processing: Electricity may be saved by raising the voltage at which it is supplied and by distributing the task across numerous branches that run in parallel.

Interleaving of data streams is one way that may be used for time-multiplexing data. Interleaving is a technique that may potentially dramatically boost efficiency in a given area by reusing data-path logic across many data streams.

Along the same lines, folding things may be an effective way to conserve space.

However, this presents a hurdle in that it is necessary to figure out how to correctly distribute pipeline registers throughout the loop to obtain maximum throughput.

The process that is referred to as "loop retiming" involves allotting the appropriate amount of delay to fundamental functional building blocks, followed by dispersing the pipeline registers that are contained within the blocks to make sure that all internal Datapath logic blocks are located in the same place.

The fifth kind of iteration is known as delayed iteration, and it takes place when the vast majority of loops have about the same latency but only a tiny percentage of loops need additional time to calculate.

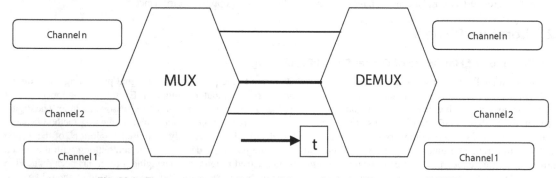

Fig. 69.1 The concept of parallelism and time-multiplexing (Banerjee et al., 1995)

2.3 Optimal VLSI Design

Technology-dependent, the best VLSI design calls for the characterization of key functional blocks in regard to speed, power, as well as area. The architectural optimization approach, which is based on this knowledge, is used to steer itself based on the algorithm throughput requirements and the capabilities of the underlying basic building blocks. Data speed and latency are the main restrictions on chip realisations. Data throughput is particularly important in terms of optimization since, for a given system, the throughput is connected with the frequency of operation. For optimization, technology-specific information is crucial, such as the energy-delay trade-off in Datapath logic. This is a critical trade-off since the quantity of energy needed to run digital logic gates affects how quickly they can work. By talking about design elements like gate size, supply voltage, and threshold voltage, a compromise is established. A new technology causes the whole Energy-Delay curve to slope downward, meaning less energy and delay are required. When the slope of the energy-delay trade-off curve (E-D) for the architecture is identical to that of the Datapath logic, we call it energy-optimal.

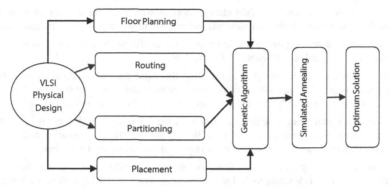

Fig. 69.2 VLSI optimal design (Hsia & Tsai, 2010)

3. Data and Variables

3.1 Study Period and Sample

All deterministic and certain random signals may be described by a set of trigonometric and conic equations, regardless of their complexity. The CORDIC processor makes solving these equations easier. For Digital Signal Processing (DSP) applications, primarily during the modulation and demodulation phase, the Coordinate Rotation Digital Computer (CORDIC) is a hardware-efficient iterative algorithm for calculating hyperbolic, exponential, logarithmic, as well as trigonometric functions such as sine, cosine, magnitude, but rather phase, with astounding precision. Due to rising quantization errors, CORDIC implementation is becoming more challenging as the number of gates and ROM capacity needed for every application rapidly increases. An appropriate Application Specific 'pipeline' in Verilog HDL is one solution proposed to address this problem. Optimizing in this way helps reduce the calculated quantization error and frees up space on the silicon substrate. Verilog HDL is used to effectively code the CORDIC design. The design is pipelined such that there is just one adder in its internal critical route. Micro-rotational counts have been fine-tuned to reduce the mistake introduced by angle estimates. Quantization errors particularly may be minimised with the use of an efficient pipelined CORDIC architecture.

3.2 Review and Design of Low-cost Digital Pulse-width Modulators Utilizing Field-Programmable Gate Arrays

This article explains the design and operation of two DPWM implementations for inexpensive FPGAs, or field-programmable gate arrays (FPGAs). Both designs use a counter comparator block to handle the MSB of the reference input, with the LSB being processed by a different set of components to improve duty-cycle resolution (LSB). The first described design has been previously published in the literature; it makes use of the on-chip PLL blocks to create fixed delays and a selector to choose the one that corresponds with the required duty cycle. To account for delay variations throughout the selector's various signal routes, post-fitting modifications to the PLL's delay are necessary. In the second design, the LSB input is thermometer-coded and then serialized using a serializer-reserialize (SERDES) module. This serialization method has wide support from FPGA manufacturers and is widely deployed for usage in high-speed serial I/O data transfer standards like LVDS. For all designs, we report experimental findings demonstrating extremely high linearity and resolutions up to 1 ns, all generated on commodity, low-cost FPGA chips. The resolution is somewhat better in the first architecture. On the other hand, the second design is far more reliable since it doesn't need any post-fitting delays.

3.3 Reconfigurability

To do comprehensive logic and connection reconfiguration in the field, most reconfigurable devices and systems feature SRAM-programmable memory. Most DSP systems need reconfiguration under a broad range of limitations, despite the large diversity of system features. Environmental considerations, such as fluctuations in signal-to-noise ratio, transmission speed, channel quality, and atmospheric conditions, might be limiting. Data traffic and interference may vary quickly, whereas elements like location and weather might change more slowly. The necessity for frequent reconfiguration is mitigated by the low frequency with which other elements influence standards across time and space change.

As new vendor firmware versions become available or as flaws in the product are discovered, the functionality of programmable devices may be updated and maintained in the field.

The need for field customization increases when considering the rapid pace at which standards and communication protocols are evolving. As opposed to ASIC implementations, reconfigurable hardware solutions don't need manual field upgrades for hardware swaps to be quickly changed depending on the needs of the application.

Reconfigurable logic-based signal processing systems may need regular updates during normal operation. This may be a time-consuming procedure. Some examples of such challenges are the effects of weather and operations on mobile communication and the structural support for several time-varying standards in fixed receivers.

Many communication processing systems benefit from the ability to rapidly reset and reevaluate parameters. Some examples of these challenges include learning to deal with fluctuating datasets, dealing with network congestion in various network topologies, and adapting to time-varying noise in communication channels.

4. Methodology and Model Specifications

The development of the Very-Large-Scale-Integration-Systems has allowed for significant progress in wireless communication. As research into cutting-edge VLSI systems proceeds, it is fascinating to see how VLSI circuits used in wireless communications have evolved. Power amplifiers based on MOSFETs (Metal Oxide Semiconductor Field Effect Transistors) form the backbone of very large-scale integration (VLSI) design systems and are responsible for the transmission of radio waves from base stations. Some of the many technologies for use in RF frequencies may be considered. When it comes to RF applications, Si-Ge Bipolar CMOS technology is quickly becoming the standard. For the many items that have stringent demands on power performance, these technologies provide affordable answers. Currently, Si-Ge Bic MOS technology is being tested for use in wire-line communications at 40 Gigabytes per second and beyond, as well as growing wireless local area networks (WLANs), automobile radar, and collision avoidance technologies operating in the 24 to 77 GHz range. RF CMOS technology is another cutting-edge development for RF applications; it can do several tasks on a single chip, which reduces manufacturing costs. RF CMOS is used in a variety of wireless communication applications due to

Table 69.1 Digital signal processing analysis and its growth in recent years (Banerjee et al., 1995)

Years	$ millions
2019	1800
2020	1900
2021	1920
2022	1960
2023	2000
2024	2010
2025	2020
2026	2050
2027	2060
2028	2065
2029	2070

its ability to strike a good balance between sensitivity, gain, and noise. When considering RF technologies for extensive communication uses, you may categorize them as cost-optimized or performance-optimized. Considering that digital CMOS serves as the foundation for RFCMOS, the digital CMOS roadmap has a significant impact on the characteristics of RF technology. Upcoming advances in VLSI Circuits will be studied in light of how they may render today's state-of-the-art technology obsolete in the realm of wireless communications.

5. Empirical Results

Sigma Delta ADCN All natural signals are continuous, and hence analog, in the early stages. For these signals to be handled by digital computational systems, they must first undergo a conversion from their original analog form to a digital one with discrete time-discrete-valued signals. Since all discrete digital systems need the conversion and processing of continuous data, ADC and DAC are fundamental. To achieve its discrete form, every analog signal must first be sampled. The so-called delta-sigma, or ADC, is one of the most cutting-edge types of ADC (using the proper Greek letter notation). The Greek letter delta is used to symbolize a change or difference in mathematics and physics, whereas the Greek letter sigma is used to denote a sum or total. The sigma-delta converter uses an integrator with an analog input voltage signal as input to generate a slope (or rate of change) in the output voltage that is proportional to the input magnitude. A comparator then evaluates this soaring voltage against the reference voltage of zero volts. The integrator's positive or negative output determines whether the comparator's one-bit (high or low) output is positive or negative, making the comparator a kind of one-bit analog-to-digital converter. The output of the comparator is sent back into the integrator through another input channel, where it is latched by a D-type flip-flop that is being timed at a high frequency.

5.1 The use of Fully Combinational Circuits for Power Optimization of Single-precision Floating-point FFT Designs

In this work, we developed a 32-bit,754 single-precision floating-point architecture for 8-point FFT. The whole thing has a combinational structure. Simulations are run in Active HDL to test the FFT layout. Simulation in MATLAB is used to check the results. Up to the twenty-two-bit level, correctness is achieved. Complex data is used to test the design (separately for real and imaginary data). To reduce power consumption, designers utilise a technique called pipelining, which consists of a forward route cutest leading to FFT stages. Architecture power is determined in Synopsys' Design Vision tool using a 45nm technology file and two steps of pipelining. With this method, we may cut down on electricity use by as much as 35%.

Table 69.2 Single core storage and compute requirements for overlapped and non-overlapped versions of N1 × N2 2D and N = N1 × N2 1DFFTs for 4-Step mode (Parhi, 1997)

FFT N1 × N2	2DNo-Ov	2D Ov	1DNo-Ov	1D Ov
Comm	$2N_1(R) + 2N_1(W)$		$4N_1(R) + 2N_1(W)$	
Local Storage	$4N_1$	$6N_1$	$6N_1$	$8N_1$
Tw. Mult. Cycl.	-	-	$6N_1/n_1^2$	$4N_1/n_1^2$
Radix-4 Cycl.	$6N_1\log_4 N_1/n_1^2$			

6. Conclusion

The study's results suggest that advancements in very large-scale integration (VLSI) technology and design tools have greatly expanded digital signal processing's domain of viable uses. These developments have taken place throughout the last decade. This research will primarily concentrate on the architectural and performance aspects of VLSI used in DSP applications such as voice processing, wireless communication, analog-to-digital converters, and so on. The exponential growth in VLSI system complexity brought on by Moore's law has created serious problems with design productivity and verification. More information has to be checked, which has led to these problems. New advances in hardware synthesis, high-level compilation, and design verification are needed to keep up with the rapid advancements being made in DSP computing right now. A system's performance may be improved in a number of ways, including by selecting an appropriate design, amount of reconfigurability, and degree of parallelism. Power consumption, space constraints, and parallelism in data processing are all factors that must be considered while designing a VLSI system for use in signal processing.

REFERENCES

1. 1997 IEEE Workshop on Signal Processing Systems. sips 97 design and implementation formerly VLSI Signal Processing. (1997). 1997 IEEE Workshop on Signal Processing Systems. Sips 97 Design and Implementation Formerly VLSI Signal Processing. doi:10.1109/sips.1997.625678
2. 1997 IEEE Workshop on Signal Processing Systems. sips 97 design and implementation formerly VLSI Signal Processing. (1997). doi:10.1109/sips.1997
3. Aoki, T., Negi, H., & Higuchi, T. (n.d.). High-radix cordis algorithms for VLSI signal processing. 1997 IEEE Workshop on Signal Processing Systems. Sips 97 Design and Implementation Formerly VLSI Signal Processing. doi:10.1109/sips.1997.626115
4. Aoki, T., Negi, H., & Higuchi, T. (n.d.). High-radix cordis algorithms for VLSI signal processing. 1997 IEEE Workshop on Signal Processing Systems. SiPS 97
5. Design and Implementation Formerly VLSI Signal Processing. doi:10.1109/sips.1997.626115
6. Author index. (1997). 1997 IEEE Workshop on Signal Processing Systems SiPS 97 Design and Implementation Formerly VLSI Signal Processing SIPS-97. doi:10.1109/sips.1997.626346
7. Gass, W. (n.d.). System integration issues for a set-top box. 1997 IEEE Workshop on Signal Processing Systems. SiPS 97 Design and Implementation Formerly VLSI Signal Processing. doi:10.1109/sips.1997.625691

8. HOUSE, D. (n.d.). VLSI implementation of the Realtime Image Processing Parallel Architecture GFLOPS. Workshop on VLSI Signal Processing. doi: 10.1109/vlsisp.1992.641049

9. Howard, D., Tyrrell, A., & Murrin, P. (n.d.). Hearing music [human peripheral hearing system]. 1997 IEEE Workshop on Signal Processing Systems. SiPS 97 Design and Implementation Formerly VLSI Signal Processing. doi: 10.1109/sips.1997.626255

10. Hsia, S., & Tsai, P. (2010). VLSI implementation of Camera Digital Signal Processor for the document projection system. 2010 2nd International Conference on Signal Processing Systems. doi: 10.1109/icsps.2010.5555444

11. Jones, R. F., & Swartzlander, E. E. (1994). Parallel Counter Implementation. Journal of VLSI Signal Processing Systems for Signal, Image and Video Technology, 7(3), 223–232. doi: 10.1007/bf02409399

12. Meyer, H. (n.d.). On core and more: A design perspective for system-on-chip. 1997 IEEE Workshop on Signal Processing Systems. SiPS 97 Design and Implementation Formerly VLSI Signal Processing. doi: 10.1109/sips.1997.625688

13. Parhi, K. (n.d.). Fast VLSI binary addition. 1997 IEEE Workshop on Signal Processing Systems. SiPS 97 Design and Implementation Formerly VLSI Signal Processing. doi: 10.1109/sips.1997.626129

14. Ruei-Xi Chen, Mei-Juan Chen, Liang-Gee Chen, & Tsung-Han Tsai. (n.d.). The system implementation of I-phone hardware by using low-bit-rate speech coding. 1997 IEEE Workshop on Signal Processing Systems. SiPS 97 Design and Implementation Formerly VLSI Signal Processing. doi: 10.1109/sips.1997.626328

15. Srikanthan, T., Bhardwaj, M., & Clarke, C. (n.d.). Implementing area-time efficient VLSI residue to binary converters. 1997 IEEE Workshop on Signal Processing Systems. SiPS 97 Design and Implementation Formerly VLSI Signal Processing. doi: 10.1109/sips.1997.626113

16. Yao, K., Reed, C., Hudson, R., & Lorenzelli, F. (n.d.). Beamforming performance of a randomly distributed sensor array system. 1997 IEEE Workshop on Signal Processing Systems. SiPS 97 Design and Implementation Formerly VLSI Signal Processing. doi: 10.1109/sips.1997.626306

17. Feiste, K., & Swartzlander, E. (n.d.). Merged arithmetic revisited. 1997 IEEE Workshop on Signal Processing Systems. SiPS 97 Design and Implementation Formerly VLSI Signal Processing. doi: 10.1109/sips.1997.626121

18. Aggoun, A. (n.d.). Radix-differential 2d FIR filters. 1997 IEEE Workshop on Signal Processing Systems. SiPS 97 Design and Implementation Formerly VLSI Signal Processing. doi: 10.1109/sips.1997.626278

19. Banerjee, S., Chau, P. M., & Fellman, R. D. (1995). Rapid prototyping methodology for multiprocessor implementation of Digital Signal Processing Systems. Journal of VLSI Signal Processing Systems for Signal, Image and Video Technology, 11(1–2), 21–34. doi: 10.1007/bf02106821

Computer Science Engineering and Emerging Technologies (ICCS-2022) – Prof (Dr.) Rajeev Sobti et al. (eds)
© 2024 Taylor & Francis Group, London, ISBN 978-1-032-52199-2

Chapter **70**

Exploratory Data Analysis of Heart Disease Using Machine Learning

Prerna Rawat[1]

M.Tech(CSE), Department of Computer Science & Engineering,
Graphic era deemed to be University, Dehradun, Uttarakhand

Prabhdeep Singh[2]

Assistant Professor, Department of Computer Science & Engineering,
Graphic era deemed to be University, Dehradun, Uttarakhand

Devesh Pratap Singh[3]

Professor, Department of Computer Science & Engineering,
Graphic era deemed to be University, Dehradun, Uttarakhand

Abstract: The healthcare industry generates a massive amount of data, or "big data," which can contain useful information such as a trend or insight that would otherwise be impossible to discern. A judgement based on the massive amount of data is more reliable than one based on gut feeling alone. EDA can be used to identify inaccuracies, locate relevant data, verify assumptions, and calculate the degree of association between explanatory factors. Data analysis without the use of conclusions or statistical models is what is meant by "EDA" in this setting. Because of its ability to reveal hidden patterns and predict the future, analytics has become a crucial tool in virtually every industry. Recent advances in data analytics have made it a practical tool for use in healthcare, where it has proven invaluable in the face of unexpected discoveries, medical emergencies, and disease outbreaks. Preventive care is made easier with the help of analytics, which is why EDA is so important when analyzing healthcare data for insights. Today, heart disease remains one of the world's leading killers. There has been a substantial shift in the underlying causes of heart disease deaths, although life expectancy has increased dramatically in the twenty-first century. The dataset used in this research is Heart Disease dataset from UCI. The heart dataset has been used to plot many different sorts of graphs, including categorical plots, grid plots, matrix plots, distribution plots Regression plots, and advanced plots. The heart dataset's many aspects have been analysed, visualised, and distilled into conclusions.

Keywords: Heart disease, Machine learning, EDA, Big data

1. Introduction

Today, heart disease remains one of the world's leading killers. Increases in education and healthcare have contributed to a substantial shift in the root causes of heart disease mortality in the twenty-first century. About 40% of the world's population lives in high-income countries, yet 28% of humanity lives in low- or moderate-income nations [1]. This continual transition is occurring around the globe, across all racial and ethnic groupings, and across all nations at a rate that is much faster than in the last century. Heart failure rates have been rising significantly in recent years due to changes in modern lifestyles.

[1]Prerna7rawat@gmail.com, [2]prabhdeepsingh.cse@geu.ac.in, [3]Devesh.geu@gmail.com

DOI: 10.1201/9781003405580-70

The huge shift in people's health status around the world is causing an increase in cardiovascular disease on a global scale. Heart disease has replaced all other causes as the leading cause of death around the world. Cardiovascular disease is on the rise all across the world as a result of a drastic shift in people's general health. A heart attack is one of the leading causes of death worldwide, and its prevalence has been steadily rising over the past two decades. The paper organisation for this paper goes as mentioned in the upcoming paragraph. After a short abstract of the paper in Section 1, we have introduced the ideas given in the paper along with what motivated us to move into this area of research in Section 2. Section 3 explains the Literature Review of past research papers, and Section 4 explains our experimental setup for this research paper. In Section 5, we have discussed the results and their analysis, and Section 6 concludes the study.

1.1 Types of Cardiac Disease

Multiple types of heart conditions have been identified. Based on the available clinical evidence, the conditions are grouped into the following basic categories: myocardial infarction, heart failure, cardiac arrhythmias, angina pectoris, cardiomyopathy, and atrial fibrillation. Numerous aspects of cardiac disease influence either the heart's ability to function or its physical make-up.

Coronary artery disease: Reduced blood flow causes pain associated with coronary artery disease. If blood flow is cut off from the heart, it will cause the veins to deteriorate and the heart to experience discomfort during its normal systolic and diastolic contractions.

Acute myocardial infarction: In medical terms, a cardiac arrest is referred to as an acute myocardial infarction. When the pace of blood flow is altered due to the presence of fatty substances, cardiac arrest occurs, causing damage to the artery walls. If the blood vessels in your body get clogged, you risk not receiving enough oxygen, which can cause a wide range of health problems.

Chest pain (Angina): Angina is the clinical term for chest pain or discomfort. Most individuals in need of medical care require immediate intervention. If we see this kind of pain, we need to get the patients on ventilators as soon as possible. As a result of the increased strain on the blood vessel walls, inadequate blood flow might influence the blood vessels themselves. Which can lead to discomfort in the chest due to increased strain on the blood vessels. This disease induces stable angina in the peritorium. An abnormal exchange of blood between the layers of the peritoris. [2]. Changes in one's way of life and patterns of behaviour are the primary contributors to unstable angina.

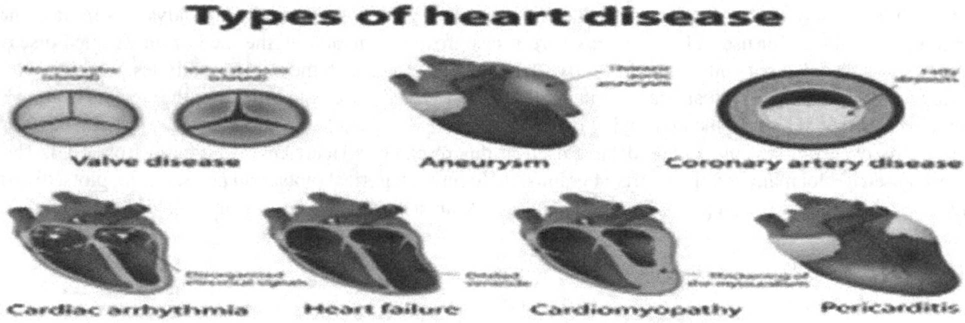

Types of heart disease

Valve disease   Aneurysm   Coronary artery disease

Cardiac arrhythmia   Heart failure   Cardiomyopathy   Pericarditis

Fig. 70.1 Types of cardiac disease

Source: Made by Author

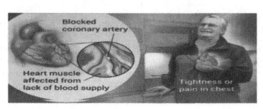

Fig. 70.2 Acute myocardial infraction

Source: Made by Author

1.2 Risk Factors of Heart Disease

Heart disease risk factors are discussed by Brijian et al. in their paper. There are a number of factors that increase the risk of developing heart disease. Age, sex, patient history, lipid profiles, smoking habits, and glucose levels are only a few of the factors that might be considered.

Family history of patients: Heart disease risk is increased when patients have a history of symptoms including chest pain and abnormal glucose levels. High blood pressure and abnormal lipid profiles are common among the obese, and these factors increase the likelihood that atherosclerotic plaques may form and worsen in the arteries over time.

High blood pressure: Zanchetti explains in his paper how the risk of heart disease is increased when blood flow is erratic.

High cholesterol: In their article, Rabindranath et al. explain that healthy lipid profile fragments and paramenters play a crucial role in cell membrane integrity and overall bodily health. When blood cholesterol levels are high, it increases the risk of cardiovascular disease. Atherosclerosis is triggered by consuming high-cholesterol foods and drinks. Lipid profiles can be split into two categories. There are two types of lipid profiles: high and low.

Smoking: Heart dysfunction is greatly increased by the presence of coagulation enzymes in the blood, which is a direct result of smoking and a major risk factor for cardiac arrest.

Diabetes mellitus: The molecular mechanisms, management recommendations, and epidemiological conditions of diabetes are described by Benjamin Leon et al. Diabetic illness develops from inefficient coordination of blood sugar levels. If diabetic individuals do not take care to keep their blood sugar, blood pressure, and cholesterol levels in check, they may develop cardiovascular disease.

2. Literature Review

Early in their paper, Richter et al. demonstrate how making clinical judgements ahead of time might help doctors and other medical staff cut down on potential dangers. Doctors need to be familiar with the medical literature, but they also need to incorporate this information into a sound decision-making process that puts their patients' interests first and inspires trust in their care. It's getting harder and harder to make sound clinical judgements. Current diagnostic and treatment modalities have a continually growing menu of possibilities. [3]. As healthcare costs continue to rise, there is an increased need to weigh value when deciding on a course of treatment. Especially since the average patient visit is getting shorter, there is often less time to make decisions. Methods such as classification analysis, accuracy evaluation, sensitivity testing, and specificity testing are used to determine the diagnostic model's efficacy. This system presents a prediction model for determining the presence or absence of heart disease and offers related guidance. The models of Random Forest, Vector Machine Support, Naive Bayes Classifier, Gradient Boosting, and Logistic Regression are evaluated against one another on the regional dataset used to accurately forecast cardiovascular disease. We have a long way to go before various diseases may be treated in individuals using current medical practises. Heart problems are particularly perilous since they are invisible to the naked eye and strike suddenly when the heart is stressed to its limit. [4]. If a patient dies as a result of subpar medical care, the hospital will be financially devastated. An effective and reasonably priced computer-based therapy and support system can be created to aid in decision-making. [5]. The healthcare sector is widely recognised as "information rich," yet it is regrettable that not all the data required to identify hidden patterns is being mined. In the medical industry, cutting-edge data mining tools are employed to make the best possible decisions. A lot of effort has been put into predicting heart disease using Machine Learning, Deep Learning, and Data Mining. Researchers employ a variety of datasets, algorithms, and approaches to better diagnose cardiovascular illness, and they report on their findings and plans. Research into the development of models for the prognosis of cardiovascular disease has been conducted on a global scale throughout the last several decades. Cardiovascular disease automated prediction and diagnosis is the most pressing medical issue in the actual world. Early detection of cardiac disease is essential for effective therapy. Researchers from all around the globe have tried a variety of methods to foresee the onset of heart disease. [6]. M.Akhil Jabbar et al.: A model fusing KNN and a genetic algorithm was suggested in the research. The dataset is from the UCI machine learning repository. However, owing to irrelevant and duplicated features in the dataset, the suggested model was not effective for primary tumours or breast cancer. The research demonstrates an improvement in accuracy when predicting cardiovascular illness, and the data suggest that the cross-over rate for the genetic algorithm is 60% KNN. [7]. Abderrahmane Ed-Daoudy et al. The focus of this research is on creating a monitoring system for data processing with the help of Spark and Cassandra frameworks.

There are three main components to the proposed system: streaming processing, data storage, and data display. The dataset was pulled from the UCI machine learning repository and has 14 characteristics and 303 entries. There are two stages to the process of incorporating a Random Forest model into an existing system; the first is an examination of a healthcare dataset used to construct a machine learning model. In the next phase, we put this model to work in the real world by making predictions with the help of the Matplotlib machine learning toolkit. This strategy will be much more effective in the future when combined with other big data technologies. [8]. Monika Gandhi et al.: The focus of this research is on creating a system to track how well data processing is going in real time, and it does so by making use of the Spark and Cassandra frameworks. There are three main components to the proposed system: streaming processing, data storage, and data display. [9]. The dataset was pulled from the UCI machine learning repository and has 14 characteristics and 303 entries. There are two stages to the process of incorporating a Random Forest model into an existing system: the first is an examination of a healthcare dataset used to construct a machine learning model. In the next phase, we put this model to work in the real world by making predictions with the help of the Matplotlib machine learning toolkit. This strategy will be much more effective in the future when combined with other big data technologies. [10] M. Nikhil Kumar et al. Decision tree, Random forest, Naive Bayes, K-Nearest Neighbour, Vector support system, and the method for the Logistic System Tree are all examples of algorithms that may be used for this purpose. [11] Naive Bayes performed well, unlike other algorithms. In order to track your heart's health, you accessed the UCI server. J48 required less time to develop than competing algorithms. Several algorithms, including the K-nearest neighbour, the Naive Bayes, and the Help vector machine, were compared by Amandeep Kaur et al. for their ability to predict cardiovascular disease. Logistic regression, gradient boosting, neural networks, and random forest were the four machine learning techniques employed by Stephen F. Weng et al. [12].

3. Experimental Setup

The following flowchart shows the Experimental setup used in this research paper proceeding. The dataset used in this research is Heart Disease dataset from UCI.

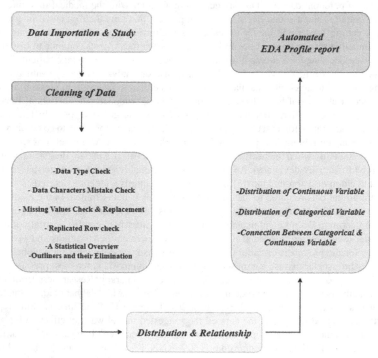

Fig. 70.3 EDA outline description

Source: Made by Author

4. Results and Analysis

1. Data Importation & Study,
2. Cleaning of Data,
3. Data Type Check,
4. Distribution and Relationship
   (a) target variable distribution,
   (b) Age variable distribution

   The average age of a patient is in their 60s. Now, let's take a brief look at some rudimentary data. The range of ages included in this sample is rather wide, from 29 years old at the youngest to 77 years old at the oldest, giving a mean age of around 54 years with a standard deviation of 9.08 years.

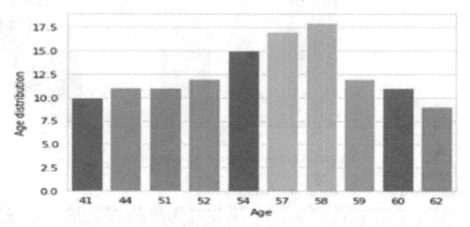

Fig. 70.4   Age distribution

Source: Image snapshot by author

   (c) Gender distribution w.r.t. target variable

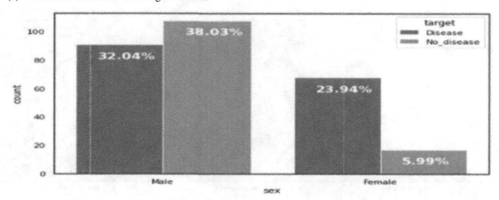

Fig. 70.5   Sex distribution according to target

Source: Image snapshot by author

   The bar chart clearly shows that males account for a larger proportion of illness patients than females.

(d) Chest pain distribution w.r.t. target variable

Angina or chest pain occurs when the heart muscle doesn't get enough oxygen-rich blood, causing pain in the arms, shoulders, neck, etc. Looking at the bar graph above, more healthy individuals have typical angina.

Chest discomfort is subjective and varies by gender, stress, and physical activity. Women and the elderly have unusual illness symptoms.

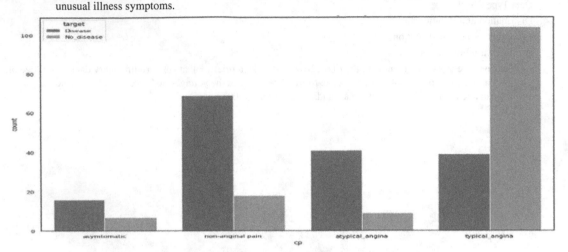

Fig. 70.6 Chest pain distribution according to target

Source: Image snapshot by author

(e) Fasting blood sugar distribution according to target Variable

Diabetic status is denoted by a fasting blood sugar (fbs) value more than 120 mg/d (True class). Specifically, we can see that the true class has a smaller total than the false class does. However, if we take a closer look, we see that there is a greater percentage of patients with heart disease who do not have diabetes. This suggests that fbs is not a reliable indicator of whether a person has heart disease or not.

(f) Slope distribution according to target variable

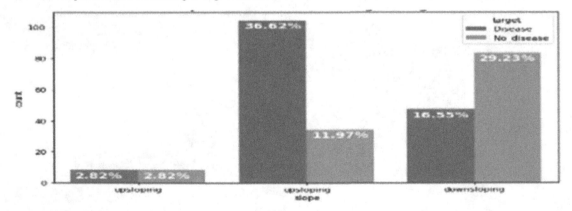

Fig. 70.7 Slope distribution according to target

Source: Made by Author

(g) Distribution plot on continuous variables

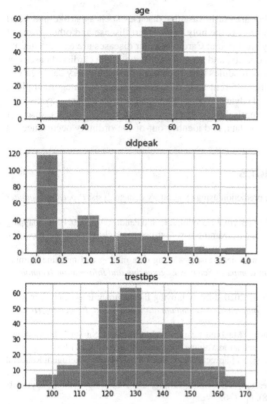

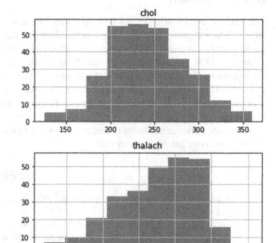

Fig. 70.8

Source: Made by Author

(h) Sns pair plot to visualize the distribution.

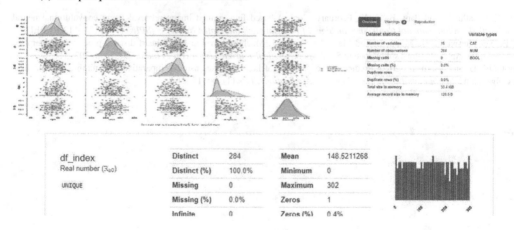

Fig. 70.9

Source: Made by Author

5. Conclusion

The leading causes of mortality and disability in the world today are cardiovascular diseases such as stroke and heart attack. When it comes to diagnosing cardiac disease, chest discomfort is the holy grail. Heart disease and other forms of cardiovascular disease (CVD) cause 17.9 million deaths annually worldwide. Cardiovascular diseases are exacerbated by a number of risk factors, including high blood pressure, diabetes, obesity, and poor dietary habits. The cardiac dataset was subjected to an exploratory analysis in this article. Python's Seaborn modules have been used for exploratory data analysis in the PANDA IDE. The heart dataset has been used to plot many different sorts of graphs, including categorical plots, grid plots, matrix plots, and distribution plots. Regression plots, and advanced plots. The heart dataset's many aspects have been analysed, visualised, and distilled into conclusions. To summarise the key aspects of the cardiac dataset, discover relationships between attributes to better comprehend patterns in the data, and identify out-of-the-ordinary occurrences in the data, analysis has been performed.

REFERENCES

1. Indrakumari, R., Poongodi, T. and Jena, S. R., 2020. Heart disease prediction using exploratory data analysis. *Procedia Computer Science*, *173*, pp. 130–139.
2. Segar, M. W., Patel, K. V., Ayers, C., Basit, M., Tang, W. W., Willett, D., Berry, J., Grodin, J. L. and Pandey, A., 2020. Phenomapping of patients with heart failure with preserved ejection fraction using machine learning-based unsupervised cluster analysis. *European journal of heart failure*, *22*(1), pp. 148–158.
3. Kumar, M. N., Koushik, K. V. S. and Deepak, K., 2018. Prediction of heart diseases using data mining and machine learning algorithms and tools. *International Journal of Scientific Research in Computer Science, Engineering and Information Technology*, *3*(3), pp. 887–898.
4. Samhitha, B. K., Priya, M. S., Sanjana, C., Mana, S. C. and Jose, J., 2020, July. Improving the accuracy in prediction of heart disease using machine learning algorithms. In *2020 International Conference on Communication and Signal Processing (ICCSP)* (pp. 1326–1330). IEEE.
5. Himanshu Sharma, M. A. Rizvi, "Prediction of Heart Disease using Machine Learning Algorithms: A Survey" ,International Journal on Recent and Innovation Trends in Computing and Com munication,Volume 5, Issue-8, pp. 99–104, 2017
6. Manjunath K., Noor Basha, Ashok Kumar P. S., Venkatesh P., Analysis and Forecasting of Heart Syndrome by Intelligent Retrieval Approach, ICTIDS-2019, Malaysia
7. Nishadi, A. T., 2019. Predicting heart diseases in logistic regression of machine learning algorithms by Python Jupyterlab. *International Journal of Advanced Research and Publications*, *3*(8), pp. 1–6.
8. Lei, Y., Yang, B., Jiang, X., Jia, F., Li, N. and Nandi, A. K., 2020. Applications of machine learning to machine fault diagnosis: A review and roadmap. *Mechanical Systems and Signal Processing*, *138*, p. 106587.
9. Jasti, V., Kumar, G. K., Kumar, M. S., Maheshwari, V., Jayagopal, P., Pant, B., Karthick, A. and Muhibbullah, M., 2022. Relevant-based feature ranking (RBFR) method for text classification based on machine learning algorithm. *Journal of Nanomaterials*, *2022*.
10. Kumar, V., Tripathi, V. and Pant, B., 2020, February. Content based fine-grained image retrieval using convolutional neural network. In *2020 7th International Conference on Signal Processing and Integrated Networks (SPIN)* (pp. 1120–1125). IEEE
11. Maini, E., Venkateswarlu, B., Maini, B. and Marwaha, D., 2021. Machine learning–based heart disease prediction system for Indian population: An exploratory study done in South India. *Medical Journal Armed Forces India*, *77*(3), pp. 302–311.
12. Ananey-Obiri, D. and Sarku, E., 2020. Predicting the presence of heart diseases using comparative data mining and machine learning algorithms. *International Journal of Computer Applications*, *176*(11), pp. 17–21.

Computer Science Engineering and Emerging Technologies (ICCS-2022) – Prof (Dr.) Rajeev Sobti et al. (eds)
© 2024 Taylor & Francis Group, London, ISBN 978-1-032-52199-2

Chapter **71**

Recommending Future Collaborations Using Feature Selection Technique for Scholarly Network

Shilpa Verma[1], Sandeep Harit[2], Rajesh Bhatia[3]
Department of Computer Science & Engg.,
Punjab Engineering College, Chandigarh

Abstract: Academic networks have significant difficulties in developing techniques to predict associations as a result of the rapid expansion of diversity in the research community. There have been more advancements of several prediction algorithms based on machine learning and deep learning which use semantic and topological data. However, the requirement to utilize content-based data severely limits the usefulness of existing works. On the other hand, prediction would help propose better researchers to respond to the question of "With Whom I should collaborate?". Our primary focus is to understand the relative effectiveness of network proximity measures adapted from techniques like node based topological similarity and path based topological similarity. As a result, it minimizes the damage posed by possible delays in future collaborations. Beyond the discussion of content-based feature approaches in this study, we analysed a supervised machine learning model to efficiently automate the process of predicting researcher collaboration based on a wide range of other features. The results have been evaluated using various standard metrics like accuracy, precision, recall, AUC-roc curves.

Keywords: Recommending authors, Random forest, Neo4j, Machine learning

1. Introduction

Link prediction is a way to estimate how likely a relationship is to form in the future, or whether it should already be in our graph but is missing due to incomplete data. Since networks are dynamic and can fairly grow quickly, being able to predict links that will soon be added has broad applicability, from product recommendations to drug re-targeting and even inferring criminal relationships. A network enables the computation of a variety of metrics to evaluate certain aspects of the network topology. Some social network measures that were initially developed for measuring connections are now widely used in a variety of other domains. Connected features from graphs are often used to improve link prediction using basic graph features as well as features extracted from centrality and certain algorithms. Network structure alone may contain enough latent information to detect node proximity/similarity and outperform more direct measures. There can be a large number of use cases of this in the academia as well. We will be focusing on co-authorship network connections. For example, there are many reasons, pertaining to the network, why two scientists/authors who have never written a paper together will do so in the next few years: for example, they may happen to become geographically close if one of them changes institutions. Such collaborations are hard to predict but are hinted at the topology of the network.

Co-authorship networks can be basically built given a corpus of literature, with nodes denoting researchers and interconnections denoting co-authorships. Topological properties in co-authorship networks, such as Common Neighbors,

---

[1]shilpa@pec.edu.in, [2]sandeepharit@pec.edu.in, [3]rbhatia@pec.edu.in

DOI: 10.1201/9781003405580-71

clustering, degree etc. provide a good method for predicting the future co-authorship interactions between authors of the network. In other words, if we could reasonably estimate the formation of fresh interconnections between two existing authors in co-authorship networks, these new links might be credible ideas for future research collaborations. In this paper, we combined the fundamental topological features with textual feature from co-authorship networks, and supervised model is used to determine the various topological features for determining co-author relationships. We tested our method on co-authorship networks in the computer science domain, and the result showed that co-author relationships depend on the combination of topological and textual formations of the network. Furthermore, supervised learning methods can be used to take advantage of this dependence when predicting the future about co-author relationships.

In our model, we consider both textual information: such as an author's current topic of interest in which the author is an expert and associated structural information from neighbours. As a result, we investigated a link prediction model for authors of the academic network, which offers a different approach on comprehending and researching scholarly relationships. The paper's original contributions are: (i) In this article, we examine a machine learning technique for obtaining textual and structural data from academic metadata and adding network science to it. (ii) In a heterogeneous network with nodes and relationships between them, we highlight the importance of certain features for forthcoming collaboration. (iii) We perform and present the evaluation results based on the AUC-ROC curve using actual academic data.

The remainder of the paper is laid out as follows. The related work of the scholarly data and features involved in large scholarly networks along with the link prediction fundamentals are summarised in Section 2. Section 3 describes the proposed methodology of system incorporating network features, textual feature and machine learning classifier. Section 4 discusses data set used, experimental setup and performance evaluation methods. Results are discussed in section 5 followed by conclusion.

2. Related work

2.1 Scholarly Data and Features for Scholarly Network

Managing and interpreting scholarly knowledge has become difficult with the quick growth of digital publishing. The rapidly growing field of scholarly data, which includes information on millions of authors, papers, institutions, as well as scholarly graphs and scholarly knowledge graphs, has been given the name "scholarly data". papers such as [1] and [2] investigates current trends, challenges and latest research areas in the domain of scholarly data. Some of the basic scholarly digital libraries such as Arnetminer[3], CiteSeerX[4], DBLP[5] are some of the free to access scholarly data platforms which provides wide variety of scholarly metadata in structured as well as unstructured formats. Analyzing the statistical characteristics of scholarly networks, such as network scope, number of articles published per scholar, average number of co-authors per researcher, and average number of authors per publication, has been the focus of numerous research areas. Additionally, some academics have investigated into the evolution of academic social networks as well. Authors in [6] have addressed the issue of measuring collaboration strength in co-authorship networks by defining a new tieness metric. A combined scientometric oriented analysis of scholarly network is presented in [7] which investigates the network of individuals by using bibliographic data of all articles published. Scholarly networks have a number of structural features that can use to evaluate how strongly related they are. Some of these features include Triangle and Clustering Coefficients, Preferential Attachment, Total Neighbors, Label Propagation, and Louvain Algorithms for Community Detection. These measures operate on a pair of nodes and gives some results based on some algorithms. These can either produce outcomes on their own or can be used as input to a machine learning model that will predict binary classes. In [8] and [9], authors explored the scientific productivity and level of collaboration using network science approach.

2.2 Link Prediction and Machine Learning Models

In network science, Link prediction is the problem which is applied to predict missing links among the nodes. For example, in [10] links are predicted for wikipedia and in [11] links are predicted for connections based on social media data. Authors in [12] is one of the core surveys on link prediction state-of-the-art methods. Link Prediction problem has stated as the collaborator recommendation problem in a number of studies such as [13] and [14]. For example, [15] have used coauthorship statistics and author profiles, academic information from specific institution to recommend and predict multidisciplinary connections. In [16], authors have used Random forest classifier to predict paper acceptance by combining different types of features from authors and their affiliations. [17] discusses and compares the decision trees, neural network, statistical and clustering algorithms. It discusses trade-off between various parameters and conditions used data mining products for their decision support systems. A weighted network is constructed in [18] and random classifier is used to determine the relative merit of predictors and generated recommendations for future collaborations. Authors in [19] predicted author collaborations using machine learning models based on network features.

3. The proposed Approach

In this study, we work with a heterogeneous network made up of several sorts of nodes (like venues, study fields, authors, and articles) and linkages (like co-authors, cites, written by, and belongs to). By examining existing collaborations and employing a diversity of link prediction approaches in a heterogeneous network, we aim to be able to predict future collaborations. We have performed feature selection, feature engineering and classification. A few pre-modeling steps that can enhance the performance of the model have also been shown in flow diagram Fig. 71.1.

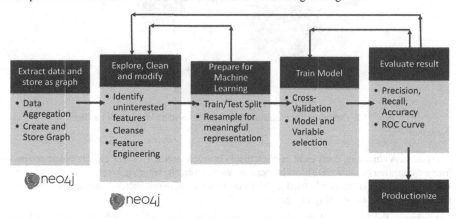

Fig. 71.1 Machine learning workflow

Source: Made by Author

3.1 Feature Selection

These features are fed incrementally into the model and the results are noted down. The introduction of node features makes the feature set a hybrid model containing both node and edge features. The analysis of co-authorship connections is facilitated by the use of the following well-known metrics.

Keywords: Similarity scores based on TF-IDF model for field of studies for authors. (Taken 10 per author at a time).

Common Neighbors: The idea that two strangers who have a common friend might be connected by that friend is captured by the common-neighbor predictor. This introduction seems like a process similar in everyday life and has the effect of "closing a triangle" in the graph. In collaboration network, smaller research groups or communities are detected by disjoint groupings of connected nodes in the network, according to the definition. This measurement helps us understand the size and density of the network's communities.

$$CN_{xy} = |\Gamma(x) \cap \Gamma(y)| \tag{1}$$

where x and y are author nodes and $\Gamma(x)$ is the set of nodes adjacent to x and $\Gamma(y)$ is the set of nodes adjacent to y. A value of 0 indicates two nodes are not close, while greater values indicate two nodes are closer.

Preferential Attachment: It multiplies the number of co-authors, each author has to generate a score for each pair of collaborators. It is logical that authors choose to work with someone who has already co-authored variety of works.

$$PA_{xy} = |\Gamma(x) * \Gamma(y)| \tag{2}$$

where x and y are author nodes and $\Gamma(x)$ is the set of nodes adjacent to x and $\Gamma(y)$ is the set of nodes adjacent to y. A value of 0 indicates two nodes are not close, while greater values indicate two nodes are closer.

Triangle and Clustering Coefficients: A community detection graph approach called triangle counting is used to count the number of triangles that pass through each node in the graph. A triangle is composed of three nodes, each of which is

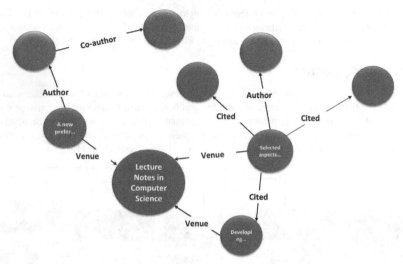

Fig. 71.2 Instance of co-author, Venue-article and article-author relations

Source: Made by Author

connected to the others. A clustering coefficient in graph theory is a measurement of how closely connected nodes in a graph tend to be. Triangle counting became well-liked in social network research, where it is employed to find communities and evaluate their cohesiveness. It is frequently used in the computation of network indices, such as the clustering coefficient, and can also be used to assess the stability of a graph.

The correlation between the feature and the class label serves as the essential principle of supervised feature selection, which is frequently focused on classification problems. Importance measurements can be used to assess the significance of the attributes. The supervised model seeks to identify the best feature subset $S(|S| = k)$ that maximises classification accuracy for a given data set $A = (X, C)$, with a feature set $X = x_1, x_2, ..., x_n$ and class label C. The ensemble of base classifiers trained on various feature spaces obtained by selecting features is known as ensemble feature selection. The efficiency of the obvious classifiers can be improved by using this approach, which can also increase the stability of feature selection. Given that it trains base classifiers on many feature subsets, the random forest [20] method in this study could be viewed as an ensemble feature selection method.

3.2 Machine Learning Classifier

Using the supervised learning method, a granular analysis is carried out in this part to identify feasible interpretations for the emergence of a relation between two authors. When raw data is provided, the results of supervised learning are derived using the previously learnt data. Another method to describe supervised learning is by an output variable that tracks its progress. A non-linear ensemble learning technique called random forest aggregates the classification results of various de-correlated decision trees that have been gathered into a "forest" to get a classification result. Every independent attribute's GINI importance is calculated for each node in the scientific network. As a result, the primary independent variable may be found by comparing the average information gain obtained by each independent variable. Additionally, it is the most adaptable algorithm where a forest is supposed to be stronger the more trees it has. On randomly chosen data samples, random forests generate decision trees, obtain predictions from each tree, and vote for the best option. Additionally, it provides a relatively accurate indicator of the feature's relevance.

Using randomly chosen data samples, random forests generate K decision trees, obtain predictions from each tree, and then vote on the best answer. An ideal division property of the present node is taken into account in accordance with the GINI index to produce a single decision tree. It should be highlighted that a small number of decision trees have a limited capacity for classification, and that only a large amount of decision trees can yield reliable classification outcomes. This method ensures unpredictability as each tree grows even without pruning and performs well on large datasets. By selecting

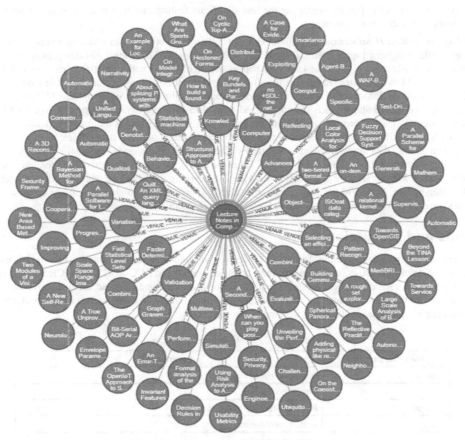

Fig. 71.3   Instance of venue-article relations

Source: Made by Author

the most appropriate number of trees using the sample data and the random forest algorithm, the suggested technique used the random forest algorithm for feature importance selection.

4. Evaluation method, Data and Experimental Results

In this section, several performance metrics, including precision, recall, and F1-score, are used to compare and quantify the classification performance of the RF. In classification applications, let positive represent the preferred class and negative represent other classes; for each class, four basic measures, including true positives (TP), false positives (FP), true negatives (TN), and false negatives (FN), can be formulated.

The **precision** of an interested class can be used to quantify the correct classification results of this class as:

Precision = TP/(TP + FP)

High precision correlates to a low rate of false positives for our model.

Recall: Recall is used to calculate the frequency of all false conditions in the class and represents as: Recall= TP/(TP+FN)

It correlates to the sensitivity of the classifier.

AUC-ROC: ROC curve is used to plot TPR and FPR at several classification thresholds and AUC represents the 2-Dimentional area under the ROC curve which scales from 0 to 1. We also calculated the feature's importance, which is estimated by the relevant classifier. By neglecting the less significant features, such an evaluation of feature importance results in fine-tuning of the entire system.

Data and Implementation Details In our algorithm, Aminer Citation Dataset is used in which two versions v10 and v11 are freely available containing papers from DBLP, ACM, MAG sources. v10 contains 3,079,007 papers and 25,166,994 citation relationships whereas v11 contains 4,107,340 papers and 36,624,464 citation relationships as shown in Table 1. In implementation, v11 is used extracting details from two different venues such as Lecture Notes in Computer Science and IEEE Transactions on Information Theory. Our filtered graph contains 63800 Author nodes, 146804 Article nodes and 120775 coauthor relationships which are constructed from dataset using Cypher queries. *Neo4j*, Graph database management system, is used to provide structure to the network in which *Cypher* is the querying language for Graph DBMS. Neo4j has a flexible structure determined by recorded associations between data entries, as opposed to typical databases, which arrange data in rows, columns, and tables. Each data record, or node, in Neo4j holds direct pointers to all the other nodes to which it is connected. Utilizing Cypher for Neo4j, all graphs (co-author, citation, etc.) are created. Additionally, Spark's Mllib is used for constructing our Machine Learning models along with the *py2neo* library to work with neo4j within python. Azure VM has been used to run the Neo4j instances remotely. A co-author network and venue-wise network generated from database are shown in Figs. 2 and 3, respectively.

5. Results and Discussion

The outcomes for each incrementally added feature are presented (with and without field of study). Our models are assessed using a variety of defined measures, including accuracy, precision, recall, and AUC-ROC curves. Clearly, the importance and correlations of all scholarly network feature variables can be quantified and analysed using the proposed RF-based method. The plots for feature importance are also shown for each model to see how well each feature is performing in that particular model giving us a better idea of the working of our models.

Table 71.1 Dataset attribute description

Metadata Attribute	Description
Paper ID	Unique identifier assigned to the publication
Paper Title	Title of publication
Field of Study	Areas of research of the publication
Author ID	Unique identifier assigned to author
Author Name	Name of the author
Venue ID	Unique identifier assigned to each Venue
Venue Name	Name of the Venue where papers are published

Source: Made by Author

RQ1: How to manage the large class imbalance?

Link prediction problems attempt to predict the future formation of interconnections. Our data set is preferable for this purpose because the articles contain dates that can be used to segment our data and 2006 appears to be a favorable year so far for splitting. Approximately 60% of the papers were published prior to 2006, with the remaining 40% published during or after 2006 as shown in Fig. 71.4. This is a reasonably balanced data split for our training and testing. Positive examples will be nodes with Co-author relationships between them, but we will also need to create some negative examples. The majority of real-world networks are sparse, with clusters of relationships, and this graph is no exception. The number of examples where two nodes do not have a relationship seems to be much greater than the number of examples in which they do. Precisely, it is very intuitive that negative examples will be as follow:

$$\text{No. of negative examples} = (\text{No. of nodes})^2 - (No. of relationships) - (No. of nodes) \tag{3}$$

This negative example issue must be addressed in our training and test data sets. One of these approaches is to generate negative examples by discovering nodes in our neighbourhood to which are not currently connected. We constructed negative examples by identifying pairs of nodes that are between two and three hops apart, excluding pairs that already have an association and down sample those node pairs to attain an equal number of positive and negative examples. This solves the problem of encountering a large number of negative examples in real-world graphs.

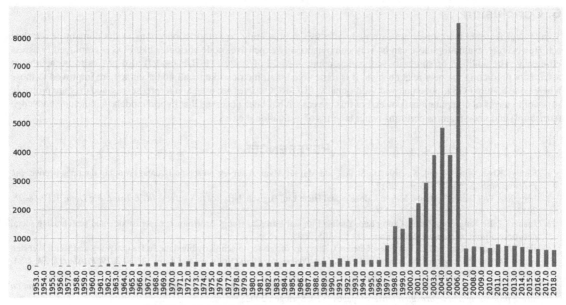

Fig. 71.4   Distribution of Papers chosen in Aminer V11 data set

Source: Made by Author

RQ2: What are the most important features to find collaboration patterns?

Figure 71.5 illustrates the importance score for each attribute. Common authors, FoS, number of triangles and clustering coefficient receive scores of 0.44, 0.33, and 0.09 and 0.05 respectively in the academic domain, ranking them the most significant variables. Combining two contextual factors textual and topological, creates the preferences parameter for author-topic interactions, disjoint set of authors and clustering. In order to evaluate the effectiveness of the system, we examine if the additional information improved its performance. We evaluated whether employing randomization in tree selection will improve predictive abilities when performing the specific recommendation task using contextual information.

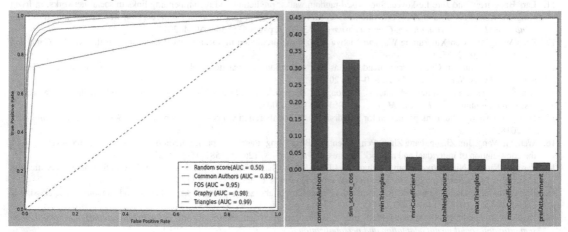

Fig. 71.5   (a) AUC for model trained with content, common authors, graphy features and maxTriangle (b) Feature importance

Source: Made by Author

6. Conclusion

Topological features themselves are extremely effective at predicting co-author connections in the domain of our data set. However, as evaluating these can be very computationally expensive, node attributes like FOS is employed to assess efficiency. The addition of similarity scores depending on field of study (TF-IDF model) also proves to be helpful in accurately predicting the new relationships. It is to be noted that, metrics like recall and accuracy are improved to those where node feature FOS is not employed. Additionally, AUC-ROC curves are used to interpret scores, and they are probably superior in terms of computational power. For this use case, it has been observed that hybrid models that include both edge (structural) and node features performs better in terms of evaluation metrics.

REFERENCES

1. Samiya Khan, Xiufeng Liu, Kashish Ara Shakil, and Mansaf Alam. A survey on scholarly data: From big data perspective. *Inf. Process. Manag.*, 53(4): 923–944, 2017.
2. Feng Xia, Wei Wang, Teshome Megersa Bekele, and Huan Liu. Big scholarly data: A survey. *IEEE Trans. Big Data*, 3(1): 18–35, 2017.
3. Juanzi Li, Jie Tang, Jing Zhang, Qiong Luo, Yunhao Liu, and MingCai Hong. Arnetminer: expertise oriented search using social networks. *Frontiers Comput. Sci. China*, 2(1): 94–105, 2008.
4. Jian Wu, Kunho Kim, and C. Lee Giles. Citeseerx: 20 years of service to scholarly big data. In Huajin Wang and Keith Webster, editors, *Proceedings of the Conference on Artificial Intelligence for Data Discovery and Reuse, AIDR 2019, Pittsburgh, PA, USA, May 13-15, 2019*, pages 1: 1–1: 4. ACM, 2019.
5. Michael Ley. The dblp computer science bibliography: Evolution, research issues, perspectives. In *International symposium on string processing and information retrieval*, pages 1–10. Springer, 2002.
6. Michele A. Brand~ao and Mirella M. Moro. The strength of co-authorship ties through different topological properties. *J. Braz. Comput. Soc.*, 23(1): 5: 1–5:11, 2017.
7. Haiyan Hou, Hildrun Kretschmer, and Zeyuan Liu. The structure of scientific collaboration networks in scientometrics. *Scientometrics*, 75(2): 189–202, 2008.
8. Mark EJ Newman. The structure of scientific collaboration networks. *Proceedings of the national academy of sciences*, 98(2): 404–409, 2001.
9. Massimo Franceschet. Collaboration in computer science: A network science approach. *J. Assoc. Inf. Sci. Technol.*, 62(10): 1992–2012, 2011.
10. Sisay Fissaha Adafre and Maarten de Rijke. Discovering missing links in wikipedia. In Jafar Adibi, Marko Grobelnik, Dunja Mladenic, and Patrick Pantel, editors, *Proceedings of the 3rd international workshop on Link discovery, LinkKDD 2005, Chicago, Illinois, USA, August 21–25, 2005*, pages 90–97. ACM, 2005.
11. Lars Backstrom and Jure Leskovec. Supervised random walks: predicting and recommending links in social networks. In Irwin King, Wolfgang Nejdl, and Hang Li, editors, *Proceedings of the Forth International Conference on Web Search and Web Data Mining, WSDM 2011, Hong Kong, China, February 9–12, 2011*, pages 635–644. ACM, 2011.
12. Peng Wang, Baowen Xu, Yurong Wu, and Xiaoyu Zhou. Link prediction in social networks: the state-of-the-art. *Sci. China Inf. Sci.*, 58(1): 1–38, 2015.
13. Xin Li and Hsinchun Chen. Recommendation as link prediction in bipartite graphs: A graph kernel-based machine learning approach. *Decis. Support Syst.*, 54(2): 880–890, 2013.
14. Xiaoming Liu, Johan Bollen, Michael L. Nelson, and Herbert Van de Sompel. Co-authorship networks in the digital library research community. *Inf. Process. Manag.*, 41(6): 1462–1480, 2005.
15. Haeran Cho and Yi Yu. Link prediction for interdisciplinary collaboration via co-authorship network. *Soc. Netw. Anal. Min.*, 8(1): 25, 2018.
16. Wenyan Wang, Jun Zhang, Fang Zhou, Peng Chen, and Bing Wang. Paper acceptance prediction at the institutional level based on the combination of individual and network features. *Scientometrics*, 126(2): 1581–1597, 2021.
17. Pardeep Kumar, Nitin, Vivek Kumar Sehgal, and Durg Singh Chauhan. A benchmark to select data mining based classification algorithms for business intelligence and decision support systems. *CoRR*, abs/1210.3139, 2012.
18. Raf Guns and Ronald Rousseau. Recommending research collaborations using link prediction and random forest classifiers. *Scientometrics*, 101(2): 1461–1473, 2014.
19. Ilya Makarov and Olga Gerasimova. Predicting collaborations in co-authorship network. In *2019 14th international workshop on semantic and social media adaptation and personalization (SMAP)*, pages 1–6. IEEE, 2019.
20. Leo Breiman. Random forests. *Mach. Learn.*, 45(1): 5–32, 2001.

Computer Science Engineering and Emerging Technologies (ICCS-2022) – Prof (Dr.) Rajeev Sobti et al. (eds)
© 2024 Taylor & Francis Group, London, ISBN 978-1-032-52199-2

Chapter

72

Applications of SPT (Squeeze Pack and Transfer) and Other Lossless Compression Algorithms in IoT: A Comparative Study

Shiv Preet[1]

Senior IT Faculty, iNurture Education Solutions

Chirag Sharma[2]

Associate Professor, Lovely Professional University, Jalandhar - Delhi,
Grand Trunk Rd, Phagwara, Punjab

Abstract: Data compression is the panacea for the clogging network. It helps in the optimum productivity of wireless and mobile networks. Bandwidth to transfer data is usually limited, so an overflow of data at one point can lead to data loss on the other point if the recipient point's speed is slow compared to the sender point. IoT devices are booming in the modern era, and their applications will soon increase. IoT devices consume only a tiny chunk of data, but the exponential growth of these devices poses a problem of network congestion on wireless networks. Compression helps in improving the data transfer rate along with its accuracy. This review paper compares popular lossless algorithms and their efficacy in transferring massive datasets.

Keywords: Lossless compression algorithms, SPT algorithm, Binary keys, Compression ratio, Lossy compression algorithms, Huffman coding, Run length encoding, Limpel-Ziv-Welch algorithm, IoT

1. Introduction

Information technology is the driving force in the current world. Everyone connects to the internet to share information or resources through text or multimedia. IT (Information Technology) is not only helping the organisms used on the earth but also is an evolving technique for interplanetary communication [1]. The data transfer rate in the wireless networks is much lower than the data generation, even for the current 4G or upcoming 5G technologies. Data overflow at the time of the data creation results in data loss at the time of data transfer. The following mathematical equations explain it with clarity [2].

$$XX = \{x|x \text{ } iis \text{ } a \text{ } set \text{ } ooo \text{ } elements \text{ } created \text{ } while \text{ } generatiing \text{ } data, \text{ } also \text{ } 0 \leq Y \leq XX\}.$$

$$Y = \{y|y \text{ } iis \text{ } the \text{ } set \text{ } ooo \text{ } elements \text{ } whiich \text{ } are \text{ } used \text{ } iin \text{ } the \text{ } data \text{ } transooer, \text{ } also \text{ } XX \geq Y \geq 0\}.$$

Here $0 \leq Y \leq X$. It specifies that Y is the set of elements used in data transfer and is always smaller than the set X created at the time of data generation. IoT devices and applications are growing by leaps and bounds in the modern world. Though IoT device uses a tiny chunk of data for network communication, the number of IoT devices and their data transactions coalesced into a massive disjoint dataset on its own. Compression technology is the savior for these tiny transactions so they can use existing network bandwidth optimally. There are two broad categories of compression algorithms, lossless and lossy. Lossless compression algorithms are the only solution for sensitive information where even a tiny loss could have disastrous consequences [3]. Lossy compression algorithms are helpful where a little data loss does not matter to the user.

[1]saishivam@gmail.com, [2]chiragsharma1510@gmail.com

DOI: 10.1201/9781003405580-72

Images and videos codecs come in this category. This paper is divided into three subsections. Lossless compression and its methodology are introduced in the first section. The second section describes popular compression technologies, including the SPT algorithm. A final section provides the efficacies of various lossless algorithms in conclusion.

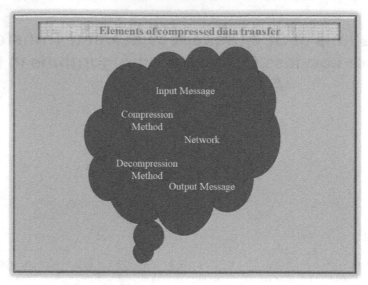

Fig. 72.1 Elements of compressed data transfer

1.1 Methodology

In any compressed data transfer, there are five elements as shown in Figure 1, input message, which is for the receiver; compression method which compresses that message, the network to transfer that message, the decompression method to decompress that message; and finally, the output message to the receiver [4] [5]. In a real-world scenario, compression takes more time than decompression. In general, if CT is the time taken for compressing a file and DCT is the time taken for decompressing a file, then CT is always greater than DCT. *In general* $0 < DCT < CT\ or\ CT >$

$DCT > 0$. This paper discusses some popular lossless compressions and their relative merits and demerits.

1.2 Run Length Encoding

Run Length Encoding is a lossless compression algorithm that converts long lengths of symbols into smaller data values. It helps in reducing the space required to store data files. RLE can be understood with a simple mathematical example in which a set DD is used, which contains some numeric symbols [6].

$$DD = \{1,1,1,1,1,1,1,1,1,1,3,3,3,3,3,3,3,3,3,3,5,5,5,5,5,5,5,7,7,7,7,7\}$$

Where DD is a set of some repeated numeric symbols, this set consumes thirty-one bytes (1 byte for each character). RLE compresses it so that DD consumes only eight bytes after compression. Four bytes are used for storing unique four characters, and four additional bytes store the number of occurrences of each character [7].

$$RLE = \{\{1,10\}, \{3,9\}, \{5,7\}, \{7,5\}.\}$$

Figures 72.2 and 72.3 describe the compression comparison of the RLE compression algorithm used on the DD symbol Set. It is evident that with the help of the RLE compression algorithm, there is a saving in the storage of 23 bytes (one byte is consumed for storing one character). Table 72.1 gives an in-depth review of the RLE compression algorithm on the DD symbol set. DD symbol set has a storage requirement of 31 bytes in its uncompressed form, while after applying the RLE compression algorithm, its storage requirement is reduced to eight bytes only [8].

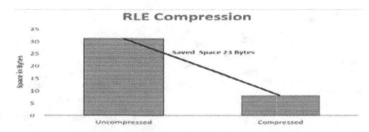

Fig. 72.2   Comparison of RLE Compression with the uncompressed dataset

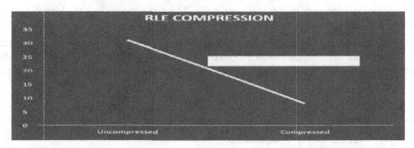

Fig. 72.3   Memory requirement reduction with RLE compression algorithm

Table 72.1   RLE compression test matrices

Uncompressed data for DD symbol set (in bytes)	Compressed data for DD symbol set (in bytes)	Saved space (in bytes)	Saved Space %	Compression factor
31	8	23	287.5	3.875

1.3 Huffman Coding

Huffman coding is one of the most popular lossless data compression algorithms. It assigns variable length codes to different symbols based on their occurrence. Huffman coding is understandable with a simple example of a data file that contains text, "this text is an example data file is used to demonstrate Huffman coding." First of all, the frequency of each character is measured. The frequency of each character corresponds to the number of times that character is repeated in a given data file [9].

Table 72.2   Frequency chart for Huffman Coding (abridged chart)

S. No.	Character	Frequency	Code Assigned	Code Length	Total bits consumed byeach symbol
1	Space (" ")	12	0	1	12
2	E	7	100	3	21
3	T	7	101	3	21
.	.	.	.	.	.
18	P	1	1111111101	10	10
19	R	1	1111111111	10	10

Table 72.2 describes frequency charts of Huffman coding. It is evident that a space character has the highest frequency, and its code is 0, while characters having the least frequency count got lengthy codes. Huffman coding achieves the balance between long and small codes with the help of frequency count [10].

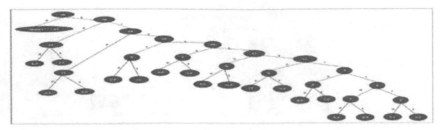

Fig. 72.4 Huffman coding for assigning codes to symbols

Figure 72.4 describes the Huffman code tree. It is evident in Fig. 72.4 that symbols with the highest frequency count tend to be near the root node, while symbols with the least frequency count are farthest from the root node [11].

Table 3 describes Huffman's coding efficiency for the example data file. The original uncompressed file version consumes 568, whereas the compressed data file consumes 326 and saves 242 bits. Figure 72.5 describes how Huffman coding saved the storage space using codes instead of actual symbols. There is a visible reduction in the storage requirement for 242 bits [12].

Table 72.3 Huffman coding algorithm efficiency

Original data inbits	Compresseddata in bits	Reduction instorage requirement	Compression %	Compressionfactor	Compression ratio
568	326	242	43	1.74	284:163

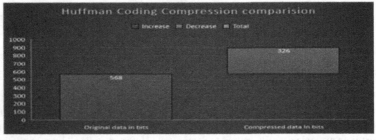

Fig. 72.5 Comparison of uncompressed and compressed data using Huffman coding

1.4 Delta Encoding

Delta encoding is a lossless compression technique that does not store the whole data of a file but only stores the difference in the sequence. It keeps the initial value of a file, and later on, the only difference of the data value concerning the initial value is stored. This type of encoding is used to encode signal files. This technique is used in modern televisions and set-top boxes to upscale the video quality of data from SD to HD or 4K or even 8K.

Figure 72.6 depicts the use of delta encoding on an audio file segment. The segment is digitized to 8 bits, and its sampling rate varies between –200 to +128. The file segment on the left side is without any encoding. On the right side, delta encoding has lowered the amplitude of the file segment without reducing its quality.

Table 72.4 shows the functioning of data encoding. The first-row original data file shows the actual sampling rate. In the third row, data is encoded by using only the difference between the initial value and the preceding data samples. 25 is the initial value in the original file, as shown in the first row of the table. All other preceding values are differences from the original initial value and following values (10 depicts 35 while -10 depicts 15 and so on). This way, the Whole data file can be reconstructed from the compressed file using the Delta encoding technique. It is evident from the heights of the bars of data-encoded sample rates in Fig. 72.6 that they utilize much less space than the original sample rates in the data files.

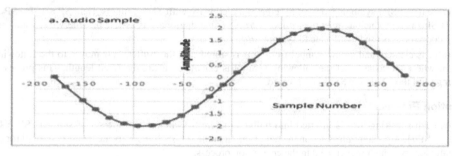

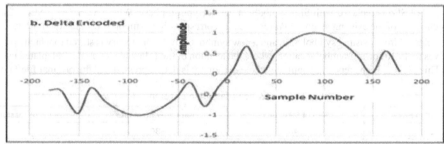

Fig. 72.6 Use of Delta Encoding [15]

Table 72.4 Delta encoding with example data [13]

Original data	25	35	15	20	30	30	45	...
	←————————————— Delta Encoding (Δ) —————————————→							
Delta encoding	25	10	-10	-5	5	5	20	...

1.5 LZW Algorithm

LZW or Lempel-Ziv-Welch algorithm is a lossless algorithm that uses the dictionary of codes to replace recurring patterns of strings. The LZW algorithm has a table of 4096 codes used for compressing the file. The LZW algorithm has certain mathematical assumptions, making it one of the best lossless algorithms.

Assumption 1: Source file SF represents arrays of strings α, which belong to an infinite set of symbols. SF $= \{\alpha_0, \alpha_1, \alpha_2, \alpha_3, ..., \alpha_\infty\}$ where $\alpha_0, \alpha_1, \alpha_2, \alpha_3, ..., \alpha_\infty$ are symbols of source file SF.

Assumption 2: A substring SL is a subset of symbols from file SF and is defined as SL (a, b), where a is the starting index of the symbol and b is the last index. For SL, $a \leq b$ or, in other words, for a finite substring SL (a, b), $0 \leq a \leq b$.

Assumption 3: DL is the distance between a and b for substring SL (a, b) and calculated by calculating the difference between b and a. $D = b - a$, also known as length L of substring SL (a, b).

Assumption 4: Each SL substring is of fixed length, and each SL substring is converted into fixed cipher code SP. Fixed cipher code length LSP of cipher code SP calculated using the following formula [14].

$LSP = 1 + [log\ log\ (n - SL)] + [log\ log\ SL]$. Here n is the size of the Buffer in the algorithm for encrypting the substring SL.

1.6 Encryption Process

1. Initially, each substring SLα is inserted into buffer b where SLα belongs to the set of symbols SL $= \{SL_1, SL_2, SL_3, ..., SL\alpha\}$. A pointer *ptr set on the next symbol in the set SL. It helps in locating the next symbol for encryption.

2. Already assigned SPα symbols from set SP creates a dictionary with SLα symbols. Here SP = {SP$_1$, SP$_2$, SP$_3$, ..., SPα}. If SLα is reproducible, then the symbol SPα from that dictionary is assigned. Otherwise, a new string from symbol code space is used to allocate to symbol SPα.

3. Old Buffer is cleared, and a new symbol from *ptr is stored into the Buffer. *ptr moves to the following symbol location, where the location of the following symbol is calculated using the fixed length. This process keeps on repeating until the whole file SF is compressed.

1.7 Decryption Process

1. Initially, each substring SPα is inserted into buffer b where SPα belongs to the set of symbols SP = {SP$_1$, SP$_2$, SP$_3$, ..., SPα}. A pointer *ptr is set on the next symbol in the set SP. It helps locate the next symbol for decryption for the dictionary, which was created in the encryption process.

2. Every symbol SPα is replaced with SLα symbols in the decryption phase. Where SL = {SL$_1$, SL$_2$, SL$_3$, ..., SL$_\alpha$}. Each occurrence of the existing symbol SPα replaced its corresponding symbol SLα in the dictionary.

3. Buffer is cleared from existing symbol SPα, and a new symbol from the dictionary is stored to which *ptr is pointing. *ptr moves to the following symbol location, where the location of the following symbol is calculated using the fixed length. This process keeps repeating until the whole dictionary is decompressed and the original file SF is restored.

Table 72.5   LZW compression on example data

Size of SF in bits	Size of SP in bits	Space Saving in bits	Compression %
1120	240	880	78.57

Table 72.5 describes LZW compression on SF data files. This file contains 1120 bits in its uncompressed form, and the algorithm compresses this file into 240 bits. It shows a space-saving of 880 bits and a compression percentage of 78.57 percent [15].

Figures 72.7 and 72.8 describe how LZW compression has reduced the space required to store SF data files. Figure 72.7 illustrates that LZW compression can achieve a compression ratio of 78.57 percent, while Fig. 72.8 describes the reduction in the space required to store SF data files. The LZW algorithm has shown a saving of 880 bits with the help of a declining slope between the original SF file and its compressed version.

Fig. 72.7   LZW algorithm compression percentage

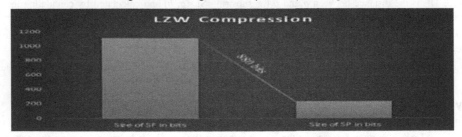

Fig. 72.8   LZW algorithm saving of space in bits

2. Squeeze Pack and Transfer Algorithm (SPT)

SPT algorithm is a lossless compression algorithm that uses binary values instead of standard regular string patterns. It works on the basic principle that computers understand only machine language. Any file stored in it will always get converted into binary codes before processing. SPT algorithm finds binary patterns and provides codes to them [16].

2.1 Compression Process

The compression and decompression process is relatively simple in the SPT algorithm. In the compression process, binary patterns are extracted from the source file, and codes are assigned to those binary patterns.

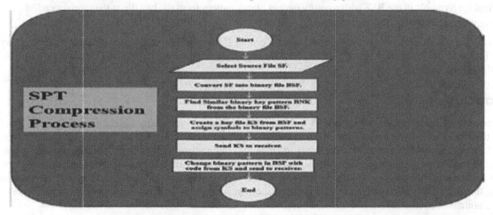

Fig. 72.9 SPT Compression process

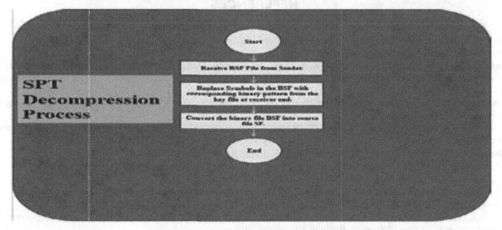

Fig. 72.10 SPT Decompression process

Figures 72.9 and 72.10 describe the compression and decompression process in SPT algorithm.

Steps:

1. Select the source file SF to transfer to the receiver and convert Source File SF into binary file BSF.
2. Find a Similar binary key pattern BNK from the binary file BSF.
3. Create a key file KS by storing regular binary patterns from binary file BSF and assigning codes to them.
4. Send key file KS to the receiver.

5. Replace every occurrence of binary pattern in the BSF with the corresponding code in the key file
6. Send BSF to the receiver.

2.2 Decompression Process

In the decompression process as shown in Figure 10, the key file at the receiver end replaces all codes in the compressed file with the binary pattern to convert it back to the source file [17].

Steps:

1. Receive BSF File from Sender.
2. Replace Symbols in the BSF with a corresponding binary pattern from the key file at the receiver end.
3. Convert the binary file BSF into the source file SF.

SPT algorithm has the potency to compress all kinds of formats if they are convertible into binary files. SPT algorithm is relatively new in the IT industry, but it promises a lot for improving network congestion and increasing data transfer rate by lossless compression.

3. Conclusion

This review paper has thoroughly discussed a few of the popular compression algorithms which IoT devices and applications can use for data transfer over the wireless or mobile network. This research also advises that algorithms like the SPT algorithm will become more prevalent in usage in the coming time as these algorithms can compress almost all types of formats. This review paper has also discussed RLE extensively, Huffman coding, Delta encoding, and the LZW algorithm. In a nutshell, all these algorithms are best in their respective applications. IoT devices and applications need compression algorithms as they emit constant bursts of short data transactions. Each algorithm has its advantages as well as shortcomings.

REFERENCES

1. Athira Gopinath, Ravisankar. M, "Comparison of Lossless Data Compression Techniques," IEEE, 2020.
2. Wu, W. W., "Future Satellite & Space Communications," IEEE, 2006.
3. Wu, W. W., "Satellite Communications," IEEE, 1997.
4. Pritchard, W. L., Suyderhoud, H. G., Nelson, R. A., "Satellite Communication Systems Engineering," Prentice-Hall, 1993.
5. Shiv Preet et al., "An overview of the Internet of Things and its Research Issues," "In Inter-national Journal of Computer Technology and Applications," IJCTA, 2016.
6. Shiv Preet et al., "Comparison of Various Routing and Compression Algorithms: A Comparative Study of Various Algorithms in Wireless Networking," Springer, 2016.
7. Shiv Preet, Dr. Amandeep Bagga, "Lempel-Ziv-Oberhumer: A critical evaluation of loss-less algorithm and its applications," ICCS, 2018.
8. Weigang Li, "Optimize Genomics Data Compression with Hardware Accelerator," IEEE, 2017
9. Zhang Xiaohong, Ju Shui, Jiao Zhibin, "A Scheduling Method Based on Deadlines in MapReduce," Springer, 2011.
10. Huitema et al., "IPv6: The New Internet Protocol", Prentice Hall PTR, 1996.
11. Zhu, S., He, Z., Meng, X., Zhou, J., & Zeng, B., "Compression-dependent transform-domain downward conversion for block-based image coding.", IEEE Transactions on Image Processing, 2018
12. Amro, I., "Higher Compression Rates for Conjugate Structure Algebraic Code Excited Linear Prediction", IEEE Third International Conference on Consumer Electronics -Berlin (ICCE-Berlin), 2013.
13. Wu, W. W., "Blockage Mitigation Techniques in Satellite Communications," IEEE, 2005.
14. Xiao, X. and Ni, L. "Internet QoS: A Big Picture," IEEE, 1999.
15. Dr. Amandeep Bagga, Shiv Preet, "Squeeze Pack and Transfer Algorithm: A new over-the-top compression application for Seamless data transfer over the wireless network," IJITEE, 2019.
16. Dr. Amandeep Bagga, Shiv Preet, "A MapReduce approach to automatic key file updates for SPT (Squeeze Pack and Transfer) algorithm," Springer, 2019.
17. Bhaskar Prasad Rimai et al., " Mobile data offloading in FiWi enhanced LTE-A heterogeneous networks," IEEE, 2017.

Note: All Images and Tables are made by Author

Computer Science Engineering and Emerging Technologies (ICCS-2022) – Prof (Dr.) Rajeev Sobti et al. (eds)
© 2024 Taylor & Francis Group, London, ISBN 978-1-032-52199-2

Chapter **73**

Call Centre Resource Optimization Using Applied Operations Research: A Linear Programming Approach

Pawan Kumar[1]
Associate Professor, Computer Applications,
Lovely Professional University, India

Varun Kumar[2]
Associate Professor, Mathematics,
Lovely Professional University, India

Kajal Rai[3]
Assistant Professor, Computer Applications,
G. L. Bajaj Institute of Technology and Management, Greater Noida, India

Vandana Sharma[4], Rahul Kamboj[5]
Department of Communications, Lovely Professional University, India

Abstract: Call centres are emerging as the preferred choice of organizations to reach their customers and maintain connections to retain these customers. The problem of ensuring the availability of 'just enough' agents to handle the queries of the customers is an important concern for call centre managers. In this work, the problem of resource optimization at a call centre has been modelled as a linear programming problem in operations research. The results showed an overall improvement of 5.4% in daily productivity of the call centre by adopting OR-based approach for optimal utilization of resources. Sensitivity analysis of the obtained optimal solution has also been done to check the robustness of the solution against possible changes in the availability of resources. The outcomes of this study are important for staffing and scheduling of resources at a call centre, especially in an academic setup.

Keywords: Call centre, Resource optimization, Intelligent computing, Linear programming, Sensitivity analysis, Operations research

1. Introduction

A call centre is a centralized department that handles inbound and outbound calls from current and potential customers. Most of the organizations maintain a dedicated call center or outsource their call center requirement to a vendor. The aim is to provide resolution to the queries of the customers quickly and efficiently. An important concern in managing a call center is to ensure that representatives are available when customers call for service or support. Also, almost every call center uses a dialer software for handling inbound or outbound calls. Number of representatives in a call center which can login at the same time is directly proportional to the availability of the number of the licenses that calling software can support. The number of licenses of this software is usually limited and is a planning issue due to cost involved per license.

[1]pawan.11522@lpu.co.in, [2]varun.kumar@lpu.co.in, [3]kajal_saraswat@rediffmail.com, [4]vandana.sharma@lpu.co.in, [5]rahul.22280@lpu.co.in

DOI: 10.1201/9781003405580-73

So, agents and licenses are an important resource to manage at a call center from financial perspective. The management of these resources makes it a use case for resource optimization.

Operations research (OR) is a field that helps optimizing operations. OR is a method of solving any given problem and making decisions that are useful in the functioning of any organization. The problem is divided into basic requirements and then it is solved by a few defined steps by mathematical analysis. In simple words, OR can be defined as an analytical method of problem solving, testing each solution on the model and analyzing its success and executing the outcomes.

With the advancement of computer science, particularly in the field of intelligent computing, educational institutes have also started making use of these technologies. Some of the recent applications include anticipating placement status of students (Kumar et al, 2019), predicting joining behaviour of enrolled students (Kumar et al, 2020) and analysing academic performance (Kumar and Sharma, 2020).

Related Work: Due to the rise in importance of call centres as an alternative to reach out to customers and maintaining customer service, the research community has contributed to this field in several dimensions including resource optimization while staffing and scheduling manpower, motivating call centre employees and applications of concepts like queueing models and intelligent computing.

Stochastic queuing models have been used to optimize resource optimization at call centers taking into account expected waiting time, the number of customers, probability of a calling customer to wait and call center service level (Brezavšček, A., & Baggia, A. (2014).). A rationale and scientific method are the basis for understanding how to improve call center performance. The methods range from basic Erlang formulas to advanced techniques like skill-based routing and multi-channel environments (Koole, 2013). Genetic Algorithms have been used to build a mathematical model to describe the staff scheduling problem at a call center with the objective of minimizing the gap between maximizing performance (Ma & Liu, 2012). A bicriteria approximation algorithm has been proposed for maximizing the number of time slots where the minimum manpower requirement count is satisfied (Dhesi et al, 2011), using non-trivial properties of an optimal solution to solve the LP relaxation problem. The use of Discrete-event Simulation has been promoted for modeling call center operations and functions (Akhtar & Latif, 2010). The task of getting the "Just Right" count of staff is one of the most important concerns in managing a call center (Reynolds, 2010). The task of forecasting the workload accurately is the key to the success of managing call center operations.

Contribution of this research: In this work, the problem of managing resources at a call center has been modeled as an OR problem. The case study under investigation was the contact center of a reputed university in North India. It has a limited number of advisors (or agents) and a limited number of licenses of the dialing software. The problem was to identify an optimal way of utilizing these two resources. This work demonstrates how the task of resource optimization can be solved using OR tools. The problem of ensuring optimal utilization of agents and software licenses has been modeled as a Linear programming problem (LPP) (Dantzig, 2002). The importance of this work lies in demonstrating the application of OR in resource optimization at a call center. The outcomes help the organization concerned in planning when and how many resources are to be scheduled in order to maximize the objective function value. In this work, the case study is of a call center in an academic setup where agents (or advisors) include academic experts and skill required is of domain knowledge of education domain. To the best of our knowledge, this is the first of kind study in terms of the domain under study. Moreover, the objective is to incorporate unique requirements like avoiding sudden changes in working hours, night shifts and swapping of teams between Morning and Evening Shifts.

Organization of the paper: The rest of the paper is organized as follows: Section 2 describes the problem statement and its modeling as an LPP in OR. Section 3 discusses the optimal solution obtained. Section 4 perform sensitivity analysis to anticipate the impact of changes in resources or objective functions on the optimal solution. Section 5 concludes the outcomes of this study and provides directions for future extension of this work.

2. Problem Statement

In order to model an optimization problem as an OR problem, it is required to identify resources, specify constraints and frame an objective function. In the context of the call center under study, the resources include agents who handle the calls and number of licenses available for the dialing software. The aim is to identify how many agents should be working in each shift so that productivity of the call center (number of calls handled) is maximized.

Resources:

(i) *Agent:* An agent is a human advisor or counsellor who handles incoming or outgoing calls and is responsible for providing necessary information to the customers as per their needs, resolving their doubts, and ensuring a quick and accurate solution to the queries of students or parents. Every agent is trained professionally regarding use of the software interface as well as usage of different channels like WhatsApp or email for sharing information with candidates.

(ii) *Licenses:* When you purchase a Call Center agent license, that license is tied to the individual user. It is a permission, a permit, a document that states a particular individual or agent is qualified or allowed to do work (Calling) against that particular license.

(iii) *Constraints:* The software (Ameyo) used for dialing calls supported 330 licenses at a time. It means, maximum 330 agents can work at a time. If any agent tries to login beyond this limit, he or she will be unable to login. The total number of agents available was 400. Due to limited licenses, all 400 agents cannot work at the same time. So, the idea was to call them in shifts so that both the resources (agents and licenses) are utilized to the maximum. Simply dividing the team into two shifts (200 agents in each shift) was also not optimal as licenses were more than 200. Also, it was a practice of the organization that the Morning and Evening shift agents required to be swapped after every month, so count of agents in these shifts required to be same. Table 1 gives the shift-wise work timings, auto-call requirement and number of agents.

Let X_1 = Number of agents called in Morning (or Evening) shift

Let X_2 = Number of agents called in Regular shift

Table 73.1 Shift timings and auto-call on requirement

Shift	Timings	Auto-call requirement	Number of agents
Morning (M)	8 AM – 2:30PM	6 hours	X_1
Evening (E)	2:30 PM – 9PM	6 hours	X_1
Regular (R)	9 AM–6 PM	6 hours 30 minutes	X_2

Source: Made by Author

(a) *Constraint due to limited agents:* The total number of agents allocated in Morning, Evening and Regular shifts taken together should not exceed 400 (the total number of agents).

$$2X_1 + X_2 <= 400 \tag{A}$$

(b) *Constraint due to limited licenses:* The total number of agents logged in at a time should not exceed 330 (the number of licenses of the dialer software).

$$X_1 + X_2 <= 330 \tag{B}$$

(iv) *Objective Function:* To maximize the overall productivity in terms of number of calls handled, it is equivalent to maximizing the total auto-call on duration of the team for all the agents across all the shifts. To maximize the number of auto-call on hours, the objective function is framed as below:

$$\text{Maximize } Z = 12X_1 + 6.5X_2 \tag{C}$$

3. Result (Optimal Solution)

The OR problem modeled in Section 3 is an LPP and can be solved using Simplex method in operations research (Dantzig, 1990). The solution of the LPP is presented in Tables 73.2, 73.3 and 73.4:

Table 73.2 Optimal value

Objective Function	Original Value	Final Value
Total Auto-call Hours	0	2530

Source: Made by Author

Table 73.3 Optimal solution

Variable	Original Value	Final Value
X_1	0	70
X_2	0	260

Source: Made by Author

Table 73.4 Constraints status

Constraint	Value	Status	Slack
Total Advisors	400	Binding	0
Total Licenses	330	Binding	0

Source: Made by Author

The optimal solution satisfying our constraints says that 70 agents should be called during Morning and Evening shifts and 260 agents should be called during Regular shift. This will lead to total of 2530 auto-call on hours daily. Note that both the constraints are declared to be 'Binding' as slack value is zero in each case. They are also termed as 'tight' in that they are satisfied with equality ('=' instead of '<=') at the LP optimal. Figure 73.1 presents the graphical solution of this two-dimensional LPP. As clear from the figure, this LPP has a bounded solution and optimal solution is presented by point A (70,260).

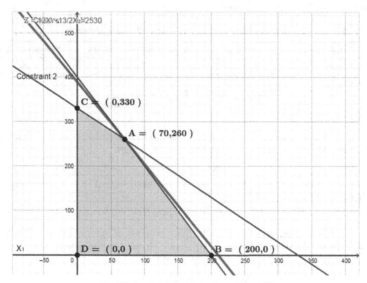

Fig. 73.1 Graphical Solution of the LPP

Source: Made by Author

Comparison with the earlier approach: Prior to using this optimal solution approach, the organization used to equally divide agents into two shifts whenever the number of agents exceeded the number of licenses available. Going by this approach, calling agents in two shifts gives us 200 * 6 + 200 * 6 = 2400 hours of auto-call duration. There is an improvement of (2530 – 2400)/2400 = 5.4% in overall productivity.

Table 73.5 Improvement over the earlier approach

Approach	Morning (X_1)	Evening (X_1)	Regular (X_2)	Auto-call on hours)
OR Approach	70	70	260	2530
Earlier Approach	200	200	0	2400

Source: Made by Author

4. Sensitivity Analysis

The resources, constraints and objective function in a typical OR problem are subject to changes due to the dynamics of the real environment and the problem under study is no exception. The number of agents may increase due to new hiring or may decrease due to agents quitting the job without serving a notice period. The number of licenses may also increase due to new purchase or may decrease if a subset of licenses is kept reserved for a crucial task. Changes in any of these will lead to change in the constraints. Also, there may be a change in objective function whenever there is a change in the auto-call requirement for agents in a particular shift. Due to this dynamic environment, it is important to anticipate in advance the impact of such changes on our optimal solution. Sensitivity analysis gives us insights on sensitivity of our optimal solution in response to these changes (Nilu and Bhuiyan, 2021). The importance of sensitivity analysis has been validated by the evolution of software packages to perform sensitivity analysis along with tools for solving LPP (Jansen et al., 1997).

(a) Changes in the objective function coefficient?

As neither of the two variables X_1 or X_2 has a zero value in the optimal solution, so changes in the coefficient of X_1 or X_2 in the objective function is going to result in a change in the optimal value of the objective function. Table 73.6 gives the possible range for objective function coefficients without affecting the optimal values of X_1 and X_2.

Table 73.6   Sensitivity report—Objective function coefficients

Variable	Final Value	Objective Coefficient	From	To
X_1	70	12	6.5	13
X_2	260	6.5	6	12

Source: Made by Author

However, as long as the coefficient or X_1 remains between 6.5 and 13 or the coefficient of X_2 remains between 6 and 12, the optimal values of variables will remain same. Although, the optimal value of the solution will change due to change in coefficient of X_1 or X_2 in the objective function. In terms of the problem under study, it means that the decision to call 70 advisors in Morning or Evening shift shall remain unaffected even if number of auto-call hours per advisor ranges between 6.5 hours and 13 hours. Similarly, the decision to call 260 advisors in the regular shift shall remain unaffected even if number of auto-call hours per advisor ranges between 6 hours and 12 hours.

(b) Changes in the Constraints RHS?

(i) Change in the number of Advisors

(ii) Change in the number of Licenses

Table 73.7   Sensitivity report—Change in RHS of constraints

Constraint name	Final value	Shadow price	Constraint RHS	From	To	Change	Change in optimal value
Total Advisors	400	5.5	400	330	660	a	5.5*a
Total Licenses	330	1	330	200	400	b	1*b

Source: Made by Author

Table 73.7 compiles the possible impact of change in RHS of the constraints. The column headed 'Shadow Price' gives a measure of the impact of change in the final optimal value corresponding to change in RHS of the constraints. If there is a change of 'a' units in number of Advisors, the optimal value is subject to change of 5.5*a. Similarly, if there is a change of 'b' units in number of Licenses, the optimal value is subject to change of 1*b. For example, if number of advisors is increased from 400 to 410, the final optimal solution changes from 2530 to 2530+5.5*10 = 2585.Similarly, if number of Licenses are increased from 330 to 335, the final optimal solution changes from 2530 to 2530+5*1 i.e. 2535. So, an increase in advisor count seems more beneficial in comparison to an additional license, as long as change is within permissible range assuming they are otherwise same on other parameters of concerns like Advisor salary against license cost.

The solution of the LPP was implemented using R software, a software for statistical programming (Ihaka and Gentleman, 1996). For sensitivity analysis, the 'lpSolve' package in R was used (Berkelaar, 2015).

5. Conclusion and Future Work

The task of resource allocation at a call center can be modeled as an OR problem. The use of OR approach led to an increase of 5.4% in the overall daily productivity. Assuming daily call volume as 20k, it amounts to handling additional 1k calls daily or additional 30k calls every month. Modeling this problem as an OR problem also helped better utilization of licenses and agents. Sensitivity analysis helps anticipate the impact of changes in resources or objective function on the overall optimal solution. It can be very helpful while going for making a choice in revising the resource count.

There are several interesting directions for future research. In this work, the variation in the call flow was not taken into consideration. However, in practice, this is not the case. The flow of calls also keeps on increasing or decreasing during different hours of the day. In future work, we want to keep this flow into consideration and decide resource allocation on a more continuous manner rather than shifts. This is expected to help us improve the daily productivity further. Moreover, we intend to use forecasting and machine learning techniques to predict call flow on more continuous basis (at least hourly) and then allocating resource optimally using a combination of machine learning and OR approach.

REFERENCES

1. Akhtar, S., & Latif, M. (2010). Exploiting simulation for call centre optimization. In Proceedings of the World Congress on Engineering (Vol. 3, pp. 2963–2970).
2. Berkelaar, M. (2015). Package 'lpSolve'.
3. Brezavšček, A., & Baggia, A. (2014). Optimization of a call centre performance using the stochastic queueing models. Business Systems Research: International journal of the Society for Advancing Innovation and Research in Economy, 5(3), 6–18.
4. Dantzig, G. B. (1990). Origins of the simplex method. In A history of scientific computing (pp. 141–151).
5. Dantzig, G. B. (1991). Linear programming. History of mathematical programming, 19–31.
6. Dantzig, G. B. (2002). Linear programming. Operations research, 50(1), 42–47.
7. Dhesi, A., Gupta, P., Kumar, A., Parija, G. R., & Roy, S. (2011, June). Contact center scheduling with strict resource requirements. In International Conference on Integer Programming and Combinatorial Optimization (pp. 156–169). Springer, Berlin, Heidelberg.
8. Ihaka, R., & Gentleman, R. (1996). R: a language for data analysis and graphics. Journal of computational and graphical statistics, 5(3), 299–314.
9. Jansen, B., De Jong, J. J., Roos, C., & Terlaky, T. (1997). Sensitivity analysis in linear programming: just be careful!. European Journal of Operational Research, 101(1), 15–28.
10. Koole, G. (2013). Call center optimization. Lulu. com.
11. Kumar, P., Sharma, M., & Sood, S. (2019). Anticipating placement status of students using machine learning. *J Gujarat Res Soc*, *21*(6), 374–8588.
12. Kumar, P., & Sharma, M. (2020). Predicting Academic performance of international students using machine learning techniques and human interpretable explanations using LIME—Case study of an Indian University. In *International Conference on Innovative Computing and Communications* (pp. 289-303). Springer, Singapore.
13. Kumar, P., Kumar, V., & Sobti, R. (2020, July). Predicting joining behavior of freshmen students using machine learning–A case study. In *2020 International Conference on Computational Performance Evaluation (ComPE)* (pp. 141–145). IEEE.
14. Ma, Y., & Liu, L. (2012, October). Solving Call Center Agent Scheduling Problem through Improved Adaptive Genetic Algorithm. In 2012 Fifth International Symposium on Computational Intelligence and Design (Vol. 2, pp. 27–30). IEEE.
15. Nilu, T. Y., & Bhuiyan, S. A. M. (2021). A Study of Sensitivity Analysis in Linear Programming Problem and its Implementation in Real life.
16. Reynolds, P. (2010). Call center metrics—Fundamentals of call center staffing and technologies. NAQC Issue Paper. Phoenix, 1–27.

Computer Science Engineering and Emerging Technologies (ICCS-2022) – Prof (Dr.) Rajeev Sobti et al. (eds)
© 2024 Taylor & Francis Group, London, ISBN 978-1-032-52199-2

Chapter **74**

Role of Machine Learning in Developing the Effectiveness of Digital Marketing Aspects in Emerging Economies

Harihara Sudhan R.[1]
Associate Professor, School of Liberal Arts and Applied Science,
Hindustan University, Chennai

A. Shameem[2]
Professor, AMET Business School, AMET University

Pavithra V.[3]
Associate Professor & HoD, Department of Management Studies,
Villa Marie College for Women, Hyderabad

Tanvi Jindal[4]
Assistant Professor, Chitkara Business School, Chitkara University, punjab, India

Jeidy Panduro-Ramirez[5]
Professor, Universidad Tecnológica Del Perú

José Luis Arias Gonzáles[6]
Business Department, Pontifical Catholic University of Peru

Abstract: All company sectors, especially communications, where customers are the most erratic and brand loyalty is at an all-time low, are being significantly impacted by the digital revolution of businesses. By partnering with cashback services, many major retail firms attempt to keep their customer base engaged. These websites are built on a particular form of affiliate marketing where users can access a variety of retailers and earn money according to their actions. The word-of-mouth promotional method employed by cashback networks, which is based on financial rewards for individuals who suggest others to these sites, helps them boost existing customers' engagement while also attracting new target consumers. Digital technology has an influence on people. "Artificial intelligence and machine learning" are widely employed to alter businesses. Both input and output have an impact on a machine's capacity for learning; the latter's outputs are constantly improved. "Machine intelligence and artificial intelligence" are the two key computational models nowadays that are revolutionising people's lives everywhere. A secondary analysis has been done for this paper to gather relevant data related to research topic.

Keywords: "Machine learning", "Digital marketing", Economics, Technology, "Deep learning"

1. Introduction

Machine learning is a revolutionary strategy in digital marketing that records, examines, and utilises views and comments regarding brands to understand the thoughts related to the brand. With the use of this data, merchants may customise their

[1]rhsudan@hindustanuniv.ac.in, [2]shameemanwar2003@gmail.com, [3]pavichandra@gmail.com, [4]anglebirth1990@gmail.com, [5]C21289@utp.edu.pe, [6]joseariasgon6@gmail.com

DOI: 10.1201/9781003405580-74

customer care calls for every potential consumer and adjust solutions for individuals. By categorising various responses to businesses on a more individualised basis, machine learning-powered services can increase consumer engagement. In order to fully appreciate the potential of big data, researchers advise dedicating the time necessary to produce one's own statistical data before diving into a technique. The enormous cache of data obtained is divided into various segments and analysed to develop patterns via machine learning relating to digital service users. In this approach, one may educate himself about the facts so that he can employ (or train) a technique that is appropriate for the circumstance when the time comes. The research aims at organizations that have started to create new business models, procedures, and technologies. Through courageous innovation initiatives, the majority of people are already aware of the promise of tech transformation (Pandey *et al*. 2020). Directors are crucial in developing strategies that will improve corporate results and influence the trend going forward. A minimal focus has been given to machine learning.

Digital marketing may reach new heights thanks to deep learning algorithms, with artificial intelligence making all the difference. This research aims to ascertain the effects of customers' reactions to programs across various demographics and their capacity to promote, which may be through digital marketing. Researchers noticed that by taking into consideration customer attitude, activity, and decisions, software developers' conceptual design in collaboration with marketing executives who use machine learning algorithms. Since salespeople will soon have easy access to accurate information about customers, this should be extremely advantageous to companies (Akpan *et al*. 2022). Utilizing only a conceptual framework and multiple regressions, the effectiveness of the machines in various scenarios is characterised. Additionally, it offers practically applicable, doable, and realistic research-based solutions to almost all business-related problems.

2. Literature Review

The online transformation has been reimagined by machine learning, which has altered how value is produced. They have alternatives now on online platforms, as well as a market that is quite crowded, machine learning may assist marketers to connect consumers with the proper offering. A widespread technology that affects everyday activities is deep learning. The development of machine learning has opened up new prospects for businesses involved in digital marketing. Consumers now have chances in the services sector, particularly in online marketing, due to this analysis. Perfect examples of how deep learning may advance online marketing are social network sites, Flipkart and Amazon (Panwar *et al*. 2021). From online bookstores to constructing a platform where both employers and employees may interact, researchers start by linking individuals to the connecting groupings of participants.

2.1 Customer Attitude Analysis

Effective promotional research is based on the psychological insights of the consumer. Marketers that develop their tactics depending on their target audience may modify their offerings and choose the frequency and timing of their advertising to clinch deals. Marketers must choose the best digital service to reach their target audience with relevant information and data because there are many of them and each includes millions of individual consumers. The computers that produce promotional presentations must comprehend the customer's digital existence and give it significance (Jain and Pandey, 2019). Customers' purchasing decisions are significantly influenced by online brand communities. Machines are capable of deciphering the behaviour of these groups and grouping them according to a variety of criteria, such as their spending capacity and preferences, into different clusters. The robots give data on these groups using deep learning that also analyses the personalities of the people who make up these communities. Machines use a variety of analytical methods to evaluate internet users and create customer-specific digital adverts. The advertising is tailored to the stage at which potential buyers are viewing it based on the promotional mix data that the machines acquire.

Machine learning by algorithms analyses several layers of data about consumers, from a prospect to an established client, and this aids in suggesting various items to people depending on their wants. Eventually, machines may even create things with the help of consumers and make recommendations on what to purchase and when to buy them.

2.2 Behaviour Analysis

Sophisticated, human-like, and customised machines' intellectual component decodes online consumers' behaviour logically and intelligently using huge data about previous consumer behaviours. Machine learning is only currently being utilised in India to analyse consumer habits using statistics. The use of technology in promotion has not gone beyond communication customisation and targeted optimization (García-Fernández *et al*. 2018). Consumers are confronted with a diverse range of brands on a regular basis, and artificial intelligence-powered computers study consumer behaviour about each product on online platforms. Social networking is a clear representation of what consumers enjoy, and computers trawl through it to find out what consumers appreciate about particular products (Zaki, 2019). Social media exposes vast data to the systems on how clients behave online toward different companies. Algorithms might quickly analyse the characterization of online activity and record it for upcoming use and study. Focusing on views, likes, and posts, computerized solutions used by computers in marketing and advertising can characterise buyer behaviour. This communicates to the people operating the devices what the consumers are expected to do depending on their online activity. The ability of the system to deep learning has led to an increase in the usage of tools that analyse online consumer behaviour. The robots can identify the clicks and likes on social networking sites. This digital activity might be used to study consumer behaviour toward retail companies (Jain *et al.* 2019). Deep learning computers have considerably greater possibilities than how they are now employed since they can evaluate click trends in greater detail and modifications in processes and behaviour in the upcoming. According to the findings, software designers should create tools that can classify user preferences depending on businesses and items and distinguish between various behaviours over time (Jain *et al.* 2021).

More advanced machines can anticipate client wants before the consumer is able to recognise their own requirements, helping the consumer make decisions. The systems can also create algorithms that compare the time a product is exposed to a potential and the moment it is bought by consumers, allowing them to cross-check their forecasts and correlate consumer habits. Consumer behaviour, as well as consumption time, have both been studied in the past. It has been detailed how commercials are exposed, how consumers respond to them, and how sales are predicted using this information (Jain, and Pandey, 2019). The researcher looked at the proportion of brand awareness that resulted in purchases. Machines that are unable to comprehend client behaviour digitally relying on liked and shared content on social networking sites are inefficient since they are unable to provide the proper product adverts at the correct time. The businesses may better position and market their advertisements by using machines programmed to recognise context and offer a textual explanation of the activity. Machines that can decode situations engage prospects on a deeper level, thus it is important to create algorithms that are well-informed in human behaviour (Kumar *et al.* 2019).

2.3 Choice Analysis

A conceptual model has been built by researchers to examine consumer preferences. Consumers' choices might be divided into three categories: dilemma choices, where customers select the least troublesome possibilities, Hobson's choices, where consumers must select one or nothing, and Sophie's choices, where customers must select one of two appealing options. For a better knowledge of the consumer, several academics have merged all of the different decision kinds (Ballestar *et al.* 2019). Options are influenced by consumer attitude, and the sentimental model can forecast how well advertisements succeed. The reviews recommendation system may help to better describe the items and the marketers. Deep learning algorithms focus on choice-based evaluation, primarily employing social networking sites and messaging apps to decipher likes, emoticons, and other user interactions. The kind of remarks that the organizations receive are determined by corporate reputation (Jain and Pandey, 2019). Depending on the sentiments expressed by the users, the data gathered through the collection of likes and comments are divided into numerous divisions. It is possible to monitor clients' online behaviour with regard to both new and old items (Panwar *et al.* 2021). The information offered on online platforms is essential for anticipating potential brand issues, and the information gleaned from customer preferences is remarkably precise since consumers make decisions without thinking about how they will be interpreted (Mackey *et al.* 2018). Customers' decisions to like as well as share companies on social media platforms as a reflection of their preferences have a social viewpoint. Marketers may identify trends in consumer behaviour and forecast the future depending on these similarities in the selection, which represent shifting consumer emotions.

3. Research Methodology

A research technique is a way to explain the best way to go about conducting an investigation. It is a deliberate, logical approach to a research problem. A methodology outlines the steps a researcher will take to carry out the study and generate reliable, accurate results that serve their goals and purposes. It outlines the information they will collect, where they will obtain it, how they will collect it, and how they will evaluate it. A research-based methodology lends the study legitimacy and produces valid scientific findings. It also provides a comprehensive framework that helps keep researchers on track and enables a straightforward, effective, and regulated approach. By knowing the study's methodology, the reader can realize the method and techniques used to arrive at the results. In qualitative research, "textual data and spoken or written words" are gathered and analysed. It can help to construct a thorough account of a researcher's observations and may also concentrate on body language or visual components. Typically, researchers use a variety of research methods to collect qualitative data, taking into account journals, papers, and websites.

4. Data and Variables

Digital marketing may make use of the data so extracted with accurate advertising strategies and suggestions. Previous research has looked at both high-level and low-level perceptual characteristic routes. Less deep learning has been employed to analyse decisions and motivations. Some academics have employed cross-modality predictive models to examine the underlying emotions behind the decisions made by consumers.

Supervised learning is frequently used interchangeably with "predictive analytics". A solitary or a collection of algorithms that translate the readings for a number of characteristics into a specific single quantity of relevance make up a "supervised learning algorithm". The software solution of discovering variables that optimally translate extracted features to forecasts while keeping in mind that the variables of the functionalities are originally undetermined is referred to as "training" a system. Researchers design the basic framework labels for the goal outcomes to be supplied in addition to the collection of features in order to develop a classifier (Bag *et al.* 2021). This is frequently offered in historical information, wherein identifiers for the goal value, as well as its attributes, have been noted. Using the retail business as an instance, if researchers keep track of each time a consumer enters the business, researchers can look into the past and estimate the likelihood that they will return one week from now (from a particular point in time in the past). The trained model or testing set is the generated database with labelled target values. The supervised learning approach discovers variables that optimally transfer the attribute values to the labelled predicted values for all observed after being given a training data set. The supervised learning issue is mathematically defined in Equation (1) below:

$$\min_{k} g \left(f(X, K), y_{true} \right), \tag{1}$$

in which the function f(.) to forecast the specified value from such a matrices of characteristic variables X and a vector of factors k, as well as the vector of true labelled expected values y_{true}, are inputs to the error function $g()$. Therefore, the objective is to identify the values of k that minimise the inaccuracy. The user selects the error function $g(.)$ and forecast functional $f(.)$, which are problem- and data-specific (i.e., some error functions are more appropriate for some problems than others). Both computation and mathematical methods can be used to determine the appropriate variables k.

The "confusion matrix" is a key component of many error functions for binary classifier tasks. A 2-by-2 table with four elements—"true positive," "true negative," "false positive," and "false negative"—makes up the confusion matrix. Each observable can have a forecast attributed to one of the variables. False positive (FP) occurs whenever the prediction is calculated but the true label is 1, false positive (FN) occurs when the forecast is made but the real label is 0 and true negative (TN) occurs whenever the system is tested but the true label is 1.

$$Accuracy = \frac{TP + TN}{TP + TN + FP + FN} \tag{2}$$

Since it shows how frequently the system is right compared to incorrect, accuracy is a relevant metric. This quickly persuades individuals of an algorithm's efficacy because it is simple for to comprehend by humans. Accuracy is a poor statistic in practise, nevertheless, when the classes are unbalanced.

Precision can be thought of as how accurate the algorithm is when making positive predictions. Its mathematical equation is:

$$Precision = \frac{TP}{TP + FP} \tag{3}$$

The percentage of real positive findings that the program is capable of retrieving is known as recall (i.e., predict as positive). It is mathematically represented as:

$$Recall = \frac{TP}{TP + FN} \tag{4}$$

Precise measurements omit data in which the algorithm projected a negative result. Accordingly, making a naive assumption that all findings would be negative will result in low reliability if the fraction of the positive class is tiny. This is likewise true for recall, in which only facts that genuinely fall under the positive category are taken into account, and only forecasts that fall under the positive category can be true of these findings. Last but not least, the harmonized mean-based Fβ-score is employed to integrate precision and recall into a single statistic as continues to follow:

$$F_\beta \; score = (1 + \beta^2) \cdot \frac{Precision \cdot Recall}{\beta^2 \cdot Precision + Recall} \tag{5}$$

in which the variable is employed to combine the precision and recall levels. Precision and recall are taken into

account if $\beta = 1$, but differently if $\beta < 1$ or $\beta > 1$ as precision is considered more or less than recall, accordingly. The most often employed measures for binary classifier tasks requiring precise class predictions are precision, recall, and F-score. Area under the Receiver Operating Characteristics curve, sometimes shortened as "AUC," and "logarithmic loss," also known as "log loss," are two extensively used metric for assessing the accuracy of probabilistic forecasts. Following is a definition of Logless:

$$Logloss := - \sum_{i=1}^{N} (y_i^{true} \cdot \ln(y_i^{pred})) + (1 - y_i^{true}) \cdot \ln(1 - y_i^{pred}) \tag{6}$$

wherein i stands for an observation, y_i^{true} is the observation's true binary label (1 or 0), and y_i^{pred} is the observation's anticipated likelihood. It makes sense that this error measure takes into account both the true label being 1 and the true label being 0.

Assessment becomes more challenging when supervised learning systems are given more latitude to largely attributable due to regression issues. Nevertheless, because of this extra complexity, professionals have literally made evaluation criteria for regression and classification simpler and have mostly depended on metrics depending on the quantitative discrepancy between the anticipated and real label values. "Mean squared error" (MSE), which is most frequently employed, is characterised as follows:

$$MSE = \frac{1}{N} \sum_{i=1}^{N} (y_i^{true} - y_i^{pred})^2 \tag{7}$$

For each occurrence, MSE evaluates the median of the squared differences between the true and anticipated readings. The fact that MSE is continuously and distinguishable with regard to the anticipated values gives it a considerable advantage because it makes it easier for supervised learning algorithms to improve its variables. The MSE measure prefers more minor errors over larger-sized errors, similar to the Log loss measure for categorization. Regression issues are unlimited, hence MSE is less resistant to outliers because the extreme value may have a significant impact on the model's forecasts. It is typically preferable to use "mean absolute error" (MAE) as the error measure, as stated by

$$MAE = \frac{1}{N} \sum_{i=1}^{N} |y_i^{true} - y_i^{pred}| \tag{8}$$

MAE employs the exact number rather than estimating the square of variations between the expected and actual label quantities. This is more resistant to severe anomalies than MSE since it uniformly weights all ranges. Unfortunately, MAE is not a constant value, unlike the MSE, making it more difficult to optimise supervised learning systems using this measure. Whatever the size of the true label element, MSE and MAE use the same assumption that mistakes are equal. The very same inaccuracy size on lower numbers, though, might occasionally be greater than on bigger values. The error is taken into account as a percentage of the real label value via the measurement "mean average percent error" (MAPE).

$$MAPE = \frac{1}{N} \sum_{i=1}^{N} \left| \frac{y_i^{true} - y_i^{pred}}{y_i^{true}} \right| \cdot 100 \tag{9}$$

MAPE has the drawback of potentially causing precision issues for occurrences in which the true label quantity is little. The supervised learning technique might not be accurate enough even to forecast with a modest inaccuracy on views when the true value is tiny if the spectrum of true label values within a dataset is 0 to 100. (e.g., less than 5). Alternatively, use the mean of y pred I and y true I as the exponent of Solution to solve the issue (9). Last but not least, the coefficient of estimation (R2), which is defined as:

$$1 - \frac{\dfrac{1}{N} \sum_{i=1}^{N} (y_i^{true} - y_i^{pred})^2}{\sum_{i=1}^{N} (y_i^{true} - y^{-2})^2} \tag{10}$$

The range of R^2 is [−1, 1], and its conventional interpretation is the strength of the link between an algorithm's forecasts and the true label readings (0 means no relationship and 1 means perfect relationship). The orientation of the association is implied by the R^2 value, which might be positive or negative.

Numerous supervised learning algorithms have been created over the years for forecasting issues. Recency and attractiveness, it must be noted, are not indicators of an algorithm's effectiveness. A variety of complex algorithms (such as neural networks and gradient boosting) are becoming significantly more successful since their inception because of the exponential rise in availability of data and processing capacity.

Gradient boosting is the only approach utilised in this research because it is best suited for the challenges being studied. However, the purpose of this part is to give the reader a given instructions of various well-known supervised learning methods and their context.

Linear types: It is widely acknowledged that the "perceptron", the precursor to contemporary neural nets, was the first supervised algorithm for learning. The perceptron is a straightforward linear cut-off functional that can be used to categorise events.

$$y_i^{pred} = \begin{cases} 1 & \text{if } w \cdot x_i + b > 0, \\ 0 & \text{otherwise} \end{cases} \tag{11}$$

where w is a vector of weighted, b is a bias factor, and x_i is a matrix of attribute values for observation x_i. There is an algorithm process to choose w and b for a set of training data that minimises performance of the classifier. Conversely, "linear regression," the most widely used supervised training technique, was created even before machines were invented. The perceptron and linear regression are both described by:

$$y_i^{pred} = w \cdot x_i + b \tag{12}$$

Therefore, w and b are determined by minimising the mean squared error as stated in Equation (7). This problem can be solved theoretically using likelihood function or conventional least squares, or computationally using gradient descent. The weights w represents how much of an impact a unit increase in attribute x has on the desired value of y.

4.1 Social Data Analysis System Study

NLP enables AI systems to analyse the implications of millions of tweets, Facebook updates, and newsfeeds as well as blogs and consumer feedback. According to a study funded by EMC, the amount of data will increase by 50 times from the start of 2010 to 40 zettabytes by the middle of 2020. Text mining is essential to social data gathering because of the enormous amounts of usually unstructured information produced by social platforms. Retail businesses employ ML technology as a technique and accelerator to help solve market issues. Evaluating freshness, the latex identification issue, and categorization strategies are some examples of sample application scenarios. For projecting sales figures and shelf-out circumstances, prediction algorithms have been applied. Advertising, personalization, and client segmentation may all benefit from clustering techniques (Harmeling *et al.* 2017). ML has been employed to rate products and promote as well as list-objects. Content analysis is one of several types of analytics that many businesses use today to better recognize and react to what consumers are saying regarding them and their services in digital marketing. Business organisations will depend mostly on machine learning (ML) technologies and other mining approaches in the upcoming for the evaluation of dynamic information. Numerous techniques for text mining such as information retrieval and entity recognition (gender identification, gender forecasting, and sentiment classification), are used in industries including fraud prevention, share price prediction, customer engagement, and description. Following Google, "YouTube is the second-largest" online platform, the third-most-visited website, and the main platform for sharing media content globally. YouTube is widely used, which produces enormous amounts of revenue for marketing communications. This demonstrates how social networking sites dominate digital marketing. To boost performance, initiatives that combine machine learning techniques with marketing tactics might be used. AI and statistics are combined in ML. In ML, knowledge is developed as a framework for making wise judgements on unproven test data by understanding input information. In the age of microblogging, interpersonal analysis of the data has advanced significantly, and regular patterns in recurring behaviours have been discovered using unorganized data analytics. The primary analysis techniques are AI and ML (Brynjolfsson *et al.* 2017). Many technological and scientific fields, including biology, psychology, healthcare, commercial, machine learning, deep learning, and object tracking, are interested in the challenges of automatic (machine) identification, characterization, categorization, and pattern clustering.

5. Conclusion

People may draw the conclusion that the culture of the nation has a significant impact on how machine learning expertise is measured. The consumers' acceptance of learning algorithms is influenced by their line of work. Future users of machine learning may include all of the research participants. The research offers guidance to software developers working on machine learning as they estimate the parameters for cross-cultural and career profiles. By conducting beta tests and gathering user feedback, it is possible to prevent obstacles in the growth of machine learning. Furthermore, the software is created by programmers in collaboration with online marketers with an emphasis on analysing the attitudes, actions, and decisions of the target audience. According to the research, increasing the accuracy and effectiveness of digital marketing would have tremendous advantages.

REFERENCES

1. A. Jain, A. K. Pandey, (2019), "Modeling And Optimizing Of Different Quality Characteristics In Electrical Discharge Drilling Of Titanium Alloy (Grade-5) Sheet" Material Today Proceedings, 18, 182–191. https://doi.org/10.1016/j.matpr.2019.06.292
2. A. Jain, A. K. Pandey, (2019), "Modeling And Optimizing Of Different Quality Characteristics In Electrical Discharge Drilling Of Titanium Alloy (Grade-5) Sheet" Material Today Proceedings, 18, 182–191. https://doi.org/10.1016/j.matpr.2019.06.292
3. A. Jain, A. K. Pandey, (2019), "Multiple Quality Optimizations In Electrical Discharge Drilling Of Mild Steel Sheet" Material Today Proceedings, 8, 7252–7261. https://doi.org/10.1016/j.matpr.2017.07.054
4. A. Jain, A. K. Yadav & Y. Shrivastava (2019), "Modelling and Optimization of Different Quality Characteristics In Electric Discharge Drilling of Titanium Alloy Sheet" Material Today Proceedings, 21, 1680–1684. https://doi.org/10.1016/j.matpr.2019.12.010
5. A. Jain, C. S. Kumar, Y. Shrivastava, (2021), "Fabrication and Machining of Fiber Matrix Composite through Electric Discharge Machining: A short review" Material Today Proceedings. https://doi.org/10.1016/j.matpr.2021.07.288
6. Akpan, I. J., Udoh, E. A. P. and Adebisi, B., 2022. Small business awareness and adoption of state-of-the-art technologies in emerging and developing markets, and lessons from the COVID-19 pandemic. *Journal of Small Business & Entrepreneurship*, *34*(2), pp. 123–140.
7. Bag, S., Gupta, S., Kumar, A. and Sivarajah, U., 2021. An integrated artificial intelligence framework for knowledge creation and B2B marketing rational decision making for improving firm performance. *Industrial Marketing Management*, *92*, pp. 178–189.
8. Ballestar, M. T., Grau-Carles, P. and Sainz, J., 2019. Predicting customer quality in e-commerce social networks: a machine learning approach. *Review of Managerial Science*, *13*(3), pp. 589–603.
9. Brynjolfsson E, Rock D, Syverson C (2017) Artifcial intelligence and the modern productivity paradox: a clash of expectations and statistics. In: Agrawal A, Gans J, Goldfarb A (eds) Economics of artifcial intelligence. University of Chicago Press, Chicago
10. García-Fernández J, Gálvez-Ruiz P, Vélez-Colon L, Ortega-Gutiérrez J, Fernández-Gavira J (2018) Exploring ftness centre consumer loyalty: diferences of non-proft and low-cost business models in Spain. Econ Res 31(1): 1042–1058 Harmeling CM, Mofett JW, Arnold MJ, Carlson BD (2017) Toward a theory of customer engagement marketing. J Acad Mark Sci 45(3): 312–335
11. Kumar, V., Rajan, B., Venkatesan, R. and Lecinski, J., 2019. Understanding the role of artificial intelligence in personalized engagement marketing. *California Management Review*, *61*(4), pp. 135–155.
12. Mackey, T., Kalyanam, J., Klugman, J., Kuzmenko, E. and Gupta, R., 2018. Solution to detect, classify, and report illicit online marketing and sales of controlled substances via twitter: using machine learning and web forensics to combat digital opioid access. *Journal of medical Internet research*, *20*(4), p.e10029.
13. Pandey, N., Nayal, P. and Rathore, A.S., 2020. Digital marketing for B2B organizations: structured literature review and future research directions. *Journal of Business & Industrial Marketing*.
14. Saura, J. R., 2021. Using data sciences in digital marketing: Framework, methods, and performance metrics. *Journal of Innovation & Knowledge*, *6*(2), pp. 92–102.
15. V. Panwar, D. K. Sharma, K. V. P. Kumar, A. Jain & C. Thakar, (2021), "Experimental Investigations And Optimization Of Surface Roughness In Turning Of EN 36 Alloy Steel Using Response Surface Methodology And Genetic Algorithm" Materials Today: Proceedings, https://Doi.Org/10.1016/J.Matpr.2021.03.642
16. V. Panwar, D. K. Sharma, K. V. P. Kumar, A. Jain & C. Thakar, (2021), "Experimental Investigations And Optimization Of Surface Roughness In Turning Of EN 36 Alloy Steel Using Response Surface Methodology And Genetic Algorithm" Materials Today: Proceedings, https://Doi.Org/10.1016/J.Matpr.2021.03.642
17. Zaki, M., 2019. Digital transformation: harnessing digital technologies for the next generation of services. *Journal of Services Marketing*.

Computer Science Engineering and Emerging Technologies (ICCS-2022) – Prof (Dr.) Rajeev Sobti et al. (eds)
© 2024 Taylor & Francis Group, London, ISBN 978-1-032-52199-2

Chapter **75**

Leveraging Cyber Hunt and Investigation on Endpoints Using Elastic XDR/EDR

Gobinda Karmakar[1]
MTech Research Scholar, LPU, Phagwara, Punjab, India
Urvesh Devendra Thakkar[2], Sakshi Kashid[3]
BTech Research Scholar, Jaywantrao Sawant College of Engineering, Pune

Abstract: The goal of this paper is to highlight the core capabilities and functioning of Elasticsearch EDR. EDR (Endpoint Detection and Response) is developed to leverage beyond detection-based, reactive cyber defense. It focuses on a proactive approach for the analysts to get the data they need to identify threats and protect the organization proactively. Elastic Security for endpoints protects against ransomware and malware, detects advanced threats, and provides critical investigative context to responders. Everything is built on an open platform and is available freely. This open accessibility of Elastic Endpoint Security makes it convenient even for small or individual businesses to adapt security monitoring and protection for the detection and prevention of critical risks.

Keywords: EDR, Endpoint protection, Attack detection and investigation, XDR

1. Introduction

As the threat landscape advances, companies are responding by integrating XDR products into their traditional SIEM systems to offer a coordinated, holistic strategy. Extended Detection and Response is a new integrated solution for endpoint protection, detection, and response for networks and the cloud. XDR promises to consolidate much of the fragmented process that security professionals are now dealing with into a single, unified solution. This significantly assists teams in automating and accelerating their analysts' workflows of triage, investigation, escalation, and reaction – eventually providing these capabilities to more users quicker to better protect enterprises from cyber assault.

Regardless of the technology used, the following are 3 core capabilities that an XDR/EDR must inculcate in its architecture:

Visibility: The exponential rise of data has made the work of security practitioners more challenging. A central repository is necessary for analysis, root cause identification, and remedy planning. XDR solutions derived from endpoint security products are typically incapable of ingesting and retaining the volume and diversity of data sources needed by enterprises.

Analysis: To construct, implement, and monitor new analytics use cases at scale, a flexible framework is necessary. There should also be a smooth interaction with analyst procedures, allowing you to prioritize and develop the attack narrative.

Response: Analysts want a straightforward, user-friendly method for collaborating on an investigation, developing a remediation plan, carrying it out, and reporting on its effectiveness. A centralized XDR system enables users to collaborate to swiftly remediate and, ideally, prevent attacks from being carried out. Native endpoint security solutions integrated into a larger XDR framework can assist in reducing the mean time to remedy (MTTR) to zero.

---

[1]gobindak2@gmail.com, gobinda.karmakar@lpu.in; [2]reach.urvesh@gmail.com; [3]sakshikashid1@gmail.com

DOI: 10.1201/9781003405580-75

Because SIEM, endpoint security, and cloud security solutions complement each other, a security leader's toolset may be far more efficient when implemented as a coordinated, synchronized whole than if organizations deployed these technologies individually. Organizations with a comprehensive understanding of the operating environment, vulnerabilities, and threats may prioritize the risk to critical digital assets better. The ability of security teams to ingest data from throughout the enterprise and examine it in a single pane of glass is perhaps the most appealing feature of Elastic Limitless XDR. The capacity to store and ingest data in a single repository reduces risk through enhanced visibility, automatic detection, and automation of regular processes that would otherwise require a large percentage of analysts' valuable time.

2. Literature Review

2.1 Endpoint Security

As businesses continue to embrace a hybrid, distributed workforce, using personal devices to complete daily professional duties has become the standard. Essential assets are frequently connected via unprotected hosts. Endpoint Detection and Response (EDR) was created to secure consumers' endpoint devices. EDR often has limited integration capabilities, resulting in only partial security monitoring, leaving other network sections vulnerable to attack if not addressed. This problem can be remedied with a more comprehensive XDR method. Endpoint security is further enhanced by Limitless XDR's in-depth prevention and detection.

Users may connect and cooperate with their team while effortlessly integrating with essential remediation providers and engaging in current workflows of varied scales with free and open case management. The API-first development and webhooks features enable easy connection with any other productivity tool to accelerate analysis and reporting, as well as other key adaptations for an organization's operations.

Elastic's logging capabilities significantly decrease the time required to investigate security incidents by allowing clients to search and filter across real-time and archival activity. Based on MITRE ATT&CK® alerts and important events, Linux native threats may be recognized and fed into the organization's SIEM - a vital component missing from most cloud security systems today.

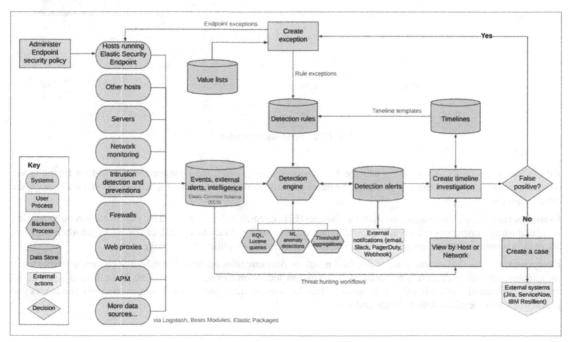

Fig. 75.1   Elastic security workflow

Image source: Elastic Security Reference Guide

Zero Trust Cloud Security Approach in Elastic: The Protect Surface method to Zero Trust identifies and prioritizes an organization's most vital assets, with safeguards deployed in priority order. Using the DAAS approach to identify critical assets reveals that most crucial cloud computing parts are based on or utilize Linux. Organizations require Linux controls like those provided in Elastic's Cloud Security Foundation, making it the optimal platform for implementing a Zero Trust cloud strategy. When authorized users get access to hosts, Elastic's cloud workload safeguards them against unauthorized, non-compliant, or malicious use. It also provides a suite of protection features, such as proactive controls to prohibit actions specified by the company, and is accompanied by threat detection and remediation capabilities. The ability to block the execution of specific commands based on custom policies and block file systems from allowing access or modification to sensitive files while providing user and role attribution for such actions achieves the goal of putting controls as close to the Protect Surface as possible.

3. Endpoint Security in Action

3.1 Fleet Management

In Kibana, Fleet provides a web-based UI for centrally managing Elastic Agents and associated rules. In Fleet, you can monitor the status of all your Elastic Agents. On the Agents page, you can see whether agents are healthy or unfit, as well as when they last checked in. You may also view the Elastic Agent executable and policy versions. Agents often check in for the most recent updates. Each agent policy can have any number of agents enrolled in it, allowing you to scale up to multiple hosts.

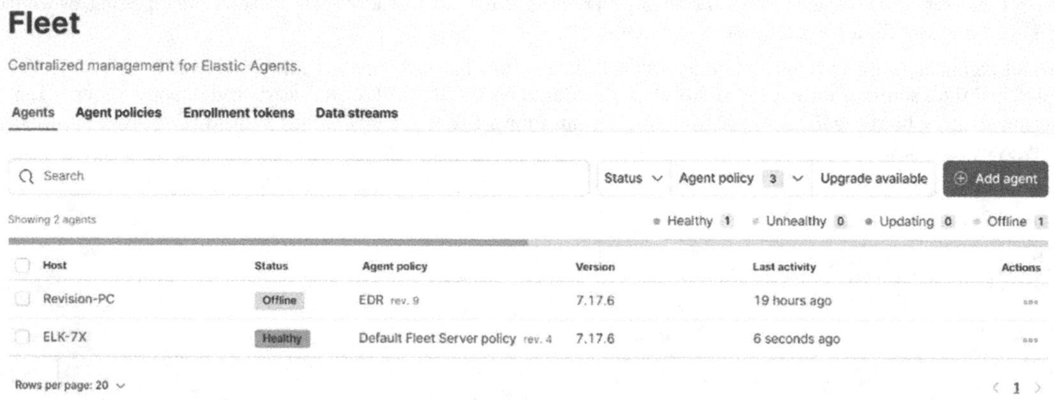

Fig. 75.2 Fleet management

Source: Author

Kibana's Elastic Security app is used to manage the Detection engine, Cases, and Timeline and administrate Endpoint and Cloud Security hosts. The engine of detection: Searches for suspicious host and network activity automatically using the following methods:

Detection rules: Search for suspicious events in the data (Elasticsearch indices) received by your hosts regularly. An alert is created when a suspicious occurrence is found. Other systems, such as Slack and email, can be leveraged when warnings are made to communicate information. You may write your own rules or utilize the pre-built ones.

Exceptions: Reduce the amount of noise and false positives. Abnormalities are linked to rules and prevent warnings when the circumstances of an exception are satisfied. Value lists include source event values that can be utilized as a part of the criteria of an anomaly. When Elastic Endpoint and Cloud Security are deployed on your hosts, the Security app allows you to add malware exceptions straight to the endpoint.

Machine learning jobs: include automatically detecting anomalies in host and network events. Anomaly scores are supplied for each host and can be used with detection criteria.

Timeline: An investigation workspace for alerts and occurrences. Timelines delve down into events connected to a single occurrence using queries and filters. Timeline templates are tied to rules when alarms are explored and employ predefined queries. Timelines may be stored, shared with others, and added to Cases.

Cases: An internal system that allows you to open, track, and share security concerns straight from the Security app. Cases can be linked to third-party ticketing systems.

Administration: View and manage hosts that are running Elastic Endpoint and Cloud Security.

4. Investigation of an Alert

4.1 Timeline Analysis

One can easily track the number of times the rule was fired, and with the help of timeline analysis, it is straightforward to observe the rule trigger rate. The timeline view provides other options to analyse the alert in a much more detailed manner.

Fig. 75.3   Timeline analysis

Source: Author

The rule analyser functionality provides a full view of the entire backend process and activities that occurred in the system. This view provides a complete time-linked graphical analysis of the backend process that followed and led to the rule trigger.

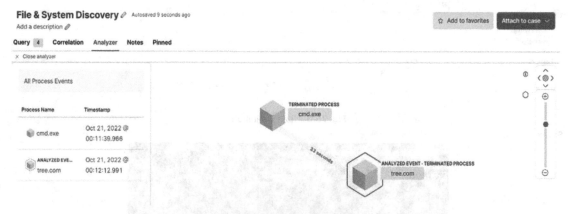

Fig. 75.4   System discovery

Source: Author

The rule description page provides complete information about the rule, including the Mitre ATT&CK mappings and rule query with unlimited modification options (Fig. 75.5).

Further, multiple rule trigger actions can send the alert notification to various mediums like Teams, Slack, Webhooks, Email, etc. An example of alert information sent in Slack is the image in Fig. 75.6.

‹ Rules

File and Directory Discovery

Activate   ⚙ Edit rule settings   ⋮

Created by: elastic on Oct 20, 2022 @ 23:01:52.327   Updated by: elastic on Oct 21, 2022 @ 00:11:36.313

Last response: ● succeeded at Oct 21, 2022 @ 19:53:26.952 ↻

About

Enumeration of files and directories using built-in tools. Adversaries may use the information discovered to plan follow-on activity.

Author	Elastic
Severity	● Low

examples	inherently malicious and noise may come from scripts, automation tools, or normal command line usage. It's important to baseline your environment to determine the amount of expected noise and exclude any known FP's from the rule.
License	Elastic License v2
MITRE ATT&CK™	Discovery (TA0007) ↗ File and Directory Discovery (T1083)
Timestamp override	event.ingested
Tags	Elastic Host Windows Threat Detection Discovery

Definition

Index patterns	logs-endpoint.events.* winlogbeat-* logs-windows.*
Custom query	sequence by agent.id, user.name with maxspan=1m [process where event.type in ("start", "process_started") and ((process.name : "cmd.exe" or

process.name : "tree.com")
[process where event.type in ("start", "process_started") and
((process.name : "cmd.exe" or
process.pe.original_file_name == "Cmd.Exe") and
process.args : "dir") or
process.name : "tree.com")
[process where event.type in ("start", "process_started") and
((process.name : "cmd.exe" or
process.pe.original_file_name == "Cmd.Exe") and
process.args : "dir") or
process.name : "tree.com")

Rule type	Event Correlation
Timeline template	None

Fig. 75.5   Rule Definition

Source: Author

Fig. 75.6   Webhook Triggering

Source: Author

5. Conclusion

Elastic Security is a system that combines SIEM threat detection features with endpoint prevention and response capabilities. These analytical and protective capabilities, enabled by Elasticsearch's speed and flexibility, allow analysts to defend their company against attacks before damage and loss occur. Elastic Security offers the following security features and benefits:

- An engine for detecting assaults and system misconfigurations.
- A location for triage and examination of events.
- Investigating process linkages with interactive visualizations.
- Case management incorporated with automatic actions.
- Signatureless attack detection using prebuilt machine learning anomaly tasks and detection rules.

REFERENCES

1. Ian Ahl (2014), The Relevance of Endpoint Security in Enterprise Networks
2. Elastic security guide, https://www.elastic.co/guide/en/security/current/es-overview.ht https://www.elastic.co/guide/en/security/current/es-overview.htmlml
3. A. Shaji George (2021), XDR: The Evolution of Endpoint Security Solutions - Superior Extensibility and Analytics to Satisfy the Organizational Needs of the Future, IJARSCT

Computer Science Engineering and Emerging Technologies (ICCS-2022) – Prof (Dr.) Rajeev Sobti et al. (eds)
© 2024 Taylor & Francis Group, London, ISBN 978-1-032-52199-2

Chapter **76**

An examination of Cloud Network Security Issues and Potential Solutions

Gobinda Karmakar[1]

Research Scholar, Department of Computer Science and Engineering,
Lovely Professional University, Phagwara, Punjab, India

Harwant Singh Arri[2], Dhiraj Kapila[3]

Associate Professor, Department of Computer Science and Engineering,
Lovely Professional University, Phagwara, Punjab, India

**Nancy Sharma[4], Siddharth Pansare[5], Jithin Govind[6],
Sahil Bhardwaj[7], Nupur Kaushik[8], Jayant Mehra[9]**

Research Scholar, Department of Computer Science and Engineering,
Lovely Professional University, Phagwara, Punjab, India

Abstract: Cloud computing is a modern method of computing in the field of computer science. A collection of resources and services known as "cloud computing" are provided through a network or the internet. Distributed and grid computing, for example, are expanded by cloud computing. Today, both the corporate and academic sectors embrace cloud computing. Through the provision of virtual resources through the internet, the cloud helps its users. New approaches are emerging as the world of cloud computing expands. The environment for cloud computing is expanding, which presents new security difficulties for cloud developers. Because cloud users save their data there, insufficient cloud security may undermine user confidence.

In this article, we will look at certain cloud security challenges, such as multi-tenancy, In this report, we'll talk about a few cloud security concerns related to things such as multi-tenancy, flexibility, availability, and so on. The presentation also covers current security methods and strategies for a safe cloud. Researchers and professionals will be able to learn about the many security risks, models, and techniques offered thanks to this study.

Keywords: Cloud computing, Cloud security, Security threats, Security techniques, Cloud security standards

1. Introduction

Internet computing is often referred to as cloud computing. The National Institute of Standards and Technology's (NIST) definition of cloud computing reads as follows: "In order to enable seamless on-demand net access to a shared pool of reconfigurable computing resources (such as networks, servers, storage applications, and services), the cloud computing concept was developed [9]. While for some, it is simply a method of accessing cloud-based applications and data, for others, it is a paradigm that offers processing power and storage. Because it offers its customers scalability, flexibility, and availability of data, cloud computing is more popular in business and academia today. Additionally, by making it possible for a business to share data, cloud computing lowers costs. A company can move its data to the cloud so that its shareholders can use it. A cloud computing example is Google Apps.

[1]gobindak2@gmail.com, [2]hs.arri@lpu.co.in, [3]dhiraj.23509@lpu.co.in, [4]nancysharma2177@gmail.com, [5]sidhu.pansare@gmail.com, [6]jithingovindkanayi001@gmail.com, [7]binny4166@gmail.com, [8]nupurkaushiknk@gmail.com, [9]jayant46mehra@gmail.com

DOI: 10.1201/9781003405580-76

Although the cloud offers a number of features and advantages, it still has certain problems with secure data access and storage. Cloud computing research difficulties include vendor lock-in, multi-tenancy, loss of control, service disruption, information loss, and others. These concerns are all connected to cloud security [2]. In this report, we examine the security concerns raised by the cloud computing concept. Studying various attack types and security measures for the cloud model is the major objective.

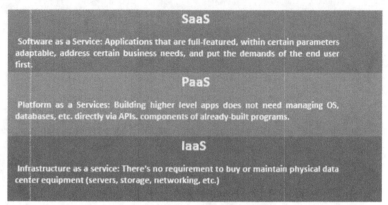

Fig. 76.1   Layers of cloud computation

Source: Author

2. Cloud Security Issues

A variety of cloud services, including IaaS, PaaS, and SaaS, and models including public, private, and hybrid, are used by organizations. These models and services suffer from a number of cloud security problems. Every service model has certain related problems. In order to ensure that the services they offer are safe and to manage consumer identification, security concerns are first viewed from the perspective of the service provider. The customer's perspective is another viewpoint that confirms the level of security of the service being used.

2.1 Multi-tenancy

A cloud model is created for things like resource sharing, shared computation, memory, and storage [2]. The effective use of resources offered by multi-tenancy keeps costs down. It means sharing computing resources, services, and applications at the provider's facilities with other tenants existing on the same physical or logical platform. As a result, it compromises data secrecy, causing information to leak, data to be encrypted, and a rise in the risk of assault.

2.2 Elasticity

Elasticity is the degree to which a system can adjust to variations in workload by automatically allocating and providing resources so that they satisfy the demand as nearly as feasible at any given time. Scalability is an elastic property. Customers may scale up or down as necessary, according to the statement. A resource that was previously assigned to another tenant can now be used by other tenants thanks to this scalability. The potential for secrecy problems exists nonetheless.

2.3 Insider Attacks

A multitenant cloud model paradigm that is managed solely by the provider. This threat materializes within the company. There are no requirements or providers for recruiting cloud workers [1]. Therefore, a third-party vendor might simply breach the data of one company, damage it, and then sell it to another company.

2.4 Outsider Attacks

Because it makes private company information public, this is one of the most alarming problems in a corporation. Clouds differ from private networks in that they have more interfaces. Therefore, hackers and assailants have an edge in taking use of the API's flaws and may disrupt connections [1]. These assaults are less dangerous than insider attacks since the latter can occasionally go undetected.

2.5 Loss of Control

Organizations can be oblivious of the location of their services and data thanks to the cloud's location transparency approach. As a result, service providers may host their services on the cloud from anywhere. In this scenario, the company may lose its data and may not be aware of the supplier's security measures.

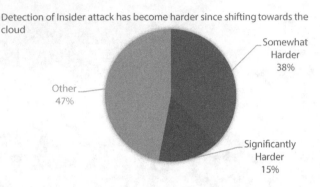

Fig. 76.2 Percentage of insiders versus outsiders

Source: Author

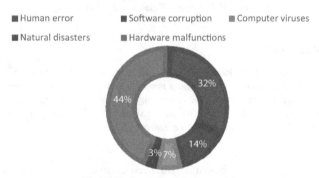

Fig. 76.3 Loss of control over data

Source: Author

2.6 Data Loss

Since there are several tenants in the cloud, data reliability and security could not be guaranteed. Records loss may cause a firm to lose customers and money. A notable illustration of this is the upgrading and deleting of data without a backup.

3. Network Security

3.1 Man in Middle Attack

In this strike, the mugger establishes a separate context and talks with the cloud's private network user under his or her complete control.

3.2 Distributed Denial of Service Attacks

A massive quantity of network traffic bringing down servers and networks during a DDOS assault prevents people from accessing a certain Internet-based service. [3]

3.3 Port Scanning

Port is the starting point for information exchange. As soon as the subscriber configures the group, port scanning begins. The security concerns are violated since port scanning happens automatically when you configure the internet [3].

3.4 Malware Injection Attack Problem

Since there is a lot of data being exchanged between cloud providers and consumers, user authentication and authorization are required [10]. Attackers may insert harmful code into data transfers between cloud providers and users. The original user might then have to wait until the fraudulently inserted job is finished.

3.5 Flooding Attack Problem

There are several servers in the cloud that exchange information and connect with one another. As soon as a request is handled, the requested jobs must first be authorised, however this authentication uses a lot of CPU and memory, causing the server to become overwhelmed and transmit the burden to another server[10]. By doing all of this, the system's regular functioning is halted, and it becomes swamped.

4. Techniques to Secure Data in Cloud

4.1 Authentication and Identity

There are several ways to authenticate people and even communication systems, but cryptography is the most widely used [8]. User authentication may happen in several different ways, such as through the use of unique passwords, security tokens, or quantifiable data like fingerprints. When an organization employs several cloud service providers (CSPs), adopting standard identification procedures in a cloud environment can be problematic [8]. Synchronizing identification information with the organization in such a use case is not scalable. When infrastructure is migrated to a cloud-based solution, additional issues with traditional identity systems appear.

4.2 Data Encryption

Use data encryption techniques if you intend to keep confidential data on a sizable data storage. Firewalls and passwords are helpful, but they may still be hacked to access your data. Data that has been encrypted cannot be decrypted or read without the encryption key. The invader can do nothing with the information. It is a method for converting data into a secret code. You need to have the encryption key, which is also known as the secret key or password, in order to read encrypted data.

4.3 Information Integrity and Privacy

Valid users can access resources and information using cloud computing. Web browsers may be used to access resources, and hostile attackers can also do so [2]. The provision of mutual trust between the supplier and the user is a practical solution to the issue of information integrity. Another option is to set up adequate authentication, authorizations, and accounting controls so that information access should go through several stages of verification to guarantee that resources are being used in a permitted manner [2]. There should be some secure access methods available, such as SSH-based tunnels and RSA certificates.

4.4 Availability of Information (SLA)

The lack of information or data availability is a significant problem with cloud computation services. Information regarding whether or not users may access network resources is provided by a service level agreement. It is a connection of trust between the customer and the supplier [2]. Having a backup plan for both the most important information and local resources is one technique to ensure resource availability. This gives the user access to resource information even when it is no longer available.

4.5 Secure Information Management

It is an information security method for gathering data into a single repository. It is made up of agents that operate on the systems that need to be monitored, sending data to a server known as the "Security Console" in the process. The administrator, a human being who oversees the security console, examines the data and responds to any alarms. Cloud security management becomes significantly more challenging as the user base, dependency stack, and number of cloud security techniques grow. It is additionally known as log management. Additionally, cloud service providers provide various security requirements, such as PCI DSS and SAS 70 [2]. Another paradigm of an information security management system is data security management maturity.

4.6 Malware-injection Attack Solution

With this method, several client virtual computers are created and kept in a single storage location. It makes use of the virtual operating system-containing FAT (File Allocation Table) [10]. The FAT table contains the programme that a client is running. Hypervisor manages and schedules all of the instances. Integrity testing is performed via the IDT (Interrupt Descriptor Table).

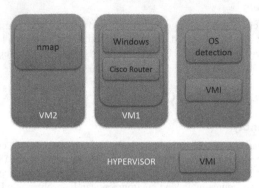

Fig. 76.4   Malware-Injection attack solution [10]

4.7 Flooding Attack Solution

The whole fleet of servers in the cloud is regarded as one server. One fleet of servers is taken into consideration for system-type requests, one for memory management, and the last one for tasks involving core compute. Each server in the fleet has communication capabilities. An additional server, known as the name server, will be utilized to update destinations and states when a server is overloaded. If a server is overloaded, a brand new one is brought in to take its place. Jobs may be managed using a hypervisor [10]. Additionally, the hypervisor handles task authorization and authentication. A PID can be used to identify a request from an authorized customer. The PID can also be encrypted using RSA.

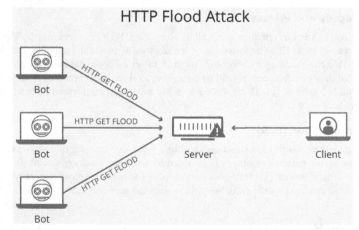

Fig. 76.5   Flooding attack solution [10]

5. Cloud computing Security Standards

Security standards provide instructions on how to develop a security program and what steps to take. Applying cloud-related operations in line with these criteria allows for the maintenance of a safe environment that offers privacy and security. Cloud security is provided via a principle known as "Defense in Depth" [3]. Layers of defense are present in this idea. As there is no single point of failure, overlapping techniques may be utilized to offer security if one of the systems breaks in this fashion. Endpoints have historically used a method of security maintenance in which the user controls access.

5.1 Security Assertion Markup Language (SAML)

Basically, SAML is utilized in commercial transactions to provide secure online partner communication. It is XML-based standard in order to authenticate and authorize partners. The principal (a user), a service provider (SP), and an the three responsibilities are identity provider (IDP), that SAML defines [3]. SAML offers XML-formatted queries and replies that allow for the specification of user attribute, authorization, and authentication data. A website that requests security information is the asking party.

5.2 Open Authentication (OAuth)

It is a technique for communicating with secured data. It primarily serves to provide developers access to data. Users can provide consumers and developers without access to information disclosing their identities [3]. OAuth is dependent on different procedures, like SSL, for protection because it cannot provide any protection on its own.

5.3 OpenID

A single-sign-on (SSO) technique is OpenID. The user just has to log in once to access all of the participating systems [3] thanks to a standard login procedure. It doesn't rely on centralized authorization for user authentication.

5.4 SSL/TLS

TLS is used to offer secure TCP/IP communication. TLS functions primarily over three phases: The choice of cyphers is negotiated between clients during the first phase. Key interchange technique is employed for authentication in the second phase [3]. These methods for key exchange use public keys. The third and final stage comprises cypher and message encryption.

6. Conclusion

This report explains a few cloud-related ideas and gives examples of their benefits, including scalability, platform independence, affordability, flexibility, and reliability. Although there are many security issues with cloud computation, we have covered some of them in this paper as well as prevention methods that may be utilized to keep communications safe and get rid of security issues. This poll is primarily being conducted to examine all of the issues, such as assaults, data loss, and unauthorized access to data, as well as solutions to those issues. The typical security results offered by the cloud ecosystem do not translate due to its virtualization settings as a result of dynamic and complicated nature of cloud computation. Organizations focused on cloud computing security include the Cloud Security Alliance (CSA) and NIST. We have discussed a few security concerns-related ideas in this article, but there are still a lot more that are in the works. As several systems operate and communicate within a cloud, some standards are also set that may be utilized to preserve security and safe communication.

REFERENCES

1. Akhil Behl (2011), Emerging Security Challenges in Cloud Computing (An insight to Cloud security challenges and their mitigation).
2. Akhil Behl & Kanika Behl (2012), An Analysis of Cloud Computing Security Issues.
3. L. Ertaul, S. Singhal & G. Saldamli, Security Challenges In Cloud computing
4. Peter Mell, Tim Grance, The NIST Definition of Cloud Computing, Version 15, October 7, 2009,
5. Cloud Computing: Benefits, Risks and Recommendations for Information Security. ENISA(European Network and Information Security Agency), Crete, 2009.
6. Cloud computing security forum http://cloudsecurity.org/
7. Cloud Computing – A Practical Approach by Velte, Tata McGraw-Hill Edition (ISBN-13:978-0-07-068351-8)
8. Yashpalsinh jadeja & kirti modi (2012) cloud computing-concepts, architecture and challenges
9. Satyendra singh rawat & Mr. Alpesh Soni (2012) ,A Survey of Various Techniques to Secure Cloud Storage
10. R. Balasubramanian, Dr.M.Aramuthan (2012) Security Problems and Possible Security Approaches In Cloud Computing

Computer Science Engineering and Emerging Technologies (ICCS-2022) – Prof (Dr.) Rajeev Sobti et al. (eds)
© 2024 Taylor & Francis Group, London, ISBN 978-1-032-52199-2

Chapter

77

Blockchain Scalability Analysis on Throughput and Long Transaction Time

Dama Vamsi Krishna[1]

Research Scholar, School of Computer Science Engineering,
Lovely Professional University, Phagwara, Punjab

Ravi Shanker[2]

Assistant Professor, School of Computer Science Engineering,
Lovely Professional University, Phagwara, Punjab

Abstract: Decentralized cryptocurrencies that operate on blockchains have received a lot of interest and have seen significant adoption in recent years. The initial blockchain application, Bitcoin, is a huge success and encourages further advancement in this area. However, Bitcoin experiences issues with limited throughput and long transaction times. It also affects other proof-of-work-related cryptocurrencies and raises fresh questions about the scaling of blockchain. The Scalability Issue in Blockchain is two-fold. Off-chain and On-chain On-chain like Block size increase, SegWit, Sharding, Proof-of-Work (PoW), Proof-of-Stake (PoS), or otherwise Off-Chain Lighting networks

Keywords: Blockchain, Scalability, Proof of work, Proof of stake, SegWit, Sharding

1. Introduction

Blockchain was proposed to support Bitcoin [1], the first decentralized cryptocurrency. After Bitcoin, other decentralized cryptocurrencies (such as Litecoin, Bitcoin Cash, and Ethereum) quickly emerged. The blockchains of these coins utilize Nakamoto's PoW method for distributed node consensus.

One big difficulty with blockchain is scalability [2] [3], which is one of its problems. Hundreds of cryptocurrencies rely on the Public blockchain for trades, mining, and record upkeep. Every cryptocurrency struggles with scaling, yet among the largest electronic payment networks worldwide, Visa Net (the Visa credit card payment network) can execute many transfers every second [4]. Due to the diverse protocols used by each cryptocurrency, transaction speeds vary. For instance, Ethereum employs Proof of stake, whereas Bitcoin uses Proof of Work to validate blocks. Ethereum [5] and Bitcoin are two well-known instances of permissionless blockchain. The processing and confirmation times for transactions in different cryptocurrencies are shown in Table 77.1.

Table 77.1 The speed of cryptocurrency transactions [5]

Cryptocurrency	Transactions each second	Transaction completion time duration on general
Bitcoin	5-6	25 min
Ethereum	14-20	2 min

[1]damavamsi622@gmail.com, [2]ravishanker@lpu.co.in

DOI: 10.1201/9781003405580-77

Cryptocurrency	Transactions each second	Transaction completion time duration on general
Bitcoin Cash	61	60 min
Litecoin	26	30 min
Neo	1000	15-20 sec
Cardano	5-7	3-5 min
Ripple	1500	4 sec
Dash	48	2-10 min
Monero	4	30 min

A unique type of distributed database is a blockchain. When all parties trust one another and do not wish to maintain duplicate recordings of the same data, a distributed system functions well. However, when there is no one entity in charge and we need a magical database that is distributed and decentralized, blockchain comes into play since there is no way for the parties to trust each other. (Figure 77.1) [6]. A blockchain's genesis block is its initial block and does not have a parent block.

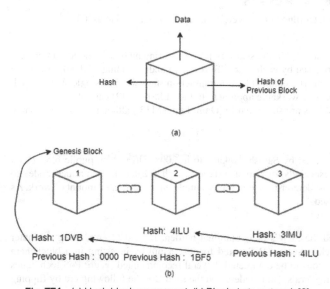

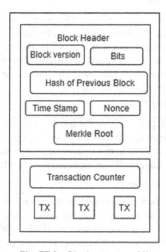

Fig. 77.1   (a) Hash block component, (b) Blockchain network [6]

Fig. 77.2   Block structure [4]

The 1 MB maximum block size may hold up to 4,000 transactions. The typical size of a bitcoin transaction is 250 bytes. Since one block is typically mined once every ten minutes, there are around 7 transactions per second (TPS).

Transactions as well as a transaction counter make up the block body. A block can store a total number of transactions. According to this block size and the amount of each operation, [7] Blockchain validates the authenticity of transactions via an asymmetric cryptography algorithm. Blockchains validatephy-based digital signatures are utilised in an unreliable scenario. Next, we give a quick example of a digital signature.

2. Literature Review

The Scalability Issue in Blockchain is two-fold. Off-chain and On-chain On-chain explanations frequently focus on scalability concerns by focusing on blockchain components, in contrast to Off-chain solutions, which prefer to carry out transactions outside of the chain.

2.1 Layer-1: On-chain Solution

Scalability problems are typically addressed through on-chain solutions by focusing on the blockchain's internal components.

1. Block-size Increase

On-chain solutions are often large in block size. According to this method, there are several important connections between the block size and the public blockchain scalability issue [8]. The huge block can surely support more transactions, which will undoubtedly increase throughput. A huge block is an example of which is Bitcoin Unlimited. However, it decreases the effectiveness of block prorogation over time and may raise the likelihood of a blockchain fork, increasing the likelihood that orphan blocks will require more care.

2. SegWit

The block size is maintained when the latest transactions are added to the block using the SegWit mechanism. To successfully create more storage for subsequent transactions, this strategy seeks to separate the digital signature information from the transaction and store it elsewhere. This method keeps the validating portion and the transaction's actual data apart [9]. By assigning a weight to each block, SegWit suggests a novel technique for figuring out the maximum block size [10].

$$BW = 3 \times BS + TS$$

where BS stands for base size and BW is the newly determined block weight. Total size is referred to as TS.

3. Sharding

The nodes are divided into several pieces known as "shards" in the sharding process. A tiny number of nodes are present in each shard. Small chunks of a transaction are processed by each shard. To reach an understanding of the transaction's status, nodes within shards apply the Byzantine consensus method [11]. If a transaction stays within a single shard, which is regarded as the biggest restriction, sharding is the only workable approach. In fact, Elastico [12] cannot conduct inter-shard transactions automatically. Inter-shard transactions are supported by Omni Ledger [13], although choosing a large shard size might be difficult.

4. Proof-of-Work

The PoW [14] concept for Bitcoin was initially launched by Satoshi Nakamoto in 2008. Since then, public blockchain technologies have adopted it as standard procedure, especially for virtual currencies such as Bitcoin. Each miner (node), to be granted the opportunity to attach a new Block, must demonstrate that it has completed an adequate amount of work. As a result, the term "PoW agreement set of rules" is used.

5. Proof-of-Stake

The PoS is a replacement method that gets around the PoW's computational burden. Instead of employing computer resources to participate in the construction of blocks, users in PoS voted for leadership by investing in a blockchain network, which reduces the time it takes for transactions to be completed. Several recommended secure PoS techniques exist. For instance, Ouroboros [15] chooses the current era's commanders and the seeds for the following era by flipping coins. In Ouroboros Praos, users use a trusted random process to produce a different value.

6. Delegated Proof of Stake

The PoS as well as the DPoS differ essentially in that one is focused on representative democracy while the other relies on democratic representation; nonetheless, this difference does not significantly improve either [16]. The block must be created, validated, and verified by the delegate, among other things. If a small number of miners (nodes) handled validation instead of the entire network, the process would go considerably more quickly. As a result, it would directly affect transaction speed. Therefore, the dishonest delegate should not be a problem. An illustration of DPoS implementation is bit-sharing.

7. Practical Byzantine Fault Tolerance (PBFT)

The PBFT consensus algorithm is frequently used by the permissioned blockchain, i.e., Hyperledger, since it can resist up to 1/3 of harmful byzantine replicas. Byzantine defects are routinely accepted by this system [17]. This model operates in rounds. Each round's principal node selection follows a set of predetermined processes. Three phases are used in the processing of the PBFT consensus protocol: pre-prepared, prepared, and commit. The server then sends a preparation response to all other replicas if it is approved [18].

2.2 Layer-2: Off-Chain Solutions

Lighting Network

The volume of Bitcoin transactions has dramatically expanded recently, exposing its flaws, such as lengthy transaction times and expensive transaction costs. To solve these problems, the Bitcoin network's engineers have recommended a novel strategy called the lightning network. The Lightning Network's core tenet is that two Bitcoin miners create an off-chain trading path via which they can execute several extremely low-latency transactions [19]. This approach comprises three phases. Creating the channel, dealing with it, and closing it when the channel is closed, the total quantity of tokens is utilized by both parties transmitted towards the main chain block on the Lightning Network is low, suggesting that the Lightning Network as it now exists is unsuitable for processing high-value transactions [20]. The widespread use of lightning networks is significantly hampered by the two mentioned drawbacks.

3. Conclusion

Over the past 20 years, the blockchain industry has grown significantly, in part due to the enormous popularity of public blockchain networks, including Bitcoin and Ethereum. Due to the underlying problem of scalability, which has grown to be a serious worry, particularly when utilizing blockchain in a real-world commercial setting, it has not, however, affected as many industries as was anticipated. Major crypto currencies are, in fact, struggling with the same scaling issue. Through this inquiry, we learned that there are several definitions of the word "scalability". Some of the factors that are associated with it are transaction throughput, the quantity of nodes, storage, memory requirements, high connections, duration, pricing, and the validation process. The most talked-about of these, transaction throughput, has a close relationship with a consensus process.

REFERENCES

1. Nakamoto, S., 2008. Bitcoin: A peer-to-peer electronic cash system. Decentralized Business Review, p. 21260.
2. Scherer, M., 2017. Performance and scalability of blockchain networks and smart contracts.
3. Bonneau, J., Miller, A., Clark, J., Narayanan, A., Kroll, J. A. and Felten, E. W., 2015, May. Sok: Research perspectives and challenges for bitcoin and cryptocurrencies. In 2015 IEEE symposium on security and privacy (pp. 104–121). IEEE.
4. Hazari, S.S., and Mahmoud, Q.H., 2019, January. A parallel proof of work to improve transaction speed and scalability in blockchain systems. In 2019 IEEE 9th annual computing and communication workshop and conference (CCWC) (pp. 0916–0921). IEEE.
5. Wood, G., 2014. Ethereum: A secure decentralised generalised transaction ledger. Ethereum project yellow paper, 151(2014), pp. 1–32.
6. Zheng, Z., Xie, S., Dai, H., Chen, X. and Wang, H., 2017, June. An overview of blockchain technology: Architecture, consensus, and future trends. In 2017 IEEE international congress on big data (Big Data congress) (pp. 557–564). Ieee.
7. Göbel, J. and Krzesinski, A.E., 2017, November. Increased block size and Bitcoin blockchain dynamics. In 2017 27th International Telecommunication Networks and Applications Conference (ITNAC) (pp. 1–6). IEEE.
8. Garzik, J., 2015. Block size increase to 2MB. Bitcoin Improvement Proposal, 102.
9. Kim, S., Kwon, Y. and Cho, S., 2018, October. A survey of scalability solutions on blockchain. In 2018 International Conference on Information and Communication Technology Convergence (ICTC) (pp. 1204–1207). IEEE.
10. Basile, M., Nardini, G., Perazzo, P. and Dini, G., 2022, August. SegWit Extension and Improvement of the BlockSim Bitcoin Simulator. In 2022 IEEE International Conference on Blockchain (Blockchain) (pp. 115–123). IEEE.
11. Yu, G., Wang, X., Yu, K., Ni, W., Zhang, J.A. and Liu, R.P., 2020. Survey: Sharding in blockchains. IEEE Access, 8, pp. 14155–14181.
12. Luu, L., Narayanan, V., Zheng, C., Baweja, K., Gilbert, S. and Saxena, P., 2016, October. A secure sharding protocol for open blockchains. In Proceedings of the 2016 ACM SIGSAC conference on computer and communications security (pp. 17–30).
13. Kokoris-Kogias, E., Jovanovic, P., Gasser, L., Gailly, N., Syta, E. and Ford, B., 2018, May. Omniledger: A secure, scale-out, decentralized ledger via sharding. In 2018 IEEE Symposium on Security and Privacy (SP) (pp. 583–598). IEEE.
14. Vukolić, M., 2015, October. The quest for scalable blockchain fabric: Proof-of-work vs. BFT replication. In International workshop on open problems in network security (pp. 112–125). Springer, Cham.
15. Kiayias, A., Russell, A., David, B. and Oliynykov, R., 2017, August. Ouroboros: A provably secure proof-of-stake blockchain protocol. In Annual international cryptology conference (pp. 357–388). Springer, Cham.
16. Liu, D., Alahmadi, A., Ni, J., Lin, X. and Shen, X., 2019. Anonymous reputation system for IIoT-enabled retail marketing atop PoS blockchain. IEEE Transactions on Industrial Informatics, 15(6), pp. 3527–3537.

17. Ferrag, M. A., Derdour, M., Mukherjee, M., Derhab, A., Maglaras, L. and Janicke, H., 2018. Blockchain technologies for the internet of things: Research issues and challenges. IEEE Internet of Things Journal, 6(2), pp. 2188–2204.
18. Garay, J. A. and Moses, Y., 1998. Fully polynomial Byzantine agreement for n> 3 t processors in t+ 1 rounds. SIAM Journal on Computing, 27(1), pp. 247–290.
19. Khan, D., Jung, L. T. and Hashmani, M. A., 2021. Systematic literature review of challenges in blockchain scalability. Applied Sciences, 11(20), p. 9372.
20. Zhou, Q., Huang, H., Zheng, Z. and Bian, J., 2020. Solutions to scalability of blockchain: A survey. Ieee Access, 8, pp. 16440–16455.

Computer Science Engineering and Emerging Technologies (ICCS-2022) – Prof (Dr.) Rajeev Sobti et al. (eds)
© 2024 Taylor & Francis Group, London, ISBN 978-1-032-52199-2

Chapter **78**

Approach Based on Machine Learning to Predict People's Intention to Use Mobile Learning Platforms

Madhavi Katamaneni[1]
Assistant Professor, Department of IT, Vrsiddhartha Engineering College, Vijayawada

Brijesh kumar Verma[2]
Research Scholar, Amity Institute of Information Technology Lucknow, Uttar Pradesh, India

Shyam Sundar[3]
Assistant Professor, Department of Educational planning,
Research and Assessment, District Institute of Education and Training,
(National capital Territory of Delhi) Ansari Road, Daryaganj New Delhi

Prachi Juyal[4]
Assistant Professor, Department of Allied Science (Mathematics),
Graphic Era (Deemed to be University), Dehradun, Uttarakhand, India

Ravi Kumar Sanapala[5]
Associate Professor, Department of Electronics and Communication Engineering,
St Martin's Engineering College, Dhulapally, Secunderabad

Firos A.[6]
Assistant Professor, Department of computer Science and Engineering Rajiv Gandhi University
(A Central University), Rono-Hills, Doimukh, Arunachal Pradesh, India

Abstract: Because of the Coronavirus pandemic issue, mobile learning has formed a significant educational stage in a few schools, universities, colleges, and other instructive foundations all around the world. Numerous understudies currently effectively utilize mobile innovation for learning because of the cruel pandemic-related conditions that have upset physical and eye-to-eye contact education procedures. Overall availability of web-based teaching and learning stages is made conceivable by mobile learning advancements. This study investigated how mobile learning stages are utilized in advanced education settings in the United Arab Emirates.

To inspect how college understudies embraced mobile learning stages for getting to course materials, looking into data online connected with their fields of study, trading information, and submitting tasks during the Coronavirus pandemic, a drawn-out innovation acknowledgment model and the hypothesis of an organized conduct model were proposed. We assembled a total of 1880 understudies from different universities in the United Arab Emirates. Our information investigation discoveries affirmed each connection that was supposed to exist inside the exploration model, as indicated by our discoveries.

Our examination found that executing remote learning stages as informative guides during the Coronavirus pandemic could emphatically affect education and learning. The value of such systems, however, can be diminished as a result of the feelings that students go through, such as anxiety about receiving subpar marks, stress from difficult personal situations,

---
[1]itsmadhavi12@gmail.com, [2]vermamtech05@gmail.com, [3]drssponia@gmail.com, [4]Prachijuyal@yahoo.com, [5]sravikumarece@smec.ac.in, [6]firos.a@rgu.ac.in

DOI: 10.1201/9781003405580-78

and sadness over losing friends. Therefore, the best way to address these challenges is to analyze the feelings that students experienced during the pandemic.

Keywords: Machine learning, Mobile learning, Covid-19, Online learning

1. Introduction

With the aid of appropriate learning platforms and resources, colleges and universities frequently work actively to build online learning environments. Additionally, these institutions of higher learning provide a variety of learning management systems that improve teaching and learning methodologies and practices in an effort to produce effective student results. Advanced education establishments have confronted various challenges because of the Coronavirus pandemic, though, since students all around the world have been feeling depressed and anxious about their academics. These feelings include anxiety, fear, and apprehension. Stigmatization is a result of these bad feelings, which is something that pupils who are psychologically influenced by fear frequently go through. After COVID-19 was proclaimed a pandemic, students also experienced prejudice, loss, and several other psychosocial problems. Students' apprehension has also been impacted by the lockdown effect, making e-learning essential after educational institutions were obliged to stop their contact teaching and learning procedures. Furthermore, students' feelings of trepidation can show up as an apprehension about falling flat, an apprehension about passing up a great opportunity, an apprehension about facing challenges, and a fear welcomed on by frailty (Morchid N. 2020). The Coronavirus lockdown has constrained colleges, universities, and establishments to carry out far-off learning with an end goal to relieve the adverse results of Coronavirus and support student learning, so students' trepidation can likewise affect innovation reception.

A sizeable portion of colleges and universities have encountered problems with respect to teachers' use of technology for instruction and learning. Students' technological aptitude is a challenge because classes must be performed using web-based tools. However, implementing remote learning technology is crucial for effectively evaluating the delivery of web-based courses. The majority of research on technology adoption claims that adoption is complicated since other aspects of teaching and learning, like learning techniques, learning settings, and innovation availability, might change as a result of technology adoption.

The reception of imaginative showing systems (for example, the utilization of versatile learning applications) because of the Coronavirus pandemic and other practically equivalent disasters has not yet been examined, regardless of the way that different researchers have zeroed in on innovation reception in their exploration. Applications for versatile learning are currently exceptionally easy to locate on both the Apple Store and Google Play Store. These stores allow users to download mobile learning apps, and they also handle their automatic updates. Additionally, people are using these apps more frequently due to the freemium business model used by app stores. Notwithstanding, it is essential to consider what teachers and understudies think about utilizing a mobile learning platform during the pandemic. Subsequently, the difficulties connected with the Coronavirus pandemic and the prerequisite for mobile learning frameworks should be addressed (Al-Emran M. 2020). There isn't sufficient focus on what mobile learning can mean for advanced education since utilizing mobile learning stages is as yet a somewhat new practice. The emotion of fear has not received enough attention when thinking about how technology would be adopted during the COVID-19 pandemic, despite the fact that the adoption of technology has been the subject of much research. Previous research has largely focused on technology aspects of teaching and learning while ignoring psychological aspects. The impact of fear on technology adoption is still not fully understood, which is frequently the cause of technology's underutilization in the education sector (Al-Maroof RS 2020).

We looked to give educational information on proper innovation use for periods when understudies and teachers are careful about innovation in the wake of considering the downsides of innovation use in schooling. This is particularly obvious in circumstances (like the Coronavirus pandemic) where utilizing innovation is vital for bettering training for the two students and educators, who are oftentimes novices at involving mechanical apparatuses for educating and learning.

Studies have shown that the theory of planned behavior (TPB) model and the technology acceptance model (TAM) joined as a half-and-half model are useful for advancing innovation reception. These models make it conceivable to measure individuals' receptiveness to embracing and using innovation (Liu Q, Geertshuis S, 2020). The TPB model and TAM, alongside two outer elements, are utilized in this review to comprehend students' and teachers' longing to utilize portable learning frameworks (i.e., subjective norms [SNs] and fear). To examine students' and educators' perspectives on the use of AI strategies all through the scattering of Coronavirus, we had the option to apply the Hat and TPB models. Moreover, there are not many investigations of dread during the Coronavirus scourge and what dread directly means for the TAM and TPB models. We set off on a mission to make a half-breed model that might distinguish the different concerns that the two students and instructors might have during the Coronavirus pandemic in the absence of proof. Our exploration article has a more prominent likelihood of furnishing instructors and application designers with the information about innovation and training they need to make and utilize new advances during the Coronavirus lockdown time since we inspected the trepidation component.

Assuming more information on the elements of AI reception at the hour of the Coronavirus scourge is gained, it will be feasible to stress the unique instructive issues that have emerged during these phenomenal times. Advanced education foundations can acquire knowledge from the coronavirus-related writing on the innovation reception region in both a hypothetical and viable sense.

2. Literature Review

Many types of fear have been the focus of earlier research studies on technology adoption. For instance, anxiety plays a significant role in managing skepticism and approval of technology. Anxiety affects how readily pupils adopt technology in the educational setting (Patil P. 2020). In addition to worry, a lack of knowledge and abilities may also affect how people use technology. The acknowledgment of innovation is hampered by nervousness, inadequate mechanical proficiency, and innovation-related fear. Subsequently, it is essential for teachers to focus on mental development and help students tolerate the utilization of innovation. Specialized status and readiness are different reasons for innovation reception uneasiness in the instructional area; both of these causes have an adverse consequence (Callum KM 2014).

There are other industries, as well as the education sector, that have shown resistance to adopting new technologies. When using technology, students in the medical industry typically perceive hazards and display negative anxiety (Meng F. 2020). Additionally, one of the main issues facing the medical community is health anxiety. Patients' apprehension and the worry of learning they have a serious illness are examples of health anxiety. Numerous fears related to clients' opinions and attitudes about technology have been identified in the banking industry. Customers do not want their data to be used for mobile transactions. Customers are adversely affected by the frauds that have happened and are afraid of using technology in mobile banking. They consequently lack both technological expertise and confidence (Bailey AA, 2019). Concerning the household sector, the biggest deterrents to utilizing technology include apprehension about using it and concern that it will add to the burden of family responsibilities.

Numerous studies have evaluated the challenges surrounding technological adoption and apprehension. These study investigations are based on the TAM (Kamal SA 2020) and a number of additional models, and the majority of them have evaluated how technology acceptance can be influenced by technology phobia. Many tech users have offered explanations for why they are afraid of using technology. For instance, a number of users have said that their dread is connected to their level of confidence. When a human is given a task, mistakes are bound to happen, and fretting excessively about this fact just makes people fearful (Gresham J. 2020). Additionally, a number of users have claimed that they avoid using technology because they feel that it takes too much time and prevents them from finishing their jobs. The impact of fear on data privacy breaches has been evaluated by a number of technology acceptance studies, which is why privacy and security awareness are prioritized in technology research investigations.

The utilization of mobile learning in United Arab Emirates (UAE) organizations has not been sufficiently explored observationally before, and the elements that influence students' real innovation use have not been considered. With regards to systems, primary condition demonstration and AI strategies have generally been utilized by specialists concentrating on innovation acknowledgment to assess theoretical models. The TAM and TPB models were joined into one hypothetical model, and we utilized ML and partial least squares structural equation modeling (PLS-SEM) calculations to approve the subsequent hypothetical model. In the wake of considering different hypothetical models, we led this review with the accompanying goals: (1) look at how students utilize mobile learning.

3. Methodology

3.1 Data Collection

The study's intended audience was college students. Students at colleges in the UAE gave the information. The Higher Colleges of Technology, The British University in Dubai, the United Arab Emirates University, the University of Fujairah, the American University in the UAE, and the University of Ajman were the seven prestigious colleges in the UAE that were at last chosen for this review. In 2020, we will assemble information from May through June. The accommodation examination technique was utilized in this review to assemble information. From a total of 2000 understudies, 1880 were taken. There were 778 ladies and 1102 men, or 58.6% and 41.4% individually.

Table 78.1 Students in participating universities (N = 1880) (Al-Maroof RAS 2018)

University	Number of students, *n*
United Arab Emirates University	569
University of Sharjah	438
Higher Colleges of Technology	366
Ajman University	286
The British University in Dubai	104
University of Fujairah	67
American University in United Arab Emirates	50

3.2 Create a Model

The exploration strategy for this study was made to integrate the SN and dread parts into two distinct kinds of hypothetical models the TAM and TPB model. We expected that the SN and dread would affect how effectively and successfully mobile learning frameworks are viewed as utilized. Furthermore, we guessed that the continuous craving to utilize portable learning frameworks will affect mentality and perceived behavioural control (PBC). Figure 78.1 shows the proposed theoretical model.

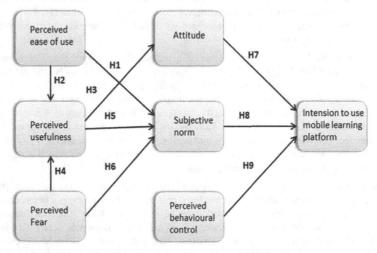

Fig. 78.1 Study model (Al-Maroof RAS 2018)

3.3 TAM

The TAM's major goal is to validate outside elements based on one's own beliefs. Since it may be used to explain why people are able to embrace technology in their educational institutions, the concept is regarded as being highly potent

(Al-Maroof RAS 2018). The TAM states that the PEOU and PU are the only types of perceptions that can be measured. This implies that the user's behavioral intentions can be directly changed. PU should be taken into account because it may be used to gauge how much a person must evaluate technology and determine whether it is beneficial enough to be adopted and accepted. The PEOU, on the other hand, refers to how much a person believes technology is controllable and reachable.

The longing of a client to utilize a framework has been characterized as a mentality with regards to innovation acknowledgment. Prior research on mobile learning has proposed an association between social goals and mentality. The expectation to utilize mobile learning frameworks might be incredibly affected by attitude, according to earlier studies.

Considering the prior presumptions, it can be concluded that consumers will continue to have a positive attitude if technology is perceived as being simple to use. User perceptions are therefore very significant. Users are predicted to adopt technology if they have a good mindset. After incorporating the earlier presumptions into the study model, the following hypotheses were put forth:

1. The PEOU will predict the SN,
2. The PEOU will predict PU,
3. The PU will predict attitude,
4. The PU will predict the SN,
5. People's attitudes will predict their intention to use a mobile learning platform (ie, H7).

3.4 SN

A strategy known as the SN, which is a kind of discernment in view of the presence of individuals who show comparable attitudes and ways of behaving toward innovation, can be utilized to measure individual discernments. The SN fortifies the TAM since it permits the TAM to consolidate client ways of behaving that are normal among a client bunch. The objective of understudies to involve mobile learning innovation for schoolmate bunch gatherings is a part of the SN, which is an outer variable.

The SN likewise influences the conduct aim, the PU, and the PEOU, as per various examinations on mechanical reception or worthiness. In a new report, Huang et al. utilized the SN and TAM as outer factors and found that the Hat implanted parts from various exploration papers showed a discernibly close relationship with outside factors. In any case, they found that different examinations had not actually or completely utilized the outer component SN. As indicated by previous research, the SN impressively affects clients' aims to utilize mobile learning frameworks (Al-Emran M 2020). In this way, it was concluded that the SN would gauge individuals' expectations to utilize a portable learning stage (i.e., H8).

3.5 Perceived Fear

The exceptional Coronavirus ailment was first seen in China in December 2019, and over the long run, it spread to the remainder of the world. As per late examinations, people have reacted with terror to the alleged threat posed by the SARS-CoV-2 virus. Fear is also at its maximum level, according to the Health Anxiety Inventory scale (Nicomedes CJ 2020). Even though people regard fear as a good thing when genuine threats are present, fear in the Coronavirus pandemic situation might be oppressive and persistent. The COVID-19 pandemic has caused a variety of fears, including worry about one's health, uncertainty, and the possibility of losing loved ones. Two crucial difficulties have emerged as a result of the COVID-19 pandemic: a high level of fear and a high likelihood of contracting the illness.

Through the use of the TAM, this study endeavored to look at the connection between the reception of innovation and the outside factor of perceived fear (PF). TAM restrictions are required to be overcome in this study. These restrictions include the application of external elements, such as PU, the PEOU, and the SN, which are particular to the analysis of a TAM for PF. In light of these considerations, the following theories were created: PF will forecast both the PU (i.e., H4) and the SN (i.e., H6).

3.6 PBC

Individuals' impression of the straightforwardness or trouble of completing an interest-related conduct is alluded to as PBC. The goal of mobile, versatile learning stages is profoundly influenced by PBC, as per a prior study. Therefore, it was theorized that PBC would estimate individuals' goals to utilize mobile learning stages (i.e., H9). The proposed research model was made utilizing our thoughts, as displayed in Figure 78.1. Machine learning strategies were utilized to look at the theoretical model, which was given as an underlying condition model.

4. Results and Discussion

Two elective techniques were utilized to survey the hypothetical model that was developed in this review. The principal strategy utilized the SmartPLS (SmartPLS GmbH) instrument and PLS-SEM. The PLS-SEM procedure was used in this work basically on the grounds that it considered the synchronous examination of the underlying and estimation models, which worked on the precision of the discoveries. For the subsequent strategy, Weka (College of Waikato) machine learning methods were utilized to figure out the reasonable model's dependent variables.

We embraced a corresponding procedure that combines the use of PLS-SEM and AI order techniques to test our recommended model. There haven't been many studies that have endeavored to gauge how portable learning frameworks will truly be utilized utilizing AI techniques. Thus, research on data frameworks that utilize a reciprocal multianalytical approach can be very compelling. Likewise, to be stressed is the way that PLS-SEM can support both the forecast of a dependent variable and the approval of a reasonable model that looks to propel a current hypothesis. Like how an independent variable can be anticipated, a dependent variable may in like manner be anticipated with the guidance of regulated machine learning calculations and free factors. The work of various arrangement calculations related to the utilization of various strategies, for example, brain organizations, affiliation rules, Bayesian organizations, and choice trees, was one more piece of our review. Our outcomes showed that the J48 choice tree frequently outflanked different classifiers. Moreover, to make homogenous subsamples from our principal test in view of the essential independent variable, we utilized a nonparametric choice tree to order both categorical and continuous (i.e., mathematical) factors. To put it another way, we utilized example substitutions chosen indiscriminately from an enormous number of subsamples to gauge the meaning of coefficients using the nonparametric PLS-SEM technique. The adequacy of sending mobile learning stages during the Coronavirus plague was upheld by genuine information from this examination.

In Table 78.2, we show the use of mobile learning platforms for prediction of intention on the basis of behavioral control, subjective norm, and attitude. The accuracy and precision of different classifiers were shown on the basis of the F factor and CCI%.

Table 78.2   Predicting the intention to use a mobile learning platform based on behaviour, perceptions of behavioural control, and attitude (Al-Maroof RAS 2018)

Classifier	Correctly classified instances	True positive	False positive	Recall	Precision	F measure
Logistic	82.23	0.813	0.372	0.814	0.759	0.753
Locally WeightedLearning	81.73	0.808	0.39	0.813	0.752	0.76
Bayes Net	82.1	0.812	0.304	0.813	0.754	0.76
AdaBoostM1	82.44	0.815	0.815	0.816	0.763	0.762
J48	87.66	0.867	0.596	0.873	0.803	0.799

Research studies have evaluated how the COVID-19 pandemic has affected contemporary technology, particularly how it has affected technology used for teaching and learning. Technology is a useful instrument that offers a fresh and practical platform for continuing instruction and learning even when the school is under lockdown. In order to examine the impact COVID-19 has on teaching practices, this study used machine learning algorithms. Our research model focused on PF's effects, which had a significant impact on measuring COVID-19's effects on student and instructor groups. Our data also allowed us to evaluate the pandemic's impact on teaching-related mobile learning technology. As a result, our study contributes to filling in the gaps in the literature and laying the groundwork for future studies on mobile learning and teaching approaches. Rewrite your content as soon as possible.

5. Conclusion

The findings of this study are consistent with past examinations of the meaning of elements in the TAM and TPB models (Teo T. 2012). We observed that students were undeniably more open to utilizing innovation during the Coronavirus pandemic, assuming mobile learning innovation was the main asset available. Our discoveries in regards to PU and the PEOU are practically identical to those of prior examinations that took a gander at what PU and the PEOU meant for students acknowledgment of mobile learning advancements. Signs of students preparation to take on mobile learning stages during the Coronavirus pandemic ought to in this manner incorporate the PU and the PEOU. Moreover, the PEOU fundamentally affected PU, exhibiting that in the event that an innovation is easy to utilize, it is likewise prone to be viewed as supportive. Our discoveries likewise uncovered a huge relationship (P.001) between understudies' reception of mobile learning innovation and the emotional standard.

Review has shown that students' reception of mobile learning innovation is fundamentally affected by their conduct in the study hall, conduct beyond the homeroom, and responses to the utilization of mobile learning innovation. The SN and students' reception of mobile learning innovation are connected, as indicated by prior investigations. Students lives in the UAE are vigorously affected by the activities of their companions. Furthermore, students' are urged to utilize mobile learning gadgets to communicate with cohorts. Furthermore, various elements outside the PEOU and PU emphatically impacted the SN. Our discoveries show that attitudes among instructors and students' likewise supported the use of mobile learning stages as a teaching device during the pandemic. When teachers and students approach mobile learning tools positively, they will see them as pleasant, helpful, and low-effort.

Our results are in line with those of earlier research. For instance, it has been claimed that feedback from peers, students, and teachers can have a positive impact on how students feel about and perceive the usefulness of technology. The COVID-19 epidemic has caused an increase in panic. Given the continued adverse effects of this on the human population, this should be viewed as a crucial area for future research.

Pandemic of Coronavirus Worldwide, there is a requirement for complete lockdown and remain-at-home strategies since the SARS-CoV-2 infection has a high capability of spreading (Zhang SX 2020). We made a model in this study that will be useful for future exploration since it tends to be utilized to check the coronavirus' effect during the pandemic. In light of the discoveries of our review and the flood of uneasiness that happened during the pandemic, we feel that mobile learning advances are critical and viable assets that guide in bringing down tension between understudies and educators. In our examination, PF altogether affected the PEOU and PU. Moreover, in light of the answers we got, there was certainly alarm all through the pestilence period. Mobile learning stages, then again, kept on keeping up with elevated degrees of PU and PEOU, which diminished uneasiness and constrained students to go to their ordinary illustrations.

REFERENCES

1. Morchid N. The Current State of Technology Acceptance: A Comparative Study. Journal of Business and Management 2020 Feb; 22(2): 1–16 [FREE Full text]
2. Al-Emran M. Mobile learning during the era of COVID-19. Revista Virtual Universidad Católica del Norte 2020 Dec; 1(61): 1–2.
3. Al-Maroof RS, Salloum SA, Hassanien AE, Shaalan K. Fear from COVID-19 and technology adoption: the impact of Google Meet during Coronavirus pandemic. Interactive Learning Environments 2020 Oct 14: 1–16 [FREE Full text]
4. Liu Q, Geertshuis S, Grainger R. Understanding academics' adoption of learning technologies: A systematic review. Comput Educ 2020 Jul; 151: 103857.
5. Patil P, Tamilmani K, Rana NP, Raghavan V. Understanding consumer adoption of mobile payment in India: Extending Meta-UTAUT model with personal innovativeness, anxiety, trust, and grievance redressal. Int J Inf Manag 2020 Oct; 54: 102144.
6. Callum KM, Jeffrey L, Kinshuk. Comparing the role of ICT literacy and anxiety in the adoption of mobile learning. Comput Human Behav 2014 Oct; 39: 8–19.
7. Meng F, Guo X, Zhang X, Peng Z, Lai KH. Examining the Role of Technology Anxiety and Health Anxiety on Elderly Users' Continuance Intention for Mobile Health Services Use. 2020 Presented at: Proceedings of the 53rd Hawaii International Conference on System Sciences; January 7-10, 2020; Maui, Hawaii p. 3297–3306 URL: https://scholarspace. manoa.hawaii.edu/bitstream/10125/64145/0325.pdf
8. Kamal SA, Shafiq M, Kakria P. Investigating acceptance of telemedicine services through an extended technology acceptance model (TAM). Technol Soc 2020 Feb; 60: 101212.
9. Bailey A. A., Pentina I., Mishra A. S., Mimoun M. S. B. Exploring factors influencing US millennial consumers' use of tap-and-go payment technology. The International Review of Retail, Distribution and Consumer Research 2019 Oct 22; 20(2): 143–163.
10. Gresham J. Manufacturing Trends in Automated Inspection Equipment: Linking Technology with Business Change Management Using the Technology Acceptance Model. ProQuest Dissertations Publishing. 2020.
11. Al-Maroof RAS, Al-Emran M. Students Acceptance of Google Classroom: An Exploratory Study using PLS-SEM Approach. International Journal of Emerging Technologies in Learning 2018 May 29; 13(6): 112–123. [doi: 10.3991/ijet.v13i06.8275]
12. Teo T. Examining the intention to use technology among pre-service teachers: an integration of the Technology Acceptance Model and Theory of Planned Behavior. Interactive Learning Environments 2012 Feb; 20(1): 3–18.
13. Al-Emran M, Arpaci I, Salloum SA. An empirical examination of continuous intention to use m-learning: An integrated model. Educ Inf Technol (Dordr) 2020 Jan 04; 25: 2899–2918
14. Huang F, Teo T, Zhou M. Chinese students' intentions to use the Internet-based technology for learning. Education Tech Research Dev 2019 Jul 17; 68(1): 575–591
15. Nicomedes CJ, Avila RM. An Analysis on the Panic of Filipinos During COVID-19 Pandemic in the Philippines. ResearchGate. Preprint posted online on March 21, 2020.
16. Zhang SX, Wang Y, Rauch A, Wei F. Unprecedented disruption of lives and work: Health, distress and life satisfaction of working adults in China one month into the COVID-19 outbreak. Psychiatry Res 2020 Jun; 288: 112958

Computer Science Engineering and Emerging Technologies (ICCS-2022) – Prof (Dr.) Rajeev Sobti et al. (eds)
© 2024 Taylor & Francis Group, London, ISBN 978-1-032-52199-2

Chapter **79**

Epileptic Seizure Detection and Classification Based on EEG Signals Using Particle Swarm Optimization and Whale Optimization Algorithm

Puja Dhar[1]

Research Scholar, Lovely Professional University, Punjab

Vijay Kumar Garg[2]

Associate Professor, Department of Computer Science Engineering,
Lovely Professional University, Punjab

Abstract: Researchers claim that as the population has grown, more people are affected by epilepsy than ever before—about 65 million people, according to a WHO report. Electroencephalogram (EEG) signals, which serve to record patient information and have the capacity to gather the signals received from electrodes, have been used in numerous investigations to identify epilepsy. The spatial distribution of particular fields, with an emphasis on the brain, is displayed along with these signals. In the current study, we used a hybrid approach that combines a Dense Convolutional Network (DenseNet201) and LSTM (Long Short-Term Memory) for identifying epileptic seizures using EEG data, and we used WOA (Whale Optimization Algorithm) and PSO to select the right features. The current study's primary goal is to shorten the time-consuming.

Keywords: PSO, Whale optimization, CNN, RNN, EEG signal

1. Introduction

The signals are observed manually, which is considered to be sensitive work that led to practical equipment for the study that is used in seizure detection diagnosis. In the majority of scenarios, EEG is considered valuable equipment that is mainly concentrated on the spatial-temporal dynamic characterization of the neuron activities taking place in the brain. Epileptic seizure detection is the main area of current research, and these subjects still require further attention. In the health sector, it is crucial to apply a variety of ML or DL techniques, such as PSO, or particle swarm optimization, CNN, or fuzzy-based concepts, among many others. Undoubtedly, several epileptic seizure detection techniques are used with EEG recordings (Slimen, et al., 2020).

Additionally, aberrant neuronal activity and improper neuronal synchronisation in the brain can be used to detect epilepsy symptoms. Millions of people worldwide are affected by this chronic neurological illness that developed in the brain as a result of excessive electrical activity, which is defined by epileptic seizures. Therefore, if not appropriately treated and recognised, these have physiological, cognitive, and neurological effects that can cause death or dizziness (Saminu et al., 2021). These investigations show that hyper-synchronous and other aberrant activity in neuron cells that has an impact on the patient's physical and mental health is the cause of this sort of disease. Electroencephalography (EEG) technologies are used to detect seizures when they occur.

[1]puja.dhar@rediffmail.com, [2]vijay.garg@lpu.co.in

DOI: 10.1201/9781003405580-79

The aberrant activities that occurred in the brain neurons that were recorded using EEG are captured in this clinical test, which is carried out under a variety of conditions. The biological signals in the recordings make them difficult to decipher, making manual investigation impossible. The absence of neurologists during lengthy EEG recordings, however, is the main problem encountered during manual EEG signal inspection. In order to accurately identify the seizures, it is a difficult and time-consuming process that requires expertise. However, using automatic EEG readings allows for the resolution of these problems. Machine Learning (ML) approaches are used to test and train the obtained datasets in order to automatically capture the signals (Qureshi, M. B et al., 2021).

The EEG also has a big impact on the medical field, particularly when it comes to diagnosing epilepsy through measuring brain activity. The subject's knowledge facilitates the analysis of EEG records to detect epileptic activity. Convolutional Neural Network (CNN) was used in (Zhou, M. et al., 2018) as an alternative to feature extraction, which has been used to distinguish between interictal, preictal, and ictaol segments for diagnosing epileptic seizures, in order to address several problems that remain in the present research.

2. Literature Review

EESC (epileptic-EEG-signal) classification has been used in studies for precise classification of various epileptic states (Gao, Y et al., 2020), which includes important information on the electrical activities that took place in the brain for investigation. This technique first converts EEG signals into PSDEDs (power-spectrum-density-energy diagrams), and then it uses transfer learning and a DCNN (Deep Convolutional Neural Network) to automatically analyse the PSDED's extracted features. Seizures, preictal states, interictal states, and other epileptic states are eventually divided into four categories. When comparing the efficiency and precision of this procedure to the alternatives, it produced effective results. When using CHB-MIT epileptic EEG data, the classification accuracy is typically 90%. To offer better epilepsy treatment, it is important to improve the EESC approach.

In Subasi, A et al. (2019), an epileptic seizure was detected using a hybrid approach that combines PSO (particle swarm optimization) and GA (genetic algorithm). In most cases, notably for the categorization of EEG data, the PSO approach aids in the creation of the SVM - Support Vector Machine optimization parameters. As a result, SVM is regarded as an efficient ML technique and has been used in a variety of applications. The accuracy of classification is influenced by the SVM kernel parameters that are processed during training. The goal of the current study was to raise the SVM parameters through optimization by using PSO and GA-based techniques. When compared to GA algorithms, PSO-based approaches are processed more efficiently. With the EEG datasets, the current hybrid SVM approach achieved 99.38% accuracy, which is better. The hybrid classifier run-time should still be minimized in the future for better performance.

In Kabir, E. et al. (2016), an analytic system that uses statistical features in line with the optimum allocation - OAT approach and the LMT - logistic model trees has been used in the research for the detection of epileptic seizures processed from EEG signals.

Additionally, DCNN has the ability to categorise and recognise epilepsy episodes based on EEG-spectrogram images. The research used an EEG dataset that is freely accessible online, and this approach led to an EEG classification accuracy of 98.22%. Convolutional neural networks, or CNNs, are the foundation of deep learning techniques used in (Abiyev, R et al.,2020) to identify epilepsy from EEG information. Therefore, CNN training to diagnose epilepsy used a four-level structure. The CNN training was also created using a cross-validation technique. The datasets from Bonn University were used to create the classification system. Eventually, specificity, sensitivity, and accuracy for the simulation results were determined to be 98.83%, 97.67%, and 98.67%, respectively.

3. Data Collection

To start the experiment, the right datasets need to be gathered from the right sources. In the current study, we used datasets made up of 11500 records that were collected from several time-series and multivariate data sources and contained particular data such as Recording of Seizure Activity, Tumour-Located, Healthy-Brain-Area, Eyes closed, and Eyes-Open. These are the pre-processed data values that will be used later. The second step in the experimental process is data sampling or pre-processing. Background noise and uncertainty have been removed from the data by pre-processing the information acquired from various time-series and multivariate datasets. Here, filters like the FIR filter and the adaptive filter have been used in the experimentation process.

4. Feature Selection and Extraction

We used temporal and spectral characteristics for feature extraction and PSO and Whale optimization for feature selection in the feature extraction and selection approach. The following phase is feature selection, where a successful automated method has been created to identify epileptic seizures and categorise the EEG signals for epileptic seizures into specific occurrences, including post-seizure, seizure, and pre-seizure. These need to be properly identified and analysed. We applied PSO and whale optimization strategies during the feature selection phase. The PSO technique's key advantages are that it is straightforward, effective, simple to use, and robust when controlling parameters. The PSO algorithm is described below, and the optimal feature subset was used to predict the outcome of the ideal location.

4.1 PSO—Optimization Algorithm

Input-Feat-Original Feature-set, N1 - Defines the population size, H02 - Feature dimension, Maximum Iteration (MI) - 100 iterations, O/P (Output) - optimal-feature subset, Label (L) - Input Feature Labels

Initiate the particle presents in the population, Evaluate the correlation matrix coefficients M amidst features in Fe, Evaluate every feature contribution in Fe by Rr While - The iteration termination condition is not satisfied certain aspects.

do

For j=j to N1 do

Evaluate the particle fitness value utilizing KNN classifier Historical best-position update of the particle

end for

Velocity of the particle Update, Population Optimal position Update For j=I to N1 do

For j=1 to h02 do

Finally, the particle position Update by integrating the value v of every feature end for

end for end while

Further, WOA optimization has been utilized in the research, and it is a population-based method that can avoid certain local optima conditions to achieve a global-optimum solution. Therefore, this technique can solve various unconstrained and constrained issues that occur in the practical application without structural reformation.

4.2 WOA Optimization

Input-Feat-Original Feature-set

N1 - Defines the population size, Lb1 - lower_bound – 0, Ub1 - upper_bound - 1 Threshold_value – 1, H02 - Feature dimension, Maximum Iteration (MI) - 100 iterations, O/P (Output) - optimal-feature subset, Label (L) - Input Feature Labels Initiate the particle presents in the population

Evaluate the correlation matrix coefficients M amidst features in Fe

Evaluate every feature contribution in Fe by Rr

While

Every iteration termination condition is not satisfied

For j=j to N1 do

Fitness value Evaluation of the particle utilizing KNN-classifier,

Update the agents historical best-position

end for

Update the population optimal position

For j=I to N1 do

For j=1 to ho1 do

Feature

If (fit1 <0.5)

Update the current position search agent using equ1

elseif (fit1 <1)

Random search-agent selection (rand)

Update the current position search agent using equ2

end for

end for

end while

The current research has utilized PSO and WOA in the feature selection process in order to provide an efficient outcome that helps in the real-time application. The WOA optimization fitness graph has been represented in Fig. 79.1. The mathematical formulation of PSO and WOA at their current position has been expressed as follows:

4.3 PSO Formula

$$x_j\,(t1 + 1) = x_j\,(t1 + vj\,(t1 + 1))$$ (1)

WOA Formula

$$\vec{d} = |\,c * \vec{Y}rand - \vec{Y}|$$ (2)

$$\overrightarrow{Y(t1 + 1)} = \vec{Y}rand - \vec{B} * \vec{Y}$$ (3)

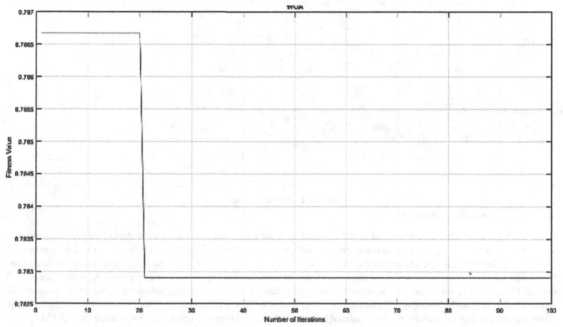

Fig. 79.1 WOA fitness graph showing fitness value vs. number of iterations

Source: Original Graph

5. Hybrid RNN(LSTM) with CNN (Densenet201)

In the current research, three primary layers have been utilized, stacked together to develop a fully connected CNN that is a dense layer, pooling layer, and convolutional layer. Firstly, the input signal has been interconnected to the convolutional layer to manage the operation utilizing a window (kernel). Therefore, the outcome of the equation, as mentioned earlier, is created as a feature map for the layer presented next. Further, the convolutional layers are presented in between, and a pooling layer will be utilized in order to minimize the feature map size; therefore, it allows fast computation. Certainly, each neuron presented in the pooling layer is interconnected with the neuron presented in the fully connected layer. Here, the high-level features are utilized in the research in input signal classification into different classes.

Moreover, this study utilizes pre-trained NN models known as DENSENET-201 in experimentation with the CNN and 201 layers deep. The total network can be trained by loading pre-trained, and it has the capability to train images captured from the ImageNet database. Certainly, the dense201 was modified into an RNN and compared with the conventional feedforward network architecture. Further, RNN has the capability to inherit the properties of strong modeling and has the capacity to study sequential data as neurons and transmit feedback signals to the next presented neuron found in the hidden layer.

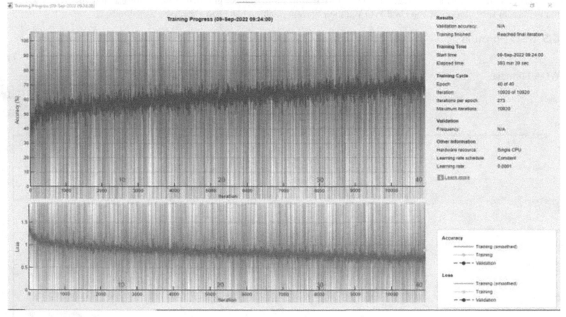

Fig. 79.2 Training image

Source: Image captured using MATLAB

Here, the high-level features are utilized in the research in input signal classification into different classes. The training image is represented in Fig. 79.2. Eventually, this research integrates the CNN and RNN by developing a DL network for information, including image sequences that include medical images or videos. The sequence input layer has been used to provide the images to the network and employed with the convolutional operations at every step. As a first step, it will convert the image sequences into arrays utilizing the folding sequence layer. Once the operation is executed, restoring the sequence structure and converting the changes arrays to image-sequence is significant. Finally, in order to transform the converted data to feature vectors, we have utilized a flattened layer and then the input vector sequence into LSTM.

6. Results and Discussions

This section compares the results of the hybrid RNN-CNN model with those of other existing techniques. The WOA and PSO feature selection and classification are compared with the Hybrid LSTM with Dense201. We utilized RNN-LSTM in the experimentation process for classification, as stated in this section. This proposed method has successfully and efficiently extracted the feature map signals and procured better results than existing research.

7. Conclusion

In the current research, a novel hybrid DL model that integrates a Dense Convolutional Network (DenseNet201) and LSTM (Long Short-Term Memory) for epileptic seizures was identified using EEG data to choose the features of PSO and WOA optimizations. The proposed method first transforms the EEG data into an Adaptive FIR filter. Therefore, it usually chooses features utilizing WOA and PSO optimization algorithms. Then, we trained the previously transformed image via a hybrid model integrating Densenet201 and LSTM. Eventually, the performance of the proposed method has procured efficient results with an accuracy of 90.34% in WOA and PSO and an accuracy of 89.02% in existing methods.

REFERENCES

1. Slimen, I. B., Boubchir, L., Mbarki, Z., & Seddik, H. (2020). EEG epileptic seizure detection and classification based on dual-tree complex wavelet transform and machine learning algorithms. Journal of biomedical research, 34(3), 151.
2. Saminu, S., Xu, G., Shuai, Z., Abd El Kader, I., Jabire, A. H., Ahmed, Y. K., ... & Ahmad, I. S. (2021). A recent investigation on detection and classification of epileptic seizure techniques using EEG signal. Brain Sciences, 11(5), 668.
3. Qureshi, M. B., Afzaal, M., Qureshi, M. S., & Fayaz, M. (2021). Machine learning-based EEG signals classification model for epileptic seizure detection. Multimedia Tools and Applications, 80(12), 17849–17877.
4. Zhou, M., Tian, C., Cao, R., Wang, B., Niu, Y., Hu, T., ... & Xiang, J. (2018). Epileptic seizure detection based on EEG signals and CNN. Frontiers in neuroinformatics, 12, 95.
5. Gao, Y., Gao, B., Chen, Q., Liu, J., & Zhang, Y. (2020). Deep convolutional neural network-based epileptic electroencephalogram (EEG) signal classification. Frontiers in neurology, 11, 375.
6. Subasi, A., Kevric, J., & Abdullah Canbaz, M. (2019). Epileptic seizure detection using hybrid machine learning methods. Neural Computing and Applications, 31(1), 317–325.
7. Kabir, E., & Zhang, Y. (2016). Epileptic seizure detection from EEG signals using logistic model trees. Brain informatics, 3(2), 93–100.
8. Abiyev, R., Arslan, M., Bush Idoko, J., Sekeroglu, B., & Ilhan, A. (2020). Identification of epileptic EEG signals using convolutional neural networks. Applied Sciences, 10(12), 4089.

Computer Science Engineering and Emerging Technologies (ICCS-2022) – Prof (Dr.) Rajeev Sobti et al. (eds)
© 2024 Taylor & Francis Group, London, ISBN 978-1-032-52199-2

Chapter **80**

Coding Sketch: Turn Your Sketch Designs into Code

Ayush Gour[1], Sankalp Sudarsan Rajguru[2], V. Shivanshu Yadav[3]
Student, Department of Computer Science and Engineering,
Lovely Professional University Phagwara, Punjab, India

Shilpa Sharma[4]
Associate Professor, Department of Computer Science and Engineering,
Lovely Professional University Phagwara, Punjab, India

Abstract: It is an online application that essentially allows you to convert a hand-drawn drawing into HTML code. Any hand-drawn plan may be instantly transformed into HTML code using artificial intelligence. This strategy is unusual and unique. This study shows how several machine-learning approaches may be crucial in building a model from scratch that can generate code from a user-supplied picture. We demonstrate two ways to automate this process: conventional computer vision approaches and state-of-the-art deep semantic segmentation networks. Finally, we release a dataset for systems analysis and training.

Keywords: HTML, Deep learning, Sketch-to-code, Artificial intelligence

1. Introduction

Web development is a multi-phase process. This also includes wireframe-based website design. The front and back codes come next. Their demands are met by the developer's completely working and enjoyable website. Every website begins with a fundamental concept and basic structure that may be outlined in a wireframe. It supplies the necessary components and gives developers suggestions for building a site structure. The responsibility of the developers is to create the boilerplate code that sets everything up correctly. Most boilerplate codes are now created by hand. Users now must write HTML code to organize items on a web page. When the structure of web pages is the same, users are more likely to save a copy of the source code for reuse. Even though the code for the HTML elements is the same, the boilerplate script for web pages frequently differs.

A machine learning model is just what we recommend using to make this process simpler. As with components that identify text from the wireframe, it will be trained to recognize certain symbols and shapes. The model is an outline of a web application's input. Processing the information is the goal. Utilize the open-source and free Computer Vision Library to find every piece in a wireframe (Open CV). Once the items on the sketch have been identified, the appropriate code is subsequently added to an HTML file. Coding Sketch uses machine learning and artificial intelligence to convert a scribbled interface design from an image to a valid HTML layout code. Learn about how Coding Sketch converts a handwritten graphic to HTML. Much imagination goes into the user interface design process, which begins on a whiteboard where designers discuss ideas. After one design is created, it is often photographed and manually converted into a functional HTML wireframe that can be seen in a web browser. Instead, it uses artificial intelligence, a web-based program that converts a handwritten user interface sketch from an image to a valid HTML markup code.

[1]ayushgour232@gmail.com, [2]sankalprajgurur1221@gmail.com, [3]shivanshu.yadav04@gmail.com, [4]shilpa.sharma@lpu.co.in

DOI: 10.1201/9781003405580-80

Making a wireframe on paper to outline the interface's structure is a preliminary stage in the development of an application (Pedro Campos and Nuno Nunes, 2007; James A. Landay, 1995). The problem for designers is turning their wireframe into code, which frequently entails handing the design off to a developer who will then create the boilerplate graphical user interface (GUI) script. This effort takes the developer a long time and is consequently expensive (T. Silva da Silva et al, 2011). Prior research has been done on the following issues related to translating designs into code: Digital drawings are transformed into application code using movements by SILK (J. A. Landay, 2001). Many of these applications do detection and classification using traditional computer vision algorithms.

2. Literature Review

To convert the wireframe setup into code, intelligent systems and the suggested model go through the process of picture analysis and pattern recognition built on an ML model (T. Silva da Silva et al, 2011). It depicts the tedious yet time-consuming job a UI designer performs while turning a Graphical User Interface (UI) design into a programmed UI application. This process will be significantly sped up by an automated system that can substitute human efforts for the simple implementation of UI ideas. The publications that advocate for such a system emphasize using UI wireframes (Pedro Campos and Nuno Nunes, 2007) rather than hand-drawn drawings as input. Because of its inherent platform neutrality, the model can be trained once and provide UI prototypes for several platforms (J. A. Landay, 2001). The design phase of a website takes much time, but the systems do not always function as planned. For this reason, only a few libraries employ specific libraries like OpenCV (Andrej Karpathy, 2014), which analyze images and other contours to decrease noise and provide a foundation for precise picture analysis. Software programmers then transform the mockup into structured HTML or another type of markup code (Pedro Campos and Nuno Nunes, 2007). The final proposal uses ML to build consistent wireframes by matching graphical user interface elements in paper sketches to their digital equivalents (T. Silva da Silva et al, 2011). As soon as the photos and patterns are identified, we can use the text detection method and built-in ML Model library (James A. Landay, 1995) to separate the pictures from the text and then develop the conversion model to provide the output. It might be difficult to extract text from intricate photos or have more colour. Textual information found in photographs may be used to structure, index, and consistently explain images. The text in each image is extracted via detecting, localizing, tracking, removing, improving, and recognizing it (Oriol Vinyals et al, 2014). A series of wireframe pictures are transmitted from an end user's device via a network to a wireframe recognition and analysis engine.

The whole output of source code is reduced into a single archive folder and made available for download to the end user's device. Once the product has been formed, the HTML code must be converted. To generate a personalized user interface, the program was constructed to transform user-generated images into HTML code (James Lin et al, 2000). This analysis shows that the deep learning technique outperforms our traditional computer vision approach and concludes that deep learning is the most effective strategy for future study (T. A. Nguyen, 2015). The present scenario addresses this reality and provides information on the automatic code-generation approaches for using various inputs to generate code in different programming languages (Chao Dong et al, 2015). These define the breadth of the available technology.

3. Computer Vision and Techniques

Image processing or technique accepts input from web cameras or real-world photos. Due to changes in current across the camera sensor, these pictures frequently have Gaussian noise. Edge detection (S. Singh and B. Singh, 2015), which we use for element detection, can perform poorly on noisy images.

1. Colour Detection: in our technique, element detection is aided by colour detection. We concentrate on threshold-based detection since it is a valuable method for handling big, homogeneous colour blobs. Red, Green, and Blue (RGB), often known as a colour space, are the three colour channels most frequently used to describe digital pictures.

2. Edge Detection: we are interested in identifying components in wireframe drawings. The icons for the wireframe elements mostly have straight edges. Therefore, we employ edge detection as a crucial method for element discovery.

3. Segmentation: wireframe elements must first be discovered before they can be categorized. Since a wireframe sketch will likely include several components, a technique for identifying element boundaries is necessary.

4. Text Detection: we employ the stroke width transform in our algorithm to identify text from drawings. It should be noted that SWT is not a text recognition program; instead, it is a quick, lightweight, and language-independent scene text detector.

4. Machine Learning Techniques

1. Deep Learning: this area of machine learning, also known as "deep learning", uses deep neural networks with several hidden layers. Deep understanding has demonstrated phenomenal performance in several sectors, frequently exceeding conventional approaches (Chao Dong et al, 2015).

2. TensorFlow: a free software library called TensorFlow exists. TensorFlow was initially created by engineers and researchers working on the Brain Team of Google within Google's Machine Intelligence research organization to conduct deep learning and machine learning research.

3. Keras: an open-source, Python-based high-level neural network framework called Keras is powerful enough to operate with TensorFlow. It is designed to be user-friendly, expandable, and modular, enabling quicker exploration with deep neural networks.

4. K Nearest Neighbor: one of the most fundamental but crucial categorization methods in machine learning is K-Nearest Neighbors. It falls under supervised learning and is heavily utilized in pattern recognition, data mining, and intrusion detection.

5. OpenCV Python: openCV is a sizable open-source library for image processing, machine learning, and computer vision. OpenCV supports Python, C++, Java, and many other programming languages. It can analyze pictures and movies to find faces, objects, and even human handwriting.

6. Methodology and Model Specifications

The main objective of this work is to develop a program that converts a wireframe into code. We developed two strategies using traditional computer vision and deep learning methods to accomplish the aim. This section explains our dataset first, followed by our generic framework, which can produce the website either way after accepting a picture of the wireframe and pre- and post-processing. Then, we go over each step of the approach. In this part, we go over our standard procedure for transforming an image of a drawing into code, which mainly relies on computer vision. This strategy includes four essential phases: Computer vision may be used for element detection to identify and categorize the locations, dimensions, and kinds of every element in the drawing. Necessary for generating identical HTML components.

6.1 Dataset Training

It would be best to have a big dataset with plenty of examples to use deep learning techniques. The dataset includes code and trained drawings. Human blunders and divergent viewpoints on the proper drawing method might help determine the dataset's quality. We consider three methods for generating the dataset: finding websites and manually drawing them, manually drawing websites, and manually creating matching websites, and finding websites and automatically drawing them (James A. Landay, 1995). To maximize accuracy on our test set, we tuned our hyper-parameters to our dataset using standard methodologies and trial and error. Two MLPs coupled together make up our model. One MLP is trained and taught to categorize using the container's x, y, width, and height. The other is taught to categorize using the sub-element element's kinds. The categorical element types are binarized using one hot encoding. The final classification is created by combining both results into a final MLP (Fig. 80.1). This model was created to give the network the best possible chance of success. We considered the Tanh (Nasser M Nasrabadi, 2007) and ReLU (Vinod Nair and Geoffrey E Hinton, 2010) activation functions for the hidden layer.

7. Conclusion

To create a tool that converts a wireframe design into a website and to compare deep learning to traditional computer vision techniques for this purpose. The study that has already been done has been expanded in this work to include the innovative field of wireframe-to-code conversion. Wireframes are converted into websites using an end-to-end framework that generates outcomes instantly. We describe how our framework was created to be simple to use by enabling the use of photographs taken using webcams or mobile devices and employing widely used wireframe symbols to reduce the need for special training. As a result, our dataset sketching method makes it possible to do empirical evaluations of converting drawings into code, which was impossible before our study. Additionally, we were not knowledgeable of any deep learning applications in this area. We anticipate that our publication and the availability of our dataset and methodology will encourage more research in this area.

```
Model: "sequential"
_____
Layer (type)            Output Shape        Param #
===============================================
conv2d (Conv2D)         (None, 70, 70, 8)       80
_____
batch_normalization (BatchNo (None, 70, 70, 8)   32
_____
activation (Activation)  (None, 70, 70, 8)       0
_____
max_pooling2d (MaxPooling2D) (None, 35, 35, 8)    0
_____
dropout (Dropout)        (None, 35, 35, 8)       0
_____
conv2d_1 (Conv2D)        (None, 35, 35, 128)   25728
_____
batch_normalization_1 (Batch (None, 35, 35, 128)  512
_____
activation_1 (Activation) (None, 35, 35, 128)    0
_____
max_pooling2d_1 (MaxPooling2 (None, 17, 17, 128)  0
_____
dropout_1 (Dropout)      (None, 17, 17, 128)     0
_____
conv2d_2 (Conv2D)        (None, 17, 17, 512)   590336
_____
batch_normalization_2 (Batch (None, 17, 17, 512) 2048
_____
activation_2 (Activation) (None, 17, 17, 512)    0
_____
max_pooling2d_2 (MaxPooling2 (None, 8, 8, 512)    0
_____
```

```
dropout_2 (Dropout)      (None, 8, 8, 512)       0
_____
conv2d_3 (Conv2D)        (None, 8, 8, 512)    2359808
_____
batch_normalization_3 (Batch (None, 8, 8, 512)  2048
_____
activation_3 (Activation) (None, 8, 8, 512)      0
_____
max_pooling2d_3 (MaxPooling2 (None, 4, 4, 512)    0
_____
dropout_3 (Dropout)      (None, 4, 4, 512)       0
_____
flatten (Flatten)        (None, 8192)            0
_____
dense (Dense)            (None, 256)          2097408
_____
batch_normalization_4 (Batch (None, 256)        1024
_____
activation_4 (Activation) (None, 256)            0
_____
dropout_4 (Dropout)      (None, 256)             0
_____
dense_1 (Dense)          (None, 512)           131584
_____
batch_normalization_5 (Batch (None, 512)        2048
_____
activation_5 (Activation) (None, 512)            0
_____
dropout_5 (Dropout)      (None, 512)             0
_____
dense_2 (Dense)          (None, 6)             3078
===============================================
Total params: 5,215,734
Trainable params: 5,211,878
Non-trainable params: 3,856
_____
```

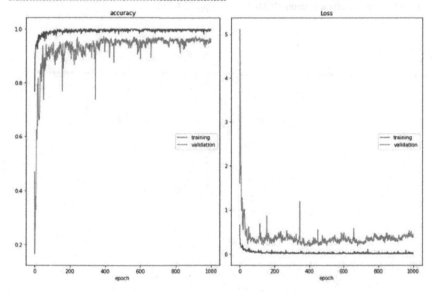

```
accuracy
        training        (min:  0.767, max:  1.000, cur:  1.000)
        validation      (min:  0.165, max:  0.973, cur:  0.964)
Loss
        training        (min:  0.001, max:  0.662, cur:  0.004)
        validation      (min:  0.181, max:  5.111, cur:  0.378)
```

Fig. 80.1 Dataset training

Source: Python program output for training dataset on Author's machine

REFERENCES

1. Pedro Campos and Nuno Nunes. "Practitioner Tools and Workstyles for User-Interface Design". In: 24 (Feb. 2007), pp. 73–80.
2. James A. Landay and Brad A. Myers. "Interactive Sketching for the Early Stages of User Interface Design". In: Proceedings of the SIGCHI Conference on Human Factors in Computing Systems. CHI '95. Denver, Colorado, USA: ACM Press/Addison-Wesley Publishing Co., 1995, pp. 43–50. ISBN: 0-201-84705-1. DOI: 10.1145/223904.223910. URL: HTTP://dx.doi.org/10.1145/223904.223910.
3. T. Silva da Silva et al. "User-Centered Design and Agile Methods: A Systematic Review". In: 2011 Agile Conference. Aug. 2011, pp. 77–86. DOI: 10.1109/AGILE.2011.24.
4. J. A. Landay and B. A. Myers. "Sketching interfaces: toward more human interface design". In: Computer 34.3 (Mar. 2001), pp. 56–64. ISSN: 0018-9162. DOI: 10.1109/2.910894.
5. James Lin et al. "DENIM: Finding a Tighter Fit Between Tools and Practice for Web Site Design". In: (Apr. 2000), pp. 510–517.
6. T. A. Nguyen and C. Csallner. "Reverse Engineering Mobile Application User Interfaces with REMAUI (T)". In: 2015 30th IEEE/ACM International Conference on Automated Software Engineering (ASE). Nov. 2015, pp. 248–259. doi: 10.1109/ASE.2015.32.
7. Chao Dong et al. "Image Super-Resolution Using Deep Convolutional Networks". In: CoRR abs/1501.00092 (2015). arXiv: 1501.00092. url: http://arxiv.org/abs/1501.00092.
8. Oriol Vinyals et al. "Show and Tell: A Neural Image Caption Generator". In: CoRR abs/1411.4555 (2014). arXiv: 1411.4555. url: http://arxiv.org/abs/1411.4555.
9. Andrej Karpathy and Fei-Fei Li. "Deep Visual-Semantic Alignments for Generating Image Descriptions". In: CoRR abs/1412.2306 (2014). arXiv: 1412.2306. url: http://arxiv. org/abs/1412.2306.
10. S. Singh and B. Singh. "Effects of noise on various edge detection techniques". In: 2015 2nd International Conference on Computing for Sustainable Global Development (INDIACom). Mar. 2015, pp. 827–830.
11. Nasser M Nasrabadi. "Pattern recognition and machine learning". In: Journal of electronic imaging 16.4 (2007), p.
12. Vinod Nair and Geoffrey E Hinton. "Rectified linear units improve restricted Boltzmann machines". In: Proceedings of the 27th international conference on machine learning (ICML10). 2010, pp. 807–814.

Computer Science Engineering and Emerging Technologies (ICCS-2022) – Prof (Dr.) Rajeev Sobti et al. (eds)
© 2024 Taylor & Francis Group, London, ISBN 978-1-032-52199-2

Chapter

81

Automatic Error Detection Using Python

Shilpa Sharma[1], Punam Rattan[2],
Banala Lakshmipathi[3], Devendra Kumar[4],
Sharan Kumar[5], Siva Ramakrishna[6]
Department of Computer Science and Engineering,
Lovely Professional University, Jalandhar, Punjab, India

Abstract: The main focus of this paper is to make the programmers fast and efficient in debugging, and it shows a number of relevant solutions to the errors that occurred in the program. Stack Overflow is a source of helpful information for software development-related queries. Since a few years, most people have been using stack overflow to find solutions to errors they have encountered, and stack over flow has become familiar to the majority of users. While we code, many times all of us will probably get struck by one or another of the different types of errors. Then the stackover flow will get into the picture for providing solutions, and in software development, the daily activity is to write code and execute the removal of errors, and the immediate action that most will take after getting encountered by an error is to search the errors manually by copying and pasting the error on a browser. In a small case, it is ok to search the errors on the browser, but just think about the case where we have to deal with a lot of errors, and yeah, I can agree with you as it is risky as well. We are going to develop a Python script that will execute the source code and detect errors during execution.

If there are errors are encountered, the tool will try to search for a stack overflow solutions that relates to the errors and open the solution pages as tabs in Chrome or any other browsers.

Keywords: Python, Query-resolving, Relevant-query output, Stack API

1. Introduction

For newcomers, debugging is a difficult chore. Programmers and developers can identify many mistakes, including logical and semantic faults, via debugging. Debugging and testing software frequently take longer than writing the software itself. Bugs and issues should be found and fixed via debugging to prevent software or system breakdowns. Programmers can ask questions and receive answers on the website Stack Overflow, which was founded by Jeff Atwood in 2008 and is geared toward both professionals and hobbyists. Most of the time, people refer to Stack Overflow as a website that is similar to a stack exchange, which means that it is an open source forum wherein students, professionals, employees, teachers, and many others can post questions and queries about problems they are having, and upon posting their questions, they can receive answers from numerous other peers who are confident in their ability to provide a solution. These peers can then

[1]shilpa13891@gmail.com, [2]punam.26558@lpu.co.in, [3]lakshmipathichari@gmail.com, [4]devendrakumar0319@gmail.com,
[5]sharankumar2007@gmail.com, [6]sivamudhiraj2@gmail.com

DOI: 10.1201/9781003405580-81

post their own questions and answers. According to statistics on stack overflow questions, 75% of registered users are the only ones who post a single question, and 65% of registered users are also only attempting to answer a single question. Additionally, 8% of registered users are able to respond to all five questions. The numbers mentioned above were observed in 2013, and they are getting better every day. At the moment, it is one of the most popular websites where all faults and solutions for all technologies can be found.

Writing code takes less time than fixing errors, which is why programmers tend to make a lot of mistakes when first starting out. We had a lot of trouble fixing the issues, and now we're attempting to search in the browser by copying and pasting the error message. There will be a website that provides solutions for issues because the majority of them are not very good at it. Actually, this question-and-answer website is the best for newcomers because it makes debugging simple. In the beginning, we, as programmers, made numerous mistakes and were unaware of this website. So, this notion was developed to make the process of solving problems simpler. Here, minimizing manual labor is the major goal in order to simplify the process.

2. Literature Review

2.1 Python

Python is a powerful programming language that is commonly interpreted, interactive, or object-oriented. Python is a powerful language with a design philosophy that emphasizes readability of code (specifically, use blank markings for split blocks of code instead of curly braces or keywords) and programmers. It also features a syntax like C++ or Java that allows you to convey a concept with a few lines of code. It establishes a framework for clear programming on both small and large scales. On a variety of operating systems, the Python interpreter is available. Python's reference implementation, Python, is open-source software with a community-based development structure, similar to practically all variant implementations. Python is managed by the Python Software Foundation, a non-profit organization. Python offers a strongly typed system as well as automatic dynamic typing and management. It supports multiple programming paradigms, including object-oriented, imperative, functional, and procedural, and has a large set with comprehensive standards.

2.2 Stack Overflow

It is a very well-known and popular website for developers. They are taking use of this site to post their query, and after posting their query, they got their solution from the professionals who were already present some time ago. We are seeing that when we post something, we get an instant result, so it does not mean that some machines have solved our question, but it is not right. The region behind it is that some have already asked a similar question, and some professionals have posted their thoughts on that point, so we are getting our answer instantaneously. It is a privet organotin, the aim of this website is to provide the right way for students and developers to improve their coding skills and to help them if they get stuck during the work. &&It has one more extra feature which is very need to any of the developer need is that if they searching anything on internet and they found some response so is it true are not for 24 | P a g e that we have a feature on this of liking od disliking of any post so if you think that it is an spam or it not correct so you can just click on the dislike and add some comment bello the post and make eyes for those who are going to see it they can just see the like and dislike button and under stan that it is not appropriate answer for this and you also repost on wrong threads which help upcoming user. There are some more interesting features that help us allot time to do them. As of now, there are more than 27 million users, 21 million asked questions, and 35 million answered questions; we are just talking about the mean question and answer. It also creates jobs for some developers. You can monetize your profile by fulfilling all the requirements of the SQ, and we charge a fee for the users who are going to see your solution. More than a million users are doing this and earning money.

2.3 Bridging the Gap Between Python Script—Stack Overflow

After the script has run, we only need a newly developed pertinent fix for the issue identified in the user-provided code file. To fill in this gap, we utilize the Stack Overflow platform, a question-and-answer site where enthusiastic programmers post their questions and receive responses from their peers. To get our query answered, we should construct a bridge between our script and stack overflow. To do this, we extract the Stack Overflow API and then add the bridge to have our query answered, making it a strong candidate for a solution. By creating a bridge using this API, our script will be able to retrieve the newly formed pertinent answers to the problem at hand. The users will learn something about their queries from this project in addition to having their questions answered. In order to quickly find the appropriate answers, the gap must be closed here.

3. Data and Variables

For programmers, constantly copying and pasting errors might result in malware infestations. The system as a whole has duplicate defects and security holes. The researchers came up with a lot of issues, many of which were straightforward security flaws. This does not, however, diminish their power. Failure to check the return value is one of the most frequent mistakes. If you don't check the return value in C++, you run the risk of breaking the reference. The process crashes as a result of this mistake, which results in a segmentation fault. It is easy to combat this problem. Verify that Singleton is the return value. But given how frequently that happens, there could be a bigger problem. If you borrow something without fully understanding what you're borrowing, you risk falling into the code reuse trap, which has potential vulnerabilities. You must first learn code if you wish to reuse it.

3.1 Dependent Variable

Stack Overflow: A Q&A website for both professionals and students is called Stack Overflow. This is the main site for the Stack Exchange Network, founded in 2008 by Jeff Atwood and Joel Sapolsky. contains queries and responses on a range of computer programming subjects. It was developed as a more accessible substitute for earlier Q&A platforms like Expert Exchange.

3.2 Independent Variable

It is one of the following techniques that aid in determining the project's optimal algorithm while also assessing the project's overall cost and time complexity.

4. Methodology and Model Specifications

As previously suggested, this prediction includes a fix for the program's faults. To fix the programming mistakes, a Python script is used to answer questions on the Stack API, which launches a browser and displays the answers. We have Stack Overflow and Python.

4.1 Model Specifications

We receive a code file from the user as input, train our model to find errors in the code, and then obtain the appropriate reformulations of solutions via the stack overflow platform. Here, after gathering information, our Python software finds errors, and if the error was discovered on Stack Overflow, it displays a default browser ad that offers the user pertinent remedies.

It offers the customer a pertinent remedy in order to Through membership and active engagement, users can vote questions and answers up or down in a manner similar to Reddit and modify questions and answers in a manner akin to a wiki. The website provides a forum for users to ask and answer questions. On Stack Overflow, users can acquire reputation and badges.

It gives the user a pertinent solution, giving them a fundamental understanding of the issue and enabling them to understand the WHAT, WHY, and HOW of the analysis.

Workflow

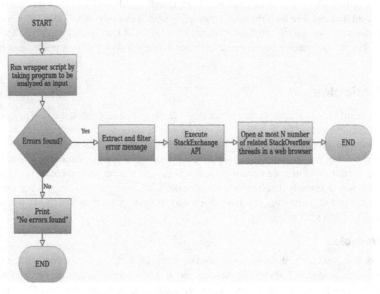

Fig. 81.1 Flow diagram of error detection

5. Results

We will pass one example of code that contains an error in this section, and we will accept that the error will cause a redirect to a browser that displays the appropriate answers.

The findings of our study are shown in the figures below. When our Python script was run, numerous solutions were displayed.

Figure 81.2 shows the fix for the unsupported operand type problem that occurred in our test case, which was created to validate our research.

Fig. 81.2 Shows the fix for the unsupported operand type problem

Figure 81.3 shows the fix for the unsupported operand type problem that occurred in our test case, which was created to validate our research.

Fig. 81.3 Depicts the problem of unsupported operand type

Figures 81.4 and 81.5 show the fix for the indentation mistake found in our test case, which was created to validate our research.

Fig. 81.4 Show the fix for the indentation mistake

Fig. 81.5 Show the fix for the Indentation mistake

5.1 Graphical Analysis

We will view the graphic analysis of our project in this section. Based on the information we are giving our project; this analysis was created. Sometimes it can even be the project report that has been tested. We are only seeing the comparison of several point values in the graph portion.

6. Conclusion

In this project, we will ensure that the user is aware of the error in the program and that the user can successfully correct the error. The main motivation for this study is to provide error detection with Stack Overflow and to provide users with reformulated and relevant things that are highly valued by programmers. The current approach requires you to make some changes and provide user errors in the solution. We have proposed and developed a model that provides a reformulated, related solution that is actively evaluated and displayed by users.

7. Future Scope

I started this project to use Python to automatically detect errors due to Stack Overflow. There are degrees for further upgrades and expansions. A progressively effective approach to integrating different highlights and features should be a major addition to deep learning and machine learning. This is a major change in related solutions for effective and accurate resolution of errors. This will be a future model for our project.

REFERENCES

1. Huang, C Chen, Z Xing, T Lin, Y Liu, "Distinguish them: Refining Innovation Contrasts from Swarm Scale Correlation Conversations", 2018 33rd IEEE/ACM International Conference on Automated Software Engineering (ASE), S. 214224, 2018. Im Kontext anzeigen Volltext des Artikels anzeigen
2. C. Chen und Z. Xing, "Minning Innovation Scene from Stack Flood", Minutes of the 10th International Symposium on ACM / IEEE Empirical Software Engineering and Measurement, S. A. 110, 2016.
3. C. Chen, Z. Xing, L. Han, "Techland: Supporting Innovation Scene Requests with Stack Flood Experience", 2016 IEEE International Conference on Software Maintenance and Evolution (ICSME), pp. x 356366, 2016.

4. Abdalkareem, E. Shihab, and J. Rilling, "What Do Designers Involve Groups? A Review Using Stack Floods," IEEE Software, vol. 34, No. 2, p. 5360, 2017.
5. X. Xia, L Bao, D. Lo, P. S. Kochhar, A. E. Hassan and Z. Xing, "What are designers looking for on the Web?", Empirical Software Engineering, vol. 22, No. 6, p. 31493185, 2017.
6. ° C Chen and Z. Xing, "Towards Related Searches and Stack Flood Questions on Google," Minutes of the 2016 IEEE 40th Annual Computer Software and Applications Conference, p. 8392, 2016.
7. Datta, D. Joshi, J, Li und JZ Wang, Picture Recovery: Ideas Impacts and Patterns of the New Age, ACM Computing Surveys, vol. 40, No. 2, p. 160, 2008. 37
8. Z. J Zha L. Yang T. Mei, M. Wang, Z. Wang, T. S. Chua, et al., "Visual Question Idea: Towards catch client target in web pictures search," ACM Transactions on Multimedia Computing Communications and Applications, vol. 6, Nr. 3, S. 119, 2010
9. C. Chen, Z. Xing und X. Wang SoloProgramming Explicit Morphological Structures Induction from Casual Conversations 2017 IEEE/ACM 39th International Conference on Software Engineering (ICSES.450461,2017
10. X. Chen, C. Chen, D. Zhang, Z. Xing, "Sethesaurus: Wordnet in computer Programming", IEEE Transactions on Software Engineering, 2019. View in context Google Scholar.
11. B. J. Jansen, D. L. Stall, A. Spink, "Examples of Query Reformulation During Web Browsing," Journal of the American Culture for Data Science and Innovation, vol. 60, no. 7, pp. 13581371, 2009.
12. M. Sloan, H. Yang, and J. Wang, "Concept-based strategies for capturing paraphrases of questions," Information Retrieval Journal, vol. 18, No. 2, p. 145165, 2015.L. Bing, W. Lam, T.-L. Wong and S. Jameel, "Web query reformulation via joint modeling of latent topic dependency and term context", ACM Transactions on Information Systems (TOIS).
13. J.-Y. Jiang, Y.-Y. Ke, P.-Y. Chien and P.-J. Cheng, "Learning user reformulation behaviour for query auto-completion", Proceedings of the 37th international ACM SIGIR conference on Research & development in information retrieval, pp. 445-454, 2014.
14. I. Sutskever, O. Vinyals and Q. V. Le, "Sequence to sequence learning with neural networks", Proceedings of Advances in neural information processing systems, pp. 3104–3112, 2014.
15. A. Sordoni, Y. Bengio, H. Vahabi, C. Lioma, J. Grue Simonsen and J.-Y. Nie, "A hierarchical recurrent encoder-decoder for generative context-aware query suggestion", Proceedings of the 24th ACM International on Conference on Information and Knowledge Management, pp. 553–562, 2015.
16. R. C. Cornea and N. B. Weininger, Providing autocompletes suggestions, Feb. 2014. C. Sadowski, K. T. Stolee and S. Elbaum, "How developers search for code: a case study", Proceedings of the 2015 10th Joint Meeting on Foundation.

Note: All figures in this document were created by Author.

Computer Science Engineering and Emerging Technologies (ICCS-2022) – Prof (Dr.) Rajeev Sobti et al. (eds)
© *2024 Taylor & Francis Group, London, ISBN 978-1-032-52199-2*

Chapter **82**

Emerging Cryptographic Techniques

Jayant Mehra[1]
Research Scholar, Department of Computer Science and Engineering,
Lovely Professional University, Phagwara, Punjab, India

Harwant Singh Arri[2]
Associate Professor, Department of Computer Science and Engineering,
Lovely Professional University, Phagwara, Punjab, India

Dhiraj Kapila[3]
Associate Professor, Department of Computer Science and Engineering,
Lovely Professional University, Phagwara, Punjab, India

**Siddharth Pansare[4], Nancy Sharma[5], Sahil Bharadwaj[6],
Jithin Govind[7], Gobinda Karmakar[8], Nupur Kaushik[9]**
Research Scholar, Department of Computer Science and Engineering,
Lovely Professional University, Phagwara, Punjab, India

Abstract: The main focus of this paper is to find out the emerging and future scope of cryptography. Using the principles of quantum physics, quantum cryptography is a revolutionary technique that enables two parties to protect network communications. The theory of quantum cryptography and how this technology improves network security are the main topics of this research study. This article encapsulates the state of quantum encryption at present, practical application implementations of this expertise, and ultimately the future course that quantum cryptography will take. The ease of authentication via fingerprint, eye, voice, palm, and other biometrics is expressly stated by biometric cryptography. Biometric verification provides more security than would be comfortably provided by conventional cryptography-based confirmation. A rapidly developing field of technology is DNA cryptography, which uses DNA computing principles.

Keywords: Quantum cryptography, Biometric encryption, DNA cryptography, Honey encryption

1. Introduction

One method of Information security is encryption. Encryption is the procedure of encoding data into a form that can only be accessed by the intended recipient. How does encryption safeguard your data from possible hackers, also referred to as "adversaries" in the cryptosphere? Using algorithms and keys, plaintext data is converted into code, or ciphertext. The very same key might be applied to several ciphertext and plaintext combinations. The original letter or keys shouldn't be viewable to hackers. A stream cipher, which essentially encodes the original source byte by byte, can be used to encrypt data. The original text and the ciphertext are both the same size. A block cipher, which encrypts specific data blocks one at a time, is another option for encryption. One could encode your information using several encryption methods. Each has benefits and drawbacks, and they can all be combined to produce a more effective encryption technology.

[1]jayant46mehra@gmail.com, [2]hs.arri@lpu.co.in, [3]dhiraj.23509@lpu.co.in, [4]sidhu.pansare@gmail.com, [5]nancysharma2177@gmail.com,
[6]binny4166@gmail.com, [7]jithingovindkanayi001@gmail.com, [8]gobindak2@gmail.com, [9]nupurkaushiknk@gmail.com

DOI: 10.1201/9781003405580-82

2. Symmetric Encryption

The first encryption method used online was symmetric encryption, often known as symmetric key encryption. By using symmetric encryption, data is converted into a cipher (encrypted code). In symmetric cryptography, information is encoded and deciphered using the same key both by the sender and the receiver; therefore, you need the key to crack the code. Symmetric encryption can swiftly process huge volumes of data since it is so straightforward. Yet, as you might expect, key sharing developed into an issue [2]. If you intend to disclose your passcode to others, kindly keep this in mind. This password can be easily detected by hackers if it is sent over SMS or email. Nearly all passwords call for passwords! Similar vulnerabilities were introduced when senders and receivers shared keys, which hackers could swiftly take advantage of. Data is encrypted using a single key that is known only to the sender and receiver with the help of secret key cryptography, often called is secret key encryption. Both the sender and the recipient must be aware of the private key, which should never be broadcast over the channel. But if a hacker gets their hands on the key, it will be simpler to decrypt the communication. When the transmitter and receiver are face-to-face at the handset, the key must be addressed. Nevertheless, this may not be the best approach. The fact that the key remains constant makes it simpler to send messages to specified recipients. The most widely used symmetric key system is the Data Encryption Framework (DES) algorithm.

As an illustration, suppose X sends Y a message he doesn't want anybody else to view. He wants the message to be encrypted. This is merely a result of X and Y exchanging the identical key. Both encryption and decryption must use the same key. How it functions: X first uses his key to encrypt the signal. His communication was both encrypted and decrypted. Anyone cannot read it. Y obtains the ciphertext and uses the same key to decrypt it in order to read the plaintext when it receives it.

2.1 Advanced Encryption Standard

The AES Encryption algorithm, often referred to as the Rijndael algorithm, is a symmetric block encryption method with just a block or chunk of 128 bits in size. It translates each of these discrete blocks using keys of 128, 192, and 256 bits. After being encoded, these chunks are concatenated to produce the encrypted message. Its foundation is a substitution-permutation network, or SP network. It comprises a number of interconnected operations, such as bit shuffles and replacements, that change inputs into particular outputs (permutations). The AES is one of many Federal Information Processing Standards (FIPS) released by NIST that must first receive approval from the U.S. Secretary of Commerce before being made public so as to comply with both the Computer Security Act of 1987 and the Information Technology Management Reform Act of 1996. The National Security Agency (NSA) has authorized only one publicly accessible block cipher for use in the transmission and encryption of sensitive and top-secret data and intelligence. Morris Dworkin, Elaine Barker, James Nechvatal, James Foti, Lawrence Bassam, Edward Roback, and James Dray Jr. wrote the AES, which was published on November 26, 2001, and the American government formally approved it in 2002. In particular, the AES algorithm is often known as Rijndael since it is a member of the Rijndael family of encryption algorithms, which was created by cryptographers Vincent Rijmen and Joan Daemen from Belgium.

3. Asymmetric Encryption

Asymmetric encryption is the next type of cryptography that can be used in this situation. Asymmetric encryption The keys of the transmitter and the recipient differ in asymmetric cryptography. Information is encrypted using one key and then decrypted using a different key. But how can you be certain that when information is given, only the right receiver may open it if two individuals have distinct passwords? Simply put, how can you instruct the appropriate parties to decrypt your code without disclosing the key? Asymmetric cryptography employs a set of two keys (public and private) for each user to address this issue. Only you have access to your public key, though others can view it. Your private key is only accessible to you. It behaves similarly to your bank's PIN. Together, both public and confidential keys function [2]. In such a transfer, the sender of the data can do so using your public key. The confidential key is then required to decrypt the information after it has been encrypted and transferred to the public key.

Asymmetric cryptography uses distinct keys for the sender and the recipient. One key is used to encrypt information, and a different key is used to decrypt it at the other end. But how can you make sure that only the right recipient may access the information when it is given if the two people actually have different passwords? In other words, how do you instruct the code to execute for the correct person without revealing keys? To address this issue, asymmetric cryptography employs a system that requires two keys per individual: a public key and a private key. Although your public key is specific to you, it is also visible to everyone else. Your private key is known only to you. It functions similarly to your bank's PIN. Together, the public and private keys function. As a result, during a transaction, the sender of the data can use your public key to transfer it. After that, you need the private key to access the information in order to decipher any messages encrypted using your public key. You would encrypt a message using its public key before sending it to that person. When that happens, only they and their private key can open it. Alternately, if someone uses their private key to add a unique identifier to a collection of data, anybody on the internet might use the public key to decipher the signature and authenticate that it is truly them.

3.1 Digital Signature Algorithm

A FIPS (Federal Information Processing Standard) for digital signatures is the Digital Signatures Algorithm. The National Institute of Standards and Technology proposed it in 1991, and the world standardized it in 1994. (NIST). It operates within the framework of discrete logarithmic problems and modular exponentiation, both of which are challenging to compute using a force-brute system.

The three advantages of the DSA Algorithm are as follows:

(a) *Message authentication:* By using the proper key combination, you can confirm the sender's identity.
(b) *Integrity verification:* Modifying the message will prevent the bundle from ever being decrypted, so you can't do it.
(c) *Non-repudiation:* If the recipient verifies the signature, the sender cannot claim they never sent the message.

4. Quantum Cryptography

Using the core beliefs of quantum physics, quantum cryptography is a revolutionary technique that enables two parties to protect network communications. These transmissions' security is based on the immutable nature of quantum physics' principles. Steven Wiesner's Conjugate Coding, which he wrote in the early 1970s, gave rise to quantum cryptography. He worked on this material for more than ten years. The two core concepts of quantum mechanics—uncertainty Heisenberg's principle and the principle of photon polarization—are the basis of quantum cryptography. According to Heisenberg's uncertainty principle, it is impossible to measure a system's quantum state without also scattering it. As established by the photon polarization principle, users can pick up unidentified qubits. The no cloning theorem, first brought forth by Wootters and Zurek in 1982, states that it is not possible to replicate an unidentified quantum state [1]. The theory of quantum cryptography and how this technology improves network security are the main topics of this research study. The current situation of quantum cryptography, actual application deployments of this technology, and perhaps the direction that quantum cryptography will go are all outlined in this research paper.

The inadequacies of classical encryption techniques, which can be defined as "public key" or "key" techniques, are what inspired the birth of quantum cryptography. The mechanics of quantum cryptography open the door to fascinating possibilities for interaction among adversaries in the arts, sciences, and cryptography. The capability to easily reverse one-way operations like parsing huge integers is a weakness in modern encryption that can be exploited by developments in computation power and mathematics. To lay a new framework for encryption in computer communications networks, there have been efforts over the past decade. However, one attempt culminated in the development of quantum cryptography, whose security is based on the principles of quantum mechanics. Utilizing the peculiar behavior of microscopic particles, quantum cryptography allows individuals to generate secret keys in a secure manner and identify listening devices. The first protocol for transferring secret keys via quantum technology was not disclosed until 1980 by Bennett and Brassard, despite the fact that Stephen J. Wisner started to work on quantum computation in the late 1960s. Quantum Key Distribution is a quantum state-based encryption technique. The benefit of quantum coding is that the final code cannot be theoretically cracked. The Heisenberg uncertainty principle as well as the photon polarization principle, which are both crucial concepts in quantum physics, are the foundations of quantum coding. According to Heisenberg's uncertainty principle, a system's distribution must be known in order to measure the quantum states of the system. The non-reproduction theory, first put forth by Wootters and Zurek in 1982, demonstrates that hackers cannot recreate unknown qubits, i.e., unknown quantum states. The spy is contrasted with the letter "E," whereas the sender and receiver are referred to throughout the text as "A" and "B," respectively.

5. Quantum Cryptography Security Issues

5.1 Polarization Shift

There is always a danger that anything could go wrong while the photon is passing forward through channel, such as an optical fibre or a change in the photon's air (wireless) polarisation.

5.2 Digital Signatures are Absent

The digital signatures enable the receiver to confirm the accuracy of the digital information. If a message includes a valid digital signature, the recipient has strong reason to trust that the information was produced by a trusted source and was not changed while in transit. The digital generation technique is composed of three algorithms: key generation, key signing, and key verification. We are conscious of the fact that developing techniques in QC is not an easy undertaking. As a result, QC lacks a number of crucial components like a digital certificate, a verified email, and the ability to solve conflicts in front of a court.

5.3 Predicament Because of the Source

When designing the source, consistency in the phase of the laser pulses is indeed a crucial factor. All emitted photons must have different levels of phase coherence, which is essential. This calls for an extraordinary phase modulator architecture that quickly alters the phase of subsequent photons. Furthermore, the multi-photon components of the suppressed laser pulses are essential because they are not single photons.

5.4 A Dedicated Channel is Required

To achieve high-speed communication using an individual photon, a high-quality, specialized channel is required. Multiplexing is against quantum principles; therefore, employing a quantum channel to deliver secret keys to a number of distinct sites is not possible. As a result, it necessitates different channels connecting the source to the various targets, implying a high cost. This is a significant disadvantage of quantum communication, particularly through optical channels.

6. Biometric Encryption

The biometric tokenization used for public-key infrastructure authentication is known as biometric cryptography (PKI). Biometric encryption in particular allows the ease of authentication via fingerprints, facial features, eyes, speech, hands, etc. without the hazards associated with making the biomarkers be in the form of a secret key. Biometric verification offers significantly higher security than would be comfortably offered by traditional encryption-based confirmation [4]. Since each person's biometric features are unique, it is difficult for outsiders to access them, and it interferes with privacy during verification because there is no reasonable chance that anyone could be spying. In this way, many modern devices now use biometric-based confirmation, which is increasingly being used in mobile, portable workstations as well as a wide range of other devices. An overview of the various encryption methods used by the face recognition biometric system is provided in this section. A method of converting plain content to figure content and then back to plain content again for the purpose of securing electronic information is known as an encryption calculation. Three encryption techniques—DES, RSA, and AES—are being used by us.

7. Biometric Encryption Techniques

Data Encryption Standard (DES): Unclassified and sensitive data are typically secured using the Data Encryption Standard algorithm.

Advanced Encryption Standard (AES): AES has the advantage of being fast.

Rivest-Shamir-Adleman (RSA): a public key encryption algorithm, is used to encrypt data.

8. DNA Cryptography

DNA cryptography is a method of data encryption based on DNA sequences. The cryptographic approach converts each individual letter in the alphabet into a unique mixture of the four bases that constitute human deoxyribonucleic acid (DNA).

DNA cryptography, which employs DNA computer concepts, is a rapidly evolving area of research [5]. The tiny nuclei of living cells contain enormous amounts of information stored in DNA. It possesses all the knowledge required to produce any life form on the planet. The parallelism and miniaturization of conventional silicon-based computers are the primary advantages of computation. For instance, whereas existing modification methods are capable of handling up to 1020 DNA strands, silicon now supports around a million transistors per square centimeter.

For this exact reason, several groups have proposed using the nucleotide order in DNA (A for 00, C for 01, G for 10, and T for 11). One solution is to simply bury the data in the DNA, using a method known as DNA steganography, rather than bothering to encrypt it at all [6]. The capacity of DNA Storage of Data ranges widely:

- Ultra-compact information storage uses a medium that can hold massive amounts of data in a small volume.
- 1021 DNA bases, or 108 Terabytes of data, are present in one gram of DNA.
- All the information in the world may be stored in a few grams of DNA.

8.1 Benefits of DNA Cryptography

1. DNA computing supports a high degree of parallelism, which aids in increasing computational speed.
2. DNA molecules are transmission media with a high capacity.
3. Low power consumption.

9. Honey Encryption

The honey cryptographic technique, which deceives an attacker into thinking he has hacked the codebase, represents one of the modern cryptography defences against brute-force attacks. Repeated decryption using keys created at random is the foundation of a brute-force attack. When using the incorrect key to decipher the ciphertext created by Honey's encryption, the result is a set of trustworthy but deceptively transparent encryption keys. This makes it more difficult for an intruder to determine if their estimate was correct or not. In 2014, honey encryption was created by Thomas Ristenpart of the University of Wisconsin and Ari Juels of the Cornell Institute [7]. Honey's encryption technology is used to safeguard private data in practical applications like SMS messaging and credit card transactions. It is currently in the planning stages.

9.1 Method of Defence

In a brute-force attack, data is repeatedly decrypted using random keys, a technique that entails taking random plaintexts out of an endless pool of equally dispersed plaintexts. This works well because most plaintexts are quite rare to just be reliable, despite the attacker having an equal chance of viewing any given plaintext; in other words, the allocation of trustable plaintexts is not random. Such attacks are defeated by honey encryption by first transforming the plaintext together into a space where the distribution of valid plaintexts is uniform. As a result, a key-guessing intruder will regularly come across plaintexts that appear to be legitimate and infrequently come across plaintexts that appear to be random. This makes it difficult to determine when the correct key has already been guessed. In reality, honey encrypts fictitious information as a result of every incorrect password guess.

Honey encryption's security depends on the encrypting party's capacity to predict the probability that an intruder will view a plaintext as valid at the moment of encryption. In some cases, for instance, where plaintext space is indeed very wide or the text distribution is unpredictable, honey encryption can be difficult to employ. So it indicates that honey encryption can be vulnerable to brute-force attacks if this probability is estimated incorrectly. For example, if the attacker knows a cot that such a plaintext must match in order to be acceptable, they can brute force perhaps honey-encrypted data if the encryption does not take the cot into account. Due to this, it is prone to known plaintext hacks.

10. Conclusion

Since Steven Wiesner's Conjugate Coding was published in the early 1970s, quantum cryptography has already been put to the test. According to Heisenberg's uncertainty principle, it is difficult to assess a system's quantum state without also dispersing it. The principle of photon polarization shows that eavesdroppers can detect unknown qubits. Biometric verification offers significantly higher security than would be comfortably offered by conventional cryptography-based confirmation. Cyberbiosecurity benefits from the ongoing computerization of contemporary biological research. The foundation of modern digital biotechnology is the electronic storage of genetic data. With the growing use of technology in cyberbiosecurity and the ability to alter DNA strands, there is a greater risk of maliciously damaging biological machinery and the production of dangerous biological materials. We need to be aware of any potential downsides of technological advances as DNA cryptography develops. When using the incorrect key to decrypt the ciphertext created by honey encryption, a trustworthy but seemingly transparent encryption key is revealed. As a result, it is challenging for attackers to determine whether they accurately predicted the mail.

REFERENCES

1. M. S. Sharbaf, "Quantum Cryptography: A New Generation of Information Technology Security System," 2009 Sixth International Conference on Information Technology: New Generations, 2009, pp. 1644–1648, doi: 10.1109/ITNG.2009.173.
2. S. Chandra, S. Paira, S. S. Alam and G. Sanyal, "A comparative survey of Symmetric and Asymmetric Key Cryptography," 2014 International Conference on Electronics, Communication and Computational Engineering (ICECCE), 2014, pp. 83–93, doi: 10.1109/ICECCE.2014.7086640.
3. W. Diffie and M. Hellman, "New directions in cryptography," in IEEE Transactions on Information Theory, vol. 22, no. 6, pp. 644–654, November 1976, doi: 10.1109/TIT.1976.1055638.
4. A. Thawre, A. Hariyale and B. R. Chandavarkar, "Survey on security of biometric data using cryptography," 2021 2nd International Conference on Secure Cyber Computing and Communications (ICSCCC), 2021, pp. 90–95, doi: 10.1109/ICSCCC51823.2021.9478120.
5. S. Pramanik and S. K. Setua, "DNA cryptography," 2012 7th International Conference on Electrical and Computer Engineering, 2012, pp. 551–554, doi: 10.1109/ICECE.2012.6471609.
6. Xiao, G., Lu, M., Qin, L. et al. New field of cryptography: DNA cryptography. CHINESE SCI BULL 51, 1413–1420 (2006). doi :10.1007/s11434-006-2012-5
7. A. Juels and T. Ristenpart, "Honey Encryption: Encryption beyond the Brute-Force Barrier," in IEEE Security & Privacy, vol. 12, no. 4, pp. 59–62, July-Aug. 2014, doi: 10.1109/MSP.2014.67.

Computer Science Engineering and Emerging Technologies (ICCS-2022) – Prof (Dr.) Rajeev Sobti et al. (eds)
© 2024 Taylor & Francis Group, London, ISBN 978-1-032-52199-2

Chapter

83

Mixed Language Text Classification Using Machine Learning: Cyberbullying Detection System

Pankaj Shah[1], Shivali Chopra[2]

Lovely Professional University, Jalandhar, Phagwara, Punjab

Abstract: The use of the internet has been increasing every day, and after COVID-19, we can see a sudden growth in the use of the internet. Because of the COVID-19 pandemic, people were forced to switch their work from offline to online mode. Many organizations and corporate industries have switched to online due to lockdown during the COVID-19 pandemic, like schools, colleges, different offices, and industries. That has also boosted the amount of unstructured data available online. That resulted in praise for the cyberbullying rate on the internet. During online classes and meetings during those days, not just students but also the teachers faced the Cyberbullying issue. So, keeping that in mind, many researchers and authors have conducted many surveys as well as research on this issue. This review paper contains what methods and algorithms those researchers have proposed and what methodology and algorithms those researchers have used to overcome this issue, along with the research gap and what other researchers can do to fill those research gaps.

Keywords: Machine learning (ML), Artificial intelligence (AI), Natural language processing (NLP)

1. Introduction

Machine learning (ML) is a type of artificial intelligence (AI) that produces more accurate predictions and output without being explicitly programmed or with very few human interactions. Arthur Samuel, a pioneer in the fields of artificial intelligence and computer gaming, first used the term "machine learning" in 1959. In the early 1960s, Raytheon Company created Cybertron, an experimental "learning machine" with punched tape memory that could be used to analyze speech patterns, electrocardiograms, and sonar signals. It was frequently "trained" by a human teacher or operator to recognize patterns, and a "goof" button was provided to make it reevaluate poor decisions. The book Learning Machines by Nilsson, which mainly discussed machine learning for pattern categorization, is a good example of machine learning research from the 1960s. In 1981, research on teaching methods to enable a neural network to recognize 40 characters (26 letters, 10 digits, and 4 special symbols) via a computer terminal was made public. Open-ended text is categorized into several specified categories using the machine learning technique known as text classification. It can be used to organize, structure, and categorize just about any type of text, including files from the web, medical research, and documents. It was introduced in the early 1960s. Text classification was effectively accomplished using machine learning techniques in the late 1990s [17].

A mixed language is a language that is made up of a combination of two or more languages. When people use two or more different languages to communicate, this is known as mixed language. It is mainly used in south Asian countries like India, Bangladesh, Nepal, Bhutan, etc., for example, when communicating with other people through online platforms using different apps like WhatsApp, Facebook Messenger, Instagram, etc. People text each other in their native Language but use English text to type those messages. So, the typing is in English, but the pronunciation is in their native language [16].

[1]pankaazshah3622@gmail.com, [2]shivali.19259@lpu.co.in

DOI: 10.1201/9781003405580-83

The study of how to give computers the ability to understand spoken and written words similarly to humans is known as natural language processing (NLP), which is a branch of computer science and, more specifically, an area of artificial intelligence (AI). NLP powers computer algorithms that summarize huge amounts of information quickly, even in real time, translate text across languages, respond to spoken requests, and translate text between languages [18].

2. Literature Review

A research paper purposed by Justin W. Patching et al. (2022) has collected data from 2007 to 2021 from middle and high school students since 2004. They have gathered more than 30,000 students 'data for this survey, and it is found that the average cyberbullying victimization rate, or people who have been bullied, is 29.3%, and the average cyberbullying offense rate, or people who bully others, is 15.6%. But among the percentage of Average Cyberbullying Victimization Rate the 11.8% Cyberbullying was reported occurred within 30 days before surveying and the total percent of people who bullies other is 6%. So, the researchers and authors have been trying to find the best method to identify cyberbullies through different methods. [1]

In one of the research papers by Xiaoyu Luo (February 21, 2021), he stated that the text classification method is the best approach to classifying the kinds of documents he tried to classify. He has used a support vector machine on around 1033 text documents with 90% accuracy. In the same way, other authors have also published their own methods of identifying cyberbullying or tried to Build a cyberbullying detection System. [2]

Marcin Micha Mironczuk et al. (March 28, 2018) used the most recent text categorization components. The six basic elements of text classification are described, including data gathering, data processing for labeling, feature generation and balancing, feature extraction and projection, building a classification method, and result validation. [3]

Another study by M. Ikonomakis et al. (August 2017) elaborates that text classification plays a vital role in information gathering, identifies several theoretical issues, and helps researchers guide their research in beneficial directions. They also stated that many researchers have done different research using different Machine learning algorithms, but This is still a crucial area for research because those researchers are unable to explain a good strategy and the performance of existing automatic text classifiers can still be improved. [4]

In the same way, another paper published by MD. Rajab Hossain et al. (17 April 2021) said they have used CNN-based Text classification to assign the different language texts into their category, like Bengali Language. They used four basic functionalities: training, validation, embedding model development, and text-to-feature representation. They performed it with a 9,779-test dataset and got 96.85% accuracy. [5]

Charles Malafosse (February 25, 2019) used a dataset of different languages, like English tweets, Spanish tweets, French tweets, Italian tweets, and German tweets. They tried Sentiment Analysis and found that its accuracy was 80%. [6]

A Survey by Kamran Kowsari et al. (23 April 2019) discusses various text feature extraction approaches, dimensionality reduction strategies, current algorithms and methods, and evaluation procedures. Each technique's limitations are explored, as well as how it might be used to solve actual situations. [7].

Another research paper on the same topic by Aurangzeb Khan et al. (February 2010) says that their research focuses on solving the documentation problem by giving a more effective and simple way to concentrate on using key methods and strategies used in the classification of text texts. [8]

Karishma Borkar et al. (June 2017), which shows the Nave Bays method to classify the text. [9]

Kshitija Deshmukh et al. (March 2018) In his paper, he shows a review of the different authors who used different approaches, like the filter approach and the wrapper approach. He also says the author introduced a new divergence method called Jeffrey's multi-hypothesis divergence. [10]

Sayar Ul Hassan et al. (April 2022) say they used five algorithms in their paper: SVM, K-NN, LR, MNB, and the RF method to classify the text and can obtain 95.5% accuracy. [11]

Neha Rani et al. (March 2018) in their paper compared different classifiers like SVM, Nave Bayes, Neural networks, etc. [12]

Kshitija Deshmukh et al.'s (March 2018) research paper shows they have used the Nave Bayes method to get the output and classify the text into its relevant category. [13]

Dr. K. Meenakshi Sundaram et al. (September 2014) say they tried to filter the emails and newspapers and organize the Documents and their retrieval in their paper. They also used Opinion mining, News monitoring, and Narrow Casting for the classification of the text. [14]

Marcin Micha Mironczuk et al. (2018) In their study, the authors presented a comprehensive summary of the most recent text classification components. They help readers know the required information about elements and the techniques that can be used. They show the data acquisition and labeling of data, along with data representation and solution evaluation. [15]

In the latest paper from Sayar Ul Hassan et al. (April 2022), they have used different machine learning algorithms like SVM, K-NN, LRM Nave Bayes, and RF algorithms. In their paper, the authors have also reviewed other research papers related to their work along with methodologies and their findings. They simply took the text data, tokenized it, and passed it to pre-processing. After that, the data was sent for future engineering and modeling, and then they evaluated the text. [16]

3. Research Questions

1. What Machine Learning Algorithms and Methods are being used to perform the multi-language text classification?

The answer to this question are listed billow in the Table 83.1

Table 83.1 List of different technique and algorithms used by different authors

Authors name and date	Algorithms or methods used	Research findings
Marcin Michał Mironczuk et al. (28 March 2018) [3]	Qualitatively analyse, quantitatively analyse	There were six stages to the research process: data collection, categorization training, extraction of features and projecting, features construction and weighing, data processing and tagging, and result validation.
Xiaoyu Luo (21 February 2021) [2]	Support Vector Machines, Naïve Bayes, DT, NN, SVM, Hybrid techniques	These methods can also be used with BBC English.
Nawal Aljedani et al. (22 September 2020) [19]	Hierarchy Of Multilabel Classifier (HMATC) model, Hierarchy of Multilabel Classifier (HOMER) algorithm	Arabic dataset with several labels that was introduced in a suitable format for public use.
Zhuo Chen et al. (2020) [20]	KNN-based classification method	Dimensionality reduction and data normalisation were carried out to enhance the classification effect.
Sayar Ul Hassan et al. (April 2022) [11]	SVM, k-NN, LR, MNB, and RF	According to the results of the suggested system, While Logistic Regression and Support Vector Machine surpass the other models for the IMDB dataset, K-NN surpasses them for the SPAM dataset.
M. Ikonomakis et al. (August 2017) [4]	Support Vector Machines, K-NN	The proposed system's results show that K-NN beats the other models in the SPAM dataset while Logistic Regression and Vector Support Machine beat the other models in the IMDB dataset.
Karishma Borkar et al. (June 2017) [9]	Naïve Bayesian model	Study shows how a novel probabilistic translation of tied term weighting could lead to a better understanding of measurable positioning devices.
Aurangzeb Khan et al. (February 2010) [8]	Bayesian classifier, Decision Tree, K-nearest neighbour (KNN), Support Vector Machines (SVMs)	With an emphasis on the available literature, this study offers a discussion of text analytics and documents categorization theories and practice.
Neha Rani et al. (March 2018) [12]	SVM, Naïve Bayes, Neural Networks	Tabular structure was used to discuss various classifier algorithms that have gained popularity recently.
Dr. K. Meenakshi Sundaram et al. (September 2014) [14]	K-Nearest Neighbour, Decision tree, Support Vector Machine	Employing the internal patterns assessment approach, which helps to resolve the text categorization problem with low frequency.

Source: Author's compilation

2. What Datasets are used to perform the purposed research Methodology and Algorithms?

The datasets used in these research papers are: (2411 news articles in 7 categories, 1490 papers as training samples, 239 papers in cities) [20], (1400 records with 8 classes) [9], (Facebook dataset, Arabic dataset, News content) [12], (tweets collected from twitter.com.) [21].

3. What are the common Research Gaps?

In south Asian countries like India, Nepal, Bangladesh, Bhutan, etc., people use English typing while communicating in their native or mother tongue language, or simply, we can say mixed language, for example, "Hinglish (English text but Hindi pronunciation), Nepanrasy (English text but Nepali pronunciation)." There are no algorithms or classification methods mentioned to classify these types of texts in their papers. Similarly, unlike other text-formatted data like PDFs, Word documents, and.txt files, multimedia files (i.e., Videos, photos, audios, etc.) are a little more difficult to classify into text categories. The classification of online streaming data is difficult because those data are directly transmitted from source to destination. It is based on a real-time data transmission system. So, the classification process for this kind of data is also not covered in their papers.

4. Conclusion and Future Scope

After analyzing the research papers from the authors, which are mentioned in the literature review, We can conclude that the authors have used different techniques and methods to categorize the text into its relevant category. They have published their research findings, and they tried to find the best way possible to resolve the research problems in their papers, but there are some gaps that went unnoticed by them.

That gives the new researchers a great opportunity to make some progressive changes in this related field. They can now fill those gaps that these researchers may not have noticed. They can work on these gaps that remained unfilled, improve accuracy, or find their own methodology to resolve the research gap questions raised by analyzing the research paper related to this topic.

REFERENCES

1. A. Azaria et al, Medrec: Using blockchain for medical data access and permission management, 2016 2nd International Conference on Open and Big Data (OBD), IEEE, 2016.
2. Xiaoyu Luo, Hunan University of Technology and Business, China
3. Marcin Michał Mironczuk ´, Jarosław Protasiewicz, National Information Processing Institute, al. Niepodległo´sci 188 b, 00-608 Warsaw, Poland
4. M. IKONOMAKIS Department of Mathematics University of Patras, GREECE ikonomakis@mailbox.gr S. KOTSIANTIS Department of Mathematics University of Patras, GREECE sotos@math.upatras.gr V. TAMPAKAS Technological Educational Institute of Patras, GREECE tampakas@teipat.gr
5. Ana Cardoso-Cachopo, Arlindo L. Oliveira, An Empirical Comparison of Text Categorization Methods, Lecture Notes in Computer Science, Volume 2857, Jan 2003, Pages 183–196
6. Phani, S., Lahiri, S., Biswas, A.: A supervised learning approach for authorship attribution of Bengali literary texts. ACM Trans. Asian Low Resour. Lang. Inf. Process 16(4), 1–15 (2017)
7. Xie, J., Hou, Y., Wang, Y., et al.: Chinese text classification based on attention mechanism and feature-enhanced fusion neural network. Computing 102, 683–700 (2020)
8. Aurangzeb Khan, Baharum Baharudin, Lam Hong Lee*, Khairullah khan Department of Computer and Information Science, Universiti Teknologi PETRONAS, Tronoh, Malaysia. *Faculty of Science, Engineering and Technology, Universiti Tunku Abdul Rahman, Perak Campus, Kampar, Malaysia. (E-mail: aurangzebb_khan@yahoo.com, baharbh@petronas.com.my,leelh@utar.edu.my,khairullah_k@yahoo.com)
9. Karishma Borkar1, Prof. Nutan Dhande2 1 Department of CSE,ACE Nagthana,Maharastra,India 2 Department of CSE,ACE Nagthana,Maharastra,India
10. Jiawei Han and MichelineKamber "Data Mining Concepts And Techniques" ,Morgan kaufman publishers, San Francisco, Elsevier, 2011, pp. 285-351
11. Sayar Ul Hassana , Jameel Ahameda,∗ , Khaleel Ahmada a Department of Computer Science & Information Technology, Maulana Azad National Urdu University, Hyderabad, Telangana, India
12. Neha Rani Apex Institute of Technology Chandigarh University, Mohali nhrajput.24@gmail.com Aanchal Sharma Apex Institute of Technology Chandigarh University, Mohali aanchal08107@gmail.com Dr. Sudhir Pathak Apex Institute of Technology Chandigarh University, Mohali

13. Dr. K. Meenakshi Sundaram, Associate Professor of Computer Science, Erode Arts and Science College, Erode-638009, India. e-mail: lecturerkms@yahoo.com

14. Dr. K. Meenakshi Sundaram, Associate Professor of Computer Science, Erode Arts and Science College, Erode-638009, India. e-mail: lecturerkms@yahoo.com K. Ramya, Research Scholar of Computer Science, Erode Arts and Science College, Erode-638009, India. e-mail: anuramgowri.msc@gmail.com

15. Sayar Ul Hassana , Jameel Ahameda,* , Khaleel Ahmada, Department of Computer Science & Information Technology, Maulana Azad National Urdu University, Hyderabad, Telangana, India

16. From website: https://en.wikipedia.org/wiki/Mixed_language

17. From website: https://en.wikipedia.org/wiki/Machine_learning

18. From webpage: https://www.ibm.com/cloud/learn/natural-language-processing#:~:text=Natural%20language%20processing%20 (NLP)%20refers,same%20way%2 0human%20beings%20can. , https://en.wikipedia.org/wiki/Natural_language_processing

19. Nawal Aljedani , Reem Alotaibi, Mounira Taileb Department of Information Technology, Faculty of Computing and Information Technology, King Abdulaziz University, Jeddah 21589, Saudi Arabia

20. Zhuo Chen1 , Lan Jiang Zhou2,*1 , Xuan Da Li4 , Jia Nan Zhang 4 , Wen Jie Huo5 1 School of Information Engineering and Automation, Kunming University of Science and Technology, Kunming 650500, China 2 The Key Laboratory of Intelligent Information Processing, Kunming University of Science and Technology, Kunming, Yunnan 650500, China 3 School of Information Engineering and Automation, Kunming University of Science and Technology, Kunming 650500, China 4 Information Engineering University, Kunming team of the three schools 650500, China 5 School of Information Engineering and Automation, Kunming University of Science and Technology, Kunming, Yunnan 650500, China

21. Arvind Singh Raghuwanshi M.Tech, Computer Science and Engineering Department Samrat Ashok Technological Institute Vidisha(M.P.), India e-mail: arvindraghuwanshi1411@gmail.com Satish Kumar Pawar Asst. prof., Computer Science and Engineering Department Samrat Ashok Technological Institute Vidisha(M.P.), India

Computer Science Engineering and Emerging Technologies (ICCS-2022) – Prof (Dr.) Rajeev Sobti et al. (eds)
© 2024 Taylor & Francis Group, London, ISBN 978-1-032-52199-2

Chapter 84

A Systematic Review on Thalassemia Using Neural Network Techniques

Gurbinder Kaur[1]

Research Scholar, School of Computer Science and Engineering,
Lovely Professional University

Vijay Kumar Garg[2]

Associate Professor, School of Computer Science and Engineering,
Lovely Professional University

Abstract: The genetic blood disorder thalassemia is brought on by a lack of haemoglobin synthesis, the primary protein found in RBCs. Its function is to distribute oxygen to all of the body's organs from the lungs. Haemoglobin is composed of four chains of globin, which are two β-chains and two α-chains. Clinicians perform a CBC test as well as a haemoglobin test to identify thalassemia. Machine learning has been the subject of extensive early study. Several machine learning methods, including K-nearest neighbour, decision trees, support vector machines, and naive Bayes, perform better in their respective fields. Currently, one of the hottest research areas in medicine is neural networks. In this research, different neural network methods for thalassemia diagnosis are reviewed, including artificial neural networks, convolutional neural networks, radial basis functions, multilayer perceptrons, etc. These algorithms have better accuracy, sensitivity, and specificity as compared to machine learning. This survey in medical diagnostics is primarily intended to serve as a roadmap for researchers as they create the most practical, user-friendly, and affordable technologies, methods, and clinical approaches.

Keywords: Thalassemia, Multilayer perceptron, Convolutional neural network, Radial basis function, Artificial neural network

1. Introduction

Thalassemia is a group of genetic diseases that are perpetuated by a decline in the production of haemoglobin or its chain. [1]. Among human single-gene genetic illnesses, it is one of the most prevalent. The consequences of an imbalance in the ratio of globin chains include inefficient or insufficient erythropoiesis, persistent hemolytic anaemia, hypercoagulability, compensatory increased intestinal iron absorption, and hematopoietic expansion [2]. Red blood cells include a major protein called haemoglobin that transports oxygen to the tissues of the body via the lungs, and a shortage of haemoglobin results in thalassemia, a genetic blood disorder [3]. The three types of thalassemia are (a) major, (b) intermediate, and (c) minor. A person with thalassemia major will suffer from a severe type of anaemia and require lifelong transfusions of blood [4]. A mild-to-severe form of anaemia known as thalassemia intermedia occasionally necessitates blood transfusions. On the other hand, people with thalassemia minor typically have good health and very little need for blood transfusions [5]. Analysing the blood characteristics is necessary to make the diagnosis. The first step in making a thalassemia diagnosis in a lab is a complete blood count. The CBC counts the red blood cells and other types of blood cells, including haemoglobin, in a blood sample. Thalassemia patients have less haemoglobin and a lack of healthy RBCs in their blood [6]. The outcomes

[1]gurucs135@gmail.com, [2]vijay.garg@lpu.co.in

DOI: 10.1201/9781003405580-84

of the thalassemia screening included data from the peripheral blood analysis, high-performance liquid chromatography (HPLC), and complete blood count (CBC). Hematocrit, haemoglobin, platelets, MCHC, MCV, MCH, and leukocytes are the CBC's constituent parts. The Hb components of the HPLC are RDW HbA2 and HbF as well [7]. Artificial intelligence (AI) is a subset that employs algorithmic methods to enable computers to deal with challenges alone without the use of complex computer programming. Additionally, several neural network techniques are being used to identify thalassemia.

2. Neural Network Techniques

The ability of neural networks to learn complex nonlinear connections between input and output, consecutive training techniques, and data adaptability are among their key characteristics. Neural networks analyse data in a manner comparable to the human brain. Neurons, which are the processing units in the network, are numerous and intricately connected, and they work together to concurrently handle a specific problem. Neural network configurations can take many different forms.

2.1 Artificial Neural Network (ANN)

Artificial neurons connect their inputs and outputs via weighted directed edges, acting as nodes in a weighted directed graph. [11]. The notation x(n), which stands for n number of inputs, is used to identify these inputs. The related weights are multiplied by each input and used to evaluate an issue that indicates how closely connected neurons are to one another by weight in neural nets. [16]. There are studies that use ANNs to identify TM patients from healthy populations.

Table 84.1 Artificial neural nework

Author	ANN Model	Accuracy (Ac) Specificity (Sp) Sensitivity (Se)	Application Domain
Hirimutugod a, Y. M. et al. [11]	Light microscopy images of blood samples have the ability to quickly and accurately automate the diagnosis of aberrant red blood cells. Image processing techniques were coupled with two 3-layer and 4-layer back propagation artificial neural network models.	Ac = 86.54%	Detection of thalassemia
Barnhart-Ma gen, Guy, et al. [13]	The study included 526 patients, 185 cases of TM that had been verifid. The control group includes patients with iron deficiency anemia, sufferers of myelodysplastic syndrome (MDS) and normal healthy people. The best-optimized ANNs were used to find TM patients based on the variables MCV, RBDW and RBC.	Sp = 100% Se = 96%	Diagnose thalassemia minor and classify TM and malaria parasite
M. Baldini et al. [17]	ANN model use the dataset of 180 samples to define degree of relationship between variables in any dataset, auto-contractive map algorithm to graphically illustrate links	Ac = 92.51%	Detection of thalassemia
Kabootariza deh, Leila et al. [18]	The data set was retrieved using the Complete Blood Count (CBC) test parameters of 268 individuals. This model has 70 neurons and input with 4 factors.	Ac = 92.5% Sp = 92.33% Se = 93.13%	Classification between IDA and Beta-Thalassemia
F. Yousefian et al. [19]	The dataset of 1575 patients used in model with 50 neurons in middle layer and 65 neurons in 2nd middle layer. The middle layer and output layer have used sigmoid function.	Ac = 80.78%	Diagnose β-thalassemia major
A. Jahan et al. [22]	Suggested the back-propagation type ANN and uses C4.5 and NB. The Japanese Sysmex Corporation's (Bio-Rad Labs , USA) VARIANT-II device dataset is used for research.	Ac = 84.95%	Diagnose β-thalassemia trait
Azarkhish et al. [26]	ANN model and the Neuro-fuzzy system used lab data of MCHC, Hb, MCH, MCV to predict level of iron serum and to diagonse IDA.	--	Identify IDA

Source: Made by Author

2.2 Convolution Neural Network

Convolutional neural networks have enabled substantial advancements in a variety of pattern recognition-related fields during the past 10 years, including speech recognition and image analysis. The greatest favourable aspect of CNNs is that they require less ANN parameters. This achievement has encouraged researchers and developers to adopt more complex models to tackle challenging issues that were earlier difficult to address with conventional ANNs. Three layers make up

ConvNet: (i) convolutional, (ii) pooling, and (ii) fully connected. [9]. The representation between the inputs and outputs is mapped with the aid of the FC layer. [8]. The CNN provides best result in classification of medical image dataset.

Table 84.2 CNN model

Author	CNN Model	Accuracy (Ac) Specificity (Sp Sensitivity (Se)	Application Domain
Tyas, Dyah Aruming, et al. [16]	Histogram equalisation was used during the preprocessing step, followed by morphological operation during the segmentation stage, and feature extraction at the end.	Ac = 92.55%	Classify abnormal blood to detect thalassemia
Lin, Yang-Hsien et al. [21]	To discriminate between thalassemia RBCs and segments of individual RBCs with the aim of characterising single RBCs, a convolutional neural network that is mask region-based, or Mask R-CNN, was developed.	Ac = 97.8%	Distinguishes between RBCs of thalassemic (tRBCs) and RBC of healthy persons (hRBCs).
Abdulhay, Enas Walid et al. [23]	After the training phase, the photographs are processed using the Convolutional Neural Networks (CNN) technology, which classifies the images into normal blood cells, sickle cell anemia, malaria, thalassemia or megaloblastic anemia.	Ac = 93.4%	Identify and differentiate malaria from anaemia (Megaloblastic anemia, Sickle Cell, and Thalassemia)
Purwar, Shikha, et al. [24]	This research use principal component analysis (PCA) to eliminate feature redundancy and thereby reduce computational complexity. Clinical variables are combined with features extracted from blood pictures using the CNN model.	Ac = 99.1% Sp = 99.0% Se = 100%	Diagnose thalassemia

Source: Made by Author

Multilayer Perceptron

A directed graph, in which the signal only moves in one way across the nodes, is what distinguishes a multilayer perceptron from other neural networks. All nodes have a nonlinear activation function, excluding the input nodes. A supervised learning technique that an MLP uses is called back propagation. The Multilayer Perceptrons' neurons are trained using the back propagation learning algorithm. [13]. A non-linearly separable problem can be solved with multilayer perceptrons, which are built to approximate any continuous function.

Table 84.3 Multilayer perceptron

Author	MLP Model	Accuracy (Ac) Specificity (Sp Sensitivity (Sc)	Application Domain
Paokanta, Patcharaporn, et al. [12]	The suggested study analyses the effectiveness of machine learning techniques using feature selection based on Principal Components Analysis (PCA). This work seeks to reduce the dimensions of the data before classification. The Multi-Layer Perceptron (MLP) is the most effective strategy, according to the results.	Ac=86.61%	Screening genotypes of thalassemia
N. ChidozieE gejuru et al.[20]	suggested MLP for classification of thalassemia using dataset includes 99 photos of normal erythrocytes and 725 images of diseased erythrocytes.	Ac=98.11%	Classification of thalassemia
Eshpala, Rahil, Hosseini, et al. [15]	The statistical population consisted of 395 individuals' CBC results. With four inputs, one hidden layer, and 100 neurons, the proposed system was constructed using a multilayer perceptron technique.	Ac=93.4% Sp=92% Se=94%	Diagnose and classify TM and IDA

Source: Made by Author

Radial Basis Function

An artificial neural network with radial basis functions as activation functions is known as a radial basis function network. The network's output is produced linearly by integrating the input's radial basis functions and the neurons' parameters. Since the architecture is feed-forward, in the same layer, connecting nodes are not connected to each other. [10]. The processing components of the nonlinear hidden layer is static Gaussian activation function [15]. Recent studies have given significant focus to radial-basis function-based disease diagnosis.

Table 84.4 Radial basis function

Author	RBF Model	Accuracy (Ac) Specificity (Sp) Sensitivity (Sc)	Application Domain
Masala, Giovanni Luca, et al. [14]	PCA used as dimension reduction tool on 28 samples collected out of which 15 were male and control set with 13 healthy people with parameter of HbA2.	Ac = 100% (carrier) Ac = 93% (normal) Ac = 91% (T-carriers)	Identifying T-carriers and classification of sick and normal
Wirasati, Ilsya, et al. [25]	Using a support vector machine (SVM) with a linear, polynomial, and gaussian radial basis function (RBF), data on thalassemia are categorised. The optimum technique is determined to be gaussian RBF kernel with SVM.	Ac = 99.63%	Classification of thalassemia

Source: Made by Author

3. Result and Discussion

The goal of this research was to analyse various neural approaches adopted for thalassemia diagnosis, detection, and classification purposes, such as MLP, CNN, RBF, and ANN. Table 84.5 shows that out of 16 cases, 7 cases of ANN, 4 cases of CNN, 3 cases of MLP, and 2 cases of RBF were used to diagnose and classify thalassemia patients. These investigations demonstrated the value of the neural network approach and were able to distinguish different thalassesmia kinds from CBC generic datasets.

Table 84.5 Reported results of some similar methods

Application	Model			
	ANN	CNN	MLP	RBF
Detection	3	-	-	-
Diagnose	2	1	2	-
Classification	2	3	1	2
Aggregate	7	4	3	2

Source: Made by Author

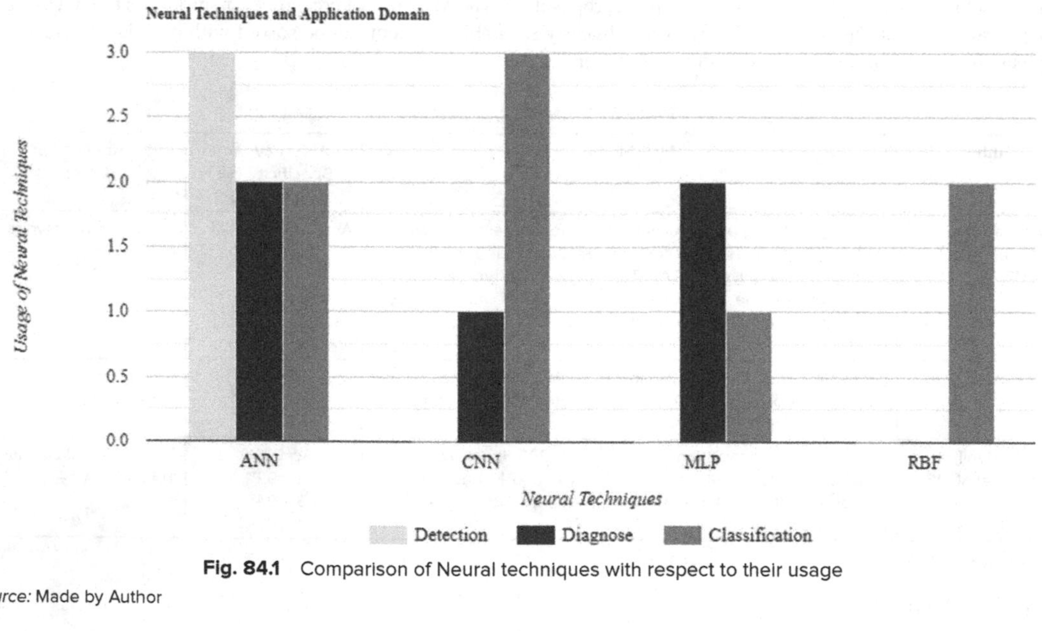

Fig. 84.1 Comparison of Neural techniques with respect to their usage

Source: Made by Author

4. Conclusion

Thalassemia is considered one of the most life-threatening diseases. For thalassemia to be effectively treated, a proper early diagnosis is essential. Various machine learning algorithms are now available to correctly diagnose thalassemia. Many researchers have recently shown interest in developing neural network methods to identify thalassemia. This paper summarises previous research on the diagnosis and detection of thalassemia disorders employing different neural network approaches implemented by various authors. Depending on the datasets and characteristics chosen, among other things, each neural network technique has some positive and negative results. Despite the fact that neural network approaches offer a good classification rate, they require a lot of training. Future research may find that by adding more neurons to the hidden layer, neural networks' accuracy can be improved. To enhance the performance of the classifier, different rules can be used when training neural networks.

REFERENCES

1. Y. Chen, "Thalidomide for the Treatment of Thrombocytopenia and Hypersplenism in Patients With Cirrhosis or Thalassemia," *Frontiers in Pharmacology*, vol. 11, 2020, doi: 10.3389/fphar.2020.01137.
2. Taher, Ali T., David J. Weatherall, and Maria Domenica Cappellini, "Thalassaemia," *The Lancet*, 2018, pp. 155–167.
3. Mohammed, Muna Qais, and Jamal Mustafa Al-Tuwaijari, "A Survey on various Machine Learning Approaches for thalassemia detection and classification," *Turkish Journal of Computer and Mathematics Education (TURCOMAT)*, 2021, pp. 7866–7871.
4. Thompson, Alexis A., Mark C. Walters, Janet Kwiatkowski, John EJ Rasko, Jean-Antoine Ribeil, Suradej Hongeng, Elisa Magrin et al., "Gene therapy in patients with transfusion-dependent β-thalassemia," *New England Journal of Medicine*, 2018, pp. 1479–1493.
5. C. D.Asadov, "Immunologic Abnormalities in β-Thalassemia," *Prime Arch. Immunol.*, 2020, doi:10.37247/pai.1.2020.1a.
6. Susanto, E. R., A. Syarif, K. Muludi, R. R. W. Perdani, and A. Wantoro, "Implementation of Fuzzy-based Model for Prediction of Thalassemia Diseases," *Journal of Physics: Conference Series*, vol. 1751, 2021.
7. Mustafa, I., Firdous, N., Shebl, F. M., Shi, Z., Saeed, M., Zahir, Z., & Zayed, H., "Genetic epidemiology of beta-thalassemia in the Maldives: 23 years of a beta-thalassemia screening program," *Gene*, vol. 741, 2020, doi: 10.1016/j.gene.2020.144544.
8. Dutta, Aniruddha, Tamal Batabyal, Meheli Basu, and Scott T. Acton, "An efficient convolutional neural network for coronary heart disease prediction," Expert Systems with Application, vol. 159, 2020.
9. Mehmood, Awais, Munwar Iqbal, Zahid Mehmood, Aun Irtaza, Marriam Nawaz, Tahira Nazir, and Momina Masood, "Prediction of heart disease using deep convolutional neural networks," *Arabian Journal for Science and Engineering,* vol. 46, 2021.
10. Hannan, Shaikh Abdul, "Prediction of heart disease medical prescription using radial basis function," *IEEE International Conference on Computational Intelligence and Computing Research.* IEEE, 2010.
11. Hirimutugoda, Y. M., and Gamini Wijayarathna, "Image analysis system for detection of red cell disorders using artificial neural networks," *Sri Lanka Journal of Bio-Medical Informatics,* 2010.
12. Paokanta, Patcharaporn, Napat Harnpornchai, Somdat Srichairatanakool, and Michele Ceccarelli, "The Knowledge Discovery of [beta]-Thalassemia Using Principal Components Analysis: PCA and Machine Learning Techniques," *International Journal of e-Education, e-Business, e-Management and e-Learning,* 2011.
13. Barnhart-Magen, Guy, Victor Gotlib, Rafael Marilus, and Yulia Einav, "Differential diagnostics of thalassemia minor by artificial neural networks model," *Journal of clinical laboratory analysis,*2013, pp. 481–486.
14. Masala, Giovanni Luca, Bruno Golosio, R. Cutzu, and Roberto Pola, "A two-layered classifier based on the radial basis function for the screening of thalassaemia," *Computers in biology and medicine,* 2011, pp. 1724–1731.
15. Eshpala, Rahil Hosseini, Mostafa Langarizadeh, Mehran Kamkar Haghighi, and Banafsheh Tabatabaei, "Designing an expert system for differential diagnosis of β-Thalassemia minor and Iron-Deficiency anemia using neural network," *Hormozgan Medical Journal,* 2015.
16. Tyas, Dyah Aruming, Tri Ratnaningsih, Agus Harjoko, and Sri Hartati, "The classification of abnormal red blood cell on the minor thalassemia case using artificial neural network and convolutional neural network," In *Proceedings of the International Conference on Video and Image Processing,* 2017, pp. 228–233.
17. Baldini, Marina, Enzo Grossi, Maria Domenica Cappellini, Carmelo Messina, Alessia Marcon, Elena Cassinerio, Lorena Airaghi, Giuseppe Guglielmi, and Fabio Massimo Ulivieri, "The role of trabecular bone score and hip geometry in Thalassemia Major: a neural network analysis," *British Journal of Research,* 2017, pp. 1–9, doi: 10.21767/2394-3718.100025.
18. Kabootarizadeh, Leila, Amir Jamshidnezhad, and Zahra Koohmareh, "Differential diagnosis of iron-deficiency anemia from β-thalassemia trait using an intelligent model in comparison with discriminant indexes," *Acta Informatica Medica*, 2019.
19. F. Yousefian, T. Banirostam, and A. Azarkeivan, "Predicting the Risk of Diabetes in Iranian Patients with β-Thalassemia Major / Intermedia Based on Artificial Neural Network," *Signal Processing and Renewable Energy*, 2019, pp. 23–33.
20. N. Chidozie Egejuru, S. Olayinka Olusanya, A. OnyenonachiAsinobi, O. Joseph Adeyemi, V.Oluwatimilehin Adebayo, and P.

Adebayo Idowu, "Using Data Mining Algorithms for Thalassemia Risk Prediction," Int. J. Biomed. Sci. Eng., vol. 7, no. 2, 2019, p. 33, doi: 10.11648/j.ijbse.20190702.12.

21. Lin, Yang-Hsien, Ken Y-K. Liao, and Kung-Bin Sung, "Automatic detection and characterization of quantitative phase images of thalassemic red blood cells using a mask region-based convolutional neural network," *Journal of Biomedical Optics*, 2020.

22. A. Jahan, G. Singh, R. Gupta, N. Sarin, and S. Singh, "Role of Red Cell Indices in Screening for Beta Thalassemia Trait: an Assessment of the Individual Indices and Application of Machine Learning Algorithm," *Indian J. Hematol. Blood Transfus.*, 2020, pp. 3–7, doi: 10.1007/s12288-020-01373-x.

23. Abdulhay, Enas Walid, Ahmad Ghaith Allow, and Mohammad Eyad Al-Jalouly, "Detection of Sickle Cell, Megaloblastic Anemia, Thalassemia and Malaria through Convolutional Neural Network," *Global Congress on Electrical Engineering,* 2021.

24. Purwar, Shikha, Rajiv Tripathi, Ravi Ranjan, and Renu Saxena, "Classification of thalassemia patients using a fusion of deep image and clinical features," In *2021 11th International Conference on Cloud Computing, Data Science & Engineering (Confluence)*, 2021, pp. 410–415.

25. Wirasati, Ilsya, Zuherman Rustam; Aurelia, Jane Eva; Sri Hartini, Glori Stephani Saragih",Comparison some of kernel functions with support vector machines classifier for thalassemia dataset." *IAES International Journal of Artificial Intelligence*, 2021

26. Azarkhish, Iman, Mohammad Reza Raoufy, and Shahriar Gharibzadeh, "Artificial intelligence models for predicting iron deficiency anemia and iron serum level based on accessible laboratory data.", *Journal of medical systems* 36.3, 2012, pp. 2057–2061.

Computer Science Engineering and Emerging Technologies (ICCS-2022) – Prof (Dr.) Rajeev Sobti et al. (eds)
© 2024 Taylor & Francis Group, London, ISBN 978-1-032-52199-2

Chapter

85

Cryptographic Applications in Blockchain

Sahil Bhardwaj[1]

Research Scholar, Department of Computer Science and Engineering,
Lovely Professional University, Phagwara, Punjab, India

Dhiraj Kapila[2]

Assistant Professor, Department of Computer Science and Engineering,
Lovely Professional University, Phagwara, Punjab, India

Harwant Singh Arri[3]

Associate Professor, Department of Computer Science and Engineering,
Lovely Professional University, Phagwara, Punjab, India

**Siddharth Pansare[4], Nancy Sharma[5], Gobinda Karmakar[6],
Jithin Govind[7], Nupur Kaushik[8], Jayant Mehra[9]**

Research Scholar, Department of Computer Science and Engineering,
Lovely Professional University, Phagwara, Punjab, India

Abstract: Blockchain is a cutting-edge application framework that combines decentralised data storage, peer-to-peer connections, consensus procedures, digital encryption technology, and other computer technologies. It is safe, decentralised, and information-disclosing. Digital encryption technology is a key component of the blockchain. A requirement for the promotion of blockchain is the security of user data and transaction data. Blockchain growth is both facilitated and constrained by the advancement of cryptographic technology. Hash functions play an important role in the blockchain as they restrict the ability to overwrite the content that is in the blockchain. Hash functions were first used in cryptology in the late 1970s as a technique to safeguard data integrity. They quickly proved to be a very helpful foundation for addressing further security issues in telecommunications and computer networks. A hash function is a function that accepts an input of mostly arbitrary size and produces an output of a predetermined size. When implemented properly, some hash functions' characteristics may be utilised to significantly strengthen the security of a system administrator's network. A basic introduction to the fundamentals of encryption technology is given, including the hash function, asymmetric cryptosystem, and digital signature. It examines how cryptography is used at every level of the blockchain, including the data layer, network layer, consensus layer, etc. It demonstrates how cryptography permeates the whole blockchain system. The analysis of blockchain's current security issues indicates the route that future research should take.

Keywords: Blockchain, Cryptography, Cryptocurrency, Bitcoin, Digital signatures, Ethereum, Hyperledger

1. Introduction

A distributed database having the characteristics of decentralisation, traceability, immutability, security, and dependability is called a blockchain. It combines the P2P (Peer-to-Peer) protocol with additional technologies, including smart contracts, consensus mechanisms, and digital encryption. Abandoning the traditional central node's maintenance mode in favour

[1]binny4166@gmail.com, [2]dhiraj.23509@lpu.co.in, [3]hs.arri@lpu.co.in, [4]siddhu.pansare@gmail.com, [5]nancysharma2177@gmail.com, [6]gobindak2@gmail.com, [7]jithingovindkanayi001@gmail.com, [8]nupurkaushiknk@gmail.com, [9]jayant46mehra@gmail.com

DOI: 10.1201/9781003405580-85

of the technique of numerous users maintaining each other's work in order to achieve information supervision among many parties and protect the accuracy and reliability of the data. Public chain, private chain, and alliance chain are three subcategories of the blockchain platform. The private chain rigorously restricts the eligibility of participating nodes, while the alliance chain is jointly administered by a number of collaborating universities. All nodes in the public chain are free to join or exit at any time. The most popular example of digital money and the most common use of blockchain is Bitcoin, which was first suggested by Nakamoto in 2008. The blockchain has also demonstrated its capacity to change society and has broadened the scope of its special application value in many areas. Blockchain has high criteria for its security performance since it keeps all user transaction information there. A decentralised peer-to-peer network is what blockchain is. There is no central node, and nodes do not have to trust one another. As a result, in order to preserve transaction integrity, transactions on the blockchain must also guarantee the security of transaction information through unsafe networks. It is clear that the blockchain places the most emphasis on cryptographic technologies. Cryptography technology is primarily employed in blockchain to safeguard data integrity, user privacy, and transaction information. The hash algorithm, asymmetric encryption algorithm, and digital signature are a few of the cryptographic techniques that are briefly introduced in this paper. It also elaborates on the blockchain infrastructure, the blockchain structure, bitcoin addresses, digital currency trading, and other blockchain technologies, and it explains in detail how cryptography technology protects privacy and transaction maintenance in the blockchain.

2. Blockchain Architecture

Blockchain technology has undergone two phases, according to Melanie Swan, the Blockchain Science Institute's founder. The first is the blockchain 1.0 phase, which is represented by Bitcoin and is a multi-technology portfolio innovation. The second is the blockchain 2.0 phase, which is represented by Ethereum and involves the transfer of digital assets. Blockchain technology is typically used for things like Bitcoin, Ethereum, Hyperledger, etc. The underlying design shares a lot of similarities, even though the implementations vary. The blockchain platform may be separated into five tiers, as illustrated in Table 85.1: the network layer, the consensus layer, the data layer, the contract layer, and the application layer.

Table 85.1 Blockchain architecture

	Bitcoin	**Ethereum**	**Hyperledger**
Application layer	Bitcoin trading	Ethereum trading	Enterprise blockchain
Network layer	TCP-based P2P	TCP-based P2P	HTTP/2-based P2P
Contract layer	Script	Solidity/Script EVM	Go/Java Docker
Consensus layer	PoW	PoW/PoS	PBFT/SBFT
Data layer	Merkle tree	Merkle patricia tree	Merkle Bocket tree

To maintain the integrity of data storage, the data layer mostly employs the block data structure. Each node in the network stores the data transactions it has received over time in a block of time-stamped data that is linked to the longest primary blockchain at the moment. The primary block storage, chain structure, hash algorithm, Merkle tree, time stamp, and other methods are included in this layer.

The primary component of the consensus layer is a consensus mechanism that enables every node in the decentralised system to agree on the veracity of block data. PoW, PoS, PBFT, and SBFT make up the majority of the consensus process. The foundation of the blockchain programmable feature is the smart contract, which is primarily present in the contract layer. The blockchain stores code and data sets that make up the computer software that can automatically carry out the provisions of the contract. Blockchain nodes spread the distributed execution of smart contracts that are triggered by time or events. Signatures or other external data messages activate the coding, automated settlement, and triggering of all pertinent clauses. Different data transmission methods and verification techniques are included at the network layer. A typical P2P network is the blockchain. There are no core nodes and a flat topology connects every node. A node can join or leave the network at any moment, and any two nodes can freely trade with one another. The blockchain's P2P protocol is primarily used to transfer data between nodes. The major components of the application layer are Hyperledger, Ethereum, and Bitcoin. Bitcoin is mostly used for digital money exchanges. Decentralized apps based on digital money are added by Ethereum. Hyperledger is primarily used for enterprise-level blockchain applications and does not permit transactions in digital currency.

3. Block Structure and Hash Functions

The hash algorithm is a function that reduces a string of any length messages to a shorter fixed-length value. It is characterised by susceptibility, unidirectionality, collision resistance, and high sensitivity. Hash is typically used to ensure data integrity, or to confirm that the data hasn't been improperly altered. The hash value of the tested data adjusts as the data changes. As a result, even in a dangerous setting, the integrity of the data may be determined using its hash value.

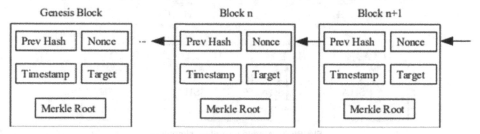

Fig. 85.1 Block structure in blockchain

3.1 SHA

The National Institute of Standards and Technology (NIST) released the cryptographic hash function known as SHA, which possesses the fundamental properties of a cryptographic hash function. The SHA256 algorithm creates a 256-bit message digest and is a subclass of the SHA-2 algorithm cluster. The main loop and message preparation are the two steps in the algorithm's computation process. Any length of information is subjected to binary bit filling and message length filling during the message preparation step, and the filled message is then broken into several 512-bit message blocks. Each message block is handled by a compression function during the main loop phase. The original message's hash value is the output of the previous compression algorithm, which is the input for the current compression process.

3.2 RIEPMD

The COSI research team at the University of Leuven in Belgium created the hash function algorithm known as RIEPEMD, which is a summary of the RACE original integrity check message. The most popular RIPEMD version is RIPEMD-160. Message complement is the initial stage of the algorithm, and the complement technique is the same as the SHA series algorithm. The compression function, which is a loop with 16 step functions inside each loop, forms the basis of the processing algorithm. The processing of the method is split into two separate instances using different original logic functions in each loop, with five of the two original logic functions executing in reverse order. The hash value of the original message is produced as a 160-bit output following the completion of all 512-bit packet processing. Hash functions may be used on blockchains to perform block and transaction integrity checks. Any user may compare the computed hash value with the stored hash value in the blockchain since the hash value of the data from the previous block is stored in the header of each block. The information in the previous block is then checked for integrity. Public-private key pairs can also be created using the hash function.

3.3 Time Stamp

According to the blockchain method, the node must include a timestamp in the header of the current data block to show when the block data was really written. On the main chain, the blocks are ordered according to time. The timestamp may be utilised to establish a blockchain database that is impenetrable and unforgeable by serving as evidence of the block data's existence.

3.4 Merkle Tree

The renowned cryptographer Merkle first suggested the Merkle Tree, a hash binary tree, as a rapid way to check the accuracy of huge amounts of data. The block's transaction database, the block header's root hash, and each branch leading from the underlying block data to the root hash are commonly included in the Merkle tree. Typically, the Merkle tree operation organises the block's data and adds the freshly created hash value to the Merkle tree. It is ultimately built into a tree structure up to the last root hash is left and recorded as the Merkle root of the block header.

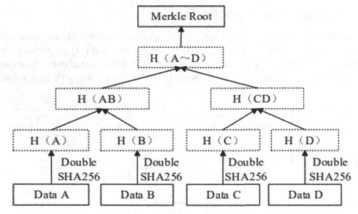

Fig. 85.2 Merkle root of blockchain

4. Public Key System and Digital Signatures in Currency Trading

Symmetric and asymmetric encryption are two of the primary cryptographic technologies. Public key encryption, or asymmetric encryption, can effectively address the issue of early key distribution in symmetric encryption. When using an asymmetric encryption technique, the encryption key and the decryption key are distinct and are referred to as a public key and a private key, respectively. In most cases, a random number algorithm is required to produce the private key, and an irreversible technique is used to determine the public key. Separate public and private keys, which may be sent through insecure channels, are a benefit of the asymmetric encryption technique. The asymmetric encryption technique based on mathematical puzzles also has the drawbacks of slow processing speed and weak encryption, so security must be maintained. The Bitcoin system uses a key pair that consists of a private key and a public key that is exclusively derived from it. Public key encryption is used to create the key pair. A public key, also known as the bitcoin address, which is the payee, is used to produce the recipient's address in the payment link of bitcoin transactions. The public key is created by encrypting the private key using elliptic curve multiplication. The private key is a number that is often chosen at random. Additionally, the public key is utilised to build the bitcoin address using a single-entry encrypted hash function. Elevated Curves Common public key encryption algorithms are used in cryptography. The degree of security is based on how difficult the discrete logarithm problem for elliptic curves is. Secp256k1 in the elliptic curve is the public key encryption technique used in the blockchain. The foundation for secp256k1 is an elliptic curve over a finite field. Its unique structure enables its optimum use to outperform other curves by 30%. Backdoors are successfully prevented by the constant secp256k1.

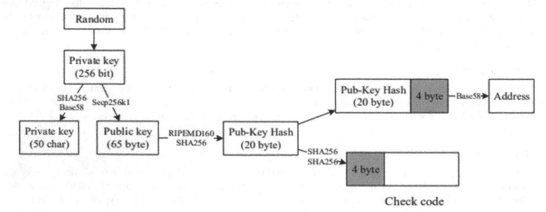

Fig. 85.3 Bitcoin address generation process

A signature algorithm plus a verification algorithm often makes up the digital signature system. A digital signature is created using a signature algorithm, which is generally controlled by a signature key. Both the signature algorithm and the signature key are kept private and are within the signer's control. The message's digital signature can be efficiently validated using the verification method, and the message may also be checked independently of the signature. The verification method is often managed by the verification key, but both the algorithm and the key are available to the public, making it simple for the person who has to validate the signature to do so. The owner of the digital currency hashes the content of the previous transaction order of the digital currency and the address of the subsequent owner in a cryptocurrency system where the blockchain is the underlying technology. The recipient receives the data that has been digitally signed using the sender's private key and is attached to the end of the transaction list. The recipient must confirm the information they have received in order to demonstrate that it is accurate and then confirm the owner of the transaction. The blockchain keeps track of the currency's present owner, former owner, and subsequent owner for each transaction. As a result, it is possible to track the flow of money from start to finish, thereby preventing multiple payments, fraudulent transactions, and other problems.

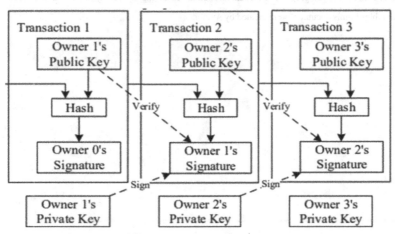

Fig. 85.4 Working of digital signature in currency trading

5. Security Issues in Blockchain

Any node that joins the blockchain network has access to a complete copy of the global ledger, which blockchain technology uses to record transaction data. Potential attackers may put the user's transaction privacy and identity privacy at risk by examining the transaction records in the global ledger. By exchanging privacy risks, an attacker can gain access to sensitive data by reviewing transaction logs. For instance, the balance of funds and transaction information for a certain account, the movement of a certain amount of money, etc. By integrating certain basic understandings based on an analysis of the transaction data, the attacker can learn the identity information of the trader, according to the identity privacy threat. We frequently employ coinjoin, ring signature, zero-knowledge proof, and other techniques to defend against this attack. Dash utilises a coin measure, which hides the connection between the payment address and the payment address by combining many transactions into a single transaction via a coin node. However, the impact of the coin is overly reliant on the number of users using it, and the volume of transactions is easily compromised.

6. Conclusion

It is clear that the characteristics of cryptographic hash functions have a wide range of uses in the field of computer security, and one of them is in blockchain for making it secure. The primary uses of cryptography in the blockchain are described in this paper, which also examines current issues. First, the blockchain technology is made simpler by beginning with the blockchain infrastructure. The blockchain is further developed with the introduction of cryptographic technologies. Finally, an analysis of the blockchain's current security issues is performed. It demonstrates how digital encryption technology, which is the foundation of the blockchain system, permeates the whole network. This essay highlights the critical impact that research in cryptography has had on the growth of the blockchain and discusses possible future directions for blockchain research.

REFERENCES

1. Eastlake, Motorola, Jones. "RFC 3174 - US Secure Hash Algorithm 1 (SHA1)"
2. RSA Laboratories. "What is a hash function?"
3. Nakamoto, S. (2008) Bitcoin: A peer-to-peer electronic cash system
4. Zhu, Y., Gan, G. H., Deng, D. (2016) Security Research in Key Technologies of Blockchain.
5. Shen, Y., Wang, G. (2017) Improved preimage attacks on RIPEMD-160 and SHA-160. Ksii Transactions on Internet & Information Systems.
6. Yuan, Y., Wang, F. (2016) Current Status and Prospects of Blockchain Technology Development. Acta Automatica Sinica.
7. Wang, H.Q., Wu, T. (2017) Cryptography in Blockchain. Journal of Nanjing University of Posts and Telecommunications.

Note: All figures and tables in this document were created by Author.

Computer Science Engineering and Emerging Technologies (ICCS-2022) – Prof (Dr.) Rajeev Sobti et al. (eds)
© 2024 Taylor & Francis Group, London, ISBN 978-1-032-52199-2

Chapter **86**

Use of Blockchain Technology Toward Green IoT and its Impact on Smart City Development

S. K. UmaMaheswaran[1]
Professor, Department of Mathematics,
Sri Sai Ram Engineering College, Chennai, T.N. India

Ankur Kulshreshtha[2]
Principal, NIMS School of Robotics and Artifical Intelligence, NIET,
NIMS University, Jaipur, Rajasthan

Bipin Kumar Srivastava[3]
Associate Professor, Department of Applied Sciences,
Galgotias College of Engineering and Technology Greater Noida, U.P.

Sunil Babu Melingi[4]
Professor, Department of Electronics and Communication Engineering,
Dhanekula Institute of Engineering and Technology, Ganguru, Krishna District, A.P, India

Rajani Mahendra Mandhare[5]
Assistant Professor, Arvind Gavali College of Engineering Satara,
Anurag',Rayat Colony,Saidapur Satara

José Luis Arias Gonzáles[6]
Department of Business, Pontifical Catholic University of Peru

Abstract: Blockchain highly empowers different kinds of IoT devices for enhancing security as well as bringing a significant level of transparency to several IoT ecosystems. Block chain extensively offers a decentralised and scalable environment for IoT devices and applications. Additionally, Green IoT highly represents impediments to diminishing energy consumption for IoT devices. It is also an energy-efficient process that can effectively minimise the emission of CO_2 and the effect of greenhouse gases. Due to this reason, it can create an eco-friendly environment that can be considered sustainable for various smart cities. It is highly capable of addressing techniques as well as strategies to reduce traffic waste, pollution hazards, and the usage of resources. For perspective, some examples of IoT devices include webcams, detectors, Scanners, controllers, drones, smartphones, etc. All of them have the capacity to cooperate and communicate in order to accomplish shared objectives. Smart devices are positioned to offer a wide range of real-time surveillance applications, such as pollution management, e-healthcare, mobility automation, industrial modernization and mechanisation, and building automation, with the help of such elements and modern communications.

Keywords: Blockchain, Technology, CO_2, Smart city, Development, IoT, ICT

[1]umamaheswaran.maths@sairam.edu.in, [2]ankurkulsh@nimsuniversity.org, [3]bipin.srivastava@galgotiacollege.edu, [4]sunil.babu.m@gmail.com, [5]rajanimandhare80@gmail.com, [6]joseariasgon6@gmail.com

DOI: 10.1201/9781003405580-86

1. Introduction

The "things" that surround people are being interconnected to enable a variety of smart city applications, boosting the overall quality of life as a result of the enormous progress in connectivity and sensing technology. The "Internet of Things (IoT)" is a term used to describe the connectedness between objects in the smart city. Everything else in smart cities can be linked to the internet of things (IoT) at any time, any place, and through any channel. IoT components are becoming smarter as a result of an adaptable communication system, computation, evaluation, and storage as IoT technologies continue to advance. IoT also makes it possible for software components to exchange information, decide together, and perform jobs in the best way possible. IoT can gather and distribute enormous volumes of data using cutting-edge technological tools, which may then be evaluated for wise decision-making. To enable IoT to be widely used, big data requires storage space, cloud technology, and high communication bandwidth [1]. IoT systems use a lot of energy to analyse and send all of this information. But employing clever and effective methods could result in a reduction in power usage. IoT may, however, improve the standard of living in smart cities as well as help make the world a healthier, more ecological, and overall safer living environment by combining practical methods to lower the power efficiency of big data storage and transmission [2].

In order to develop sustainable, environmental, and smart cities, specialists highlighted the link between green IoT and big data. They explained how this connection reduces the risks of pollution, lowers energy consumption, and promotes resource efficiency. Using cutting-edge technology like machine learning, smart cities have the possibility of growing even better than they already are. Smart city elements, such as sensor-integrated modern transportation infrastructure, webcams in smart surveillance systems, and others, provide illustrations of this. The key components of the prospective green infrastructure in 2020 were introduced by experts. These cities will be places where things are made sophisticated through design for sustainability, building automation, smart transport, smart citizens, sophisticated infrastructure, smart environments, smart technology, as well as digital education and governance [3]. IoT has a significant impact on the improvement of smart cities in a variety of ways, including by improving community evolution, lowering traffic congestion, developing cost-effective public works, maintaining residents safe and healthy, lowering energy consumption, getting better surveillance systems, and improving air quality. Researcher's interest has been drawn to IoT environmental challenges, such as power consumption, carbon emissions, energy savings, trade, carbon labelling, and footprint [4].

As a result, a summary of solutions based on IoT for reducing carbon dioxide emissions and fuel efficiency is provided. The paper talks about IoT technologies that enable in-the-moment cognitive sensing of the environment and produce and gather data on energy use throughout the manufacturing process. Green IoT is a crucial technology to reduce carbon emissions and electricity consumption in order to achieve the aims of green infrastructure and conservation. Energy use rises as there are more IoT devices on the market. IoT devices, for instance, now have wake-up procedures and sleep cycles to control their resources and energy usage [5, 6]. The researchers offered methods for reducing IoT energy usage, including efficient information centre energy, data transfer from IoT systems, and the implementation of energy-efficient rules.ICT (information and communication technology)" consequences on carbon emissions and power use in smart cities are also discussed by the writers.

2. Related Literature Work

The early research on green IoT-based smart cities is fragmented, which results in a lack of appreciation for its significance. In-depth explanations of the enabling technologies for IoT networks in smart buildings that can lower CO_2 emissions, minimise energy consumption, improve QoS, and enable ICT seem to be lacking in the present body of research. The tactics and strategies for establishing sustainable smart cities are not fully covered in the surveys that are currently available. There isn't existing research that examines the methods and strategies for sustainable green infrastructure, including enabling ICT, lowering energy consumption, cutting CO_2 emissions, enhancing durability, and minimising waste management. Researchers contrasted green IoT with a focus on reducing energy use [7]. Developing energy-efficient network infrastructure, energy-efficient regulations, and data transfer from Internet of Things devices are the only topics covered in the research. Although the research will concentrate on approaches and tactics, it does not contain all of the suitable alternatives for using IoT to enhance smart cities' efficiency and eco-friendliness. The paper that was given examined the drawbacks of IoT technology and offered suggestions to lessen them. This research covered certain IoT drawbacks, such as energy consumption and greenhouse gas emissions. The research looked at how green IoT works to enhance smart city ecosystems, economic expansion, and life satisfaction. It provided evidence that the green IoT may help the sustainable use of natural resources in forestry, fisheries, and farming [8]. The researchers did not, meanwhile, cover all of the possible drawbacks of IoT technology in diverse applications. As a result, this research focuses on using green IoT to enhance eco-friendliness and sustainable development for green infrastructure, in addition to covering a wider range of negative effects.

In this, the researchers discuss methods for reducing energy usage for green IoT and, as a result, propose the sustainable ICT principle. They also presented IoT for smart cities. The researchers, moreover, did not go into additional detail about green ICT for IoT systems in green infrastructure. This study will thus close this gap in the existing literature. In order to achieve a green IoT, professionals demonstrated how to effectively implement IoT technologies. They found IoT applications that can use less energy and benefit the environment [9]. Several methods for allowing the IoT to promote energy efficiency have been presented. The idea of IoT for smart cities and its potential benefits, features, and many applications were explored by the writers. The research concentrated primarily on the application of IoT for smart cities, including climate and pollution control, smart housing, smart parks, and smart transportation. The research does not include the methods for increasing IoT to increase the eco-friendliness and viability of smart cities; instead, the researchers concentrated on the advantages and uses of IoT for digital infrastructure [10]. Table 86.1 provides a comparison between previous surveys and the current research.

Table 86.1 Comparison of existing surveys and the present work [4]

"Survey	
[20] (2017)	Designing energy-efficient polities for IoT data transmission and data centres.
[21] (2012)	Exploring the principles of green IoT to enhance quality of life, safety environment and economic growth
[22] (2015)	The principle of green ICT for smart cities
[23] (2017)	Applying techniques for enabling green IoT for energy efficiency
[24] (2017)	IoT concepts and advantages for different applications of smart cities
[25] (2019)	Enabling techniques for green IoT in smart cities
[26] (2020)	Fog computing and enabling technologies for sustainable smart cities based on IoT environments.
[38] (2021)	UAV-assisted green IoT application in smart cities based on BSG networks
Our Work	Focuses on techniques and strategies which lead to reduce emissions, reduce traffic, improve waste management, reduce resource usage, reduce energy consumption and enhance QoS of communication networks for making smart cities more liveable, sustainable, and more environmentally friendly".

2.1 The scope of Study and Structure

IoT is essential for enhancing living quality, a supportive environment, conservation, and ecology in a modern city. The methods and approaches utilised to make smart cities more environmentally friendly and ecological will be explored in this study. The writers concentrate on methods that minimise pollutants, congestion, wastewater treatment, consumption of resources, energy use, and contamination, as well as the quality of service (QoS) of network technologies [11]. Relevant needs can be identified, and although the approaches are designed for different problems, relevant work will be presented.

2.2 Overview of Blockchain and Green IoT

However, each failure exposes numerous devices, vast amounts of individual private data, suppliers and distributors, and the broader community due to security flaws in the IoT platform. Major problems include devices that connect, verify, or expend improperly with other devices. Devices are linked through a centralised cloud computing and storage platform, which is not long-term sustainable since the number of devices connected and the amount of information are expanding quickly. The centralised design suffers as a result, creating redundancies and constraints. Recent advances in blockchain technology have enabled peer-to-peer contract behaviour, eliminating the need for middlemen in Internet of Things (IoT) transactions, which has been a very consistent response to the difficulties of confidentiality and security, confidence, trustworthiness, singular point of failure, as well as configurability [12]. It offers a decentralised system that allows multiple technologies to immediately transfer assets like money or data thanks to safe and dependable contract negotiation. Any hacker would have to get over the second layer of protection that depends on some of the strongest encrypted communications now in use if accessibility to IoT device data were managed via blockchain [13]. Furthermore, because there is no centralised authority, the single-point-of-breakdown issue will vanish irrespective of the platform's density. Blockchain networks make it feasible to design arrangements that will only be carried out when specific requirements are satisfied.

In plain terms, a company must improve operational efficiency and cut expenses if it desires to increase earnings while altering its goods or advertising plan. In order to enable customers to track the effectiveness of their activities and make necessary adjustments, IoT applications may be connected to the web and utilised to capture and rebroadcast data. But the IoT gadget's adaptability greatly exceeded what had been anticipated [14]. A sustained environment now faces new issues as a result of the expanding number of IoT device modifications in smart homes, smart businesses, smart cities, and other applications. In order to establish a healthy ecological setting, researchers must thus concentrate their research efforts on the requirement for a green IoT. The key traits and elements that must be prioritised in order to create an IoT ecosystem that is more environmentally friendly are covered in the following section.

3. Methodology

Research methodology can be considered as specific procedures as well as techniques that have been used to detect, select, process, and analyse information about a definite topic. This section remarkably helps the reader make a critical evaluation of the validity and reliability of a study. In this context, secondary qualitative data collection methods have been followed to extract authentic information about the usage of blockchain in green IoT. Empirical research has also been followed, where different kinds of mathematical expressions have been included, and different tables have also been attached to support this technology for smart city development.

4. Analysis and Discussion

4.1 The Role of Blockchain in the Green IoT

By offering a private communications system and dependable connections, blockchain technology subsequently created a new foundation for the Internet of Things (IoT), preventing risks to centralised control architectures. The blockchain is already being utilised by many stakeholders, such as banking, industrial companies, and agricultural organisations, to support IoT systems that call for sensing devices and mechanisation. Blockchain networks build a safe, low-power infrastructure that can directly supervise operations without the use of central cloud infrastructure, establishing a more ecologically responsible IoT ecosystem. The conventional computer method has had a more significant impact on the world's power systems as networking has expanded. One excellent illustration of a green ecosystem is a virtual currency. Several businessmen who are concerned about the planet have embraced their technology platform and altered it to make a positive impact instead of damaging it [14, 15]. For instance, unlike huge, conventional centralised generation that must carry electricity thousands of metres across the grid, microplants may be put practically everywhere and function autonomously. By distributing assets to shareholders, several companies are utilising the blockchain to enable people to take part in the expansion of greener fuel efficiency. The significance of blockchain technology for the development of a resilient, greener environment is covered in this subsection.

The block chain system is only one of many uses for blockchain technologies, which might also support the fundamental requirements of green infrastructure as a framework for the distributed storage of information. Big data technologies must be used by smart cities in order to integrate the acquired data and provide unique value. The administration provides a framework for players in smart cities to assume the function and utility of big data since it is the regulator and executive inspector. One advantage is that each member might get access to a lot of data to cut expenses and boost service quality [16]. However, individuals are also sufficiently motivated to provide their data to smart cities. Researchers devised a model to confirm the amount of smart city development based on the TOPSIS technique. The assessment variables are systematically given weight by the entropy technique. The intensity of the indicator reports is used to calculate each indication's weight [17]. The extreme value approach, which can be classified into positive indexing and inverse indexing, is used to standardise this work. These are the precise techniques:

Positive indicator

$$X'_{ij} = \frac{X_{ij} - \min(X_{1j}, X_{2j}, \ldots . X_{nj})}{\max(X_{1j}, X_{2j}, \ldots , X_{nj}) - \min(X_{1jj}, X_{2j}, \ldots . , X_{nj})} + 1 \tag{1}$$

$$i = 1,2, \ldots . , ; j = 1,2, \ldots , m$$

Reverse index

$$X'_{ij} = \frac{\max(X_{1j}, X_{2j}, \ldots . , X_{nj}) - X_{ij}}{\max(X_{1j}, X_{2j}, \ldots , X_{nj}) - \min(X_{1jj}, X_{2j}, \ldots . , X_{nj})} + 1 \tag{2}$$

$$i = 1,2, \ldots . , ; j = 1,2, \ldots , m$$

The calculation formula for calculating the proportion of the indicator-I in the area-J is as follows

$$P_{ij} = \frac{X_{ij}}{\sum_{i=1}^{n} X_{ij}} \ (i = 1, 2, \ldots \ldots, n, j = 1, 2, \ldots \ldots, m) \tag{3}$$

$$E_{ij} = 1/\ln m * (\sum_{i=1}^{m} P_{ij} \ln P_{ij}) , i = 1,2, \ldots \ldots, n, j = 1,2, \ldots \ldots m \tag{4}$$

$$D_{ij} = 1 - E_i , i = 1,2, \ldots \ldots, n \ j = 1,2, \ldots \ldots m \tag{5}$$

$$W_{ij} = \frac{D_{ij}}{\sum_{j=1}^{m} D_{ij}}, i = 1,2, \ldots n \ j = 1,2, \ldots m \tag{6}$$

A technique of multi-attribute judgement is TOPSIS. For a small number of applications, it mostly performs multi-objective assessment and decision theory. Depending on how closely the assessment systems resemble the ideal positive and negative outcomes, this assessment approach rates the assessment methods. Find the equation for the ideal positive and negative responses.

$$V_j^* = max_i(V_{ij}) \tag{7}$$

$$V_j^\nabla = min_i(V_{ij}) \tag{8}$$

Calculate the Euclidean distance.

$$S_i^* = \sqrt{\sum_{j-1}^{m} (V_{ij} - V_j^*)^2}, i = 1,2, \ldots n, j = 1,2, \ldots \ldots m \tag{9}$$

$$S_i^\nabla = \sqrt{\sum_{j-1}^{m} (V_{ij} - V_j^\nabla)^2}, i = 1,2, \ldots n, j = 1,2, \ldots \ldots m \tag{10}$$

Calculate the closeness c value of each object to the ideal solution

$$Ci = \frac{S_i^\nabla}{S_i^* + S_i^\nabla} \tag{11}$$

C_i ranges from 0 to 1, and the greater the figure, the more advanced the state of developing smart cities that year. The amount of smart city construction in a given year is inversely correlated with the C value.

4.2 ICT Technology for Smart Cities

Intelligent devices, cams, applications, analytics, and data centres in smart cities are the foundation of the Internet of Things (IoT), worldwide, ambient communication systems, integrated programming environments, and undetectable system software. The researchers suggested using IoT to create an energy-efficient, sustainable campus environment. IoT aspects have been introduced despite earlier proof being offered, where the advantages of IoT and ways to build a green space by using effective strategies were highlighted. The writers of this article examined many technical approaches to achieving a future green Internet. As a result, IoT reduces costs, minimises the technical effect on the environment as well as people's health, and saves the national environment. Green IoT so emphasises environmentally friendly production, design, usage, and disposal [16]. Each of the aforementioned categories and their significance for enhancing smart cities was explored by the writers. Additionally, in order to complete the technological world with the resilience of intelligent things, alternatives for green IoT include lowering CO_2 emissions and IoT power consumption.

Designing and utilising green components are part of green IoT. Designing computer devices, power efficiency, modulation schemes, and connectivity topologies are some of the design components of green IoT. Utilizing the IoT component will save Emissions of carbon dioxide and improve energy efficiency. Discovering new resources, utilising environmental preservation, reducing the use of existing funds as well as prices, and minimising IoT's detrimental consequences for human health and the ecosystem are all part of the process of "greening" IoT [17]. (e.g., CO_2 emission, NO_2 and other pollution). The researchers of the offered information on the long-term effects of industrial pollutants on the environment.

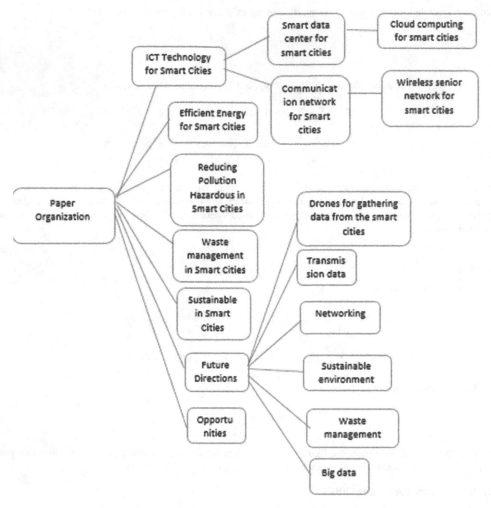

Fig. 86.1 Framework of paper organization [3]

In order to improve the environment, IoT platform energy usage must be reduced. In addition, promoting sustainable ICT technologies contribute to economic development and environmental protection, making the world greener and smarter as a result of rising IoT technology [18].

4.3 Communication Network for Smart Cities

Rendering the Internet of Things (IoT) greener depends heavily on remote monitoring technology. Sustainable, resource-, power-, and ecologically sound communications are referred to as "green communications." Minimised energy use, low radiation doses, and lower Carbon emissions are all considered characteristics of a "green" communication network. The authors recommend an evolutionary algorithm improvement for system modelling, and the results demonstrated much lower exposure to radiation and CO_2 costs. Research in 2014, which confirmed the hypothesis, described methods to increase data rates and decrease Emissions of CO_2 in cognitively impaired WSNs. Researchers also offered a number of models for assessing the energy usage and Carbon intensity of wireless communications networks in addition to their study [18]. To reduce energy usage, "Vehicular Ad hoc NETworks" (VANETs) were suggested by scholars. Three areas, namely theory frameworks, applications, and technological advancements, are examined in the examination of the fuel efficiency of 5G-based mobile communications networks. Furthermore, scholars have demonstrated the impact of developing technologies that boost "Next Generation Networks" (NGN) technology's energy savings. To ease congestion, boost data rates, and improve NGN QoS, fuel efficiency and CO_2-reducing emissions must be adopted.

Numerous scientists have concentrated on solar for conserving energy and QoS enhancement, including dependable storage for energy efficiency. Additionally, the "stochastic geometry" technique is used to preserve QoS and boost energy efficiency. The convenience of the dynamic duty cycle method also made a case for reducing latency, boosting energy savings, and maintaining a long life span. Nevertheless, "the hypertext transfer" protocol was employed to reduce the waiting period and lengthen the period for reliable service. The advancement of wireless communication will improve the effectiveness of a "next-generation network" in accordance with the demands centred on lowering energy consumption, lowering Carbon dioxide emissions for maintaining a safe atmosphere, and creating greener communities. The goal of 5G is to use less energy, which leads to communication that is green and beneficial for the ecosystem [19]. According to the environmental connection forecast for 2020, all communication methods and products will be able to interact effectively and economically for a green and healthy lifestyle. In order to increase communication dependability and QoS between machines and people, 5G technology is crucial. Additionally, the 5G technique improves connectivity over a wider region, lowers latency, consumes less energy, and offers faster data rates.

5. Conclusion

The twenty-first century has seen incredible advancements in a diverse range of technologies that have enhanced living in smart cities. IoT research has rapidly shown increased advantages in improving the quality of life in intelligent cities. Conversely, the creation of new technology necessitates a large amount of energy and results in unintended releases of pollutants and e-waste. This study looked at ways to make cities smarter, better, more ecological, and healthier while also enhancing the quality of life. Researchers focused on the green IoT in particular for its efficient material use, creation of durables, reduction of emissions, reduction of contamination, and reduction of e-waste. The key components of advanced technologies make smart objects in smart cities intelligent, so they can complete their jobs on their own. To make the neighbourhood eco-friendly and viable, these objects connect with each other and with people while utilising broadband and power efficiently, minimising toxic gases, and generating less e-waste. In order to create eco-friendly and viable smart city initiatives, researchers also highlighted problems and potential directions for future research. In order to establish a green IoT environment, blockchain technology may also improve the administration of energy systems, the currency sector, e-governance, and smart cities. It provides safe, open, and untouchable interactions and participates increasingly actively in the creation and use of sustainable power. Blockchain is quickly replacing older technologies in IoT research and innovation because it can get around obstacles and inefficiencies. In order to develop a greener IoT ecosystem, this paper analyses the crucial elements that may be tackled by utilising blockchain technology. It also discusses the importance of blockchain technology in progressing towards an ecologically sound IoT ecosystem. This paper contributes to the debate by giving a thorough and comprehensive analysis of the blockchain in the green IoT. While building an ecologically sound IoT environment, attention ought to be concentrated on addressing open concerns and the strategic development of studies. The limitless deployment possibilities of blockchain technology and its capacity for real concern will fundamentally alter the dynamics of creating a green, viable IoT ecosystem. In order to better grasp the arising occurrences at the intersection of Blockchain technology and the green IoT ecosphere, investigators will be urged to investigate in greater detail the potential application of research hypotheses. The research area for this work will establish the foundation for future studies in this field.

REFERENCES

1. Sharma, P. K., Kumar, N. and Park, J. H., 2020. Blockchain technology toward green IoT: Opportunities and challenges. *IEEE Network, 34*(4), pp. 263–269.
2. Ferrag, M. A., Shu, L., Yang, X., Derhab, A. and Maglaras, L., 2020. Security and privacy for green IoT-based agriculture: Review, blockchain solutions, and challenges. *IEEE access, 8*, pp. 32031–32053.
3. Ahmed, I., Zhang, Y., Jeon, G., Lin, W., Khosravi, M. R. and Qi, L., 2022. A blockchain-and artificial intelligence-enabled smart IoT framework for sustainable city. *International Journal of Intelligent Systems.*
4. Almalki, F., Alsamhi, S. H., Sahal, R., Hassan, J., Hawbani, A., Rajput, N. S., Saif, A., Morgan, J. and Breslin, J., 2021. Green IoT for eco-friendly and sustainable smart cities: future directions and opportunities. *Mobile Networks and Applications*, pp. 1–25.

5. Wong, P.F., Chia, F.C., Kiu, M.S. and Lou, E.C.W., 2020, March. The potential of integrating blockchain technology into smart sustainable city development. In *IOP Conference Series: Earth and Environmental Science* (Vol. 463, No. 1, p. 012020). IOP Publishing.

6. Sun, M. and Zhang, J., 2020. Research on the application of block chain big data platform in the construction of new smart city for low carbon emission and green environment. *Computer Communications*, *149*, pp. 332–342.

7. V. Panwar, D. K. Sharma, K. V. P. Kumar, A. Jain & C. Thakar, (2021), "Experimental Investigations And Optimization Of Surface Roughness In Turning Of EN 36 Alloy Steel Using Response Surface Methodology And Genetic Algorithm" Materials Today: Proceedings, https://Doi.Org/10.1016/J.Matpr.2021.03.642

8. A. Jain, A. K. Pandey, (2019), "Modeling And Optimizing Of Different Quality Characteristics In Electrical Discharge Drilling Of Titanium Alloy (Grade-5) Sheet" Material Today Proceedings, 18, 182–191. https://doi.org/10.1016/j.matpr.2019.06.292

9. Treiblmaier, H., Rejeb, A. and Strebinger, A., 2020. Blockchain as a driver for smart city development: application fields and a comprehensive research agenda. *Smart Cities*, *3*(3), pp. 853–872.

10. A. Jain, A. K. Yadav & Y. Shrivastava (2019), "Modelling and Optimization of Different Quality Characteristics In Electric Discharge Drilling of Titanium Alloy Sheet" Material Today Proceedings, 21, 1680–1684. https://doi.org/10.1016/j.matpr.2019.12.010

11. A. Jain, A. K. Pandey, (2019), "Modeling And Optimizing Of Different Quality Characteristics In Electrical Discharge Drilling Of Titanium Alloy (Grade-5) Sheet" Material Today Proceedings, 18, 182–191. https://doi.org/10.1016/j.matpr.2019.06.292

12. Treiblmaier, H., Rejeb, A. and Strebinger, A., 2020. Blockchain as a driver for smart city development: application fields and a comprehensive research agenda. *Smart Cities*, *3*(3), pp. 853–872.

13. Pee, L.G. and Pan, S.L., 2022. Climate-intelligent cities and resilient urbanisation: Challenges and opportunities for information research. *International Journal of Information Management*, *63*, p. 102446.

14. Karmakar A and Sahib U 2017 Smart Dubai: Accelerating Innovation and Leapfrogging EDemocracy: In E-Democracy for Smart Cities (Singapore: Springer pp 197–257)

15. Ølnes S, Ubacht J and Janssen M 2017 Blockchain in government: Benefits and implications of distributed ledger technology for information sharing. Government Information Quartely 34 355–364

16. Rebrisoreanu M, Rus C, Leba M and Ionica A 2018 Exploring the Possibilities of Blockchain Use in a Smart City. Int J Syst Appl Eng Dev 12 164–167.

17. A. Jain, A. K. Pandey, (2019), "Multiple Quality Optimizations In Electrical Discharge Drilling Of Mild Steel Sheet" Material Today Proceedings, 8, 7252–7261. https://doi.org/10.1016/j.matpr.2017.07.054

18. V. Panwar, D. K. Sharma, K. V. P. Kumar, A. Jain & C. Thakar, (2021), "Experimental Investigations And Optimization Of Surface Roughness In Turning Of EN 36 Alloy Steel Using Response Surface Methodology And Genetic Algorithm" Materials Today: Proceedings, https://Doi.Org/10.1016/J.Matpr.2021.03.642

19. Pieroni A., Scarpato N., Di Nunzio L., Fallucchi F. and Raso M. 2018 Smarter city: smart energy grid based on blockchain technology. Int J Adv Sci Eng Inf Technol 8 (1) 298–306

20. A. Jain, C. S. Kumar, Y. Shrivastava, (2021), "Fabrication and Machining of Fiber Matrix Composite through Electric Discharge Machining: A short review" Material Today Proceedings. https://doi.org/10.1016/j.matpr.2021.07.288

Computer Science Engineering and Emerging Technologies (ICCS-2022) – Prof (Dr.) Rajeev Sobti et al. (eds)
© 2024 Taylor & Francis Group, London, ISBN 978-1-032-52199-2

Chapter

87

Automated Smart Agriculture Using Machine Learning

Tarun Kumar[1], Cherry Khosla[2], Manik Rakhra[3]
Computer Science and Engineering,
Lovely Professional University, Phagwara, India

Abstract: Agriculture is a basic need for human survival, but these days it has become very hard to farm on a large scale because of the increase in desert areas. It is very important to make this area farmable again. To do so, we must plant trees and use new technology to protect them. This paper uses new-tech sensors to check the quality of the environment and Image processing to create an ideal condition for plant growth in a desert area. This project is semi-automated, where a level of danger to plants can be resolved by the system itself, and if the danger level reaches a very high level, it will send a distress signal to the user on its app or mobile. This project also includes weeding, bird, animal, or intruder scaring, spraying, keeping vigilance, and irrigation with controlled chemical combinations with water for proper growth of plants.

Keywords: Sensor, Drone, Image processing, Microprocessor, Microcontroller

1. Introduction

Agriculture in India plays a vital role, as 70% of households are farming-based. Thus, issues like low production, soil desertification, low level of ground water plays an important role in country growth. This paper is about solving problem of desertification with very less resources and automatic system which learns and decide for issues it faces in the field. Because of desertification, the production of crops is declining in quality and quantity, and this area is increasing day by day. This paper suggests using sensors to get data in the surrounding area, drones to analyse the field in real time, and machine learning and artificial learning algorithms to solve the problem with minimum resources and maximum benefits. The same process can be used in non-desert areas, but this project shows its maximum efficiency in desert areas. The sensors like temperature, moisture, NPK, etc. will send the data of respective elements like temperature, water in the soil, and amount of nitrogen and phosphorus to the main processor, which decides if the value is lower than the critical value or if it is higher and decides the action. The action can be divided into three parts, which are based on signals that occur in different situations, like in the case of a deficiency, an intruder, or a disease. We have a yellow signal, which the system will try to solve. If it is solved signal will go to green and it will start storing data on cloud. If the system is not able to solve the problem, the signal will turn red, and the system will send an emergency signal to the user.

2. Literature Review

The decrease in water level, drying of wells and rivers, and very little rain have given us a scenario to utilise the water we have. To do so, different processes have been used, and one of the most popular is the sensor-based approach [2], where temperature, humidity, and moisture sensors are used with suitable algorithms and monitoring locations. The algorithm used in the approach is programmed with threshold values for different sensor inputs and programmed in a microprocessor

[1]tarunsharma080997@gmail.com, [2]cherry.khosla86@gmail.com, [3]Rakhramanik786@gmail.com

DOI: 10.1201/9781003405580-87

or microcontroller to control the quantity of water given to plants. The technology for wireless communication makes it very easy to communicate with devices very far away from the microprocessor.

One of the most important aspects of farming is soil quality. It includes Nitrogen, phosphorus, and Potassium as important elements, and different properties of soil like Electrical Conductivity, ph level, and temperature affect the growth of plants. So, it is necessary to keep them in balance. We can use a soil quality sensor [5] and microcontroller to adjust the critical values for the soil and use various fertilisers effectively. [6]

Disease control for such farming is not a difficult task. It is a difficult task to find the disease a plant is suffering from. It can be done by Image Processing and Machine Learning, where the photos are taken by a drone. Since the start of project will be cold start, we can use all the data to find anomaly and give a signal of distrust to call for human help [7].

3. System Overview

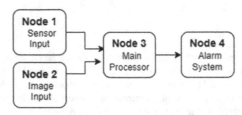

Fig. 87.1 System overview

Source: Author's compilation

This paper is divided in four sections: Node 1, Node 2, Node 3, and Node 4. Each node in the above diagram deals with problem of the project, which are very small project. The main goal of the project is to protect the plants individually and if any problem occurs deals with it and take appropriate action.

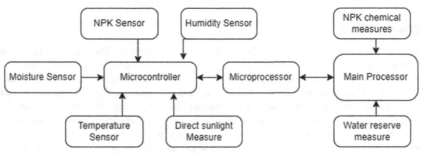

Fig. 87.2 Block Diagram for sensor signals

Source: Author's compilation

The first section or Node 1 represents the sensor input system as shown above. It is made up of an AVR microcontroller, NPK sensor, temperature sensor, humidity sensor, moisture sensor, sunlight measure, water reserve measure, chemical reserve measurer. This section will use different hardware to measure the different attributes such as Nitrogen, moisture in the air etc. We will use different hardware as given below:

NPK Sensor

This sensor is used to measure the quantity of nitrogen (N), phosphorus (P), and potassium (K) in the soil. Since nitrogen, phosphorus, and potassium are main source of nutrients for any plant, they are the deciding factor if the soil is fertile or not.

Humidity Sensor

The air's humidity affects the growth of plants. Some plants need a very humid environment, but some plants require very humid air. The humidity sensor returns the humidity value in the air in analogue signals to the processor, which calculates the percentage of humidity in the air.

Moisture Sensor

The moisture sensor senses the amount of water present in the soil. The amount of water in the soil is a main component of a plant's growth.

Temperature Sensor

The temperature of the surrounding area of the plant is very important, as it increases or decreases the intake of water for any plant. If the temperature around a plant is very high, the plant may die because of the low water quantity it requires, as it needs a high water quantity in a high-temperature area.

Sunlight Measure

The sunlight falling directly on the plant is also responsible for the early death of plants. It is the main problem with the dehydration of plants, as they lose water through their leaves. Too little sunlight will decrease the food-making process for the plants, making it very dangerous for them.

Microprocessor

The microprocessor is the brain of the circuit, which can take input from different sensors and process it. The data is saved or is used to calculate if we can grow plants in the specific area or how much it will cost us to do it.

The second section of this paper refers to the Image collection part of the project, where a drone is used to access images of different plants at different times. It helps the main processor understand the situation on the farm. These images can be used to detect diseases using Image processing [8–13] and to detect any intruder using object detection [14–19]. The drone takes images of the plants and other areas and sends them to the main processor. The main processor checks them up and finds any possibility of disease or intruder.

The third section, or node, is the main processor, which takes the data from different systems around the field and decides on appropriate measures.

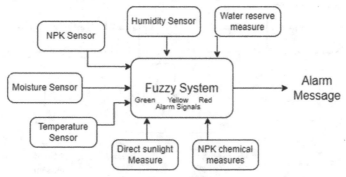

Fig. 87.3 Fuzzy System for Alarm

Source: Author's compilation

The fourth section has the responsibility of giving out the signal based on which appropriate action can be taken. The paper divides it into three parts: Green, Yellow, and Red.

Green: If the fuzzy system is giving out this signal, it means that there is no problem with the system or the field; thus, do nothing and continue the loop and save the data sent by the different sensors and drone.

Yellow: If the Fuzzy system is giving out a yellow signal, the problem can be solved by the system. It is generated by either an intruder in the farm or any anomaly of weed that can be solved, like the weed system, which will start the weed-removing rover, and for any intruder, it will start the siren and noise-producing system, which will make it run away.

Red: The red signal is generated if the problem cannot be solved by the system itself and needs human interference, for example, if the level of water or chemicals in their respective containers is very low or if the plants are infected by some type of disease. The system will immediately send a distress signal to the user via any communication system.

Table 87.1   Rule base for sensor input

Sensor	Low	Intermediate	High	Results
Temperature/NPK/ Humidity/Moisture	Yes	NO	No	Yellow
	No	Yes	No	Green
	No	No	Yes	Yellow

Source: Author's compilation

Table 87.2   Rule base for Image processing

Intruder/Low level of water, chemical container	Yes	Red Alert
	No	Green Alert

Source: Author's compilation

The above tables are the proposed rule base for fuzzy system, which will give different alarm system at different combination of sensors and image processing values and evaluation.

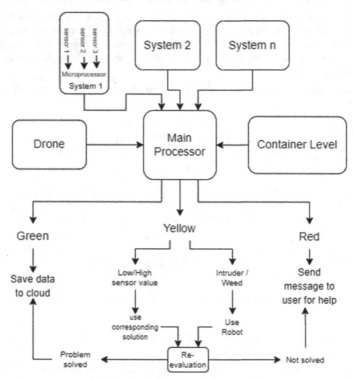

Fig. 87.4   Flow chart for the system working

Source: Author's compilation

The above flow chart showcases the process of automation of the crops of trees in desert areas. Since these projects are very large and in a desert area with very little population, we can't take care of these trees all the time. So, we use modern time technology to resolve this issue by keeping a watch over the trees. Here a tree or plant is watched over by a system of sensors; these plants can be in succession to each other or at a constant distance from each other, and the data obtained can be interpolated for all the other trees nearby.

4. Conclusion

The paper creates a system that can take input from different sensors and images, send their respective alarm signals, and solve any problem with very little human interference. The main problem came out because of the cold start, that is, we have no initial ideas about the threshold values and limiting values about temperature, NPK, etc., so we must take some initial values at random and by observation. Over time, the values can be adjusted for every farm and crop based on previous results and data. This system will handle different diseases, any shortage of chemicals and water, and intruders on its own.

REFERENCES

1. G. Eason, B. Noble, and I. N. Sneddon (1955). On certain integrals of Lipschitz-Hankel type involving products of Bessel functions.
2. Gondchawar, Nikesh, and R. S. Kawitkar. (2016) IoT based smart agriculture. 5.6 838-842.
3. JoaquínGutiérrez, Juan Francisco Villa-Medina, Alejandra Nieto-Garibay, and Miguel Ángel Porta-Gándara (2013) Automated Irrigation System Using a Wireless Sensor Network and GPRS Module.
4. Chung, Hsi-Hao, and Sun Lu (2003) Contrast-ratio analysis of sunlight-readable color LCDs for outdoor applications
5. Masrie, Marianah, et al. (2017) Detection of nitrogen, phosphorus, and potassium (NPK) nutrients of soil using optical transducer.
6. Madhura, U. K., et al. (2017) Soil quality management using wireless sensor network
7. Fang, Yi, and Ramaraja P. Ramasamy (2015). Current and prospective methods for plant disease detection
8. Zang Chuanlei, Zang Shanwen, Yang Jucheng, Shi Yancui and Chen Jia (2017) Apple Leaf Identification Using Genetic Algorithm and Correlation Based Feature Selection Method
9. Jobin Francis, Anto Sahaya Dhas and Annop B. K (2016) Identification of Leaf Diseases in Pepper Plants Using Soft Computing Techniques", In proc. of IEEE Conference on Emerging Devices and Smart Systems, pp. 168–173, 2016.
10. Manisha Bhange and H. A. Hingoliwala (2015) Smart Farming: Pomegranate Disease Detection Using Image Processing
11. Ashwini Awate, Damini Deshmankar, Gayatri Amrutkar, Utkarsha Bagul and Samadhan Sonavane (2015) Fruit Disease Detection using Color, Texture Analysis and ANN
12. Tejal Deshpande, Sharmila Sengupta, and K. S. Raghuvanshi (2014) Grading & Identification of Disease in Pomegranate Leaf and Fruit
13. Sudhir Rao Rupanagudi, Ranjani B.S., Prathik Nagaraj and Varsha G. Bhat (2014). A Cost Effective Tomato Maturity Grading System using Image Processing for Farmers
14. T. Y. Lin, M. Maire, S. Belongie, J. Hays, P. Perona, D. Ramanan, P. Dollár, and C. L. Zitnick, Microsoft COCO (2014) Common Objects in Context
15. D. Hoiem, S.K. Divvala and J.H. Hays, Pascal VOC 2008 Challenge (2009) WORLD LITERATURE TODAY.
16. R. Girshick, J. Donahue, T. Darrell, and J. Malik (2014). Rich Feature Hierarchies for Accurate Object Detection and Semantic Segmentation
17. N. Chumerin (2015). convolutional neural network.
18. Y. Lecun, Y. Bengio and G. Hinton (2015) Deep learning.
19. A. S. Razavian, H. Azizpour, J. Sullivan, and S. Carlsson, CNN Features Off-the-Shelf (2014). An Astounding Baseline for Recognition
20. Kounalakis, Tsampikos, Georgios A. Triantafyllidis, and Lazaros Nalpantidis (2018). Image-based recognition framework for robotic weed control systems

Computer Science Engineering and Emerging Technologies (ICCS-2022) – Prof (Dr.) Rajeev Sobti et al. (eds)
© 2024 Taylor & Francis Group, London, ISBN 978-1-032-52199-2

Chapter

88

A Review on Classification of Covid-19 and Pneumonia Disease Using Machine Learning

Vikram Sharma[1], Anurag Anand[2], Sushant Kumar[3],
Pabitra Kumar Panda[4], Makul Mahajan[5]

School of Computer Science and Engineering,
Lovely Professional University Phagwara, Punjab India

Abstract: Coronavirus is one of the severe diseases spreading over the globe. Due to this, the entire world was shut down for more than a year, which shows the level of risk it is imposing. The major target of this virus is the lungs, which cause respiratory issues that further lead to death. It is very important to detect it in its infancy. There is one more such disease that causes the lungs to malfunction, i.e., Pneumonia, and its types are Viral and Bacterial. This creates a lot of confusion among the doctors, i.e., It is a coronavirus or pneumonia. To solve this problem, this research paper will help them do the best prediction using their knowledge and the machine's knowledge of analysing the X-rays and City scan images and then giving the possibilities like 99% Coronavirus, etc. This is done by doing a regression comparative analysis between different neural network architectures like VGG16, Dense-Net-50, ResNet50, Xception, Squeeze Net, and EffectiveNetB0.

Keywords: Covid, SARS-CoV-2, VGG16, DenseNet-50, ResNet50, Xception, SqueezeNet, EfficientNetB0, DNN, GAN, Google Net

1. Introduction

In the month of December 2019, in Wuhan, Hubei, China, the sudden and unexpected emergence of a mysterious disease along with its misinformation and disinformation regarding its treatments, preventions, and origin led to a worldwide pandemic crisis. This disease was later termed as Coronavirus Disease 2019 (CORONAVIRUS) and the virus responsible to cause this disease was termed Severe Acute Respiratory Syndrome Coronavirus 2 (SARS-CoV-2). Time by Time, COVID proved itself to be a lethal disease. On January 30, 2020, the Director General of the World Health Organisation (WHO), which is the leading health concern organisation, declared CORONAVIRUS a Public Health Emergency of International Concern. According to the statistics provided by Google and Wikipedia, as of April 22, 2022, the total number of COVID cases was 507 million. The total number of deaths caused by COVID is 5.21 million.

Several tests were designed to detect COVID, among which RT-PCR proved much more effective and accurate than the Antigen test, but still, due to the average accuracy of 60%–70% of RT-PCT, we needed a much more effective way than RT-PCT to detect COVID. CT Scans generate radiographic images that can be evaluated by a radiologist for the diagnosis of COVID. A similar aim can also be achieved by the X-Ray report of an infected chest. Scans on a regular basis of the patient confirm the presence of the SARS-CoV-2 virus.

Experts from the fields of Artificial intelligence and machine learning started contributing their valuable deeds to help the medical industry in the fight against COVID. Several Deep learning Convolutional Neural Network (C. NNET) models

[1]vikramsh2002@gmail.com, [2]anuraganand7618@gmail.com, [3]000sushantkumar@gmail.com, [4]pkpdps2000@gmail.com, [5]makul.14575@lpu.co.in

DOI: 10.1201/9781003405580-88

have been proposed till now for the detection of CORONAVIRUS so that it can be treated and prevented from causing much harm at a very early stage by the physicians. The most common techniques used to train and detect COVID through the AI model are taking x-ray or radiography images of the infected chest. To make the model much more effective and acceptable, multi-class models are proposed for the detection of COVID-infected pneumonia, bacterial pneumonia, viral pneumonia, and COVID-negative pneumonia. Some of the most popular deep convolutional neural network architectures available for COVID detection are Xception, ResNet50, VGG-16, SqueezeNet, and DenseNet.

In this review paper, several case studies on the already existing COVID detection deep learning model have been reviewed to provide a better understanding and prove an efficient catalyst in the research field.

2. Literature Review

Militante et al. 2020 [1] proposed the C. NNET. model to detect Coronavirus and Pneumonia with various classes like normal, bacterial, and pneumonia.

For this analysis, datasets are taken from the Radiology Society of North America (RSNA) and Kaggle's chest X-Ray images, which are then pre-processed with various data augmentation methods. For the C. NNET. architecture, researchers have used VGG-16. For activation of the middle layer, this paper used ReLU with a batch size of 32 images by applying the Adam optimizer with a learning rate of 0.0001 for 100 epochs. In this methodology, the researcher achieved 95% accuracy with a precision of 1.0 for Normal, 0.95 for CORONAVIRUS, 0.97 for Bacterial pneumonia, and 0.94 for Viral Pneumonia.

Sohaib Asif 2020 [2] researcher published a paper based upon X-Ray images and CT scan images. For image pre-processing, researchers resized images to 299*299*3 with various augmentation techniques like vertical flip, noise, horizontal flip, translation, blur, and rotation. For Model building, they used the transfer learning approach. Here, the researcher chose the Inception V3 model at the first layer, followed by Convolution with a max pooling layer, and its subsequent layer comprises recursive blocks of convolution and max pooling layers, which were followed by Average pooling and dropout, and finally connected with a fully connected layer to generate three-class output for Coronavirus, normal pneumonia, and Viral pneumonia. The result after analysis of the model was 97% for training data and 93% for validation data.

Mohammad Rahimzadeh 2020 [3] describes experiments based upon CT scans and X-ray images. Datasets are collected from the GitHub repo, which includes images of Coronavirus, SARS, streptococci, ARDS, pneumocystis, and other types of pneumonia. Researchers also include datasets from Kaggle's RSNA Challenge for Pneumonia Detection. Then we augmented the dataset with various techniques like zoom range, rotation range, width and height shifting, shift range, and lastly, rescaling them to normalise. Architecture used in this paper to classify Coronavirus, pneumonia, and Normal based upon the concatenation of Xception and Res-Net50V2 architecture Initially, both architectures partially get images, which extract the deep hidden features from images, and both produce volumes of 10*10*2048 convolution blocks. Later, these two blocks of Xception and ResNetV2 are concatenated to produce the resultant block as 10*10*4096 conv2D, through which 1 conv2D is applied with kernel size = 1, no padding, and no activation, then Flatten it by applying dropout at the next layer of 50% to produce output with SoftMax into three classes. Model performance for CORONAVIRUS class, Pneumonia class, and Normal class of Xception is 99.48%, 91.52%, and 91.62%; for ResNet50V2, it is 99.25%, 90.07%, and 90.25%; and for the concatenated model, it is 99.50%, 91.60%, and 91.71%, respectively.

Mizuho Nishio 2020 [4] has solved the multi-classification problem, i.e., 3 classes that are coronavirus with pneumonia, non-Coronavirus pneumonia, and Healthy. Here transfer learning is used as a base, and on top of different well-known architectures, new layers are added, such as the global average layer, pool layer, NNET layer, dropout layer, and NNET layer (output with 3 neurons). After testing it with different pre-trained models, the following result was achieved: VGG16 (Loss: 0.4682 ± 0.0289, Accuracy: 83.682.00), ResNet-50 (Loss: 0.5237 0.0161, Accuracy: 77.761.18), Mobile Net (Loss: 0.49190.0300, Accuracy: 78.723.22), Dense Net-121 (Loss: 0.52760.0082, Accuracy: 78.242.23), Efficient Net (Loss: 0.52060.0177, Accuracy: 78.401.82). The best performer is VGG16, with an accuracy of 83.68%.

Asif Iqbal Khan 2020 [5] proposed a deep learning-based approach to originate a C. NNET. model to detect two different types of pneumonia, i.e., bacterial and viral, also CORONAVIRUS. The proposed model was named CoroNet based on Xception architecture. The Xception model is used with a flatten layer, a dropout layer, and two NNETs, which were added at the very end of the architecture layer. Multiple sources were used to collect and build the appropriate dataset, including a GitHub repository by Joseph that contained around 290 chest x-ray images, and the others were obtained from the Kaggle repository "chest x-ray images (pneumonia)". In total, 1300 images were taken of normal, bacterial pneumonia, viral pneumonia, and COVID cases to train the model. Then they resized it to 224 x 224 pixels with a resolution of 72 dpi. The accuracy obtained by the CoroNet model on different classification categories for 2-class classification was 99%, for 3-class classification it was 95%, and for 4-class classification it was 89.6%.

Tulin Ozturk 2020 [6] proposed the C. NNET. model DarkCovidNet, which was based upon the C. NNET. model Darknet-19. The total number of dataset images was 1125 (112 were COVID positive, 500 were negative, and 500 were pneumonia). In the proposed DarkCovidNet model, it consists of 19 convolutional layers, including a conv2D layer, max pooling layers, batch Normalisation, leaky RELU, flatten, and a linear layer. Evaluation of the model was performed using a 5-fold cross-validation procedure, and the average accuracy achieved by the binary class classification was 98.08% and by the triple class classification was 87.02%. The model was designed to provide assistance to reduce the workload and perform an accurate diagnosis faster, so specialists can shift their focus to more critical cases. And in addition, researchers have used the gradient-weighted Class activation mapping (Grad-CAM) heat map approach to produce heatmaps, which could help radiologists identify the unhealthy regions of the patient's lungs through his or her chest X-rays.

Shervin Minaee 2020 [7], a sourced dataset formed from two publicly available sources, consists of 2084 training and 3100 test images. Researchers named this dataset the COVID-Xray-5K dataset. The two sources that were used for dataset collection were the COVID-chestxray-dataset on GitHub and the CheXpert dataset for image pre-processing. Data augmentation was performed to create transformed versions of CORONAVIRUS sample datasets. Techniques include minor rotations, flipping, and adding small amounts of distortion. The main intention was to increase the number of dataset samples by a factor of 5 for pre-processing. The Four popular C. NNET. models, which proved highly acceptable by throwing promising results during recent years, are used. The models are ResNet18, ResNet50, SqueezeNet, and DenseNet-161. In this research paper, researchers have analysed their performance only for a 2-class classification. Instead of defining and training a whole new model, they just tweak and customise the last few layers of the pre-trained model on a sample dataset of the COVID-Xray-5k dataset. A further heatmap of COVID-infected lung regions was generated by using a deep visualisation technique. The sensitivity achieved by these models is 98%.

Muhammad E. H. Chowdhury 2020 [8] proposed a C. NNET.-based transfer learning system to automatically detect CORONAVIRUS and pneumonia. Eight different well-known and widely reported C. NNET-based research algorithms are trained, validated, and evaluated to differentiate normal patients with pneumonia using chest X-ray images. DenseNet201 exceeded many other C. NNET. networks while image enhancement was used to train C. NNET. models. The different CheXNet Dense net was more efficient than others, while image enhancement could be used. This highlights the fact that performance reported on a smaller website should be evaluated on a larger, extended website. The classification accuracy, precision, sensitivity, and specificity of normal, CORONAVIRUS, and viral pneumonia were 97.9%, 97.95%, 97.9%, and 98.8%, respectively.

In Wanshan Ning 2020 [9], the model proposed is termed asHust19, i.e., In which a 13-layer C. NNET. predicts the individual CT (Chest computed tomography) images and then another 13-layer C. NNET. trans-forms this individual image-based prediction to the patient-based prediction, then further a 7-layer DNN predicts the result based on CFs (from Clinical Features) and SARS-CoV-2 laboratory test results, and further these predictions are combined using the PLR-Algorith The average age accuracy of CT-base is 79.626%, CF-base is 79.676, and hust19 is 81.083%. As a result, hust19 is clearly the best performer, with an average of 81.083% accuracy, 84.3% specificity, and 70.59% sensitivity.

Md. Jahid Hasan 2021 [10], In this paper, researchers analysed various open-source datasets from J. P. Cohen's Spain hospital, which consist of 1587 for Normal, 4283 for pneumonia, and 701 for CORONAVIRUS. For the analysis, researchers used Grad-CAM, which is an ensemble technique to visualise the region at which predictions can be made. The proposed pipeline for the model is to take input images and pass them to Grad-CAM with other ensemble techniques, then U-Net segmentation is performed to find the mask for the actual place that causes diseases. After taking the predicted mask, it is subjected to lung images, which are later used to do classification. The C. NNET. architectures analysed for this classification are Ensemble Model, ResNet50, and the 17-layered C. NNET. model. To get the best results, researchers process the Ensemble Classification Model as the concatenation of EfficientNetB0, DenseNet121, and VGG19, which then passes to Ensemble Grad-CAM and U-Net Segmentation to get feature extraction to generate output to classify classes. The accuracy achieved in this experiment was 99.2% for the proposed Ensemble Model, 93.3% for Res-Net50, and 87.8% for the 17-layered C. NNET model.

Himadri Mukherjee [11], In this paper, a typical 2-class classification COVID detection model was described, which was a lightweight deep neural network-based C. NNET model with 9 layers, with 3 pairs of convolution and pooling layers followed by 3 dense layers. The output dimensions of the three convolution layers were 32, 16, and 8 with filters of 5*5, 4*4, and 3*3. Each convolution layer used the ReLU activation function. Moreover, the pooling window was a 2*2 filter size with a max pooling function and 3 dense layers of network size dimensions 256, 50, and 2 for output classification. Multiple sources were used for gathering sufficient amounts of data; 336 X-rays and 336 CT scans were used in total, of which 168 in each category were COVID and 168 were non-COVID. The 10-fold cross-validation approach was followed with 400 iterations, and finally they achieved an accuracy of 96.28%. At last, for validation, the data in terms of accuracy were compared with other existing DNN models such as Inception V3 (71.88%), MobileNet (82.89%), ResNet (90.77%), and the proposed model (96.28%).

Sharmila V. J. [12] proposed a method to solve a multiclass problem. The three classes considered are pneumonia, Coronavirus, and normal. This new method is proposed in which, after pre-processing on CXR-images, DCGAN (Deep Convolutional Generative Adversarial Network) is used, followed by different pretrained models and its own architecture. The average accuracy of Pretrained models is: Alex Net Training Accuracy is 94.3%, Testing Accuracy is 94.9%, Google Net Training Accuracy is 91.95%, Testing Accuracy is 93.45%, and Proposed DCGAN-C. NNET. Training Accuracy is 96.1%, and testing accuracy is 97.125%. Therefore, the best performer is the proposed model, i.e., DCGAN-C. NNET, with 97.125% testing accuracy.

Kanakaprabha [13] presented a paper based upon the identification of CORONAVIRUS and Pneumonia and within pneumonia classes like bacterial and Viral Pneumonia. The dataset is collected from the SIRM and includes 219 images of CORONAVIRUS, 1341 X-Ray images for normal, and 1345 X-Ray images for Pneumonia. For image pre-processing, researchers first read images and convert them to grayscale, apply the N-CLAHE (Normalised Contrast Limited Adaptive Histogramme Equalisation) for the pixel correction, and then convert images back to RGB mode by applying the default resize size with Image augmentation. The researcher's proposed architecture takes input images (after applying pre-processing), and in the first layer of convolution, it has 64 filters with a 3*3 kernel size; in the second layer, it has 64 filters with a kernel size of 3*3 followed by max pooling layers of 2*2; in the next layer, it has 512 filters with a kernel size of 3*3 followed by max pooling layers of 2*2; and in the last convolution block, it has 256 filters with avirus and pneumonia (bacterial and viral separately). After 50 epochs, Normal X-Ray medical images have an accuracy of 88%, and infected X-Ray images have an accuracy of 90%, with a sensitivity of 95%, a specificity of 93%, and a whole accuracy of 93.9%.

Emtiaz Hussain [14] used Coro-Det, a C. NNET. model having 22 layers, which consist of 9 convolution layers followed by 9 max pooling layers, 2 dense layers, and a leaky ReLU activation function. The main motive was to achieve higher accuracy, and the researcher chose an attribute to make it happen by taking the largest dataset of all time to train the model (8 publicly available datasets, 7390 images). Data labelling for multi-class classification was considered by the researchers in the categories of 2-class classification, 3-class classification, and 4-class classification. The accuracy of 2 class classifications (CORONAVIRUS and normal), 3 class classifications (CORONAVIRUS, normal, non-covid pneumonia), and 4 class classifications (covid, normal, bacterial pneumonia, and viral pneumonia) came out to be 99.1%, 94.2%, and 91.2%, respectively. All the C. NNET. architectures used the 5-fold cross-validation technique to ensure the better accuracy of the model and divided the dataset into 5 subsets (4 for training and 1 for validation).

Rahib H. Abiev's [15] paper was intended to improve C. NNET, which will assist in the diagnosis of cases of CORONAVIRUS and non-CORONAVIRUS viral pneumonia using chest X-ray images. Due to the lack of CORONAVIRUS chest X-ray image case data, the researcher showed that the learning method of transfer can be used. The two models of C. NNET. are trained on two different data sets; the first model was trained in binary separation (pneumonia or normal) from the original site, which contained only cases of pneumonia and chest X-ray images. On the other hand, with the help of the transfer learning method, the second model used the first model as the basic model and was trained in the second, which contained CORONAVIRUS, pneumonia, and common chest X-ray images of 3 stage structures (CORONAVIRUS, pneumonia, and common). After the use of the model, the results found with the detection of CORONAVIRUS and pneumonia were 98.3%, 97.9%, 98.3%, and 98.0% with accuracy, recall, precision, and F1 scores, respectively; therefore, the model has been shown to be effective in diagnosing CORONAVIRUS and pneumonia. The Grad CAM is also shown to help the researcher visualise when a model is looking at X-ray images of the chest to form a differentiating function.

Mainuzzaman Mahin [16], a researcher, trained three transfer learning models: MobileNetV2, VGG19, and Inceptionv3. There are 4,237 pneumonia chest X-rays and 1,142 CORONAVIRUS X-rays in the collection. In the dataset, these models have given excellent results. MobileNetV2 and VGG19 performed well. Next, we created an easy-to-use VNG-based C. NNET. model with only six layers, including ReLU functionality, fall performance, and mass integration layers, to see the edges of real photos or maps of the previous feature. The discovery indicates that the proposed model exceeds C. NNET's model designs with an accuracy rate of 98%. Feature recognition and classification worked well, and model validation confirmed that the findings were valid models that could detect CORONAVIRUS and lung disease using a simple chest X-ray image. MobileNetV2, VGG19, and Inceptionv3 showed accuracy of 98%, 92.82%, and 96.92%, respectively.

Rubina Sarki [17] proposed two scenarios: Normal vs. Coronavirus classification and Normal vs. Coronavirus vs. Pneumonia classification. The dataset used for model building was taken from the repository of Cohen, which includes Coronavirus X-ray images, and for pneumonia, the author used the Kermany repository, and later they merged to perform analysis. For the creation of C. NNET. models, this paper used a transfer learning approach with pre-trained models like Inception V3, VGG-16, and Xception architecture with top equal to false, which means they did not provide the pre-defined final activation layer to classify the various classes; instead, the researcher added VGG-16 and Proposed C. NNET. models for top to classify the provided class output. The C. NNET. model that is proposed by them includes an input image of (224, 224, 3), 5 Conv2D blocks, 5 Pooling blocks, and some NNET. with a dropout layer. Model performance for normal CORONAVIRUS on testing was 97.67%, and for normal COVID/Pneumonia on testing data, it was 97.75%.

Zohreh Mousavi [18] have proposed involved various steps followed that are pre-processing on images under this image are resized to 224×224×3 and then normalised between 0 and 1. To make the data balanced, the Data Augmentation method is used. The proposed model is a combination of long-short-term memory and C. NNET, such that 5 Convolutional and 3 long-short-term-memory layers are used to automatically detect pneumonia from the different classes, and leaky relu is used as an activation function. At last, an NNET with 50 neurons plus leaky relu and 4 neurons with softmax for the output The accuracy of the processed model is best, i.e., 99.4%, and even the recall and precision are the same, i.e., 99.4%.

3. Comparative Analysis

After compiling all survey, comparative table is designed to demonstrate how various models achieves to classify their objectives.

Table 88.1 Comparative analysis of different models in Literature review

Reference Paper	Dataset	Diseases Class	Model	Accuracy
[1]	RSNA, Kaggle Chest X-ray	CORONAVIRUS, Pneumonia (Normal, Bacterial, Viral)	VGG-16	95%
[2]	SIRM, Joseph Cohen	CORONAVIRUS, Pneumonia (Normal, Viral)	Inception V3	93%
[3]	RSNA, GitHub Covid Chest X-ray	CORONAVIRUS, Pneumonia, Normal	Xception, ResNet50V2, Xception + ResNet50V2	94.20% 93.19% 93.93%
[4]	RSNA, Covid-chest x -ray dataset	CORONAVIRUS, Pneumonia, Non-CORONAVIRUS	VGG-16 ResNet50 DenseNet121 EfficientNet	83.68% 77.76% 78.24% 78.40%
[5]	Joseph's GitHub, Kaggle Chest X-ray	Bacterial pneumonia, Viral pneumonia CORONA -VIRUS.	CoroNet (based upon Xception)	89.6%
[6]	Cohen JP Dataset, ChestX-ray8 dataset by wang et al.	CORONAVIRUS+, CORONAVIRUS-, Pneumonia	DarkCovidNet (based on Dark-Net19)	87.02%
[7]	GitHub Covid Chest X-ray, CheXpert	CORONAVIRUS positive, Normal	ResNet18 ResNet50 SqueezeNet DenseNet161	Specificity 90.7% 89.6% 92.9% 75.1% Sensitivity-98%
[8]	GitHub Covid Chest X-ray, CheXpert	CORONAVIRUS Pneumonia	DenseNet201	99.7%

Reference Paper	Dataset	Diseases Class	Model	Accuracy
[9]	CXR images	Coronavirus, Pneumonia, Normal	CT-base CF-base hust19	79.626% 79.676% 81.083%
[10]	J.P Cohen, Spain Hospital	CORONAVIRUS, Normal, Pneumonia	Ensemble (EfficientNetB0, DenseNet121 and VGG19)	99.2%
[11]	LUNA, MedPix, Pub-Med Central, and Ra-diopedia	Coronavirus and Non Coronavirus	Inception V3 MobileNet ResNet Proposed model	71.88% 82.89% 90.77% 96.28%
[12]	COVID (X-ray, Chest X-ray, Radiography), and CoronaHack-Chest X-Ray	CORONAVIRUS, Normal, Pneumonia	Google Net, Alex Net, DCGAN	93.45% 94.9% 97.125%
[13]	SIRM	CORONAVIRUS and Pneumonia (Bacterial and Viral)	Researcher proposed	Normal – 88% Infected – 90%
[14]	Chest Xray and CT scan images	Coronavirus, Normal, Bacterial Pneumonia and Viral Pneumonia	Proposed C. NNET.	91.2%
[15]	GitHub Covid Chest X-ray	CORONAVIRUS, Pneumonia, Normal	Proposed C. NNET.	98.3%
[16]	GitHub, Kaggle Covid Chest X-ray	CORONAVIRUS, Pneumonia	MobileNetV2 VGG19 Inceptionv3	98%, 92.82% 96.92%
[17]	Cohen and Kermany repository	CORONAVIRUS/Normal Normal/Covid/Pneumonia	(Inception V3, VGG-16 and Xception) + VGG-16	97.67% 97.75%
[18]	Chest-Xray	Coronavirus, Viral Pneumonia, Bacterial Pneumonia, Normal	Model (LSTM +C. NNET.)	99.4%

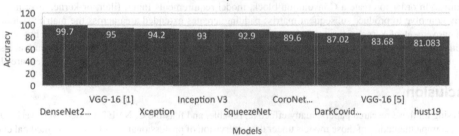

Fig. 88.1 Accuracy analysis of different models 2020

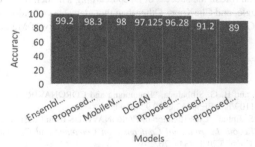

Fig. 88.2 Accuracy analysis of different models 2021

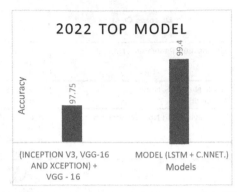

Fig. 88.3 Accuracy analysis of different models 2022

4. Outcome

After performing comparative analysis, we can conclude the most accurate model from the list of models we analysed. DenseNet201 has a high accuracy of 99.7% in the categories of 2-class classification, COVID-positive, and pneumonia. Followed by the ensemble model with 99.2% accuracy in 3-class classification and then by the LSTM + C. NNET model with 99.4% accuracy in 4-class classification.

5. CNN Model Classification

Convolution A neural network is a network of deep layers. The term convolution is a mathematical operation for convolving the matrices. It gains popularity over traditional neural networks due to the deep and shallow level of feature extraction by sharing parameters of the vertical and horizontal edge detector with the next layer while creating a sparsity matrix, which reduces complexity. CNN model produces good results on the image of the RGB channel by convolving with matrixvolumes. In order to create a Convolution block, model requirements Input, filter, or kernel size: matrix through image array convolve to produce subsequent matrix; padding: creates extended area across the matrix; stride: define the amount of movement of kernel size; number of filters: define the number of channels the volume has. Each layer of convolution required weight and bias updating by backpropagating through volumes of convolutions and, at last, required an activation function to classify the various objects. With these, output pooling and fully connected layers are also needed.

6. Conclusion

After analysing all these research papers, many effective, reliable, and feasible C. NNET. models were verified. The real-time practical implementation of those models under the supervision of professional radiologists and medical experts came into play and proved very productive. In cases like COVID, which is a very serious issue around the globe, achieving high accuracy and precision is mandatory and cannot be tolerated or negotiated. Therefore, it became a necessity to achieve acceptable accuracy in the automated COVID detection models. To make the model accurate enough to be accepted by physicians, datasets played a crucial role in the success of Deep Learning's model. Some trusted dataset sources used were open repositories on GitHub, Kaggle, and CheXpert. Other than that, datasets were also taken from the Radiology Society of North America (RSNA), J. P. Cohen, Spain Hospital, and the Italian Society of Medical and Interventional Radiology (SIRM).

REFERENCES

1. S. v. Militante, N. v. Dionisio, and B. G. Sibbaluca, "Pneumonia and CORONAVIRUS Detection using Convolutional Neural Networks," Oct. 2020. doi: 10.1109/ICVEE50212.2020.9243290.
2. S. Asif, Y. Wenhui, H. Jin, and S. Jinhai, "Classification of CORONAVIRUS from Chest X-ray images using Deep Convolutional Neural Network," in *2020 IEEE 6th International Conference on Computer and Communications, ICCC 2020*, Dec. 2020, pp. 426–433. doi: 10.1109/ICCC51575.2020.9344870.

3. M. Rahimzadeh and A. Attar, "A modified deep convolutional neural network for detecting CORONAVIRUS and pneumonia from chest X-ray images based on the concatenation of Xception and ResNet50V2," *Informatics in Medicine Unlocked*, vol. 19, Jan. 2020, doi: 10.1016/j.imu.2020.100360.

4. M. Nishio, S. Noguchi, H. Matsuo, and T. Murakami, "Automatic classification between CORONAVIRUS pneumonia, non-CORONAVIRUS pneumonia, and the healthy on chest X-ray image: combination of data augmentation methods," *Scientific Reports*, vol. 10, no. 1, Dec. 2020, doi: 10.1038/s41598-020-74539-2.

5. A. I. Khan, J. L. Shah, and M. M. Bhat, "CoroNet: A deep neural network for detection and diagnosis of CORONAVIRUS from chest x-ray images," *Computer Methods and Programs in Biomedicine*, vol. 196, Nov. 2020, doi: 10.1016/j.cmpb.2020.105581.

6. T. Ozturk, M. Talo, E. A. Yildirim, U. B. Baloglu, O. Yildirim, and U. Rajendra Acharya, "Automated detection of CORONAVIRUS cases using deep neural networks with X-ray images," *Computers in Biology and Medicine*, vol. 121, Jun. 2020, doi: 10.1016/j.compbiomed.2020.103792.

7. S. Minaee, R. Kafieh, M. Sonka, S. Yazdani, and G. Jamalipour Soufi, "Deep-COVID: Predicting CORONA-VIRUS from chest X-ray images using deep transfer learning," *Medical Image Analysis*, vol. 65, Oct. 2020, doi: 10.1016/j.media.2020.101794.

8. M. E. H. Chowdhury *et al.*, "Can AI Help in Screening Viral and CORONAVIRUS Pneumonia?," *IEEE Access*, vol. 8, pp. 132665–132676, 2020, doi: 10.1109/ACCESS.2020.3010287.

9. W. Ning *et al.*, "Open resource of clinical data from patients with pneumonia for the prediction of CORONAVIRUS outcomes via deep learning," *Nature Biomedical Engineering*, vol. 4, no. 12, pp. 1197–1207, Dec. 2020, doi: 10.1038/s41551-020-00633-5.

10. M. Hasan Jahid, M. Alom Shahin, and M. Ali Shikhar, "Deep Learning based Detection and Segmentation of CORONA-VIRUS Pneumonia on Chest X-ray Image," in *2021 International Conference on Information and Communication Technology for Sustainable Development, ICICT4SD 2021 - Proceedings*, Feb. 2021, pp. 210–214. doi: 10.1109/ICICT4SD50815.2021.9396878.

11. H. Mukherjee, S. Ghosh, A. Dhar, S. M. Obaidullah, K. C. Santosh, and K. Roy, "Deep neural network to detect CORONAVIRUS: one architecture for both CT Scans and Chest X-rays," *Applied Intelligence*, vol. 51, no. 5, pp. 2777–2789, May 2021, doi: 10.1007/s10489-020-01943-6.

12. S. v J and J. F. D, "Deep Learning Algorithm for CORONAVIRUS Classification Using Chest X-Ray Images," *Comput Math Methods Med*, vol. 2021, p. 9269173, 2021, doi: 10.1155/2021/9269173.

13. S. Kanakaprabha and D. Radha, "Analysis of CORONAVIRUS and Pneumonia Detection in Chest X-Ray Images using Deep Learning," Jun. 2021. doi: 10.1109/ICCISc52257.2021.9484888.

14. E. Hussain, M. Hasan, M. A. Rahman, I. Lee, T. Tamanna, and M. Z. Parvez, "CoroDet: A deep learning based classification for CORONAVIRUS detection using chest X-ray images," *Chaos, Solitons and Fractals*, vol. 142, Jan. 2021, doi: 10.1016/j.chaos.2020.110495.

15. R. H. Abiyev and A. Ismail, "CORONAVIRUS and Pneumonia Diagnosis in X-Ray Images Using Convolutional Neural Networks," *Mathematical Problems in Engineering*, vol. 2021, 2021, doi: 10.1155/2021/3281135.

16. M. Mahin, S. Tonmoy, R. Islam, T. Tazin, M. Monirujjaman Khan, and S. Bourouis, "Classification of CORONAVIRUS and Pneumonia Using Deep Transfer Learning," *Journal of Healthcare Engineering*, vol. 2021, 2021, doi: 10.1155/2021/3514821.

17. R. Sarki, K. Ahmed, H. Wang, Y. Zhang, and K. Wang, "Automated detection of CORONAVIRUS through convolutional neural network using chest x-ray images," *PLoS ONE*, vol. 17, no. 1 January, Jan. 2022, doi: 10.1371/journal.pone.0262052.

18. Z. Mousavi, N. Shahini, S. Sheykhivand, S. Mojtahedi, and A. Arshadi, "CORONAVIRUS detection using chest X-ray images based on a developed deep neural network," *SLAS Technol*, vol. 27, no. 1, pp. 63–75, Feb. 2022, doi: 10.1016/j.slast.2021.10.011.

Note: All figures in this document were created by Author.

Computer Science Engineering and Emerging Technologies (ICCS-2022) – Prof (Dr.) Rajeev Sobti et al. (eds)
© 2024 Taylor & Francis Group, London, ISBN 978-1-032-52199-2

Chapter

89

A Systematic Review on Machine Learning-based Fraud Detection System in E-Commerce

Ankush Kumar Shah[1]

M.Tech (CSE), Lovely Professional University, Phagwara, Punjab

Parminder Singh[2]

Assistant Professor (CSE), Lovely Professional University, Phagwara, Punjab

Abstract: The use of the internet practically everywhere in the world has become a new trend as digitalization advances. The majority of users are making day-to-day purchases of goods using e-commerce platforms such as Flipkart, Amazon, Myntra, etc., but there will be certain dangers associated with payment. Due to the fact that we consider it secure while making payments and have a decreased likelihood of spotting fraud, we are able to develop transaction processing systems, such as Internet-based banking, in a safe manner. However, there are significant hurdles that come along with learning about and having access to the advantages and benefits that are provided by E-Commerce systems. Security is one of the main problems that we can encounter presently. Internet traffic has been increasing daily because people are spending more time on these online platforms. One of the most important elements and difficulties of online transactions is fraud detection. Online fraud is now on the rise, along with the number of transactions, and it is even more difficult to identify the fraud transactions. By utilising some approaches, such as Information Fusion Technology (IFT), Big Data Mining (BDM), Logistic Regression, Support Vector Machine (SVM), Random Forest, etc., we can stop fraudulent actions in E-Commerce Systems. Fraudulent behaviours may be analysed and found with great accuracy by machine learning. So the main goal of this paper is to offer an examination of e-commerce system security.

Keywords: Information fusion technology, Big data mining, Support vector machine, Random forest

1. Introduction

In the past, e-commerce systems were created in 1999 by Gordon and Gordon, which began as an online firm on August 11, 1994. A compact disc (CD) was sold to the customers during this transaction by a person using a website. As an American store named Egger emerged in the year 2000, sales and purchases took place via the internet. [1] It might be regarded as the first instance of a user making a purchase via the Worldwide Web (WWW), which was initially named by John et al. in the year 2000. [1] E-commerce is called so because it can exist on the Internet, however E-Commerce Systems are useless without the Internet. E-commerce refers to the practise of buying and sellInternet; howeveruce-commercensystems grow their online business, they can grow it quickly by using communication tools like commercials, broadcasting their ads on radio and television, etc. [2] Business-to-business (B2B), business-to-business-to-consumer (B2B2C), business-to-government (B2G), consumer-to-business (C2B), direct-to-consumer (D2C), and consumer-to-consumer are some of the different types of e-commerce businesses that can be expressed when we are expanding our businesses through online business (C2C).

[1]ankush7431@gmail.com, [2]parminder.27942@lpu.co.in

DOI: 10.1201/9781003405580-89

In 2019, it is anticipated that 4 billion individuals will use Internet services globally, according to the most recent data. [1] As e-commerce grows, more problems are being created daily that are used in online businesses. These problems will have a significant impact on the e-commerce management system and will not provide security for the user(s) if they are not acknowledged or adequately addressed (GooglePay, Patym, Phonepe, etc.). [3] The fraud detection systems for e-commerce only have a few elements that allow us to assess or analyse transactions to see if they are fraudulent or not. One fantastic method for identifying fraudulent activity is machine learning. Every system or website is required to analyse credit card data that has been authorised by an internal team member or risk team member. This analysis can lead to machine learning fraud prevention. [4]

E-commerce is experiencing a period of immense prosperity due to the development of artificial intelligence (AI) technologies. [5] Customers are being introduced to new levels of trends in new formats, in part thanks to e-commerce. Every year, millions of people have their identity cards (IDs) stolen, but neither they nor the thieves can be found. In addition to measuring accuracy through the heart rate and skin electrical conduction, traditional lie detectors also require face-to-face acknowledgment. [5] Data mining (DM), natural language processing (NLP), and machine learning (ML), the three main components of AI, can help e-commerce businesses grow quickly. AI makes manual tasks for company strategy decision-makers possible. The internet market in China experienced over 6 trillion RMB in transactions in 2017 and is projected to reach approximately 7.5 trillion RMB in 2018 [5], according to research consulting statistics. The following categories will be used to classify this paper's main contributions:

- There will be a distribution of papers by year (2012–2022) in the literature study on e-commerce security.
- Numerous issues and current research directions.
- Statistics on current dangers and security.

2. Literature Review

We can provide the statistics of articles on different assaults on e-commerce systems during the previous 11 years in this subject (2012-2022). [7]

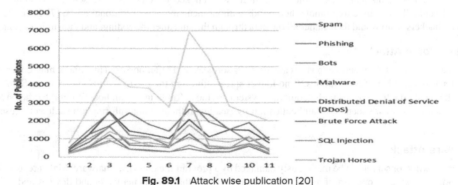

Fig. 89.1   Attack wise publication [20]

Because the banking sector is the one most frequently targeted by cyberattacks, e-commerce businesses are chosen. Even if e-commerce is growing thanks to effective marketing and attractive web design, there are still cyberattacks in the corporate world. The progression of financial fraud assaults, which were followed by brute force attacks, bot attacks, spam attacks, etc., is now more obvious. Additionally, it can be used to counter the fewest number of attacks, such as SQL Injection and distributed denial of service (DDOS). This study has the potential to undermine concepts related to security concerns, including SQL Injection. As a result, additional study is required in the area of global cyber-attack risks.

2.1 Financial Fraud Attack

Financial fraud assaults are one form of attack that typically takes place during financial transactions, i.e., when we are dealing with very large transactions. Financial fraud, which includes identity fraud, ransomware attacks, email assaults, credit card attacks, and other payment-related scams like Phonepe, Paytm, UPI, GooglePay, etc., is the act of earning financial gains through profit-driven attacks. [7] Investors or business people lose a lot of money if the hacker steals unapproved transactions. The following is a list of some typical financial fraud attack types:

- Loan fraud, credit fraud, and bank scams are all caused by identity theft.
- Tax preparation and return fraud involving fake checks, cashier's checks, or "Ghost" checks
- credit card theft
- takeover of a financial account
- Fraud in small business (employee theft, housing theft, etc.)
- Scams involving the butchering of pigs or romance.

2.2 Brute Force Attack

A brute force attack is one of those assaults in which hackers attempt to guess the password before using the website's authentication method to get into the account and access the system's secret data. This kind of attack involves repeatedly making attempts before successfully breaching the system. This approach is currently very outdated. Hackers may also employ this technique. We can also state that "the cracking approach is another name for the brute force attack." [7]

2.3 Bot Attacks

Current data show that bot traffic makes up nearly 40% of all web traffic, 60% of which is malicious bot traffic. Some malicious bots are frequently employed for nefarious activities like credential stuffing, DDoS assaults, data theft, and unauthorised crawling, among other things that harm enterprises. [7] Bots are automated jobs that we may programme to carry out with little to no internet use, giving us greater speed, agility, precision, and performance when performing repetitive chores.

2.4 Spam Attack

Spam attacks are ones that send thousands of consumers unwelcome messages using IoT devices. These messages typically contain false advertisements and links to the actual users who clicked on them and are sent by fraudulent or hacked individuals. Eventually, it is used to promote their goods without incurring any operational costs. [7] Their website might be hacked by hackers, who would then gather all the data through the site, alter the coding, and then upload dangerous files.

2.5 Trojan Horse Attack

Actually, one of the most frequently exposed categories of software is Trojan horses. This attack may cover up some of the computer's inherent harmful operations. It no longer spreads through the use of worms and viruses. Some specialists claim that the most effective viruses in the computer system are those found in Trojan horses. On the other side, a Trojan horse can attack the system's method of authentication by stealing authentication information such as the username and password.

2.6 Malware Attack

A computer, network, or server can be maliciously damaged by a programme known as malware. Malware, usually referred to as malicious software, is one sort of attack. Malware is software that infects networks and devices and is intended to negatively impact people, networks, and devices in some way. One major cyber issue that impacts e-commerce systems is malware. [7] Its primary goal is to steal credit card information. This harm may manifest itself differently to the user and end points depending on the sort of malware and its objectives. Malware can have both very minor and upsetting effects on different people.

2.7 Phishing Attack

One such assault is phishing, in which hackers try to persuade users to take "the wrong action," like clicking a malicious link that downloads malware or sends them to a dubious website. One form of social engineering assault designed to collect user information, such as login information and credit card details, is phishing. [7] The infected link is misled into being clicked by the receiver, and once it is, it may install malware, freeze the computer, launch a ransomware assault, or reveal important data.

2.8 Distributed Denial of Service (DDos) Attack

A distributed denial of service assault (DDos) is a malicious attempt to obstruct a server, service, or network's regular traffic by saturating the target or infrastructure with internet traffic. DDos attacks are successful because they make use of numerous compromised computer systems as the attack source for traffic. One of the main attacks that are employed as a big danger to the e-commerce system is the DDos attack. DDos attacks are escalating daily, according to Kaspersky's DDos security data. Attacks have increased to 84%, which is nearly twice as many and can last for more than 60 minutes. [7]

2.9 SQL Injection Attack

Web security vulnerabilities that allow attackers to interact with database queries made by applications are known as SQL injection attacks.

3. Different Types of Techniques to Detect the Frauds

3.1 Support for Information Fusion Technology (IFT)

In the software development and systems engineering sectors, fusion technology offers a wide range of services and assistance. Along with our numerous dependable commercial or economic partners, we provide support to several federal government and private sector customers in order to provide value, accomplish system objectives, and ensure the accomplishment of our customers' missions. [7] Information fusion technology is the technique of combining information processes from the source of the same object or scene in order to produce more intricate, trustworthy, and correct information. To achieve inferences that will be more tailored than if they were achieved by using diverse [7] sources, there is a different exchange of data from numerous sources and aggregating that information into discrete, actionable items. Image fusion in computer vision refers to the procedures used to merge pertinent data from two or more images into a single image.

3.2 Large-scale Data Mining (BDM)

Huge Data By mining and analysing vast amounts of data acquired from many applications, mining and analytics seek out hidden patterns, corrections, knowledge, and insights. [7] Big data is generated via a variety of applications, including social media, sensors, the Internet of Things (IOT), scientific applications, surveillance, video, and audio. Big data analytics is now a performance that the mining sector seldom employs. Sensors installed throughout mining operations are the best resource BDM has for achieving this objective. These sensors can instantly assert status and operational data, as well as provide a large number of geostatistics. Real-time data collection is now possible from the point of extraction all the way up to the final shipping of one or two plants thanks to Wi-Fi and network speeds. [7] Massive parallel computing, as well as quicker dissemination of intelligence among stakeholders, can be used to analyse this data.

3.3 Logistic Regression (LR)

When there are several explanatory variables, the odds ratio is calculated using logistic regression. With the exception of the binomial response variable, the process is quite similar to multiple linear regression. The outcome is how each variable affects the odds ratio of the observed important event. By examining the connection of all variables together, the key benefit is to prevent confounding effects.

3.4 Random Forest

These are combinations of different decision trees, and they make up a random forest. Both classification and regression can be done with it. More than one output can be found in a random forest. Information can be offered as a result since accuracy and variability are significant variables. A random forest is a set of classifiers made up of k randomly distributed random forests, where k is the set of tree structural classifiers. An assortment of samples from the training datasets that we are using during class distribution are pulled at random by a random seed that is determined at random.

3.5 Support Vector Machines (SVM)

Support vector machines are a cutting-edge approach to machine learning that is based on the notion of statical learning. Support vector machines are now the subject of research on machine learning skills. The various parts of supervised learning techniques known as support vector machines are mostly utilized for classification, regression, and more straightforward outlier detection. [9] These various tasks are all typical of machine learning. Based on the millions of instructions you need to anticipate the well-fitted regression models, SVM can be used to identify malignant cells. Because SVM uses boundary values that maximize the distance from all classes' nearest data points, it can differ from other classification algorithms in this regard. By drawing a straight line between two locations, a straightforward linear SVM classifier operates. The expansion of the data points on one side shows that they stand for various lines of code that fall under various categories. The various numbers lines selected from the machine learning components can also be included in this task.[9]

3.6 Decision Trees

Decision trees are shown as a flowchart-like structure with internal and leaf nodes, internal nodes and leaf nodes representing a class label (decision can be fetched after computing all features) and branches representing conjunctions of features that lead to class labels. Internal nodes are tests on the feature (e.g., whether we can drop a die and there is a chance to come 1 to 6), leaf nodes are class labels. [7] Basic decision-making flow diagrams with labels, such as "Rain (yes), No Rain (no)," are among them.

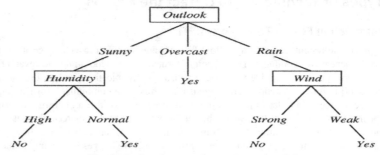

Fig. 89.2 Decision tree for predicting rain [21]

A decision tree is a frequently used technique in data mining, as well as for creating classification schemes based on numerous variables or when creating prediction schemes as a goal. Large datasets can be mined for information, which can then be shown in an interpretive way. Data mining is the process of identifying values that are simple to use, clear of ambiguity, and resilient in the face of missing values. The goal or independent variables can both use discrete and continuous variables. [7] The following are typical characteristics of decision tree models:

* Variable selection
* Assessing the relative importance of variables
* How to handle missing values
* Prediction
* Manipulation of data

3.7 Neural Network

Artificial neural networks (ANNs), or simulated neural networks, are networks that are also referred to as neural networks (SNNs). They are also the core of deep learning algorithms and a subset of machine learning. Their design takes cues from the way organic neurons communicate with one another in the human brain. The node layers that make up simulated neural networks (SNNs) each have an input layer, one or more hidden layers, and an output layer. Each artificial node, or node, is linked to a corresponding threshold and weight. The node is activated when it reaches the specified threshold value and then delivers information to the network's next tier. Data is either sent to another network or device.

The neural networks whose boundaries we can control by enhancing training data and learning the notion that we can enhance their accuracy over time. These ideas are particularly potent in computer science and artificial intelligence once they have been adjusted for correctness, and they also enable those clusters to process data quickly.

4. Conclusion

The development of e-commerce platforms, particularly in marketplace-oriented domains, has received significantly more attention over the past few years due to their growing popularity. Because they protect their customers from dishonest vendors. All of these online marketplaces regard reputation as a crucial quality. An e-commerce system can be thought of as a crucial part of any online transaction between a vendor and a buyer. Electronic transactions are required for this type of transaction. So, we have analysed and reviewed various ideas and studies from the past five years where the user's initial transaction can be fraudulent due to a number of different variables. A study shows that these fraudulent transactions can be identified with various techniques. It has been observed that supervised techniques are used by the majority of fraud detection systems. Artificial neural networks (ANN), support vector machines (SVM), rule-induction approaches, decision trees, logistic regression, and meta-heuristics like evolutionary algorithms are also some of the most frequently utilised fraud detection tools. It is noticed that there is still scope for improvement to increase the accuracy of fraud detection in the area of e-commerce, which can be improved by applying the support vector machine with a combination of decision tree, logistic regression, and meta-heuristics techniques. Additionally, we can examine the various theories pertaining to numerous fraud detection systems that may be created based on the use of different machine learning approaches as time and technology advance.

REFERENCES

1. Badotra, Sumit and Amit Sundas. "A systematic review on security of E-commerce systems." International Journal of Applied Science and Engineering 18 (2021): 1–19.
2. Aithal, Sreeramana. (2016). A Review On Various E-Business And M-Business Models & Research Opportunities. International Journal of Management, IT and Engineering (IJMIE). 6. 275–298. 10.5281/zenodo.161146.
3. K, A. K. Pani, M. M and P. Kumar, "An Approach for Detecting Frauds in E-Commerce Transactions using Machine Learning Techniques," 2021 2nd International Conference on Smart Electronics and Communication (ICOSEC), pp. 826–831, 2021.
4. R. Jhangiani, D. Bein and A. Verma, "Machine Learning Pipeline for Fraud Detection and Prevention in E-Commerce Transactions," 2019 IEEE 10th Annual Ubiquitous Computing, Electronics & Mobile Communication Conference (UEMCON), 2019, pp. 0135–0140, doi: 10.1109/UEMCON47517.2019.8992993.
5. Li, J. (2022). E-Commerce Fraud Detection Model by Computer Artificial Intelligence Data Mining. Computational Intelligence and Neuroscience, 2022. https://doi.org/10.1155/2022/8783783
6. Adi Saputra & Suharjito: "Fraud Detection using Machine Learning in e-commerce", International Journal of Advanced Computer Science and Applications, Vol 10, No.9, 2019
7. Badotra, S., Sundas, A. 2021. A systematic review on security of E-commerce systems, International Journal of Applied Science and Engineering, 18, 2020323. https://doi.org/10.6703/IJASE.202106_18(2).010
8. Sperandei, S. (2014). Understanding logistic regression analysis. Biochemia Medica, 24(1), 12–18. https://doi.org/10.11613/BM.2014.003
9. Evgeniou, Theodoros & Pontil, Massimiliano. (2001). Support Vector Machines: Theory and Applications. 2049. 249-257. 10.1007/3-540-44673-7_12.
10. International Research Journal of Modernization in Engineering Technology and Science (IRJMETS) | 2582-5208 | IRJMETS
11. H. Weng et al., "Online E-Commerce Fraud: A Large-Scale Detection and Analysis," 2018 IEEE 34th International Conference on Data Engineering (ICDE), pp. 1435–1440, 2018
12. E. Caldeira, G. Brandao and A. C. M. Pereira, "Fraud Analysis and Prevention in e-Commerce Transactions," 2014 9th Latin American Web Congress, pp. 42–49, 2014.
13. J. Shaji and D. Panchal, "Improved fraud detection in e-commerce transactions," 2017 2nd International Conference on Communication Systems, Computing and IT Applications (CSCITA), pp. 121–126, 2017.
14. M. Mary, M. Priyadharsini, K. K and M. S. F, "Online Transaction Fraud Detection System," 2021 International Conference on Advance Computing and Innovative Technologies in Engineering (ICACITE), pp. 14–16, 2021.
15. Fabrizio Carcillo, Andrea Dal Pozzolo, Yann-Aël Le Borgne, Olivier Caelen, Yannis Mazzer, Gianluca Bontempi, SCARFF: A scalable framework for streaming credit card fraud detection with spark, Information Fusion, Volume 41, 2018, Pages 182–194, ISSN 1566–2535, https://doi.org/10.1016/j.inffus.2017.09.005.
16. Saputra, Adi & Suharjito, Suharjito. (2019). Fraud Detection using Machine Learning in e-Commerce. 10.14569/IJACSA.2019.0100943.
17. Saputra, Adit Rangga and Suharjito -. "Fraud Detection using Machine Learning in e-Commerce." International Journal of Advanced Computer Science and Applications (2019): n. pag.
18. Tax, N., de Vries, K. J., de Jong, M., Dosoula, N., Akker, B. V., Smith, J., Thuong, O., & Bernardi, L. (2021). Machine Learning for Fraud Detection in E-Commerce: A Research Agenda. arXiv. https://doi.org/10.48550/arXiv.2107.01979
19. Ge Zhang, Zhao Li, Jiaming Huang, Jia Wu, Chuan Zhou, Jian Yang, and Jianliang Gao. 2022. EFraudCom: An E-commerce Fraud Detection System via Competitive Graph Neural Networks. ACM Trans. Inf. Syst. 40, 3, Article 47 (July 2022), 29 pages. https://doi.org/10.1145/3474379
20. Badotra, Sumit and Amit Sundas. "A systematic review on security of E-commerce systems." International Journal of Applied Science and Engineering 18 (2021): 1–19.)
21. Wei Wei1, Mingwei Hui1, Beibei Zhang1, Rafal Scherer2, Robertas "Research on Decision Tree Based on Rough Set." Research on Decision Tree Based on Rough Set 1385)

Computer Science Engineering and Emerging Technologies (ICCS-2022) – Prof (Dr.) Rajeev Sobti et al. (eds)
© 2024 Taylor & Francis Group, London, ISBN 978-1-032-52199-2

Chapter

90

A systematical Reviewing of Prediction Models During Aggravation of Asthma and its Validation

Tarun[1]

Research Assistant & Assistant Professor, School of Computer Science and Engineering,
Lovely Professional University, Phagwara, Punjab, India;

Vijay Kumar Garg[2]

Associate Professor, School of Computer Science and Engineering,
Lovely Professional University, Phagwara, Punjab, India

Varsha[3]

Assistant Professor, School of Computer Science and Engineering,
Lovely Professional University, Phagwara, Punjab, India

Abstract: Smart healthcare is the most promising application created towards offering enhanced disease detection and prediction tools. Recent studies have developed a number of detection and predictive models for various diseases, that incorporate machine-learning techniques and other disease-causing characteristics. Numerous triggers, such as individual and environmental factors, might aggravate asthma. This research often employs conventional machine learning methods, predictive tools, and visualisation processes depending on a constrained set of triggers. The prediction of asthma attacks is dependent on the use of an extensive range of patient records and several environmental triggers. A systematic study of recommendation systems and a comparison of different prediction models are introduced.

Keywords: Smart healthcares, Triggers, Asthma, Predictive models

1. Introduction

The World Health Organization identifies illness as a physical or psychological problem characterized simply by symptoms (such as discomfort or pain), malfunction, or tissue damage that leads potential clients to poor wellness. Acute diseases (those that arise abruptly, for a brief period of time, are intense, and are severe) are usually distinguished from persistent diseases (those that will endure for some time plus have long-term influences ranging from reasonable to extreme problems) and, in several situations, from both. Persistent illnesses are the most serious wellness issue confronting modern society today. Chronic health problems refer to troubles with human wellness that last for a long period of time or deteriorate over time. When the particular span of an illness lasts greater than three months, this is said to be chronic. Asthma, diabetes, arthritis, malignancy, chronic renal conditions, and chronic obstructive pulmonary disease are usually common chronic problems. Asthma is a respiratory condition that makes breathing difficult because the lungs are affected and the airways become congested and irritated. [11]. People of all ages can get asthma, and it frequently begins in childhood. The pollen, weather's condition, and air quality are examples of environmental factors [12].

[1]tjangwal@gmail.com, tarun.24044@lpu.co.in, [2]vijay.garg@lpu.co.in, [3]barkhabright@gmail.com, varsha.28384@lpu.co.in

DOI: 10.1201/9781003405580-90

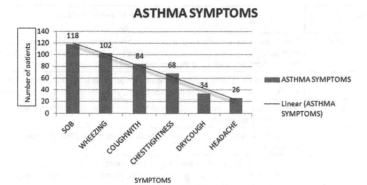

Fig. 90.1 Symptoms of asthma

According to reports, air pollution is a primary cause of asthma. Road traffic, fossil fuels consumed in factories, and particular industries are the leading causes of air pollution in metropolitan areas. Urban areas are primarily home to several pollutants, including PM10, SO_2, O_3, NO_2, and CO. Air pollution with weather variations, such as humidity, chilly air, and rain, might exacerbate an asthma attack. [13]. Patients with severe asthma are more likely to be affected by the weather and air pollution since their airways are already inflamed. Due to the presence of wet air, humidity promotes shortness of breath and makes breathing harder. It needs a method that can assist people in managing their illness and avoiding things that could set off an asthma attack.

2. Literature Review

A number of recommendation systems and prediction models were introduced in several studies on asthma attacks. The majority of these models were created using merely individual triggers. Some of them used common person-dependent triggers like Peak Expiratory Flow Rate (PEFR) if the person has a cold, exercise, sleeping disorders, or respiratory illnesses. Anumber of others had employed mutually general and unique person-dependent triggers, like the condition of their asthma or their blood eosinophil levels. The frequency of asthma attacks in the past, smoking status, obesity, concomitant conditions, and medication use These findings suggest that using both particular and generic personal triggers is crucial for enhancing model performance. The research overview of the triggers utilized in these models is shown in Table 90.1.

Table 90.1 Literature survey

Ref No.	Author	Research Summary
1	Alberto Alvarez-Perea, et al.	The Authors have concluded that all are those who have indirectly or directly benefitted because of modern advancements in electronic healthcare show that these innovations hold great potential for treatment customisation and illness monitoring, and their positive impact on patient education, symptom monitoring, comorbidities management, and medication adherence
2	Jagriti Saini et al.,	The authors present the state of the art new way of predicting indoor concentration of PM10 in this paper. Four alternative performance indicators, including hybrid FIST + GA and three additional models, were used to examine the model's performance. They were logged by a monitoring system based on IoT to find indoor PM10.
3	Elizabeth A. Campbell, et al.	This thesis presents a technique for mining temporal conditions to tackle the sparse existence Usage of electronic health records of coded condition definition.
4	Dinh-Van Phan, et al.	The authors processed records from 2002 to 2010, in order to predict sleep disturbances of asthma cohort, they investigated 1 million samples from Taiwan's National Health Insurance Research Database (NHIRD).
5	M.Mozaffarinya et al.	The authors have created a questionnaire which needs to be filled out by patients, and hence on the basis of that data, the author has ranked various parameters according to their impact on asthma.

Ref No.	Author	Research Summary
6	Anne M. Fitzpatrick, et al.	The Authors have concluded that there are minimal objective asthma intensity quantification methods. The Asthma Severity Scoring System (ASSESS) measures four asthma domain and can be beneficial for quantifying medical responses in study contexts.
7	Samir Gupta, et al.,	To order to cope with significant health issues and to determine the effects on asthma-related adults, they have created the computerized clinical decisions support systems (EAMS).
8	B.N. Zamora-Mendoza, et al.	The authors used immunoassay and SRS on asthmatic children's saliva to find bio-markers of bronchial inflammations.
9	Xin Zhang, et al.	The authors performed tentative analysis of asthma in clinical medicine with MOF-based logical platforms.
10	Young Juhn, et al.	This short analysis addresses the latest developments Secondary usage literature of EHR information for asthma, allergy and clinical research Immunology highlight a potential, complexities and implication of NLP technique.
11	Hillary A. Cuesta, et al.	This study demonstrates the possible utility of data mining in understanding Complex issues relating to public health.
12	Neda Kaffash-Charandabi, et al.,	There are different arguments for the model proposed Prediction techniques and processes. The model is sufficiently robust to foresee potential patients with asthmatic disorders. The overall accuracy of 93%.
13	Roghaye Khasha et al.	The goal of this study was to create a unique ensemble learning technique for detecting the control level of asthma utilising supervised learnings and rule-based classifiers.
14	Julie L. Harvey et al.	In this paper, we developed predictive models to analyze a child's asthma health dataset.
15	Soobia Saeed, et al.	This paper compares patients data using an algorithm with the help of decision trees and created models for predicting right treating methods of patient data.
16	WASIF AKBAR, et al.	In this study, data from patients' prior medical records were mined to develop an efficient technique for asthma illness prediction.
17	Roghaye Khasha et al.	Author has created a data base of various asthmatic patients in tehran and also gathered the data of pollution and air quality of that region. He then developed a web-based application for generation of the maps which tells the various areas prone to asthma due to environmental factors.
18	Almin Badnjevic, et al.	They developed diagnostics systems which helps distinguish between people suffering from asthma, COPD or people with normal lung functions, also with patient symptom data.
19	S. Indulakshmi, et al.	The paper shows a portable system that tracks and sends these data on cloud to control environmental exposure of people suffering from asthma. A suitable approach has been suggested to detect asthma causes to better determine a certain person's factors triggering asthma.
20	Md. Ariful Islama, et al.	For this paper, normal and asthmatic people have been categorized by their posterior lung signals, 403 reported using a new 4-channel data acquisition method.
21	Alharbi, Eman, et al.	It is proposed to construct SHC systems to anticipate asthmatic attack in people suffering from asthma and to display level of danger caused dew to airborne pollution in order to inform customer and give pollution free paths which keep users distant to keeps him away from any.

3. Analysis of Existing Techniques

In this paper, by examining the visualization systems with asthmatic triggers along with the current predictive model, it addressed a variety of problems. These models contain a variety of restrictions, such as the use of a few triggers during the prediction process, which reduces the models' accuracy. Additionally, the majority of these models forecast the attack without taking action after this prediction. The majority of the current asthmatic attacks, according to predictions from the model, got developed by means of a small number of triggers. Few of the writings employed only a few features while combining both trigger types. The majority of predictions from the model used conventional machine-learning and data-mining techniques, as reviewed in this study, and their prediction accuracies were under 0.87. The performance of these models can be improved by utilizing cutting-edge machine learning methods, like deep learning, that offer several benefits over conventional machine-learning methods. Utilizing a comprehensive list of asthma triggers to forecast the attack.

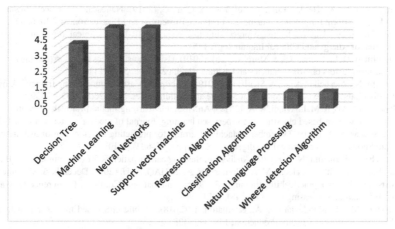

Fig. 90.2   Different predictive models

In Fig. 90.2, many predictions from model are using machine-learning, neural network along with decision tree as compared to the rest of the prediction models. Table 90.2 represents prediction model algorithm with count in research papers.

4. Conclusion

It is crucial to build SHC systems for forecasting asthmatic symptoms in people suffering from asthmatic conditions and envisioning their likelihood with airborne pollution. Airborne pollution data channels cause various issues on patients depending on their condition and level of asthma, among other factors. Map visual graphics must therefore be designed specifically for the customer's situation. The specific suggested SHC platform offers a number of facilities that will offer superior asthmatic attack prevention along with prediction techniques. Each of the hazard factors is usually extra varied, and they are obtained from several sources. Additionally, some reasoning-based signaling systems are recommended to inform the client and provide a path that is pollution-safe and keeps your pet far from asthmatic triggers. Additionally, the visualization service will offer user maps to track the high-risk locations for asthma triggers and an air pollution visual picture chart to keep track of the high-risk locations for asthma causes.

REFERENCES

1. Alvarez-Perea, A., Dimov, V., Popescu, F. D., & Zubeldia, J. M. (2021). The applications of eHealth technologies in the management of asthma and allergic diseases. Clinical and Translational Allergy, 11(7), e12061.
2. Saini, J., Dutta, M., & Marques, G. (2021). Fuzzy inference system tree with particle swarm optimization and genetic algorithm: a novel approach for PM10 forecasting. Expert Systems With Applications, 183, 115376.
3. Campbell, E. A., Bass, E. J., & Masino, A. J. (2020). Temporal condition pattern mining in large, sparse electronic health record data: A case study in characterizing pediatric asthma. Journal of the American [3] Medical Informatics Association, 27(4), 558–566.
4. Phan, D. V., Yang, N. P., Kuo, C. Y., & Chan, C. L. (2021). Deep learning approaches for sleep disorder prediction in an asthma cohort. Journal of Asthma, 58(7), 903–911.
5. Mozaffarinya, M., Shahriyari, A. R., Bahadori, M. K., Ghazvini, A., Athari, S. S., & Vahedi, G. (2019). A data-mining algorithm to assess key factors in asthma diagnosis. Revue Française d'Allergologie, 59(7), 487–492.
6. Fitzpatrick, A. M., Szefler, S. J., Mauger, D. T., Phillips, B. R., Denlinger, L. C., Moore, W. C., ... & Jarjour, N. N. (2020). Development and initial validation of the Asthma Severity Scoring System (ASSESS). Journal of Allergy and Clinical Immunology, 145(1), 127–139.
7. Gupta, S., Price, C., Agarwal, G., Chan, D., Goel, S., Boulet, L. P., ... & Straus, S. E. (2019). The Electronic Asthma Management System (eAMS) improves primary care asthma management. European Respiratory Journal, 53(4).
8. Zamora-Mendoza, B. N., Espinosa-Tanguma, R., Ramírez-Elías, M. G., Cabrera-Alonso, R., Montero-Moran, G., Portales-Pérez, D., ... & Gonzalez, C. (2019). Surface-enhanced raman spectroscopy: A non invasive alternative procedure for early detection in childhood asthma biomarkers in saliva. Photodiagnosis and Photodynamic Therapy, 27, 85–91.

9. Zhang, X., Fang, L., Jiang, K., He, H., Yang, Y., Cui, Y., ... & Qian, G. (2019). Nanoscale fluorescent metal–organic framework composites as a logic platform for potential diagnosis of asthma. Biosensors and Bioelectronics, 130, 65–72.

10. Juhn, Y., & Liu, H. (2019). Natural language processing to advance EHR-based clinical research in Allergy, Asthma, and Immunology. Journal of Allergy and Clinical Immunology, 145.

11. Cuesta, H. A., Coffman, D. L., Branas, C., & Murphy, H. M. (2019). Using decision trees to understand the influence of individual- and neighborhood-level factors on urban diabetes and asthma. Health & place, 58, 102119.

12. Kaffash-Charandabi, N., Alesheikh, A. A., & Sharif, M. (2019). A ubiquitous asthma monitoring framework based on ambient air pollutants and individuals' contexts. Environmental Science and Pollution Research, 26(8), 7525–7539.

13. Khasha, R., Sepehri, M. M., & Mahdaviani, S. A. (2019). An ensemble learning method for asthma control level detection with leveraging medical knowledge-based classifier and supervised learning. Journal of medical systems, 43(6), 1–15.

14. Harvey, J. L., & Kumar, S. A. (2019, December). Machine learning for predicting development of asthma in children. In 2019 IEEE Symposium Series on Computational Intelligence (SSCI) (pp. 596–603). IEEE.

15. Saeed, S., Abdullah, A., & Jhanjhi, N. Z. (2019). Analysis of the lung cancer patient's for data mining tool. IJCSNS, 19(7), 90.

16. Akbar, W., Wu, W. P., Faheem, M., Saleem, M. A., Golilarz, N. A., & HAQ, A. U. (2019, December). Machine learning classifiers for asthma disease prediction: a practical illustration. In 2019 16th International Computer Conference on Wavelet Active Media Technology and Information Processing (pp. 143–148). IEEE.

17. Khasha, R., Sepehri, M. M., Mahdaviani, S. A., & Khatibi, T. (2018). Mobile GIS-based monitoring asthma attacks based on environmental factors. Journal of Cleaner Production, 179, 417–428.

18. Badnjevic, A., Gurbeta, L., & Custovic, E. (2018). An expert diagnostic system to automatically identify asthma and chronic obstructive pulmonary disease in clinical settings. Scientific reports, 8(1), 1–9.

19. Indulakshmi, S., Adithya, M., Anirudh, A. R., & Jawahar, A. (2018, March). Design and development of prototype model for asthma trigger detection. In 2018 International Conference on Wireless Communications, Signal Processing and Networking (WiSPNET) (pp. 1–5). IEEE.

20. Islam, M. A., Bandyopadhyaya, I., Bhattacharyya, P., & Saha, G. (2018). Multichannel lung sound analysis for asthma detection. Computer methods and programs in biomedicine, 159, 111–123.

21. Alharbi, E., Nadeem, F., & Cherif, A. (2021, March). Smart Healthcare Framework for Asthma Attack Prediction and Prevention. In 2021 National Computing Colleges Conference (NCCC) (pp. 1–6). IEEE.

Note: All figures and tables in this document were created by Author.

Computer Science Engineering and Emerging Technologies (ICCS-2022) – Prof (Dr.) Rajeev Sobti et al. (eds)
© 2024 Taylor & Francis Group, London, ISBN 978-1-032-52199-2

Chapter

91

Cyber Crimes: An Interdisciplinary Perspective

Nidhi Sagarwal[1]

Research Scholar, Department of Forensic Science,
Lovely Professional University, Punjab

Rachit Garg[2]

School of Computer Science and Engineering,
Lovely Professional University, Punjab

Bhupendra Kumar[3]

Professor, Department of Accouting & Finance, College of Business & Economics,
Debre Tabor University, Amhara, Ethiopia, East Africa

S. Praveenkumar[4]

Assistant Professor & Research supervisor, Centre for Tourism and Hotel management,
Madurai Kamaraj University, Madurai, Tamilnadu, India

Dharmesh Dhabliya[5]

Professor, Department of Information Technology,
Vishwakarma Institute of Information Technology, Pune, Maharashtra, India

Yagnam Nagesh[6]

Professor, Department of Information and Technology,
Debre Tabor University, Ethiopia, Africa

Ankur Gupta[7]

Assistant Professor, Department of Computer Science and Engineering,
Vaish College of Engineering, Rohtak, Haryana, India

Abstract: It is difficult to relate the statistics to the increase in the rate of cybercrime in countries such as India, where literacy rates are 65% and digital literacy is almost nonexistent. With the advent of technology in all spheres of life, it becomes important to realize the causative agents responsible for this menace. Journalism has played a substantial part in bringing this issue into the mainstream, providing much-needed support to victims of cybercrimes. Even though scholars from various disciplines have put forward different theories in this regard, an interdisciplinary approach may help distinguish the micro and macro factors responsible for crimes.

Keywords: Cybercrime, Interdisciplinary, Law

[1]nidhi.11816304@lpu.in, [2]rachit.garg@lpu.co.in, [3]drbkumar@dtu.edu.et, [4]s.praveenkumarus@gmail.com, [5]dharmesh.dhabliya@viit.ac.in, [6]nageshyagnam1@gmail.com, [7]ankurdujana@gmail.com

DOI: 10.1201/9781003405580-91

1. Introduction

Internet users in India crossed the 500 million mark in November 2019, as per the Digital in India report of the Internet and Mobile Association of India (IAMAI) [14]. Though the word 'cybercrime' has nowhere been defined in Indian legislation, the National Cyber Crime Reporting Portal defines cybercrimes as *"any unlawful act where a computer, communication device, or computer network is used to commit or facilitate the commission of crime"* [6]. The motives of cybercrimes are quite similar to the motives of traditional crimes. Some of the common motives involve financial gain, fraud, revenge, political motives, terrorist activities, etc. According to *Crime in India 2019*, fraud was the top motive, followed by sexual exploitation [5].

Table 91.1   Number of cybercrime cases according to motive [5]

Motive	Cases reported in 2019
Fraud	26891
Others	7578
Sexual exploitation	2266
Causing disrepute	1874
Extortion	1842
Prank	1385

According to Crime in India 2019 [5], there was a significant increase in the number of cyber-crime cases under the IT Act. Several news articles also reported a surge in cybercrimes during the COVID pandemic, with a splurge in cases of UPI and payment frauds, ATM frauds, etc. The reasons for these surges were cited as an increase in digital activity and general fear and misinformation among the public.

2. Interdisciplinary Perspectives

Since its commercialization, the internet has grown rapidly, and the number of internet connections is growing at a rapid rate in developing countries, though the major consumers remain in developed countries. The trends of internet usage often represent differential access within traditional lines of social exclusion within individual countries. The differentiating factors include education, income, employment status, etc. [4]. These social inequalities point out the factors contributing to cybercrime and cybercriminals. Some studies conceptualize cybercrime as those computer-mediated activities that are either illegal or considered illicit by certain parties and which can be conducted through global electronic networks (Thomas and Loader, 2000) [23].

Table 91.2   Dashora's Classification based on target of cybercrimes [7]

Type of cybercrime	Examples
Crime against individual	Fraud, email spoofing, cyber stalking, defamation, etc.
Crime against their property	Computer vandalism, transmitting virus etc.
Crime against organization	Unauthorized access to other computer systems, cyber terrorism etc.
Crime against society	Child pornography, financial crimes, etc.

Table 91.3   Wall's Classification of cybercrimes [24]

Type of crime	Explanation
Cyber trespass	Cracking/hacking (gaining illegal/ unethical access into someone's computer)
Cyber deception	Deception/thefts which was most similar in nature to traditional crimes
Cyber pornography	The exchange of pornographic materials in cyberspace
Cyber violence	Inciting hate or violence against a certain individual or social or political group in cyberspace. It includes cyber stalking, cyber bullying, harassment, hate speech, etc.

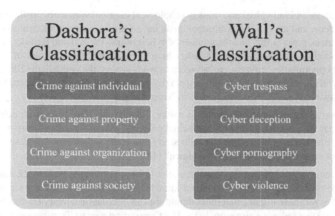

Fig. 91.1 Classification of cybercrimes by Dashora [7] and Wall [24]

Cybercrime is such a dynamic discipline that it is common for criminologists to have different views. Some scholars believed that cybercrimes are quite similar to traditional crimes because the basic motivation behind both is the same, i.e., material or financial gain, and were of the view that these differed only in operational aspects. While another group of scholars believed that cybercrime fundamentally differed from traditional crimes and should be treated as such [21], Stalans & Donner (2010 believed that the criminological and psychological theories applicable to traditional crimes would not be able to explain all cybercrimes [21].

To deal with similar problems and to introduce an independent discipline that presented cybercrimes from a social science perspective, K. Jaishankar (2007) coined the term cyber criminology [9, 15]. Grabosky (2000) referred to Cybercriminals as computer Criminals. He said that though the motivations were diverse, they were not new. The computer criminals were driven by "time-honoured motivations, the most obvious of which are greed, lust, power, revenge, adventure, and the desire to taste forbidden fruit". He believed that most criminals committed crimes just for the simple power and gratification of being able to affect larger systems [8].

Since the incidence of Cybercrime is multiplying manifold, it is crucial to develop technology to deal with the complications that ensue because of its misuse or its application in illegal activities. It is for this reason that it becomes quite necessary to get perspectives from various disciplines to get a fairer view of the extent of the problem, loopholes in the existing law, and solutions.

The American Psychological Association defines forensic psychology as the application of clinical psychology to the legal arena [22, 24]. While the American Academy of Psychiatry and the Law (AAPL) defines forensic psychology as 'a medical subspecialty', which includes both research and clinical practice in the many areas in which psychiatry is applied to legal issues [22, 24], understanding criminal psychology helps an investigator understand the human element of the crime. Many psychologists have also agreed that, though it is difficult to verify the effectiveness and utility of offender profiling (Alison and Kebbell, 2006; Alison et al., 2003), several other forensic psychologists [Gudaitis (1998); Nykodym et al. (2005); Rogers (2003)] have agreed that offender profiling might be useful in cybercrime cases, especially in the investigation part [3].

Criminal profiling is a psychological assessment of the criminal made without actually knowing his identity. It contains a set of characteristics that are common to those who commit similar types of crimes. It not only narrows down the suspect pool but also helps in evaluating the possibility that a particular criminal committed the crime. The job of a criminal psychologist includes studying criminal cases to see if there is a pattern, analyzing suspect behavior, and predicting their moves based on their behavioral profile.

Joshi and Singh (2003) discussed the anthropological aspects of cybercrime. They cited socio-educational, socio-economic, and techno-ideological factors and their expressions as causes of cybercrimes. They believed that instability in the educational structure may lead to deviant behavior. People who had psychological troubles with their socioeconomic status also used the internet as an outlet for their criminal activities, such as theft, hate, violence, child pornography, etc. With regards to techno-ideological factors, Joshi and Singh (2013) warned that one must consider sites and networks aimed at propaganda, destabilization, and individual and mass psychological manipulation using methods that involve the digital processing of images, videos, and audio [16]. Anthropologists have found a close relationship between socio-economic factors such as unemployment, poverty, etc. and the number of cybercrimes (Ilievski and Bernik, 2016) [11]. One such case is that of a small town called Jamtara in Madhya Pradesh, which is considered the epicenter of cybercrime in India. The geography, lack of career opportunities, poverty, etc. all seem to work against the youth here [20]. This year, after millions lost jobs due to mass layoffs, a surge in cybercrimes, especially tech support frauds, was seen. Other examples of such communities are the Sahawa boys and Yahoo Yahoo boys in Nigeria [2].

The damages due to cybercrimes are mostly financial in nature. Economists have time and again estimated the kind of damage a person or firm has suffered due to loss of intellectual property, loss of reputation, corporate espionage, and other such incidents. Florencio and Herley (2012) found in their study that every single report was subject to upward bias and that "cybercrime estimates are wildly, ridiculously overblown" [18].

Lawyers and Law enforcement officials believe that there should be a regulatory framework and training. The biggest problems faced by Police officers are a lack of technical knowledge, the use of redundant technologies, and a lack of expertise. [19,22] Many lawyers have insisted that India should sign an international treaty for cooperation on Cybercrimes. Seth (2003) observed in [13] that India is a signatory to the UN Convention against Transnational Organized Crime, which applies to criminal matters in general but not cybercrime cases. India is not a signatory to any Cybercrime Convention or a Mutual Legal Assistance Treaty (MLAT) for cooperation in matters of cybercrime, so it is quite difficult for India to deal with such cases where a foreign national is involved in cybercrime and could not be prosecuted until assistance from his country of residence [13].

2.1 Loopholes in Existing Laws

"When you know there is no clear law about what is offensive the fear goes away" (Baweja) [24]. The offenses defined in the IT Act, 2000, are not comprehensive. The subjectivity of the law risks the arbitrariness of the investigating officers. Most of the offenses have been left open to interpretation, which can lead to arbitrariness and disproportionate actions on the part of law enforcement officers. The IT Act of 2000, in its present form, does not cover various kinds of cybercrimes and Internet-related crimes and needs to be inclusive in terms of ever-emerging technology and newer crimes. The most serious concern about the Indian Cyber Law relates to its implementation. India is one of the few countries that has dedicated legislation dealing with cyberlaws. However, it also has some drawbacks that need to be addressed so that the legislation can become a strong tool to deter cybercriminals.

3. Conclusion

In June 2018, the Ministry of Women and Child Development proposed amendments to the Indecent Representation of Women Act 1986 to include virtual spaces. The proposed amendments also included recommendations to define the term publish and widen the scope of the word 'publish' to include distribute, or cause to publish and distribute [12, 17].

Various scholars, like Higgins and Marcum (2011) and Holt and Bossler (2014), have emphasized bringing together the various theoretical perspectives in an attempt to better explain the reasoning behind criminal behavior. Combining these attempts with real-life cases would be especially helpful in understanding why people commit cybercrimes [10].

REFERENCES

1. Adesina, O. S. (2017). Cybercrime and Poverty in Nigeria. *Canadian Social Science*, *13*(4), 19–29.
2. Bada, M., & Nurse, J. (n.d.). *The Social and Psychological Impact of Cyber-Attacks*.
3. Castells, M., & Himanen, P. (2002). *The Information Society and the Welfare State: The Finnish Model* (pp. 208–223). Oxford University Press.
4. Council of Europe. (2001). *"Convention on Cybercrime" Details of Treaty No.185*. Council of Europe.
5. *Crime in India 2019 | National Crime Records Bureau - Volume II*. (2019). Ncrb.gov.in; NCRB.
6. *Cyber Crime Portal*. (2021). Cybercrime.gov.in.
7. Dashora, K., & Patel, P. (2011). Cyber Crime in the Society: Problems and Preventions. *Journal of Alternative Perspectives in the Social Sciences*, 3(1), 240–259.
8. Grabosky, P., Smith, R. G., & Dempsey, G. (2010). *Electronic Theft: Unlawful Acquisition in Cyberspace* (1st ed.). Cambridge University Press.

9. Halder, D., & Jaishankar, K. (2010). Cyber Victimization in India: A Baseline Survey Report (2010). *SSRN Electronic Journal.*

10. Holt, T. J., & Bossler, A. M. (2013). Examining the Relationship Between Routine Activities and Malware Infection Indicators. *Journal of Contemporary Criminal Justice, 29*(4), 420–436.

11. Ilievski, A., & Igor, B. (2016). SOCIAL-ECONOMIC ASPECTS OF CYBERCRIME. Innovative Issues and Approaches in Social Sciences, 9(3).

12. *Indecent Representation of Women | Ministry of Women & Child Development.* (2017). Wcd.nic.in.

13. *India needs to sign a Cybercrime Convention: Karnika Seth.* (2014).

14. Internet and Mobile Association of India. (2020). *DIGITAL IN INDIA 2019 -ROUND 2 REPORT.* Internet and Mobile Association of India.

15. Jaishankar, K. (2018). Cyber Criminology as an Academic Discipline: History, Contribution and Impact. *Zenodo.* https://doi.org/10.5281/zenodo.1467308

16. Joshi, Y., & Singh, A. (2013). A Study on Cyber Crime and Security Scenario in INDIA. *International Journal of Engineering and Management Research, 3.*

17. *Law Against Indecent Representation of Women on Digital Platforms in the Works.* (2018). The Wire.

18. Madrigal, A. C. (2012, April 16). *Economists: Cybercrime Estimates Are Wildly, Ridiculously Overblown.* The Atlantic

19. Mastrofski, S. D. (2007). *Document Title: Police Organization and Management Issues for the Next Decade.*

20. Roser, M., Ritchie, H., & Ortiz-Ospina, E. (2019). *Internet.* Our World in Data.

21. Stalans, L. J., & Donner, C. M. (2010). Explaining Why Cybercrime Occurs: Criminological and Psychological Theories. In H. Jahankhani & A. Al-Nemrat (Eds.), *Cyber Criminology* (pp. 573–583).

22. Stephens, D. W. (2011). *New Perspectives in Policing Police Discipline: A Case for Change Executive Session on Policing and Public Safety.*

23. Thomas, D., & Brian, L. (2000). *Cybercrime Law Enforcement, Security and Surveillance in the Information Age* (p. 8). Routledge.

24. Viano, E. C. (2017). *Cybercrime, Organized Crime, and Societal Responses* (E. C. Viano, Ed.; p. 5). Springer International Publishing.

Computer Science Engineering and Emerging Technologies (ICCS-2022) – Prof (Dr.) Rajeev Sobti et al. (eds)
© 2024 Taylor & Francis Group, London, ISBN 978-1-032-52199-2

Chapter **92**

Blockchain Based Framework for E-Governance: A Review of the Literature

Ajinkya Panday[1], Vikas Verma[2], Arun Malik[3]

School of Computer Science and Engineering, Lovely Professional University, Punjab, India

Abstract: A ledger system known as blockchain technology serves as the foundation of the Bitcoin cryptocurrency. Since its inception, the literature has praised the potential positive uses of blockchain in other digital industries and questioned the difficulties associated with those applications. This study assesses the literature for frameworks and examples that fully realize the usefulness of blockchain technologies. E-government, supply chain management, healthcare, and finance were among the most frequently recorded digital sectors in this context. This evaluation lists use cases where blockchain technologies have been attempted to deploy in each industry. The main goal of this article is to examine each industry's level of adoption of blockchain technology and list the specific advantages and difficulties that come with doing so. The results demonstrate that, despite an increasing acceptance of blockchain technologies, their implementation within these four sectors is still in its infancy since the use cases lack specific assessments of their efficacy and viability.

Keywords: Blockchain, Distributed ledger, E-Government, E-Governance

1. Introduction

The Bitcoin cryptocurrency's underlying technology, the blockchain, is a decentralized ledger that allows for the integrity of exchange data to be preserved. The technology's ledger is distributed and decentralized, with digital records for all transactions, agreements, and controls [1]. The transfer's specifics are listed on a public ledger that is accessible to everyone on the network [2]. Since the birth of Bitcoin, a number of enhancements have been suggested to address some of the shortcomings of the blockchain, such as scalability and lack of privacy [3]. It decentralizes the regulation of financial services that are typically centralized and run by an authoritative client, such as the registration of transactions, identity verification, and contract completion [4].

Numerous researchers have also looked at how the application of blockchain technology is possible in a number of digital fields. This expanded interest includes corporate, governmental, and cross-industry applications in a number of different fields. By maintaining a shared database of data, blockchain technology has the capacity to revitalize long-standing business operations, for example in sectors like supply chain management and healthcare, to address concerns about security, privacy, and shareability. Various leading nations in the field, like Israel, the UK, Estonia, the USA, and New Zealand, have launched blockchain initiatives for future-ready information exchange infrastructures [5]. From a technological point of view, broad summaries of blockchain development have been undertaken to evaluate ongoing research subjects, difficulties, and upcoming prospects. (e.g., [6], [7], [8], [9]).

The blockchain can be considered a common ledger that stores transactional data and is dispersed over decentralized network nodes [10]. It creates openness and mutual trust between parties and allows one-to-one exchange of information

---

[1]ajinkyapanday@gmail.com, [2]vikas.verma@lpu.co.in, [3]arun.17442@lpu.co.in

DOI: 10.1201/9781003405580-92

without the requirement of a middleman [11]. The blockchain technology that supports the Bitcoin digital payment system was initially introduced by Nakamoto in 2008 [12]. Being a network where participants may trade information without the aid of a middleman, the technology is decentralized [13]. Under specific access control circumstances, network users have access to examine the complete ledger and add new entries [14].

Each block is connected to the one before it (the parent block) via the hash value of the previous block in its header. There are various procedures involved in adding a new block to the blockchain. The transaction block is initially created and digitally signed by the sender. After that, the fresh block is transmitted to all connected users. Once the majority of users accept the new block as genuine, it will be added to the blockchain. To secure the consistency of the distributed ledger across the network, A consensus procedure is required for the approval of a new block; POW consensus, for example, is employed for Bitcoin. [15]. A blockchain, unlike Bitcoin, can either have a private infrastructure (mining is carried out by a singular node) or a consortium infrastructure (nodes defined previously are only allowed to mine) [16].

1.1 Blockchain Advantages

Blockchain does away with the need for third parties to control transactions, which saves time and effort. In addition, the risks of a singular point of failure and traffic congestion are eliminated by blockchain's decentralization. Blockchain technology also provides finality because there is just one blockchain platform that is utilized as a trustworthy benchmark for block verification [17]. The technique makes auditability easier since each block has a timestamp and a mention of its parent block. Each transaction block is required to be digitally signed using the private key of the owner and given a hash in order to maintain integrity. Additionally, the ledger is permanent, making it unchangeable and impervious to tampering, which guarantees integrity.

Table 92.1   The Advantages of using blockchain in various sectors

Advantages	Governance	Supply chain	Healthcare	Finance
Accountability	✓		✓	✓
Adaptability	✓	✓	✓	✓
Anonymity		✓		
Auditability	✓	✓	✓	✓
Availability	✓		✓	✓
Credibility	✓		✓	✓
Confidentiality	✓	✓	✓	✓
Decentralization	✓	✓	✓	✓
Immutability	✓	✓	✓	✓
Integrity	✓	✓	✓	✓
Provenance	✓	✓	✓	✓
Transparency	✓	✓	✓	✓
Trust	✓	✓	✓	✓

Source: Author's compilation

1.2 Blockchain Disadvantages

Despite the advantages described above, implementing blockchain technology comes with a number of difficulties. The capacity of the blockchain to scale is one of the biggest problems. A blockchain network's whole ledger, which is composed of vast numbers of transaction blocks, is stored on each network node. Restricted node storage is a result of this. Another drawback is that the consensus method results in a very low throughput rate and a very significant latency when compared to a typical system. A transaction block has to be approved by the majority of network nodes through a consensus method like the proof-of-work mechanism before it can be added to the ledger. In actuality, it takes up to 10 minutes on average to authenticate and register each transaction. It might be argued that the blockchain mining method is a waste of resources because it necessitates a significant amount of processing and energy [18]. This inevitably brings up privacy issues, particularly when it comes to public ledgers.

Table 92.2 The Disadvantages of using blockchain in various sectors

Disadvantage	Governance	Supply chain	Healthcare	Finance
Computational Overhead	✓	✓	✓	✓
Interoperability		✓	✓	
Latency	✓	✓	✓	✓
Privacy		✓	✓	✓
Scalability	✓	✓	✓	✓
Storage	✓	✓	✓	✓

Source: Author's compilation

2. Review Design

This report provides a summary of fully developed and recorded blockchain application examples in an effort to identify patterns. Hence, it is demonstrated that the fundamental concepts of blockchain technology are useful in a variety of settings. However, this evaluation solely takes into account studies that focus on the unique aspects and difficulties of applying blockchain technology.

2.1 Research Questions

The subsequent research questions (RQs) were developed in order to fulfill the objective of the review:

RQ1: What are the fields of blockchain application which can be used for e-governance? Identification of blockchain technology use in not just cryptocurrencies and financial services but also in other fields is the key research subject. This query identifies the key contexts where blockchain has been applied as a remedy.

RQ2: What is the blockchain architecture applied inside each application? The goal of this inquiry is to pinpoint the fundamental elements of blockchain as they are applied in a specific setting. These factors comprise the kind of blockchain, the kind of data kept on it, and the methods used for mining and storing data.

RQ3: What possible benefits may blockchain adoption have in each setting? The use of blockchain technology may have several advantages, which have been extensively covered in the literature. With this query, the evaluation draws attention to the immediate gains that result from a particular environment's requirements and blockchain's benefits.

RQ4: What are the challenges with using blockchain within every setting? This question provides a contrast to RQ3 with the aim of highlighting the particular difficulties presented by blockchain technology in each of the above situations.

3. E-Governance

Utilizing ICT to give people access to public services is known as electronic government, or e-government [19]. Their objectives are to design services around individuals and locals, improve access to government services, take social factors into account, distribute information responsibly, and efficiently employ resources [20]. Additionally, governments have shown a lot of interest in implementing and improving their overall e-government programs [21]. Lately, a lot of emphasis has been placed on the use of blockchain technology to get around different obstacles and enhance the delivery of services [22].

To encourage the use of blockchain among its services, the government of the UAE likewise took action by forming a Global Block-chain Council [5]. A few of the project reports involving blockchain are concentrated on specific governmental programs, like e-democracy [23], land registration, or e-residency. A new technological initiative called the Dubai Blockchain Strategy Project seeks to promote the UAE as a global distributor that deals with everything from smart tourism to e-democracy [24]. The first and biggest permitted blockchain network now in use is the European network Trusted Chain. Along with other applications, it helps e-government [17]. But significant efforts, including new laws and standardization, will be needed to achieve its global acceptance. Blockchain technology is now being used by the Republic of Estonia to manage a number of e-government initiatives. Projects like the Estonian land registry, data sharing, and e-residency are examples [5]. They are made to give data owners direct control of their data so that an accessible, fair, and safe infrastructure can increase public confidence.

4. Supply Chain Management

Globally, billions of items are produced each day and delivered to end users. Operations can be disrupted by a supply chain breakdown, which may result in losses in money and reputation and also harm to the ecosystem. Owing to supply chain management's intricacy, transparency and traceability are required in order to reduce risk by raising understanding of cause-and-effect relationships [10]. The risks connected with technological information storage reliability, compatibility, confidentiality, and the information's privacy are raised in present practice when reliable information is held centrally by a third-party institution. Integrating blockchain technology may improve process flows, supplier and customer responsibility, and consumer accountability [13]. A manufacturing supply chain may benefit from a blockchain system. A private blockchain architecture was suggested. For network entry and privacy protection, members can obtain private keys and public keys via a registration service. A privately owned system of blockchain called OriginChain is intended to be flexible in response to shifting conditions and laws [13]. Four different categories of nodes—Suppliers or merchants, testing facilities, suppliers of traceability services, and plant or cargo inspectors—provide data to OriginChain. To enable various parties to use the blockchain, administration personnel evaluate requests from parties and issue certificates of access, plant inspectors verify the qualifications of producers, and cargo examiners check goods and supervise the packing and sealing of goods. By means of smart contracts and agreements among supply chain participants, all data is registered and confirmed.

5. Healthcare

A new generation of coordinated, smart healthcare delivery approaches that are comprehensive, individualized, and even mobile are being made possible by information and communication technology (ICT) [6]. However, patient satisfaction necessitates collaborative, well-informed decision-making among healthcare professionals. Only seamless access to pertinent siloed data stored in separate electronic medical record (EMR) systems may do this [6]. However, due to their variability and the disparities in security policies and access control models among EMR systems, present systems fall short [6]. Blockchain technology is generating growing attention in healthcare because it is considered to have the potential to usher in a technological revolution. There are some encouraging concepts that may help to provide individualized treatment with blockchain-based EMR systems, even though the modest work disclosed is currently preliminary. This will prioritize patient engagement in their treatment and cut down on third-party direct involvement, which should eventually alleviate misunderstandings between patients and healthcare professionals. A decentralized blockchain-based approach for keeping records that is connected with the patient's medical professionals manages a unified patient-centered EMR.

EMR systems were revolutionized by implementing more stringent access control security mechanisms [25], [26], and [27]. Healthcare Data Gateway (HGD) is a blockchain approach suggested by Yue et al. [25] that grants patients access rights and control over their medical data. A blockchain-based storage system is used by HGD to administer the EMRs, and all data access requests are authenticated using the purpose-centered information security concept. To allow other parties to evaluate patient data without compromising their privacy, it also uses secure Multi-Party Computation (MPC) technology. In the meantime, AlOmar et al. [26] developed a system that revolutionizes EMR systems by employing safe solutions for authentication but with a stronger focus on participant identification. It is akin to HGD in this regard. Then again, Xia et al. [28] introduced MeDShare. It adds an extra degree of protection by monitoring who accesses data from a system that holds it with malicious intentions.

6. Discussion

6.1 E-Governance

Administrative divisions in government sectors run the risk of isolating information about individuals and organizations. In situations when data access is restricted, these records' preservation, transparency, and decentralization promote reliable and efficient data interchange. Blockchain technology encourages accountability and transparency, which in the public sector helps overcome administrative flaws. By reducing paperwork, cheating, and bribery in the supply of public services, the use of blockchain technology can significantly assist truly networked governments. Despite this, several technical and legal restrictions continue to prevent the broad use of blockchain technology by government sectors since its applications are still in their infancy. The latest security incident involving Bitcoin has increased worries about security and privacy, which are two obstacles to the adoption of the blockchain. It has been suggested that giving citizens authority over their ledger will help alleviate the security issue [17].

6.2 Supply Chain Management

A decentralized approach is particularly beneficial for supply chains for perishable items since it guards against fraud and extortion by ensuring data security, dependability, and transparency [10]. When data is shared independently by different stakeholders in the supply chain, its immutability and irrevocability act as a diversified source of reality. This overcomes the lack of comprehensive visibility, which, in the absence of it, would raise the risk of fraud [30]. Despite these advantages, maintaining a supply chain system using blockchain technology calls for a specific technological infrastructure at each party's location [31]. Utilizing technology like sensors to successfully improve information continuity is one way to overcome the difficulties of keeping current records and interoperability. Despite these benefits, sustaining a supply chain system based on blockchain technology necessitates a certain technological setup for each stakeholder [31].

6.3 Healthcare

Blockchain technology has the ability to fully complement a patient-centered healthcare delivery method, even if most of the work on it only started in 2016. The majority of digital immigrants lack basic technology skills, and if patients lack these skills, the success of the new blockchain-based healthcare system won't be as high. On the other hand, user-centered interaction is becoming more and more in demand, particularly among digital natives, and as a result, the time will come sooner or later. Very few alternatives make an evolutionary shift toward patient-centeredness in an effort to address the problems with conventional EMR systems. The other frameworks, which seem to be in favor, take a radical approach and switch out obsolete, traditional EMR systems with adaptable, scalable blockchain-based replacements. However, solutions adopting the former strategy are so much more liberal in terms of their protection that they accept weak, inflexible EMR technology, whereas the latter concepts have better flexibility to increase their security countermeasures. This is understandable given that EMR systems are often effectively protected inside their local physical perimeters by access control and local organization-oriented policies [29].

7. Conclusion

This study presents the findings of a survey of the literature on the advancement of blockchain value beyond theory in often discussed corporate, governmental, and cross-industry settings. Due to its distinctive features, blockchain technology offers the potential to transform the E-governance, supply chain management, healthcare, and finance sectors. A literature review was conducted for each of these digital businesses to uncover instances of blockchain technology being used and assess its potential. Additionally, the benefits and challenges of all of these digital fields were identified using the literature. By emphasizing existing research and thereby exposing potential research gaps that, if properly addressed, may be helpful to industry, this study enhances the body of knowledge on blockchain technology. There are still questions regarding the usefulness of blockchain technology in terms of user experiences, namely those of end users at the opposite end of the continuum.

REFERENCE

1. Bhutta, M. N. M., Khwaja, A. A., Nadeem, A., Ahmad, H. F., Khan, M. K., Hanif, M.A., Song, H., Alshamari, M., and Cao, Y. (2021). A survey on blockchain technology: evolution, architecture and security. IEEE Access 9, 61048–61073.
2. Dashkevich, N., Counsell, S., and Destefanis, G. (2020). Blockchain application for central banks: A systematic mapping study. IEEE Access 8, 139918–139952.
3. Fernandez-Carames, T. M., and Fraga-Lamas, P. (2020). Towards Post-Quantum Blockchain: A Review on Blockchain Cryptography Resistant to Quantum Computing Attacks. IEEE Access 8, 21091–21116.
4. Ferrag, M. A., Shu, L., Yang, X., Derhab, A., and Maglaras, L. (2020). Security and Privacy for Green IoT-Based Agriculture: Review, Blockchain Solutions, and Challenges. IEEE Access 8, 32031–32053.
5. Jagrat, C. P., and Channegowda, J. (2020). A Survey of Blockchain Based Government Infrastructure Information. 2020 International Conference on Mainstreaming Block Chain Implementation (ICOMBI), 1–5.
6. Khatri, S., Alzahrani, F. A., Ansari, M. T. J., Agrawal, A., Kumar, R., and Khan, R. A. (2021). A systematic analysis on blockchain integration with healthcare domain: scope and challenges. IEEE Access 9, 84666–84687.

7. Shodhganga@INFLIBNET: Social Media Adaptation Framework for E Governance Available at: http://hdl.handle.net/10603/336573 [Accessed September 29, 2022].
8. Shodhganga@INFLIBNET: Study of factors influencing the use of blockchain technology in student information system at universities Available at: http://hdl.handle.net/10603/394073 [Accessed September 29, 2022].
9. Shodhganga@INFLIBNET: Application of a blockchain model for effective e governance in the university system Available at: http://hdl.handle.net/10603/396816 [Accessed September 29, 2022].
10. Bodkhe, U., Tanwar, S., Parekh, K., Khanpara, P., Tyagi, S., Kumar, N., and Alazab, M. (2020). Blockchain for industry 4.0: A comprehensive review. IEEE Access *8*, 79764–79800.
11. Vafiadis, N. V., and Taefi, T. T. (2019). Differentiating Blockchain Technology to optimize the Processes Quality in Industry 4.0. In 2019 IEEE 5th World Forum on Internet of Things (WF-IoT) (IEEE), pp. 864–869.
12. Zhang, R., Xue, R., and Liu, L. (2019). Security and privacy on blockchain. ACM Comput. Surv. *52*, 1–34.
13. Abou-Nassar, E. M., Iliyasu, A. M., El-Kafrawy, P. M., Song, O.-Y., Bashir, A. K., and El-Latif, A. A. A. (2020). DITrust Chain: Towards Blockchain-Based Trust Models for Sustainable Healthcare IoT Systems. IEEE Access *8*, 111223–111238.
14. Bai, Y., Hu, Q., Seo, S.-H., Kang, K., and Lee, J. J. (2022). Public participation consortium blockchain for smart city governance. IEEE Internet Things J. *9*, 2094–2108.
15. Franciscon, E. A., Nascimento, M. P., Granatyr, J., Weffort, M. R., Lessing, O. R., and Scalabrin, E. E. (2019). A systematic literature review of blockchain architectures applied to public services. In 2019 IEEE 23rd International Conference on Computer Supported Cooperative Work in Design (CSCWD) (IEEE), pp. 33–38.
16. Tasca, P., and Tessone, C. J. (2019). A taxonomy of blockchain technologies: principles of identification and classification. ledger *4*.
17. Haque, A. B., Islam, A. K. M. N., Hyrynsalmi, S., Naqvi, B., and Smolander, K. (2021). GDPR compliant blockchains–a systematic literature review. IEEE Access *9*, 50593–50606.
18. Fernandez-Carames, T. M., and Fraga-Lamas, P. (2018). A review on the use of blockchain for the internet of things. IEEE Access *6*, 32979–33001.
19. e-government - Wikipedia Available at: https://en.wikipedia.org/wiki/E-government [Accessed October 13, 2022].
20. Commission, E., Directorate-General for Communications Networks, C., Technology, Dogger, J., Enzerink, S., Wennerholm-Caslavska, T., Noci, G., Geilleit, R., Linden, N., Marchio, G., *et al.* (2020). eGovernment Benchmark 2020 : eGovernment that works for the people : insight report (Publications Office).
21. European Commission, Directorate-General for Communications Networks, C. and T., Noci, G., Geilleit, R., Marchio, G., Linden, N., Dogger, J., Wennerholm-Caslavska, T., Enzerink, S., Claps, M., *et al.* (2020). eGovernment benchmark 2020 : eGovernment that works for the people : background report (Publications Office).
22. Commission, E., Directorate-General for Communications Networks, C., Technology, Linden, N., Marchio, G., Noci, G., Geilleit, R., Enzerink, S., Wennerholm-Caslavska, T., Dogger, J., *et al.* (2020). eGovernment Benchmark 2020 : eGovernment that works for the people : method paper for the benchmarking exercises (comprehensive rules from 2012 to 2019) (Publications Office).
23. Ølnes, S., Ubacht, J., and Janssen, M. (2017). Blockchain in government: Benefits and implications of distributed ledger technology for information sharing. Gov. Inf. Q.
24. How Dubai is Becoming the Blockchain Capital of the World Available at: https://newsroom.ibm.com/IBM-blockchain?item=30730 [Accessed October 13, 2022].
25. Yue, X., Wang, H., Jin, D., Li, M., and Jiang, W. (2016). Healthcare Data Gateways: Found Healthcare Intelligence on Blockchain with Novel Privacy Risk Control. J. Med. Syst. *40*, 218.
26. Al Omar, A., Rahman, M. S., Basu, A., and Kiyomoto, S. (2017). Medibchain: A blockchain based privacy preserving platform for healthcare data. In Security, privacy, and anonymity in computation, communication, and storage Lecture notes in computer science., G. Wang, M. Atiquzzaman, Z. Yan, and K.-K. R. Choo, eds. (Cham: Springer International Publishing), pp. 534–543.
27. Vora, J., Nayyar, A., Tanwar, S., Tyagi, S., Kumar, N., Obaidat, M.S., and Rodrigues, J.J.P.C. (2018). BHEEM: A Blockchain-Based Framework for Securing Electronic Health Records. In 2018 IEEE Globecom Workshops (GC Wkshps) (IEEE), pp. 1–6.
28. Xia, Q., Sifah, E. B., Asamoah, K. O., Gao, J., Du, X., and Guizani, M. (2017). MeDShare: Trust-Less Medical Data Sharing Among Cloud Service Providers via Blockchain. IEEE Access *5*, 14757–14767.
29. Amponsah, A. A., Adekoya, A. F., and Weyori, B. A. (2022). Improving the Financial Security of National Health Insurance using Cloud-Based Blockchain Technology Application. International Journal of Information Management Data Insights *2*, 100081.
30. Guo, H., and Yu, X. (2022). A Survey on Blockchain Technology and its security. Blockchain: Research and Applications, 100067.
31. Suhail, S., Malik, S. U. R., Jurdak, R., Hussain, R., Matulevičius, R., and Svetinovic, D. (2022). Towards situational aware cyber-physical systems: A security-enhancing use case of blockchain-based digital twins. Computers in Industry *141*, 103699.

Computer Science Engineering and Emerging Technologies (ICCS-2022) – Prof (Dr.) Rajeev Sobti et al. (eds)
© 2024 Taylor & Francis Group, London, ISBN 978-1-032-52199-2

Chapter

93

Segmentation of Skin Cancer Images Applying Background Subtraction with Midpoint Analysis

Uzma Saghir[1]

Research Scholar, Lovely Professional University, Punjab

Shailendra Kumar Singh[2]

Assistant Professor, Lovely Professional University, Punjab

Abstract: Skin cancer affects people of all ages and is a commonly occurring disease. Death toll with Skin cancer increases in case of late detection. An automated mechanism for skin cancer detection at an early stage is required to reduce the death rate. Visual examination with scanning or screening images is a common mechanism of detection of this disease, but due to its resemblance with other diseases, this mechanism shows the least accuracy. A novel segmentation mechanism that works on the ISIC dataset for the partitioning of Skin images into critical and non-critical sections is presented in this paper. The entire phase of segmentation is partitioned into separation, extraction, removing the background, and extracting the region of interest. Segmentation parameters include symmetry, color, size, shape, and many more. These are used to segment skin cancer and to distinguish benign skin cancer from melanoma. The ground truth for the validation of segmentation is accomplished by comparing the segmented images with validation data provided with the ISIC dataset. Validation and test results corresponding to segmentation show an accuracy of 96% and above.

Keywords: Hair-removal, Image Enhancement, Segmentation, Skin-cancer

1. Introduction

Skin cancer can adversely impact the lifestyle of humans. The extreme impact of skin cancer can cause death as well. The importance of skin elements in the human body is shown by the fact that even little changes in their functioning can have an impact on other body parts and organs [1]. The skin is exposed to the environment. As a result, skin infections and contamination are more common. Skin cancer caused by melanoma affects millions of people. Skin cancer is caused by harmful ultraviolet radiation and the abnormal growth of skin cells called melanocytes [2]. Since skin lesions and healthy skin are so similar, a visual examination during a physical screening of skin lesions might lead to an incorrect diagnosis. Dermoscopy has been used to help doctors improve the screening for melanoma skin lesions during the past few decades [3]. Even though the technique enhances diagnosis accuracy over the visual examination, dermatologists still find it difficult to screen through dermoscopy images due to the prevalence of artifacts and reflections in the images [4]. Since many cancer boundaries are undetectable or hazy, visual identification is challenging, time-consuming, subjective, and error-prone [5]. Therefore, the need for an automated system that ensures accurate segmentation of melanocyte lesions and avoids errors due to manual detection is very much needed.

Image segmentation is used to determine the boundary between the lesion and the skin around it. The overall goal of segmentation is to clearly distinguish groups of related pixels within a region of interest (ROI) so that structural transitions

---

[1]uzmasaghir211@gmail.com, [2]drsksingh.cse@gmail.com

DOI: 10.1201/9781003405580-93

between these groups can be detected more easily. It is critical to accurately segment the lesion to ensure low error rates for subsequent quantification of the shape, border, and size features of the skin lesion [6]. Different segmentation methods for medical imaging analysis are thresholding-based, edge-based, region-based, artificial intelligence-based, and active contour-based.

- *Thresholding-based:* These techniques involve the determination of one or more histogram threshold values that distinguish the objects from the background [7].
- *Edge-based:* These techniques use edge operators to identify the borders between the regions [8].
- *Region-based:* Pixels are grouped into homogeneous regions by merging, splitting, or both [9].
- *Artificial intelligence based:* These methods model images as random fields whose parameters are determined by various optimization procedures [10].
- *Active contours:* Using curve evolution, these methods detect object contours [11].

2. Related Work

For the past few years, different cancer detection methods have been developed in this research field by segmenting and extracting multiple dermoscopic features. **Al-Masni et al. (2018)** [12] presented a novel segmentation algorithm based on full-resolution convolutional networks (FrCN) without the need for pre- or post-processing. Artificial Bee Colony (ABC)) was developed by **Aljanabi et al. (2019).** [13] **Improved** melanoma detection can be achieved through the use of skin lesion segmentation as a means of identifying lesions in dermoscopy images. **Chouhan et al. (2019)** [10] Chauhan et al. conducted a comprehensive survey for skin lesion segmentation using computational intelligence techniques, including fuzzy C-means convolutional neural networks and genetic algorithm (GA) research. These approaches are widely used to segment images in medical imaging, scientific analysis, engineering, and the humanities. **Monika et al. (2020)** [14] Color-based k-means clustering is used for segmentation since color is a significant characteristic in determining the kind of malignancy. **Kaymak et al. (2020)** [15] FCN-8, FCN-16, FCN-32, and FCN-Alex Net are four FCN architectures generated by using the CNN model for segmentation of skin cancer images. The network was first put through its paces on the ISIC 2017 dataset. Plot and Jacquard coefficients are employed to assess the degree of agreement between the partitioned result and the actual ground truth. Even though the multiple FCN frameworks performed proportionately well, FCN-8 was discovered to be more effective in terms of segmentation. **Mohakud and Dash (2021)** [16] For dermoscopic image segmentation, the author proposes a hyperparameter optimized Full Convolutional Encoder-Decoder Network (FCEDN). The new Exponential Neighborhood Gray Wolf Optimization (EN-GWO) algorithm was used to optimize the network hyperparameters. The neighborhood search strategy in EN-GWO is determined by combining the individual wolf hunting strategy with the global search strategy, and it reflects the appropriate balance of exploration and exploitation. **Murugan et al. (2021)** [17] The median filter is applied in the pre-processing phase, and for the separation of the region of interest, the mean shift method is used.

The proposed approach corresponds to different phases, including pre-processing and segmentation. The main contribution of this paper is to propose a technique that categorizes the skin images within dermoscopic images as normal or abnormal based on segmentation. The model decides about acute cancer based on the number of abnormal skin cells detected within the sample.

3. Proposed Method

The proposed method for the segmentation of cancer images is achieved in two phases. The initial phase is preprocessing, which includes resizing the image to a standard size, hair removal, and contrast enhancement. During pre-processing, a low-hat filter was applied to tackle noise in terms of hairs. During noise tackling, the image can become distorted. To tackle the issue, restoration, in terms of color slicing and enhancement, is applied. The entire image may not be useful for skin lesion detection, so it is mandatory to extract the region of interest. This is done within segmentation through region of interest extraction with background elimination. The next phase is finding the region of interest (ROI) from the preprocessed image, which is achieved by region properties and background elimination.

4. Segmentation

Segmentation using the multiphase approach followed in the proposed mechanism uses the ISIC dataset. The segmentation phase is used to divide the image into critical and non-critical parts. The segmentation phase in the proposed work is done in terms of separation, extraction, removing the background, and extracting the region of interest. Lesion separation is critical as it will be used for the analysis of abnormalities. The novelty in the region separation phase is in terms of the direction of processing. Normally, processing in the region separation phase is performed through an inside-outside test that classifies the edge within the image. The issues are discussed in [18], but in the proposed work, this process is reversed. Contemporary region separation-based mechanism boundary identification is an issue. Thus, cancerous region extraction may not be appropriate. The extracted regions with and without the proposed approach are given in the table under Figure 4. The advantage of reversing the direction includes the last time in the identification of the region of interest in the proceeding pass in the segmentation. Starting the process from inside and moving towards the outside cannot be terminated until the boundary is encountered, but using the proposed approach, control will move from the boundary of the region and, in other words, towards the nucleus, establishing threshold points where variation in intensity levels occurs. If no deviation is detected while scanning 50% of the region, the entire region will be labeled as non-critical.

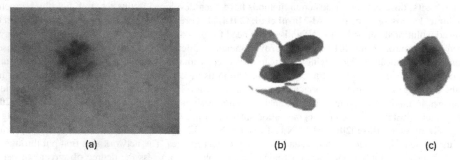

| (a) | (b) | (c) |

Fig. 93.1 (a) Original Image, (b) Contemporary region separation, (c) Proposed approach

Region separation phases initially identify the boundary (B) through the color intensity (clr) levels. To identify the region (R), color plays a vital role. The identification of colour is given through equation 1.

$$B_{xx_i, y_i} = \begin{cases} clr_i\ != clr_i + 1 & R\_B \\ 0 & \text{othrwise} \end{cases} \tag{1}$$

The color comparison with the neighbouring pixel identifies the region boundary (RB) and is stored within the $B_{x,y}$ variable where B is the boundary. Since there are multiple regions, multiple boundaries corresponding to different regions will be detected. Therefore, we need the subscripted variable 'I' with the boundary variable. The diameter of the region is estimated to obtain the dimension of the region. The dimension of the region will be divided by "2" to obtain the radius, and this will give the nucleus (N_i) of the region.

$$N_i = \begin{cases} (\max(B_{x_i, y_i}) - \min(B_{x_i, y_i}))/2 & > 0 \\ \le 0 & RB \text{ extraction not possible} \end{cases} \tag{2}$$

The region's boundaries will give the Centre of the region. The normal flow of the system will now be from the $\max(B_{x_i, y_i})$ nucleus.

The region extraction phase is critical in the process of proposed segmentation. The process first identifies the critically labelled segments. The region corresponding to the critical part has boundary values. A set of intensity (Int) values will be stored within a buffer (Bf_i) corresponding to these boundary values. These intensity values corresponding to the region will be used in the background elimination and to extract the region of interest. The primary equations used for the same region extraction are based on the valid nucleus determination given within equation 2. The nucleus intensity values will be stored within the buffer for further processing.

$$Bf_i = \begin{cases} \text{Int}(N > 0), & \text{Valid nucleaus values will be stored within buffer} \\ \text{Discard Int}(N \le 0) & \text{Invalid intensities will be rejected} \end{cases} \tag{3}$$

The result in terms of region separation and extraction is more accurate through improved inside-outside tests and region extraction mechanisms shown in Fig. 93.2 [21].

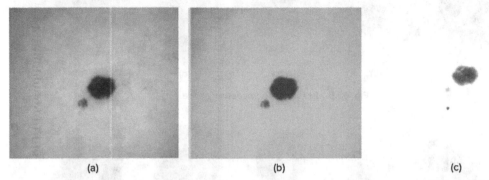

(a)   (b)   (c)

Fig. 93.2   (a) Original Skin Image, (b) After initial segmentation, (c) After overlapped object elimination

For the skin cell segmentation procedure, the object is represented individually by the centroid, major and minor axes. Figure 93.3 depicts the outcome of this phase [21].

(a)   (b)   (c)

Fig. 93.3   (a) Input image, (b) First object extraction, (c) Second object extraction

A background subtraction mechanism is used to remove the background (Bg_i) color and the foreground image is retained. The background colour with the skin image has a maximum of 255 intensity levels. The region extracted from the region separation and the intensities extracted from the region separation are used in the background subtraction process. This is expressed in equation 4.

$$\text{Without}_{Bg_i} = 255 - \text{Int}(Bf_i) \tag{4}$$

This intensity will be subtracted from the rest of the image to obtain an image without a background. After subtracting the background, the region of interest is obtained. The highest-correlated segments are obtained using a correlation-based mechanism. The most positively correlated segments will be retained, and the rest of the segments will be rejected. The relationship between the components is extracted using bwconncomp. The coordinates of the region with the highest correlation are obtained using Regionprops.

5. Results and Discussion

Figure 93.4 depicts the original input images [19]. Figure 93.5 depicts the experimental outcome of preprocessing phase. Figure 93.6 depicts the experimental result of the segmentation phase. This is accomplished by implementing background subtraction with a midpoint and region prop mechanism. The Skin images, normal and abnormal separation mechanism encloses the abnormal shape with boundaries.

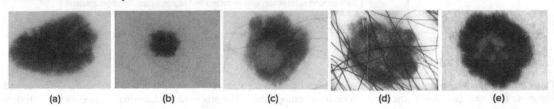

(a)   (b)   (c)   (d)   (e)

Fig. 93.4   Original input images

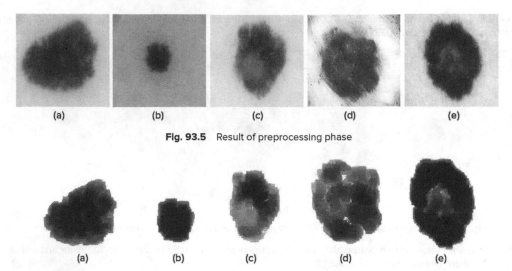

Fig. 93.5 Result of preprocessing phase

Fig. 93.6 Result of segmentation phase

The Jacobi index is used to evaluate segmentation performance. The Jacobi index compares the true and estimated results. Jacobi index is given as under

$$JI = \frac{TP}{TP + FN + FP} \tag{5}$$

The JI index ranges from 0 to 1. True positive values were set to 1 if both the estimation and the fact were 1. In the incident of an inappropriate prediction, the false-positive and negative values are determined to 1. The proposed method has TP = 25, FN = 1, TN = 1, and a segmentation accuracy of 92.0. In some cases, the accuracy is even greater than 100%.

Table 93.1 Comparison of segmentation accuracy with the existing approach [21]

Authors	Datasets	Techniques	Accuracy %
Carrera and Dominguez (2018) [19]	ISIC	Dilation approach and histogram equalization for preprocessing The optimal threshold for segmentation SVM, DT for classification	75.00
Thaajwer and Ishanka (2019) [20]	ISIC	Hough transformation for hair removal Otsu segmentation and Watershed method for segmentation NN, SVM, CNN	85.00
Kassem, Hosny, and Fouad (2020) [21]	ISIC	Google net for feature extraction Multiclass SVM for classification	81.00
Murgan et al. (2021) [17]	ISIC	A median filter for pre-processing Mean shift method for segmentation SVM, probabilistic NN, and random forests for classification	89.00
Proposed System	ISIC	Bottom hat filter and DCT for preprocessing Background subtraction with midpoint and region props for segmentation DAA for feature extraction SVM, KNN, RF, Naïve Bayes, DT	96.21

6. Conclusion and Future Scope

Due to image quality, several segmentation approaches based on early detection of melanoma fail to extract the entire and complete structures (noise, low contrast, or intensity inhomogeneity). The proposed mechanism of segmentation considers multiple phases, including separation, extraction, background removal, and region of interest. This multivariate approach helps in accurately portioning the image into critical and non-critical sections with an accuracy of 96.5. Features from the critical section will be extracted. These features will be used to identify the abnormal images. Features extracted from the critical parts will enable the successful labelling of images. In the future, labelling information generated through the segmentation process can be used to accurately classify the images into the appropriate class.

REFERENCES

1. Nivedita Singh and Shailendra K. Gupta, 'Recent Advancement in the Early Detection of Melanoma Using Computerized Tools: An Image Analysis Perspective', *Skin Research and Technology*, 25.2 (2019), 129–41 <https://doi.org/10.1111/srt.12622>.
2. Xufeng Wu and John A. Hammer, 'Melanosome Transfer: It Is Best to Give and Receive', *Current Opinion in Cell Biology*, 29.1 (2014), 1–7 <https://doi.org/10.1016/j.ceb.2014.02.003>.
3. Junji Kato and others, 'Dermoscopy of Melanoma and Non-Melanoma Skin Cancers', *Frontiers in Medicine*, 6.August (2019), 1–7 <https://doi.org/10.3389/fmed.2019.00180>.
4. Catarina Barata and others, 'Two Systems for the Detection of Melanomas in Dermoscopy Images Using Texture and Color Features', *IEEE Systems Journal*, 8.3 (2014), 965–79 <https://doi.org/10.1109/JSYST.2013.2271540>.
5. M. E. Vestergaard and others, 'Dermoscopy Compared with Naked Eye Examination for the Diagnosis of Primary Melanoma: A Meta-Analysis of Studies Performed in a Clinical Setting', *British Journal of Dermatology*, 159.3 (2008), 669–76 <https://doi.org /10.1111/j.1365-2133.2008.08713.x>.
6. Parvathaneni Naga Srinivasu and others, 'Classification of Skin Disease Using Deep Learning Neural Networks with Mobilenet v2 and Lstm', *Sensors*, 21.8 (2021), 1–27 <https://doi.org/10.3390/s21082852>.
7. Roberta B. Oliveira and others, 'Computational Methods for the Image Segmentation of Pigmented Skin Lesions: A Review', *Computer Methods and Programs in Biomedicine*, 131 (2016), 127–41 <https://doi.org/10.1016/j.cmpb.2016.03.032>.
8. Nida M. Zaitoun and Musbah J. Aqel, 'Survey on Image Segmentation Techniques', *Procedia Computer Science*, 65.Iccmit (2015), 797–806 <https://doi.org/10.1016/j.procs.2015.09.027>.
9. Rabia Javid and others, 'Region-Based Active Contour JSEG Fusion Technique for Skin Lesion from Dermoscopic Images', *Biomedical Research*, 30.6 (2019), 1–10.
10. Siddharth Singh Chouhan, Ajay Kaul, and Uday Pratap Singh, *Soft Computing Approaches for Image Segmentation: A Survey*, *Multimedia Tools and Applications* (Multimedia Tools and Applications, 2018), LXXVII <https://doi.org/10.1007/s11042-018-6005-6>.
11. Kashan Zafar and others, 'Skin Lesion Segmentation from Dermoscopic Images Using Convolutional Neural Network', *Sensors (Switzerland)*, 20.6 (2020), 1–14 <https://doi.org/10.3390/s20061601>.
12. Mohammed A. Al-masni and others, 'Skin Lesion Segmentation in Dermoscopy Images via Deep Full Resolution Convolutional Networks', *Computer Methods and Programs in Biomedicine*, 162 (2018), 221–31 <https://doi.org/10.1016/j.cmpb.2018.05.027>.
13. Mohanad Aljanabi and others, 'Skin Lesion Segmentation Method for Dermoscopy Images Using Artificial Bee Colony Algorithm', *Symmetry*, 10.8 (2018) <https://doi.org/10.3390/sym10080347>.
14. M. Krishna Monika and others, 'Skin Cancer Detection and Classification Using Machine Learning', *Materials Today: Proceedings*, 33.xxxx (2020), 4266–70 <https://doi.org/10.1016/j.matpr.2020.07.366>.
15. Çağrı Kaymak and Ayşegül Uçar, *A Brief Survey and an Application of Semantic Image Segmentation for Autonomous Driving*, *Smart Innovation, Systems and Technologies*, 2019, CXXXVI <https://doi.org/10.1007/978-3-030-11479-4_9>.
16. Rasmiranjan Mohakud and Rajashree Dash, 'Skin Cancer Image Segmentation Utilizing a Novel EN-GWO Based Hyper-Parameter Optimized FCEDN', *Journal of King Saud University - Computer and Information Sciences*, xxxx, 2022 <https://doi.org/10.1016/j.jksuci.2021.12.018>.
17. A. Murugan and others, 'Diagnosis of Skin Cancer Using Machine Learning Techniques', *Microprocessors and Microsystems*, 81.October 2020 (2021), 103727 <https://doi.org/10.1016/j.micpro.2020.103727>.
18. Pablo A. Flores-Vidal and others, 'A New Edge Detection Method Based on Global Evaluation Using Fuzzy Clustering', *Soft Computing*, 23.6 (2019), 1809–21 <https://doi.org/10.1007/s00500-018-3540-z>.
19. Enrique V Carrera B and David Ron-dom, *Technology Trends*, ed. by Miguel Botto-Tobar and others, Communications in Computer and Information Science (Cham: Springer International Publishing, 2019), DCCCXCV <https://doi.org/10.1007/978-3-030-05532-5>.
20. M. A. Ahmed Thaajwer and U. A. Piumi Ishanka, 'Melanoma Skin Cancer Detection Using Image Processing and Machine Learning Techniques', *ICAC 2020 - 2nd International Conference on Advancements in Computing, Proceedings*, 2020, 363–68 <https://doi.org/10.1109/ICAC51239.2020.9357309>.
21. Mohamed A. Kassem, Khalid M. Hosny, and Mohamed M. Fouad, 'Skin Lesions Classification into Eight Classes for ISIC 2019 Using Deep Convolutional Neural Network and Transfer Learning', *IEEE Access*, 8.June (2020), 114822–32 <https://doi.org/10.1109/ACCESS.2020.3003890>.

Computer Science Engineering and Emerging Technologies (ICCS-2022) – Prof (Dr.) Rajeev Sobti et al. (eds)
© 2024 Taylor & Francis Group, London, ISBN 978-1-032-52199-2

Chapter

94

Computational Social Interactions and Trust Models in Virtual Societies

Aseem Kumar[1]

Research Scholar, Lovely Professional University

Arun Malik[2]

Associate Professor, Lovely Professional University

Abstract: In this study, an exploratory examination of the works done in the context of social interaction with trust as the central element has been presented. It was found that no generic model can be established to fully comprehend the dynamics of social trust, but domain-specific computational models or algorithms can be constructed. Each studied computational social interaction model has its own limitations and benefits; however, it is recommended that a hybrid computational model be constructed to advance research work, as multiple parameters from different schools of thought can be added to the model or simulation, allowing us to create the best heuristic model possible in this context. For the sake of illustration, a social trust algorithm that takes inspiration from sociological theories and psychological factors such as sentiment bias has been presented.

Keywords: Trust Models, Covid-19, Sentiments, Digital societies

1. Introduction

As per the dictionary definition of trust, it requires one party (the Trustor) to be willing to put themselves in a vulnerable position in the expectation that the other person (the Trustee) will act in their best interest [1], [2]. In the field of computer science, this concept refers to the capacity of a single piece of software or an agent (Party A) to compute a particular issue in such a way that it satisfies the functional obligation of the system (Party B). It is generally accepted in the social sciences that a trustee does not have direct influence or control over his or her activities. As a consequence of this, it is challenging to "Trust" the other person [3]. Scholars in the field of research study differentiate between generalised trust, also referred to as 'social trust', which is an extension of the core concept of trust but applied to larger and unfamiliar social circles or groups. For instance, during periods of rare and unpresented events, such as unprovoked wars, the trust of the people at large is impacted. The sentiment of trust also gets impacted in cases where the 'effect' of an incident spreads like a fire in the woods and the social fabric of society shifts into new paradigms. In simple words, the level of 'social trust' shifts into something new that society as a whole has never experienced.

In the digital social sciences (the study of digital societies and communities such as Twitter),, the intricacies of 'digital trust' are a topic of continuous research [4]–[6]. In psychology, trust is a measure of a person's or group's belief in another's honesty, fairness, or generosity. The term "confidence" correctly expresses a belief in the 'competence' of the other party that improves the trust level. A breach of trust may be more easily forgiven if it is viewed as a lack of competence or skill rather than a lack of honesty. Frequently, economics defines trust as transactional dependability. In

[1]Aseem.kumar@gmail.com, [2]Arun.17442@lpu.co.in

DOI: 10.1201/9781003405580-94

almost all circumstances, trust is a heuristic judgement rule that helps humans manage complexities that would require infeasible logical effort. To some extent, autonomous algorithm-driven machines also need to make heuristic decisions that need some kind of 'computational trust' as fundamental entities that run the whole ecosystem of humans and machines.

The occurrences such as COVID-19, market crashes, or an unintentional event that changes owing to the course of history and needs careful interpretation are misinterpreted, and sometimes the erroneous connotation floats in society, which generates a tremendous deal of distrust in either society or the market. There is a great deal of background noise surrounding the event, which makes it difficult to obtain clarity, particularly when the source is of a digital nature, such as Twitter. The passage of time is the only thing that enables us to accurately determine which pieces of information ultimately turn out to be crucial. The transmission of false information or an incorrect interpretation of an event occurs at such a breakneck speed over digital platforms for social media that it causes structural shifts in society. Lessons that can be gained from history might not be able to be applied very well to the world as it is today because the structure of the past might be very different from the structure of the future. Researchers, policymakers, and scientists all continue to try their best to generate accurate forecasts of the future. It has been demonstrated numerous times through empirical research that when someone tries to foresee the future, the movement changes and becomes practically impossible to predict. Constructing 'conceptual models' or 'mental models', on the other hand, allows for a certain level of comprehension as well as the accurate interpretation of the issues that are present in particular scenarios. With the assistance of computer simulation models or algorithms, certain situations can be comprehended in order to facilitate improved decision-making. One of these scenarios involves fostering greater trust between two parties, such as the general populace and their respective governments.

In this paper, an attempt will be made to comprehend trust-based digital social interaction models and associated concepts. The following section presents evidence that is connected to the existing ideas, algorithms, models, and conceptions of digital society, including Twitter, Facebook, and other similar platforms. When it comes to the modelling of digital societies, the methodology section provides XXX and the final interpretations, lessons, and conclusions drawn from the research.

2. Literature Review

Literature from modern journals and associated material demonstrates that the notion of "social trust" encompasses a variety of different aspects and must be re-examined in light of the proliferation of new forms of digital technology, alterations in geopolitical situations such as the conflict between Ukraine and Russia, and general behavioural shifts throughout society [7].

It has been determined through narrative and meta-analysis of the numerous research papers on the topic of "social trust" that there are four distinct categories of trust. The very first instance of a "generalised trust" . Facebook is a digital platform where people generally know each other and trust each other to share their personal and family images, whereas Twitter is a platform where the degree of trust between users is lower. As a result, users are less likely to share images of themselves or their families on Twitter. Simply due to the fact that Twitter users communicate with a sizable number of total strangers who are digitally linked. Therefore, the maxim "generalised trust is more," which applies to Twitter, does not hold true for Facebook, while the maxim "In group trust" does apply. Generalised trust, also known as trust in strangers, is an important type of trust in today's modern digital culture because it involves a significant number of social contacts between individuals who have not previously met. The ability of a person to place their faith in their own people or those who are very close to them is referred to as "In-group Trust [8]." "Out-group trust" refers to the trust that an individual has in individuals who belong to a different community or group. This could refer to people of a different racial or ethnic group, as well as people who are citizens of a different country. People from different nations are more likely to interact digitally with one another through the use of platforms such as Twitter and LinkedIn. This is something that can be witnessed here as well. Trust in one's neighbourhood is another type of trust that is prevalent in the real world but not as prevalent in the digital world, due to the fact that in the digital world, a person needs only to "unfollow" or "block" a connection or friend in order to withdraw their trust in that person. This level of trust is more prevalent in the real world. It is abundantly clear that people's feelings and the ways in which they connect digitally with one another as a part of digital society are distinct from the ways in which they interact physically in physical society. As a result, it is possible to draw the conclusion that the interaction dynamics of social trust' will be different in the virtual and physical worlds by making the following inference:

Several publications and the results demonstrated that there is a persistent, albeit minor, negative relationship between ethnic diversity and social trust in the physical world. A similar correlation can be estimated for virtual societies, as there is limited work in this context [9]. The most detrimental effect that ethnic diversity has on trust between neighbours, within groups, and in general is generalised mistrust [10].. Further, it was found that it did not seem to have a major impact on the trust that people had in other groups [11]–[13].

In terms of psychology, the concept of social trust can be understood in the form of the feelings of security and optimism that one feels, thereby alleviating the levels of trust, while failure is characterised by a paradigm of insecurity and mistrust [14]. It's a given that, content with a feeling of trust, individuals are adept at cultivating positive relationships, and this is why trust is a key ingredient in achieving high levels of social well-being.

According to the science of According to the science of psychology, there are three main components to "trust." According to the first definition, trusting someone means opening up or being vulnerable to them, even when you know they won't hurt you. In addition to reliability, trustworthiness is a crucial factor in establishing rapport. The quality that causes somebody to have high hopes for you Third is the "Trust propensity," which is how likely you are to trust someone [15], [16]. The propensity to expose oneself to potential harm at the hands of others Recent studies have shown that this overall tendency can shift over time in response to significant life events. If one of these three conditions is broken, trust will be broken forever. As a result, there is an obvious imbalance between the efforts put into fostering trust and those put into destroying it. Parallels between the real world and online communities like Twitter exist.

Facial resemblance, social identity, In-group favouritism [17], place of origin, and the thought of being from the same tribe or club also increase levels of trust, as per new studies.

According to the research that has been conducted on the topic of interpersonal trust, "trust diagnostics" offer individuals a method by which they can evaluate or adjust the level of trust that exists within their relationships [18]. The term "strain test" refers to an exercise that determines a person's capacity to act in a manner that is beneficial to another person or to a relationship while simultaneously rejecting an alternative that would be in that person's own best interest. Trust diagnostics fall under this category. Trust diagnostic situations can be encountered in everyday interactions, but they can also be created deliberately by those who are curious about how much they can put their faith in another person or in a group. Such trends persist even in the sphere of digital media.

3. Problem Formulation

While trust is crucial to personal and interpersonal well-being, little is understood about its origins, evolution, and maintenance, especially in digital communities like Twitter. Even though trust is crucial to the healthy functioning of individuals and communities, this is not the case in the realm of digital societies. At the same time, it can also be said in reverse that when it comes to the formation of relationships with probable parties who are worthy of trust, human beings have a natural tendency to trust other persons or groups of humans and things, as well as to evaluate the trustworthiness of these entities. The construction of a computer model of "social trust" and the investigation of the influence that concept has on society are difficult tasks. However, the researchers have an advantage when it comes to the study of the dynamics of social trust on platforms such as Twitter because digital platforms have an enormous storehouse of 'written utterances' from which a great deal of inferences can be drawn and a computational model can be constructed, allowing for significant policy-making decisions to be made during times of crisis such as COVID 19. Hence, this work revolves around constructing a computational algorithm for understanding the 'trust dynamics' of visual societies such as Twitter in the wake of unprecedented events such as COVID-19.

4. Methodology

In this section, a theoretical computation model is proposed to understand the dynamics of social trust on virtual platforms such as Twitter. For a better understanding of the research flow, the block diagram can be referred to. The block diagram makes it abundantly clear that the suggested computational model entails capturing how information flows and modifies the dynamics of social trust in the event of an occurrence such as COVID-19 in a digital informal society such as Twitter.

In the same vein, the findings of the literature review make it abundantly evident that there is no one accurate definition of trust; hence, it is not simple to develop a universal or generic computation model. This is one of the reasons why this is the case. In addition, several fields of study, such as economics, philosophy, sociology, and behaviour science, amongst others, each have their own unique perspectives and conceptual models for understanding the concept of "social trust.". Therefore, the following steps are proposed for constructing the computation model:

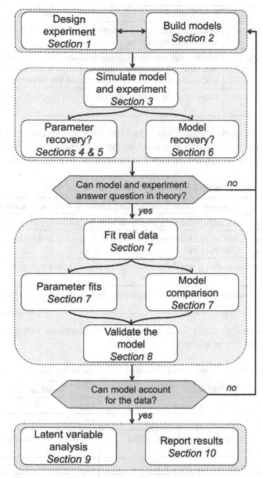

Fig. 94.1 Computational model to understand the dynamics of the social trust in virtual platforms

The issue with which we are primarily concerned is the analysis of "behaviour data," or textual utterances from digital platforms such as Twitter. The analysis of the behavioural data must give us insights into the emotions and sentiments related to the 'trust' of the people. Table 94.1 gives information on the possible types of trust models, useful parameters, and assumptions with respect to the domain from which the computational model may take inspiration.

Table 94.1 Basis and types of trust models or algorithms

S. No	Model Type	Description
1	Sociology [19] [20]	The Social Trust Computational model accounts for the use of contextual elements such as religion, ethnicity, family, physical status, social hierarchy, level of education, digital utterances and geographical location.
2	Psychological Behaviour. [21] [22]	Psychological Influence, Psychological State, digital utterances, vulnerability
3	Economics [23], [24]	When economic transactions take place between two parties, each of those party's current economic standing as well as other relevant elements, such as credit rating, are taken into consideration as the basis for building what is called a "Trust Model".
4	Law & Legal [25], [26]	When aspects such as legal accountability and legal authority, as well as digital utterances and legal environments, play a part in the construction of a computational trust model.

S. No	Model Type	Description
5	Computer Science [27], [28] ,	When interaction and tractions between Man-Machine, Machine-Machine Communication for the basis of trusting
6	Physiological Behaviour [29]	When variations in pulse, blood pressure, breathing rhythm, brain activity, body temperature, and other physiological characteristics are examined as a basis for developing a **trust** model, the model can be broken down into several categories.
7	Combinational Model or Custom Model	When multiple variables are considered for construction of the trust model.

For the sake of constructing the trust mathematical model from real life data, specific conditions and assumptions need to first be accounted for. Hence, a table of statements that make up the problem is given in Table 94.1. With the help of these statements, a computational parameter estimation process can be initiated to construct the sociological trust model.

Table 94.2 Observations on social trust

S. No	Observations on Trust Emotion based on Sociological Aspects
1	The value of trust 't' between two parties is directly proportional to the frequency of their interactions.
2	The value of trust between two or more parties increases when they belong to the same community, place of origin, gender group, ethnicity aggregation , and interests.
3	The value of trust between two parties is directly proportional to the frequency of their interactions in the physical and digital world.
4	The value of trust between two parties or more is directly proportional to the number of 'positive sentiments' expressed in their digital utterances.

By using the observations mentioned in Table 94.2, the variables (exogenous variables) that impact the overall trust (endogenous variable) of the society can be assessed.

Table 94.3 Exogenous variables that impact the 'Social Trust'

Parameter	Definition	DataType	Limits and Ranges
$X1$ = Age	Age of the digital society member	Integer	$18 <= X1 < 100$
$X2$ = Gender	Gender of a person	Enum	Male , Female , Unmentioned
$X3$ = Ethnicity	A state of belonging to a common regional or cultural tradition.	List of enthnic groups	String
$X4$ = places of origins	Place where the person had lived or is living.	List of places of groups	5
$X5$ = hobbies	Interests such as books, sports etc of the person,	List of interests	5
$X6$ = Number of interactions	Number of times a person had conversations with the other party.	Integer	$1 <= X6 < 100$
$X7$ = 'Number of Positive Sentiment Utterances'	From '$X6$' number of interactions, how many digital utterances were positive in nature.	Integer	$X7 = \{1,2,3,.,n\}$, where n= number of positive interactions

With the help of these seven variables, following equations can be formulated between each independent variable ($X1,X2,X3,X4,X5,X6,X7$) and dependent variable (social trust). The X4 and X5 variables have a max range of 5 , which implies that five pieces of evidence are required to determine the trust value.

5. Construction of Algorithm

Let $f(t)$ define the ' 'multiplier effect" function that increases or decreases when the seven independent variables are changed due to the trigger of some event such as covid 19.

Let 'n' be the total number of members of digital society, each member ' having six (computable and observable attributes as explained in Table 94.2 and Table 94.3.

Table 94.4 Variable and Equations used to design the model

Eq. No	Variable	Equation /Condition
1	X1 = Age	if($xa1$ in range($xa1$) = true, then $ts + 1$, where $xa = l$th party, $xb = l$th + 1 party, ts = social trust value, If both parties are the same age, then the level of trust between them will be greater
2	X2 = Gender	$f(tl)$ = if(($xa2l \cap xb2(l + 1)$) = ($xa2l \mid xb2(l + 1)$)) then $ts + 1$ $xa = l$th party, $xb = l$th + 1 party, ts = social trust value, If both partners are of the same gender, their level of trust will be higher
3	X3 = Ethnicity	$f(tl)$ = if(($xa3i \cap xb3(l + 1)$) = ($xa3l \mid xb3(l + 1)$)) then $ts + 1$ $xa = l$th party, $xb = l$th + 1 party, ts = social trust value, If both parties share the same ethnic background, their level of trust will be increased.
4	X4 = places of origins	$f(tl)$ = if(($xa4i \cap xb4(l + 1)$) = ($xa4l \mid xb4(l + 1)$)) then $ts + 1$ $xa = l$th party, $xb = l$th + 1 party, ts = social trust value, If both partners were born or raised in the same location, they will have a higher level of trust compared to those who were born or raised elsewhere
5	X5 = hobbies	$f(tl)$ = if(($xa5l \cap xb5(l + 1)$) = ($xa5l \mid xb5(l + 1)$)) then $ts + 1$ $xa = l$th party, $xb = l$th + 1 party, ts = social trust value, If both people connect with one another and share similar interests, such as reading comparable types of books, their level of trust will increase.
6	X6 = Number of interactions	$f(tl)$ = if(unique($xla6, xb6(l + 1)$) > Threshold, then $ts + 1$ $xa = l$th party, $xb = l$th + 1 party, ts = social trust value, If both parties interact on a digital network such as Twitter, they have incentive to trust one another.
7	X7 = 'Number of Positive Sentiment Utterances'	$f(tl)$ = if(unique($xla7, xb7(l + 1)$) > Positive Threshold,then $ts + 1$ $xa = l$th party, $xb = l$th + 1 party, ts = social trust value. //As both sides connect on a digital network such as Twitter, they will have a motivation to trust one another, and their trustworthiness will rise if they exchange good speech acts.

5.1 Pseudo Logic

$ts = 0$, where ts = social trust.

for each member 'm' in digial$_{society}$, compute 'ts'

    If (Equation1)==true

        $ts = ts + 1$

    If (equation2)==true

        ts = $ts + 1$

    If (equation3)==true

        $ts = ts + 1$

    If (equation4)==true

        $ts = ts + 1$

    If (equation5)==true

        $ts = ts + 1$

    If (compute equation6)>interaction_threshold

        $ts = ts + 1$

    If (Sentiment Analysis)>PositiveSentiment_Threshold

    end for

    return ts .

Tables 94.1, 94.2 and 94.3 and the section on pseudo logic provide information on how to design the model or algorithm for computing the trust score [19]; the algorithm can be expanded to extract more insights from the acquired data. In case , there is a need to find or discover the different levels of 'social trust' the people hold with each other clustering algorithm such as k means can be used and inferences can be drawn from it.

6. Limitations of the Research Work

This work presents foundational notions for developing mathematical reasoning for the purpose of constructing realistic algorithms of 'social trust.' These seven equations and associated operations derive their inspiration from theories presented in recent literature in the fields of sociology, economics, psychology, and other areas. An illustration of how the social trust model or algorithm can be constructed has been provided, which would help aspiring researchers in this field develop higher order mathematical thinking skills. However, the actual implementation of these equations and algorithms or their simulation is outside the purview of this research paper and therefore is not covered in any detail here.

7. Conclusions and Inferences

An exploratory investigation of the various models of social interaction in the context of trust is presented and analysed in the main body of work. It was discovered that a generic model cannot be produced to fully grasp the dynamics of social trust,' but at the same time, it was discovered that domain-specific computational algorithms may be developed with the help of axioms and assumptions taken from domain-specific variables. However, it is better to use a combinational approach, as the algorithm considers multiple parameters from different fields to give a more realistic model of the behaviour. In the case presented here, a psychological factor, i.e., sentiment bias, has been incorporated into the sociologically based variable model to construct a comprehensive algorithm. The extension of this work can further add multiple parameters from different schools of thought and construct realistic heuristic models in this context.

REFERENCES

1. R. J. Zhang, "Social trust and satisfaction with life: A cross-lagged panel analysis based on representative samples from 18 societies.," *Social Science & Medicine*, vol. 251. Elsevier, Mar. 07, 2020.
2. R. M. Kramer and E. M. Uslaner, *Ingroup-Outgroup Trust*. 2017.
3. S. M. Ghafari *et al.*, "Modeling Personality Effect in Trust Prediction," *Journal of Data Intelligence*, vol. 2, no. 4. Rinton Press, pp. 401–417, Nov. 01, 2021.
4. V. Kumar and P. Pradhan, "Trust Management: Social vs. Digital Identity," *International Journal of Service Science Management Engineering and Technology*, vol. 11, no. 4. IGI Publishing, pp. 26–44, Oct. 01, 2020.
5. Z. Yan and S. Holtmanns, "Trust Modeling and Management: From Social Trust to Digital Trust," 2008, pp. 290–323.
6. P. Pradhan and V. Kumar, "Trust Management Models for Digital Identities," *International Journal of Virtual Communities and Social Networking*, vol. 8, no. 4. IGI Publishing, pp. 1–24, Oct. 01, 2016.
7. E. M. Uslaner and E. M. Uslaner, *The Study of Trust*. 2017.
8. B. L. Hughes, N. Ambady, and J. Zaki, "Trusting outgroup, but not ingroup members, requires control: neural and behavioral evidence.," *Social Cognitive and Affective Neuroscience*, vol. 12, no. 3. Oxford University Press, pp. 372–381, Mar. 01, 2017.
9. M. A. Painter and C. Flagg, "Trust and White Ethnic Diversity in Small Town Iowa," *Sociological Quarterly*, vol. 62, no. 2. Taylor & Francis Group (Informa), pp. 234–257, Apr. 03, 2021.
10. P. T. Dinesen, M. Schaeffer, and K. M. Sønderskov, "Ethnic Diversity and Social Trust: A Narrative and Meta-Analytical Review," *Annual Review of Political Science*, vol. 23, no. 1. Annual Reviews, pp. 441–465, May 11, 2020.
11. P. T. Dinesen, K. M. Sønderskov, and E. M. Uslaner, *Ethnic Diversity and Social Trust*. 2017.
12. P. T. Dinesen and K. M. Sønderskov, "Ethnic Diversity and Social Trust: Evidence from the Micro-Context," *American Sociological Review*, vol. 80, no. 3. SAGE Publishing, pp. 550–573, Apr. 21, 2015.
13. B. Gundelach and M. Freitag, "Neighbourhood Diversity and Social Trust: An Empirical Analysis of Interethnic Contact and Group-specific Effects," *Urban Studies*, vol. 51, no. 6. SAGE Publishing, pp. 1236–1256, Aug. 02, 2013.
14. L. Joskowicz-Jabloner and D. Leiser, "Varieties of trust-betrayal: emotion and relief patterns in different domains: Varieties of trust-betrayal," *Journal of Applied Social Psychology*, vol. 43, no. 9. Wiley, pp. 1799–1813, Aug. 21, 2013.
15. J. B. Bernerth and H. J. Walker, "Propensity to Trust and the Impact on Social Exchange: An Empirical Investigation," *Journal of Leadership & Organizational Studies*, vol. 15, no. 3. SAGE Publishing, pp. 217–226, Oct. 30, 2008.
16. L. van der Werff, Y. Freeney, C. E. Lance, and F. Buckley, "A Trait-State Model of Trust Propensity: Evidence From Two Career Transitions.," *Frontiers in Psychology*, vol. 10. Frontiers Media S.A., Jan. 01, 2019.
17. W. Li, L. M. W. Li, and M. Li, "Residential mobility reduces ingroup favouritism in prosocial behaviour," *Asian Journal Of Social Psychology*, vol. 22, no. 1. Wiley, pp. 3–17, Sep. 06, 2018.
18. A. C. Weinschenk and C. T. Dawes, "The genetic and psychological underpinnings of generalized social trust," *Journal of Trust Research*, vol. 9, no. 1. Taylor & Francis Group (Informa), pp. 47–65, Jan. 02, 2019.
19. J. Golbeck, "Introduction to Computing with Social Trust," 2009, pp. 1–5.

20. R. Hardin, "Trust: A Sociological Theory, Piotr Sztompka. Cambridge University Press, 1999, xii + 214pages.," *Economics and Philosophy*, vol. 18, no. 01. Cambridge University Press, pp. 183–204, Mar. 14, 2002.
21. E. CHOI and J. WOO, "The Origins of Political Trust in East Asian Democracies: Psychological, Cultural, and Institutional Arguments," *Japanese Journal of Political Science*, vol. 17, no. 3. Cambridge University Press, pp. 410–426, Aug. 12, 2016.
22. A. Hidayat, "Effect of Information Quality, Social Psychological Distance, and Trust on Consumer Purchase Intentions on Social Commerce Shopee," *Archives of Business Research*, vol. 10, no. 1. Scholar Publishing, pp. 158–172, Jan. 28, 2022.
23. A. Tatarko, "Personal trust and economic behavior in a social dilemma," *Theoretical Economics*, no. 3. INSTITUTE OF ECONOMICS RAS, Theoretical Economics Issues, pp. 75–87, Jan. 01, 2021.
24. "The rationality of trust: Trust and Trustworthiness," *International Journal of Social Economics*, vol. 32, no. 3. Emerald Group, pp. 268–269, Mar. 01, 2005.
25. K. Vallier, "Social and Political Trust: Concepts, Causes, and Consequences," 2020, pp. 49–87.
26. R. Tao, D. L. Yang, M. Li, and X. Lu, "How does political trust affect social trust? An analysis of survey data from rural China using an instrumental variables approach," *International Political Science Review*, vol. 35, no. 2. SAGE Publishing, pp. 237–253, Jul. 12, 2013.
27. A. Grüner, A. Mühle, M. Meinig, and C. Meinel, "A Taxonomy of Trust Models for Attribute Assurance in Identity Management," 2020, pp. 65–76.
28. S. Y. Lim, O. B. Musa, B. A. S. Al-Rimy, and A. Almasri, "Trust Models for Blockchain-Based Self-Sovereign Identity Management: A Survey and Research Directions," 2022, pp. 277–302.
29. S. R. Potts, W. T. McCuddy, D. Jayan, and A. J. Porcelli, "To trust, or not to trust? Individual differences in physiological reactivity predict trust under acute stress.," *Psychoneuroendocrinology*, vol. 100. Elsevier, pp. 75–84, Sep. 25, 2018.

Note: All figures and tables in this document were created by Author.

Computer Science Engineering and Emerging Technologies (ICCS-2022) – Prof (Dr.) Rajeev Sobti et al. (eds)
© 2024 Taylor & Francis Group, London, ISBN 978-1-032-52199-2

Chapter

95

Scheduling Techniques for Convergecast in Multichannel Wireless Sensor Networks: A Review and Issues

Vishav Kapoor[1]

Research Scholar, Department of Electronics & Communication,
Lovely Professional University, Punjab, India

Daljeet Singh[2]

Assistant Professor, Department of Electronics &Communication,
Lovely Professional University, Punjab, India
Faculty of Medicine, Research Unit of Health Sciences and Technology,
University of Oulu, Finland

Abstract: In today's highly competitive environment, consumers have limited tolerance for long information-gathering procedures. This has restricted researchers ability to gather data in a timely manner. Convergecast transmission is a potential technique for rapid communication. In convergecast, each sensor node transmits its own packet straight to the sink node, bypassing the intermediate node. Multichannel allocation is one of the most important aspects of efficiency enhancement. This paper describes and examines the various scheduling techniques used to achieve convergecast efficiency in WSN. On the basis of parameters such as energy, length of schedule, and robustness, a comparative assessment of scheduling strategies has been performed. Additionally, open research issues have been established so that convergent mechanisms in WSN might be researched in the future.

Keywords: Wireless sensor networks, Convergecast, Multichannel, Scheduling, TDMA, MAC

1. Introduction

Wireless sensor networks (WSNs) are made up of low-power, low-capacity nodes that communicate with each other using radio waves. Sensor nodes are devices that work with other devices in a network to do something, like monitor the environment. In the last ten years, the number of connected devices has grown rapidly [1]. It's hard to go anywhere these days without running into at least one device that's connected to the internet. WSNs [2] are a part of this trend that can be used in more than one way. Different MAC protocols are a key part of making sure that these networks meet their needs for power use and latency. Power utilization and delay are two of the biggest problems with WSN, especially when it comes to business processes. In wireless communications, it is hard to use the least amount of power while maintaining a high throughput and no data loss. Power consumption is a big problem because sensors often need to run for weeks or even decades without human help or battery replacement.

In recent years, there have been a number of research developments focused on making these kinds of algorithms in order to solve these different problems. These scheduling techniques are classified as centralized [3], distributed [4], and independent [5–6]. With centralized scheduling, all of the network information is gathered in one place, and the link schedules are made from there. But when the topology changes, the base node may get too busy and slow down updates to

[1]vishavkapoor55@gmail.com, [2]daljeet.23804@lpu.co.in

DOI: 10.1201/9781003405580-95

network information. In the past few years, WSNs have come a long way. Nodes close to a MWSN have access to different channels for sending and receiving data. Each channel is made up of a pair of nodes. With MWSNs, it is possible to collect more data at a faster rate because more data can be transferred at once. Multiple channels on different nodes need to switch channels often, which wastes time and energy. MWSNs use channels and time slots that work together to avoid scheduling conflicts.

In the first part of the paper, the introduction is given. In the second section, it is explained what other researchers have done. In the third part of the paper, a comparison has been made between scheduling and multichannel algorithms based on different factors. In the 4th section, the open research issues are discussed, and the 5th section is the conclusion and future work.

2. Related Works

In this section, we describe the work that other researchers have done in the field of convergecast related to the scheduling algorithms in WSN. Some of the most important works have been discussed here.

In centralized systems, network data is sent to a central organization, which then schedules connections. In TASA, the schedule is made by a single node [7]. The network's layout and current traffic levels are taken into account to determine the schedule followed by each node. CLS [3] allocates and releases slots without modifying the whole schedule every CLS to decrease idle flow, resulting in efficient multi-hop schedules with a small number of centralized control messages. In [8], the authors introduced Multichannel Optimized Delay Time Slot Assignment (MODESA), which is a centralized raw convergecast type. DeTAS [4] deals with networks that have a lot of sink nodes. In [9], the authors suggest a method for scheduling that is based on waves. Each sending node is allotted a certain amount of time in a specific channel for sending its packets during each wave. In [10], a proposal was made for DeAMON, which is a decentralized mechanism for 6TiSCH wireless networks. Later on, a distributed divergence cast scheduling method called DIVA [11] was made.

Autonomous scheduling is better for the network than centralized and distributed scheduling because it uses less bandwidth. Orchestra [5] began auto-scheduling TSCH. Orchestra is a new way for TSCH to schedule jobs that uses basic criteria to speed up the rate of delivery. Escalator [12] is an autonomous scheduling method that uses Orchestra. It makes a sequential timeslot plan along the packet transmission pipeline to cut down on latency. Also, in [6], the authors tried to cut down on orchestra delays by changing the order in which they played. The authors of [13] propose a deterministic TDMA scheduling technique for dispersed networks.

FlexiTP, presented in [14], is a unique TDMA protocol that provides a synchronized and flexible slot structure. A distributed and scalable scheduling accessing approach was presented in [15], which can accommodate some mobility and reduces the amount of data lost in data-intensive sensor networks. Some other relevant work has been done by researches in context of scheduling in multichannel WSN [16-20]. Some recent work has also been done in this context [21-22].

3. Comparative Analysis of Scheduling Techniques

In this section, a comparison of the different ways that convergecast is done in WSN has been made. As already discussed about, convergecast is being put into three categories: aggregate, raw, and general. Also, the energy used, the length of the schedule, and the ability to handle problems are the most important things to look at when evaluating how well the different convergecast techniques work. In this direction, Table 95.1 shows a comparison of different things.

Table 95.1 Metric based evaluation of convergecast techniques

Reference	Aggregate Convergecast	Raw Convergecast	General Convergecast	Energy	Schedule Length	Robustness
[16]	✗	✗	✓	✗	✗	✓
[13]	✗	✗	✓	✗	✗	✗
[14]	✗	✓	✗	✗	✗	✗
[17]	✓	✗	✗	✓	✗	✗
[15]	✗	✗	✓	✗	✗	✗
[18]	✓	✗	✗	✓	✗	✗
[19]	✗	✓	✗	✓	✗	✗
[20]	✗	✓	✗	✗	✓	✗

Based on the scheduling algorithms and fault-tolerance methods listed above, it can be said that joint scheduling or general convergecast algorithms are better than other methods. The length of the schedule would be short on a small network. But the length of schedules would be long on a big network. If something happens in one part of the network, the nodes in a big network will have to wait longer for their turn to send. Some ways could be made to support data transmission based on priority. That is, nodes usually send data in the slot that was given to them. But if urgent information needs to be sent, it should be sent quickly. It can be assumed that the schedules for aggregate methods are shorter and that they use less energy. On the other hand, there are no robust features. So, for faster data transfer, researchers need to come up with methods that use less energy, can handle mistakes, and have the shortest schedules.

4. Open Issues

In the field of multichannel convergecast, researchers still need to learn more about a lot of things. Majorly channeled allocation, designing of convergecast framework, and energy-efficient methods are the main problems that need to be solved. But there are other unanswered questions that need more research.

Changing channels: For the radio to alter stations, it needs time. The changeover time should fit into the size of the time slot, and the extra time needed to make the switch is small.

Blended Approach: A blended strategy is best for raw convergent. It might be interesting to make a blended joint scheduler for raw convergecast in which each node initially selects a slot to send its own packet and afterwards selects slots to send its children's notifications.

Data Security: Security is a crucial thing to think about when gathering a lot of data. This is because, when dealing with these kinds of problems, aggregators often give out wrong information.

Dynamic Environment: However, things like the unpredictability of wireless connections, the mobility of nodes, and changes in traffic conditions make it hard to build multichannel WSNs.

Power Management: Using multiple transceivers on the sensor nodes and figuring out how much energy the current multi-channel protocols use could be important areas of research.

5. Conclusion and Future Work

In this paper, we discuss some of the problems that arise when there are multiple channels of communication in converged networks. When many channels are used, the convergecast algorithm has much less delay and works much better. We have compared and contrasted many approaches for covergecast scheduling in multichannel WSN based on metrics like energy, schedule length, and robustness. From the above literature review, it can be inferred that channel assignment is one of the most important things that affects how well a convergecast strategy works. It can be assumed that the schedules for aggregate methods are shorter and that they use less energy. On the other hand, there are no robust features. So, for faster data transfer, researchers need to come up with methods that use less energy, can handle mistakes, and have the shortest schedules. Since energy use is one of the biggest concerns in sensor networks, future research will look at ways to save even more energy by using more than one channel. Energy will also be saved by looking into ways to manage transmission power on the nodes, and the security of the information that is sent will be researched further.

REFERENCES

1. Balazka, S. D., & Rodighiero, D. (2020). Big data and the little big bang: an epistemological (R) evolution. *Frontiers in Big Data, 3.*
2. Kandris, D., Nakas, C., Vomvas, D., & Koulouras, G. (2020). Applications of Wireless Sensor Networks: An up-to-date survey. *Applied System Innovation, 3*(1), 14.
3. hoi, K.-H., & Chung, S.-H. (2016). A new centralized link scheduling for 6TiSCH wireless industrial networks. In *Lecture Notes in Computer Science* (pp. 360–371). Springer International Publishing.
4. Accettura, N., Palattella, M. R., Boggia, G., Grieco, L. A., & Dohler, M. (2013). Decentralized Traffic Aware Scheduling for multi-hop Low power Lossy Networks in the Internet of Things. *2013 IEEE 14th International Symposium on "A World of Wireless, Mobile and Multimedia Networks" (WoWMoM).*
5. Duquennoy, S., Nahas, B., Landsiedel, O., & Watteyne, T. (2015). Orchestra: Robust mesh networks through autonomously scheduled TSCH. In *Proceedings of the 13th ACM conference on embedded networked sensor systems* (pp. 337–350).

6. Rekik, S., Baccour, N., Jmaiel, M., Drira, K., & Grieco, L. A. (2018). Autonomous and traffic-aware scheduling for TSCH networks. *Computer Networks, 135*, 201–212.
7. Palattella, M. R., Accettura, N., Dohler, M., Grieco, L. A., & Boggia, G. (2012). Traffic aware scheduling algorithm for reliable low-power multi- hop IEEE 802.15. 4e networks. In *2012 IEEE 23rd International Symposium on Personal, Indoor and Mobile Radio Communications- (PIMRC)* (pp. 327–332). IEEE.
8. Soua, R., Minet, P., & Livolant, E. (2012). MODESA: An optimized multichannel slot assignment for raw data convergecast in wireless sensor networks. *2012 IEEE 31st International Performance Computing and Communications Conference (IPCCC)*.
9. Soua, R., Minet, P., & Livolant, E. (2016). Wave: a distributed scheduling algorithm for convergecast in IEEE 802.15. 4e TSCH networks. *Transactions on Emerging Telecommunications Technologies, 27*, 557–575.
10. Aijaz, A., & Raza, U. (2017). DeAMON: A decentralized adaptive multi- hop scheduling protocol for 6TiSCH wireless networks. *IEEE Sensors Journal, 17*(20), 6825–6836.
11. Demir, A. K., & Bilgili, S. (2019). DIVA: a distributed divergecast scheduling algorithm for IEEE 802.15. 4e TSCH networks. *Wireless Networks, 25*(2), 625–635.
12. Oh, S., Hwang, D., Kim, K.-H., & Kim, K. (2018). Escalator: An autonomous scheduling scheme for convergecast in TSCH. *Sensors (Basel, Switzerland), 18*(4).
13. Wang, Y., & Henning, I. (2007). A deterministic distributed TDMA scheduling algorithm for wireless sensor networks. *2007 International Conference on Wireless Communications, Networking and Mobile Computing*.
14. Lee, W. L., Datta, A., & Cardell-Oliver, R. (2008). FlexiTP: A flexible- schedule-based TDMA protocol for fault-tolerant and energy-efficient wireless sensor networks. *IEEE Transactions on Parallel and Distributed Systems: A Publication of the IEEE Computer Society, 19*(6), 851–864.
15. Lin, C.-K., Zadorozhny, V., Krishnamurthy, P., Park, H.-H., & Lee, C.-G. (2011). A distributed and scalable time slot allocation protocol for wireless sensor networks. *IEEE Transactions on Mobile Computing, 10*(4), 505–518.
16. Rhee, I., Warrier, A., Min, J., & Xu, L. (2006). DRAND: distributed randomized TDMA scheduling for wireless ad-hoc networks. In *Proceedings of the 7th ACM international symposium on Mobile ad hoc networking and computing* (pp. 190–201).
17. Wu, F.-J., & Tseng, Y.-C. (2009). Distributed wake-up scheduling for data collection in tree-based wireless sensor networks. *IEEE Communications Letters: A Publication of the IEEE Communications Society, 13*(11), 850–852.
18. Yu, C., Fiske, R., Park, S., & Kim, W. T. (2012). Many-to-one communication protocol for wireless sensor networks. *International Journal of Sensor Networks, 12*(3), 160.
19. Bagaa, M., Younis, M., Ksentini, A., & Badache, N. (2013). Multi-path multi-channel data aggregation scheduling in wireless sensor networks. *2013 IFIP Wireless Days (WD)*.
20. Zeng, B., & Dong, Y. (2014). A collaboration-based distributed TDMA scheduling algorithm for data collection in wireless sensor networks. *Journal of Networks, 9*(9).
21. Sah, D. K., Amgoth, T., & Cengiz, K. (2022). Energy efficient medium access control protocol for data collection in wireless sensor network: A Q- learning approach," Sustain. *Sustain. Energy Technol. Assessments, 53*(102530).
22. Hammoudi, S., Ourzeddine, H., Gueroui, M., Harous, S., & Aliouat, Z. (2022). A collision-free scheduling algorithm with minimum data redundancy transmission for TSCH. *Wireless Personal Communications, 124*(4), 3159–3188.

Computer Science Engineering and Emerging Technologies (ICCS-2022) – Prof (Dr.) Rajeev Sobti et al. (eds)
© 2024 Taylor & Francis Group, London, ISBN 978-1-032-52199-2

Chapter

96

A Survey on User Stories Using NLP for Agile Development

Bodem Niharika[1], Shivali Chopra[2]

Lovely Professional University, Phagwara

Abstract: The team of developers needs to learn as much as possible about the software at the initial phase of the procedure so that they can create a solid strategy. Members of the team should also properly examine any data associated with the change. Estimating how long it will take to create software is a common problem in the software engineering industry and is known as software development effort estimation (SDEE). Each iteration of an agile methodology project delivers a collection of specifications recognized as the product backlog. In agile projects, user stories are commonly used as objects for documenting customer needs. They are relatively brief fragments of writing that have a semi-structured style and demonstrate specific needs. Implementations that make use of user stories could benefit from NLP methods. This paper gives an overview of research in natural language processing studies of product backlogs. The search showed the main research articles about NLP methods in user stories. Most of this research employed natural language processing methods to retrieve (who, what, and why) details from backlogs. The goals of natural language processing research on backlogs are varied and can include finding bugs, creating software artifacts, pinpointing the stories' central abstractions, and following the threads connecting the frameworks and the stories themselves. Domain experts could use natural language processing to control and manage story points. There are a variety of advantages and disadvantages to integrating NLP into user stories. To produce high-quality studies, researchers need to learn about and experiment with various NLP methods and then subject those results to thorough assessment processes. In the field of natural language processing, context understanding remains a formidable obstacle.

Keywords: User stories, Story point estimation, Natural language processing, NLP approaches, and Agile software development

1. Introduction

The introduction of user stories into the software project is becoming incredibly common, particularly within the realm of agile software development. The user story is the object that is utilized most frequently in the development of agile software [1] [2], and it is used to convey necessities from the perspective of the customers.

User stories are a form of initial planning that is expressed in natural language and adopts a semi-structured format. Important aspects of the specifications are: WHO needs it, WHAT is estimated from the device, and WHY it is significant [3] [4].

This field of research has seen an influx of practitioners and researchers in recent years due to the growing popularity of agile methodology [1], [5], and [6]. The user stories that are used in developing agile projects are the objects that are employed the most, and exploring them can be difficult.

[1]niharikabkr@gmail.com, [2]shivali.19259@lpu.co.in

DOI: 10.1201/9781003405580-96

Which are written in human-understandable language, making it very simple for anyone involved in the process to comprehend them. On the other hand, specifications written in natural language have a number of flaws, including uncertainty, inaccuracy, and imperfection [7], [8], [9].

Methodologies that use natural language processing (NLP) have the capability to provide benefits that could help improve the overall standard of product backlogs. The data from user stories can be tokenized, derived, or evaluated with the help of NLP. In the field of computing, it has seen widespread application as a useful tool such as controlling technical specifications [10], testing is the process [13], collecting actors and activities from technical specifications [11], and collecting technical capabilities [12].

The NLP methodology, when applied to product backlog, has been used in some studies as a means of speeding up the process of determining system specifications. As natural language processing research on the user story path is still relatively new, it would be exciting to gain a comprehensive awareness of its path. This study intends to provide practitioners and researchers with insights regarding recent research based on NLP and product backlog development.

In addition to that, the findings of this study point the way for potential future research concerning user stories. This review of literature is being performed to attain these goals in order to coincide with the agile methodology, which calls for the discovery of more effective ways of producing software. Our particular goals include gaining an understanding of the research methods and tools that have been applied to the various user story research questions that have been investigated. In addition to that, difficulties encountered during NLP research will be highlighted in user stories.

2. Literature Review

In this paper, M. R. Hossain et al. use CNN to classify Bengali text. The classified text produced 96.85% accuracy, which is superior to existing approaches [14]. We offer a CNN-based model with "fast text" embedding for resource-constrained languages. Bengali texts are used to evaluate the suggested model's performance. Different CNN hyperparameters are applied to enhance categorization. The proposed strategy outperformed existing strategies on test datasets. Data can include more textual document classifications. Elmo and BERT are other word embedding approaches to explore. Future research is needed [14]. The agile approach evaluates specific tasks simultaneously, not full projects. We estimate story points using RNNs and CNNs. We assess a user story's forward and RNN-CNN models built backwards. The suggested system used BiLSTM, RNNs, and CNNs to estimate a user story point by Sardar M. N. Islam. BiLSTM forward and backward feature learning will maintain the network, and CNN and sequence data will improve extractions.

This study identified the RNNs-CNNs method for story point prediction [15]. It produced 74.2% accuracy. In the further development, we will include Multiple channels and multiple to encode user tale descriptions simultaneously [15].

Among the many possible methods for creating statistical methods for predicting the time and effort required to create agile software, the story point method stands out. Beginning with the project's overall pace and the number of story points, analysis was taken into account to determine how much work would be needed to create agile software. Next, several neural networks, including GRNNs, PNNs, GMDH networks, and cascade networks, are used to improve the resulting values [16].

The study concludes with an empirical validation and comparison of the results produced by several neural network models. The results show that the cascading network is the most effective. MATLAB was used to carry out the calculations necessary for the previous approaches and get the resulting data. It is possible to further develop this method by using more ML strategies like SGB (stochastic gradient boosting), RF (random forest), etc. [16].

In this study, we will explore scrum as a case study to talk about agile approaches, with a particular emphasis on the prediction of work and its impact on the project as measured by a variety of indicators. Budget, effort, and difficulty are the primary areas of focus when making estimates during a project's life cycle. Measures will make it simpler and more reliable for teams to monitor and assess software development progress and provide software in a consistent and timely manner. Because of this [17], the following article will highlight factors that are frequently overlooked by production staff while estimating.

Measures play a crucial part in teamwork because they allow you to monitor the teams' progress up until the point where they deliver the product. It is still necessary to investigate and implement more metrics linked to scrum and estimation into the existing development situation in order to further strengthen the agile team and process. In addition, this paper features the graphical representations of each statistic using Jira by Atlassian, an organization that is actively promoting agile software development [17].

Tawosi et al. [18], discussed here, 9LHC-SE is a unique way to estimate Story Points. In this paper, LHC and LDA methods are used for story point estimations. This model assumes that grouping comparable data points reduces variance and boosts model accuracy. We expect these poor results to push experts to develop better story point estimation algorithms.

- Advanced data cleaning and analysis before model development.
- Using alternative NLP text representation models beyond LDA.
- Collecting and exploiting issue-report-derived effort-informative features.
- Instead of baseline estimators, utilize machine learning on each cluster [18].

Alaa El-deen Hamoud introduces a technique and approach for scaling software with user stories in agile. The story point is used for the organization, not the project [19]. After integrating agile story points in CMMI businesses, size accuracy enhances. To conclude the prediction process, a story-point-based effort estimation enhancement is introduced and tested. The proposed methodology improves estimating accuracy from 28% to 5.9% [19].

Karner's model [28] Nonfunctional requirements are also undervalued. To overcome these constraints, machine learning was developed. It reduces the effort estimation error by 34% to 12%.

Zahraoui et al. [20] and Mohammed et al. both updated user story point computations utilizing priority, size, and complexity factors to generate more accurate effort and time estimations (CF). We recommended using Adjusted Story Points (ASP) to estimate a scrum project's total effort (SP). This paper shows how to leverage [2]'s Adjusted Story Point (ASP) to improve the estimation of scrum [20].

Choetkiertikul et al. [21] proposed story point estimation techniques using LSTM and Recurrent Highway networks. Our prediction system is "end-to-end". The evaluation of our methodology will be aided by increasing our evaluation to include industrial software and major projects that are open-source. We also model the evolution of teams over time using team analytics and incorporate that data into our forecasting framework. As part of our model development, we intend to learn a syntactic description of the source code [21]. We'll also try sliding windows for incremental learning. We'll also study how to incorporate issue metadata (such as priority and type) while maintaining our model's end-to-end nature.

A future study will compare the LSTM model against others, such as paragraph2vec [25] and Convolutional Neural networks [26]. We have described our work with agile and story-point-estimating software developers. Our prediction system was liked by all.

In this article, Macarious Abadeer and Mehrdad Sabetzadeh evaluate story points in an industrial development. It contains 4,727 stories by IQVIA's 27-person ASD team. Our results show that model effectiveness relates to story qualities like detail, depth, and vagueness. Before introducing the ML approach to estimate agile development, firms should embrace agile best practices, especially story point writers and estimation by experts [22].

Future affinity estimations will use a classification-based methodology. We would like to repeat our study after putting the lessons from our ongoing work into practice by using understandable artificial intelligence Methods like integrated gradients [24] to measure ambiguous words and specific sensations in model predictions.

Michael Fu and Chakkrit Tantithamthavorn [23] introduced GPT2SP is an agile transformer-based story point estimation method. Our GPT2SP model is a pre-trained model that specifies syntax and logic and is transferable and easy to interpret. We found that our GPT2SP methodology is 34-57% more accurate than existing baseline methods for within-project predictions and 39-49% more accurate for cross-project predictions. Our approach's GPT2 technology improves Deep-SE by 6%-47%, exhibiting AI for story point estimation [23]. Sixteen Agile practitioners told us that AI-based story point estimation with reasons is more credible. 69% of participants consider implementing AI-based Agile Story Point Estimations if coupled to modern software development tools like JIRA, proving the need for our Explainable AI-based story point estimation technique [23].

In this Review paper, user stories and NLP techniques are determined for text classification. For future scope, we need to use machine learning and AI for accurate results. Because ML and AI produce good results, future work

3. Prediction System

In this prediction process we are going to see some basic questions which is related to our study on user stories and natural language processing.

3.1 Research Related Questions

1. Which algorithms and methods are used for prediction of user stories using NLP?
2. Which algorithms are accurate to perform?
3. What type of datasets available for user stories in web?

Now we are going to see the research related questions overview prediction on user stories using NLP.

1. Which algorithms and methods are used for prediction of user stories using NLP?

Many verities of algorithms and methods are used in Agile Methodology. Below Table 96.1. Determines the different factors in the table and give the clear representation.

Table 96.1   Algorithms already used for prediction of user stories in NLP

Authors	Algorithms	Publication
[16]	GRNN	2015
[16]	PNN	2015
[16]	GMDH	2015
[16]	Cascade-correlation neural networks	2015
[22]	LSTM	2021
[21]	LSTM+RF	2019
[21]	LSTM+SVM	2019
[21]	LSTM+ATLM	2019
[21]	LSTM+LR	2019
[23]	GPT2SP	2022
[15]	BiLSTM	2020
[15]	RNN	2020
[15]	CNN	2020
[14]	Word2Vec	2021
[14]	CNN	2021

Source: Author's compilation

2. Which algorithms are accurate to perform?

The Following Table 96.2. Show the accuracy of the different works.

Table 96.2   Accuracy of different techniques

Papers	Algorithms	Accuracy
[14]	Word2Vec, GloVe and CNN.	96%
[16]	GRNN, PNN, GMDH and Cascade-correlation neural networks.	95%
[15]	BiLSTM, RNN and CNN.	74%
[22]	LSTM.	60%
[23]	GPT2SP.	53%

Source: Author's compilation

3. What type of datasets available for user stories in web?

In the following Table 96.3. We are discussing about the datasets available in web for the user stories.

Table 96.3   Available user stories datasets

Datasets	Papers
9,779 tested information.	[14]
16 open-source software projects.	[15]
21 SW projects datasets Implemented by 6 SW organizations by Zia9.	[16]
09 open-source projects which uses JIRA Issue Tracking System.	[21]
4,727 stories developed by 27 member's team at HealthCare Company IQVIA.	[22]
16 open-source projects by JIRA.	[23]

Source: Author's compilation

In Table 96.4, all the work which is discussed in literature review of our paper is represented as prediction system as follows:

Table 96.4   Overview of user stories using NLP

Titles	Approches used	Metodology or related study	Accuracy
[23]	- GPT2SP.	Explainable AI-based.	57%
[22]	-Deep-Se -LSTM.	Machine Learning-based.	60%
[21]	-LSTM	Deep Learning -based.	40% to 60%
[15]	-BiLSTM -RNN -CNN.	Deep Learning – based.	74.2 %
[14]	-Word2Vec -GloVe -CNN.	Deep Learning-based.	96.85%
[16]	-GRNN -PNN -GMDH -CNN	Machine Learning-based	95%
[20]	-PF -SF -CF.	Planning poker	-
[19]	-MER.	Machine Learning-based	Error decreases from 28% to 5.9%.
[18]	-LDA -LCH.	Machine Learning-based	-
[17]	-Scrum Approach.	JIRA used for diagrammatic representation	-

Source: Author's compilation

In this section we have seen prediction of algorithms, accuracies and datasets which are used by the researches to solve the problems in works. So, the next section determine the overview of our research.

4. Conclusion

This research provides a systematic literature review (SLR) illustration of how NLP is being used in user stories. After that, we conducted an assessment of the research. Here are some of the most important takeaways from the SLR: So many works are viewpoints that illustrate thoughts by illustrating how concepts can be put into practice, suggesting that more research is imminent. Abstractions, identifications of user story points, and the creation of methods or artifacts from user story points are common types of studies. Although POS tags remain the most popular NLP technique, semantic approaches are making inroads. The use of a case study in the evaluation of research is widespread. As research progresses, however, the precision-recall approach will become standard practice. Like other areas of NLP study, this one has a lot of work to do in terms of comprehending the bigger picture of a sentence. We think the results of this study can inform future NLP research involving user stories. Based on our analysis, further investigation into this area of study is needed. More varied and helpful outcomes may be attainable with further refinement of the NLP application. Several natural language processing research findings on user stories also demonstrated solid groundwork, including abstract concepts retrieval of story points, SW OBJ from user story points, user story point's comparison, prioritized, scale prediction, valuable user story points, and story point retrieval. In the end, we wish that this research would also be a place of success for those on the ASD spectrum. It's possible that studies of more general topics, like planning and specification protection upkeep, would also inspire enthusiasm. Both academics and professionals can benefit from increased industry participation.

REFERENCES

1. E. M. Schön, J. Thomaschewski, and M. J. Escalona, "Agile requirements engineering: A systematic literature review," Comput. Stand. Interface, vol. 49, pp. 79–91, 2017, doi: 10.1016/j.csi.2016.08.011.
2. R. Noel, F. Riquelme, R. M. Lean, E. Merino, C. Cechinel, T. S. Barcelos, R. Villarroel, and R. Munoz, "Exploring collaborative writing of user stories with multimodal learning analytics: A case study on a software engineering course," IEEE Access, vol. 6, pp. 67783–67798, 2018, doi: 10.1109/ACCESS.2018.2876801.
3. Y. Wautelet, S. Heng, M. Kolp, and I. Mirbel, "Unifying and extending user story models," in Advanced Information Systems Engineering (Lecture Notes in Computer Science), vol. 8484. New York, NY, USA: Springer, 2014.
4. G. Lucassen, F. Dalpiaz, J. M. E. M. van der Werf, and S. Brinkkemper, "Improving agile requirements: The quality user story framework and tool," Requirements Eng., vol. 21, no. 3, pp. 383–403, Sep. 2016, doi: 10.1007/s00766-016-0250-x.
5. I. Inayat, S. S. Salim, S. Marczak, M. Daneva, and S. Shamshirband, "A systematic literature review on agile requirements engineering practices and challenges," Comput. Hum. Behav., vol. 51, pp. 915–929, Oct. 2015, doi: 10.1016/j.chb.2014.10.046.
6. M. Younas, D. N. A. Jawawi, M. A. Shah, A. Mustafa, M. Awais, M. K. Ishfaq, and K. Wakil, "Elicitation of nonfunctional requirements in agile development using cloud computing environment," IEEE Access, vol. 8, pp. 209153–209162, 2020, doi: 10.1109/access.2020.3014381.
7. H. Meth, M. Brhel, and A. Maedche, "The state of the art in automated requirements elicitation," Inf. Softw. Technol., vol. 55, no. 10, pp. 1695–1709, Oct. 2013, doi: 10.1016/j.infsof.2013.03.008.
8. A. R. da Silva, "Linguistic patterns and linguistic styles for requirements specification (I): An application case with the rigorous RSL/business-level language," in Proc. 22nd Eur. Conf. Pattern Lang. Programs, Jul. 2017, pp. 1–27, doi: 10.1145/3147704.3147728.
9. H. Dar, M. I. Lali, H. Ashraf, M. Ramzan, T. Amjad, and B. Shahzad, "A systematic study on software requirements elicitation techniques and its challenges in mobile application development," IEEE Access, vol. 6, pp. 63859–63867, 2018, doi: 10.1109/ACCESS.2018.2874981.
10. M. Arias, A. Buccella, and A. Cechich, "A framework for managing requirements of software product lines," Electron. Notes Theor. Comput. Sci., vol. 339, pp. 5–20, Jul. 2018, doi: 10.1016/j.entcs.2018.06.002.
11. A. Al-Hroob, A. T. Imam, and R. Al-Heisa, "The use of artificial neural networks for extracting actions and actors from requirements document," Inf. Softw. Technol., vol. 101, pp. 1–15, Sep. 2018, doi: 10.1016/j.infsof.2018.04.010.
12. T. Johann, C. Stanik, A. M. B. Alizadeh, and W. Maalej, "SAFE: A simple approach for feature extraction from app descriptions and app reviews," in Proc. IEEE 25th Int. Requirements Eng. Conf., 2017, pp. 21–30, doi: 10.1109/RE.2017.71.
13. V. Garousi, S. Bauer, and M. Felderer, "NLP-assisted software testing: A systematic mapping of the literature," Inf. Softw. Technol., vol. 126, Oct. 2020, Art. No. 106321, doi: 10.1016/j.infsof.2020.106321.
14. Md. Rajib Hossain, Mohammed Moshiul Hoque(B), and Iqbal H. Sarker," Text Classification Using Convolution Neural Networks with Fast Text Embedding,"in springer link., 20th international conference on HIS 2021, vol.1375, pp. 120–132, doi: 10.1007/978-3-030-73050-5.
15. Marapelli, Bhaskar, Anil Carie, and Sardar MN Islam. "RNN-CNN MODEL: A bi-directional long short-term memory deep learning network for story point estimation." *2020 5th International Conference on Innovative Technologies in Intelligent Systems and Industrial Applications (CITISIA)*. IEEE, 2020.
16. Panda, Aditi, Shashank Mouli Satapathy, and Santanu Kumar Rath. "Empirical validation of neural network models for agile software effort estimation based on story points." *Procedia Computer Science* 57 (2015): 772–781.
17. Ahmed, Ali Raza, et al. "Impact of story point estimation on product using metrics in scrum development process." *International Journal of Advanced Computer Science and Applications* 8.4 (2017).
18. Tawosi, Vali, Afnan Al-Subaihin, and Federica Sarro. "Investigating the Effectiveness of Clustering for Story Point Estimation." IEEE, 2022.

19. Hamouda, Alaa El Deen. "Using agile story points as an estimation technique in cmmi organizations." *2014 agile conference*. IEEE, 2014.

20. Zahraoui, Hind, and Mohammed Abdou Janati Idrissi. "Adjusting story points calculation in scrum effort & time estimation." *2015 10th International Conference on Intelligent Systems: Theories and Applications (SITA)*. IEEE, 2015.

21. Choetkiertikul, Morakot, et al. "A deep learning model for estimating story points." *IEEE Transactions on Software Engineering* 45.7 (2018): 637–656.

22. Abadeer, Macarious, and Mehrdad Sabetzadeh. "Machine Learning-based Estimation of Story Points in Agile Development: Industrial Experience and Lessons Learned." *2021 IEEE 29th International Requirements Engineering Conference Workshops (REW)*. IEEE, 2021.

23. Fu, Michael, and Chakkrit Tantithamthavorn. "GPT2SP: A Transformer-Based Agile Story Point Estimation Approach." *IEEE Transactions on Software Engineering* (2022).

24. Mukund Sundararajan, Ankur Taly, and Qiqi Yan. Axiomatic attribution for deep networks. In ICML'17, 2017.

25. Q. Le and T. Mikolov, "Distributed representations of sentences and documents," in Proc. 31st Int. Conf. Mach. Learn., vol. 32, pp. 1188–1196, 2014.

26. N. Kalchbrenner, E. Grefenstette, and P. Blunsom, "A convolutional neural network for modelling sentences," in Proc. 52nd Annu. Meet. Assoc. Comput. Linguistics, 2014, pp. 655–665.

27. Z. K. Zia, S. K. Tipu and S. K. Zia, "An effort estimation model for agile software development," Advances in Computer Science and its Applications, vol. 2, no. 1, pp. 314–324, 2012.

28. Ali Bou Nassif, Luiz Fernando Capretz and Danny Ho, Estimating Software Effort Using an ANN Model Based on Use Case Points, 11th International Conference on Machine Learning and Applications, 2012.

Computer Science Engineering and Emerging Technologies (ICCS-2022) – Prof (Dr.) Rajeev Sobti et al. (eds)
© 2024 Taylor & Francis Group, London, ISBN 978-1-032-52199-2

Chapter **97**

Scheduling Techniques for Convergecast in Multichannel Wireless Sensor Networks: A Review and Issues

Vishav Kapoor[1]

Research Scholar, Department of Electronics & Communication,
Lovely Professional University, Punjab, India

Daljeet Singh[2]

Associate Professor, Department of Electronics &Communication,
Lovely Professional University, Punjab, India

Abstract: In today's highly competitive environment, consumers have limited tolerance for long information-gathering procedures. This has restricted researchers' ability to gather data in a timely manner. Convergecast transmission is a potential technique for rapid communication. In convergecast, each sensor node transmits its own packet straight to the sink node, bypassing the intermediate node. Multichannel allocation is one of the most important aspects of efficiency enhancement. This paper describes and examines the various scheduling techniques used to achieve convergecast efficiency in WSN. On the basis of parameters such as energy, length of schedule, and robustness, a comparative assessment of scheduling strategies has been performed. Additionally, open research issues have been established so that convergent mechanisms in WSN might be researched in the future.

Keywords: Wireless sensor Networks, Convergecast, Multichannel, Scheduling, TDMA, MAC

1. Introduction

Wireless sensor networks (WSNs) are made up of low-power, low-capacity nodes that communicate with each other using radio waves. Sensor nodes are devices that work with other devices in a network to do something, like monitor the environment. In the last ten years, the number of connected devices has grown rapidly [1]. It's hard to go anywhere these days without running into at least one device that's connected to the internet. WSNs [2] are a part of this trend that can be used in more than one way. Different MAC protocols are a key part of making sure that these networks meet their needs for power use and latency. Power utilization and delay are two of the biggest problems with WSN, especially when it comes to business processes. In wireless communications, it is hard to use the least amount of power while maintaining a high throughput and no data loss. Power consumption is a big problem because sensors often need to run for weeks or even decades without human help or battery replacement.

In recent years, there have been a number of research developments focused on making these kinds of algorithms in order to solve these different problems. These scheduling techniques are classified as: centralized [3], distributed [4], and independent [5-6]. With centralized scheduling, all of the network information is gathered in one place, and the link schedules are made from there. But when the topology changes, the base node may get too busy and slow down updates to network information. In the past few years, WSNs have come a long way. Nodes close to a MWSN have access to different

[1]vishavkapoor55@gmail.com, [2]daljeet.23804@lpu.co.in

DOI: 10.1201/9781003405580-97

channels for sending and receiving data. Each channel is made up of a pair of nodes. With MWSNs, it is possible to collect more data at a faster rate because more data can be transferred at once. Multiple channels on different nodes need to switch channels often, which wastes time and energy. MWSNs use channels and time slots that work together to avoid scheduling conflicts.

In the 1st part of the paper, the introduction is given. In the 2nd section explains what other researchers have done. In the 3rd part of the paper, a comparison has been done on scheduling, multichannel algorithms based on different factors. In the 4th section, the open research issues are discussed, and the 5th section is the conclusion and future work.

2. Related Works

In this section, we describe the work that other researchers have done in the field of convergecast related to the scheduling algorithms in WSN. Some of the most important works have been discussed here.

In centralized systems, network data is sent to a central organization, which then schedules connections. In TASA, the schedule is made by a single node [7]. The network's layout and current traffic levels are taken into account to determine the schedule followed by each node. CLS [3] allocates and releases slots without modifying the whole schedule every CLS to decrease idle flow, resulting in efficient multi-hop schedules with a small number of centralized control messages. In [8], the authors introduced Multichannel Optimized Delay Time Slot Assignment (MODESA), which is a centralized raw convergecast type. DeTAS [4] deals with networks that have a lot of sink nodes. In [9], the authors suggest a method for scheduling that is based on waves. Each sending node is allotted a certain amount of time in a specific channel for sending its packets during each wave. In [10], a proposal was made for DeAMON, which is a decentralized mechanism for 6TiSCH wireless networks. Later on, a distributed diverge cast scheduling method called DIVA [11] was made.

Autonomous scheduling is better for the network than centralized and distributed scheduling because it uses less bandwidth. Orchestra [5] began auto-scheduling TSCH. Orchestra is a new way for TSCH to schedule jobs that uses basic criteria to speed up the rate of delivery. Escalator [12] is an autonomous scheduling method that uses Orchestra. It makes a sequential timeslot plan along the packet transmission pipeline to cut down on latency. Also, in [6], the authors tried to cut down on orchestra delays by changing the order in which they played. The authors of [13] propose a deterministic TDMA scheduling technique for dispersed networks.

FlexiTP, presented in [14], is a unique TDMA protocol that provides a synchronized and flexible slot structure. A distributed and scalable scheduling accessing approach was presented in [15], which can accommodate some mobility and reduces the amount of data lost in data-intensive sensor networks. Some other relevant work has been done by researches in context of scheduling in multichannel WSN [16-20]. Some recent work has also been done in this context [21-22].

3. Comparative Analysis of Scheduling Techniques

In this section, a comparison of the different ways that convergecast is done in WSN has been made. As already discussed about, convergecast is being put into three categories: aggregate, raw, and general. Also, the energy used, the length of the schedule, and the ability to handle problems are the most important things to look at when evaluating how well the different convergecast techniques work. In this direction, Table 97.1 shows a comparison of different things.

Table 97.1 Metric based evaluation of convergecast techniques

Reference	Aggregate Convergecast	Raw Convergecast	General Convergecast	Energy	Schedule Length	Robustness
[16]	✗	✗	✓	✗	✗	✓
[13]	✗	✗	✓	✗	✗	✗
[14]	✗	✓	✗	✗	✗	✗
[17]	✓	✗	✗	✓	✗	✗
[15]	✗	✗	✓	✗	✗	✗
[18]	✓	✗	✗	✓	✗	✗
[19]	✗	✓	✗	✓	✗	✗
[20]	✗	✓	✗	✗	✓	✗

Source: Made by Author

Based on the scheduling algorithms and fault-tolerance methods listed above, it can say that joint scheduling or general convergecast algorithms are better than other methods. The length of the schedule would be short in a small network. But the length of schedules would be long in a big network. If something happens in one part of the network, the nodes in a big network will have to wait longer for their turn to send. Some ways could be made to support data transmission based on priority. That is, nodes usually send data in the slot that was given to them. But if urgent information needs to be sent, it should be sent quickly. It can be assumed that the schedules for aggregate methods are shorter and that they use less energy. On the other hand, there are no robust features. So, for faster data transfer, researchers need to come up with methods that use less energy and can handle mistakes and have the shortest schedules.

4. Open Issues

In the field of multichannel convergecast, researchers still need to learn more about a lot of things. Majorly channeled allocation, designing of convergecast framework, and energy-efficient methods are the main problems that need to be solved. But there are other unanswered questions that need more research.

Changing channels: For the radio to alter stations, it needs time. The changeover time should fit into the size of the time slot, and the extra time needed to make the switch is small.

Blended Approach: A blended strategy is best for raw convergent. It might be interesting to make a blended joint scheduler for raw convergecast in which each node initially selects a slot to send its own packet and afterwards selects slots to send its children's notifications.

Data Security: Security is a crucial thing to think about when gathering a lot of data. This is because, when dealing with these kinds of problems, aggregators often give out wrong information.

Dynamic Environment: However, things like the unpredictability of wireless connections, the mobility of nodes, and changes in traffic conditions make it hard to build multichannel WSNs.

Power Management: Using multiple transceivers on the sensor nodes and figuring out how much energy the current multi-channel protocols use could be important areas of research.

5. Conclusion and Future Work

In this paper, we discuss some of the problems that arise when there are multiple channels of communication in converged networks. When many channels are used, the convergecast algorithm has much less delay and works much better. We have compared and contrasted many approaches for covergecast scheduling in multichannel WSN based on metrics like energy, schedule length, and robustness. From the above literature review, it can be inferred that channel assignment is one of the most important things that affects how well a convergecast strategy works. It can be assumed that the schedules for aggregate methods are shorter and that they use less energy. On the other hand, there are no robust features. So, for faster data transfer, researchers need to come up with methods that use less energy, can handle mistakes, and have the shortest schedules. Since energy use is one of the biggest concerns in sensor networks, future research will look at ways to save even more energy by using more than one channel. Energy will also be saved by looking into ways to manage transmission power on the nodes, and the security of the information that is sent will be researched further.

REFERENCES

1. Balazka, S. D., & Rodighiero, D. (2020). Big data and the little big bang: an epistemological (R) evolution. *Frontiers in Big Data*, *3*.
2. Kandris, D., Nakas, C., Vomvas, D., & Koulouras, G. (2020). Applications of Wireless Sensor Networks: An up-to-date survey. *Applied System Innovation*, *3*(1), 14.
3. Hoi, K.-H., & Chung, S.-H. (2016). A new centralized link scheduling for 6TiSCH wireless industrial networks. In *Lecture Notes in Computer Science* (pp. 360–371). Springer International Publishing.
4. Accettura, N., Palattella, M. R., Boggia, G., Grieco, L. A., & Dohler, M. (2013). Decentralized Traffic Aware Scheduling for multi-hop Low power Lossy Networks in the Internet of Things. *2013 IEEE 14th International Symposium on "A World of Wireless, Mobile and Multimedia Networks" (WoWMoM)*.
5. Duquennoy, S., Nahas, B., Landsiedel, O., & Watteyne, T. (2015). Orchestra: Robust mesh networks through autonomously scheduled TSCH. In *Proceedings of the 13th ACM conference on embedded networked sensor systems* (pp. 337–350).

6. Rekik, S., Baccour, N., Jmaiel, M., Drira, K., & Grieco, L. A. (2018). Autonomous and traffic-aware scheduling for TSCH networks. *Computer Networks, 135*, 201–212.
7. Palattella, M. R., Accettura, N., Dohler, M., Grieco, L. A., & Boggia, G. (2012). Traffic aware scheduling algorithm for reliable low-power multi-hop IEEE 802.15. 4e networks. In *2012 IEEE 23rd International Symposium on Personal, Indoor and Mobile Radio Communications-(PIMRC)* (pp. 327–332). IEEE.
8. Soua, R., Minet, P., & Livolant, E. (2012). MODESA: An optimized multichannel slot assignment for raw data convergecast in wireless sensor networks. *2012 IEEE 31st International Performance Computing and Communications Conference (IPCCC)*.
9. Soua, R., Minet, P., & Livolant, E. (2016). Wave: a distributed scheduling algorithm for convergecast in IEEE 802.15. 4e TSCH networks. *Transactions on Emerging Telecommunications Technologies, 27*, 557–575.
10. Aijaz, A., & Raza, U. (2017). DeAMON: A decentralized adaptive multi-hop scheduling protocol for 6TiSCH wireless networks. *IEEE Sensors Journal, 17*(20), 6825–6836.
11. Demir, A. K., & Bilgili, S. (2019). DIVA: a distributed divergecast scheduling algorithm for IEEE 802.15. 4e TSCH networks. *Wireless Networks, 25*(2), 625–635.
12. Oh, S., Hwang, D., Kim, K.-H., & Kim, K. (2018). Escalator: An autonomous scheduling scheme for convergecast in TSCH. *Sensors (Basel, Switzerland), 18*(4).
13. Wang, Y., & Henning, I. (2007). A deterministic distributed TDMA scheduling algorithm for wireless sensor networks. *2007 International Conference on Wireless Communications, Networking and Mobile Computing*.
14. Lee, W. L., Datta, A., & Cardell-Oliver, R. (2008). FlexiTP: A flexible-schedule-based TDMA protocol for fault-tolerant and energy-efficient wireless sensor networks. *IEEE Transactions on Parallel and Distributed Systems: A Publication of the IEEE Computer Society, 19*(6), 851–864.
15. Lin, C.-K., Zadorozhny, V., Krishnamurthy, P., Park, H.-H., & Lee, C.-G. (2011). A distributed and scalable time slot allocation protocol for wireless sensor networks. *IEEE Transactions on Mobile Computing, 10*(4), 505– 518.
16. Rhee, I., Warrier, A., Min, J., & Xu, L. (2006). DRAND: distributed randomized TDMA scheduling for wireless ad-hoc networks. In *Proceedings of the 7th ACM international symposium on Mobile ad hoc networking and computing* (pp. 190–201).
17. Wu, F.-J., & Tseng, Y.-C. (2009). Distributed wake-up scheduling for data collection in tree-based wireless sensor networks. *IEEE Communications Letters: A Publication of the IEEE Communications Society, 13*(11), 850– 852.
18. Yu, C., Fiske, R., Park, S., & Kim, W. T. (2012). Many-to-one communication protocol for wireless sensor networks. *International Journal of Sensor Networks, 12*(3), 160.
19. Bagaa, M., Younis, M., Ksentini, A., & Badache, N. (2013). Multi-path multi-channel data aggregation scheduling in wireless sensor networks. *2013 IFIP Wireless Days (WD)*.
20. Zeng, B., & Dong, Y. (2014). A collaboration-based distributed TDMA scheduling algorithm for data collection in wireless sensor networks. *Journal of Networks, 9*(9).
21. Sah, D. K., Amgoth, T., & Cengiz, K. (2022). Energy efficient medium access control protocol for data collection in wireless sensor network: A Q-learning approach," Sustain. *Sustain. Energy Technol. Assessments, 53*(102530).
22. Hammoudi, S., Ourzeddine, H., Gueroui, M., Harous, S., & Aliouat, Z. (2022). A collision-free scheduling algorithm with minimum data redundancy transmission for TSCH. *Wireless Personal Communications, 124*(4), 3159–3188.

Computer Science Engineering and Emerging Technologies (ICCS-2022) – Prof (Dr.) Rajeev Sobti et al. (eds)
© 2024 Taylor & Francis Group, London, ISBN 978-1-032-52199-2

Chapter **98**

Architectural Sustainability in Computer Design: A mirror Review

Ayush Gour[1], Sankalp Sudarsan Rajguru[2*]
Student, Department of Computer Science and Engineering,
Lovely Professional University Phagwara, Punjab, India

Gursharan Singh[3*], Gurpreet Singh[4*], Balwinder Kaur[5*]
Assistant Professor, Department of Computer Science and Engineering,
Lovely Professional University Phagwara, Punjab, India

Abstract: Computer designers have focused on boosting processing speed and arithmetic capability while maintaining strict weight and power restrictions as a necessity for long-term system stability, which may radically alter the structure of the onboard computer. While this industry is driven by application development and technology improvements, the demand for high multimedia performance, simplicity of design, and power-efficient computing environments is increasing. This study examines and summarises recent developments and trends in sustainable computer designs. The challenge for computer designers and architects is to make microprocessor layout recommendations that both meet the demands of upcoming applications and efficiently utilise this large transistor budget. In order to strike the correct balance in favour of the organisation and its facilities for long-term development, this article concentrates on longer-term trends in computer architecture and design as well as their viability.

Keywords: Computer architecture, Sustainability, Green computing

1. Introduction

Environmental sustainability is an important challenge to humanity that necessitates concerted action from all sectors of society, including business. The globe has experienced a sharp increase in computing demand over the past 20 years, driven by new edge and cloud-scale applications. Unfortunately, this increase has primary global energy and environmental costs. A collection of rules and techniques used to describe computer system performance, structure, and application is known as computer architecture in computer engineering. Other definitions of architecture state that it represents, without mentioning a prototype version, the scripting language and characteristics of a system. According to some accounts, the development of implementations, microcontrollers, logics, and performance all fall under the umbrella of computer architecture (Hennessy et al., 2011).

As per modern computers, a computerised platform's effectiveness, productivity, pricing, and trustworthiness must all be controlled. The illustration of advanced microcontroller bus architecture may be used to illustrate how these opposing forces might coexist. More complex implementations let developers develop more spatial programmes since a single command may communicate a relatively high conceptualization (Null et al., 2018). In contrast, longer and even more

*Corresponding Authors: [2]sankalprajgurur1221@gmail.com, [3]gursharan.dhot@gmail.com, [4]gurpreet.17671@lpu.co.in, [5]balwinder.25673@lpu.co.in
[1]ayushgour232@gmail.com

complicated directions take a lot longer for the Central processing unit to digest and might even incur additional costs to accomplish correctly. Combined circuitry, container, transmission, and refrigeration are all included in the implementation. Topology efficiency requires knowledge of interpreters, desktop software concept layout, or bundling (Mallo Jr., 2017).

One billion transistors will soon be possible to combine on a single chip thanks to advancements in integrated circuit technology. It will be difficult for technology engineers and designers to propose microcontroller designs that efficiently utilise this substantial pixel expenditure and meet the requirements of potential developments. Unfortunately, because it concentrates on desktop and server applications, modern computer architecture research will be in the past. However, the personal mobile computing sector will dominate technology in the next ten years. This paradigm's actual computer or communication gadgets are battery-operated and capable of multimedia functions, including speech recognition. These gadgets might change the focus of computer architecture research and place new demands on microprocessors.

2. Literature Review

According to the design levels of the networks, the current work on energy management can be divided into four categories: Where to stack nodes on installation to conserve energy, Where to play as an intermediary at the level of congestion to minimise the number of cluster members, adjusting system throughput in response to traffic volume at the urban traffic intensity, Where to adjust the available bandwidth to conserve energy somewhere at the distribution level, changing agile methodologies at the fundamental level in order to achieve efficiency improvements, depending on the power generation used by each procedure and its characteristics of the system at the mechanism tier, depending mostly on energy utilisation within each directive now at the tier of either the directive.

Our sector is influenced by application developments and technological advancements, increasing the demand for power-efficient computing environments (Tan et al., 2001). Today's computer market (cell phones, laptops, tablets, and games) is more advanced than it was thirty years ago, and as a result, battery life is a crucial design consideration. In the past, outdated designs were incorporated into new workflows. Power is also more important than corporate distributions, which are at the other extreme (Tiwari et al., 1994). Numerous high-end servers are housed in data centres, frequently constrained by their capacity to provide enough power and cooling to give the needed execution throughput. As a result, technological and application forces have brought us to a situation where energy-efficient processing, which is essential to the sustainability of future computer systems, is becoming more challenging to achieve.

Table 98.1 A literature review of computer architecture for sustainable design

Citation	Methodology	Outcomes	Limitation
(Khan, et al, 2021).	General Problem Solver, Theorem-Power, Natural Languages Processors	Through the use of numerous demarcation line and matrix postprocessing, it reached a fresh level of efficiency and speed.	Due to the constraints on information processing, storage, and computing capacity, it served as the basis for artificial.
(Bianzino, et al, 2010).	Simultaneous powered modelling through use calls.	In an endeavor to promote "clean connectivity," as the practice of reducing wastages in frame relay.	Most digital phones have restricted computing capacity and can only work with constrained maximum input charges, thus restricting the amount of simultaneous power generation they can consume.
(Gupta, et al, 2021)	Key Performance Indicators Qualitative Data with the PRSM Model.	The impact of the established system is on the ecological objectives of the company.	Consulted members first from organization and application developers, who constitute the primary users of proposed platform, to lessen this restriction.
(Zhong, et al, 2010)	Utilized in conjunction with current program engineering development and evaluation techniques.	The method outlined in this research can predict how much resource a program utilizes when operating on a certain Central processing unit or chipset.	Whereas if aggregate reflexes or capacity of types of networks is identical or nearly the same, but one utilizes less energy compared from another.
(Själander, et al, 2014)	Design to focus on investigating different types of synchronization.	This can be deemed useful for a postgraduate pupil with the fundamental knowledge of parallel computing and construction models but hasn't had much exposure to power difficulties.	Progress has been achieved expansion and Mitchell's Legislation advancements have halted, and the difficulties of developing highly tuned computer servers have increased.

Citation	Methodology	Outcomes	Limitation
(Gupta, et al, 2022)	Focus on different types of methods such as encouraged produce hypotheses and the techniques used in green marketing.	Fundamental correction factor including productivity, capacity, surface, but also economy, ecology must be taken into account in forthcoming and equipment building phases.	There are some limitations in energy balance analysis and Life cycle analysis tools.

3. Optimization of Sustainable Architecture

In general, computer systems have come to a fascinating crossroads. For more than ten years, power has been a primary design limitation for architects. The initial response targets per-module work to increase design complexity, power efficiency, microprocessor power, and green computing methods. Unfortunately, these efforts have only had the impact of turning off the lights in empty rooms in one's home, which is prudent but must be employed more effectively to alter the development of the environment for strength drastically.

3.1 Power Efficiency

The Grand Challenge is how to control the electricity demand of contemporary computer systems. All electronic systems are influenced by electricity, whether slightly elevated workstations, processing power, our handsets' power consumption and productivity, or the computational resources of our big data centres. An introduction to power as a significant problem may appear recent to today's computer builders. However, it is a fact that power issues plagued the very first computer systems. Computer systems profited from technological advancements that increased circuit performance, cost, and power (Bell et al. 1997). For instance, in Gordon Moore's projections of technological growth, integration levels were connected to manufacturing costs.

3.2 Green Computing

Green computing is getting more attention because of its climate impact and escalating fuel costs. Hardware and software concepts, which are examined regarding throughput, consistency, serviceability, and protection, play a major role across both systems. Nonetheless, the research focusing on microcontroller power utilisation necessitates additional work (Balabanian, N., 1994). Systems that rely on a specific data structure consume less power than crucial systems since most communication systems must operate continuously. In addition, the electrical characteristics of the transistors used in a processor and the number of active transistors determine how much energy the processor uses. Any electrical device will lose energy in the following ways:

$$P = V * I \tag{1}$$

V stands for voltage and current is I, Additionally, typical energy use is equivalent to the following:

$$E = P * t \tag{2}$$

t is appropriate time, and P is the device's power dissipation.

If the Control Processing Unit clock speed is S, a switch S,000,000 several repetitions in a moment. Therefore, the amount of energy consumed by a digital circuit every millisecond is:

$$E_{per\_sec} = V * I * t * S \tag{3}$$

3.3 Microprocessors

These personal mobile computing devices require a CPU that combines general-purpose processing with digital signal processing and has the latter's power budget. Such microprocessors must meet four critical criteria: High multimedia performance, Energy and power efficiency, Portability, and simplicity of design.

The fundamental requirements for a processor to handle media-centric applications were instantaneous reactions. Processors must deliver worst-case assured performance that enables simultaneous sensory judgement in software via streaming rather than maximal peak performance on small-scale parallelism. The same operation must be performed over data sequences in Integration of visuals, acoustics, and transmissions is a single-processor utility. Wide-bandwidth networks are required to stream data from external sources, such as video or photos.

3.4 Design Complexity

Physical design complexity, which comprises the time spent developing, validating, and testing an integrated circuit, is the last problem. Creating an advanced microprocessor requires over four years and several hundred engineers. These activities now make up most of the processor development work due to the increasing testing complexities and practical and electrical verification efforts. Extreme statistical information forecasting, in operation, multicore, trade, and industry designs, makes it difficult for new, and multiple core engines are some sophisticated techniques that make these problems harsher. Along with manageability, there is another issue in the Consumer electronics industry. Not just in terms of physical design but also in terms of performance, an architecture should scale effectively (Tremblay et al., 1998). For instance, many designers believe that lengthy on-chip interconnects will constrain future CPU development.

4. Conclusion

The industry's task is to build electricity components capable of more effectively satisfying the rising energy requirements of upcoming cloud services and calculate how much energy a programme utilises while operating on a specific processor. This concept may be used in conjunction with current programme structure development and evaluation techniques. Computer designers and developers can benefit from this approach when power consumption or "sustainable technology" becomes increasingly important. There is a large amount of work that must be carried out on the subject of green computing in the future. In addition, corporate organisations must take more green initiatives. Otherwise, humans will face severe problems in the coming years. As such, this survey has no limitations, although it is expected that there will be much research related to these issues in the coming years. Future work will include using the direction in sustainable architecture to evaluate the actual hyperparameters of various designs and compare the findings with those estimated by these strategies.

REFERENCES

1. Hennessy, J. L., & Patterson, D. A. (2011). *Computer architecture: a quantitative approach*. Elsevier.
2. Null, L., & Lobur, J. (2018). *Essentials of Computer Organization and Architecture*. Jones & Bartlett Learning.
3. Mallo Jr, S. (2017). The Challenges of Lecture Delivery of Arm X86, Cisc and Risc in the Teaching of Coursecsc303 (Computer Architecture) in the University of Jos, Nigeria: an Overview.
4. Tan, T. K., Raghunathan, A., Lakshminarayana, G., & Jha, N. K. (2001, June). High-level software energy macro-modeling. In *Proceedings of the 38th Design Automation Conference (IEEE Cat. No. 01CH37232)* (pp. 605-610). IEEE.
5. Tiwari, V., Malik, S., & Wolfe, A. (1994). Power analysis of embedded software: A first step towards software power minimization. *IEEE Transactions on Very Large Scale Integration (VLSI) Systems*, 2(4), 437-445.
6. Khan, F. H., Pasha, M. A., & Masud, S. (2021). Advancements in microprocessor architecture for ubiquitous AI—An overview on history, evolution, and upcoming challenges in AI implementation. *Micromachines*, 12(6), 665.
7. Bianzino, A. P., Chaudet, C., Rossi, D., & Rougier, J. L. (2010). A survey of green networking research. *IEEE Communications Surveys & Tutorials*, 14(1), 3-20.
8. Gupta, S., Lago, P., & Donker, R. (2021, March). A framework of software architecture principles for sustainability-driven design and measurement. In *2021 IEEE 18th International Conference on Software Architecture Companion (ICSA-C)* (pp. 31-37). IEEE.
9. Zhong, B., Feng, M., & Lung, C. H. (2010, December). A green computing based architecture comparison and analysis. In *2010 IEEE/ACM Int'l Conference on Green Computing and Communications & Int'l Conference on Cyber, Physical and Social Computing* (pp. 386-391). IEEE.
10. Själander, M., Martonosi, M., & Kaxiras, S. (2014). Power-efficient computer architectures: Recent advances. *Synthesis Lectures on Computer Architecture*, 9(3), 1-96.
11. Gupta, U., Elgamal, M., Hills, G., Wei, G. Y., Lee, H. H. S., Brooks, D., & Wu, C. J. (2022, June). ACT: designing sustainable computer systems with an architectural carbon modeling tool. In *Proceedings of the 49th Annual International Symposium on Computer Architecture* (pp. 784-799).
12. Bell, G., & Gray, J. (1997). Beyond Calculation: The Next 50 Years of Computing.
13. Balabanian, N. (1994). *Electric circuits*. McGraw-Hill.
14. Tremblay, M., Grohoski, G., Burgess, B., Killian, E., Colwell, R., & Rubinfeld, P. I. (1998). Challenges and trends in processor design. *Computer*, 31(1), 39-48.

Computer Science Engineering and Emerging Technologies (ICCS-2022) – Prof (Dr.) Rajeev Sobti et al. (eds)
© 2024 Taylor & Francis Group, London, ISBN 978-1-032-52199-2

Chapter **99**

Comprehensive Analysis of IEEE 802.11 WLAN Performance Optimization Strategies

Simarjit Singh Malhi[1]
Ph.D Research Scholar, Computer Science Engineering, RIMT University;
Assistant Professor, Lovely Professional University

Raj Kumar[2]
Associate Professor, Computer Applications, RIMT University

Abstract: A wireless network without a fixed infrastructure is known as a Wireless LAN (WLAN). Due to its unique characteristics, load balancing is a crucial challenge. If the loads on the APs are not balanced, the throughput of the entire network may be significantly reduced. One of the main issues with wireless LANs is boosting network throughput while maintaining fairness. There are many load-balancing algorithms presented. A broad study of several load balancing algorithms in WLAN is presented in this paper. These are evaluated in terms of various constraints like packet delivery ratio, throughput, end-to-end delay, total energy expended, standardized routing load, packet loss cost, etc.

Keywords: WLAN, Load balancing, Throughput, Delay, Packet loss

1. Introduction

In order to provide users of such devices with a seamless experience, it is important to thoroughly examine various aspects of computer networks in general and wireless local area networks in particular. This is because the current state of affairs calls for even the smallest task to be completed through digital devices using the internet, which is dynamically characterized by real-time switching from one network channel to another. Load balancing in the network is a crucial subject that must never be overlooked from the aforementioned angle.

As put forth by Krishan and Laxami (2015), "For the higher throughput and increased performance of the network, the proposed algorithm executes the users load balancing on each AP which leads to raise the network throughput."

2. Research Method

The process of reading literature is essential because it creates a solid foundation for the advancement of knowledge and makes it easier to find areas that warrant further investigation. In order to represent the current state of WLAN and its performance issues, this paper objects to a thorough analysis of the literature. The evaluation process looked at the key tactics for leading a real literature review.

[1]simarmalhi@gmail.com, simarjit.28260@lpu.co.in, [2]raj.kumar@rimt.ac.in

DOI: 10.1201/9781003405580-99

3. Literature Search Process

The literature exploration procedure of this analysis involves intricately inquiring into eminent scholarly literature databases (ACM digital library, IEEE Explore, IEEE Transactions, INDERSCIENCE Online, ScienceDirect, Springer, Taylor & Francis). The said databases, which access high-quality peer-reviewed conference publications and top journals, as well as online databases, are suitable and hands-on bases for studying the literature around WLAN performance. The search standard was restricted to the article's title to guarantee the significance of the articles. The terms used for penetrating said databases are 'WLAN performance' in grouping with 'load balancing. This resulted in 21 research papers in total. An outline of the exploration process is shown in Table 99.1 and Fig. 99.1.

Table 99.1 An outline of the exploration process

Literature databases	Search query	Search results
ACM (Digital Library)	(Title:"WLAN" and Title:"load balancing*")	3
IEEE Xplore	(("Document Title":"WLAN") AND "Document Title":"load balancing*")	7
IEEE Transactions	(("Document Title":"WLAN") AND "Document Title":"load balancing*")	3
INDERSCIENCE Online	(Title:"WLAN" and Title:"load balancing*")	1
ScienceDirect	TITLE("WLAN") and TITLE(load balancing*)	1
Springer	(Title:"WLAN" and Title:"load balancing*")	3
Taylor & Francis	(Title:"WLAN" and Title:"load balancing*")	3
Total		21

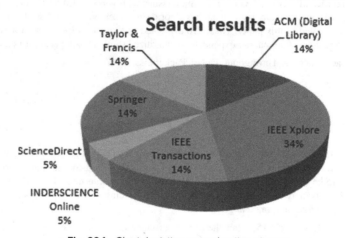

Fig. 99.1 Chart depicting an exploration process

4. Analyzing the Literature

4.1 Wireless Local Area Network

WLAN, often known as wireless LAN, is a type of Local Area Network (LAN) that uses high-frequency radio waves rather than physical connections to transmit data between two or more devices and frequently includes an access point that connects to the Internet. Users of wireless local area networks can access the internet from a variety of locations, including their homes, offices, and other buildings, while maintaining network connectivity through wireless network communication rather than conventional network cable.

4.2 Operation of WLAN

Components in WLAN

Wireless Local Area Networks are constructed by using a node known as an access point (AP), which connects to the node of a fixed network. Through a wireless network connector, user nodes are linked to the access point (AP).

Routers manage signals going to and from access points (APs). Different types of devices, including workstations, desktop computers, laptops, IP phones, mobile phones, smartphones, and tablets, may be used by users.

Load Balancing in WLAN

Velayos Hector et al. (2004) They had projected a load-balancing approach for overlying wireless LAN cells. With the help of periodic broadcasts, the load on each AP had been analyzed via agents running on each access point. They had shown through experimental evaluation how the network throughput increases.

Bejerano Yigal et al. (2004), According to recent studies, the user load was unequally dispersed between different access points in WLAN. They had observed that unstable loads and unfair bandwidth distribution were intelligently dispersed over APs using association control. They had introduced an efficient algorithmic approach that ensured fair bandwidth allocation.

Brickley, Olivia, et al. (2005), authors said that real-time applications that are sensitive, like streaming voice over IP and multimedia, are increasing. The authors attempted to augment the experienced superiority in the 802.11b model of WLAN by matching the load among different access points while altering the exposure area of every access point, a method usually recognized as cell breathing.

Abusubaih Murad et al. (2008), Which AP had to be selected was the main concern of the authors. In IEEE 802.11, AP selection also led to load imbalance between numerous APs, and throughput also s suffered. he mechanisms improved the quality of service moreover best usage of network resources concerning stability and offer their performance enhancement in thicker or lighter network configurations.

Bejerano Yigal and Han Seung-Jae (2009), In this paper, they proposed a new balancing of load method by adjusting the WLAN cell size. The planned arrangement does not indulge in any modifications to the IEEE 802.11 standard or the user side. They had established a set of polynomial-time procedures to overcome the congested AP by finding optimal beacon power settings.

In Ye Xiao Guo et al. (2011), the authors introduced a new adaptive load-balanced routing algorithm (ALB), which depends on the cross-layer design principle and minimum interference and is implemented in detail. The results of the simulation depicted that the projected adaptive routing procedure can efficiently evade the existence of Link overload, reduce packet loss rates, and improve network throughput.

Le Yuan et al. (2011), In this paper, they had formulated an optimization problem, and the objective of this problem was to lessen the load alteration of the APs. The said issue was NP-complete, so they had proposed two greedy heuristics to originate AP associations for balancing the load.

Suresh Lalith et al. (2012) They had presented Odin, which was a SDN framework that introduced programmability in enterprise WLANs. The facilities and functionalities comprise accounting, authorization, authentication, interference management, mobility, policy, and balancing the load. To be precise, access point (AP) association choices were built by clients. The client management was simplified by Odin, which was based on a light virtual AP abstraction.

Xue Guangtao et al. (2013) In this paper, they focused on the social relationships of users while balancing the load on AP by proposing an online greedy procedure. Contrasting with the state-of-the-art technique, a balancing performance gain of around 64.7 percent during normal peak hours on working days was achieved.

In Rong Hui Hou et al. (2014), the authors proposed a utility-based access point selection arrangement that provides the users with proper bandwidth by selecting the best AP. The experimental result shows the accuracy and convergency of belief propagation in balancing the load problem.

Krishan Ram and Laxami Vijay (2015), authors, talked about the best AP selection criteria in a WLAN along with balancing the load over each AP. Their procedure energetically balanced the load on the network by spreading the users between access points (APs). The network performance enhancement parameters, such as load, throughput, and data dropped on an AP, were identified, and the projected procedure displayed the efficacy of the distributed load and increased the performance of the network.

Bhuwania Anshu et al. (2016) showed how a network of different access points was implemented using Particle Swarm Optimization (PSO) to cover the maximum area. The access points were only positioned in rooms over the walls for security reasons. Signal strength loss because of free space and walls had been taken into consideration. Simulation outcomes also showed the perfection of the procedure.

Breskovic Damir and Begusic Dinko (2017), authors, presented a techno-economic analysis of a fiber wireless access network. With the greater bandwidth volume of the gigabit passive optical network and the cost-effectiveness of higher-throughput 802.11ac WLANs that permit user movement in the wireless segment, fiber-wireless access networks can be regarded as a substitute for the fiber-to-the-home architecture for succeeding generation access networks.

Comparison table of different research papers

Table 99.2 Comparison table of different research papers

Title/Authors	Issues addressed/ Problems	Methodologies/ Techniques	Results/Limitations/Future Work
Balachandran Anand, et. al. (2002)	Performance of network and behavior of user	Parametrized model	Load distribution was uneven and was not matched with the quantity of users. Will perform behavior of user and performance of network in different and similar wireless networks in future
Velayos Hector, et. al. (2004)	Overloaded Aps	Two-step process	Enhances the total network throughput and reduces the cell delay
Bejerano Yigal, et. al. (2004)	Uneven distribution of user load	Approximation algorithms	Network throughput was enhanced. Will aim to implement a practical management system based on the theoretical foundation
Brickley Olivia, et. al. (2005)	Quality of Service (QoS) restrictions for applications (multimedia and voice over IP)	Cell breathing	Decrease the cell load, Future effort will purpose to achieve the cell breathing method in a WLAN 802.11e standard
Gowrishankar and Satyanarayana P. S. (2008)	Quality of Service (QoS), Load balancing	Recurrent Radial Basis Function Network (RRBFN), Echo state network (ESN), Fractional Auto Regressive Integrated Moving Average (FARIMA) model	Traffic prediction accurateness was in the range of 96.4% to 98.3% and 78.5% to 80.2%
Gong Huazhi and Kim JongWon (2008)	Unfair bandwidth distribution among mobile users (MUs)	Distributed association algorithm	Recover, or sometimes nearly double, the amount of throughput fairness between the MUs with low overhead
Abusubaih Murad, et. al. (2008)	AP selection	Decision metric, Two new selection mechanisms	Improved mean quality of service and better utilisation of network resources
Scully Ted and Brown Kenneth N. (2008)	Quality of service (QoS) and load distribution and in congested networks	Micro-genetic and standard genetic algorithm approaches	Enhancement in performance over present techniques. In future, examine the performance of the projected procedures when escorted with greedy initialization approaches
BejeranoYigal and Han Seung-Jae (2009)	Network-wide min max AP load balancing	Min-max algorithm	Performance was superior to the superlative existing methods
Lin Cheng-Han, et. al. (2012)	Quality of video transmissions	Enhanced Random Early Detection Forward Error Correction (ERED-FEC) apparatus	In future, the recovery performance of the ERED-FEC apparatus will be further improved by using an FEC interleaving/ de-interleaving strategy
Suresh Lalith, et. al. (2012)	Access point (AP) association decisions	Odin, an SDN framework	Observed the time delay among AP associations. The average delay for a handoff within the identical channel was about 190 ms. this was smaller than 1 ms from the supplication of the LVAP-handoff call

Title/Authors	Issues addressed/ Problems	Methodologies/ Techniques	Results/Limitations/Future Work
Xia Yang and Yeo Chai Kiat (2012)	Traffic redirection and forwarding	Network based local mobility management scheme	Removed slightly longer handover delay
Xue Guangtao, et. al. (2013)	AP selection and load balance	Online greedy AP selection algorithm	64.7 percent balancing performance gain on normal throughout peak hours in working days
Xu Shibo, et. al. (2013)	Load imbalance and performance	Simple scheme with aggregated traffic patterns	According to two groups of simulations, fairness and throughput affected
Rong Hui Hou, et. al. (2014)	Access point selection	Utility-based access point selection scheme, belief propagation	Conducted numerical tests to evaluate the convergency and accuracy variations of the belief propagation in load balancing problem
Krishan Ram and Laxami Vijay (2015)	Unbalanced load distribution, performance degrades	Load balancing algorithm	The rate of data dropped was decreased to 600 (bits/sec) and 1.5 times greater throughput. Future work will extend different performance parameters and additional multifaceted scenarios
Bhuwania Anshu, et. al. (2016)	Number of access points	Particle Swarm Optimization (PSO) technique	Simulation results displayed the effectiveness of the algorithm
Kim Hye-Young (2016)	Load balancing, energy consumption of the sensor nodes	Scheme using analytical models	Sensor nodes operated with each other for full network lifetime and highest usage of the usable energy of the wireless sensor network

5. Research Limitations

In their work on the selection of a preferred Access Point, Xu et al. (2013) considered only UDP traffic and all traffic from stations to the AP and did not take into account TCP flows. So the present research envisages bridging this gap by considering TCP flows while analyzing load balancing in WLANs.

In their work on enhancing the performance of WLAN by balancing the load, Krishan and Laxami (2015) considered the Data Dropped, throughput, and Load on an AP as performance parameters. Further, they proposed that future work can be prolonged by seeing different parameters of performance and more multifaceted hotspot environmental scenarios. The type of data to be transceived has not been considered in their study as a performance parameter, which also plays a significant role from the perspective of load balancing in the WLAN and its performance enhancement. So this work will take into account the type of data to be transceived as one of the parameters in studying load balancing in the WLAN.

In order to bridge the above-identified gaps, this thesis attempts to provide new acumen pertaining to load balancing in WLAN by commissioning a more inclusive and significant study by incorporating load balancing in the network.

6. Literature Findings

To bridge the limitations as identified in analyzing the literature, these limitations envisage to a Comprehensive Framework for IEEE 802.11 WLAN Performance Optimization. The main outcome of the literature survey is to look at the various factors for load balancing in a WLAN for network performance optimization.

7. Conclusion

The expected outcome of future research would be that our proposed algorithm can efficiently allocate mobile users to each access point so that we can achieve load balancing among available access points with respect to different parameters, resulting in network performance. The proposed dynamic scheme will minimize the load on the network and user congestion as well by analyzing and balancing the mobile device load on access points (APs).

REFERENCES

1. Balachandran, A., Voelker, G. M., Bahl, P., & Rangan, P. V. (2002, June). Characterizing user behavior and network performance in a public wireless LAN. In ACM SIGMETRICS Performance Evaluation Review (Vol. 30, No. 1, pp. 195–205). ACM.

2. Velayos, H., Aleo, V., & Karlsson, G. (2004, June). Load balancing in overlapping wireless LAN cells. In 2004 IEEE International Conference on Communications (IEEE Cat. No. 04CH37577) (Vol. 7, pp. 3833–3836). IEEE.

3. Bejerano, Y., Han, S. J., & Li, L. E. (2004, September). Fairness and load balancing in wireless LANs using association control. In Proceedings of the 10th annual international conference on Mobile computing and networking (pp. 315–329). ACM.

4. Brickley, O., Rea, S., & Pesch, D. (2005, May). Load balancing for qos optimisation in wireless lans utilising advanced cell breathing techniques. In 2005 IEEE 61st Vehicular Technology Conference (Vol. 3, pp. 2105–2109). IEEE.

5. Gowrishankar, & Satyanarayana, P. S. (2008). Neural network based traffic prediction for wireless data networks. International Journal of Computational Intelligence Systems, 1(4), 379–389.

6. Gong Huazhi and Kim Jong Won (2008), "Dynamic Load Balancing through Association Control of Mobile Users in WiFi Networks", IEEE Transactions on Consumer Electronics, Vol. 54, No. 2.

7. Abusubaih, M., Wiethoelter, S., Gross, J., & Wolisz, A. (2008). A new access point selection policy for multi-rate IEEE 802.11 WLANs. International Journal of Parallel, Emergent and Distributed Systems, 23(4), 291–307.

8. Scully, T., & Brown, K. N. (2008, December). Wireless LAN load-balancing with genetic algorithms. In International Conference on Innovative Techniques and Applications of Artificial Intelligence (pp. 3-16). Springer, London.

9. Bejerano, Y., & Han, S. J. (2009). Cell breathing techniques for load balancing in wireless LANs. IEEE Transactions on Mobile Computing, 8(6), 735–749.

10. Ye Xiao Guo, Lv Kang Meng, Wang Ru Chuan and Sun Li Juan (2011), "Adaptive Load-Balanced Routing Algorithm", Second International Conference on Digital Manufacturing & Automation, IEEE, pp. 155–158.

11. Le, Y., Ma, L., Yu, H., Cheng, X., Cui, Y., Al-Rodhaan, M. A., & Al-Dhelaan, A. (2011, August). Load balancing access point association schemes for ieee 802.11 wireless networks. In International conference on wireless algorithms, systems, and applications (pp. 271–279). Springer, Berlin, Heidelberg.

12. Lin Cheng-Han, Shieh Ce-Kuen and Hwang Wen-Shyang (2012), "An Access Point-Based FEC Mechanism for Video Transmission Over Wireless LANs", IEEE TRANSACTIONS ON MULTIMEDIA, VOL. 15, NO. 1, pp 195–206.

13. Suresh, L., Schulz-Zander, J., Merz, R., Feldmann, A., & Vazao, T. (2012, August). Towards programmable enterprise WLANS with Odin. In Proceedings of the first workshop on Hot topics in software defined networks (pp. 115–120). ACM.

14. Xia Yang and Yeo Chai Kiat (2012), "Enabling Network Based Local Mobility With Cooperative Access Points", IEEE.

15. Xue Guangtao, He Qi, Zhu Hongzi, He Tian and Liu Yunhuai (2013), "Sociality Aware Access Point Selection in Enterprise Wireless LANs", IEEE TRANSACTIONS ON PARALLEL AND DISTRIBUTED SYSTEMS, VOL. 24, NO. 10, pp 2069–2077.

16. Xu Shibo, Ren Fengyuan, Xu Yinsheng, Lin Chuang and Yao Min (2013), "Selecting a Preferable Access Point with More Available Bandwidth", IEEE ICC 2013 - Wireless Networking Symposium, pp 633–6316.

17. Rong Hui Hou, Jian Dong LI, Min Sheng and Chun Gang Yang (2014), "Access point selection in heterogeneous wireless networks using belief propagation", Science China Press and Springer-Verlag Berlin Heidelberg.

18. Krishan Ram and Laxami Vijay (2015e), "IEEE 802.11 WLAN Load Balancing for Network Performance Enhancement", 3rd International Conference on Recent Trends in Computing 2015 (ICRTC-2015), Procedia Computer Science 57 (2015), ELSEVIER, pp 493–499.

19. Bhuwania Anshu, Subba Pritam and Roy Uttam Kumar (2016), "Positioning WiFi Access Points Using Particle Swarm Optimization", Second International Conference on Research in Computational Intelligence and Communication Networks, IEEE, pp 112–115.

20. Kim Hye-Young (2016), "An energy-efficient load balancing scheme to extend lifetime in wireless sensor networks", Cluster Comput, Springer, pp 279–283.

21. Breskovic, D., & Begusic, D. (2017). Techno-Economic Analysis of FiWi Access Networks Based on 802.11 ac WLAN and NG-PON2 Networks. Fiber and Integrated Optics, 36(3), 127–143.

Note: All the tables and figures in this chapter were made by the author.

Computer Science Engineering and Emerging Technologies (ICCS-2022) – Prof (Dr.) Rajeev Sobti et al. (eds)
© 2024 Taylor & Francis Group, London, ISBN 978-1-032-52199-2

Chapter **100**

Review Paper for Detection and Prevention of Cyber Attacks

Malik Rasool Magry[1]
Scholar, Lovely Professional University, Phagwara, Punjab, India

Gurpreet Singh*
Assistant Professor, Lovely Professional University, Phagwara, Punjab, India

Abstract: The current trend of cyber-attack detection, identification, and removal is related to the advancement and application of informational technologies. Intrusion Detection Systems are used to detect and identify computer threats. There has been a rise in internet connectivity, and with this greater connectivity has come an increase in security problems. Cyberattacks can result in the loss or theft of sensitive information, disruptions to business operations, and regulatory penalties. In order to protect against these threats, organizations must implement a comprehensive strategy for preventing and detecting cyberattacks. In addition to technical measures, security awareness training is also critical for preventing cyberattacks. Educating users about the risks of cyberattacks and how to recognize and avoid them can help prevent attacks from occurring. This document addresses the various network threats and how to monitor and prevent them. Cyberattacks are a growing concern for individuals and organizations alike as the reliance on technology continues to increase. Detection and prevention of these attacks are crucial in order to protect sensitive information and maintain the integrity of systems. Detection methods include network monitoring, intrusion detection systems, and endpoint protection software. These tools can detect potential threats and alert security teams to take action. Prevention methods include security best practices such as implementing strong passwords and regularly updating software, as well as utilizing firewalls and virtual private networks. Additionally, incident response plans can be put in place to quickly respond and mitigate the effects of a successful attack. It is important for individuals and organizations to stay informed about the latest cyber threats and implement a comprehensive security strategy to protect against them.

Keywords Cyber attacks, Intrusion detection, Intrusion prevention, Cyber crime, Cyber-security

1. Introduction

Cyberattacks are deliberate attempts to compromise computer systems, technology-dependent enterprises, and networks. Every day, thousands of websites and applications are targeted because of the vulnerability of files, attachments, and improper configurations on servers. When cyberattacks are carried out, malicious code is used to alter the code, logic, or data of computer systems. This can lead to cybercrime and other negative repercussions, such as information and identity theft, which can compromise critical data. Cybercrime refers to any wrongdoing that involves a computer and a network. The computer could be used to carry out the assault, or it could be the target device [1]. Cybercrime refers to criminal activity that uses the internet or other forms of digital communication technology. Examples of cybercrime

---

*Corresponding author: Gurpreet.17671@lpu.co.in
[1]malikmagry@gmail.com

DOI: 10.1201/9781003405580-100

include hacking, identity theft, online fraud, and the distribution of malware. Cybercrime can cause significant harm to individuals, businesses, and governments and can be difficult to detect and prevent. [2] [3]

Computer assaults against information and communication infrastructure can pose major problems on a regional or national scale. These effects could be caused by purposeful hacker attacks or by unintentional personnel faults within a system. To prevent possible incidents, implement a comprehensive security strategy that includes several key elements. Identifying and assessing the potential risks and vulnerabilities of the network and systems is the first step in preventing cyberattacks. Also, implementing technical measures such as firewalls, intrusion detection and prevention systems, anti-virus software, vulnerability scanning, and penetration testing can help prevent cyberattacks from being successful. Educating users about the risks of cyberattacks and how to recognize and avoid them can help prevent attacks from occurring. Regularly monitoring and updating security measures, including software, hardware, and policies, can help to prevent new vulnerabilities and ensure that the network and systems are protected against the latest threats. [7] [13]

Finally, regularly testing security measures and incident response plans through simulated attacks can help organizations identify weaknesses and improve their readiness for a real-world attack.

2. Literature Review

2.1 Common Methods of Detection and Prevention for Some Major Attacks

1. Man in the Middleattack

Man-in-the-middle (MitM) attacks involve an attacker intercepting and modifying communications between two parties. Here are a few methods that can be used to detect and prevent MitM attacks: [7] [13]

- **SSL/TLS certificate validation:** When a client establishes a secure connection with a server, the server's SSL/TLS certificate is presented to the client for validation. By verifying the certificate's authenticity, the client can ensure that it is communicating with the correct server and not an attacker who is impersonating the server.
- **ARP spoof detection:** ARP spoofing is a common technique used in MitM attacks, and can be detected by monitoring ARP traffic and identifying ARP packets that contain unusual or unexpected information.
- **Network traffic monitoring:** By monitoring network traffic, it is possible to detect MitM attacks by identifying abnormal patterns of traffic or unusual connections.
- **Antivirus software:** Some antivirus software can detect and prevent MitM attacks by monitoring network traffic and identifying malicious software or activity.
- **Two-factor authentication:** By adding an extra layer of security like two-factor authentication, it can make it much more difficult for an attacker to successfully perform a MitM attack.
- **VPN:** By using a VPN service, all the traffic is encrypted and passed through a secure tunnel, thus making it more difficult for an attacker to intercept the communication.

2. Distributed Denial of Service Attacks (DDoS)

DDoS (Distributed Denial of Service) is a type of cyberattack in which an attacker uses a network of compromised devices (such as computers or IoT devices) called a Botnet to flood a target website or server with an overwhelming amount of traffic. The goal of a DDoS attack is to disrupt the normal functioning of the targeted website or server by overwhelming its resources and making it unavailable to legitimate users. Here are a few methods that can be used to detect and prevent MitM attacks. [2] [7]

Network Monitoring

Regularly monitoring network traffic for unusual spikes or patterns can help detect a DDoS attack in progress. Here are a few ways that network monitoring can aid in the detection of DDoS attacks:

- **Traffic analysis:** Network monitoring tools can analyze traffic patterns and identify abnormal spikes in traffic that may indicate a DDoS attack.
- **Protocol analysis:** Network monitoring tools can monitor and analyze network traffic at the protocol level, which can help detect malicious traffic that is using specific protocols or ports to launch an attack.

Firewalls

Firewalls can help in the detection and mitigation of DDoS attacks by providing several key features:

- **Traffic filtering:** Firewalls can be configured to filter incoming traffic based on a set of rules, which can be used to block or limit traffic from known malicious IP addresses or ranges.
- **Intrusion detection and prevention:** Firewalls can include built-in intrusion detection and prevention systems (IDPS) that can detect and block malicious traffic before it reaches the network.
- **Rate limiting:** Firewalls can be configured to rate-limit traffic, which can help prevent DDoS attacks that rely on overwhelming the network with a high volume of traffic.
- **Alerts:** Firewalls can be configured to send alerts to administrators when they detect suspicious traffic, which can help quickly identify and respond to a DDoS attack.

Anti-DDoS Services

Anti-DDOS services are designed to protect websites and servers from overwhelming traffic that can cause them to crash. Some examples of anti-DDOS services include Cloudflare, Akamai Technologies, Incapsula, Imperva, Arbor Networks, etc.

These services use a variety of techniques to mitigate DDOS attacks, such as traffic filtering, traffic shaping, and network congestion control. Some of these services can be used as cloud-based solutions, while others are offered as hardware or software solutions that can be installed on-premises.[6] [12]

3. Backdoor Attack

A Backdoor attack is a cyberattack in which an attacker gains unauthorized access to a system or network and establishes a way to bypass normal authentication and gain access in the future. Here are a few methods for the detection and prevention of Backdoor attacks:

- **Intrusion detection systems (IDS):** An IDS can help detect Backdoor attacks by monitoring network traffic for suspicious activity and alerting administrators when it detects any unusual patterns.
- **Antivirus software:** Antivirus software can detect and prevent Backdoor attacks by identifying and removing malware that is used to establish a Backdoor on a system.
- **File integrity monitoring:** By monitoring the changes made to files and system settings, it is possible to detect Backdoor attacks by identifying any unauthorized changes.
- **Patch management:** Keeping software and systems up-to-date with the latest security patches can help prevent Backdoor attacks by closing vulnerabilities that attackers can exploit.
- **Log monitoring:** Regularly monitoring system logs can help detect Backdoor attacks by identifying any unusual or unauthorized access attempts. [2] [4][9]
- **Strong authentication:** By implementing strong authentication methods such as multi-factor authentication or passwordless authentication, it can make it more difficult for an attacker to gain unauthorized access.

It is important to note that, no single method is foolproof and a combination of these methods can help to provide a more comprehensive defense against Backdoor attacks.

3. Related Work

3.1 Classification of Cyber Attacks

There are several ways to classify cyberattacks. One strategy is below:

(A) Cyberattacks Against an Individual

Phishing: This is a type of social engineering attack in which an attacker sends an email or message that appears to be from a legitimate source, such as a bank or a social media platform, in order to trick the recipient into providing sensitive information, such as login credentials or credit card information.

Spear Phishing: This is a targeted phishing attack that is directed at specific individuals or organizations. The attacker will often do research on the target in order to craft a more convincing message.

Ransomware Attack: This is a type of malware that encrypts the files on a victim's computer, making them inaccessible. [5][8] The attacker then demands a ransom payment in order to provide the decryption key.

Identity theft: This is a type of cyberattack in which an attacker steals a victim's personal information, such as their Social Security number or credit card information, in order to open bank accounts, make purchases, or commit other types of fraud.

Cyber Stalking: Cyber stalking is the use of the internet, email, social media, or other electronic means to harass, threaten, intimidate, or stalk an individual. Cyber stalkers may use a variety of tactics to target their victims, including:

1. Sending threatening or harassing emails or messages.
2. Posting personal information or false information about the victim online.
3. Creating fake social media profiles to impersonate the victim.
4. Posting embarrassing or compromising photos or videos of the victim.
5. Tracking the victim's online activity using spyware or other tracking tools. [6]

(B) Cyber-attack against Property

Credit Card Frauds: It is a type of financial crime in which an individual uses someone else's credit card or personal information to make unauthorized purchases or withdraw money.

Intellectual Property Crimes: These crimes refer to illegal activities that involve the unauthorized use, reproduction, or distribution of protected IP such as patents, trademarks, copyrights, and trade secrets. Some examples of IP crimes include: Copyright infringement, Trademark infringement, Patent infringement, Trade secret theft, Software Piracy. [7][11]

Internet of Things (IoT) attacks: These are attacks on devices connected to the internet, such as smart home devices or connected cars. These attacks can disrupt the normal functioning of the device, or allow an attacker to take control of the device and use it to launch further attacks.

(C) Cyber-attack against Organizations

Denial of Service Attack: A DoS attack is a type of cyberattack that aims to make a particular service, network, or website unavailable to its intended users.

Advanced Persistent Threats (APTs): These are a type of cyber-attack that are specifically designed to gain access to an organization's sensitive information over an extended period of time. APTs are typically carried out by nation-states, criminal organizations, or other highly-skilled and well-funded attackers. [7][10]

(D) Cyber-attack against Society

Forgery: Forgery refers to the creation of a false document or instrument with the intent to deceive or defraud. This includes creating fake currency, falsifying official documents, or imitating the signature of another person.

Cyber Terrorism: This refers to the use of cyber-attacks to create fear, panic, or chaos among the population. It is a global issue with both domestic and international implications.[6][9] Distributed denial of service attacks are the most common type of terrorist assault on the internet.

Web Jacking: It is a type of cyberattack that involves unauthorized access and control of a website. This can be accomplished through a variety of methods, such as exploiting vulnerabilities in the website's code, stealing login credentials, or redirecting the domain name to a different server.

Once a website has been hijacked, an attacker can use it to spread malware, steal sensitive information, or launch further attacks.

4. Conclusion and Future Scope

In conclusion, cyberattacks have become a significant threat to organizations and individuals in recent years. The detection and prevention of these attacks is crucial in order to protect sensitive information and maintain the integrity of systems. Various techniques and tools have been developed to detect and prevent cyberattacks, including intrusion detection systems, firewalls, and antivirus software. However, it is important to note that no single solution can provide complete protection, and a combination of methods is often necessary. Additionally, it is crucial to stay up to date on the latest threats and to implement best security practices to minimize the risk of a successful attack. Overall, the ongoing development and improvement of detection and prevention methods is crucial in the fight against cybercrime.

The field of cyber security is constantly evolving, and new threats and technologies are continuously being developed. Therefore, there are several areas of research and development that can be explored in the future to improve the detection and prevention of cyberattacks.

One area of research is the use of artificial intelligence and machine learning for the detection and prevention of cyberattacks. These technologies have the potential to significantly improve the ability to detect and respond to cyber threats in real-time. Additionally, they can be used to analyze large amounts of data and identify patterns that may indicate an attack.

Another area of research is the development of more advanced encryption techniques to protect sensitive information. As cyber criminals become more sophisticated, traditional encryption methods may become less effective. Therefore, it is important to continue researching and developing new encryption methods to ensure the security of sensitive information.

Moreover, the Internet of Things (IoT) and other connected devices are becoming increasingly prevalent in our lives, and as a result, securing these devices is of paramount importance to prevent cyberattacks. Therefore, future research can be focused on developing secure and efficient protocols for IoT and other connected devices.

REFERENCES

1. Indre and C. Lemnaru, "Detection and prevention system against cyber attacks and botnet malware for information systems and Internet of Things," 2016 IEEE 12th International Conference on Intelligent Computer Communication and Processing (ICCP), 2016, pp. 175–182, doi: 10.1109/ICCP.2016.7737142.
2. A. M. Kandan, G. JaspherWillsie Kathrine and A. R. Melvin, "Network Attacks and Prevention techniques - A Study," 2019 IEEE International Conference on Electrical, Computer and Communication Technologies (ICECCT), 2019, pp. 1–6, doi: 10.1109/ICECCT.2019.8869077.
3. Y. V. Alpeev, A. N. Stadnik and I. D. Korolev, "Analysis of Methods and Systems of Computer Attacks Detection and Probabilistic Representation of Conditions to Respond," 2020 International Youth Conference on Radio Electronics, Electrical and Power Engineering (REEPE), 2020, pp. 1–5, doi: 10.1109/REEPE49198.2020.9059126.
4. D. Liu et al., "Research on Network Attack Detection Technology based on Reverse Detection and Protocol Analysis," 2019 6th International Conference on Information Science and Control Engineering (ICISCE), 2019, pp. 490–494, doi: 10.1109/ICISCE48695.2019.00104.
5. Kumar, V., Sinha, D. A robust intelligent zero-day cyber-attack detection technique. *Complex Intell. Syst.* **7**, 2211–2234 (2021). https://doi.org/10.1007/s40747-021-00396-9
6. A. S. Choudhary, P. P. Choudhary and S. Salve, "A Study On Various Cyber Attacks And A Proposed Intelligent System For Monitoring Such Attacks," 2018 3rd International Conference on Inventive Computation Technologies (ICICT), 2018, pp. 612–617, doi: 10.1109/ICICT43934.2018.9034445.
7. C. Herringshaw, "Detecting attacks on networks," in Computer, vol. 30, no. 12, pp. 16–17, Dec. 1997, doi: 10.1109/2.642762.
8. M. Baykara, U. Gurturk and R. Das, "An overview of monitoring tools for real-time cyber-attacks," 2018 6th International Symposium on Digital Forensic and Security (ISDFS), 2018, pp. 1–6, doi: 10.1109/ISDFS.2018.8355339.
9. Khraisat, A., Gondal, I., Vamplew, P. *et al.* Survey of intrusion detection systems: techniques, datasets and challenges. *Cybersecur* **2**, 20 (2019). https://doi.org/10.1186/s42400-019-0038-7
10. E. Mousavinejad, F. Yang, Q. -L. Han and L. Vlacic, "A Novel Cyber Attack Detection Method in Networked Control Systems," in IEEE Transactions on Cybernetics, vol. 48, no. 11, pp. 3254–3264, Nov. 2018, doi: 10.1109/TCYB.2018.2843358.
11. V. A. Greiman, "Cyber attacks: the fog of identity," 2016 International Conference on Cyber Conflict (CyCon U.S.), 2016, pp. 1–13, doi: 10.1109/CYCONUS.2016.7836617.
12. A. M. Shabut, K. T. Lwin and M. A. Hossain, "Cyber attacks, countermeasures, and protection schemes—A state of the art survey," 2016 10th International Conference on Software, Knowledge, Information Management & Applications (SKIMA), 2016, pp. 37–44, doi: 10.1109/SKIMA.2016.7916194.

Computer Science Engineering and Emerging Technologies (ICCS-2022) – Prof (Dr.) Rajeev Sobti et al. (eds)
© 2024 Taylor & Francis Group, London, ISBN 978-1-032-52199-2

Chapter **101**

A Concise Review on the Vision-Based Moving Vehicle Detection System by Deep Learning Approaches

Vaibhav Pandilwar[1]
Research Scholar, School of Computer Science and Engineering,
Lovely Professional University

Navjot Kaur[2]
Assistant Professor, Department of Computer Science and Engineering,
Lovely Professional University

Abstract: Applications, planning, and surveillance In a variety of contexts, the process of detecting vehicles on the road is used to achieve goals, like the methods and analysis tools applied in the development of the aforementioned applications, which included developing traffic surveillance systems. In order to better understand the traffic systems, we divided the processing techniques into three groups and contrasted them with other reviews. Vision-based vehicle detection is a key technology that not only plays a significant role in the implementation of active safety features for motor vehicles but also plays a significant role in the monitoring of traffic on roadways using video. In circumstances such as these, the traditional approach to identifying vehicles, which is based on simplified models of such vehicles, is not currently in a position to fulfill the need for accurate vehicle recognition. In this study, a new vehicle identification system that uses deep learning and the deep residual visual geometry group network (DRVGGN) classifier is developed. In this work, the image was retrieved and pre-processed using the contrast stretch median filter, and then the background could be subtracted using the spatio-temporal lasso algorithm. Finally, the proposed DRVGGN architecture detects the vehicle in a precise manner. The whole experimentation was carried out in a Caltech 1999 database. On-road experimental findings show that the algorithm outperforms the most cutting-edge vehicle recognition algorithm in testing data sets. This was shown by the experiments that were conducted on roads. The findings of the comparative assessment indicated that the recommended model performed better than the other models that were evaluated and was able to predict vehicles with an extremely high level of accuracy.

Keywords: Tracking, Occlusion, Shadowing, Traffic monitoring and Classification of vehicles, Vision-based vehicle detection, Deep residual vision geometry group network (DRVGGN), Spatio temporal algorithm

1. Introduction

The primary use of Traffic surveillance is using systems that use video to monitor traffic. For many years, researchers have studied the applications of ITS (Vision-Based Intelligent Transportation System), transportation planning, and traffic engineering in order to gather precise and practical traffic data for traffic image analysis and flow control. Vehicle tally, flow, trajectory, and tracking are a few examples of these applications, as are license plate recognition and traffic density and velocity [1]. In the past, the automated toll levy system employed vehicle identification. For the purpose of calculating

[1]123vaibhavpandilwar@gmail.com, [2]navjot.20506@lpu.co.in

DOI: 10.1201/9781003405580-101

the fee for various vehicle types, segmentation and tracking technologies were used. Vehicle identification systems are now being utilized to identify vehicles, traffic lanes, and vehicle classes on highways, including buses, automobiles, motorcycles, vans, and heavy goods trucks (HGVs) [2].

These systems' effectiveness depends on effective methods for detecting, following, and categorising vehicles in traffic image analysis [3]. Traditional vehicle systems, on the other hand, may be declining as they are difficult to identify because they are hidden by other cars or backdrop obstructions like trees, road signs, or adverse weather, among others. The techniques for segmenting and detecting moving vehicles are covered [4].

2. Literature Review

The suggested dataset, in contrast to the currently available publicly accessible datasets, offers the whole data foundation for vehicle recognition based on deep learning and includes annotated small items in the picture. The newly suggested segmentation methodology, which is essential for enhancing vehicle recognition, divides the highway road surface in the picture into a remote zone and a proximal area. This division is used in the proposed vehicle identification and counting method. The YOLOv3 network then utilizes the two aforementioned zones to determine the kind and position of the vehicle [5]. The final output of the ORB algorithm is the vehicle trajectories, which can be used to calculate the number of automobiles and the direction that each one is going. Numerous highway surveillance recordings based on different circumstances are used to verify the offered approaches. The experimental results are consistent with the hypothesis that using the proposed segmentation technique may improve detection precision, especially when hunting for small vehicle objects [6]. Additionally, while detecting the direction of movement and counting the number of automobiles, the novel technique described in this work performs quite well. This research takes a wide, practical approach to the management and regulation of roadway scenery [7]. Recent Feature engineering methods in vision-based Detection of Vehicles: The authors have provided a description of how, by adjusting the vertices for the best fit, the cuboid was used to fit different vehicle image sizes and types [8]. Therefore, modifying height while taking prior photos into account may effectively accomplish vehicle identification, segmentation, and tracking [9].

Author has advocated a single multi-vehicle tracking and classification method for numerous vehicle kinds, including motorbikesvideo sequences of cars, was used in this study. Measurement was made possible by the vehicles' 3D geometric shapes [10]. Based on a probabilistic border feature grouping, a novel framework for 3D model-based vehicle identification and portrayal has been proposed by the author [11]. This framework is utilized for vehicle detection and tracking processes. This framework provided beneficial qualities such flexibility since it detects cars from more diagonal viewpoints and is free from the scale issue, in addition to being quick when applied to many different applications. The item may be distinguished from the backdrop using a variety of methods, including one that uses trainable object detection. This learning-based strategy identifies the traits of the extracted objects using a set of labeled training data. Additionally, it uses the support vector machine classifier for classification and the Haar wavelet approach for feature extraction. This technique has also been tested on datasets of static images of people, objects, and vehicles [12]. A subregion is a method for identifying regional traits that are utilized to identify partly and completely obscured and non-occluded cars. Both the principal components and the coefficient vector of independent component analysis (ICA) analysis (PCA) were produced by subregions and used to pattern the high-frequency components. This approach uses state-of-the-art statistical techniques that rely on regional characteristics in three subregions to automatically recognize the cars [13]. Additionally, a multistate transformation employs image frame elements that are indexed by position, measure, and orientation criteria. This technique, known as the curve-let transform, also has Wavelets' time-frequency localization characteristics that are very directed and anisotropic. Has been suggested a revolutionary vehicle detection system that leverages the curve let transform as a feature extraction method. According to the authors, there are three main types of classifiers: support vector machines (one versus one) and k closest neighbours are employed in this work to recognize vehicles (one versus all). Finally, the testing results demonstrated the great performance of the vehicle identification procedure [14]. The usage of computer graphics (CG) model pictures in conjunction with a local-feature point setup approach has been presented. The Eigen-window technique is used in this study because it offers a number of benefits, including the ability to identify cars even if they alter their course owing to swerving out of lanes or if some of their components are obscured. Additionally, the CG model photographs outperformed real-world car images in the process of recognizing automobiles. And the CG model simplifies the time-consuming and challenging job of gathering actual photographs of all target cars [15].

Classification approaches in the vision-based Detection of Vehicles CNN: A deep learning model known as CNN is used to analyze data with a grid pattern, such as images. Animal visual cortex organization served as a model for how CNN was designed to automatically and adaptively learn spatial hierarchies of information, from low-level to high-level patterns [16]. A typical CNN is composed of three distinct layers (or "building blocks") that advance in complexity in a hierarchical and progressive manner. Using optimization techniques like back propagation and gradient descent, among others, training is the process of optimizing kernels and other parameters to reduce the difference between outputs and ground truth labels [17]. RNN: Recurrent neural networks, often known as the previous words. In order to tackle this issue, RNN was created, which made use of a Hidden Layer. The Hidden state, which retains some information about a sequence, is the most crucial and fundamental aspect of RNNs [18]. VGG: The VGG is a typical convolutional neural network architecture. It was based on research into how to deepen these networks. The network makes use of tiny 3-by-3 filters. The network is distinguished by its simplicity otherwise; the only additional elements are pooling layers and a fully connected layer [19].

Table 101.1 Comparative study of related work

Author	Title	Algorithm used
[12] M. P. D. Jolly	Vehicle Segmentation and Classification Using Deformable Templates.	YOLO V3
[18] A. Monnet	Background Modeling and Subtraction of Dynamic Scenes.	CNN (Convolutional Neural Network)
[21] W. Weiqiang	Modeling Background and Segmenting Moving Objects from Compressed Video.	VGG (Visual Geometry Group)
[22] J. Goo	Tracking and Segmentation of Highway Vehicles in Cluttered and Crowded Scenes.	DNN (Deep Neural Network)
[32] D. R. Magee	Tracking Multiple Vehicles Using Foreground, Background and Motion Models.	SURF (Speed-Up Robust Features)

Source: Made by the Author

A classifier receives as inputs the top-ranked 3678 features (30% of all features) determined using multi-objective ACO. These derived characteristics lessen the possibility of overfitting and expedite training (and testing). In this experiment, a deep neural network with the following dimensions was utilized for classification: 3678, 500, 250, and 6. The output layer was a softback layer with 6 nodes, which correspond to 6 classifications: 5 car classes plus background. The layers of the deep neural network were initialized using several auto-encoders that had been trained. These numerous auto encoders were known as stacked auto encoders in the Mat Lab toolbox. The phrase "stacked auto-encoder neural network" has several connotations depending on the context; hence, for the purposes of this research study, the term "Deep Neural Network (DNN)" itself will be used [20].

All other classifiers were consistently outperformed by the deep neural network's stacked auto-encoder. Another series of studies included selecting features using various optimizers, which were subsequently provided as inputs to a stacked auto-encoder deep neural network. In Section 4, each of the aforementioned experiments is thoroughly explained. Below is a quick general explanation of neural networks and autoencoders. A neural network may be mathematically characterized and generally consists of an input and output layer as well as many hidden layers [21]. Benchmark dataset associated with the detection of vehicles: One of the fundamental technologies for autonomous driving is the ability to detect moving objects and describe their location and orientation in three dimensions. Methods for 3D vehicle recognition that are just dependent on monocular RGB photos have recently grown in favor. A number of new datasets and benchmarks have been produced to help with this effort as well as to compare and evaluate cutting-edge techniques. Lidar point clouds are often used to produce ground truth annotations for vehicles; however, these point clouds frequently include inaccuracies because of poor calibration or synchronization between the two sensors [22]. In order to do this, we suggest Cityscapes 3D, an extension of the original Cityscapes dataset that adds 3D bounding box annotations for all different kinds of vehicles. In contrast to previous datasets, our 3D annotations cover all nine degrees of freedom and were labeled using just stereo RGB pictures. In comparison to lidar-based methods, this results in a greater range of annotations and a pixel-accurate projection in the RGB picture. We provide a coupling of 2D instance segments with 3D bounding boxes to facilitate multitasking. Additionally, based on the additional annotations and metrics described in this study, we added 3D vehicle identification to the Cityscapes benchmark suite. Online resources for the benchmark and data set [23] Autonomous vehicle systems (AVS) have developed exponentially over the last ten years, in large part because of advances in artificial intelligence. The future of transportation networks as well as social and vehicular safety have all been greatly impacted by this. The AVS is still a long way from being mass manufactured, however, because of the innovative combinations used to deal with unpredictability on roads. Since they increase production, reduce dependency on sensors, and enhance research, the literature is investigated for final representative results that may be represented in things like enhanced navigation and early warning. due to road markings and increased safety due to pedestrians and vehicles overlapping in poor visibility to lessen collisions. The literature review's contribution includes a thorough overview of the most cutting-edge deep learning techniques that solely depend on RGB camera vision as opposed to the intricate creation of workable, affordable solutions [24].

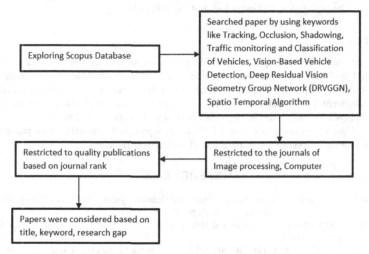

Fig. 101.1 Paper search approach

Source: Made by the Author

3. Research Gap

Many applications, including image processing, make use of the neural network, which plays a significant role in these applications. They have also provided a neural-boundary-based vehicle identification and classification method, which is a noteworthy addition. By combining the outcomes, vehicle numbering and vehicle type are removed. Seed-filling is the name of this distinctive knowledge mining method. Once that was done, the extracted feature was employed as input data into a neural network to accurately identify and categorize vehicles [25]. Additionally, the author has developed an approach for recognizing vehicles in traffic views that is based on fuzzy integrals [26]. The method uses the Hough transform to extract the car's contour boundaries, lowers noise, and improves the shape of the entity regions using morphological processes. It also makes use of the fuzzy integral and calculates it using the data gathered during the recognition process [27].

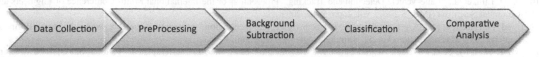

Fig. 101.2 Workflow Diagram

Source: Made by the Author

4. Suggestions and Future Recommendations

This section discusses the detection of a vehicle in front vision. A novel approach using maximizing a posterior probability and Markov chain Monte Carlo (MCMC) approaches has been put forward by the authors. The Markov chain is designed to iteratively sample edge information from road and vehicle model simulations. Thereafter, sequential vehicle recognition is carried out using the MAP approach in front-view static pictures with frequent occlusions [28]. Additionally, the segmentation approach requires background reduction and shade removal as complicated pre-processing procedures that are not provided. Many statistical methods are employed in image processing as well [29]. A computerized system for monitoring traffic on the highway based on higher-order statistics for classifying and identifying automobiles in photos is provided. In this study, test patterns are classified as cars by learning from example photos, and HOS data about the vehicle class is gleaned and used as a decision-making tool [30].

Additionally, it has proposed a strategy for segmenting mobile vehicles, which are dispersed. A Bayesian system will then be used to categorize the mobile in the views, which strengthens and improves the suggested technique and roughly satisfies its criteria using the expectation-maximization (EM) algorithm [31].

5. Conclusion

The suggested strategies that have been applied to traffic videos are summarized in this article. With the appearance of shadows and partial occlusion, it concentrates on three areas: vehicle identification, tracking, and classification. Additionally, we propose and categorize traffic surveillance systems into three groups based on the distinct techniques that were used in their development. These kinds of demonstrations demonstrate in detail how image processing techniques and analytic tools were employed by traffic surveillance systems to identify, classify, and track moving objects. Additionally, issues with shadow and partial occlusion are covered, along with potential remedies. More precisely, this assessment clarifies the problems with traffic monitoring systems and identifies their remedies.

REFERENCES

1. H. Chung-Lin and L. Wen-Chieh, "A vision-based vehicle identification system," in Pattern Recognition, 2004. ICPR 2004. Proceedings of the 17th International Conference on, 2004, pp. 364–367 Vol.4.
2. Z. Wei, et al., "Multilevel Framework to Detect and Handle Vehicle Occlusion," Intelligent Transportation Systems, IEEE Transactions on, vol. 9, pp. 161–174, 2008.
3. N. K. Kanhere and S. T. Birchfield, "Real-Time Incremental Segmentation and Tracking of Vehicles at Low Camera Angles Using Stable Features," Intelligent Transportation Systems, IEEE Transactions on, vol. 9, pp. 148–160, 2008.
4. N. K. Kanhere, "Vision-based detection, tracking and classification of vehicles using stable features with automatic camera calibration," ed, 2008, p. 105.
5. A. H. S. Lai, et al., "Vehicle type classification from visual-based dimension estimation," in Intelligent Transportation Systems, 2001. Proceedings. 2001 IEEE, 2001, pp. 201–206.
6. Z. Zhigang, et al., "A real-time vision system for automatic traffic monitoring based on 2D spatio-temporal images," in Applications of Computer Vision, 1996. WACV '96., Proceedings 3rd IEEE Workshop on, 1996, pp. 162–167.
7. W. Wei, et al., "A method of vehicle classification using models and neural networks," in Vehicular Technology Conference, 2001. VTC 2001 Spring. IEEE VTS 53rd, 2001, pp. 3022–3026 vol.4.
8. R. Rad and M. Jamzad, "Real time classification and tracking of multiple vehicles in highways," Pattern Recognition Letters, vol. 26, pp. 1597–1607, 2005.
9. Y. Iwasaki and H. Itoyama, "Real-time Vehicle Detection Using Information of Shadows Underneath Vehicles," in Advances in Computer, Information, and Systems Sciences, and Engineering, K. Elleithy, et al., Eds., ed: Springer Netherlands, 2006, pp. 94–98.
10. K. H. Lim, et al., "Lane-Vehicle Detection and Tracking," Proceedings of the International Multi-Conference of Engineers and Computer Scientists (IMECS 2009), vol. 2, pp. 5–10, 2009.
11. J. M. Ferryman, et al., "A generic deformable model for vehicle recognition," presented at the Proceedings of the 1995 British conference on Machine vision (Vol. 1), Birmingham, United Kingdom, 1995.
12. M. P. D. Jolly, et al., "Vehicle segmentation and classification using deformable templates," Pattern Analysis and Machine Intelligence, IEEE Transactions on, vol. 18, pp. 293–308, 1996.
13. N. D. Matthews, et al., "Vehicle detection and recognition in greyscale imagery," Control Engineering Practice, vol. 4, pp. 473–479, 1996.
14. T. Kato, et al., "Preceding vehicle recognition based on learning from sample images," Intelligent Transportation Systems, IEEE Transactions on, vol. 3, pp. 252–260, 2002.
15. F. M. Kazemi, et al., "Vehicle Recognition Using Curvelet Transform and SVM," in Information Technology, 2007. ITNG '07. Fourth International Conference on, 2007, pp. 516–521.
16. B. Han, et al., "Motion-segmentation-based change detection," SPIE Defence & Security Symposium 2007, pp. 65680Q-65680Q, 2007.
17. S. Gupte, et al., "Detection and classification of vehicles," Intelligent Transportation Systems, IEEE Transactions on, vol. 3, pp. 37–47, 2002.
18. A. Monnet, et al., "Background Modeling and Subtraction of Dynamic Scenes," presented at the Proceedings of the Ninth IEEE International Conference on Computer Vision - Volume 2, 2003.

19. G. Monteiro, et al., "Robust segmentation for outdoor traffic surveillance," in Image Processing, 2008. ICIP 2008. 15th IEEE International Conference on, 2008, pp. 2652–2655.
20. [20] P. Spagnolo, et al., "Moving object segmentation by background subtraction and temporal analysis," Image and Vision Computing, vol. 24, pp. 411–423, 2006.
21. W. Weiqiang, et al., "Modeling Background and Segmenting Moving Objects from Compressed Video," Circuits and Systems for Video Technology, IEEE Transactions on, vol. 18, pp. 670–681, 2008.
22. J. Goo, et al., "Tracking and Segmentation of Highway Vehicles in Cluttered and Crowded Scenes," in Applications of Computer Vision, 2008. WACV 2008. IEEE Workshop on, 2008, pp. 1–6.
23. L. Vasu, "An effective step to real-time implementation of accident detection system using image processing," Master of Science, Oklahoma State University, USA, 2010.
24. C. R. Wren, et al., "Pfinder: real-time tracking of the human body," Pattern Analysis and Machine Intelligence, IEEE Transactions on, vol. 19, pp. 780–785, 1997.
25. G. C. De Silva, "Automation of Traffic Flow Measurement Using Video Images," Master of Engineering, University of Moratuwa, Sri Lanka, 2001.
26. C. P. Papageorgiou and T. & Poggio, "A Trainable System for Object Detection in Images and Video Sequences," Massachusetts Institute of Technology Center for Biological and Computational Learning, vol. 1673., 2000.
27. W. Chi-Chen Raxle and J. J. J. Lien, "Automatic Vehicle Detection Using Local Features—A Statistical Approach," Intelligent Transportation Systems, IEEE Transactions on, vol. 9, pp. 83–96, 2008.
28. T. Yoshida, et al., "Vehicle Classification System with Local-Feature Based Algorithm Using CG Model Images," IEICE Trans. on Information and Systems, vol. vol.E85--D, pp. 1745–1752, 2002.
29. T. M. Deng and B. Li, "A Detection Method of Traffic Parameters Based on EPI," Procedia Engineering, vol. 29, pp. 3054–3059, 2012.
30. Z. Tao and R. Nevatia, "Car detection in low resolution aerial image," in Computer Vision, 2001. ICCV 2001. Proceedings. Eighth IEEE International Conference on, 2001, pp. 710–717 vol.1.
31. D. Koller, et al., "Towards robust automatic traffic scene analysis in real-time," in Decision and Control, 1994., Proceedings of the 33rd IEEE Conference on, 1994, pp. 3776–3781 vol.4

Computer Science Engineering and Emerging Technologies (ICCS-2022) – Prof (Dr.) Rajeev Sobti et al. (eds)
© 2024 Taylor & Francis Group, London, ISBN 978-1-032-52199-2

Chapter **102**

Automation and Robotics in Healthcare Industry for Monitoring Patients in Critical Care Unit

Manish Kumar Thimmaraju*
Head of the Department-Pharmaceutical Analysis,
Balaji Institute of Pharmaceutical Sciences, Narsampet, Warangal, Telangana India

Mohammed Asif Hussain[1]
Professor, Pathfinder Institute of Pharmacy Education and Research,
Beside Mamnoor camp, Khammam Road, Warangal Telangana India

Anil Kumar Garige[2]
Head of the Department-Pharmaceutical Chemistry,
Jayamukhi Institute of Pharmaceutical sciences, Narsampet, Warangal, India

Vijitha Chandupatla[3]
Head of the Department-Pharmacognosy,
Vaagdevi Institute of Pharmaceutical sciences, Bollikunta, Warangal Telangana India

A. Mohathasim Billah[4]
Professor of Pharmacy Practice,
Thanthai Roever College of Pharmacy, Perambalur, Tamilnadu India

Abstract: Customarily, progress in automated innovation has been made in the assembling business because of the requirement for cooperative robots. Nonetheless, this isn't true in the help area, particularly in the medical care area. The absence of accentuation put on the medical care area has prompted new doors to open in creating administration robots that help patients with ailments, perception difficulties, and handicaps. Besides, the Coronavirus pandemic has served as an impetus for the improvement of administration robots in medical services, which are trying to conquer the challenges and difficulties brought about by this infection. The utilization of administration robots is profitable as they not only forestall the spread of disease and decrease human mistakes, but they additionally permit frontline staff to lessen direct contact, concentrate on higher-need errands, and make a partition of straight openness to contamination. This essay provides an overview of several mechanical developments and their applications to the field of medical care.

Keywords: Automation, Healthcare, Monitoring, Critical care, Robotics

1. Introduction

Throughout the long term, the field of administrative mechanical technology has fundamentally developed, particularly in the business area. In any case, less consideration has been given to the medical care area than to other areas, maybe because of the difficulties related to giving relational consideration and the actual idea with the help. Albeit this has frustrated the

*Corresponding Author: manishcancer@gmail.com
[1]drasifhussainp@gmail.com, [2]anilkumargarige@gmail.com, [3]cvijitha@gmail.com, [4]billahs@yahoo.co.uk

DOI: 10.1201/9781003405580-102

improvement of robots that can assist with customer consideration demands, things have mostly changed after COVID's resurgence. Automated innovation is generally rapidly re-examined and used to assist with forestalling the spread of infections and microbes through sterilization, coordinated operations, and telehealth (Kosa *et al.*, 2022). Moreover, there is an interest in administration robots to help medical caretakers and medical care laborers increase efficiency by limiting one person from coming into contact with another while compensating for a critical increase in the shortage of medical workers due to the illness's utterly alluring character. Robot innovation can be used in many different fields, but it might have a significant impact on clinical considerations. Mechanical implementations could provide the commitment of a viable and economical medical services arrangement without compromising the character of care (Holland *et al.*, 2021).

For example, robots could be utilized for estimating temperatures using warm touch to fabricate the viability of plates. Also, numerous nations have depended on gathering pharyngeal and nasopharyngeal swabs for the exhibition testing of COVID. This habitually requires the selection, handling, transferring, and testing of many things, which can be laborious. A computerized interaction could diminish the risk of contamination and human error and could likewise permit bleeding-edge staff to concentrate on higher-need undertakings (Ferre *et al.*, 2021). One may argue that the coronavirus could serve as a catalyst for the development of mechanical systems that medical professionals can quickly transport and use to forestall the spread of infection and reduce pollution. In any case, the quarantine assumptions that have been set up all over the world have guessed that individuals will carry on with their lives disconnected from their loved ones. Both physical and mental health are impacted by this. Subsequently, administration robots could be utilized as friendly colleagues, offering useful help for regular exercises. They could likewise go about as friends, partaking in friendly connections to advance actual work and checking close to home states (Panwar *et al.*, 2021).

2. Literature Review

The demand for skilled help robots to assist medical services staff is expected to reach 38 billion Annually by 2022, despite the fact that the field of mass drug advanced mechanics is still relatively young. Robots will not only reduce the responsibility of medical care staff but additionally aid troublesome assignments that should be finished. The essential assistance robot definition was generated in 1993 by specific examiners at the Foundation for Collecting Planning and Automation. An assistance robot is an uninhibitedly programmable kinematic contraption that performs organizations tasks semi-or totally (Gupta and Arora, 2022). Organizations are tasks that don't add to the advanced collection of items yet are the execution of supportive work for individuals and equipment. From there on out, various definitions have been proposed; the Worldwide Standardization Affiliation portrays the phrase as an AI that performs critical undertakings for people or hardware, with the exception of current computerization applications, though the Worldwide League of Mechanical Technology underscores the autonomy of the robot according to their definition: "*a helping robot is a robot that works semi-or completely independently to perform administrations valuable to the prosperity of people and gear, barring producing tasks*" (Jain and Pandey, 2019).

As the expression "Administration Robot" has kept on advancing, its definition has been obscured because of the hybridization between industry and administration areas. For example, portable robots and computer-directed vehicles are utilized in modern mechanization applications and as administration robots in new conditions like medical clinics. Most of this paper will zero in on help robots intended for the medical services area and thusly sort a helping robot as one that does errands, either to some degree or completely independently in a clinical setting (Khamis *et al.*, 2021). On account of the subsection on friendly consideration, we give instances of how individual help robots can be utilized to moderate forlornness and advance efficiency during social detachment.

As one can give exact control of instruments, keep up with well-being, screen patients, and perform different diagnostics, they have a key role in medical care. Generally speaking, these robots share the climate with people, and in that capacity, they ought to have the option to perceive faces, signals, and discourse as well as articles. The fruitful comprehension of these assignments brings about deterrent aversion and correspondence in view of feeling. Essentially, administration robots are machines that can do a progression of activities. They are equipped for independent dynamics in light of the information they gain through their sensing, photos, and propaganda outlets, and they can modify their behavior in response to the situation (Javaid and Haleem, 2019). Many assistance robots are linked to larger frameworks, for example, cloud-based frameworks that store data like the client's data and exchange information. When combined with biometrics, for example, face recognition, administration robots can recognize individuals and customize their administration at a minor expense. While depicting the portrayal of a helping robot, we will generally consider them either machine-like by all accounts or human-like for all intents and purposes, having a few humanlike elements, frequently stylized. Concerning the kinds of undertakings that they complete, obligations can either be calculated (functional assignments for transportation), insightful (picture investigation for the conclusion), or profound (straightforwardly managing individuals) (Hager *et al.*, 2020).

Besides security, it is critical to confirm that there are no bogus positive or adverse outcomes while being utilized for discovery or determination, as this can be a hazardous gamble for general well-being. Accordingly, it is with the greatest possible level of significance that continuous mechanical advancements in sensors and actuators are finished and further research into new advancements and interpersonal cooperation is conducted.

3. Methodology

Because different research methodologies can be used in a variety of contexts, it is crucial to understand which technique is most appropriate for a certain hypothesis or topic. In fact, using the wrong study methodology could make the findings meaningless. A variety of notions are used in research techniques to ascertain a situation's reality through objective analysis. Research methodologies describe the methodological approach to gathering data and analyzing it to derive significant findings. This is a crucial procedure that aids in conflict resolution and strategic decision-making. It allows managers to focus their efforts on coming up with ideas the right way. The effectiveness and dependability of the study project will be determined by the methodology used. The two basic problems that method addresses in investigation are how the data utilized for the project was obtained and how it was analyzed to produce the findings.

4. Analysis and Discussion

An enormous collection of writing is given to portray various ways to deal with Mechanical technology as well as breaking down their belongings. An overall agreement exists on Mechanical technology being useful, and thus, it ought to be integrated into everyday clinical practice. To wrap things up, past creating significant clinical enhancements for ICU patients, Mechanical technology lessens expenses for clinics. Nonetheless, the writer additionally considers a few things that need to be taken into account. Basically, it is difficult for professionals to adhere to a specific Mechanical technology convention due to the broad variety of conventions and the diverse characteristics of ICU patients (Blick, 2013). Additionally, they prevent experts from accurately focusing on the advantages and assets of Advanced mechanics. Further research on activation time and power will be necessary in this area to advance patient results, especially in unambiguous ICU populaces. Besides, there are various components that are seen as boundaries to the inescapable execution of Advanced mechanics, which are examined straightaway.

Alongside the standing execution of ICT in the medical services space, urban areas began to furnish their systems with ICT to address both urbanization issues, such as the increase of people moving from rural to urban areas, and segment difficulties, for example, the total populace expansion in the future (Jain *et al.* 2019). ICT develops urban areas with detecting and examination capacities ready to accumulate and take advantage of information progressively to assist leaders with reworking assets all the more productively and upgrade the personal satisfaction of residents. Therefore, urban communities are consistently being transformed into savvy urban communities, where residents can collaborate with their nearby climate. By summing up this idea, conditions fit for adjusting to clients' requirements are ordinarily known as setting mindful conditions. Brilliant homes, savvy structures, shrewd clinics, and savvy urban communities are instances of setting mindful conditions (Jain and Pandey, 2019). The regular collaboration between well-being and m-wellbeing combined with the development of savvy urban communities and setting mindful conditions propelled brilliant medical care, presented as "the arrangement of wellbeing administrations by utilizing the setting mindful organization and detecting framework of shrewd urban areas". Albeit the given definition was enlivened by the extent of brilliant urban areas, the idea goes beyond their limits, and it very well may be summed up as setting mindful conditions. Notwithstanding the patient-driven viewpoint utilized by both e-wellbeing and m-wellbeing standards, s-wellbeing additionally presents a natural/logical methodology, as it considers information coming from the detecting framework of the setting mindful climate and adjusts its way of behaving as needs are met. The combined use of low-impression sensors and the Web of Things, which can amass vast amounts of pertinent data with reduced registered capacity and energy consumption, can contribute to the enormous transmission of smart, setting mindful health service arrangements at large (Reddy *et al.* 2019).

In the realm of surgery, automation and medicine have a close working relationship that greatly benefits doctors' hands. General surgery, minimally invasive surgical procedures, remote patient monitoring, preoperative preparation and rehearsal, intraoperative navigation, and post-operative evaluations are all included in the technology integrated into surgical care.

Robotic surgery speeds up the participant's recovery since it lowers operational trauma and epithelial tissue loss (Watson *et al.* 2020). This is because these devices are tremor-free and produce accurate micromotions with predetermined microforces. In "computer assisted surgery (CAS)", the computer interface helps the surgeon operate the operation suite remotely, whereas "robotic assisted surgery (RAS)" uses a motorized system to manage the mobility of the intervention. CAS is typically used for tool detection, path planning, cut recognition, cancer cell identification, and other applications. As shown in Fig. 102.1, RAS comprises a robot at the patient's side called a "patient side manipulator (PSM)", which can be operated independently or via telemetry by a device called a "master tool manipulator (MTM)" (Verma *et al.* 2018).

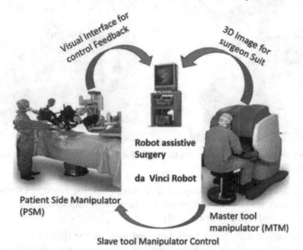

Fig. 102.1 Robot assistive surgery (Kosa et al., 2022)

Surgeons can examine the operating room surroundings and even practice before completing specific surgeries with the help of simulation technologies. They assist in preparing new surgeons to operate in real-world situations without any reluctance by educating them in virtual environments. Robotic simulators offer a superior framework for viewing human conscious and unconscious psychology that directly affects physiological wellbeing when combined with virtual reality (VR) innovations (Holland *et al.,* 2021). Some people's phobias have a profound impact on their psychology and many biological processes, which can lead to heart failure at a young age, hormone imbalances, and mental instability. Doctors can benefit from the combination of robotic emulators and VR by asking patients to sit, stand, or lay down on the simulator while donning the VR goggles. Patients who do this may find it easier to face and conquer their concerns (Panwar *et al.,* 2021). Distinct biochemical parameters are recorded and maintained on patients' identities instantly through the Internet of Things (IoT) throughout that operation for doctors and patients to examine as well as to generate recordings for later use (Jain *et al.,* 2021).

The various emulators used to treat various diseases as well as track, record, and manage various real-time biological parameters are shown in Fig. 102.2.

A mechanical slant table that permits early preparation of out-of-commission patients by balancing their body tendencies and leg development is introduced. These boundaries are naturally set by a self-learning fluffy regulator that ceaselessly screens and balances out the cardiovascular boundaries of patients, for example, pulse and circulatory strain, to safe reaches. The proposed framework is meant to restore the reconditioned cardiovascular framework after a prolonged period of chronic in patients who are not in active treatment. Although the system was tested on healthy volunteers, during the acceptance of early activation exercises, the vascular boundaries were successfully maintained within therapeutically acceptable levels. The results were sufficiently encouraging to focus on the framework's suitability for patients who were laid up for a long period of time (Guntur *et al.* 2019). Comparatively, an original slant table with a coordinated mechanical venturing instrument for inactive mobilizations The proposed framework is meant to recuperate the cardio-pneumonic arrangement. Many patients who have had terrible brain injuries or spinal cord injuries have disconnected developments in their lower extremities. It's interesting to note that the altered virtualization and venturing network of the device enabled

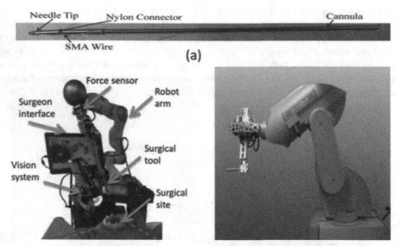

Fig. 102.2 Pre-programmed or semi-autonomous robot. (a) Self-actuating flexible needle system. (b) STAR. (c) Acrobot (Panwar et al., 2021)

the era of physiologically burdensome designs (Arajo *et al*. 2020). Albeit the outcomes showed an immediate impact of the latent second on the circulatory framework, further investigations with additional patients and assessing the drawn-out impacts of the treatment are required (Antony *et al*. 2020).

Mechanically assisted care is undoubtedly being used more and more in the field of medical service robotization, from walking exoskeletons to end-effector robots, including innovative mechatronic wearable systems that aim to execute uninvolved mobilizations. They are useful for computerizing medical services because they can prepare tedious and serious tasks, offer assistance as needed, and provide input. Whatever the case, their high cost may act as a barrier to their integration into medical care robotization protocols (Jain and Pandey, 2019).

5. Conclusion

According to the analysis, there are fewer papers on automotive medical technology services that consider the use of electronic devices and ICT. Additionally, the current proposals for ICT-related arrangements related to physical technology used in health services only focus on the use of a single innovation rather than offering a comprehensive solution for further developing better biomechanics in medical care practice. In this line, the recommendations in certain articles are portrayed as innovation-centered settings, and the impacts of utilizing a particular sort of innovation in any case, sadly, don't depict how the Mechanical technology IN Medical services practice could be upgraded with procedures, for example, information mining, process mining, or cutting-edge AI. Just proposes the utilization of man-made reasoning and the gained information to survey the level of accomplishment and adherence to the booked schedules. In any case, the surveyed innovations could be coordinated into a worldwide situation for Mechanical technology IN Medical care, upgraded using the shrewd medical services worldview. Additionally, a portion of the proposition that was at first chosen for Set 3 but was sifted through during the screening stage could be considered for this situation.

References

1. A. Jain, A. K. Pandey, (2019), "Modeling And Optimizing Of Different Quality Characteristics In Electrical Discharge Drilling Of Titanium Alloy (Grade-5) Sheet" Material Today Proceedings, 18, 182–191. https://doi.org/10.1016/j.matpr.2019.06.292
2. A. Jain, A. K. Pandey, (2019), "Multiple Quality Optimizations In Electrical Discharge Drilling Of Mild Steel Sheet" Material Today Proceedings, 8, 7252–7261. https://doi.org/10.1016/j.matpr.2017.07.054
3. A. Jain, A.K. Yadav & Y. Shrivastava (2019), "Modelling and Optimization of Different Quality Characteristics In Electric Discharge Drilling of Titanium Alloy Sheet" Material Today Proceedings, 21, 1680–1684. https://doi.org/10.1016/j.matpr.2019.12.010
   A. Jain, A. K. Pandey, (2019), "Modeling And Optimizing Of Different Quality Characteristics In Electrical Discharge Drilling Of Titanium Alloy (Grade-5) Sheet" Material Today Proceedings, 18, 182–191. https://doi.org/10.1016/j.matpr.2019.06.292

4. A. Jain, C. S. Kumar, Y. Shrivastava, (2021), "Fabrication and Machining of Fiber Matrix Composite through Electric Discharge Machining: A short review" Material Today Proceedings. https://doi.org/10.1016/j.matpr.2021.07.288
5. Antony, M., Parameswaran, M., Mathew, N., Sajithkumar, V.S., Joseph, J. and Jacob, C.M., 2020, June. Design and implementation of automatic guided vehicle for hospital application. In *2020 5th International Conference on Communication and Electronics Systems (ICCES)* (pp. 1031–1036). IEEE.
6. Araújo, N.M.F., 2020. Impact of the Fourth Industrial Revolution on the health sector: A qualitative Study. *Healthcare informatics research, 26*(4), pp. 328–334.
7. Blick, K.E., 2013. Providing critical laboratory results on time, every time to help reduce emergency department length of stay: how our laboratory achieved a Six Sigma level of performance. *American Journal of Clinical Pathology, 140*(2), pp. 193–202.
8. Ferre, M., Batista, E., Solanas, A. and Martínez-Ballesté, A., 2021. Smart Health-Enhanced Early Mobilisation in Intensive Care Units. *Sensors, 21*(16), p. 5408.
9. Guntur, S. R., Gorrepati, R. R. and Dirisala, V. R., 2019. Robotics in healthcare: an internet of medical robotic things (IoMRT) perspective. In *Machine learning in bio-signal analysis and diagnostic imaging* (pp. 293–318). Academic Press.
10. Gupta, V.P. and Arora, A.K., 2022. Automation in healthcare services. In *Research Anthology on Cross-Disciplinary Designs and Applications of Automation* (pp. 285–303). IGI Global.
11. Hager, G., Kumar, V., Murphy, R., Rus, D. and Taylor, R., 2020. The role of robotics in infectious disease crises. *arXiv preprint arXiv:2010.09909.*
12. Holland, J., Kingston, L., McCarthy, C., Armstrong, E., O'Dwyer, P., Merz, F. and McConnell, M., 2021. Service robots in the healthcare sector. *Robotics, 10*(1), p. 47.
13. Holland, J., Kingston, L., McCarthy, C., Armstrong, E., O'Dwyer, P., Merz, F. and McConnell, M., 2021. Service robots in the healthcare sector. *Robotics, 10*(1), p. 47.
14. Javaid, M. and Haleem, A., 2019. Industry 4.0 applications in medical field: A brief review. *Current Medicine Research and Practice, 9*(3), pp. 102–109.
15. Khamis, A., Meng, J., Wang, J., Azar, A.T., Prestes, E., Takács, Á., Rudas, I.J. and Haidegger, T., 2021. Robotics and intelligent systems against a pandemic. *Acta Polytechnica Hungarica, 18*(5), pp. 13–35.
16. Kosa, G., Morozov, O., Lehmann, A., Pargger, H., Marsch, S. and Hunziker, P., 2022. Robots and Intelligent Medical Devices in the Intensive Care Unit: Vision, State of the Art and Economic Analysis.
17. Reddy, S., Fox, J. and Purohit, M.P., 2019. Artificial intelligence-enabled healthcare delivery. *Journal of the Royal Society of Medicine, 112*(1), pp. 22–28.
18. V. Panwar, D. K. Sharma, K. V. P. Kumar, A. Jain & C. Thakar, (2021), "Experimental Investigations And Optimization Of Surface Roughness In Turning Of EN 36 Alloy Steel Using Response Surface Methodology And Genetic Algorithm" Materials Today: Proceedings, https://Doi.org/10.1016/J.Matpr.2021.03.642
19. V. Panwar, D. K. Sharma, K. V. P. Kumar, A. Jain & C. Thakar, (2021), "Experimental Investigations And Optimization Of Surface Roughness In Turning Of EN 36 Alloy Steel Using Response Surface Methodology And Genetic Algorithm" Materials Today: Proceedings, https://Doi.Org/10.1016/J.Matpr.2021.03.642
20. Verma, V., Chowdary, V., Gupta, M. K. and Mondal, A. K., 2018. IoT and robotics in healthcare. In *Medical Big Data and Internet of Medical Things* (pp. 245–269). CRC Press.
21. Watson, D., Womack, J. and Papadakos, S., 2020. Rise of the robots: Is artificial intelligence a friend or foe to nursing practice?. *Critical Care Nursing Quarterly, 43*(3), pp. 303–311.

Computer Science Engineering and Emerging Technologies (ICCS-2022) – Prof (Dr.) Rajeev Sobti et al. (eds)
© 2024 Taylor & Francis Group, London, ISBN 978-1-032-52199-2

Chapter **103**

A Review of Various System-on-Chip Technologies for Multiprocessor Systems

Sankalp Sudarsan Rajguru[1], Ayush Gour[2]
Student, Department of Computer Science and Engineering,
Lovely Professional University Phagwara, Punjab, India

Gursharan Singh[3]*, Gurpreet Singh[4]*, Makul Mahajan[5]*, Salil Batra[6]*
Assistant Professor, Department of Computer Science and Engineering,
Lovely Professional University Phagwara, Punjab, India

Abstract: Low-level languages are effective tools for creating applications for some embedded devices. Nevertheless, high-level languages offer a fantastic environment for the creation of programming tools. A multiprocessor is a computer system with two or more central processing units. A heterogeneous multiprocessor is created by combining digital logic, mixed-signal circuits, and a multiprocessor system-on-chip. Teams working on MPSoC design face a significant obstacle as a result of this technology combination. We also discuss various difficulties faced by MPSoC designers in terms of hardware and software. A system-on-chip with several processors that only interact locally is a target device. That share complete access to RAM. Increasing system execution speed is the main goal of employing several processors; additional goals include fault tolerance and application customisation. This paper discusses the present condition, difficulties, and developments of MPSoC technology. The study also discusses prospective advances in MPSoC technology and how they can affect computer design in the future.

Keywords: Multiprocessor, Multiprocessor system-on-chip (MPSoC), Unified modeling language (UML), Real-time operating systems (RTOSs)

1. Introduction

A multiprocessor is a computer system with two or more CPUs that has full access to a single RAM. The key advantages of using several processors are quicker system execution, application customization, and fault tolerance. Multiprocessors are available in two types: distributed and shared-memory multiprocessors. The performance, scalability, and reliability of each Control Processing Unit (CPU) have significantly increased, making them a crucial component of computer design. Recent multiprocessor breakthroughs include the creation of novel designs, the use of novel technologies, and the incorporation of several processors into a single system (J. Backus et al., 1978). Multiprocessing is frequently employed in embedded computer systems because it helps us meet our performance, cost, and energy/power consumption objectives. However, heterogeneous embedded multiprocessors are usually made up of several kinds of processors. To fully utilise these multiprocessors, complicated applications must be suitably designed. For instance, all CPUs in shared memory multiprocessors share a common memory, but each CPU in distributed memory multiprocessors has its own private memory.

*Corresponding authors: [3]gursharan.dhot@gmail.com, [4]gurpreet.17671@lpu.co.in, [5]makul.14575@lpu.co.in, [6]salil.16836@lpu.co.in
[1]sankalprajgurur1221@gmail.com, [2]ayushgour232@gmail.com

DOI: 10.1201/9781003405580-103

Since the 1960s, when multiprocessor computers were first developed, they have advanced significantly. The development of multiprocessor systems has significantly accelerated with the rise in demand for high-performance computing. By allowing parallel processing and enhancing performance, multiprocessor system-on-chip (MPSoC) technology has changed the area of computer architecture. On a single chip, MPSoCs combine several different parts, including CPUs, memory, and I/O interfaces. Due to this, MPSoCs are becoming more common in a range of applications, including embedded systems, mobile devices, and high-performance computing.

Multiprocessor systems-on-chips (MPSoCs) had already started to become more readily available in subsequent decades and are likely to be delivered in a significantly wider diversity in the forthcoming years. A comprehensive integrated system is produced by an MPSoC, which integrates embedded CPUs, specialised digital hardware, and frequently mixed-signal circuits. MPSoCs are challenging to build in part because they accomplish complex functionalities and in part because they employ such a diverse range of technologies. We will now examine the difficulties that MPSoC designers now encounter in both hardware and software.

2. Existing System

We will first discuss the current state of the art before moving into the future of MPSoC design. Following a brief discussion of MPSoC applications, we also outline various hardware and software difficulties faced by MPSoC designers.

2.1 Multiprocessor System-on-Chip (MPSoC)

A multiprocessor system-on-chip (MPSoC) implements the system using several CPUs as well as additional hardware subsystems. Over the past ten years, a variety of MPSoC designs have been created. We look at a few of the technical developments that influenced MPSoC design (Xu, J., et al., 2006). It represents a significant and distinctive multiprocessor branch. They are not just conventional multiprocessors that have been compressed into a single chip; rather, they were created to meet the particular demands of embedded applications. Compared to multicore processors, MPSoCs have been in production for a significantly longer time.

Although there is a pressing need for low-level programming tools, it is occasionally unavoidable. Currently, the only resources available to programmers to make use of the potential parallelism of programmes with typical data requirements on their MPSoCs are local connections and distributed memory (Rowen et al., 2005). Even if a programmer is given the perfect solution, which can be successfully translated to the right MPSoC using a systolic method, the programmer will probably only be able to use a few low-level languages.

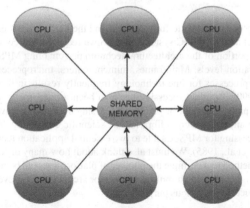

Fig. 103.1 Access of shared memory in multiprocessor architecture

Source: Drawn by the Author

Depending on how the restricted capabilities of the Keep the Level tool, which was designed exclusively for this device, are combined By allowing parallel processing and enhancing performance, MPSoC technology has transformed computer architecture. On a single chip, MPSoCs combine several different parts, including CPUs, memory, and I/O interfaces. Due to this, MPSoCs are becoming more common in a range of applications, including embedded systems, mobile devices, and high-performance computing. Power consumption, communication, and load balancing are only a few of the difficulties involved in the design and implementation of MPSoCs. We have included a table (Table 103.1) of the many processors and chip types currently available on the market.

Table 103.1 Types of processors and their characteristics

S. No	Processors/Chips	# Cores	Turbo maximum frequency	Base processor frequency	Smart cache
1	Intel Core i9-13900T Processors	24	6.00 GHz	-	36 MB Intel Smart Cache
2	Intel Core X-series Processors	10	4.50 GHz	3.70 GHz	19.25 MB Intel Smart Cache
3	Intel Core i7-1365U Processors	10	5.20 GHz	1.50 GHz	12 MB Intel Smart Cache
4	Intel Core i5-13500H Processors	12	4.70 GHz	1.50 GHz	18 MB Intel Smart Cache
5	Intel Core i3-1215UL Processors	6	4.40 GHz	1.20 GHz	10 MB Intel Smart Cache

2.2 Software/Hardware Design

Only a few computationally intensive, real-time applications can be solved using software. However, there are only a limited number of uses for dedicated hardware. A strong foundation can be built in the area positioned halfway between these two extremes. Integrated general-purpose hardware and software. The main goals to

- enhance software development,
- offer a versatile gadget,
- easier performance measurement, and
- promote the development of real-time, computationally intensive applications.

The register transfer and gate levels of hardware are expressed by designers using Hardware Description Languages (HDL) (Henkel et al., 2001). A hardware engineer must have a better grasp of programming as hardware grows more complex, but a programmer must also have a greater understanding of hardware design. As a result, developing hardware and software separately is getting more expensive and difficult. Hardware and software designs are developed together. The Unified Modelling Language (UML) is a common modelling tool. UML structure diagrams are used to describe models of a parallel computer. After a cursory analysis of hardware architecture, UML provides a reliable framework for software development.

Hardware Challenges

We need to ask ourselves two questions in order to fully comprehend the hardware issues that multiprocessor systems-on-chips provide to us: What is novel about MPSoC systems, and do we require a variety of MPSoC platforms? In order to start, we must ascertain what proportion of the architectural technologies enabling MPSoCs have already been produced for devices made at lower integration levels. Mainframes, minicomputers, microprocessors, and other technologies are instances of how the creation of processes for one technology frequently results in the creation of procedures for other technologies (Patterson et al., 1990). Parallel processing has also been around for a very long time, going all the way back to the invention of the computer. The bulk of parallel processing systems, however, were developed for tasks that are very distant from embedded computing, such as libraries and scientific computing. We will need to reevaluate various aspects of traditional parallel processing for MPSoCs due to two essential application features: real-time operation and low power/energy operation (Rodgers et al., 1985). We must also think about how many different MPSoC technologies should eventually be utilised. A simple method to determine the number of platforms would be to sort issues according to data rate (Wolf, W., et al., 2008). We could then develop a multiple processor architecture for every data transfer rate. Technology often helps to modify the infrastructure for various purposes.

Software Challenges

The fact that hardware designers must consider software design from the outset when they transition to MPSoC design is perhaps the hardest adjustment for them to make. A machine cannot be built by a hardware architect and thrown over a wall for someone else to programme. To determine what may be removed from the hardware and what must be kept, the architects must have a thorough understanding of the application. The properties of the application software that have an impact on real-time and low-power operation must also be understood by the architects. The design of an MPSoC depends heavily on software because the chip is useless without it. However, the best understanding of software difficulties related to MPSoCs starts with a simulation model before moving towards the technology itself.

Development Environments and Tools

Coders and programmers must have development environments to write the logic code for the different systems whenever the chip is in the making phase. When we talk about a development environment, we typically think of the host software, but the target hardware is also a part of the environment. Software development will be unacceptably delayed when the developing phase needs a whole chip to function with the different logics. To create approaches that enable them to create the most software feasible without a functional MPSoC, software and hardware designers must collaborate.

Operating Systems and Middleware

For embedded computer devices, various real-time operating systems (RTOS) are developed. The majority of commercial RTOSs, on the other hand, were created for industries like automotive, industrial, or other sectors that value utility above size. Contrarily, due to speed and memory constraints, MPSoCs often demand that their fundamental operations be implemented in a relatively small amount of software.

Embedded System Security

The programmable system had the potential to have security issues. However, MPSoCs will be more susceptible to various security vulnerabilities when they begin to have Internet connectivity (Wolf, W., et al., 2004). Whenever MPSoCs are used in protection activities like ships and aircraft, those security concerns should always be given the highest consideration by the grads. Sometimes, in non-safety-critical devices like home entertainment, a lack of adequate protection here on the MPSoC might render the device unusable.

3. Emerging Trends and Future Directions

Multiprocessor architecture is constantly evolving to meet the changing demands of high-performance computing. Heterogeneous processing has gained popularity in recent years because it provides for a better balance between performance and power usage. Multiprocessor systems have gained new prospects as a result of the development of the Internet of Things (IoT), since they can now process the enormous volumes of data produced by IoT devices. Future developments in multiprocessor architecture are probably driven by the creation of fresh applications like machine learning and autonomous systems. In addition, the integration of various components, such as memory and I/O interfaces, is expected to increase, resulting in more compact and efficient MPSoC systems.

4. Conclusion

Multiprocessor systems-on-chips have a promising future. Some of the most important electrical items in the coming decade will include them. The Multiprocessor System-on-Chip (MPSoC) technology, which has changed computer design by enabling parallel processing and enhanced performance, may teach us a lot. High performance and low power consumption will increasingly be prioritised in MPSoC development, it is predicted. With various possible changes anticipated to take place in the upcoming years, including more integration, higher performance, increased energy efficiency, emergent applications, and breakthroughs in heterogeneous computing, the future of MPSoC technology appears optimistic. The many improvements in multiprocessors covered in this paper serve as evidence of continuous work to enhance these systems and increase their functionality and effectiveness. Further research is needed to continue the development of these systems and explore new applications for multiprocessors in computer architecture.

REFERENCES

1. Backus, J. (1978). Can programming be liberated from the von Neumann style? A functional style and its algebra of programs. Communications of the ACM, 21(8), 613–641.
2. Patterson, D. A., Hennessy, J. L., & Goldberg, D. (1990). Computer architecture: a quantitative approach (Vol. 2). San Mateo, CA: Morgan Kaufmann.
3. Mei, B., Vernalde, S., De Man, H., & Lauwereins, R. (2003). Design and optimization of dynamically reconfigurable embedded systems. IMEC vzw.
4. De Michell, G., & Gupta, R. K. (1997). Hardware/software co-design. Proceedings of the IEEE, 85(3), 349–365.

5. Rowen, C. (2005). Performance and flexibility for multiple-processor soc design. In Multiprocessor Systems-on-Chips (pp. 113–151). Morgan Kaufmann.
6. Dutta, S., Jensen, R., & Rieckmann, A. (2001). Viper: A multiprocessor SOC for advanced set-top box and digital TV systems. IEEE Design & Test of Computers, 18(5), 21–31.
7. Jerraya, A., & Wolf, W. (2004). Multiprocessor systems-on-chips. Elsevier.
8. Xu, J., Wolf, W., Henkel, J., & Chakradhar, S. (2006). A design methodology for application-specific networks-on-chip. ACM Transactions on Embedded Computing Systems (TECS), 5(2), 263–280.
9. Rodgers, D. P. (1985). Improvements in multiprocessor system design. ACM SIGARCH Computer Architecture News, 13(3), 225–231.
10. Henkel, J., & Ernst, R. (2001). An approach to automated hardware/software partitioning using a flexible granularity that is driven by high-level estimation techniques. IEEE transactions on very large scale integration (VLSI) systems, 9(2), 273–289.
11. Wolf, W. (2004). Modern VLSI design. Computing Reviews, 45(6), 324.
12. Wolf, W., Jerraya, A. A., & Martin, G. (2008). Multiprocessor system-on-chip (MPSoC) technology. IEEE Transactions on Computer-Aided Design of Integrated Circuits and Systems, 27(10), 1701–1713.

Computer Science Engineering and Emerging Technologies (ICCS-2022) – Prof (Dr.) Rajeev Sobti et al. (eds)
© 2024 Taylor & Francis Group, London, ISBN 978-1-032-52199-2

Chapter **104**

Detailed Investigation of Role of Machine Learning Techniques in Agricultural Development in Future

Khongdet Phasinam[1]
Faculty of Food and Agricultural Technology,
Pibulsongkram Rajabhat University, Phitsanulok, Thailand

Priyanka P. Shinde*
Department of MCA,
Government College of Engineering, Karad, India

Thanwamas Kassanuk[2]
Faculty of Food and Agricultural Technology,
Pibulsongkram Rajabhat University, Phitsanulok, Thailand

Chetan M. Thakar[3]
Department of Mechanical Engineering,
Savitribai Phule Pune University, Pune

Abstract: To enable an enthusiastic framework for definitive disorder across the board, a number of factors related to disorganization in plants utilizing substantial learning techniques should be taken into account. Numerous studies have recently looked at the effectiveness of important learning frameworks for accurate development. Despite this, there are still a number of gaps in plant jumble research that need to be filled in order to alleviate the problem on ranches. In order to help drive the development of devices that meet ranchers' needs, it is necessary to spread out a database of existing apps and understand the prompts and prospective opportunities.

This study gives a circumspect summary of 70 studies on major learning applications, together with the concepts relating to their use in jumble discovery and the cultivation of pioneers. The framework is turned around to provide a point-by-point analysis and considerations for developing significant learning-based devices for plant tangled mess end as seven key requests interacting with (I) dataset requirements, transparency, and comfort; (ii) imaging sensing and communication blend levels; (iii) critical learning strategies; (iv) speculation of meaningful learning concepts; (v) pollution reality evaluations; and (vi) significant learning and living person accuracy evaluations.

Keywords: Machine learning, "Convolutional neural networks or CNN", Technology, Agriculture, Plant

1. Introduction

Plant diseases pose a threat to crop output issues, which clearly affect the public and usually food production structures and result in financial mishaps. According to the Agriculture and Food Alliance (FAO), pest infestations and plant problems account for 20% to 40% of catastrophes in the general food production industry. Overall Plant Risk Show for the Countries

*Corresponding Author: ppshinde.gcek@gmail.com

[1]phasinam@psru.ac.th, [2]thanwamas.k@psru.ac.th, [3]cthakar12@gmail.com

DOI: 10.1201/9781003405580-104

A typical 13% of commonly reported yield incidents are caused by plant concerns. These evaluations take into account how crucial it is to identify plant diseases in order to alleviate crop problems. Despite this, it's important to first comprehend the factors responsible for plant contamination. The host, a perfect climate, and the organism are the three factors that aid in the improvement of disease in plants. The plant pathogen triangle is made up of these components.

Pollution typically has delayed effects and affects a plant from the ground up. Numerous plant diseases spread over the affected area. In that position, harvests ought to be regularly inspected, as early identification of the ailment will help stop its spread. Plant illnesses that manifest in this way appear at a later time after preparedness in a couple of instances. Plant diseases come in many forms and affect numerous plant parts (Shaikh *et al.*, 2022). Plant pathologists' ability to visually analyze plant diseases is particularly acute when they result in foliar messes or unintentional effects on leaves. Particularly, up to half of supply mishaps are caused by irrepressible defilements.

As a result, the majority of modern assessments use images of plant leaves to detect illnesses using PC vision, intelligent systems, and important learning frameworks. Solid plant disease disclosures will include early-season plant disease undeniable evidence, the identification of various problems in different yields and various synchronous issues, estimation of the truth of the muddying, looking over the appropriate volume of fungicide to apply, and significant steps taken to try to guide responsibility to limit its spread. The precision of agriculture and plant phenotyping depends on being able to identify plant contamination (Pallathadka *et al.*, 2022). Both of these professions have been advanced by information, data, and advancement. Standard plant disease end and checking methods are laborious, reliant on knowledgeable authorities, and hence unsuitable for precise cultivation because they combine a manual visual assessment. Additionally, it appears that these approaches will be impacted by human fatigue and propensity, resulting in decreased accuracy. Studies have investigated the usage of picture-managing approaches utilizing plant images to circumvent these delicate structures for hardship apparent proof (Wani *et al.*, 2022). Perhaps the first analyses that utilized standard picture treatment for plant ailments were those of a robotized illness evaluation device using really separate images and records of approaches in a location with clipped tomatoes and cloudy vegetation plants.

2. Literature Review

In the area of machine vision, plant disease and irritation recognition are huge research topics. In a development, images are obtained using machine vision devices to determine whether there are defects and bugs in the acquired plant images. Currently, machine vision-based plant diseases and bothering area equipment have been first used in agribusiness and have partially replaced traditional independent eye ID. Standard picture taking care of computations or manual arranging of features aside from classifiers are frequently used for machine vision-based plant sullying and annoyance acknowledgment procedures. This type of method, which is important to ensure photos with uniform lighting, often employs the various qualities of plant diseases and disturbances to develop the imaging plan, choose a suitable light source, and take position. However, correctly constructed imaging plans can amazingly minimize the complexity of a standard compute setup while also raising the cost of the application (Ahmad *et al.*, 2022). However, it is consistently irrational to rely on outdated estimates that were designed to ignore the effects of transitions on the outcome of affirmation in a typical daily environment.

Plant disorders and discomfort acknowledgement are thwarted in the certification complex natural environment by a number of issues, such as the small distance between the sensitive area and the establishment, the lack of contrast, the vast variations in the size of the knee problem locale and various types, and the significant uprisings in the sensitive image (Al Kafy *et al.* 2021). In a similar vein, social events, plant disorders, and irritant images taken in normal lighting can have a lot of disruptive effects. At this time, it is challenging to get better acknowledgment results, and the conventional old-style tactics frequently seem to be ineffective.

"Convolutional neural networks (CNNs)" have recently gained popularity in many fields of computer vision (CV, PC vision), including busy street, clinical picture affirmation, situation text new discovery, outlook affirmation, face affirmation, etc., due to the successful application of deep learning models. In plain cultivating practice, a few plant diseases and troublesome identifiable proof techniques with in-depth study are used. Wechat applets and picture affirmation application programming focused on significant learning-based plant illnesses and pests have been supported by a few local and new groups (Shaikh *et al.*, 2022). Similar to this, the identification of pests and plant diseases using deep learning has enormous potential for market application as well as for educational assessment.

Given the lack of a comprehensive and direct discussion on plant challenges and aggravation recognizing evidence systems taking profound understanding, this study summarizes and brushes the significant work normally done from 2014 to 2020 and the need to aid specialists in handling the crucial procedures and motions in this field quickly and purposefully. The following facilitates the overview's main points: The *"Image acknowledgement development concerning profound learning"* region is based on a point-by-point presentation of picture validation development considering profound learning, and the *"Plant illnesses and bugs implicit acceptance procedures considering profound learning"* region depicts the importance of plant diseases and disturbance area issues (Panwar *et al*. 2021).

"Dataset and execution partnership" chapter presents some data sources of plant pollution and vermin area and considers the lecture of the flow assessment methods; "Challenges" region drives the challenges of plant illnesses and aggravations area; and "Dataset and operation relationship" section evaluates the three types of plant abnormalities and aggravations availability of different techniques taking profound advancing into account according to organizational structure, which include course of action, area, and division association (Jain and Pandey, 2019). Plant diseases and disturbances in computer vision tasks will frequently be based on human knowledge rather than a straightforward mathematical characterization. The demands of plant sickness and annoyance recognition are very extensive, as contrasted with the unmistakable collecting, area, and division undertakings in PC vision (Jain *et al*. 2021). The fundamentals of it can be divided into three distinct levels: what, where, and how. In the main stage, "what" refers to the PC vision task of depiction.

At the end of the day, determining which article exists in which position in a picture is the most obvious way that object disclosure differs from item demand. Regardless of element explanation, a group portrays the picture typically through highlight elaboration and, a short while later, decides whether there is a specific kind of thing in the photograph using depiction activity (Liu and Wang, 2021). In other words, whereas structure education is the major evaluation criterion for the blending of article revelation, highlight articulated is the main research line of item need. However, the appropriate underlying principles and emphasis points of the different plant disease and irritability revelation periods differ. The three phases can be switched between and are generally broad. As an illustration, the "why" in the successive stage contains the direction of the "what" in the beginning phase, and the "where" in the third step can completely accomplish the control of the "where" as in the successive level. Additionally, the "what" in the crucial stage might use clear-cut tactics to achieve the goals of the third and second phases (Singh *et al.,* 2022). As stated in the accompanying text, the subject of this inquiry is entirely related to the spread of diseases and bug confirmation; nevertheless, the issue separates when various affiliation designs and works are used.

3. Research Methodology

This research paper has discussed ML techniques for agricultural development in the future. In this context, different methods are discussed. Secondary data analysis methods have been used to gather relevant information. We give a thorough analysis of machine learning's use in agriculture. There are several pertinent publications that highlight important and distinctive characteristics of well-known ML models. The current work is organized as follows: The most common learning models and techniques were originally covered in the analysis section, along with the nomenclature, definition, learning problems, and evaluation of ML.

4. Analysis and Discussion

A publication published in science in 2006 by Hinton et al. served as the catalyst for the possibility of Significant Learning (DL). A convolution is used to lower the risk elements, and low-level features are then combined to produce dynamic, unquestionable-level aspects, which can effectively alleviate the neighborhood least-squares problem (Jain and Pandey, 2019). The basic idea behind significant learning is that results can be concluded to be isolated by various mystery layers, each of which can be viewed as a perceptron.

Deep learning has drawn the attention of an ever-increasing number of academics since it outperforms conventional estimations, which rely on incorrectly organized information. Currently, it has been successfully used in proposition systems, traditional language handling, plan affirmation, talk affirmation, and PC vision (Jain and Pandey, 2019).

The main components of manual course-of-action elements can be disengaged by standard picture soliciting and certification systems, but it is difficult to do away

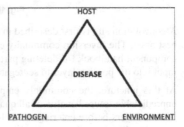

Fig. 104.1 Disease triangle (Ahmad et al., 2022)

with the major and sophisticated picture that includes data. A substantial learning mindset can also remove this roadblock. It can clearly organize free acquisition from the primary image to provide a stunning image with information such as low-level components, generally interesting components, and obvious semantic highlights.

Common plant maladies and irritants for genuinely arranged features, area estimations typically use the image affirmation method, which is troublesome because it relies on experience and reputation and cannot therefore acquire and think elements from the source image. In actuality, considerable obtaining typically enables the acquisition of highlights from massive data without manual control (Hasan *et al.*, 2021). The model is created employing various layers, each of which has the amazing autonomy to study and integrate clarifying restraints as well as typically erase them to the maximum extent possible for picture soliciting and confirmation.

Therefore, significant learning can anticipate playing a particularly important role in the fields of plant concerns and irksome picture certification. The *"substantial inclination relationship"*, *"significant Habsburg machine"*, "stack power autoencoder", and *"significant multilayer mind association"* are currently some of the exceptionally significant brain network models created using significant learning techniques.

The use of these important mind network models to perceive automated clear extraction from high-layered consolidating space gives a great deal of advantages over manual standard plans, including extraction procedures in the field of picture certification. Furthermore, when processing power and the number of arranging tests increase, the representation capability of key brain networks typically reaches a higher level. The impact of substantial learning is currently dominating academia and industry, and the presentation of significant underlying neural models is fundamentally superior to ordinary models (Virnodkar *et al.* 2020). Significant convolutional brain associations have become the most prominent learning structure in recent years.

4.1 Convolutional Neutral Network or CNN

"Convolutional neutral networks,", often known as CNN, are convolution-capable and have an unusual hierarchical structure. The neural mind networking model is created utilizing the foregoing convolutional pooling layer, complete alliance layer, and outcome layer, as shown in the linked figure. In one model, the fully connected layers and the convolution are substituted twice or more. When the convolution layer's neurons are connected to the pooling layer's neurons, a full association is not necessary (Panwar *et al.*, 2021).

On the subject of important learning, CNN is a preeminent role model. The reason is that CNN is able to contribute to picture attestation thanks to its enormous model limit and sophisticated data obtained by its core hidden abilities. CNN's successes in PC vision tasks have simultaneously aided in the development of considerable learning.

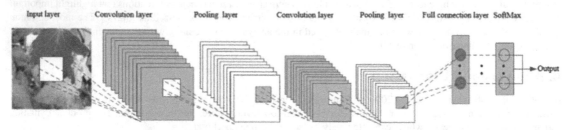

Fig. 104.2 Basic structure of CNN (Shaikh et al., 2022)

A convolution site is first described in the convolution layer. The closest responsive field is the convolution community's best asset. The inversion community can be thought of as a local open field. The convolution community glides on the component handbook for deleting part of the utilized while taking care of data information. The neurons are once again input into the pooling layer to segregate the parts after the convolution layer's component extraction.

At this juncture, the commonly employed pooling algorithms combine to determine the mean, most extreme, and unpredictable future benefits of all qualities in the nearby open field. The input then enters a number of convolutions and pooling layers before entering the full-association layer, where the neurons are fully correlated with those in the higher layer. Finally, the softmax approach can set up all the data in the full-connection layer, and later, the characteristics are transferred to the result layer to provide results.

4.2 Parametric Yield Model

Plant growth is closely tied to the amount of time spent exposed to particular temperatures when there are no external pressures. The "growing-degree day (GDD)", which calculates the entire amount of time spent inside a specific temperature range, can be used to evaluate this. "Schlenker and Roberts' (2009)" primary models included OLS regressions in GDD, fixed effects, and controls, similar to the following:

$$y_{it} = \alpha_i + \sum GDD_{rit}\,\beta_r + X_{it}\beta + \epsilon_{it} \tag{1}$$

When first described, this model disclosed significant negative reactions to temperatures around 30°C in maize, allowing different temperature bands to have distinct impacts on plant growth. A better statistical approach to the interaction between demand and supply of water has been established in later work, and it has also substantiated the declining resilience to high "vapor pressure deficit (VPD)" over time. These studies have also identified the role of "vapor pressure deficit (VPD)" in describing much of the adverse response to a large temperature. When viewed as merely predictive tools, models like (1) that were created for the purpose of parameter estimation about maximum temperature thresholds have room for improvement (Jain *et al.*, 2021). Its implicit presumptions—additive separability between "regressors", "time-invariance of the impact of heat exposure", and exclusion of other potential yield-influencing factors—improve parsimony, comprehensibility, and consequently knowledge of underlying mechanisms. But they, like any simplistic characterization of a complicated phenomenon, will bias predictions to the point where they are inaccurate in practice. But rather than completely replacing these models, we modify ML techniques to improve them.

Additionally, the four widely popular cross-platform deep learning open-source devices support "Linux, Windows, iOS, Android, and other operating systems". When building large CNN networks on ***GPU, Light/PyTorch, and Tensorflow***," offer the fastest planning speed and support the greatest number of training libraries and important association structures. Plant diseases and bugs are disclosed using methods that consider profound learning. This section provides a summary chart of plant diseases and bug-obvious proof methods for considering important learning. Plant diseases and bothersome affirmation systems taking important learning into account should be observable as the utilization of crucial conventional linkages in the domain of cultivation, as the target achieved with the Computer vision task is entirely dependable. According to the various hierarchical designs, the association can also be divided into an organized association, a region association, and a division network, as shown in the picture. The graphic below should make it clear that this paper is separated into various sub-methods that take into account the characteristics of each type of technique.

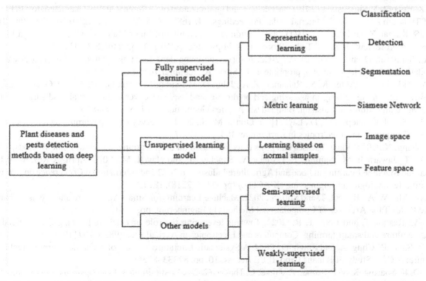

Fig. 104.3 Framework of plant diseases and pests detection methods based on deep learning (Wani et al., 2022)

4.3 Plan Organization

In the certified normal environment, the unprecedented differentiation in shape, size, surface, assortment, establishment, plan, and imaging lighting up of plant sicknesses and vermin makes the affirmation an irksome endeavor. Because of the solid part extraction cut-off of CNN, the social occasion of a CNN-based assembling network has changed into the most customarily elaborate arrangement for plant illnesses and unsettling influences. There are several appraisals that have organized network structures for thinking about reasonable issues. By contributing a test picture to the solicitation association, the association explores the information picture and returns an engraving that bundles the picture. As exhibited by the separation of undertakings accomplished by the depiction network framework, it very well may be isolated into three subcategories: the association as a part extractor, including the association for social events straightforwardly, and the association for wounds locale.

5. Conclusion

In this study, 70 assessments of plant disease were examined. These assessments included outline papers, image management, deep learning, and significant learning checks. There was considerable attention paid to the seven key evaluation questions. Interesting images of plant contamination were analyzed from a range of freely accessible sources. Different image sensors and information blending stages were looked at for the purpose of identifying plant illnesses. Finally, we considered the possibility of substantial learning algorithms to outperform humans under hypothetical circumstances. We think that a thorough analysis of the reality of the sickness will lead to a run-by-robots, start-to-finish plant issue in the design of the center. This will effortlessly distinguish different yields and their own issues throughout the season.

REFERENCES

1. A. Jain, A. K. Pandey, (2019), "Modeling And Optimizing Of Different Quality Characteristics In Electrical Discharge Drilling Of Titanium Alloy (Grade-5) Sheet" Material Today Proceedings, 18, 182–191. https://doi.org/10.1016/j.matpr.2019.06.292
2. A. Jain, A. K. Pandey, (2019), "Modeling And Optimizing Of Different Quality Characteristics In Electrical Discharge Drilling Of Titanium Alloy (Grade-5) Sheet" Material Today Proceedings, 18, 182–191. https://doi.org/10.1016/j.matpr.2019.06.292
3. A. Jain, A. K. Pandey, (2019), "Multiple Quality Optimizations In Electrical Discharge Drilling Of Mild Steel Sheet" Material Today Proceedings, 8, 7252–7261. https://doi.org/10.1016/j.matpr.2017.07.054
4. A. Jain, A.K.Yadav & Y. Shrivastava (2019), "Modelling and Optimization of Different Quality Characteristics In Electric Discharge Drilling of Titanium Alloy Sheet" Material Today Proceedings, 21, 1680–1684. https://doi.org/10.1016/j.matpr.2019.12.010
5. A. Jain, C. S. Kumar, Y. Shrivastava, (2021), "Fabrication and Machining of Fiber Matrix Composite through Electric Discharge Machining: A short review" Material Today Proceedings. https://doi.org/10.1016/j.matpr.2021.07.288
6. Ahmad, A., Saraswat, D. and El Gamal, A., 2022. A survey on using deep learning techniques for plant disease diagnosis and recommendations for development of appropriate tools. Smart Agricultural Technology, p.100083.
7. Al Kafy, A., Al Rakib, A., Akter, K. S., Rahaman, Z. A., Jahir, D. M., Subramanyam, G., Michel, O. O. and Bhatt, A., 2021. The operational role of remote sensing in assessing and predicting land use/land cover and seasonal land surface temperature using machine learning algorithms in Rajshahi, Bangladesh. Applied Geomatics, 13(4), pp. 793–816.
8. Hasan, A. M., Sohel, F., Diepeveen, D., Laga, H. and Jones, M. G., 2021. A survey of deep learning techniques for weed detection from images. Computers and Electronics in Agriculture, 184, p. 106067.
9. Liu, J. and Wang, X., 2021. Plant diseases and pests detection based on deep learning: a review. Plant Methods, 17(1), pp. 1–18.
10. Pallathadka, H., Jawarneh, M., Sammy, F., Garchar, V., Sanchez, T. and Naved, M., 2022, April. A Review of Using Artificial Intelligence and Machine Learning in Food and Agriculture Industry. In 2022 2nd International Conference on Advance Computing and Innovative Technologies in Engineering (ICACITE) (pp. 2215–2218). IEEE.
11. Shaikh, T. A., Mir, W. A., Rasool, T. and Sofi, S., 2022. Machine Learning for Smart Agriculture and Precision Farming: Towards Making the Fields Talk. Archives of Computational Methods in Engineering, pp. 1–41.
12. Shaikh, T. A., Rasool, T. and Lone, F. R., 2022. Towards leveraging the role of machine learning and artificial intelligence in precision agriculture and smart farming. Computers and Electronics in Agriculture, 198, p. 107119.
13. Singh, A. P., Sahu, P., Chug, A. and Singh, D., 2022. A Systematic Literature Review of Machine Learning Techniques Deployed in Agriculture: A Case Study of Banana Crop. IEEE Access, 10, pp. 87333–87360.
14. V. Panwar, D. K. Sharma, K. V. P. Kumar, A. Jain & C. Thakar, (2021), "Experimental Investigations And Optimization Of Surface Roughness In Turning Of EN 36 Alloy Steel Using Response Surface Methodology And Genetic Algorithm" Materials Today: Proceedings, https://Doi.Org/10.1016/J.Matpr.2021.03.642

15. V. Panwar, D. K. Sharma, K. V. P. Kumar, A. Jain & C. Thakar, (2021), "Experimental Investigations And Optimization Of Surface Roughness In Turning Of EN 36 Alloy Steel Using Response Surface Methodology And Genetic Algorithm" Materials Today: Proceedings, https://Doi.Org/10.1016/J.Matpr.2021.03.642

16. Virnodkar, S. S., Pachghare, V. K., Patil, V. C. and Jha, S. K., 2020. Remote sensing and machine learning for crop water stress determination in various crops: a critical review. Precision Agriculture, 21(5), pp. 1121–1155.

17. Wani, J. A., Sharma, S., Muzamil, M., Ahmed, S., Sharma, S. and Singh, S., 2022. Machine learning and deep learning based computational techniques in automatic agricultural diseases detection: Methodologies, applications, and challenges. Archives of Computational Methods in Engineering, 29(1), pp. 641–677.

Computer Science Engineering and Emerging Technologies (ICCS-2022) – Prof (Dr.) Rajeev Sobti et al. (eds)
© 2024 Taylor & Francis Group, London, ISBN 978-1-032-52199-2

Chapter **105**

Emerging Microfluidic Devices and Fabrication Methods in Various Domains

Manoj B. Mandake*
Department of Chemical Engineering,
Bharati Vidyapeeth College of Engineering Navi Mumbai

Ravi W. Tapre[1]
Assistant Professor, Department of Chemical Engineering,
Datta Meghe College of Engineering, Airoli, Navi Mumbai, Maharashtra, India

Ashwini G. Thokal[2]
Department of Chemical Engineering,
Bharati Vidyapeeth College of Engineering, Navi Mumbai

4Yaser Qureshi[3]
Assistant Professor, Zoology,
Govt. College Khertha Distt. Balod (Chhattisgarh)

Sandhya Jadhav[4]
Professor, Bharati Vidyapeeth College of Engineering Navi Mumbai

Chetan M. Thakar[5]
Department of Mechanical Engineering,
Savitribai Phule Pune University, Pune.

Abstract: The concepts of liquid dynamics, microelectronics, material science, physics, chemistry, and biology are all united in the fairly young discipline of microfluidics. Different polymers could be manufactured from miniature circuits with nano-scale pathways and rooms. These structures may be produced using a variety of techniques that may achieve the appropriate dimensions, structure, and geometry. Microfluidic circuits could be utilized for cell examination, diagnostics, and cultures, as well as for the creation of nanoparticles, medicine entrapment, delivery, and focusing, and tissue evaluation. This study discusses microfluidic technologies in regards to the manufacturing methods and foundation elements that are now accessible, with a particular emphasis on the amazing gadgets' uses in biomedicine.

Keywords: Microfluidics, Diagnostic, Methods, Devices

1. Introduction

Microfluidics includes the research and development of machines that function as well as control tiny volumes of liquids, employing networks with diameters of tens to hundreds of micrometers, thus making George Whitesides one of the most

*Corresponding Author: manojkumar.mandke@bharatividyapeeth.edu
[1]ravitapre40@gmail.com, [2]ashwini.thokal@ bharatividyapeeth.edu, [3]dryaserqureshi@gmail.com, [4]sandhya.jadhav@bharatividyapeeth.edu,
[5]cthakar12@gmail.com

DOI: 10.1201/9781003405580-105

significant figures in such a subject. Technology and ideas from many well-known fields, including chemicals, physics, biology, mechatronics, hydrodynamics, and microsystems, came together to form the field of microfluidics. Although the area of microfluidics is relatively young, the idea of microfluidic devices has long been a part of fluidized bed combustor and the glasses or quartzite capillaries that make up gas filtration and single beam technology. As a result, starting in the 1980s, increasingly advanced designs for directing fluid level along microfluidics were recorded in inventions. However, this introduction of microfluidic technology is thought to have occurred in the 1990s, yet ever since, it has really grown exponentially, becoming a strong instrument with limitless scope for advancement.

Those very nanoscopic miniaturized machines can be important tools for executing conduct processes via reactors, division, or chemical identification. Microfluidic devices are commonly referred to as microreactors, lab-on-a-chips, or organ-on-a-chips within research, according to their functionality and functioning characteristics (Zhao et al. 2020). Microfluidic chips may be made of all kinds of elements and use a variety of manufacturing techniques, depending on their intended functions. This same promise for innovations in the subject of microfluidics grows drastically as various production approaches have previously been published in literature and used in reality, opening up new opportunities for not only the domains of academia and industry. Some industrially accessible equipment is also now being used in at-home pregnancy checking, virus timely checking (for example, for HIV, Coronavirus Disease 19 (COVID-19), and blood sugar monitoring), so the said innovation is also encouraging during daytime proposal areas.

The goal of this paper is to provide a full explanation of microfluidic technologies from the standpoint of silicon production, including the primary uses of both gadgets that are produced.

2. Literature Review

2.1 Instruments for Microfluidic Fabrication

(a) Ingredients for Microfluidic Devices: Choosing the best material for board designs represents one of the key tasks in microfluidic technologies. The platform substance is anticipated to have an impact on the characteristics of produced nanomaterials since attributes are significantly higher on a microscopic-level surface. Particularly, short treatment durations, vertical rushes, improved energy and gravity transfers, and surface area proportions cause localized features to occur in microvascular microfluidics. A number of benefits that alloys offer make them excellent materials for the production of microchips. They can tolerate extreme temperature demands, high intensity, and dangerous substances (Fernandez-la-Villa et al. 2019). They are also inexpensive, accessible, and simple to manufacture. Additionally, their ability to withstand rough handling is advantageous for mopping.

According to its own easy accessibility, nontoxicity, and stability, silica provides one of the top options when it comes to the creation of microfluidic devices. Silica is the best material for microfluidic devices due to its simplicity of production, adaptability in terms of structure, highly conductive qualities, and potential for border alterations (Reyes et al., 2021).

Glass is thermally conductive, robust, has chemical resistance, is acceptable with living things, and is simple to functionalize its surfaces. Due to these characteristics, crystal microreactors may be used to conduct chemical changes that call for elevated heat, heavy forces, and harsh solutions.

Microfluidic platforms might well be made with limited porcelain. Ceramics' surface reactivity, remarkable resilience to hostile environments, and outstanding stabilization at extreme temperatures are the qualities that make them a viable choice for silicon chips.

The manufacture of microfluidic devices is transitioning beyond silica and glass devices as a result of composites' adaptability. Polymers benefit from simpler and less efficient manufacturing methods than bulk nanoparticles and are relatively affordable (Jain et al., 2021). Opportunities for polymer microfluidic systems range from fluid management to the generation of nanoparticles.

(b) Chemical Methods: Glass and silicon microfluidic pathways have been created for a very long time using a variety of chemical production techniques. Wet etching and dry etching, as well as electrolytic discharging manufacturing, are the chemistry methods that are more frequently utilized.

Due to its quick etching rate and capacity to handle several plates at once, moist embossing has gained popularity. For mass transfer, this method calls for powerful solvents, and hydrogen chloride acid is frequently used as an etchant. Due to the severe health and safety risks associated with prone corrosion color removal, this is a restriction of this production technology (Niculescu et al., 2021).

An electrocatalyst produces sparks on a work piece in the relatively unconventional production method known as electrolytic discharging grinding. Glasses and porcelain are two examples of non-cconducting materials that can be used with the method.

(c) Mechanical Methods: Another of the very earliest recognized techniques for creating microfluidic devices was micromachining, which has been adapted only from the electronics sector. In order to produce materials without cracks, materials must maintain acceptable layered precision and surface finish. These methods work well for processing silicon and glasses, although they might be used to create the replicating standard for urethane products.

(d) Sensor Methods: Although lasers are often costly instruments, they are thought of as a more available manufacturing approach in comparison to sanitary facility expenditures. Additionally, magnetron sputtering enables the fast and flexible production of microfluidic circuits on a wide range of substrates without the risks connected to traditional manufacturing techniques. Lasers' basic operating mechanism is the controlled emission of infrared energy, which optically amplifies sight. The mechanical deterioration impact engraves the area of success of projects by creating a nanoscale (Carrell et al. 2020).

(e) The printing of 3 dimensions: A recent yet effective method for creating microfluidic pathways is 3-dimensional printing. Particularly for systems needing complex microfluidic architectures, it provides the capacity to produce a wide range of chip shapes. Various production techniques, including suspension fluid algebraic photography, ink cartridge printing, fused, and a number of co-publishing, have taken advantage of the benefits that 3D publishing offers. The widespread use of 3D printers in the production of microfluidics is nevertheless constrained by a few factors. The limits in the precise manufacture of the emptiness and vacuum parts, the poor z-resolution of 3D printers, the constrained selection of visible light, the requirement for highly polished material properties, and these restrictions are all significant (Panwar et al. 2021).

(f) Technology hybrids: The difficulties and restrictions of any stand-alone manufacturing technique were solved through battery technology. In doing so, scientists improved the construction accuracy of the building phase while still doing away with the requirement for costly and momentary work areas.

Kojic et al. put forth a different hybrid approach by combining the advantages of thermal lamination and xurography into a 3D printing process. Their manufacturing technique allowed for efficient and reliable production with the possibility to scale the process up by running different parts of the entire operation (Jain and Pandey, 2019).

3. Methodology

One of the solid pillars of a given research study is its technique. It has a clear explanation supported by methodical and logical analysis in line with the numerous techniques used by researchers to collect primary and secondary data. The post-positivist concept has been used in the current research approach to explore study findings in a trustworthy manner. This study philosophy makes it possible to investigate microfluidic devices and fabrication methods in various domains. The third pillar that can be effectively applied in this research, based on original scientific hypotheses, is the "deductive research approach." On the other hand, "exploratory research design" has been widely used to effectively address diverse issues and their background repercussions. According to the approach utilized to acquire the data, a qualitative secondary method was used, which involved using reliable books, journals, and appropriate research articles from Google Scholar and other internet sources. Through transparent rational reasoning and the use of actual data from real-world situations, an empirical analysis of the entire study has been noted.

4. Analysis and Discussion Results

Numerous uses for microfluidic devices may be found in efforts to go around or circumvent problems with conventional tests. The research indicates significant promise in DNA sequencing, customised medicine, illness diagnostics, biochemical screenings, tissue culture, unit segregation, and cells therapy. Additionally, the particulates that may be produced in microfluidic devices can really be employed in a variety of fields, including microbiology, biomedical imaging, biosensor, and controlled release, as well as computing, power, and clothing.

4.1 Diagnostic Tools

With the use of microfluidic technology, a variety of samples, including plasma, spit, or biological sections, may be analysed to quickly and accurately diagnose an illness.

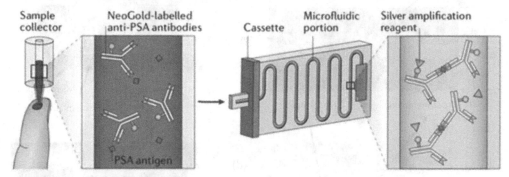

Fig. 105.1 This illustration of a microfluidic diagnostic tool which can identify PSA in under fifteen minutes (Carrell et al., 2020)

To find harmful bacteria, microgels for microbial extraction have already been built and integrated with a variety of testing techniques. In particular, flying viruses are being captured via a microfluidic chip. Creatinine is just another chemical that may be identified using microfluidic technology. Its content is crucial in identifying diseases such as glomerulonephritis, developmental disorders, and kidney problems.

The solution to better Coronavirus Illness 19 (COVID-19) diagnosis may potentially lie in microfluidic technologies. Using connected nanopores covalently using vertically stacked Au/Ag-coated nanomaterials or reusable hydrogel sensor membranes, Amit Jadhav et al. suggested a diagnostic framework that focuses on edge Raman spectroscopy and computer chips (Panwar et al., 2021).

The greatest outcomes will be obtained using samples that are clean or even less than one milligram in size, or the outcome is visible with the naked eye. Additionally, its DNA collection chip may be used in conjunction with specialized resume software to enable local police organizations to see if a subject's possession and DNA profiles found in unexplained criminal situations correspond.

4.2 Media for Cell Culture

Miniaturized culture methods have emerged as a possible alternative because cells grown in petri dishes and culturing bottles experience environmental cues that are vastly different from those experienced by normal tissues inside a 3-dimensional ECM. Microfluidic systems can provide important biochemical and biophysical signals to grown organisms in a precise and repeatable way by precisely controlling fluid flows. As a result, studying tissue development, regeneration, and illness is achievable without encountering issues unique to in vivo investigations (Niculescu et al., 2021).

Liver-on-a-chip systems may simulate in vivo settings by replicating the laminar shape of this system, preserving excellent cell growth and biological phenotypes, and simulating the functionalities of real tissues. To understand the course of liver problems, make medical creation easier, and enable toxicology assessments, a range of models have now been created and are accessible (Jain and Pandey, 2019).

There have been developments in Gut-on-a-chip microchannels, via one scenario given by Actually et al., who produced a hydrodynamic mouse intestine culturing paradigm that can preserve the shape of proximal tubules for up to 192 hours for a quarter of the inoculums (Fig. 105.2).

Microfluidic systems that simulate the surroundings of genuine renal cells, such as kidney-on-a-chip, have indeed garnered a lot of interest. PDMS microchannels and permeable walls were combined into a three-layer microfluidic organ chip created by Yin et al. They also created a supported hydrodynamic culture environment that allowed again for lengthy cultivation of renal tubules (Fig. 105.3). The gadget is valuable for embryonic investigations since the researchers found that it performed better over lymphocytes cultivated in Agar plates in regards from both cellular proliferation and medication hepatotoxicity assessment (Jain et al. 2019).

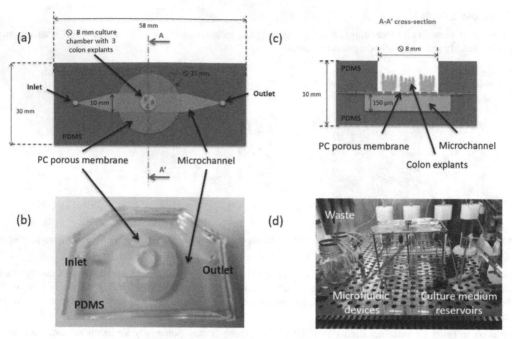

Fig. 105.2 Gut-on-a-chip microfluidic device (Lai et al., 2019)

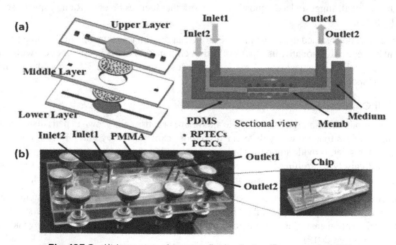

Fig. 105.3 Kidney-on-a-chip microfluidic device (Reyes et al., 2019)

4.3 Delivery Methods for Drugs

The advancement of drug delivery methods is now particularly interesting due to the immense promise of microfluidics. Precision dose, tailored administration, prolonged and managed drug dissolution, the ability to administer several doses, and the presence of very benign side effects are all benefits of this microfluidic delivery method. Microfluidic devices can carry a variety of cargos, including medicines, sensing capabilities, and/or targeting molecules. Microfluidics, which has a potential colloidal stability of 100%, marks a significant shift in the creation of sophisticated delivery systems (Lai et al. 2019).

Adolescent substance provider microfluidics, drug vehicle deterministic science department technologies, and entering the code pharmaceuticals are the three primary categories of microfluidic delivery systems. As shown in Fig. 105.4, there could be subgroups within each kind of device.

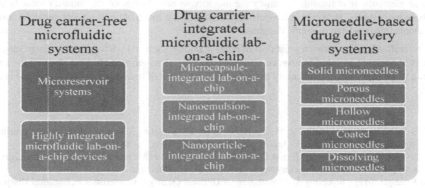

Fig. 105.4   Types of microfluidic devices for drug delivery. On information gathered from with a scientific referenced while creating (Zhao et al., 2020)

4.4 Systems for Nanomaterial Synthesis

Unquestionably, the emergence of nanotechnology has transformed several facets of contemporary medicine, particularly in the areas of medicines, diagnoses, selective medication delivery, and biosensing. Because of their uniform thickness, limited size distribution, enhanced repeatability, and higher adsorption effectiveness, microfluidic devices are good manufacturing platforms for a variety of nanomaterials. These particles may then be used in a wide range of industries (Liao et al. 2019).

The market finds microfluidics synthesized interesting because it enables the manufacture of less expensive, more potent, and more widely available medication formulations. Like sildenafil, an active substance used to treat acute myocardial infarction, compounds (APIs) resulting from extremely thermal processes can be produced in microchannels.

4.5 Upcoming and Emergent Solutions

Although there are now a number of applications accessible, the advancement of microfluidics is only getting started. The technological innovation could be further enhanced; products may be even more downsized; chips could be combined with some other device types; fabrication operations can indeed be better regulated; different reaction routes can be explored; and unique possibilities might well emerge.

The invention of "template stickers," which can be chosen and merged according to the demands of every response, is just an emerging technique. A toolkit is filled with a set of uniform labels, each of which represents a part of the finished machine. The resulting microfluidics offer well-defined characteristics, excellent performances, and the potential to be customized, while a production method is portable, affordable, and useful (Wongkaew et al. 2019).

Microfluidics and machine intelligence as a merged discipline represent an additional example of constructive integration. The majority of microfluidic devices are now handled physically; however, multifunctional equipment can be developed and integrated.

The above enables the creation of autonomous systems and even the analysis of experiments via machine learning. Other creative pairings of microfluidics with fresh fields, such as intelligent systems, heterostructures, and machine vision technology, might result in historically significant technical advances in the coming days.

5. Conclusion

In conclusion, microfluidics is a young, diverse area of investigation with a wide range of implications. Those wafers are excellent for implementations including stage in the game gadgets, wearing biomaterials, forensic analysis, medicine transportation methods, medicine screening technologies, and upgradeable for this in the presence of synthesized diverse chemicals because of their low cost, portability, and ephemeral aspect. There are innumerable options for creating microfluidic chips because of the large variety of elements that are currently available and the complex manufacturing options for those elements. It is feasible to satisfy the majority, if not always, of the industry's needs by linking and customizing these two aspects. However, microgels may eventually be manufactured on a commercial level thanks to a number of developments in related scientific domains.

In conclusion, microfluidics has drawn a great deal of interest among scientists while still in its early stages. As a result, this discipline is anticipated to rapidly advance our understanding of nanomaterials as well as nano- and biomedical sciences, leading to game-changing innovations that might address a few of today's most urgent medical issues.

REFERENCES

1. Carrell, C. S., McCord, C. P., Wydallis, R. M. and Henry, C. S., 2020. Sealing 3D-printed parts to poly (dimethylsiloxane) for simple fabrication of microfluidic devices. *Analytica Chimica Acta, 1124*, pp. 78–84.
2. Fernandez-la-Villa, A., Pozo-Ayuso, D.F. and Castaño-Álvarez, M., 2019. Microfluidics and electrochemistry: An emerging tandem for next-generation analytical microsystems. *Current Opinion in Electrochemistry, 15*, pp. 175–185.
3. Jain, A. K. Pandey, (2019), "Modeling And Optimizing Of Different Quality Characteristics In Electrical Discharge Drilling Of Titanium Alloy (Grade-5) Sheet" Material Today Proceedings, 18, 182–191. https://doi.org/10.1016/j.matpr.2019.06.292
4. Jain, A. K. Pandey, (2019), "Multiple Quality Optimizations In Electrical Discharge Drilling Of Mild Steel Sheet" Material Today Proceedings, 8, 7252–7261. https://doi.org/10.1016/j.matpr.2017.07.054
5. Jain, A.K.Yadav & Y. Shrivastava (2019), "Modelling and Optimization of Different Quality Characteristics In Electric Discharge Drilling of Titanium Alloy Sheet" Material Today Proceedings, 21, 1680–1684. https://doi.org/10.1016/j.matpr.2019.12.010
6. Jain, C. S. Kumar, Y. Shrivastava, (2021), "Fabrication and Machining of Fiber Matrix Composite through Electric Discharge Machining: A short review" Material Today Proceedings. https://doi.org/10.1016/j.matpr.2021.07.288
7. Lai, X.; Lu, B.; Zhang, P.; Zhang, X.; Pu, Z.; Yu, H.; Li, D. Sticker Microfluidics: A Method for Fabrication of Customized Monolithic Microfluidics. Acs Biomater. Sci. Eng. 2019, 5, 6801–6810.
8. Liao, S.; He, Y.; Chu, Y.; Liao, H.; Wang, Y. Solvent-resistant and fully recyclable perfluoropolyether-based elastomer for microfluidic chip fabrication. J. Mater. Chem. A 2019, 7, 16249–16256.
9. Niculescu, A.G., Chircov, C., Bîrcă, A.C. and Grumezescu, A.M., 2021. Nanomaterials synthesis through microfluidic methods: an updated overview. *Nanomaterials, 11*(4), p. 864.
10. Niculescu, A.G., Chircov, C., Bîrcă, A.C. and Grumezescu, A.M., 2021. Fabrication and applications of microfluidic devices: A review. *International Journal of Molecular Sciences, 22*(4), p. 2011.
11. Reyes, D. R., van Heeren, H., Guha, S., Herbertson, L., Tzannis, A. P., Ducrée, J., Bissig, H. and Becker, H., 2021. Accelerating innovation and commercialization through standardization of microfluidic-based medical devices. *Lab on a Chip, 21*(1), pp. 9–21.
12. V. Panwar, D. K. Sharma, K. V. P. Kumar, A. Jain & C. Thakar, (2021), "Experimental Investigations And Optimization Of Surface Roughness In Turning Of EN 36 Alloy Steel Using Response Surface Methodology And Genetic Algorithm" Materials Today: Proceedings, https://Doi.Org/10.1016/J.Matpr.2021.03.642
13. V. Panwar, D. K. Sharma, K. V. P. Kumar, A. Jain & C. Thakar, (2021), "Experimental Investigations And Optimization Of Surface Roughness In Turning Of EN 36 Alloy Steel Using Response Surface Methodology And Genetic Algorithm" Materials Today: Proceedings, https://Doi.Org/10.1016/J.Matpr.2021.03.642
14. Wongkaew, N.; Simsek, M.; Griesche, C.; Baeumner, A. J. Functional Nanomaterials and Nanostructures Enhancing Electrochemical Biosensors and Lab-on-a-Chip Performances: Recent Progress, Applications, and Future Perspective. Chem. Rev. 2019, 119, 120–194.
15. Zhao, Q., Cui, H., Wang, Y. and Du, X., 2020. Microfluidic platforms toward rational material fabrication for biomedical applications. *Small, 16*(9), p. 1903798.

Computer Science Engineering and Emerging Technologies (ICCS-2022) – Prof (Dr.) Rajeev Sobti et al. (eds)
© 2024 Taylor & Francis Group, London, ISBN 978-1-032-52199-2

Chapter **106**

Computation of Cuckoo Search Algorithm and its Implementation in Active Noise Cancellation

Balpreet Singh[1], Harpal Thethi[2]
Department of ECE, SCEE, Lovely Professional University Jalandhar, Punjab, India

Santosh Nanda[3]
Techversant Infotech Pvt Ltd, Trivandrum, Kerala, India

Abstract: This paper proposes an evolutionary and metaheuristic Cuckoo search algorithm (CS) to implement the Active noise controller. The purpose is to develop a computational algorithm and an adaptive filter, eliminating the chance of local minima convergence of the adaptive algorithm and providing a more robust algorithm for time-varying and nonlinear noise signals. Moreover, in a practical environment, the acoustic path changes abruptly. The classical method of adaptive filters fails to perform, especially in Linear ANC systems like Fx-LMS, where prior estimation of the secondary path decides the algorithm's efficiency. On the contrary, the bio-inspired algorithms do not require secondary path estimation and solve convergence to local minima. This paper presents the systematic implementation of CS-based ANC. It compares the simulation result with FxLMS, Particle Swarm Optimization, and Genetic algorithms.

Keywords: Active noise control, Cuckoo search algorithm, Filtered-LMS (Fx-LMS), Genetic algorithm (GA), Least mean square, Narrowband noise, Particle swarm optimization (PSO)

1. Introduction

Noise pollution in urban areas has increased exponentially, resulting in hearing impairment, stress, anxiety, and mental illness. Thus, in the current scenario, the development of Noise reduction techniques is our utmost priority for comfortable living for humankind and all the species on earth. Broadly, the two noise reduction techniques are passive noise reduction and active noise reduction [1]. The passive noise reduction techniques select materials (silencers in automobiles, cushions used in headphones) to absorb unwanted high-frequency noise. However, it does not seem reliable because of its inefficiency in reducing low-frequency noise. The weight, dimension, and material costs increase with an increase in the bandwidth of noise reduction. In contradiction, active noise control (ANC) is a cost- and space-efficient noise elimination technique for a broader range of frequencies. [2] Active Noise Control systems work on the principle of destructive interference and generate an anti-noise signal of amplitude equal to the input signal but in the opposite phase [3] [4]. It consists of a reference microphone, an error microphone, an adaptive controller, and an anti-noise speaker. The reference microphone senses the noise signal and feeds it to an adaptive controller to generate anti-noise. Further, the error microphone takes residual noise as input and leads the adaptive filter to adapt its weight accordingly. The primary path of the noise signal is the acoustic path between the reference microphone and loudspeaker and the anti-noise speaker. The path between the speaker and the error microphone is known as the secondary path. Figure 106.1 shows a block diagram of Active Noise

[1]balpreet.15731@lpu.co.in, [2]thethi@lpu.co.in, [3]santoshnanda@live.in

DOI: 10.1201/9781003405580-106

Control based on the Filtered Least Mean Square (FxLMS) algorithm. The input signal x(n) travels through the impulse response of the primary path P(z) and generates the desired signal d(n) for noise cancellation.

Meanwhile, the ANC algorithm W(z) generates y(n). The output of the ANC algorithm y(n) is fed to secondary path transfer function S(z) to generate the antinoise signal. At cancellation juncture, the error microphone senses the error sign e(n), which is fed to the adaptive algorithm [in case of FxLMS, Least Mean Square] along with x'(n). The x'(n) is output from passing input signal x(n) to the inverse of secondary path transfer function S'(z). The adaptive algorithm aims to update the

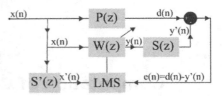

Fig. 106.1 Block diagram of feedback ANC system[7]

Weight W(z) to minimize the mean square error e(n). The secondary path is modelled priorly. It consists of a digital-to-analog converter, reconstruction filter, power amplifier, loudspeaker, the acoustic path between the canceling loudspeaker, the error microphone preamplifier, the antialiasing filter, and the error microphone preamplifier analog-to-digital converter

Despite the affordable hardware implementation of Fx-LMS, practical performance is not significant because of the non-linearity of the primary and secondary paths [8]. Furthermore, the time-varying nature of noise, nonlinear noise, non-Gaussian noise, colored noise, pink noise, deterministic or stochastic noise, and a chance for an adaptive algorithm to converge to local minima Subsequently, this led to the development of Nonlinear adaptive algorithms and metaheuristic adaptive algorithms.

Even though nonlinear and linear adaptive filters can solve the minimization problem, the non-linearity and time-varying nature of the acoustic medium and a noise signal probably confine the adaptive filter to local minima. Moreover, finding an optimal convergence rate for every delta change in paths and noise characteristics is tedious and cumbersome. Indeed, bio-inspired algorithms' capability to find global optimum solutions motivates the development of bio-inspired algorithms with mean square error as a cost function. Besides finding the global solution capability of the heuristic algorithm, there is no need to find the secondary path, thereby improving the system's overall stability.

In the notion of subject, Wangler et al. were the first to propose a bio-inspired Genetic Algorithm to implement the ANC system in 1994. Moreover, Cheng-Yuan Chang et al. proposed the Genetic algorithm-based ANC system, which utilizes GA instead of the FxLMS algorithm. The proposed algorithm uses GA as an inherent solution for nonlinear noises and the problem of local minima compared to Fx-LMS. A genetic algorithm is an evolutionary algorithm that mimics natural selection to optimize the solution.

Further, Rout et al. proposed a PSO-based ANC [6]–[10] system with and without secondary path estimation. Nitin V. George et al. proposed feedforward ANC based on the Wilcoxon norm and PSO that identify and remove outliers in the secondary path estimation [9] and eliminate impulse or abrupt noise in error microphones.

It is valuable to note that the potential of the bio-inspired algorithm is immense, but at the cost of the high dimensionality of search space and time-consuming iterations. This paper evaluates and compares the Cuckoo Search performance and particle swarm optimization [10], [11], and [12] based on computational complexity and space-time efficiency.

2. Literature Review

2.1 Cuckoo Search Algorithm

Yang and Deb first proposed Cuckoo Search (CS) in 2009, inspired by the holoparasite reproduction strategy of the Cuckoo bird [13]. The cuckoo bird lays eggs in a host nest for their upbringing. Due to almost the same texture, shape, and color, the host bird raises a cuckoo chick as his child. However, there is a probability that the host bird will find the alien egg and abandon the cuckoo's egg and nest. As far as developing an evolutionary algorithm goes, the objective is to maximize the chance of survival of a cuckoo's egg with the minimum investment. In order to mathematically model the CS [14], let's assume there are N numbers of cuckoos and nests, assuming that the cuckoos lay one egg in one host nest only for simplicity. The position of the egg is the solution vector x to the optimization problem. Further, to make evolutionary algorithms programable, there are the following assumptions:

- A cuckoo select a nest randomly and lay one egg.
- The probability that the host discovered the egg as an alien egg and abandoned the nest with . The valuedepends on upon total population and changes with every iteration.

- The cost function evaluates the fitness of an egg. The minimum of the population is the best solution for the next generation.

In the literature, there are two processes used to update the solution. The first process aims to reduce the dissimilarity between eggs by updating the egg-laying approach.

$$x_i^{t+1} = x_i^t + \alpha s \oplus H(p_a - \varepsilon) \oplus (x_j^t - x_k^t) \tag{1}$$

where as x_i^t is the current position selected randomly $(x_j^t - x_k^t)$ is the dissimilarity of two population from $i = 1,2,3......$ N. The probability that host will discover the contaminated egg is defined by of step function $H(p_a - \varepsilon)$, by comparing p_a with random number ε between [0,1]. In addition, α & s is scaling factor and differences of solution selected by random permutation respectively. $\oplus$ is element-wise multiplication of two vectors.

The second process uses the concept of Levy's flight and enables host to builds it nest at distant place to avoid contamination of nest. The host bird update new position by adding Levy's step size (which is Levy's distribution) to its previous position. But, the generation of pseudorandom number in Levy's flight is cumbersome and it is recommended to use power law distribution where $0 \le \beta \le 2$.

$$x_i^{t+1} = x_i^t + \alpha L(s, \beta) \tag{2}$$

$$L(s, \beta) \sim \frac{\beta \Gamma(\beta) \sin(\pi \beta/2)}{\pi} \cdot \frac{1}{s^{1+\beta}} \tag{3}$$

$$\Gamma(q) = \int_0^\infty z^{q-1} e^{-u} du \tag{4}$$

Mantegna et al. proposed algorithm to generate random number that follows the Levy's distribution[14]. Levy's flight step size is as follows[14]

$$s = \frac{u}{|v|^{1/\beta}} \tag{5}$$

Where, u, v are Normal distribution with following characteristics.

$$u \sim N(0, \sigma_u^2); v \sim N(0, 1) \tag{6}$$

And,

$$\sigma_u = \left\{ \frac{\Gamma(1+\beta)\sin(\pi\beta/2)}{\beta\Gamma[(1+\beta)/2] \times 2^{(\beta-1)/2}} \right\}^{1/\beta} \tag{7}$$

Since, the calculation of variance involves the gamma function and its calculation is cumbersome. Moreover, for approximation σ_u is considered as fixed value of 0.01 for $\beta = 1.5$. Thus, with approximation the step size is updated as follows.

$$s = \frac{u}{|v|^{1/\beta}} \quad \text{and} \quad \beta = 1.5 \tag{8}$$

$$\alpha = x_i - x_{\text{best}}; \text{ Since the change will leads to } x_i \tag{9}$$

$$\text{stepsize} = \alpha L(s, \beta) = 0.01(x_i - x_{\text{best}}) \cdot \frac{u}{|v|^{1/\beta}} \tag{10}$$

2.2 Proposed Algorithm

Figure 106.2 presents a block diagram of CS-based ANC Feedback ANC with a Finite Impulse Response (FIR) filter. Specifically, the performance of any ANC system relies on the controller's configuration, mainly finite-impulse response (FIR) and infinite-impulse response (IIR) [1], and algorithm to cope with a dynamic system. However, the IIR system requires less computational time for a complex system, but its instability, slower convergence, and chance to converge to local minima make FIR a favorable configuration. FIR filters use delays, multipliers, and adders to produce the output. Figure 3 shows the basic structure of the N-length FIR filter: z^{-1} represents the delay of one-input samples, k is the weight multiplied by the inputs, and output is the sum of delayed input samples multiplied by corresponding weights. The weights of the FIR filter are pivotal in determining the desired output, and hence the algorithms that adjust the weight are the heart of the ANC system.

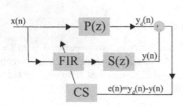

Fig. 106.2 The Block diagram for cuckoo search based ANC system[10]

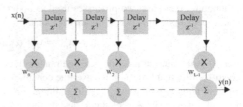

Fig. 106.3 Schematic of finite impulse response (X denotes multiplication)

Source: Made by Author

$x(n)$ = input noise Signal

$p(n)$ = Primary path transfer function

$y_d(n)$ = desired noise signal

W = Adaptive filter weight vector of length of $L = [W_0, W_1, W_2, \ldots\ldots W_{L-1}]$

$s(n)$ = Secondary path transfer function

$y(n)$ = Output signal from loudspeaker

$e(n)$ = Error signal frons error microphone

LMS = Least mean Square (cost function)

$$y_d(n) = x(n) \otimes y(n) \tag{11}$$

$$y(n) = s(n) \otimes (W^T x(n)) \tag{12}$$

or $$y(n) = s(n) \otimes \{x(n)\, W_0 + x(n-1)\, W_1 + \cdots \cdots \cdots \cdots \cdots + x(n-L+1)\, W_L\} \tag{13}$$

$$e(n) = y_d(n) - y(n) \tag{14}$$

$$MSE = \frac{1}{N} \sum_{n=0}^{N} e^2(n) \tag{15}$$

where, N is the length of input Sequence $x(n)$ and $\otimes$ is the convolution operation

The objective of cost function is to find optimum weight vector W of length L subjected to minimum MSE.

Hence; Cost function, $MSE = f(W)$ (16)

The foremost objective of CS algorithm in ANC system is to minimize the error at error microphone such that the residual noise is approximately equals to zero. Moreover, for the implementation of CS in ANC optimization, consider the coefficient of nest or population as N adaptive filter, and initial solution for ANC. Generally, L is filter length or dimension of problem, and using each row the corresponding value of cost function is calculated for minimizing. The pseudocode is shown below.

$$\text{Nest/population} = \text{Weight } W = \begin{bmatrix} w_L^0 & w_1^2 & w_1^2 & \ldots w_1^{L-1} \\ w_2^0 & w_2^1 & w_2^2 & \ldots w_2^{L-1} \\ w_N^0 & w_N^1 & w_N^2 & \ldots w_N^{L-1} \end{bmatrix} N \times L \tag{17}$$

Input: Read Population size N, probability p_a, Levy's Exponent β and maximum iteration maxitr

Output: Print: Display Global best value

Calling Function: Cost function to calculate the fitness of nest.

1. Set a population of N nest as x_i where $i \in 1,2,3\ldots N$ of size $[N \times D]$
   for $i = 1$:*maxitr*

2. Select random cuckoo/nest from the population
3. Calculate the new Levy's Flight solution using Equation 2
4. Determine the fitness value of each solutions using CALL Cost Function $f_i\,(x_i)$
   Randomly select the nest from n nest (f_j)
   If $f_i < f_j$ (in case of minimization) then
   Update $x_j = x_i$
   End if
5. Discard the worst nest by fraction = p_a
6. Generate the new nest using Equation 1
   End For
7. Display Best solution x_j

The performance of evolutionary algorithms substantially depends upon the number of parameters. Contrary, to other bio -inspired algorithms Cuckoo search algorithm require minimum numbers of parameters. hence, add advantage of comfortable turning of algorithm.

3. Simulation Result

This section of the paper evaluates the performance of CS based ANC system with MATLAB R2018a simulation. The objective is to calculate the performance of proposed ANC configuration under various conditions. The primary path for the experiment is taken as p(n)=[0.01 0.25 0.5 1 0.5 0.25 0.01]; and secondary path s(n)=0.25*p(n)[1]. Moreover, dimension of cost function is equal to the length L of weight of adaptive filter W. The lower and upper bound for CS algorithm is taken as [-5,5] respectively. The other parameters for CS algorithm are as follows β=1.5, p_a=0.25, population size N=25 and the maximum iteration is 200. In order to implement the CS in MATLAB.

Case I: The effectiveness of CS based ANC with respect to length of FIR filter.

The length/order of ANC filter is the length of FIR filter, initially the optimum weight of filter is unknown. Further, the experiment is conducted for various filter lengths from L=6 to 40, and the fitness value of cost function (MSE) for 1000 Iterations is plotted in Fig. 106.4. It has been observed that for filter length L greater than 10 the convergence degrades, because as the number of weight vector increases the number of parameters for optimization also increase eventually leads to poorer performance. However, at N=10, the algorithm converges faster and steady state error also stabilizes before 200th iteration as shown in Fig. 106.5. Hence, ANC with filter length L=10 is preferred for rest of experiment.

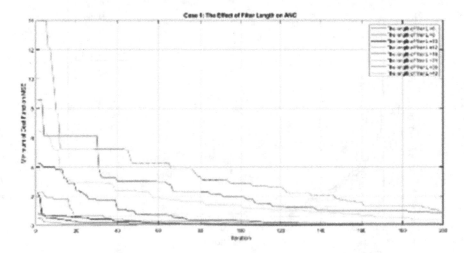

Fig. 106.4 The value of error square of different length of FIR filter

Source: Made by Author

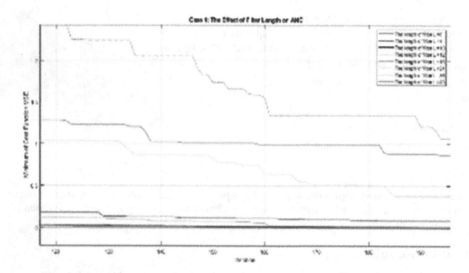

Fig. 106.5 The zoomed graph of error square of different filter length

Source: Made by Author

Case II: The effect of fitness value of cost function and population size.

In order to determine the optimum number of populations or nests N, an experiment is conducted to find the MSE for different population sizes. Figure 106.6 depicts the graph of the fitness value of the cost function vs. 200 Iterations for different N, and Fig. 106.7 presents the graph of the cost function and 1000 Iterations for the various values of N. Further, as N increases, the CS algorithm converges faster and gives stable steady-state values. However, the more significant the value N, the more parameters are required to optimize, which eventually decreases the overall ANC system's time-space efficiency. Hence, a trade-off value of N = 30 is considered for the rest of the experiment.

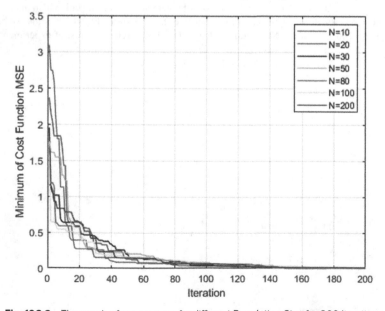

Fig. 106.6 The graph of error square for different Population Size for 200 Iterations

Source: Made by Author

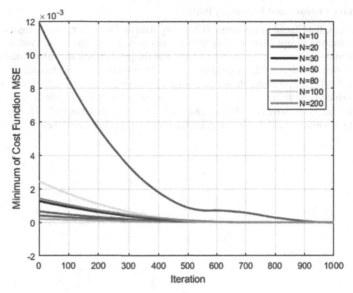

Fig. 106.7 The graph of error square for different Population Size for 1000 Iterations

Source: Made by Author

Case III: Time Varying Noise Signal

In most of the practical cases, the noise signal does not always vary with the same frequency and phase, but due to the continuous changing environment like change in speed of the fan, change of load on motor/generators, or change in speed of the vehicle the characteristics of noise varies with time. For instance, this experiment considers the case of periodic and sinusoidal noise at different frequencies from 10 - 200 Hz. The parameters of CS are as follows population N = 30, Weight of filter L = 10, and Iteration =1000. From Fig. 106.8, the result is evident that the CS-based ANC system works efficiently for periodic noise, non-stationary noise, and broadband no

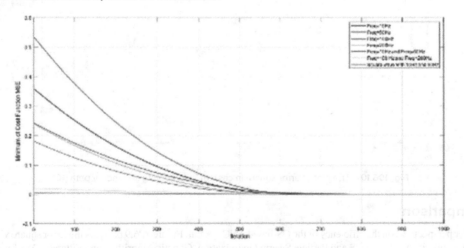

Fig. 106.8 The Error square for periodic noise signal

Source: Made by Author

Case IV: Non-Stationary Primary and Secondary Path[10]

In a Practical ANC system, the change in environment (primary path and secondary path) degrades the system's overall performance. For instance, the abrupt change in speed of the fan or sudden opening of windows or doors changes the living room's environment, which eventually results in a change in the primary and secondary path[10]. In this simulation, firstly, the impulse response of Primary Path p(n)=[0.01,0.25,0.5,1,0.5,0.25,0.01] has changed abruptly at 500th Iteration to p(n)=[-0.01,0.25,0,1,-0.5,0.5,0.1] Second, the secondary path has changed to s(n)=0.25*p(n)to s(n)=0.5*p(n) at 500th iteration. Lastly, both primary and secondary path has been changed as per above impulse responses—the fitness of cost function i.e., error square has been plotted for all three cases in Figs 106.9, 106.10 and 106.11, respectively. The CS-based ANC system works all the variations efficiently and converges to a global minimum effectively

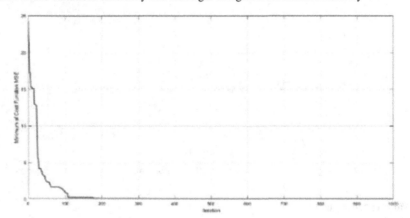

Fig. 106.9 The plot of error square in case of time varying primary path [10]

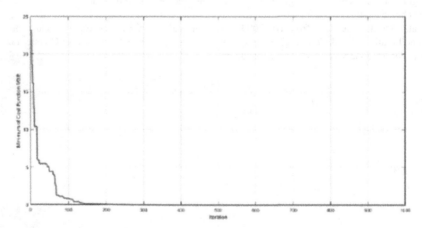

Fig. 106.10 The plot of error square in case of time varying secondary path [10]

4. Comparison

For broader perspectives on the efficiency of the CS-based ANC system, Figure 106.9 presents the Error square vs. Iteration graph and comparison between CS and Particle Swarm Optimization, Genetic Algorithm, and Filtered-LMS for sinusoidal noise signals, and Figure 106.10 plots error square at log scale. The parameters table for the various algorithms is as follows:

The PSO algorithm converges best compared to CS, GA, and FxLMS, and the CS convergence rate to steady state is better than that of GA and FxLMS. However, the number of parameters required in PSO is greater than in CS, which is a foremost advantage to CS because the more optimization parameters, the more space and tunic are needed. However, Fx-LMS has shown substantial performance, but the risk of a bad secondary path is profound, whereas bio-inspired algorithms show better results without secondary path estimation.

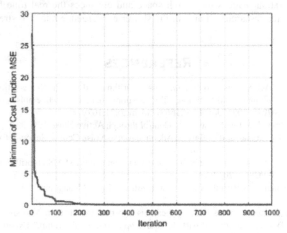

Fig. 106.11 The plot of error square in case of time varying primary and secondary path together [10]

Table 106.1 Optimization parameters for various algorithms

Algorithm	Parameters
Cuckoo Search	Population = 30
	Dimension/Filter Length = 10
	Iterations = 1000
Particle Swarm Optimization	Population = 30
	Dimension/Filter Length = 10
	Iterations = 1000
	Inertia Coefficient = 0.7298
	Damping Ratio of Inertia Coefficient = 1
	Personal Acceleration Coefficient = 1.4692
	Social Acceleration Coefficient = 1.4692
Genetic Algorithm (Roulette Wheel Selection)	Population = 30
	Dimension/Filter Length = 10
	Iterations = 1000
	Crossover Rate = 1
	Mutation Rate = 1
	Tournament Size = 3

Source: Made by Author

5. Conclusion

In conclusion, this paper presents the computation of the Cuckoo search algorithm to implement the ANC system. Further, the results are promising in all the conditions of broadband noise, periodic, sinusoidal noise signals, and time-varying primary and secondary paths. However, the proposed algorithm shows slower convergence than PSO. Still, the lesser required parameter for optimization reduces the search space and enhances the real-time high-performance capability of the algorithm [15]. Further, the research to improve the slower convergence rate will strengthen the efficiency of the algorithm manifold.

REFERENCES

1. S. M. Kuo and D. R. Morgan, "Active Noise Control Systems Algorithms and DSP Implementations," 1996.
2. B. Lam, W. Gan, D. Shi, M. Nishimura, and S. Elliott, "Ten questions concerning active noise control in the built environment," Build. Environ., vol. 200, p. 107928, 2021, doi: 10.1016/j.buildenv.2021.107928.
3. A. Raghav, "Noise Control through Active Noise Noise Control through Active Noise," 2012.
4. D. Veeravasantarao, S. Ajay, P. P. kumar, and L. Behera, Adaptive Active Noise Control Schemes for Headset Applications, vol. 41, no. 2. IFAC, 2008.
5. N. Nakrani, "Feed-forward and Feedback Active Noise Control System using FxLMS algorithm for Narrowband and Broadband Noise," no. 1, 2012, doi: 10.1109/CSNT.2012.130.
6. D. J. Krusienski and W. K. Jenkins, "A Particle Swarm Optimization – Least Mean Squares Algorithm for Adaptive Filtering," pp. 241–245, 2004.
7. N. V George and G. Panda, "Expert Systems with Applications Short communication A robust evolutionary feedforward active noise control system using Wilcoxon norm and particle swarm optimization algorithm," Expert Syst. Appl., vol. 39, no. 8, pp. 7574–7580, 2012, doi: 10.1016/j.eswa.2012.01.038.
8. N. K. Rout, D. P. Das, and G. Panda, "Particle swarm optimization based nonlinear active noise control under saturation nonlinearity," Appl. Soft Comput. J., vol. 41, pp. 275–289, 2016, doi: 10.1016/j.asoc.2016.01.011.
9. N. K. Rout, D. P. Das, and G. Panda, "PSO based adaptive narrowband ANC algorithm without the use of synchronization signal and secondary path estimate," Mech. Syst. Signal Process., vol. 114, pp. 378–398, 2019, doi: 10.1016/j.ymssp.2018.05.018.
10. N. K. Rout, D. P. Das, and G. Panda, "Particle Swarm Optimization Based Active Noise Control Algorithm Without Secondary Path Identification," vol. 61, no. 2, pp. 554–563, 2012.
11. L. Lu et al., "A Survey on Active Noise Control in the Past Decade – Part II: Nonlinear Systems," 2020, doi: 10.1016/j.sigpro.2020.107929.
12. Z. G. Diamantis, D. T. Tsahalis, and I. Borchers, "Optimization of an active noise control system inside an aircraft, based on the simultaneous optimal positioning of microphones and speakers, with the use of a genetic algorithm," Comput. Optim. Appl., vol. 23, no. 1, pp. 65–76, 2002, doi: 10.1023/A:1019924707917.
13. X.-S. Yang and S. Deb, "Cuckoo Search via Levy Flights," pp. 210–214, 2010, [Online]. Available: http://arxiv.org/abs/1003.1594.
14. X. Yang and X. He, Bat algorithm and cuckoo search algorithm. Elsevier Ltd, 2020.
15. A. Adnan, "A Comparative Study of Particle Swarm Optimization and Cuckoo Search Techniques Through Problem-Specific Distance Function," pp. 88–92, 2013

Computer Science Engineering and Emerging Technologies (ICCS-2022) – Prof (Dr.) Rajeev Sobti et al. (eds)
© 2024 Taylor & Francis Group, London, ISBN 978-1-032-52199-2

Chapter

107

Development of Evaluation Protocol for Anti-Forensics Encryption Tool Using Software Reverse Engineering Techniques

Zakariyya Hassan Abdullahi[1]
Research Scholar, Department of Computer Science and Engineering,
Lovely Professional University, Phagwara, Punjab, India

Shailendra Kumar Singh[2]
Assistant Professor, Department of Computer Science and Engineering,
Lovely Professional University, Phagwara, Punjab, India

Moin Hasan[3]
Assistant Professor, CSE, Jain University

Abstract: Encryption software has become increasingly popular in recent years, but it has raised concerns about security and privacy, particularly when it comes to law enforcement and digital investigations. Protocol reverse engineering (PRE) is a process by which a protocol specification is analyzed to identify its components and source code, but it can also raise concerns about the security of the software. To address these concerns, researchers have developed a number of PRE methodologies and properties that can help ensure the security and reliability of encryption software. Additionally, access hiding is the practice of deliberately concealing data or other information from investigators, which can impede their ability to solve crimes and bring perpetrators to justice. To address this challenge, investigators may need to use specialized tools and techniques to uncover hidden data or break encryption keys.

Keywords: Reverse engineering, Encryption, Protocol

1. Introduction

In the digital world we are living in, virtually everything is digital. It is supported by digital data. Numerical data is present in these fields, which reflects the presence of technology in those disciplines. Digital data is used by people, companies, and governments for a number of purposes, including cybercrime, terrorism, and everyday crimes where digital data may provide useful information. The development of digital forensics has contributed to this expansion (Rogers & Seigfried, 2004) (Majed et al., 2020). On the other hand, the existence of digital forensics tools also served as a warning to hackers and threat actors, as well as to parties concerned with privacy, to create anti-forensics tools in order to protect the capacity of forensics tools (FT) to be useful in recovering useful and pertinent information. The forensic examiner is assisted in gathering evidence from a device by the use of computer forensic tools (CFT) and Mobile forensic Tools (MFT).

Anti-forensics tools and tactics are used to attack the availability and utility of digital evidence by modifying, disturbing, and destroying the evidence's scientific validity (Gül & Kugu, 2017). (Conlan et al., 2016) Depending on the use and goal, AFT might take on various forms: Through advances in technology, forensic experts are now using modern methods to

[1]Hassanzakariyya78@gmail.com, [2]drsksingh.cse@gmail.com, [3]mmoinhhasan@gmail.com

DOI: 10.1201/9781003405580-107

perform their inquiries quickly, accurately, and conclusively. But on the other hand, cyber criminals are also exploiting the same advances in technology to implement advanced, personalized techniques to confuse forensic inquiry (Pimenidis, 2016). Although the term "anti-forensics" is not conceptually new, there is no clear definition of the same from any engineer or educator. The authors here have attempted to define the term. It may be deduced that anti-forensics may be defined as attempts to adversely affect the existence, quantity, and/or quality of evidence from a crime scene or make it difficult or impossible to perform the review of facts. (Kessler, 2007) ,an expert and investigator in digital forensics, describes AF as "attempts to adversely impact the nature, amount and or quality of evidence from a scene of the crime, professionals of anti- forensic methods and tools, find a somewhat darker definition: ' application of the scientific process to digital media in order to nullify information for judicial scrutiny.(Mothukur et al., 2019).

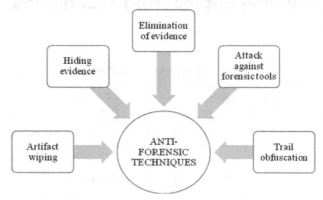

Fig. 107.1 Classification of anti forensics techniques

Source: 978-1-7281-6939-2/20/2020 IEEE, 10.1109/ISDFS49300.2020.9116399

1.1 Encryption

Data Encryption is used to prevent access to stored data. Encryption can be applied to an individual file, database, email, or entire disk using several encryption algorithms. In today's computing environment, data encryption is one of the most important aspects. Security attacks are vulnerable to user data contained in electronic devices, including laptops, personal digital assistants, flash drives, smart phones, and external hard drives. In a report published in 2017 by Intel Corporation, nearly 50 percent of stolen laptops had no encryption mechanisms to protect the data. (Bari & Siddique, 2017) For every person, data and information security are important departments in today's world. People spend hundreds of dollars to secure their Data information for competitive survival, and any leakage of crucial data could lead to unrecoverable loss. (Hou et al., 2009), dataInformation security is the most critical type of security—more important than network security—since only securely encrypted data can be safely transmitted.

VeraCrypt is an open-source OTFE software that fully supports Windows XP and provides plausible deniability. TrueCrypt 1.0 supports Windows 98/ME and Windows 2000/XP, while 2.0a removed Windows 98 and ME support. (Miao, 2010).

1.2 Contribution of this Article

The article contributes to the strategy the novelist uses to create higher-level abstract representations of a system. It consists of calculating exact subsystem interfaces as well as locating important components and interconnections inside multilayer subsystem hierarchies. The steps in this approach, which is based on the principles of software reverse engineering, include using offline analysis and finding modules and components. The system-level technique typically decomposes a system more effectively than an automatic process, which is what the majority of earlier studies employed. Offline code analysis is a potent strategy because it offers a clear picture of the program and makes it simple to look for certain functions of interest.

2. Literature Review

Software reverse engineering has been used for a long time to try and understand the logic, architecture, and design of the code. By reverse engineering an application, the code design can be discovered. Restored to a certain extent. Malware authors are interested in later app cloning via code reuse and repackaging. Malware writers target these apps because of the openness of the Machine App Market and the inadequate security testing performed by app developers to develop and disseminate movable malware. Gonzalez and others (Gonzalez et al., 2015) explore a few offline and online repackaging detection methods in depth that identify software similarities using various attributes and metrics. Including Lim et al. (Lim et al., 2016) With the help of communication analysis, protocol reverse engineering (PRE) aims to approximate the protocol definition. Contrary to reverse engineering of executable program binaries (software), which focuses on getting source code or comprehending a program's implementation, PRE's inference purpose is to draw conclusions about the program's behavior. However, PRE-is not only restricted to this kind of analysis and may also utilize software reverse engineering to infer communication. Techniques for reverse engineering software are fundamentally distinct from traffic analysis. Software reverse engineering approaches need to be used with specific tools, methods, and analysis processes, and the analyst must have a certain level of background knowledge. Beyond PRE, the techniques required for entity analysis are also widely used and well understood. (Schwartz & Avgerinos, 2010) When reverse engineering a node implementation using software, entity analysis infers the protocol (e.g., Narayan et al., 2015). To employ techniques for software control flow analysis and memory introspection, entity analysis requires access to the program and its execution environment. Obtaining the program or a sufficient execution environment for it frequently proves to be impossible; in both situations, entity analysis approaches are inapplicable. Contrasted with traffic, Traffic trace analysis is still an option when reverse engineering the executable program is not practical since trace analysis just looks at the communication that is visible in the link between entities. Such trace analysis is non-invasive and does not need to have control over any entity, even if it can only learn information from what can be seen on the communication link. Rauch [12] discussed PRE-automation in 2006 and outlined the procedures required to lessen repetitive work performed by humans throughout the Pre-process. Since the tool he demonstrated at Blackhat was never made public, the PRE-field was unable to continuously advance. The standard Pre-process is still being carried out manually more than ten years later, even though many methods with varying degrees of automation have been put out in the interim. Stroulia, Eleni, et al. Focusing on program understanding and modeling the structure of a program by examining its COBOL and C codes (Stroulia & Systä, 2002) Reverse engineering produces higher-level abstractions and provides architectural views of the large-scale structure of software. (Cordes & Brown, 1991), Several techniques have been developed to automate the rating of sources and code snippets, but regrettably, many algorithms miss and undervalue the source code features. To overcome the aforementioned problem, Diamantopoulos et al. (2016).

2.1 Reverse Engineering

Reverse engineering is a vital collection of methods and equipment for discovering the true nature of software. Specifically, it is "the process of evaluating a subject system to discover the system's components and their interrelationships and to build representations of the system in another form or at a higher level of abstraction" (Chikofsky, E., & Cross, I., 1990). We are able to see the software's architecture, modes of operation, and features that influence its behavior as a result. We now have a practical means to comprehend the complexity of software and discover its truth through the use of automated tools for software assessment and analytical techniques. Reverse engineering has been around for a while. Every time someone examines another person's code, they are engaging in the conceptual Reversing process. However, it can also happen when a developer reviews their own code after a few days have passed since it was written. A process of discovery is called reverse engineering. When we analyze and learn from code that has been written by ourselves or others, we may not expect to see certain things. (Eilam, 2011). Reverse engineering a protocol (PRE) aims to deduce by being mindful of communication in comparison to other inference goals, such as reverse engineering executable program binaries for software (software), which prioritizes obtaining source code or learning about the application of software. However, PRE may use It is not restricted to these, though. This paper describes a reverse engineering process and a reverse engineering tool that are used to analyze the way signatures are matched by network-based intrusion detection systems. The results of the analysis are used to either generate variations of attacks that evade detection or produce non-malicious traffic that overstimulates the sensor (Mutz et al., 2005). Various methods of analysis are used to assess communication. Consequently, there are two primary ways to understand how a There will be two distinct protocols: entity analysis and trace analysis. [19], as shown in Fig. 107.2.

IDA Pro disassembles binary programs to create maps of their execution, showing instructions in assembly language. Assembly language is hard to make sense of, so advanced IDA Pro has techniques to make it more readable.(Summary & Pro, 2009).

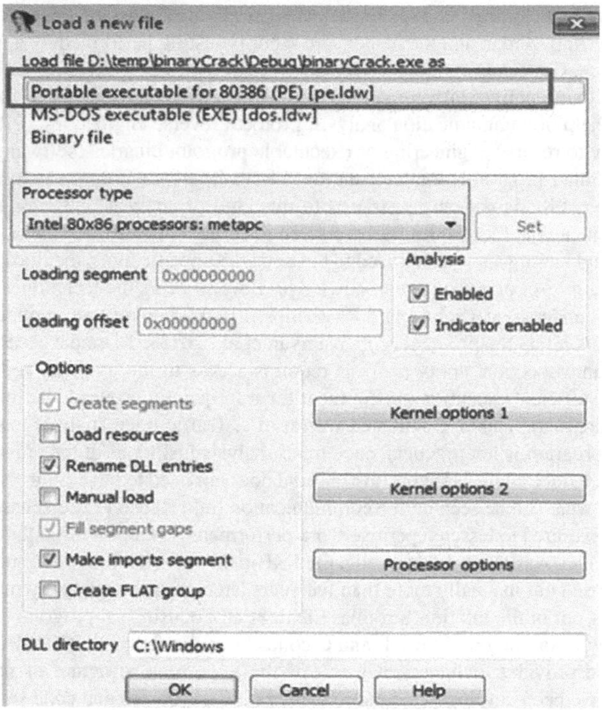

Fig. 107.2 IDA Pro shows three file types that can be reversed: binary files, DOS executable files, and PE files

Source: www.c-sharpcorner.com.Ajayadav123, 2020

3. Results and Discussion

The source code for the VeraCrypt encryption program as well as binary executable forms are anticipated outcomes. Static analysis and dynamic analysis are the two routes for the programmer.

Static analysis is a technique for learning as much as you can without actually executing a binary. (Sihwail et al., 2018). Reverse engineering and disassembly techniques are used to achieve this. Other, more focused analysis methods include string analysis, obfuscation, restricted execution settings, reverse engineering, packaging, and so forth. Static analysis comprises disassembling the internal workings of the malware, putting the executable file into IDA Pro, and looking over the program's manual to determine what it does (Sikorski & Honig, 2012). A debugger is employed in dynamic analysis to look into the internal state of an active malicious attack (Or-Meir et al., 2019; Sikorski & Honig, 2012). A debugger is a piece of hardware or software used to check another program's functionality. A dynamic analysis technique is employed to obtain the program's detailed information. Three well-known botnet detection debuggers include In contrast to other approaches that are more difficult to comprehend, the article offered a thorough reverse engineering technique in a straightforward manner to understand the internal and interpretational behavior of software programs.

4. Conclusion

The Veracrypt software's Reverse engineering was the main focus of this paper. In order to find the source code for various modules, this form was carefully inspected, and its description was divided into blocks. The method for creating a protocol for an existing software system has been detailed in this paper. The program's design was viewed and recorded using this process. Utilizing the recovered design, which was saved in a software development setting, a new implementation of the program can be made. Descriptions of the interactions and new discoveries made while working on this protocol development are provided in the portions. The list of issues that have been found is summarized in the sentences that follow. The focus of the research is on evaluating an anti-forensic encryption tool. The evaluation protocol for the tool has been

Fig. 107.3   A selection of extracted source codes for encryption algorithms

Sources: www.socinvestigation.com>tools

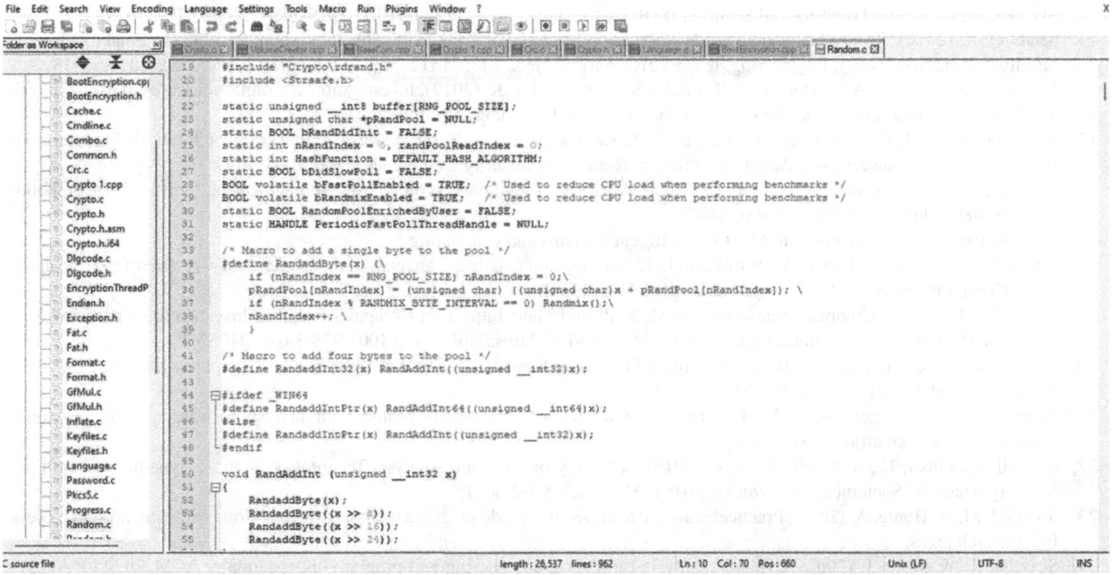

Fig. 107.4   A selection of random pool enriched extracted source codes

Sources: www.socinvestigation.com>tools

developed using software reverse engineering techniques. The aim of the evaluation protocol is to assess the effectiveness of the anti-forensic encryption tool. The use of software reverse engineering techniques in the evaluation protocol suggests that the tool is being tested by examining its code and behavior. The development of an evaluation protocol is an important step in assessing the security and effectiveness of encryption tools, particularly those that are designed to evade forensic analysis and their ability to evade digital forensic analysis.

REFERENCES

1. Bari, M. S., & Siddique, A. T. (2017). Study on different Cryptography Algorithm a Critical Review. International Journal of Advanced Research in Computer Engineering & Technology (IJARCET) Volume 6, Issue 2, February 2017, ISSN: 2278 – 1323 Study, 6(2), 177–182.
2. Chikofsky, E., & Cross, I., J. H. (1990). Reverse Engineering and Recovery A Taxonomy. IEEE Software, 7(1), 13-17.
3. Conlan, K., Baggili, I., & Breitinger, F. (2016). Anti-forensics: Furthering digital forensic science through a new extended, granular taxonomy. DFRWS 2016 USA - Proceedings of the 16th Annual USA Digital Forensics Research Conference, 18(December 2015), S66–S75. https://doi.org/10.1016/j.diin.2016.04.006
4. Cordes, D., & Brown, M. (1991). The Literate-Programming Paradigm. Computer, 24(6), 52–61. https://doi.org/10.1109/2.86838
5. Diamantopoulos, T., Thomopoulos, K., & Symeonidis, A. (2016). Reusability-aware Recommendations of Source Code Components. 488–491. https://doi.org/10.1145/2901739.2903492
6. Eilam, E. (2011). R. secrets of reverse engineering (1st ed.). J. W. & S. (2011). Reversing: Secrets of Reverse Engineering. Wilely Publishing.
7. Gonzalez, H., Kadir, A. A., Stakhanova, N., Alzahrani, N., & Ghorbani, A. A. (2015). Exploring reverse engineering symptoms in android apps. Proceedings of the 8th European Workshop on System Security, EuroSec 2015. https://doi.org/10.1145/2751323.2751330
8. Gül, M., & Kugu, E. (2017). A Survey On Anti-Forensics Techniques. International Artificial Intelligence and Data Processing Symposium (2017).
9. Hou, F., Xiao, N., Liu, F., & He, H. (2009). Secure disk with authenticated encryption and IV verification. 5th International Conference on Information Assurance and Security, IAS 2009, 2, 41–44. https://doi.org/10.1109/IAS.2009.48
10. Kessler, G. C. (2007). Anti-forensics and the digital investigator. Proceedings of the 5th Australian Digital Forensics Conference, 1–7.
11. Lim, K., Jeong, Y., Cho, S. J., Park, M., & Han, S. (2016). An android application protection scheme against dynamic reverse engineering attacks. Journal of Wireless Mobile Networks, Ubiquitous Computing, and Dependable Applications, 7(3), 40–52.
12. Majed, H., Noura, H. N., & Chehab, A. (2020). Overview of Digital Forensics and Anti-Forensics Techniques. 8th International Symposium on Digital Forensics and Security, ISDFS 2020, June. https://doi.org/10.1109/ISDFS49300.2020.9116399
13. Miao, Q. X. (2010). Research and analysis on Encryption Principle of TrueCrypt software system. 2nd International Conference on Information Science and Engineering, ICISE2010 - Proceedings, 1409–1412. https://doi.org/10.1109/ICISE.2010.5691392
14. Mothukur, A. R., Balla, A., Taylor, D. H., Sirimalla, S. T., & Elleithy, K. (2019). Investigation of Countermeasures to Anti-Forensic Methods. 2019 IEEE Long Island Systems, Applications and Technology Conference (LISAT), 1–6.
15. Mutz, D., Kruegel, C., Robertson, W., Vigna, G., & Kemmerer, R. a. (2005). Reverse Engineering of Network Signatures. In Proceedings of the Auscert Asia Pacific Information Technology Security Conference, Gold, i, 1–86499.
16. Narayan, J., Shukla, S. K., & Clancy, T. C. (2015). A survey of automatic protocol reverse engineering tools. ACM Computing Surveys, 48(3). https://doi.org/10.1145/2840724
17. Rasmita Panigrahi - Academia. Advances in Intelligent Systems and Computing.
18. Or-Meir, O., Nissim, N., Elovici, Y., & Rokach, L. (2019). Dynamic malware analysis in the modern era—A state of the art survey. ACM Computing Surveys, 52(5). https://doi.org/10.1145/3329786
19. Pimenidis, E. (2016). Computer Anti-forensics Methods and Their Impact on Computer Forensic Investigation Computer Anti-forensics Methods and Their Impact on. August 2009, 145–155. https://doi.org/10.1007/978-3-642-04062-7
20. Rogers, M. K., & Seigfried, K. (2004). The future of computer forensics: A needs analysis survey. Computers and Security, 23(1), 12–16. https://doi.org/10.1016/j.cose.2004.01.003
21. Schwartz, E. J., & Avgerinos, T. (2010). All you ever wanted to know about dynamic taint analysis forward symbolic execution (but might have been afraid to ask). 1–5.
22. Sihwail, R., Omar, K., & Ariffin, K. A. Z. (2018). A Survey on Malware Analysis Techniques: Static , Dynamic , Hybrid and Memory Analysis. September. https://doi.org/10.18517/ijaseit.8.4-2.6827
23. Sikorski, M., & Honig, A. (2012). Practical malware analysis: the hands-on guide to dissecting malicious software. no starch press. In No starch press.
24. Stroulia, E., & Systä, T. (2002). Dynamic analysis for reverse engineering and program understanding. ACM SIGAPP Applied Computing Review, 10(1), 8–17. https://doi.org/10.1145/568235.568237
25. Summary, E., & Pro, I. D. a. (2009). Executive Summary : IDA Pro – at the cornerstone of IT security What is IDA Pro ? How is IDA Pro useful ? Who are IDA Pro users ? PC Magazine.
26. H. Majed, H. N. Noura, and A. Chehab, "Overview of Digital Forensics and Anti-Forensics Techniques," 8th Int. Symp. Digit. Forensics Secur. ISDFS 2020, no. June, 2020, doi: 10.1109/ISDFS49300.2020.9116399.
27. Y. Ajay, Applied Reverse Engineering with IDA Pro, Dec,03, 2020.

Computer Science Engineering and Emerging Technologies (ICCS-2022) – Prof (Dr.) Rajeev Sobti et al. (eds)
© 2024 Taylor & Francis Group, London, ISBN 978-1-032-52199-2

Chapter

108

Latest Trends in Non-Destructive Document Examination Using Hyperspectral Imaging

Nidhi Sagarwal[1]
Research Scholar, Department of Forensic Science,
Lovely Professional University, Punjab

Rachit Garg[2]
School of Computer Science and Engineering,
Lovely Professional University, Punjab

Abstract: Non-destructive document examination has become a major focus in forensic science, particularly in the area of digital imaging. It has been recognized as a method to examine documents without tampering with the original. This paper mainly focuses on the research work done in relation to document examination using hyperspectral imaging since 2018. The authors observed that the results obtained in the research are quite promising, but to be used by document experts, the methods used for data analysis in conjunction with hyperspectral imaging have to go a long way before becoming routine. Cost effectiveness is another major concern.

Keywords: Hyperspectral imaging, Non-destructive, Document examination, Spectroscopy, Forensic

1. Introduction

Non-destructive methods in forensic document examination are a recently trending topic, as they examine documents without damaging them. Forensically, it is critical to preserve the evidence for further study and for various relevant purposes, including expert examination. Sometimes, the examiner has to rely on destructive methods (requiring sample preparation) or other intrusive processes like Fourier transform infrared spectroscopy (FTIR) and ultraviolet (UV) fluorescence, which literally destroy the value of evidence and have many adverse consequences in the procedure [11, 12]. Nonetheless, there has been an effort amongst forensic scientists to develop non-destructive methods like hyperspectral imaging that can be used to examine the documents without changing their physical constitution, thus preserving them completely for future analysis. For court cases, non-destructive methods are often preferred over destructive methods as they allow for the re-examination of original documents, if necessary, and the respondent has the opportunity to rebut any findings [11, 12].

Historically, several different techniques have been used for non-destructive examination, such as optical microscopy, ultraviolet (UV) light analysis, and infrared (IR) imaging. However, these techniques have several limitations. For example, optical microscopy can only be used to examine small sections [3, 11, 12]. UV light analysis can be used to identify certain types of inks, but it is often difficult to obtain detailed images of documents using this technique. IR imaging can be used to examine the entire surface of a document, but it is generally not as effective as other methods for identifying hidden features or determining the order of layers in a document. Hyperspectral imaging (HSI), on the other hand, is a relatively

---
[1]nidhi.11816304@lpu.in, [2]rachit.garg@lpu.co.in

DOI: 10.1201/9781003405580-108

new technique that is being increasingly used for non-destructive examination [10, 12, 16]. HSI is a type of imaging that captures images of an object at different wavelengths of light. This allows for the analysis of an object's spectral signature, which can provide information about its chemical composition [11, 12].

The term hyperspectral imaging was coined by Jerry Solomon in 1985 [5]. Since then, the method has been used commercially in real-world applications such as agriculture, remote sensing, astronomy, molecular biology, forensic science, etc., and recently has been of interest to document examiners. In forensic document examination, it gets its fame due to its non-destructive nature and rapid results. It is used for ink discrimination, forgery detection, analysis and restoration of historical documents [19, 20, 22].

HSI has many advantages over traditional document examination techniques. Firstly, HSI can be used to examine documents in their entirety, rather than just small sections at a time. Secondly, HSI can provide information about the three-dimensional structure of a document, which can be useful for determining the order of layers in a document or identifying hidden features. In this regard, a hyperspectral camera is different from a traditional camera, which can only capture images in RGB and hence provides only one-dimensional data. Thirdly, HSI is non-destructive, meaning that documents can be examined multiple times using the same technique. [3, 11, 12].

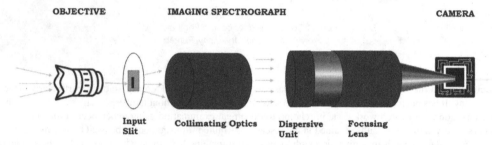

Fig. 108.1 The basic structure of a line hyperspectral camera

Source: Created by Author

Hyperspectral cameras capture data in many ways, but area scanning and line scanning are the most popular and suitable for forensic purposes. Hyperspectral imaging uses an imaging spectrometer to collect spectral information. This spectral information is recorded using a hyperspectral camera. The data is collected in the form of bands. In hyperspectral imaging, there are 11 to several hundred bands. A hyperspectral camera measures hundreds of spectra and collects them to form an image of the target in such a way that each pixel is a complete spectrum. Hyperspectral imaging provides three-dimensional data known as data cubes." It answers what, based on the spectrum, and where, based on location.

The present paper is an attempt to highlight the benefits of hyperspectral imaging and suggests that, combined with data analysis software such as k-means, CNN, etc., it could be used as a tool for non-destructive document examination. However, we have found that very limited research exists in this area. The available [as of the time of the report] hyperspectral digital cameras cost a great deal of money and are fairly large, making them difficult to transport to the crime scene. The future holds significant promise for non-destructive document examination using hyperspectral imaging and data analysis algorithms. If these systems become more compact, cheaper, and easier to use, we could witness an increase in their use as new tools to assist forensic document examiners [9, 10, 16, 18, 19].

2. Literature Review

Ostrum (2006 [15] was one of the first to discuss the application of hyperspectral imaging in problems of Forensic Document Examination. Later, a detailed literary mention was found in the book entitled Forensic Document Examination by Jane A. Lewis, published in 2014 [12]. There are commercially available instruments available to forensic document examiners that offer multispectral and hyperspectral imaging. The main difference between multispectral and hyperspectral imaging is the number of bands. Multispectral imaging usually has 4–10 bands. Some of the commercially available hyperspectral devices are ChemImage, ForensicXP, SEPIA, Surface Optics, Video Spectral Comparator, etc., which have been discussed in detail by Qureshi (2016 [17]).

Morales et al. (2014 [14] attempted to develop an automated system for discriminating between things based on their optical properties. The experiment included 25 pens of four different ink types, including viscous ink, ink color gel, and Marker Pen ink. These pens were used to create two data sets: system design and validation. For data acquisition, a spectrograph along with a CCD (charge-coupled device) camera was used to obtain the hyperspectral image. The image was scanned using a line camera, and then the background noise was removed. Next, hyperspectral curves were extracted and then smoothed using a moving averaging filter. The classifiers used in this experiment were the least squares SVM classifications. The results indicated an accuracy of 100% in detecting forgeries in cases where different inks were used and an accuracy of 80% when the same inks in different pens were used.

Ciortan et al. (2015 [2] acquired hyperspectral images using HySpec line scanning cameras in VNIR (very near infrared) at 1600 nm. The research aimed to compare and identify a better technique between color and hyperspectral imaging for ink discrimination and ink segmentation in four documents of historic importance. In these four documents, the first labeled M1 had purple and black mixed ink. M2 had writings in black ink by two different writers and possibly different inks. M4 had ink bleeding to the front of the paper, and M5 had barely visible watermarks. For different uses, the color signal would have a different shape, and the distance function to be used is a Spectral Correlation Mapper. In cases where the inks have similar hues but different lightness, the Euclidean Distance Function should be employed. For color distance, the sample was sent to the CIELAB Color Space, and the color difference was computed. M1 showed different spectral reflectance signals. In M2, the results indicated that the spectral shapes are only different by magnitude, so the writings may be identical. In M4, the spectral approach yields better results than CIELAB and HSV. In M5, the fading ink was better visible in spectral imaging as compared to traditional The watermark in M5, on the other hand, was not at all visible with color processing but was more visible in the NIR (near infrared) region of hyperspectral imaging.

Vora et al. (2018 [23] compared simulated smudged documents containing typewritten text, thermally printed text, seal impressions, and fingerprints. The samples were analyzed at various wavelengths under VSC 6000/HS. The discriminative power of the instrument for given samples was found to be 0.93.

Islam et al., 2019 [7] used The UWA WIHSI database consists of 14 spectral data cubes with 33 spectral channels in the visible range. Each of these cubes contains five lines of text written using five same-colored pens. The hyperspectral image of these documents was obtained, and the spectral responses of text pixels were extracted from them. These text pixels were then organized into three data sets: blue, black, and both blue and black ink pixels. To make sure that the spectral response of text pixels was compatible with a 2D CNN (Convolutional Neural Network), the researchers converted it into the proper format. The five different CNN architectures tested with the combination parameters selected the most suitable architecture and set of parameters for the purpose of identifying the writer. The research found promising results and could benefit from a larger database.

Qureshi, 2019 [17], laid out the steps of pre-processing required by hyperspectral images. The common challenges in the pre-processing of hyperspectral imaging include spike removal, dead pixel removal, and compression. Pre-processing reduces noise from images, corrects any illumination defects, and enhances relevant information. Spikes are caused by abrupt changes in an instrument or environment. For the removal of spikes, interpolation and modified Wiener filters are used. Dead pixels are caused by defects in the detector, which cause the pixels to be replaced by zero or their maximum value. This can be removed by doing a histogram analysis. A HSI contains more than 12 million data points, which would require a lot of memory. Its size can be reduced significantly by using principal component analysis (PCA) or multivariate curve analysis.

Qureshi et al., 2019 [17], also discussed the challenges of acquiring high-quality spectral images. These were image acquisition, direction of image illumination, signal-to-noise ratio, etc. If the image was not properly illuminated from all directions, the non-uniform illumination pattern would be visible in the image. In cases where the light source in a hyperspectral camera was high-power halogen lamps, a major issue was the concentration of illumination at the center of the image. Which resulted in a circular illumination pattern.

Devassy, George, and Hardeberg, 2019 [13], compared the ability of popular similarity measures used for classification in hyperspectral imaging to discriminate between inks. These are: binary encoding (BE), Euclidean Distance (ED), Spectral Angle Mapper (SAM), Spectral Correlation Mapper (SCM), and Spectral Information Divergence (SID). The image acquisition was done using a line camera, and then radiometric calibration was performed. The data set was created using ten different inks, which included ballpoint pen inks, gel pens, and ink pens. After this, the spectra of ten different ink classes labeled C1 to C10 were compared using five different similarity measures. The results indicated that blue ballpoint ink looks similar in shape but differs in magnitude. The accuracy was lowest in SCM and ED. SAM had the highest accuracy, and SID and BE had almost similar accuracy [13].

Yaseen et al., 2020, examined hyperspectral image documents provided to them in order to identify the number of inks in different bands [24]. They used a Python program to display the 1st, 10th, and 30th bands and performed K-means clustering to identify the number of inks used in the document. K-means displays images in different clusters based on the spectral image, and therefore the number of inks can be identified.

Huang et al., 2022 [6] did a thorough review of the literature covering the role of hyperspectral imaging in the examination of counterfeits. The various types of counterfeit works covered by them included counterfeit currencies, documents, holograms, paintings, artworks, etc.

3. Conclusion

The review papers by Qureshi, 2019 [17] and Huang, 2022 [6] have shed light on application, challenges, future prospects, and recent advances in the use of hyperspectral imaging for the detection of counterfeits. The present review reiterates the legal significance of non-destructive methods and focuses on research done in the domain of document examination using hyperspectral imaging.

It was observed that hyperspectral imaging presents a unique solution to the field of forensic science, particularly forensic document examination, due to its non-destructive nature. Combined with a data analysis algorithm, hyperspectral imaging can offer added benefit to the document examiner in court. Despite the huge potential and commercially available hyperspectral imaging systems, the method is still not being utilized to its fullest potential. One of the reasons behind this may be the cost incurred or the lack of technical expertise. The authors believe that the potential of hyperspectral imaging in conjunction with the latest algorithms like k-means clustering, FCM, CNN, etc. [1, 8, 9, 18] needs to be explored further.

Non-destructive methods in forensic document examination have been an immense help to the legal system. However, the authors feel that they still have a long way to go before they become commonly used in the mainstream. Only through continuous research will they be able to achieve this.

REFERENCES

1. Chen, H., Meng, H., & Cheng, K. (2017). A Survey of Methods Used for the Identification and Characterization of Inks.
2. Ciortan, I., Deborah, H., George, S., & Hardeberg, J. Y. (2015). Color and hyperspectral image segmentation for historical documents. 2015 Digital Heritage.
3. de Koeijer, J. (2013). Analytical Methods. Encyclopedia of Forensic Sciences, 342–350.
4. Francis, J., Madathil, B., George, S. N., & George, S. (2022). A Comprehensive Tensor Framework for the Clustering of Hyperspectral Paper Data With an Application to Forensic Document Analysis. IEEE Access, 10, 6194–6207.
5. Goetz, A. F. H., Vane, G., Solomon, J. E., & Rock, B. N. (1985). Imaging Spectrometry for Earth Remote Sensing. Science, 228(4704), 1147–1153.
6. Huang, S.-Y., Mukundan, A., Tsao, Y.-M., Kim, Y., Lin, F.-C., & Wang, H.-C. (2022). Recent Advances in Counterfeit Art, Document, Photo, Hologram, and Currency Detection Using Hyperspectral Imaging. Sensors, 22(19), 7308.
7. Islam, A. U., Khan, M. J., Khurshid, K., & Shafait, F. (2019). Hyperspectral Image Analysis for Writer Identification using Deep Learning. 2019 Digital Image Computing: Techniques and Applications (DICTA).
8. Khan, M. J., Khan, H. S., Yousaf, A., Khurshid, K., & Abbas, A. (2018). Modern Trends in Hyperspectral Image Analysis: A Review. IEEE Access, 6, 14118–14129.
9. Khan, M. J., Yousaf, A., Khurshid, K., Abbas, A., & Shafait, F. (2018). Automated Forgery Detection in Multispectral Document Images Using Fuzzy Clustering. 2018 13th IAPR International Workshop on Document Analysis Systems (DAS).
10. Khan, Z., Shafait, F., & Mian, A. (2013). Hyperspectral Imaging for Ink Mismatch Detection. 2013 12th International Conference on Document Analysis and Recognition.
11. Koppenhaver, K. M. (2010). Forensic Document Examination. Humana Press.
12. Lewis, J. (2014). Forensic document examination : Fundamentals and current trends. Elsevier Academic Press.
13. Melit Devassy, B., & George, S. (2020). Dimensionality reduction and visualisation of hyperspectral ink data using t-SNE. Forensic Science International, 311, 110194.
14. Morales, A., Ferrer, M. A., Diaz-Cabrera, M., Carmona, C., & Thomas, G. L. (2014). The use of hyperspectral analysis for ink identification in handwritten documents. 2014 International Carnahan Conference on Security Technology (ICCST).

15. Ostrum, B. (2006). Application of Hyperspectral Imaging to Forensic Document Examination Problems. Journal of American Society of Questioned Document, 9(2).
16. Pereira, J. F. Q., Silva, C. S., Braz, A., Pimentel, M. F., Honorato, R. S., Pasquini, C., & Wentzell, P. D. (2017). Projection pursuit and PCA associated with near and middle infrared hyperspectral images to investigate forensic cases of fraudulent documents. Microchemical Journal, 130, 412–419.
17. Qureshi, R., Uzair, M., Khurshid, K., & Yan, H. (2019). Hyperspectral document image processing: Applications, challenges and future prospects. Pattern Recognition, 90, 12–22.
18. Rahiche, A., & Cheriet, M. (2020). Forgery Detection in Hyperspectral Document Images using Graph Orthogonal Nonnegative Matrix Factorization. 2020 IEEE/CVF Conference on Computer Vision and Pattern Recognition Workshops (CVPRW).
19. Seon Joo Kim, Shaojie Zhuo, Fanbo Deng, Chi-Wing Fu, & Brown, M. (2010). Interactive Visualization of Hyperspectral Images of Historical Documents. IEEE Transactions on Visualization and Computer Graphics, 16(6), 1441–1448.
20. Silva, C. S., Pimentel, M. F., Honorato, R. S., Pasquini, C., Prats-Montalbán, J. M., & Ferrer, A. (2014). Near infrared hyperspectral imaging for forensic analysis of document forgery. The Analyst, 139(20), 5176–5184.
21. SWGDOC Standard for Non-destructive Examination of Paper. (n.d.). Retrieved October 28, 2022, from https://www.swgdoc.org/documents/SWGDOC%20Standard%20for%20Non-destructive%20Examination%20of%20Paper.pdf
22. Tahtouh, M., Despland, P., Shimmon, R., Kalman, J. R., & Reedy, B. J. (2007). The Application of Infrared Chemical Imaging to the Detection and Enhancement of Latent Fingerprints: Method Optimization and Further Findings. Journal of Forensic Sciences, 52(5), 1089–1096.
23. Vora, H. (2018). Hyper Spectral Imaging as a Tool For Fraudulent Document Investigation. International Journal of Current Advanced Research, 7(1(A)), 8742–8746.
24. Yaseen, M., Ahmed, R. A., & Mahrukh, R. (2020). Forgery Detection in a Questioned Hyperspectral Document Image using K-means Clustering. ArXiv.org.

Computer Science Engineering and Emerging Technologies (ICCS-2022) – Prof (Dr.) Rajeev Sobti et al. (eds)
© 2024 Taylor & Francis Group, London, ISBN 978-1-032-52199-2

Chapter **109**

Adaptive Cloud Service Optimization Using Drone Swarm Methodology

Rajesh Kumar[1]
CSE, Chandigarh University, Chandigarh, India

Vani Agrawal[2]
Department of CSA, ITM University Gwalior, Gwalior, India

Sumit Kumar[3]
CSE, College of Engineering, Roorkee, Uttrakhand, India

Manikandan R[4]
CSE, Madanapalle Institute of Technology & Science, Andhra Pradesh, India

Juan Carlos Cotrina-Aliaga[5]
CSE, Cesar Vallejo,Perú, Lima, PE

Sarvesh Kumar[6]
CSE, BBD University, Lucknow, India

Abstract: Cloud computing gives on-request framework administration to huge quantities of partners. It upholds enormous quantities of equal solicitations and synchronous get-to by partners in a powerful way to distinguish or foresee sickness in the shortest time. The antenna array system is composed of multiple single-antenna drones. By using the drone swarm optimization methodology, the cloud services are easily followed. This system also helps cloud service providers track the services of the cloud. The principal results exhibit that the calculation offloading approach permits us to give a lot higher throughput (i.e., outlines per second) when contrasted with the edge processing approach, notwithstanding the bigger correspondence delays.

Keywords: Cloud computing, Drone swarms, Networked control systems, Wireless networks, Drone scheduling; Drone authentication; Particle swarm optimization

1. Introduction

Cloud computing plays a huge part in medical service administration, particularly in clinical applications. In distributed computing, the most ideal decision of virtual machines plays a fundamental part in the quality improvement of distributed computing by limiting the execution season of clinical questions from partners and amplifying the use of restorative assets. Cloud computing will truly change the engineering of robots and entirely work on flying robots," said Guinn. "When the robot has low dormancy, high transmission capacity, and an exceptionally dependable association with the cloud, it just needs to convey sensors; it doesn't need to convey process power. In addition, the most ideal decision of VM helps the

[1]rajeshkumarmuj1@gmail.com, [2]vaniagrawal.cse@itmuniversity.ac.in, [3]mail2dr.sumit@gmail.com, [4]maniarunai2011@gmail.com,
[5]jcotrinaal@ucvvirtual.edu.pe, [6]Kr.sarvi91@gmail.com

DOI: 10.1201/9781003405580-109

partners to diminish the absolute execution season of clinical solicitations through the time required to circle back, boost computer chip use, and hold up time.

The issue of way arranging is not simply restricted to looking for a suitable way from the beginning stage to the objective, but is additionally connected with how to pick an optimal way among every accessible way and give a component to crash evasion. By considering how to develop the best way, a few related issues should be considered that connect with wellbeing, snag evasion, reaction speed to surpass deterrents, and so on. Swarm optimization calculations have been utilized to give wise display to rambling way arranging and empower to fabricate the best way for each robot. This is followed by the preparation and coordination aspects among the multitude of individuals. With the help of cloud computing, multiple drones can effectively provide wireless service to end users. The cloud service time is also minimized by optimizing the wireless transmission time and control time needed for the movement and stabilization of drones. In cloud technology, synchronization with GPS would allow precise localization. By using drones in cloud technology, the low mass, mechanical simplicity, directing energy into a spot, higher efficiency, and better autonomous flight duration will be beneficial for the cloud services.

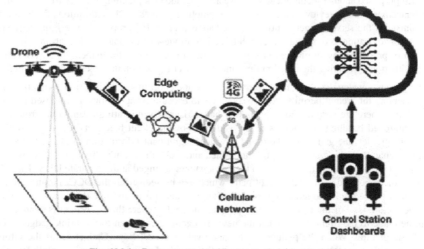

Fig. 109.1   Basic structure of Drone in cloud services [8]

A portion of the multitude of knowledge approaches utilized for ideal VM choice is honey bee colony optimization (BCO), Ant colony optimization (ACO), bat streamlining [1, 5, 6], and particle swarm optimization (PSO). In any case, most of these methodologies can't utilize equal figuring. BCO is a populace-based calculation that is motivated by the shrewd way of behaving of bumble bees yet has two fundamental weaknesses: (1) it has slow union and (2) many control boundaries. The subterranean insect is utilized to distinguish the ideal arrangement from a bunch of arrangements, in view of the way insects behave when examining food. All things considered, doing an equal hunt in a population isn't proper. Molecule swarm streamlining is utilized to track down the best arrangement from a bunch of arrangements by utilizing particles to re-enact the populace and multitude to arrive at an answer. In any case, it additionally does not utilize equal calculation, and it can't deal with the issue of dissipating. Computerized reasoning, specifically profound learning, and Automated Elevated Frameworks are the two most conspicuous advances over the most recent five years [1].

There is an interconnected Cloud-based world where Robots are utilized to gather information, later to be put away in the Cloud. A Robot is fundamentally an independent actual innovation that can be utilized to accumulate information, mention observable facts from a distance, and much more. On-request PC assets by means of the web are referred to as distributed computing. Whatever is expected to keep the association running—servers, information bases, programming, and investigation—may be generally included. By utilizing cloud-based figuring assets, it is easy to make and change programming custom-made to a client's necessities. IoT infers that IoT gadgets have insignificant computational and energy necessities. They simply require an organization, an association, and a few sensors or actuators to expand their field life expectancy. The computational power that is available to the gadget might prompt more convoluted and faster exercises to be finished. In any case, the burden is that the devices will become subject to an organization's association, which may not generally be accessible [6].

2. Literature Review

Later, it will go from the robots' imaging sensors directly to the cover over 5G to be handled and put away in the cloud," said Guinn, who is likewise the pioneer behind Storage Innovation and was the previous President of DJI in North America. "You'll have a quicker time to acknowledge exact bits of knowledge and data, and ongoing choices can be made in the air. In [2], the creators created ideal joint availability, stockpiling, and registering assets as the executive's framework for vehicular organizations. The profound support learning approach with the multi-time scale system is intended to advance asset assignment. In [3], creators bring haze processing into a multitude of robots and develop an errand portion enhancement issue that mutually thinks about idleness, dependability, and energy utilization to limit the energy utilization of the multitude of robots when dormancy and unwavering quality prerequisites exist.

Almezeini et al. [5] proposed another technique to improve and upgrade task planning for a distributed computing climate utilizing lion enhancement. In this review, the creators are attempting to work on the exhibition of VM and augment asset usage while diminishing the server's energy utilization. Chaurasia et al. [6] proposed an original strategy to pick the ideal VM position for relocation, prompting server solidification, in view of the Pareto Ideal arrangement and the Fuzzy technique for order of preference by similarity to the ideal solution (TOPSIS). In this paper, the creators are attempting to pick the best VM situation by limiting the reaction time and the power utilization in servers while expanding asset usage.

Cloud ideas are vigorously materialized in drone correspondence and coordinated with various organizational designs for enhancement. Dispersing the weight permits more IoT gadgets to execute computations, as opposed to everything being finished on the cloud. There are various cloud plans that have arisen. By migrating estimations from the cloud, these plans utilize the improved handling capabilities of the gadgets. For the client blackouts identified by brilliant meters, the OMS framework predicts the gadget blackout and advances significant information to DCC. Here, the focal group will distinguish the separate docking stations to be summoned and make the robot's flight plan in view of the area to be studied by the robot. The flight plan is then driven to the brink gadget arranged at the separate DDS. The GCS framework at the edge will fly the robot and control the flight path, which can be seen from the DCC. Picture information caught by the robot is driven to the brink gadget, which performs an examination to approve the nature of the picture. On the off chance that the picture isn't of the right quality, it informs the DCC, where the equivalent is examined and essential adjustments can be made to the flight plan. When the new arrangement is driven to the brink gadget, a drone is flown again to re-catch the pictures. When the picture quality approval succeeds, Edge Gadget sends the information to the picture investigation application. Here the flawed gadget is distinguished utilizing man-made intelligence (ML), and the abnormality information is sent to handle versatility or Work The board Framework (WMS) for dispatching the team to the field for a shortcoming goal The experiences with the shortcoming assist the team with getting a better comprehension of the issue and conveying essential apparatuses and hardware to the field to empower the ideal goal. When the shortcoming is fixed and power is re-established, a separate blackout is cleared in the OMS framework. Along these lines, DCC helps the team stay away from numerous field trips by independently and precisely recognizing broken gadgets and empowering speedier blackout reclamation.

The essential difficulties talked about in this paper are as follows:

- To begin with, the robot needs to follow the path. For this, the way ought to be characterized and, furthermore, be a framework that controls the engines and the body of the UAVs for the way to follow.
- Furthermore, as far as possible, There are certain levels for UAVs to fly at that are chosen by legitimate bodies. It restricts the region and, furthermore, the way decisions and proficiency are made, as there must be a consistent way where level does not increment, but the UAVs push ahead.
- The UAVs are programmed. The machine ought to be equipped for making choices about when to begin, rise or slide, or simply move straight.
- As there are no aides or drivers, the machine ought to be self-propelled. The air is loaded with traffic, both natural and man-made, with structures likewise taking off past creative minds up high. The UAVs should be introduced with an artificial intelligence or directing framework to survive boundaries, insurance, and harm control, and furthermore, unambiguous circumstances with regards to when to initiate what framework. This should be disregarded by artificial intelligence, which is intricate to create.

- As the UAV is programmed and its improvement will bring about an increment, there should be some global positioning frameworks that persistently send and store particle servers with every one of the progressions during the excursion until the excursion is finished, and during a crisis, it ought to be found without any problem.

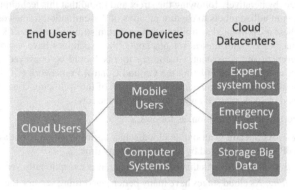

Fig. 109.2   Cloud service storage using drone [9]

3. Drone Optimization Models

Commonly, drones present extraordinary qualities, being dynamic, lithe, simple to fix and send, and offering the possibility to give data estimations at any place and at whatever point required. They provide a minimal-cost option in contrast to gathering and giving data to shrewd frameworks that can embrace the essential information examination. The advancement of cultivating, safeguarding, protection review, policing, helping, contamination checking, debacle recuperation, and bundle conveyance Cost-effective conveyance of their item has additionally been investigated by making a calculation to tackle the vehicle directing issue, which is to convey to however many clients as would be prudent in a specific set, which thusly saves the expense of robots, powers, and so forth [4]. The effective conveyance of packages has additionally been explored by considering the vehicle direction issue, which is a serious issue; however, this is settled by utilizing a few numerical conditions and charts, so conveying in a specific set is simple. They have considered preparing drones in a specific vehicle, and the vehicle remains in every one of the areas and the robots when every one of the packages is conveyed in a specific time, which saves a ton of time and is an expense-productive thought [5]. Research has been performed on battery-effective robot conveyance, which makes the robots work more proficiently and can add additional functioning hours to the conveyance of bundles.

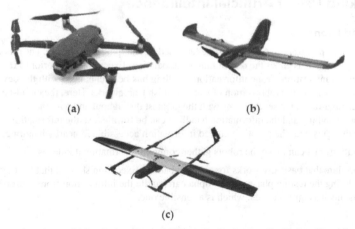

Fig. 109.3   (a) rotary-wing drone, (b) fixed-wing drone (c) fixed wind hybrid vertical take-off and landing (VTOL) drone
Source: Made by Author

Presently, I guess we have two drones for this application. Current frameworks will utilize just a single robot on this application at some random time because only one solicitation is exceptional. Bee Cluster can apply this advancement without requiring any changes to the application code. We played out an assessment with a street planning application that maps a recently built street by iteratively following the street and found that this technique lessens the execution time by 21.3%. Utilities have begun to utilize robots to capture pictures of dissemination framework resources for intermittent investigation. By and large, these are presented as 'information as administration' or 'bits of knowledge as administration' by drone administrators. Nonetheless, with drones for blackouts, the executives have various necessities. The picture-catching prerequisite is impromptu and consistent. Customary robots should be conveyed by a field group to the area of interest and require collection and routing utilizing the Ground Control Framework (GCS) at the site. Even though it decreases manual exertion in picture capture and addresses a portion of the wellbeing concerns, it actually requires field group visits to distant areas and includes manual endeavors in flying the robot.

The Cloud drone is very important for optimization, as follows:

- *Simple information access:* As Spectra is an online cloud stage, all information is put away in a concentrated vault. This information can be effortlessly accessed by any gadget at any time.
- *Handling various datasets on the double:* As this is a cloud stage, it is exceptionally versatile.
- *Quicker information handling:* As cloud stages have many better-performing servers, the information handling is a lot quicker.
- *Low upfront expense:* top-of-the-line PCs and GIS/Photogrammetry specialists are costly. A cloud stage like Spectra can decrease the upfront expense.
- GIS and photogrammetric specialists are not needed. Spectra is controlled by computer-based intelligence innovation and can subsequently assist you with handling the information without the outright need for a GIS or photogrammetry master.

Over the years, cloud gadgets, among others those that emphasize short-range remote interchanges, like radio, Zig-Honey bee, NFC, or Bluetooth, have been proposed with different correspondence principles and conventions [3]. Expanded quantities of cloud gadgets empower cloud network solutions for different cloud specialist co-ops. On-request PC assets, commonly known as cloud computing, are cloud computing. Rather than overseeing and staying aware of equipment and framework, the client is simply worried about getting to explicit assets when the need arises. Microsoft Purplish Blue, Google Cloud, and Amazon Web Services have emerged as conspicuous cloud specialist co-ops with their own contributions. They utilize mainland-spanning server farms to furnish their clients with additional assets. Because these administrations are mostly pay-per-use or pay-more only as costs arise, organizations have had the option to change rapidly and without the requirement for extra gear as they create.

4. Drones Making Use of Artificial Intelligence

4.1 Cloud-AI-Based Drones

In cloud computing service optimization, AI-based drones are used for mapping and security. The robot is controlled through Man-made consciousness, which assumes the role of human association. Execution is superior to Human Individuals. With the assistance of PC-based innovation, drone information handling has been enhanced with the development of limitless, versatile computational power and the robotization of start-to-finish frameworks. Here, the cloud-based stages can uphold any sort of information put away in the server farms with the greatest throughput and with the most extreme quality. [7] [8] [9] Eventually, the cloud handling and the information handling can be fulfilled, so the information cycle creation can start with ground-breaking thoughts with the robot's gathered information accessible in nearby handling.

This has inbuilt calculations that can make the robots gather common informational indexes.

Alpha is a current procedure that basically works for military battles. Execution showed that hostile and protective modes were more backward during the testing phases [16]. Alpha can handle the information from sensor hubs, which move for four battles with not as much as milliseconds, which is a sensible one.

Fig. 109.4   Drone based cloud services by CSPs

Source: Author

6. Conclusion

Associations are consolidating cloud computing and drone innovation to assist their organizations in prospering. The quick learning ability of the Cloud can be utilized to make drones more brilliant. Since lots of robots are working simultaneously to assemble piles of information, 5G innovation is fundamental for producing ideal cloud computing administrations for drones. The objective is that information will go from Robot to Cloud by means of 5G. It will be handled and saved in the Cloud. Ongoing choices and situational mindfulness can be made quicker, in the air, by having exact experiences from information gathered through ramblings. Prior, these tasks would depend on individuals as mediators, and it took a ton of functional free time for information to be checked out. Cloud-controlled drones are good to go to convey superb outcomes, whether in the business world by making drone conveyances or showing eco-accommodating firecrackers. This innovation is not just assisting organizations in becoming quicker, but also giving people experiences to help them.

REFERENCES

1. Alvear, O., Zema, N. R., Natalizio, E., and te, C. T. Using uav-based systems to monitor air pollution in areas with poor accessibility. Journal of Advanced Transportation 2017 (2017).
2. Bastani, F., He, S., Abbar, S., Alizadeh, M., Balakrishnan, H., Chawla, S., and Madden, S. Machine-assisted map editing. In Proceedings of the 26th ACM SIGSPATIAL International Conference on Advances in Geographic Information Systems (2018), ACM, pp. 23–32.
3. Vasisht, D., Kapetanovic, Z., Won, J.-h., Jin, X., Chandra, Farmbeats: An iot platform for data-driven agriculture. In Proceedings of the 14th USENIX Conference on Networked Systems Design and Implementation (2017).

4. Villa, T., Gonzalez, F., Miljievic, B.,Ristovski, Z., and Morawska, L. An overview of small unmanned aerial vehicles for air quality measurements: Present applications and future prospectives. Sensors 16, 7 (2016), 1072.

5. Villa, T., Salimi, F., Morton, K., Morawska, L., and Gonzalez, F. Development and validation of a uav based system for air pollution measurements. Sensors 16, 12 (2016).

6. Almezeini, N.; Hafez, A. Task Scheduling in Cloud Computing Using Lion Optimization Algorithm. Int. J. Adv. Comput. Sci. Appl. 2017, 8, 77–83.

7. Chaurasia, N.; Tapaswi, S.; Dhar, J. A Pareto Optimal Approach for Optimal Selection of Virtual Machine for Migration in Cloud. Int. J. Comput. Sci. Inf. Secur. 2016, 14, 117.

8. Tiwari, A., & Sharma, R. M. (2019). Realm Towards Service Optimization in Fog Computing. International Journal of Fog Computing (IJFC), 2(2), 13–43.

9. Tiwari, A., & Garg, R. (2021). ACCOS: A Hybrid Anomaly-Aware Cloud Computing Formulation-Based Ontology Services in Clouds. In ISIC (pp. 341-346).M. Young, The Technical Writer's Handbook. Mill Valley, CA: University Science, 1989.

10. Al-Fuqaha, M. Guizani, M. Mohammadi, M. Aledhari, and M. Ayyash, "Internet of things: A survey on enabling technologies, protocols, and applications," IEEE Communications Surveys Tutorials, vol. 17, no. 4, pp. 2347–2376, 2015.

11. Tiwari, A., Kumar, S., Baishwar, N., Vishwakarma, S. K., & Singh, P. (2022). Efficient Cloud Orchestration Services in Computing. In Proceedings of 3rd International Conference on Machine Learning, Advances in Computing, Renewable Energy and Communication (pp. 739-746). Springer, Singapore.

12. Tiwari, A., & Garg, R. (2022). Adaptive Ontology-Based IoT Resource Provisioning in Computing Systems. International Journal on Semantic Web and Information Systems (IJSWIS), 18(1), 1–18.

13. J. Gubbi, R. Buyya, S. Marusic, and M. Palaniswami, "Internet of things (IoT): A vision, architectural elements, and future directions," Future generation computer systems, vol. 29, no. 7, pp. 1645–1660, 2013.

14. Nguyen, Dang Tu; Song, Chengyu; Qian, Zhiyun; V. Krishnamurthy, Srikanth; J. M. Colbert, Edward; McDaniel, Patrick (2018). IoTSan: Fortifying the Safety of IoT Systems. Proc. of the 14th International Conference on emerging Networking EXperiments and Technologies (CoNEXT '18). Heraklion, Greece. arXiv:1810.09551. doi:10.1145/3281411.3281440. arXiv:1810.09551.

15. Tiwari, A., & Garg, R. (2022). Orrs Orchestration of a Resource Reservation System Using Fuzzy Theory in High-Performance Computing: Lifeline of the Computing World. International Journal of Software Innovation (IJSI), 10(1), 1-28.

16. Tiwari, A., & Sharma, R. M. (2021). OCC: A Hybrid Multiprocessing Computing Service Decision Making Using Ontology System. International Journal of Web-Based Learning and Teaching Technologies (IJWLTT), 16(4), 96–116.

17. S. Ranger. What is cloud computing? Everything you need to know about the cloud, explained. Mar. 11, 2020.

18. Arkian, Hamid Reza; Diyanat, Abolfazl; Pourkhalili, Atefe (2017-03-15). "MIST: Fog-based data analytics scheme with cost-efficient resource provisioning for IoT crowdsensing applications". Journal of Network and Computer Applications. 82: 152–165. doi: 10.1016/j.jnca.2017.01.012.

19. Jaihyun, L. Optimization of modular drone delivery system. In Proceedings of the 2017 Annual IEEE International Systems Conference, Quebec City, QC, Canada, 24–27 April 2017.

20. Insu, H.; Michael, K.; Murray, A. A commercial drone delivery system for urban areas. IEEE Xplore. In Geocomputation; Springer: Cham, Switzerland, 2017.

21. Miae, K.; Eric, T.; Murray, A. A cost optimization model in multi-agent system routing for drone delivery. In International Conference on Practical Applications of Agents and Multi-Agent Systems; Springer: Cham, Switzerland, 2017.

22. Luigi, D.P.P.; Francesca, G.; Giusy, M. Using Drones for Deliver Process. ISM. 2019.

23. Taner, C. Optimization of battery swapping infrastructure for e-commerce drone delivery. Comput. Commun. 2020, 168, 146–154.

24. Okan, D.; Bahar, Y.K.; Tolga, B. Minimizing energy and cost in range- limited drone deliveries with speed optimization. Transp. Res. Part C Emerg. Technol. 2021, 125, 102985.

25. Shashank, A.; Vincent, R.; Sivaraman, A.K.; Balasundaram, A.; Rajesh, M.; Ashokkumar, S. Power Analysis of Household Appliances using IoT. In Proceedings of the 2021 International Conference on System, Computation, Automation, and Networking (ICSCAN), Puducherry, India, 30–31 July 2021; pp. 1–5.

26. Qadir Md, A.; Vijayakumar, V. Combined preference ranking algorithm for comparing an initial ranking of cloud services. Recent Adv. Electr. Electron. Eng. 2020, 13, 260–275.

27. Nex, F.; Remondino, F. Unmanned Aerial Vehicles for 3D mapping applications: A review. Appl. Geomat. 2014, 6, 1–15.

28. Zhang, C.; Kovac, J.M. The application of small unmanned aerial systems for precision agriculture: A review. Precis. Agric. 2012, 13, 693–712.

29. Goodchild, A.; Jordan, T. Delivery by drone: An evaluation of unmanned aerial vehicle technology in reducing CO2 emissions in the delivery service industry. Transp. Res. Part D Transp. Environ. 2018, 61, 58–67.

Computer Science Engineering and Emerging Technologies (ICCS-2022) – Prof (Dr.) Rajeev Sobti et al. (eds)
© 2024 Taylor & Francis Group, London, ISBN 978-1-032-52199-2

Chapter

110

Efficient Security Enhancement of Key Management System (KMS) in Cloud Environment

Harish Reddy Gantla[1]
CSE, Vignan Institute of Technology and Science, Telangana, India

V. Akilandeswari[2]
Department of IT, Sethu Institute of Technology, Tamil Nadu, India

Nancy Arya[3]
CSE, Shree Guru Gobind Singh Tricentenary University, Gurugram, India

Kusum Yadav[4]
CSE, College of Computer Science and Engineering,
University of Ha'il, Ha'il, Saudi Arabia

Sayed Sayeed Ahmad[5]
Rochester Institute of Technology, Dubai Campus, Dubai, UAE

Dhiraj Kapila[6]
Department of Computer Science & Engineering,
Lovely Professional University, Phagwara, Punjab, India

Abstract: The term cloud computing suggests any kind of work with an organization passed on over the web. These organizations every now and again integrate servers, databases, programming, associations, examinations, and other abilities that can be managed in the cloud. The cloud is basically a decentralized spot to share information through satellite associations. Each cloud application has a host, and the association is obligated to stay aware of the monstrous server cultivates that give the key-based security, storing breaking points, and figuring power expected to stay aware of every one of the pieces of information clients transport off the cloud. Cloud security ensures that your data and applications are quickly opened to supported clients by using a key management system. They consistently have a trustworthy procedure to get to cloud applications and information, helping with quickly acting on any potential security issues. The execution of this solid cycle is finished in the MATLAB Stage. The reproduction results of the proposed framework have been contrasted with the ordinary strategies as far as private rate, information move rate, encryption time, asset use, key management, and unscrambling time are concerned. The correlation shows that the created model has the best security capability over the current procedures.

Keywords: Cloud parameters, Resource issues, Fuzzy logic, Mathematical parameters, Approximation process, Cloud simulation

[1]harsha.rex@gmail.com, [2]akilandeswari.v2015@gmail.com, [3]nancy_feat@sgtuniversity.org, [4]y.kusum@uoh.edu.sa, [5]saeed.ks@gmail.com, [6]dhiraj.23509@lpu.co.in

DOI: 10.1201/9781003405580-110

1. Introduction

Cloud computing engineering is the transfer of IT assets for specific administrations to clients. With regards to cloud computing, the cloud specialist co-op is known as a cloud supplier, which is an association that provides distributed computing administration. Then again, the association that gets the cloud computing administration is known as the cloud client [1–2] and is the fundamental premise for overseeing and controlling the delivered administrations. Service level agreement measurements are accordingly used to survey the help level between cloud suppliers and their clients and act as the reason for administration improvement [2].

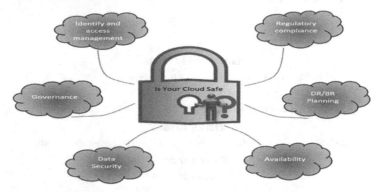

Fig. 110.1 Basic structure of cloud service security system

Source: Copied from anonymous source

Cloud computing alludes to a model for empowering helpful, on-request network admittance to a common pool of configurable figuring assets that can be quickly provisioned and delivered with negligible administration exertion or specialist co-op cooperation [3].

1.1 Objectives of Cloud Service Security

The set goals of the review which will coordinate towards accomplishing our point are to:

  (i) Recognize significant data security credits for distributed computing.
 (ii) Recognize data security dangers for distributed computing.
(iii) Select a structure reasonable for creating security measurements.
 (iv) Recognize SLA-based data security measurements in distributed computing lined up with the system.

Cloud computing has been planned to permit access to a lot of information in a completely virtualized way. Cloud computing considers the sharing and versatile sending of administrations from practically any area, for which the client can be charged considering genuine use. Security is required against unapproved access and to decrease the dangers of information theft. The primary point of safety is to give accessibility, classification, and respectability to the information [5]. There are so many risks related to the cloud organization, like the fact that information can be hacked by an unapproved individual. Information can be changed by an outsider while moving it. Accordingly, to give security to cloud information, we proposed a framework that can accomplish secure key conveyance and information sharing for dynamic gathering.

2. Literature Review

The cloud plan of action upholds on-request, pay-for-use, and economies-of-scale IT administrations over the Web. The virtualized server farms join to frame the web cloud [11]. To improve the numerous information sources on a similar cloud, the cloud should be intended to be secure and private since security breaks will prompt information to be compromised. Cloud stages are progressively worked through virtualization with provisioned equipment, programming, organizations, and informational collections [15]. The thought is to relocate work area processing to a centrally located stage utilizing virtual server groups at server farms. The cloud services want to recognize best practices for financially savvy security upgrades in distributed computing, and watermarking has been examined to fit into this classification [18]. Expanding the public cloud's use with security upgrades like utilizing computerized watermarking strategies assists in improving the cloud's income by overhauling suppliers and clients.

Computerized watermarking is a strategy that can be applied to safeguard records, pictures, videos, programming, and social databases. These methods safeguard shared information objects and hugely dispersed programming modules. This, combined with information shading, can prevent information objects from being harmed, taken, changed, or erased. Safeguarding server farms should initially get cloud assets and maintain client protection and information respectability [22]. The new methodology could be savvier than utilizing conventional encryption and firewalls to get the mist. This can be carried out to safeguard server farm access at a coarse-grained level and secure information access at a fine-grained record level. This can be interlinked with security as a service (SECaaS) and information data as a service (DPaaS) and be broadly utilized for individual, business, finance, and computerized government information [18–19]. It shields client confirmation and fixes the information access control openly. It guarantees privacy, respectability, and accessibility in a multi-occupant climate. Figuring mists with upgraded protection controls requires omnipresence, productivity, security, and reliability.

3. Cloud Computing Security Challenges and Issues

Powerful trust among executives, sure-fire security, client security, information respectability, portability backing, and copyright insurance are essential to the widespread acknowledgment of the cloud as a universal help. Powerful, less-expensive use of public mists prompts fulfilled clients. Because of the extraordinary nature of the organization, different sorts of safety assaults are conceivable. Different upgraded security methods had been proposed in earlier years to beat the issues of different assaults, yet there is no such strategy that gives full security since every day new threats are shown up. The crossover strategy in cloud security is upgraded security procedures that give better security to cloud gadgets. Cloud security engineering depicts all the equipment and innovations intended to safeguard information, jobs, and frameworks inside cloud stages. Fostering a technique for cloud security engineering ought to start during the outline and configuration process and ought to be coordinated into cloud stages starting from the earliest stage. Repeatedly, cloud planners will zero in completely on execution first and then endeavor to bolt security on sometime later. The IaaS security upgrade from an entrance control perspective IaaS requires an entrance control model that can adapt to its dynamic and versatile highlights. Trait-based admission Control is distinguished as the most fitting model that can uphold IaaS highlights. Secure distributed computing design includes three center capacities: classification, trustworthiness, and accessibility. Seeing every capacity will assist with directing your endeavors toward arranging a safer cloud send.

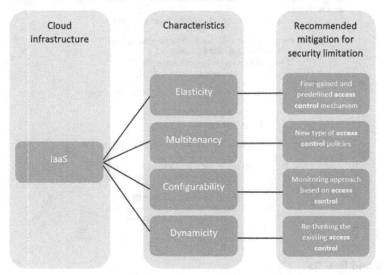

Fig. 110.2 Some of IaaS cloud security challenges

Source: Made by author based on today's challenges for cloud security

Classification is the capacity to keep information quiet and incomprehensible to individuals who should not approach it, for example, aggressors or individuals inside an association without the legitimate access level. Classification likewise incorporates security and trust, or when a business vows mystery in taking care of their clients' information. Uprightness is the possibility that the frameworks and applications are precisely the things you anticipate that they should be, and capability is precisely the way you anticipate that they should work. If a framework or application has been compromised to deliver an obscure, unforeseen, or misdirected yield, this can prompt misfortunes.

4. Proposed Methodology

We are proposing a crossover algorithm for calculation. Now this encipher text from DES is given to AES calculation as decoded text, and the encipher text is returned encoded using the key given before the coded text length, which is presently 704 pieces in length. Then right 0 is apportioned to left 1, and the result of AES is given to the right parts; for example, right 1.1088 pieces of encoded information are laid out after attacking left 1 and right 1 sections. We follow the required change activity to get decoded text. First, we have observed that key calculations deal with the security framework. So, to make cloud administration security safer, there is a need for mixture calculation. That is why we have developed new calculations for cloud security. Our half-breed calculation accommodates top-notch keys to limit encryption time, solid code text development, and high encryption procedures for cloud information wellbeing throughout the organization. In cryptography, the torrential slide impact implies how much distinction changes when plain text is expanded. At the point when information is changed tolerably, a torrential slide impact is self-evident. There are not many changes in the great, either in the key or in the plaintext; there is an additional adjustment of the code text. While working out the torrential slide impact, look at it. Two code texts are created from plain text, which utilizes slide contrast, and text that utilizes the string correlation capability. Torrential slide works out the impact separately for AES, DES, RSA, and cross-breed AES, DES, and RSA and charts it on the histogram. Build the half-and-half calculations that are so great for AES. Consider that for future requirements in security, it finishes up crossover calculations and is superior to other cryptography.

Algorithm: Crossover Algorithm (This proposed algorithm is the combination of RSA, DES and AES).

Input: The cloud services are taken as an input to perform the Crossover Algorithm.

Output: Getting the best Secured services of cloud computing.

1: **procedure** (Methods :)
2:      *If* (Cloud services come form the CSP to the end users)*then*
3:      {
4:          Perform the RSA algorithm check for the cloud services.
5:      *If* $\left(\begin{array}{c}\text{It was found that by passing}\\ \text{the RSA checks Cloud Services are}\\ \text{not Secure}\end{array}\right)$ *then*
6:              {
              Perform the DES algorithm check for the cloud services.
7:                  {
8:              *If* $\left(\begin{array}{c}\text{It was found that by passing}\\ \text{the DES checks Cloud Services are}\\ \text{not Secure}\end{array}\right)$ *then*
9:              Perform the AES algorithm check for the cloud services.
              {
10:                  *If* (Service is Highly attacked)*then*
11:                  *Step1: Do not use the cloud service*
                          provided by the CSP
                  If (Service is Highly secured)*then*
                  Step2: The cloud service provided
                          by the CSP is 100% Secure.
12:              }
          end if

4.1 Experiments and Results

In cryptography, the torrential slide impact implies how much contrast changes when plain text is expanded. At the point when information is changed modestly, the torrential slide impact is self-evident. There are not many changes in the great, either in the key or in the plaintext; there is an additional adjustment to the code text. While working out the torrential slide impact, look at it. Two types of code text are generated: one that uses slides and one that uses the string examination capability. Torrential slide computes the impact separately for AES, DES, RSA, and cross-breed. AES, DES, RSA, and crossover chart it on the histogram. Develop cross-breed calculations that are great for AES. Consider that for future imperative security, it finishes up mixture calculations and is superior to other cryptography.

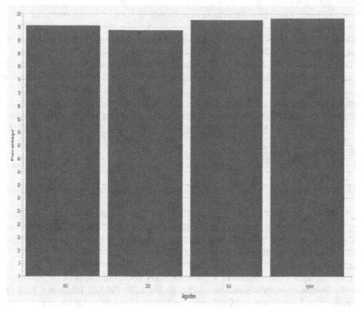

Fig. 110.3   Result analysis of the proposed algorithm

Source: Made by Author

5. Conclusion and Future Work

As indicated by a report, "Overall and Local Public IT Cloud Administrations 2012-2016 Figure," delivered by IDC, cloud administrations will see as much as 41% development from 2013 to 2016. Spending on IT cloud administrations overall will edge toward $100 billion by 2016. Furthermore, in this cloud development, security will play a key role. AES encryption is the quickest technique that has adaptability and versatility, and it is effectively executed. Then again, the necessary memory for the AES calculation is not exactly the Blowfish calculation. The AES calculation has an exceptionally high security level because the 128, 192, or 256-digit keys are utilized in this calculation. It shows obstruction against various attacks, for example, square assaults, key assaults, key recuperation attacks, and differential assaults. Hence, the AES calculation is an exceptionally solid encryption strategy. Information can likewise safeguard against future crimes, for example, crush assaults. AES encryption calculations have negligible extra room and superior execution with practically no shortcomings or constraints, while other symmetric calculations have a few shortcomings and contrasts in execution and extra room. This is a strong foe of interest in data sharing schemes for dynamic get-togethers in the cloud. In this arrangement, the clients can securely get their classified keys from a pack of chiefs with no statement-trained professionals and secure correspondence channels. In like manner, this plan can uphold dynamic get-togethers. Capably, when another client partakes in the social occasion or a client is revoked from the social occasion, the confidential keys of various clients shouldn't even worry about being recomputed and revived. Moreover, this plan can achieve secure client revocation; the renounced clients can't have the choice to get the extraordinary data records at whatever point they are denied, whether they plot with the untrusted cloud.

REFERENCES

1. Ian Foster, Yong Zhao, Ioan Raicu, Shiyong Lu. "Cloud Computing and Grid Computing 360-Degree Compared", Grid Computing Environments Workshop, 2008, GCE'08, 12–16 Nov. 2008.
2. John Harauz, Lori M. Kaufman, Bruce Potter, " Data Security in the World of Cloud Computing", IEEE Security and Privacy, July/Aug. 2009, vol. 7, no. 4, pp. 61–64 .
3. Wayne Jansen, Timothy Grance, "Guidelines on Security and Privacy in Public Cloud Computing (Draft)", NIST, NIST Special Publication 800–144; Jan. 2011.
4. Siqin Zhao, Kang Chen, Weimin Zheng, "The Application of Virtual Machines on System Security", Fourth ChinaGrid Annual Conference, chinagrid; 2009, pp. 222–229.
5. Kamble, S., Saini, D. K. J., Kumar, V., Gautam, A. K., Verma, S., Tiwari, A., & Goyal, D. (2022). Detection and tracking of moving cloud services from video using saliency map model. Journal of Discrete Mathematical Sciences and Cryptography, 25(4), 1083–1092.
6. Xuan Zhang, Nattapong Wuwong, Hao Li, Xuejie Zhang, " Information Security Risk Management Framework for the Cloud Computing Environments", cit. 10th IEEE International Conference on Computer and Information Technology; 2010,
7. Tiwari, A., Sah, M. K., & Malhotra, A. (2015, September). Effective service Utilization in Cloud Computing exploitation victimisation rough pure mathematics as revised ROSP. In 2015 4th International Conference on Reliability, Infocom Technologies and Optimization (ICRITO)(Trends and Future Directions) (pp. 1–6). IEEE.
8. Tiwari, A., & Sharma, R. M. (2019). Realm Towards Service Optimization in Fog Computing. International Journal of Fog Computing (IJFC), 2(2), 13–43.
9. Tiwari, A., Mahrishi, M., & Fatehpuria, S. (2014). A Broking Structure Originated on Service accommodative Using MROSP Algorithm.
10. Tiwari, A., & Garg, R. (2021). ACCOS: A Hybrid Anomaly-Aware Cloud Computing Formulation-Based Ontology Services in Clouds. In ISIC (pp. 341–346).M. Young, The Technical Writer's Handbook. Mill Valley, CA: University Science, 1989.
11. Tiwari, A. Dr. A. Nagaraju and Mehul Mahrishi, An Optimized Scheduling Algorithm for Cloud Broker Using Cost Adaptive Modeling. In 3rd IEEE (International Advanced Computing Conference-2013).
12. Al-Fuqaha, M. Guizani, M. Mohammadi, M. Aledhari, and M. Ayyash, "Internet of things: A survey on enabling technologies, protocols, and applications," IEEE Communications Surveys Tutorials, vol. 17, no. 4, pp. 2347–2376, 2015.
13. Tiwari, A., Kumar, S., Baishwar, N., Vishwakarma, S. K., & Singh, P. (2022). Efficient Cloud Orchestration Services in Computing. In Proceedings of 3rd International Conference on Machine Learning, Advances in Computing, Renewable Energy and Communication (pp. 739-746). Springer, Singapore.
14. Tiwari, A., & Garg, R. (2022). Adaptive Ontology-Based IoT Resource Provisioning in Computing Systems. International Journal on Semantic Web and Information Systems (IJSWIS), 18(1), 1–18.
15. J. Gubbi, R. Buyya, S. Marusic, and M. Palaniswami, "Internet of things (IoT): A vision, architectural elements, and future directions," Future generation computer systems, vol. 29, no. 7, pp. 1645–1660, 2013.
16. Tiwari, A., & Garg, R. (2022). Orrs Orchestration of a Resource Reservation System Using Fuzzy Theory in High-Performance Computing: Lifeline of the Computing World. International Journal of Software Innovation (IJSI), 10(1), 1–28.
17. Tiwari, A., & Sharma, R. M. (2021). OCC: A Hybrid Multiprocessing Computing Service Decision Making Using Ontology System. International Journal of Web-Based Learning and Teaching Technologies (IJWLTT), 16(4), 96–116.
18. S. Ranger. What is cloud computing? Everything you need to know about the cloud, explained. Mar. 11, 2020.
19. Nouri, Seyed; Han, Li; Srikumar, Venugopal; Wenxia, Guo; MingYun, He; Wenhong, Tian (2019). "Autonomic decentralized elasticity based on a reinforcement learning controller for cloud applications". Future Generation Computer Systems. 94: 765–780. doi: 10.1016/j.future.2018.11.049.
20. Arkian, Hamid Reza; Diyanat, Abolfazl; Pourkhalili, Atefe (2017-03-15). "MIST: Fog-based data analytics scheme with cost-efficient resource provisioning for IoT crowdsensing applications". Journal of Network and Computer Applications. 82: 152–165. doi: 10.1016/j.jnca.2017.01.012.
21. Tiwari, A., Sharma, V., & Mahrishi, M. (2014). Service adaptive broking mechanism using MROSP algorithm. In Advanced Computing, Networking and Informatics-Volume 2 (pp. 383–391). Springer, Cham.
22. Tiwari, A., & Garg, R. (2022). Reservation System for Cloud Computing Resources (RSCC): Immediate Reservation of the Computing Mechanism. International Journal of Cloud Applications and Computing (IJCAC), 12(1), 1–22.
23. Dawei Sun, Guiran Chang, Qiang Guo, Chuan Wang, Xingwei Wang., "A Dependability Model to Enhance Security of Cloud Environment Using System-Level Virtualization Techniques", First International Conference on Pervasive Computing, Signal Processing and Applications pcspa; 2010, pp. 305–310.
24. Qian Liu, Chuliang Weng, Minglu Li, Yuan Luo, "An In-VM Measuring Framework for Increasing Virtual Machine Security in Clouds", IEEE Security and Privacy, vol. 8, no. 6, pp. 56–62, Nov./Dec. 2010.

25. M. Sharif et al, "Secure In-VM Monitoring Using Hardware Virtualization", Proc. 16th ACM Conf. Computer and Communications Security; ACM Press, 2009, pp. 477–487.
26. Tiwari, A., & Sharma, R. M. (2019). A Skywatch on the Challenging Gradual Progression of Scheduling in Cloud Computing. In Applications of Computing, Automation and Wireless Systems in Electrical Engineering (pp. 531–541). Springer, Singapore.
27. Jia Xu, Jia Yan, Liang He, Purui Su, Dengguo Feng. "CloudSEC: A Cloud Architecture for Composing Collaborative Security Services" , 2nd IEEE International Conference on Cloud Computing Technology and Science cloudcom; 2010, pp. 703–711.
28. Cloud Security Alliance. Security Guidance for Critical Areas of Focus in Cloud Computing V2.1; 2009,
29. Luigi, D.P.P.; Francesca, G.; Giusy, M. Using Drones for Deliver Process. ISM. 2019.

Computer Science Engineering and Emerging Technologies (ICCS-2022) – Prof (Dr.) Rajeev Sobti et al. (eds)
© *2024 Taylor & Francis Group, London, ISBN 978-1-032-52199-2*

Chapter

Machine Learning-based Cloud Optimization System

Pankaj Agarwal[1]
K.R Mangalam University, Gurgaon, India

Abolfazl Mehbodniya[2]
Kuwait College of Science and Technology (KCST), Doha, Kuwait

Julian L. Webber[3]
Kuwait College of Science and Technology (KCST), Doha, Kuwait

Radha Raman Chandan[4]
School of Management Sciences, Varanasi, Uttar Pradesh, India

Mohit Tiwari[5]
Bharati Vidyapeeth's College of Engineering, Delhi, India

Dhiraj Kapila[6]
Lovely Professional University, Phagwara, Punjab, India

Abstract: AI and Models for Advancement in Cloud's principal point is to meet the client's necessity with great administration, the least time for calculation, and high unwavering quality. With expansion in administrations relocating to cloud suppliers, the heap over the cloud increments, bringing about issues and different security disappointments in the framework and diminishing unwavering quality. Cloud guarantees speed, nimbleness, and cost reserve funds, yet understanding the full worth of cloud requires settling troublesome difficulties like information gravity, security, consistency with guidelines, cost administration, and the requirement for authoritative change. HPE's cross-breed cloud arrangements can assist your business with exploring cloud intricacies and speed up your computerized change through a demonstrated procedure for changing individuals, cycles, and innovation.

Keywords: Cloud technology, Machine learning, Resource allocation, Wireless communications

1. Introduction

Machine Learning (ML) is a discipline of computerized reasoning that furnishes machines with the capacity to naturally gain from information and previous encounters while recognizing examples to make expectations with negligible human intervention. AI techniques empower PCs to work independently without unequivocal programming. ML applications are taken care of with new information, and they can freely learn, develop, create, and adjust. AI gets smart data from huge volumes of information by utilizing calculations to distinguish designs and learn in an iterative cycle [1]. ML calculations use calculation strategies to advance straightforwardly from information as opposed to depending on any foreordained condition that might act as a model. The exhibition of ML calculations adaptively improves with an expansion in the

---
[1]pankaj.agarwal7877@gmail.com, [2]a.niya@kcst.edu.kw, [3]j.webber@kcst.edu.kw, [4]rrcmiet@gmail.com, [5]mohit.tiwari@bharatividyapeeth.edu, [6]dhiraj.23509@lpu.co.in

DOI: 10.1201/9781003405580-111

quantity of accessible examples during growing experiences. For instance, profound learning is a sub-space of AI that trains PCs to imitate regular human qualities, like learning from models [4]. It offers preferred execution boundaries over regular ML calculations.

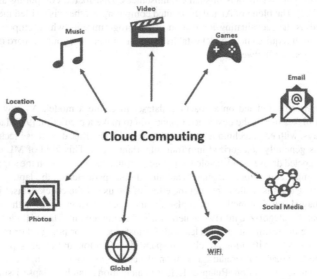

Fig. 111.1   Basic Services of ML using Cloud technology [7]

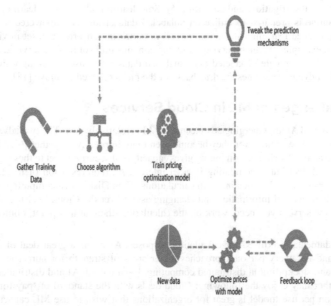

Fig. 111.2   Cloud-based ML structural model [9]

In this innovation-driven time, Machine Learning and Distributed computing are the most remarkable advances around the world [7]. Both of these innovations assume a vital role in helping small and large associations develop their organizations. AI assists clients with making forecasts and fosters calculations that can naturally advance by utilizing verifiable information. Nonetheless, different AI calculations, for example, Direct Relapse, Strategic Relapse, SVM, Choice Tree, Gullible Bayes, K-Means, irregular woodland, Slope Helping calculations, and so on, require a monstrous measure of capacity that becomes quite trying for an information researcher as well as AI experts. Distributed computing turns into a unique advantage for conveying AI models in such circumstances. Distributed computing assists with upgrading and extending AI applications [12]. The blend of AI and distributed computing is otherwise called the smart Cloud. Distributed computing is characterized as the reevaluating innovation of PC programming, which empowers us to remotely get to applications and information. It requires no product establishment or capacity on your PC hard drive. You just need to join to partake in the administrations on the web.

2. Related Work

Machine learning algorithms are modeled on a coaching dataset to create a model. As new records are added to the educated ML algorithm, it makes use of the developed mannequin to make a prediction [9]. Machine-learning algorithms can be studied in many ways, with each technique having its pros and cons. Based on these techniques and approaches to learning, computer study is generally categorized into four important types: This kind of ML entails supervision, where machines are educated on labeled datasets and enabled to predict outputs based totally on the supplied training. The labeled dataset specifies that some input and output parameters are already mapped. Hence, the laptop is educated with the input and corresponding output. A gadget is made to predict the effect of the use of the check dataset in subsequent phases. The essential target of the managed learning method is to plan the information variable (a) with the result variable (b) [11]. Administered AI is additionally categorized into two general classes: Arrangement: These allude to calculations that address characterization issues where the result variable is clear-cut; for instance, yes or no, valid or misleading, male or female, and so on. The true uses of this classification are clear in spam identification and email separation. Some known order calculations incorporate the Irregular Timberland Calculation, the choice tree calculation, the strategic relapse calculation, and the backing vector machine calculation. Relapse: Relapse calculations handle relapse issues where information and result factors have a straight relationship. These are known to be consistent result factors. Models incorporate climate expectations, market pattern investigation, and so forth [15]. Solo learning alludes to a learning method that is without oversight. Here, the machine is prepared to utilize an unlabeled dataset and is empowered to foresee the result with next to no oversight. An unaided learning calculation intends to bunch the unsorted dataset in view of the information's similitudes, contrasts, and examples. Semi-supervised studying contains traits of both supervised and unsupervised laptop learning. It makes use of the aggregate of labeled and unlabeled datasets to instruct its algorithms. Using each kind of dataset, semi-supervised studying overcomes the drawbacks of the picks referred to above [18].

3. Research Challenges of ML in Cloud Services

Although cloud computing and AI are emerging advancements, AI is relatively new. The two advances assume significant roles in organizations' development; however, they become even more impressive together [6]. AI makes smart machines or programming, and then again, distributed computing gives capacity and security to get to these applications. The primary association between AI and distributed computing is asset interest. AI requires a ton of handling power, information capacity, and numerous servers, all while dealing with calculations. Then Distributed computing assumes a critical role in giving new servers pre-characterized information and changing assets over the Cloud (web). Utilizing cloud computing, you can turn up quite a few servers you need, work on the calculation, then, at that point, obliterate the machines again when it's complete [9].

Cloud computing is fundamentally utilized for calculation purposes; AI needs a great deal of computational ability to make test information; and not every person approaches major areas of strength for numerous reasons. AI finds (here and there) task booking and stockpiling in distributed computing. Even though AI and distributed computing enjoy their benefits separately, together they enjoy the following: Cloud deals with the standard of 'pay for what you really want'. The Cloud's compensation per-use model is great for organizations that wish to use ML capacities for their businesses without a lot of use. It furnishes the adaptability to work with AI functionalities without having advanced information science abilities [10]. It assists us with simplicity of investigation with different ML innovations and scales up as activities go into creation and request increments. There are so many cloud-specialized organizations that propose bunches of ML innovations for everybody without having earlier information on man-made intelligence and ML. Reinforcement-based knowledge-gaining is a feedback-based process. Here, the AI element mechanically takes inventory of its environment by means of the hit-and-run method, takes action, learns from experiences, and improves performance. The factor is rewarded for every exact motion and penalized for each incorrect move. Thus, the reinforcement of getting to know things pursues maximizing the rewards by performing accurate actions [20].

4. Features and Architecture of Machine Learning based Technology

Although there are so many distributed computing stages accessible on the web, not many of them are generally famous for AI. How about we examine them exhaustively. Amazon Web Services (AWS) is one of the most well-known distributed computing stages for AI, created by Amazon in 2006 [16]. There are such countless items given by AWS as follows [19]:

- Amazon Sage Maker: This item fundamentally assists with making and train AI models.
- Amazon Gauge: This item helps increment the figure precision of ML models.
- Amazon Make an interpretation of: Deciphering dialects in NLP and ML is utilized.
- Amazon Customize: This item makes different individual suggestions in the ML framework.
- Amazon Polly: It is utilized to change over text into a discourse design.
- AWS Profound Learning Ami's: This item is basically used to take care of profound learning issues in ML.
- Amazon Expanded computer-based intelligence: It executes human survey in ML models.

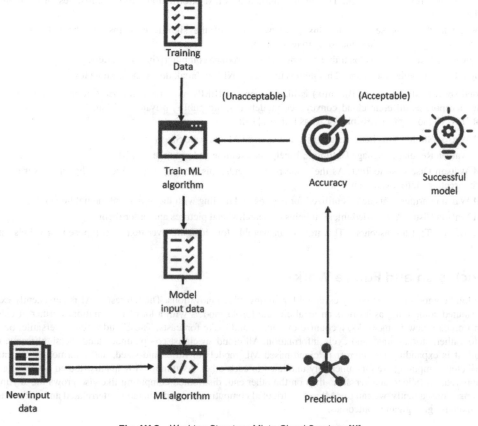

Fig. 111.3 Working Structure ML in Cloud Services [11]

Microsoft Sky blue is likewise a well-known distributed computing stage presented by Microsoft in 2010. It is famous among information researchers and AI experts for information examination necessities. There are some Microsoft Sky blue items accessible for AI as follows [21]:

- Microsoft Purplish blue Mental Assistance: This item assists you with offering clever mental types of assistance for ML applications.
- Microsoft Purplish blue Bot Administration: This item fundamentally centers around making savvy and shrewd bot administrations for ML applications.
- Microsoft Purplish blue Databricks: This item gives Apache Flash based investigation.
- Microsoft Purplish blue Mental Hunt: This item centers around portable and web applications in AI.
- Microsoft Sky blue AI: This item is liable for sending ML models overcloud.

Google Cloud or Google Cloud Stage is a distributed computing stage that is an auxiliary of Tech Goliath Google created in 2008. It gives its framework to clients to creating AI models overcloud. There are a couple of Google Cloud items accessible for AI as follows [18]:

- Google Cloud Vision man-made intelligence: This item permits AI applications to effectively incorporate vision location highlights, for example, picture marking, text recognition, face identification, labeling, and so on.
- Google Cloud man-made intelligence Stage: This item creates, test, and oversee AI models.
- Google Cloud Text-to-Discourse: This item communicates text information into discourse design for preparing AI models.
- Google Cloud Discourse to-Text: This is likewise one of the significant items that help 120+languages for communicating discourse information into text design.
- Google Cloud AutoML: It helps train an AI model and produce computerizing AI models.
- Google Cloud Regular Language: This item is utilized in NLP to break down and arrange text.

IBM Cloud (previously known as Bluemix) is likewise one of IBM's most famous open-source distributed computing stages. It incorporates different cloud conveyance models that are public, private, and half-breed models. There are a couple of IBM Cloud items accessible for AI as follows [14]:

- IBM Watson Studio: This item creates, run, and oversee AI and Fake Savvy models.
- IBM Watson Regular Language Getting it: It helps us examine and group text in NLP.
- IBM Watson Discourse to-Text: As the name recommends, this item is answerable for changing over discourse or voice directions into text design.
- IBM Watson Partner: This item is utilized for making and dealing with the individual menial helper.
- IBM Watson Visual Acknowledgment: it helps AI search visual pictures and order them.
- IBM Watson Text-to-Discourse: This item is answerable for changing over text or composed directions into voice design.

5. Conclusion and Future Work

AI with cloud computing is extremely essential for cutting-edge innovations. The interest in AI is persistently expanding with distributed computing, as it offers an ideal climate for AI models with a lot of information. Further, it tends to be utilized to prepare new frameworks, recognize examples, and make forecasts. The Cloud offers a versatile, on-demand climate to gather, store, curate, and cycle information. All cloud specialist co-ops understand the significance of AI in the Cloud; it is expanding the interest in cloud-based ML models to little, mid-sized, and enormous associations. AI and distributed computing are fundamentally unrelated to each other. Assuming AI helps distributed computing become more improved, proficient, and versatile, then on the other end, distributed computing likewise grows the skyline for AI applications. Consequently, we can say Ml and distributed computing are unpredictably interrelated and utilized together; they can likewise give gigantic outcomes.

REFERENCES

1. Broy, M.: Software engineering — from auxiliary to key technologies. In: Broy, M., Dener, E. (eds.) Software Pioneers, pp. 10–13. Springer, Heidelberg (2002)
2. Dod, J.: Effective substances. In: The Dictionary of Substances and Their Effects. Royal Society of Chemistry (1999) Available via DIALOG.
3. H. Alipour and Y. Liu, "Online machine learning for cloud resource provisioning of microser- vice backend systems," 2017 IEEE International Conference on Big Data (Big Data), Boston, MA, 2017, pp. 2433–2441, doi: 10.1109/BigData.2017.8258201.
4. T. V. T. Duy, Y. Sato and Y. Inoguchi, "Performance evaluation of a Green Scheduling Al- gorithm for energy savings in Cloud computing," 2010 IEEE International Symposium on Parallel Distributed Processing, Workshops and Phd Forum (IPDPSW), Atlanta, GA, 2010, pp. 1–8, doi: 10.1109/IPDPSW.2010.5470908.
5. Tiwari, A., Sharma, R. M., & Garg, R. (2020). Emerging ontology formulation of optimized internet of things (IOT) services with cloud computing. In Soft Computing: Theories and Applications (pp. 31–52). Springer, Singapore.
6. Zhang, Jihua Xie, N. Zhang, X. Yue, K. Li, Weidong Kumar, D.. (2018). Machine learning based resource allocation of cloud computing in auction. Computers, Materials and Continua. 56. 123–135. 10.3970/cmc.2018.03728.
7. Tiwari, A., & Sharma, R. M. (2019). Realm Towards Service Optimization in Fog Computing. International Journal of Fog Computing (IJFC), 2(2), 13-43.
8. Buyya, R., Yeo, C. S., Venugopal, S., Broberg, J., and Brandic, I. (2009). Cloud computing and emerging IT platforms: Vision, hype, and reality for delivering computing as the 5th utility. Future Generation computer systems, 25(6), 599–616.
9. Lee, Y.C., Zomaya, A.Y. Energy efficient utilization of resources in cloud computing systems. J Supercomput 60, 268–280 (2012).
10. Tiwari, A., Sah, M. K., & Malhotra, A. (2015, September). Effective service Utilization in Cloud Computing exploitation victimisation rough pure mathematics as revised ROSP. In 2015 4th International Conference on Reliability, Infocom Technologies and Optimization (ICRITO)(Trends and Future Directions) (pp. 1–6). IEEE.
11. Rajkumar Buyya and Amir Vahid Dastjerdi. 2016. Internet of Things: Principles and paradigms. Elsevier.
12. Tiwari, A., Sharma, V., & Mahrishi, M. (2014). Service adaptive broking mechanism using MROSP algorithm. In Advanced Computing, Networking and Informatics-Volume 2 (pp. 383–391). Springer, Cham.
13. Rajaraman, V. Cloud computing. Reson 19, 242–258 (2014).
14. Tiwari, A., & Sharma, R. M. (2016, August). Potent cloud services utilization with efficient revised rough set optimization service parameters. In Proceedings of the International Conference on Advances in Information Communication Technology & Computing (pp. 1–7).
15. Tiwari, A. Dr. A. Nagaraju and Mehul Mahrishi, An Optimized Scheduling Algorithm for Cloud Broker Using Cost Adaptive Modeling. In 3rd IEEE (International Advanced Computing Conference-2013).
16. Varghese, B., and Buyya, R. (2018). Next generation cloud computing: New trends and research directions. Future Generation Computer Systems, 79, 849–861.
17. Sweeti , Nivedita M (2016), Similarity Based Technique and Text document classification, International Journal of Advance Engineering Research and Technology(IJAERT), volume 4, Issue 2, 23–30.
18. Liu, Ning Li, Zhe Xu, Zhiyuan Xu, Jielong Lin, Sheng Qiu, Qinru Tang, Jian Wang, Yetang. (2017). A Hierarchical Framework of Cloud Resource Allocation and Power Man- agement Using Deep Reinforcement Learning.
19. Tiwari, A., & Garg, R. (2022). Reservation System for Cloud Computing Resources (RSCC): Immediate Reservation of the Computing Mechanism. International Journal of Cloud Applications and Computing (IJCAC), 12(1), 1–22
20. Tiwari, A., & Garg, R. (2022). Orrs Orchestration of a Resource Reservation System Using Fuzzy Theory in High-Performance Computing: Lifeline of the Computing World. International Journal of Software Innovation (IJSI), 10(1), 1–28.
21. Tiwari, A., & Sharma, R. M. (2021). OCC: A Hybrid Multiprocessing Computing Service Decision Making Using Ontology System. International Journal of Web-Based Learning and Teaching Technologies (IJWLTT), 16(4), 96–116.
22. Bartłomiej Nawrocki, Piotr Wilk, Michal Jarzab, Marcin Zielinski, Krzysztof. (2019). VM Reservation Plan Adaptation Using Machine Learning in Cloud Computing. Journal of Grid Computing. 17. 10.1007/s10723-019-09487-x.
23. Singh, S., Chana, I. " QRSF: QoS-aware resource scheduling framework in cloud computing." J Supercomput 71, 241–292 (2015).

Computer Science Engineering and Emerging Technologies (ICCS-2022) – Prof (Dr.) Rajeev Sobti et al. (eds)
© 2024 Taylor & Francis Group, London, ISBN 978-1-032-52199-2

Chapter

Multi Objective Eagle Optimization Feature Selection for Cloud Systems

Gaurav Kumar Arora[1]
Sr. Solution Architect, IBM India Pvt. Ltd., Greater Noida, Uttar Pradesh, India

Rahul Koshti[2]
SVKM'S NMIMS, Hyderabad, India

G. Swamy[3]
Vignana Bharthi Institute of Technology, Hyderabad, India

Abolfazl Mehbodniya[4]
Kuwait College of Science and Technology (KCST), Doha, Kuwait

Julian L. Webber[5]
Kuwait College of Science and Technology (KCST), Doha, Kuwait

Ashish Tiwari[6]
Amity University, Lucknow, India

Abstract: Cloud computing is the on-request conveyance of IT assets through the web with pay-to-utilize charges. Rather than purchasing and keeping up with PC items and administrations, you can pay to utilize a distributed computing administration. It saves you the time, exertion, and cost of doing everything without anyone else. Different systems exist for building a rational framework that reaches from the public to the private cloud. These procedures depend on cooperation instruments that are not difficult to introduce, utilize, and enable in existing correspondence environments. Multi-objective improvement has been applied in many areas of science, including design, financial matters, and strategies where ideal choices should be taken within the context of compromises between at least two clashing goals. Limiting expense while boosting solace while purchasing a vehicle and expanding execution while limiting fuel utilization and the emanation of poisons from a vehicle are instances of multi-objective enhancement issues, including two and three goals, separately. In down-to-earth issues, there can be multiple goals.

Keywords: Cloud computing, Task scheduling, Multi-objective optimization, Load balance, Resource allocation, Resource performance matching distance

1. Introduction

In designing and financial matters, numerous issues include different goals that are not describable as the more the better or minimizing; all things considered, there is an ideal objective incentive for every goal, and the craving is to get as close as conceivable to the ideal worth of every goal [1] [3]. The streamlining burden for a solitary objective varies from that of bi-

[1]gaurav@gaurav-arora.com, [2]rahul.koshti@nmims.edu, [3]swamygachi2010@gmail.com, [4]a.niya@kcst.edu.kw, [5]j.webber@kcst.edu.kw,
[6]er.ashish.tiwari89@gmail.com

DOI: 10.1201/9781003405580-112

targets and multi-goals. On account of single-objective streamlining, the response to the difficulty is found through finding an extraordinary solution to the difficulty, and for that, the improvement inconvenience is taken as both an expansion or minimization objective issue. On account of multi-objective streamlining findings, one excellent response will at this point not be sufficient as unmistakable objectives have unprecedented necessities that need to be upgraded simultaneously to get the best choices for the problem [8]. In multi-objective advancement issues, there are clashing objectives that stop the synchronous enhancement of every goal. The choices give higher results in an objective than others. These choices are perceived as non-ruled choices as they overwhelm various choices somewhere around one goal. The choices that are ruled by various choices are perceived as overwhelming arrangements [11]. The customary cloud asset distribution strategies don't uphold the rising mode in ensuring the practicality and streamlining of the asset portion. This paper proposes an asset distribution calculation for emergent requests in distributed computing. After building the need for asset designation and the matching distances of asset execution and asset extent to answer emanant asset requests, a multi-objective streamlining model of cloud asset distribution is laid out in view of the base number of actual servers utilized and the base matching distances of asset execution and asset extent [15].

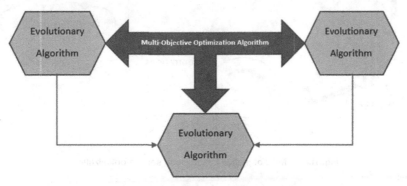

Fig. 112.1 Structure of Multi objective optimization system

Source: Made by Author

Cloud computing innovation offers an assortment of cloud administrations to clients. The cloud client faces the test of picking the assistance that can meet his prerequisites. Consequently, the choice of a methodology that can think about and select the best assistance as indicated by the prerequisite is an issue. A few methodologies, calculations, and systems have been proposed and planned that will help the client pick the best administration. Enhancing the planning procedure just from a solitary viewpoint can't address the issues of forced business. Simultaneously, the power data framework conveyed on the security cloud will confront various kinds of business traffic, and every business traffic has different risk levels. Be that as it may, the current examination has not been directed in that frame of mind from this angle, so it is hard to get the ideal booking plan. As of late, with the top-to-bottom improvement of force informatization, an ever-increasing number of strong applications and undertakings are conveyed in the cloud [16]. For the purpose of safeguarding the power data framework and forestalling information spillage, the security cloud can constantly give visual and exceptionally dependable security administrations on a case-by-case basis, including firewall, interruption discovery, interruption counteraction, and other security administrations. With an ever-increasing number of strong organizations sent to the security cloud, the assignment planning of the security cloud is confronting difficulties. In a protected cloud, task booking is a combinatorial improvement issue. The errand plan influences the proficiency of the entire secure cloud office and plays a key role in further developing the helping nature of the power business [19].

2. Related Work

A mix of nearby information handling that is straightforwardly underway, down to the computerization level, and handling in the cloud can be the ideal arrangement here and open up colossal potential for the industry, particularly in the space of shrewd assembly. This mix offers producers the chance to make the most of the cloud while still satisfying business sector needs for the greatest adaptability and responsiveness. At the point when a lot of information is handled by edge computing, an organization's stockpiling and transmission costs are diminished since only significant information is moved to a cloud or IT framework. To manage gigantic undertakings, sensibly apportion errands to the server in the most

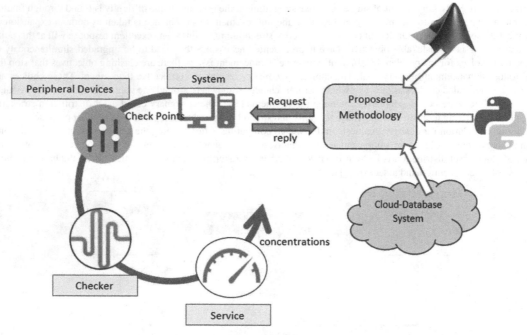

Fig. 112.2 Multi objective based cloud service optimization

Source: Made by Author

limited fulfillment time, and understand the heap equilibrium of the server, Chiang et al. [8] proposed a novel dispatching calculation called the Progressed Max Suffrage calculation, which can further develop the dispatching productivity in the distributed computing organization. Focusing on heterogeneous multi-cloud climates, Panda et al. [9] proposed two errand planning calculations considering general SLA: administration level understanding least finish time (SLA-MCT) and administration level arrangement min (SLA Min). The proposed calculations support the three degrees still up in the

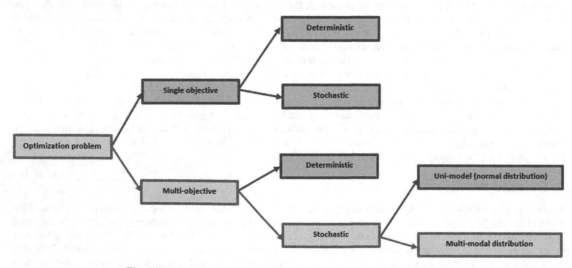

Fig. 112.3 Types of optimization problems in service selections of cloud

Source: Made by Author

air by the clients and accomplish a fitting harmony between assembling time and administration gain cost. Mao et al. [10] proposed Decima, a universally useful booking administration for information handling positions with subordinate stages. Decima picks up planning approaches through experience utilizing present-day support learning (RL) and brain organization. The exploratory outcomes show that Decima further develops normal work culmination time by something like 21% over hand-tuned booking heuristics, accomplishing up to 2% enhancements during times of high group load.

The researcher [19] had proposed a nice video copyright framework for the executive's framework in view of a decentralized blockchain to assist the substance makers' hobby for a high-quality technique for overseeing DRM. In the proposed conspiracy, the proper holders themselves have some control over the framework, which relies on the instrument. In this procedure, the headers of magnificently excessive video content material are scrambled and unscrambled to alter the cryptographic costs associated with encryption and decoding activities. In any case, the framework would not have a motivation machine for mining calculation power. Furthermore, it does not supply cross-stage handing over or get admission to the management of the media record. Abualigah et al. [19] presented a clever antlion calculation for dealing with multi-objective undertaking planning issues in distributed computing conditions. In the proposed method, the multi-target nature of the issue has a similar time limit as the makespan while supporting resource use. The proposed calculation was updated by involving first-class-based differential progression as a local pursuit methodology to further develop its abuse limit and to try not to become trapped in neighboring optima. To summarize, it very well may be found that the current examination has gained extraordinary headway in the errand planning of distributed computing, particularly in the streamlining of significant markers, for example, task fruition time, execution cost, and burden adjusting. In any case, the power data framework conveyed on the protected cloud will confront various kinds of business traffic, and every business traffic has different risk levels. The above research work has not been directed in that frame of mind. Thusly, we constructed a safe cloud task-booking model that, joined with the power data framework, characterizes the risk level of business traffic and the goal capability of undertaking planning. On this premise, we utilize the MOOAFSA to accomplish task booking on the safe cloud [23].

3. Research Challenges in Multi Objectives

Specialists study multi-objective enhancement issues from various perspectives, and, in this manner, there exist different ways of thinking and objectives while setting and settling them. The objective might be to track down a delegate set of Pareto ideal arrangements or potentially measure the compromises in fulfilling the various targets, as well as track down a

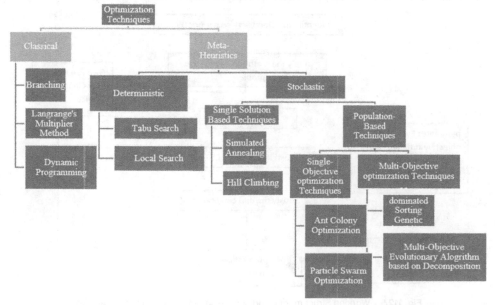

Fig. 112.4 Research Techniques of multi objective function in cloud service selectio

Source: Made by Author

solitary arrangement that fulfills the emotional inclinations of a human leader [21]. In financial matters, numerous issues include various targets along with requirements on what blends of those goals are achievable. For instance, the purchaser's interest in different products is not set in stone by the course of the expansion of the utilities got from those products, but is dependent upon an imperative in view of how much money is accessible to spend on those merchandise and on the costs of that merchandise [25]. This limitation permits a greater amount of one great to be bought exclusively at the expense of consuming less of another great; hence, the different targets (more utilization of every great is liked) are in struggle with one another.

In finance, a continuous difficulty is choosing a portfolio when there are two clashing objectives: the wish to have the anticipated expense of portfolio returns be as essential and over the top as could really be expected, and the wish to have risk, routinely estimated via the favored deviation of portfolio returns, be as low as could really be expected [24]. This inconvenience is consistently addressed through a sketch in which the climate accommodating boondocks propose the quality combinations of danger and expected returns that are accessible and in which lack of concern bends show the financial backer's inclinations for various gambles anticipated to bring mixes back. The difficulty of enhancing a component of the anticipated cost and the notable deviation of portfolio return is known as a two-second decision model [26]. Multi-objective streamlining has been progressively utilized in synthetic design and assembly. In 2009, Fiandaca and Fraga utilized the multi-objective hereditary calculation to upgrade the strain swing adsorption process. The planned issue included the double boost of nitrogen recuperation and nitrogen virtue. The outcomes gave a decent estimate of the Pareto wilderness, with OK compromises between the targets.

4. Working Architecture of Multi Objectives Scheduling

Accordingly, the asset allotment calculation is changed into the arrangement of a multi-objective numerical model. This multi-objective numerical issue is NP-hard on the grounds that its answer isn't exceptionally distinct, that is to say, it isn't single yet numerous. These arrangements can be obtained by utilizing a multi-objective developmental calculation, but they didn't measure up. In this planning model, the assistance traffic in the board module gets administration traffic undertakings presented by clients and arranges and distinguishes them [9]. It isolates the unusual and advances them to the planning community alongside the boundaries. Then the traffic data framework decides the sort and request and produces a planning plan set. Then, the multi-objective improvement process is run for planning plan sets, which are then shipped off to the timetable assessment module. The ideal timetable plan is chosen by the assessment measurements. At last, each is distributed to the VSCRs in every security part asset pool as per the ideal timetable plan [15].

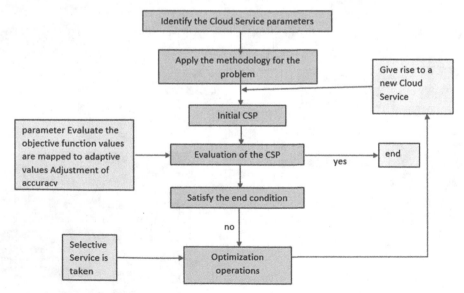

Fig. 112.5 Working Structure of cloud service selection using multi objectives

Source: Made by Author

A multi-objective enhancement issue improves at least two targets while fulfilling the imperatives characterized by the issue. In a genuine application, the goals characterized are in many cases clashing, which implies that the enhanced arrangement obtained with one goal may not give the best outcome with another objective, which leads to a clashing circumstance [17]. For multi-objective streamlining issues, hereditary calculation is broadly utilized for tracking down the ideal arrangement. The calculation assesses and looks at an alternate arrangement of arrangements accessible and afterward tracks down the ideal outcome for the issue. The hereditary calculation is an effective calculation for dealing with circumstances where the issue is perplexing, non-arched, and intermittent. The calculation finds the arrangements that are non-overwhelming and are investigated further utilizing hybrid and transformation administrators. The hereditary calculation doesn't include human mediation, like the contribution of clients in focusing on loads, and this element makes the calculation a well-known heuristic methodology for giving answers for handling the issue connected with the multi-objective enhancement issues [23].

5. Conclusion and Future Work

With the improvement of distributed computing, enormous information, and counterfeit knowledge, cloud asset requests show the qualities of variety, burst, and vulnerability. Without a doubt, cloud stages frequently experience such new asset requests, which should be distributed as assets rapidly and ideally. This paper proposes a multi-objective streamlining of cloud asset allotment calculations for emanant requests. The need for asset distribution is first planned to answer developing requests, and asset execution and asset extent matching distances are laid out to acknowledge asset streamlining and the adjusted use of a wide range of assets. In future work, we will concentrate on adaptation to non-critical failure in a solid cloud climate and consider how to join adaptation to internal failure with the calculation proposed in this paper to improve the unwavering quality of STT booking for a safe cloud.

REFERENCES

1. Luo, X.; Zhang, S.; Litvinov, E. Practical Design and Implementation of Cloud Computing for Power System Planning Studies. Smart Grid. IEEE Trans. Smart Grid 2018, 10, 2301–2311.
2. Anushree, B.; Arul Xavier, V.M. Comparative Analysis of Latest Task Scheduling Techniques in Cloud Computing environment. In Proceedings of the Second International Conference on Computing Methodologies and Communication (ICCMC 2018), Erode, India, 15–16 February 2018; pp. 608–611.
3. Han, P.; Du, C.; Chen, J. A DEA Based Hybrid Algorithm for Bi-objective Task Scheduling in Cloud Computing. In Proceedings of the 5th IEEE International Conference on Cloud Computing and Intelligence Systems (CCIS 2018), Nanjing, China, 23–25 November 2018; pp. 63–67.
4. Fu, M.; Fei, T.; Zhang, L.; Li, H. Research on Location Optimization of Low-Carbon Cold Chain Logistics Distribution Center by FWA-Artificial Fish Swarm Algorithm. In Proceedings of the International Conference on Communications, Information System and Computer Engineering (CISCE 2021), Beijing, China, 14–16 May 2021; pp. 529–533.
5. Chiang, M.L.; Hsieh, H.C.; Tsai,W.C.; Ke, M.C. An improved task scheduling and load balancing algorithm under the heterogeneous cloud computing network. In Proceedings of the 2017 IEEE 8th International Conference on Awareness Science and Technology (iCAST), Taichung, Taiwan, 8–10 November 2017; pp. 290–295.
6. Panda, S.K.; Jana, P.K. SLA-based task scheduling algorithms for heterogeneous multi-cloud environment. J. Supercomput. 2017, 73, 2730–2762.
7. Mao, H.; Schwarzkopf, M.; Venkatakrishnan, S.B.; Meng, Z.; Alizadeh, M. Learning Scheduling Algorithms for Data Processing Clusters. In Proceedings of the ACM Special Interest Group on Data Communication, Beijing, China, 19–23 August 2019; pp. 270–288.
8. Tiwari, A., Sharma, R. M., & Garg, R. (2020). Emerging ontology formulation of optimized internet of things (IOT) services with cloud computing. In Soft Computing: Theories and Applications (pp. 31-52). Springer, Singapore.
9. Li, J.Q.; Han, Y.Q. A hybrid multi-objective artificial bee colony algorithm for flexible task scheduling problems in cloud computing system. Clust. Comput. 2020, 23, 2483–2499
10. Tiwari, A., & Sharma, R. M. (2019). Realm Towards Service Optimization in Fog Computing. International Journal of Fog Computing (IJFC), 2(2), 13-43.
11. Buyya, R., Yeo, C. S., Venugopal, S., Broberg, J., and Brandic, I. (2009). Cloud computing and emerging IT platforms: Vision, hype, and reality for delivering computing as the 5th utility. Future Generation computer systems, 25(6), 599-616.
12. Abualigah, L.; Diabat, A. A novel hybrid antlion optimization algorithm for multi-objective task scheduling problems in cloud

computing environments. Clust. Comput. 2021, 24, 205–223.

13. Tiwari, A., Sah, M. K., & Malhotra, A. (2015, September). Effective service Utilization in Cloud Computing exploitation victimisation rough pure mathematics as revised ROSP. In 2015 4th International Conference on Reliability, Infocom Technologies and Optimization (ICRITO)(Trends and Future Directions) (pp. 1-6). IEEE.

14. Rajkumar Buyya and Amir Vahid Dastjerdi. 2016. Internet of Things: Principles and paradigms. Elsevier.

15. Tiwari, A., Sharma, V., & Mahrishi, M. (2014). Service adaptive broking mechanism using MROSP algorithm. In Advanced Computing, Networking and Informatics-Volume 2 (pp. 383-391). Springer, Cham.

16. Wu, C.; Toosi, A.N.; Buyya, R.; Ramamohanarao, K. Hedonic Pricing of Cloud Computing Services. IEEE Trans. Cloud Comput. 2021, 9, 182–196.

17. Tiwari, A., & Sharma, R. M. (2016, August). Potent cloud services utilization with efficient revised rough set optimization service parameters. In Proceedings of the International Conference on Advances in Information Communication Technology & Computing (pp. 1–7).

18. T. I. Kiviat, ``Beyond bitcoin: Issues in regulating blockchain transaction,'' Duke Law J., vol. 65, p. 569, 2015.

19. Tiwari, A. Dr. A. Nagaraju and Mehul Mahrishi, An Optimized Scheduling Algorithm for Cloud Broker Using Cost Adaptive Modeling. In 3rd IEEE (International Advanced Computing Conference-2013).

20. Varghese, B., and Buyya, R. (2018). Next generation cloud computing: New trends and research directions. Future Generation Computer Systems, 79, 849–861.

21. Sweeti , Nivedita M (2016), Similarity Based Technique and Text document classification, International Journal of Advance Engineering Research and Technology(IJAERT), volume 4 , Issue 2, 23–30.

22. Jiang, M.; Luo, Y.P.; Yang, S.Y. Stochastic convergence analysis and parameter selection of the standard particle swarm optimization algorithm. Inf. Process. Lett. 2007, 102, 8–16.

23. Barham P, Dragovic B, Fraser K et al (2003) Xen and the art of virtualization, ACM SIGOPS. Operating Syst Rev 37(5): 164–177.

24. Armbrust M, Fox A, Griffith R et al (2009) Above the clouds: a Berkeley view of cloud computing. University of California, EECS Department, University of California, Berkeley. In: UCB/EECS-2009-28.

25. Tiwari, A., & Garg, R. (2022). Reservation System for Cloud Computing Resources (RSCC): Immediate Reservation of the Computing Mechanism. International Journal of Cloud Applications and Computing (IJCAC), 12(1), 1–22

26. Tiwari, A., & Garg, R. (2022). Orrs Orchestration of a Resource Reservation System Using Fuzzy Theory in High-Performance Computing: Lifeline of the Computing World. International Journal of Software Innovation (IJSI), 10(1), 1–28.

27. Tiwari, A., & Sharma, R. M. (2021). OCC: A Hybrid Multiprocessing Computing Service Decision Making Using Ontology System. International Journal of Web-Based Learning and Teaching Technologies (IJWLTT), 16(4), 96–116.

28. Pradhan P, Behera PK, Ray NNB (2016) Modified round Robin algorithm for resource allocation in cloud computing. Proc Comp Sci 85: 878–890

29. Shirvastava S, Dubey R, Shrivastava M (2017) Best fit based VM allocation for cloud resource allocation. Int J Comp Appl 158(9): 25–27

30. Katyal M, Mishra A (2014) Application of selective algorithm for effective resource provisioning in cloud computing environment. Int J Cloud Computing 4(1): 1–10

Computer Science Engineering and Emerging Technologies (ICCS-2022) – Prof (Dr.) Rajeev Sobti et al. (eds)
© 2024 Taylor & Francis Group, London, ISBN 978-1-032-52199-2

Chapter **113**

The impact of Anti-forensic Techniques on Forensic Investigation Challenges

Zakariyya Hassan Abdullahi[1]
Research Scholar, Department of Computer Science and Engineering,
Lovely Professional University, Phagwara, Punjab, India

Shailendra Kumar Singh[2]
Assistant Professor, School of Computer Science and Engineering,
Lovely Professional University, Phagwara, Punjab, India

Moin Hasan[3]
Department of Computer Science and Engineering,
Jain Deemed-to-be-University Bengaluru, India

Abstract: This paper explores the increasing complexity of investigating and prosecuting computer crimes, primarily due to the growing use of digital artifacts in forensic investigations. Perpetrators of computer crimes are becoming more knowledgeable about digital forensics and are using anti-forensic techniques to hinder investigations. These methods make it difficult, time-consuming, and expensive to conduct an effective investigation, which can lead to a digital forensics' expert giving up on the case. This project examines how criminals utilize various anti-forensic techniques to impede digital forensic investigations, with a focus on data encryption. The article provides a multi-level analysis of the anti-forensic dilemma, both conceptually and practically. By highlighting the challenges of digital forensic investigations and the techniques used to impede them, this paper aims to raise awareness of the importance of staying up to date on anti-forensic techniques and developing effective countermeasures.

Keywords: Anti-forensic methods, Disk forensics, Digital crime, Digital forensic investigation

1. Introduction

Digital evidence refers to any information, data or material that is processed, stored, or transmitted through electronic devices, and which is of relevance to an investigation. The concept of digital evidence is based on Locard's principle, which suggests that every exchange between two objects, including the offender and the scene of a crime, leaves some material trace that can be used to link the culprit to the criminal act. Digital forensic investigators collect and analyse this evidence to uncover the nature and course of the crime and to identify the perpetrators (G. C Kessler and G. H Carlton 2017).

The increasing use of digital gadgets such as smartphones and personal computers has led to the growth of the alphanumeric society. However, this growth has also resulted in a corresponding increase in online crime, commonly known as cybercrime. Cybercrime leaves digital fingerprints that investigators can use to analyse and determine how the crime was committed, enabling them to build a case to potentially bring criminals to justice. The digital forensics procedure aims to discover

[1]Hassanzakariyya78@gmail.com; [2]drsksingh.cse@gmail.com, shailendra@27293@lpu.co.in; [3]moin.hasan@jainuniversity.ac.in

DOI: 10.1201/9781003405580-113

digital fingerprints or events and generally involves the documentation, gathering, examination, and presentation of digital evidence.

Digital evidence is typically stored on hard disks and memory as log files and other components. The evidence may be encountered on computer solid drives, and it is important to understand when a specific event happened, who performed the act, and what kind of evidence will be encountered. However, anti-forensics techniques are specifically designed to mask or change computer evidence, rendering it ineffectual in litigation (Ramine et al. 2020). The lack of adequate hypothetical inquiries is primarily due to anti-forensics, as opposed to more traditional modern forensic analysis methods.

Anti-forensics techniques are used by cybercriminals to interfere with the forensic process and electronic evidence. For example, encryption is commonly used as a technique to protect confidential information. At the same time, intruders use cryptography to prevent forensic inquiry (Garfinkel 2006). The goal of anti-forensics may include avoiding finding any form of suspicious behaviour that has occurred, disrupting knowledge collection by making it almost impossible for the forensic prosecutor to find any evidence against them, and increasing the examiner's time to settle a case where an impediment is put on the investigation's path.

However, the experimental validity and legal observability of digital evidence expose and accept its value, where complete, credible and accurate proof is required. The modern forensic investigation has some drawbacks that should be taken into consideration. Using technical instruments for forensic operations is primarily based upon resources, which are vulnerable to conflict and thereby influence the reliability and legitimacy of the findings of testimony. Individuality is also an issue when performing investigations as each forensic investigator uses a variety of methods. The usefulness of either approach can vary based on factors such as knowledge and experience, as well as the investigator's intellect and understanding.

The limitations of modern forensic investigations highlight the need for continued development of forensic techniques and tools to keep up with the evolving nature of cybercrime. The use of digital evidence in legal proceedings requires a thorough understanding of the forensic process and the principals involved in collecting, analysing, and presenting digital evidence. The integration of digital forensic techniques into the overall investigative process is essential to ensure that digital evidence is not overlooked or mishandled.

Digital forensics aims to discover digital fingerprints or events and involves the documentation, gathering, examination, and presentation of digital evidence (Kent et al. 2006) (Harris 2006). However, anti-forensics techniques are specifically designed to mask or change computer evidence, rendering it ineffectual in litigation.

This article focuses on the anti-forensic techniques, anti-forensic tools and research gaps.

2. Anti-forensic Techniques

The act of concealing digital evidence can take various forms and has been used for over two thousand years. One common method is steganography, which involves hiding data within carrier files such as images, audio, and videos. Low-tech steganography techniques can also be used, such as hiding an image or text block under a picture in a PowerPoint or Influence visual presentation. Morse code messages can even be embedded within an image. The goal is to make it difficult for forensics tools to detect the hidden data. (Harris 2006)

Another technique is artifact wiping, which involves deleting data from a system to ensure that no tool can retrieve it. Simply deleting a file does not completely remove its contents from the disk, as the file's "MFT" or "INOD" may still be present (By and Panwar n.d.). Wiping, on the other hand, ensures that no tool can retrieve the file. It is the digital equivalent of wiping fingerprints from a weapon or cleaning residue from a crime scene.

Elimination of evidence involves removing any traces of digital evidence from a system, which can be difficult as any attempt to do so may itself generate evidence of tampering (Harris 2006). Attack against forensic tools involves exploiting vulnerabilities in forensics tools to bypass their mechanisms. This can be done using custom software and various techniques such as file signature alteration, hash-flooding, and nested directories. (Wundram, Freiling, and Moch 2013) (Newsham, Street, and Art 2007).

Trail obfuscation aims to confuse and deceive forensics systems by inserting fake evidence. Techniques such as spoofing, log cleaner, and Trojan commands (Hilley 2007) can be used, as well as altering timestamps and file headers. Encryption is also a common tactic used by computer criminals to protect data from unauthorized access and to make it unreadable to investigators. This can be done using file-based encryption, where the file material is translated into ciphertext that can only be read with the correct decryption key, or disk encryption, which encrypts the entire storage partition containing the data.

Steganography, the practice of hiding data within plain documents or messages, has been used since ancient times. It can be used to conceal data within video/audio files, pictures, and records, but its use is easily detected by authorities, and there are readily available cracking tools such as the Forensic Toolkit (FTK). (Bagaskara 2017)

Overall, digital evidence can be hidden or eliminated using a range of techniques, making it difficult for forensics tools to detect and analyse. However, these techniques are not fool proof and may generate evidence of tampering or lead to the discovery of the perpetrator.

3. Anti-forensics Tools

Data security methods can be mainly categorized in: disk encryption, file encryption, data encryption, steganography, VeraCrypt sophisticated encryption method, runs readily on all popular computer functioning systems Windows, Linux and Mac OS. It offers a number of encryption methods, including: Sophisticated Coding Standard (AES), Serpent coding, and TwoFish; In accumulation to the above methods of encryption, VeraCrypt also enables the development of secret and encrypted volumes inside certain existing volumes (Free Open source disk encryption with strong security for the Paranoid - IChannel Technologies [online] Available https//www.veracrypt.fr/en/home.html n.d.).

Table 113.1 Classification of common anti-forensic methods (nt. Artif. Intell. Data Process. Symp., 2017)

Sr. No.	Method	Methodology	Outcomes
1	MACE alterations	Destroying	Erasing MACE information or overwriting with useless data
		Counterfeiting	Overwriting with data which provides misleading information to investigators
2	Removing/wiping files	Destroying	Overwriting contents with useless data
		Hiding	Deleting file (overwriting pointer to content)
3	Data encapsulation	Hiding	Hiding by placing files inside other files
4	Account hijacking	Counterfeiting	Evidence is created to make it appear as if another person did the "bad act"
5	Archive/image bombs	Counterfeiting	Evidence is created to attempt to compromise the analysis of an image
6	Disabling logs	Eliminating source	Information about activities is never recorded

In another experiment, an attempt was made to recover hidden data. 65% of the manipulated signatures were effectively recognized by forensics software using the FTK1.71 (trial version) computer forensics set. In the forensics code, manually concealed information in the file slack space was fully revealed and fully readable. In terms of computer forensics tools for steganography the information was not re-established, but the entropy test. (Pimenidis 2016) (Toolkit 2015). Suspicion was raised. Encryption has also succeeded in hiding the data in such a way that forensic technology has not retrieved actual data but is also suspicious.

Table 113.2 Analysis of results

Sr. No.	Technique Used	FTK	ProDiscover	Results	Efficiency of Technique
1	Steganography: Hiding files within another file	could not detect	Could not detect info	Both the tools could not detect the hidden content.	This is an efficient technique, no external software needed.
2	Changing file attributes	Could detect	Could detect	Both tools could detect the files and its contents.	This is an inefficient technique.
3	Password Protected Files and Folders	Could not find the files when in protected mode.	Could not find the files when in protected (locked) mode.	FTK and ProDiscover could not find the drive when the drive was locked and hidden	This technique is efficient as the complete drive is protected and could not be identified by Forensic tools.

Sr. No.	Technique Used	FTK	ProDiscover	Results	Efficiency of Technique
4	Hiding Partitions Could not fine drive.	Could not find the drive.	Could not find the drive.	FTK and ProDiscover could not find the drive for examining.	This method is considered one of the calmest and best ways to hide information.
5	Data Deletion Could not retrieve the information after the file is deleted.	Could not retrieve the information after the file is deleted.	Could not find the drive.	FTK and ProDiscover could not show the contents of the deleted files.	This is a good way to erase all marks making it clean.
6	File Fragmenting Could identify the file and its contents.	Could identify the file and its contents.	–	FTK and ProDiscover could display the source file name controlled in each piece of the fragment.	This technique is a week technique of hiding information.
7	Rename folder to system predefined	Could detect the contents of folder	Could retrieve the contents of folder	FTK and ProDiscover	This is a good way to rename the folder. Not an efficient technique.
8	Bit Shifting the fillings of the file	Could not retrieve the file contents.	Could not detect the file contents.	FTK and ProDiscover could not indicate that the file content has undergone shifting, or reveal the original content	This is an efficient technique and a good way to hide information.
9	File slack Could retrieve the contents	Could detect the contents	Could not detect the file contents.	FTK and ProDiscover could detect the contents of the file slack	This is not an efficient technique as the information can be detected.

Source: Made by Author

It is conceivable that more experiments Utilize programs like Outguess or Steg detect would have exposed secret information through stenography or authentication, but forensics technology on its own was incapable to do it.

4. Conclusion

A significant area of research and development is computer forensics. Disk forensics must carefully consider its methods since computer anti-forensic success renders digital evidence inadmissible in court. Determining the effect of anti-forensics on digital forensic research was the main goal of this investigation. The results of the investigations undertaken indicate that not all sophisticated counter-forensics are effective when used in conjunction with forensics technology. Tools have frequently failed to conceal or remove crucial data. The likelihood of the forensics' recognition rate is very high. As demonstrated by the instances of encryption and steganography, where systems and techniques become significantly more complicated than those utilized in this research, technology depends on the sophistication of the counter forensic methods deployed. Data encryption is another efficient anti-forensic technique, as it prevents forensic investigations into encrypted volumes from continuing in the absence of a decryption key. This study only examined a small number of forensic and anti-forensic approaches; a larger, more thorough investigation is required to determine the simple and conclusive effects of anti-forensic methodologies.

REFERENCES

1. AxCrypt. 2016. "AxCrypt - File Security Made Easy, online." Http://Www.Axcrypt.Net/. http://www.axcrypt.net/.
2. Bagaskara, Jordy Ardian. 2017. "Analysis of JPEG Image Steganography Using Spread Spectrum Method." 12(23): 13944–50.
3. Berinato, Scott. "The Rise of Anti-Forensics, A." Cso. https://www.csoonline.com/article/2122329/the-rise-of-anti-forensics.html.
4. By, and Narendra Panwar. "Anti-Forensics Analysis of File Wiping Tools." Msc Thesis, Cyber Security.
5. Cohen, Fred. 2012. "The Science of Digital Forensics: Recovery of Data from Overwritten Areas of Magnetic Media." Journal of Digital Forensics, Security and Law 7(4): 7–20.

6. Conlan, Kevin, Ibrahim Baggili, and Frank Breitinger. 2016. "Anti-Forensics: Furthering Digital Forensic Science through a New Extended, Granular Taxonomy." DFRWS 2016 USA - Proceedings of the 16th Annual USA Digital Forensics Research Conference 18(December 2015): S66–75. http://dx.doi.org/10.1016/j.diin.2016.04.006.

7. Dahbur, Kamal. 2011. "The Anti-Forensics Challenge."." Proceedings of the 2011 International Conference on Intelligent Semantic Web-Services and Applications. ACM, 2011. 2.

8. Ferguson, Niels. 2006. "AES-CBC + Elephant Diffuser: A Disk Encryption Algorithm for Windows Vista.": 1–22. http://download.microsoft.com/download/0/2/3/0238acaf-d3bf-4a6d-b3d6-0a0be4bbb36e/BitLockerCipher200608.pdf.

9. "Free Open-Source Disk Encryption with Strong Security for the Paranoid - IChannel Technologies [Online] Available Https//Www.Veracrypt.Fr/En/Home.Html."

10. G. C Kessler and G. H Carlton. 2017. "Exploring Myths in Digital Forensics_ Separating Science From Ritual_ International Journal of Interdisciplinary Telecommunications and Networking_ Vol 9, No 4.": p 1–9.

11. Garfinkel, Simson. 2006. "Anti-Forensics: Techniques , Detection and Countermeasures.": 77–84.

12. Harris, Ryan. 2006. "Arriving at an Anti-Forensics Consensus: Examining How to Define and Control the Anti-Forensics Problem." Digital Investigation 3(SUPPL.): 44–49.

13. Hilley, S. 2007. "Anti-Forensics with a Small Army of Exploits." 4: 13–15.

14. Kent, Authors Karen, Suzanne Chevalier, Tim Grance, and Hung Dang. 2006. "Guide to Integrating Forensic Techniques into Incident Response." (August).

15. Kessler, Gary C. 2007. "Anti-Forensics and the Digital Investigator." Proceedings of the 5th Australian Digital Forensics Conference: 1–7.

16. Kessler, Gary C., and Gregory H. Carlton. 2017. "Exploring Myths in Digital Forensics." International Journal of Interdisciplinary Telecommunications and Networking 9(4): 1–9.

17. Losavio, Michael M., Musa Hindi, Roman Yampolskiy, and Deborah Wilson Keeling. 2011. "Boundary Conditions for the Digital Forensic Use of Electronic Evidence and the Need for Forensic Counter-Analysis." 2011 6th IEEE International Workshop on Systematic Approaches to Digital Forensic Engineering, SADFE 2011.

18. Majed, Hussein, Hassan N. Noura, and Ali Chehab. 2020. "Overview of Digital Forensics and Anti-Forensics Techniques." 8th International Symposium on Digital Forensics and Security, ISDFS 2020 (June).

19. Mothukur, Abhinav Reddy et al. 2019. "Investigation of Countermeasures to Anti-Forensic Methods." 2019 IEEE Long Island Systems, Applications and Technology Conference (LISAT): 1–6.

20. Newsham, Tim, Sansome Street, and Prior Art. 2007. "Breaking Forensics Software: Weaknesses in Critical Evidence Collection.": 1–30.

21. Pimenidis, Elias. 2016. "Computer Anti-Forensics Methods and Their Impact on Computer Forensic Investigation Computer Anti-Forensics Methods and Their Impact On." (August 2009): 145–55.

22. Qureshi, Muhammad Ali, and El Sayed M. El-Alfy. 2019. "Bibliography of Digital Image Anti-Forensics and Anti-Anti-Forensics Techniques." IET Image Processing 13(11): 1811–23.

23. Ramine, Tambue, Etow Supervisor, Ola Flygt Semester, and Computer Science. 2020. "IMPACT OF ANTI-FORENSICS TECHNIQUES ON DIGITAL Author: Tambue Ramine Etow." 4: 1–10.

24. Sabir, Maha F, and James H Jones. 2018. "A Non-Algorithmic Forensic Approach for Hiding Data in Image Files.": 60–64.

25. Toolkit, Forensic. 2015. "AccessData AccessData Legal and Contact Information." AccessData Corporation, FTK manual v 1.71 –Entropy test User Guide 2015.

26. Wundram, Martin, Felix C Freiling, and Christian Moch. 2013. "Anti-Forensics : The Next Step in Digital Forensics Tool Testing." Seventh International Conference on IT Security Incident Management and IT Forensics Anti-Forensics:: 83–97.